The IDG SECRETS™ Advantage

DOS 6 SECRETS is part of the *InfoWorld SECRETS* series of books, brought to you by IDG Books Worldwide, The designers of the *SECRETS* series understand that you appreciate insightful and comprehensive works from computer experts. Authorities in their respective areas, the authors of the *SECRETS* books have been selected for their ability to enrich your daily computing tasks.

The formula for a book in the *SECRETS* series is simple: Give an expert author a forum to pass on his or her expertise to readers. A *SECRETS* author, rather than the publishing company, directs the organization, pace, and treatment of the subject matter. *SECRETS* authors maintain close contact with end users through column feedback, user group participation, and consulting work. The authors' close contact with the needs of computer users gives the *SECRETS* books a strategic advantage over most computer books. Our authors do not distance themselves from the reality of daily computing, but rather, our authors are directly tied to the reader response stream.

We believe that the author has the experience to approach a topic in the most efficient manner, and we know that you, the reader, will benefit from a "one-to-one" relationship, through the text, with the author. The author's voice is always present in a *SECRETS* series book. Some have compared the presentation of a topic in a *SECRETS* book to sitting at a coffee break with the author and having the author's full attention.

And, of course, the author is free to include or recommend useful software, both shareware and proprietary, in a *SECRETS* series book. The software that accompanies a *SECRETS* book is not intended as casual filler. The software is strategically linked to the content, theme, or procedures of the book. We expect that you will receive a real and direct benefit from the included software.

You will find this book comprehensive whether you read it cover to cover, section to section, or simply a topic at a time. As a computer user, you deserve a comprehensive and informative resource of answers that *DOS 6 SECRETS* delivers.

David Solomon
Publisher

INFO WORLD

DOS 6 SECRETS

INFO WORLD

DOS 6 SECRETS

by Robert D. Ainsbury

Foreword by George Yates,
President of The Houston Area League of PC Users, Inc.

IDG BOOKS

IDG Books Worldwide, Inc.
An International Data Group Company

San Mateo, California ✦ Indianapolis, Indiana ✦ Boston, Massachusetts

DOS 6 SECRETS

Published by
IDG Books Worldwide, Inc.
An International Data Group Company
155 Bovet Road, Suite 310
San Mateo, CA 94402

Library of Congress Catalog Card No.: 93-77602

ISBN 1-878058-70-3

Printed in the United States of America

10 9 8 7 6 5 4 3 2 1

Distributed in the United States by IDG Books Worldwide, Inc.

Distributed in Canada by Macmillan of Canada, a Division of Canada Publishing Corporation; by Woodslane Pty. Ltd. in Australia and New Zealand; and by Computer Bookshops in the U.K. and Ireland.

For information on translations and availability in other countries, contact Marc Jeffrey Mikulich, Foreign Rights Manager, at IDG Books Worldwide. Fax: 415-358-1260.

For sales inquiries and special prices for bulk quantities, write to the address above or call IDG Books Worldwide at 415-312-0600.

Dedication

To Mum and Dad with love

Acknowledgments

My fabulous wife, Erica, for supporting me throughout the six-month ordeal and for keeping the business afloat while I was running in protected mode. George Bean, for all the moral support and for the painstaking research on various hardware platforms. Oh, and Uncle Charles, for the secrets that got away.

The folks at Microsoft, especially Andy Thomas and Ben Slivka. True professionals.

The fantastic IDG team. I submitted a donut and they transformed it into a *gateaux!* The marshalls: Mary Bednarek, Terrie Lynn Solomon, and David Solomon. The wordsmiths: Sandy Blackthorn, Diane Steele, Becky Whitney, Chuck Hutchinson, Julie King, and Tricia Reynolds. The Shareware sultans: Laurie Smith and Darrin Strain. The production posse: Cindy Phipps, Beth Baker, and Mary Briedenbach. The cover girl: Polly Papsadore. And Linda Slovick, for all the technical support, corrections, and suggestions.

It was a pleasure working with y'all.

(The publisher would like to give special thanks to Patrick J. McGovern, without whom this book would not have been possible.)

About IDG Books Worldwide

Welcome to the world of IDG Books Worldwide.

IDG Books Worldwide, Inc., is a division of International Data Group (IDG), the world's largest publisher of computer-related information and the leading global provider of information services on information technology. IDG publishes over 190 computer publications in 60 countries. Thirty million people read one or more IDG publications each month.

If you use personal computers, IDG Books is committed to publishing quality books that meet your needs. We rely on our extensive network of publications, including such leading periodicals as *Macworld, InfoWorld, PC World, Computerworld, Publish, Network World*, and *SunWorld*, to help us make informed and timely decisions in creating useful computer books that meet your needs.

Every IDG book strives to bring extra value and skill-building instruction to the reader. Our books are written by experts, with the backing of IDG periodicals, and with careful thought devoted to issues such as audience, interior design, use of icons, and illustrations. Our editorial staff is a careful mix of high-tech journalists and experienced book people. Our close contact with the makers of computer products helps ensure accuracy and thorough coverage. Our heavy use of personal computers at every step in production means we can deliver books in the most timely manner.

We are delivering books of high quality at competitive prices on topics customers want. At IDG, we believe in quality, and we have been delivering quality for over 25 years. You'll find no better book on a subject than an IDG book.

John Kilcullen
President and C.E.O.
IDG Books Worldwide, Inc.

About the Author

Bob Ainsbury is the vice president of software development for TechnoJock Software, Inc., a Houston-based software company specializing in the development of programming libraries for DOS and Windows. He recently was the lead developer on the SmartPak product for 1-2-3 for Windows for Lotus Development Corporation.

Although Bob received a degree in Civil Engineering from the University of Manchester, England, he recently had trouble building a BBQ pit.

When Bob isn't coding or writing, he enjoys shooting pool, playing the drums, and avoiding home-maintenance projects. His favorite film is *The Commitments,* and his favorite clothes are baggy.

Credits

Publisher
David Solomon

Acquisitions Editor
Janna Custer

Managing Editor
Mary Bednarek

Project Editors
Sandra Blackthorn
Laurie Smith
Terrie Lynn Solomon
Diane Graves Steele

Editors
Julie King
Darrin Strain
Rebecca Whitney

Technical Reviewer
Linda Slovick

Editorial Assistant
Patricia R. Reynolds

Proofreader
Charles A. Hutchinson

Production Manager
Beth J. Baker

Production Coordinator
Cindy L. Phipps

Production Assistant
Mary A. Briedenbach

Indexing
Steve Rath

Illustrations
Matt Tyndall Design

Production
Beth J. Baker
Cindy L Phipps
Mary A. Briedenbach

Book Design and Production
Peppy White
Francette M. Ytsma
Tracy Strub
(University Graphics, Palo Alto, California)

university **G** raphics

Contents at a Glance

Foreword xxvi

Introduction 1

Part I: Secrets for an Effective Beginning 1

    Chapter 1: Taking an Aerial View of DOS 6 13

    Chapter 2: Mastering the Top DOS Commands 39

    Chapter 3: Protecting and Recovering That Irreplaceable Data 71

Part II: Secret Weapons for Your Hardware 107

    Chapter 4: Making Your Hard Disk Faster, Bigger, and Safer 109

    Chapter 5: Maximizing Memory 159

    Chapter 6: Taking Control of the Display and Keyboard 217

    Chapter 7: Juggling IRQs, DMAs, Buses, Device Drivers,
        and Other "What's Its" 241

    Chapter 8: Power System Configuration Techniques 261

Part III: Secrets for Automating DOS 283

    Chapter 9: Putting DOSKEY to Work 285

    Chapter 10: Moving Beyond Basic Batch Files 305

    Chapter 11: Demystifying DEBUG 337

Part IV: The Complete DOS 6 Command Reference 367

Part V: Bob's Better-Than-DOS Shareware Collection 603

xiv

Part VI: Appendixes **807**

Appendix A: Installing DOS 6 809
Appendix B: DOS Command Quick Reference 815
Appendix C: ANSI.SYS Quick Reference 825
Appendix D: Interacting with Workgroups and Networks 831
Appendix E: Additional DOS Information Sources 879

Index 883
Installing Bob's Better-Than-DOS Shareware Collection Disks 952

Table of Contents

Foreword xxvi

Introduction 1

Part I: Secrets for an Effective Beginning....................................1

Chapter 1: Taking an Aerial View of DOS 6 13
  Something to Write Home About 13
  Configuration Flexibility 14
    Configuration menus 14
    Interruption keys 16
    A new switch for device drivers 17
  On-Line Help 17
  Advanced Memory Management 19
    Memory optimization tools 20
    EMM386 enhancements 23
  Virus Protection 24
  Heavy-Duty Disk Utilities 25
    DoubleSpace disk compression 25
    DBLSPACE.BIN 26
    The DBLSPACE command 27
    A real backup program 29
    Disk defragmentation 31
    New undeletion tools 32
    Improved cache performance 33
  Windows-Hosted Utilities 33
  Laptop Tools 35
  Other Goodies 35
  What's Gone? 36

Chapter 2: Mastering the Top DOS Commands 39

So Many Commands, So Little Time 39
Getting the Best HELP 40
   Running help searches 40
   Solving help conflicts with 4DOS and NDOS 42
   Help tricks for Microsoft C programmers 43
   Using the /? switch 44
   Using FASTHELP 45
   Applications help 46
Kicking the COPY Habit 47
Using the New MOVE Command 49
Deleting Files 50
Zap It with DELTREE 52
DIR — Yes, DIR 53
   Listing subdirectories 53
   Displaying all files, including hidden and system files 53
   Searching for files 54
   Creating a smarter filemask 54
   Searching for a partial directory name 55
   Setting default DIR switches 56
   Shareware alternatives to DIR 57
Directory Navigation Commands 59
A Smarter PATH 61
MSD, the Administrator's Friend 61
Making the DOSSHELL Work 62
   File viewing 64
   Diverse file selection and management 64
   Task switching 67

Chapter 3: Protecting and Recovering That Irreplaceable Data ... 71

The DOS 6 Defensive Arsenal 71
Backup Tips, Traps, and Truths 73
   Using the DOS 6 backup software 74
     Comparing MSBACKUP and MWBACKUP 74
     Selecting files to back up 75
       Using point and click 76
       Using include/exclude clauses 76

Selecting the backup type 78
Special file-selection options 79
Make sure that your backup is good 80
Optimizing backup speed 81
Files created and used by the backup 81
Restoring files from a backup 84
Backup size limitations 86
Backing up DoubleSpace drives 86
Developing a backup strategy 86
"Must Do" Data-Protection Precautions 88
Guarding against accidental file deletion 88
Installing deletion protection 89
Understanding UNDELETE.INI 90
DEFRAG — yes, DEFRAG 91
Check your disks 92
The case of the missing MIRROR 92
Recovering Lost Files and Data 93
Undeleting files 93
Recovering from an accidental disk format 95
Restoring hard disk partition data 97
Deliberate Data Destruction 97
Vital Virus Measures 98
The virus phenomenon 98
Understanding how viruses spread 99
Potential virus damage 100
Defending against and identifying viruses 101
Scanning for virus infection 101
Where did those CHKLIST.CPS files come from? 101
Getting rid of those checksum files 102
Guarding against destructive viruses 102
Removing viruses from an infected system 103
Comparing MSAV and MWAV 104
On-line virus information 104
On a Lighter Note 104

Part II: Secret Weapons for Your Hardware 107

Chapter 4: Making Your Hard Disk Faster, Bigger, and Safer 109
The Brawn Behind the Brain 109
The Mechanics of a Hard Disk..110
   Inside a hard disk 110
   The role of disk controllers 112
Data Storage Schemes 113
   Tracks 114
   Sectors 114
   Clusters 115
   How to check your drive characteristics 116
   The file allocation table 117
   Directories 118
   How DOS reads, writes, and deletes files 119
      Reading a file 119
      Deleting a file 119
      Writing a file 120
How to Prepare a New Hard Disk 120
   Low-level formatting 120
   Disk partitioning 121
The Role of CHKDSK 123
Faster, Faster, Faster 126
   Optimizing the interleave 126
      Drive alignment problems 128
      Disk surface deterioration 128
   Improving throughput with caches 129
      Using SMARTDRV 129
         How much memory should you assign to the cache? 129
         Do you need double buffering? 131
         Is delayed write caching appropriate? 132
      Resolving communications problems with SMARTDRV 133
      Using SMARTDRV with DoubleSpace drives 134
      Avoiding bad cluster problems..134
      Using SMARTDRV with CD-ROMs 134

Using Fastdisk with Windows 135
Using RAM drives 135
Using FASTOPEN 136
Reviewing the benefits of defragmentation 136
  Using DEFRAG 137
  Solving memory problems 139
Bigger, Bigger, Bigger with DoubleSpace 142
  Reviewing DoubleSpace mechanics 143
    Understanding the compressed volume file 144
    Compressing an entire drive 144
  Installing a DoubleSpace drive 146
    Express setup 146
    Custom setup 146
    The DoubleSpace files 148
    The DoubleSpace booting process 148
    Problems with swap files 149
    Drive-mounting problems caused by file fragments 150
    How to defragment DoubleSpace volumes 150
  Resizing a DoubleSpace drive 151
  Removing a DoubleSpace drive 152
  Removing the DoubleSpace device driver from memory 152
  Changing drive letter assignments 153
  Understanding drive compression ratios 155
  Caching compressed drives with SMARTDRV 156
  Compressing data on floppies 156

Chapter 5: Maximizing Memory **159**
Photographs and Memories 159
The Memory Crunch 160
Memory Terms, Types, and Tidbits 161
  ROM vs. RAM 161
  ROM-BIOS 162
  Memory hardware 162
    The DRAM chip 163
    The SRAM chip 164
    SIMMs 165

The CMOS chip 165
Memory speed issues 166
Memory addressing 167
Hexadecimal numbers 167
Segments and offsets 169
Major types of memory 171
How to check your system 171
Base and upper memory 172
Expanded memory 175
Extended memory 176
High memory 182
Other memory terms 183
Memory managers 183
DOS extenders 183
Upper memory blocks 184
Shadow RAM 184
Stealth and BIOS compression 184
Virtual memory 184
How to Maximize Memory with DOS 6 185
Reviewing the DOS 6 memory arsenal 185
Full steam ahead with the 80386 186
Options for 286 systems 186
Bad news for 8086 owners 186
Alternatives for 8086 and 286 owners 186
Reviewing your memory settings with MEM 187
Using the big gainers 189
Load DOS high 189
Use the UMBs 190
Shifting from RAM cram to UMB cram 192
Identifying potential UMB space 192
Controlling load order and location 193
Tweaking UMB memory allocation 194
Loading DBLSPACE.BIN high 195
Letting MEMMAKER do the work 195
Looking at MEMMAKER in action 196
Running MEMMAKER 198
Optimize upper memory for use with Windows 200
Use the monochrome region 201

Understanding how MEMMAKER works 201
Helping MEMMAKER succeed 204
    Avoid using a multiple configuration menu in CONFIG.SYS 204
    Don't call programs from other batch files 205
    Don't call programs in IF statements 205
    Exclude some programs from analysis and execution 206
Saving every drop of base memory 207
    Minimizing the environment size 208
    Tuning the FILES statement 209
    Tuning the BUFFERS statement 209
    Optimizing the STACKS command 209
    Minimizing the FCBS allocation 210
    Being frugal with LASTDRIVE 210
    Minimize MSCDEX base memory consumption 210
Maximizing extended memory 210
Managing expanded memory 211
Solving memory conflicts 212
    Running MEMMAKER locks up the system 212
    The new configuration locks up the system 213
    A program causes system lockup 214
    A program runs more slowly 214
    The system doesn't respond to Ctrl-Alt-Del 214

Chapter 6: Taking Control of the Display and Keyboard 217
We Want a Color TV! We Want a Color TV! 217
Reviewing ANSI.SYS Techniques 218
    Sending instructions to ANSI.SYS 218
        Using batch files 219
        Using the TYPE command 220
        Using PROMPT 220
        Sending multiple escape sequences 221
    Determining whether ANSI.SYS is loaded 222
Jazzing Up the Display 223
    Setting foreground and background colors 224
    Setting display attributes 225
    Positioning the cursor 226
    Pulling it all together 227
    Creating fancy prompts 230

Customizing the Keyboard 232
  Key codes 232
  How to remap keys 237
  How to assign strings or commands to keys 237
Going Beyond ANSI.SYS...239

Chapter 7: Juggling IRQs, DMAs, Buses, Device Drivers, and Other "What's Its" 241

Looking under the Hood 241
Understanding Interrupts and IRQ Conflicts 242
  Interrupting the microprocessor 242
  Interrupt vectors 243
  Interrupt request lines 244
  Reviewing your IRQ assignments 246
Understanding DMA 247
Which Bus Is Best: ISA, MCA, or EISA? 248
  The role of the bus 249
  The ISA bus 249
  The MCA bus 251
  The EISA bus 252
  Recent bus innovations 255
    The local bus 255
    SCSI, the UnBus 256
    What's next? 257
Deciphering Device Drivers 257

Chapter 8: Power System Configuration Techniques 261

Interrupting and Controlling the Boot Cycle 261
  Using the clean-start key 262
  Using the interactive start key...263
  Forcing a [Y/N] prompt 264
  Controlling start keys with the SWITCHES command 264
Creating Multiboot Configurations 265
  Defining menus 266
    Setting menu defaults 268

Changing menu colors 268
Changing menu headings 269
Combining common commands 269
Using multimenu configurations 272
Providing an escape option 274
Prompting for user confirmation 275
Configuring AUTOEXEC.BAT 276
Checking CONFIG.SYS...278
Checking AUTOEXEC.BAT 281

Part III: Secrets for Automating DOS 283

Chapter 9: Putting DOSKEY to Work 285

Installing DOSKEY 285
Setting Insert Mode 286
Setting the buffer size 286
Reinstalling DOSKEY 287
Using DOSKEY as a Command-Line Manager 287
Editing the command line 287
Using the command history 288
My top five (forgotten) DOSKEY commands 288
Selecting commands by number 288
Using characters to select commands 289
Saving a command without executing it 289
Executing two or more commands at a time.................290
Erasing the entire command history 290
Using DOSKEY Macros 290
Accessing command-line switches 291
Piping and redirection with DOSKEY 292
Entering multiple commands 293
Building a macro builder 293
Comparing DOSKEY Macros to Batch Files 294
My Favorite DOSKEY Macro Tricks 295
Question-mark help 295
Replacing, enhancing, and disabling DOS commands 296

Intercepting drive changes 297
Supporting multiple filenames 297
Extending the search path 298
And some quickies to finish 298
Going Beyond DOSKEY with ANARKEY 299
Command-line editing 299
Environment editing..300
History lists 301
Macros 302
The MegaKey and MenuKey shortcuts 302

Chapter 10: Moving Beyond Basic Batch Files 305
The Tools of the Trade 305
A batch file command summary 306
It's about time we had a choice 308
Editor tips 311
Power Techniques That Use Redirection and Pipes 313
Just say yes 314
Just be quiet 315
Displaying command output selectively 316
Environment Innovations 317
Temporarily changing the search path 318
Managing the TEMP variable 320
Saving and restoring the environment 320
Uppercasing input 321
Dates, Times, and Batch Files 323
Waiting for a while 323
What day of the week is it?...324
What time is it? 324
Waiting for a specific time 325
Running batch files once a day 327
A Batch File Potpourri 328
Does a directory exist? 328
Checking for wildcards 329
Checking the DOS version 330
Checking for TSRs 330
Saving the current directory 331

Using Batch Files with Windows 3.1 332
   Controlling DOS session settings 332
   Exploiting WINSTART.BAT 333
   Using the new command /K switch 334
   Checking for Windows 3.1 334
Batch File Enhancers 335
   Adding pizzazz with Batutil 335
   Putting batch files in overdrive with TURBOBAT 336

Chapter 11: Demystifying DEBUG 337
Understanding VCRs, Understanding DEBUG 337
Getting Acquainted with DEBUG Editing Capabilities 338
Using DEBUG Commands 339
   DEBUG command reference 339
      The ? (help) command 340
      The A command 340
      The C command 341
      The D command 341
      The E command 342
      The F command 342
      The G command 342
      The H command 342
      The I command 343
      The L command 343
      The M command 343
      The N command 344
      The O command 344
      The P command 344
      The Q command 344
      The R command 344
      The S command 345
      The T command 345
      The U command 345
      The W command 345
      The XA command 346
      The XD command 346
      The XM command 346
      The XS command 346

How to enter DEBUG commands 346
  Taking a test drive 347
  Creating ASCII script files 349
Patching Programs with DEBUG 350
  Changing the CHOICE command 350
  Patching the default EDIT filemask 352
Creating Useful Utilities with DEBUG 355
  Returning to DOS and setting an ERRORLEVEL 355
  Working with dates 356
  Writing keyboard management utilities 358
    Checking and changing the state of special keys 358
    Rebooting the PC 361
    Waiting for a function key 361
  Creating disk and drive utilities 363
    Abort, Retry, Fail? Not! 363
    A script to determine the boot drive 365

Part IV: The Complete DOS 6 Command Reference 367

Part V: Bob's Better-Than-DOS Shareware Collection 603

Part VI: Appendixes 807

Appendix A: Installing DOS 6 809
Upgrading to DOS 6 809
Installing to Floppies 810
Installing a Minimum Configuration 811
Installing the Windows Components of DOS 6 812
Installing DOS 6 Manually 812
Installing to a Nonboot Drive 812
Uninstalling DOS 6 813

Appendix B: DOS Command Quick Reference 815
Standard DOS 6 Files 815
Files Installed Only When an Older Version of the File Is Present
  on the System 822
Files Used by SETUP but Not Installed 823
Old Files Available on the DOS 6 Supplemental Disk 823

Appendix C: ANSI.SYS Quick Reference 825

   Color Display Codes Used with Esc[codem 825
   Display Attribute Codes Used with Esc[codem 826
   Text Erasing Codes 826
   Cursor-Control Codes 826
   Display Mode Control Codes 827
   Keyboard Control Codes 828

Appendix D: Interacting with Workgroups and Networks 831

   The InterLink Connection 831
     Wiring the two computers together 831
     Establishing an InterLink connection 832
       How to install INTERLNK 832
       How to install INTERSVR 833
       Three easy steps to successful linking 833
     Using server resources 834
     Understanding InterLink limitations 835
   Workgroup Wizardry 835
     Installing the network software 836
     Reviewing network commands 838
     Connecting to a network 838
       Network entries in CONFIG.SYS 839
       How to log on to the network 841
       Password management 842
     Using network resources 843
       Using the Pop-Up utility 843
         Loading and running Pop-Up 843
         Connecting to directories 845
         Connecting to shared printers 846
       Using the command-line utilities 846
         Viewing resources with NET VIEW 846
         Accessing remote directories and printers 847
         Reviewing directory examples 848
         Reviewing printer examples 849
       Accessing CD-ROMs 850
   Mail Secrets 850
     Installing Mail 850
     Running Microsoft Mail 852
     Locating your mail files 852

Receiving new mail 853
Forgetting your password or mailbox name 855
Workgroup Connection Command Reference 855
MAIL 856
  Description 856
  Usage 856
  Options and switches 856
  Remarks 858
  Examples 858
  Additional information 858
MICRO 858
  Description 858
  Usage 858
  Options and switches 858
  Remarks 859
  Examples 860
  Additional information 860
NET 860
  Description 860
NET CONFIG 861
  Description 861
  Usage 861
  Options and switches 861
  Remarks 862
  Example 862
NET LOGOFF 862
  Description 862
  Usage 862
  Options and switches 862
  Remarks 862
  Example 863
NET LOGON 863
  Description 863
  Usage 863
  Options and switches 863
  Remarks 863
  Examples 864
  Additional information 864

NET PASSWORD 865
   Description 865
   Usage 865
   Options and switches 865
   Remarks 865
   Examples 865
   Extended use 866
NET PRINT 866
   Description 866
   Usage 866
   Options and switches 866
   Remarks 867
   Examples 867
   Additional information 868
NET START 868
   Description 868
   Usage 868
   Options and switches 868
   Remarks 869
   Examples 869
   Additional information 870
NET STOP 870
   Description 870
   Usage 870
   Options and switches 870
   Remarks 871
   Examples 871
NET TIME 871
   Description 871
   Usage 871
   Options and switches 871
   Remarks 872
   Example 872
NET USE 872
   Description 872
   Usage 872
   Options and switches 872
   Remarks 874
   Examples 874
   Additional information 875

NET VER 876
    Description 876
    Usage 876
    Options and switches 876
    Remarks 876
NET VIEW 876
    Description 876
    Usage 876
    Options and switches 876
    Remarks 877
    Examples 877

Appendix E: Additional DOS Information Sources **879**
Microsoft Telephone Support 879
Magazines and Periodicals 879
PC User Groups 880
On-Line Sources 880
Information for Users with Disabilities 881

Index **883**

Disclaimer page **952**

Introduction

DOS 6 began shipping nearly twelve years after the introduction of the first version of DOS in August 1981. During this time, PCs have ascended from humble beginnings to today's systems sporting 128 megabytes of memory and gigabytes of storage space.

The only significant changes in DOS from August 1981 to November 1988 (DOS 4.0) were hardware related, such as adding support of 3½-inch disk drives and networks. DOS 5 was the first version of the operating system that provided significant end-user enhancements — a full-screen editor ousted EDLIN, for example, and DOS 5 came with a reasonable help system to provide users with on-line help.

Interestingly, Microsoft's improved *user orientation* on DOS upgrades came at a time when another vendor, Digital Research (now part of Novell Inc.), was having significant market success with a competitive *friendlier* operating system, DR DOS. As is often the case in the computer business, we, the users, have benefited from vendor competition.

Microsoft has continued its user focus with the introduction of DOS 6. There are plenty of all-new facilities, such as virus protection, sophisticated memory optimization, and on-the-fly disk compression, as well as major improvements to some old war horses like BACKUP.

DOS 6 is packed with new features, utilities, and enhancements, and every DOS user should seriously consider upgrading. For the first time ever, I really enjoyed upgrading my version of DOS.

Why Another DOS Book?

The shelves in computer bookstores are weighed down with DOS books, but *DOS 6 SECRETS* is different from the rest of them.

DOS 6 SECRETS goes beyond a command reference (although a very rich and exhaustive command reference is included); in this book, you are given guidance as to the *importance* and *value* of each command.

DOS 6 SECRETS doesn't go into excruciating detail on obscure and little-used features. You won't find twenty pages discussing the various EDLIN commands, and CTTY is given a lot less coverage than CHOICE. Nor will you have to trudge through lengthy explanations of well-known concepts, such as how to create and change directories or what a filename extension is.

This book shows you how to use DOS in the real world, using practical examples and insights. Throughout the editorial process, everybody involved in *DOS 6 SECRETS* has strived to make sure that the information is not just accurate but that it is *relevant* to the PC user.

The Audience for This Book_____

DOS 6 SECRETS is written for a broad base of PC users, ranging from the infrequent user all the way to a DOS Jedi Master. I do, however, assume that you are familiar with the basic tenets of using DOS, such as editing files, creating and managing directory hierarchies, and so on. If you have never used a PC before or you are just in the early learning stages, I recommend that you first cut your teeth on the excellent IDG book *DOS For Dummies,* 2nd Edition. The target audience for *DOS 6 SECRETS* is quite simply current DOS users who want to learn more.

If you have been using a computer for some time but feel that you are not getting the best results, or you have used a computer that has been installed and set up by someone else and you want to learn more, then *DOS 6 SECRETS* is for you.

This book is also valuable to long-time DOS users who first started using DOS in the early 1980s. Very often these users are experts in the commands that have been around since DOS 1.0. Typically, they have used commands like COPY, DEL, and DIR hundreds of thousands of times. The trouble is, many of the original commands have been improved since the mid 1980s. For example, the old timers know that the /W and /P switches can be used to improve the readability of the output from DIR, but how many realize that the /A switch can be used to display all files — including system and hidden files — or that the /S switch can be used to search all subdirectories?

Finally, if you are an experienced DOS 5 user, remember that DOS 6 is packed with new, very useful features, such as virus protection, on-the-fly disk compression, multiple boot-up configurations, and much more. Particular care has been taken to ensure that these new features are covered in depth.

Armed with *DOS 6 SECRETS,* you'll soon become a DOS 6 Jedi Master.

How This Book Is Organized

The book is organized into five main parts. The first two parts concentrate on how to use the primary DOS commands and how to get the most from your hardware. The third part explains how programming enables complex operations to be reduced to single commands and how routine tasks can be automated. Part IV is an exhaustive command reference to each and every command and option available in DOS. DOS, however, doesn't have all the answers, so the fifth and final part examines a wealth of Shareware and public domain programs that further empower the user. All the programs and utilities discussed in Part V are included on the Bob's Better-Than-DOS Shareware Collection disks.

The appendixes include information on how to install DOS 6, along with at-a-glance command summaries, and information about other ways to increase your DOS knowledge.

Part I: Secrets for an Effective Beginning

The first part of the book focuses on those features of DOS that are mostly used on a regular and frequent basis. The *eighty/twenty rule* states that 80 percent of the time you will use 20 percent of the DOS commands. The primary goal of Part I is to make sure that you are an expert in the most-used 20 percent. You will also learn how to use DOS efficiently and make DOS work for you — and you will pick up good habits to avoid data loss.

Chapter 1, "Taking an Aerial View of DOS 6," provides a flight over the DOS 6 terrain. This chapter discusses each major component of the operating system with particular emphasis on the new features introduced in DOS 6, such as virus protection and data compression. After reading this chapter, you will be ready to enter the DOS 6 inner circle.

Chapter 2, "Mastering the Top DOS Commands," offers an in-depth discussion of the everyday DOS commands. This chapter describes how to get the most from the most popular and frequently used commands like XCOPY and DOSKEY. Some of the best Shareware alternatives are also introduced.

Chapter 3, "Protecting and Recovering That Irreplaceable Data," is a must for every PC user. The data stored in your computer is valuable — probably more valuable than you realize. As my sister used to say, "You'll miss me when I'm gone!" This chapter explains all the measures you should take to ensure that your data is safe and secure. You will learn how specific preventive measures can alert you to problems before they occur as well as how to recover files after disaster has struck. No chapter on data security would be complete without a discussion of backups. This chapter provides detailed guidance on how to establish an efficient, nondisruptive regimen to keep valuable file backups.

Part II: Secret Weapons for Your Hardware

Most of us want more for less. In the case of your PC, you may already have more but don't know it. The second part of *DOS 6 SECRETS* focuses on how to fine-tune DOS so that you really can leverage the performance of your computer hardware. A DOS Jedi must use the power of the hardware. Part II explains how to find and use every nook and cranny of your memory and hard disk, along with ways to jazz up the boring gray and black DOS screen.

Chapter 4, "Making Your Hard Disk Faster, Bigger, and Safer," as the title suggests, explains how to squeeze every last drop of performance and capacity from your hard disk. Improving hard disk performance is the single most effective way of improving your system's overall performance, and this chapter shows you how. You'll learn how a hard disk physically works as well as how DOS and the disk controller maintain detailed records about every file's data. This chapter also explains how to double your storage capacity with the all-new DoubleSpace utility and how to dramatically improve disk performance using a disk cache.

Chapter 5, "Maximizing Memory," starts by explaining all the various memory issues in plain terms. You will learn how the memory *warehouse* stores base, high, upper, extended, and expanded memory. The chapter goes on to explain how you can tune your system using the all new MEMMAKER program to dramatically increase the memory available to your applications.

Chapter 6, "Taking Control of the Display and Keyboard," shows you how ANSI.SYS can be used to give the DOS display a much-needed facelift. This chapter also discusses techniques for customizing the keyboard.

Chapter 7, "Juggling IRQs, DMAs, Buses, Device Drivers, and Other 'What's Its'," explains, in layman's terms, important hardware facts that can help you to overcome conflicts between various devices. For example, your fax board might fight with your scanner for the CPU's attention. This chapter shows you why these conflicts occur and what steps can be taken to resolve them.

Chapter 8, "Power System Configuration Techniques," concludes Part II and explains how to organize your CONFIG.SYS and AUTOEXEC.BAT file to meet all your requirements. Techniques for building boot-up menus (allowing you to choose from more than one configuration set) are presented, together with a checklist of all the items you should include in your boot-up files.

Part III: Secrets for Automating DOS

Computers are meant to automate and simplify tasks. If you find yourself frequently repeating a series of commands or writing cheat-sheet instructions on how to do specific operations, you ought to be thinking of a better way. There is one. Part III explains how to use DOS's own tools to automate and program your computer.

Chapter 9, "Putting DOSKEY to Work," explains how DOSKEY enhances command-line input and shows how DOSKEY's macro facility provides a powerful and easy programming tool. You'll learn how to integrate batch files with DOSKEY, how to save your favorite DOSKEY settings, and how to avoid some of the DOSKEY pitfalls.

Chapter 10, "Moving Beyond Basic Batch Files," shows how to leverage the most power from batch files. You will learn how to prompt the user for input, how to manage the DOS environment, and how to use the batch file programming statements like IF and FOR. The chapter concludes with a look at a variety of batch files that should be in every DOS user's arsenal.

Chapter 11, "Demystifying DEBUG," shows how to make the terse and grumpy DEBUG program work for you. You'll learn how to build very small, compact programs to perform a variety of low-level functions, such as rebooting the system, checking whether a disk is in the drive, and more.

Part IV: The Complete DOS 6 Command Reference

This part of the book provides a complete and thorough reference to all the DOS device drivers and programs. Part IV goes beyond a clinical command reference and provides explanations of how and when each command should be used. Each command is awarded a score on "Bob's Scorecard" indicating its value and merit. The awards range from 10, indicating a very valuable command, to 0, which indicates the command should be locked away in the basement.

Part V: Bob's Better-Than-DOS Shareware Collection

As good as DOS 6 is, there are still many areas where third-party utilities are superior. For example, consider the EDIT command. There is no doubt that EDIT is a great improvement on EDLIN, but it is still lacking in some areas. The Shareware program QEDIT is far superior to EDIT, providing multifile editing, column manipulation for easy indenting, file merging, a macro language, and much more.

DOS 6 SECRETS includes two disks packed with the cream of the Shareware crop. Part V explains how to install the Shareware programs and includes thorough documentation on each program.

Part VI: Appendixes

Appendix A, "Installing DOS 6," provides detailed instructions on how to install and uninstall DOS 6.

Appendix B, "DOS Command Quick Reference," includes a handy quick reference of all the DOS commands and device drivers.

Appendix C, "ANSI.SYS Quick Reference," provides quick references for ANSI.SYS.

Appendix D, "Interacting with Workgroups and Networks," explains how the InterLink commands can be used to connect two PCs and how the Workgroup Connection software can be used with DOS 6 to access devices such as disks, CD-ROMs, and printers on other computers.

Finally, **Appendix E, "Additional DOS Information Sources,"** suggests other sources where you can gain further information on DOS and Shareware in general.

Versions of DOS

From a marketing perspective, it might have been desirable to write this book in such a style that it could be read by users of any version of DOS. But who cares about EDLIN now that there is EDIT or about BACKUP now that there is MSBACKUP! Consequently, this book concentrates on the features available in DOS 5 and, especially, DOS 6. The features newly implemented in DOS 6 are clearly marked with an icon so that users of earlier versions of DOS will know what they are missing.

If you don't know which version of DOS you are using, enter the command ver; DOS will respond with the version number. To be honest, if you are running a system with an earlier version of DOS, you really ought to upgrade to DOS 6.

What's on the Disks?

Good though DOS 6 is, there are still some excellent Shareware programs that run rings around their DOS counterparts. *Bob's Better-Than-DOS Shareware Collection* disks are packed full of the best Shareware utilities available today. In addition to programs which are better than COPY, MOVE, FORMAT, and DIR, you'll find programs for duplicating disks, managing your hard disk, listing files, compressing files and directories, compiling batch files, and much, much more.

Having completed the book, we didn't simply throw a few programs onto the disks and bundle them with the book. The Shareware programs have been carefully selected because, in my opinion, they provide better functionality and performance than the DOS 6 commands. Throughout the text, you will find references to these Shareware programs with clear explanations as to why they have an edge over DOS.

Remember that most of these utilities are Shareware and are not free. Copies have been included on the disks so that you can evaluate them. Use them one or two times; if you want to continue to use them, you should register them. Quite simply, Shareware is a try-before-you-buy honor system. For further information on the Shareware system, along with comprehensive documentation of each program, refer to Part V.

Complete installation instructions appear on the last page of the book.

Conventions Used in This Book _____

Important facts, tips, and suggestions appear in the text with eye-catching icons in the margin. Here is a comprehensive list of the icons scattered throughout the book:

 This icon highlights a special point of interest about the topic under discussion.

 This icon points to a useful hint that might save you time or trouble.

 This icon alerts you to potential problems.

 This icon, which is used in Part IV, "The Complete DOS 6 Command Reference," points to a more complete discussion of the commands in the chapters of the book and also points you to related commands.

This icon highlights information that gives you some special insight into the topic under discussion.

This icon alerts you that the item under discussion is included on Bob's Better-Than-DOS Shareware Collection disks packaged with the book.

This icon alerts you to a subject that is new to DOS 6.

This icon points to information that is not available in the DOS documentation.

This icon highlights explanations of error messages that DOS displays when problems occur.

This icon points to technical discussions that you may want to read to be a well-rounded DOS Jedi.

This icon, which is used in Chapter 1, identifies text that discusses some of DOS 6's trouble spots.

Sidebars

Sidebars are often used to discuss an item in greater detail. For example, one sidebar explains how file undeletion actually works, whereas the main text just explains how to undelete a file. Other times, the sidebars are more anecdotal and provide some general background material, such as the history of the UART chip. If you don't want to delve too deeply into a subject, just read the body of the text and skip most of the sidebars.

How Commands Are Explained

Listed next are some of the conventions used to identify commands and keystrokes:

- All DOS commands mentioned within a paragraph are displayed in UPPERCASE letters.

- Key combinations in which you hold down one key and press another are shown in hyphenated format. Ctrl-F10, for example, indicates that you hold down the Ctrl key while you press F10.

- Key combinations pressed in sequence are separated by commas (Ctrl-PgUp, down arrow, down arrow).

- *Italic* type is used for new terms or emphasis, as well as variable items in command syntax lines.

- For commands selected from DOS-based menus, **bold** is used to indicate the letter the user presses to choose the command (**O**ptions⇨Help **P**ath). For commands selected from Windows-based menus, an <u>underline</u> is used to indicate the letter the user presses to choose the command (<u>F</u>ile⇨<u>N</u>ew⇨<u>G</u>roup).

- On-screen information and batch file listings appear in a `special typeface`.

- Literal commands that you type appear in a `bold special typeface`.

Most of the DOS commands can accept varying numbers and types of options or switches. For example, when you execute the change directory command, CD, with no options, DOS displays the default directory. However, when you specify a directory path, DOS tries to change the default directory to the specified path.

Although this makes for a flexible command mechanism, it is a pain to document. A special syntax is used to define each command and its switches. For example, the syntax for the CD command is defined as follows:

```
cd [drive:][path] or [..]
```

I admit that the syntax is daunting at first, but once understood, it provides a very convenient and concise way to document a command.

At the beginning of Part IV you will find a thorough explanation of the syntax. In brief, optional commands are included in square brackets, and required command components are not in brackets. If all the options and switches are themselves surrounded by square brackets, the command can be executed without any of them, as is the case in the preceding CD example. Note also that variable elements appear in italics.

Note: This syntax is very similar to that used in the DOS 6 on-line help.

Give Us Feedback

The best products in the computer marketplace are the ones that have been molded and shaped by user feedback. And so it is for computer books. We sincerely solicit your feedback and criticism. Please write to me in care of IDG Books at the following address:

IDG Books Worldwide
3250 N. Post Road, Ste. 140
Indianapolis, IN 46226

Or you can contact me through CompuServe. My CompuServe ID is 74017,227.

By the way, I'd especially like to hear *your* DOS secrets.

Enough preliminaries, let's get busy.

Part I:
Secrets for an Effective Beginning

Page 13 ◇ **Chapter 1**
Taking an Aerial View of DOS 6

Page 39 ◇ **Chapter 2**
Mastering the Top DOS Commands

Page 71 ◇ **Chapter 3**
Protecting and Recovering That
Irreplaceable Data

Chapter 1

Taking an Aerial View of DOS 6

In This Chapter

▶ Introduction to the new and improved DOS

▶ A look at some DOS 6 drawbacks

▶ A quick guide to using important DOS 6 commands and programs

Something to Write Home About

Past upgrades of DOS left me cold. They seemed to offer few real improvements — just a new switch for FORMAT here, support for 3 ½-inch drives there, and maybe an occasional extra switch. Every now and then, an upgrade provided something interesting, such as a full-screen editor or the ability to load DOS high, but more often than not, upgrades were incremental and often hardware related. They were necessary, no doubt, but not a lot to excite most users.

The DOS 6 upgrade is different. It offers a bevy of new applications and features, such as a real backup system, anti-virus tools, on-the-fly disk compression, and a lot more. This new, user-oriented version of DOS embraces many functions previously left to the third-party utilities market.

Of course, DOS 6 does have some warts. One flaw is that the keystrokes used to perform certain functions vary depending on the situation. For example, you sometimes press Alt-X to quit, but other times you press Ctrl-F4. Another blemish is that programs such as XCOPY still don't take advantage of extended memory. But despite these and other drawbacks, DOS 6 is well worth writing home about.

This chapter provides a summary of the most interesting new features introduced in DOS 6 and also discusses some of its trouble spots.

 The special thumbs-down icon is used in this chapter to identify text that discusses some of those DOS 6 warts!

Configuration Flexibility

Several new enhancements make CONFIG.SYS far more flexible than ever before. The most-publicized improvement is the support of new start-up menu commands. Other enhancements include new keys to interrupt the normal boot cycle and control command execution, plus a new ? switch to force a confirmation prompt before a device driver is loaded.

Configuration menus

With so many add-on hardware devices installed in PCs these days, many users resort to multiple configuration files. One CONFIG.SYS and AUTOEXEC.BAT pair might be used to install a scanner and digitizing tablet for desktop publishing, and another pair might load a mouse and log on to a network for normal day-to-day activities. Prior to DOS 6, users either had to purchase a third-party utility that supported multiple configurations or write batch files to copy the appropriate configuration files to the root directory and reboot.

Now, DOS provides special menu commands that enable you to place all your diverse configuration commands in a single copy of CONFIG.SYS. When the system boots, you are presented with a list of menu choices. You select a menu option, and DOS executes the specific commands associated with that option. The following is a typical boot menu:

```
MS-DOS 6 Startup Menu
========================


      1. Clean (Most Memory)
      2. Laptop Connection
      3. Standard
```

You can control the format of the menu using the new commands described in Table 1-1.

The following CONFIG.SYS file created the menu shown earlier:

```
[menu]
menuitem=Clean,Clean (Most Memory)
menuitem=Interlink,Laptop Connection
menuitem=Normal,Standard

[common]
BUFFERS=15,0
FILES=30
LASTDRIVE=G
```

Table 1-1	New Menu Commands
Command	**Description**
[MENU]	Marks the beginning of the menu definition block.
MENUITEM	Creates an item on the menu and identifies the name of the associated configuration block. When the user selects the menu item, DOS executes the commands in the specified configuration block.
SUBMENU	Creates a branch to a secondary menu, thereby providing nested or multilevel configuration menus.
[*BLOCKNAME*]	Every blockname specified with the MENUITEM and SUBMENU commands must have a corresponding block defined. The commands following the menu block are executed when the user selects the corresponding menu item.
MENUDEFAULT	Sets the default item in a menu and, optionally, the number of seconds DOS waits for user input before applying the default.
INCLUDE	Includes the commands from one configuration block in another.
MENUCOLOR	Sets the display colors for the menu.

```
[Clean]
FCBS=4,0

[Normal]
DEVICE=C:\DOS\HIMEM.SYS
DEVICE=C:\DOS\EMM386.EXE RAM
DOS=HIGH,UMB
FCBS=4,0
SHELL=C:\DOS\COMMAND.COM C:\DOS\  /p
DEVICEHIGH /L:1,47296 =C:\DOS\DBLSPACE.SYS

[InterLink]
DEVICE=C:\DOS\HIMEM.SYS
DEVICE=C:\DOS\EMM386.EXE RAM
DOS=HIGH,UMB
DEVICE=C:\DOS\INTERLNK.EXE /DRIVES:5
```

 All configuration commands placed in a special block called [COMMON] are executed no matter which option is selected.

DOS 6 provides no specific enhancements to AUTOEXEC.BAT that are related to the multiple configuration feature, but it does give you an easy way to synchronize AUTOEXEC.BAT and CONFIG.SYS. When you make a selection from the start-up menu, DOS creates an environment variable with the name CONFIG and assigns it the name of the selected menu option. By testing the value of the CONFIG variable, you can branch to a specific part of AUTOEXEC.BAT as follows:

```
goto %CONFIG%
```

Refer to Chapter 8 for a thorough discussion of the new multiple configuration feature.

Interruption keys

If you ever pounded on the Ctrl-Break key to try to stop DOS from executing the start-up commands during system boot, you will be pleased to hear that DOS 6 provides you with two special keys that make it easy to suspend, stop, or selectively execute the start-up commands.

When the system boots, DOS displays the following message for approximately 2 seconds:

```
Starting MS-DOS...
```

If you press F5 (or hold down the Shift key) while this message is displayed, DOS ignores all the commands in CONFIG.SYS and AUTOEXEC.BAT and immediately displays the DOS prompt. This procedure is referred to as *clean booting*.

If you want to execute some, but not all, start-up commands, you can press F8 when the Starting MS-DOS... message is displayed. DOS then displays each command in turn and prompts you to press Y or N to indicate whether the command should be executed. After all the CONFIG.SYS commands are processed, DOS asks for confirmation before executing AUTOEXEC.BAT.

If you step through some commands and then want to exit without processing any more CONFIG.SYS commands, you can take a shortcut: Press the F5 key while DOS is prompting for confirmation. Similarly, if you are stepping through the CONFIG.SYS commands and decide that you want to execute all remaining commands along with AUTOEXEC.BAT, you can simply press Esc. DOS stops prompting you for confirmation and executes all remaining commands.

The SWITCHES configuration command (which is used in CONFIG.SYS) was enhanced so that you can disable the interruption keys, ensuring that all CONFIG.SYS commands are executed without user intervention. The /F switch instructs DOS to proceed without pausing for 2 seconds when the message Starting MS-DOS... is displayed. The /N switch instructs DOS to ignore the interruption keys F5, Shift, and F8.

A new switch for device drivers

You can instruct DOS 6 to prompt you for confirmation before it executes statements in CONFIG.SYS. You can force a [Y/N] confirmation prompt on any statement (except switches) by inserting a question-mark character (?) before the equals character (=) in the statement. After you make this change, DOS always prompts you for confirmation before executing the statement.

Suppose, for example, that sometimes you load a device driver for a CD-ROM but other times you don't. The following statement installs the device driver with the new ? switch:

```
device?=c:\proaudio\tslcdr.sys /d:MVCD001 /r /p:3
```

If you use such a statement, DOS prompts you for confirmation before loading the device driver. I wish the same feature were available in batch files.

Further details about the new boot interruption keys and the enhancements to SWITCHES are provided in Chapter 8.

On-Line Help

DOS 5 introduced the notion of an on-line help system for DOS commands. When you entered the HELP command and a command name, DOS displayed a single screen of information about the specified command.

DOS 6 takes this idea further. It provides a full-blown hypertext help system that offers pages of useful information about almost every command and device driver. If you enter the command HELP with no switches, a full-screen menu is displayed, as illustrated in Figure 1-1.

You can request information about specific commands by clicking on the command name with the mouse or by tabbing to a command and pressing Enter. You can even search for all topics that contain a specific word or phrase. Most commands and device drivers have three sections of help: syntax, notes, and examples. Figure 1-2 shows part of the notes for the XCOPY command.

To exit the help system, press Alt-F, X.

The FASTHELP command provides an additional help resource. If you enter the FASTHELP command, DOS displays a brief list that shows each DOS command along with the supported switches. You can access additional switch information by entering a specific command followed by the /? switch. For example, to display the switches supported by XCOPY, you enter the following command:

```
xcopy /?
```

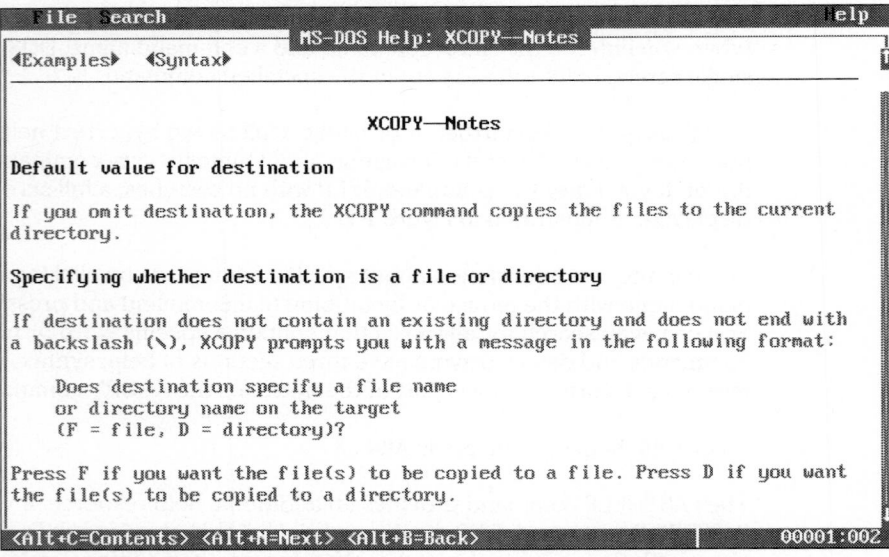

```
 File  Search                                                      Help
┌──────────────────── MS-DOS Help: Command Reference ────────────────────┐
│Use the scroll bars to see more commands. Or, press the PAGE DOWN key. For│
│more information about using MS-DOS Help, choose How to Use MS-DOS Help   │
│from the Help menu, or press F1. To exit MS-DOS Help, press ALT, F, X.    │
│                                                                          │
│  <ANSI.SYS>              <Erase>              <Multi-config>             │
│  <Append>                <Exit>               <Nlsfunc>                  │
│  <Attrib>                <Expand>             <Numlock>                  │
│  <Batch commands>        <Fasthelp>           <Path>                     │
│  <Break>                 <Fastopen>           <Pause>                    │
│  <Buffers>               <Fc>                 <Power>                    │
│  <Call>                  <Fcbs>               <POWER.EXE>                │
│  <Cd>                    <Fdisk>              <Print>                    │
│  <Chcp>                  <Files>              <Prompt>                   │
│  <Chdir>                 <Find>               <Qbasic>                   │
│  <Chkdsk>                <For>                <RAMDRIVE.SYS>             │
│  <CHKSTATE.SYS>          <Format>             <Rd>                       │
│  <Choice>                <Goto>               <Rem>                      │
│  <Cls>                   <Graphics>           <Ren>                      │
│  <Command>               <Help>               <Rename>                   │
│  <CONFIG.SYS commands>   <HIMEM.SYS>          <Replace>                  │
│  <Copy>                  <If>                 <Restore>                  │
│<Alt+C=Contents> <Alt+N=Next> <Alt+B=Back>            N 00006:002        │
└──────────────────────────────────────────────────────────────────────────┘
```

Figure 1-1: The Help menu.

```
 File  Search                                                      Help
┌──────────────────── MS-DOS Help: XCOPY—Notes ─────────────────────┐
│ ◄Examples►  ◄Syntax►                                              │
│                                                                    │
│                        XCOPY—Notes                                 │
│                                                                    │
│Default value for destination                                       │
│                                                                    │
│If you omit destination, the XCOPY command copies the files to the  │
│current directory.                                                  │
│                                                                    │
│Specifying whether destination is a file or directory               │
│                                                                    │
│If destination does not contain an existing directory and does not  │
│end with a backslash (\), XCOPY prompts you with a message in the   │
│following format:                                                   │
│                                                                    │
│     Does destination specify a file name                           │
│     or directory name on the target                                │
│     (F = file, D = directory)?                                     │
│                                                                    │
│Press F if you want the file(s) to be copied to a file. Press D if  │
│you want the file(s) to be copied to a directory.                   │
│<Alt+C=Contents> <Alt+N=Next> <Alt+B=Back>           00001:002      │
└────────────────────────────────────────────────────────────────────┘
```

Figure 1-2: An example of Help notes.

In general, the DOS 6 help system is excellent, but it presents a few minor irritations. The help information for some topics, for example, extends beyond one screenful. You can scroll down to read all the text, but when you jump from topic to topic, you encounter an annoying feature. Suppose that you're reading a lower part of the help screen for one topic and then jump to the help screen for a second topic. If you jump back to the first topic (by pressing Alt-B), DOS sends you back to the top line of that topic's help text, even though you were viewing a lower part of the text originally. Few other hypertext help systems, including that for Windows, suffer from this ailment.

Also, if you are viewing the main help index (or contents) and press a character, DOS jumps the cursor to the first command that begins with that letter. So far, so good. But if you immediately type a second character, DOS jumps to a command that begins with the new letter instead of homing in on a command that matches the first two characters. If you want to jump to the EDIT command, for instance, you might press the E key. DOS jumps to ECHO, the first command beginning with E. If you then press the D key, DOS jumps to the DATE command, the first command beginning with D. It should jump to EDIT, the only command beginning with the letters ED. Ah, well.

The main on-line help code is contained in the QBASIC.EXE file. Behind the scenes, HELP.COM calls QBASIC with the /QHELP switch (which must be uppercase). If you delete QBASIC.EXE, you won't be able to use the HELP command. Also, the help text is stored in the binary file HELP.HLP in the DOS directory. This file cannot be directly edited. However, if you have the Microsoft C Compiler version 6 or later, you can customize the help text. This technique is discussed further in the next chapter.

Advanced Memory Management

Computer users want to get the most value from installed memory. With past versions of DOS, most *power* users resorted to third-party memory managers, such as QEMM, from Quarterdeck Office Systems, or 386MAX, from Qualitas, to make the best use of the 640K base memory. DOS 6, however, offers memory management capabilities similar to those provided by third-party memory managers. The new memory management tools come in the form of MEMMAKER and enhanced versions of EMM386.EXE, LOADHIGH, and DEVICEHIGH. These enhanced programs can squeeze more than 100K of extra upper memory out of a system — much more than was possible with DOS 5.

The bad news is that these tools only function on 386+ systems.

Although DOS seems to be leaving AT-class users behind, some terrific third-party utilities are available for these older systems. Bob's Shareware Collection disks include the excellent memory manager UMB_DRVR.SYS, from Christopher Blum. Among other things, UMB_DRVR.SYS can take advantage of the shadow

RAM on many of the 286 chip sets and can offer as much as 224K of upper memory on 286 systems. What's more, UMB_DRVR.SYS provides considerable advantages for 386 users, including the ability to load HIMEM.SYS high.

Memory optimization tools

The art of memory optimization involves pushing as many programs and device drivers into upper memory as possible. The DEVICEHIGH and LOADHIGH commands are responsible for loading such software into upper memory. Both DEVICEHIGH and LOADHIGH are enhanced in DOS 6 with switches that enable you to control the precise amount and region of upper memory used for installation of a device driver or program.

You use the /L switch to identify the upper memory region where the software should be loaded. If the program needs more memory to install than it does to run, you can use the /S switch to shrink the memory allocation after the software is installed.

To help with memory analysis, the MEM command was enhanced so that it displays the amount of free UMBs when you use the /FREE switch. Also, MEM's /D switch shows which upper memory regions are occupied by each program.

Making optimum use of installed memory can be a complicated business. Even the order in which devices are loaded into upper memory can have a profound impact on the number of programs that can be loaded high. All these new switches are of little use if you can't determine which software should be loaded where and how much memory the programs need after they are installed.

Fortunately, DOS 6 has a very practical and effective solution to this problem. The program MEMMAKER analyzes your system, experiments a little, and then configures your system to make the best use of memory. All you have to do is configure your CONFIG.SYS and AUTOEXEC.BAT files so that your normal device drivers and programs are loaded — you don't need to worry about loading them high. If you then run MEMMAKER, DOS assesses your system and reconfigures it to make the most of installed memory.

You can run MEMMAKER in Express Mode or Custom Mode. In Express Mode, MEMMAKER asks only one question before proceeding with the optimization: whether any programs need expanded memory support. If so, MEMMAKER automatically configures EMM386 to provide an EMS page frame in upper memory. Otherwise, that 64K of upper memory is used to create UMBs to load device drivers and programs high.

Selecting Custom Mode usually provides the highest degree of optimization and therefore increases the amount of available conventional memory. In Custom Mode, you can specify six advanced options (see Figure 1-3) that control many of the EMM386.EXE settings. One quick way to increase upper memory space on systems equipped with color displays is to set the Use monochrome region for running programs option to Yes.

After you make your selections, MEMMAKER moves ahead with the optimization procedure. Its primary objective is to determine how much memory device drivers and programs need. To perform this analysis, MEMMAKER uses two special utilities: CHKSTATE.SYS and SIZER.EXE.

MEMMAKER modifies CONFIG.SYS and adds a new line to the beginning of the file to load the CHKSTATE device driver. If the HIMEM.SYS, EMM386, and DOS=UMB statements are missing, MEMMAKER adds them. Each device statement is modified so that SIZER.EXE is used to load the device drivers and to observe them as they are loaded. AUTOEXEC.BAT is also modified so that SIZER.EXE can observe each program as it loads.

After the configuration files are modified, MEMMAKER reboots the system, and CHKSTATE.SYS and SIZER.EXE observe and gather statistics as the device drivers and programs are loaded. Using this data, MEMMAKER calculates which programs should be loaded into upper memory, in what order they should be

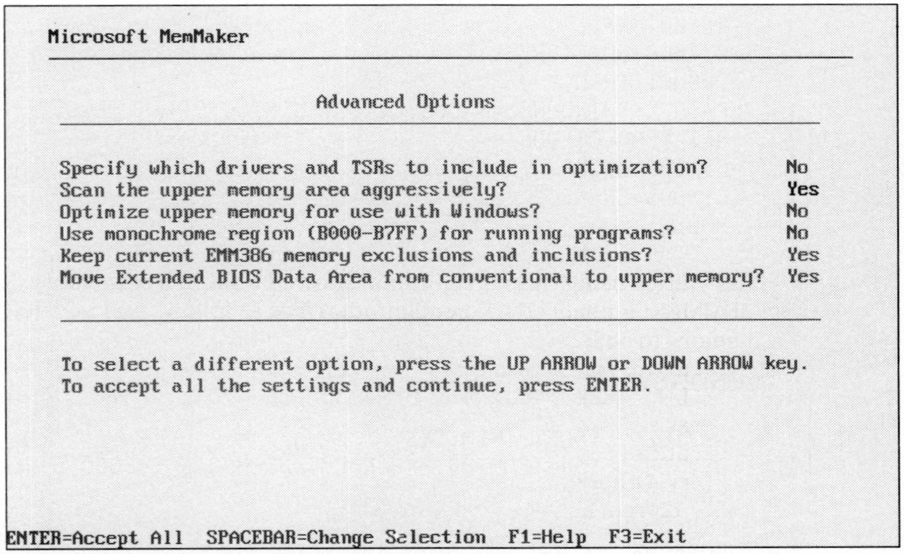

```
 Microsoft MemMaker


                          Advanced Options


     Specify which drivers and TSRs to include in optimization?    No
     Scan the upper memory area aggressively?                      Yes
     Optimize upper memory for use with Windows?                   No
     Use monochrome region (B000-B7FF) for running programs?       No
     Keep current EMM386 memory exclusions and inclusions?         Yes
     Move Extended BIOS Data Area from conventional to upper memory? Yes



     To select a different option, press the UP ARROW or DOWN ARROW key.
     To accept all the settings and continue, press ENTER.



 ENTER=Accept All  SPACEBAR=Change Selection  F1=Help  F3=Exit
```

Figure 1-3: Advanced MEMMAKER options.

loaded, and how much memory they need. In some extreme cases, MEMMAKER may compute more than 20,000 different configuration permutations before identifying the optimum one. Based on these computations, further edits are made to the configuration files, and the system is rebooted. Bingo, your system is optimized.

You can use the file MEMMAKER.INF, located in the DOS directory, to control which device drivers and programs are not analyzed or executed by MEMMAKER. This file contains a list of programs and device drivers and can be easily customized with EDIT. Any program preceded by an asterisk is not modified by MEMMAKER but is executed. All other programs are completely ignored by MEMMAKER and are not run during the optimization process.

Listed next are the configuration files from a typical (not very well-configured) system:

CONFIG.SYS:

```
DEVICE=C:\DOS\HIMEM.SYS
DEVICE=C:\DOS\EMM386.EXE
DEVICE=C:\DOS\DBLSPACE.SYS /MOVE
BUFFERS=15,0
FILES=30
DOS=HIGH
```

AUTOEXEC.BAT:

```
@ECHO OFF
C:\DOS\SMARTDRV.EXE
PROMPT $P$G
PATH C:\WINDOWS;C:\DOS;C:\;C:\U\MISC;C:\BATFILES
SET TEMP=C:\DOS
C:\DOS\DOSKEY /BUFSIZE=1024
C:\DOS\SHARE
MOUSE
```

The system using this configuration showed 515K of free memory. Running MEMMAKER changed the configuration files as follows and boosted the free memory to 589K:

CONFIG.SYS:

```
DEVICE=C:\DOS\HIMEM.SYS
DEVICE=C:\DOS\EMM386.EXE NOEMS HIGHSCAN I=B000-B7FF
BUFFERS=15,0
FILES=30
DOS=UMB
```

```
LASTDRIVE=I
FCBS=16,8
DEVICEHIGH /L:2,44432 =C:\DOS\DBLSPACE.SYS /MOVE
DOS=HIGH
```

AUTOEXEC.BAT:

```
@ECHO OFF
LH /L:0 C:\DOS\SMARTDRV.EXE
PROMPT $P$G
PATH C:\WINDOWS;C:\DOS;C:\;C:\U\MISC;C:\BATFILES
SET TEMP=C:\DOS
LH /L:1,6400 C:\DOS\DOSKEY /BUFSIZE=1024
LH /L:1,13984 C:\DOS\SHARE
LH /L:2,56928 MOUSE
```

 Unfortunately, MEMMAKER is not adept at handling a CONFIG.SYS file with multiple configurations. The only practical solution is to run MEMMAKER several times, changing CONFIG.SYS and AUTOEXEC.BAT each time to reflect a different configuration option. After optimizing each configuration separately, you can then rebuild a consolidated CONFIG.SYS and AUTOEXEC.BAT. Ugh.

EMM386 enhancements

Before DOS 6, you could use the MEMORY switch to instruct EMM386 to reserve part of extended memory to emulate expanded memory. The main weakness of this approach was that the memory literally was reserved and could be used only for expanded memory.

The DOS 6 version of EMM386 offers significant improvements over its predecessor, as it provides expanded and extended memory from a *pool*. If a program needs expanded memory, memory is taken from the pool and presented to the program as expanded memory. Similarly, if extended memory is required, it too can be allocated from the common memory pool.

In earlier versions of DOS, EMM386 defaulted to providing EMS only, and the RAM switch was used explicitly to instruct EMM386 to provide EMS *and* UMB support. With DOS 6, EMM386 defaults to provide EMS and UMB support.

Also, EMM386 now automatically includes the region c000-efff.

Chapter 5 explores all the new memory management features and explains a variety of techniques for optimizing the amount of available memory.

Virus Protection

A software virus is a program that is designed to propagate from system to system undetected. After some trigger event, such as booting the system on or after a specific date, many virus programs try to destroy valuable data by damaging the FAT, formatting the disk, or randomly writing to disk sectors. Virus programs are unwanted and harmful. Although it is true that far more data is destroyed by user error, every prudent user should take measures to protect against virus infection.

For the first time, DOS includes anti-virus tools. The MSAV program can search for and remove viruses, and the memory-resident VSAFE program can guard against infection and protect the disk areas commonly attacked by viruses.

 A Windows version of MSAV, called MWAV, is discussed in a later section.

MSAV is a full-screen program that provides two options. You can just search for viruses, or you can perform the search and eradicate any viruses that are discovered (see Figure 1-4). These processes are referred to as *scanning* and *cleaning,* respectively.

Most known viruses leave a specific pattern of bytes, known as *virus signatures,* in an infected file. MSAV searches for these signatures in all files on the selected drive(s). New virus strains are discovered every month, so MSAV must be

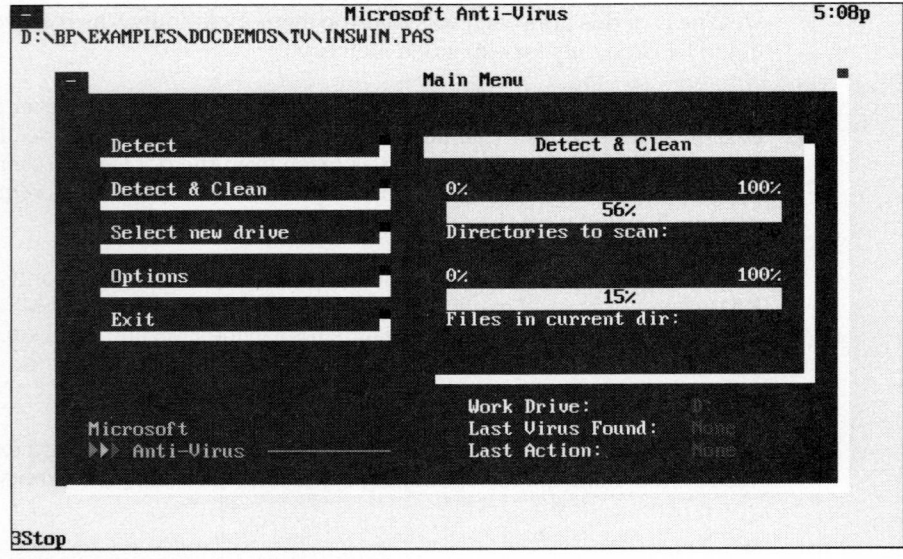

Figure 1-4: The full-screen MSAV program.

updated on a regular basis to look for these signatures. You can update the DOS virus programs by downloading the updated signature files from a dedicated bulletin board system. Further details are explained in Chapter 3.

MSAV also offers an optional generic virus-identification method that uses *checksums* to identify suspicious changes in a program file. A checksum is a numerical value derived by applying a special algorithm to the individual bytes in a file. When a file is changed, so is the checksum. By comparing a file's current computed checksum to a checksum created previously, you can ascertain whether the file has been changed.

MSAV is designed to scan an entire drive and cannot be configured to scan an individual directory. Bob's Shareware Collection disks include SCAN, from McAfee Associates. SCAN is a very flexible and fast virus-detection utility and is part of the renowned anti-virus tools from McAfee Associates. Refer to Part V for further information.

VSAFE is a memory-resident program that monitors program and disk activity. If some program tries to make a suspicious change to the disk (such as modifying the boot sector or an EXE file), VSAFE displays a dialog box to alert you and prompts you for confirmation before allowing the change to occur. VSAFE does not check for specific brands of viruses. It protects the areas usually infected by viruses and so provides generic protection against all viruses.

Heavy-Duty Disk Utilities

Until recently, DOS provided third-rate tools for managing data stored on hard disks. BACKUP and RESTORE were jokes, the disk cache was one of the slowest on the market, and programs such as RECOVER did more harm than good.

Many software developers built large corporations by creating products that filled the gap in the DOS hard-disk arsenal. At long last, Microsoft has acknowledged that the operating system needs to provide real disk utilities and has introduced some industrial-strength disk utilities in DOS 6. In fact, the UNDELETE and BACKUP tools (as well as the anti-virus tools discussed earlier) were licensed from some of the major disk-utility companies. If you can't beat 'em, join 'em.

DoubleSpace disk compression

One of the most eagerly anticipated features of DOS 6 was the all-new DoubleSpace disk compression facility. Like SuperStor, from Addstor Inc., and Stacker, from Stac Electronics, DoubleSpace uses space on an existing drive to create a new compressed drive. For example, DoubleSpace can take 20MB of free space on a drive and create a new drive that can hold about 40MB of files. Similarly, it can compress a 100MB C drive to provide storage for approximately 200MB of files.

A DoubleSpace drive actually is a large hidden file that is stored in the root directory of a physical drive. The DoubleSpace device driver DBLSPACE.BIN tricks DOS into thinking that there is an additional hard drive, in much the same way that RAMDRIVE.SYS makes DOS believe an area of memory is a disk.

Whenever a program (including DOS) tries to save data to a compressed drive, DoubleSpace intercepts the request, compresses the data, and then saves the compressed data in the hidden file. When a program tries to read a file from the compressed drive, DoubleSpace reads the data from the hidden file, decompresses the data, and then passes it on to the program. The programs are oblivious to the data compression tasks taking place behind the scenes.

You might think that all this behind-the-scenes compression and decompression would significantly slow down your system, but that isn't usually true. One of the slowest procedures in a PC is the physical reading and writing of data to the surface of the disk. In many cases, the delay incurred while DOS compresses and decompresses data is offset by the time that is saved because 50 percent less data must be physically accessed on the disk surface. Although the exact impact of disk compression varies from system to system, a broad average seems to be that systems operate approximately 5 to 10 percent slower when accessing a compressed drive.

DBLSPACE.BIN

DoubleSpace is arguably the easiest to use of all the disk compression tools, especially when you want to compress your boot drive (for example, drive C). Because DOS accesses the hidden files MSDOS.SYS and IO.SYS during system boot, DOS must boot from an uncompressed drive. After all, DOS wouldn't be able to read these system files if they were compressed.

Most third-party tools maintain two copies of CONFIG.SYS (and sometimes AUTOEXEC.BAT). One copy of CONFIG.SYS is on the uncompressed drive and contains the statement to load the disk compression device driver. As soon as the device driver is loaded, the compressed drive is activated and swapped with the boot drive. The physical boot drive is assigned a new letter (for example, F), and the compressed drive is assigned the letter C.

So far, so good. The problem is that most software (not to mention most users) expects drive C and not drive F (or whatever) to contain the CONFIG.SYS and

AUTOEXEC.BAT files. Two copies of CONFIG.SYS are maintained by the disk compression software. One copy is on the compressed drive (drive C), and another is on the boot drive. Whenever the system boots, the disk compression utility compares the two copies and keeps them synchronized. Sometimes, this requires a second boot during start-up.

DoubleSpace is smarter. There is no device driver entry in CONFIG.SYS for DBLSPACE.BIN, the disk compression device driver. Before even looking at CONFIG.SYS, IO.SYS searches the root directory of the boot drive, looking for the device driver file. If the file is found, it is automatically loaded. Only after the device driver is loaded and the physical boot drive is swapped with the compressed drive does IO.SYS look for CONFIG.SYS. The result is that the real CONFIG.SYS and AUTOEXEC.BAT files reside on the compressed drive.

Because DBLSPACE.BIN is loaded into memory before CONFIG.SYS is processed, it must be loaded into conventional memory. The upper memory area can be used only after HIMEM.SYS and EMM386 are installed. DBLSPACE.BIN is initially loaded at the top of memory, adjacent to the memory area occupied by IO.SYS.

DOS provides another DoubleSpace device driver, called DBLSPACE.SYS, whose purpose is to transfer DBLSPACE.BIN from base memory to upper memory. This device driver is loaded from CONFIG.SYS in the normal manner, using a DEVICE or DEVICEHIGH statement. If CONFIG.SYS contains a statement loading DBLSPACE.SYS with DEVICE, DBLSPACE.BIN is moved to the bottom of base memory. If DBLSPACE.SYS is loaded with DEVICEHIGH, DBLSPACE.BIN is moved to upper memory.

The DBLSPACE command

The DBLSPACE command is used to manage compressed drives. The first time you execute DBLSPACE, it guides you through the process of creating a compressed drive. Like MEMMAKER, DBLSPACE offers an Express Mode and a Custom Mode, and both are very easy to use. In Express Mode, DBLSPACE compresses the boot drive along with all the files on it. In Custom Mode, you can choose which drive is to be compressed, indicate whether existing files should be compressed or left on an uncompressed drive, and control the size and drive letter of the compressed drive.

After you create at least one compressed drive on your system, you can use DBLSPACE to maintain and manage the compressed drives. DBLSPACE can be executed as a command-line utility or as a full-screen utility. For example, you can use the DBLSPACE /LIST command to see a summary of all the drives on your system. The following is a sample of such a summary:

```
Drive   Type                       Total Free   Total Size  CVF Filename
- - - - - - - - - - - - - - - - - - - - - - - - - - - - - - - - - - - - - - - - -

  A     Removable drive          No disk in drive
  B     Floppy drive                  0.04 MB      0.69 MB
  C     Local hard drive              7.79 MB    201.97 MB
  D     Local hard drive             29.87 MB    165.11 MB
  E     Local hard drive             14.82 MB    159.32 MB
  F     Available for DoubleSpace
  G     Available for DoubleSpace
  H     Available for DoubleSpace
  I     Compressed hard drive        29.31 MB     37.00 MB E:\DBLSPACE.001
  J     Compressed hard drive        43.65 MB     43.65 MB D:\DBLSPACE.001
```

Notice that in this example, the compressed drives I and J are actually hidden files called DBLSPACE.001 on drives E and D, respectively.

DoubleSpace allocates space on a sector-by-sector basis, whereas DOS allocates space by clusters. Like standard hard drives, a compressed drive has a boot sector, FAT, and root directory. It also maintains a sector allocation table that maps standard FAT clusters to DoubleSpace sectors.

The hard disk maintenance tools, such as CHKDSK and DEFRAG, are enhanced in DOS 6 so they can perform work on compressed drives. If you execute such utilities on a compressed drive, DOS automatically calls the DoubleSpace versions after the versions that work on the host drive are done.

You can execute DBLSPACE with no switches to launch the full-screen application, as shown in Figure 1-5. From the DoubleSpace menu, you can perform maintenance tasks, such as running CHKDSK or defragmenting files; create new compressed drives; and delete or change the size of existing compressed drives.

Chapter 4 explores many different ways to take full advantage of the new DoubleSpace tools.

 DoubleSpace does support compression of data on diskettes but only in a clumsy way. Even if you don't have any compressed drives on the hard disk, you must boot your system so that the DoubleSpace device driver is installed — that is, with DBLSPACE.BIN in the root directory of the boot drive — just to have compressed data on floppies. This occupies more than 40K of precious RAM. Even more cumbersome is the way you have to mount (with DBLSPACE) each and every compressed diskette before you can access the data on it.

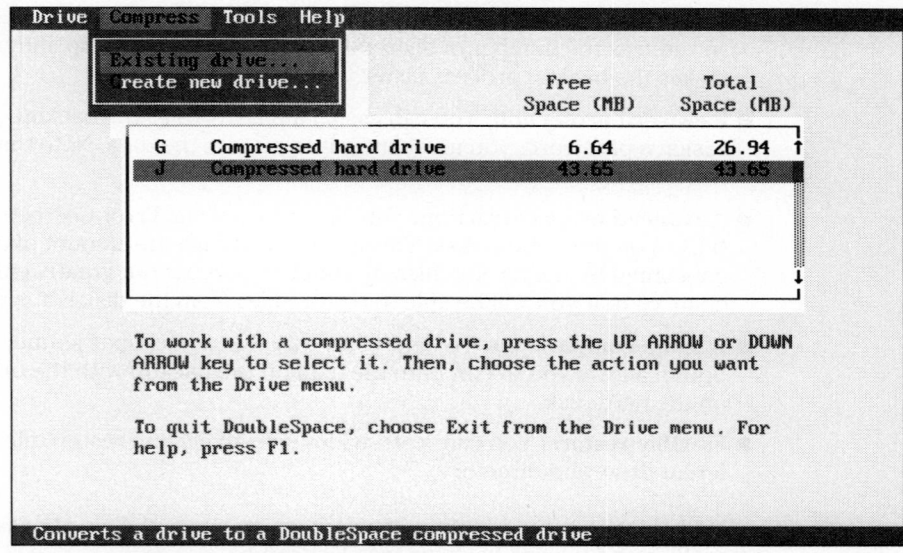

Figure 1-5: The full-screen DBLSPACE utility.

A real backup program

For a long time, the DOS utilities BACKUP and RESTORE were totally outclassed by third-party backup utilities. Experienced DOS users were forced to use non-DOS backup programs because the DOS offerings were so inadequate. Finally, with the introduction of version 6, DOS users are given a practical and powerful backup program.

The long-standing DOS program BACKUP is replaced by two new backup programs: MSBACKUP for DOS and MWBACKUP for Windows. Both programs are licensed from Symantec, the makers of Norton Backup.

Both backup programs offer the following features:

■ **Backup options:** Full, incremental, and differential backups are supported. A full backup creates a backup of all selected files, an incremental backup makes a backup of all selected files that were changed (or added) since the last full or incremental backup, and a differential backup makes a backup of all selected files that were changed since the last full backup.

■ **Flexible file selection:** You can select files to back up in different ways. You can select individual directories and files from a directory tree, or you can specify include and exclude lists that use paths and filemasks to identify the file selection. You also can use a combination of both methods.

- **Data compression:** Data can be compressed before it is saved to disk. Doing so reduces the number of disks needed to store the backup and often makes the backup process faster.

- **Password protection:** You can assign a password to the backup. After you assign a password, you must enter it to restore the data. Note that the password *is* case sensitive.

- **Advanced error correction:** You can store special Error Correction Codes (ECCs) on the backup disk. These codes increase the amount of disk space consumed by the backup files by about 10 percent but greatly enhance the chances that you will be able to restore files from the disk if it is damaged.

- **Backup comparisons:** To help you verify that a backup is sound, a compare option allows you to compare the data on the backup with the original data on the hard disk.

- **Flexible restore:** You can restore files selectively and restore files to a different drive and directory.

MSBACKUP uses a combination of pull-down menus and dialog boxes for selecting options and making backups (see Figure 1-6).

The Windows version of the backup program, MWBACKUP, is discussed later, in the section titled "Windows-Hosted Utilities."

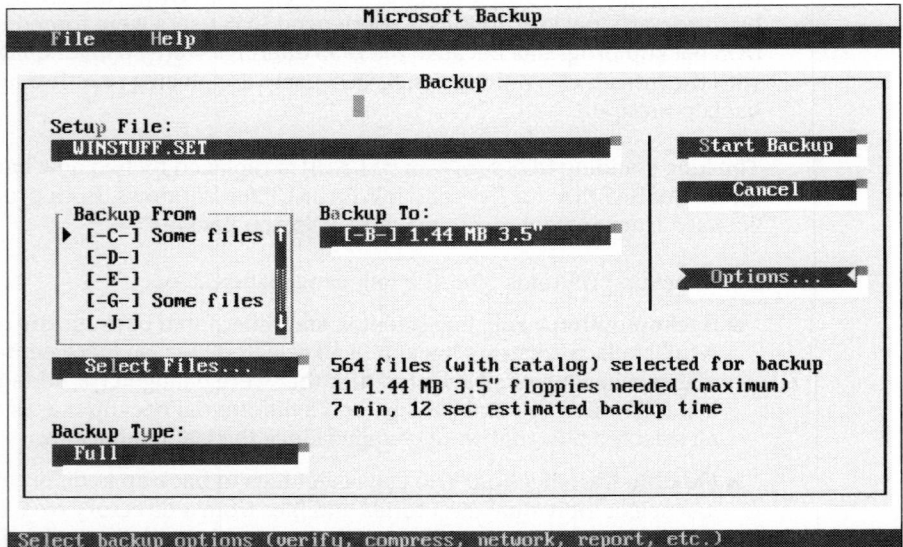

Figure 1-6: The MSBACKUP dialog box.

Unfortunately, you cannot execute MSBACKUP solely from the command line using switches, so you can't ordinarily invoke a full backup from a batch file.

STACKEY, an excellent utility from CtrlAlt Associates, is included on Bob's Shareware Collection disks. STACKEY can stuff almost any sequence of keystrokes into the keyboard buffer. If you want to create an automated backup routine, you can use STACKEY to stuff the buffer with a set of backup commands, such as Enter to select the Backup option from the main menu and Alt-S to choose Start Backup. If you then start MSBACKUP, STACKEY passes the keystrokes to MSBACKUP as though you entered them directly from the keyboard. Magic.

Chapter 3 explains the ins and outs of using MSBACKUP and MWBACKUP to back up and restore files.

The backup programs have one significant weakness: They cannot back up to tape devices. They can back up only to standard DOS devices, such as floppy disks, hard disks, network drives, and removable drives. With the increasing popularity of huge drives, more and more systems are equipped with tape drives expressly for data backup. DOS backup products really need to support tape drives. No sensible third-party vendor would dream of releasing a new backup program that didn't support tape drives.

Disk defragmentation

A file is said to be *fragmented* when it is not stored in contiguous clusters. Although DOS can manage and handle fragmented files reliably, you should always strive to minimize file fragmentation. It takes longer to access fragmented files than contiguous files because the disk read-write heads must move around the disk surface accessing the different locations where various pieces of the file are stored. What's more, the data recovery tools UNDELETE and UNFORMAT are much more likely to be successful if the files they are trying to recover are not fragmented.

DOS 6 provides a defragmentation tool called DEFRAG, which is licensed from Symantec. DEFRAG can defragment files on any drive by rearranging the clusters on the disk. If you execute DEFRAG with no switches, you can use the program interactively, selecting commands and options from menus. Figure 1-7 shows the main DEFRAG screen, which provides a graphical representation of the disk fragmentation.

By using switches, you can control the entire defragmentation process from the command line. You can specify the optimization method, choose the sort order for directories, and even instruct DEFRAG to reboot the system when it finishes.

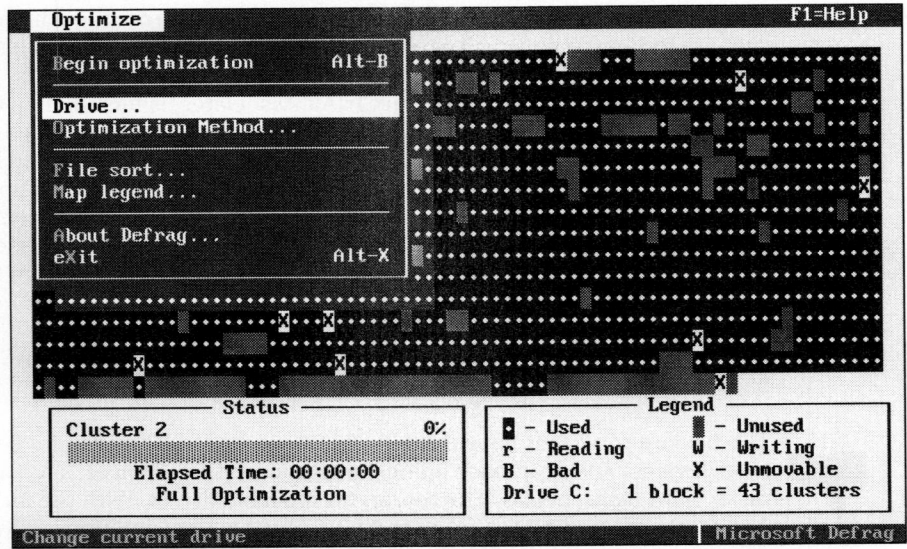

Figure 1-7: A DEFRAG disk map showing the locations of free space on a fragmented disk.

 DEFRAG uses only conventional memory to defragment a disk. Because every directory and file is loaded into memory, DEFRAG doesn't have enough memory to handle large drives with many files and directories. As a rule of thumb, drives less than 400MB in size can be defragmented.

Disk OrGanizer™ (DOG for short), from Soft GAM's Software, is included on Bob's Shareware Collection disks. DOG™ provides all the functionality of the DOS DEFRAG command and then some. For example, DOG™ uses EMS and so can defragment disks with as many as 32,000 files.

New undeletion tools

Microsoft licensed UNDELETE and MWUNDEL from Central Point Software to provide the primary DOS data-recovery tools. (The UNFORMAT and MIRROR commands also are licensed from Central Point Software.)

UNDELETE is a DOS command-line utility that enables you to protect against accidental file deletion and to recover files after they have been deleted. When loaded as a TSR, UNDELETE consumes approximately 14K of RAM and monitors all file-deletion activity. Whenever a file is deleted, UNDELETE saves information that enables you to recover the file. UNDELETE offers the following two methods of protecting files:

■ **Delete Sentry:** Copies of deleted files are stored in a hidden directory named \SENTRY. This method provides the most secure form of protection because the file can be undeleted just by moving it from the deleted directory back to the original directory.

■ **Delete Tracker:** The name of the deleted file, along with a list of all the clusters where the file's data was stored, is kept in a hidden file named PCTRACKR.DEL. This method doesn't offer as much protection as the Delete Sentry method because the clusters still can be overwritten by other files. However, it consumes much less disk space.

You can use the UNDELETE and MWUNDEL commands to recover a deleted file. They attempt to recover a deleted file even if the sentry or tracker defense mechanisms are not loaded. If you have Windows installed, use MWUNDEL — it is much more visual and easier to use than UNDELETE.

Refer to Chapter 3 for a thorough explanation of how to use UNDELETE and MWUNDEL to protect and recover files, along with other techniques for guarding against data loss.

Improved cache performance

One of the most effective ways to improve the performance of a system is to use a disk cache. DOS 6 includes version 4.1 of the Microsoft disk cache SMARTDRV. Not all disk caches are alike, and in the past, SMARTDRV tended to be one of the poorer performers. To give SMARTDRV a performance boost, Microsoft added support for *write buffering*. When a program saves data to disk, SMARTDRV stores the data in a memory cache. The program, thinking that the file has been saved, can then proceed with other operations while the disk cache software saves the data to disk in the background. There is, however, an increased chance for data loss if the system is rebooted (deliberately or by a power failure or system crash) before the cache has saved the data to disk.

Thanks to write buffering and other enhancements, SMARTDRV is now a viable disk cache for the power user.

 SMARTDRV cannot cache CD-ROM drives. If you want to cache a CD-ROM drive, you must use a different cache program.

Windows-Hosted Utilities

More and more PCs are running Windows. For the first time in the history of DOS, some Windows-hosted utilities are included with the operating system. The three main utilities are MWAV, MWBACKUP, and MWUNDEL, which provide anti-virus, file backup, and file-undeletion facilities, respectively. All three

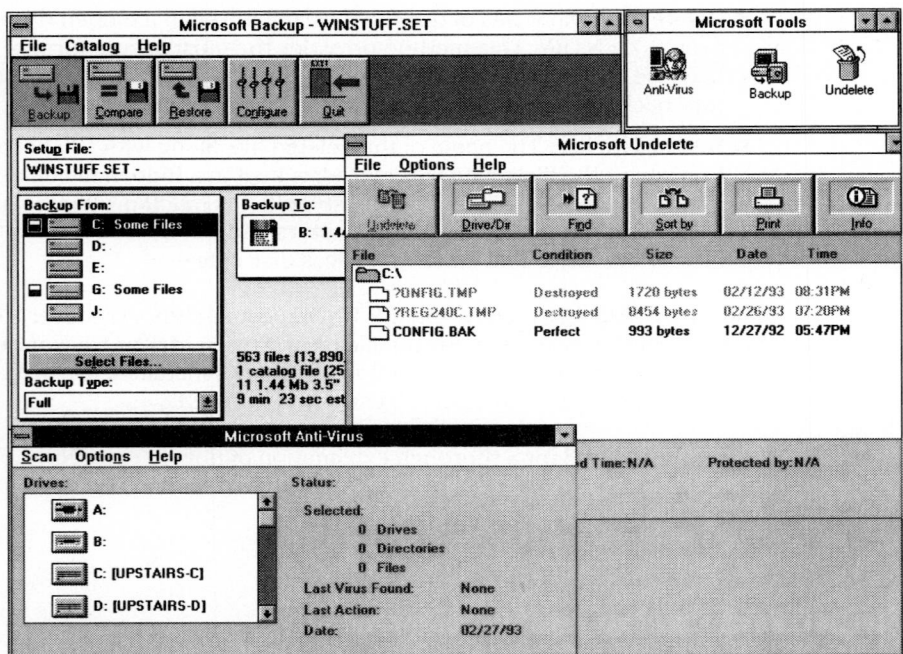

Figure 1-8: The Windows tools providing anti-virus, backup, and file-undeletion support.

programs have text-mode counterparts, and when you install DOS 6, you can elect to install only the Windows version of the programs, only the DOS version, or both. In general, the DOS and Windows programs offer similar features, and the choice is purely a cosmetic one. Most Windows users, however, opt to use the Windows-hosted versions.

Figure 1-8 shows the three Windows applications and the Microsoft Tools group created by SETUP.

A small Windows utility, SMARTMON, also is included with DOS 6. SMARTMON visually displays the effectiveness of the SMARTDRV disk cache and enables you to alter the cache mode of any drive.

Laptop Tools

DOS 6 provides the InterLink programs INTERLNK.EXE and INTERSVR.EXE to connect two PCs together for transferring files or sharing a printer. One computer runs INTERLNK as a device driver, and the other runs the program INTERSVR. Although designed primarily for laptop users, these programs can link any two computers that are wired together by a bidirectional parallel cable, a three-wire serial cable, or a seven-wire null modem serial cable.

You can't use the host computer to perform any other tasks while it's running INTERSVR (even if INTERSVR is executed from within Windows), but the computer that loaded INTERLNK can access the drives and printers on the host. The drives and printers on the host are assigned to additional drive letters and LPT ports on the computer running INTERLNK.

Data can be transferred to and from the computers using standard DOS commands. Programs treat the remote drives as additional local drives.

Refer to Appendix D for a detailed explanation of how to link two computers using InterLink. The appendix also explains how to connect a DOS 6 computer to a network using Microsoft's Workgroup Connection software.

InterLink is considerably slower than many similar third-party offerings. It is fine for low-volume file transfers and print jobs but is very sluggish when large data transfers are involved.

In addition to the InterLink programs, DOS 6 provides POWER.EXE, which is both a device driver and an executable program. You can use POWER to conserve battery power on battery-powered computers that support the industry-standard Advanced Power Management (APM) specification.

Other Goodies

Other commands introduced in DOS 6 include the following:

■ **CHOICE:** By using the CHOICE command in a batch file, you can prompt a user to press a key to select an option. CHOICE sets the ERRORLEVEL to indicate which key was pressed.

Chapter 10 provides a whole suite of examples explaining how to use CHOICE in batch files. CHOICE can be enhanced with DEBUG to accept keys like Esc and Enter. Chapter 11 explains how to customize CHOICE with DEBUG.

- **DELTREE:** This powerful and potentially destructive command removes a directory, all of its subdirectories, and all files contained in the directories.

  Even if the read-only attribute is set on a file or directory, DELTREE will cheerfully blow it away without even asking for confirmation. Always use this command with caution.

- **MOVE:** You can use this command to move files from one directory to another.

- **MSD:** MSD is short for Microsoft System Diagnostics. This excellent program was introduced in Windows 3.1 and was so popular it was added to the DOS command set. It provides detailed information about your system's hardware and software configuration.

What's Gone?

Some DOS commands have been atrophying for a number of years, and Microsoft finally decided to remove them. These commands are still available on the DOS 6 Supplemental disk, which you can obtain directly from Microsoft. Programs dropped from the main DOS package include the following:

ASSIGN.COM

BACKUP.EXE

COMP.EXE

CV.COM

EDLIN.EXE

EXE2BIN.EXE

GRAFTABL.COM

JOIN.EXE

MIRROR.COM

MSHERC.COM

PRINTFIX.COM

PRINTER.SYS

If you are upgrading from an earlier version of DOS, SETUP does not remove old copies of these programs. After you upgrade to DOS 6, the old versions of these commands remain in the DOS directory. If you try to use some of these old programs (such as ASSIGN, EDLIN, and JOIN) you get the `Incorrect DOS version` error message. You can avoid this problem by loading SETVER before executing the commands. Better still, get the Supplemental DOS 6 disk. The only difference between the DOS 5 versions of the programs and versions on the Supplemental disk is that the new versions do not generate the error message.

Most of these commands will not be missed. I, for one, will not mourn EDLIN. However, you should continue to use MIRROR. Much of the functionality of MIRROR was replaced by UNDELETE, but two important data-protection features are not supported by the standard DOS commands. The MIRROR command creates vital data recovery information and should be used in AUTOEXEC.BAT to make copies of the partition table and copies of the FAT and root directory for each hard drive. For example, the following two commands make a copy of the FAT and root directory for drives C, D, and E and make a copy of the hard disk partition table:

```
mirror c: d: e:
mirror /partn
```

Summary

DOS version 6.0, arguably the biggest upgrade in DOS history, offers many significant new features. This chapter provided an overview of DOS 6 and highlighted its strengths and weaknesses. The following points were discussed:

▶ By defining configuration menus and using special boot interruption keys, you can easily control which device drivers and commands are executed at system start-up.

▶ The new on-line help system provides detailed information on virtually every command and device driver.

▶ Enhancements to the memory management commands, coupled with the memory optimizer MEMMAKER, give DOS 6 industrial-strength memory management tools.

▶ By adding DoubleSpace disk compression, defragmentation tools, and a *real* backup program, DOS now provides users with an excellent set of disk management tools.

▶ The DOS data-protection arsenal was strengthened by the addition of anti-virus tools and enhanced UNDELETE and UNFORMAT programs.

▶ A number of old commands were dropped, including the DOS 5 MIRROR command. Even though MIRROR is not included in DOS 6, you should continue to use it to protect the FAT and partition table. If you don't have access to DOS 5, you can obtain the old commands by ordering the Supplemental DOS 6 disk from Microsoft.

▶ The anti-virus, file-undeletion, and backup programs are available in DOS and Windows versions. The versions share similar feature sets, but most Windows users will, no doubt, opt to use the Windows-hosted programs.

▶ Good as DOS 6 is, it has a number of disappointing weaknesses, such as the lack of support for tape drives, the cumbersome way that compressed diskettes must be handled, and SMARTDRV's inability to cache CD-ROM drives.

Chapter 2 investigates some of the more popular and frequently used commands and explains how to use some lesser-known switches to leverage the most power from these commands.

Chapter 2

Mastering the Top DOS Commands

In This Chapter

▶ So many commands, so little time

▶ Getting the best help

▶ Kicking the COPY habit

▶ Using the new MOVE command

▶ Deleting files

▶ Zapping it with DELTREE

▶ Using DIR — yes, DIR

▶ Looking at directory-navigation commands

▶ Creating a smarter PATH

▶ Using MSD, the administrator's friend

▶ Making the DOSSHELL work

So Many Commands, So Little Time

"Whoa — what did you just type?"

Have you ever sat down next to a colleague who's using a PC and seen a command switch being used that you didn't know about? With more than 70 commands and device drivers, and some of them sporting 10 or more switches, it's no wonder that no one remembers them all.

Fortunately, the 80/20 rule applies to DOS — 80 percent of the time, you will use only 20 percent of the commands. This chapter focuses on these most frequently used commands and explains how to get the most productivity from them.

You will also learn about some shareware programs, included on Bob' Shareware Collection disks, that outperform and outsmart their DOS cousins.

Getting the Best HELP

The DOS 6 on-line help feature is excellent. You may recall that the help table of contents is displayed whenever you enter the HELP command with no switches, as follows:

```
help
```

You can jump directly to a specific topic by executing the HELP command followed by a command name. The following command, for example, displays help for using the CHOICE command:

```
help choice
```

You can also jump directly to a submenu of commands, in addition to the standard commands and device drivers, by entering one of the following help topic strings:

Help Topic	Description
batch	Batch file commands
config	CONFIG.SYS commands
international	Commands for international configurations
multi-config	Commands for creating a multiboot CONFIG.SYS menu

To display a menu that details all the batch file commands, for example, enter the following:

```
help batch
```

Running help searches

You can search for a specific string in the body of the help text by selecting the **F**ind option from the **S**earch menu. Figure 2-1 shows the Find dialog box that is displayed when you press Alt-S,F. You can enter a string of any length, from a single character to a complete sentence, and you can optionally specify whether the search should be case sensitive. Case-sensitive searches are usually about 20 percent faster than case-insensitive ones.

HELP searches for the string beginning at the cursor position and moving forward through the help file, and accesses each command in alphabetical order. When the last command has been searched, HELP continues searching from the beginning of the help file. HELP displays the search progress in a very subtle manner: In the lower right corner, you will notice the cursor line number being updated as the search progresses. When the text is found, the cursor is positioned beneath the matching text. A full search can take as long as two minutes on some systems (I wish that it would beep when it finds the text).

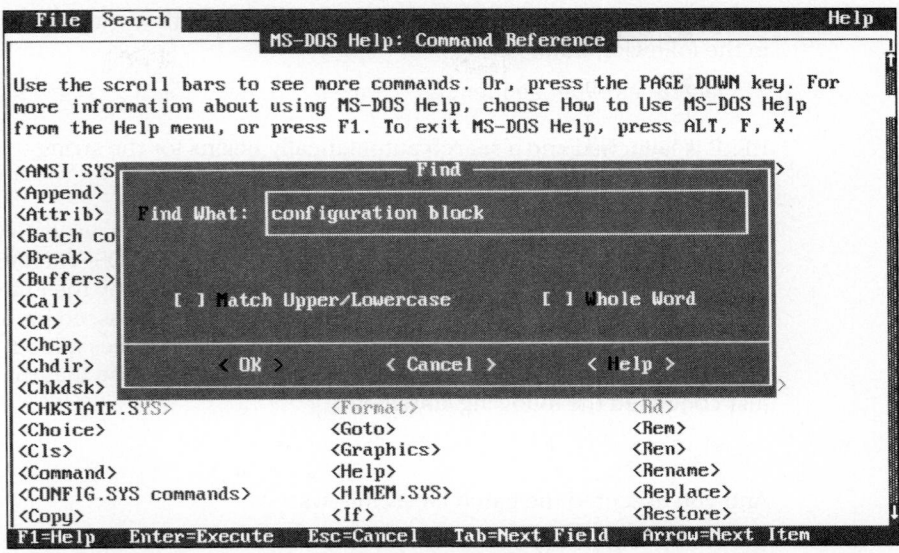

Figure 2-1: HELP's Find dialog box is used to search for a character, word, or phrase.

There is nothing earth-shattering about HELP's search facility. When you combine the search option with STACKEY, however, you can create a quick and very functional help search engine.

The STACKEY utility (included on Bob's Shareware Collection disks), from CtrlAlt Associates, can be used to stuff keystrokes into the keyboard buffer. The following batch file, FHELP.BAT, uses STACKEY to pass a search string to the Find dialog box:

```
@echo off
if "%1"=="" goto plainhelp
stackey W36 @S "F"
if not "%1"=="" if "%2"=="" stackey "%1" CR
if not "%2"=="" if "%3"=="" stackey "%1 %2" CR
if not "%3"=="" if "%4"=="" stackey "%1 %2 %3" CR
if not "%4"=="" if "%5"=="" stackey "%1 %2 %3 %4" CR
if not "%5"=="" if "%6"=="" stackey "%1 %2 %3 %4 %5" CR
if not "%6"=="" if "%7"=="" stackey "%1 %2 %3 %4 %5 %6" CR
if not "%7"=="" if "%8"=="" stackey "%1 %2 %3 %4 %5 %6 %7" CR
if not "%8"=="" if "%9"=="" stackey "%1 %2 %3 %4 %5 %6 %7 %8" CR
if not "%9"=="" stackey "%1 %2 %3 %4 %5 %6 %7 %8 %9" CR
:PLAINHELP
help
```

To use this batch file, just enter FHELP, followed by the string to search for, as in the following example:

```
fhelp escape sequences
```

HELP is launched and a search automatically begins for the string escape sequences. Neat.

The first STACKEY command, on line three of the batch file, waits for 2 seconds (W36) and then sends the Alt-S,F keystroke sequence to DOS. Then the passed parameters are stuffed into the keyboard buffer, followed by the Enter key (CR). The series of IF statements are necessary because every passed parameter must be separated by a space; there must be no extra spaces added, however, to separate null (unused) parameters. For example, suppose that the batch file just contained the following statement:

```
stackey "%1 %2 %3 %4 %5 %6 %7 %8 %9" CR
```

And you executed the batch file as follows:

```
fhelp terminal
```

The string passed to the Find dialog box would be terminal followed by eight spaces. By using the IF statements as shown in the preceding batch file, the string passed to FHELP would be terminal with no spaces after it.

Refer to Part V of this book for more information about STACKEY.

Normally, when you enter the HELP command with a topic name, the name must correspond exactly with the first word of the entry in the main help contents; otherwise, the following message is displayed:

```
Match not found
```

By using the FHELP batch file, you can use a partial name to select a topic. When you enter the following command, for example, the XCOPY command is highlighted:

```
fhelp xco
```

Solving help conflicts with 4DOS and NDOS

If you use 4DOS (from J. P. Software) or its hybrid, NDOS (from Symantec Corporation), to replace COMMAND.COM as the command interpreter, you may experience problems in accessing the DOS HELP command. When you enter the command HELP, 4DOS (or NDOS) invokes its own internal help rather than DOS's help.

You can maintain access to both help systems by using the 4DOS alias command, to substitute one command for another. The following command, for example, invokes the DOS help system when you enter the command DHELP:

```
alias dhelp=c:\dos\help.com
```

Better still, you can enter the following command to take advantage of the capability of 4DOS to recognize partial commands by using an asterisk:

```
alias dh*elp=c:\dos\help.com
```

By embedding the asterisk after the letters DH in the ALIAS command, you can invoke the DOS help system by entering DH, DHE, DHEL, or DHELP.

Alternatively, you can use the following ALIAS command to assign HELP to DOS:

```
alias he*lp=c:\dos\help.com
```

You can then invoke the 4DOS or NDOS help by entering the command 4HELP or NHELP, respectively.

Help tricks for Microsoft C programmers

Although you can print every individual help page, there is no convenient way to print the entire help text for all commands. Furthermore, there is no way to customize the help text. No way, that is, unless you have the Microsoft C compiler (version 6 or later).

The entire help text for the HELP command is stored in the file HELP.HLP in the DOS directory. This file was created by using the Microsoft C Helpmake utility. You can use the Helpmake program, included in the BIN directory of the C compiler, to decode the HELP.HLP file and convert it to ASCII text. You can then print the text file or make modifications to the file and re-create a revised binary help file.

To see a summary of Helpmake's switches, enter the following command:

```
helpmake /h
```

The following command creates a file called HELP.TXT that contains the source text for the DOS help:

```
helpmake /d help.hlp /ohelp.txt
```

If you want to make enhancements to the on-line help, you can edit the text file and then use the /E switch to rebuild the HELP file. Refer to the *Microsoft C Environment and Tools* manual for additional information about Helpmake.

Using the /? switch

The HELP command is not the only way in which DOS provides command assistance. If you enter a command followed by the /? switch, DOS displays a brief summary of the command usage, including a list of all the switches the command supports. The following output, for example, was generated from the command CHOICE /?:

```
Waits for the user to choose one of a set of choices.

CHOICE [/C[:]choices] [/N] [/S] [/T[:]c,nn] [text]

/C[:]choices Specifies allowable keys. Default is YN
/N           Do not display choices and ? at end of prompt string.
/S           Treat choice keys as case sensitive.
/T[:]c,nn    Default choice to c after nn seconds
text         Prompt string to display

ERRORLEVEL is set to offset of key user presses in choices.
```

If you are writing batch files for other users, you should consider writing them to support the /? switch. The following modified version of FHELP.BAT has been enhanced to support /? (the boldface areas indicate the commands that provide the /? support):

```
@echo off
rem Finds a string using DOS HELP command.
if "%1"=="/?" goto commandhelp
if "%1"=="" goto plainhelp
stackey W36 @S "F"
if not "%1"=="" if "%2"=="" stackey "%1" CR
if not "%2"=="" if "%3"=="" stackey "%1 %2" CR
if not "%3"=="" if "%4"=="" stackey "%1 %2 %3" CR
if not "%4"=="" if "%5"=="" stackey "%1 %2 %3 %4" CR
if not "%5"=="" if "%6"=="" stackey "%1 %2 %3 %4 %5" CR
if not "%6"=="" if "%7"=="" stackey "%1 %2 %3 %4 %5 %6" CR
if not "%7"=="" if "%8"=="" stackey "%1 %2 %3 %4 %5 %6 %7" CR
if not "%8"=="" if "%9"=="" stackey "%1 %2 %3 %4 %5 %6 %7 %8" CR
if not "%9"=="" stackey "%1 %2 %3 %4 %5 %6 %7 %8 %9" CR
:PLAINHELP
help
goto quit
:COMMANDHELP
echo Searches for a string in the DOS on-line help.
echo.
echo FHELP [/?] [text]
```

```
echo.
echo When no switches are specified, the help contents are displayed
echo /?      Displays this help text
echo text    Specifies the text to search for
echo.
:QUIT
```

Using FASTHELP

The FASTHELP command might have been more appropriately named HELPLITE because it provides a brief description of each DOS command.

FASTHELP used to be called DOSHELP, and you can still enter the command DOSHELP if you prefer. It was renamed to avoid confusion with the new HELP command.

If you enter the FASTHELP command with no switches, nearly five screens full of information that summarize each command are displayed. If you enter the FASTHELP command followed by a command name, more detailed information about the specific command is presented. Behind the scenes, FASTHELP simply executes the command with a /? switch.

The text displayed by FASTHELP is stored in the ASCII file DOSHELP.HLP in the DOS directory. Because HELP now provides the real on-line help for DOS commands, you might consider replacing the data in DOSHELP.HLP with information about your favorite batch files and utilities.

The format of DOSHELP.HLP is straightforward. Any line beginning with the @ character is ignored — it is used to add comments to the file. The help text for commands should be added in alphabetical order, and the command name should begin in the first column. To add more than one line of text, make sure that the second and subsequent lines begin with one or more spaces. Otherwise, DOS treats the line as a new command.

The following custom version of DOSHELP.HLP describes some custom batch files:

```
@ Custom on-line help for batch files. Accessed by FASTHELP
CHKFRAG    Checks the fragmentation of a set of files.
EDITBAT    Launches EDIT and prepares a new batch
           file for editing.
FHELP      Searches for a string in the DOS on-line help.
HEXMATH    Uses DEBUG to provide a simple HEX calculator.
SAVEENV    Saves the active environment. Execute OLDENV to
           subsequently restore the old environment.
SET25      Sets screen into 25 line mode.
SET43      Sets screen into 43 line mode.
SET50      Sets screen into 50 line mode.
```

There is one problem with customizing FASTHELP. Even if you add /? support to your batch files, FASTHELP does not display custom help when you pass the name of the batch file as a FASTHELP switch. For example, when you enter the command

```
fasthelp fhelp
```

DOS responds with the message

```
Help not available for this command
```

FASTHELP calls only COM or EXE files and (stupidly) ignores batch files.

TURBOBAT, which is included on Bob's Shareware Collection disks, is a batch-file compiler that can convert BAT files to COM files. I use TURBOBAT, part of the ExtraDOS Toolbox (from Foley Hi-Tech Systems) all the time. If you compile your batch file and locate the new COM file somewhere on the search path, FASTHELP calls it with the /? switch.

Applications help

In addition to the on-line help available with the HELP command, the DOS programs in Table 2-1 feature their own extensive help systems.

Table 2-1	DOS Programs That Have Their Own Help System
Command	*Description*
DBLSPACE	DoubleSpace disk compression
DEFRAG	File defragmenter
DOSSHELL	Full-screen file and task manager
EDIT	Text editor
MEMMAKER	Memory optimizer
MSAV	DOS anti-virus utility
MSBACKUP	DOS backup utility
MWAV	Windows anti-virus utility
MWBACKUP	Windows backup utility
MWUNDEL	Windows undelete tools
QBASIC	Basic language interpreter
SMARTMON	Windows SMARTDRV monitor

Kicking the COPY Habit

Old habits die hard. If you began using DOS many years ago, you are probably a dedicated COPY command user. The truth is that XCOPY is much better than COPY.

From its name, you might think that XCOPY is the former or ex-COPY command. Nothing could be further from the truth. XCOPY, the next generation of COPY, was introduced with DOS 3.2. The name stands for *extended copy*. It's smarter and faster than COPY. Blue Bashers might be interested in knowing that IBM, not Microsoft, programmed XCOPY.

The following list shows some reasons you should use XCOPY rather than COPY:

- XCOPY uses a memory buffer to store multiple files. If you are copying more than one file, XCOPY reads as many files as it can into the buffer; when the buffer fills, XCOPY writes the files to the target location. This technique makes XCOPY much faster than COPY, especially when you are copying from a floppy or remote drive.

    There is one exception to the rule. If you are copying a single file that is less than 64K in size (COPY's buffer size), COPY is faster than XCOPY. This anomaly exists because COPY is an internal command that is already loaded in memory; XCOPY is external and must be loaded in memory before the file is copied.

- You can use the /S switch with XCOPY to copy an entire subdirectory tree.

- If you are copying a large set of files to multiple floppy disks, first use the ATTRIB command to set all the archive bits on (ATTRIB FILEMASK +a, for example) and then use the /M switch with XCOPY. This switch instructs XCOPY to copy only files that have the archive bit set. After each file has been copied, the archive bit is turned off. When the first floppy disk is full, DOS displays this message:

```
Insufficient disk space
```

    Just change disks and reissue the same XCOPY command. Because the files that already have been copied have their archive attribute turned off, they are ignored and XCOPY recommences with the correct file.

- Other switches supported by XCOPY but not by COPY are /D, to copy files that have been modified on or after a specified date, and /P, which prompts for confirmation before creating each file copy.

- Use XCOPY in batch files because it returns an ERRORLEVEL indicating whether the copy was a success; COPY does not.

Enough said.

As good as XCOPY is, it pales in comparison to PCOPY. PCOPY is part of the Patriquin Utilities, from Patri-Soft. An evaluation copy is included on Bob's Shareware Collection disks. The following list shows just a few of the PCOPY features:

- Enables you to save older versions of files with new names before replacing them.
- Deletes the original file if /X is specified.
- Enables you to pause processing at any time by pressing any keyboard key. After the program is stopped, you can terminate it by pressing Esc.
- Allows commands to be tested so that you can be sure that commands are specified as you desire.
- Optionally prompts for confirmation before overwriting existing files.

You can execute PCOPY as a command-line utility or in full-screen mode (see Figure 2-2).

The PocketD program D.EXE is also included on Bob's Shareware Collection disks. One of D's primary functions is copying files, and it includes many unique features. Unlike PCOPY, D is solely a command-line utility (although a full-screen utility is under development) and is controlled by using switches. By using a few simple switches, you can invoke some extremely powerful copy operations.

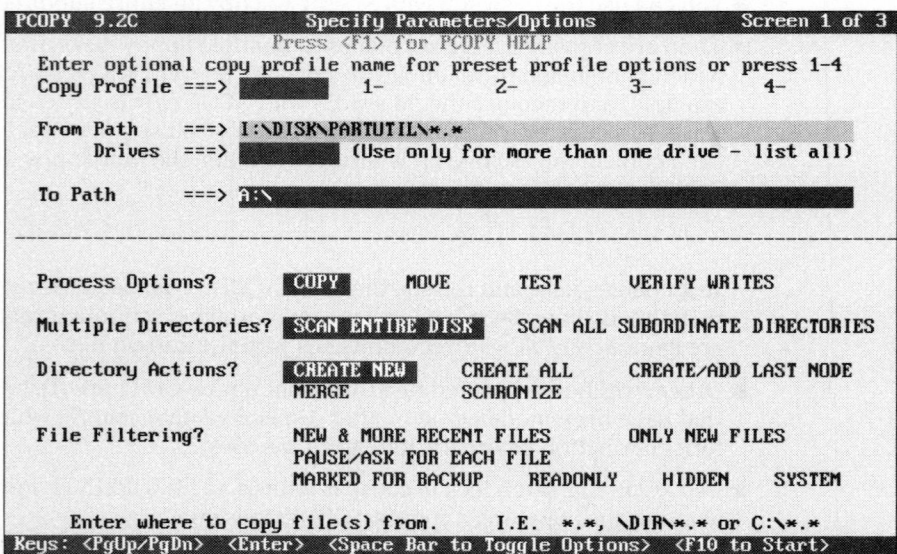

Figure 2-2: You can use PCOPY in full-screen mode to select each switch visually before copying the files.

To copy a series of files to the \STUFF directory, you might issue a command like the following:

```
d *.c *.h *.asm /c \stuff
```

The following command copies all the files in the default directory and in all subdirectories to drive A and creates the same directory structure on the floppy disk:

```
d /cp a:\
```

D has an excellent feature for network users. A common problem in copying a large number of files on a network is that another user has already opened some of the files to be copied. D can skip these files and automatically return to them later and try again. That's smart.

D supports many more copy-related switches; see Part V of this book for more information.

Using the New MOVE Command

DOS finally has a MOVE command to move one or more files from one directory to another. If the files are moved to another directory on the same drive, MOVE is smart enough to just change each file's directory entries (the file data is not physically moved). When files are moved to a different drive, however, the files are copied to the target location and then the original is deleted.

The syntax for MOVE is similar to COPY but not exactly the same. Refer to Part IV, "The Complete DOS 6 Command Reference," for a full explanation of the syntax.

One nice feature of MOVE is that it allows multiple source filenames to be specified. The following command, for example, moves all files with DOC and SAM to the DOCS directory:

```
move *.doc,*.sam \docs
```

Unlike COPY, MOVE insists that you specify a source filename. You cannot, for example, move all the files in the STUFF directory to the TRASH directory by using the following command:

```
move \stuff \trash
```

MOVE tries to move the STUFF *file* from the root directory to the TRASH directory or (if TRASH doesn't exist) tries to rename the STUFF directory to TRASH. The correct use of the command is as follows:

```
move \stuff\*.* \trash
```

Or, using the briefer dot notation, you can type the following:

```
move \stuff\. \trash
```

Another difference between COPY and MOVE is that MOVE requires you to specify the target directory. You cannot move files to the current directory by omitting the target directory from the command line.

One quirk of the MOVE command, which Microsoft calls a feature, is that it can be used to rename a directory. Well, kinda. You cannot move a directory to another location in the directory hierarchy, but you can assign it a new name. To rename the \TRASH directory to \JUNK, for example, enter the following command:

```
move \trash \junk
```

One final note: If you specify only one file as the source and one file as the target, you can rename the file when it is moved. To move the file IQUIT.DOC from the DOCS directory to RESIGN.DOC in the BADDAY directory, for example, enter the following command:

```
move \docs\iquit.doc \badday\resign.doc
```

We have been waiting ten years for a MOVE command, and I, for one, am disappointed with Microsoft's offering. Both of the excellent shareware programs PocketD and PCOPY provide superior move facilities. These programs provide the same functionality to move operations as they do to copy operations (discussed earlier in this chapter).

By adding the /X switch to any PCOPY command or the M switch to D, the operation instantly becomes a move rather than a copy.

Deleting Files

There is not much mystery about the DEL (or ERASE) command. Even though DEL supports only one switch, most users don't remember it. The /P switch prompts for confirmation before deleting each file.

Normally, DEL allows you to specify only a single filemask. The following batch file, DELMANY.BAT, however, enables you to delete multiple filemasks with one command:

```
@echo off
for %%f in (%1 %2 %3 %4 %5 %6 %7 %8 %9) do del %%f /p
```

To delete all the files with a BAK or $$$ extension, just enter the following command:

```
delmany *.bak *.$$$
```

Chapter 9 shows how you can use a similar technique to create a DOSKEY macro that deletes multiple files.

 When DOS deletes a file, the file's data is not physically deleted; a data recovery program, such as UNDELETE, might be capable of restoring the file. To erase a confidential or classified file and make sure that no one can undelete it, use RELDEL from Tardis DP Consultants. RELDEL, included on Bob's Shareware Collection disks, goes to considerable lengths to ensure that the file's data cannot be recovered.

 You can use the PocketD utility D.EXE (discussed earlier in this chapter) to traverse every directory on a hard disk and delete any files that match one or more file specifications. The following command deletes all files with a BAK extension on the current drive:

```
d *.bak /WFzz
```

The following command uses the qz switch to prompt for confirmation before deleting each file; it optionally enables you to view the file before responding:

```
d *.bak *.del *.$$$ *.tmp /WFqz
```

 An evaluation copy of PDEL, another program in the Patriquin Utilities (from Patri-Soft), is included on Bob's Shareware Collection disks. PDEL is a command-line utility for deleting files. In addition to all the standard features, it can delete files based on their date or size, begin deleting files when a specific filename is encountered in the directory, stop deleting files when another file is reached, exclude files from specified filemasks, and much more.

 The ExtraDOS Toolbox, from Foley Hi-Tech Systems, offers a number of tools that simplify file-deletion chores, including the ones in this list:

ALLSUB   Executes any command in the current directory and in all nested subdirectories. (ALLSUB can be used with any command, not just with DEL.) To delete all files beginning with the letters *BUD* on drive C, for example, enter the following command from the root directory of drive C:

```
allsub del bud*.*
```

CLEANUP   A full-screen utility for analyzing a drive, identifying duplicate or unused files, and optionally deleting them.

NO Enables you to exclude a specified file or groups of files from a command. The following command, for example, deletes all the files in the current directory *except* files with a DOC extension:

```
no *.DOC del *.*
```

Multiple NO statements can be used. The following command, for example, deletes all files except programs and batch files:

```
no *.bat no *.exe no *.com del *.*
```

Zap It with DELTREE

DOS 6 includes the powerful and destructive DELTREE command, which removes a directory, all its subdirectories, and all the files contained in these directories.

DELTREE can erase thousands of files with one simple command. Always be cautious when you use DELTREE. Stop and think before you press Enter and make sure that you have specified the correct directory path.

You can use the /Y switch to bypass the standard confirmation prompt, but — because of the destructive nature of the command — I don't recommend that you use it.

In DELTREE's normal format, you pass a single pathname that identifies the parent directory to be expunged. The following command, for example, removes all the files in the BACKUP directory and below:

```
deltree c:\backup
```

Unlike DEL, DELTREE deletes hidden, system, and read-only files. You can delete any single file, regardless of the file's attributes, by specifying a filename rather than a directory path. To delete the hidden file DBLSPACE.BIN in the root directory of drive C, for example, enter the following command:

```
deltree c:\dblspace.bin
```

DELTREE supports filemasks, but you should use them with extreme caution. When a filemask is specified, DELTREE deletes all matching files and all matching directories in addition to *any* files stored in the matching directories.

DIR — Yes, DIR

Few people take advantage of the switches recently added to the ever-popular DIR command. The full syntax of the DIR command is explained in Part IV of this book, but a few practical tips might illustrate some of the less well-known features.

Listing subdirectories

I often see experienced DOS users entering the following command to display a list of all the directories in the current directory:

```
dir *.
```

This command displays a list of all (nonsystem and nonhidden) files in the current directory that do not have an extension. Because most users do not create directory names that have extensions, the command lists all the directories. Unfortunately, the command lists any file that doesn't have an extension.

In its day, `dir *.` was a useful shortcut; thanks to the /A (for *attribute*) switch, however, there is now a foolproof way to list all directories regardless of their name. Simply use the identifier d with the /A switch to indicate that you want to view all files that have the directory attribute set:

```
dir /ad
```

Displaying all files, including hidden and system files

Another problem with plain DIR is that it normally doesn't list hidden or system files. If you want to see all the files in a directory, just use the /A switch with no identifier, as follows:

```
dir /a
```

You can also specify a filemask with the /A switch. To display all hidden files in the root directory of drive C that have a BIN extension, for example, just enter the following command:

```
dir *.bin /a
```

Searching for files

My favorite switch of all time is the /S switch for DIR. The /S switch instructs DOS to read the specified directory and all subdirectories when it displays a directory listing.

To search the entire hard drive for a file or files, just specify the appropriate filename or filemask in addition to the /S switch. To search the entire drive C for the file GIRLFRND.BUK, for example, enter the following command:

```
dir \girlfrnd.buk /s
```

Similarly, to list all files that have an extension of ASM, enter the following command:

```
dir \*.asm /s
```

 The new MSD command can search for, and optionally display, any file. This feature is discussed in more detail later, in the section "MSD, the Administrator's Friend."

 The use of the /S switch to help find files is useful, but QFIND (from Bruce Gavin), which is included on Bob's Shareware Collection disks, is more flexible and much, much faster. QFIND searches for any file or filemask on the current drive or all drives, and does so at breakneck speed. If a lot of files are found, you can scroll through a list of all matching files. You can even search for files that have a certain set of characters somewhere in the filename. The following command, for example, displays all the files that have *bud* in their name:

```
qfind *bud*.*
```

Creating a smarter filemask

 If a filemask begins with an asterisk, DOS assumes that you want to list *all* files. If you enter the following command, for example, DOS lists all files, not just the ones with the characters 93 in their name:

```
dir \*93*.* /s
```

By using the FIND filter, you can work around this DOS shortcoming. FIND searches for any string anywhere on a line. By reading the output from DIR, FIND displays only the names of files that contain the specified string.

The FIND command is explained fully in Chapter 10.

The following batch file, FLEXDIR.BAT (for *flex*ible *dir*ectory), uses this technique and provides a convenient way to search for files when you can remember only part of the name:

```
@echo off
if "%1"=="" goto noparam
echo Searching for matching files....
dir *.* %2 %3 %4 %5 %6 %7 %8 %9|find "%1" /i
goto quit
:NOPARAM
dir *.* /a
:QUIT
```

To display all files in the current directory that include the characters 93, you enter the following command:

```
flexdir 93
```

To search the entire drive, you enter the following command from the root directory:

```
flexdir 93 /s
```

Searching for a partial directory name

By using a technique similar to the flexible directory lister discussed in the preceding section, you can search for any directory that contains a specified set of characters.

The batch file FINDDIR.BAT uses the /S and /AD switches with DIR to list all directories on the drive. The output from DIR is redirected to FIND, which searches for any line that contains the word *Directory*. A second FIND command searches these lines for the user-specified characters. Here are the contents of FINDDIR.BAT:

```
@echo off
echo Searching for directories....
if "%1"=="" goto noparam
dir \ /s /ad | find "Directory" | find "%1" /i
goto quit
:NOPARAM
dir \ /s /ad | find "Directory"
:QUIT
```

The following command shows FINDDIR being used to search for any directory that contains the characters ICO:

```
finddir ico
```

FINDDIR responds, on my system, by displaying the following output:

```
Searching for directories....
Directory of C:\123W\GRAPHICO
Directory of C:\123W\SHEETICO
Directory of C:\AMIPRO\ICONS
Directory of C:\WINDOWS\ICONS
```

Setting default DIR switches

By assigning specific DIR switches to the environment variable DIRCMD, you can define your own custom defaults. To always sort your directory listings in date order, for example, with the newest files first, you ordinarily use a command like this one:

```
dir /o-d
```

You can make the /O-D switch the default by adding the following command to AUTOEXEC.BAT:

```
set dircmd=/o-d
```

Whenever you enter DIR, the /O-D switch then is applied.

On the odd occasion when you don't want the default to apply, you should precede the entire switch with the minus character (–). To instruct DIR to ignore the DIRCMD setting and display an unsorted directory listing, for example, you enter the following command:

```
dir /-o
```

I find this override approach to be unnecessarily awkward, especially when multiple switches have been set. The following PDIR.BAT (for *plain DIR*) batch file temporarily disables the DIRCMD settings, executes a standard DIR command that ignores the defaults, and then reactivates the default settings:

```
@echo off
if "%dircmd%"=="" goto notset
set dirtemp=%dircmd%
set dircmd=
dir %1 %2 %3 %4 %5 %6 %7 %8 %9
set dircmd=%dirtemp%
set dirtemp=
goto quit
```

```
:NOTSET
dir %1 %2 %3 %4 %5 %6 %7 %8 %9
:QUIT
```

The following example command uses PDIR to display a directory listing in wide format and pause after every screen:

```
pdir /p /w
```

Shareware alternatives to DIR

Let's face it — DIR is dull. Two excellent utilities on Bob's Shareware Collection disks significantly improve on DOS's directory listing capabilities.

HotDIR Plus, from Robert Woeger, is an elegant and easy-to-use utility that colorizes directory listings based on the file extension. It's amazing how much more legible a directory listing is when like-files are displayed in the same color (yellow for batch files and green for DOC files, for example). In addition to colorizing the output, HotDIR Plus can sort files, and it supports column formats that range from one to six columns (see Figure 2-3).

```
C:\WORD55>
C:\WORD55>hdir /4
HotDIR Plus 7.2                                       (c) 1992 by Robert Woeger
Path: *.*                                             HDIRPLUS /H for help

POSTSCRP PRD   22839 RESUME   STY    1024 WORD_RTF DOC    1578 WORD     PIF     545
POSTSCRP INI   12471 ACADEMIC STY    1536 RTF_OS2  EXE  110433 MW341280 TMP    2048
MACRO5   GLY    3584 SAMPLE   STY    1024 MW       HLP  270360 MW473092 TMP    2048
MACROCNV EXE  105372 SIDEBY   STY    1024 DCA_RTFP EXE  144083 MW241151 TMP    2048
CONTRACT GLY    6144 MAKEVID  EXE    8727 WORD_DCA EXE   25533 MW462528 TMP   10240
WORK_RTF EXE   61207 MACRO    GLY   42496 WORD_DCA DOC    3608 MW065995 TMP    3072
WORD     ICO     288 MSD      EXE   64475 RTF_DOS  EXE  107741 MW180726 TMP    9216
MACROCNV DOC    7676 CHARTEST DOC    5120 MAKEPRD  EXE   61567 MW282527 TMP    9216
CAPTURE  COM   59247 OS2_NOTE DOC    2509 PRINTERS DOC    3118 CHKLIST  MS      351
THES-AM  LEX  329707 SEMI     STY    1536 DOSBOOK       <dir> MW565587 TMP    9216
OUTLINE  STY    1024 STATE    STY    1024 .             <dir> MW173383 TMP    4096
HYPH     DAT   24072 FULL     STY    1536 ..            <dir> UPDAT-AM CMP    1956
APPEALS  STY    1024 README   DOC   11229 SCREEN   VID  15942 MW       INI     309
SPELL-AM LEX  161337 DCA_RTF  EXE  140527 WORD     EXE  738281 MW482162 TMP    9216
TYPOS    DOC    2560 MERGEPRD EXE  126116 REMEM-AM COR     23

      59 files totaling 2754299 bytes, 13340672 bytes free on Drive C:

C:\WORD55>
```

Figure 2-3: HotDIR Plus displays a colored directory in four-column format.

```
Volume UPSTAIRS-C 11/12/92  C:\WORD55\DOSBOOK   v2.00  Type D /? for HELP
   : ECHO IBMVIR NU SAVE$YL% \SCREENS
bat: ANSIATTR ANSIAUTO ANSICODE ANSIHELP ANSIOK ANSIOUCH ANSIPRMT ANSISET
     APPLE BCD BLCKGREN BROWNCLR BUTIL BYPASS CHKDIR CHKFRAG CLEAR CYANBLUE
     DELALL DELAY DELMANY DIRSIZE DOSPRMPT EDITBAT FHELP FINDDIR FLEXDIR
     GETDAY GETMOUSE HEXMATH INMEM ISDOS6 ISWILD JUMPHELP JUMPTO LINEWRAP
     MACROS MCD MENUCHCE NEWPATH OLDPRMT ONLYONCE PDIR RN SAVEENV SAVEPRMT
     SET25 SET43 SET50 SETDATE SETMACRO SETTEMP SWAPSEM2 SWAPSEMI TCD TEMP
     TESTA TESTBOUT TESTFUNC TOPRIGHT UPPER2 UPPERIT WAITFOR WINSTART WONCE
     WRITEAT YELLOW
bob: DS00RA10
com: BOOTDRV CAPSOFF CAPSON CHOICE12 CHOICEA2 CURSFAT CURSNORM DRIVEAOK
     DRIVEBOK FHELP GETFUNCY KEYSTATE REBOOT WEEKDAY WHATDAY WHATMON WHATYEAR
del: TEMP
doc: BOB CMDBLANK DS00RA01 DS00RA02 DS00RA04 DS00RA05 DS00RA06 DS00RA07
     DS00RA08 DS00RA09 DS00RA10 DS00RA11 DS00RA12 DS00RA14 DS00RAAE DS00RAFN
     DS00RAIN DS00RAOZ DSCH11 EXPAND MIRROR MOVE MSCDEX TEMP TEMBAK
exe: PREFIX
ms : CHKLIST
out: CHOICE12 DEBUG QBASIC
pas: PREFIX
red: TYPE
scr: BOOTDRV CAPSOFF CAPSON CHOICE12 CHOICEA2 CURSFAT CURSNORM DRIVEAOK
     DRIVEBOK GETFUNCY KEYSTATE REBOOT REBOOT2 TEMP TEST WEEKDAY WHATDAY
...MORE ? (h=help)
```

Figure 2-4: PocketD can display a large number of files in a compact manner by using Tiny Mode.

The versatile PocketD utility already has been mentioned a number of times in this chapter. The main PocketD program D.EXE is, among other things, a flexible directory listing tool. In addition to its support of multiple columns, D can display listings in Tiny Mode and show files sorted by directory in such a way that you can view hundreds of files on one screen (see Figure 2-4).

PocketD also supports flexible wildcards, such as *BUD*.*, to list all filenames that include the letters *BUD*. You can specify multiple filemasks on the command line and exclude specific filemasks from the listing. The following command, for example, displays all filenames that begin with F or that have an extension of DOC and excludes any files with a BAK extension:

```
d F* *.DOC /-*.BAK
```

Another unique feature of PocketD is that it can analyze the size of files categorized by file type and display a graph indicating its findings. Figure 2-5 shows a bar chart that identifies which directories consume the most space on a hard disk. It didn't surprise me that WINDOWS was at the top.

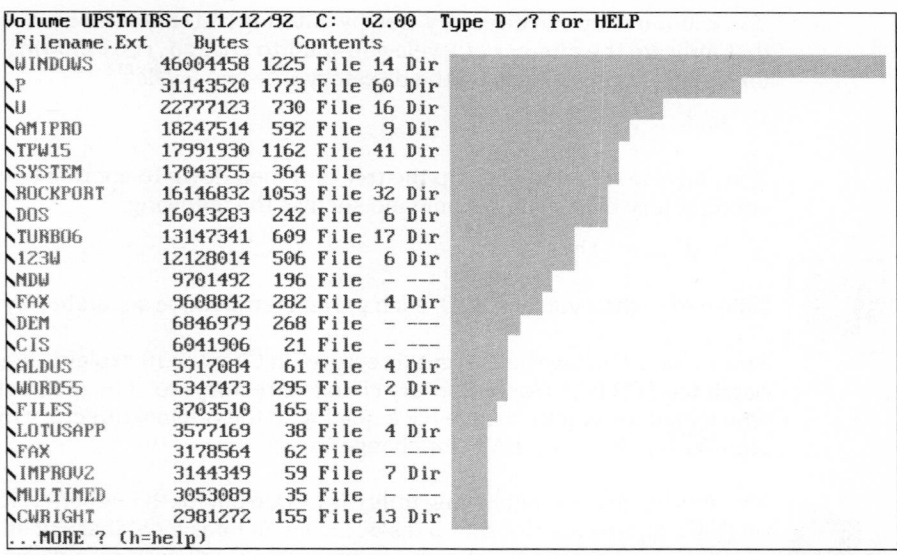

```
Volume UPSTAIRS-C 11/12/92  C:   v2.00   Type D /? for HELP
 Filename.Ext    Bytes     Contents
\WINDOWS       46004458 1225 File 14 Dir
\P             31143520 1773 File 60 Dir
\U             22777123  730 File 16 Dir
\AMIPRO        18247514  592 File  9 Dir
\TPW15         17991930 1162 File 41 Dir
\SYSTEM        17043755  364 File  - ----
\ROCKPORT      16146832 1053 File 32 Dir
\DOS           16043283  242 File  6 Dir
\TURBO6        13147341  609 File 17 Dir
\123W          12128014  506 File  6 Dir
\MDW            9701492  196 File  - ----
\FAX            9608842  282 File  4 Dir
\DEM            6846979  268 File  - ----
\CIS            6041906   21 File  - ----
\ALDUS          5917084   61 File  4 Dir
\WORD55         5347473  295 File  2 Dir
\FILES          3703510  165 File  - ----
\LOTUSAPP       3577169   38 File  4 Dir
\FAX            3178564   62 File  - ----
\IMPROV2        3144349   59 File  7 Dir
\MULTIMED       3053089   35 File  - ----
\CWRIGHT        2981272  155 File 13 Dir
...MORE ? (h=help)
```

Figure 2-5: A bar chart generated by PocketD shows the amount of space used by files in every directory.

Directory Navigation Commands

Let's be honest — CD (or CHDIR) is a crude and unfriendly way to change directories. You have to either know the name of the directory you want to change to or hunt around for the directory name by using DIR or TREE.

There aren't many ways to enhance the CD command, but you might find the following BCD.BAT (for *backward change directory*) batch file useful. You may know that the command CD.. changes directories to the parent directory of the current directory. Some network operating systems and replacements for COMMAND.COM support extensions to the double-dot shortcut by changing directories two levels back when three dots are specified. BCD.BAT provides DOS with similar capabilities:

```
@echo off
if "%1"=="" cd
if "%1".."=".." cd..%2
if "%1"=="..." cd..\..%2
if "%1"=="...." cd..\..\..%2
if "%1"=="....." cd..\..\..\..%2
```

You can move up the directory tree by entering BCD followed by a series of dots that indicate the number of levels you want to change. The following command, for example, moves back up the directory tree two levels:

```
bcd ...
```

You can also traverse back up the tree and then down to another specific subdirectory by issuing a command such as the following:

```
bcd ... \this\that
```

Unlike CD, when you use BCD, each parameter must be separated by a space.

The section "Saving the current directory" in Chapter 10 explains how to use the batch file TCD.BAT (for *temporary change directory*) to change directories, which enables you to change back quickly to the original directory by executing another batch file, CB.BAT (for *change back*).

My favorite directory-changing utility is LCD, from Keith Ledbetter; it is included on Bob's Shareware Collection disks. LCD maintains a database of all directories on all drives. When you enter the command LCD followed by a directory name, or even by a partial directory name, LCD changes to the appropriate directory. If you enter a partial directory name and more than one match is found, a pop-up dialog box lists all the matching directory names (see Figure 2-6). Just choose the directory you want from the list, and it is made the default directory.

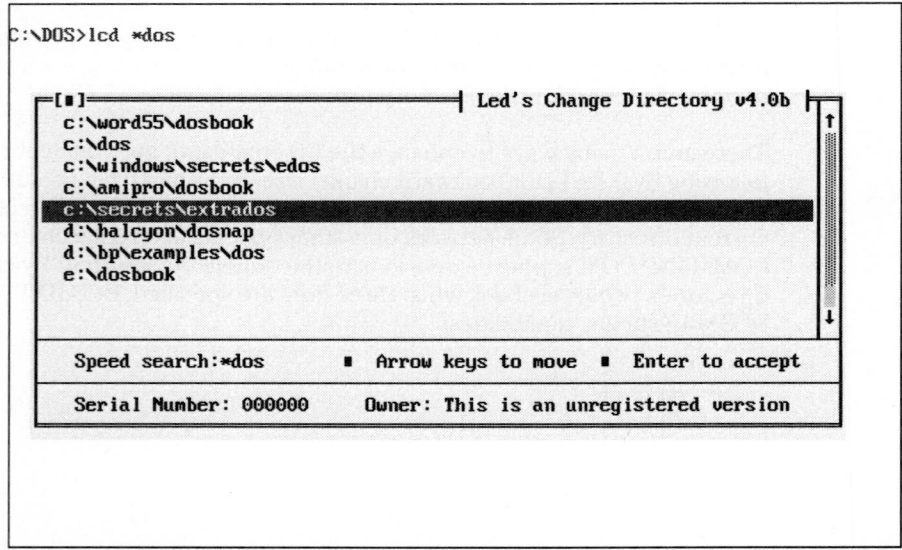

Figure 2-6: LCD shows all directories with the characters *DOS* somewhere in the directory name.

McAfee Associates (best known for its anti-virus products) is taking responsibility for LCD and actively developing an enhanced version of LCD that will be called MCD.

A Smarter PATH

It seems that nearly every program wants to be included on the search path. On most systems, the path is cluttered with directory names and is far too long. Every time you enter an external command, DOS begins its search for the program file. The longer the path, the more directories have to be searched for the program.

By adding the entries \ and ..\ to the search path, you can instruct DOS to search in the root directory of the current drive and in the parent of the default directory. Because most people store data files in subdirectories below each main program directory, the ..\ entry ensures that DOS will find the main program files when one of its data directories is the default.

The following entry from AUTOEXEC.BAT uses this technique:

```
path c:\dos;c:\windows;c:\windows\ndw;c:\batfiles;\;..\
```

MSD, the Administrator's Friend

The DOS program MSD, short for Microsoft System Diagnostics, provides valuable information about your system's hardware and software configuration. MSD displays information about the system board, memory, video, operating system, mouse, disk drives, ports, and related items.

Although MSD is most often used interactively by a user trying to solve a problem, you can also use it from the command line to generate detailed configuration reports. This feature makes it ideal for technical-support staff members who have to diagnose someone else's system problem over the phone or by electronic mail.

Used with the /F switch, MSD analyzes the system and writes a detailed report on the complete system configuration, in addition to the contents of CONFIG.SYS, AUTOEXEC.BAT, and the main INI files, such as WIN.INI, SYSTEM.INI, and DBLSPACE.INI. Before the report is created, MSD prompts the user for a name, an address, and a one-line comment. These details are written at the top of the report.

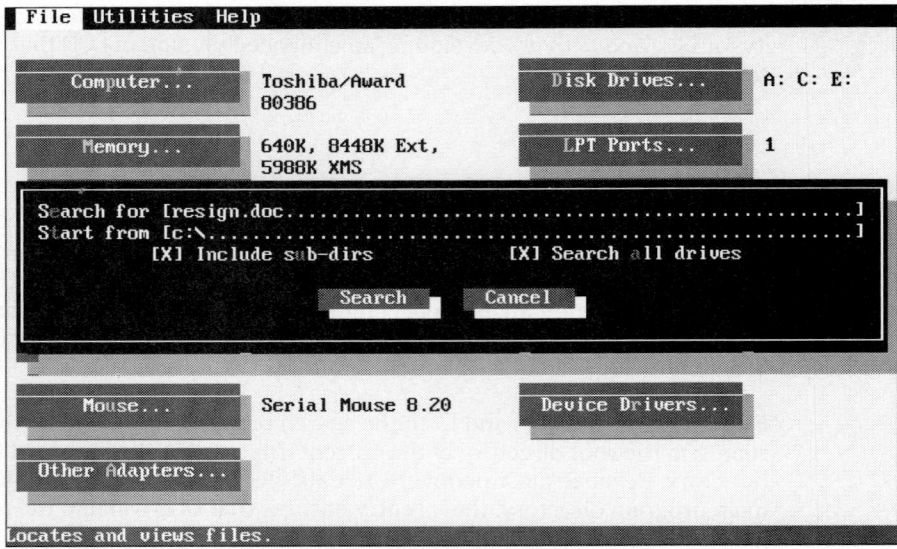

Figure 2-7: MSD can search for files across multiple drives.

The following command, for example, prompts for the user details and then generates a detailed report in the ASCII file MSD.OUT:

```
msd /fmsd.out
```

Having entered this MSD command, the user can then send the MSD.OUT file to you by mail or e-mail for analysis.

One surprising and little-known feature of MSD is that it includes a decent file-finding and -browsing tool. You can search for any file by first selecting File⇨Find File from the main MSD menu and then entering the file details in the dialog box (see Figure 2-7). All the files MSD finds during the search are displayed in a scrollable list. You can view the contents of any file by selecting it from the list.

Making the DOSSHELL Work

The DOS Shell was introduced with DOS 5.0, and Microsoft tried hard to convince users that it was a major new feature. The DOS Shell provides file-management, program-launching, and task-switching capabilities from a full-screen application that supports the mouse. Figure 2-8 shows a typical DOS Shell display with a menu bar and four activity windows.

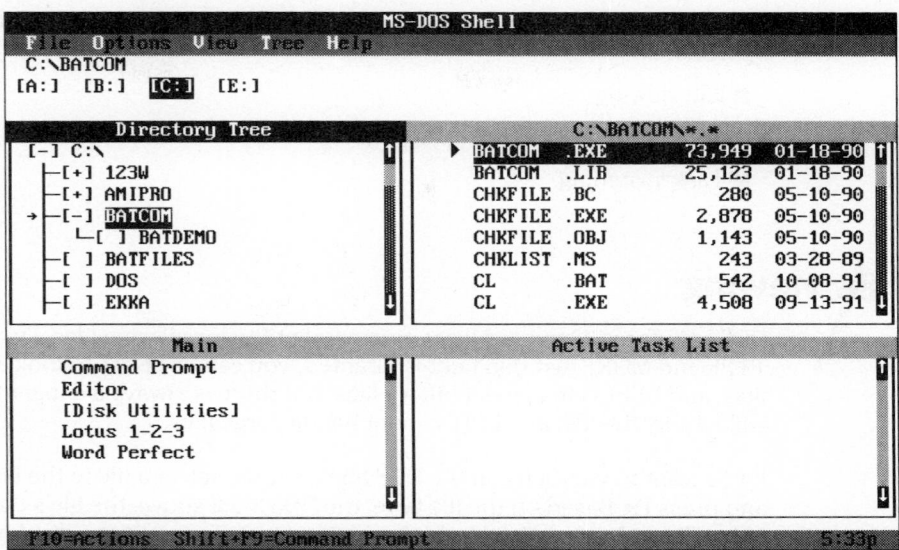

Figure 2-8: The primary interface of the DOS Shell program.

The DOS Shell was Microsoft's attempt to shield users from the terse command prompt and provide an easy-to-use environment for running programs and managing files. In reality, however, only a small percentage of users embraced the new program.

There are two main reasons for the user community's lackluster response: The program is slow, and it arrived too late, at a time when Windows was gaining popularity. Windows certainly provides all the features of DOSSHELL and then some. It is interesting to note that the DOS Shell is no longer being pushed by Microsoft, and it has not been significantly enhanced for DOS 6. Furthermore, the DOS Shell gets less than three pages in the *MS-DOS User's Guide*. Microsoft is clearly placing less emphasis on the DOS Shell. I hope that it's because it is working on providing improved file management and task switching in the core of a future version of DOS. Time will tell.

Some people used to use the DOS Shell solely to perform tasks that couldn't be performed with other DOS commands — namely, renaming directories and moving files. Now these tasks can be performed by the use of the new MOVE command.

If you use Windows, it is highly unlikely that you will need the DOS Shell. There are still some things, however, the DOS Shell does better than plain DOS does. If you don't use Windows, you might be tempted to use the DOS Shell for these operations:

- File viewing
- Diverse file selection and management
- Task switching

File viewing

DOS still doesn't have a decent command utility for viewing files. I'm afraid that TYPE and MORE just don't cut it. Granted, you can use EDIT to look at ASCII files, and DEBUG to inspect binary files, but there is always a danger that you will modify the file, and EDIT cannot handle large files.

If you want to view a file in the DOS Shell, simply select a file in the File Window and press F9. Based on the file type, the DOS Shell shows the file's contents in either Text Mode or Hex Mode (for binary files). To toggle the display to the other mode, press F9 again.

Bob's Shareware Collection disks include the excellent file-viewing program LIST, from Buerg Software. LIST can quickly display any file of any size, and it offers features such as an optional ruler bar, customizable colors, user-placed bookmarks, text searching, printing, and condensed mode display. To put it bluntly, LIST is the king of file-viewing utilities.

Diverse file selection and management

The standard DOS commands enable you to manage a block of files only if they all conform to a common filemask. There is no way, for example, to copy with one DOS command all the files that have an EXE, a COM, and a BAT extension. The DOS Shell enables you to select a mixed set of files regardless of the filemask and then perform common file operations such as copying, moving, and deleting them.

If you are planning to use the DOS Shell for file management, make the file and tree windows larger by choosing **View**⇨**Single** File List from the DOS Shell menu. Select the menu option **Options**⇨File Display Options to work with files that match a particular filemask. Otherwise, leave it set at *.*. Also, if you want to be able to select a set of files that span more than one directory, you must select **Options**⇨Select **Across** Directories and make sure that a dot appears next to the menu item to indicate that the option is active.

To select a contiguous block of files from the list, move the cursor to the first or last file in the block, hold down the Shift key, and press either the up- or down-arrow key to extend the selection block. To select various files from around the list, press Shift-F8 to change to Add Mode (the ADD indicator illuminates in the lower right corner) and then press the arrow keys to navigate around the list. Press the spacebar to toggle the selection status of the file at the cursor. All selected files are displayed in reverse video (see Figure 2-9). Having selected the files, you can then select the appropriate file operation from the File menu.

There are a couple of shortcuts for mouse users. You can select the files by clicking the left mouse button. To move all the selected files, place the mouse cursor over one of the selected files, press and hold down the left mouse button, and then drag the mouse cursor to the target directory or drive and release the mouse button. To copy files (rather than move them), hold down the Ctrl key during the drag operation.

Another useful feature of the DOS Shell file manager is that you can display all the files on the entire drive in one contiguous list. You then can sort the list in any of the standard ways. To delete all the files with a BAK extension from your hard disk, for example, you can follow these steps:

1. Choose **Options**⇨**File Display Options** and then enter *.BAK.

2. Choose **View**⇨**All Files.**

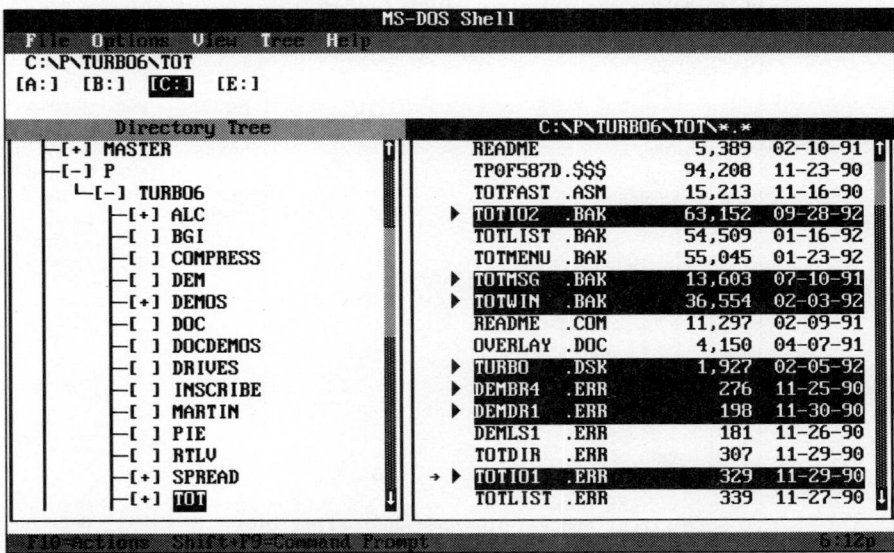

Figure 2-9: You can select diverse files, and they are displayed in reverse video.

3. Choose **File**⇨Select All.

4. Choose **File**⇨Delete.

You can bypass the repetitive confirmation prompts by choosing **O**ptions⇨**C**onfirmation and unchecking the Delete field.

If you are using the DOS Shell for file management, I have good news for you. Bob's Shareware Collection disks include the excellent file manager CMFILER, from NovaSoft. CMFILER is a lightning-fast, full-screen utility that makes the DOS Shell look primitive.

CMFILER can display two directories side by side or display a directory tree in one window and a file list in the other (see Figure 2-10). In addition to enabling you to copy, move, delete, and rename files, you can browse, edit, and concatenate files. You can even add notes or comments to any file. CMFILER can print files or directory listings in the background, which enables you to continue with other file-management tasks and not wait for the print task to finish.

CMFILER also acts as a command center for executing programs, and you can optionally assign programs to the function keys. See Part V of this book for a detailed description of CMFILER.

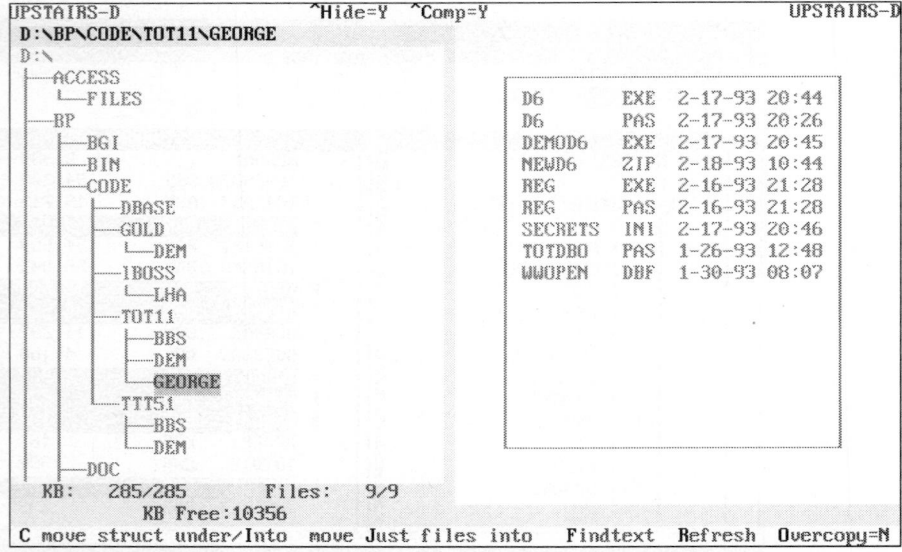

Figure 2-10: CMFILER can display a directory tree in one window and a directory list in the other.

Task switching

The DOS Shell includes a task switcher that enables you to run more than one program at a time and then switch or jump from one active program to another. You may have both your word processor and your spreadsheet running at the same time, for example. Note that, unlike Windows, the DOS Shell does not allow one program to run in the background (to recalculate a spreadsheet, for example) while another application is being used. As soon as you switch from one application to another, the old application is suspended.

Although the DOS Shell task switcher has been criticized for being slow, it may well be much faster than having to repeatedly shut down one program and then launch another.

To run multiple programs, you must enable task switching by selecting **O**ptions⇨Enable Task Swapper. A dot appears next to the menu option when task switching is enabled. Many of the ways to launch programs and swap between them are the same as in Windows. This section shows some guidelines for how to perform the following main task-switching operations:

■ Add programs to the menu

■ Start programs

■ Load programs

■ Swap between programs

■ Terminate programs

Adding programs to the menu. To add a program or submenu to the menu window (which is in the lower left quadrant of the display — refer to Figure 2-9), activate the window and select **F**ile⇨**N**ew. You then can create a new program entry by selecting Item or create a new submenu by selecting Group.

All the DOS Shell configuration details are stored in the file DOSSHELL.INI. If you have upgraded from DOS 5 to DOS 6, the setup procedure does not overwrite the existing DOSSHELL.INI file. The default options in the DOS 5 version of DOSSHELL.INI included a Disk Utilities menu that called the outdated DOS BACKUP and RESTORE programs. If you have not customized the DOS Shell and you want to use the new DOS 6 factory defaults (which call DEFRAG, MSBACKUP, and the other new programs), delete DOSSHELL.INI before installing DOS 6.

If you have already installed DOS 6, you can manually load an updated initialization file from Disk 1 of the DOS 6 installation disks. Be aware that any changes you already have made to customize the DOS Shell will be overwritten. Three files contain copies of DOSSHELL.INI: MONO.IN_, CGA.IN_, and EGA.IN_; these files are for monochrome, CGA, and EGA/VGA systems, respectively. Select the file that corresponds to your system's video display type. (Remember that you can use MSD to ascertain your display type if you don't know what it is.)

Because these files contain compressed data, they must be *expanded*, not copied, to the DOS directory. To expand the appropriate file (assumed to be EGA.IN_), insert Disk 1 into the drive (assumed to be drive A) and enter the following command:

```
a:expand a:ega.in_ c:\dos\dosshell.ini
```

The next time you run the DOS Shell, you see the new DOS 6 menu options.

Starting programs. You can start a program by using a variety of methods. The most obvious way is to select the item from the Program menu. Another way is to double-click the mouse on any program or batch file in the file list or highlight the program and press Enter. If you have *associated* a file extension with a specific program, you can select any file with that extension, and the associated program will be launched. You can also launch a program by selecting File⇨Run from the menu.

Loading programs. If you want to load a program but not start using it right away, hold down the Shift key before pressing Enter or clicking the left mouse button. The program is added to the Active Task List window, but the main DOS Shell window remains displayed.

Swapping between programs. You can return to the DOS Shell application from any program by pressing Ctrl-Esc, but be patient because it can take a few seconds. To use a different program, simply select it from the Active Task List. You can rotate from program to program by holding down the Alt key and pressing Tab. If you keep the Alt key pressed down, you can press Tab additional times to rotate through the list of programs. Release the Alt key when you reach the program you want. You can also assign a unique hotkey to any application when you first add the program to the menu, or later, by highlighting the menu item and selecting File⇨Properties.

Terminating programs. The normal way to remove a program from the Active Task List is to swap to the program and quit the application in the normal manner. You can also terminate a program by highlighting the program in the Active Task List and pressing the Del key. Remember, however, that the application is terminated just as though you had turned the computer off; no files are saved, and the program does not follow its normal exit procedures. Avoid using Del, except when a program cannot be terminated in the normal manner.

Summary

In this chapter, I have described some of the ways you can leverage maximum power from the most frequently used DOS commands. The important features you learned about in this chapter are shown in this list:

▶ The HELP command is packed with useful information about DOS commands and device drivers, and includes a search option for scanning for any text.

▶ You should use XCOPY in preference to COPY because, in most cases, it is faster and more versatile.

▶ The new MOVE command can move multiple files in a single operation, but, unlike COPY, a source filemask and a target path must always be specified. You can also use MOVE to rename directories.

▶ The new command DELTREE can erase an entire set of directories and files in one command, and it should be used with caution. DELTREE can delete hidden, system, and read-only files.

▶ Most users don't tap the power of DIR: By using the /S switch, you can search for files; by using the /A switch, you can list files that match a specific attribute; you can use the DIRCMD environment variable to customize DIR's default settings.

▶ The system diagnostic program MSD analyzes your system's hardware and can generate a comprehensive report that documents all aspects of the system's configuration. MSD can be used also to search for files.

▶ Although the DOS Shell is slow and a little clunky, you might consider using it for file viewing, task switching, and managing blocks of files that don't share a common filemask.

▶ Many excellent shareware programs included on Bob's Better-than-DOS Shareware Collection disks provide more power, functionality, and flexibility than do their DOS counterparts.

In Chapter 3, you learn which precautions you should take to avoid data loss and ways to recover from accidental file deletion, disk formatting, and virus infection.

Chapter 3

Protecting and Recovering That Irreplaceable Data

In This Chapter

▶ The DOS 6 defensive arsenal

▶ Backup tips, traps, and truths

▶ "Must do" data-protection precautions

▶ Lost file and data recovery

▶ Deliberate data destruction

▶ Vital virus measures

▶ A lighter note

The DOS 6 Defensive Arsenal

More and more businesses and livelihoods depend on the data stored in PCs. The loss of this data can be a real catastrophe. Fortunately, DOS 6 provides an arsenal of tools to help you protect against data loss and tools to help you recover if data loss occurs.

The following list summarizes the data-protection tools available in DOS 6:

MIRROR: Using the /PARTN switch, MIRROR saves a copy of the hard disk partition table to disk. This program is available on the DOS 6 Supplemental disk.

MSAV: The Microsoft Anti-Virus utility for identifying and removing (or cleaning) computer viruses. You can execute MSAV as a full-screen application or directly from the command line by using switches.

MSBACKUP: The Microsoft Backup utility for backing up *and* restoring files. The MSBACKUP full-screen utility does not support full execution directly from the command line.

MWAV: The Windows version of the Microsoft Anti-Virus utility. The core utility functions are the same as MSAV, but MWAV takes advantage of Windows' rich graphical environment.

MWBACKUP: The Windows version of the Microsoft Backup utility. The core features of both backup utilities are identical, and backups performed with MWBACKUP and MSBACKUP are compatible and interchangeable.

MWUNDEL: This Windows version of UNDELETE is used to recover accidentally deleted files.

UNDELETE: This tool provides mechanisms for enhancing the chances of recovering deleted files and provides tools to undelete files that have been deleted.

UNFORMAT: This tool recovers files and directories destroyed by an accidental format.

VSAFE: This tool loads the anti-virus TSR to monitor disk activity and protect against virus infection and damage.

Refer to Part IV, "The Complete DOS 6 Command Reference," for a full description of each of these commands.

When you install the Windows applications, SETUP automatically adds to the File Manager a Tools menu item with Backup and Anti-Virus menu options. If you install Windows after you install DOS 6, you can update File Manager with the new menu by running SETUP with the /E switch:

```
setup /e
```

Users of Norton Desktop for Windows (NDW) 2.0 or earlier may be irritated by the appearance of two (count 'em) Tools menus on the desktop. One is the NDW standard Tools menu, and the other one is the Tools menu created by DOS 6. NDW reads the [ADDONS] section of WINFILE.INI and, like File Manager, uses this information to create additional menus. You can instruct NDW to ignore the menu add-ons (and therefore eliminate the extra Tools menu) by adding the following entry to the [DEFAULTS] section of NDW.INI:

```
MaxWinFileExtensions=0
```

DOS 6 SETUP also creates a program group labeled Microsoft Tools that provides quick access to the three Windows-based applications: Anti-Virus, Backup, and Undelete. This group is defined in the file WNTOOLS.GRP in the DOS directory. NDW users should manually create a Microsoft Tools group by selecting the main menu options File⇨New⇨Group and using the browse facility to select the WNTOOLS.GRP file from the DOS directory.

When you use the Anti-Virus, Undelete, or Backup utilities from a shared network drive, you may find that another network user has reconfigured the tools. All three data-protection utilities access INI files — namely, MSAV.INI, MWAV.INI, UNDELETE.INI, and MSBACKUP.INI — to determine their default characteristics.

By creating an environment variable called MSDOSDATA, you can instruct these utilities to access the INI file in a specific directory. Just set the environment variable MSDOSDATA equal to the specific directory in which the personal INI file is located. You should add the following command, for example, to AUTOEXEC.BAT to force DOS to load the INI files from the C:\INIFILES directory:

```
msdosdata=c:\inifiles
```

When you customize a utility's configuration, the changes are stored in your personal INI file.

Backup Tips, Traps, and Truths

The best way to deal with data loss is to be prepared for it, which leads us to the first truth:

Truth 1: At one time or another, an important file will be destroyed.

Although you may be able to use a utility program to recover a deleted file, in many cases the file is destroyed and cannot be recovered. If you accidentally overwrite a file by using the same name to copy or move another file into the same directory, for example, the chances that you can recover the overwritten file are slim to none. Your only option is to restore a copy of the file from a backup disk. Obviously, you can restore the file from a backup only if you *have* a backup.

It is all too easy to destroy a valuable file by using the COPY or MOVE command. One of the many valuable features of the shareware program PCOPY (part of Patriquin's Hard Disk Utilities) is that it prompts you before overwriting a file during a copy or move operation. You can, of course, instruct PCOPY to overwrite files automatically, but by default (thankfully), it doesn't.

Even with first-class data-recovery tools at your disposal, up-to-date file backups are essential.

Using the DOS 6 backup software

With the release of version 6, DOS backup tools suddenly got much better, and it's about time. Thankfully, the much-criticized BACKUP and RESTORE programs have been replaced by an all-new backup utility, which comes in two flavors: MSBACKUP for character-mode DOS and MWBACKUP for Windows.

Although the RESTORE program ships with DOS 6, it is provided only so that you can restore files made with DOS's old BACKUP program.

Comparing MSBACKUP and MWBACKUP

Other than their obvious cosmetic differences, the two backup utilities MSBACKUP and MWBACKUP are very similar. They feature the same backup options, use similar terminology and menus, and offer similar performance. What's more, backups created with one product can be restored with the other. Figures 3-1 and 3-2 show the similarities between the two products highlighted in the Backup dialog boxes.

Use whichever utility you are most comfortable with.

The backup programs can back up files only to a standard DOS device, such as a floppy disk, hard disk, network drive, or removable drive (a Bernoulli box, for example). A major drawback is that the programs cannot back up files to tape devices. I anticipate that this feature will be added in a future DOS release.

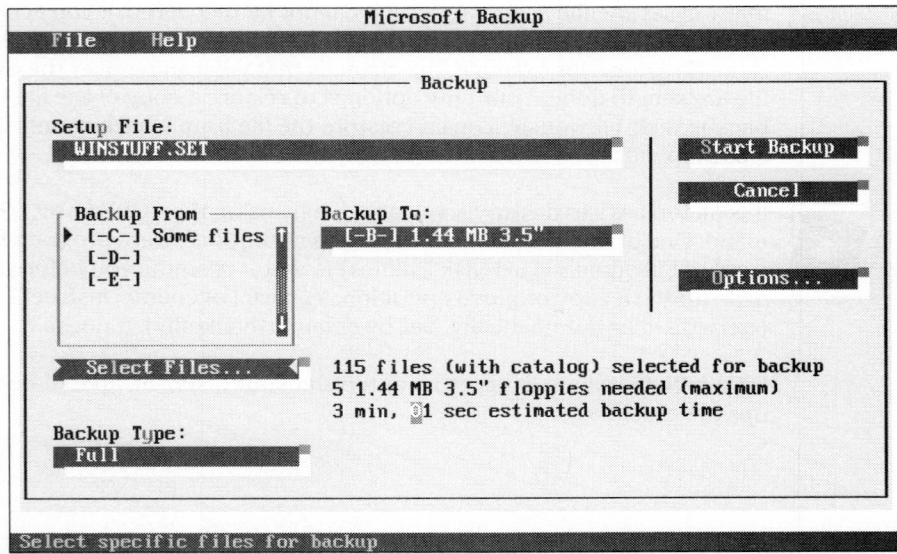

Figure 3-1: The Backup dialog box from MSBACKUP, the Text Mode backup utility.

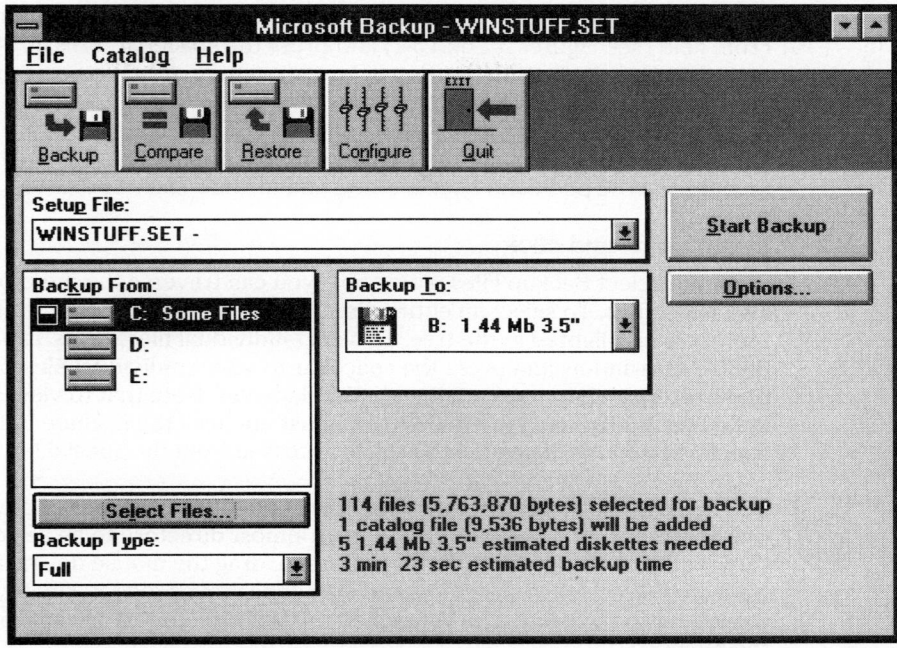

Figure 3-2: The Backup dialog box from MWBACKUP, the Windows backup utility.

The first time you run the backup software, you must go through a configuration process. During the configuration, the backup program backs up a little more than one floppy disk full of files and then runs a comparison to verify that the files were backed up successfully. Be prepared to have two disks and don't use disks that have valuable data on them.

If your system has more than one floppy drive, you can choose which drive is used for the minibackup. Be sure to select the drive you normally use for backups — normally, the highest capacity drive.

Selecting files to back up

As bizarre as it may sound, most people have difficulty selecting which files to back up. If you think you just execute the program and select the backup button, think again!

The list of files you select to back up is stored in a SETUP file that has a SET extension. By default, the backup program loads the file DEFAULT.SET.

You must have at least one file tagged for backup before you can run a backup. If no files are tagged for backup, the Start Backup button is grayed.

A quick way to select all the files on a drive is to highlight a drive in the Ba**c**kup From field (see Figures 3-1 and 3-2) and press the spacebar. Pressing the spacebar again toggles the setting from all files to no files. You can select files from multiple drives in a single backup.

To select some but not all files from a drive, you can choose from two distinct techniques: the point-and-click method and include/exclude clauses.

Using point and click

From the Select Backup Files dialog box, you can traverse the directory tree and select files. To select an entire directory, press the spacebar while the directory is highlighted in the tree. To select individual files, press Tab to move to the file list window and press the spacebar to select individual files. You can press the spacebar a second time to deselect files. Note that to view all files, including hidden and system files, you must uncheck the Exclude options in the Special Selections dialog box, which is accessed from the **S**pecial button.

You can use the mouse to select multiple contiguous branches of the tree in one operation. First double-click on the topmost directory to be selected and then, while you keep the left button pressed, drag the mouse downward. Each traversed directory is selected as you drag the mouse over it. Finally, release the left button when you have reached the last directory you want to select in the block.

Selected files are identified by a check mark ( ). When a file is selected individually but is excluded because of an overriding exclusion clause or because it doesn't match the backup type, a dot (·) is displayed. Files that display a dot are not backed up.

Although the two backup programs are virtually identical, file selection is one area in which the Windows program has the edge. The use of the + and - keys expands and collapses the directory tree and makes it easy to select an entire drive by collapsing the root directory. You cannot collapse the tree in MSBACKUP.

Using include/exclude clauses

My preferred method of file selection is to include and exclude directories explicitly by using the Edit Include/Exclude List dialog box (or the Include/Exclude Files dialog box in the Windows version). In the DOS backup program, you should click on either the **In**clude or **Ex**clude button and then immediately select the **E**dit Include/Exclude List button to bypass the next dialog box (which doesn't appear in the Windows version). Figure 3-3 illustrates this dialog box.

By specifying filemasks and directories, you can create a list of included and excluded files. You should note that the backup programs read the list in top-down order. If two conditions conflict (one clause says to include some files,

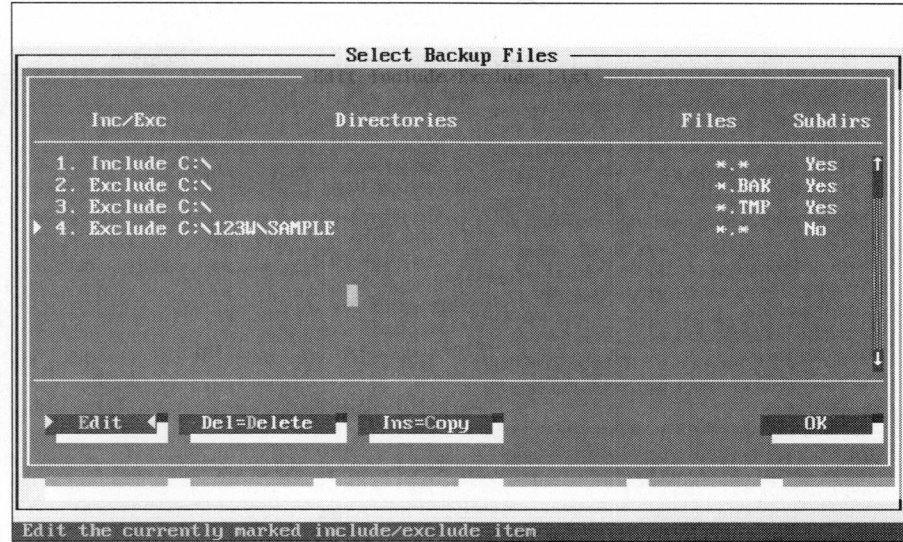

Figure 3-3: The Edit Include/Exclude List dialog box from MSBACKUP.

and another clause says to exclude the same files, for example), the clause that is lower down the list is honored. Consider the following clause list:

```
INCLUDE D:\                                   Yes *.*
EXCLUDE D:\ACCESS                             Yes *.*
EXCLUDE D:\.............................Yes *.BAK
```

The preceding clause list includes all files in drive D except files in the \ACCESS subdirectory (and its subdirectories) and any files with a BAK extension.

If the order of the list is changed, however, the meaning is very different. Consider the following list:

```
EXCLUDE D:\ACCESS                             Yes *.*
EXCLUDE D:\.............................Yes *.BAK
INCLUDE D:\                                   Yes *.*
```

Because the last statement in the list includes all files on drive D, the two preceding EXCLUDE items are overwritten (ignored). This list results in the inclusion of all drive D files.

Figure 3-4 shows the Include/Exclude Files dialog box in the Windows-based backup program. I can't count the number of times I have seen a user define an include or exclude clause and then promptly lose it by pressing Enter. Only the items listed in the lower dialog box field titled Include/Exclude List are applied.

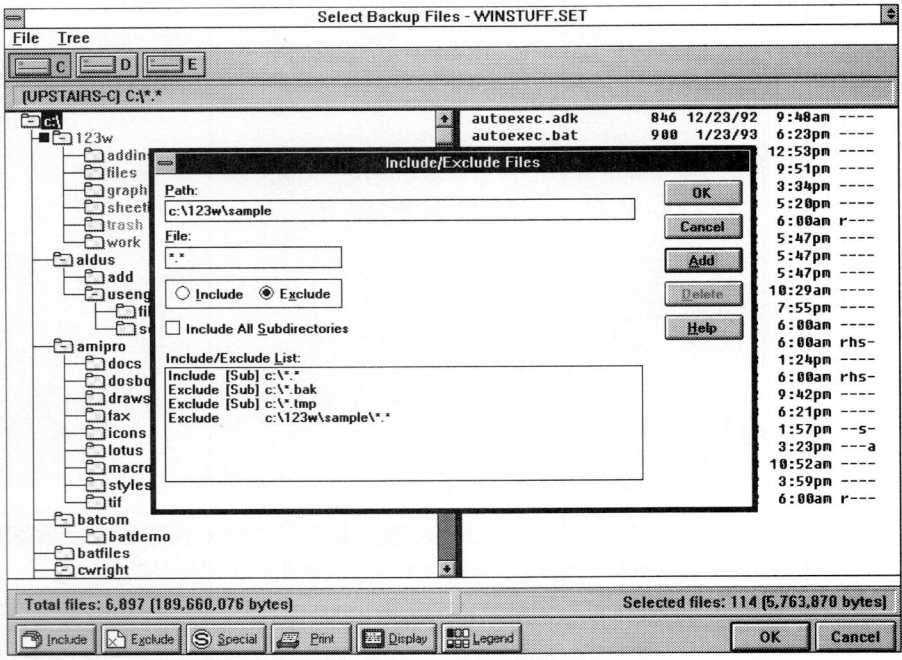

Figure 3-4: The Include/Exclude Files dialog box from MWBACKUP.

After you have entered a new clause in the top fields, you must click on the Add button — pressing Enter simply selects the OK button, which ignores the last entry and removes the dialog box. Crazy.

When you return to the main backup window, a summary of the number of selected files is displayed in the lower right quadrant of the window (refer to Figure 3-1).

Having gone through the pain of selecting the files you want, you can save the selection in a SET file. The next time you want to back up the same collection of files, just load the SET file from the File menu. I keep a variety of SET files to handle all my backup needs: one saves all my programming source files, for example, and another one saves all the files used in the creation of this book.

Selecting the backup type

In addition to the selection of individual files, the backup programs support these three types of backups:

■ Full

■ Incremental

■ Differential

As its name suggests, a *full* backup creates a backup of all *selected* files.

An *incremental* backup makes a backup of all files that have been changed (or added) since the last full or incremental backup. This backup type references the file archive bit to determine whether the file should be included in the backup. If the archive bit is set, the file is backed up; otherwise, the file is not backed up. When the file has been backed up, the archive bit is turned off.

 Do not use the same backup disks for saving every incremental backup. You can restore the complete file system from only the previous full backup and *each* subsequent incremental backup. Always use fresh disks for each incremental backup, until the next full backup is taken.

A *differential* backup makes a backup of all files that have been changed since the last full backup. Like an incremental backup, a differential backup uses the archive bit to determine which files should be backed up. The main difference between these two backup types is that the archive bit is not turned off after a differential backup. A complete backup disk set comprises a full backup and the last differential backup.

 Between full backups, you should perform either incremental backups or differential backups. Do not mix the two backup types. The task of restoring a complete file set is significantly complicated when you have used both partial backup types.

You can change the backup type by using the Backup Type field in the main Backup window.

Special file-selection options

In addition to individual file selection and the backup type, a set of special options narrows the file selection. You can confine the backup to include only files with a date that falls within a specific range or exclude files based on their read-only, hidden, and system attributes.

The Special Selections dialog box is displayed when you select the Special button in the Select Backup Files window (see Figure 3-5).

The dialog box is self-explanatory except for the five fields in the lower right quadrant. These fields are designed for specifying copy-protected files that should not be backed up. They enable you to specify as many as five files that are not backed up from any directory if the Exclude Copy Protected Files field is checked.

 Thankfully, copy-protected files are less prevalent nowadays. One file I always want to avoid backing up is the Windows permanent swap file 386SPART.PAR. This file is invaluable for increasing the capacity of Windows, but it contains no data that has to be backed up. A sure-fire way to always exclude this file from a backup is to identify it as a copy-protected file in the Special Selections dialog box.

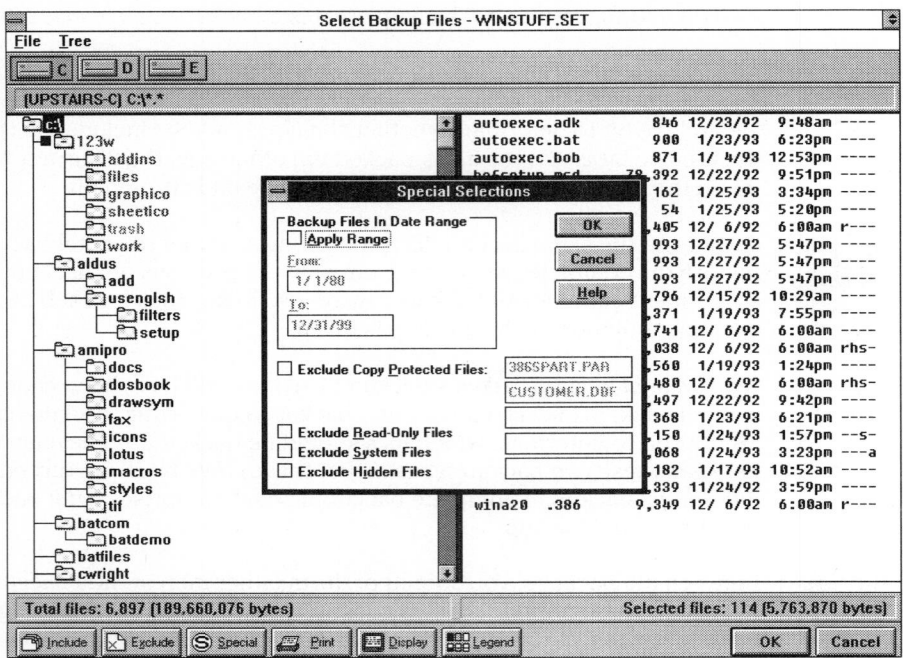

Figure 3-5: The Special Selections dialog box from MWBACKUP.

Make sure that your backup is good

Truth 2: Many people don't discover that their backups are useless until they try to recover an important file.

Both backups provide a Compare option for verifying that the backed-up data is the same as the source data on the hard disk. For the first few backups, run the Compare option to verify that you are making good backup copies. This option takes time, but there is no point in wasting time backing up files if you cannot restore them later.

As an acid test, you should consider restoring a single file from a backup to make sure that, in a real emergency, you can do likewise. Pick a single file to restore as a test and rename that file on the hard disk. Then try to restore the file from the backup.

Optimizing backup speed

In my book, the faster the backup, the better. The longer a backup takes, the less frequently I make them. Follow these steps to maximize backup speed:

- Use high-density floppy disks.

- Turn off data verification (from the Options menu). There is, of course, a trade-off between performance and safety. Use the Compare option a number of times to occasionally spot-check that the backup is sound. If you are using new disks for a backup, turn on data verification for the first backup.

- Turn on data compression. It takes less time to compress the data and write fewer bytes to the disk than it does to blindly save the uncompressed file to disk.

- Turn off error correction. Again, there is a trade-off between speed and safety here. By storing error-correction data on the backup disk, the chances of restoring files from the disk (after the disk has been damaged) are greatly enhanced. The error-correction information requires approximately 10 percent additional disk space.

- In the Windows environment, keep the other active applications to a minimum. The more applications asking for a slice of the CPU's attention, the longer the backup takes.

Both backup programs use a special Error Correction Code (ECC) data-storage technique, pioneered by Symantec. This technique enhances your chances of restoring data from a damaged disk. This damage can occur when you make the backup with the Data Verification option disabled and the disk has some bad sectors, or when the disk becomes physically damaged after the backup is made.

The ECC system involves storing a group of sectors to the end cylinder of the disk. When you are restoring data, you can use the ECC section to rebuild as many as four damaged sectors.

When you use MWBACKUP, make sure that you do not run another application that accesses the floppy drives — data can be destroyed. This restriction applies to all floppy drives, not just to the one being used for the backup.

Files created and used by the backup

A variety of files are created and accessed by the backup programs. The following list shows the main files, which are discussed in this section:

- SET
- SLT
- Catalog

- CAT
- 00*n*
- INI
- LOG

SET files. SET files store a full definition of a backup, including which drives to back up, which files to back up, which target drive to back up to, the backup type (full or incremental, for example), and the special options. SET files are stored in the DOS directory and are plain ASCII files. You can readily print and review them by using the File⇨Print menu option.

SLT files. An SLT file holds the list of directories and files that were selected for backup using the keyboard and mouse (rather than an include/exclude list). The file uses the same eight-character name as the SET file, but with an SLT extension.

Catalog files. A catalog file is created for every backup. The catalog file is binary and stores complete information about the structure of the drive (or drives) that was backed up, in addition to a complete list of all backed-up files. One copy of the file is stored in the DOS directory, and another copy is stored at the end of the backup data on the backup disks.

A simple convention is used to build the catalog filename. The eight-character filename details the backup source and date by using the following conventions:

Character 1   The letter of the first drive that had files backed up.

Character 2   The letter of the last drive that had files backed up.

Characters 3–7   The date when the backup was made using the format YMMDD, where Y is the last digit of the year when the backup was made (4 for 1994, for example).

Character 8   A letter that identifies the order of the backup. This character really is used to ensure that every catalog has a unique name. If the backup program sees that a catalog already exists with the same first seven digits (and the same extension), the next available letter of the alphabet is used in character position 8.

 If the Keep Old Catalogs option is turned off, the eighth character always is A, and any existing catalog with the same name is overwritten.

The catalog filename extension indicates the type of backup and is FUL, INC, or DIF.

CAT files. A master catalog (CAT) file is created for every backup set. The file-name comprises the first eight characters of the SET filename and has a CAT extension. This (ASCII) file contains a record of when the last full backup was made and a chronological history of every subsequent incremental or differential backup. This file is accessed during the restore process. Every time a new full backup is taken, the file is cleared and the new backup is recorded as the first entry.

00*n*. The files created on the backup disks with a 00*n* extension format are the files in which the backed-up data is stored. The first backup disk has the extension 001; the second, 002; and so on. The eight-character filename is built by using the same conventions as the catalog file. The date and time stamp on the file indicates the date and time the backup was made. You can use old backup disks that were formatted by the BACKUP program as general-purpose DOS disks.

The volume label of a backup disk provides more information about the backup. The first part of the volume label is the name of the setup file (without the SET extension) that was used to define the backup options. The last three characters of the volume label indicate the backup type and are FUL, INC, or DIF.

INI files. MSBACKUP creates the binary (noneditable) file MSBACKUP.INI, which defines the primary backup configuration and system characteristics (DMA transfer type and installed drives, for example). If this file is not present, you must configure MSBACKUP before you can use it.

LOG files. The temporary file MSBACKUP.LOG contains (in binary format) the directory structure of all the drives that were logged in the last MSBACKUP session. This file is created when MSBACKUP displays the message that it is reading disk information.

Any floppy disk used for a backup can be used later as a standard DOS floppy disk for copying files and other tasks. If you try later to use the old disk in a new backup, the backup program presents a warning message that the disk was used in a previous backup. This message is displayed even when you have deleted the old backup files and changed the volume label.

You may wonder how the backup program knows that the disk has been used in an earlier backup. The backup program records the backup details (including the SET name, the date and time of the backup, and the floppy disk number) behind the scenes in part of the boot sector. This area is erased only when you format the disk. Whenever you insert a new disk, BACKUP checks the boot sector to see whether the disk has already been backed up to. This defensive mechanism stops you from inadvertently inserting the wrong floppy disk during a backup session.

Restoring files from a backup

Truth 3: A backup is useless if you can't restore any files from it.

You can restore files only after the backup program has loaded the backup's corresponding catalog file. When the backup is made, one catalog file is saved in the DOS directory, and the other is saved on the last backup disk.

Figure 3-6 shows the catalog-selection options presented in the Select Catalog dialog box. You can display this dialog box by selecting the **Catalog** button in the Restore window. Although MWBACKUP does not provide a catalog dialog box, you can select the same options from the Restore main menu (see Figure 3-7).

You can access a catalog in one of these three ways:

Load   The CAT file is retrieved from the hard disk.

Retrieve   The CAT file is restored from the last floppy disk in the backup set.

Rebuild   The backup program examines the contents of every floppy disk in the backup series and re-creates the CAT file.

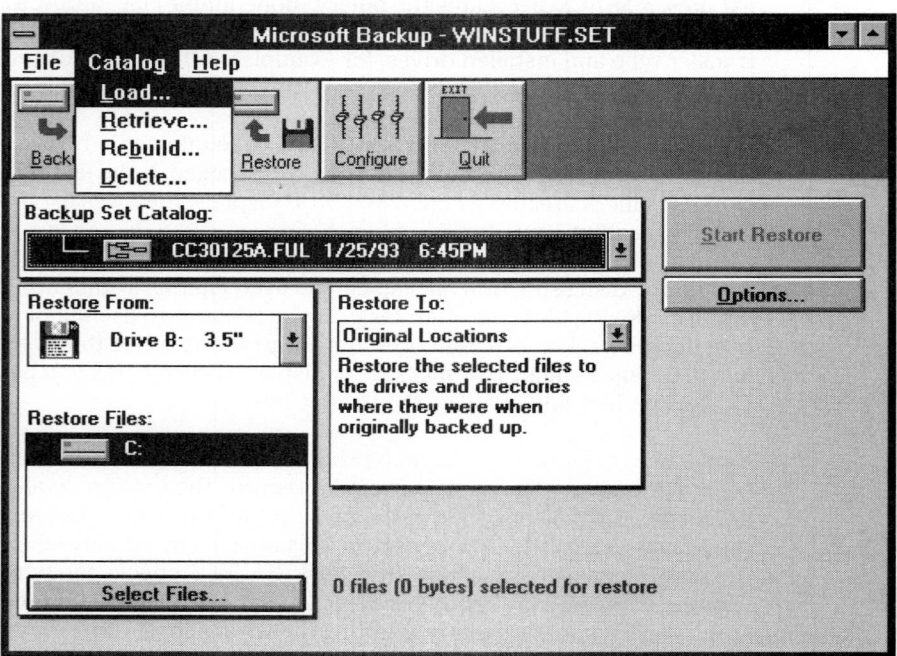

Figure 3-6: The Select Catalog dialog box from MWBACKUP.

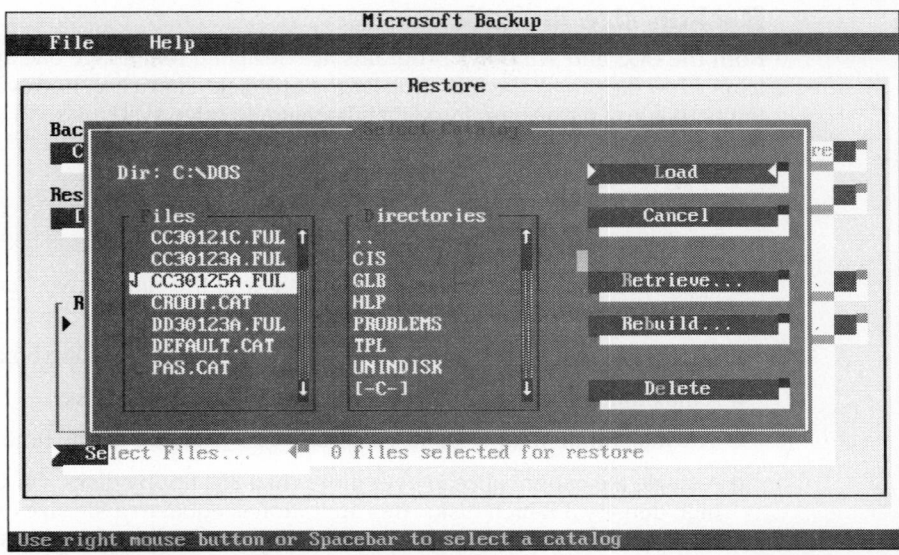

Figure 3-7: The catalog menu options in MSBACKUP.

Normally, you should try to load the catalog. If you can't find the CAT file, try to retrieve the catalog from the backup set. If the file is damaged or you can't find the last disk in the backup, rebuild the catalog from the disks you have.

After loading the catalog, you choose the files to be restored by using the same techniques you used to choose files to be backed up (discussed earlier in this chapter), except that you cannot use include and exclude lists. When you choose the Select Files button from the Restore menu, the directory tree reflects the directory structure of the disk when the files were backed up, and it can differ from the current directory structure.

If you have not selected any files, the Start Restore button is grayed and inactive.

By default, the backup program does not restore files that are read-only, hidden, or system. If you back up all the files on drive C, format the drive, and then use default settings to restore the files, for example, your drive will not be bootable because all the read-only, hidden, and system files will be missing. Select the Special button from the Select Restore Files dialog box and uncheck the exclude fields to ensure that all files are restored regardless of their attribute values.

Backup size limitations

Both the DOS and Windows programs are designed to manage backups ranging from a few files to all the files on a large hard disk. There are, however, some limits that you may bump into when backing up huge systems such as a file server.

This list shows some of the backup program's operating limits:

- The maximum number of entries in an include/exclude list is 50.
- There is a maximum of 26 backups per day of the same drives using the same backup type.
- A maximum of 49 setup (SET) files can be listed in the dialog boxes.
- A maximum of 1,023 directories can be logged for any drive.
- The maximum number of files that can be backed up at one time is 65,535.
- A single file cannot spread over more than 254 floppy disks. On 1.44MB high-density 3 ½-inch disks, this limitation is equal to a file size of 730MB when maximum compression is used. Using 360K floppies with no compression, however, drops the maximum file size to a mere 90MB.

Backing up DoubleSpace drives

All the files and directories on a DoubleSpace drive are stored in a single (humongous) hidden file on the host drive.

You could, in theory, back up the DoubleSpace files in one of two ways. You could back up the host drive and be sure to include hidden files in the backup. The drawback to this technique is that all the DoubleSpace files are stored in a single backup file. If, for some reason, this large file cannot be restored because of a minor data error, you could not restore any of the DoubleSpace files hidden within. You will have put all your eggs in one huge, fragile basket.

A better way is to back up the files on the DoubleSpace drive individually, like any other standard drive. Then, if a data error occurs, it probably will affect only one or two files.

Developing a backup strategy

No discussion of backup tools is complete without a discussion of backup strategy.

Truth 4: The older your backup, the more likely it is that you will lose some important data.

You can adopt many different backup strategies. The frequency of data changes generally dictates how frequently you should back up. On a little-used system, you can do a full backup every month and an incremental backup every week. If you use your system on a full-time basis, you should make a full backup at least every week and make an incremental or differential backup every day.

Truth 5: If you don't follow a strict backup regime, you will make backups less and less frequently.

Don't set unrealistic backup goals, such as making a full backup twice a day. It isn't necessary. I prefer to make a full backup twice a week and then do daily differential backups. I prefer differential backups over incremental backups because the floppy disk sequence is easier to manage and the restoration process is simpler. I'm a great believer in KISS (Keep It Simple, Stupid).

 I also use PCOPY (the shareware utility) to keep, on floppy disks, a simple file copy of important files (such as the DOC file for this chapter!).

Truth 6: One backup copy is not enough.

Imagine that you realize you edited the wrong worksheet last week and updated the master budget files rather than the monthly forecast files. You have to get the original budget file back, so you try to restore the original file from a backup. The only problem is that you took the last backup after you made the changes, so the backup contains the modified budget file as the one on the system. This scenario occurs more often than you can imagine.

The solution is to keep multiple backup sets. You may keep four old sets of backups, for example, one for each of the past four weeks. Every time you make a full backup, you overwrite the oldest backup disk set.

Truth 7: If you keep your backup floppy disks near your computer, you are courting disaster.

Always, always keep backup files in a different location from your computer, and preferably off-site. If your office (or home) gets damaged by fire or water, your backup will be destroyed with your computer.

 If you have classified or confidential information on your computer, guard your backup floppy disks with the same fervor as you guard your system. There is little point in keeping your system secure when snoopers can restore on their system your files from the backup. I keep a complete backup in a safety-deposit box at the bank. Not only is it secure, but also the chances of the bank going up in flames at the same time as my office is remote enough for me.

Truth 8: If making backups isn't convenient, you probably won't make them.

Backing up a 500MB disk drive to floppy disks is downright impractical. If you have a large hard drive, you should set up an alternative to floppy disks.

If you are a network user, for example, you may be able to back up your local drives to the file server. As a bonus, the network administrator can keep back copies of all server volumes on tape.

If you are not connected to a network, consider installing a removable drive device, such as a Bernoulli drive.

More and more power users are installing tape-backup devices. Larger systems can hold 250 or 500 megabytes on a matchbox-size cassette. Unfortunately, the DOS backup programs do not (yet) support tape devices. If you are a heavy PC user with no other cost-effective alternative, you should consider installing a tape unit and buying a third-party backup program that supports tape drives. It may be the best $300 you spend.

"Must Do" Data-Protection Precautions

No one takes a backup every 15 minutes. By implementing a few sound practices, you can put in place a defensive mechanism that will help you to survive unexpected system crashes, accidental file deletions, and virus attacks.

This section discusses some of the main precautions you should consider implementing. Don't forget, however, that there is no substitute for frequent data backups.

Guarding against accidental file deletion

The most common cause of data loss is not by a virus attack or malice, or even by hardware failure: It is by you and me — human error. Put simply, we delete things by mistake.

DOS 6 provides the UNDELETE program to help protect against data loss caused by accidental file deletion. UNDELETE provides both data protection and data recovery. You can load it as a TSR that consumes about 14K of RAM and configure it to use one of the following two primary methods of deletion protection:

- Delete sentry
- Delete tracker

In the *delete sentry* method, a hidden directory named \SENTRY is used to store copies of deleted files. The TSR portion of UNDELETE monitors all file-deletion activity and substitutes a file move operation in place of the file deletion. This method provides the most secure form of protection because you can undelete the file just by moving it from the deleted directory back to the original directory. The problem with delete sentry is that it can hog disk space. After all, you don't recover any disk space when you delete a file because the file isn't really deleted.

The *delete tracker* method uses a hidden file named PCTRACKR.DEL in the root directory of the monitored drive to store vital data recovery information. This file contains the name of the deleted file and a list of all the clusters in which the file's data was stored. This method doesn't offer as much protection as the delete sentry method because other files can still overwrite the clusters. The primary advantage is that much less disk space is consumed. What's more, the chances of file recovery are good if there has been limited activity since the file was deleted.

 Avoid using ASSIGN, JOIN, and SUBST in conjunction with the delete tracking method.

Installing deletion protection

If you have plenty of free disk space, use the delete sentry method. One way to install delete sentry is to load UNDELETE using the /S switch. To install delete sentry protection for drive C, for example, add the following statement to your AUTOEXEC.BAT file:

```
undelete /sc
```

If, like me, you tend to have full disks, use the delete tracker method. To install delete tracker protection for drive D, add the following statement to AUTOEXEC.BAT:

```
undelete /td
```

Delete tracker records details on only a limited number of deleted files. The default number of files depends on the size of the hard disk and ranges from 100 on a 20MB drive to 300 on 30MB drives and larger. A 300-entry file consumes less than 60K of disk space. You can explicitly specify the number of entries (in the range from 1 to 999) when you install UNDELETE using the syntax entries. To track the maximum number of files on drive D, for example, revise the entry in AUTOEXEC.BAT as follows:

```
undelete /td-999
```

Understanding UNDELETE.INI

When you install UNDELETE, settings are recorded in the UNDELETE.INI file in the DOS directory. Rather than remember cumbersome command switches, you can edit UNDELETE.INI to configure your settings and then enter the following command to install UNDELETE using these settings:

```
undelete /load
```

The following file is an example of an UNDELETE.INI file:

```
[configuration]
archive=FALSE
days=7
percentage=20
[sentry.drives]
C=
D=
[mirror.drives]
C=
D=
[sentry.files]
s_files=*.* -*.TMP -*.VM? -*.WOA -*.SWP -*.SPL -*.RMG -*.IMG
-*.THM -*.DOV
[defaults]
d.sentry=TRUE
d.tracker=FALSE
```

The UNDELETE.INI file contains the following five sections:

> [configuration]
>
> [sentry.drives]
>
> [sentry.files]
>
> [mirror.drives]
>
> [defaults]

The [configuration] section contains three entries that define whether the archive bit is set when the secret copy is made, the total number of days deleted files are retained in the \SENTRY directory, and the maximum percentage of the total drive space the files in the \SENTRY directory can consume.

The [sentry.drives] section specifies the drives that will be protected by using the delete sentry method when that method is installed. If the delete tracker method is used, this section is ignored. Every drive letter is specified on a separate line and is followed by an equal-sign character. The following three entries, for example, protect drives C, D, and F:

```
C=
D=
F=
```

Use the [sentry.files] section to control which files are monitored and protected when the delete sentry method is used. This section is normally a list of filemasks. Precede a filemask with a minus sign if you want to exclude a set of files. The following entry, for example, protects all files except files with a BAK extension or an extension beginning with TP:

```
*.* -*.BAK -*.TP?
```

The [mirror.drives] section specifies the drives that are protected by using the delete tracker method when that tracker method is installed. (The name is a legacy from the time when Central Point Software, the original developer of UNDELETE, distributed the product.) Use the same syntax as in the [sentry.drives] section.

The [defaults] section controls which method of file protection is implemented when you execute the UNDELETE /LOAD command. One entry must be set to false and the other to true, as shown in this example:

```
d.sentry=FALSE
d.tracker=TRUE
```

 UNDELETE, as a minimum, always protects the drives specified in the UNDELETE.INI file, even if fewer drives are specified with the /S or /T switch when UNDELETE is loaded.

If you edit the UNDELETE.INI file, you must unload UNDELETE by using the /U switch and then reload it by using /LOAD. If you loaded another TSR after UNDELETE, you must reboot for the new configuration to take effect.

DEFRAG — yes, DEFRAG

If you do not use the UNDELETE TSR, your chances of successful data recovery using after-the-fact techniques improve significantly if your disk is not fragmented. Unassisted file recovery is much simpler when a file's data is stored in adjacent (or contiguous) clusters.

Use DEFRAG on a frequent (probably weekly) basis to keep files unfragmented. It not only enhances your chances of data recovery but also improves your system's overall performance. See Chapter 4 for a full discussion of fragmentation.

Check your disks

Run CHKDSK at least once a week and, preferably, once a day, just to ensure the integrity of the file allocation table. The sooner you know about a file-structure logic error, the better.

Unfortunately, DOS doesn't provide a real disk-analysis tool that verifies the physical integrity of the disk. You may consider supplementing the DOS tools with a third-party disk utility — I use Norton Disk Doctor, which is bundled with Symantec's Norton Desktop for Windows.

The case of the missing MIRROR

Microsoft surprisingly decided to drop the MIRROR utility introduced in DOS 5. New commands replace much of the MIRROR functionality, but two important MIRROR features are missing from the replacement tools — the capacity to make a copy of the hard disk partition table and record unformat details for each hard drive.

MIRROR is available on the DOS 6 Supplemental disk, and I suggest that you use it, but only for saving the partition and hard drive unformat information.

One of the worst system tragedies occurs when a drive's partition table is accidentally scrambled. The damage can be caused by a program bug that writes to the wrong area of memory or by an unwise user directly editing disk sectors with DEBUG.

 You can protect your partition table from accidental — and intentional — destruction by using the anti-virus tool VSAFE (discussed later in this chapter).

To save the partition table, execute this MIRROR command:

```
mirror /partn
```

A copy of the hard disk partition table is then stored on a floppy disk, in the file PARTNSAV.FIL.

Every DOS 6 user should also use MIRROR to make copies of the FAT and root directory for each hard drive. This data is vital for recovery from an accidental disk format and is stored in some hidden files on the hard disk.

To save the FAT and root directory details for drives C and D, add the following MIRROR command to AUTOEXEC.BAT:

```
mirror c: d:
```

Recovering Lost Files and Data _____

Accidents happen. If you delete a file by accident or format a drive by mistake, or if an errant program destroys your hard disk partition table, you may still be able to recover the data by using one of the DOS data-recovery tools.

Undeleting files

You did it. You accidentally deleted a file you need. Even if your backup is only one day old, it is worth trying to recover the deleted file to avoid losing a day's work.

The technique you use to recover a deleted file depends on the deletion-protection method you have implemented and whether you have Windows installed. DOS includes two programs for restoring deleted files: UNDELETE, a DOS command-line utility, and MWUNDEL, for Windows users. I much prefer the Windows program — it is easier to use, it can search a drive to look for deleted files, and it can undelete directories as well as files. Refer to Part IV, "The Complete DOS 6 Command Reference," for a full description of the use of each command.

Figure 3-8 shows the main MWUNDEL window listing all the deleted files in the active directory. By clicking on the Info button, you can display additional information about the selected file.

Every file in the list includes a Condition field that indicates your probable success in restoring the file. Every file has one of the following conditions:

Perfect	You can undelete the file automatically. This category is reserved for files that have been protected with the delete sentry method.
Excellent	Because all the file's clusters are consecutive and none of them has been used, the file in all likelihood can be recovered successfully.
Good	It seems that all the file's clusters are available, although they are not contiguous. You should be able to undelete the file.
Poor	The first file cluster is being used by another file. The chances of recovery are slim to none.
Destroyed	All the file's clusters have been reused. You have no chance of recovering the file.
Recovered	You have undeleted the file in this session.

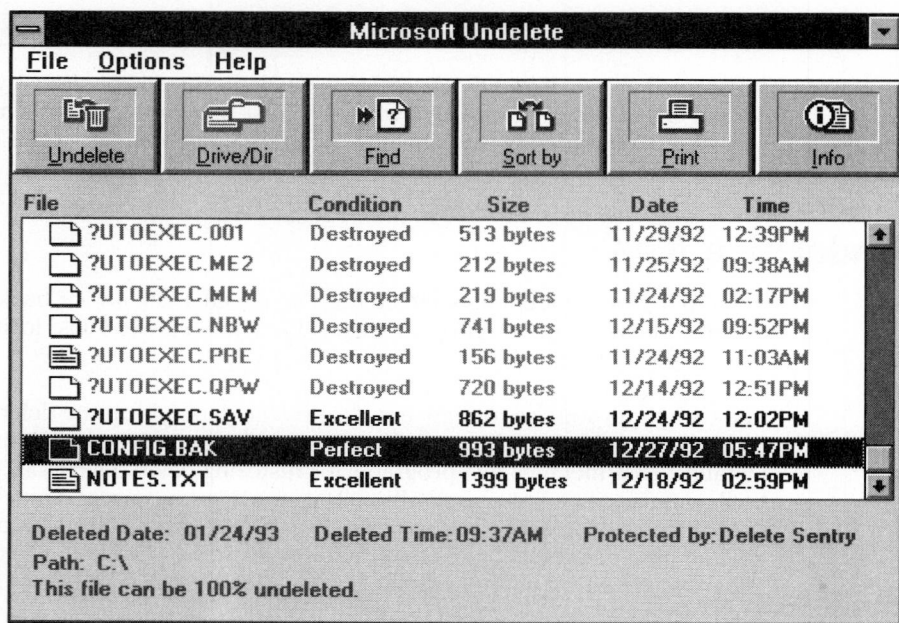

Figure 3-8: A list of deleted files displayed by MWUNDEL.

Neither UNDELETE program can undelete files categorized as poor or destroyed.

Note that any file listed with a question mark as the first character was not protected by delete sentry or delete tracker when it was deleted. You can undelete these files only by using the DOS method; these files will never have a classification better than Good.

 Unlike MWUNDEL, the DOS command-line utility UNDELETE is not very forthcoming in providing information about deleted files. By combining two switches, however, you can get UNDELETE to list deleted files by category. To see a list of all the deleted files that can be recovered only by using the DOS method, enter the following command:

```
undelete /list /dos
```

Filenames listed with a double-asterisk prefix cannot be recovered. Replace the /DOS switch with /DS or /DT to list the files protected by delete sentry and delete tracker, respectively.

How DOS Undeletion Works

When a file is deleted (without deletion-protection installed), DOS replaces the first character of the filename with the sigma character ( ). DOS does not list any files that begin with sigma. All the clusters used by the file are marked as available in the file allocation table (FAT). The important point is that no data is deleted.

Because the file's clusters are marked as available, DOS can reuse them to create another file or to expand the size of an existing file and thereby destroy the deleted file's data. The good news is that, because DOS typically uses clusters beyond its most recently saved data cluster, for a while at least, there is a reasonable chance that the deleted file's clusters will remain intact. The longer the file remains deleted, however, the more likely the file's data will be overwritten. Always try to recover an accidentally deleted file as soon as possible after the accident.

DOS maintains the deleted file's name (minus the first character), its starting cluster number, and the number of clusters allocated to the file. By searching a directory for files that begin with the sigma character and analyzing the directory entry, an undelete program can reconstruct the file — assuming that the clusters are still available. The chances of recovering a file are greatly enhanced when the file occupies only a single cluster or when all the file's clusters are stored in a contiguous area. You therefore enhance your chances of recovering larger deleted files by keeping your disk defragmented. If there are fewer contiguous free clusters than the file was using, you cannot recover the file.

If you choose to restore a file, the undelete program prompts for a replacement first character and then modifies the FAT to indicate that the file's cluster (or clusters) is in use.

Note: Some third-party file-recovery utilities enable you to reconstruct a file by browsing through all the unused clusters on a drive and selecting the ones that seem to be part of the file. This technique can be successful with ASCII files, but it is very tedious with binary files.

Recovering from an accidental disk format

If you accidentally format a disk, you can try to recover it using the UNFORMAT command. Just issue the command that identifies the drive to be unformatted, as in this example:

```
unformat a:
```

There is a chance you can unformat a disk that does not contain the hidden unformatting files. UNFORMAT attempts to reconstruct the missing data. Don't expect miracles, though — the process is far from fool-proof. The DOS UNFORMAT command, in fact, is less reliable than many competitive third-party products, such as PC Tools and the Norton Utilities. All these programs use similar techniques, but — as my father says — "Some are dumber than others." If the data is important and you know that no mirror files exist, you should consider using a third-party unformatting tool rather than the DOS UNFORMAT command.

You can determine easily whether a disk contains the hidden mirror files by using the /J switch. To check whether the floppy disk in drive A includes the unformat information, for example, enter the following command:

```
unformat a: /j
```

UNFORMAT must try to rebuild the FAT. First, it scours the disk, cluster by cluster, looking for data that resembles a directory file. This process can take as long as 30 minutes for a floppy disk. The directory files are then recovered. Unfortunately, all the root-level directory entries are destroyed by the FORMAT command, so UNFORMAT assigns these root-level directories the names SUBDIR.1, SUBDIR.2, and so on. All lower level subdirectory names can normally be recovered.

How Unformatting Works

Most versions of the FORMAT command (including the version in DOS 6) by default do not destructively format the entire drive. They simply rebuild the FAT and the root directory. All other sectors on the disk remain intact.

Note: Some OEM versions of DOS perform destructive formats, including Compaq DOS through v3.2, AT&T DOS through v3.1, and some versions of Burroughs' DOS.

To unformat a disk, the FAT and root directory must be restored. To make life easier, the FOR-MAT command tries to save all this information in two hidden files: MIRORSAV.FIL and MIRROR.FIL. If you try to view these hidden files on a newly formatted disk, you won't find them. Because the files are created before the FAT and root directory are erased, the file details disappear with all the other files that were on the disk before formatting.

MIRORSAV.FIL, which is always located on the last available cluster of the disk, is small enough to fit on a single cluster. At the beginning of the file is a special string composed of the characters AMSESLIFVASRORIMESAEP, which, when you read it backward, translates loosely to PLEASE MIRORSAV.FIL SESAME. The remainder of the file contains information that identifies the location and size of the MIRROR.FIL file. MIRROR.FIL contains the copy of the FAT and the root directory.

When you execute the UNFORMAT command, the program scours the disk, starting at the last cluster and working backward, looking for the special string. When the special string is located, UNFORMAT reads the location of the MIRROR.FIL file, jumps to the starting cluster, and retrieves the FAT and root directory information. Just like magic. The more a formatted disk is used, of course, the less chance you have of successfully unformatting it. Eventually, the data in the mirror files and in the original files will be overwritten.

If you try to format a disk that is full or that has very little free space, FORMAT cannot create the two mirror files. When this occurs, FORMAT warns you that the UNFORMAT details cannot be saved and prompts for confirmation before proceeding.

If you like to experiment, format an old disk that contains some (no longer needed) files. Then immediately unformat the disk and use UNDELETE to recover the mirror files. You can browse these two files with a binary viewer or DEBUG and see the secrets for yourself.

After recovering the directories, UNFORMAT uses the same techniques as UNDELETE to recover the files in every directory. UNFORMAT cannot recover root directory files or any fragmented files. This instance is just one more that illustrates the advantages of keeping your disks unfragmented.

If you want to use UNFORMAT on a disk that is missing the mirror files, you may consider using the /TEST switch. This switch instructs FORMAT to perform a dry run and not make the modifications, and it gives you a good estimate of the success of the unformat.

Some of UNFORMAT's additional limitations are shown in this list:

■ You cannot unformat a disk that has been formatted with the /U switch.

■ You can unformat only drives with 512, 1,024, or 2,048 bytes per sector. Note that you can determine a drive's sector size with MSD.

■ You cannot unformat network drives.

Restoring hard disk partition data

If you used MIRROR to make a copy of the hard disk partition table (discussed earlier in this chapter), you can restore it with the UNFORMAT command by using the /PARTN switch. In most cases, if the partition table is damaged, the system will not boot, so it is a good idea to keep the partition file PARTNSAV.FIL, and UNFORMAT.COM, on a bootable floppy disk.

To restore the partition table, just enter the following command:

```
unformat /partn
```

After the partition table is restored, reboot and — hopefully — your system is back in action.

Deliberate Data Destruction

To destroy files that contain confidential or personal information, you should do more than just delete the file or format the floppy. As the previous sections of this chapter have shown, there are ways and means to recover "deleted" data.

If you really want to erase files and make sure that no one can recover them, use RELDEL, from TARDIS DP Consultants, or PDELETE, part of Patriquin's Hard Disk Utilities. Both of these programs are included on Bob's Shareware Collection disks.

To delete files with RELDEL, simple execute RELDEL and specify a filename or filemask. The following command, for example, will destroy all the files with a PRV extension in the current directory:

```
reldel *.prv
```

One of the many useful switches that make PDELETE much better than DOS's DEL command is /WI, for wipe. When you use the /WI switch, PDELETE erases the file and destroys the data the file contained. The following command, for example, deletes the file HATEBOSS.DOC:

```
pdelete hateboss.doc /wi
```

But remember, when it's gone, it's really gone.

Vital Virus Measures

As with dieting, there is much more talk about viruses than there is action. Unless you live in a cave, you have heard horror stories about computer viruses. Although the truth is that viruses are a reality and they do destroy data, operator error causes much more data loss. Nonetheless, every prudent user should take measures to protect against virus infection, and DOS 6 makes it easy with the following anti-virus tools:

MSAV   The Microsoft Anti-Virus utility for finding and removing viruses. This DOS application can be run in full-screen interactive mode or directly from the DOS prompt by using switches.

MWAV   Although this Windows version has features that are similar to MSAV, it is much more graphical and provides a couple of useful extra features.

VSAFE   This anti-virus TSR monitors disk activity looking for potential virus activity. VSAFE can prevent modifications to some key data areas, such as a disk's boot sector and FAT.

The virus phenomenon

In simple terms, a *computer virus* is a program that uses devious techniques to propagate, undetected, from system to system. A program's capability to propagate was the reason that the term "computer virus" was coined. Stimulated by some event, such as executing the program on April 1 or running a program for the tenth time, for example, the virus program makes its presence known. Although the program may do this by simply displaying a message, all too often the virus attempts to destroy your files and data.

There are no good or innocent viruses. All viruses modify your system in some way. In my humble opinion, viruses are written by irresponsible programmers who should be prosecuted. Some 1,200 known virus programs exist. As virus-detection techniques improve, new strains of virus programs are written that strive to avoid detection.

To gain an appreciation for the number of different strains, run the MWAV application in Windows and select Scan⇨Virus List from the menu. MWAV displays a list of all the specific viruses it can detect. Select the Info button to see a full description of the highlighted item (see Figure 3-9).

Understanding how viruses spread

When a virus-infected program is executed, the virus program is loaded into memory along with the host program. After the virus program is installed in memory, it can — like any program — access drives, files, and printers. Usually, the virus program tries to attach itself to other program files and infect them. These newly infected programs then infect other programs when they are executed, and the virus spreads.

A common misconception is that viruses spread only in EXE and COM files. Viruses are found in all types of executable code, including EXE and COM files, SYS device drivers, Windows DLL files, and overlay files (usually with the letter *O* or *V* in the extension). Viruses cannot spread in nonexecutable files, such as plain ASCII files.

Because a virus spreads only when infected code is executed, you can easily see that your system can become infected only by running programs from other sources. In theory, if you never install new software or run programs from floppies, networks, or via modem, then your system cannot become infected. Unfortunately, most PCs frequently access remote programs (when you load new software from floppy disks, download programs from bulletin boards, and access programs on a network, for example). All these tasks can infect your system.

MWAV identifies the various propagation methods in the Type column (refer to Figure 3-9). Every virus is classified as one of the following types:

File   This type adds the virus code to executable programs such as COM, EXE, and DLL files. Some viruses override existing program code rather than append themselves to the end of a program.

Boot   A boot virus appends itself to the boot sector of a hard disk or bootable floppy. Every time the system boots from the infected disk, the virus is loaded into memory, where it can propagate to other disks.

If you are given a boot disk, always check it for viruses before booting your system from it. If you accidentally leave a nonbootable disk in the drive and power up the system, do not press a key and try to boot

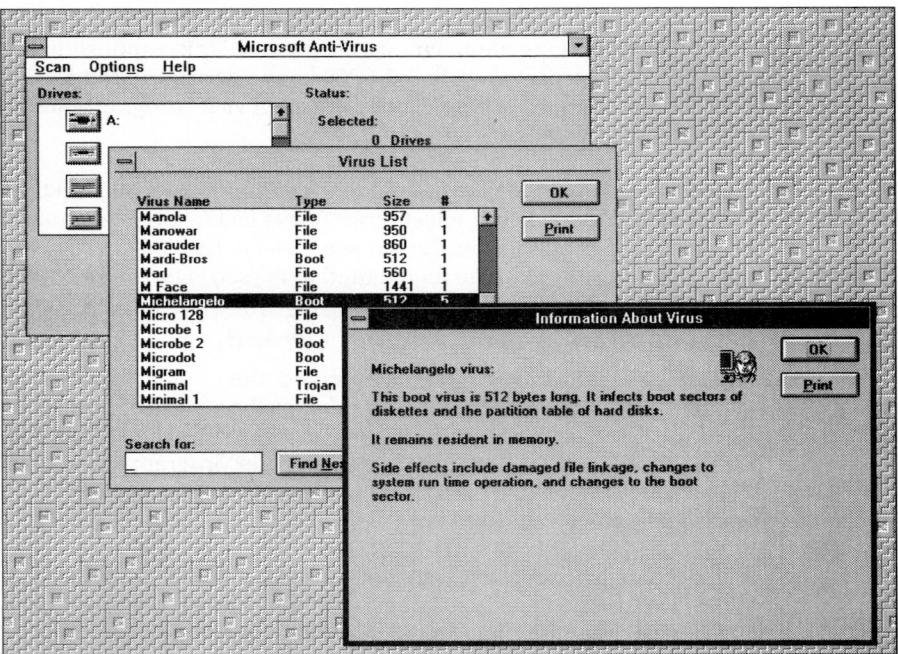

Figure 3-9: MWAV details the characteristics of more than 1,200 known viruses.

again when DOS reports the "non-system disk" error message; immediately remove the disk, power down the system, and try again. Even an aborted boot attempt can infect your system.

Trojan   Technically, a Trojan horse program is not a virus. It is a program that disguises its real (destructive) purpose by providing some other function. A seemingly innocent biorhythm program, for example, may include some code to erase your hard disk.

Potential virus damage

A virus can damage your system in two ways. First, the code used to propagate the virus can modify a program or the boot sector and affect the program's functionality and performance. Even when the virus is removed, the program can malfunction. This type of damage is simply a by-product of the propagation algorithm.

Second, the virus can attempt to damage your system when a trigger event occurs. Most malevolent viruses attempt to damage your system in one of the following ways: destroy the hard disk partition table, destroy or corrupt the FAT, or overwrite files with meaningless characters. Needless to say, all these actions are highly destructive.

Defending against and identifying viruses

Because a virus program must propagate undetected before it tries to damage your system, a good chance exists that you can identify the infection before any major damage is done.

The following telltale symptoms can provide an indication of virus infection:

- Available memory may decrease.

- Program files may increase in size and reduce free disk space.

- Your system may operate more slowly, become less stable, and crash with greater and greater frequency.

Unfortunately, a memory shortage, a lack of disk space, and system crashes are commonplace; at least on my computers they are. That is why it is important to scan your system frequently to look for viruses.

Scanning for virus infection

Both MSAV and MWAV can scan your system looking for viruses. Just select the Detect button to scan the selected drive for viruses.

Most known viruses leave a specific pattern of bytes in an infected file, which is sometimes referred to as *virus signatures*. During the scan, the program searches for these signatures in all the files on the selected drive or drives.

You should consider scanning for viruses at least once a week — I do it immediately before running my full backup.

As new virus strains are analyzed, new signatures are identified and added to the signature list. You can update the MSAV and MSAW signature lists via modem by downloading signature updates from a Microsoft-supported bulletin board. Refer to Appendix D of the Microsoft *MS-DOS User's Guide* for further details.

 Unlike some third-party anti-virus products, you cannot configure the DOS anti-virus programs to scan an individual directory. The Windows program MWAV, however, supports limited file drag-and-drop in Windows 3.1. To check one or more individual files for viruses, launch File Manager and select the files. Then drag the files off the File Manager window and drop them on the Anti-Virus icon in the Microsoft Tools group. MWAV then launches, scans for viruses in memory, and checks the specific files you dropped on the icon. Neat.

Where did those CHKLIST.CPS files come from?

Obviously, scanning for signatures identifies only known viruses. The anti-virus programs can optionally use a clever method, *checksums*, for identifying suspicious activity. A checksum is a number value derived by applying a special algorithm to the individual values in a file. When a file is changed, so too is the checksum. By comparing a file's current computed checksum to a checksum created earlier, you can ascertain whether the file has been changed.

To enable checksum scanning, select Options and make sure that the Verify Integrity and Create New Checksums options are checked.

The option settings are stored in an INI file in the DOS directory. The anti-virus programs do not share the same settings: The DOS settings are stored in MSAV.INI, and the Windows settings in MWAV.INI.

Change the options from the main program rather than directly edit the INI files.

The next time you scan a drive, the anti-virus program creates a file named CHKLIST.CPS in every directory. This file records a checksum value for every file in the directory that contains executable code (files with the EXE, COM, or DLL, for example). During future scans, the checksum in the CHKLIST.CPS file is compared with the newly computed checksum.

Some viruses deploy a technique known as Stealth (which is not associated with the QEMM Stealth memory feature) that makes them less vulnerable to detection by using the checksum method. You can instruct the Anti-Virus program to perform a more rigorous scan, however, by selecting the Anti-Stealth item in the Options dialog box.

Getting rid of those checksum files

The CHKLIST.CPS files provide a valuable anti-virus function, but you can delete them if you want. Rather than laboriously go through every directory and delete every file, you can delete them easily by using one of the following methods:

- If you are a Windows user, just select the option Delete CHKLIST Files from the MWAV Scan menu.

- If you don't have Windows, use the PocketD program D.EXE supplied on Bob's Shareware Collection disks, by entering the following command:

```
d chklist.cps /WFzz
```

Guarding against destructive viruses

You can load the TSR program VSAFE into memory to monitor program and disk activity. VSAFE does not check for specific brands of viruses. It protects the areas usually infected by viruses and provides generic protection against all viruses.

Refer to Part IV, "The Complete DOS 6 Command Reference," for a full explanation of the switches.

If a program tries to make a suspicious change to the disk (such as modifying
the boot sector or changing an EXE file), VSAFE pops up a dialog box to alert
you and prompts for confirmation before allowing the change to occur. If you
use Windows with VSAFE installed, you must load the DOS 6 program
MSAVTSR.EXE. This program enables VSAFE to pop up a Windows-style dialog
box to ask for confirmation. Ideally, add the following statement to WIN.INI to
load the program automatically every time Windows is started:

```
load=c:\dos\msavtsr.exe
```

When you are using Windows, always disable VSAFE's option 3, which intercepts all hard disk writes and prompts for approval before proceeding —
Windows frequently writes directly to the hard disk, and you will never get any
work done because of all the confirmation prompts.

Removing viruses from an infected system

Both MSAV and MWAV can remove virus infections from the system. This process is referred to as *cleaning*. To remove viruses from your system, simply
select the Detect and <u>C</u>lean button.

If the Anti-Virus program detects that a virus is in memory, take the following
steps:

1. Turn off your computer.

2. Reboot the computer from a bootable floppy disk that you know is virus
   free.

   Obviously, you must prepare for this procedure by creating a bootable
   floppy. If your hard disk includes DoubleSpace drives, this floppy should
   include the appropriate drivers for DoubleSpace (see Chapter 4). Also, copy
   the MSAV.EXE, MSAV.INI, and VSAFE.EXE files from your DOS directory for
   the next step. Execute MSAV to make sure that the floppy disk is virus free
   and then cover the write-protect tab on the floppy disk to prevent more
   changes to the disk.

3. Run the anti-virus program MSAV from the floppy and select the Detect and
   <u>C</u>lean option.

4. Reboot the computer from the hard disk, insert the bootable floppy into a
   disk drive, and install VSAFE (discussed earlier in this chapter) in memory
   from the floppy.

5. Some of the files that were infected may be damaged and unusable. If so, you must reload the files from the backup. Be aware that the files on the backup can also be infected. As soon as you have restored the files, run a thorough scan to ensure that the restored files are not infected.

6. Virus-scan all your floppy disks.

7. Immediately warn other computer users with whom you have been in contact, especially people with whom you have exchanged files. If you are a network user, contact your network administrator.

During the next few weeks, you should continue to run VSAFE in a high-protection mode to alert you against reinfection from the same source. You should also perform a complete scan of all your hard disks daily.

Comparing MSAV and MWAV

Although the two MSAV and MWAV anti-virus programs are similar, a few features are available in one that aren't in the other. This list shows the main differences:

- MSAV can be executed from the command line and supports a variety of switches for automated running. This capability makes MSAV well suited to unattended execution or inclusion in AUTOEXEC.BAT.

- MSAV supports the storing of information in a report file with the /R switch.

- MWAV includes an option to delete all the checksum files from a drive.

On-line virus information

If you are interested in more information about viruses and you are a member of the CompuServe Information Service, I recommend that you access the excellent Virus Forum by entering the command **GO VIRUSFORUM**. This forum is managed by McAfee Associates, the much respected virus busters. Also, to get the latest updates to MSAV and MWAV, access the Central Point Software forum by entering the command **GO CENTRAL**.

On a Lighter Note

Data loss is a serious matter we all take too lightly. In keeping with that spirit, I thought you may be interested in some trivia.

If you suffer a system problem and lose valuable data, suddenly everything seems to remind you of your woes. Even movie titles remind you of data loss. Here are but a few:

Indiana Jones and the PC of Doom

Discablanca

Star Wars: The Disk Strikes Back

Crashanova

Here are some CDs (or *records,* for you old-time mainframers) that should constantly remind you to look after your precious files:

Fifty Ways to Lose Your Data, by Paul Simon

Bit out of Hell, by Meat Loaf

Pray, by Hammer

Get Back(up), by the Beatles

Backing Up Is Hard to Do, by Neil Sedaka

Summary

This chapter described many of the preventive measures you can take as insurance against data loss and some ways to recover data if disaster strikes. The chapter discussed these subjects:

▶ How to select files to be backed up by using the point-and-shoot method or by creating an include/exclude list.

▶ The importance of using the Compare option to verify the integrity of a backup.

▶ How to restore files by using the backup catalog, including how to reload or rebuild a catalog when it has been removed from the hard disk.

▶ Essential data-protection precautions, including deletion protection with UNDELETE and saving hard disk partitions with MIRROR.

▶ Data-recovery procedures using UNDELETE, UNFORMAT, and MIRROR.

▶ Understanding how viruses spread and how MSAV and MWAV can identify and eradicate a virus infection.

Chapter 4 begins Part II, "Secret Weapons for Your Hardware." The chapter explores hard disks and explains the all-new DoubleSpace file-compression tools.

Part II:
Secret Weapons for Your Hardware

Page 109 ◇ **Chapter 4**
Making Your Hard Disk Faster, Bigger, and Safer

Page 159 ◇ **Chapter 5**
Maximizing Memory

Page 217 ◇ **Chapter 6**
Taking Control of the Display and Keyboard

Page 241 ◇ **Chapter 7**
Juggling IRQs, DMAs, Buses, Device Drivers,
and Other "What's Its"

Page 261 ◇ **Chapter 8**
Power System Configuration Techniques

Chapter 4

Making Your Hard Disk Faster, Bigger, and Safer

In This Chapter

▶ Hard disk mechanics

▶ Data storage schemes

▶ How to prepare a new hard disk

▶ The role of CHKDSK

▶ Ways to increase hard disk speed

▶ How to use DoubleSpace to make your hard disk bigger

The Brawn Behind the Brain

If the microprocessor is the PC's brain, the hard disk is its muscle.

Short of buying new hardware, the most effective way of boosting your PC performance is to fine-tune the hard disk. You often can double or triple the effective throughput of hard disks by taking a few simple measures.

You may have heard the argument that hard disks have a significant impact on performance only when you use disk-intensive applications, such as database or CAD programs. The truth is that in the 90s, *all* major software applications are disk-intensive, even programs that traditionally were disk-shy. Word processors access dictionaries, spreadsheets access add-ins and overlay files, and as for Windows programs — well, you know. . . .

The point is that any user today can benefit from a faster and larger hard disk. In this chapter, you first learn how hard disks work. Then you learn how to use DOS 6 to improve the performance of your hard disk.

The Mechanics of a Hard Disk

One of the few mechanical components in a PC — and clearly the most important — is the hard disk.

It is important that you acquaint yourself with the physical components of the hard disk, including the disk platters and disk heads, and also that you understand the role of the hard disk controller. If you understand the basic mechanics of a hard disk, the whole process of recognizing, diagnosing, and fixing performance problems is simplified. In other words, to be a DOS Jedi, you need to know how a hard disk works.

Inside a hard disk

Hard disks come in a variety of shapes and sizes, but they all share some common elements and characteristics. Figure 4-1 shows the inside of a typical hard disk.

The largest component of a hard disk is the *platter*. A platter is a hard circular disk (hence the name *hard disk*), usually made of aluminum. The number of platters in a disk varies but typically ranges from four to sixteen. The platters are mounted in a column, like a stack of records.

A disk platter is similar to a floppy disk. Its surface is coated with a magnetic oxide that is used to store the data. To maximize the storage capacity of the hard disk, both the top and bottom sides of the platter are used. The top side is referred to as *side 0* and the bottom side as *side 1*. You may have noticed that the FORMAT command reports which side, 0 or 1, is being formatted when you format a floppy disk.

Data is transferred to and from the hard disk by a disk *read-write head*. The read-write head is located on a very light armature that pivots across the platter. When placed very close to the platter surface, the head can read or modify the tiny electrical charges in the magnetic oxide — similar to the way a tape recorder reads and records sound on a digital cassette tape.

When data is written to or read from the hard disk, a read-write head must be positioned directly over the appropriate location on the disk. One of the main time delays that occurs when the system accesses data on a hard disk is incurred when the hard disk moves a read-write head to the correct position over the platter surface. To minimize such delays, hard disks have one read-write head for every platter surface. A hard disk with ten platters, for example, has twenty read-write head armature assemblies. This avoids the delay that would occur if an armature had to move from one platter to another. Some of the most

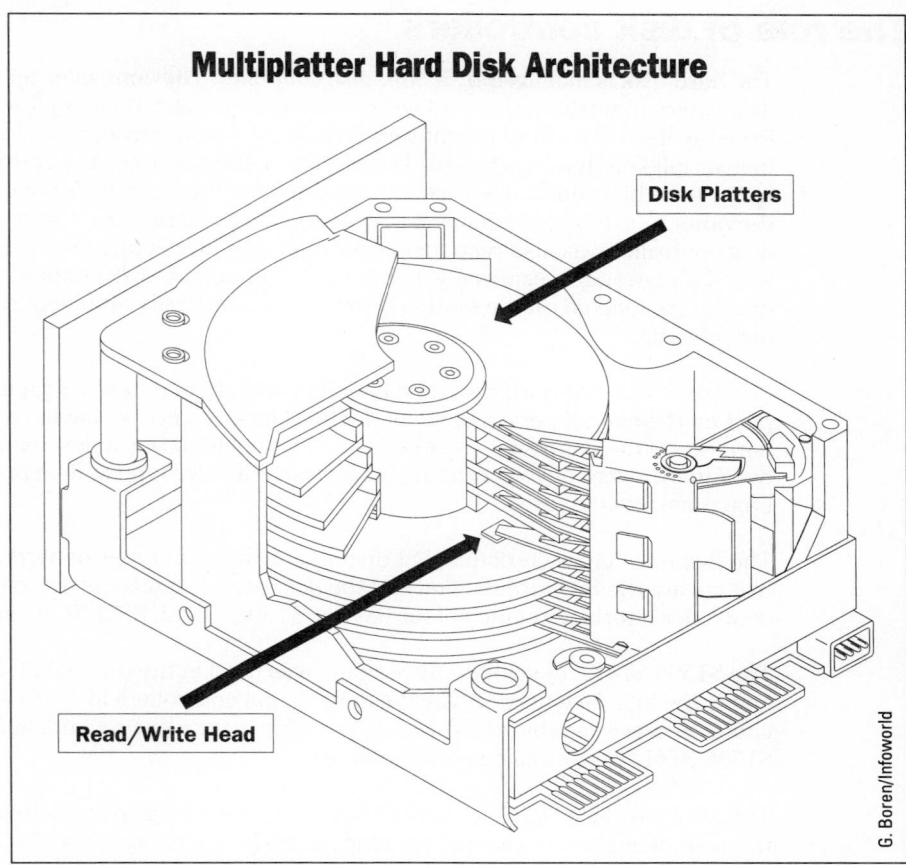

Figure 4-1: The inside of a hard disk.

modern disk designs actually have two heads for each surface. Although this offers potential gains on performance, it presents significant design challenges and therefore has not been widely adopted.

A hard disk is not complicated to understand but is challenging to engineer. In a modern hard disk, the disk platters rotate at 3,600 revolutions per minute, and the read-write heads move across the surface of the hard disk just one ten-thousandth of an inch above the platters. If a head were to touch the surface (called a *head crash*) or if a head were not positioned correctly, the data would be at best unreliable and at worst destroyed. Needless to say, any dirt or particles in a hard disk wreak havoc. Hard disks therefore are sealed and have a special filtered air inlet.

The role of disk controllers

The hard disk is managed by a *hard disk controller*. The controller tells the hard disk where to position the read-write head and manages the data flow to and from the hard disk. Until recent times, the hard disk controller was located on a half- or full-length adapter card. Two ribbon cables ran from the controller card to the hard disk; one cable was dedicated to running the transfer of data and the other to sending mechanical instructions to the hard disk. Often, the hard disk controller was also responsible for managing the floppy drives in the same way. To save space, especially in notebook computers, disk controllers now usually are located on the motherboard or are physically attached to the hard disk chassis.

Controllers are the hard disk data handlers and as such have a significant impact on the overall performance of the hard disk. It's no use having a very fast hard disk if the controller can't keep up. If you plan to buy a new hard disk, you need to be aware of your existing hard disk controller type and be prepared to upgrade it if necessary.

The two main characteristics that distinguish different types of hard disk controllers are the *interface method* and the *data encoding scheme.* Hard disk controller interfaces come in four flavors: ST506/ST412, ESDI, SCSI, and IDE.

The ST506/ST412, developed by Seagate, was used in the original PC hard disk and is the interface used by the Western Digital controllers in PC XTs. Such controllers are capable of a throughput of 5 megabits per second. In a word, the ST506/ST412 performance is *conservative.*

The ESDI interface *(Enhanced Small Device Interface)* was popularized by Compaq, which used it on the company's 386 line of computers. The ESDI really is a variation of the ST506/ST412 that nearly doubles the throughput. Note that an ESDI controller cannot be used on a disk designed for the ST506/ST412.

The emerging interface standard is SCSI *(Small Computer System Interface).* A SCSI (pronounced *scuzzy*) controller can control as many as eight devices, including hard disks, CD-ROMs, and tape drives, and is designed primarily for high-performance computers with a 386 or better microprocessor. The throughput can exceed 20 megabits per second.

The IDE controller interface *(Integrated Drive Electronics)* was originally developed in the mid-80s to save to an expansion slot. ESDI and SCSI drives are actually IDE drives. As the name implies, an IDE drive has the disk controller directly attached to the hard disk — in other words, the controller and the hard disk are a single unit. The IDE controller attaches to a special IDE connector located on the system board, thereby avoiding the need to plug a separate disk controller into an expansion slot. Even the lowly XT system board had an IDE connector, but the signal system was changed for AT-class systems. If you have an XT system, then you can only use an XT-class IDE drive. Nearly all new systems use IDE drives.

As well as establishing the interface protocol, a controller governs the way data is physically stored on the disk surface. The storage method used by the controller is referred to as the data encoding scheme. By using data compression techniques, today's controllers can reduce the amount of bits that must be physically written to and from the hard disk. Such techniques are referred to as *data encoding schemes*. It should come as no surprise that the original PC controllers used an encoding scheme that did not employ data compression. Instead, they used a scheme called *modified frequency modulation,* or *MFM,* which transferred every bit of data from the controller to the hard disk.

MFM encoding was eclipsed by the *run length limited,* or *RLL,* encoding scheme. In this scheme, the controller uses data compression algorithms to reduce the amount of data stored on the disk surface. RLL controllers also pack the data more closely on the disk surface, further increasing the capacity of the hard disk. These techniques increase performance and can double the effective data throughput.

Since its introduction, the RLL encoding scheme has been enhanced with an improved compression technique. Often referred to as *advanced run length limited,* or *ARLL,* this encoding scheme is the most widely used today.

Data Storage Schemes

Data integrity and performance are the two primary concerns for a hard disk. The way data is physically stored on the hard disk has a profound effect on both of these issues. When you save a file from your word processor (and by the way, you should save your file more frequently!), the operating system goes through a whole series of computations to decide where to store the data so that it can be retrieved again later. A lot happens when you select **File** and then **Save**.

A hard disk is like a warehouse for storing computer data. If items in a warehouse were stored in a haphazard way, havoc would ensue — you'd never be able to find anything. To prevent this confusion, warehouses use numbering or addressing schemes that enable users to locate any item in the warehouse quickly. A warehouse typically is divided up into bays, bays are subdivided into racks, and racks are further subdivided into storage bins or shelves.

Hard disks use a similar scheme, but the nomenclature is different. Disk storage areas are organized by *tracks, sectors,* and *cylinders.*

Tracks

Because each disk platter continually rotates (usually at 3,600 revolutions per minute), a disk read-write head can access the entire circumference of a thin band of the platter without moving. By moving inward toward the center of the disk or outward toward the edge of the disk, the read-write head can access the entire surface of the platter, reading or writing data in a series of concentric circles. These concentric circles, which are the width of the read-write head, are referred to as *tracks*. A platter can have a thousand tracks or more per inch. Each track is given a unique number, with the outermost track assigned the number 0.

Every platter surface has the same track-numbering scheme. Track 3 on one surface is vertically aligned with track 3 on each of the other surfaces, for example. The term *cylinder* refers to the vertical column of tracks.

Sectors

On some systems, a single track is large enough to store 27K or more of data. It would be wasteful to consume (or allocate) an entire track for a file smaller than 27K. Storing only one file per track would also pose a problem for files larger than 27K. If a file were 57K in size, for example, 24K of space would be wasted, because a total of three tracks would be needed to store the file.

To make more efficient use of the available space, each track is subdivided into a series of individual sections called *sectors*. Each sector can store 512 bytes of data. The number of sectors in a track depends on the capacity of the track but usually ranges from 17 to 55. Figure 4-2 illustrates a disk platter organized into tracks and sectors.

Breaking the 1,024 Cylinder Barrier

DOS 6 and all of its predecessors do not support a drive with more than 1,024 cylinders. Most hardware vendors that provide disks using more than 1,024 cylinders also provide a device driver and disk-formatting software that tricks DOS into accessing the additional cylinders.

One strategy is to hook into interrupt 13 and advise DOS that the disk has more heads and fewer cylinders so that the total number of tracks is accurate but the number of reported cylinders is within DOS's range. Many of the newer IDE drives take advantage of the close integration of the controller and the drive to mask the real cylinder count, without having to intercept DOS interrupts.

You may find that the Window's Fastdisk utility (discussed later) is not reliable on systems where the real cylinder count exceeds 1,024.

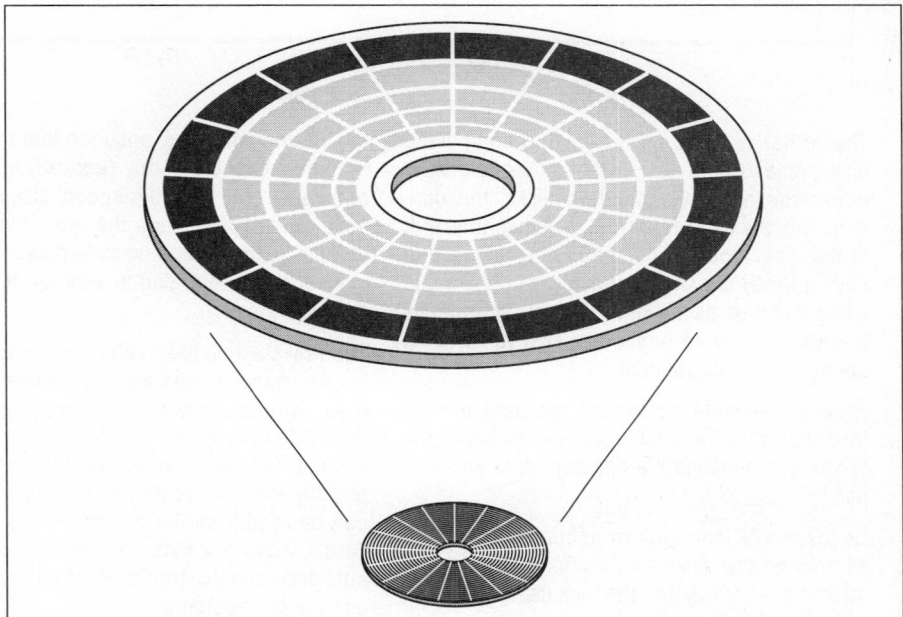

Figure 4-2: Disk tracks and sectors.

Although the outermost tracks have a larger diameter and therefore a larger surface area, most disks allocate the same number of sectors to the outermost (longer) tracks as are allocated for the innermost tracks. However, to increase the storage capacity, some newer disks use a technique called *zone bit recording,* which squeezes more sectors onto the outer tracks.

Clusters

One of the primary functions of DOS is to know which sectors are in use and which are available. Managing all these sectors is a burden. A 300MB hard disk, for instance, has more than half a million sectors.

To make the hard disk more manageable, DOS manages blocks of contiguous sectors together. Each block of sectors is referred to as a *cluster.* The number of sectors in a cluster varies and typically ranges from 4 to 16. In a system configured with 8 sectors per cluster, DOS has to worry about only one-eighth of the storage areas, so performance is significantly improved.

Zone Bit Recording

The farther away a track is from the center of the disk, the faster the disk surface spins below the read-write head. On standard disks, the data density of the outermost tracks is lower than that of the inner tracks. The sectors are longer but have a lower density, so they contain the same amount of data as the inner sectors. This means that the read-write heads are always handling the same data throughput.

It seems wasteful to reduce the data density (and therefore the total storage capacity of the drive) just to maintain a constant data through-put.

Conceptually, one way to accommodate more sectors on the outermost tracks is to store the information throughout the disk using the same data density. The controller would then rotate the disk at lower speeds when reading or writing

the outermost tracks, ensuring that the disk surface moves below the read-write head at a constant rate. Variable-speed disks, however, have slow access times; the system must wait for the disk to speed up and slow down as the head moves from one region to another. It's just not a practical solution.

The real solution lies in electronics, not mechanics. By changing the frequency of operation of the read-write head electronics, the system can read and write data at different throughput rates. If the same data density is used throughout the platter and the head frequency is changed, more data can be read from the outermost tracks. In other words, more 512 byte sectors can be squeezed onto the outermost tracks. This technique is known as zone bit recording.

The tradeoff is that space is allocated in single, cluster-size chunks. The larger the cluster size, the more space is potentially wasted. On a system with 8 sectors per cluster, space is allocated in 4K chunks. A 50-byte batch file uses up 4K of space, and a 37K file uses 40K.

DOS can only manage a limited number of clusters (65,518 to be precise), and so the cluster size is larger on high-capacity drives to ensure that all the available disk space can be addressed. If the cluster size is too large, space is wasted. On the other hand, if the cluster size is too small, files become too fragmented and disk throughput is reduced. As a general rule, you should use one of the following cluster sizes: 2,048, 4,096, or 8,192 bytes.

How to check your drive characteristics

The DOS 6 diagnostic program MSD provides some useful information about your hard disk(s). Execute MSD and select the **D**isk Drives option. When you select this option, the Disk Drives window, shown in Figure 4-3, appears. The characteristics of each disk (including floppy drives) are displayed. DOS reports the number of cylinders (tracks), heads (platter surfaces), bytes per sector, and sectors per track. The total capacity of each logical drive along with the amount of free space is displayed as well.

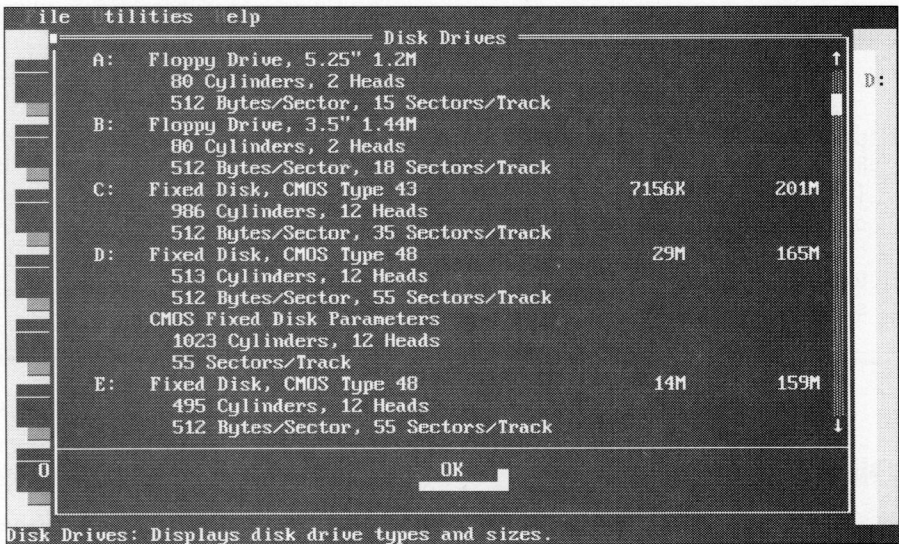

Figure 4-3: The MSD Disk Drives window.

The file allocation table

Every DOS drive has a *file allocation table*, or *FAT*. In fact, because the FAT is so important, DOS maintains two copies of it, just in case one gets damaged. The FAT is responsible for keeping records about every cluster on the drive. At the beginning (or outside edge) of each drive is a boot record, the FAT, and root directory, followed by the general data storage area.

The FAT assigns a unique number to each cluster. The first cluster in the data area (immediately following the root directory) is assigned the value 2. That's right — the first data cluster is numbered 2. The next cluster is assigned number 3, and so on. The FAT can keep track of 65,518 individual clusters.

In the FAT, there is a two-byte *status field* for every cluster. The cluster status indicates that the cluster is in one of the following five states:

- The cluster is unused and available (value 0).
- The cluster is reserved (values FFF0 to FFF6).
- The cluster is bad and should not be used (value FFF7).
- The cluster is the last one in a file (value FFF8 to FFFF).
- The cluster is in use (the value is the cluster number of the next cluster in the chain).

12-bit versus 16-bit FATs

Originally, DOS created a FAT that used only 1½-byte fields (12 bits) to store the cluster details, limiting the maximum number of clusters to 4,078. These 12-bit FATS severely limited the capability of DOS to handle larger drives. The only real way to increase the addressable area of a disk was to increase the cluster size, which led to wasted space.

Since the introduction of version 3, DOS has supported both 12-bit and 16-bit FATs. DOS decides which size FAT to use when the drive is formatted. Drives 16MB or less in size use a 12-bit FAT, and all larger drives use a 16-bit FAT.

Directories

In conjunction with the FAT, DOS uses directories to maintain further information about each file. For every file, there is one 32-byte entry in a directory. Each file's directory entry contains the information listed in Table 4-1.

When a drive is formatted, DOS creates a root directory with a fixed number of entries. The total number of entries depends on the size of the disk but usually ranges from 112 on 360K floppies to 512 on larger hard disks. Obviously, it would be very limiting to be able to store only 512 files on any one disk. The solution lies in directories and subdirectories.

Table 4-1	Directory File Information
Entry Description	**Size in Bytes**
Filename	8
Extension	3
Attribute	1
Reserved	10
Time	2
Date	2
Starting FAT Entry	2
File Size	4

When you create a directory, DOS creates a special file in the parent directory to keep track of all the files in that directory. The contents of the special file are organized in the same way as the root directory; however, the number of directory entries is unlimited. There is one directory file for every unique subdirectory on the system.

How DOS reads, writes, and deletes files

By using the information in the directories and the FAT, DOS can read, write, and delete files reliably. The following sections provide an overview of how DOS performs each of these tasks.

Reading a file

A lot of activity takes place behind the scenes when you ask DOS to open and read a file. For example, when you select **F**ile and then **O**pen in EDIT, a file open request is passed to DOS.

After DOS receives the request, its first task is to locate the file's directory entry. Suppose that the filename is C:\BUDGET\LOWCASE\USA\NOTES.TXT. DOS goes to the root directory of drive C and locates the subdirectory file named BUDGET. DOS opens the file BUDGET and searches for the location of the LOWCASE subdirectory file. DOS then opens the LOWCASE file and searches for the USA entry. Finally, DOS opens the USA subdirectory file and reads the entry for NOTES.TXT. The directory entry for NOTES.TXT contains the starting cluster number of the file's data. Stage one is then complete.

DOS next switches its attention to the FAT. Using the starting cluster number as an index into the FAT, DOS reads the FAT entry for NOTES.TXT. If the 2-byte status code has a value in the range FFF8 to FFFF (the last-cluster codes), the entire file's data is held in one cluster; DOS simply reads the data from the single cluster, and the file is loaded. However, if the status code points to a second cluster, DOS must read the first cluster and then move to the second cluster's FAT entry. It reads the data in the second cluster, and if the second cluster's FAT entry points to a third cluster, the process continues. DOS reads the data from each cluster in the chain until it reads the file's last cluster — that is, the cluster that has a 2-byte status code in the range FFF8 to FFFF in the FAT. *Phew.*

Deleting a file

When you delete a file, DOS changes the first character in the directory entry to the sigma character, which has the ASCII value 229. The FAT entries for the file's clusters are then updated with the cluster-available code. That's all there is to it.

Apart from the first character of the filename, no data is actually destroyed when you delete a file. For a thorough discussion of file deletion and undeletion, refer to Chapter 3.

Writing a file

When you save a new file to disk, DOS tries to use clusters on the innermost unused part of the disk. This strategy increases the chances that the entire file can be saved in adjacent clusters — in other words, not fragmented — and enhances the chances of data recovery using UNDELETE because a deleted file's clusters are not immediately overwritten. If no free space exists in this region, DOS starts to save the file using the first free cluster indicated in the FAT. If the entire file fits in one cluster, DOS marks the FAT entry with a last-cluster code, and the process is complete. If the file is too large to fit in one cluster, DOS locates the next free cluster by scanning the FAT and then records the second cluster entry in the first cluster's status code, thereby creating a *cluster chain*. If the remainder of the file fits in the second cluster, the cluster's FAT entry is marked with the last-cluster code. Otherwise, the process continues until all the data is written to disk. DOS then creates the directory entry for the file and records the starting cluster number in it.

If the file has previously been saved to disk, DOS uses a different methodology. It uses the directory entry and FAT to locate the file's clusters, similar to the way it does when reading a file. DOS attempts to use the same clusters to store the updated data. If the revised file is smaller than the original file, DOS marks the unused clusters as free in the FAT and marks the file's last cluster entry with a last-cluster code. If the revised file is larger than the original, DOS scans the FAT for the next free cluster and extends the cluster chain until the file is completely saved.

How to Prepare a New Hard Disk_____

Three levels of preparation are required before a hard disk is ready to store files. These stages are typically referred to as *low-level formatting, partitioning*, and *high-level formatting*.

Low-level formatting

Every sector on the disk has a unique address. This address is simply a combination of the platter (or head) number, the track (or cylinder) number, and the sector number within the track. At the beginning of every sector, there is a special header section in which, among other things, the sector address is stored. When data needs to be retrieved from the hard disk, the read-write head is positioned over the appropriate track and the sector addresses are read. As soon as the correct address is found, the data is read from the sector that follows. This addressing scheme is referred to as *soft sectoring*.

The low-level formatting process divides the disk into sectors and then records the sector address in each sector header. Low-level formatting also is responsible for verifying the integrity of the disk surface. If any sectors are found to be defective, they are marked as unusable.

Disk partitioning

Because low-level disk formatting usually is performed at the factory, the first stage of disk preparation in which users typically become involved is disk partitioning. A single physical disk can be subdivided, or *partitioned,* into smaller logical drives. For example, a single 500MB hard disk might be partitioned into three logical drives: drive C with 200MB, drive D with 175MB, and drive E with 125MB. Each of these drives is referred to as a partition.

 It is now commonplace for a computer to be delivered ready to run. In some cases, popular software packages, such as Windows, are already installed as well. Rest assured that if your computer arrives with software installed, the disk is low-level formatted, partitioned, and high-level formatted.

Even if you want to use a hard disk as one logical drive, the disk still must be partitioned, albeit with a single partition.

In the past, one of the most common reasons to partition a disk into several logical drives was related to a DOS shortcoming known by many as the "32MB limit." Before the release of DOS 4.0 (or 3.3 for some DOS strains), DOS could only access drives up to 32 megabytes in size. This meant that someone who owned a 100-megabyte disk, for example, could only access the first 32 megabytes. The solution was to partition the disk into multiple drives, with each one being 32MB or less in size. The new size limit for drives is 2 gigabytes (2,048MB). Even with the rapid pace of change in this industry, I suspect that this limit will suffice for some time to come.

 Prior to the release of DOS 4.0, a 16-bit number was in the boot record to store sector details, which meant that DOS could only handle 65,536 sectors. Because each sector is 512 bytes in size, the maximum storage space that could be managed was 65,536 x 512 bytes, which is 32MB. With the introduction of DOS 4.0, two 16-bit numbers were used to store sector details in the boot record, shattering the 32MB limit.

Following are the main reasons that you might consider organizing a single physical disk into several partitions:

- Although the vast majority of PCs use the DOS operating system, not all do. Some of the most popular alternatives are UNIX, XENIX, and OS/2. Partitioning enables you to install more than one operating system on a single disk. Each disk partition can accommodate a different operating system.

- With today's large hard disks, subdividing a disk into smaller drives is often done just to make it more manageable or to reduce the space wasted by saving small files to large clusters. Also, really big drives choke DEFRAG (see "Solving memory problems" later in this chapter). Anyone who has forgotten the name of a file and spent hours trying to find it on a 500MB hard disk knows that there are a lot of places to look. Partitioning provides a convenient way to avoid this problem. For example, you might use drive C for all programs associated with word processing and desktop publishing and use drive D for all the other program files, such as spreadsheets and databases.

DOS provides the program FDISK for partitioning a hard disk. FDISK is responsible for storing the disk partition information on the hard disk. This information is stored in the *master partition table*, located in the first sector of the first track on the first platter. Refer to Part IV, "The Complete DOS 6 Command Reference," for more information about using FDISK.

Huge Disks and Small FATs

Aside from making drives easier to manage, there is one more compelling reason to organize huge disks into several logical drives: to save space. That's right — to *save* space.

The FAT has room to manage 65,518 individual clusters. The number of bytes per cluster is always a value of 2 to a power, as well as an even multiple of 512 bytes (the standard sector size). This results in cluster sizes of 512, 1,024, 2,048, 4,096, 8,192, 16,284, and 32,768 bytes.

Consider the cluster organization of a 1 gigabyte drive — in other words, a 1,073,741,824 byte drive. Because the total number of cluster entries is 65,518, each cluster must be at least 16,389 bytes large. Rounding up to the next available cluster size results in a cluster size of a whopping 32,768 bytes. Imagine every batch file consuming 32K!

Because each drive has its own FAT, dividing a huge disk into several drives can reduce the cluster size and thereby increase the real storage capacity. In this example, if the 1 gigabyte disk is organized into four 250MB drives, the cluster size falls to a respectable 8,192 bytes. Better still, five 200MB drives can use a cluster size of 4,096.

The moral of this analysis is that smaller is sometimes bigger.

The master partition table informs the system of the way the disk is partitioned. It also contains the starting and ending sector of each partition, a code indicating the operating system for each partition, and information about which partition should be used to boot or start the computer. When the computer is first booted, the partition table is inspected and then attention is turned to the boot partition, from which the appropriate operating system is loaded. The partition used to boot the computer is referred to as the *active partition*.

You can easily check the status of partition table by executing the following command:

```
fdisk /status
```

This new switch displays the partition settings, detailing the number of installed disks and the logical drives associated with each disk.

Clearly, the partition table is a very important element of the hard disk. If the partition table gets damaged, you may not even be able to boot the computer from the hard disk. Refer to Chapter 3 for information about using MIRROR to keep a copy of the partition table.

Some disks are configured with an odd number of platters — seven, for example. In such situations, the odd platter, known as the *servoplatter,* is used, but not to store user data. The platter contains sector addressing information, which ensures that any sector can be accurately located even when the platters expand and contract due to operating temperature fluctuations. This accurate location of each sector reduces reseeking and thereby speeds up disk access. Newer *embedded servo* technologies have eclipsed this once popular technique.

The Role of CHKDSK

As the name suggests, the CHKDSK command (short for *check disk*) checks the integrity of the disk. CHKDSK doesn't check the physical condition of the disk; it merely analyzes the directory entries and the FAT and then identifies inconsistences and problems. If you execute CHKDSK with the /F switch, DOS tries to correct any problems it encounters. Otherwise, it reports problems but makes no attempt to correct them.

CHKDSK is not very adept at recovering data when a problem occurs. Its main focus is to remove the cause of the errors, not to recover data that was lost as a result of those errors. You should consider purchasing a third-party data recovery package, such as Norton Utilities, from Symantec, or PC Tools, from Central Point Software, to name just two. These packages might be worth the purchase price the first time a valuable file is damaged. Nonetheless, CHKDSK does act as a valuable file-integrity barometer and can solve some simple problems.

The following paragraphs explain the main error messages reported by CHKDSK:

- *filename* is cross-linked on allocation unit *x*

  Two or more files both claim ownership of a specific cluster. CHKDSK is unable to solve this problem even when it is used with the /F switch. You might be able to solve the problem by copying the files to another drive, deleting the original files, and then copying the files back to their original directories. In all likelihood, one file will be correct and the other will be corrupted. Check both files by loading them into an appropriate application and determine which file is damaged. You probably will need to restore a copy of the damaged file from backup.

  If you encounter cross-linked errors on valuable files, you should consider using a third-party data recovery program such as The Norton Utilities or PC Tools.

- *x* lost allocation units in *y* chains

  Some clusters are marked in the FAT as being in use, but no file claims ownership of them. That is, they are not in the chain of any file. When you use the /F option, DOS can optionally create one file in the root directory for each lost chain, giving you an opportunity to see what data is stored in these clusters. The files are given standard names, using the syntax file*nnnn*.chk, where *nnnn* is a sequential number — for example, FILE0001.CHK, FILE0002.CHK, etc.

- Insufficient room in the root directory

  The root directory of a hard drive is limited to 512 files. The limit is even lower on floppies and RAM disks. CHKDSK displays this error message when trying to create the FILE*nnnn*.CHK files (discussed previously) from the lost chains. To solve the problem, move some files into a subdirectory and then execute CHKDSK /F a second time.

- File allocation table bad, drive *x*:

  This message means what it says. The FAT is corrupted and cannot be read. If you regularly use MIRROR to keep a copy of the FAT, as recommended in Chapter 3, you can restore the FAT using UNFORMAT. Otherwise, you should consider using a third-party FAT rebuilding tool. If all else fails, try to copy all of your important files to another disk and then restore your entire drive from backup.

- First allocation unit is invalid, entry truncated

  The first cluster specified in a file's directory entry does not exist. When used with /F, CHKDSK changes the file's size to 0, indicating that there is no corresponding data.

■ `Has invalid allocation unit, file truncated`

One of the cluster entries in the file's cluster chain points to a cluster that does not exist. When used with /F, CHKDSK reduces the file's size and marks the last sensible cluster in the chain as the last cluster.

■ `Allocation error, size adjusted`

By comparing the file size in the directory entry with the total number of clusters allocated to the file's cluster chain, CHKDSK determined that too many clusters were allocated. CHKDSK assumes that the file-size entry in the directory is correct. When the /F switch is used, CHKDSK computes how many clusters are needed, changes the FAT status code for the real last cluster and assigns it the last-cluster code, and marks all subsequent clusters as available.

■ `Disk error reading FAT n`

`Disk error writing FAT n`

Two copies of the FAT are maintained at the beginning of the drive. This message indicates that one of the copies cannot be accessed. If the other copy were to become damaged, you would have a serious problem. Treat this message as a critical warning. One sure solution is to back up your entire drive, reformat, and then restore the files from backup.

■ `CHDIR .. failed, trying alternate method`

CHKDSK is unable to use the ".." file to traverse to the parent directory. To resolve the problem, CHKDSK goes to the root and searches downward for a directory that contains a directory file pointing to the subdirectory with the missing ".." file.

■ `Directory is totally empty, no . or ..`

A directory does not even contain the standard "." and ".." files. Remove the directory using RD and try CHKDSK again.

■ `Cannot recover .. entry`

There is a problem with the special ".." file. CHKDSK can normally correct these problems when you use the /F switch.

■ `Cannot CHDIR to *directory*, tree past this point not processed`

No matter how it tries, CHKDSK cannot access a directory. This is an indication of a corrupted directory file and is best resolved using a third-party data recovery tool.

■ `Cannot CHDIR to root. Processing cannot continue`

A serious corruption of the directory structure has occurred. Again, the problem is best resolved by using a third-party data recovery tool.

■ Unrecoverable error in directory. Convert directory to file (Y/N)?

CHKDSK identified a major error in the drive's directory structure. If you press Y, CHKDSK effectively deletes all the files stored in the bad directory. I recommend that you respond by pressing N and try to resolve the problem with a third-party data recovery program.

You may be wondering how problems such as these occur. They can happen when the system loses power in the middle of writing a file — for example, if you turn the computer off by mistake. Other causes include program bugs and computer viruses.

 When you run CHKDSK on a DoubleSpace drive, it performs exactly the same checks as it does on a standard drive. After all, the FAT structure and directory entries are the same for both drive types. However, when CHKDSK finishes checking a DoubleSpace drive, DOS automatically invokes the command DBLSPACE /CHKDSK. DBLSPACE /CHKDSK verifies the integrity of the additional DoubleSpace data structures, including the MDFAT, which maps a FAT cluster to the location in the DoubleSpace drive where the compressed cluster is stored.

Faster, Faster, Faster

You can use many software tools to enhance the performance of your hard disk. The most effective measure is to install a software disk cache, but other alternatives include setting the optimum interleave, using Fastdisk in Windows, and defragmenting files. If you haven't personally taken these measures, the chances are that with a few simple steps, you can increase the speed of your hard disk. Don't just assume that your hard disk is working at full throttle.

Optimizing the interleave

During low-level formatting, a disk is organized into sectors. You might expect the sectors to be numbered in ascending order — with sector 1 followed by sector 2, sector 3, and so on around the circumference of the track. This isn't always the case.

The sector numbering scheme can have a profound influence on disk performance. To understand why, you need to consider how data is actually transferred to and from the drive.

Suppose that you want to save a 10K file to disk. The file is too large to fit in a single sector, so it must be saved in several sectors. Usually, the file is saved in adjacent sectors. The read-write head moves over the appropriate track, reads the sector headers, and looks for the address of the first sector where the file is to be stored. As soon as the sector is located, the first 512 bytes are saved. The system then prepares the next batch of 512 bytes and saves it in the next sector. However, the disk platter is spinning at 3,600 revolutions per minute. If the sectors are numbered sequentially, by the time the read-write head starts looking for the next sector, that sector may already be spinning past the head. If so, the disk must wait for almost one complete revolution before the target sector is once again below the read-write head.

If the system is not fast enough to write two adjacent sectors one after the other, it does not make sense to number the sectors sequentially. The solution is to separate sector 2 from sector 1 by one or more sectors. That way, by the time the system is ready to save the data, the target sector is just rotating under the read-write head.

The term *disk interleave* refers to the sector numbering scheme used on a hard disk. An interleave of 1:1 indicates that the sectors are numbered in sequential order — that is, 3 follows 2, 2 follows 1, etc. Only high-performance systems have a 1:1 interleave, which means that as soon as one sector is written, the system is ready to write the next 512 bytes in the next sector. On a disk with a 2:1 interleave, sector numbers are ordered alternately, as shown in Figure 4-4.

The interleave setting is established during low-level drive formatting. If your drive is configured with the wrong interleave, performance is adversely affected. The drive must rotate an unnecessary number of times to read or write data.

The programs SpinTest and SpinTime, from Gibson Research Corporation, are included on Bob's Shareware Collection disks. Use these programs to report the interleave setting of your hard disk and identify the optimal interleave setting.

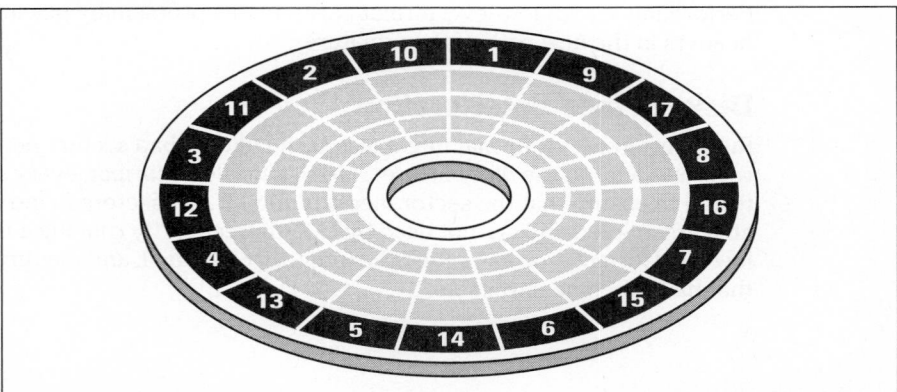

Figure 4-4: Interleave settings for a hard disk with 17 sectors per track and a 2:1 interleave.

If you discover that your disk has an inappropriate setting, DOS won't be able to help you. Drives are normally low-level formatted at the factory or by the dealer. DOS, therefore, does not provide any low-level formatting tools. You must use a third-party tool, such as SpinRite, from Gibson Research Corporation. In general, these programs determine the optimum interleave prior to performing a low-level format.

 A destructive low-level format will, as the name implies, destroy all the data on the disk; both the sector IDs and the general data area of each sector are rewritten. Some disk drives can be rendered useless (except, perhaps, as a paperweight) if they are destructively formatted because the format will destroy vital drive statistics that are stored on the drive itself. Some of the early SCSI drives, for example, store important data on the disk. SpinRite can perform a nondestructive low-level format, where the data is left intact and only the sector IDs are rewritten. If you do not get the low-level formatting program directly from the drive manufacturer, always use a nondestructive formatting tool like SpinRite.

You may also need to low-level format a drive if you experience frequent error messages saying that sectors were not found. These messages may be caused by drive alignment problems or by disk surface deterioration.

Drive alignment problems

Like all devices with moving parts, a disk drive is subject to wear. When the sector address information is first recorded on the hard disk, the drive is new and the head armature is accurately positioned above each track. As the disk ages, the armature mechanism can wear slightly, causing the read-write head to shift so that the original sector header is not located directly below the head. When the armature drift is large enough, the sector heads are too far from the head position, and the sector address information cannot be read. This is usually the cause when DOS presents the `Sector not found` message.

Performing a fresh low-level format corrects this problem by placing new sector headers in the new path of the armature.

Disk surface deterioration

Running a low-level format might also be justified if bad sectors develop due to wear and tear on the disk surface. During a low-level format, every sector is tested to ensure that the sector media is sound. Any sectors found to be unreliable are marked and are not used by DOS thereafter. By running a fresh low-level format, you can retest the integrity of the disk and identify any sectors that have become unreliable.

Improving throughput with caches

One of the most dramatic ways to improve the performance of a disk is to install a software disk cache. All PC users, in fact, should use a disk cache. DOS's disk cache program is SMARTDRV.

Before DOS 6, the DOS disk cache program was called SMARTDRV.SYS and was always loaded as a device driver in CONFIG.SYS. Now, the disk cache is named SMARTDRV.EXE and is both a device driver and an executable program. If you have an entry in CONFIG.SYS for SMARTDRV.SYS, make sure that you replace it with SMARTDRV.EXE.

The DOS 6 SMARTDRV does not support an expanded memory cache, only an extended memory cache.

Using SMARTDRV

When using SMARTDRV, you need to consider the issues outlined in the following few sections.

The complete syntax for SMARTDRV is detailed in Part IV, "The Complete DOS 6 Command Reference."

How much memory should you assign to the cache?

We all know that memory is a precious commodity, and few of us are using systems with more than 20MB of RAM (yet). As a general rule, the cache size should be as large as possible. There is, of course, a direct trade-off between the size of the cache and the amount of extended memory available to applications software.

Ideally, the cache size should range from 0.5MB to 2MB, depending on the amount of installed memory. If your system has 4MB or less of extended memory, a cache of 0.5MB to 1MB is appropriate. Systems with 4MB to 8MB of installed memory might use a cache in the range 1MB to 2MB. There are diminishing performance improvements when you increase the disk cache size much beyond 2MB — the cache hit rate reduces and the cache management algorithms take longer to compute.

A little trial and error is often the best way to determine the optimum cache size. Try using various cache sizes and time how long disk-intensive tasks take.

Contrary to popular belief, SMARTDRV memory allocation is not truly dynamic; the cache cannot lend memory to any application that needs it. The one exception is Windows. When you launch Windows, SMARTDRV can automatically reduce the size of the cache, leaving more extended memory available to Windows. When you subsequently leave Windows, SMARTDRV reclaims the extended memory, increasing the cache to its original size.

How Disk Caches Work

All disk cache software is based on one simple truth: Memory access is a lot faster than disk access. Without an active disk cache, a computer system takes the following steps to process data from disk:

1. The microprocessor asks the hard disk controller for some data.

2. The disk controller determines precisely where on the disk the data is stored.

3. The disk controller moves the read-write head over the appropriate cylinder.

4. Each sector header is read until the target sector is located.

5. The data is read from the sector and passed to the disk controller.

6. The disk controller decodes the data and passes it via the bus to memory.

7. The data is passed from memory to the microprocessor via the bus.

No wonder it seems to take so long. Disk caches use three main techniques to improve file-reading performance:

■ **File mirroring:** The first time you read a file into memory, the disk cache software keeps a copy of the file, by sector, in the memory cache. The next time a program tries to access the same file, the disk cache software can intercept the request and pass the file directory from the memory cache, avoiding another time-consuming trip to the disk. Eventually, the cache memory fills up with data. The better cache programs use a sophisticated algorithm to determine which cache data should be overwritten when the cache is full, but basically, they discard the least used sectors.

■ **Track buffering:** More often than not, the system reads one block of data in one request and then immediately initiates a second request for the adjacent block of data. The concept behind track buffering is simple: While the system is reading one sector, it might as well read the remaining sectors on the track and keep them in a memory cache. The read-write head is already in position over the next sector, so the overhead of reading the additional sectors is minimal. If a request is made for the next sector, the disk cache software can supply the sector data directly from RAM. Track buffering can speed up all file accesses, even the first time you access a file.

■ **Write buffering:** Write buffering is similar in principle to print buffering. The disk cache software stores in a memory cache data that a program is trying to save to disk. The main application program, thinking that the file has been saved, can then proceed with other operations while the disk cache software saves the data to disk in the background. When a system reads a file, the order in which sectors are processed is important, but during file saving, the order in which sectors are written to the disk is not important, provided that all the sectors are saved in a timely fashion. The more advanced disk cache programs analyze the data in the write cache and reorganize the sector-saving sequence so that the data is written in the most efficient way. This strategy reduces read-write head movement and reduces the delays incurred while the system waits for the correct sector to spin beneath the heads. Although this does speed things up, there are risks associated with having unwritten information left in memory; there's more to lose during a crash or power failure, for example.

If your hard drive already has a hardware cache, adding a software cache will not improve your throughput much and will likely slow things down. Try out your favorite programs with and without the cache to see whether you really get an improvement.

Windows, like any disk-intensive program, benefits from a disk cache. However, the less extended memory available to Windows, the more Windows must access the disk. Make the cache too big, and Windows must use the disk more; make the cache too small, and Windows doesn't get much benefit from it. Catch-22 — or maybe Cache-22. As a simple rule of thumb, you should probably reduce the cache size by 50 percent when running under Windows.

When you launch SMARTDRV, specify the normal cache size, followed by the Windows cache size in kilobytes. The following command, for example, creates a 4MB standard cache with a 2MB Windows cache:

```
smartdrv 4096 2048
```

If you don't specify a cache size, SMARTDRV uses a default value based on the total of installed memory. Table 4-2 shows the default cache sizes.

Do you need double buffering?

The only reason to install SMARTDRV as a device driver in CONFIG.SYS is to enable *double buffering*. Double buffering can resolve conflicts between the disk controller and the memory manager. If your system locks up when you are installing device drivers into upper memory or running Windows in Enhanced Mode, double buffering may provide the solution.

When you enable double buffering, data is moved first from the disk cache to a conventional memory buffer and then off to disk. This technique is needed on some systems that use a bus-mastering disk controller. The problem is most common on older SCSI devices, but some ESDI drives and MCA hard disk controllers may also exhibit the problem. Most systems do not need double buffering.

Fortunately, there is an easy way to determine whether or not you need the double buffering system. Install SMARTDRV.EXE with the /DOUBLE_BUFFER switch in CONFIG.SYS and in AUTOEXEC.BAT. Also make sure that your system is configured to use upper memory; use EMM386 and the DOS=UMB statement.

Table 4-2	SMARTDRV Default Cache Sizes	
Extended Memory	*DOS Cache Size*	*Windows Cache Size*
1MB (or less)	All extended memory	0K
2MB (or less)	1MB	256K
4MB (or less)	1MB	512K
Less than 6MB	2MB	1MB
More than 6MB	2MB	2MB

Refer to Chapter 5 for more information on upper memory.

Use your system for a while and then execute SMARTDRV with no switches. A summary of the cache status, similar to the following, is displayed:

```
Microsoft SMARTDrive Disk Cache version 4.1
Copyright 1991,1993 Microsoft Corp.

Cache size: 2,097,152 bytes
Cache size while running Windows: 2,097,152 bytes

              Disk Caching Status
 drive    read cache    write cache    buffering
----------------------------------------------

   A:        yes           no            no
   B:        yes           no            no
   C:        yes           yes           no
   D:        yes           yes           no
   E:        yes           yes           no

For help, type "Smartdrv /?".
```

If "no" appears in the buffering column for every drive, you do not need double buffering, and you can remove the SMARTDRV.EXE statement from CONFIG.SYS. However, if any drive has a "yes" entry, you must continue to use double buffering.

If the double buffer column has a "-" entry, there has been insufficient activity for SMARTDRV to assess whether double buffering is needed. Perform some additional tasks on the PC and try again. Eventually, the "-" entry will be replaced by "no" or "yes."

Do not use the DEVICEHIGH statement with SMARTDRV in CONFIG.SYS; load SMARTDRV low, using DEVICE. It only consumes about 2K of conventional memory.

Is delayed write caching appropriate?

The reason for installing a disk cache is to improve hard disk performance. Clearly, write caching enhances the performance more than basic read caching does. The only drawback is that chances for data loss increase, because data is not immediately written to disk. However, data loss occurs only if you lose power to your system, press the Reset button, or a program locks up while a file-saving operation is in progress. SMARTDRV is smart enough to intercept a Ctrl-Alt-Del reboot and flush the buffers (save the data) before rebooting.

If you use a third-party utility in a batch file to reboot the system, you might consider adding the following statement to flush the buffers before rebooting:

```
smartdrv /c
```

Because SMARTDRV saves the data within a few seconds, the odds of losing data are not great. If you use a PC in an environment where power failures or program crashes are common, you might consider disabling the delayed write cache. Personally, I like speed and always use write caching.

Resolving communications problems with SMARTDRV

If you use SMARTDRV on a system that has DoubleSpace installed, you may experience intermittent problems running communications at 9600 baud and above. The problems may be related to the 8250 UART communications controller, which is unable to handle the interrupt bombardment. You can easily determine your UART type using MSD. If you select the **C**OM Ports option from the main menu, MSD displays (on the bottom line) the UART model.

One quick solution might be to disable the write-caching feature of SMARTDRV. For example, if you are caching drives C and D, specify the drives (without the + or – switch) as follows:

```
smartdrv c d
```

If you specify a drive letter with the plus (+) character, SMARTDRV enables read caching and write caching. If you specify the drive letter with a minus (–) character, SMARTDRV disables caching altogether on that drive. However, if you specify the drive without a plus or minus character, read caching is enabled and write caching is disabled.

If it irks you to disable write caching or if it simply doesn't fix the problem, consider upgrading the UART chips to the much more capable 16450 model or, better still, the 16550A model. They cost anywhere from $25 to $35.

A Brief History of the UART Chip

Each serial port on a PC has a *Universal Asynchronous Receiver/Transmitter* (UART) chip. This chip acts as a translator, converting incoming serial communications into the parallel input that the main PC circuits use. Similarly, it converts parallel data into serial signals for communication to the attached serial device.

The original PC used the 8250 UART chip. Even back then, this chip had a reputation for being slow and awkward. Surprisingly, many of today's PCs still use this antiquated chip (my 33 MHz 486 included). This chip was never designed to accommodate today's high-speed communications. In 1984, manufacturers started to replace the 8250 with the 16450 chip, and then in 1987, the 16550 took the throne. The latest incarnation is the 16550A UART, which includes a tiny, 16-byte buffer that enables it to handle high-speed bursts of data.

Using SMARTDRV with DoubleSpace drives

To optimize cache efficiency, always configure SMARTDRV (or any other disk cache, for that matter) to cache the host drive and do not cache the DoubleSpace drive. For example, if the host drive is D and the DoubleSpace drive is C, use the following switches to install SMARTDRV:

```
smartdrv e+ c-
```

Avoiding bad cluster problems

SMARTDRV's track buffering may cause a problem in one situation. When you enable track buffering using default settings, SMARTDRV, after reading a requested cluster, reads the additional clusters on a track in anticipation of a future request for them. SMARTDRV does not analyze the FAT when reading these extra clusters, and on occasion, it tries to read bad clusters — that is, clusters that contain unreliable sectors. Some hard disk controllers deal with this situation gracefully, and others bump and grind for a second or two, but some retry for a significant period of time.

If you experience problems that may be related to SMARTDRV reading bad clusters, configure SMARTDRV so that track buffering is disabled. Set the read-ahead buffer to 0 by using the /B:0 switch and set the element size equal to your disk's cluster size. Assuming the cluster size is 4,096, the following command resolves the track buffering problem:

```
smartdrv /b:0 /e:4096
```

If you don't know the cluster size, run CHKDSK and review the line *nnnn* bytes in each allocation unit. The cluster size is the *nnnn* value.

Using SMARTDRV with CD-ROMs

Time for the bad news: SMARTDRV cannot cache CD-ROM drives. Ironically, CD-ROMs are slow and desperately need a cache performance boost. But if you want to cache a CD-ROM, you need to use a cache program other than SMARTDRV.

Never cache a DoubleSpace drive. Always cache the host drive — the drive that contains the hidden DoubleSpace volume file DBLSPACE.*nnn*. SMARTDRV has a built-in safety feature that prevents you from caching a DoubleSpace drive, but most third-party cache programs do not.

Using Fastdisk with Windows

Under normal circumstances, all disk I/O is handled by the BIOS, which can function only in Real Mode. When a Windows program is running in Protected Mode, it must throttle down into Real Mode to perform file I/O and then switch back into Protected Mode to proceed. Needless to say, this takes time.

To improve Windows performance in Enhanced Mode, Microsoft introduced Fastdisk, a form of device driver that reduces the amount of Protected- to Real-Mode switching during file I/O. To be specific, the swap file I/O is performed in Protected Mode, but standard disk I/O still requires a switch into Real Mode. Additional benefits of Fastdisk include the ability to run more DOS-based applications simultaneously and improved performance when a DOS application is running in the background. The benefits of Fastdisk are most apparent on systems with low RAM (5MB or less) and systems that run multiple DOS sessions.

To activate Fastdisk, you must open the Windows Control Panel, select the 386 Enhanced icon, and then select the Virtual Memory button. When the Virtual Memory dialog box is displayed, select Use 32-Bit Disk Access to enable Fastdisk.

Fastdisk is very hardware specific and only functions with controllers that are compliant with the Western Digital 1003 controller interface standard. This standard was selected because the vast majority of IDE drives are compliant. If you use a SCSI system or any drive that uses device drivers to exceed DOS's 1,024 cylinder limit (discussed earlier), you should not use Fastdisk. Many vendors of high-capacity, high-performance drives are supplying their own variations of Fastdisk to provide Protected Mode access. Adaptec, the dominant SCSI force, has not yet released a Fastdisk-style driver for Windows, but other SCSI vendors have.

 If you are unable to run Windows after activating Fastdisk, you are probably using an incompatible disk controller. If Windows won't even start, edit the SYSTEM.INI file and turn the 32-Bit Disk Access off by using the following command:

```
32bitdiskaccess=off
```

Using RAM drives

As the name suggests, a RAM drive (or RAM disk) is a disk drive that exists in memory. A RAM drive performs like any other disk drive, with two exceptions:

- A RAM drive is in memory and so is very fast.
- The files stored on a RAM drive are lost when you turn off or reboot the system.

RAM disks gained popularity in the mid- to late 1980s, when many power users had systems equipped with a few megabytes of RAM but had no applications software that could take advantage of it. By using RAMDRIVE.SYS (or its variant, VDISK) to create a RAM disk in extended memory, they could at least use some of the expensive hardware and get a performance boost as a bonus.

RAM drives are fast, but they have too many limitations. In truth, a disk cache using delayed-write buffering is a far more flexible and effective way to use RAM than a RAM drive. With a disk cache, you don't have to copy files from the hard disk to the RAM drive; you don't have to worry about having too little room on the drive; and you don't have to make sure that data is copied back from the RAM drive to the hard disk before rebooting.

To put it bluntly, don't use a RAM drive; use a disk cache instead.

Using FASTOPEN

FASTOPEN was first introduced in DOS 3.3. It was designed to enhance disk performance by keeping directory information about recently accessed files in a memory buffer. The second time a file is read, DOS can get the file details from RAM rather than having to access the directory and FAT on disk. Although the concept sounds good, tangible performance gains are realized only when you use programs that open and close files frequently, such as database applications.

You realize far greater performance gains if you use SMARTDRV or a third-party disk cache. These programs cache the file data along with the location details. In short, use SMARTDRV instead of FASTOPEN.

Reviewing the benefits of defragmentation

Not all files are stored neatly in consecutive clusters. When you save a file, DOS tries to save the file in one contiguous block on the unused part of the disk. However, if the disk is near capacity and there isn't room for the entire file, DOS accesses the FAT and starts to save the file in the first available cluster. DOS then checks the FAT again to find the next free cluster and saves the file's second cluster in that space. The process continues until the entire file is saved to disk.

When a file is saved in noncontiguous clusters like this, it is said to be *fragmented*. If you have a disk that is nearly full (whose isn't?), and you regularly delete and create or copy files, there is a good chance that some of your files will be fragmented.

Fragmented files have a negative effect on performance and data recovery. When a file is fragmented, the read-write heads must jump from cluster to cluster to save or load the file. All this head movement takes time. It can take more than twice as long to access a heavily fragmented file than it does to access a file stored in contiguous clusters.

In addition, your chances of recovering a fragmented file that has been accidentally formatted or deleted are greatly reduced. Only when a file is stored in contiguous clusters is there a reasonable chance that you can recover data using UNFORMAT or UNDELETE (when delete sentry or delete tracker are not enabled).

For more information on data recovery and the benefits of defragmentation, refer to Chapter 3.

A quick and easy way to see whether a file is fragmented is to use CHKDSK. If you specify a filename or filemask with the CHKDSK command, DOS reports the overall disk status and lists any files matching the filemask that are fragmented. For example, the following output was generated by issuing the command CHKDSK *.* in the directory E:\DOC:

```
Volume UPSTAIRS-E  created 11-16-1992 1:35p
Volume Serial Number is 1996-B0AA


  167059456 bytes total disk space
   48533504 bytes in 3 hidden files
     598016 bytes in 143 directories
   80965632 bytes in 2035 user files
   36954112 bytes available on disk


       4096 bytes in each allocation unit
      40786 total allocation units on disk
       9022 available allocation units on disk


     655360 total bytes memory
     586000 bytes free

E:\DOC\READ.ZIP Contains 3 non-contiguous blocks
E:\DOC\DS00RAFN.DOC Contains 2 non-contiguous blocks
E:\DOC\DS00RA0Z.DOC Contains 2 non-contiguous blocks
E:\DOC\DS00RA06.DOC Contains 5 non-contiguous blocks
```

Using DEFRAG

By rearranging the clusters on a disk, you can reorganize fragmented files so that they occupy contiguous clusters. This process is known as *defragmentation*. DOS 6 includes the program DEFRAG for analyzing and defragmenting files.

DEFRAG supports a variety of switches, allowing you to execute the entire defragmentation process from the command line. Using switches, you can specify the optimization method and the sort order for directories, and even instruct DEFRAG to reboot the system when it finishes. The full syntax for DEFRAG is included in Part IV, "The Complete DOS 6 Command Reference."

If you execute DEFRAG with no switches, you can use the program interactively, selecting commands and options from the menu. When DEFRAG is executed interactively, the hard disk is analyzed and DEFRAG reports the most appropriate optimization method (see Figure 4-5).

Defragmentation takes time, so DEFRAG offers two defragmentation methods:

- **Full Optimization:** This method takes the longest amount of time (from 30 to 60 minutes in some cases) but offers the most performance improvements. All directories are moved to the beginning of the disk — in other words, the outermost tracks, near to the FAT. This means that a file's starting cluster can be determined with minimum head movement. All the files are unfragmented and then moved to the outermost part of the disk, leaving the entire free space on the disk in one contiguous free block.

- **Files Only:** This method is a lot faster, but it only defragments the files. Directories are not moved to the beginning of the disk; files are not moved to the outside of the disk; and unused free clusters remain scattered about the disk. When you use this method, new files tend to be fragmented more quickly, as they tend to occupy the noncontiguous clusters.

Figure 4-5: Running DEFRAG interactively.

DEFRAG displays a form of road map that details the fragmentation of a disk. Compare the disk in Figure 4-6, which was fully optimized, with the one illustrated in Figure 4-7, which was optimized with the Files Only option. Notice all the empty clusters scattered around the disk on the second disk.

 If a large section of the disk map is marked with Xs, it probably indicates a DoubleSpace volume or a Windows swap file. DEFRAG automatically defragments a DoubleSpace drive, and the Windows swap file is always stored in a contiguous block and so doesn't need defragmenting.

During the defragmentation procedure, you can sort directory entries so that files are listed in order by name, extension, date, or size. This doesn't affect the physical location of a file — simply the order that it appears in directory listings.

Because fragmented files impair performance and reduce the chances of error recovery, you should run DEFRAG on your hard disks at least once a week.

Solving memory problems

DEFRAG only uses conventional memory to defragment a disk. Sad but true. You may experience insufficient memory problems trying to run DEFRAG on big drives (400MB+) that have large numbers of directories and files.

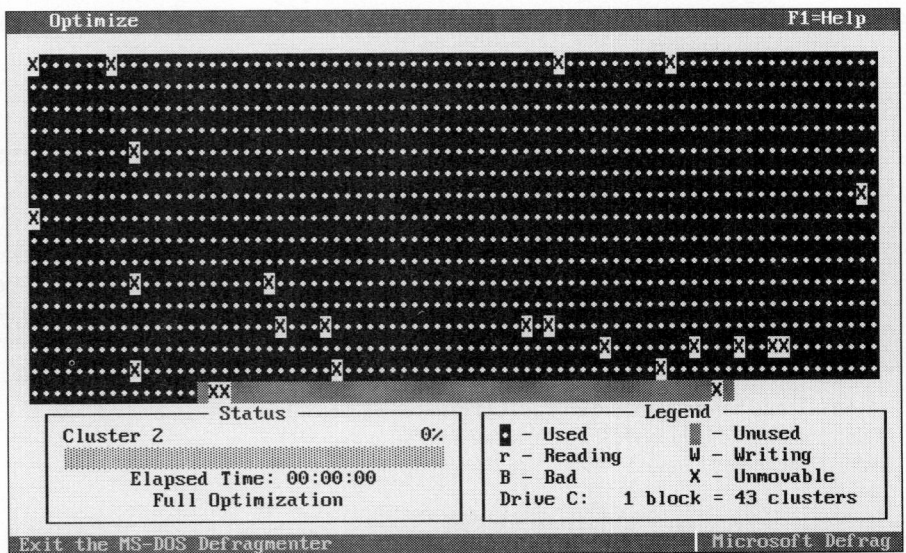

Figure 4-6: A disk defragmented using the Full Optimization method.

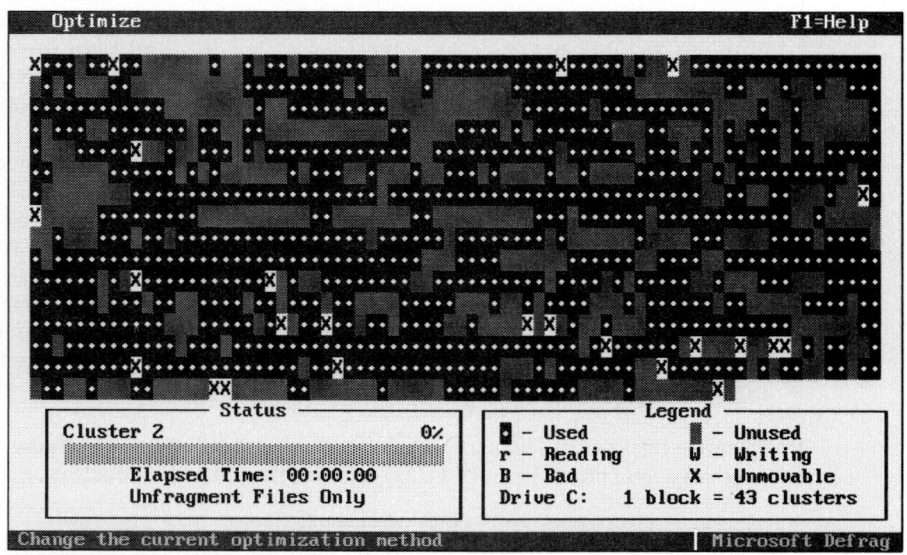

Figure 4-7: A disk defragmented using the Files Only method.

In case you are interested, DEFRAG consumes 16 bytes for every file on the system and 48 bytes for every directory, plus some room for itself and the two copies of the FAT. What's left is used for buffering the clusters during the reorganization.

Defragmenting Hidden Files

By default, DEFRAG does not move hidden files. A hidden file may be part of a copy-protection scheme, and the associated application may not execute if the hidden file's clusters are moved to a different location.

You can and normally should instruct DEFRAG to defragment the hidden files. To do this, execute the /H switch as follows:

```
defrag /h
```

If you suspect that some of your hidden files may be part of a copy-protection scheme, do not use the /H switch. To see a list of all the hidden files on your system, execute the following DIR command:

```
dir \ /ah /s
```

One approach to solving the memory problem is to boot with a configuration that maximizes the amount of free conventional memory. If you have a 386 or better system, try booting with an empty AUTOEXEC.BAT and with the following entries in CONFIG.SYS:

```
dos=high
dos=umb
device=c:\dos\himem.sys
device=c:\dos\emm386.exe noems ia000-b7ff
```

Add the following line if you are using a DoubleSpace drive:

```
devicehigh=c:\dos\dblspace.bin /move
```

When you boot the system, you should have 675K or more of base memory. That's right — more than 640K! This trick uses some of the graphics memory as base memory. Be sure not to run any graphics applications when the system is configured this way.

After you maximize memory, run DEFRAG with the /U switch to force a Files Only optimization. Finally, run DEFRAG a second time with the /F switch to attempt a full optimization.

If this doesn't work, try deleting all the anti-virus CHKLIST.CPS files, using the MWAV program (discussed in the preceding chapter), and run DEFRAG again. As a last resort, you might delete some files and directories (having made a backup first) to reduce the information DEFRAG has to manage.

A more practical solution is to use a third-party defragmenter that can take advantage of expanded or extended memory.

Included on Bob's Shareware Collection disks is an excellent utility called Disk OrGanizer™ (or DOG, for short), from Soft GAM's Software. As well as providing all the functionality of the DOS DEFRAG command, DOG™ has additional power and flexibility. DOG™ can use EMS and can defragment disks with as many as 32,000 files.

Some of the additional switches for DOG™ give you the ability to exclude specific files; to move select files and directories, based on the PATH setting, to the outermost tracks; to physically place files on the disk in the order of creation; and to move specific files to the outermost or innermost tracks. The defragmentation options can be recorded in an ASCII file.

In addition, DOG™ can perform a test to analyze the disk without actually moving any clusters. Use the following command to instruct DOG™ to perform a dry run on drive C:

```
dog c: /test
```

DOG™ provides four different defragmentation methods, each offering a different balance of speed and defragmentation completeness. The /FILL switch invokes the maximum defragmentation option. The following is a sample output from the command DOG C: /FILL:

```
DOG - Disk OrGanizer, Version 3.17 - April 17, 1992
Copyright (C) 1992, G. Allen Morris III,  All rights reserved.

Analyzing disk ...Reading File Allocation Table ...Testing
File Allocation Table ...
Reading directories ...Testing file allocation ...
Drive C: Volume "UPSTAIRS-C" has:
   136 areas of free disk space.
     1 volume label.
    82 null files.
  6495 user files that are contiguous.
    21 user files that are fragmented with 51 extra fragments.
     2 system files that are contiguous.
     2 system files that are fragmented with 6 extra fragments.
   178 user directories that are contiguous.
     1 hidden directory that is contiguous.

Reading order file.Analyzing disk organization. Please wait...
717 clusters need to be moved to organize this disk.
    10 directories need to be packed.
Is it OK to write to the disk?
```

If you press Y, DOG™ defragments the disk; otherwise, it returns you to the DOS prompt.

 If you use a third-party defragmenting tool, make sure that you do not try to run it from within Windows or any other multitasking program.

Bigger, Bigger, Bigger with DoubleSpace

One of the major new features introduced in DOS 6 is DoubleSpace. DoubleSpace is a combination of device drivers and utilities that can almost double the storage capacity of a standard hard drive. If you are forever running out of disk space, DoubleSpace offers a very economical way of increasing your disk capacity without having to buy a new hard disk.

DoubleSpace saves disk space by compressing data before saving to disk. To take advantage of DoubleSpace, you must create at least one DoubleSpace drive. You can create a DoubleSpace drive by using free space on an existing drive or by compressing the data already stored on a drive. For example, DoubleSpace can take 30MB of free space on a drive and create a new drive that can hold about 60MB of files.

All files stored on a DoubleSpace drive are compressed, and the total storage capacity of the drive is almost double that of a conventional drive — hence the name *DoubleSpace*.

You use the command DBLSPACE to create and manage the compressed DoubleSpace drives. The full syntax for DBLSPACE is described in Part IV, "The Complete DOS 6 Command Reference." Although DBLSPACE supports a wide variety of switches, you also can use DBLSPACE in a full-screen, menu-driven mode by executing DBLSPACE with no switches.

 The first time you execute DBLSPACE, DOS runs a setup procedure to install at least one compressed drive. You can use the full-screen DBLSPACE utility only if you have at least one DoubleSpace drive.

Reviewing DoubleSpace mechanics

A device driver named DBLSPACE.BIN is the brain behind DoubleSpace. When DOS tries to save data to a DoubleSpace drive, DBLSPACE.BIN intercepts the task, compresses the data on the fly, and then saves the compressed data to disk. When that data is read back from the DoubleSpace drive, DBLSPACE.BIN decompresses the data and passes it to DOS in uncompressed form.

The concept of data compression is not new. The basic approach is to analyze the source data and identify repeated sequences or patterns of bytes (or characters). These repeated sequences are then replaced with markers indicating the location of each matching sequence. The repeated sequence is stored only once, and because the marker is smaller than the full character sequence, space is saved.

Some compression techniques provide optimal compression for text files, and others are designed to compress binary program files the most. Recently, compression algorithms were developed to compress video image and sound files. The algorithms used by DoubleSpace are based on methods first introduced by the compression experts Lempel and Ziv. The Lempel-Ziv method employs a general compression algorithm that offers the best overall compression for a mixture of file types — text files, program files, clip art, etc. Some files compress better than others, but as a rule of thumb, DoubleSpace compressed files are half the size of the normal (uncompressed) files.

The primary difference between DoubleSpace and file compression tools such as PKZIP and ARJ (which is included on the enclosed disk) is that DoubleSpace files are compressed in real time. That means that the files are compressed and uncompressed automatically by the device driver; you do not need to manually compress the files or to decompress or extract them before they can be used.

Also, because DoubleSpace must compress and uncompress more quickly than the manual compression utilities, it trades off squeezing that last little bit of compression for additional speed.

Understanding the compressed volume file

DoubleSpace creates one or more additional drives to store files. Any files that are saved to a DoubleSpace drive are automatically compressed.

Each DoubleSpace drive actually is a large hidden file stored on a normal drive. The file is called a *compressed volume file* (or CVF-) and has the filename DBLSPACE.*nnn*, where *nnn* is a sequence number (DBLSPACE.000, DBLSPACE.001, and so on).

Suppose that your system has two hard disks installed, and you decide to dedicate 20MB of physical drive D to be a DoubleSpace drive. DoubleSpace creates a 20MB hidden file in the root of drive D and also tricks DOS into thinking that there is a new drive — drive J, for example. Drive J appears to have about 40MB of free space. The drive that stores the hidden CVF is said to be the *host* drive. In the example, drive D is the host of drive J.

Whenever you save a file on drive J, DBLSPACE.BIN compresses the file and stores it in the large hidden file on drive D. Similarly, when you load a file from drive J, DBLSPACE.BIN extracts the file from inside the hidden file on drive D and passes it to DOS.

In a way, the CVF is like a giant ZIP or ARJ file that is accessed behind the scenes whenever DOS tries to load a file from the compressed drive.

A CVF file contains all the normal drive structures, including a boot sector, FAT, and root directory. A CVF also includes a sector allocation table that maps standard FAT clusters to DoubleSpace sectors. DBLSPACE.BIN allocates data on a sector-by-sector basis, unlike DOS, which uses clusters. In addition to saving space by compressing data, DoubleSpace sector-based allocation saves space by avoiding the normal waste that occurs when every small file must occupy at least one cluster.

Compressing an entire drive

When you want to compress an existing drive, files and all, DoubleSpace operates a little differently. For example, consider a system that has only one installed hard disk: drive C.

DoubleSpace creates a CVF in the root directory of drive C and then compresses and transfers all the files from the original drive C to the new CVF. You might expect that after the compression, the original drive C would hold just a few files and the new drive (probably drive H) would contain all the compressed files that used to be on drive C. Not so!

Whenever you compress an existing drive, DoubleSpace automatically *swaps* the drive letters of the physical drive and the compressed drive. So, in this example, the real drive C (the host) appears to be drive H, and the drive that contains all the compressed files appears to be drive C.

Although this drive swapping may seem odd, it is done for a very good reason. After you compress drive C, the newly compressed files still appear to DOS and other programs as if they are on drive C. Imagine the chaos that would ensue if suddenly everything that used to be on drive C were now on drive H. You would need to reconfigure all your programs to run from drive H. It might take days just to edit the Windows INI files.

 Whenever you create a CVF on drive C, the drive letter of the physical drive C is swapped so that the DoubleSpace drive is assigned the letter C. Even if you create a new CVF using the free space on drive C, DoubleSpace still swaps the drive letter assignments for drive C and the compressed drive.

You can use the switch /LIST with the DBLSPACE command to review the drive letter assignments.

The following output was generated from a system with three physical drives: C, D, and E. The compressed drive I was created using free space on drive D, and the compressed drive J was created using the free space on drive E. Notice that no drive swapping occurred because the DoubleSpace drives were created using free space on existing drives.

```
Drive  Type                    Total Free   Total Size  CVF  Filename
-----------------------------------------------------------------------

  A    Removable drive         No disk in drive
  B    Floppy drive                0.04 MB      0.69 MB
  C    Local hard drive            7.79 MB    201.97 MB
  D    Local hard drive           29.87 MB    165.11 MB
  E    Local hard drive           14.82 MB    159.32 MB
  F    Available for DoubleSpace
  G    Available for DoubleSpace
  H    Available for DoubleSpace
  I    Compressed hard drive      29.31 MB     37.00 MB  E:\DBLSPACE.001
  J    Compressed hard drive      43.65 MB     43.65 MB  D:\DBLSPACE.001
```

The following output from a DBLSPACE /LIST command was generated on a system with only one physical drive. DoubleSpace was used to compress the drive. Notice that the drive letters have been swapped so that the compressed drive is C and the physical drive is I.

Drive	Type	Total Free	Total Size	CVF Filename
A	Removable-media drive	No disk in drive		
C	Compressed hard drive	46.34 MB	139.93 MB	I:\DBLSPACE.000
D	Available for DoubleSpace			
E	Available for DoubleSpace			
F	Available for DoubleSpace			
G	Available for DoubleSpace			
H	Available for DoubleSpace			
I	Local hard drive	6.31 MB	80.52 MB	

 When you compress an existing drive, the CVF filename is always DBLSPACE.000. The 000 extension indicates that the drive letters of the host and the compressed drive should be swapped. When a drive is created from free space on an existing drive, the CVF filename has an extension of 001 or of the next free value if it is not the first CVF on the drive.

Installing a DoubleSpace drive

Creating a DoubleSpace drive is a snap. If you are running DBLSPACE for the first time, you are prompted to select either the custom or express setup.

Express setup

The express option compresses the existing drive C and creates a new host drive, which is usually assigned the letter H. The process involves running CHKDSK on drive C, defragmenting the drive, and creating an empty CVF in the root directory of drive C. In turn, each existing file is read from drive C and compressed. The CVF is then expanded, and the file is written to the CVF. Finally, the originally uncompressed file is deleted. Measures are taken to ensure that there will be no loss of data if the system loses power or is rebooted during the compression procedure. The entire process can take several hours.

Custom setup

The custom option allows you to select which drive you want to compress and identify whether you want to create a new empty drive or compress an existing drive. You also can select the drive letter that you want to assign to the new drive (see Figure 4-8) as well as the amount of free space you want to leave on the host drive.

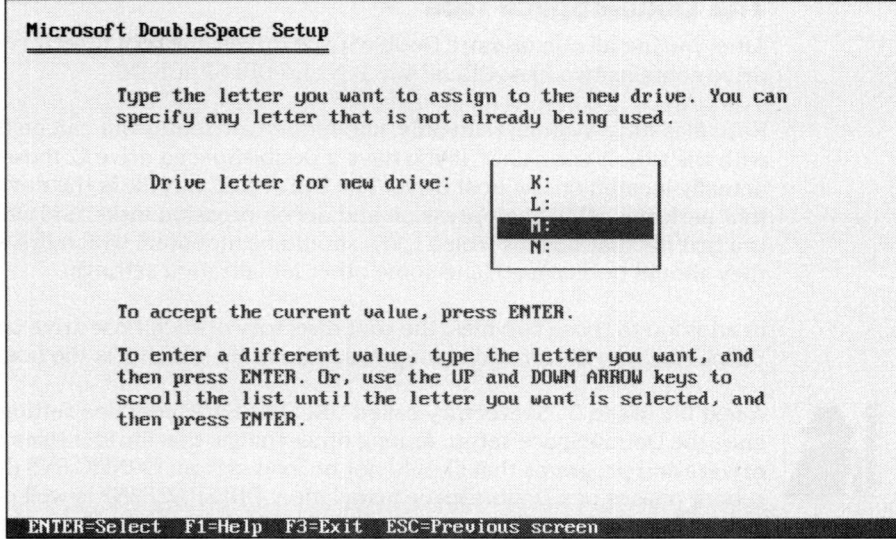

```
Microsoft DoubleSpace Setup

          Type the letter you want to assign to the new drive. You can
          specify any letter that is not already being used.


          Drive letter for new drive:        K:
                                             L:
                                             M:
                                             N:


          To accept the current value, press ENTER.

          To enter a different value, type the letter you want, and
          then press ENTER. Or, use the UP and DOWN ARROW keys to
          scroll the list until the letter you want is selected, and
          then press ENTER.




 ENTER=Select   F1=Help   F3=Exit   ESC=Previous screen
```

Figure 4-8: Custom setup allows you to select the drive letter for the new drive.

Choose the custom setup if you want to compress any drive other than C. You also should use the custom option if you want to compress drive C but control the drive letter of the new host for C, or if you want to specify the amount of free space to be left on the host.

If your drive was already compressed using Stacker (a third-party compression tool), DoubleSpace recognizes that fact and automatically converts the Stacker file to DoubleSpace format. Don't expect the conversion to be fast; it usually takes several hours.

If you install a DoubleSpace drive, you are not able to restore your previous version of DOS using the UNINSTALL command. You may want to run DOS 6 for a few sessions before installing DBLSPACE. When you are confident that you want to keep DOS 6 (and I think you will), you can go ahead and create a DoubleSpace drive. While you are at it, you might as well save some more disk space by deleting the OLD_DOS.1 directory — a quick way to do this is by executing the DELOLDOS command. This directory is used by UNINSTALL to restore the previous version of the operating system. Because UNINSTALL won't work, there is no need to keep the OLD_DOS.1 files.

Although DBLSPACE works on huge drives (those larger than 1 gigabyte), the maximum size of a compressed drive is 512MB. Assuming an approximate 2 to 1 compression ratio, this means that you should not use more than 250MB of drive space to create a CVF.

The DoubleSpace files

After you install one or more DoubleSpace drives, the root directory of the boot drive contains two files: DBLSPACE.BIN and DBLSPACE.INI.

Both files have system, read-only, and hidden attributes but can be displayed with the DIR /A command. If you have a DoubleSpaced drive C, these files are actually located on the host drive. The DBLSPACE.BIN file is the device driver that performs all the compression and decompression tasks, and DBLSPACE.INI is a text file that defines which CVFs should be mounted, which drive letters they should be assigned, and some other initialization settings.

In addition to these two files, the root directory of each host drive contains one DBLSPACE.*nnn* file for each compressed drive for which it is the host.

A text file in the DOS directory called DBLSPACE.INF contains settings that influence the DoubleSpace setup. Among other things, this file identifies device drivers and programs that should not be loaded from CONFIG.SYS during the reboot phases of a DoubleSpace installation. DBLSPACE.INF is well commented, and each section is clearly explained in the file. Browse the file for further information.

The DoubleSpace booting process

Although DBLSPACE.BIN is the device driver for compressed drives, you will not find a DEVICE= entry in CONFIG.SYS to load DBLSPACE.BIN, for one very good reason. If CONFIG.SYS itself is stored on a compressed drive, DOS must load the device driver before it is able to read CONFIG.SYS. To work around this problem, IO.SYS searches the root directory of the boot drive looking for the hidden file DBLSPACE.BIN. If it finds the file, it is installed as a device driver. DBLSPACE.BIN is initially loaded at the top of memory, adjacent to the memory area occupied by IO.SYS. After the device driver is installed, the CONFIG.SYS file can be read, and booting proceeds normally.

The drawback to this approach is that the device driver cannot be loaded directly into upper memory because the UMBs are not available so early in the booting cycle. DOS provides another DoubleSpace device driver, called DBLSPACE.SYS, whose sole purpose is to transfer the DBLSPACE.BIN device driver from base memory to upper memory.

DBLSPACE.SYS is not a device driver for DoubleSpace drives; it is a device driver to move the DBLSPACE.BIN device driver into upper memory.

To place both DBLSPACE.SYS and DBLSPACE.BIN into upper memory, use the following command in CONFIG.SYS:

```
devicehigh=c:\dos\dblspace.sys /move
```

If CONFIG.SYS does not contain a DBLSPACE.SYS driver, DBLSPACE.BIN is moved to the bottom of base memory after all the CONFIG.SYS statements are processed.

Technically, only the boot drive needs a copy of the DOS start-up files IO.SYS and MSDOS.SYS. In other words, these files could reside on drive C's host drive and do not need to be on the compressed drive C. However, some applications programs search the root directory of a drive looking for the hidden start-up files to determine which drive should contain the configuration files AUTOEXEC.BAT and CONFIG.SYS. To trick these programs into using the correct CONFIG.SYS and AUTOEXEC.BAT files, DoubleSpace copies IO.SYS and MSDOS.SYS to the compressed C drive, even though they are not accessed in the booting process.

If you compress drive C, consider copying some of the external DOS programs to the host drive. If you ever have any difficulty mounting drive C, you can use these tools to solve the problem. Specifically, create a \DBLTOOLS directory on the host drive and copy the following files to it from the \DOS directory:

- ATTRIB
- CHKDSK
- DBLSPACE.BIN
- DBLSPACE.SYS
- DBLSPACE.EXE
- DBLSPACE.HLP
- DEFRAG.EXE
- DEFRAG.HLP
- EDIT.COM
- EDIT.HLP
- QBASIC.EXE
- MSD.EXE

Problems with swap files

To improve performance, Windows bypasses DOS and the DoubleSpace device driver when accessing swap files. Swap files, therefore, cannot be located on a compressed drive. When creating a compressed drive, DoubleSpace automatically identifies the presence of a Windows swap file and makes sure that it is situated on the host drive.

If you get a corrupted swap file message from Windows soon after you compress an existing drive, it is probably because the swap file now resides on the host drive and Windows is looking on the compressed file. For example, Windows may be looking at drive C, when the swap file is actually on drive I. You can remove the old swap file and create a new one using the <u>V</u>irtual Memory option in the 386 Enhanced dialog box, accessed via the Control Panel.

You may think that a quick solution to the situation just described is to edit the SYSTEM.INI file and change the drive letter in the `PermSwapDOSDrive` entry, but this only solves part of the problem. You would also need to modify the binary file SPART.PAR (using DEBUG or a programmer's editor) to change the drive entry for 386SPART.PAR. It's far easier to let Windows do the work.

If you plan to install Windows after compressing a drive, be sure to leave enough space on the host (10MB or so) for a swap file. By default, DoubleSpace does not leave sufficient room on the uncompressed drive.

Drive-mounting problems caused by file fragments

If you get an error message such as `DoubleSpace cannot mount drive n because of an unrecognized error (assertion 105)`, the problem is probably too many fragmented files on the CVF. To correct the problem, you must edit the DBLSPACE.INI file in the root directory of the boot drive and add or modify the `maxfilefragments` entry, using the following procedure:

1. Change directories to the root of the boot drive (the drive containing DBLSPACE.BIN).

2. Change the attributes of DBLSPACE.INI using the following command:

   ```
   attrib -s -r -h dblspace.ini
   ```

3. Edit the DBLSPACE.INI file and make sure that the following line exists:

   ```
   maxfilefragments=1000
   ```

4. Change the file attributes using the following command:

   ```
   attrib +s +r +h dblspace.ini
   ```

5. Reboot the system and, when the CVF is successfully mounted, run DBLSPACE and defragment the file.

6. Edit the DBLSPACE.INI file once more (changing the attributes before and after) and set the `maxfilefragments` entry back to 115.

How to defragment DoubleSpace volumes

DEFRAG does not normally move a DoubleSpace compressed volume file (CVF) on a host drive because the file is marked as a system and hidden file. If the CVF is located in the middle of the disk, you might want to trick DEFRAG into including the CVFs in the optimization process. Doing so improves the overall optimization.

A DoubleSpace volume is a hidden file containing all the files and directories that appear to be stored on the DoubleSpace drive. The files are stored in the root directory of the host drive. Filenames follow the convention DBLSPACE.*nnn,* where *nnn* is 000, or 001, or 002, etc.

To include a CVF in the optimization process, you must remove the system attribute from the CVF file, run DEFRAG with the /H option, and then reboot the system. The following batch file defragments the host drive I using this technique:

```
@echo off
attrib -s dblspace.000
defrag i: /h /b
```

Resizing a DoubleSpace drive

Using DBLSPACE, you can easily increase or decrease the size (capacity) of a DoubleSpace drive. Figure 4-9 shows the dialog box in which you change the size of a DoubleSpace drive. The dialog box is displayed when you choose **Drive**⇒Change-**S**ize from the main menu.

The only editable field in the dialog box is the New free space field for the Uncompressed or host drive. The default value is the current amount of free space on the host. To increase the size of the DoubleSpace drive, make the amount of free space smaller than the default. The size of the Double Space drive increases by approximately 2MB for every 1MB you reduce the free space.

If you want to decrease the size of the DoubleSpace drive and increase the free space on the host drive, defragment the DoubleSpace drive before resizing. After you defragment the drive, enter a value larger than the default. Note that

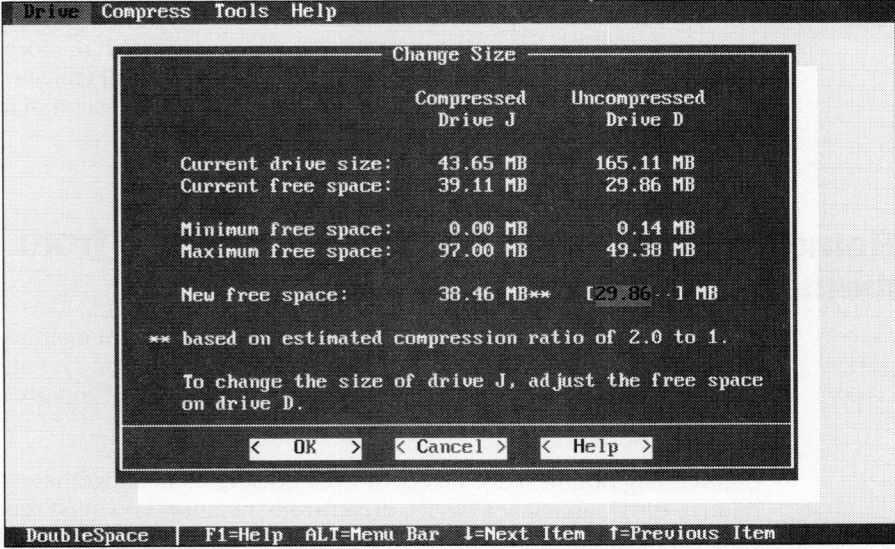

Figure 4-9: The Change Size dialog box.

the value cannot exceed the size listed in the Maximum free space field in the Uncompressed column. You cannot reduce the DoubleSpace drive by more than this amount because of the number of files stored on the compressed drive.

Removing a DoubleSpace drive

You probably will be disappointed to learn that there is no convenient way to remove a DoubleSpace drive. Well, to be accurate, there is no convenient way to remove a DoubleSpace drive without losing all files stored on the drive. Although DoubleSpace can take all files on an existing drive and compress them, creating a new compressed drive, it cannot uncompress a drive and return the files to the original (host) drive.

 If you select the **Drive**➪**D**elete option from the DBLSPACE menu, the drive is deleted, as are all files stored on the drive.

One way to uncompress a drive is to back up all files on the compressed drive, delete the drive using DBLSPACE, and then restore all files from backup to the original drive.

Alternatively, you can copy as many directories as will fit onto the host, delete the directories from the compressed drive, and then shrink the size of the compressed drive as much as possible. By shrinking the compressed volume, you create more space on the host drive. Keep repeating the copy-delete-shrink operation until all the files are transferred to the host drive. You can then delete the compressed drive.

Both techniques assume that the host drive is large enough to store all the compressed drive files. If not, you must delete some files or transfer them to a different drive. As my mother would say, "You can't get a gallon of milk into a pint jug."

Removing the DoubleSpace device driver from memory

The DoubleSpace device driver consumes a valuable 41K of memory. Note that the memory consumed does not vary. In other compression systems, the amount of memory consumed is affected by the number of compressed drives, but this is not true with the DoubleSpace system.

Unmounting DoubleSpace drives or even erasing them altogether does not remove the DoubleSpace device driver from memory. You must remove the DBLSPACE.BIN file from the root directory of the boot drive to stop IO.SYS from automatically loading it into memory.

Because a copy of DBLSPACE.BIN is stored in the DOS directory, you can simply delete the file in the root directory. The file's attributes are set to read-only, hidden, and system, so if you want to use the DEL command, you should first change the attributes using ATTRIB.

Alternatively, you can delete the file using DELTREE — yes, DELTREE. If you specify a particular file rather than a directory, DELTREE can delete the file, regardless of the file attributes. To delete the two primary DoubleSpace files and stop them from being loaded into memory, you can use the following two commands (assuming that the boot drive is H):

```
deltree h:\dblspace.bin
deltree h:\dblspace.ini
```

Remove DoubleSpace from memory in this way only after you delete any DoubleSpace volumes.

Changing drive letter assignments

To most users (including me) the way DoubleSpace assigns drives seems odd.

If you have only one hard disk installed, DoubleSpace assigns the letter H to the host. If you have two drives installed (C and D), DoubleSpace assigns the letter I to the host of the first drive to be compressed and H to the second. If you have three drives installed, the first host drive is assigned the drive letter J, and so on.

If you don't like the drive assignments, you can modify them. Remember, however, that you can always specify the desired drives when you first create them using the custom setup (see Figure 4-8, discussed earlier).

The easiest way to change drive letter assignments is to use DBLSPACE's command-line switches. The basic approach is to use /UNMOUNT to unmount the drive and then use /MOUNT and /NEWDRIVE to remount the drive and assign a new drive letter.

One of the example configurations discussed earlier had a host drive E that managed the compressed drive I. The following commands change the compressed drive letter to G:

```
dblspace /unmount i:
dblspace /mount=001 e: /newdrive=G:
```

The =001 switch is used with /Mount because the CVF filename to be mounted as drive G is DBLSPACE.001.

Behind the scenes, DoubleSpace modifies the DBLSPACE.INI file in the root directory of the boot drive. In this example, the INI file had the following contents:

```
MaxRemovableDrives=2
FirstDrive=F
LastDrive=J
MaxFileFragments=128
ActivateDrive=I,E1
ActivateDrive=J,D1
```

After the unmount and remount procedure, the INI file changed to the following:

```
MaxRemovableDrives=2
FirstDrive=F
LastDrive=J
MaxFileFragments=128
ActivateDrive=G,E1
ActivateDrive=J,D1
```

If you want to change the host drive letter (rather than the DoubleSpace compressed drive letter), you need to use a different tactic. You must manually edit the DBLSPACE.INI file. Consider a system in which the C drive is compressed and the host drive is I. The contents of the DBLSPACE.INI file will be similar to the following:

```
MaxRemovableDrives=2
FirstDrive=D
LastDrive=I
MaxFileFragments=115
ActivateDrive=I,C0
```

The following command changes the file attributes:

```
attrib -h -s -r dblspace.ini
```

You can then edit the file and change the ActivateDrive line that contains the C0 entry to the desired drive. In this example, the following INI file contents change the drive to D:

```
MaxRemovableDrives=2
FirstDrive=D
LastDrive=I
MaxFileFragments=115
ActivateDrive=D,C0
```

You could use the following command to set the file attributes back and then reboot:

```
attrib +h +s +r dblspace.ini
```

The host drive changes to D, and the compressed drive stays as C.

Understanding drive compression ratios

The amount a file is compressed, referred to as the *compression ratio,* depends on the specific file contents. A BMP file, for example, can be compressed a lot more than an EXE file, and a ZIP file can hardly be compressed at all.

On average, the compression ratio is about 2:1, indicating that when a file is compressed, it occupies about half the number of bytes as it did originally. You can use the new /C switch with the DIR command to look at the actual compression ratio of files stored on a compressed drive. The following listing illustrates the output from a DIR /C command:

```
Volume in drive G is COMPRESSED
Volume Serial Number is 1BE8-3A0F
Directory of G:\

CMFILER   ZIP     155953 02-14-93   8:54p   1.0 to 1.0
CMFILER   DOC     203348 11-12-92   5:45a   1.7 to 1.0
DUNES     BMP     308278 05-26-92   1:00a   1.5 to 1.0
CUSTOMER  DBF    1660706 11-27-92   3:56p   3.8 to 1.0
MAIN123W  EXE    1687360 11-02-92   9:25a   1.4 to 1.0
                   1.9 to 1.0 average compression ratio
         6 file(s)    4015645 bytes
                     25968640 bytes free
```

DoubleSpace maintains an average compression ratio for each compressed drive. At boot time, DOS automatically adjusts each DoubleSpace drive's compression ratio based on the compression ratio of each drive's existing files.

The amount of data that can be stored on a compressed drive depends on the type of files that are to be stored on the drive. For example, there might be room for 10MB of database files (because they compress so well) but only 2.5MB for ZIP files. To provide an average figure, DOS reports the amount of free space available on a DoubleSpace drive by multiplying the physical free space by the compression ratio.

You can use DBLSPACE to modify the compression ratio temporarily. By selecting the **Drive**⇨Change-**R**atio option from the DBLSPACE menu, you can alter the ratio to any value in the range 1.3 to 4.5. However, if you use the command switch /RATIO, you can change the ratio to any value in the range 1.0 to 16.0.

You should realize that modifying the compression ratio doesn't actually change the amount of free space; it simply changes the amount of free space that is reported by DOS. You may want to do this in a few rare circumstances. Suppose that you want to install a road map program onto a compressed drive, and the current drive compression ratio is low (say 1.5) because the drive is used to store a graphics application loaded with large executables and BMP files. When you try to install the new map program, the installation aborts, and a message appears stating that you need 10MB of free space and only 8MB are available. However, you know that in reality, DoubleSpace will have plenty of room because the map data files can be highly compressed. The solution is to doctor the compression ratio to something in the neighborhood of 4:1 so that DOS reports more than 10MB free space to the map installation program.

Caching compressed drives with SMARTDRV

SMARTDRV is tightly integrated with DoubleSpace. When caching a host drive, SMARTDRV automatically caches each compressed drive supported by the host. What's more, SMARTDRV caches the compressed clusters rather than the standard (uncompressed) clusters. This means that a 1MB cache can effectively cache 2MB worth of data. Smart.

Compressing data on floppies

The concept of compressing data on floppies has real merit; being able to store nearly 3MB of data on a 3½-inch floppy is very appealing. Unfortunately, the way that DoubleSpace handles compressed floppies is far from graceful. The two major problems follow:

- Even if you don't have a compressed hard drive, the entire DoubleSpace device driver must be installed at boot time to handle compressed floppies. That's 41K of RAM. To make a situation worse, there is no convenient way to use the multiple-boot facility to optionally load DoubleSpace from a menu. You have to manipulate the hidden file DBLSPACE.BIN as discussed earlier.

- To access data on a compressed drive, you must insert the diskette in a drive and then use DBLSPACE to mount the diskette. DOS cannot automatically mount a DoubleSpace drive. In other words, you can't simply put the disk in the drive and start using it. Worse still, every time you change compressed diskettes, you must mount the newly inserted diskette.

 If you try to access a compressed diskette without first mounting it, all you will see is a single file called READTHIS.TXT. If you type or browse the file, you will see that it contains a message informing you that the drive must be mounted using DBLSPACE.

If you already have compressed drives and so would be loading DBLSPACE.BIN anyway, and you don't mind mounting each floppy, you probably will find compressed floppies valuable. I think I'll wait for the next release!

Summary

This chapter covered all the different ways to get the best performance and capacity from your hard disks. You learned the following points:

▶ A disk comprises a stack of metal plates coated with metal oxide and a set of read-write heads that transfer data to and from the platter surfaces.

▶ The data stored on a disk is organized into tracks, sectors, and clusters. A vertical column of aligned tracks is known as a cylinder.

▶ DOS uses a combination of a directory entry and the FAT to locate the clusters occupied by a file. You can verify the integrity of the data stored in these areas using the DOS command CHKDSK.

▶ A disk's interleave setting controls the order in which sectors are numbered around the track. Using the optimum interleave setting can have a profound impact on disk performance.

▶ The DOS disk cache SMARTDRV provides the best way to use RAM to increase disk performance.

▶ A file is fragmented when its data is not stored in adjacent clusters. Defragmenting files improves performance and enhances the chances of recovering from an accidental format or file deletion.

▶ You can almost double the capacity of your hard disks by using DoubleSpace. The DoubleSpace device driver DBLSPACE.BIN compresses files when they are saved to disk and decompresses (or expands) them when they are read from disk.

▶ DoubleSpace can compress existing drives or use the free space on a drive to create a new drive. As a safety measure, you should copy the key DoubleSpace files and ATTRIB.EXE onto the host drive when compressing the boot drive.

▶ To remove DoubleSpace from memory, you must delete the hidden file DBLSPACE.BIN from the root directory of the boot drive.

▶ Although DoubleSpace is an excellent hard disk utility, it is cumbersome to use on floppy disks.

The next chapter explains how to improve your system performance even more by making the best use of memory. The chapter provides information about different memory types as well as instructions on how to use the new DOS memory management tools.

Chapter 5

Maximizing Memory

In This Chapter

▶ Memory terms, types, and tidbits

▶ The DOS 6 memory arsenal

▶ How to check your memory settings with MEM

▶ The big memory gainers

▶ From RAM Cram to UMB Cram

▶ How to load DBLSPACE.BIN high

▶ How to save every drop of base memory, maximize extended memory, and manage expanded memory

▶ Ways to solve memory conflicts

Photographs and Memories

When I was a boy scout, I took some photographs at our annual camp and so did another scout's father. A few weeks later, all the scouts were looking at the photographs. Mine were appalling; the other man's were superb. I was mortified. I told the man that he was very talented to master such a difficult subject, and his response was simple yet profound: "It's easy once it's explained to you."

That man later gave me a lesson in photography. He taught me that the shutter speed controls how long the film is exposed to the light, and the aperture controls how much light gets through at any given time. To take good photographs, you simply assess the available light and adjust the shutter speed and aperture accordingly. He was right; it is easy once it's explained!

The same is true for computer memory. At first, the subject can seem daunting, and for good reason. You must deal with DRAMs, SIMMs, RAM, ROM, UMB, HMA, and other CMAs (confusing memory acronyms). But after someone explains the concepts and terms involved, you'll find it hard to imagine why you were so confused.

There's one other parallel between photography and memory. Many people know how to snap a picture but don't know enough about how the camera works to use it to its full potential. Similarly, many people have a working knowledge of memory but don't understand it well enough to use their computers to their best advantage. To squeeze the most from your system, you must learn to make optimum use of all your computer's memory.

In this chapter, you learn the basics of memory — what it is, what it does, and why you can't compute without plenty of it. You also learn more advanced memory concepts that enable you to push your computer to its maximum potential.

The Memory Crunch _____

All programs need computer memory to run. An operating system needs memory, a pop-up calendar needs memory, a disk cache needs memory, a mouse driver needs memory — you get the idea. In general, the more functional and feature-laden the program, the more memory it consumes.

All computers have a basic, 640K memory allotment, which is referred to as *conventional* or *base* memory. Many applications can use this standard memory only. Such programs cannot utilize anything but the base memory even if your system has 16MB of memory. The problem with this is that by the time you load start-up programs such as the operating system (COMMAND.COM), mouse and network drivers, and a disk cache, conventional memory may be reduced to 550K or less. (The good news is that DOS 6 provides ways to load many of these start-up programs in memory outside of the 640K memory area, thereby leaving as much precious conventional memory available as possible.)

It is a common misconception to assume that the more memory you install in your system, the more programs you can run. Although there is no doubt that having more memory is desirable, you cannot assume that your programs can utilize all the memory in your computer system. All memory is not alike, and memory can be configured to operate and behave in different ways. For example, on 286 and later systems, you usually can configure memory as *expanded* or *extended memory*. Some programs can use only expanded memory, some can use only extended memory, and some can use either. Lotus 1-2-3 Release 2.4 uses expanded memory, for instance, whereas Lotus 1-2-3 Release 3.4 uses extended memory.

You can use many different techniques to make sure that every nook and cranny of free memory is put to good use. Before exploring these techniques in detail, however, you need to understand some basic memory concepts.

Memory Terms, Types, and Tidbits_____

If you are already familiar with memory hardware, memory addressing schemes, and the major memory types (base, upper, high, expanded, and extended), you may want to skip to the next major section, "How to Maximize Memory with DOS 6." Otherwise, I suggest that you read this section because it explains important memory principles that will help you to leverage the most potential from your system.

To fully understand today's confusing memory melee, you need to take a look at the history of the PC.

Since the introduction of the first PC in the early '80s, users (and programs) yearned for more and more memory. People resolved memory shortages by buying more memory chips and adding them to their PCs but soon reached a fundamental design limit — the 640K ceiling. The original 8088/8086 computers, such as the IBM PC and the IBM PC-XT, were designed to provide a maximum of 640K of read/write memory.

In the drive to break through this barrier, vendors formed alliances (such as the Lotus-Intel-Microsoft committee), working together to find ways to go beyond 640K. At about the same time, manufacturers introduced new chips that could address up to 16MB of memory. Standards started to dissolve. The memory techniques used on XT computers often were not appropriate or necessary on AT-class computers. When 386 computers were introduced, further memory options surfaced.

Over the years, a lack of standards and market drive led to a melting pot of terms and techniques.

ROM vs. RAM

The two most basic classifications of memory are *read-only memory* (ROM) and *random-access memory* (RAM).

When you first turn on your PC or reboot the system, the PC goes through a special initialization process. You may have noticed the memory check being displayed or the disk drives spinning before DOS is loaded. The instructions that guide this process are stored in ROM. As its name implies, read-only memory is read but never modified. The instructions are fused into the memory chips during manufacturing and are permanent.

By contrast, random-access memory, or RAM, is initially empty (at least, it contains no meaningful data). Your computer uses RAM to store programs and data temporarily. RAM is the lifeblood of computer programs.

ROM is similar to a book, in which the text is preprinted and cannot be changed. RAM, on the other hand, is like a chalkboard onto which data can be written, erased, and rewritten.

As a PC user, your interest lies in gaining effective use of RAM. The instructions stored in ROM are indispensable, and your computer won't work without them, but in general, you do not need to understand or configure ROM. Most of your energy will be focused on optimizing RAM. Some utilities even convert unused ROM memory addresses to trick programs into thinking ROM is RAM. More about that later.

ROM-BIOS

In addition to start-up ROM, which controls the booting process, there is ROM-BIOS, which stands for *read-only memory — basic input/output system.* DOS uses ROM-BIOS to perform low-level tasks such as retrieving a sector of data from the disk or outputting data to a COM port. ROM-BIOS is therefore very hardware dependent.

If you add new hardware to an older system — for example, if you add a new hard drive to a Compaq Deskpro 286 — you may find that you also need to replace the ROM-BIOS chips. These memory chips are not soldered into the circuit board; you can simply pull out the old chips and push in the new ones.

The hidden DOS file IO.SYS, located in the root directory of the boot disk, includes patches, updates, and extensions to ROM-BIOS. This file provides a convenient mechanism for extending a PC's BIOS capabilities without replacing the ROM-BIOS chips.

When the first IBM PCs were distributed, they included proprietary ROM-BIOS code developed by IBM. Following the emergence of non-IBM PCs, known as *clones* or *PC compatibles,* a number of vendors began developing their own versions of ROM-BIOS. Some of the best known BIOS developers are American Megatrends, Award, and Phoenix Technologies.

Every ROM-BIOS includes the manufacturer's name, a version number, and the date when the BIOS was written. Use the DOS 6 utility MSD.EXE to review the type of ROM-BIOS installed on your PC.

Memory hardware

All memory chips, which are used to store individual bits of data, work on the same basic principle. Each bit of data has either of two values, 0 or 1. The presence of a small electrical charge indicates that the bit is *on* and therefore has a value of 1. If a bit has no charge, it has a value of 0. You may recall that 8 bits comprise a *byte,* and it takes one byte to store a single character.

Over the past ten years, the demand for memory soared. Technology reacted to meet that demand with a great variety of different memory chips. The following is a listing of the chips that dominate the market.

The DRAM chip

The most common memory chip in PC, XT, and AT computers is the *dynamic random-access memory* (DRAM) chip. The DRAM chip has sixteen metal pins that protrude downward from the bottom of the chip, as shown in Figure 5-1. To install a DRAM chip, you push these pins into sockets or solder them onto the motherboard or memory add-on board.

The memory storage capacity of DRAM chips can range anywhere from 16K bits to 4,096K bits and beyond. The 16K bit chips were placed in the original IBM PCs, but today, the most commonly used size is 1,024K bits. (Note that the memory sizes are stated in bits and not bytes. Each DRAM chip stores one bit of a byte. When the CPU requests data from memory, it accesses eight chips simultaneously; each chip provides one-eighth of the data.)

DRAM memory is arranged in banks of nine chips. Eight of the chips store a single bit of each byte, and the ninth bit stores a cross-check or *parity value.* This parity value ensures that the chips are functioning correctly. (For a more detailed explanation of this setup, see the sidebar titled "How Parity Checks Work.")

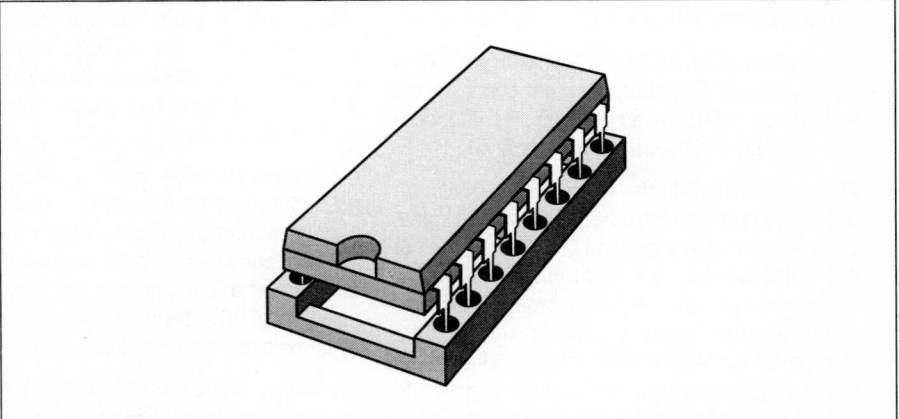

Figure 5-1: A DRAM chip.

Like all PC memory chips, a DRAM chip stores data as an electrical charge of about five volts. The charge in a DRAM chip fades over time, and the chip loses its memory — hence the name, *dynamic* RAM. For the DRAM chip to maintain accurate data, the charge must be refreshed every few thousandths of a second. This can lead to delays: Before the CPU can save data on the chip, it may be forced to wait until the chip's charge is refreshed.

The SRAM chip

Dynamic RAM chips do not require much power, but their charges must be refreshed frequently. The *static* RAM chip, or SRAM, requires more power but doesn't need to be refreshed. SRAM chips are somewhat power-hungry and expensive to produce, but they are very fast. The CPU doesn't have to wait for charges to be refreshed.

In the last chapter, you learned that disk caches can significantly increase overall system performance because memory access is much faster than disk access. Well, as you now know, some types of memory are faster than others — SRAM chips are a lot faster than DRAM chips. In high-performance systems, SRAM chips often are used as a memory cache. They cache memory data in much the same way that a disk cache stores disk data. The SRAM cache is used

TECHNICAL STUFF

How Parity Checks Work

Nobody wants a computer to make mistakes. PC designers added a simple cross-check mechanism to PC memory to help identify memory hardware errors. Here's how that system works.

Eight chips hold eight bits of data, with each chip storing one bit. Together, the eight chips store a single byte of data. On a ninth chip, the PC stores one more bit of data, called the *parity bit.*

The value stored on the ninth chip depends on the values stored in the other eight. As you know, each bit can have a value of 0 or 1. If the sum of the eight data bits is an odd number, then the value of the parity bit is 1. Conversely, if the sum of the eight data bits is an even number, the parity bit is set to zero. This scheme is known as the *even parity system,* because when you add the value of the parity bit to the sum of the other eight bits, the result is always an even number.

If the system finds that the sum of the nine bits is an odd number, it knows that a hardware failure has occurred — that is, that one of the memory chips is bad. Your PC then generates a *memory parity error.* The system halts and you see an appropriate error message displayed on-screen. It's then time to start your diagnosis to find and replace the rogue chip.

It is possible to have two or more bad chips that go undetected by the parity check. The parity check mechanism does not notice the problem if an even parity is coincidentally maintained. The chances of this happening are very remote, so the original PC's designers decided a single parity bit was more than adequate.

For further reading on this subject, I highly recommend Caroline Halliday's book *PC SECRETS,* published by IDG Books Worldwide.

to store frequently or recently accessed memory data. When the CPU requests some data, the SRAM cache is checked first. If the data is available in the cache, the SRAM chips pass the information to the CPU very quickly.

Systems that use SRAM chips for a cache usually are referred to as having *cache memory.* Such systems consistently outperform similar systems that don't have cache memory. Although systems with cache memory are a few hundred dollars more expensive, the performance gains are significant. (In fact, the performance improvements from even a small memory are so significant that Intel built an on-board 8K memory cache directly into the 486 chip.) The bigger the cache, the better. Cache memory added to the system board between memory and CPU is usually 64K to 256K in size.

To date, no PCs provide a way to add cache memory after the fact. The cache memory must be installed during manufacturing. If you want a high-performance system, get one that uses cache memory because you won't be able to install it later.

SIMMs

DRAM chips were ideal in the early PC days, when memory was an expensive luxury and users only added small amounts of it — 256K on this machine and 384K on that one. Nowadays, users add memory in chunks of 4MB or more. That's a lot of chips and circuit-board real estate. And as you can imagine, it's easy to bend the pins on DRAM chips during installation — I know I've bent my share.

As high-memory systems became more popular, manufacturers began shipping DRAM memory chips already installed on small circuit boards. The motherboards had special memory sockets designed to receive these small memory boards. These chips-on-a-board are referred to as *single in-line memory modules,* or SIMMs for short. The printed circuit usually holds 4 or 9 soldered DRAM chips (see Figure 5-2) that have a storage capacity ranging from 1 to 8MB. SIMMs are installed in much the same way as general PC add-on boards, such as network cards and internal modems, thereby eliminating all those bent pins.

The CMOS chip

All 286 or better PCs have a special memory chip known as the CMOS chip. CMOS stands for *complementary metal-oxide semiconductor.* The CMOS chip is a special memory chip that requires very little power to maintain its charge. Although several CMOS chips are installed in today's PCs, one specific chip is always considered to be *the* CMOS chip.

The data on the CMOS chip records basic information about your system, such as the date and time, the floppy disk configuration, the number and type of hard disks installed, etc. If you install some new equipment or modify your system configuration, you can update this information from the main SETUP program.

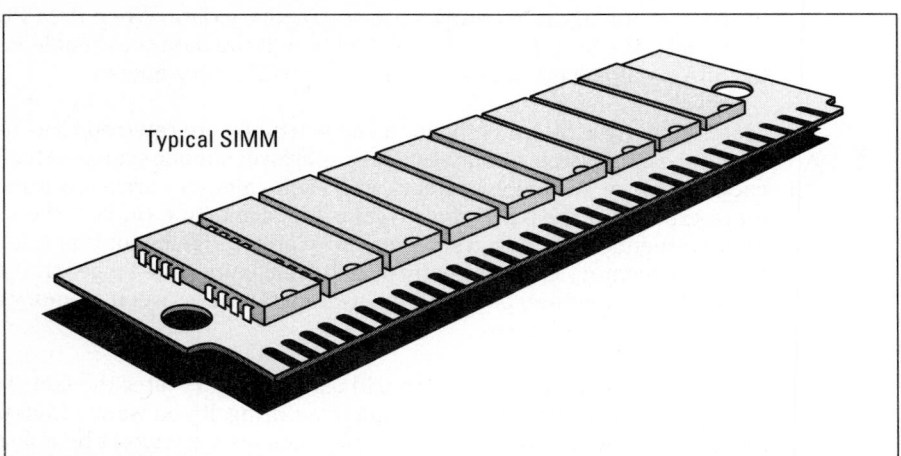

Figure 5-2: A SIMM board.

A small battery inside the PC chassis supplies power to the CMOS chip. (Often, the battery is attached with a Velcro strip.) That's how the computer remembers the date and time even though you turn off the power supply. The battery can last as long as two years.

Memory speed issues

Some types of memory are fast, and some are not so fast. The speed of a memory chip is rated in *nanoseconds* (NS for short). One nanosecond equals one-billionth of a second.

The general speed rating is referred to as the chip's *access time.* The smaller the rating, the faster the chip. PC memory access times can range anywhere from 140NS, at the very slow end of the spectrum, to 60NS or better at the other.

It's not always sensible to install the fastest memory available. As my grandfather would say, there is little use in hiring a faster mortar-mixer if you've got a slow bricklayer. The same goes for memory chips. You're wasting your money to buy memory chips that are too fast for the speed of the CPU; the chips will simply sit idle longer. Look in your computer handbook or consult with the PC manufacturer before buying memory chips to upgrade your system.

The CPU speed, referred to as *clock speed,* is rated in *megahertz* (MHz). The original IBM PC AT was rated at 6 MHz; now, it is not impossible to see 66 MHz PCs in the home. The clock speed controls the tempo at which the CPU performs operations. The faster the clock speed, the more quickly the CPU completes tasks. Although we have witnessed a huge increase in PC clock speed, we have not seen the same improvements in memory-chip speed.

Sometimes, when the CPU needs to get data from memory or put data into memory, it must wait for the memory chips to respond. The memory may be just plain slow, or the refresh cycle may be to blame. (Remember, while a DRAM chip is being refreshed, it cannot save data.) The average number of *clock cycles* (or *ticks*) the CPU has to wait while the memory does its share is called the *wait state*. The optimum PC has zero wait states, which indicates that the CPU is never delayed waiting for the memory chips to respond.

After data is accessed from a specific memory location, the chip must prepare itself for the next access. The delay incurred while the chip prepares for con-current access is referred to as the *precharge time*.

A few years ago, PC designers faced a dilemma: Even the fastest DRAM chips couldn't keep pace with the fastest CPUs, and SRAM chips were too expensive and too power-hungry. Rather than make a faster chip, manufacturers solved the problem by redesigning the memory storage architecture to improve per-formance. The concept of memory *interleaving* was introduced.

Interleaved memory is organized on the principle that memory is most often accessed in contiguous blocks. For example, the CPU requests data from memory location 10000 and then immediately accesses the memory at location 10001. To get around precharge time delays, the memory is divided into two major parts: even memory locations and odd memory locations. With inter-leaved memory, the system accesses one chip to get data from address 10000 and another chip to get data from address 10001, thereby avoiding the precharge delay.

It appears that systems engineers have exhausted the configuration tricks that can be used to squeeze the most out of DRAM-based memory chips. Power-hungry users, myself included, eagerly anticipate the introduction of the successor to DRAM chips. Only with a fundamental change in technology will memory chips be able to keep pace with the improvements in CPU perfor-mance.

Memory addressing

The process of optimizing memory involves telling the memory manager to include or exclude specific memory locations when you load certain programs. Every memory location has an address, just like every house on a street has an address. To master the memory manager, you need to understand the PC memory addressing scheme. And to understand that scheme, you must first understand hexadecimal numbers.

Hexadecimal numbers

Most people are familiar with the decimal, or base 10, numbering scheme, in which any single digit can represent ten different values, zero through nine. If we had been created with eight fingers on each hand, instead of five, we might have adopted a 16-based numbering scheme.

The memory addressing scheme in PCs uses a 16-based numbering system known as *hexadecimal* or *hex*. In this numbering scheme, each digit can represent one of sixteen unique values.

In Latin-based languages, we use special characters to denote numbers: a circle represents a zero (0), a vertical line represents a one (1), a curly line with a flat base represents a two (2), and so forth. The same is true for hexadecimal numbers, but there is a problem for the six numbers greater than nine. What characters do we use to represent them? Trust mathematicians to come up with a boring solution.

In the case of hexadecimal numbers, the letters A through F are used to represent the numbers 10 through 15. So the sixteen numbers that represent the base hexadecimal numbers are 0, 1, 2, 3, 4, 5, 6, 7, 8, 9, A, B, C, D, E, and F.

In the decimal system, we represent numbers larger than nine by using digits to represent the tens, hundreds, thousands, etc. For example, the number 625 means 6 hundreds, 2 tens, and 5 singles. Most people find this scheme intuitive and never really think about it. The same scheme applies to hexadecimal numbers. In decimal, the numbers increase in tens; in hexadecimal, the numbers increase in units of sixteen — 16s, 256s, 4096s, etc.

The hexadecimal number 235 means two 256s, three 16s, and 5 singles. That translates to the decimal number 565. The following list shows some hexadecimal numbers and their decimal equivalents:

Decimal	*Hexadecimal*
3	3
9	9
10	A
13	D
17	11
55	37
256	100
266	10A

As you can see, it is difficult, if not impossible, to distinguish hexadecimal numbers from decimal ones when no letters are used. There are, however, a few popular conventions for identifying hexadecimal numbers. One convention is to place the characters *0x* or *$* before the number. Alternatively, the lowercase letter *h* is used as a suffix to the number. For example, the hexadecimal equivalent of the decimal 55 can be written as *0x37, $37,* or *37h.*

Most programmers and systems engineers are conversant in hexadecimal arithmetic. I know some people who can add up their grocery bill in hex. Fortunately, you really only need to understand the numbering scheme in principle in order to manage PC memory. By the way, I'm 24 years old in hexadecimal!

Segments and offsets

The original IBM PC used Intel's 8088 microprocessor (or CPU). Shortly after the IBM PC was released, the 8086 microprocessor gained popularity. It was installed in some IBM PC compatibles as well as in the IBM PS/2 model 25 and model 30.

The 8088 uses an 8-bit data bus, whereas the 8086 uses a 16-bit data bus (more about buses later). In all other respects, the 8086 and 8088 chips are identical. They form the foundation of the entire PC family of CPUs, and all newer Intel microprocessors, including the 80486, can emulate and operate like fast 8086s.

The 8086 chips use a set of *registers* to manage and manipulate data. For example, suppose that you want to multiply two whole numbers. Each number is moved into a different register, and the CPU is instructed to multiply them together. Each register is 16 bits in size.

The registers are also used to access data stored in memory, but the largest value a 16-bit number can have is 64K, so a single register can only access 64K worth of single-byte memory addresses. This value is actually 2 to the power of 16, or 65,536 to be accurate. Even the original PC engineers recognized that a PC with 64K of memory wouldn't be very functional, so they decided to use two registers to store memory addresses. They devised a system that allows 1,048,576 bytes (one megabyte) of memory to be accessed. Surely no program would ever need to address more memory than that!

Here's how the system works. Every byte in memory has a unique address, just like every office in a building has a unique address. A PC memory address comprises two parts, the *segment* and the *offset.* These are similar to the floor and office number of an office building.

The 1MB of memory is subdivided into major blocks called *segments.* Each segment starts 16 bytes beyond the previous one. To identify a specific memory location, you first identify the segment. This is like specifying the floor on which a particular office is located. The *offset* specifies how many bytes there are between the beginning of the segment and the precise memory location. This is like specifying the room number of the office.

To specify a memory address, you must identify both the segment and the offset. Normally, you indicate the segment and offset as follows: *segment:offset.* A colon (:) separates the segment and offset values. The CPU stores the segment in one 16-bit register and the offset in another.

Values are specified in hexadecimal, and the numbers are usually zero-padded to four digits. For example, the memory address at segment B800, offset 0 is written as *B800:0000,* and the memory address at segment 40, offset 17 is written as *0040:0017.* (Although the numbers are hexadecimal, the 0x, h, or $ symbols are often not added because memory addresses are always specified in hexadecimal.)

Some memory management tasks are performed on a range of memory rather than on a single location. If you see two four-digit numbers separated by a minus (–) sign, the address actually identifies a memory range. The value before the minus sign indicates the first segment in the range, and the second value indicates the last segment in the range, as follows: *StartSegment-EndSegment.*

Multiple Memory Addresses

In the *segment:offset* scheme, one specific memory location can have multiple addresses. In other words, many different addresses can point to the same memory location.

There is a new segment address every 16 bytes: Segment 0000 starts at the beginning of addressable memory; segment 0001 starts at the 16th byte; segment 0002 starts at the 32nd byte, and so on. The memory offset value can range from 0 to FFFF (65,536 in decimal). So the address 0002:0004 is the same as 0001:0014 because they both point to an address 14 bytes (20 decimal — 16 + 4) from the beginning of addressable memory.

Imagine an office tower that has 16 offices per floor. The 7th office on the 20th floor would normally have the address *Floor 20, Room 7.* If the building used a scheme similar to PC memory addressing, the office could also have the address *Floor 19, Room 23,* or even *Floor 18, Room 39.* Wild.

Behind the scenes, the actual memory address is linear. The first byte of memory has address 0, and the last byte has address 1,048,575. When the CPU needs to access a specific byte of data, the segment:offset address is converted to a linear address. This is achieved by multiplying the segment by 16 and adding the offset, which yields a 20-bit number identifying the precise linear memory location.

For example, the memory address 1000:2345 can be converted to a linear address by multiplying 1000h by 16. Sixteen in hexadecimal is 10h, so the result is 10000h. The offset of 2345h is added to 10000h, resulting in a linear address of 12345h.

Using the office analogy again, you can convert the address of the 7th room on the 20th floor to a linear room number by multiplying the floor number (20) by 16, because there are 16 rooms on each floor, and then adding 7. The resulting linear room number is 327. It's a good thing this scheme isn't used in airport parking lots; I'd never find my car.

If you don't intend to do any programming, you may be wondering why you need to know how the CPU addresses memory. The answer is that you may encounter these memory addresses when you install device drivers for specialty hardware or add commands to your CONFIG.SYS file to fine-tune the memory manager. For example, the following line is extracted from my CONFIG.SYS file:

```
device=c:\dos\emm386.exe ram win=dd00-dfff win=da00-dcff
```

The WIN statements at the end of the line instruct the memory manager EMM386 to reserve the specified area of memory for use by Windows. Later in the chapter, you learn much more about EMM386 and its options.

Memory addresses using the segment and offset notation can range from 0000:0000 to FFFF:FFFF. (Remember, addresses are specified in hexadecimal, and the highest hexadecimal number is F.)

Major types of memory

The 8086 family of microprocessors uses a 20-bit addressing scheme that yields a maximum addressable memory of 1MB. When Intel introduced the 80286 (or 286 for short), they added new memory capabilities, but they also made sure that the 286 could function just like a fast 8086 chip. There would have been a riot if software that used to run on the 8086 would not run on the 80286. Some new applications were written that utilized the memory scheme introduced in the 286, but users with 8086 systems could not run these applications. You may be aware of software that will only run on 286s or better — for example, Lotus 1-2-3 Release 3.

Even with the added memory capabilities of the 286, users still wanted more. The 386 family of microprocessors was introduced, sporting yet more advanced memory management features. Once again, the chip had to be backward-compatible — this time, with the 286 and 8086 microprocessors. Over time, software was written to take advantage of the 386 memory management capabilities. Windows 3.1 (in Enhanced Mode), Paradox 386, and even some features of DOS are examples of such programs.

Memory comes in a variety of flavors, and some applications require memory that is configured a certain way. In this section, you learn about the various memory architectures available on each CPU platform. The model of a memory warehouse is used to help clarify the various options.

How to check your system

How much you can improve your system depends on how much memory you have installed and the type of CPU in your system. If you are not sure about your hardware base or your current memory setup, you can use the DOS 6 program MSD to find out.

If you use an earlier version of DOS, you may have the MSD program and not know it — it was included in the Windows 3.1 package. (There were even fledgling versions of MSD shipped with Microsoft Word 5.5.) If you have DOS 6 (or DOS 5), you can search for MSD on your hard disk by entering the following command:

```
c:\> dir \msd.exe /s
```

 Alternatively, you can use the QFIND program on Bob's Shareware Collection disks to search for MSD.EXE.

To run MSD, simply enter the MSD command without any options, as follows:

```
c:\> msd
```

After MSD snoops around your system, it prompts you to press a key and then presents you with the main menu.

To find out your processor type, select the Computer option by clicking on it with the mouse or by pressing P and looking at the Processor entry. To review your memory configuration, select the Memory option in a similar manner. Figure 5-3 illustrates sample displays of the information generated by MSD for the Computer and Memory options.

Base and upper memory

Most DOS users have heard about the 640K barrier or ceiling. This ceiling represents the most memory a program can use, and it continues to be a source of frustration to this day. But wait a minute — in the last section, you learned how the original PC engineers devised a memory addressing system that allowed the CPU to access 1MB of memory. So why is there a 640K ceiling rather than a 1MB ceiling?

Although there is 1MB of addressable memory in a PC, not all of it is directly available to DOS programs. The area between 640K and 1MB is reserved for use by special adapter boards and ROM-BIOS. Some memory, for example, is reserved for the video display. This reserved area of memory from 640K to 1MB is known as *upper memory.*

It is safe to say that the amount of memory address space dedicated to upper memory is very generous, especially when you consider how precious base memory is. In many cases, one third or more of upper memory is not used at all. If you have a 386 or later system, you can steal this area of memory and use it for storing DOS programs. You learn how to do so later in this chapter.

 Over the past few years, there have been many changes in memory technology. Unfortunately, there have been just as many changes in memory terminology. Some memory terms used in the late 1980s now have a different meaning. For example, in old literature, you may see upper memory referred to as *high*

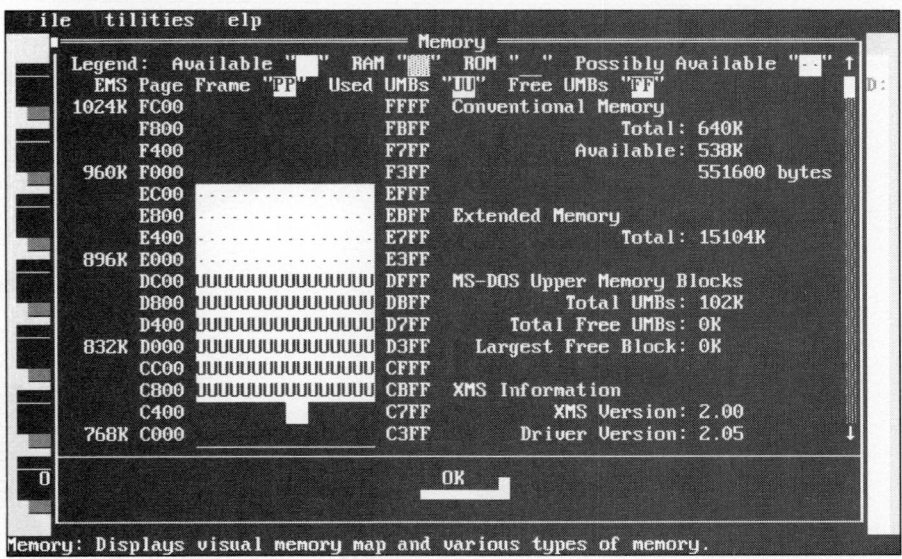

Figure 5-3: Computer and memory displays from MSD.

memory. Worse still, the term high memory now has a different meaning. This can be a real source of confusion. The good news is that it appears terminology has finally matured, so you should always use the terms as I describe them in this chapter.

To understand the memory management scheme used in PCs, it helps to think of it in terms of a "memory warehouse." Figure 5-4, a sketch of the memory warehouse, shows the structure of base and upper memory.

The memory warehouse in Figure 5-4 illustrates a number of important details:

■ The DOS command interpreter, COMMAND.COM, automatically uses the first portion of the 640K base memory. This leaves less than 640K for your programs.

■ Device drivers (such as mouse and network drivers) and other TSR programs use up still more of your base memory.

■ Although 8086 computers can address 1,024K of memory, most computers do not actually have that much general-purpose RAM installed. The memory addresses in upper memory are reserved for memory located elsewhere. For example, the ROM-BIOS memory is located on the ROM chips, and the video memory is located on the video card. In Figure 5-4, they are shown as storage containers that occupy part of the warehouse space.

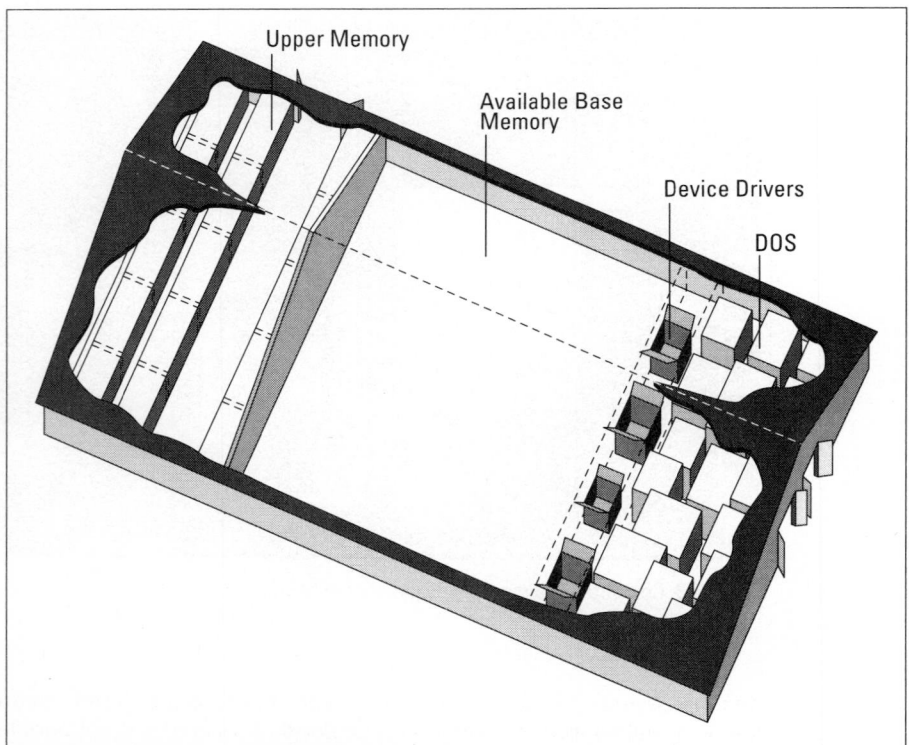

Figure 5-4: The standard memory warehouse.

■ Some areas of upper memory are not occupied. These areas are available for use by additional hardware devices, but in many situations, this memory is wasted and not used.

When a program is executed, it is loaded into the bottom of base memory, and the remaining base memory is available for data. In the case of Lotus 1-2-3, the data is the spreadsheet, and in WordPerfect, the data is a letter or document.

When you load a large program like Lotus 1-2-3, it may occupy 200K or more of memory, and the size of data area often is reduced to 300K or less.

Expanded memory

Arguably the most successful PC program and the one that first put PCs on the desktops of corporate America was Lotus 1-2-3. But corporate America soon demanded bigger spreadsheets, and PCs simply didn't have enough memory to do the job.

The History of EMS

The original expanded memory specification was developed by Lotus and Intel and called LI-EMS. Believe it or not, this first specification was dubbed EMS version 3.0. Presumably, the authors believed we would give more credence to a third-generation product. The original specification detailed how memory hardware should be engineered and how software should communicate with it.

Microsoft joined forces with Lotus and Intel to produce a revised specification known as LIM-EMS version 3.2. The primary change in the specification between 3.0 and 3.2 was the removal of strict hardware controls, which in turn allowed more vendors to produce expanded memory products.

A number of other PC vendors believed that LIM-EMS 3.2 was too conservative and didn't utilize the full potential of expanded memory. Ashton-Tate (now part of Borland International), Quarterdeck Office Systems (the DESQview folks), and board-maker AST Research banded together and developed a better mousetrap, called the *Enhanced Expanded Memory*

Specification, known as EEMS. (Aren't you glad they didn't call it the ATQOSASTR-EMS?)

EEMS supported all the features of LIM-EMS 3.2 and then some. The most important new feature was the capability to load and run programs from the EMS page frame. The original specification was really oriented to managing data and not programs in expanded memory. By adding support for programs, EEMS provided an excellent vehicle for *multitasking* programs — that is, running more than one program at a time and switching between them.

While all this was taking place, other vendors, such as IBM, were developing their own EMS enhancements. The final chapter in the EMS story was written by the LIM team. In a cooperative effort to settle on one standard, the LIM team took the best features of all the hybrid EMSs and introduced LIM-EMS version 4.0. This specification incorporated most of the features of EEMS, EMS 3.2, and other vendors' variations. Today, LIM-EMS 4.0 stands as the dominant expanded memory specification for the PC industry.

Three major companies in the PC business got together to devise a way to make more memory available: Lotus Development Corporation was the spreadsheet company, Microsoft Corporation was the operating system company, and Intel Corporation was the hardware manufacturer. They called their solution *expanded memory*.

As Figure 5-4 illustrates, there is a lot of wasted space in upper memory. The obvious solution to the memory shortage problem was to make better use of upper memory. But upper memory could only offer a few hundred thousand extra bytes at most, and it was becoming clear that users wanted spreadsheets that were two or three megabytes in size. The answer to this dilemma was *memory paging*.

Lotus, Intel, and Microsoft designed the *expanded memory specification,* or EMS. This specification often is called the *LIM-EMS,* named after the three main contributors (Lotus, Intel, and Microsoft). The theory behind LIM-EMS is quite simple. A 64K area of upper memory is reserved for use as expanded memory. This area, called the *EMS page frame,* is subdivided into four 16K pieces. Those four pieces can be taken from a pool of 32MB of memory.

A program cannot access all the expanded memory at one time. Rather, it must manage the data in 16K pieces. The process of assigning different blocks of memory into the page frame is known as *bank switching*.

In the memory warehouse sketch shown in Figure 5-5, the expanded memory pool is represented by 16K container trucks. This memory is separate from the main 1MB warehouse and must be shunted in small pieces into the warehouse before DOS can access it.

The truck analogy isn't quite accurate because the 16K pieces of expanded memory aren't actually moved into upper memory. A memory manager fools DOS into thinking the memory is located in upper memory. When DOS tries to manipulate the data in the expanded memory area, the memory manager intercepts the task and makes the real changes directly to the real memory, which is located somewhere in the 32MB expanded memory area.

The expanded memory solution for 8086 computers is, at best, a work-around. Although it provides a lot more memory to applications, the bank switching process is not efficient. Dealing with memory in small 16K pieces is restrictive and time-consuming. Ideally, software needs to access huge blocks of contiguous memory.

Extended memory

When Intel developed the 80286 microprocessor (286), the company decided to implement a new memory architecture that provided access to large volumes

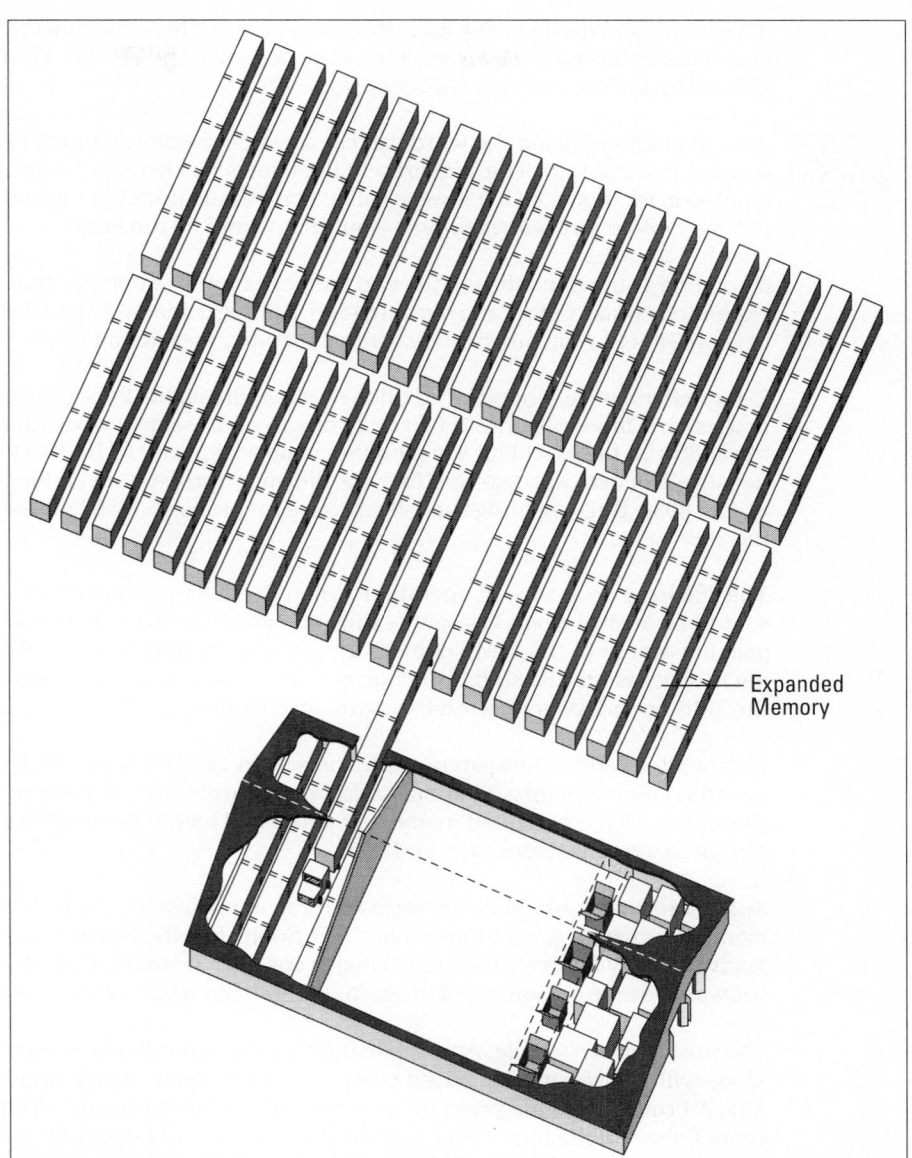

Figure 5-5: Expanded memory is divided into 16K pieces and accessed from a 64K area of upper memory.

of memory and didn't suffer from the restrictions of bank-switched EMS. The new memory architecture was called *extended memory*. The PC AT was the first IBM PC to use the 286 microprocessor.

 Why the industry used the word *extended,* which sounds so much like *expanded,* is a mystery. The similarity of the names has been the source of confusion for years. I wish it were called something more distinguishable, like *286 memory* or *auxiliary memory* — but that would be too easy.

If you find yourself confusing the two memory types, remember that the *p* in expanded comes before the *t* in extended. Another, somewhat backward, memory jogger is to remember that e*x*tended memory was not available on the *XT*.

Extended memory blows the lid off the 1MB addressable limit suffered by 8086 processors. Internally, the 286 uses 24 bits to address memory, compared with the 8086's 20 bits, yielding a maximum memory capacity of 16MB. However, because it is backward-compatible, the 286 microprocessor can function just like an 8086, thus ensuring that all software that runs on an 8086 also runs on the 286.

The 286 has two modes of operation. When the 286 is emulating the 8086, it is said to be in *Real Mode*. (I know — they should have called it *8086 Mode*.) To gain full access to the 15MB of memory beyond the traditional 1MB limit, the microprocessor must shift into *Protected Mode*. Note that the memory above the 1MB boundary is referred to as *extended memory*.

In Protected Mode, the system enjoys access to 16MB of memory, if the PC has that much memory. That makes for a big warehouse, as you can see in Figure 5-6. All the extended memory is contained within the warehouse and doesn't need to be trucked in and out.

Applications that run in Protected Mode can enjoy fast access to 16MB of memory — which is a lot more than 1MB. Soon after the 286 was introduced, many industry figures expected all major software vendors to start writing software to take advantage of Protected Mode. But it just didn't happen.

The problem was simple. Any application written specifically to use Protected Mode will not run on 8086-based computers — in other words, original PCs and XTs. A Protected-Mode program is useless to a PC or XT owner. For the first few years following the introduction of the 286, the majority of the PC marketplace was still dominated by the 8086 computers, and that was too large a market to ignore. Nonetheless, a few companies did introduce products written exclusively for Protected Mode. Lotus 1-2-3 Release 3 was the most popular. Even though Lotus Development introduced Release 3, the company made it clear that it would continue to enhance the Release 2 version of the product to keep 8086 customers happy.

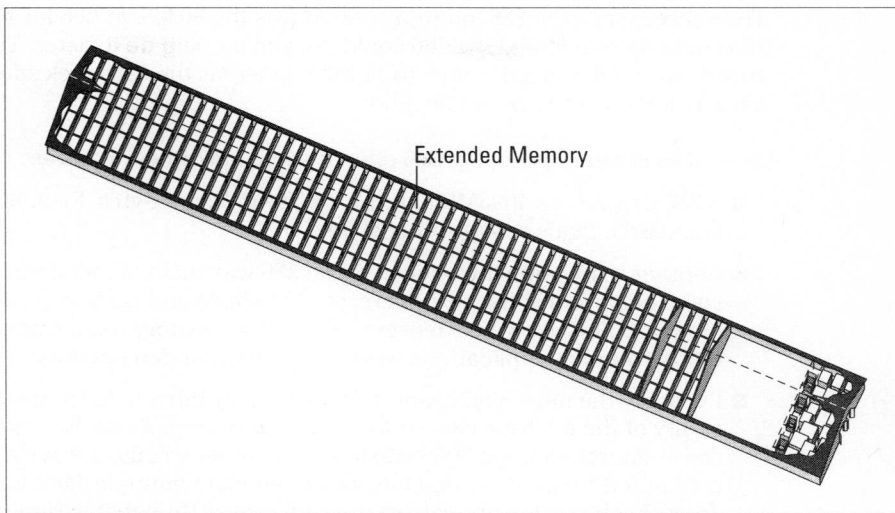

Extended Memory

Figure 5-6: In Protected Mode, a 286-based computer can access 16MB of memory: the standard 1MB plus 15MB of extended memory.

DOS is a Real-Mode application and is still limited to accessing the first megabyte of memory. A Protected-Mode program is launched from DOS in Real Mode. The program must then switch the microprocessor into Protected Mode to access extended memory. When the user quits the application, the microprocessor is switched back into Real Mode and control is passed back to DOS.

Why is DOS 6 a Real-Mode program? If you are thinking that it would make sense to create a Protected-Mode operating system, you're right. OS/2 is the best known Protected-Mode operating system. Although originally developed by Microsoft, OS/2 is now developed and supported by IBM. Meanwhile, Microsoft provides Protected-Mode support in Windows and probably will do so in a future version of DOS.

As a Real-Mode application, DOS had no control or interest in Protected Mode, and so Protected Mode was a free-for-all, with each program doing as it saw fit. A sort of extended-memory anarchy prevailed. In 1988, some four years after manufacturers shipped the first 286 computers, the major PC vendors got together to develop some industry standards on the use of extended memory. The folks that were most involved in expanded memory (Lotus, Intel, Microsoft, and AST) released a new specification for extended memory. Not surprisingly, this specification was dubbed the *extended memory specification,* or XMS.

The successor to the 286 microprocessor was the 80386, or 386 for short. The 386 could do everything the 286 could do, and it could do it faster. The clock speed of the 286 ranged from 6 to 12 MHz, whereas the 386 clock speed ranged from 16 MHz to 33 MHz and beyond.

As well as greater speed, the 386 offered some major new features:

- A 386 can access 4096MB of RAM. Yes, four billion bytes. Even by today's standards, that's a b-i-g spreadsheet.

- Another innovation introduced in the 386 was that extended memory, with some help from software drivers, could behave and act like expanded memory. This allowed 386 users with lots of memory to take advantage of this memory in applications written to use expanded memory.

- Probably the most significant new technology introduced in the 386 was the ability of the microprocessor to run in *Virtual 8086 Mode*. In this mode, the 386 supports multiple 8086 sessions — in other words, the system can be configured to use extended memory to emulate multiple 640K base memory areas. Each session appears to the software as though it is running in Real Mode. Products such as DESQview 386 and Windows 3.*x* in Enhanced Mode take advantage of this capability, allowing you to run multiple DOS sessions concurrently.

- The unused memory blocks in the upper memory area can be filled with extended memory. DOS can then access this memory to store itself, TSRs, and device drivers, freeing precious base memory for applications software.

The Protected-Mode Addressing Scheme

Just like the 8086, the 286 microprocessor uses two 16-bit registers for storing memory addresses. You may recall that the 8086 uses one register to store the memory segment and the other to store the memory offset. In Protected Mode, a similar scheme is used, but the segment register is used to store an index into a *segment descriptor table*. The descriptor table, which is stored in memory, contains a list of 24-bit linear memory addresses. A specific linear memory address is obtained by looking up the 24-bit segment in the descriptor table and adding the offset to it.

In addition to the linear segment address, the descriptor table includes a description of the type of information stored in memory — whether the data is program code or program data, whether the data is read-only or can be modified, and so on.

The 386 and 486 microprocessors offer a further advancement. The same basic addressing scheme is employed; however, the segment and offsets use 32-bit registers, providing access to 2^{32} bytes or 4096MB of memory. That's a huge warehouse.

The next generation of operating systems is by-passing the 286 Protected-Mode scheme and going directly to the 32-bit system. Windows NT and OS/2 3.0 are two prime examples.

All these new features essentially divided the user community into two camps: those who have 386 systems and those who don't. More and more programs and operating systems that run only on 386 or later systems are being developed.

After the 386, Intel introduced the 486 microprocessor. The 486 offers a faster clock speed than its predecessor, a built-in math coprocessor, and numerous other technological advances, but in terms of memory management, the 486 is the same as the 386.

SX, DX, and DX2 Microprocessors

During the late 1980s, computer-purchasing habits changed. Instead of buying higher priced PCs from the main vendors such as IBM and Compaq, consumers switched to budget-priced PCs. In many cases, people simply compared prices of comparable PCs and bought the cheapest one.

To provide a broader price spectrum of microprocessors and to encourage users to buy 386 computers rather than 286s, Intel introduced the 80386SX. To avoid confusion between the 80386 and the 80386SX, Intel added a DX suffix to the standard 80386 processor. So now we have the 80386SX and the 80386DX.

Internally, the 80386SX is the same as the 80386DX, and software that runs on one chip also runs on the other. The difference lies in the way the microprocessor communicates with the other devices in the system. The standard 80386DX uses a 32-bit bus interface, whereas the 80386SX uses a 16-bit interface. Because the 8086 and 80286 chips used 16-bit interface, the supporting circuitry is cheaper for a 16-bit microprocessor. Manufacturers can therefore produce 80386SX computers for less than 80386DX systems. The down side is that an 80386SX system is slower than an 80386DX system. You get what you pay for.

Continuing the theme of offering microprocessor price/performance options, Intel introduced the i486DX and i486SX. The *i* prefix in the name

indicates that the product is manufactured by Intel and is used to differentiate Intel chips from those produced by other vendors. With 486 microprocessors, the difference between the DX and the SX system is not the bus interface. Both systems use a 32-bit interface. Believe it or not, the i486SX is exactly the same as the i486DX, but the on-board math coprocessor is disabled. Yes, the SX chip costs the same to manufacture as the DX, but it is sold for less. Imagine disabling the anti-lock brakes on a car and selling it for less. Marketing madness.

Along with the standard 486 chips, Intel offers an *overdrive* option. Chips in the overdrive family internally process instructions at twice the clock speed. In terms of overall throughput, a system equipped with overdrive runs approximately 50 percent faster than it does with the standard chip. It may even handle some numeric operations many times faster than that.

When the overdrive option was first introduced for i486SX systems, a second processor (or overdrive) chip had to be installed on the system board next to the i486SX chip. Later, an i486DX2 chip designed to replace existing i486DX chips was introduced. If you have a PC with an i486DX microprocessor, you can probably significantly upgrade your system by pulling out the i486DX chip and replacing it with the i486DX2.

High memory

The 286 and later processors can access extended memory by switching the microprocessor into Protected Mode. DOS, however, cannot run in Protected Mode, so the extra memory doesn't help standard DOS applications.

Thanks to a quirk in the 286 chip design, almost the entire first 64K of extended memory can be accessed without switching into Protected Mode. In other words, DOS in Real Mode can access nearly 64K extra bytes on systems with a 286 processor. Although 64K doesn't sound like much, it's an extra 10 percent that's well worth having. In fact, to qualify as a DOS Jedi, you *must* use it.

The first 64K of extended memory is called the *high memory area,* or HMA. Quarterdeck first exploited this area of memory; DOS has supported it directly since version 5.0. You use the DOS device driver HIMEM.SYS to make this high memory available to DOS. Although mainstream applications such as Lotus 1-2-3 and WordPerfect cannot directly use the HMA, you can load the DOS kernel into the HMA. Doing so frees up as much of the base 640K as possible. Windows can also take advantage of the HMA.

How the HMA Is Addressed

The 286 and later computers use a 20-bit memory address, providing access to 2^{20} or 1MB of memory. Twenty pins, numbered A0 to A19, connect the CPU to the memory bus. The twenty-first pin, A20, is used as a toggle switch to indicate whether the CPU is in Real or Protected Mode. If the CPU is in Real Mode and a program tries to access memory beyond the 1MB range, the address is wrapped around to the low memory. It's like a 12-hour digital clock: After you reach the time 11:59, the value wraps around to 00:00. On the other hand, a 24-hour clock moves to 12:00 and beyond — you might call this a Protected-Mode clock!

By twiddling with the A20 pin, you can trick DOS into accessing the high memory area. With the A20 pin high, DOS actually thinks that it is addressing FFFF:0010 to FFFF:FFFF, which is 16 bytes short of 64K, but it is actually addressing the memory from 10000:0000 to 10000:FFEF.

As you can imagine, manipulation of the A20 pin is very hardware dependent, and some systems respond differently than others. HIMEM.SYS tries to determine the precise hardware model and then configures itself accordingly. You can use the /MACHINE switch to specify the hardware when HIMEM.SYS doesn't recognize the system.

Other memory terms

The following section provides brief descriptions of other memory terms you may encounter in software manuals or magazines.

Memory managers

Memory managers are utility programs that are responsible for managing the diverse memory needs of applications software. Typically, they control how installed memory is configured — that is, whether it is expanded or extended, where software is loaded, and how memory is allocated to applications when they request it.

Memory management products usually include more than one program. For example, one program may be responsible for expanded and extended memory allocation, and another for managing the HMA. Memory managers often include a program that analyzes all the software you installed and adjusts the CONFIG.SYS and AUTOEXEC.BAT files to help make optimum use of memory.

Two of the most popular third-party memory managers are Quarterdeck's Expanded Memory Manager and Qualitas' 386MAX. Many of the features offered in these products are now available in DOS 6.

DOS extenders

Writing Protected-Mode applications is complicated. Believe me — I've done it. To shield the programmer from the nitty gritty complications of writing Protected-Mode applications, a number of companies that specialize in programming tools release libraries of Protected-Mode routines. These program libraries provide a layer between the application program and DOS and are known as *DOS extenders*. The programmer makes simple calls to the library, and the DOS extender makes the low-level calls to the operating system or hardware.

Two of the better known libraries are DOS-Extender from Phar Lap software and DOS/16M from Rational Systems. As a DOS user, you wouldn't ordinarily care about these behind-the-scenes tools, but occasionally a program written with one of these libraries may generate a DOS extender error message.

The industry developed a set of programming standards called the *DOS Protected Mode Interface,* or DPMI. Most Protected-Mode applications now comply with DPMI version 0.9. These standards ensure that different applications can cooperatively use Protected Mode. For example, Windows 3.1 and Lotus 1-2-3 Release 3 can run simultaneously, thanks to the DPMI standard.

One other programming standard you may encounter is called the *Virtual Control Program Interface,* or VCPI. This standard identifies an approach for converting expanded memory back to extended memory, when the expanded memory is really extended memory that has been configured as expanded. *Phew!*

Upper memory blocks

Upper memory is reserved for video memory, ROM-BIOS, and other hardware memory, but much upper memory goes unused. The 386 and later systems can map extended memory into these unused areas and store device drivers and other TSRs in them. The areas of extended memory mapped into unused upper memory are referred to as *upper memory blocks,* or UMBs.

Shadow RAM

In general, ROM is much slower then RAM. When DOS needs to access a disk drive, write to video memory, or access many other hardware services, it must execute code in the ROM-BIOS. To speed up these operations, some PCs implement a system known as *shadow RAM.* When the computer first boots, a copy of ROM-BIOS is transferred to RAM, which is a lot faster than ROM. When DOS tries to access ROM-BIOS, it is diverted into reading the copy of ROM in extended memory.

Stealth and BIOS compression

In the battle for RAM-squeezing supremacy, some of the leading memory management vendors developed ingenious techniques to find every last byte of unused upper memory.

QEMM-386 v6.0, from Quarterdeck Office Systems, uses a special ROM-switching technique known as *Stealth.* Stealth hides ROM-BIOS, video ROM, and even disk ROM, and fills the vacated addresses with UMBs. This approach is very machine-dependent and does not work on all systems.

386MAX, from Qualitas, identifies unused areas of BIOS and converts it to UMBs. This technique, called *BIOS compression,* can yield up to 32K extra bytes on Compaq and IBM systems.

Virtual memory

Virtual memory provides a way for applications to access more memory than is physically installed in the PC. If all the physical memory is already being used and an application requests more memory, a virtual memory manager can temporarily store some of the data held in memory in a file on disk, thereby freeing up that memory area for the new application. When the owner of the disk-based memory tries to access its memory area, the data must be swapped back from disk to RAM.

As you might imagine, virtual memory is much slower than RAM because it is stored on disk. However, if you don't have the memory, slow is better than stop.

Windows is the best-known application that supports virtual memory. The infamous swap file serves as temporary storage for virtual memory.

How to Maximize Memory with DOS 6

Now that you have learned the theory, it's time to put your knowledge to practical use. In this section, you learn how to use DOS commands such as HIMEM.SYS, EMM386.EXE, and MEMMAKER to maximize your memory utilization.

Reviewing the DOS 6 memory arsenal

DOS 6 provides some first-class memory management tools. Table 5-1 provides a brief description of each of the memory management tools available in the DOS 6 arsenal.

The amount of memory you can utilize depends on the type of microprocessor and the type and quantity of memory installed in your system.

Table 5-1	**DOS Memory Management Tools**
DOS Tool	*Use*
HIMEM.SYS	The extended memory manager, responsible for policing the use of extended memory; among other things, HIMEM.SYS enables you to load DOS *high* (into the HMA)
EMM386.EXE	Uses extended memory to simulate expanded memory and allows extended memory to be used as UMBs for loading programs and device drivers
DOS=HIGH	Instructs DOS to load itself into the HMA
DOS=UMB	Instructs DOS to manage the programs in the UMBs
MEM.EXE	Displays the status of installed memory, including the location of programs in memory and the amount of memory programs are using
MSD.EXE	Displays diagnostic information about the PC's hardware, BIOS, and software
DEVICEHIGH	Loads device drivers into the UMBs
LOADHIGH	Loads programs into the UMBs
MEMMAKER	Assesses your system's memory utilization and modifies CONFIG.SYS and AUTOEXEC.BAT to make better use of available memory

Don't forget, you can use the MSD.EXE program to determine your micro-processor type and your installed memory (see the section "How to check your system" earlier in the chapter).

Full steam ahead with the 80386

If you have a 386 or later computer system, you can take full advantage of all the memory tools available in DOS 6.

These tools help you maximize base memory by filling unused upper memory with extended memory (UMBs), into which you can then load device drivers and terminate-and-stay-resident programs (TSRs). In Real Mode, you can access the first 64K of extended memory as high memory (HMA) and then load DOS into HMA. On 386+ systems, EMM386 can also use extended memory to emulate expanded memory.

Options for 286 systems

Many of the DOS 6 memory management features take advantage of hardware introduced in the 386 microprocessor. For example, the primary management tool, EMM386, runs on 386+ systems only, as its name implies. Without EMM386, there is no support for UMBs. MEMMAKER's primary function is to optimize the use of UMBs, and so it, too, only runs on 386+ systems.

However, 286 systems such as IBM PC ATs and compatibles do support ex-tended memory and the HMA. You can therefore use HIMEM.SYS to manage the HMA and load DOS high. But that's all, folks.

Bad news for 8086 owners

If you own an 8086 system such as the original IBM PC or IBM PC XT, I've got some bad news for you. You cannot create UMBs, and you do not have access to the HMA because your computer can't access extended memory. In other words, none of the memory-increasing tools provided with DOS 6 work with 8086 systems.

Alternatives for 8086 and 286 owners

Although DOS 6 shortchanges 8086 and 286 owners as far as memory manage-ment capabilities are concerned, a number of third-party products do provide useful memory management tools. These products provide many of the UMB facilities by exploiting the capabilities of specific 80286 chip sets, such as NEAT, AT/386, and LEAP CHIPSet from Chips and Technologies. Many third-party memory management tools also can utilize LIM-EMS 4.0 expanded memory hardware. Two of the most popular products are QRAM from Quarterdeck Office Systems and MOVE'EM from Qualitas. Both QRAM and MOVE'EM bring UMB capabilities to these older systems.

Bob's Shareware Collection disks include the excellent memory manager UMB_DRVR.SYS from Christopher Blum. UMB_DRVR.SYS is a versatile memory device driver, which can use the shadow RAM on many of the 286 chip sets and can provide more than 200K of upper memory on 286 systems.

Reviewing your memory settings with MEM

The process of fine-tuning your PC's memory configuration involves some degree of trial and error. You look at the memory available, change some settings, reboot the system, and see whether you increased the free memory.

You can use the DOS 6 command MEM to review your memory usage. The amount and type of detail displayed by MEM depends on which switches you use. If you run MEM without any switches, the display will be a brief summary, as follows:

```
Memory Type          Total =   Used   +   Free
- - - - - - - - - - - - - - - - - - - - - - - - - - - -
Conventional          640K      87K       553K
Upper                  59K      59K         0K
Adapter RAM/ROM       325K     325K         0K
Extended (XMS)      15104K   14080K      1024K
- - - - - - - - - - - - - - - - - - - - - - - - - - - -
Total memory        16128K   14551K      1577K

Total under 1 MB      699K     146K       553K

EMS is active.
Largest executable program size      553K   (565952 bytes)
Largest free upper memory block        0K       (0 bytes)
MS-DOS is resident in the high memory area.
```

You also can use the following switches with the MEM command:

/C   Shows how much base and upper memory is being used by each active program and device driver and displays a summary of overall memory usage. The long form of this switch is /CLASSIFY.

/D   Shows detailed information about each active program and device driver, including the item's size, segment address, and memory type. The long form of this switch is /DEBUG.

/F   Displays the free base and upper memory regions. The long form of this switch is /FREE.

/M   Provides complete memory information about a specific program. You must specify the name of the program or device driver following the /M switch. The long form of this switch is /MODULE.

/P   Instructs MEM to pause when the display is filled. (In other words, it stops MEM output from scrolling off the screen.) To restart the display, you press any key. You won't be surprised to hear that the long form of this command is /PAUSE.

 The DOS 5 version of MEM does not support the same switches as DOS 6. In DOS 5, /P is an abbreviation for /PROGRAM, which instructs MEM to display detailed information about each program loaded in memory. On DOS 5 systems, use the |MORE pipe as an alternative to /PAUSE. The /C and /D switches are supported, but in general, the MEM command in DOS 6 provides more information than its predecessor.

For a full description of the MEM switches, refer to Part IV, "The Complete DOS 6 Command Reference."

When I tune a PC's memory, I primarily use the /C and /P switches. If a program is experiencing memory problems, I use the /D switch to obtain more detailed information. The following listing shows the output from the MEM command when the /C switch is specified:

```
Modules using memory below 1 MB:

Name          Total       =    Conventional   +    Upper Memory
--------------------------------------------------------------------
MSDOS         18605    (18K)     18605   (18K)        0       (0K)
HIMEM          1200     (1K)      1200    (1K)        0       (0K)
EMM386         3072     (3K)      3072    (3K)        0       (0K)
SETVER          624     (1K)       624    (1K)        0       (0K)
SATISFAX       4032     (4K)      4032    (4K)        0       (0K)
SMARTDRV      30832    (30K)     30832   (30K)        0       (0K)
PROTMAN         128     (0K)       128    (0K)        0       (0K)
COMMAND        3088     (3K)      3088    (3K)        0       (0K)
win386        16096    (16K)     12112   (12K)     3984       (4K)
WIN            1664     (2K)      1664    (2K)        0       (0K)
SHARE          5248     (5K)      5248    (5K)        0       (0K)
CASMGR         5504     (5K)      5504    (5K)        0       (0K)
COMMAND        3360     (3K)      3360    (3K)        0       (0K)
MOUSE         17120    (17K)         0    (0K)    17120      (17K)
MVSOUND        9184     (9K)         0    (0K)     9184       (9K)
TSLCDR        12768    (12K)         0    (0K)    12768      (12K)
EXP16          8976     (9K)         0    (0K)     8976       (9K)
WORKGRP        4400     (4K)         0    (0K)     4400       (4K)
DOSKEY         4144     (4K)         0    (0K)     4144       (4K)
Free         565968   (553K)    565968  (553K)        0       (0K)
```

```
Memory Summary:

    Type of Memory         Size         =        Used       +        Free
    - - - - - - - - - - - - - - - - - - - - - - - - - - - - - - - - - - - - - - - - - - - - - - - -
    Conventional          655360    (640K)       89392     (87K)     565968    (553K)
    Upper                  60576     (59K)       60576     (59K)          0     (0K)
    Adapter RAM/ROM       332640    (325K)      332640    (325K)          0     (0K)
    Extended (XMS)      15466496  (15104K)    14417920  (14080K)    1048576   (1024K)
    - - - - - - - - - - - - - - - - - - - - - - - - - - - - - - - - - - - - - - - - - - - - - - - -
    Total memory       16515072  (16128K)    14900528  (14551K)    1614544   (1577K)

    Total under 1 MB     715936    (699K)      149968    (146K)     565968    (553K)

    EMS is active.
    Largest executable program size          565952    (553K)
    Largest free upper memory block               0     (0K)
    MS-DOS is resident in the high memory area.
```

Using the big gainers

There are some very simple ways of dramatically increasing the amount of available base memory on a 386 system. Before worrying about squeezing out 1K of memory here and another 2K there, you should take advantage of the "big gainers."

PC memory is configured and controlled by the start-up files CONFIG.SYS and AUTOEXEC.BAT. You can realize big gains in memory usage by making a few simple changes in CONFIG.SYS.

Load DOS high

The first item of business is to take advantage of the HMA capabilities and load DOS high. This is the only DOS 6 feature available to 286 users. To load DOS high, you must install HIMEM.SYS. You then can instruct DOS to load itself high by adding the statement DOS=HIGH in CONFIG.SYS. If DOS is loaded high, the BUFFERS also are loaded high.

The following typical CONFIG.SYS file illustrates this technique:

```
FILES=50
BUFFERS=15
DEVICE=C:\WINDOWS\MOUSE.SYS /Y
DEVICE=C:\DOS\SMARTDRV.EXE /DOUBLE_BUFFER
```

When I boot my PC with the preceding plain CONFIG.SYS, MEM indicates that there are approximately 571,000 bytes of base memory free. That's not much memory, considering that only DOS, a disk cache, and a mouse driver are loaded. MEM shows that the memory is consumed by these programs as follows:

```
Name          Total      =   Conventional   +   Upper Memory
-------------------------------------------------------------------
MSDOS         60093   (59K)       60093   (59K)        0   (0K)
MOUSE         17088   (17K)       17088   (17K)        0   (0K)
SMARTDRV       2480    (2K)        2480    (2K)        0   (0K)
COMMAND        5024    (5K)        5024    (5K)        0   (0K)
Free         570704  (557K)      570704  (557K)        0   (0K)
```

After the CONFIG.SYS file is modified to load DOS high, it appears as follows:

```
DEVICE=C:\DOS\HIMEM.SYS
DEVICE=C:\WINDOWS\MOUSE.SYS /Y
DEVICE=C:\DOS\SMARTDRV.EXE /DOUBLE_BUFFER
BUFFERS=15,0
FILES=50
DOS=HIGH
```

Just by adding the HIMEM.SYS and DOS=HIGH statements, the free memory jumps to nearly 616,000 bytes, and MEM reports the following memory usage:

```
Name          Total      =   Conventional   +   Upper Memory
-------------------------------------------------------------------
MSDOS         15757   (15K)       15757   (15K)        0   (0K)
HIMEM          1200    (1K)        1200    (1K)        0   (0K)
MOUSE         17088   (17K)       17088   (17K)        0   (0K)
SMARTDRV       2480    (2K)        2480    (2K)        0   (0K)
COMMAND        2960    (3K)        2960    (3K)        0   (0K)
Free         615920  (601K)      615920  (601K)        0   (0K)
```

Notice that when DOS is loaded high, a 15K stub is left in base memory.

Use the UMBs

You may recall that upper memory is designed for video memory, BIOS, and plug-in hardware extensions, but that much of the upper memory often goes unused. The second big gainer is to allocate some of the system's extended memory to fill the unused portions of upper memory — creating upper memory blocks, or UMBs for short.

You can use the EMM386.EXE program to create UMBs by adding an EMM386 statement to CONFIG.SYS. EMM386 performs many functions, and the RAM switch must be used to instruct EMM386 to convert extended memory to UMBs.

Having installed EMM386, you can instruct DOS to manage the UMBs by changing the DOS= statement in CONFIG.SYS to DOS=HIGH,UMB.

 If you are using a third-party memory management program instead of EMM386.EXE, you usually should not use the DOS=UMB statement. The memory manager will manage the UMB space independently.

 When you review existing CONFIG.SYS files, you may find two different DOS= statements. One line will say DOS=HIGH and the other DOS=UMB. These two separate statements have the same effect as the single statement DOS=HIGH,UMB. These separate statements are often created by the DOS memory optimizer, MEMMAKER (discussed later). MEMMAKER adds a second DOS= statement if it finds that the UMB component is missing.

Having created UMBs, you can now take advantage of them by loading device drivers and programs into the UMBs. Programs loaded into UMBs are said to be *loaded high.* The DOS commands DEVICEHIGH and LOADHIGH are used to load device drivers and programs high, respectively. In the example configuration, the only device driver being loaded is MOUSE.SYS, but it can be loaded into the UMBs simply by changing the DEVICE statement to DEVICEHIGH.

The example CONFIG.SYS file is therefore updated to utilize UMBs as follows:

```
DEVICE=C:\DOS\HIMEM.SYS
DEVICE=C:\DOS\EMM386.EXE RAM
DEVICE=C:\DOS\SMARTDRV.EXE /DOUBLE_BUFFER
BUFFERS=15,0
FILES=50
DOS=HIGH,UMB
DEVICEHIGH=C:\WINDOWS\MOUSE.SYS /Y
```

The effects of these changes on free memory are summarized by MEM as shown in the following listing:

Name	Total		=	Conventional		+	Upper Memory	
MSDOS	15757	(15K)		15757	(15K)		0	(0K)
HIMEM	1200	(1K)		1200	(1K)		0	(0K)
EMM386	3072	(3K)		3072	(3K)		0	(0K)
SMARTDRV	2480	(2K)		2480	(2K)		0	(0K)
COMMAND	2960	(3K)		2960	(3K)		0	(0K)
MOUSE	17120	(17K)		0	(0K)		17120	(17K)
Free	706080	(690K)		629920	(615K)		76160	(74K)

```
Memory Summary:

 Type of Memory        Size        =       Used      +       Free
 -----------------------------------------------------------------------
 Conventional        655360   (640K)        25440   (25K)      629920   (615K)
 Upper                93280    (91K)        17120   (17K)       76160    (74K)
 Adapter RAM/ROM      299936  (293K)       299936  (293K)           0     (0K)
 Extended (XMS)     15466496 (15104K)      589824  (576K)    14876672 (14528K)
 -----------------------------------------------------------------------
 Total memory       16515072 (16128K)      932320  (910K)    15582752 (15218K)
```

As you can see, EMM386 consumes 3K of base memory, but it is more than offset by the 17K saved by loading the mouse driver into UMBs. What's more, an additional 74K of UMBs are available for other device drivers and programs like SHARE, network shells, DOSKEY, etc.

Shifting from RAM cram to UMB cram

In the 8086/286 days, everybody complained about RAM cram. With DOS, TSRs like Sidekick, and large programs, there was never enough RAM. Along came UMBs, and suddenly RAM cram was a thing of the past.

If you ever moved into a larger apartment or house, you might remember wondering what you were going to do with all the space. But it wasn't long before you filled the place up and started complaining about the lack of room. The same goes for UMBs. Now people complain about UMB cram — too many programs and too little UMB space in which to put them.

Making the best use of the available UMBs memory is not as straightforward as you might think.

Identifying potential UMB space

The upper memory area is a memory mine field — here's ROM-BIOS, there's empty space, over there is video memory, and down there is another empty space. To complicate things even more, the organization of upper memory varies from system to system. Figure 5-7 shows how upper memory is organized on the most common systems. As a general rule, ROM-BIOS is located in the F000-FFFF range, the range A000-BFFF is used for video memory, and the C000-CFFF range is used for video and disk BIOS.

 EMM386 is responsible for mapping extended memory into the unused portions of upper memory. You can instruct EMM386 to include or exclude specific areas of upper memory with the I= and X= directives, respectively.

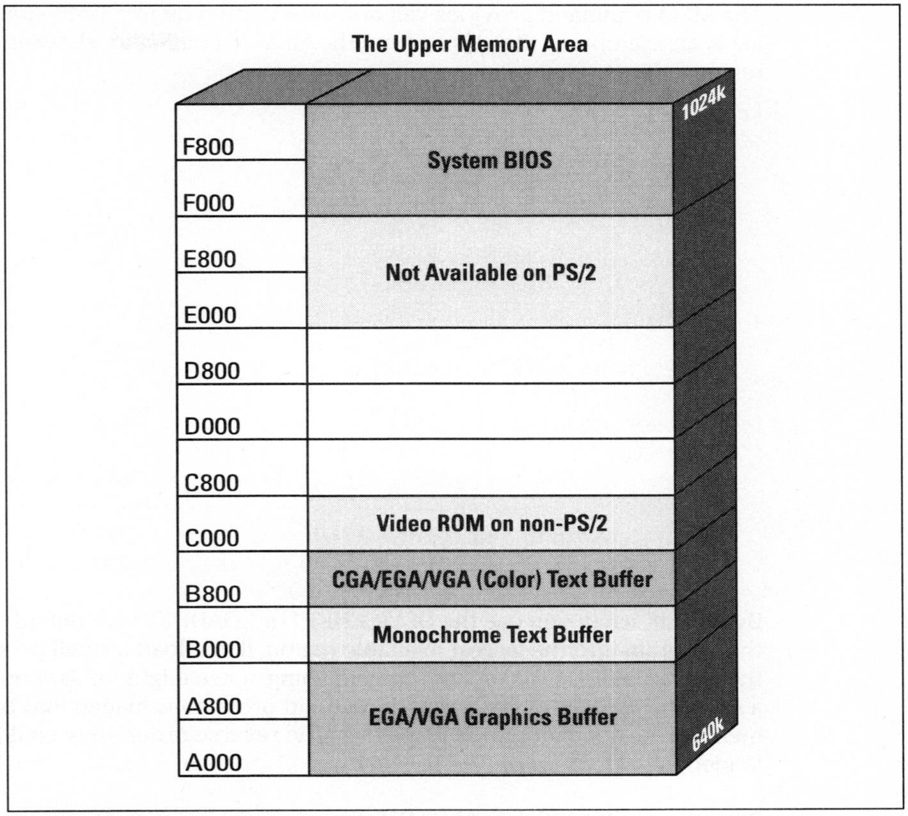

The Upper Memory Area

Address	Region
F800	System BIOS
F000	
E800	Not Available on PS/2
E000	
D800	
D000	
C800	
C000	Video ROM on non-PS/2
B800	CGA/EGA/VGA (Color) Text Buffer
B000	Monochrome Text Buffer
A800	EGA/VGA Graphics Buffer
A000	

1024k ... *640k*

Figure 5-7: How upper memory is utilized on popular systems.

By default, the DOS 5 version of EMM386 only supported upper memory in the range C000-DFFF. The I= switch had to be used to instruct EMM386 to access the other areas. Many books and magazines recommended using the switch I=E000-EFFF to get an extra 64K of UMB space. Starting with DOS 6, EMM386 now supports the range E000-EFFF by default, so you no longer need to explicitly include it.

Controlling load order and location

Because UMBs are mapped into the unused portions of upper memory, they are fragmented, with some blocks of memory at one address and other blocks of memory at another. These different areas of UMBs are referred to as *regions*.

The MEM command provides valuable information on free UMB space. Following is an example of the output from the MEM /F command, showing 2 UMB regions of free space:

```
Free Conventional Memory:

    Segment         Size
    -------------------------
    00624            80     (0K)
    0063A           208     (0K)
    00647         87376    (85K)
    01B9C        542256   (530K)

    Total Free: 629920   (615K)

Free Upper Memory:

    Region   Largest Free     Total Free      Total Size
    ----------------------------------------------------------
       1     27696  (27K)    27696  (27K)    27696  (27K)
       2    146720 (143K)   146720 (143K)   163840 (160K)
```

By default, when you use the DEVICEHIGH or LOADHIGH command, DOS loads the program into the largest available region. If you load a small program first, the largest region is used, and the remaining space might not be enough to load a second, bigger program. If so, the second program is loaded into base memory. If you loaded the programs in the reverse order, they could both be loaded high.

Both the DEVICEHIGH and LOADHIGH commands provide the /L switch so you can specify the specific region(s) where a program is loaded.

By fine-tuning the order in which programs are loaded and by using the /L switch, you can make optimum use of the available UMBs.

Tweaking UMB memory allocation

Effective UMB management is further complicated by the fact that some programs require more memory when they are loaded, but then shrink their memory requirements after successful installation. It's like a building that needs a whole block during construction but only occupies half a block after it's built. The reverse is also true; some programs require less space to load than they do to operate.

The DEVICEHIGH and LOADHIGH /L switch optionally enable you to identify the minimum amount of memory that must be available in the region for the program to be loaded high. This is necessary for programs that require less memory to load than they require to run. You can use the /S switch in conjunction with the /L switch to instruct DOS to shrink the program to its minimum size when loaded.

Loading DBLSPACE.BIN high

You must use a special technique to load the disk compression driver DBLSPACE.BIN into UMBs.

The device driver DBLSPACE.SYS, included with DOS 6, has one purpose in life: to move DBLSPACE.BIN into upper memory. The DBLSPACE.SYS statement should be added to CONFIG.SYS and can either be loaded into conventional memory with a DEVICE= statement or into upper memory with a DEVICEHIGH= statement:

```
DEVICEHIGH=C:\DOS\DBLSPACE.SYS /MOVE
```

The /MOVE switch is really a comment. Any switches specified with DBLSPACE.SYS actually are ignored. The DOS developers added the /MOVE switch to provide a hint about the purpose of the device driver. Remember that it is not a device driver for DoubleSpace drives; it is a device drive to *move* the DBLSPACE.BIN device driver into upper memory.

 During system boot-up, IO.SYS loads DBLSPACE.BIN before CONFIG.SYS is even looked at. It is initially loaded at the top of memory, adjacent to the memory area occupied by IO.SYS. It must load into base memory because the UMBs are not available so early in the booting cycle. If CONFIG.SYS does not contain a DBLSPACE.SYS driver, DBLSPACE.BIN is moved to the bottom of base memory after all the CONFIG.SYS statements are processed.

Letting MEMMAKER do the work

Fully optimizing the use of UMBs is a painstaking, complicated, and laborious process. In fact, it's the kind of work a computer should be doing!

Fortunately, DOS engineers agreed and added a brand new program, MEMMAKER, to DOS 6. The sole purpose of MEMMAKER is to analyze your PC's memory usage and reconfigure the CONFIG.SYS and AUTOEXEC.BAT files for optimum memory usage. It's an excellent program.

Looking at MEMMAKER in action

Listed next are typical CONFIG.SYS and AUTOEXEC.BAT files from a 386 system that is not configured very well:

CONFIG.SYS:

```
FILES=50
BUFFERS=15
DEVICE=C:\WINDOWS\MOUSE.SYS /Y
DEVICE=C:\DOS\SETVER.EXE
LASTDRIVE=M
```

AUTOEXEC.BAT:

```
@ECHO OFF
PATH C:\DOS;C:\;C:\WINDOWS;C:\WINDOWS\NDW;C:\BATFILES
PROMPT $P$G
DOSKEY
SET SAGEEDIT=C:\SPE
SET NU=C:\U\NORTON
SET TEMP=C:\TEMP
```

Using these configuration files, MEM reports 567,520 bytes of free memory as follows:

```
Memory Type        Total =  Used  +  Free
-------------------------------------------
Conventional        640K     86K     554K
Upper                 0K      0K       0K
Adapter RAM/ROM     384K    384K       0K
Extended (XMS)    15104K  15104K       0K
Expanded (EMS)        0K      0K       0K
-------------------------------------------
Total memory      16128K  15574K     554K

Total under 1 MB    640K     86K     554K

Largest executable program size       554K  (567520 bytes)
Largest free upper memory block         0K     (0 bytes)
The high memory area is available.
```

After running MEMMAKER in Express Mode, the configuration files have been modified as follows:

CONFIG.SYS:

```
DEVICE=C:\DOS\HIMEM.SYS
DEVICE=C:\DOS\EMM386.EXE RAM WIN=DD00-DFFF WIN=D800-DCFF
BUFFERS=15,0
FILES=50
DOS=UMB
LASTDRIVE=M
FCBS=4,0
DEVICEHIGH /L:1,55168 =C:\WINDOWS\MOUSE.SYS /Y
DEVICEHIGH /L:1,12048 =C:\DOS\SETVER.EXE
```

AUTOEXEC.BAT:

```
@ECHO OFF
PATH C:\DOS;C:\;C:\WINDOWS;C:\WINDOWS\NDW;C:\BATFILES
PROMPT $P$G
LH /L:1,6400 DOSKEY
SET SAGEEDIT=C:\SPE
SET NU=C:\U\NORTON
SET TEMP=C:\TEMP
```

The free memory increases to 583,216 bytes, and MEM shows the following statistics:

```
Memory Type        Total = Used +  Free
-------------------------------------------
Conventional        640K     70K    570K
Upper                59K     21K     38K
Adapter RAM/ROM     325K    325K      0K
Extended (XMS)    15104K  15104K      0K
-------------------------------------------
Total memory      16128K  15521K    607K

Total under 1 MB    699K     92K    607K

EMS is active.
Largest executable program size        570K   (583216 bytes)
Largest free upper memory block         38K   (38464 bytes)
The high memory area is available.
```

The main changes MEMMAKER made to CONFIG.SYS were to add HIMEM.SYS and EMM386 statements, to add a DOS=UMB statement, and to use DEVICEHIGH to load MOUSE.SYS and SETVER.EXE into the upper memory blocks. The only change to AUTOEXEC.BAT was the addition of the instruction to use

LOADHIGH, in its abbreviated form LH, to load DOSKEY into the upper memory blocks.

Notice that the /L switch is used in every instance of DEVICEHIGH and LOADHIGH to control the region as well as the minimum memory required by each program.

Having already learned about the big memory gainers, you may have observed one omission from the modified CONFIG.SYS file. Although HIMEM.SYS was installed, DOS was not loaded into high memory. If the DOS=UMB line is manually changed to DOS=HIGH,UMB, the free memory jumps to 631,648 bytes.

```
Memory Type          Total =  Used  +  Free
--------------------------------------------------
Conventional          640K     23K     617K
Upper                  59K     21K      38K
Adapter RAM/ROM       325K    325K       0K
Extended (XMS)      15104K    544K   14560K
--------------------------------------------------
Total memory        16128K    913K   15215K

Total under 1 MB      699K     44K     655K

EMS is active.
Largest executable program size        617K  (631648 bytes)
Largest free upper memory block         38K  (38464 bytes)
MS-DOS is resident in the high memory area.
```

You probably wonder why MEMMAKER missed such an obvious improvement. When DOS 6 is first installed, SETUP adds the statement DOS=HIGH to CONFIG.SYS. The MEMMAKER developers assumed that DOS=HIGH must have been removed on purpose, and so MEMMAKER does not add DOS=HIGH if it is missing, even in Custom Mode. Strange.

Running MEMMAKER

MEMMAKER is one of those all too rare programs that is very powerful *and* easy to use. MEMMAKER is located in the DOS directory and normally is executed without any switches or options. The only keys you need to remember are the spacebar (to toggle menu options), F3 to abort, and Enter to proceed with the selections.

Initially, MEMMAKER displays a welcome screen. After you press a key, the program presents the main option screen (see Figure 5-8), which prompts you to choose between *Express Mode* or *Custom Mode*.

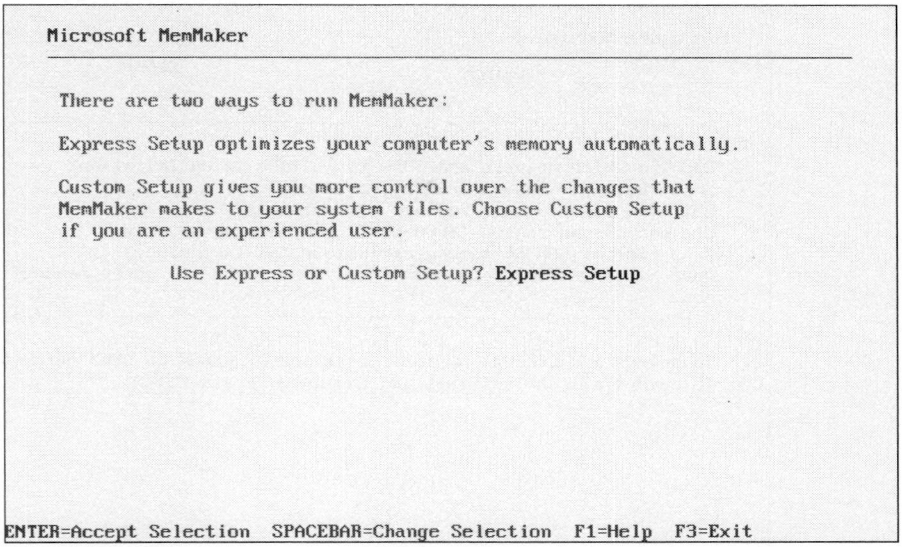

```
Microsoft MemMaker
─────────────────────────────────────────────────────────────

 There are two ways to run MemMaker:

 Express Setup optimizes your computer's memory automatically.

 Custom Setup gives you more control over the changes that
 MemMaker makes to your system files. Choose Custom Setup
 if you are an experienced user.

            Use Express or Custom Setup? Express Setup




ENTER=Accept Selection  SPACEBAR=Change Selection  F1=Help  F3=Exit
```

Figure 5-8: MEMMAKER can run in Express or Custom Mode.

No matter which mode you select, MEMMAKER asks the following question:

```
Do you use any programs that need expanded memory (EMS)?
```

One function of EMM386 is to convert extended memory to expanded memory. As you may recall, expanded memory uses a 64K page frame in upper memory for paging. If you don't run applications that take advantage of EMS, you might as well eliminate the 64K page frame and free that memory for use as UMBs. When you respond No to this question, MEMMAKER adds a NOEMS switch to the EMM386.

After the change to NOEMS is made, certain applications may run much more slowly than they used to. This is a good indication that the application did take advantage of expanded memory after all. Remove the NOEMS switch from the EMM386 statement in CONFIG.SYS, reboot the system, and see whether the applications regain their old speed. If so, you may want to re-run MEMMAKER and respond Yes to the EMS question.

When you select Express Mode, MEMMAKER just gets on with its work. If you choose Custom Mode, you can guide MEMMAKER in some areas of optimization. Figure 5-9 illustrates the options available in Custom Mode. You can use the cursor keys to change the active selection and use the spacebar to toggle the setting between Yes and No.

```
Microsoft MemMaker
─────────────────────────────────────────────────────────────────

                        Advanced Options
─────────────────────────────────────────────────────────────────

   Specify which drivers and TSRs to include in optimization?    No
   Scan the upper memory area aggressively?                      Yes
   Optimize upper memory for use with Windows?                   No
   Use monochrome region (B000-B7FF) for running programs?       No
   Keep current EMM386 memory exclusions and inclusions?         Yes
   Move Extended BIOS Data Area from conventional to upper memory? Yes

─────────────────────────────────────────────────────────────────


   To select a different option, press the UP ARROW or DOWN ARROW key.
   To accept all the settings and continue, press ENTER.




─────────────────────────────────────────────────────────────────
ENTER=Accept All  SPACEBAR=Change Selection  F1=Help  F3=Exit
```

Figure 5-9: Configuration options in the Custom Mode of MEMMAKER.

Unfortunately, MEMMAKER does not scan the existing setup before displaying the custom options. Therefore, the values presented in the configuration options may bear no resemblance to your existing CONFIG.SYS settings.

Chapter 7 of the *MS-DOS User's Guide* provides a good description of most of the custom options, but two options deserve special mention: Optimize upper memory for use with Windows and Use the monochrome region.

Optimize upper memory for use with Windows

In short, select this option if you use Windows most of the time and are not experiencing low-memory problems when using DOS outside of Windows. MEMMAKER will add one or more WIN= switches to the EMM386.EXE statement in CONFIG.SYS, indicating that the UMB space is reserved for use by Windows.

Windows must create translation buffers in the first megabyte of memory, and, for performance reasons, these translation buffers must be aligned on a 4K boundary. The buffers can, however, be situated in UMBs. Unfortunately, both EMM386 and DOS store information, called *arenas,* at the start and end of each UMB. These arenas cause the start and end of the free memory in the UMB *not* to be 4K-aligned. The first 4K and last 4K of each free UMB space cannot, therefore, be utilized by Windows for translation buffers.

If the X= EMM386 switch is used to exclude a region, Windows 3.1 will not put translation buffers there; the EMMIMPORT information from EMM386 says that the region should be excluded. The WIN= switch tells EMM386 not to map in UMBs but to tell Windows that it can use the address for translation buffers (via EMMIMPORT). This allows Windows to use the full UMB space without wasting 8K. The trade-off is that you cannot use the area for UMB memory when Windows is not in use — in a standard DOS session.

Use the monochrome region

The B area of upper memory — that is, the range from 0xB000 to 0xBFFF — is reserved for video memory. The first half of the range, 0xB000-0xB7FF, is reserved for monochrome systems, and the remainder, 0xB800-0xBFFF, is reserved for color systems. If you use a color system, you can probably fill the monochrome video area with UMBs. If you set this option to Yes, MEMMAKER adds the I=B000-B7FF to the EMM386 statement. On systems with Windows installed, MEMMAKER also adds the line DEVICE=MONOUMB2.386 to the [386enh] section of SYSTEM.INI. Without this modification, Windows will not run.

If you are a Windows user and you manually add the I=B000-B7FF statement to the EMM386 statement, make sure that you also edit SYSTEM.INI and add the statement DEVICE=MONOUMB2.386 to the [386enh] section.

In rare circumstances, MEMMAKER may make changes to your configuration files that cause your system to lock up. Refer to the section titled "Solving memory conflicts," later in the chapter, for guidance on how to proceed.

Understanding how MEMMAKER works

In the simple example discussed earlier, MEMMAKER didn't perform many miracles. However, if you have a complicated configuration with many different device drivers and programs loaded at system boot-up, MEMMAKER can work wonders. MEMMAKER may literally evaluate thousands of configuration permutations before selecting its optimum choice.

The most complicated task MEMMAKER undertakes is determining how much space is required for device drivers and programs, both at load time and thereafter. To perform this feat, MEMMAKER uses two special utilities, CHKSTATE.SYS and SIZER.EXE.

MEMMAKER modifies CONFIG.SYS and adds a new line to the beginning of the file to load the CHKSTATE device driver. If the HIMEM.SYS, EMM386, and DOS=UMB statements are missing, MEMMAKER adds them. MEMMAKER also modifies each DEVICE statement so that SIZER.EXE is used to load and observe the device drivers as they are loaded.

The following listing shows how the example CONFIG.SYS is modified by MEMMAKER during the optimization process:

CONFIG.SYS:

```
DEVICE=C:\DOS\CHKSTATE.SYS /S:SR1 /14277
DEVICE=C:\DOS\HIMEM.SYS
DEVICE=C:\DOS\EMM386.EXE RAM
BUFFERS=15,0
FILES=50
DOS=UMB
LASTDRIVE=M
FCBS=4,0
DEVICE=C:\DOS\SIZER.EXE /14277 /8 C:\WINDOWS\MOUSE.SYS /Y
DEVICE=C:\DOS\SIZER.EXE /14277 /9 C:\DOS\SETVER.EXE
```

MEMMAKER also makes modifications to the AUTOEXEC.BAT file. As it does with device drivers, MEMMAKER modifies all program execution statements, including batch files, so that SIZER.EXE is used to load them. At the end of the AUTOEXEC.BAT file, MEMMAKER adds a line to call itself so that the optimization process can proceed.

AUTOEXEC.BAT:

```
@ECHO OFF
PATH C:\DOS;C:\;C:\WINDOWS;C:\WINDOWS\NDW;C:\BATFILES
PROMPT $P$G
C:\DOS\SIZER.EXE /14277 /3 DOSKEY
SET SAGEEDIT=C:\SPE
SET NU=C:\U\NORTON
SET TEMP=C:\TEMP
C:\DOS\MEMMAKER.EXE /SESSION:14277
```

Having edited the configuration files, MEMMAKER reboots the system. Then CHKSTATE.SYS and SIZER.EXE observe and gather statistics as the device drivers and programs are loaded. Using this data, MEMMAKER calculates which programs should be loaded into upper memory, in what order they should be loaded, and how much memory they will need.

Based on these computations, MEMMAKER makes further edits to the configuration files. The main change involves removing the SIZER.EXE statements and replacing them with DEVICEHIGH and LOADHIGH statements, using the appropriate switches. The following listing shows the example configuration files after MEMMAKER made the second set of adjustments:

CONFIG.SYS:

```
DEVICE=C:\DOS\CHKSTATE.SYS /S:FR1 /27107
DEVICE=C:\DOS\HIMEM.SYS
DEVICE=C:\DOS\EMM386.EXE RAM WIN=DD00-DFFF WIN=D800-DCFF
BUFFERS=15,0
FILES=50
DOS=UMB
LASTDRIVE=M
FCBS=4,0
DEVICEHIGH /L:1,55168 =C:\WINDOWS\MOUSE.SYS /Y
DEVICEHIGH /L:1,12048 =C:\DOS\SETVER.EXE
```

AUTOEXEC.BAT:

```
@ECHO OFF
PATH C:\DOS;C:\;C:\WINDOWS;C:\WINDOWS\NDW;C:\BATFILES
PROMPT $P$G
LH L:1,6400 DOSKEY
SET SAGEEDIT=C:\SPE
SET NU=C:\U\NORTON
SET TEMP=C:\TEMP
C:\DOS\MEMMAKER.EXE /SESSION:27107
```

MEMMAKER reboots the system for a second time and then prompts you to see whether everything appears to be working correctly. If you respond Yes, MEMMAKER removes the CHKSTATE statement from the beginning of CONFIG.SYS and removes the MEMMAKER statement from the end of AUTOEXEC.BAT. A summary of your memory gains is displayed, and you are returned to the DOS prompt. You are now ready to take advantage of your newfound memory. If the system appears unstable and you respond No to MEMMAKER's question, the original configuration files can be restored and the system rebooted, leaving the system the same as it was before MEMMAKER started.

 Behind the scenes, MEMMAKER creates the file MEMMAKER.STS in the DOS directory. This file contains all the analysis performed by CHKSTATE and SIZER and provides interesting details about each program and device driver loaded at boot-up.

CHKSTATE.SYS writes the summary information at the top of the file, and then SIZER writes the detailed information for each command.

The DOS 6 diagnostic program MSD.EXE can show you how your base and upper memory is used and where programs and device drivers are physically stored in memory. Run MSD and select the **M**emory Block Display option from the Utilities menu. If you scroll through the list of installed programs, the block diagram shows where the program is situated. In Figure 5-10, the location of the WORKGRP.SYS file is identified by the |—| characters in the D400 segment.

Helping MEMMAKER succeed

Although MEMMAKER is very "smart," some relatively common situations can reduce its effectiveness. The following section describes some circumstances in which you can give MEMMAKER a helping hand.

Avoid using a multiple configuration menu in CONFIG.SYS

MEMMAKER is often less effective when the CONFIG.SYS file contains a MENU of options (discussed fully in Chapter 8).

A CONFIG.SYS file that contains more than one configuration may have multiple entries for HIMEM.SYS, EMM386.EXE, etc. When MEMMAKER encounters this situation, it copies the first occurrence of HIMEM.SYS and EMM386.EXE to the beginning of the file. If you instructed MEMMAKER to retain the existing include (I) and exclude (X) switches for EMM386, the switches for the first EMM386 statement are used. Now here's the silly part: MEMMAKER comments out (with a REM statement) all the remaining HIMEM.SYS and EMM386.EXE statements in CONFIG.SYS.

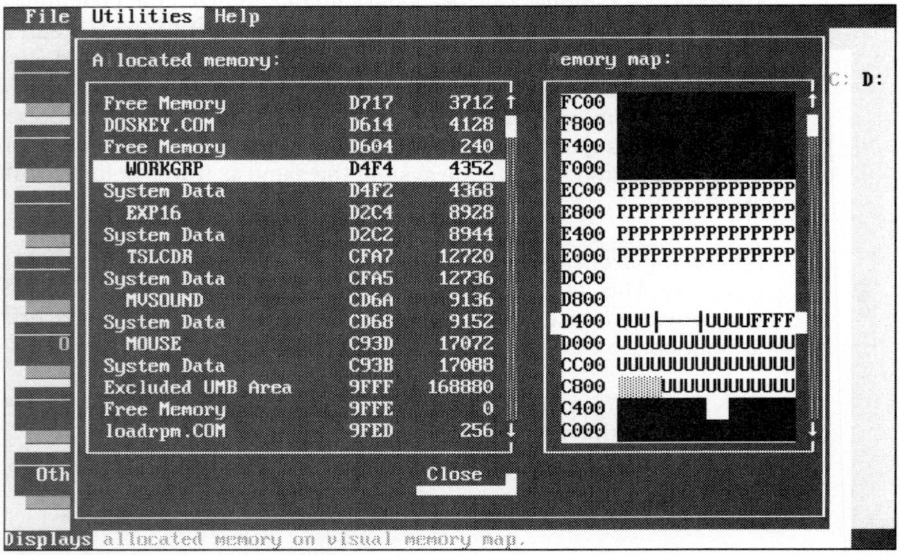

Figure 5-10: MSD shows where device drivers and programs are loaded in upper memory.

In some situations, you may want to have multiple configurations optimized by MEMMAKER. For example, you may have one configuration that doesn't load network drivers, another that loads a scanner driver, and maybe a third configuration that loads everything. On my system, that configuration is called *Enchilada*.

MEMMAKER can configure all the multiple options, but not automatically. The best approach is to make backup copies of CONFIG.SYS and AUTOEXEC.BAT and then create slimmed-down versions of them using the statements for one specific configuration or menu option. Then run MEMMAKER to optimize the configuration for that specific setup. After you do this, merge the modified AUTOEXEC.BAT and CONFIG.SYS files into the backup configuration files, replacing the original statements. Repeat this process for each configuration scenario.

If you have a device driver or program (such as DOSKEY) that is used in each configuration option, avoid placing the program statement in a [COMMON] section of CONFIG.SYS. Rather, place a copy of the statement in each individual configuration set. Remember that the DEVICEHIGH/LOADHIGH switches may be different for each configuration. Although the program is common to each configuration, the way the program is loaded high may differ depending on the other programs sharing the UMBs.

Don't call programs from other batch files

In the AUTOEXEC.BAT file, avoid calling other batch files that in turn load programs. For example, don't load DOSKEY and SHARE from a batch file that is itself called from AUTOEXEC.BAT. MEMMAKER analyzes all the programs loaded from the batch file as a single entity. Either all the programs are loaded high or none are loaded high. The solution is to modify AUTOEXEC.BAT before you run MEMMAKER. In this example, edit AUTOEXEC.BAT to call the DOSKEY and SHARE programs directly.

Don't call programs in IF statements

Avoid running a program from an IF statement in AUTOEXEC.BAT. MEMMAKER will not optimize a program that is called directly from an IF statement. For example, MEMMAKER will ignore the call to DOSKEY in the following statement:

```
if "%anarkey%"=="" doskey
```

Use a GOTO statement in the IF clause, and MEMMAKER will optimize the program's memory usage. This example can be modified as follows:

```
if %anarkey%"=="" goto loaddoskey
.....
:LOADDOSKEY
doskey
.....
```

Exclude some programs from analysis and execution

You may have some programs and device drivers that you don't want MEMMAKER to analyze — you want them to be executed as is, without any changes to their switches and so forth. There may be other programs that you do not want MEMMAKER to analyze or execute. For example, you may have a menu program, THEMENU.EXE, that is always called at the end of the AUTOEXEC.BAT to display a menu of programs and utilities. Obviously, it would be confusing if this menu program were repeatedly executed during the analysis phases of MEMMAKER.

You can use the file MEMMAKER.INF, in the DOS directory, to control which device drivers and programs MEMMAKER analyzes and executes. This file is ASCII and can be easily edited with EDIT.

Here is an example of MEMMAKER.INF:

```
;USED BY MEMMAKER
AUTOMENU
DBASE
DOSSHELL
EZMENU
LOTUS
MENU
NC
PARADOX
*PROTMAN
*SMARTDRV /DOUBLE_BUFFER
*SSWAP
*STRETCH
WORD
WP
WIN
123
```

All lines must be flush-left — that is, with no leading spaces. Any line beginning with a semicolon is ignored. The file contains a list of programs and device drivers, but the filename extension must not be specified; don't use EXE, COM, SYS, etc. Any program preceded by an asterisk is not modified by MEMMAKER but is executed. All other programs are completely ignored by MEMMAKER and are not run during the optimization process.

Saving every drop of base memory

Most DOS and Windows users want to make base memory as large as possible. The first step is to use MEMMAKER to analyze your system and make the major changes, such as running HIMEM.SYS and EMM386.EXE, and loading programs high. MEMMAKER takes care of the big issues, but you can still squeeze out a few more bytes here and there.

More and more programs and device drivers are being written in ways that conserve base memory and take direct advantage of UMBs or expanded memory. For example, the recent versions of the PCKWIK disk cache automatically loads into UMBs, and on my system, the fax board driver, SATISFAX.SYS, loads much of itself into expanded memory. In such cases, MEMMAKER does not try to directly load the program into UMBs. If you notice that MEMMAKER has not loaded a program high even though there is free upper memory, it is probably because the program loads high unassisted. You can always use the MEM command to verify where a program is being loaded and how much memory it is using.

Fine-tuning your system's memory configuration takes patience, as some changes can destabilize your system. In the event of a system lockup, you may need to retrace your steps and remove the "enhancements." Using these simple methods can help you keep track of your changes:

■ If you are just making a change to one command's switches, don't make changes to the original line. Comment out the old line with the REM command and add a new statement with the appropriate switch changes. When I use the REM command, I always add the date so I can remember when I made the change. Some problems may not surface for weeks. Here is an example of how to adjust the EMM386 command:

```
REM 02/20/93 DEVICE=C:\DOS\EMM386.EXE RAM I=B000-B7FF NOEMS
DEVICE=C:\DOS\EMM386.EXE RAM I=B000-B7FF NOEMS MIN=0
```

■ If you are making a few changes, make a backup copy of the configuration files before making the adjustments.

■ Consider using the multiple configuration facility in DOS 6 (discussed in Chapter 8). Create a new menu option (for example, an option called *Experiment*) and save your old configuration in a separate configuration block.

The following section discusses some other changes that may gain you a few more bytes of base memory. I recommend that you don't make these changes until you are sure your system is running smoothly following MEMMAKER optimization. If you make too many changes at once, it is far more difficult to diagnose problems if they occur.

Minimizing the environment size

The DOS environment is used to store the file search path, the DOS prompt format, the location of COMMAND.COM, and other information for specific programs (for example, a temporary directory for Windows). You can view your current environment settings by entering the SET command. Here is the environment on one of my systems:

```
CONFIG=NORMAL
COMSPEC=C:\DOS\COMMAND.COM
PATH=C:\DOS;C:\;C:\WINDOWS;C:\WINDOWS\NDW;C:\BATFILES
PROMPT=$P$G
SAGEEDIT=C:\SPE
NU=C:\U\NORTON
TEMP=C:\TEMP
```

More and more programs are taking advantage of the environment to store information. The default size of the environment is 256 bytes, but that often is too small. You can use the SHELL command in CONFIG.SYS to increase the environment size by specifying the COMMAND switch /E. The following statement increases the environment size to 500 bytes:

```
SHELL=C:\DOS\COMMAND.COM C:\DOS\ /E:500 /P
```

The space used by the environment is taken from base memory, so make sure that the environment isn't wasting space. Allocate only the environment space you need.

An easy way to determine the amount of environment bytes actually being used is to pipe the output of the SET command to a file. Here is an example:

```
c:\> set > sizeof.set
```

You can then use the DIR command to display the file size of the temporary file:

```
c:\> dir sizeof.set
```

The file size is a few bytes larger than the actual size of the environment data, but it provides a very close approximation.

Compare the consumed environment size with the memory allocated by the SHELL command. You may be able to save a few hundred bytes by reducing the amount allocated with the SHELL command. The environment space can range from 160 to 32,768 bytes and is always rounded up to the nearest number divisible by 16.

If you encounter the message Out Of Environment Space, you made the environment too small.

Tuning the FILES statement

The FILES statement in CONFIG.SYS specifies the maximum number of files that DOS can have open at any one time (for example, FILES=25). The more files specified, the more memory is used. Every additional file above the default setting of 8 consumes approximately 50 bytes. You should therefore tune the FILES command to make sure that you are not allocating unnecessary memory for file handles. The wasted memory soon adds up; 20 files too many wastes 1,000 bytes.

There is no hard and fast way to accurately determine the number of files you need. It depends on the specific requirements of the software you use. If you run Windows, a common setting is FILES=50. If you don't run Windows but do run a database program, FILES=30 is reasonable. If you only use word processing or spreadsheet applications, FILES=20 might be enough.

If you encounter an "out of file handles" message or a similar message, you need to increase the number of files.

Tuning the BUFFERS statement

The BUFFERS statement was originally introduced to speed up file operations. Think of it as a poor man's disk cache. You can allocate between 1 and 99 buffers; each buffer consumes approximately 500 bytes. If you load DOS high, the BUFFERS are loaded high as well.

Since its introduction, BUFFERS has been eclipsed by real disk caching software. If you use an 8086 system and don't own a disk cache, allocating about 20 buffers makes sense. Although it consumes a few thousand bytes of memory, it improves disk performance. However, if you own a 286 or later system, use DOS SMARTDRV or a third-party disk cache and reduce the buffers to 4. There is no advantage to having more than 4 buffers if a disk cache is used. In fact, having too many buffers can interfere with the disk cache and reduce the overall performance of your system.

Optimizing the STACKS command

The STACKS command in CONFIG.SYS allocates memory to manage hardware interrupts. STACKS accepts two arguments: the number of stack frames and the size (in bytes) of each frame. Here is an example:

```
STACKS=9,256
```

This stacks statement consumes more than 2,000 bytes of base memory. Not all systems need to allocate memory for stacks, and so the memory is wasted. If no STACKS command is specified, DOS defaults to 9 stack frames of 128 bytes each.

Try using a STACKS=0,0 statement to remove all stack frame allocation. In most cases, your system will run fine. If you encounter stack error messages such as `Internal Stack Overflow`, you need to reinstate the STACKS command. Start with a low value, such as 9,128. If you still have a problem, increase the allocation to 9,256. If the problem persists, try 12,128, then 12,256, and so on, until the trouble is resolved.

Minimizing the FCBS allocation

File control blocks are a legacy from the first version of DOS. Unless you are running some old (and probably very outdated) software, you do not need file control blocks. Conceptually, FILES is a modern version of FCBS.

When I removed the statement FCBS=20 from my CONFIG.SYS, I recovered an additional 944 bytes of memory. Even when there is no FCBS statement in CONFIG.SYS, however, DOS uses a default of FCBS=4. To minimize the FCBS allocation, add the statement `fcbs=1`. On my system, this produced a net saving of 1,120 bytes.

Being frugal with LASTDRIVE

The LASTDRIVE command is used in CONFIG.SYS to allow for additional logical drives, such as network drives and RAM disks. For example, the statement LASTDRIVE=M instructs DOS to allocate enough memory for each drive up to the letter M. Because each drive consumes about 80 bytes, avoid allocating memory for drives that are never used. If you don't use RAM disks or networks, you might even omit the LASTDRIVE statement altogether.

Minimize MSCDEX base memory consumption

MSCDEX, the CD-ROM driver, uses anywhere from 16K to 5K for sector buffers, depending on the configuration. If your system is configured for expanded memory, you can conserve base memory (or upper memory if MSCDEX is loaded high) by specifying the /E switch with MSCDEX. The /E switch instructs MSCDEX to place the CD-ROM buffers in expanded memory.

With default settings, MSCDEX will consume 35K of memory (high or base), but when /E is specified, the memory usage drops to 16K.

Maximizing extended memory

The primary memory goal for users of DOS applications is to maximize the amount of free base memory. However, Windows users have a different goal: maximizing *extended* memory. In Real Mode, Windows uses expanded memory, but in Standard and Enhanced Modes, Windows thrives on extended memory.

In short, the most effective way to increase the amount of available extended memory is to install more memory. You can quickly ascertain how much extended memory is available by executing the MEM command. But don't run the command from within Windows because it will probably report that all the extended memory is in use (by Windows). If you find that no extended memory is available, make sure that the HIMEM.SYS and EMM386 statements are included in the CONFIG.SYS file.

Most of the previously discussed techniques for maximizing base memory do not adversely affect Windows performance. In fact, they improve the free memory available to applications when Windows launches a DOS program.

Some programs reserve extended memory for themselves, thereby preventing Windows from using that reserved memory. In the past, disk caches and expanded memory managers fell into this category, but both SMARTDRV and EMM386 can share extended memory cooperatively with Windows. For example, if Windows needs more extended memory to perform a certain operation, SMARTDRV automatically releases some of its extended memory to Windows. If you use a program that takes too much extended memory, such as a disk cache, refer to the program documentation to determine how to reduce the amount of extended memory it reserves.

If you run Windows on a system with minimal extended memory installed — say 2 to 4 megabytes — you may want to trade off the amount of free base memory for more extended memory, as follows:

- If you use EMM386 and you have not specified the NOEMS switch, EMM386 can convert extended memory to expanded. By default, EMM386 automatically converts some extended memory to expanded when it is loaded. If you specify the switch min=0, EMM386 conserves the extended memory and only converts it to expanded when a program requests it.

- If you use the NOEMS switch with EMM386, you can save additional extended memory by adding the NOVCPI switch. This removes support for VCPI compliant applications. As a rule of thumb, if you don't use EMS, you don't need VCPI support either.

- The HMA consumes 64K of extended memory, and the UMBs are created by mapping extended memory into upper memory. By disabling the EMM386 and DOS=HIGH commands from CONFIG.SYS, you free this memory for use by Windows. The amount of free conventional memory is likely to drop significantly because DOS, device drivers, and TSR programs are forced to reside in base memory. But, if you need extended memory, it's a trade-off worth considering.

Managing expanded memory

The way EMM386 simulates expanded memory is significantly improved in DOS 6.

If your computer uses expanded memory hardware, you must use a third-party expanded memory device driver, such as EMM.SYS. DOS 6 does not provide direct expanded memory managers — only ways to simulate expanded memory with extended.

With earlier versions, you could instruct EMM386 to reserve part of extended memory to emulate expanded memory using the MEMORY switch. The main weakness of this approach was that the memory was literally reserved and could only be used for expanded memory.

DOS 6's EMM386.EXE is a significant improvement over its predecessor because it allows a 386 or later computer to share memory from a *pool.* If a program needs expanded memory, memory is taken from the pool and presented to the program as expanded memory. Similarly, if a program requires extended memory, it too can be allocated from the common memory pool.

Provided that EMM386 is specified without the NOEMS switch, expanded memory is directly supported.

The EMM386 MEMORY switch sets the maximum amount of expanded memory that is provided, and the MIN= switch sets the minimum. Five other switches also are used to manage the EMS page frame: MX, FRAME=, /P, PN, and H=. For further information on these switches, refer to Part IV, "The Complete DOS 6 Command Reference."

Solving memory conflicts

"Lockup happens" — what a perfect bumper sticker. When juggling software configurations and program-loading sequences, you will eventually run into a situation where the system stops behaving. A program refuses to run, or worse still, the system won't respond. My favorite techno-slang for this situation is *hosed,* but *locked up* and *hung* are also popular.

The following paragraphs describe some common ailments and suggested remedies.

Running MEMMAKER locks up the system

First, reboot the system. MEMMAKER normally recognizes that there has been a problem and restores your original configuration files. If MEMMAKER locks up second time, reboot again and press F5 when you see the message Starting MS-DOS... to *clean boot.* Change to the DOS directory and execute the following command:

```
memmaker /undo
```

MEMMAKER then restores your old configuration files and reboots your system. Try running MEMMAKER again, but this time choose the custom option. Then change the Scan Upper Memory Aggressively? option to No and try again.

The new configuration locks up the system

If the system is locked at the DOS prompt or repeatedly hangs after a few simple commands, there probably is a memory conflict. You need to do some detective work to isolate the true cause of the problem.

If the system refuses to run and you recently changed CONFIG.SYS or AUTOEXEC.BAT, it is likely that one of the recent changes caused the problem. To identify the specific cause, try reverting back to the previous configuration and making the changes one by one.

If you don't know which changes were made recently, take a methodical approach to isolate the problem. One tactic is to strip the CONFIG.SYS and AUTOEXEC.BAT files down to the bare bones and start including statements one by one until the problems start occurring. If you like to play a hunch, you might go in the opposite direction and remove individual statements until the problem goes away. Remember that you can use the F8 key at start-up to interactively select which statements execute. Often, problems are caused by a conflict in the UMBs. Rather than remove device drivers altogether, you might change the DEVICEHIGH statements to `device`.

If you are unable to isolate the specific program that is causing the trouble, EMM386 may be to blame. By adjusting the EMM386 switches, you should be able to isolate the problem.

Start by removing the HIGHSCAN switch if it is present. HIGHSCAN instructs EMM386 to use an aggressive technique to identify every free UMB space. This can cause problems on some systems, especially those that use SCSI device drivers, like ASPI4DOS.

Many ISA (industry standard architecture) bus systems equipped with SCSI drives cannot handle more than 16MB of memory. The problems arise because the DMA (direct memory access), used by SCSI device drivers, on ISA systems can only access 16MB of RAM. Unfortunately, the common solution is to change the CMOS to recognize only the first 16MB of installed memory, thereby disabling the additional installed memory. Refer to Chapter 7 for a thorough discussion of ISA and DMA.

If HIGHSCAN wasn't the problem, try adding the NOMOVEXBDA switch to stop EMM386 from relocating the extended BIOS data area. If that doesn't work, remove the switch, along with any include (I=) statements. If it does work, isolate the problem memory area by adjusting the I= statements until the problem returns.

Lockup may also be caused by EMM386 mapping extended memory into an active area of upper memory. A quick way to isolate this kind of problem is to exclude all upper memory with the statement X=A000-FFFF. If the problem appears to be fixed, try excluding a smaller area — for example, use X=A000-DFFF. Keep whittling the memory region down until you isolate one specific region of memory. You can use the resulting X switch to stop EMM386 from using that area of upper memory.

A program causes system lockup

Some programs do not like being loaded into upper memory. If a program locks the system when it is executed, try loading it in base memory by removing the LOADHIGH (or LH) statement.

If the program wasn't being loaded high in the first place, you may need to isolate the conflict in the ways described in the last section. In other words, start from a simple configuration that works with the program and keep expanding the statements until the program locks up again.

You should, of course, refer to the program documentation to determine whether there are known conflicts. It is also worth calling the vendor's technical support line to ask for guidance.

A program runs more slowly

This problem might occur when the NOEMS switch is added to EMM386. If that is the case, the program probably uses expanded memory to speed operations. Remove the NOEMS switch and see whether the speed improves.

If the speed doesn't improve, check to see whether the disk cache has been disabled or reduced in size. Also, make sure that you don't have two disk caches loaded because this too slows the system down.

Once again, if you can't seem to find the cause of the slowdown, start with a bare-bones configuration and add the statements one by one. You should be able to isolate the cause of the problem.

The system doesn't respond to Ctrl-Alt-Del

Add the ALTBOOT switch to the EMM386 statement in CONFIG.SYS if your system doesn't reboot when you press Ctrl-Alt-Del or if your system responds to the keystrokes in an erratic way.

Summary

This chapter explored PC memory, one of the most important topics for today's DOS user. You learned some of the following points:

▶ The most common PC memory chip is the DRAM chip. High-capacity chips are soldered onto compact circuit boards known as SIMMs. High-performance SRAM chips are used for memory caches, but their power demands are too high for general-purpose RAM.

▶ Each memory location has a segment:offset address. On 286 and later systems, the segment is used in a lookup table to determine the physical address. This technique increases the maximum addressable memory to 16MB on a 286 and all the way to 4 gigabytes on 386+ systems. (On 8086 systems, the maximum addressable memory is 1MB.)

▶ The first megabyte of memory is separated into base memory and upper memory. Additional memory is either expanded or extended memory.

▶ On 286+ systems, you can use HIMEM.SYS to remap the first 64K of extended memory as *high* memory. The majority of DOS can be loaded into high memory.

▶ On 386+ systems, unused areas of upper memory can be filled with extended memory, creating UMBs.

▶ MEMMAKER analyzes your system and modifies CONFIG.SYS and AUTOEXEC.BAT to make optimum use of your system's memory.

▶ You cure memory lockup by methodically revising the configuration files until you isolate the cause of the problem.

Chapter 6 shows how you can use DOS device drivers to brighten the display and customize the keyboard.

Chapter 6

Taking Control of the Display and Keyboard

In This Chapter

▶ A more colorful way to look at DOS

▶ ANSI.SYS techniques

▶ Ways to jazz up the screen display

▶ How to change display lines and modes

▶ How to customize the keyboard

▶ Alternatives to ANSI.SYS

We Want a Color TV! We Want a Color TV!

In the 60s, my sisters and I put our father under a lot of pressure. Every night, we begged him to buy a color TV. Eventually, we got one. It appears that, unlike my sisters and I, the DOS developers had a monochrome upbringing. Let's face it — DOS is not very pretty.

If you have been wanting a colorful version of DOS, you might be surprised to hear that you already have one. By using the DOS device driver ANSI.SYS, you can add a lot of pizazz to your DOS sessions. As well as offering color support, ANSI.SYS provides ways to reposition the cursor and customize the keyboard. You can assign keystroke sequences to the function keys, for example. ANSI.SYS is powerful, yet it takes less than 5K of memory.

Reviewing ANSI.SYS Techniques

To take advantage of ANSI.SYS, you must install it as a device driver in CONFIG.SYS. You can load it using either DEVICE or DEVICEHIGH.

ANSI.SYS supports two switches, both of which are related to extended (101-key) keyboards. On extended keyboards, you can use more than one key to perform some operations. For example, two keys enter the plus (+) character, and two keys perform the Page Up function. The /X switch instructs ANSI.SYS to treat these keys independently. With this switch in effect, you can remap the keys so that each has a different purpose.

If you have a nonstandard extended keyboard and experience problems remapping keys, use the /K switch to instruct ANSI.SYS to treat the keyboard as a traditional 84-key keyboard. You cannot use the /X and /K switches together.

 If you specified /K in a SWITCHES entry in CONFIG.SYS, load ANSI.SYS with the /K switch. If you use /K with SWITCHES, you must also use it with ANSI.SYS.

The following command from CONFIG.SYS loads ANSI.SYS into upper memory and specifies individual key support on extended keyboards:

```
devicehigh=c:\dos\ansi.sys /x
```

Sending instructions to ANSI.SYS

Whether you want to change display colors, position the cursor, or remap keys, you need to communicate with ANSI.SYS. You give instructions to ANSI.SYS by sending special escape codes to the standard output device (that is, the display).

The escape codes all begin with two specific *signature characters:* the Esc character, which has the ASCII value 027, and the left square-bracket character ([ ), which has the ASCII value 019. The characters you place after the signature characters depend on the task you want to perform; the character sequence 33m, for example, sets the text foreground color to brown.

ANSI.SYS intercepts characters sent to the standard output device (the display) but does nothing unless it receives the signature characters. When it receives the signature characters, ANSI.SYS jumps into action and responds to the instructions that follow.

The DOS commands ECHO, PROMPT, and TYPE all send characters to the standard output device, so you can use them to send escape sequences to ANSI.SYS. You need to be aware of some conditions, however.

Suppose that you want to change the foreground color to brown. You might think that the following command would do the job:

```
echo Esc[33m
```

In the examples, Esc represents the Esc key (ASCII code 027); don't enter the literal characters *E, s,* and *c.*

It isn't quite that straightforward. When you press Esc, DOS thinks that you want to undo the partially entered command, and so it clears the command before you have a chance to enter the [33m characters. In many situations, holding down the Alt key and pressing the 3-digit ASCII value on the numeric keypad provides an alternate way of entering a special key. If you use this technique on the command line, however, DOS reacts as if you pressed Esc directly — it clears the command. Shucks.

How do you solve this problem? Read on.

Using batch files

One way to get around the problem described in the preceding paragraphs is to create a batch file that contains the ECHO statement(s). The following batch file, for example, changes the text color to brown:

```
@echo off
echo ←[33m
```

This approach presents another challenge, however. When you press the Esc key in EDIT, nothing happens. The same goes for entering the Alt three-key sequence. You can use a simple trick to solve the problem. In EDIT, you can enter a special character by pressing Ctrl-P and then holding down the Alt key and entering the two or three digits identifying the character's ASCII value. Entering the Esc key is even easier: Just press Ctrl-P and then press the Esc key.

Note that EDIT displays the Esc character as a left-pointing arrow (←).

After creating a batch file containing the ANSI.SYS escape sequences, just execute the batch file, and ANSI.SYS responds. If you issue the command just discussed in the example, the foreground color changes to brown.

More often than not, you want to send more than one escape sequence to ANSI.SYS. You might want to change the foreground and background colors and clear the screen, for example. The following batch file, ANSICODE.BAT, makes it easy to send one or more commands to ANSI.SYS:

```
@echo off
:LOOP
if "%1" == "" goto quit
```

```
echo ←[%1
shift
goto loop
:QUIT
```

If you use this neat little batch file, you don't have to worry about entering the Esc[character sequence because it is already embedded in the batch file. To change the foreground color to brown, all you need to do is enter the following command:

```
ansicode 33m
```

Better still, ANSICODE.BAT can send several ANSI codes in one command. The following command, for example, changes the foreground to brown and the background to green and clears the screen:

```
ansicode 33m 42m 2J
```

One of the special ANSI.SYS escape sequences is Esc[2J, which clears the screen and moves the cursor to the home position. (Also, the Esc[K command erases the line starting at the cursor position.)

For more information about batch files, refer to Chapter 10.

Using the TYPE command

Instead of using the ECHO statement in batch files, you can just enter the commands into a plain file and then use TYPE to write the commands to the display. For example, you can use EDIT to create a single-line text file, BROWN.COL, that contains the following characters:

```
←[33m
```

Then, by entering the following command, you can direct the escape sequence to ANSI.SYS:

```
type brown.col
```

Using PROMPT

Like EDIT and TYPE, PROMPT sends characters to the display, so you can use it to communicate with ANSI.SYS. One of the special meta-characters supported by PROMPT is $e, which represents the Esc character.

For a complete list of all the meta-characters supported by PROMPT, refer to the PROMPT entry in Part IV, "The Complete DOS 6 Command Reference."

Using the same example discussed earlier, you could change the text foreground color to brown by entering the following command:

```
prompt $e[33m
```

Although ANSI.SYS correctly intercepts the commands, this approach does have an irritating drawback: It changes the system prompt, usually to a null (or characterless) prompt. After using PROMPT to send ANSI.SYS one or more instructions, call PROMPT again to reset the DOS prompt. The following batch file, ANSIPRMT.BAT, makes life a little easier. It saves the old prompt in a batch file and then restores it after the ANSI.SYS instructions are processed:

```
@echo off
set|find "PROMPT" > oldprmpt.bat
:LOOP
if "%1"=="" goto stop
prompt $e[%1
@echo on
echo.
@echo off
shift
goto loop
:STOP
call oldprmpt
del oldprmpt.bat
```

Again, don't worry if some of the batch file statements seem like Greek to you. All will be revealed in Chapter 10.

If you know the system's default prompt, you can simplify matters by adding the default prompt settings to the end of the ANSI.SYS commands. For example, if you normally use the pg prompt, which displays the current directory as the prompt, you can set the color to brown and reset the prompt to normal in one command, as follows:

```
prompt $e[33m$p$g
```

Sending multiple escape sequences

You do not need to confine each ANSI.SYS instruction to a single line. You can send multiple instructions on a single line by preceding each new instruction with the standard Esc[sequence.

After changing the foreground color to brown, you can clear the screen by using the 2J command as follows:

```
@echo off
echo ←[33m
echo ←[2J
```

Alternatively, you can combine the two commands into a single statement:

```
@echo off
echo ←[33m←[2J
```

The letters used in ANSI.SYS commands are case sensitive. If you enter the 2J sequence as 2j, the screen does not clear.

Determining whether ANSI.SYS is loaded

If ANSI.SYS is not installed, DOS does not react very gracefully to all the obscure escape sequences. Although nothing untoward happens, the escape code gibberish is written to the screen and looks very unprofessional. A sophisticated display screen that relies on ANSI.SYS to change colors and attributes, position the cursor, and redefine keys looks dreadful if ANSI.SYS is not installed. If you write a batch file that uses ANSI.SYS features, you must check to see whether ANSI.SYS is loaded.

With earlier versions of DOS, you had to write a program, using DEBUG or another programming language, to determine whether ANSI.SYS was installed in memory. Thanks to the introduction of the MEM /M switch, this is no longer necessary. DOS displays the details of where ANSI.SYS is installed in memory if you enter the following command:

```
mem /m ansi
```

If ANSI.SYS is not installed, the program responds with the following message:

```
ansi is not currently in memory.
```

You can use FIND to search for the output "not currently" and then test FIND's ERRORLEVEL to determine whether ANSI.SYS is or is not installed.

The following batch file, ANSIOK.BAT, displays a message that indicates whether ANSI.SYS is installed:

```
@echo off
mem /m ansi|find "not currently" /i > nul
if errorlevel 1 goto loaded
:NOTLOADED
echo ANSI.SYS is not in memory
goto quit
:LOADED
echo ANSI.SYS is loaded
rem Insert your ANSI statements here

:QUIT
```

You also can employ the technique of using MEM /M together with FIND to test whether any specific program, such as Share, Windows, or DOSKEY, is loaded in memory. The approach is explored in detail in Chapter 10.

You can improve the ANSICODE.BAT file discussed earlier by adding a test to determine whether ANSI.SYS is loaded, as follows:

```
@echo off
mem /m ansi|find "not currently" /i > nul
if errorlevel 1 goto loaded
:NOTLOADED
echo ANSI.SYS is not in memory
goto quit
:LOADED
:LOOP
if "%1" == "" goto quit
echo ←[%1
shift
goto loop
:QUIT
```

Jazzing Up the Display

You just learned a half-dozen ways to set the text color to brown. You will, no doubt, be pleased to hear that you can do a lot more. For example, you can set the foreground and background colors of the text, write any characters in any

The History of ANSI Commands

You might be wondering who dreamed up the awkward notion of sending commands to the screen by using obscure character sequences that can't even be typed on the command line. It was the American National Standards Institute (ANSI). In fairness to ANSI, however, I should explain that these commands were standardized long before DOS came on the scene.

The commands were drawn up primarily for the benefit of mini- and mainframe computers. When CRTs (monitors) were first implemented on the larger computers, they basically behaved like paper-fed terminals. The typical workstation was just a CRT and a keyboard, with no independent computational capability. The primary role of these workstations was to display computer prompts and send keyboard input to the main computer. Such workstations were often called

dumb terminals. Everything was drawn on a line-by-line basis, and old commands just scrolled off the top of the screen — no support was provided for full-screen editing or data entry. The ANSI standards defined a command set that allowed the CRT to behave like a full-screen terminal rather than a line-oriented Teletype. I, for one, was excited at the time.

The latest ANSI command set was ratified in 1979 and is called *ANSI standard X3.64.* Similar standards were implemented for printers in order to standardize such commands as line feed and form feed.

The ANSI.SYS device driver implements the screen-related commands that were originally developed for the mini- and mainframe dumb terminals.

position on the screen, and change the display attribute of any text to bold, blink, and reverse video.

Setting foreground and background colors

You can set the foreground and background display colors using the m command set. The syntax of the command is as follows:

```
Esc[codem
```

You replace the variable *code* with a two-digit number identifying the desired color. Table 6-1 lists all the valid color codes.

The following batch file sets the display color to cyan text on a blue background:

```
@echo off
echo ←[36m
echo ←[44m
```

If you are entering multiple m commands, you can issue them in one instruction by using the following syntax:

```
Esc[code;code; ...m
```

For example, the following line from a batch file sets the display colors to black text on a green background:

```
echo ←[30;42m
```

Table 6-1	ANSI.SYS Display Codes	
Color	*Foreground Code*	*Background Code*
Black	30	40
Red	31	41
Green	32	42
Brown	33	43
Blue	34	44
Magenta	35	45
Cyan	36	46
Light gray	37	47

Setting display attributes

The ANSI.SYS m command provides a set of single-digit codes for changing the text display attribute. Table 6-2 lists the valid codes.

The most commonly used attribute code is 1, which changes the dull default colors into bright high-intensity colors; brown becomes yellow, light gray becomes bright white, etc.

When executed, the following batch file, ANSIATTR.BAT, illustrates each of the attribute effects:

```
@echo off
echo ←[2J
echo ←[0m All attributes off
echo ←[0;1m Bright intensity
echo ←[0;4m Underline (monochrome systems only)
echo ←[0;5m Blinking text
echo ←[0;7m Reverse Video
echo ←[0;8m Hidden or invisible
echo ←[1;33m
```

The attribute 8m hides the text and the cursor. If this is the last command in the batch file, the system prompt and the cursor are invisible after the batch file finishes. This is a useful trick in some instances — for example, when you want to suppress the display of program or batch file activity. The preceding ANSIATTR.BAT batch file, however, sets the text foreground color to yellow (bright brown) before terminating.

Table 6-2	ANSI.SYS Display Attribute Codes
Code	**Attribute**
0	All attributes off
1	Bright intensity
4	Underline (monochrome systems only)
5	Blinking text
7	Reverse video
8	Hidden or invisible

Positioning the cursor

Every PC programming language provides ways to write text in any color at any location on the screen. Normally, DOS positions the cursor at the line following an ECHO statement, making it impossible to write text on lines above the cursor without clearing the screen first. Impossible, that is, unless ANSI.SYS is installed.

The ANSI.SYS H commands support the positioning of the cursor anywhere on the display. After you position the cursor, any subsequent text you enter with the ECHO command is written to the display starting at the cursor location.

The syntax of the H command is as follows:

```
Esc[row;colH
```

The *row* variable is the row or line number, starting with 1 at the top of the screen and ending with 25, 43, or 50 at the bottom. The *col* parameter is the column or X coordinate, starting with 1 at the left and ending with 40 or 80 at the right.

The following batch file writes a string to the top right corner of the display:

```
@echo off
echo ←[1;69HPretty Neat
```

The only problem with this batch file is that the cursor remains at the top of the display. After the batch file finishes, the DOS prompt rests at the top of the display, in the middle of old commands. Very ugly.

Two more ANSI.SYS commands can resolve this problem. The s command saves the current cursor position, and the u command moves the cursor back to the position it held when the last s command was executed.

The following batch file, WRITEAT.BAT, provides a generic routine for writing text at any location on the screen and then returns the cursor to its prior location:

```
@echo off
if "%1"=="" goto quit
echo ←[s
echo ←[%1;%2H%3 %4 %5 %6 %7 %8 %9
echo ←[u
:QUIT
```

In addition to the position, save, and restore commands, ANSI.SYS also supports column- and row-based cursor movement commands relative to the active cursor position. Table 6-3 summarizes all the cursor-related commands supported by ANSI.SYS.

Table 6-3	ANSI.SYS Cursor Control Codes	
Escape Sequence	*Description*	*Action*
Esc[*row*;*col*H	Absolute	Moves the cursor to the specific row and column. If only one value is specified (without a semicolon), it is assumed to represent the column, and the row defaults to 1.
Esc[s	Save	Saves the active cursor position.
Esc[u	Restore	Repositions the cursor to the position it occupied when the last s (save) command was issued.
Esc[*pos*A	Up	Moves the cursor up the number of rows specified by the *pos* variable. The cursor stops when it reaches the first row.
Esc[*pos*B	Down	Moves the cursor down *pos* rows. The cursor stops when it reaches the last row.
Esc[*pos*C	Right	Moves the cursor to the right *pos* columns. The cursor stops when it reaches the last column.
Esc[*pos*D	Left	Moves the cursor left *pos* columns. The cursor stops when it reaches the first column.

Note: The f command has the same meaning and syntax as the H command for moving the cursor to a specific address.

Pulling it all together

By giving you the ability to change colors and attributes, position the cursor, and write text, ANSI.SYS provides all the tools you need to create a very snazzy and professional display. These displays are well suited to batch files for help systems, menus, and the like.

The following statements are extracted from the batch file, ANSISET.BAT, which is a derivative of ANSICODE.BAT, discussed earlier:

```
@echo off
if "%1"=="?" goto help
if "%1"=="/?" goto help
mem /m ansi | find "not currently" /i > nul
if errorlevel 1 goto loaded
:NOTLOADED
echo ANSI.SYS is not in memory
goto quit
```

```
:LOADED
:LOOP
if "%1" == "" goto quit
echo ←[%1m
shift
goto loop
:HELP
rem Clear the screen with a blue background and draw banner
echo ←[1;37;44m←[2J
echo ←[2;23H ┌─────────────────────────────────┐
echo ←[3;23H | ←[3;54H |
echo ←[4;23H └─────────────────────────────────┘
echo ←[3;29HAnsiSet On-Line Help
echo ←[3;25H←[0;35;44m♦←[37;44m♦←[36;44m♦
echo ←[3;50H←[0;36;44m♦←[37;44m♦←[35;44m♦
rem Draw Box shadow
echo ←[5;24H←[0;30;44m█████████████████████████
echo ←[3;55H█←[4;55H█
echo ←[1;37;44m
echo ←[7;10H┌──────────────────────────────────────┐
echo ←[8;10H║ ←[59C∫
echo ←[9;10H║ ←[59C∫
echo ←[10;10H║ ←[59C∫
echo ←[11;10H║ ←[59C∫
echo ←[12;10H║ ←[59C∫
echo ←[13;10H║ ←[59C∫
echo ←[14;10H║ ←[59C∫
echo ←[15;10H║ ←[59C∫
echo ←[16;10H║ ←[59C∫
echo ←[17;10H║ ←[59C∫
echo ←[18;10H║ ←[59C∫
echo ←[19;10H║ ←[59C∫
echo ←[20;10H└──────────────────────────────────────┘
echo ←[1;33;44m←[8;12HEnter one of the following codes to change the display
echo ←[9;12Hcolors of the DOS Session:
echo ←[11;20H←[1;37;44mColor        Code Fgnd.   Code Bgnd.
echo ←[12;20H←[0;30;44mBlack          30           40
echo ←[13;20H←[0;31;44mRed            31           41
echo ←[14;20H←[0;32;44mGreen          32           42
echo ←[15;20H←[0;33;44mBrown          33           43
```

```
echo ←[16;20H←[0;34;40mBlue          34        44
echo ←[17;20H←[0;35;44mMagenta       35        45
echo ←[17;20H←[0;36;44mCyan          36        46
echo ←[17;20H←[0;37;44mLightgray     37        47
echo ←[22;13H←[1;37;44m
echo ←[22;54H←[1;37;44m
echo ←[22;28H←[5;36;44mPress any key to continue
rem Wait for a key
pause > nul
rem Position cursor at bottom of screen, set colors, and quit
echo ←[23;1H←[0;1;37;44m
:QUIT
```

The code creates a fancy help screen that is displayed if the user executes the batch file with the /? or ? switch. Figure 6-1 shows the display that is generated when this batch file is executed.

The preceding batch file, along with all the others mentioned in the book, are included on the Bob's Shareware Collection disks. Run it for yourself to see the kind of colorful effects you can create.

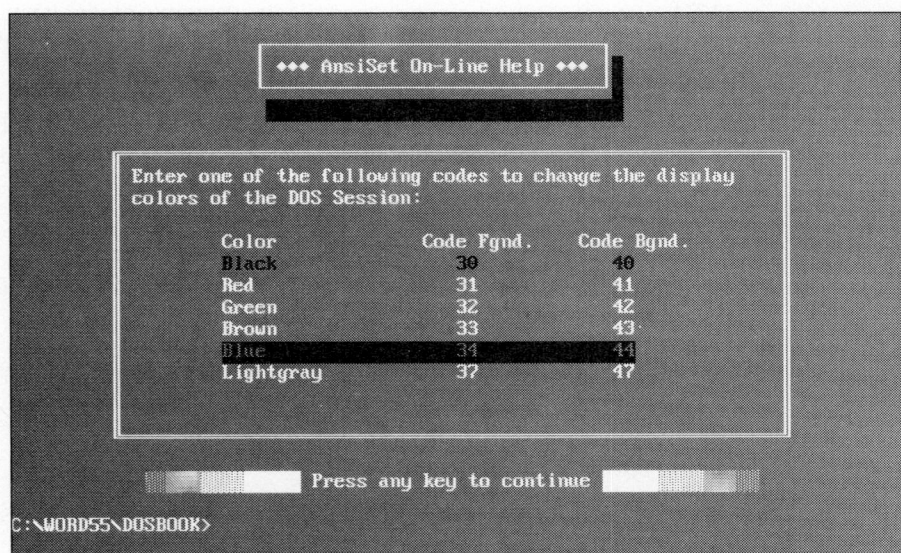

Figure 6-1: The help screen that appears when ANSISET.BAT is executed with the /? switch.

Creating fancy prompts

You can use ANSI.SYS escape codes to colorize your system prompt. As a Houston resident, I consider it my unwritten duty to use the infamous Texas Lone Star flag as an example.

The following prompt statement (located in TEXAS.BAT) is mandatory in Texas:

```
@echo off
PROMPT $e←[0;44m*$e←[41m|$e←[40;36m $p$g $e←[1;33;40m
```

The Californian bear prompt is not quite as easy!

You Bill the Cat lovers will enjoy the following prompt (located in BILLCAT.BAT):

```
@echo off
prompt $e[6C/$b$_    \'o.0'$_
$q(___)$q$_$e[1;5;31mU$e[0;37m$_ACK!PFFTTT!$_$P$G
```

Changing Display Lines and Modes

More and more PCs are using EGA and VGA display systems. Because these EGA and VGA systems support a condensed display, capable of displaying 43 or 50 lines of text, respectively, Microsoft enhanced ANSI.SYS (starting with DOS 5) to support them.

To set your PC to run DOS in Condensed Mode, you execute the MODE command (ANSI.SYS must be installed). The syntax of the MODE command for changing the display lines is as follows:

```
mode con: lines=xx
```

The *xx* parameter represents the desired number of display lines and can have the value 25, 43, or, on VGA systems, 50.

The following batch file, SET43.BAT, sets the display to 43-line mode:

```
@echo off
mem /m ansi|find "not currently" /i > nul
if errorlevel 1 goto loaded
:NOTLOADED
echo ANSI.SYS is not in memory
goto quit
:LOADED
mode con: lines=43
:QUIT
```

You also can use the MODE command to set the number of characters per line to 40 or 80. Refer to Part IV, "The Complete DOS 6 Command Reference," for further details.

You can use the ANSI.SYS =h command to set any of the display modes listed in Table 6-4.

The odd entry in Table 6-4 is the =7h entry, which enables line wrapping. It is the complement to the =7l (lowercase L) command, which disables line wrapping.

When line wrapping is disabled, any text that extends beyond the right edge of the display is not displayed. With line wrapping enabled, however, the text is written at the beginning of the next line. The following batch file, LINEWRAP.BAT, illustrates the use of the line wrapping commands:

```
@echo off
echo ←[1;37;41m←[2J
echo ←[=7l
echo ←[2;70HThis is too long to fit
echo ←[=7h
echo ←[5;70HThis is too long to fit
echo ←[20;1H
```

Table 6-4	ANSI.SYS Display Mode Control Codes
Escape Sequence	**Description**
Esc[=0h	Text — monochrome, 40 columns by 25 lines
Esc[=1h	Text — color, 40 columns by 25 lines
Esc[=2h	Text — monochrome, 80 columns by 25 lines
Esc[=3h	Text — color, 80 columns by 25 lines
Esc[=4h	Graphics — 4-color, 320 by 200 pixels
Esc[=5h	Graphics — monochrome, 320 by 200 pixels
Esc[=6h	Graphics — monochrome, 640 by 200 pixels
Esc[=7h	Enables line wrapping
Esc[=13h	Graphics — color, 320 by 200 pixels
Esc[=14h	Graphics — 16-color, 640 by 200 pixels
Esc[=15h	Graphics — monochrome, 640 by 350 pixels
Esc[=16h	Graphics — 16-color, 640 by 350 pixels
Esc[=17h	Graphics — monochrome, 640 by 480 pixels
Esc[=18h	Graphics — 16-color, 640 by 480 pixels
Esc[=19h	Graphics — 256-color, 320 by 200 pixels

Figure 6-2: ANSI.SYS allows line wrapping to be turned on and off. The top right line was written with wrapping off and is truncated. The line below was written with wrapping on, and so the text spills over to the beginning of the next line.

Figure 6-2 shows the display generated by the batch file.

Disabled line wrapping has an eccentric feature: Characters that extend beyond the right of the screen are all written (in turn) to the rightmost character position. Notice in Figure 6-2 that the first line displays the string This is tot. The last character, *t*, is actually the character from the end of the original string — it's the *t* from *fit*.

Customizing the Keyboard

One of the most valuable features of ANSI.SYS is its capacity to remap keys and assign commands (or strings) to keys. For example, using ANSI.SYS, you can reverse the arrangement of the semicolon and colon keys, assign the HELP command to the F1 key, assign the EDIT command to F2, and so on.

Key codes

The key (pun intended) to using ANSI.SYS to customize the keyboard is knowing the scan codes for each key. Each keystroke you type is identified by a one- or two-digit *scan code*. The uppercase J has a single-byte scan code value of 74, for instance, and the F10 key has a two-byte scan code of 0 and 69. Most of the special or nonalphanumeric keys are assigned two-byte scan codes, with the first byte having a value of 0.

Understanding the Mechanics of Scan Codes

The keyboard unit includes a keyboard controller, which is responsible for monitoring and reporting keyboard activity. When you press a key on the keyboard, two events are reported: the key being pressed and the key being released. Each key is assigned two codes, with one code representing the key press and the other representing the key release. These single-byte codes are sometimes referred to as the *make code* and the *break code,* respectively. The make code for the J key is 24h, and the break code is A4h.

Although most keys generate single-byte codes, some of the new extended keys generate double-byte codes. A code of E0h indicates that an extended key was pressed, and a second code indicates the specific key. For example, the gray PgUp key on the extended keypad is identified by the byte pair E0h and 49h; the gray Home key has the byte pair E0h and 47h. Each physical key on the keyboard has a unique code.

When you press or release a key, the keyboard controller generates interrupt 9h, which advises the microprocessor that keyboard activity is taking place. The interrupt handler for interrupt 9h is in ROM-BIOS. This interrupt handler interprets the stream of bytes and then converts the codes into two-byte scan codes, which identify the key.

Before making the conversion, the interrupt handler must check the status of the three shift keys (Ctrl, Alt, and Shift) and the toggle keys (Caps Lock and Num Lock). The status of these special keys is recorded in ROM-BIOS at location 0040:0017. This enables the system to assign different scan codes based on the status of the shift and toggle keys. For example, the interrupt handler might receive two separate codes, 24h followed by A4h, indicating that the J key was pressed and released. The interrupt handler then checks the status of the shift keys and the Caps Lock key to determine whether J, j, Ctrl-J, or Alt-J should be returned as the scan code.

 In Chapter 11, you learn how to write compact utilities for checking and setting the data at memory location 0040:0017. Using these utilities, you can set the value of the Caps Lock and Num Lock keys. In a batch file, you can test whether the Alt key is pressed and, if so, skip past confirmation prompts, suppress the display of messages, or perform other useful tasks.

After making the translation, the ROM-BIOS interrupt handler places the scan codes into the keyboard buffer, which is located at memory address 0040:001E. Programs (including DOS) access this buffer to determine user input.

During the translation process, the interrupt handler looks for one of the following four special key combinations: Ctrl-Alt-Del, Shift-PrtScr, Ctrl-Num Lock, and Ctrl-Break. When one of these key sequences occurs, ROM-BIOS immediately invokes an interrupt to alert the microprocessor instead of placing the keystrokes into the keyboard buffer.

All that for a simple key press. *Phew!*

Note: The subject of interrupts and interrupt handlers is discussed in detail in the next chapter.

When using ANSI.SYS to manage the keyboard, you must specify the key you want to redefine or modify. When you specify two-byte codes, separate each byte with a semicolon. Table 6-5 details all the scan codes supported by ANSI.SYS.

Table 6-5	ANSI.SYS Keyboard Control Codes			
Key	**Standard**	**With Shift**	**With Ctrl**	**With Alt**
A	97	65	1	0;30
B	98	66	2	0;48
C	99	67	3	0;46
D	100	68	4	0;32
E	101	69	5	0;18
F	102	70	6	0;33
G	103	71	7	0;34
H	104	72	8	0;35
I	105	73	9	0;23
J	106	74	10	0;36
K	107	75	11	0;37
L	108	76	12	0;38
M	109	77	13	0;50
N	110	78	14	0;49
O	111	79	15	0;24
P	112	80	16	0;25
Q	113	81	17	0;16
R	114	82	18	0;19
S	115	83	19	0;31
T	116	84	20	0;20
U	117	85	21	0;22
V	118	86	22	0;47
W	119	87	23	0;17
X	120	88	24	0;45
Y	121	89	25	0;21
Z	122	90	26	0;44
1	49	33	N/A	0;120
2	50	64	0	0;121

(continued)

Table 6-5 ANSI.SYS Keyboard Control Codes *(continued)*				
Key	*Standard*	*With Shift*	*With Ctrl*	*With Alt*
3	51	35	N/A	0;122
4	52	36	N/A	0;123
5	53	37	N/A	0;124
6	54	94	30	0;125
7	55	38	N/A	0;126
8	56	42	N/A	0;126
9	57	40	N/A	0;127
0	48	41	N/A	0;129
-	45	95	31	0;130
=	61	43	N/A	0;131
[	91	123	27	0;26
]	93	125	29	0;27
Spacebar	92	124	28	0;43
;	59	58	N/A	0;39
'	39	34	N/A	0;40
,	44	60	N/A	0;51
.	46	62	N/A	0;52
/	47	63	N/A	0;53
`	96	126	N/A	0;41
Enter (keypad)	13	N/A	10	0;166
/ (keypad)	47	47	0;142	0;74
* (keypad)	42	0;144	0;78	N/A
- (keypad)	45	45	0;149	0;164
+ (keypad)	43	43	0;150	0;55
5 (keypad)	0;76	53	0;143	N/A
F1	0;59	0;84	0;94	0;104
F2	0;60	0;85	0;95	0;105
F3	0;61	0;86	0;96	0;106
F4	0;62	0;87	0;97	0;107
F5	0;63	0;88	0;98	0;108
F6	0;64	0;89	0;99	0;109

(continued)

Table 6-5   ANSI.SYS Keyboard Control Codes (continued)

Key	Standard	With Shift	With Ctrl	With Alt
F7	0;65	0;90	0;100	0;110
F8	0;66	0;91	0;101	0;111
F9	0;67	0;92	0;102	0;112
F10	0;68	0;93	0;103	0;113
F11	0;133	0;135	0;137	0;139
F12	0;134	0;136	0;138	0;140
Home	0;71	55	0;119	N/A
Up arrow	0;72	56	0;141	N/A
PgUp	0;73	57	0;132	N/A
Left arrow	0;75	52	0;115	N/A
Right arrow	0;77	54	0;116	N/A
End	0;79	49	0;117	N/A
Down arrow	0;80	50	0;145	N/A
PgDn	0;81	51	0;118	N/A
Insert	0;82	48	0;146	N/A
Delete	0;83	46	0;147	N/A
Print Screen	N/A	N/A	0;114	N/A
Pause	N/A	N/A	0;0	N/A
Backspace	8	8	127	0
Enter	13	N/A	10	0
Tab	9	0;5	0;148	0;165
Home (gray key)	224;71	224;71	224;119	224;151
Up arrow (gray key)	224;72	224;72	224;141	224;152
PgUp (gray key)	224;73	224;73	224;132	224;153
Left arrow (gray key)	224;75	224;75	224;115	224;155
Right arrow (gray key)	224;77	224;77	224;116	224;157
End (gray key)	224;79	224;79	224;117	224;159
Down arrow (gray key)	224;80	224;80	224;145	224;154
PgDn (gray key)	224;81	224;81	224;118	224;161
Ins (gray key)	224;82	224;82	224;146	224;162
Del (gray key)	224;83	224;83	224;147	224;163

Notice that key combinations share the same codes as some single keys. Ctrl-H is the same as the Backspace key, for example. Try entering a command at the DOS prompt and press Ctrl-H; the previous character is removed, as if you pressed Backspace. Furthermore, some key combinations are not supported. DOS does not support Shift-Enter, for instance.

How to remap keys

By using the ANSI.SYS p command, you can reassign the meaning of a key. The syntax of the p command is as follows:

    Esc[*keycode*;*newcode*p

Replace the *keycode* variable with the scan code for the key you want to redefine. The *newcode* parameter represents the replacement key code. (Other uses of the p command are discussed in the next section.)

Here's an example: You can swap the semicolon and the colon keys so that the colon is the unshifted key and the semicolon is the shifted key. If you refer back to Table 6-5, you can see that the semicolon has the value 59, and the colon (which is normally Shift-semicolon) has the value 58. The following batch file, SWAPSEMI.BAT, swaps these keys:

```
@echo off
echo ←[59;58p
echo ←[58;59p
```

If the key is a standard ASCII keyboard character (that is, not an Alt or a Ctrl key combination, a function key, etc.), you can specify the key as a string instead of specifying the scan or ASCII code. Using string literals rather than scan codes makes a batch file much clearer. For example, you could write the batch file in the preceding example as follows:

```
@echo off
echo ←[';';':'p
echo ←[':';';'p
```

Usually, when you use ANSI.SYS to change keystrokes, only the characters typed at the command line are affected. Most programs, including EDIT, ignore such reassignments. Shucks.

How to assign strings or commands to keys

You can use the p command to assign more than one character or keystroke to a key. You can specify multicharacter strings and ASCII code, provided that each entry is separated by a semicolon. The following ANSI.SYS command, for example, assigns the string *apple* to the uppercase A key:

```
echo ←['A';'Apple'p
```

When uppercase A is pressed, *Apple* is written to the keyboard buffer. It's best to avoid mapping the standard characters, such as letters of the alphabet and numbers because doing so can result in a lot of frustration. Imagine typing *A:* and seeing *Apple:* appear on the display.

The function keys, along with the Alt- and Ctrl- key combinations are good candidates for reassignment. The following batch file assigns the DOS HELP command to the F1 function key:

```
@echo off
echo ←[0;59;'help';13p
```

The 0;59 entry identifies the key to be remapped — F1. When F1 is pressed, ANSI.SYS substitutes the letters *help* followed by 13, which is the code for the Enter key. After the assignment is made, pressing F1 is the same as pressing the four characters *h,e,l,* and *p,* and then pressing Enter.

Similarly, the following batch file remaps the F2 key to launch EDIT:

```
@echo off
echo ←[0;60;'edit';13p
```

Do not assign more than 200 characters to a single key. ANSI.SYS only allocates 200 bytes for the key buffer. If you assign more characters, they have a nasty habit of overriding COMMAND.COM code. When this occurs, the system hangs, forcing a reboot.

A simple but effective antitampering device is to remap the Enter key when your system boots and then assign an unmap function to a secret key. The following extract from AUTOEXEC.BAT illustrates the approach:

```
echo ←[13;8p
echo ←[24;13p
echo ←[0;133;'prompt $e[13;13p$p$g';13;13p
echo ←[0;134;'prompt $e[13;8p$e[2J';13;13p
```

The first line assigns the Backspace function to the Enter key. When someone presses Enter, all that happens is that the last character on the command line is deleted. The second line assigns the Enter function to Ctrl-X; when you want to enter a command, you just press Ctrl-X.

The third line assigns to the F11 key a prompt command that reassigns the Enter command to the Enter key. After the system boots, you press F11 to set everything back to normal. The F12 key is assigned a prompt command that sets the Enter key as Backspace again. If you want to leave your office for a few minutes, you simply press F12. The Enter key is remapped, the screen is cleared, and the prompt disappears. When you return, press F11 and you are back in business. It's far from foolproof, but it deters the casual snoop.

Going Beyond ANSI.SYS

The idea of providing a device driver to enhance the keyboard and display is a good one. But, with its roots in dumb mainframe terminals, ANSI.SYS doesn't go far enough. The folks at Hersey Micro Consulting Inc. developed an excellent replacement for ANSI.SYS, which is called FANSI-Console. Like ANSI.SYS, FANSI-Console provides a device driver (called FCONSOLE.DEV) that supports all the ANSI.SYS codes and a whole lot more.

FANSI-Console offers a variety of additional keyboard and display options, some of which follow:

- Sets the screen into super-dense mode, which supports up to 60 lines on VGA systems and even 50 lines on CGA

- Dramatically increases the screen-drawing speed

- Increases the size of the keyboard type-ahead buffer to 255 characters

- Supports a single-finger typing mode. Ideal for handicapped users, this mode enables the Ctrl and Alt keys to act as toggles affecting the next key typed. For example, you press the Alt key once and then press the X for Alt-X instead of holding down Alt and pressing X simultaneously.

- Sets Caps Lock to work as it does on a standard typewriter, where the Caps Lock key is disabled the next time the standard Shift key is pressed

- Provides a tactile clicking sound when keys are pressed

- Through a feature called *scroll recall,* enables you to look at text (such as output from DIR) that scrolled off the screen

- Enables keyboard reassignments to function within programs such as EDIT as well as on the command line

Because a Shareware version of FANSI-Console is included on Bob's Shareware Collection disk set, you can try it out for yourself.

Summary

This chapter explained ways to use ANSI.SYS to enhance the display and keyboard. You learned the following points:

▶ You must load ANSI.SYS in CONFIG.SYS using the DEVICE or DEVICEHIGH statements.

▶ You send commands to ANSI.SYS using a special two-character signature that comprises the Esc and [characters. You communicate commands via the ECHO, PROMPT, or TYPE commands.

▶ When writing batch files to communicate with ANSI.SYS, you should use the MEM and FIND commands to first ascertain whether ANSI.SYS is loaded in memory.

▶ Using the m command, you can control the foreground and background display colors and display attributes.

▶ ANSI.SYS provides commands for positioning the cursor as well as for saving and subsequently restoring the cursor position.

▶ Although you can use the p command to redefine the purpose of keys and assign commands to keys, be careful not to assign more than 200 characters to a key.

More and more devices are being incorporated into PCs, and more and more compatibility issues are surfacing. Chapter 7 explores the ways that hardware devices use IRQs, DMA channels, and the bus to integrate with the main system.

Chapter 7

Juggling IRQs, DMAs, Buses, Device Drivers, and Other "What's Its"

In This Chapter

▶ Looking under the hood

▶ Understanding interrupts and IRQ conflicts

▶ Understanding DMA

▶ Deciding which bus is best: ISA, MCA, or EISA

▶ Deciphering device drivers

Looking under the Hood

Back in the good old days, computer users were blissfully ignorant of the PC's inner workings. They just installed the software and it worked. The most challenging task was to configure the dip switches on a new internal card to make sure that they were configured to use a unique LPT or COM port. Boy, have things changed.

With the constant desire to push PC hardware to its limits, conservative standards have been usurped, and everyone is getting "down to the metal" and accessing hardware directly. The latest software and hardware products do whatever it takes to get the best performance, such as bypass BIOS and access PC components directly. Although the upside is improved performance and greater capabilities, the downside is greater complexity and increased hardware conflicts.

Most PCs are now more than mere word processors and calculators. You can configure them with fax cards, modems, scanners, digitized tablets, tape-drive units, CD-ROMs, speakers, two monitors, sound cards, and network cards. With this array of hardware, it's no wonder that you have to look "under the hood" and understand how a PC uses IRQs and how DMAs and other mechanisms work to ensure that one product does not conflict with another.

Understanding Interrupts and IRQ Conflicts ___

The brain of the personal computer is the *microprocessor,* or *central processing unit (CPU).* The microprocessor differs from most of the other chips on the system board because it can perform numerical computations.

The early Intel microprocessors were not adept at performing high-speed floating-point computations. Many users of math-intensive software (such as spreadsheet and CAD applications) installed a math (or numeric) coprocessor to improve performance. Software written to take advantage of the math coprocessor can instruct the microprocessor to pass floating-point calculations to the math coprocessor; it in turn returns the result. With the introduction of the 80486 microprocessor, Intel incorporated the math coprocessor into the main microprocessor chip.

Another unique feature of the microprocessor chip is that it is the system board's grand marshall: It controls the communications on the system board by passing data and signals to and from other devices.

Because many of the ancillary computing tasks are performed by supporting *controller* chips, the microprocessor can focus on the primary management and computational tasks. Some controllers are dedicated to serving the disk drives and the keyboard, for example, and some I/O controllers manage input and output to external devices. The organization is similar to an operating room, in which the microprocessor is the surgeon and many important (but subordinate) functions are performed by the support team, such as the anesthesiologist, the equipment technician, and nurses.

Interrupting the microprocessor

The microprocessor must be notified when certain events occur or when a device needs attention. When you press the Ctrl-Break key combination, for example, the keyboard controller must inform the microprocessor immediately. Similarly, if you receive a fax while you are recalculating a spreadsheet, the microprocessor must ensure that the data coming in through a serial port can be saved to disk. These signals to the microprocessor for attention are called *interrupts.* Hundreds of interrupts can occur every second (even more interruptions than an author gets).

Interrupts are classified in two major categories: *hardware* and *software.* A hardware interrupt is generated by the microprocessor, another chip, or a device that needs the microprocessor's attention. Disk drive, keyboard, and system timer controllers all generate hardware interrupts. As its name suggests, a software interrupt is generated by a program. *Software interrupts* provide ways for a program to interact with DOS and ROM BIOS.

Interrupt vectors

When a microprocessor is interrupted, it must suspend its current task, save all the data stored in the registers, and respond to the interrupt. When the interruption has been serviced, the saved data is restored to the registers, and the original task resumes.

The data saved before a hardware interrupt is serviced is stored on the stack. Every time a hardware interrupt occurs, DOS allocates a stack from a stack pool. With the potential for hundreds of interrupts per second, DOS can run out of stacks, or a stack can run out of space and generate a *stack overflow.* If you encounter these problems, use the STACKS command in CONFIG.SYS to increase the number and size of the interrupt stacks. See Part IV, "The Complete DOS 6 Command Reference," for more details about the STACKS command.

Every interrupt, whether it is a hardware interrupt or a software interrupt, is assigned a unique interrupt number. Instead of every interrupt shouting "Oy!" to get the CPU's attention, the interrupt shouts its assigned interrupt number ("Interrupt 10!" for example). When the microprocessor is interrupted, the code at a specific address (known as the *interrupt vector*) is executed. In Chapter 11, you learn how to use DEBUG, for example, to change the cursor shape by calling interrupt 10h (16 decimal). The code invoked in response to an interrupt is known as an *interrupt service routine,* or ISR.

Interrupt vectors can be redirected to point to different vectors. This technique is known as *installing an interrupt handler.* Normally, when a DOS critical error occurs, for example, an interrupt 24 is generated and DOS invokes the code that displays the infamous message to choose Abort, Retry, or Fail. By redirecting interrupt 24 to some custom code, you can avoid the ugly message and handle the error more gracefully. This approach is used in Chapter 11 to test whether a disk is in drive A without generating a critical-error message.

 Every interrupt has a corresponding interrupt vector that is the *segment:offset* of the code that is executed when the interrupt occurs. The area of memory that stores the table of interrupt addresses is known as the *interrupt vector table.* At boot time, BIOS sets the location of the interrupt vector table to the beginning of RAM at address 0000:0000. The vector table contains one record for every interrupt, starting with interrupt 0 (CPU division by zero), followed by interrupt 1 (single-step execution), and so on. Every record in the table contains two words (a *word* is an unsigned integer that occupies two bytes of memory). The first word is the vector offset, and the second word is the vector segment. When an interrupt occurs, the corresponding record in the interrupt vector table is accessed, the offset value is loaded into the IP register, and the segment value is loaded into the CS register.

Not all entries in the interrupt vector table point to executable code. Some vectors point to data structures. Interrupt 41h, for example, points to the fixed disk drive parameter table.

Interrupt request lines

Electronic anarchy would occur if the microprocessor had to handle every interrupt immediately. A special support chip, the *programmable interrupt controller (PIC),* is responsible for managing hardware interrupts. The PIC manages the queue of hardware interrupts and passes them one at a time to the CPU.

Every hardware device that needs to interrupt the microprocessor must be assigned an *interrupt request line,* often called an IRQ. The interrupt request line is a direct line to the PIC from the hardware device. In the original PC and XT systems, the PIC could accommodate a maximum of only 8 different IRQs; when the 80286-based systems were introduced, two PIC chips were used to expand this limit to 15.

If you think that 8, or even 15, IRQs is not a sufficient number, you're right. In addition to standard devices, such as the hard disk controller, the math coprocessor, the video system, IO ports, and the real-time clock, additional hardware devices, such as a fax card, mouse, sound board, and scanner, also want an IRQ.

Over time, de facto standards for assigning IRQs have evolved. Tables 7-1 and 7-2 show these standard IRQ assignments for 8086 and 80286+ systems, respectively.

Table 7-1	IRQ Assignments for 8086-/8088-Based Systems
IRQ	**Device Description**
0	IRQ timer
1	Keyboard
2	IRQ cascade
3	COM2
4	COM1
5	Hard disk controller
6	Floppy disk controller
7	LPT1

Table 7-2	IRQ Assignments for 80286-Based Systems and Higher	
IRQ	**Device Description**
0	IRQ timer
1	Keyboard
2	IRQ cascade
3	COM2 and COM4, or bus mouse
4	COM1 and COM3
5	LPT2
6	Floppy disk controller
7	LPT1
8	Real-time clock
9	Remapped IRQ from IRQ2
10	Available
11	Available
12	Mouse (on IBM PS/2 systems)
13	Math coprocessor
14	Hard disk controller
15	Available

TECHNICAL STUFF

Connecting Two Interrupt Controllers

The programmable interrupt controller used in the original PCs and XTs was Intel's 8259A controller chip. Two 8259A chips are used in 80286+ systems, in which the first chip's IRQ2 line is redirected from the system bus to the second 8259A interrupt controller, and the real IRQ2 line is redirected to IRQ9. All interrupts received by the second controller are passed to the first controller by way of IRQ2 and then are passed to the microprocessor.

On PC and XT systems, the order of the IRQ numbers controls the interrupt priority. IRQ0 has a higher priority than IRQ1, and so on, through to IRQ7, with the lowest priority. The situation is a little more complicated on 80286+ systems. Because all interrupts on the second chip are redirected to IRQ2 on the first chip, all the interrupts on the second chip (IRQ8 through IRQ15) have priority over the interrupts in the range from IRQ3 to IRQ7.

Reviewing your IRQ assignments

DOS 6 includes the invaluable utility MSD (for Microsoft System Diagnostics), which can help you to ascertain your current IRQ use. Figure 7-1 shows a typical display that is generated when you execute MSD and click on the IRQ button, or press Q, to select it.

The second column details the interrupt vector (the code that is executed when the interrupt occurs). The third column contains a generic description of the IRQ port; the third and fourth columns show whether the IRQ line is in use and, if so, the corresponding program or device.

Any free lines have an entry of No in the Detected column, or the column is empty. Not all IRQs with an empty Detected column, however, are available. In Figure 7-1, for example, IRQ10 is not detected, and yet it is used by the network card.

To make sure that an IRQ line is available, check the third *and* fourth columns. If the Handled By column does not say BIOS or Default Handlers, it is probably in use. In the example, the network device driver EXP16$ is identified as the handler for IRQ10.

```
 ile  tilities  elp
                          ══════ IRQ Status ══════
  IRQ   Address   Description      Detected            Handled By
  ───────────────────────────────────────────────────────────────
    0   0BFD:03E0  Timer Click      Yes                 RPM
    1   0BFD:03FF  Keyboard         Yes                 RPM
    2   058A:0057  Second 8259A     Yes                 Default Handlers
    3   058A:006F  COM2: COM4:      COM2:               Default Handlers
    4   C803:02C9  COM1: COM3:      COM1: COM3: Serial MMS$MOUSE
    5   058A:009F  LPT2:            No                  Default Handlers
    6   058A:00B7  Floppy Disk      Yes                 Default Handlers
    7   0070:06F4  LPT1:            Yes                 System Area
    8   058A:0052  Real-Time Clock  Yes                 Default Handlers
    9   F000:9C67  Redirected IRQ2  Yes                 BIOS
   10   D18A:0A1E  (Reserved)                           EXP16$
   11   058A:00E7  (Reserved)                           Default Handlers
   12   058A:00FF  (Reserved)                           Default Handlers
   13   F000:9C58  Math Coprocessor Yes                 BIOS
   14   058A:0117  Fixed Disk       Yes                 Default Handlers
   15   F000:FF53  (Reserved)                           BIOS

                              ─── OK ───
Press ALT for menu, or press highlighted letter, or F3 to quit MSD.
```

Figure 7-1: MSD displays the system's IRQ configuration.

As Table 7-2 illustrates, some devices share an IRQ line. Both COM1 and COM3, for example, are assigned to IRQ4. IRQ lines are a popular item. The PC engineers believed that, because no one is likely to use both COM1 and COM3 simultaneously, it makes sense for COM1 and COM3 to share a line. After all, who would run two modems simultaneously from one PC? A potential for conflict does exist, however, when one port is used for a mouse and its sister port is used for a modem. A mouse and a modem are likely to be in use simultaneously. If you have a mouse and a modem attached, make sure that they use COM ports on different IRQ lines.

Every hardware device normally needs a dedicated IRQ line. If you install a fax card, for example, you must configure the card to use a specific IRQ.

Before you buy new hardware, make sure that your system can accommodate it. You must determine, specifically, whether your system has an available IRQ line and whether the new hardware can use the IRQ line. Eight-bit boards, and even some 16-bit boards, can access only the first eight IRQs. Check with your hardware vendor to determine for which IRQs their hardware can be configured.

To accommodate a new hardware device, you may have to disable an unused COM or LPT port, or even reconfigure existing devices to use different IRQs, so that a new, less flexible device can be assigned an appropriate IRQ line.

Understanding DMA

The microprocessor, arguably the busiest chip in the PC, is clearly a performance bottleneck. The more tasks other chips can handle, the better.

One common and time-consuming task is the transfer of data to and from memory. Not all memory operations have to be managed by the microprocessor. When data is being transferred directly from the hard disk to a floppy disk, for example, no computations have to be performed, and the microprocessor therefore does not have to be directly involved. A special chip called the *direct memory access (DMA)* controller can transfer data directly to and from memory. Although the microprocessor does not perform the memory transfer, it still manages or oversees the memory transfer, and its burden is reduced significantly.

The original PC- and XT-compatible systems used a single Intel 8237A-5 DMA controller chip that provided four DMA channels. In theory, every channel can be used concurrently to move data to and from memory. One of these channels is dedicated to refreshing system memory, which leaves three channels for general-purpose memory moves. This chip unfortunately can handle only 8-bit memory transfers and can address only one megabyte of memory.

A second 8237A chip was added to 80286 and subsequent systems. Like the twin-interrupt controller configuration discussed earlier in this chapter, the second DMA controller hooks into one of the first DMA controller's channels and provides, therefore, a total of seven channels. The second chip can handle 16-bit memory transfer and therefore provide access to the full memory potential of the 80286 system and improve overall performance.

Generally, only one DMA channel at a time is used. The most notable exception is in backup software, in which two channels often are used simultaneously. One channel manages memory transfers to the hard disk, and the other channel manages memory transfers to the floppy disk. The concurrent use of two DMA channels often is referred to as *concurrent read-write* or *dual DMA*.

Some third-party backup systems offer three modes of backup speed:

- **High speed.** The DMA controller chip performs concurrent read-write operations.

- **Medium speed.** The DMA chip is used for memory transfers, but only one channel at a time is used.

- **Low speed.** The DMA controller is not used, and the backup program uses the microprocessor for standard I/O transfers.

The new DOS 6 backup programs MSBACKUP and MWBACKUP support, unfortunately, only medium-speed (single DMA) and low-speed options.

The memory manager EMM386 includes the D switch to control the size of the DMA buffer. The DMA buffer size, set to 16K by default, normally is appropriate. If you encounter the message that the DMA buffer size is too small or something similar, use the D switch to increase the buffer size. Any (kilobyte) value in the range from 16 to 256 is allowed.

Which Bus Is Best: ISA, MCA, or EISA?

One of the primary reasons that the IBM PC became so popular (other than the IBM brand name) was that the PC was designed with an open architecture. The most tangible aspect of the open architecture was the use of generic expansion slots connected to the microprocessor and ancillary circuitry by a bus. Independent vendors could create expansion cards, such as internal modems, video display cards, and memory cards, that could plug in to the system board and therefore expand the system's capabilities. This open architecture ironically led to the fierce competition that forced IBM to implement a new bus design known as the *Micro Channel Architecture*. IBM chose to move away from its open architecture policies of the past and tried to impose large royalties on would-be copycats.

The role of the bus

The bus is the computer's main highway that links all expansion cards to the microprocessor. The bus is a series of parallel "wires," called *circuit pathways*. As on a a multilane freeway, data moves down every pathway simultaneously. Generally, the more pathways, the greater the throughput and the better the performance. When you plug in an expansion card on the system board, the circuitry on the expansion card is connected directly to the bus.

The primary purpose of the bus is to transfer data to and from the microprocessor or from device to device by way of the DMA controller. With all expansion cards sharing the same pathways, data must be moved in a regimented and controlled manner. The bus is divided into these four main parts:

- Power lines
- Control lines
- Address lines
- Data lines

Not surprisingly, the power lines provide power to the expansion cards. The control lines are used to transmit timing signals from the system clock and to signal interrupts. Before any data is transmitted, the destination address is transmitted along the data lines and therefore alerts the receiving location that some data is ready to be shipped to it. The microprocessor then checks to see whether there is a ready signal (on the I/O Channel Ready line). If all is well, the data is transmitted along the data lines.

The number of lines dedicated to the *address* bus dictate the amount of total addressable memory. Twenty address lines, for example, can access one megabyte of memory. The number of bus lines dedicated to the *data* bus dictates the overall data throughput of the bus. As a rule, optimum performance is achieved when the number of data lines corresponds with the data lines in the microprocessor. The number of data lines is the most quoted characteristic of a PC bus. A 16-bit bus, for example, means that the bus uses 16 data lines.

In the PC world, buses come in three main flavors: ISA, MCA, and EISA. You can determine your system's bus flavor by running MSD and pressing C to display the computer settings (see Figure 7-2).

The ISA bus

Naming PC bus architectures is a little like naming cough drops or colas. When a company starts selling a new cherry-flavored cough drop, the company feels compelled to give the old cough drop some sort of name, such as *original flavor*

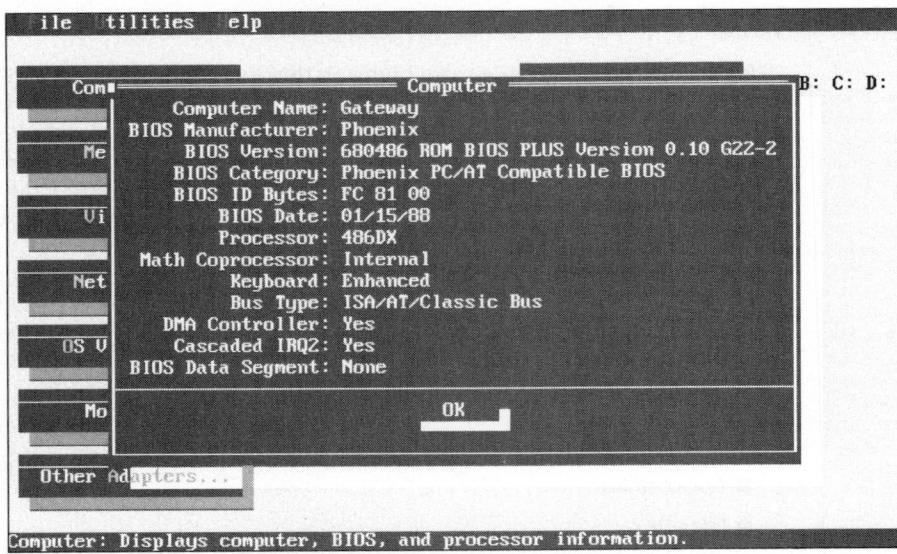

Figure 7-2: The MSD Computer option shows the system bus type.

or *classic*. Originally, the bus used in PCs and XTs didn't have a name. There was only one bus type, so it didn't need a special distinguishing name. After the introduction of alternative PC bus architectures, the old-fashioned PC bus architecture was awarded the name *Industry-Standard Architecture,* or ISA. To be accurate, the bus used in the IBM PC AT (80286) defines the ISA bus.

The bus used in the first PCs had 62 lines; 20 of them were address lines, and 8 were data lines. The bus was limited to accessing 1MB of memory, and data was transferred in single-byte (8 bit) packets. The bus clock speed was the same as the microprocessor clock speed (4.77 MHz).

The original bus design clearly was conservative. While the PC engineers were developing the IBM-PC AT to use an 80286 processor, they expanded and enhanced the bus. The most obvious change in bus design was the installation of additional address and data lines.

To preserve compatibility with the original PC bus and therefore ensure that all (or most) existing expansion cards would work in the new bus, the additional lines were accessed through a second connector on the system board. The original bus used a 3.2-inch connector with 31 contacts along each edge. The AT bus supported a second 2-inch connector that provided an additional 16 contacts along each edge (see Figure 7-3).

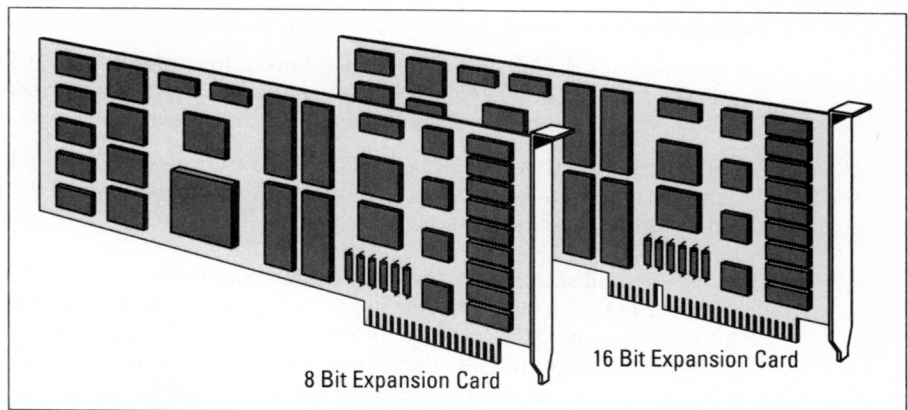

Figure 7-3: The AT bus used a second connector block to maintain backward compatibility with 8-bit expansion cards designed for the original PC.

This second connector provided four additional address lines, which made the total 24 address lines. A total of 16 megabytes of memory (the same as the 80286 processor) therefore could be addressed. Because eight data lines were added, data could be moved 16 bits at a time.

The engineers also made an important change to the bus timer design. The bus and the microprocessor originally used the same timer chip and therefore were forced to run at the same speed. Although the bus could run comfortably at 6 or 8 MHz, it could not keep pace at 12 or 16 MHz — the projected full speed of the 80286. In anticipation of ever-increasing microprocessor speeds, the AT bus was designed to run from a separate timer chip, which enabled it to run at a different (slower) speed than did the microprocessor.

The MCA bus

In the mid-1980s, the ISA bus seemed to be the system bottleneck. Memory chips and microprocessors were getting increasingly faster, but the bus wasn't. IBM decided to release a family of computers, the PS/2, that used a completely new bus architecture designed to radically improve system throughput and engineered to accommodate microprocessor advances for at least ten years. IBM called this new bus the *Micro Channel Architecture* (MCA).

The first PCs to sport this new bus were released in 1987. IBM anticipated that, thanks to performance improvements and the IBM name, customers would demand MCA-based systems. MCA has yet to dominate the marketplace, however.

Two factors contributed to the lackluster response from users:

■ The new bus design was physically different from the ISA bus. Cards designed for the ISA bus could not be used in MCA systems, and vice versa. MCA adapter cards were smaller, and the connector design was different.

■ In anticipation that its competitors would be compelled to adopt the MCA standard in their systems, IBM imposed a hefty royalty on all vendors who built MCA-based systems.

From a technical standpoint, the MCA design contained a wealth of improvements over ISA. The most notable improvement was a 32-bit data bus and a 32-bit address bus. Data could be moved around in 4-byte packets, and a huge 4 gigabytes of data could be addressed. Because IBM also redesigned the signal and power lines to reduce interference, the bus could run at speeds greater than 10 MHz.

Significantly, the MCA bus included features that enable independent devices to take cooperative control of the bus. The concept of enabling another device to take control of the bus from the microprocessor is known as *bus mastering,* which enables two or more independent devices to communicate and not involve the microprocessor. Additionally, the bus-mastering design enabled MCA systems to support multiple (parallel) microprocessors (a system may have four 386 microprocessors installed on an expansion card, for example). The utilization of parallel microprocessors unfortunately presents major software-development challenges; no mainstream applications take advantage of parallel processors.

Another innovation in the MCA bus was the abolition of expansion-card dip switches. The technique that was used is similar to the way a PC can remember the hard disk and memory configuration by using battery-sustained CMOS memory. An MCA system can remember its expansion-card configuration. This neat feature enables you to configure expansion cards by using software and the keyboard rather than a screwdriver.

Clearly, the MCA architecture is technically superior to ISA.

The EISA bus

While IBM was pushing the all-new MCA bus, the other major PC vendors (including such giants as Compaq, Hewlett Packard, and AST Research) decided to provide an alternative high-performance bus. After seeing the adverse consumer reaction to the lack of compatibility between ISA and MCA expansion cards, a primary goal was to ensure that the new bus would be fully compatible with ISA expansion cards. The result was the *Extended Industry Standard Architecture (EISA).*

In short, the EISA bus has a set of features similar to MCA. As you might expect, EISA provides 32 address lines and 32 data lines. Enhancements made to the DMA controllers allowed 32-bit DMA-driven memory transfers. Like MCA, the bus speed is controlled by a separate bus clock, which enables the bus and the microprocessor to run at different speeds. EISA also supports the all-important bus mastering.

In comparing MCA and EISA, the most significant difference is not electrical; it is physical. EISA has a major marketing advantage over MCA because ISA expansion cards can be used in EISA-based systems but not in MCA-based systems.

The backward compatibility is achieved through a clever yet simple connector design. The EISA connector is organized into two distinct levels (see Figure 7-4), with the bottom-level "teeth" serving as the new EISA connections. When a traditional ISA card is pushed into the EISA bus, the teeth do not extend low enough to make contact with the EISA-specific connections.

Although an EISA board physically fits in an ISA system, you should never insert one. EISA boards are not compatible with ISA buses, and you can damage both the system board and the EISA board.

Figures 7-5, 7-6, and 7-7 are examples of typical ISA, EISA, and MCA expansion boards, respectively. The ISA and EISA cards are similar, with the EISA

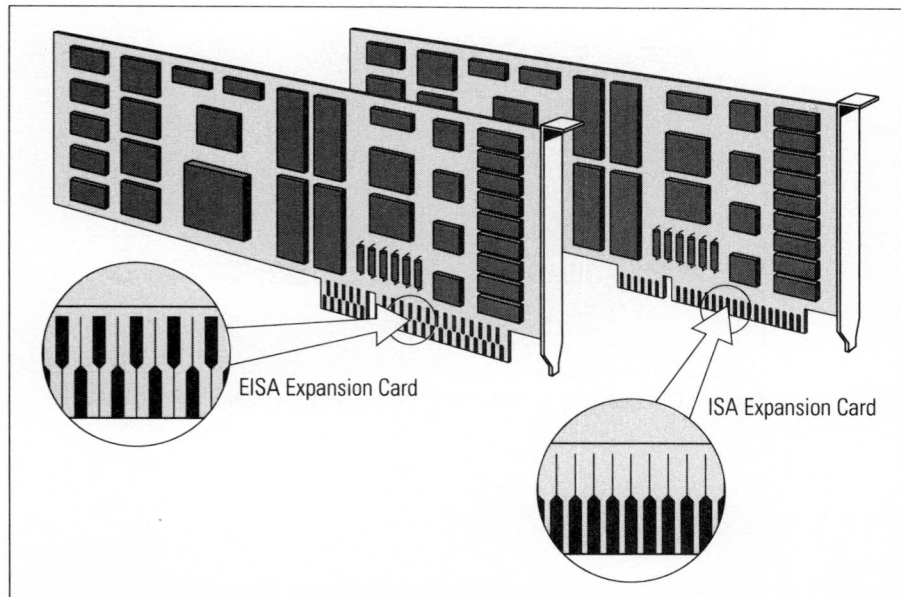

EISA Expansion Card

ISA Expansion Card

Figure 7-4: EISA expansion boards use two-tier connections compared with the single connection on ISA boards.

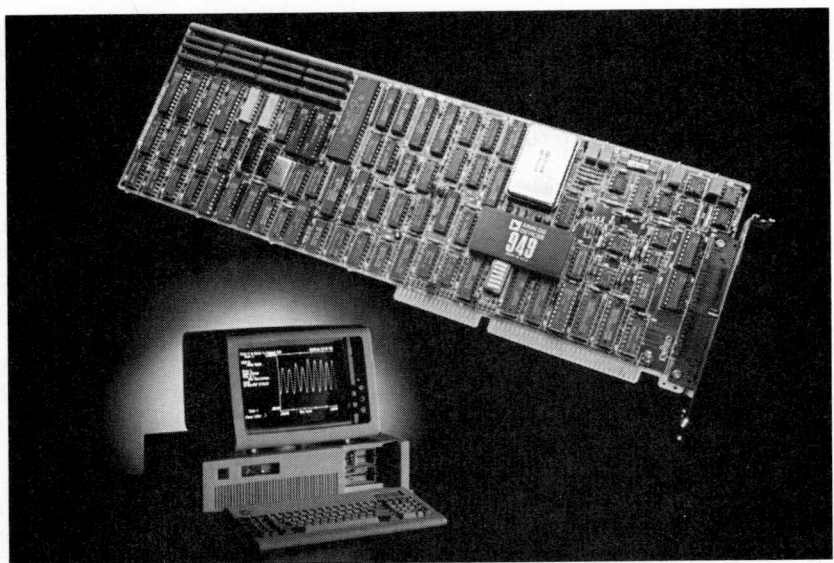

Figure 7-5: A typical 16-bit ISA expansion board. (Photo courtesy of Analog Devices Inc.)

Figure 7-6: A typical EISA expansion board. (Photo courtesy of Anco Corp.)

Figure 7-7: A typical MCA expansion board. (Photo courtesy of Genoa Systems Corp.)

connectors being slightly larger, but the MCA card is completely different in size, shape, and its unique connector design.

Recent bus innovations

Although the MCA and EISA vendors have engaged in a major marketing war for dominance, the ISA bus has been quietly enhanced and improved with some significant and powerful innovations. ISA is proving to be much more resilient and hardy than many PC engineers anticipated.

The local bus

If you had conducted a survey recently that asked users which hardware component most needed a speed boost, the resounding reply would be "video." With the enormous success of Windows and other graphical applications, the video display system has become the hardware bottleneck. It's no wonder, when the microprocessor has to transfer megabytes of data to the display. Even EISA and MCA bus systems have difficulty managing such video data loads because these buses still tend to operate at only about 10 MHz.

The solution lies in a *local bus*. This 32-bit bus is connected directly to the microprocessor and uses the same timer chip. It operates, therefore, at the same speed as the microprocessor. Few, if any, adapter cards originally could handle 33 or 50 MHz bus speeds; but, where there is a will, there is a way. A band of hardware manufacturers with primarily video-specific interests developed the VESA (Video Electronics Standards Association) VL-bus standard.

VESA-compliant video boards can plug into VL-bus-equipped PCs to obtain stunning video performance at a fraction of the cost of video cards equipped with video coprocessor chips. Increasingly more ISA PCs are being developed with local bus connectors, and new VESA video boards surface every month.

The maximum number of devices that now can be attached to the local bus is three. The primary candidates for these slots are video, network, and storage devices.

The local bus engineering has been so successful that, at the time this book was written, Intel is finishing its own local bus specification, the *Peripheral Component Interconnect (PCI)*.

SCSI, the UnBus

"When is a bus not a bus?" Yoda asked. "When it's a SCSI," replied the DOS Jedi.

The *Small Computer System Interface (SCSI)*, pronounced "skuzzy," is a high-speed system for connecting such devices as hard disks, CD-ROMs, and tape drives. Many people think of the SCSI controller as just another hard disk controller, but it is much more.

Several devices (to a maximum of seven) all are connected in parallel by using a single-ribbon cable that in turn is connected to a SCSI controller. The SCSI cable is really an expansion bus for connecting high-speed storage devices and scanners. SCSI devices can communicate and transfer data between themselves and not involve the microprocessor or use the standard system bus. Imagine being able to save hard disk files to tape and not slow down the system. The SCSI design can work with any of the three ISA, MCA, and EISA standard bus types.

The original SCSI design used a 50-bit (or -line) bus and had 8 data bits. The SCSI-2 specification released in 1991 additionally supported 16 and 32 data lines that sported impressive data-transfer rates of more than 40MB per second. Even with the revised standard, SCSI is not free from problems. Not all SCSI devices cooperate with each other, and two detailed programming specifications currently vie for acceptance: the *Common Access Method Committee (CAM)* and the *Advanced SCSI Programming Interface (ASPI)*.

Engineers are developing SCSI controllers that will attach to an ISA local bus. That's performance. Who said ISA was dead?

What's next?

With memory running on one bus, peripherals using the standard bus, and video running now on a local bus, we may find that no single bus — not ISA, MCA, or EISA — will dominate the PC. A PC probably will contain a variety of buses designed to interconnect related devices at their optimum operating speed. Only time will tell.

Deciphering Device Drivers

The operating system is designed to accommodate such standard computer devices as video cards, printers, modems, and disk drives. From the earliest days of the PC, however, it was obvious that DOS would not be capable of directly supporting the myriad devices that can be connected to a PC. Starting with DOS 2, the operating system provided a software mechanism for installing special code to handle such nonstandard devices as scanners and fax cards. Software that enables DOS to communicate with a hardware device is known as a *device driver,* usually loaded in CONFIG.SYS.

Many device drivers mimic standard devices. A hard disk device driver for a nonsupported hard disk, for example, responds to DOS's disk instructions in a standard way but uses different commands to communicate in turn with the hard disk. Similarly, a joystick device driver might make the joystick appear like a keyboard to DOS. The device driver acts as a translator, or go-between, to enable a foreign device to speak DOS's language, and vice versa.

Behind the scenes, many standard DOS devices are supported by device drivers that are loaded from the hidden DOS file IO.SYS.

You execute MSD and press R to see a list of the device drivers installed on your system. Figure 7-8 shows a typical device driver list.

Device driver routines normally are invoked by a software interrupt. When a device driver is installed, it adds in the interrupt vector table an entry that points to the device driver's main code. Column 4 of the MSD device driver listing displays the starting address of the main device driver code. DOS maintains a chain, or list, of device drivers, in which each device driver points to the next one in the list. The first device driver in the chain is the NUL device.

You can display additional device-driver details, such as the driver size, by using the MEM /D command. To filter out superfluous data, use this command in conjunction with the find filter:

```
mem /d | find "device" /i
```

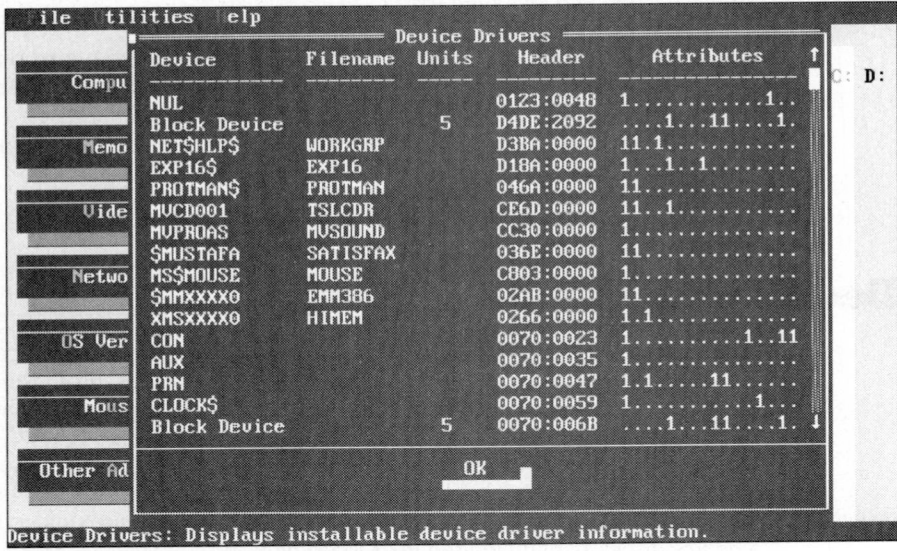

Figure 7-8: MSD displays installed device drivers.

The command produces a listing similar to the following:

```
                      CON        System Device Driver
                      AUX        System Device Driver
                      PRN        System Device Driver
                      CLOCK$     System Device Driver
                      A: - E:    System Device Driver
                      COM1       System Device Driver
                      LPT1       System Device Driver
                      LPT2       System Device Driver
                      LPT3       System Device Driver
                      COM2       System Device Driver
                      COM3       System Device Driver
                      COM4       System Device Driver
     1088    (1K)     XMSXXXX0   Installed Device=HIMEM
     3104    (3K)     $MMXXXX0   Installed Device=EMM386
     4016    (4K)     $MUSTAFA   Installed Device=SATISFAX
      112    (0K)     PROTMAN$   Installed Device=PROTMAN
    17072   (17K)     MS$MOUSE   Installed Device=MOUSE
     9136    (9K)     MVPROAS    Installed Device=MVSOUND
    12720   (12K)     MVCD001    Installed Device=TSLCDR
     8928    (9K)     EXP16$     Installed Device=EXP16
     4352    (4K)     NET$HLP$   Installed Device=WORKGRP
```

Device drivers are in two basic categories: character drivers and block drivers. Character device drivers are single-byte-oriented devices, such as printer ports. These devices include the standard DOS-supplied devices, such as AUX, CON, LPT, and NUL. Block devices manage blocks of data and usually are used for disks, CD-ROMs, and other data-intensive drivers. Every block device is assigned a logical drive letter. The rightmost column, labeled Attributes, in MSD's device driver window provides more information about the device driver format. Table 7-3 lists the meaning of every attribute.

Device drivers do not have to be oriented to a specific hardware device. ANSI.SYS, for example, is a device driver that enhances the capabilities of the standard keyboard and display. Also, you can load some device drivers as TSRs rather than as standard devices in CONFIG.SYS. In the most notable example, the Microsoft Mouse driver, you can either load MOUSE.SYS in CONFIG.SYS or execute MOUSE.COM from the command line.

To save conventional memory, you can use DEVICEHIGH and LOADHIGH to load device drivers and TSRs, respectively, into upper memory. Refer to Chapter 5 for more information about loading device drivers HIGH.

Table 7-3		Device Driver Attributes
Bit Position	*Attribute*	*Meaning*
0	1	Standard input device
1	..............1.	Standard output (character) device
2	..............1..	NUL device
3	.............1...	Clock device
4	............1....	Driver services interrupt 29
5	...........1.....	Reserved
6	..........1......	Driver supports generic IOCTL (I/O Control)
7	.........1.......	Reserved
8	........1........	Reserved
9	.......1.........	Reserved
A	......1..........	Reserved
B	.....1...........	Open/close/removable media not supported
C	....1............	Reserved
D	...1.............	Either a character device that does not support output-till-busy operation or a block device that does not use IBM block format
E	..1..............	IOCTL supported
F	.1...............	Character device — block device when empty

Summary

This chapter has examined many hardware factors related to configuring and using add-on devices. It has examined the following key points:

▶ The microprocessor tasks are governed by interrupts, and the interrupts are classified as hardware and software. When an interrupt occurs, the microprocessor executes an interrupt service routine whose address is stored in the interrupt vector table.

▶ All hardware interrupts are managed by the programmable interrupt controller, which is connected to the hardware devices by way of IRQ lines. Normally, every separate device must have a unique IRQ line.

▶ Memory moves can by expedited by using the DMA (direct memory access) controller chip. DMA moves theoretically can be executed along multiple channels, but usually only backup software uses more than one channel at a time.

▶ The expansion bus is used to connect add-on devices to the microprocessor and related circuitry. The primary bus types evident in PCs are ISA, MCA, and EISA. ISA has been given fresh life, thanks to local bus technology.

▶ Device drivers act as translators that enable foreign devices to communicate with DOS and the microprocessor. You can review installed device drivers with the MSD and MEM commands.

DOS 6 introduced a set of new commands to support multiple boot configurations. Chapter 8 describes how to use these commands to create start-up menus and how to identify common configuration commands.

Chapter 8

Power System Configuration Techniques

In This Chapter

▶ Ways to interrupt and control the boot cycle

▶ How to create multiboot configurations

▶ A CONFIG.SYS checklist

▶ An AUTOEXEC.BAT checklist

Many of today's PCs are packed full of add-on goodies such as fax cards, scanners, CD-ROMS, sound cards and the like. Unfortunately, most of these add-ons need special device drivers or programs, which in turn reduce the amount of available memory left to run applications programs.

Several enhancements in DOS 6 enable you to precisely control which programs and device drivers are loaded when your system boots. If you don't use the CD-ROM every session, for example, you can easily configure the system to prompt for confirmation before installing the CD-ROM device driver. This chapter explains how to take advantage of all the new DOS 6 configuration options and provides a checklist of the most beneficial CONFIG.SYS and AUTOEXEC.BAT commands.

Interrupting and Controlling the Boot Cycle

Before DOS 6, the most common way to halt the boot process was to thump the Ctrl-Break key repeatedly until DOS, somewhere in AUTOEXEC.BAT, responded with the prompt

```
Terminate batch job (Y/N)?
```

If a rogue statement in CONFIG.SYS caused the system to hang, about the only solution was to boot from a floppy and then edit the offending CONFIG.SYS statement(s).

Thankfully, DOS 6 provides a few more graceful and effective ways to interrupt and control the commands executed during the system boot.

Using the clean-start key

In the initial boot phase, before CONFIG.SYS entries are processed, DOS displays the following message by default:

```
Starting MS-DOS...
```

When this message appears, you have a couple of seconds to press and release the F5 function key. When you press F5, the system ignores all commands in CONFIG.SYS and AUTOEXEC.BAT and performs a *clean boot*; that is, the system boots without processing any of the commands in the CONFIG.SYS or AUTOEXEC.BAT files. This feature saves you from having to create (and later find) a DOS 6 boot diskette. And it makes you wonder why it wasn't implemented a long time ago. By the way, if you hold the F5 key down too long, @ characters will cascade down the screen until you release the key.

If you are a little heavy-handed, as I am, or get tense waiting for the right moment to press and release F5, I have good news. Instead of waiting poised over the F5 key, you can just hold down one of the Shift keys. DOS clean boots just as if you pressed F5, and you don't get all the @ symbols spilling down the display because you held the F5 key down too long.

Better still, if you configured your system with a start-up menu, you can just press F5 when the menu is displayed. DOS ignores the menu options and clean boots.

Be aware that *none* of your CONFIG.SYS and AUTOEXEC.BAT commands are executed when you clean boot the system. No memory manager, no COMSPEC, no PATH, no PROMPT — as my sister would say, "No nothin'." If you need to make some corrections to the boot files, start by entering something similar to the following two commands:

```
prompt $p$g
path c:\dos
```

In addition, if COMMAND.COM is not located in the root directory, enter the following command (specifying the appropriate path to COMMAND.COM):

```
set comspec=c:\dos\command.com
```

You should consider creating a multiboot menu (discussed later in the chapter) that includes a *Clean Start* item that executes these basic commands.

If your drive C is a DoubleSpace volume, the system still boots successfully using the clean-boot technique. The device driver responsible for mounting the DoubleSpace volume is installed (by IO.SYS) before the commands in CONFIG.SYS are processed.

If you are using a third-party disk compression product, such as Stacker, however, the clean-boot technique bypasses the driver responsible for mounting your compressed volume; you are left looking at your host drive instead of the one containing the compressed files. If you're using a third-party compression product, you should consider creating a start-up menu that includes a Clean Start item that loads the disk compression device driver and nothing else. Start-up menus are thoroughly discussed later in the chapter.

Using the interactive start key

Although the clean-start key is useful, more often than not you want to execute some, but not all, commands. For example, you may want to load only HIMEM.SYS, EMM386.EXE, and MOUSE.SYS. In such circumstances, press the F8 key as soon as the boot message Starting MS-DOS... is displayed. DOS prompts for confirmation before executing each command in CONFIG.SYS. If the first line of CONFIG.SYS loads HIMEM.SYS, DOS prompts you as follows:

```
device=c:\dos\himem.sys [Y,N]?
```

If you press Y, the statement executes; if you press N, the statement is bypassed. DOS then proceeds to the next statement in CONFIG.SYS and prompts you for confirmation before executing it. The process is repeated for every statement in CONFIG.SYS.

When all the CONFIG.SYS commands are processed, DOS prompts you with the following message:

```
Process AUTOEXEC.BAT [Y,N]?
```

If you press Y, AUTOEXEC.BAT is executed as normal. If you press N, the entire AUTOEXEC.BAT file is bypassed. Unfortunately, you cannot instruct DOS to individually step through each command in AUTOEXEC.BAT. Maybe next time.

If your system is configured with a start-up menu, the F8 key behaves differently. When the start-up menu is presented, the status of the F8 key is displayed at the bottom of the display as follows:

```
F8=Confirm each CONFIG.SYS line [N]
```

If you press F8, the status changes to [Y]; pressing the F8 key toggles the setting between [Y] and [N]. After you set the F8 switch as desired, you must then choose a menu item before proceeding. After all, DOS needs to know which configuration commands to step through.

If you step through some commands and want to exit without processing any more CONFIG.SYS commands, a shortcut is to press the F5 key while DOS is prompting for [Y,N]. DOS ignores the current command, all subsequent commands, and AUTOEXEC.BAT and drops you to the DOS prompt without further ado.

Similarly, if you are stepping through the CONFIG.SYS commands and want to execute all remaining commands along with AUTOEXEC.BAT, just press Esc. DOS stops prompting you and executes all remaining commands in one fell swoop.

If your system will not boot, the F8 key provides a very simple debugging tool. By stepping through the individual commands, you can ascertain precisely when the system locks up. The last command executed before lockup may be causing the problem. Try booting a second time using F8 and press N when you are prompted to confirm the suspect statement. If everything appears to boot normally, you have a good idea about the cause of the problem.

Forcing a [Y/N] prompt

If you only want to load a specific command in CONFIG.SYS occasionally, you can force a [Y/N] confirmation prompt by inserting a question mark character (?) before the equal sign (=) in the statements. This instructs DOS to prompt for confirmation before executing the statement. The ? character is supported by all CONFIG.SYS commands except SWITCHES.

For example, you can use the ? command with the device driver for a hand-held scanner. You don't use the scanner everyday, so you don't want to waste memory loading the device driver. But you also don't want to edit CONFIG.SYS and reboot every time you want to load the scanner. If you add a ? to the device statement, DOS prompts you to confirm execution of the device driver every time you boot the system. Here's an example of how to write such a statement:

```
device?=c:\scanman\hhscand.sys /a=280 /i=1
```

If you press Esc when prompted to confirm execution of a device installed with the ? option, DOS assumes that your response to the prompt is Y. It also assumes that your response to all remaining prompts is Y and bypasses them.

Controlling start keys with the SWITCHES command

If you are responsible for configuring computers for other users, you may be concerned that they will be able to press F5 (or Shift) and F8 to bypass the start-up commands, possibly causing mayhem. Fear not. By using the SWITCHES statement in CONFIG.SYS, you can enable or disable the start-up interruption keys.

The SWITCHES command serves a variety of purposes, and the full syntax is explained in Part IV, "The Complete DOS 6 Command Reference." However, two switches are directly related to the booting process:

/F   Instructs DOS to boot immediately, without pausing for the normal two seconds when the message `Starting MS-DOS...` is displayed. If drive C is a DoubleSpace volume, there is still a perceptible delay as DOS mounts the DoubleSpace volume — it is just two seconds shorter.

/N   Instructs DOS to ignore the F5 (and Shift) and F8 interruption keys. The user cannot bypass CONFIG.SYS or step through each command individually.

Normally, if you use the /N command, you should also use /F because there is no reason to delay the boot for two seconds. The following is an example CONFIG.SYS that cannot be interrupted:

```
SWITCHES=/F/N
DEVICE=C:\DOS\HIMEM.SYS
DEVICE=C:\DOS\EMM386.EXE RAM I=B000-B7FF WIN=B300-B7FF
BUFFERS=15,0
FILES=40
DOS=UMB
LASTDRIVE=M
```

 You do not have to locate the SWITCHES statement at the beginning of CONFIG.SYS. DOS is smart enough to peruse the entire file looking for a SWITCHES statement. In fact, if you are trying to stop users from tampering with the configuration setup, you should consider burying the SWITCHES statement in the body of the main commands. The casual user is much less likely to find and modify it.

Creating Multiboot Configurations

A great new feature of DOS 6 is that it gives you the ability to define multiple start-up configurations in CONFIG.SYS. DOS can display a menu of start-up options and then only execute the commands defined for the option you select. For example, the following menu is displayed on my notebook system:

```
MS-DOS 6 Startup Menu
=====================

    1. Clean
    2. InterLink
    3. Normal
```

You define start-up menus in CONFIG.SYS using the commands in Table 8-1.

Table 8-1	Start-Up Menu Commands
Command	**Description**
[MENU]	Identifies the beginning of a series of menu items and commands that define the start-up menu.
INCLUDE	Includes the commands from one configuration block in another.
MENUCOLOR	Sets the foreground and background display colors for the menu.
MENUDEFAULT	Sets the default item in a menu and (optionally) the number of seconds to wait for user input before applying the default.
MENUITEM	Creates an item on the menu and identifies the name of the associated configuration block. When the user selects the menu item, DOS executes the commands in the specified configuration block. The order of the MENUITEM commands in CONFIG.SYS defines the order of the menu options.
NUMLOCK	Because the user can select a menu item by pressing the menu number, this command was added to provide a convenient way to turn off Num Lock.
SUBMENU	Creates a branch to a secondary menu, thereby providing nested or multilevel configuration menus.
[*BLOCKNAME*]	Every block specified with the MENUITEM command must have a corresponding block defined. This approach is similar to the batch file command GOTO, where the GOTO name must have a corresponding label elsewhere in the file.

Defining menus

The following CONFIG.SYS file, which was used to create the three-option menu presented in the preceding section, provides a complete example of how to create start-up menus:

```
[menu]
menuitem=Clean
menuitem=InterLink
menuitem=Normal
numlock=off

[Clean]
BUFFERS=15,0
FILES=30
LASTDRIVE=G
FCBS=4,0

[Normal]
DEVICE=C:\DOS\HIMEM.SYS
DEVICE=C:\DOS\EMM386.EXE RAM
DOS=HIGH,UMB
```

```
BUFFERS=15,0
FILES=30
LASTDRIVE=G
FCBS=4,0
SHELL=C:\DOS\COMMAND.COM C:\DOS\  /p
DEVICEHIGH /L:1,47296 =C:\DOS\DBLSPACE.SYS

[InterLink]
DEVICE=C:\DOS\HIMEM.SYS
DEVICE=C:\DOS\EMM386.EXE RAM
DOS=HIGH,UMB
DEVICE=C:\DOS\INTERLNK.EXE /DRIVES:5
BUFFERS=15,0
FILES=30
LASTDRIVE=G
```

The anatomy of a multiconfiguration CONFIG.SYS file is straightforward. One [MENU] section includes a set of MENUITEM statements that define each menu option. The body of CONFIG.SYS contains configuration blocks, with each *blockname* identified by the MENUITEM name and enclosed in square brackets.

When the user selects a menu item, DOS proceeds to the appropriate configuration-block heading — for example, [InterLink] — and executes the commands that follow. DOS executes all the commands up to the next configuration-block heading or the end of the file, whichever comes first.

A blockname can be up to 70 characters long but must not include embedded spaces or any of the following characters:

$\backslash$ / [ ] = ; ,

Note that any spaces preceding or following the blockname are ignored.

DOS displays a maximum of nine entries in any single menu.

If a menu item is clearly listed in CONFIG.SYS but does not show up in the start-up menu, it's likely that the problem is related to the [*blockname*] entry. If DOS cannot find a menu item's corresponding configuration block, the MENUITEM statement is ignored. Check that the blockname specified with the MENUITEM statement is the same as the blockname specified in the body of CONFIG.SYS. Blocknames are not case sensitive.

Specify an optional MENUITEM title when you don't want the single word *blockname* to be used as the title. To specify a more descriptive MENUITEM title, use the following syntax:

menuitem=*blockname*[,*menudescription*]

You could enhance the [MENU] section in the example as follows:

```
[menu]
menuitem=Clean,Plain boot with nothing loaded
menuitem=InterLink,Standard Setup with InterLink loaded
menuitem=Normal,Normal Configuration Settings
numlock=off
```

After you make these enhancements, DOS displays the start-up menu at system boot as follows:

```
MS-DOS 6 Startup Menu
=======================

    1. Plain boot with nothing loaded
    2. Standard Setup with InterLink loaded
    3. Normal Configuration Settings
```

Setting menu defaults

The MENUDEFAULT command controls the default menu item — that is, the item that is highlighted when the menu is first displayed — and optionally specifies a timeout period. If the user does not press a key within the timeout period, DOS proceeds as though the default item was selected. The timeout period can range from 0 to 90 seconds. Locate the MENUDEFAULT statement in the [MENU] section and use the following syntax:

```
menudefault=blockname[,timeout]
```

The following [MENU] section of CONFIG.SYS defines the third item in the example menu as the default and assigns a timeout period of 10 seconds:

```
[menu]
menuitem=Clean,Plain boot with nothing loaded
menuitem=InterLink,Standard Setup with InterLink loaded
menuitem=Normal,Normal Configuration Settings
numlock=off
menudefault=Normal,10
```

If the MENUDEFAULT command is not used, the first menu item is highlighted as the default, and DOS waits for the user to make a selection and press the Enter key.

Changing menu colors

DOS has never been great with colors, and the new start-up menu facility is no exception. But you can at least change the basic display colors. You can modify the standard foreground and background menu colors by adding a MENUCOLOR statement to the [MENU] section. Use the following syntax:

```
menucolor=f[,b]
```

Table 8-2	Color Codes for the MENUCOLOR Command		
Code	**Color**	**Code**	**Color**
0	Black	8	Dark Gray
1	Blue	9	Light Blue
2	Green	10	Light Green
3	Cyan	11	Light Cyan
4	Red	12	Light Red
5	Magenta	13	Light Magenta
6	Brown	14	Yellow
7	Light Gray	15	White

The *f* variable is the foreground text color code, and *b* is the background color code. The color code must be a value in the range 0 to 15. Table 8-2 shows the codes along with the corresponding colors.

Some systems do not support background colors in the range 8 through 15. If you get blinking or flashing text, change the background color to a code in the range 0 to 7. Unless, of course, you want blinking text!

Unfortunately, you cannot change the heading colors or the color of the highlight bar. The highlight bar is always light gray, so avoid using a light gray background (code 7), or the highlight bar will not be visible.

The color settings apply to the output generated by AUTOEXEC.BAT commands and other DOS commands. Add a `cls` command at the beginning of the AUTOEXEC.BAT file to clear the display and set the colors back to the default light gray on black.

Changing menu headings

Bad news: There is no easy way to change the bland `MS-DOS 6 Startup Menu` menu heading. The menu heading is a constant in the hidden IO.SYS file. Although you can hack around in IO.SYS and change the title, I don't recommend it.

Combining common commands

If every configuration block shares one or more configuration statements, you don't need to repeat the commands in every block. The special configuration block called [COMMON] provides a useful shortcut. All commands included in a [COMMON] block are executed no matter which menu item the user selects.

In the example CONFIG.SYS file, all three blocks included the following commands:

```
BUFFERS=15,0
FILES=30
LASTDRIVE=G
```

You can simplify the entire CONFIG.SYS file by adding the commands to a common section, as follows:

```
[menu]
menuitem=Clean
menuitem=InterLink
menuitem=Normal
numlock=off

[common]
BUFFERS=15,0
FILES=30
LASTDRIVE=G

[Clean]
FCBS=4,0

[Normal]
DEVICE=C:\DOS\HIMEM.SYS
DEVICE=C:\DOS\EMM386.EXE RAM
DOS=HIGH,UMB
FCBS=4,0
SHELL=C:\DOS\COMMAND.COM C:\DOS\ /p
DEVICEHIGH /L:1,47296 =C:\DOS\DBLSPACE.SYS

[InterLink]
DEVICE=C:\DOS\HIMEM.SYS
DEVICE=C:\DOS\EMM386.EXE RAM
DOS=HIGH,UMB
DEVICE=C:\DOS\INTERLNK.EXE /DRIVES:5
```

You can place more than one [COMMON] block in a CONFIG.SYS file. All commands situated in common blocks are processed *after* the commands for the block selected by the user. Multiple common blocks are executed in the order they are entered in CONFIG.SYS.

One disadvantage of the [COMMON] block is that its commands are always executed. If you have a menu option for a clean boot configuration, avoid using the [COMMON] feature. After all, it wouldn't be a clean boot if all the common commands were executed.

If you add commands to the beginning of CONFIG.SYS, prior to the first MENU or [*blockname*] statement, the commands will be assumed to be part of a COMMON block and so will be executed no matter which menu option is selected.

If you have one or more commands that are shared by some but not all menu items, you can use the INCLUDE command to incorporate the shared commands in selective blocks. The syntax of the include statement is as follows:

```
include=blockname
```

When DOS encounters an INCLUDE statement, processing branches to the specified block. When all the commands in the block are processed, DOS returns to the statement on the line following the INCLUDE statement.

In the example configuration, the [Normal] and [Interlink] sections both load HIMEM.SYS and EMM386. The file can be modified to include a new section, [MEMSTUFF], as follows:

```
[menu]
menuitem=Clean
menuitem=InterLink
menuitem=Normal
numlock=off

[common]
BUFFERS=15,0
FILES=30
LASTDRIVE=G

[memstuff]
DEVICE=C:\DOS\HIMEM.SYS
DEVICE=C:\DOS\EMM386.EXE RAM

[Clean]
FCBS=4,0

[Normal]
INCLUDE=MEMSTUFF
DOS=HIGH,UMB
FCBS=4,0
SHELL=C:\DOS\COMMAND.COM C:\DOS\  /p
DEVICEHIGH /L:1,47296 =C:\DOS\DBLSPACE.SYS

[InterLink]
INCLUDE=MEMSTUFF
DOS=HIGH,UMB
DEVICE=C:\DOS\INTERLNK.EXE /DRIVES:5
```

Many software installation programs make modifications to CONFIG.SYS, and few of them (as yet) are aware of DOS 6's multiconfiguration facility. Usually, the installation programs add their commands to the end of the file. Consider adding a [COMMON] statement to the end of CONFIG.SYS. With this statement, CONFIG.SYS is better suited to accommodate ad-hoc commands added to the end of CONFIG.SYS by installation software. If an installation program subsequently adds commands to the end of CONFIG.SYS, they will be situated in this COMMON section; therefore, the commands will be executed no matter which item the user selects from the start-up menu.

Better still, if one menu item is used as the "business as usual" option, add a custom blockname statement, say [DEFAULT], to the end of CONFIG.SYS and then use the INCLUDE menu command to insert the following statement at the end of the business-as-usual block:

```
include=default
```

Whenever the user selects the business-as-usual option from the start-up menu, the commands situated at the end of CONFIG.SYS (after the [DEFAULT] line) will automatically be executed.

It is not always beneficial to place common commands in a [COMMON] block or to share them with an INCLUDE statement, especially if you are optimizing your system for memory usage. The load order for device drivers and the load position in an upper memory region probably differ from configuration to configuration. In one configuration, you may load MOUSE.SYS in upper memory with DEVICEHIGH, but in another configuration, when other, larger programs may make better use of upper memory, you may load MOUSE.SYS low with a DEVICE statement.

Furthermore, MEMMAKER (the DOS 6 memory-optimization program) is not very adept at dealing with CONFIG.SYS files that contain menu blocks. Refer to Chapter 5 for more information on memory optimization and how to optimize multiconfiguration systems.

Using multimenu configurations

Because there is a limit of nine items in each menu, you may want to use the SUBMENU command to create submenus. Even if you don't fill all nine item slots, you can use SUBMENU to organize your menu system into a hierarchy.

By using the SUBMENU command in place of MENUITEM, you instruct DOS to display another menu rather than execute standard CONFIG.SYS commands. When the user selects a menu item defined with SUBMENU, a secondary menu is automatically displayed. The syntax of the SUBMENU command is as follows:

```
submenu=blockname[,menudescription]
```

The block specified by the *blockname* argument is a configuration block that
defines another menu. The submenu configuration block can include MENUITEM,
MENUCOLOR, MENUDEFAULT, NUMLOCK, and even further SUBMENU commands. You can nest menus at least ten levels deep, but if you nest menus more
than two or three levels, you probably are in need of counseling.

The following CONFIG.SYS file defines a two-menu system (with commands related to the submenu in bold):

```
[menu]
menuitem=Clean
menuitem=InterLink
menuitem=Normal
submenu=Graphics,Publishing Menu
menucolor=14,2
numlock=off

[common]
BUFFERS=15,0
FILES=30
LASTDRIVE=G

[memstuff]
DEVICE=C:\DOS\HIMEM.SYS
DEVICE=C:\DOS\EMM386.EXE RAM

[Clean]
FCBS=4,0

[Normal]
INCLUDE=MEMSTUFF
DOS=HIGH,UMB
FCBS=4,0
SHELL=C:\DOS\COMMAND.COM C:\DOS\   /p
DEVICEHIGH /L:1,47296 =C:\DOS\DBLSPACE.SYS

[InterLink]
INCLUDE=MEMSTUFF
DOS=HIGH,UMB
DEVICE=C:\DOS\INTERLNK.EXE /DRIVES:5

[Graphics]
menuitem=Scanner,Install Scanner
menuitem=Tablet,Install Digitizing Tablet
menuitem=ScanTab,Install Scanner and Tablet
submenu=menu,Return to Main Menu
menucolor=15,4
```

```
[Scanner]
DEVICE=C:\SCANMAN\HHSCAND.SYS /A=280 /I=1

[Tablet]
DEVICE=C:\BUSTER\TABSCMD.SYS /P /W=54 /T=3

[ScanTab]
INCLUDE=SCANNER
INCLUDE=TABLET

[common]
```

When the system boots, DOS displays the following menu:

```
MS-DOS 6 Startup Menu
=========================

    1. Clean
    2. InterLink
    3. Normal
    4. Publishing Menu
```

If the user selects option 4, the following submenu is displayed in a different color:

```
MS-DOS 6 Startup Menu
=========================

    1. Install Scanner
    2. Install Digitizing Tablet
    3. Install Scanner and Tablet
    4. Return to Main Menu
```

Providing an escape option

Unlike the majority of menu systems, DOS, for some odd reason, does not allow you to escape from a submenu back to the main menu. Once you choose an option that displays a submenu, you are stuck there.

If you create a boot menu system that includes submenus, always add a final menu option called *Return to Main Menu*. Although it is not documented, if you specify *menu* as the blockname, DOS jumps back to the initial menu. To provide the user with an easy way to return to the main menu, just add the following statement to the end of each submenu definition:

```
submenu=menu,Return to Main Menu
```

Prompting for user confirmation

You can use the submenu facility in an unconventional way: to instruct DOS to prompt the user for confirmation before proceeding with the selected option. The approach is best explained by example.

When setting up a menu system, you may want to give the user a chance to tell DOS to abort before it executes a particular configuration. Suppose, for example, that you want to remind users that they must attach a scanner to the system and turn it on before installing the scanner's device driver.

You can instruct DOS to display a submenu with the two options Yes and No, prompting the user for confirmation before it proceeds. The following CONFIG.SYS file defines a menu with two options, Normal and Scanner:

```
[menu]
menuitem=Normal
submenu=Scanner,Activate Scanner
menucolor=14,2
numlock=off

[normal]
BUFFERS=15,0
FILES=30
DEVICE=C:\DOS\HIMEM.SYS
DEVICE=C:\DOS\EMM386.EXE RAM
DOS=HIGH,UMB

[Scanner]
menuitem=LoadIt,Yes: The scanner is connected and turned on
submenu=menu,No:  I forgot to get the scanner. Abort
scanner load
menucolor=15,4

[LoadIt]
include=normal
DEVICE=C:\SCANMAN\HHSCAND.SYS /A=280 /I=1

[common]
```

When the system boots, the following menu is displayed:

```
MS-DOS 6 Startup Menu
=======================

    1. Normal
    2. Activate Scanner
```

If the user selects the Scanner option, the following confirmation menu is displayed:

```
MS-DOS 6 Startup Menu
========================

    1. Yes: The scanner is connected and turned on
    2. No:  I forgot to get the scanner. Abort scanner load
```

When the user selects Yes, the scanner is installed and the system boots. When the user selects No, the main menu is displayed again.

Note: The program does not limit the number of menus and submenus that you can branch to.

Configuring AUTOEXEC.BAT

As yet, DOS does not offer a built-in feature that enables you to display a full-screen menu from AUTOEXEC.BAT. However, you can edit AUTOEXEC.BAT so that it determines which item the user selected from the CONFIG.SYS menu and then executes the appropriate batch file statements.

When a user makes a choice from a start-up menu, DOS creates an environment variable to indicate which item the user selected. The name of the environment variable is CONFIG, and the value is the selected blockname. For example, if the user chose the Normal option in the previous example, DOS would create the following environment variable:

```
CONFIG=Normal
```

A batch file can evaluate the value of the environment variable by using the expression %*varname*%. To test the value of the CONFIG environment variable, use the syntax %config%. After executing some standard AUTOEXEC.BAT statements, such as PATH and PROMPT, you can test the value of CONFIG with an IF statement. Here is an example:

```
path c:\dos;c:\windows;c:\batfiles
prompt $p$g
set temp=d:\temp
c:\dos\doskey
if not "%config%"=="Scanner" goto quit
c:\scanman\scanstrt /1
:quit
```

If you have several menu options, you might consider using a GOTO statement rather than several IF statements. By adding a GOTO %CONFIG% statement, you can branch to a specific label in the batch file, based on the user's menu selection. The following batch file illustrates this approach:

```
path c:\dos;c:\batfiles
prompt $p$g
goto %config%
:Interlnk
echo Execute InterSvr on Desktop to start Interlnk
goto quit
:Normal
c:\dos\doskey
goto quit
:Windows
path=c:\windows;%path%
set temp=c:\wintemp
win
goto quit
:Clean
echo Maximum Memory Configuration Installed
:Quit
```

If the message Label not found is sometimes displayed when you boot the system, it is caused, not surprisingly, by a missing label. Check and make sure that you have one label for every possible menu selection in CONFIG.SYS.

Because DOS automatically creates a CONFIG environment entry, you might consider freeing some environment space by adding the following command to the end of AUTOEXEC.BAT:

```
set config=
```

You can take this approach to extremes and use the multimenu facility in CONFIG.SYS solely as a front-end menu for AUTOEXEC.BAT. The following CONFIG.SYS file displays a menu, but all the executable commands are stored in the COMMON section:

```
[menu]
menuitem=Mouse,Use the standard mouse
menuitem=Tablet,Use the digitizing tablet
menuitem=Trackball,Use the trackball
numlock=off

[common]
BUFFERS=15,0
FILES=30
```

```
LASTDRIVE=G
DEVICE=C:\DOS\HIMEM.SYS
DEVICE=C:\DOS\EMM386.EXE RAM
DOS=HIGH,UMB
FCBS=4,0
SHELL=C:\DOS\COMMAND.COM C:\DOS\  /p
DEVICEHIGH /L:1,47296 =C:\DOS\DBLSPACE.SYS
[Mouse]
[Tablet]
[Trackball]
[common]
```

No matter which menu item the user chooses, the same configuration commands are executed. The reason for making the user choose an option is so that specific AUTOEXEC.BAT commands can be executed based on the value of %CONFIG%, as follows:

```
path c:\dos;c:\batfiles
prompt $p$g
goto %config%
:Mouse
c:\dos\mouse
goto quit
:Tablet
c:\tb\starttb /x=640 /y=480
goto quit
:Trackball
c:\ltech\tball
:quit
```

Don't forget that you can use the CHOOSE batch command to generate single-line prompts that request user input. For more information about CHOOSE, IF, and other batch file techniques, refer to Chapter 10.

Checking CONFIG.SYS

The precise entries in CONFIG.SYS vary from system to system. Apart from the menu-related commands, CONFIG.SYS supports nearly 20 other configuration commands. Table 8-3 provides a summary of the primary configuration commands. Use it to verify that you have addressed each area in your system's configuration.

Table 8-3		The Most Common CONFIG.SYS Entries
Category	*Command*	*Description*
Devices	DEVICE	Loads a device driver. Usually, the device driver is loaded into base memory, but some device drivers, such as INTERLNK, automatically load into upper, expanded, or extended memory.
	DEVICEHIGH	Loads a device driver into upper memory. If there isn't enough room or if no upper memory is available, the device is loaded in base memory.
Memory	DOS	Use with the HIGH (on 286+ systems) and UMB (on 386+ systems) switches to load DOS into high memory and to instruct DOS to manage the upper memory area, respectively.
	HIMEM.SYS	On 286+ systems, load HIMEM.SYS, using DEVICE, to manage extended memory and provide access to the high memory area (HMA).
	EMM386.EXE	Provides advanced memory management capabilities on 386+ systems.
	INSTALL	Loads memory-resident programs from CONFIG.SYS and avoids allocating unnecessary environment space for them.
	FCBS	Specifies the maximum number of file control blocks DOS can have open at any given time. Only very old programs use file control blocks. To minimize the FCBS allocation and save memory, use the statement `FCBS=1`.
	DBLSPACE.SYS	Transfers the DoubleSpace device driver into upper memory.
	STACKS	Allocates memory to manage hardware interrupts. If you encounter stack error messages, such as `Internal Stack Overflow`, you may need to add a STACKS statement to CONFIG.SYS or increase the number and size of the stack frames.
Files/drives	FILES	Specifies the number of files DOS can have open concurrently. Use a value in the range 20 to 50.
	BUFFERS	Specifies the number of disk buffers used by DOS when reading files. If you use a disk cache program (such as SMARTDRV), set the buffers to a small value, such as 4. Otherwise, use a value in the 20 to 40 range, depending on memory requirements.
	LASTDRIVE	Controls how many logical drives are recognized by DOS. Do not assign drives you don't need; it wastes base memory.
	RAMDRIVE.SYS	Creates a virtual hard drive using base, extended, or expanded memory.

(continued)

Table 8-3	The Most Common CONFIG.SYS Entries *(continued)*	
Category	**Command**	**Description**
International	COUNTRY.SYS	Configures the country language conventions for your system. Areas affected by COUNTRY.SYS are the date and time display, the characters of the alphabet, the symbol used to denote currency, and the sort order of files. If you do not have a COUNTRY entry in CONFIG.SYS, your system is automatically configured as a U.S.A. system.
	DISPLAY.SYS	Provides international character support by allowing code-page switching. You only need to use this device driver if you configure your system for international use.
Miscellaneous	ANSI.SYS	A device driver that provides ways to improve DOS display capabilities, control the cursor location, and assign special functions to keys.
	BREAK	Enables or disables checking for Ctrl-Break during disk access and other nondisplay activity.
	SHELL	Sets the options for COMMAND.COM or allows a different command processor to be loaded. SHELL is most often used with the /E switch to control the memory allocated for the environment.
	SWITCHES	Controls four configuration switches for customizing the behavior of the operating system.

As a rule of thumb, your CONFIG.SYS should include at least the following entries:

HIMEM.SYS (on 286+ systems)

EMM386.EXE (on 386+ systems)

DOS=HIGH,UMB (on 286+, 386+ systems)

FILES

FCBS

BUFFERS

LASTDRIVE

SHELL

You probably will also have a collection of DEVICE and DEVICEHIGH statements that load other device drivers, such as MOUSE.SYS. The following is a typical CONFIG.SYS file from a 386 system that uses Workgroup Connection:

```
DEVICE=C:\DOS\HIMEM.SYS
DEVICE=C:\DOS\EMM386.EXE RAM I=B000-B7FF WIN=B300-B7FF
BUFFERS=15,0
FILES=40
DOS=HIGH,UMB
```

```
LASTDRIVE=M
FCBS=1
STACKS=9,256
;Set Environment size
SHELL=C:\DOS\COMMAND.COM C:\DOS\ /e:431 /p
;Install network drivers
DEVICEHIGH /L:2,55168 =C:\WINDOWS\MOUSE.SYS /Y
DEVICE=C:\WINDOWS\PROTMAN.DOS /i:C:\WINDOWS
DEVICEHIGH /L:2,11168 =C:\WINDOWS\EXP16.DOS
DEVICEHIGH /L:2,7280 =C:\WINDOWS\WORKGRP.SYS
DEVICEHIGH=C:\DOS\ANSI.SYS
```

Remember that DOS ignores any lines beginning with REM or the semicolon character (;). With the introduction of the menu commands, CONFIG.SYS is becoming as complicated and as intricate as batch files. Take advantage of REM and ; to add explanatory comments to CONFIG.SYS.

If you modify your configuration file, be sure to use MEMMAKER to make optimum use of memory. Refer to Chapter 5 for a full discussion of memory optimization and its impact on CONFIG.SYS.

Checking AUTOEXEC.BAT

There are almost as many different AUTOEXEC.BAT configurations as there are PCs. Nonetheless, some standard commands should be used in most cases. Table 8-4 lists some of the common AUTOEXEC.BAT entries you should consider utilizing.

Table 8-4	Common AUTOEXEC.BAT Entries
Command	*Description*
PATH	Stores, in the environment, a list of directories that DOS searches when looking for a program or batch file. Specify the most commonly accessed directories first.
PROMPT	Defines, in the environment, the default command prompt. The most common prompt argument is pg, which represents the default drive and directory.
MOUSE	If your mouse is not installed as a device driver, execute MOUSE.COM.
SET TEMP=	More and more programs are referencing a TEMP environment variable to determine where to store temporary files. Specify a drive and directory, and if you have more than one hard disk, specify a directory on the fastest disk.
DOSKEY	Installs the DOS keyboard macro utility.
SMARTDRV	Configures and starts the DOS disk cache program. Use this if you aren't using another third-party disk cache.
MIRROR	Use the DOS 5 command MIRROR to make a backup copy of the hard disk partition table and record UNFORMAT details for each hard drive.

Summary

To get the most from your system, you must optimally configure CONFIG.SYS and AUTOEXEC.BAT. In this chapter, you examined the following points:

▶ You can *clean boot* the system (bypassing CONFIG.SYS and AUTOEXEC.BAT) by pressing F5 when DOS displays the message `Starting MS-DOS...` or by holding down the Shift key.

▶ You can selectively execute commands by pressing F8 when DOS starts or by placing a question mark (?) before the equals character (=) in a configuration command.

▶ If you want to ensure that all CONFIG.SYS commands are executed without user intervention, you can use the SWITCHES command to disable the F5 and F8 keys.

▶ You can use the new menu commands to create start-up menus. Each menu can contain as many as nine items, and each menu can branch to another menu. You should consider adding a *Return to Main Menu* option to each submenu.

▶ Although AUTOEXEC.BAT menus are not directly supported, the CONFIG environment variable can be tested to determine which menu item the user selected.

▶ Configuration files differ from system to system, but the majority of systems use a common set of commands. By looking at typical configuration files, you can determine whether anything obvious is missing from your system configuration.

▶ If you change CONFIG.SYS and AUTOEXEC.BAT, re-run MEMMAKER to optimize the new configuration.

Now you are ready to begin Part III of this book, in which you learn how to use DOS tools ranging from DOSKEY to DEBUG to automate your tasks and improve your productivity.

Part III:
Secrets for Automating DOS

Page 285 ◊ **Chapter 9**
Putting DOSKEY to Work

Page 305 ◊ **Chapter 10**
Moving Beyond Basic Batch Files

Page 337 ◊ **Chapter 11**
Demystifying DEBUG

Chapter 9

Putting DOSKEY to Work

In This Chapter

▶ Installing DOSKEY

▶ Reinstalling DOSKEY

▶ Using DOSKEY as a command-line manager

▶ Using DOSKEY macros

▶ Comparing DOSKEY macros to batch files

▶ My favorite DOSKEY macro tricks

▶ Moving beyond DOSKEY with ANARKEY

Installing DOSKEY

DOSKEY is a versatile tool that provides three primary and very useful functions: the ability to recall previous commands to save retyping, command-line editing (no more backspacing), and a simple and effective macro utility.

DOSKEY uses less than 4K of memory, and even that small amount can be loaded high. Because of DOSKEY's low memory demands and the features it provides, every DOS user should use DOSKEY or a similar third-party utility such as ANARKEY (discussed later in this chapter).

Installing DOSKEY couldn't be easier; you just enter the DOSKEY command with no switches, and DOSKEY is loaded as a TSR. I recommend that you add a DOSKEY statement to your AUTOEXEC.BAT file to install DOSKEY every time you boot.

Setting Insert Mode

Command-line editing is set by default to Overtype Mode. If you prefer the default to insert characters, enter the DOSKEY command as follows:

```
doskey /insert
```

You can always press the Ins key to toggle Insert Mode when you are entering an individual command. The next time you type a command, however, the default insertion mode is reinstated. After DOSKEY has been installed, you can change the default by reexecuting DOSKEY with either the /INSERT or /OVERSTRIKE switches. Believe it or not, you must type the entire switch (these long switches cannot be abbreviated). To set DOSKEY in Overtype Mode, for example, enter the following command:

```
doskey /overstrike
```

Note that this command does not change any of the other DOSKEY settings (it does not clear the command history or erase any macros).

Setting the buffer size

DOSKEY uses a buffer to store the history of executed commands and user-defined macros. By default, 512 bytes of memory are reserved for this buffer. The /BUFSIZE switch can be used to allocate a different buffer size when you first execute DOSKEY. The following command installs DOSKEY in Insert Mode and creates a 1,024-byte buffer:

```
doskey /insert /bufsize=1024
```

The smallest buffer size is 256 bytes, and you can make it as large as you want. A buffer size of 512, 1,024, or 2,048 bytes, however, generally should meet most needs.

If you are unable to recall old commands (by pressing the up-arrow key), DOSKEY has probably run out of buffer space. If you then try to assign a new DOSKEY macro (discussed later in this chapter), the following error message is displayed:

```
Insufficient memory to store macro. Use the DOSKEY command
with the /BUFSIZE switch to increase available memory.
```

Having seen the error message, you might be tempted to execute a command such as DOSKEY /BUFSIZE=1024, but that doesn't work either. The following error message is displayed:

```
Cannot change BUFSIZE.
```

The solution to these problems is to reinstall DOSKEY.

Reinstalling DOSKEY

After DOSKEY has been installed, it cannot be uninstalled, but you can reinstall it by specifying new parameters. To reinstall DOSKEY, execute the DOSKEY command with the /REINSTALL switch and any other command switches, such as /BUFSIZE and /INSERT, as shown in this example:

```
doskey /reinstall /insert /bufsize=1024
```

Unfortunately, when you reinstall DOSKEY, the command history and macros are erased. Later in this chapter, in the section "Building a macro builder," you learn how to automatically create a batch file to re-create the macros.

Using DOSKEY as a Command-Line Manager

Although DOSKEY serves a number of purposes, the vast majority of users use it for just two reasons: to edit the command line and to recall old commands. If DOSKEY served no other purposes than to edit and recall commands, it still would be a valuable tool.

Editing the command line

Sometimes the simple things in life are the most rewarding. So it goes for DOSKEY. When you enter a command, pressing the left-arrow key moves the cursor one position to the left, but, unlike in plain DOS, the character is not erased. In other words, the left-arrow key doesn't act like the Backspace key — it works just like the left-arrow key in EDIT.

In addition to being capable of moving the cursor to the left and right one character, DOSKEY supports a variety of other editing keys (see Table 9-1).

Table 9-1	The Editing Keys in DOSKEY
Key	*Purpose*
Left arrow	Moves the cursor one position to the left
Ctrl-left arrow	Moves the cursor to the beginning of the word to the left
Right arrow	Moves the cursor one position to the right
Ctrl-right arrow	Moves the cursor to the beginning of the word to the right

(continued)

Table 9-1	The Editing Keys in DOSKEY (continued)
Key	*Purpose*
Home	Moves the cursor to the beginning of the command line
Ctrl-Home	Erases all the characters to the left of the cursor and moves the remaining characters to the beginning of the command line
End	Moves the cursor to the end of the command line
Ctrl-End	Erases the character at the cursor and all remaining characters on the command line
Del	Erases the character at the cursor
Backspace	Erases the character to the left of the cursor
Esc	Erases the entire command line
Ins	Toggles between Insert and Overtype Modes

Using the command history

After DOSKEY has been loaded, every command you execute is stored in a command buffer, which forms a stack of old commands. If the DOSKEY buffer fills, the oldest commands are removed to make room for the command just entered.

When you press the up-arrow key, the last command that was executed is re-typed on the command line. Press the up-arrow key a second time to display the previous command. By repeatedly pressing the up-arrow key, you can scroll through all the past commands stored in the command buffer. You can scroll forward through the command list by pressing the down-arrow key. After you have selected the command, just press Enter to execute the command or use the editing keys to modify it.

To jump to the oldest command in the buffer, press the PgUp key.

My top five (forgotten) DOSKEY commands

The five most often used DOSKEY keys are the four arrow keys and the Ins key. If you're not using some of the other keys, you probably are not being fully productive. Here are my favorite productivity boosters:

Selecting commands by number

When you press the F7 key, DOS lists all the commands stored in the history list, with every command prefixed by a number. The oldest command is assigned number 1, and the most recent command has the largest number. If you have

```
C:\>
1: win
2: d:
3: cd\hj2
4: rpm
5: c:
6: cd\amipro
7: hdirplus *.
8: cd docs
9: del *.bak
10: j:
11: dog /test
12: dog j: /test
13: c:
14: c:
15: cd\
16: cls
C:\>Line number:
```

Figure 9-1: The use of the F7 and F9 keys to list the command history and select a command by number.

more than a screen full of old commands, DOS automatically uses the MORE filter to pause the display after every screen.

After you have perused the list of old commands, you can select one by pressing F9 and then entering the command number. Figure 9-1 shows this technique being used.

Using characters to select commands

If you can remember the first few characters of a command, you can avoid having to scroll back through all the commands to look for a specific one. Just enter one or more of the command's first characters and then press F8. DOS searches back through the command stack and, as soon as it finds a match, places the entire command on the command line.

Saving a command without executing it

Have you ever typed a long command, prepared to press Enter, and then realized that you forgot to issue another command first? Reluctantly, you press Esc to erase the premature command and then enter the correct command. Finally, when that command has been executed, you type the long command a second time. I do it all the time.

Suppose that you just typed the following command to load 1-2-3 from a network drive:

```
f:\apps\dos\lotus\12324\123 \users\ainsbrd\work\taxes94.wk1
```

Then you realize that you are not logged on to the network yet. Ugh!

To save yourself from having to retype the command, press F5 rather than Esc. F5 saves the command in the DOSKEY buffer without executing it and then erases the command line. In that way, you can enter a different command and recall the long command afterward by pressing the up-arrow key twice. I love it!

Executing two or more commands at a time

A little-known DOSKEY feature is that it can execute multiple commands in one compound statement. After you have typed one command on the command line, just press Ctrl-T and enter a second command. If you don't exceed 127 characters, you can continue entering commands and separate them with the Ctrl-T sequence. After you have entered all the commands, press Enter and each command is executed in turn.

Erasing the entire command history

To start afresh and erase all the existing commands stored in the buffer, just press Alt-F7.

Using DOSKEY Macros

Although too few people take advantage of it, DOSKEY has a useful macro facility that enables you to assign one or more commands to a single command. You can assign the following FORMAT command, for example, to the new command QFA:

```
format a: /v:technojock /q
```

When you enter QFA (for Quick Format A), DOSKEY substitutes the full format expression. This is just an example of how you can reduce potentially complex commands to one easy-to-use command. You define the shortcut command name and the command set that DOSKEY executes by using the following syntax:

```
doskey macroname=[text]
```

where *macroname* is any name you want to assign to the macro and *text* is a string of one or more commands. When the user enters *macroname*, DOSKEY executes *text*.

You create the preceding FORMAT example by using the following command:

```
doskey qfa=format a: /v:technojock /q
```

You can use any name for the macro, but it cannot include spaces or any of the redirection characters (<, >, and |, for example).

The method of removing or undefining a macro is similar to the syntax for clearing an environment entry. To remove a macro, execute DOSKEY and specify the macroname followed by the equal-sign character (=). To remove the QFA macro, for example, enter the following command:

```
doskey qfa=
```

Every time you reboot the computer, you must reinstall your macro commands. You should consider creating a batch file of your favorite macros and then call that batch file from AUTOEXEC.BAT after DOSKEY has been installed. A later section of this chapter, called "Building a macro builder," describes how you can build a batch file from the active macros.

 DOSKEY is capable only of substituting an entire command with a macro. You cannot use DOSKEY to substitute parts of a command. If you frequently copy or edit WIN.INI, for example, you might assign the single character W to represent WIN.INI by using the following statement:

```
doskey w=win.ini
```

Then, if you enter one of the following commands, you want DOSKEY to replace the *W* with WIN.INI:

```
edit w
copy w \winbak
```

Nice idea, but it doesn't work that way! You can replace only an entire command with a macro. In these examples, you end up editing or copying a file named W.

Accessing command-line switches

Optional commands or switches can be passed to batch files by using the %1 through %9 identifiers. A similar approach is used with DOSKEY, except that the nine identifiers are $1 through $9 (a $ character is used in place of the % character).

The following macro creates a VC command (for Verify Copy) that adds a /V switch to the COPY command:

```
doskey vc=copy $1 $2 /v
```

If you were to execute the command vc *.* a:, DOSKEY would execute the command copy *.* a: /v.

In addition to the nine passed parameters, DOSKEY provides another identifier used to access the entire command line — namely, $*. When you specify $* in a command, DOSKEY substitutes all the switches and parameters passed on the command line, including spaces. This capability is particularly useful when user input can exceed nine parameters or when one or more parameters can include spaces, such as the prompt used in the CHOICE command.

The following example creates a macro called DF (for *defrag*), which executes the DEFRAG command and all the user-specified options and adds the /SKIPHIGH switch to force DEFRAG to load into conventional memory:

```
doskey df=defrag $* /skiphigh
```

I wish that batch files supported %*. Maybe next time.

Piping and redirection with DOSKEY

For more information about redirection and piping, refer to Chapter 10.

To include any redirection or pipe symbols in a macro, you have to use special substitution characters that represent the real redirection characters. Imagine entering the following command to report the amount of free space in the current directory:

```
doskey dsize=dir | find "file(s)"
```

The intent of the command is to pipe the output from DIR to FIND, and FIND will echo any line that contains the string "file(s)" (the line that summarizes the total amount of space used by the files in the directory). When you enter DSIZE, a summary of the directory's files is displayed.

If you try to enter this command, however, you don't get the expected results. DOS intercepts the pipe character (|) and immediately pipes the DOSKEY command to FIND. As a result, DOSKEY only stores the command DIR with DSIZE.

The solution is to use the string $b. DOSKEY interprets it as the pipe character, but DOS ignores it when you first enter the macro-definition command. The correct way to enter the command, therefore, is as follows:

```
doskey dsize=dir $b find "file(s)"
```

There are similar substitution characters for each of the redirection commands (see Table 9-2). Note that the characters can be used in upper- or lowercase.

 If you want to use the dollar character in a command, enter two dollar characters ($$). This command stops DOSKEY from interpreting the character following the $ as a substitution character.

Table 9-2	Substitutions for the Redirection and Pipe Characters
String	*Meaning*
$b	The equivalent of I, which pipes the output from one command as input to another command
$g	The equivalent of >, which redirects output to another command, device, or file
$gg	The equivalent of >>, which appends output to the end of a file
$l	The equivalent of <, which redirects the contents of a file as input to a command

Entering multiple commands

When DOSKEY is installed, it enables you to enter multiple commands on the command line by separating every command sequence with the Ctrl-T character. To use multiple commands in a DOSKEY macro, a similar approach is used. Use the substitution characters $t, however, rather than press Ctrl-T. The following command, for example, creates the macro MCD (for Make and Change Directory):

```
doskey mcd=md $1$tcd $1
```

When you enter MCD followed by a path, the MD command is executed to make the directory, and then the CD command is executed to change to the directory.

Building a macro builder

To review the current DOSKEY macro settings, use the /MACROS switch as follows:

```
doskey /macros
```

DOSKEY responds by listing all the installed macros, as shown in this example:

```
DSIZE=dir $b find "file(s)"
?=help $*
MCD=md $1$tcd $1
QFA=format a: /v:technojock /q
VC=copy $1 $2 /v
DF=defrag $* /skiphigh
```

Every time you reboot the computer or execute DOSKEY with the /REINSTALL switch, the active macros are lost. You can use the /MACROS switch as a tool to help save the existing macro settings so that they can be easily reinstalled.

By piping the output to a batch file, you have the framework of a DOSKEY macro builder. Executing the following command, for example, creates the batch file MACROS.BAT:

```
doskey /macros > macros.bat
```

The batch file has to be modified so that it can load the DOSKEY macros. Every line must be prefixed by the text `doskey` (with a space at the end). One way to make the changes is to edit the file MACROS.BAT manually; because computers are designed to automate repetitive tasks, however, why not let the computer do it?

The free program PREFIX (written by yours truly) is included on Bob's Shareware Collection disks. PREFIX reads lines from one ASCII file and writes them to another but prefixes every line with a specified command. The full syntax for the command is explained in Chapter 10. Its use in this context, however, is straightforward. To create a new batch file, SETMACRO.BAT, by taking the input from MACROS.BAT and prefixing every line with doskey (with a space at the end), enter the following command:

```
prefix macros.bat setmacro.bat doskey
```

PREFIX then creates the batch file SETMACRO.BAT with the following contents:

```
doskey DSIZE=dir $b find "file(s)"
doskey ?=help $*
doskey MCD=md $1$tcd $1
doskey QFA=format a: /v:technojock /q
doskey VC=copy $1 $2 /v
doskey DF=defrag $* /skiphigh
```

When you execute SETMACRO, the original macro commands are installed. Magic.

Comparing DOSKEY Macros to Batch Files ____

The macro facility is similar in many ways to batch files. Both techniques allow a set of commands to be stored and then executed by invoking a shorter, simpler command, and both techniques allow the passing of command-line parameters. There are some important differences, however, and understanding them can help you to decide which option is best: macros or batch files.

This list shows the most significant differences between batch files and macros:

- Unlike batch files, macros are stored in memory, not in a file, so a macro command can be executed from any directory, regardless of the path.

- Even the smallest batch file consumes at least one cluster of disk space (usually 4,096 bytes), but macros use no disk space.

■ Because macros are loaded in memory, they operate much faster than do batch files.

■ A macro cannot call another macro command, but a batch file can call another batch file.

■ A macro can call a batch file, but a batch file cannot invoke a macro command. Only commands entered directly on the command line are accessed by DOSKEY.

■ You cannot suppress the echoing of macro commands, so the user can always observe macro commands as they execute (there is no echo off facility).

■ DOSKEY does not support the IF or GOTO statements, so no conditional branching can be performed.

■ Macros cannot access environment variables. You cannot access the path, for example, by using the %path% expression.

■ Both techniques can access nine passed parameters, but macros can access the entire command line by using $* — batch files have no equivalent.

■ Macro command names can be the same as internal DOS commands in addition to program files (with an EXE or a COM extension). The macro command is always executed in preference to the DOS command or external program of the same name. Batch files are ignored, however, if they have the same name as an internal DOS command or another program in the current directory.

■ An entire macro is limited to 127 characters, but a batch file can be any length.

My Favorite DOSKEY Macro Tricks _____

DOSKEY macros really are useful and can improve your productivity and safety if you take the time to build some valuable macros. This section discusses some of my favorites.

Question-mark help

OK, this isn't rocket science, but I like to use a question-mark character rather than the HELP command. The following macro shows how:

```
doskey ?=help $*
```

Whenever you enter ?, the DOS HELP command is launched.

Replacing, enhancing, and disabling DOS commands

A DOSKEY macro command takes priority over all other commands, whether they are internal DOS commands or external programs. In other words, the macro command is always executed. This feature enables you to disable selected commands or force additional command switches to be processed.

The following macro command, for example, disables the FORMAT command:

```
doskey format=The format command is disabled.
```

If the user enters the FORMAT command, DOSKEY executes the command The format command is disabled. The command is echoed to the screen, and DOS naturally responds with the infamous bad command or file name message (see Figure 9-2).

The following command adds the /P switch to Del to make sure that the user is prompted for confirmation before deleting a file:

```
doskey del=del $1 /p
```

By using a similar technique, the following macro creates a command that substitutes an XCOPY command in place of COPY:

```
doskey copy=xcopy $*
```

Most of the macros discussed in this section are tools that enable you to configure PCs for other (less experienced) users to help them avoid "shooting themselves in the foot." These DOSKEY macros might be loaded from AUTOEXEC.BAT. To prevent simple tampering, you might also disable the DOSKEY command by entering the following line:

```
doskey doskey=The command is not available.
```

```
D:\>format
D:\>The format command is disabled
Bad command or file name

D:\>
```

Figure 9-2: A DOSKEY macro can disable DOS commands of the same name, like FORMAT.

None of these techniques is foolproof or, more accurately, Jedi-proof. A user can simply erase all the defined macros by pressing Alt-F10. Another trick is to enter a DOS command preceded by a space. Enter the command format (preceded by a space), for example, rather than format (with no space). DOSKEY ignores the command because it does not exactly match a macro name, and the command is passed directly to DOS. DOS ignores the preceding space and the FORMAT command (proper) is executed.

Intercepting drive changes

My main desktop PC has a 1.2MB drive in drive A and a 1.44MB drive in drive B. My brain is programmed to enter b: to swap to the 3½-inch drive. When I use my notebook PC, I am forever entering b: when I mean a:. My solution is to assign the macro command a: to the macro name b:, as follows:

```
doskey b:=a:
```

Whenever I enter b:, DOSKEY intercepts it and enters a: instead. To try to train myself to end the habit of entering the wrong drive letter, I used to use the following macro:

```
doskey b:=echo ^G $ta:
```

You should enter the ^G string by pressing Ctrl-G, not by entering the two separate characters.

This macro beeped at me and then changed to drive A, but it irritated me too much, so I changed it back.

You can use a similar approach for a network drive. The following macro, for example, checks whether drive F exists; if it does not exist, a log-on command is issued before changing to drive F. Otherwise, the F: command simply is executed:

```
doskey f:=if not exist f: net logon$tf:
```

The concept of using IF and EXIST to check whether a directory exists is discussed more in Chapter 10.

Supporting multiple filenames

Some of the most popular commands support only one filemask (Del). By using a FOR loop in a macro, you can expand these types of commands to accept multiple filemasks. Consider the following macro definition:

```
doskey delall=for %n in ($*) do del %n
```

When you pass multiple filenames or masks to the command DELALL, the DEL command is called once for every separate parameter. To delete all files with the extensions of DEL, BAK, TMP, and $$$, for example, you enter the following command:

```
delall *.del *.bak *.tmp *.$$$
```

The following macro uses the same technique to enhance the COPY command to support multiple filemasks:

```
doskey copyto=for %f in ($2 $3 $4 $5 $6 $7 $8 $9) do copy %f $1
```

The COPYTO command accepts the target directory as the first argument, and the remaining arguments are the source filemasks. To copy a disparate group of files to drive A, for example, you enter a command similar to the following:

```
copyto a: *.doc *.tif *.txt \wks\*.wk3
```

Extending the search path

I hate to have a huge path. It uses up the environment and slows down the system while DOS searches every path's directory for a command. If you have a directory in the path solely to make it easy to execute a specific command from any other directory, consider creating a DOSKEY macro entry instead of clogging the PATH. To launch the CMFILER program, for example, you might create the following macro:

```
doskey cmfiler=c:\utils\cm\cmfiler
```

No matter which drive and directory is the default, when you enter the command CMFILER, the program is loaded from the directory C:\UTILS\CM.

And some quickies to finish

Here are three one-character macros I use for common tasks:

I like to enter the backslash character (\) to change the directory to the root directory. The following macro makes this possible:

```
doskey \=cd\
```

I am forever editing my CONFIG.SYS and AUTOEXEC.BAT files. The following two macros launch EDIT and load a start-up file after the press of a button:

```
doskey c=edit c:\config.sys
doskey b=edit c:\autoexec.bat
```

Going Beyond DOSKEY with ANARKEY

If you like DOSKEY, you will love ANARKEY, from Moderne Software. ANARKEY is included on Bob's Shareware Collection disks and is documented in Part V of this book.

ANARKEY, a direct replacement for DOSKEY, offers all the standard DOSKEY functions and then some. The following section summarizes ANARKEY's main features and is organized by its four primary functions: command-line editing, environment editing, history lists, and macros.

Command-line editing

Like DOSKEY, ANARKEY provides command-line editing that enables you to move the cursor along the command line and change and delete characters as you go. ANARKEY goes beyond simple editing, however, by offering file and directory completion.

If you type the command COPY and then press F8 (or Ctrl-F), for example, ANARKEY searches the current directory and puts the name of the first file directly on the command line. This feature is known as *filename completion*. You can press F8 additional times to toggle through all the filenames. Better still, if you enter a command with a partial filename and then press F8, ANARKEY reports only files that match the partial name. Type the following command, for example, and press F8:

```
edit c:\co
```

ANARKEY completes the command as `edit c:\config.sys`.

Similarly, you can use ANARKEY to complete a directory name. Suppose that you enter the command `cd\`. If you press F7 (or Ctrl-D), ANARKEY inserts the first directory in the root directory. You can scroll through the directories quickly by pressing F7 additional times. As with filename completion, you can enter a partial directory name to focus ANARKEY's directory selection.

Better still, if you enter a partial command and then press Alt-F8 (or Alt-F), ANARKEY displays a pop-up selection Window (see Figure 9-3). Like all of ANARKEY's windows, the Filename Completion window offers full mouse support.

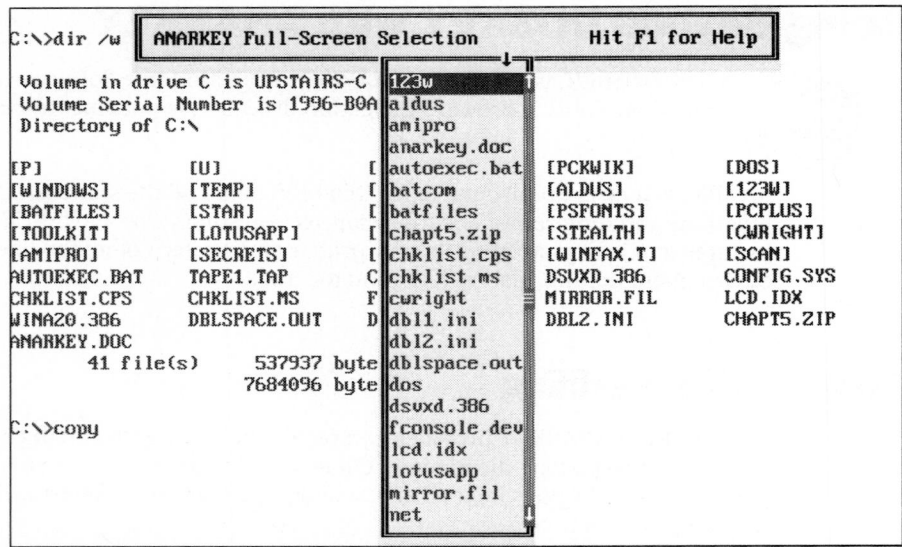

```
C:\>dir /w  | ANARKEY Full-Screen Selection        Hit F1 for Help |
                                          ┴
 Volume in drive C is UPSTAIRS-C  123w
 Volume Serial Number is 1996-B0A aldus
 Directory of C:\                 amipro
                                  anarkey.doc
[P]             [U]             [ autoexec.bat  [PCKWIK]      [DOS]
[WINDOWS]       [TEMP]          [ batcom        [ALDUS]       [123W]
[BATFILES]      [STAR]          [ batfiles      [PSFONTS]     [PCPLUS]
[TOOLKIT]       [LOTUSAPP]      [ chapt5.zip    [STEALTH]     [CWRIGHT]
[AMIPRO]        [SECRETS]       [ chklist.cps   [WINFAX.T]    [SCAN]
AUTOEXEC.BAT    TAPE1.TAP       C chklist.ms    DSVXD.386     CONFIG.SYS
CHKLIST.CPS     CHKLIST.MS      F cwright       MIRROR.FIL    LCD.IDX
WINA20.386      DBLSPACE.OUT    D db11.ini      DBL2.INI      CHAPT5.ZIP
ANARKEY.DOC                       db12.ini
        41 file(s)       537937 byte dblspace.out
                        7684096 byte dos
                                  dsvxd.386
C:\>copy                          fconsole.dev
                                  lcd.idx
                                  lotusapp
                                  mirror.fil
                                  net
```

Figure 9-3: ANARKEY displays a pop-up window that lists all matching filenames and directories when you press Alt-F8.

Environment editing

A useful extension to the command-line editing feature is the ability to edit environment strings. To edit an environment variable, enter the command set and then press F9 (or Ctrl-E). ANARKEY places on the command line the first variable in the environment. You can cycle through all the environment variables by pressing F9 additional times.

If you want to edit a specific variable and you know some or all of the environment name, just type the set command followed by the environment name (or the first part of it) and press F9. ANARKEY searches the environment and displays the first matching variable. To change the PATH command, for example, enter the command set path and press F9. ANARKEY moves the complete path statement to the command line, where you can edit it and press Enter to change it.

ANARKEY also has a pop-up environment window (see Figure 9-4) that is displayed when you press Alt-F9. The window enables you to scroll through the entire environment and select the statement you want to edit.

```
┌─────────────────────────────────────────────────────────────────┐
│ │ ANARKEY Full-Screen Selection        Hit F1 for Help │ │
│ ┌─────────────────────────────────────────────────────────┐     │
│ COMSPEC=C:\DOS\COMMAND.COM                                       │
│ CONFIG=Normal                                                   │
│ D_COL=uwcRwKWyyWw:Y*del*:g.doc:g.gde:g.hlp:y.bat               │
│ NU=C:\U\NORTON                                                  │
│ PATH=C:\DOS;C:\;C:\WINDOWS;C:\WINDOWS\NDW;C:\BATFILES;C:\U\MISC;C:\SPE;C:\U\FA│
│ PROMPT=$P$G                                                     │
│ SAGEEDIT=C:\SPE                                                 │
│ TEMP=C:\TEMP                                                    │
└─────────────────────────────────────────────────────────────────┘
```

Figure 9-4: ANARKEY displays a pop-up window that lists all the environment variables when you press Alt-F9.

History lists

Just like DOSKEY, ANARKEY maintains a history list of all the commands you have entered since ANARKEY was loaded. By pressing the up- and down-arrow keys, you can cycle through these old commands.

As you might expect, ANARKEY implements a number of features that make it more functional and useful than DOSKEY. The most visible feature is that you can display a pop-up window of the old commands by pressing Alt-F5 (or Alt-K). Figure 9-5 shows an example of a pop-up history list. You can use the arrow keys or the mouse to scroll through the commands and then press Enter to insert the command on the command line.

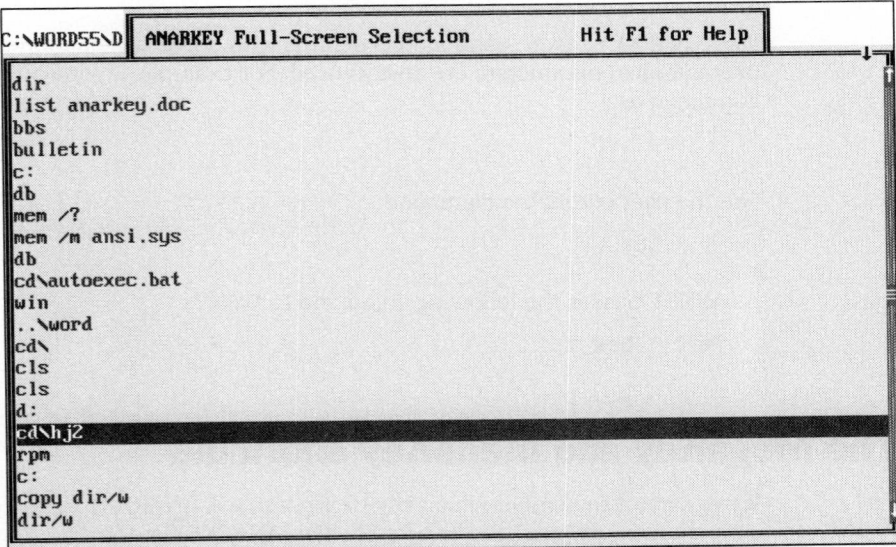

```
C:\WORD55\D │ ANARKEY Full-Screen Selection        Hit F1 for Help │
│ dir                                                              │
│ list anarkey.doc                                                │
│ bbs                                                             │
│ bulletin                                                       │
│ c:                                                             │
│ db                                                            │
│ mem /?                                                         │
│ mem /m ansi.sys                                               │
│ db                                                            │
│ cd\autoexec.bat                                              │
│ win                                                           │
│ ..\word                                                       │
│ cd\                                                           │
│ cls                                                           │
│ cls                                                           │
│ d:                                                            │
│ cd\hj2                                                        │
│ rpm                                                           │
│ c:                                                            │
│ copy dir/w                                                    │
│ dir/w                                                         │
```

Figure 9-5: Press Alt-F5 to display a history list of all the old commands.

A number of detailed enhancements make ANARKEY's buffer management easier to use than DOSKEY's — if you select a command from the buffer and execute it, for instance. The command is removed from the old position and repositioned at the head of the buffer. This procedure prevents duplicate commands from filling up the buffer as you repeatedly select and execute them. Sometimes you will want to execute a series of commands from the buffer. After you have selected and executed the first command, you simply press PgDn and ANARKEY selects the succeeding command from the buffer.

Macros

The features provided in ANARKEY's macro facility (referred to as AKA in the program documentation) are similar to those in DOSKEY's macro facility, but they use a different syntax. To install ANARKEY with macro support, you must execute ANARKEY with the -A*nnn* switch, where *nnn* is the amount of memory, in bytes, to allocate to macros.

To create an ANARKEY macro, use the following syntax:

> :*macroname* [*text*]

You can view a list of the installed macros by pressing Alt-F4, and you can erase the macros by pressing Alt-X.

DOSKEY and ANARKEY macros treat passed parameters a little differently. ANARKEY does not provide a feature to access the entire command line (like DOSKEY's $* switch); access to the nine passed parameters is by way of the symbols from %1 to %9, as in batch files, rather than from $1 to $9.

If an ANARKEY macro command is defined with no variable parameters, the user-supplied parameters are always used. For example, if you define the D command as

```
:d del /p
```

and the user enters the command

```
d *.bak
```

ANARKEY passes the following command to DOS:

```
del *.bak /p
```

The MegaKey and MenuKey shortcuts

If you cannot remember which key to press to ask ANARKEY to complete a command, just press the Tab key (which ANARKEY modestly calls the MegaKey) and ANARKEY guesses at the most appropriate command-

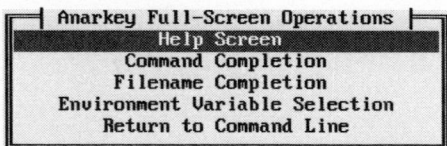

Figure 9-6: When you press Shift-Tab, ANARKEY displays a menu that provides quick access to each pop-up window.

completion technique to use (filename, directory name, or a command from the history list, for example).

Similarly, if you cannot remember which key pops up which window, just press Shift-Tab and ANARKEY displays a menu of all the windows (see Figure 9-6).

Summary

This chapter described the many uses of DOSKEY and showed how it can increase your productivity by automating tasks. The chapter discussed the following points:

▶ In addition to providing basic line editing, DOSKEY permits old commands to be recalled by using the up- and down-arrow keys.

▶ Old commands also can be displayed and reclaimed from the history list by using the lesser known F7 and F9 functions.

▶ Multiple commands can be entered on one line, if every block is separated by the Ctrl-T character.

▶ One or more commands can be stored as a DOSKEY macro and executed by entering the macro name. By using the names of existing DOS commands or programs, a macro can replace or disable a standard command.

▶ Macros can access command parameters by using the $1 to $9 expressions. The special sequence $* represents the entire command-line parameter string.

▶ DOSKEY stores the command history and macros in a buffer. The size of the buffer is 512 bytes by default, but you can use the /BUFSIZE switch to identify a custom buffer size.

▶ Although DOSKEY macros are faster than batch files and consume no disk space, batch files can contain more commands, and they access environment variables and support conditional branching.

▶ As useful as DOSKEY is, ANARKEY offers a richer set of features and sports pop-up selection windows.

In many respects, batch files pick up where DOSKEY leaves off. Chapter 10 explains how to increase productivity even more by using advanced batch-file techniques.

Chapter 10

Moving Beyond Basic Batch Files

In This Chapter

▶ Applying the tools of the trade

▶ Using power techniques with redirection and pipes

▶ Using environment innovations

▶ Determining dates and times with batch files

▶ A batch file potpourri

▶ Using batch files with Windows 3.1

▶ Enhancing batch files

The Tools of the Trade

With more than 100 commands, many with five or more switches, it's no wonder that few people take advantage of the wealth of features in DOS. The key to harnessing the power of DOS is within batch files.

AUTOEXEC.BAT, the mother of all batch files, is a great illustration of how batch files simplify DOS. Just imagine having to enter all those start-up commands every time you boot your computer. Unthinkable. It is a shame that many users don't take the time to automate tasks by creating batch files. A DOS Jedi knows better.

No one would describe the DOS batch facility as a programming language; C or Pascal it isn't. The batch file tools provided with DOS are crude, in fact. But with a little imagination and trickery, you can use these simple tools to create powerful and useful utilities that will make you more productive.

A Crash Course on Batch Files

Batch files are ASCII files that contain one or more commands. Every batch file name has an extension of BAT (short for batch). You execute all the commands listed in the batch file by simply entering the name of the batch file at the command prompt. Think of a batch file as a script or list of commands that can be executed in one easy step.

The following simple batch file, MCD1.BAT, creates the directory \DEMO with the MD command and then uses CD to change the default directory to \DEMO:

```
md \demo
cd \demo
```

You could create this batch file by running EDIT and entering the two lines of commands. To run this batch file, just enter this command:

```
c:\> mcd1
```

DOS, in turn, executes the MD and CD statements.

Batch files can do more than process standard commands, and several DOS commands are designed specifically for use in batch files. Consider the following batch file, MCD2.BAT:

```
@echo off
rem MCD2 by R D Ainsbury
rem Makes a \DEMO directory and changes to it
md \demo
cd \demo
```

The @echo off line turns off command echoing to reduce screen clutter, and the rem command is used to add comments to the file. The example batch file is still very limited because it creates only the specific directory \DEMO. You can, however, easily improve it to create any valid directory. Like many DOS commands, batch files can be executed with optional switches; within the batch file, these switches are represented by the variables %1 through %9. The enhanced version of the batch file, MCD3.BAT, uses the %1 variable to represent the first item specified after the batch filename on the command line:

```
@echo off
rem MCD3 by R D Ainsbury
rem Makes a directory and changes to it
md %1
cd %1
```

To create and change to any directory, just enter the command MCD3 and then the directory name. The directory automatically is created and made the default. To create the directory \STUFF, for example, you just enter the following command:

```
c:\> mcd3 \stuff
```

You can improve this batch file with error checking and input validation. If you use an asterisk in the directory name, for example, DOS cannot create the directory. Look at the example for the IF command in Part IV, "The Complete DOS 6 Command Reference," for an example of how to improve error checking by using other batch commands, such as IF and GOTO.

A batch file command summary

Table 10-1 contains an alphabetical list of the DOS 6 batch file commands and a brief description of each command.

In addition to the standard batch file commands, a few other DOS keywords and commands are often utilized in batch files (see Table 10-2).

Table 10-1	DOS 6 Batch File Command Summary
Command	**Description**
@	Prevents the remainder of the command line from being echoed
:LABEL	Identifies in a batch file a location where processing can branch to by using the GOTO command
CALL	Launches a second batch file; when the second batch file is completed, control returns to the calling batch file
CHOICE	Displays a prompt and waits for the user to press one key from a set of keys
ECHO	Displays a string or toggles the command-echoing status
FOR	Executes a command or statement multiple times and applies a new string or filename with every iteration
GOTO	Branches command processing to a specific location (label) in the batch file
IF	Provides a conditional branch in a batch file execution; can be used to compare two strings, test the ERRORLEVEL returned by a program, or test whether a file exists
PAUSE	Temporarily halts batch file execution and waits for any key to be pressed
REM	REM, short for remark, is designed for adding comments to batch files (and to CONFIG.SYS); any text on a line that starts with REM is ignored
SHIFT	Allows access from a batch file to more than nine passed parameters by dropping the first passed parameter and shifting all other parameters to the left one position

Table 10-2	Other Batch File Tools
Item	**Description**
FIND	Searches for the presence or absence of specific text.
SORT	Sorts ASCII data and directs the sorted output to a device or file.
%0..%9	Variables entered on the command line when the batch file was executed. Initially, %0 contains the name of the batch file, %1 contains the first parameter, %2 contains the second parameter, and so on.
%ENVVAR%	A variable whose value is equal to the contents of the environment variable with the name *ENVVAR*. For example, in a batch file, %PATH% has the value of the full path, and %COMSPEC% contains the COMMAND.COM path and filename.
ERRORLEVEL	A value in the range from 0 to 255 that a program returns to indicate success or failure. You should use IF to test the ERRORLEVELs in reverse order.

It's about time we had a choice

I won't dwell on the basic use of the batch commands — you can refer to the command reference in Part IV for a full definition and description of each command. One new batch command, however, deserves some attention.

We've been waiting ten years for a DOS batch file command that prompts for input, and — finally — we have it. The CHOICE batch command is an external command that is less than 2,000 bytes in size. Because half the file contains help text, I wonder why it took so long!

This list shows the primary features of CHOICE:

■ CHOICE displays an optional message and waits for the user to press a key.

■ By default, CHOICE waits until either Y or N is pressed, but you can optionally specify a set of valid keys.

■ You can enable case sensitivity, but keys in either case are allowed by default.

■ An ERRORLEVEL is set to indicate which key the user pressed. Usually, a CHOICE statement is followed immediately by one or more IF statements.

■ You can optionally specify a time-out period in the range from 0 to 99 seconds and a default key. After the time-out period has elapsed, CHOICE terminates and sets the ERRORLEVEL corresponding to the default key. Contrary to most other commands, CHOICE sets an ERRORLEVEL of 0 to indicate an error (a syntax error in the command or the user pressed Ctrl-Break, for example).

As useful as CHOICE is, it lacks a number of features:

■ Even though CHOICE supports most standard keys (including ;, [, and *), it does not support the spacebar, function keys, or key combinations such as Alt-X.

■ There is no easy way to set CHOICE to accept any key.

■ CHOICE supports only single-key input — there is no convenient way to enter a word or phrase.

The following example shows CHOICE used in a batch file to prompt the user to choose the type of pointing device:

```
1  @echo off
2  choice /c:mtn /t:n,10 Do you want to load the Mouse,
   Tablet or Neither
3  if errorlevel 3 goto end
4  if errorlevel 2 goto Tablet
5  mouse /y
6  goto end
7  :Tablet
8  tabk /c:345
9  :end
```

For clarity, every batch file listing in this chapter includes line numbers. These line numbers are not part of the batch file — they are used as reference points in the text. If you create these batch files, do not add line numbers.

The /C:MTN switch on line 2 instructs CHOICE to accept any one of three characters: M, T, or N. Because the case-sensitivity switch, /S, was not specified, either upper- or lowercase letters are accepted.

The ERRORLEVELs returned from CHOICE are tested (in reverse order, of course) to determine which key the user pressed. The ERRORLEVELs correspond with the order in which the keys were specified by using the /C switch. In this case, a 3 is returned if the user pressed N, a 2 if the user pressed T, and a 1 if the user pressed M.

The /T:N,10 switch on line 2 instructs CHOICE to wait for ten seconds for input. If no key is pressed, CHOICE proceeds as though the user had pressed N.

Figure 10-1 shows the prompt generated when the batch file is executed. Notice that CHOICE automatically displays the valid keys in the format [M,T,N]?. You can suppress this prompt by using the /N switch.

The prompt that displays the valid keys is always located in the first character position following the message text. Add a space at the end of the CHOICE command line to separate the message text and the prompt.

```
C:\BATFILES>getmouse
Do you want to load the Mouse, Tablet or Neither[M,T,N]?
```

Figure 10-1: CHOICE displays some message text and a list of valid keys.

If you want to include a slash mark (/) in the message text, enclose the message in quotation marks. This action prevents CHOICE from trying to interpret as a switch the character following the /. If you use a / and don't include the quotation marks, you get one of the following messages (depending on which character follows the /):

```
Invalid switch on command line
```

or

```
Only one prompt string allowed
```

 Do not use the pipe and filter characters (|, <, >, >>, and <<) in the CHOICE text, even if the text is enclosed in quotation marks.

CHOICE is ideal for building simple menu systems. The following example is a complete menu system contained in one batch file. Figure 10-2 shows the menu screen it produces.

```
1   @echo off
2   :top
3   c:
4   cd\
5   cls
6   echo
7   echo                    ┌─────────────────────────────┐
8   echo                    ‖      Buster's Main Menu      ‖
9   echo                    ‖                             ‖
10  echo                    ‖  1   Incremental Backup      ‖
11  echo                    ‖  2   Full Backup             ‖
12  echo                    ‖  3   Windows                 ‖
13  echo                    ‖                             ‖
14  echo                    ‖  Q   Quit to DOS Prompt      ‖
15  echo.                   └─────────────────────────────┘
16  echo.
17  choice /c:q123 /n "        Choose a menu option: "
18  if errorlevel 4 goto LoadWin
19  if errorlevel 3 goto FullBack
20  if errorlevel 2 goto IncBack
21  goto quit
22
23  rem Run Msbackup using inc.set
24  :incback
25  msbackup inc.set
26  goto top
27
28  rem Run Msbackup using full.set
```

```
29 :fullback
30 msbackup full.set
31 goto top
32
33 rem Change command prompt and run Windows
34 :loadwin
35 prompt Enter EXIT to return to Windows$_$p$g
36 win
37 prompt $p$g
38 goto top
39
40 :quit
```

Editor tips

Most batch files are less than a page or two long. EDIT, the full-screen editor, provides a convenient way to create and edit batch files. Although EDIT supports the normal conventions for editing files, the tips in this section can increase your productivity:

Typing special ASCII characters. To enter a nonstandard ASCII character, such as the line-drawing characters used to draw boxes, you must enter the character's ASCII value. Appendix C in the *MS-DOS User's Guide* contains a

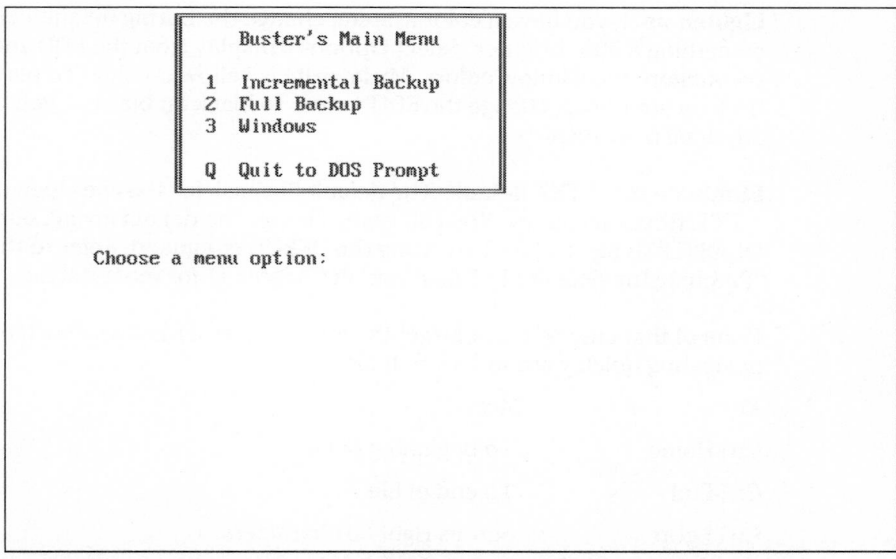

```
      Buster's Main Menu

  1  Incremental Backup
  2  Full Backup
  3  Windows

  Q  Quit to DOS Prompt
```

```
   Choose a menu option:
```

Figure 10-2: A full-screen menu that utilizes the new CHOICE batch command.

complete list of all 256 ASCII characters. After you have determined the three-digit ASCII code, follow these steps:

1. Make sure that Num Lock is enabled.

2. Hold down the Alt key.

3. Press the three digits on the numeric keypad.

4. Release the Alt key.

The special ASCII character will be inserted at the cursor position.

Use QBASIC's Editor. When you execute the EDIT command, it in turn executes QBASIC.EXE with the /EDITOR switch. The /EDITOR switch tells QBASIC to switch into edit-only mode so that many of the QBASIC-related menu options are hidden from view. Unfortunately, a couple of useful editing features also are suppressed. Try running QBASIC rather than EDIT to take advantage of the following two features:

■ Use the View⇨Split menu option to divide the screen into two separate areas. This feature enables you to view one area of the file while you are editing another area. You can press F6 to flip the cursor from window to window. Select View⇨Split a second time to return to a single edit screen.

■ Press F4 to view the DOS screen that was displayed when you launched QBASIC. This feature is very useful when you try to fix a bug in a batch file and you want to see the errors while you are editing the file.

Lighten up. If you have a color system, change the boring default colors to something a little brighter. Select Options⇨Display from the EDIT menu to reconfigure the window colors. My favorite is yellow on blue. To play a devious trick on your boss, change the EDIT colors to black on black — you can't see anything on-screen!

Eliminate the *.TXT default. The default filemask for the File Open dialog box, *.TXT, drives me crazy. You can easily change the default string, buried in the QBASIC.EXE file, to *.BAT by using the DEBUG command. Refer to the section "Patching the default EDIT filemask" in Chapter 11 for more details.

Control that cursor. Don't forget the following lesser known shortcut keys for navigating quickly around a batch file:

Key	Action
Ctrl-Home	To beginning of file
Ctrl-End	To end of file
Ctrl-PgUp	Scrolls right 80 characters
Ctrl-PgDn	Scrolls left 80 characters
Ctrl-up arrow	Scrolls up a line

Ctrl-down arrow	Scrolls down a line
Ctrl-left arrow	To the left one word
Ctrl-right arrow	To the right one word
Ctrl-Enter	To beginning of next line (without a carriage return)
Ctrl-Q,E	To top of window
Ctrl-Q,X	To bottom of window

As useful as EDIT is, there are many features it doesn't support. For example, there is no quick way to draw boxes, you can edit only one file at a time, you cannot easily import text from another file, and it does not support block column moves. If you are looking for an editor that has these additional features and much more, try Semware's excellent shareware editor, QEDIT. Refer to Part V of this book for a full description of QEDIT's features.

Power Techniques That Use Redirection and Pipes _____

The DOS redirection and piping characters play an important role in advanced batch file programming. You can, for example, pass characters to commands, create temporary files, and search or suppress command output.

Table 10-3 summarizes the redirection and pipe characters and describes their purpose.

DOS creates a temporary file behind the scenes whenever data is piped from one command to another. The output from one command is redirected to a temporary file, the temporary file then is redirected as input to the second command, and, finally, the temporary file is deleted. DOS creates the temporary file in the

Table 10-3	DOS 6 Redirection and Pipe Characters
Character	**Purpose**
>	Redirects command output to another command, device, or file; if output is redirected to a file that already exists, the original data is erased and the new output is located at the beginning of the file
>>	Redirects command output to a file but appends the output to the end of the file instead of erasing the old data
<	Redirects to a command the contents of a file as input
|	Pipes the output from one command as input to another command

directory specified with the TEMP environment variable. If no such variable exists, the file is created in the current directory.

The following section looks at a variety of real-life applications for the redirection and piping tools.

Just say yes

Some DOS commands have a habit of prompting for confirmation before proceeding with a task. For example, when you enter the command

```
del *.*
```

DOS displays this message:

```
Are you sure (Y/N)?
```

Although this message provides a valid safety feature for command-line execution, it can be annoying when a batch file pauses for confirmation part of the way through a series of commands.

By piping the output from ECHO to a command, you can trick the command into believing that a key was pressed. The following batch file shows this technique used with the DEL command:

```
1   @echo off
2   echo y | del *.*
```

If you create this batch file, make sure that you run it from a temporary directory. Don't forget that it deletes every file in the current directory and doesn't prompt for confirmation. Alternatively, you can change the echo y statement to echo n.

The use of ECHO to pipe keystrokes to a command is useful but very limited. Bob's Shareware Collection disks include the champion of key stuffers — STACKEY, from CtrlAlt Associates. This small TSR enables you to pass almost any key, key combination, or string to an application.

The following EDITBAT.BAT batch file, for example, uses STACKEY to store some keystrokes and then start EDIT. As soon as EDIT starts, STACKEY feeds these keystrokes to the editor. In this example, the keystrokes create the beginning of a new batch file:

```
1   @echo off
2   stackey W36 ES "@echo off" CR "REM Written by R D Ainsbury" CR
3   if not "%1"=="" stackey @F "S" "%1.bat" CR
4   edit
```

Line 2 instructs STACKEY to wait 36 clock ticks (2 seconds) before passing the keystrokes to the application. The ES code represents the Esc key and is used to remove the initial dialog box that EDIT displays when no filename is specified. The code CR (for *carriage return*) represents the Enter key. Line 3 checks to see whether the batch file was passed a parameter; if so, the keys Alt-F,S are passed to the editor to invoke the File⇨Save menu option. The filename then is entered.

As this example illustrates, STACKEY is a great deal more powerful than ECHO.

Just be quiet

@echo off is a great way to stop all the screen noise that occurs when batch file commands are being processed, but it doesn't stop the commands from displaying unwanted messages. If you try to rename a file and a problem occurs, for example, DOS displays the following message:

```
Invalid filename or file not found
```

To suppress these sorts of unwanted messages, you can use the following syntax to pipe the output of the command to the NUL device:

command > nul

The following commands are an extract from the RN.BAT batch file for renaming files:

```
....
5  if not exist %1 goto nosource
6  if exist %2 goto oldtarget
7  rename %1 %2 > nul
8  if not exist %2 goto failed
9  echo File Renamed!...
```

Notice that, because any messages the RENAME command on line 7 generates are redirected to the NUL device, the user doesn't see them. Refer to the IF command in Part IV of this book for the full RN.BAT listing.

To pause a batch file without displaying the standard message to press any key to continue, you can display your own message with ECHO and redirect the pause output to the NUL device:

```
1  @echo off
2  echo Press a key and we'll get busy....
3  pause > nul
```

Another way to suppress messages is to use the CTTY command to effectively turn off the screen and the keyboard. First, you execute the command

```
ctty nul
```

to redirect all I/O to the NUL device. You resume normal operations by executing this command:

```
ctty con
```

The following batch file skeleton shows this format:

```
@echo off
ctty nul
.....
.....
ctty con
```

This approach prevents having to redirect every individual command to the NUL device. Because the CTTY NUL statement effectively disables the keyboard, you should use this technique only when you are confident that the batch file is working and can handle all error conditions. The batch file ignores Ctrl-Break and any other key while CTTY is set to NUL.

Displaying command output selectively

You learned in the preceding section how to suppress all output from a command by redirecting the output to a NUL device. If you want some, but not all, of the output, you can pipe the output to FIND and limit the output to the line that contains some specified text.

You can use this technique with the DIR command to show the number of files and space a directory uses. When you enter the DIR command with no switches, the display of volume details normally is followed by a list of all the files and then a summary. The word file(s) is always printed on the line that summarizes the directory statistics. You can display this single line by searching for the "file(s)" with FIND using the batch file DIRSIZE.BAT as follows:

```
@echo off
cd
echo Directory statistics:
dir | find "file(s)"
```

Figure 10-3 shows an example of the output this simple batch file generates.

The CHKFRAG.BAT batch file uses the same approach to filter the output from the following command, which reports individual file fragmentation:

```
chkdsk filemask
```

```
C:\BATFILES>dirsize
C:\BATFILES
Directory statistics:
      21 file(s)      31828 bytes
```

Figure 10-3: You can pipe command output to FIND to enable one specific line of output to be displayed.

After checking the integrity of the drive, CHKDSK reports individual file fragmentation or reports that there was no fragmentation. In either case, the word `contiguous` is displayed so that it can be the subject of the FIND command in the following CHKFRAG.BAT batch file:

```
@echo off
rem CHKFRAG checks for file fragmentation
if "%1"=="" goto CHKALL
echo Checking the file(s) %1 for fragmentation ...
chkdsk %1 | find "contiguous"
goto QUIT
:CHKALL
echo Checking all files in current directory for fragmentation ...
chkdsk *.* | find "contiguous"
:QUIT
```

Environment Innovations_____

The DOS environment is a small storehouse for keeping general system settings that DOS and applications software use. The environment is also a useful resource for batch file programmers.

You may recall that you use the SET command to manage and view the environment. Enter SET with no switches to see the complete environment or use the following syntax to assign new data to an environment variable:

```
set varname=[string]
```

You can use the syntax %*envvar*% to access from a batch file the value of any environment variable, in much the same way you access a passed parameter by using the syntax %*n*. The following single-line batch file, for example, displays the value of the PROMPT environment variable:

```
1  @echo off
2  echo %prompt%
```

Unlike most programming languages, the batch language doesn't support the creation of temporary variables. With a little ingenuity, however, you can overcome this shortcoming by using the environment to save and restore data.

 If you encounter the message that the environment is out of space, you can increase the environment by using the /E switch with COMMAND in a SHELL statement. See the COMMAND entry in Part IV, "The Complete DOS 6 Command Reference," for more information.

Temporarily changing the search path

The PATH command does not have a switch for adding a directory to the search path. You can change PATH by editing the PATH statement in AUTOEXEC.BAT and reboot the system. Because the search path is stored in the environment, however, the following simple batch file, NEWPATH.BAT, makes the task easy:

```
1  @echo off
2  path %1;%path%
```

To add a new directory to the search path, run NEWPATH.BAT and pass the new directory as a parameter (NEWPATH C:\WP, for example). Line 2 sets the path to the passed parameter, followed by a semicolon and %path% (the current path).

You can refine the batch file by using the redirection characters > and >> to create another batch file, OLDPATH.BAT, which resets the path back to its original state:

```
1  @echo off
2  if "%1"=="" goto HELP
3  if "%1"=="/?" goto HELP
```

```
4   if exist c:\oldpath.bat goto overwrite
5   :proceed
6   echo @echo off > c:\oldpath.bat
7   path >> c:\oldpath.bat
8   echo echo The old path has been restored. >> c:\oldpath.bat
9   echo echo OLDPATH.BAT has been deleted (ignore next
message) >> c:\oldpath.bat
10  echo del c:\oldpath.bat >> c:\oldpath.bat
11  echo Enter the command OLDPATH to reset the original path
12  goto changepath
13  :overwrite
14  choice Overwrite C:\OLDPATH.BAT
15  if errorlevel 2 goto changepath
16  goto proceed
17  :CHANGEPATH
18  path %1;%path%
19  goto quit
20  :HELP
21  echo Adds a directory to the search path and creates an
OLDPATH batch file.
22  echo SYNTAX:      %1 pathdir
23  :quit
```

Lines 2 and 3 check to see whether the user failed to pass a parameter or passed the /? parameter. In either case, control jumps to line 21, which displays a brief help message.

The NEWPATH batch file dynamically creates a batch file called OLDPATH.BAT in the root directory of drive C. Line 4 uses an IF statement to determine whether the file already exists; if it does, the CHOICE command on line 14 prompts the user for confirmation before overwriting it. Line 6 uses the > redirector to create the new batch file (or overwrite the existing one) with the single line @echo off as the contents. Lines 7 through 10 use the >> redirector to add four more lines to the batch file. When you execute the temporary batch file OLDPATH, the path changes back to the original setting and the batch file deletes itself.

Finally, line 18 is executed to insert the %1 variable at the beginning of the path.

The message that the batch file is missing is displayed when you execute OLDPATH. This message appears because the batch file deletes itself while DOS is executing it.

Managing the TEMP variable

More and more programs, including Windows, are using the TEMP environment variable to ascertain where temporary files should be created. You can use the following simple batch file to assign a TEMP directory if one doesn't already exist or to prompt before changing an existing value:

```
@echo off
if "%temp%"=="" goto empty
choice Temp is currently set to %temp%. Overwrite it
if errorlevel 2 goto quit
:EMPTY
set temp=%1
Echo The TEMP environment variable is now %temp%
:QUIT
```

Saving and restoring the environment

Bob's Shareware Collection disks include a useful batch file utility called PREFIX.EXE. PREFIX reads lines from one ASCII file and writes them to another but prefixes every line with a specified command. The syntax of PREFIX is

```
prefix sourcefilename targetfilename prefixcommand
```

PREFIX sets the following ERRORLEVELs:

0 Completed successfully

1 Not enough parameters specified

2 Could not open source file

3 Could not open (or create) target file

The following batch file, SAVEENV.BAT, uses PREFIX to create a temporary batch file called OLDENV for restoring the environment:

```
1  @echo off
2  set > temp.$$$
3  echo @echo off > c:\oldenv.bat
4  prefix temp.$$$ c:\oldenv.bat set
5  del temp.$$$ > nul
6  echo del c:\oldenv.bat >> c:\oldenv.bat
```

Line 2 pipes the output from the SET command to a temporary file, TEMP.$$$. Line 3 creates in the root directory of drive C a new batch file called OLDENV.BAT and adds the line @echo off to it. Line 4 uses PREFIX to read each line from TEMP.$$$ and add each line, with the prefix "set ", to the end of the file OLDENV.BAT. The file TEMP.$$$ is deleted, and the following line is added to the end of the OLDENV.BAT file:

```
del c:\oldenv.bat
```

After you run SAVEENV.BAT to save the environment settings, you can run OLDENV to restore the old environment.

 You can use PREFIX in a variety of batch file situations. See the section "Saving the current directory," later in this chapter, for another example of PREFIX in action.

Uppercasing input

When you use the syntax %envvar% to access an environment variable from a batch file, DOS uses a case-insensitive search of the environment to determine whether the variable exists. This capability provides a sneaky way to make a case-insensitive test of parameters passed to batch files.

The following batch file fragment uses traditional techniques to check for both upper- and lowercase input:

```
. . . .
4  if "%1"=="RED" goto red
5  if "%1"=="red" goto red
. . . .
```

Unfortunately, if you enter red in another case mixture (Red, for example), the batch file doesn't recognize it. Although you can test for every possible combination of upper- and lowercase letters for a short word like *red,* testing on a longer word, such as *lightmagenta,* is totally impractical.

If you use the passed parameter to create an environment variable, you can then use the *%envvar%* syntax in an IF statement to perform a case-insensitive test. The following batch file fragment uses this technique:

```
. . . .
4  set $$%1=clever
5  if "%$$red%"=="clever" goto RED:
6  if "%$$blue%"=="clever" goto BLUE:
. . . .
20  set %1=
. . . .
```

The passed parameter is prefixed with $$ before it is added to the environment. This quick and easy method reduces the chances of overwriting an existing environment variable — I've never encountered any variable that normally begins with $$.

In the example, the text *clever* was assigned to the environment variable, and the same text is used in the IF statements. You can use any text for this purpose, but keep it short to reduce environment space consumption.

The IF statement on line 5 intercepts a parameter of red, regardless of whether it is RED, Red, red, ReD, or any case mixture.

The only drawback with this technique is that, because it uses the environment, the environment can run out of space.

An alternative is to echo the passed parameter and pipe it to the FIND command. By specifying the /I switch with FIND, you can perform a case-insensitive search. Here is an example:

```
echo %1 | find "red" /i
```

This command needs a few refinements. First, if FIND locates the text, it normally echoes the text to the screen, but this capability is not useful in this application. If FIND does not locate the text, however, a nonzero ERRORLEVEL is set. By piping the FIND output to the NUL device and testing for a nonzero ERRORLEVEL, you can implement a case-insensitive test:

```
echo %1 | find "red" /i > nul
if not errorlevel 1 echo You entered RED!
```

One more refinement is required. FIND searches for the characters red anywhere in the input parameter string. The preceding test responds in the same way to red and lightred, or any other string containing the substring red. By inserting the search string between two characters, you can ensure that there is a complete match on the full passed parameter. You can surround the string parameter in the example code with two $ characters:

```
echo $%1$ | find "$red$" /i > nul
if not errorlevel 1 echo You entered RED!
```

Enhancements to FIND

One of the more subtle enhancements to DOS 6 is the addition of ERRORLEVEL support in the FIND command. The improved FIND command returns the following ERRORLEVELs indicating whether or not the text was found:

ERRORLEVEL 0   The text was found.

ERRORLEVEL 1   The text was not found.

ERRORLEVEL 2   An error occurred and the search failed.

Although this may seem like a very minor enhancement, it provides a whole grab bag of new batch file techniques. Many of the batch files in the remainder of this chapter exploit the new ERRORLEVEL support in FIND.

Dates, Times, and Batch Files

On the surface, batch files seem to have no support for date- and time-related tasks; lurking beneath the surface, however, are a number of techniques you can use.

Waiting for a while

Many programs pause to display a message or logo for a brief time and then start executing tasks. You can implement the same facility in a batch file by using the CHOICE command to implement a fixed-period delay.

By using the /N switch to suppress the [Y,N]-style prompt, and the /T switch to specify the default key and the delay time, you suppress all output from CHOICE and make it wait a specified number of seconds. The following command pauses for five seconds and then proceeds with the next statement in the batch file:

```
choice /c:a /n /t:a,5
```

The only weakness with this approach is that the time-out period is infinite if the user presses an invalid key. To work around the problem, use the /C switch to specify all the standard keys. Then, if the user presses a key, the worst that can happen is that CHOICE will finish early and the user will continue — most users would probably see this as a useful feature.

If the user presses a nonlisted key (such as the spacebar or Enter), the batch file pauses until the user presses a standard key or Ctrl-Break.

The following batch file uses this technique to display a copyright notice:

```
@echo off
cls
echo.
echo.
echo.
echo   ┌─────────────────────────────────────────────┐
echo   ║                                             ║
echo   ║              Batch Files R Us               ║
echo   ║                  v2.05                      ║
echo   ║                                             ║
echo   ║    Copyright 1993 TechnoJock Software, Inc. ║
echo   ║                                             ║
echo   └─────────────────────────────────────────────┘
choice /c:abcdefghijklmnopqrstuvwxyz12345678790 /n /t:A,5
cls
echo Lets get busy...
....
```

What day of the week is it?

The tiny program WEEKDAY.COM sets an ERRORLEVEL to indicate the day of the week. Sunday is represented by an ERRORLEVEL of 0, Monday by 1, and through to Saturday, with an ERRORLEVEL of 6. WEEKDAY.COM, an 8-byte (count 'em) program created in a few seconds with DEBUG, is available on Bob's Shareware Collection disks. Chapter 11 explains how to use DEBUG to create WEEKDAY.COM, as well as WHATDAY.COM, WHATMON.COM, and WHATYEAR.COM.

The following skeleton batch file, TODAYIS.BAT, shows how to test the ERRORLEVEL returned by WEEKDAY.COM to determine the day of the week:

```
1  @echo off
2  weekday
3  if errorlevel 6 echo Saturday
4  if errorlevel 5 if not errorlevel 6 echo Friday
5  if errorlevel 4 if not errorlevel 5 echo Thursday
6  if errorlevel 3 if not errorlevel 4 echo Wednesday
7  if errorlevel 2 if not errorlevel 3 echo Tuesday
8  if errorlevel 1 if not errorlevel 2 echo Monday
9  if errorlevel 0 if not errorlevel 1 echo Sunday
```

What time is it?

Even a simple task like displaying the current time involves a few tricks. As you know, you use the TIME command to modify the system time. When you enter the TIME command, output similar to the following is displayed:

```
Current time is 12:00:11.86a
Enter new time:
```

Although TIME displays the current time, it waits for you to change the time or press Enter. Because ECHO commands always include a carriage return, you can use the ECHO command to feed an Enter to the TIME command:

```
echo.|time
```

The `echo.` statement instructs ECHO to draw a blank line and then enter a carriage return. This carriage return is piped to TIME to emulate your pressing Enter.

Checking ERRORLEVELs in Batch Files

The IF statement is used in batch files to test the ERRORLEVEL returned by a program. One quirk of an IF ERRORLEVEL test is that a TRUE value is applied if the ERRORLEVEL is equal to *or greater than* the test value. The important point to note is that a larger ERRORLEVEL returns a TRUE value in an IF ERRORLEVEL test. For example, if the actual ERRORLEVEL returned by a program is 2, the following expression will always ECHO true:

```
if errorlevel 1 echo true
```

One way to accommodate this characteristic of the IF ERRORLEVEL test is to test ERRORLEVELs in descending order and then branch to another location of the batch file using GOTO. The following batch file fragment illustrates this technique:

```
if errorlevel 2 goto label1
```

```
if errorlevel 1 goto label2
if errorlevel 0 goto label3
```

If you do not use GOTO in the IF ERRORLEVEL statement to branch to another location in the batch file, DOS proceeds with the next IF statement on the subsequent line. Each subsequent IF ERRORLEVEL test would also respond TRUE. If you don't use a GOTO statement, you should use two IF ERRORLEVEL statements in a single expression — one testing for a value and the other testing the next larger value. Here is an example:

```
if errorlevel 2 if not errorlevel 3 echo 2
if errorlevel 1 if not errorlevel 2 echo 1
if errorlevel 0 if not errorlevel 1 echo 0
```

The batch file TODAYIS.BAT shown in the preceding section uses this technique.

The revised TIME command still displays two lines of text, but you can filter out the second line with the FIND command. By searching for the word Current, FIND displays only the first line of the text. The complete expression for displaying the current time, therefore, becomes

```
echo.|time|find "Current"
```

When you execute this command, output similar to the following is displayed:

```
Current time is 12:00:11.15a
```

Waiting for a specific time

By using the technique outlined in the previous section, you can use the TIME command to pause a batch file until a specific time is reached. The following batch file, WAITFOR.BAT, waits until a specified time is reached before executing one or more commands:

```
 1  @echo off
 2  if "%1"=="" goto help
 3  if "%1"=="/?" goto help
 4  set $$$$TIME=is %1
 5  echo Waiting for time %1
 6  :LOOP
 7  echo.|time|find "%$$$$TIME%" > nul
 8  if errorlevel 0 if not errorlevel 1 goto ontime
 9  goto loop
10  :ONTIME
11  set $$$$TIME=
12  rem Insert the timed commands below
13  echo Alarm Alarm Alarm!!!
14  goto quit
15  :HELP
16  echo Pauses batch file execution until a specific time
17  is reached.
18  echo SYNTAX %0 HH:MM[:SS], e.g. %0 11:31
19  :QUITS
```

The batch file should be passed a single parameter that identifies the start time. The time can be passed in a format similar to the TIME command, to specify hours:minutes and, optionally, seconds.

Line 4 creates a temporary environment variable called $$$$TIME, which is set to the characters "is " followed by the user-specified time. The "is " prefix is used to ensure that FIND does not report a match if the minutes and seconds coincidentally equal the target hours and minutes. If the desired time was 10:20, for example, and TIME returned the following value, a match for is 10:20 would not be found:

```
Current time is  9:10:20.04a
```

A simple search for 10:20, however, would have erroneously returned a match.

On line 7, the output from TIME is passed to FIND, which searches for the environment variable string. This test is repeated continuously until FIND returns an ERRORLEVEL of 0, to indicate that the time has arrived. The batch file then branches to line 11, in which the environment variable is removed and the appropriate time-sensitive commands are executed.

Running batch files once a day

I like to run some programs once a day, such as a backup of some key files and a virus scan. The problem is that I reboot my system ten or more times a day, and I want to execute these commands once every day — not once every reboot. I cannot, therefore, add the commands to the AUTOEXEC.BAT file. Granted, I can add CHOICE commands to AUTOEXEC.BAT to prompt whether programs should be executed, but even responding to just two or three prompts is irritating. I can create a once-a-day batch file, but — as usual — some tricks must be used. Many of the techniques used to pause a batch file until a specified time (discussed in the preceding section) are deployed in this situation.

The key to solving the problem is to store today's date in an environment variable. The following batch file, SETDATE.BAT, stores the date in the environment variable TODAYIS:

```
1  echo off
2  echo.|date|find "Current"> $$$$DATE
3  echo @echo off > $$$1date.bat
4  echo set TODAYIS=%%5>> $$$1date.bat
5  echo @echo off > $$$2date.bat
6  prefix $$$$DATE $$$2date.bat $$$1date
7  call $$$2date
8  del $$$$DATE
9  del $$$1DATE.BAT
10 del $$$2DATE.BAT
11 :quit
```

This batch file creates three temporary files. The first file, $$$$DATE, is created on line 2 and contains the output from the first line of the DATE command, as shown in this example:

```
Current date is Sun 01-03-1993
```

Lines 3 and 4 create a second file, $$$1DATE.BAT, used to create the environment variable TODAYIS. $$$1DATE.BAT has the following contents:

```
@echo off
set TODAYIS=%5
```

The third file, $$$2DATE.BAT, is created by using the PREFIX command (included on Bob's Shareware Collection disks) by prefixing the contents of $$$$DATE with the word $$$1DATE. $$$2DATE.BAT has the following contents:

```
@echo off
$$$1date Current date is Sun 01-03-1993
```

This batch file calls the $$$1DATE batch file and passes five passed parameters. Notice that the fifth passed parameter is the system date. $$$1DATE in turn creates the environment variable TODAYIS to assign the fifth passed parameter as the contents. Finally, lines 8 through 10 delete the three temporary files. Mission accomplished.

By calling SETDATE, you can store the system date in the environment. The following batch file, ONLYONCE.BAT, uses the environment variable to execute one or more commands once a day:

```
1  @echo off
2  call setdate
3  if exist c:\%todayis%.oo$ goto quit
4  if exist c:\*.oo$ del c:\*.oo$
5  echo nul > c:\%todayis%.oo$
6  rem Insert Once a Day commands Below here
7  echo Good morning
8  :QUIT
```

ONLYONCE creates an empty file that uses the first eight characters of today's date (grabbed from the environment) for the name, with the unique extension OO$. Line 3 checks to see whether the file exists; if so, the batch file has already been run once today and therefore quits. If the file doesn't exist, all files with the OO$ extension are deleted to remove the previous day's (or days') files (see line 4), and an empty file is created by piping an ECHO NUL statement to the new file (see line 5). In this example, the text Good morning is displayed; in a real application, however, the once-a-day commands are inserted at line 7.

A Batch File Potpourri

All good programmers have a collection (or *library*) of routines in their code arsenal. This section lists a bevy of batch file routines you can add to your library.

Does a directory exist?

You can easily use the IF command to determine whether a file exists. The following extract from a batch file shows IF checking whether the file CLOCK.WCH exists:

```
....
05 if exist CLOCK.WCH goto NextStep
06 goto Error3
....
```

Checking for a directory is slightly trickier. The following batch file echoes Found only if at least one file is in the directory (excluding the . and .. "files"):

```
1  @echo off
2  if exists c:\empty\*.* echo Found
```

If no files are in the directory, the IF test fails. To determine whether a directory exists, even when it is empty, you must use IF to test for the NUL device by using the following syntax:

```
if exist [drive:]\pathname\nul command
```

The following batch file accepts a single path as a parameter and then creates and changes to the new directory:

```
1   @echo off
2   if "%1"=="" goto HELP
3   if exist %1\nul goto OK
4   md %1 > nul
5   if exist %1\nul goto OK
6   echo The directory could not be created
7   goto quit
8   :help
9   echo Syntax is %0 drive:\newpath
10  goto QUIT
11  :OK
12  cd %1
13  :QUIT
```

Line 3 determines whether the directory exists by testing the NUL device. If the directory exists, processing jumps to line 12. If it doesn't exist, an MD command is executed and the test is repeated. If the directory still doesn't exist, the directory name must have had an error. If all is well, line 12 changes the default directory to the new directory.

Checking for wildcards

The FOR command provides an easy way to determine whether a filename contains wildcards. When a wildcard is used in a FOR statement, a different specific filename is used with every iteration of the loop. If the substituted filename used in the FOR loop is exactly the same as the filename being tested, the filename being tested does not contain wildcard characters. The following batch file, TESTWILD.BAT, shows this technique in action:

```
1  @echo off
2  if "%1"=="" goto NOTWILD
3  for %%W in (%1) do if %%W==%1 goto NOTWILD
```

```
4   :ISWILD
5   echo Wildcard Entered
6   goto quit
7   :NOTWILD
8   echo No wildcard Entered
9   :QUIT
```

Checking the DOS version

If you are writing a batch file that uses new batch or DOS commands, you may want to test to ensure that the appropriate version of DOS is being used. Any batch file that uses the new CHOICE command, for example, runs only on DOS 6 systems.

The FIND command was enhanced in DOS 6 to return an ERRORLEVEL indicating whether or not the search text was found. You may recall that an ERRORLEVEL of 1 is always returned, when the text is not found. Since the FIND command for earlier versions of DOS would always return an ERRORLEVEL of zero, you can test for the presence of DOS 6 by searching for some text you know does not exist. If an ERRORLEVEL of 1 is returned, DOS 6 (or later) is being used; otherwise, an earlier version of DOS is in use.

The following example batch file, ISDOS6.BAT, shows how to use VER with FIND to search for some nonexistent text and thereby test for a specific version of DOS:

```
1   @echo off
2   ver | find "Lloyd Belcher" > nul
3   if errorlevel 1 goto OK
4   echo This Batch file requires DOS 6
5   goto quit
6   :OK
7   echo Running DOS 6
8   :QUIT
```

Line 3 sends (or pipes) the output from the VER command to FIND, which searches for the string Lloyd Belcher. (I promised I would mention Lloyd somewhere in the book!) You could search for any text that is not output from VER. Line 3 tests the ERRORLEVEL and if it returns 1, DOS 6 must be in use.

Checking for TSRs

DOS 6 introduced the /M (or /MODULE) switch for the MEM command. This switch instructs MEM to display the status of a specific program in memory. If the program is not already loaded, MEM displays this string:

progname is not currently in memory.

By piping the output from MEM /M to FIND and testing for the string not currently, a batch file can easily test to see whether a program is loaded in memory.

The following batch file uses this technique to determine whether the user-specified program is loaded in memory:

```
@echo off
if "%1"=="" goto help
if "%1"=="/?" goto help
mem /m %1|find "not currently" > nul
if errorlevel 1 goto loaded
:NOTLOADED
echo %1 is not in memory
goto quit
:LOADED
echo %1 is already loaded
goto quit
:HELP
echo Checks to see if a program is loaded in memory
echo SYNTAX %0 progname, e.g. %0 share
:QUIT
```

By using this simple technique, you can test for any memory-resident program, including DOSKEY, SHARE, EMM386, and even Windows (discussed later, in the section "Using Batch Files with Windows 3.1").

To determine the exact program name in memory, use the command MEM /D /P.

Saving the current directory

I don't know about you, but I am always changing from one directory to another and then soon after want to return to the original directory. Again, a batch file can simplify the task.

The following batch file, TCD.BAT (for *t*emporary *c*hange *d*irectory), changes directories and uses PREFIX.EXE to create a second batch file, CB.BAT (for *c*hange *b*ack):

```
1   @echo off
2   if "%1"=="" goto help
3   if "%1"=="/?" goto help
4   if exist c:\cb.bat goto overwrite
5   :PROCEED
6   echo.
7   echo Enter CB to return to the directory
```

```
 8 cd
 9 echo.
10 echo @echo off > c:\cb.bat
11 cd > $$$$TEMP
12 prefix $$$$TEMP c:\cb.bat CD
13 del $$$$TEMP
14 echo del c:\cb.bat >> c:\cb.bat
15 goto CHANGEDIR
16 :OVERWRITE
17 choice Overwrite C:\CB.BAT
18 if errorlevel 2 goto changedir
19 goto proceed
20 :CHANGEDIR
21 cd %1
22 goto quit
23 :HELP
24 echo Changes directory and creates a CB batch file to
change back.
25 echo SYNTAX: %0 newdir, e.g. %0 \DOS
26 :QUIT
```

To change to a new directory, you simply enter TCD and the directory name.
The batch file then creates a new batch file, CB.BAT, which contains the commands to change back to the original directory and delete itself (see lines 10
through 14).

Using Batch Files with Windows 3.1

Many DOS 6 users are also Windows 3.1 users. This section discusses some
batch file considerations for running batch files from within Windows 3.1.

Controlling DOS session settings

When you start a DOS session, Windows normally displays a banner to remind
you that you are running under Windows and describes some useful key combinations, such as Exit, Alt-Tab, and Alt-Enter. To suppress this default message,
edit the SYSTEM.INI file so that the following statement is located in the
[386Enh] section:

```
[386Enh]
DOSPromptExitInstruc=false
```

By adding a WINPMT environment variable before starting Windows, you can define a special prompt that is active in every DOS session. The following command in AUTOEXEC.BAT defines a special Window's prompt:

```
set winpmt=Running within Windows!$_$p$g
```

Windows 3.1 allocates by default the same environment space as defined in CONFIG.SYS. To instruct Windows to allocate a different-size environment, add a CommandEnvSize= statement to the [NonWindowsApp] section of SYSTEM.INI. The following extract from SYSTEM.INI creates an 800-byte environment in every DOS session:

```
[NonWindowsApp]
CommandEnvSize=800
```

Exploiting WINSTART.BAT

Whenever you execute WIN, Windows looks for the file WINSTART.BAT in the WINDOWS directory. Windows executes this file before shifting into graphics mode and launching the Windows shell.

The primary purpose of this file is to load TSRs that Windows requires but that are not needed by any DOS session running within Windows. All TSRs loaded before you launch Windows are installed automatically in every DOS session. By loading TSRs from WINSTART.BAT, you save memory for every DOS session. Not many TSRs are designed just for Windows, but they are usually related to networks or communications.

The standard WINSTART.BAT batch file can include any commands. On one system, I use the following commands to remind the user to enter a Bernoulli cartridge before proceeding:

```
@echo off
echo Make sure a cartridge is installed in drive D
pause
```

You can use the file also to copy the system files WIN.INI and SYSTEM.INI, just in case a pesky program decides to modify them on the fly:

```
@echo off
echo Copying system files
copy c:\windows\win.ini c:\windows\oldwin.ini
copy c:\windows\system.ini c:\windows\oldsys.ini
echo Loading Windows...
```

Using the new command /K switch

 When you launch the MS-DOS icon, Windows executes the file DOSPRMPT.PIF. Normally, this PIF file executes COMMAND.COM to start a DOS session.

DOS 6 introduced the new /K switch for COMMAND.COM, which enables you to specify the name of a batch file or program to be executed when COMMAND.COM is launched. This switch provides a convenient way to customize the DOS session. It's like having a custom AUTOEXEC.BAT for every DOS session.

To take advantage of this new switch, run PIFEDIT (from within Windows) and load the DOSPRMPT.PIF file from the Windows directory. On the Optional Parameters line, add a /K followed by a space and the name of a batch file. The batch file will be executed every time you start a DOS session.

This sample batch file changes the prompt and shows the amount of available memory:

```
1   @echo off
2   prompt RUNNING IN WINDOWS$_$P$G
3   mem | find "executable"
```

Checking for Windows 3.1

Many commands should not be run from a Windows DOS session (CHKDSK and DEFRAG, for example). You should avoid loading certain TSRs, such as disk caches and memory managers, in DOS sessions. Sometimes, therefore, you will want to know whether Windows is loaded (whether the batch file is being executed from a DOS session) before executing one or more commands.

You may have noticed that Windows automatically creates an environment variable, *windir*, in every DOS session. This variable is used to record the main Windows directory. Here's the crazy part: Windows creates the environment variable in *lowercase*. Because the command interpreter always makes environment variable names uppercase, a batch file has no way to test whether *windir* is present. Shucks.

Fortunately, you can easily test for Windows by using MEM with the new /M switch, as described in the section "Checking for TSRs," earlier in this chapter. The following batch file tests whether Windows is loaded in memory:

```
mem /m win|find "not currently" > nul
if errorlevel 1 goto WinLoad
echo Windows is not loaded
goto quit
:WINLOAD
echo Windows is loaded
:QUIT
```

Batch File Enhancers

Bob's Shareware Collection disks include two programs designed to make batch files more efficient and powerful.

Adding pizzazz with Batutil

Batutil, from CtrlAlt Associates, takes batch file programming capabilities to an entirely new level. You can create pop-up menus, add excellent sound effects, edit the environment interactively, write to the screen in full color (without ANSI.SYS), determine installed equipment, perform math, and easily manage dates and times.

The following small batch file creates the menu shown in Figure 10-4.

```
1   @echo off
2   batutil {AT 30}{CL}
3   batutil {AT 30}{BI 219}{BE $S$SBUSTER}
4   batutil {FK}{SH}{AT 0}{MH Main menu}{ME Incremental$SBackup
Full$SBackup Windows Quit}
```

BATUTIL uses two-character commands. Line 2 sets the display attribute to 30 (black on cyan) and clears the screen. Line 3 instructs BATUTIL to use *big* characters, and the command BE (for *batutil echo*) draws the string "   BUSTER" in big

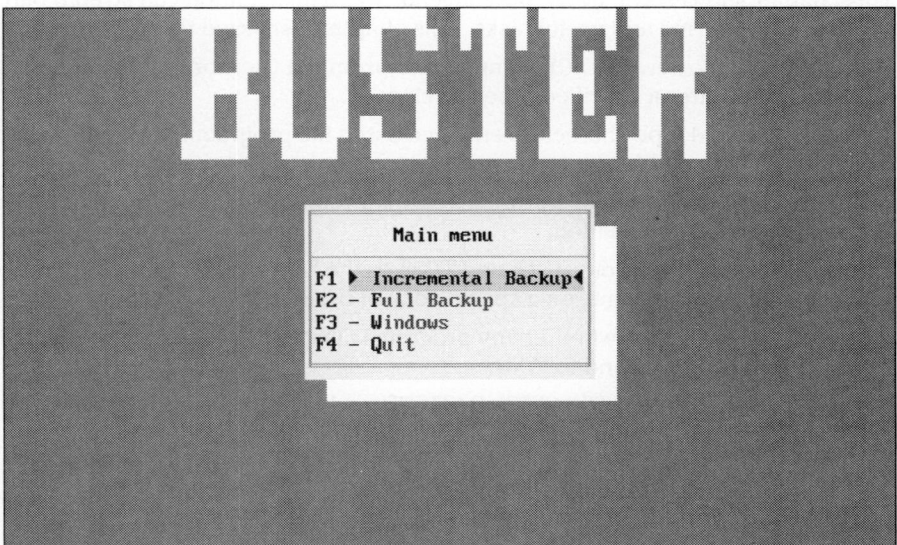

Figure 10-4: A fancy menu screen created with BATUTIL.

letters. The metastring $S denotes a space. Line 4 is responsible for displaying the menu. The commands {FK} and {SH} enable function-key support and shadows, respectively. The menu options are then defined with the {ME} command. In a real application, the ERRORLEVEL is tested to determine which option the user chose.

To gain a quick appreciation of the versatility of BATUTIL, run the BUDEMO.BAT file included with the Batutil shareware package.

Putting batch files in overdrive with TURBOBAT

TURBOBAT, part of the ExtraDOS Toolbox from Foley Hi-Tech Systems, compiles batch files into executable programs (with a COM extension). This product not only prevents users from tampering with your batch files, but it also speeds execution speed as much as 400 percent. It is a must for every batch file writer.

As if those features aren't enough, TURBOBAT also extends the batch language to include a grab bag of useful enhancements, including full color and sound support, much-improved flow control with IF, REPEAT, and WHILE statements, the capability to save multicharacter user input to an environment variable, and many more. It is firmly entrenched in my DOS bag of tricks.

Summary

This chapter showed you how a little ingenuity and imagination can stretch batch files to perform many varied and useful tasks. This chapter discussed the following points:

▶ You can use the new CHOICE command to prompt a user for input and optionally return a default value after a specified time has elapsed.

▶ Redirection and pipe characters enhance batch file programming by creating files and passing data to and from programs.

▶ The environment provides a storage place for temporary data and can be used to perform case-independent validation.

▶ By piping the output from DATE and TIME to the FIND filter, you can write batch files that execute at a specific time, on a specific day of the week, or once a day.

▶ A batch file can check whether any program is installed in memory by piping the output from a MEM /C command to FIND.

▶ The shareware utilities STACKEY, BATUTIL, and TURBOBAT are excellent tools for enhancing and extending the power of batch files.

Although you can manage DOS commands with batch files, it is not a very rich programming language. Chapter 11 describes how you can extend the power of batch files by creating compact high-performance utilities using DEBUG.

Chapter 11
Demystifying DEBUG

In This Chapter

▶ Reviewing DEBUG's many uses

▶ Getting acquainted with DEBUG editing capabilities

▶ Using DEBUG commands

▶ Patching programs with DEBUG

▶ Creating useful utilities with DEBUG

Understanding VCRs, Understanding DEBUG

Let's get one thing clear: DEBUG is useful.

I think VCRs and DEBUG have a lot in common. At first, both seem unnecessarily complicated and cumbersome, but after you learn the basic features, you can put them both to good use. Like a VCR, DEBUG has a wealth of advanced options that you probably will never need. That shouldn't stop you from exploiting the more useful features.

Ironically, DEBUG was designed to help programmers debug programs that were not operating as expected. DEBUG is rarely used for that purpose nowadays because far superior debuggers are available. But DEBUG can do a lot more than find bugs.

With DEBUG, you can edit existing programs to make small changes and enhancements, a process often referred to as *patching*. For example, you can change the default filemask in the DOS program EDIT from *.TXT to *.BAT, and you can change the default prompt characters in CHOICE.

You also can use DEBUG to create complete programs, but don't expect to write a three-dimensional spreadsheet with DEBUG. You can, however, create some very useful and compact utilities — for example, utilities to reboot the computer, to test whether Shift is held down, to determine the day of the week, and to turn the cursor off.

By the way, how do you record television shows from two different channels?

Getting Acquainted with DEBUG Editing Capabilities

As you know, EDIT is used to edit ASCII files such as batch and INI files. DEBUG also is a file editor, but it is designed to edit binary program files — that is, files with a COM or EXE extension. Unlike ASCII files, binary files are not organized into individual lines; a binary file is one homogenous blob of bytes. DEBUG does not, therefore, have a line-number orientation. File contents are displayed in blocks of bytes.

Figure 11-1 shows a typical display generated with DEBUG's D (dump) command. The display is divided into three sections. The leftmost section identifies the address (using segment:offset notation) of the first byte of data, and the middle section shows the value of 16 bytes of the file in hexadecimal. The rightmost section shows the same 16 bytes of data in ASCII format. In that section, alphanumeric characters (that is, characters with ASCII values in the range 32 to 126) are displayed; other, nondisplayable characters are represented by the period (.) character.

DEBUG can edit any type of file, not just binary ones. Consider the following bare-bones CONFIG.SYS file:

```
DEVICE=C:\DOS\HIMEM.SYS
DEVICE=C:\DOS\EMM386.EXE RAM I=B000-B7FF NOEMS
BUFFERS=15,0
FILES=40
DOS=HIGH,UMB
```

```
C:\DOS>debug find.exe
-d
14B7:0010  8B E8 8C C0 05 10 00 0E-1F A3 04 00 03 06 0C 00   ...............
14B7:0020  8E C0 8B 0E 06 00 8B F9-4F 8B F7 FD F3 A4 50 B8   ........O.....P.
14B7:0030  34 00 50 CB 8C C3 8C D8-48 8E D8 8E C0 BF 0F 00   4.P.....H.......
14B7:0040  B9 10 00 B0 FF F3 AE 47-8B F7 8B C3 48 8E C0 BF   .......G....H...
14B7:0050  0F 00 B1 04 8B C6 F7 D0-D3 E8 8C DA 2B D0 73 04   ............+.s.
14B7:0060  8C D8 2B D2 D3 E0 03 F0-8E DA 8B C7 F7 D0 D3 E8   ..+.............
14B7:0070  8C C2 2B D0 73 04 8C C0-2B D2 D3 E0 03 F8 8E C2   ..+.s...+.......
14B7:0080  AC 8A D0 4E AD 8B C8 46-8A C2 24 FE 3C B0 75 05   ...N...F..$.<.u.
-
```

Figure 11-1: The D (dump) command displays file contents in three distinct blocks.

```
C:\WORD55\DOSBOOK>debug config.sys
-d
1313:0100  44 45 56 49 43 45 3D 43-3A 5C 44 4F 53 5C 48 49   DEVICE=C:\DOS\HI
1313:0110  4D 45 4D 2E 53 59 53 0D-0A 44 45 56 49 43 45 3D   MEM.SYS..DEVICE=
1313:0120  43 3A 5C 44 4F 53 5C 45-4D 4D 33 38 36 2E 45 58   C:\DOS\EMM386.EX
1313:0130  45 20 52 41 4D 20 49 3D-42 30 30 30 2D 42 37 46   E RAM I=B000-B7F
1313:0140  46 20 4E 4F 45 4D 53 0D-0A 42 55 46 46 45 52 53   F NOEMS..BUFFERS
1313:0150  3D 31 35 2C 30 0D 0A 46-49 4C 45 53 3D 34 30 0D   =15,0..FILES=40.
1313:0160  0A 44 4F 53 3D 48 49 47-48 2C 55 4D 42 0D 0A 83   .DOS=HIGH,UMB...
1313:0170  FF FF 74 11 26 01 1D 00-A0 E2 F3 81 FA 00 F0 74   ..t.&.........t
-
```

Figure 11-2: You can use DEBUG to view and edit ASCII files.

Figure 11-2 shows a DEBUG dump of this file. Notice that the end of the first text line (shown in the middle of the second line of the dump) is followed by the two characters *0D* and *0A*. These characters are carriage return and line feed, respectively, and are used behind the scenes in ASCII files to identify the end of a new line of text.

Using DEBUG Commands

When you execute DEBUG, a single character is displayed: the minus sign (–). This character is the terse DEBUG prompt that indicates that DEBUG is waiting for you to input a command or instruction. It's not the friendliest of greetings.

DEBUG command reference

You need to remember two commands from the outset. First, the Q command quits the DEBUG program and returns you to the DOS prompt. Second, the ? command is the help command, which instructs DEBUG to display a list of all DEBUG commands along with a brief description of each one (see Figure 11-3).

As Figure 11-3 shows, DEBUG has some 23 commands. They are explained in the following paragraphs.

```
-?
assemble      A [address]
compare       C range address
dump          D [range]
enter         E address [list]
fill          F range list
go            G [=address] [addresses]
hex           H value1 value2
input         I port
load          L [address] [drive] [firstsector] [number]
move          M range address
name          N [pathname] [arglist]
output        O port byte
proceed       P [=address] [number]
quit          Q
register      R [register]
search        S range list
trace         T [=address] [value]
unassemble    U [range]
write         W [address] [drive] [firstsector] [number]
allocate expanded memory        XA [#pages]
deallocate expanded memory      XD [handle]
map expanded memory pages       XM [Lpage] [Ppage] [handle]
display expanded memory status  XS
-
```

Figure 11-3: DEBUG's help command, ?, displays a brief description of every DEBUG command.

The ? (help) command

The ? (help) command displays a summary of the DEBUG commands. The syntax is simply

> ?

The A command

The A command is the assemble command. It assembles assembly-language statements and creates machine code. The syntax is as follows:

> a [*address*]

This feature allows you to enter instructions using assembly-language notation such as

```
MOV AH,2A
INT 21
MOV AH,4C
INT 21
```

rather than directly entering the machine code bytes in the following format:

```
e 0100 B4 2A CD 21 B4 4C CD 21
```

You usually will use the A instruction to assemble a new program prior to writing it to disk. By default, DEBUG assembles from the beginning of the file or from the point where the last assemble operation stopped. Alternatively, you can specify the address of the range to be assembled. Here is an example:

```
-a0100:0108
```

The C command

This is the compare command. It compares the data stored in two memory locations and displays the byte values side by side for each location. The syntax is

```
c range address
```

The *range* parameter is the starting and ending address of the first memory location, separated by a comma. The *address* parameter identifies the starting location of the second memory address. DEBUG displays each address where the byte values differ. For example, suppose that during the editing of the sample CONFIG.SYS file shown in Figure 11-2, the following command is executed:

```
-c 0100,010f 0119
```

DEBUG produces the following display:

```
11AA:010E  48  45  11AA:0127
11AA:010F  49  4D  11AA:0128
```

The compare command instructed DEBUG to compare the data at memory location 0100 through 010f with the data starting at memory location 0119. Both of these memory locations start with the string *DEVICE=C:\DOS*, but the remaining two bytes in the comparison area are different. The first area held the bytes 48 and 49, which are the letters *HI* (the beginning of HIMEM.SYS), and the second area contained the bytes 45 and 4D, which are the letters *EM* (the beginning of EMM386.SYS).

The D command

The D (dump) command instructs DEBUG to dump (that is, to display) the data stored at a specific memory location. The command syntax is

```
d [range]
```

The dump command is used to display the file contents in Figures 11-1 and 11-2. The optional *range* parameter specifies the starting and ending addresses or the starting address and length of the area of memory that you want to view. If you do not specify a range, DEBUG dumps 128 bytes of data, starting either at the byte following the data displayed with the last dump command or at the beginning of the file. By repeatedly pressing d, you can browse through a file 128 bytes at a time.

The E command

The E (enter) command enters data into a specific memory location. The command syntax is

    e *address* [*list*]

The *address* parameter is the starting address where the data will be entered, and the optional *list* parameter is the list of byte values identifying the data to be installed. Here is an example:

    e 0100 B4 2A CD 21 B4 4C CD 21

If you don't specify any data, DEBUG shifts into Edit Mode and prompts you for input one byte at a time. DEBUG displays the existing value (followed by a period) and waits for you to enter the replacement value. I tend to use the E command for patching files but prefer to enter new programs using assembly-language mnemonics and use A to assemble them.

The F command

The F command is the fill command. It fills an area of memory with a repeated byte or set of bytes. Use the following syntax:

    f *range* *list*

The *range* variable specifies the beginning and ending addresses of the area to be filled, and *list* identifies the data that is to be filled into the area.

The G command

The G (go) command runs the program. Its syntax is

    g [*=address*] [*breakpoints*]

This feature really is designed as a debugging tool. It runs the program starting at a specific address and allows you to set up to ten breakpoints by specifying the individual breakpoint memory addresses. Just as I never use the tracking option on my VCR, I never use this command.

The H command

H is the hex command. It performs addition and subtraction of two hexadecimal numbers and displays the results. The correct syntax is

    h *value1* *value2*

The following batch file uses the H command to create a simple but effective hex calculator:

```
@echo off
echo Hexadecimal Math
echo Plus  Minus
echo h %1 %2 >$$$$TEMP.SCR
echo q >> $$$$TEMP.SCR
debug < $$$$TEMP.SCR | find "-" /v
del $$$$TEMP.SCR
```

The I command

The I (input) command reads and displays a single byte of data from a specific port. The syntax for this command is

    i *port*

The *port* variable refers to the address of the port — for example, 03f8 for COM1.

The L command

The L (load) command loads a file from disk into a specific address in memory. Use the following syntax:

    l [*address*]

By default, the file loads at the address cs:100 (100 bytes into the code segment). Typically, you will load a file by specifying the filename on the command line when you execute DEBUG. When the file has an EXE extension, the load address is ignored. EXE files include a load location in the EXE header, and DEBUG uses this address. Rename an EXE file so that the file has a different extension if you want to edit the complete file, including the EXE header bytes.

DEBUG also enables you to load specific disk sectors with the L command. But because you can create havoc writing changed data back to disk, I recommend that you ignore this feature.

The M command

The M (move) command copies a block of data from one location to another. The proper syntax is

    m *range address*

If the source and target addresses overlap, the source data is overwritten.

The N command

The N (name) command identifies the name of a file to be loaded or saved. Normally, you use this command when creating small COM file utilities. Use the N command to assign the filename prior to executing the W command to write the file to disk. The syntax is

n [*drive*:][*path*]*filename*.*ext*

The O command

The O (output) command copies a specific byte to a port, using the following syntax:

o *port datavalue*

As with the I command, *port* is the address of the port — for example, 03f8 for COM1.

The P command

The P (proceed) command instructs DEBUG to execute a program instruction. This feature is provided to support software debugging, and so you will rarely, if ever, use it. If you do, however, the syntax is as follows:

p [*=address*] [*number*]

The Q command

The Q (quit) command is everybody's favorite. It quits DEBUG and returns to the DOS prompt. Changes are not automatically saved to disk. The syntax is simply

q

The R command

The R (register) command displays a specific register and enables you to update that register. Its syntax is

r [*register*]

The following standard 80x86 registers are supported: AX, BX, CX, DX, SP, BP, SI, DI, DS, ES, SS, CS, IP, PC, and F (for flags). The AX through DX registers may also be referenced in byte-sized pieces using the high and low register components. To access AX in two sections, for example, specify AH and AL. When you execute R without a register name, the status of all registers is displayed. When you create a new COM file, the BX:CX registers must be updated with the file size before you call the W command; W looks at these registers to determine how many bytes to write.

The S command

The S (search) command searches an area of memory for a specific byte, series of bytes, or string. The correct syntax is

    s *range* *list*

Range represents the beginning and ending address of the area to be searched. *List* represents the byte (or series of bytes separated by spaces) you want to locate. Enclose strings in quotes. If you specify a single byte or a string, DEBUG displays all memory locations where a match is found. If you specify an array of bytes, the address of the first match is displayed. You can then use the D switch to display the data at that address.

The T command

The T (trace) command executes (or single-steps) a single instruction and then displays the register contents. This is another of the program debugging options you are unlikely to use, but if you do, the proper syntax is

    t [*=address*] *number*

The U command

The U (unassemble) command displays a portion of the program using assembly-language mnemonics. This process is also known as *disassembling*. The correct command syntax is

    u [*range*]

The U command is a very useful tool for inspecting small programs. You must, however, understand assembly language. If you do not specify a *range* value, 32 bytes of code are displayed, starting at the memory location immediately following the last unassembled code.

The W command

The W (write) command writes a file to disk — in other words, saves the file. The command syntax is as follows:

    w [*address*]

If you do not specify an address, the entire file is written. If you want to write a new file to disk, you must use the N switch to assign a name to the file and store the file's size in the BX:CX registers before executing W.

You also can use the W command to write data to specific disk sectors. Because this technique bypasses DOS and could destroy valuable data, however, I recommend that you ignore this feature.

The XA command

The XA (allocate expanded memory) command allocates expanded memory pages and displays the handle number if successful. Unless you want to tool around with XMS for fun, you will find little use for the XA switch and the ones that follow. If you want to use them, however, the syntax is

```
xa [count]
```

The XD command

The XD (deallocate expanded memory) command deallocates expanded memory and makes the pages available for other applications. The command syntax is

```
xd [handle]
```

The XM command

The XM (map expanded memory pages) command maps a logical page to a physical page. Use the following syntax:

```
xm [logpage] [realpage] [handle]
```

The XS command

The XS (expanded memory status) command shows the current status of expanded memory. Of all the XMS debug switches, this is the most interesting because it gives a snapshot of XMS usage. The correct syntax is simply

```
xs
```

The DOS 6 on-line help system includes comprehensive help on the debug commands. To get help, enter the command `help debug`.

How to enter DEBUG commands

DEBUG is not very particular about spaces in commands. In general, you do not need to separate a DEBUG command from the command parameters. If you prefer, however, you can separate the command and the parameters by a space or a comma for clarity. For example, the following three statements all have the same meaning:

```
-nutil.com
-n util.com
-n,util.com
```

You must specify memory ranges or addresses when using many of DEBUG's commands. Enter addresses in the *segment:offset* format and specify them in hexadecimal. (Refer to Chapter 5 for a discussion of segments, offsets, and

hexadecimal numbers.) All DOS programs have two special segment addresses: the code segment and the data segment. These segments identify the starting address of a program's code and data. DEBUG supports the segment aliases CS and DS, respectively. For example, the memory address that is 200 bytes into the code segment is CS:0200.

If you specify a single address (without a colon), DEBUG assumes that it is the memory offset and applies a default segment. The default segment is the code segment when you use commands A, G, L, T, U, and W; the default is the data segment for all other commands.

Taking a test drive

Enough theory, already. It's time to put DEBUG to use. As is the case with most programming languages, the best way to learn about DEBUG is to use it.

By default, the DOS cursor is a thin blinking line located at the bottom of the text. You can use DEBUG to create a small program that makes the cursor a large block. Figure 11-4 shows the DEBUG session used to create the program CURSFAT.COM.

To create the program, follow the steps listed in Table 11-1.

Voilà! you have created the program CURSFAT.COM. Execute it, and the cursor changes to a large block. In the next section, you create the program

```
C:\DOS>debug
-n cursfat.com
-a 100
1313:0100 mov ah,01
1313:0102 mov ch,01
1313:0104 mov cl,0c
1313:0106 int 10
1313:0108 ret
1313:0109
-r cx
CX 0000
:9
-w
Writing 00009 bytes
-q

C:\DOS>
```

Figure 11-4: Using DEBUG to create CURSFAT.COM.

Table 11-1		Creating the CURSFAT.COM Program
Step	*Input*	*Description*
Step 1.	debug	Enter the DEBUG command at the DOS prompt to start a DEBUG session.
Step 2.	n cursfat.com	Assign the filename CURSFAT.COM.
Step 3.	a 100	Instruct DEBUG to start assembling code beginning at address CS:0100, which is the beginning address for COM programs. As soon as you enter this command, DEBUG shifts into Assemble Mode and waits for assembly-language mnemonics to be entered.
Step 4.	mov ah,01	To change the cursor, first set the value of AH to 01.
Step 5.	mov ch,01	This step sets the CH register to the starting cursor line — that is, the scan line position of the top of the cursor.
Step 6.	mov cl,0C	This step sets the CL register to the ending cursor scan line. *Note:* A color system uses 14 scan lines per character block, but a monochrome system uses only 8 scan lines. The scan lines are numbered 0 to C (13 decimal) and 0 to 7, respectively. Enter mov cl,07 if you are writing this program for a monochrome system.
Step 7.	int 10	Invoke the DOS interrupt 10h. When you do so, DOS inspects the AH register to determine which task to perform. In this case, it finds the value 01, which is the code to change the cursor size.
Step 8.	ret	This step passes control back to DOS.
Step 9.	Press Enter.	Press Enter to stop the assemble session and return to the DEBUG prompt.
Step 10.	r cx	Enter this command to instruct DEBUG that you want to change the value of the CX register. DEBUG displays the current register value (0000 in this case) and waits for you to enter a new value.
Step 11.	9	Identify the size of the program. This program is only 9 bytes long, because each of the instructions entered in steps 4 through 7 consumes two bytes, and the RET instruction in Step 8 uses 1 byte.
Step 12.	w	Write the program (all 9 bytes) to disk.
Step 13.	q	Exit DEBUG and return to the DOS prompt.

CURSNORM.COM to restore the normal cursor style. Meanwhile, use the command mode co80 (or bw80) to restore the normal cursor style.

The key to writing small programs with DEBUG is knowing which DOS features to use. In CURSFAT.COM, DOS interrupt 10h (the BIOS services interrupt), subfunction 01h is used to change the cursor size. The cursor dimensions had to be stored in the CH and CL registers before the interrupt was invoked. Unless you are an experienced DOS programmer, you will not know details such as these. If you are interested in writing your own utilities, you need a DOS programming reference guide that documents all of the DOS interrupts. My favorite reference book is *PC Interrupts,* written by Ralph Kyle and Jim Brown.

Creating ASCII script files

Writing DEBUG programs interactively (as you did for CURSFAT.COM) is practical only for very small programs. When you create larger programs, entering an incorrect instruction can be extremely frustrating. Although you can make corrections with the E switch, it is far from smooth sailing, and often the process becomes so confusing that you give up, start over, and reenter all the instructions.

Another option is to use EDIT or any editor to create an ASCII file and add one command per line. After you create and verify the commands, you can redirect the statements to DEBUG and create the program. ASCII files containing DEBUG commands often are referred to as *script files.*

The following script file, called CURSNORM.SCR, contains all the instructions to create the program CURSNORM.COM, which sets the cursor back to the normal thin style:

```
n cursnorm.com
a 100
mov ah,01
mov ch,0c; use ch,06 on monochrome
mov cl,0d; use cl,07 on monochrome
int 10
ret

r cx
9
w
q
```

When DEBUG is in Assemble Mode, any characters entered after a semicolon are ignored. This feature provides a convenient way to annotate script files.

When you create a script file to use with DEBUG, check the statements carefully to make sure that they are correct. Executing the wrong statement may lock up your system or, in extreme cases, damage files or the FAT. The two most common errors are forgetting the blank line after the RET (or last INT 21) statement and forgetting the Q command. Be sure to double-check for these.

After creating the script file, you can use the < character to redirect the file contents as input to DEBUG. Use the following command to create the CURSNORM.COM file:

```
debug < cursnorm.scr
```

Patching Programs with DEBUG

One common use of DEBUG is to edit or *patch* an existing program. Using DEBUG alone, you can perform tasks such as fixing a program bug, changing error messages, or modifying program colors. Before you change a program, make a backup copy of the file just in case you don't get the expected results.

To modify a program, you first must locate the specific data you want to change. To change an ASCII file with a text editor, you would probably use PgUp and PgDn to locate the text or, better still, use a search command. You can use the same approach for a program file, but the equivalent DEBUG commands are D (dump) and S (search).

After you identify the specific memory location, use the E (edit) command to modify the data and the W (write) command to save the data to disk. Because the file was loaded by DEBUG, you can use the W command without first storing the file size in the BX:CX registers. DEBUG assumes that the file is the same size as it was when it was loaded.

For an illustration of the approach, you can make some changes to two popular DOS commands.

Changing the CHOICE command

By default, the CHOICE batch command prompts you to press either Y or N. With DEBUG, you can easily change these default keys. You can assign 1 and 2 as the default keys, for example.

To do this, copy the CHOICE.COM program (in the DOS directory) to CHOICE12.COM. Then load the new program into DEBUG by entering the following command:

```
debug choice12.com
```

At DEBUG's - prompt, issue the D command to dump the first 128 bytes. The following output is displayed:

```
0E4D:0100   E9 32 04 59 4E 00 00 00-00 00 00 00 00 00 00 00   .2.YN...........
0E4D:0110   00 00 00 00 00 00 00 00-00 00 00 00 00 00 00 00   ................
0E4D:0120   00 00 00 00 00 00 00 00-00 00 00 00 00 00 00 00   ................
0E4D:0130   00 00 00 00 00 00 00 00-00 00 00 00 00 00 00 00   ................
0E4D:0140   00 00 00 00 00 00 00 00-00 00 00 00 00 00 00 00   ................
0E4D:0150   00 00 00 00 00 00 00 00-00 00 00 00 00 00 00 00   ................
0E4D:0160   00 00 00 00 00 00 00 00-00 00 00 00 00 00 00 00   ................
0E4D:0170   00 00 00 00 00 00 00 00-00 00 00 00 00 00 00 00   ................
```

The memory segment address (displayed in the first column) may differ on your system.

Notice the characters Y and N on the first line; these are actually the defaults used when you execute CHOICE without the /C switch. To change the values to *1* and *2,* enter the following command:

```
-e 0103 31 32
```

This command instructs DEBUG to edit data starting at offset 0103 and change the first two bytes to values 31 and 32, which are the hexadecimal ASCII values for the characters 1 and 2. To visually verify the changes, enter the following command:

```
d 0100
```

The final step is to save the changes with the W command and then press q to exit DEBUG.

In just a few simple steps, you change the default values of CHOICE from Y and N to 1 and 2.

To be thorough, however, you need to modify the help text so that it says *12* rather than *YN.* Launch DEBUG with the following command:

```
debug choice12.com
```

The S (search) command can search through the file looking for any additional YN references. At the DEBUG prompt, enter the following command and be sure to specify uppercase YN (the SEARCH command is case sensitive):

```
-s 0100 FFFF "YN"
```

This command instructs DEBUG to search the entire code segment for all occurrences of the "YN" string. DEBUG responds by displaying all addresses where the text is found. DEBUG should respond with one address similar to the following:

```
11CC:0228
```

 The code segment (11CC in this example) may be different on your system.

Enter the D (dump) command to display the data in this general area:

```
-d 0220
```

DEBUG displays the data, and you see that the "YN" entry is indeed part of the help text. Enter the following EDIT command to change the help text to "12":

```
-e 0228 31 32
```

Finally, use the W command to save your changes and the Q command to quit DEBUG. You can view your handiwork by entering the following command:

```
choice12 /?
```

You may have noticed that there is a lot of empty space at the beginning of the CHOICE.COM program. If you are wondering whether these 00s can be replaced with additional default keys, the answer is yes. You can even add special keys that are not directly supported by CHOICE, such as the spacebar and Enter, on the command line. In other words, you can use DEBUG to alter CHOICE so that it accepts the input of the spacebar or Enter key.

The following script file, CHOICEAZ.SCR, changes the default CHOICE keys to the spacebar, Enter, 0–9, and A–Z.

```
n choiceaz.com
l
d
e 0103 20 d 30 31 32 33 34 35 36 37 38 39
e 0110 40 42 43 44 45 46 47 48 49 4A 4B 4C 4D 4D 4F 50
e 0120 51 52 53 54 55 56 57 58 59 5A
d 0100
w
q
```

Copy CHOICE.COM to CHOICEAZ.COM and then run the following command to redirect the script to DEBUG and update CHOICEAZ.COM:

```
debug < choiceaz.scr
```

The CHOICEAZ command is an ideal option when you have batch files and you want the system to pause for the user to press any key but then to proceed after a specified timeout period if no key is pressed. For example, you can use the following statement to pause a batch file for 10 seconds or until the user presses a key (including the spacebar or Enter), whichever occurs first:

```
choiceaz /n /T:A,10
```

Patching the default EDIT filemask

I mainly use EDIT to build and modify batch files. One thing that irritates me about the editor is the default *.TXT filemask used in the File Open dialog box. However, with a little help from DEBUG, you can easily change the prompt to *.BAT.

EDIT.EXE is not actually the program that provides the full screen-editing functions. When you enter the EDIT command, EDIT in turn calls the QBASIC.EXE program with the switch /EDITOR. It is QBASIC.EXE that provides all the editing tools, and lurking deep inside QBASIC.EXE is the default filemask of *.TXT.

DEBUG does not support the editing of files that have an EXE extension; DEBUG loads an EXE in a special way, so the data loaded is not an exact facsimile of the file. The workaround is to copy QBASIC.EXE and give the copy a name with a different extension, say QBASIC.DBG.

After you do that, start the DEBUG session by entering the following command:

```
debug qbasic.dbg
```

In the example discussed in the preceding section, you used the DEBUG search command to locate the "YN" string. You might think that a similar approach would work in this instance. To test this theory, enter the following command to search for *.TXT (use uppercase):

```
-s 0100 FFFF "*.TXT"
```

DEBUG does not find any occurrences of "*.TXT", and so no memory addresses are displayed. Why? The search command only searched the first 64K of memory, and QBASIC.EXE is almost 200K in size. DEBUG did not find the filemask because it wasn't stored in the first 64K. To instruct DEBUG to search the next 64K requires a little hexadecimal arithmetic.

The first step is to determine the specific address of the code segment. Enter the D command to dump the first 128 bytes of QBASIC.EXE. Output similar to the following is displayed:

```
11CC:0100   B8 EE 44 BA 69 2F 05 DC-11 3B 06 02 00 72 1B B4   ..D.i/...;...r..
11CC:0110   09 BA 18 01 CD 21 CD 20-4E 6F 74 20 65 6E 6F 75   .....!. Not enou
11CC:0120   67 68 20 6D 65 6D 6F 72-79 24 2D 20 00 8E D0 2D   gh memory$- ...-
11CC:0130   25 00 90 8E C0 50 B9 23-01 33 FF 57 BE 44 01 FC   %....P.#.3.W.D..
11CC:0140   F3 A5 CB 90 FD 8C DB 53-81 C3 39 00 03 DA 8C CD   .......S..9.....
11CC:0150   8B C2 80 E4 0F B1 04 8B-F2 D3 E6 D3 EA FE C6 8B   ................
11CC:0160   CE D1 E9 4E 4E 8B FE 2B-E8 2B D8 8E C5 8E DB F3   ...NN..+.+......
11CC:0170   A5 B8 00 10 B5 80 FE CE-75 ED FC 8E DD 07 06 BF   ........u.......
```

 The remaining steps involve working with segment addresses. The specific address may be different on your system, so be sure to use the address displayed on your system rather than the example addresses used in this text.

You can use the DEBUG hex calculator to find a segment address for the next 64K. Add 0FFFh to the code segment — each segment address is multiplied by 16 (decimal) to get a linear address. Use the H command, specifying the segment address and 0FFF. Here is an example:

```
-h 11CC 0FFF
```

DEBUG responds by displaying two values. The first value is the sum of the two numbers, and the second is the difference between the two numbers. Here is an example:

```
21CB 01CD
```

The first value represents the beginning segment of the next 64K of QBASIC.DBG (or whatever name you used for the copy of QBASIC.EXE). Use this value in another search command as follows:

```
-s 21CB:0000 FFFF "*.TXT"
```

Once again, no match is found. Use the H command to compute the beginning segment for the next 64K. Here is an example:

```
-h 21CB 0FFF
```

In my case, the value returned was 31CA. Try the search one more time, searching the third 64K block of QBASIC.EXE. Here is an example:

```
-s 31CA:0000 FFFF "*.TXT"
```

Bingo! DEBUG responds with a single address indicating that it found the text:

```
31CA:DD1A
```

You can view this area using the dump command as follows:

```
-d 31CA:DD10
```

The biggest challenge was finding the "*.TXT" string. Changing the string is easy using the EDIT command. To make things simple, use the specific address displayed by the search command (for example, 31CA:DD1A) and change the first five characters to *.BAT as follows:

```
-e 31CA:DD1A 2A 2E 42 41 54
```

Save the file and quit DEBUG by entering the W and Q commands.

```
C:\DOS>debug qbasic.dbg
-d
1313:0100  4D 5A 0F 01 7C 01 01 00-08 00 94 15 FF FF 71 2F   MZ..|.........q/
1313:0110  00 02 00 00 00 01 F0 FF-52 00 00 00 0F 21 50 4B   ........R....!PK
1313:0120  4C 49 54 45 20 43 6F 70-72 2E 20 31 39 39 30 2D   LITE Copr. 1990-
1313:0130  39 32 20 50 4B 57 41 52-45 20 49 6E 63 2E 20 41   92 PKWARE Inc. A
1313:0140  6C 6C 20 52 69 67 68 74-73 20 52 65 73 65 72 76   ll Rights Reserv
1313:0150  65 64 07 00 00 00 1B 01-F8 01 00 00 20 00 2C 06   ed.......... .,.
1313:0160  FF FF D8 40 80 00 00 00-12 00 D9 3D 1E 00 00 00   ...@.......=....
1313:0170  01 00 00 00 00 00 00 00-00 00 00 00 00 00 00 00   ................
-s 0100 FFFF "*.TXT"
-h 1313 0fff
2312  0314
-s 2313:0000 FFFF "*.TXT"
-h 2313 0fff
3312  1314
-s 3312:0000 FFFF "*.TXT"
3312:DD8A
-e 3312:DD8A 2A 2E 42 41 54
-w
Writing 2F70F bytes
-q

C:\DOS>
```

Figure 11-5: Changing the QBASIC.EXE default wildcard from *.TXT to *.BAT.

Before renaming QBASIC.DBG to QBASIC.EXE, rename QBASIC.EXE to QBASIC.BAK (just in case you didn't make the correct modifications). After you rename the files, EDIT uses the default wildcard of *.BAT. Figure 11-5 shows a complete session summarizing how to change the filemask.

Creating Useful Utilities with DEBUG

DEBUG is a great tool for creating compact, high-performance utilities. In this section, you learn how to create programs for returning the system date and for interacting with the keyboard. You also learn how to create disk drive utilities.

Returning to DOS and setting an ERRORLEVEL

Many utilities created with DEBUG are designed to be used in batch files. Because the IF statement can test a program's ERRORLEVEL, many of the utilities set an ERRORLEVEL to pass information to the batch file.

Use interrupt 21h, subfunction 4Ch (rather than RET) to pass control back to DOS and set an exit code (ERRORLEVEL). The following two assembly-language instructions show the basic technique:

```
mov ah,4c
int 21
```

The ERRORLEVEL returned by a program that terminates in this way corresponds with the value in the AL register. This technique is used in many of the following examples.

Working with dates

Interrupt 21h, subfunction 2Ah provides information on the system date. When this interrupt is invoked, DOS places the day of the week in register AL, the day of the month in register DL, the month in register DH, and the four-digit year in register CX.

Armed with this knowledge, you can easily use DEBUG to create some very useful date routines.

The following script file, WEEKDAY.SCR, returns the day of the week as an ERRORLEVEL:

```
n weekday.com
a 100
mov ah,2a
int 21       ;day of week is now in AL
mov ah,4c
int 21

r cx
8
w
q
```

To create the WEEKDAY.COM program, execute the following command:

```
debug < weekday.scr
```

WEEKDAY.COM sets an ERRORLEVEL to indicate the day of the week. Sunday is represented by an ERRORLEVEL of 0, Monday by an ERRORLEVEL of 1, and so on through Saturday, which has an ERRORLEVEL of 6.

Refer to Chapter 10 for an example of how to use WEEKDAY.COM in a batch file.

The following script file, WHATDAY.SCR, creates the program WHATDAY.COM, which determines the day of the month and returns an ERRORLEVEL in the range 1 to 31:

```
n whatday.com
a 100
mov ah,2a
int 21
mov al,dl   ;return day of month as error level
mov ah,4c
int 21

r cx
A
w
q
```

This script file is similar to WEEKDAY.SCR, but the day of the month is returned in register DL, and this has to be moved to register AL so it can be returned as the ERRORLEVEL. The additional instruction changes the file size to A (10 decimal) bytes.

The following script file, WHATMON.SCR, creates the program WHATMON.COM, which determines the month and returns an ERRORLEVEL in the range 1 to 12:

```
n whatmon.com
a 100
mov ah,2a
int 21
mov al,dh   ;return month as error level
mov ah,4c
int 21

r cx
A
w
q
```

This script is almost identical to WHATDAY.SCR. The only difference is that the month value is returned in register DH.

The final script in the quartet of date utilities is WHATYEAR.SCR, which returns the year as an ERRORLEVEL. DOS returns the four-digit year in the CX register. However, ERRORLEVELs are only supported in the range 0 to 255. By moving the year to the AX register and subtracting 1980 from it (7CB in hexadecimal), the ERRORLEVEL is set to the year since 1980. For example, 1994 is returned as ERRORLEVEL 14. The WHATYEAR.SCR file is as follows:

```
n whatyear.com
a 100
mov ah,2a
int 21
mov ax,cx    ; move year (format YYYY) to AX
sub ax,07bc  ; subtract 1980
mov ah,4c    ; year since 1980 now in AL
int 21

r cx
D
w
q
```

Writing keyboard management utilities

The DOS batch file language provides very few ways of obtaining user input or checking the keyboard status. The utilities in this section fill this void in the language.

Checking and changing the state of special keys

Tucked away in BIOS, at the address 0040:0017, is a very useful byte of information. This byte indicates the status of the special keys Left Shift, Right Shift, Ctrl, Alt, Scroll Lock, Num Lock, Caps Lock, and Ins. Each of the eight bits is set to *on* or *off* to indicate whether each of the special keys is being held down or, in the case of lockable keys, is set on. By returning this byte as an ERRORLEVEL, a small utility can inform a batch file of the status of these special keys.

You can use the following script file, KEYSTATE.SCR, to create KEYSTATE.COM:

```
n keystate.com
a 100
mov ax,0040
mov ds,ax
mov al,[17] ; returns the keyboard status bit as errorlevel
mov ah,4c
int 21

r cx
C
w
q
```

When [ ] brackets are used in a MOV statement, DEBUG interprets the value to be a memory location and moves the data at the specified memory location into a register. In this example, the 17th byte in the data segment (which points to segment 0400) is moved into the AL register.

The ERRORLEVELs set by each key are listed in Table 11-2.

KEYSTATE provides a great way to add shortcuts to batch files. For example, consider the following batch file, BYPASS.BAT:

```
1  @echo off
2  keystate
3  if errorlevel 16 if not errorlevel 17 goto jump
4  choice "Do you really want to delete all *.BAK files "
5  if errorlevel 2 goto quit
6  :JUMP
7  del *.BAK
8  :QUIT
```

Line 5 checks to see whether the Scroll Lock key is on (because KEYSTATE sets an ERRORLEVEL of 16 if Scroll Lock is on) and, if it is, skips the confirmation prompt and gets on with the file deletion.

If more than one special key is active or held down, the ERRORLEVEL returned by KEYSTATE is the sum of the individual key ERRORLEVELs. For example, if Caps Lock is on and the Alt key is held down, the ERRORLEVEL is set to 72.

Table 11-2	ERRORLEVELs Set by KEYSTATE.COM
ERRORLEVEL	*Key Status*
0	No keys are active.
1	Right Shift is held down.
2	Left Shift is held down.
4	Ctrl is held down.
8	Alt is held down.
16	Scroll Lock is active.
32	Num Lock is active.
64	Caps Lock is active.
128	Ins is held down.

By changing the value of the byte at address 0040:0017, you can alter the state of the Caps Lock, Num Lock, and Scroll Lock keys. The following script file creates CAPSOFF.COM, which turns off the Caps Lock:

```
n capsoff.com
a 100
mov ax,40
mov ds,ax
mov al,[17]
and al,BF     ; set bit 1 off
mov [17],al
ret

r cx
E
w
q
```

The following script file creates CAPSON.COM, for turning Caps Lock on:

```
n capson.com
a 100
mov ax,40
mov ds,ax
mov al,[17]
or al,40     ; Set bit 1 on
mov [17],al
ret

r cx
E
w
q
```

The AND and OR statements in these two script files turn the Caps Lock bit off and on, respectively. You can use similar techniques to create utilities to set Num Lock and Scroll Lock on or off. The following statements create on and off utilities for Num Lock and Scroll Lock:

`and al,df`	Turns Num Lock off
`or al,20`	Turns Num Lock on
`and al,ef`	Turns Scroll Lock off
`or al,10`	Turns Scroll Lock on

Rebooting the PC

You can use the following script file, REBOOT.SCR, to create the utility REBOOT.COM:

```
n reboot.com
a 100
mov ah,0d       ; flush disk cache
int 21          ; Call Interrupt
mov ax,0040
mov ds,ax
mov ax,1234
mov [72],ax
jmp FFFF:0000

r cx
14
w
q
```

When you execute REBOOT.COM, your system reboots.

This small program first calls sets AH equal to 0 and calls interrupt 21h, to en-sure that any data in a write-delayed disk cache is saved to disk. See Chapter 4 for a discussion of write-delayed caching. Next, the value 1234h is moved to the address 0040:0072 and then executes the code at address FFFF:0000, which is the power-on self test (POST) BIOS code used at system boot time. When the POST instructions are executed, the value stored at 0040:0072 is inspected, and if it has a value of 1234h, a warm reboot is performed. If that memory location has any other address, a cold boot is performed. You can modify REBOOT.SCR to perform a cold boot by replacing the MOV AX,1234 statement with MOV AX,ABCD.

 When REBOOT.COM is executed in a Windows DOS session, Windows does not trap the reboot attempt as it does when you press Ctrl-Alt-Del. The system simply reboots.

Waiting for a function key

Call me old fashioned, but I like function keys. Unfortunately, CHOICE does not provide function key support. The following script, GETFUNCY.SCR, creates the program GETFUNCY.COM:

```
n getfuncy.com
a 100
jmp 0108     ; skip the beep
mov dl,7     ; the beep meister
```

```
mov ah,2     ; sub-function 2
int 21       ; beep
mov ah,00    ; sub-function 0
int 16       ; wait for keyboard input
cmp al,00    ; is it an extended key
ja 0102      ; not extended—go get another key
cmp ah,3b    ; compare with 59 decimal (F1)
jl 0102      ; too small—go get another key
cmp ah,44    ; compare with 68 decimal (F10)
ja 0102      ; too large—go get another key
sub ah,3a    ; subtract 58 decimal from key value
mov al,ah    ; set key value as errorlevel
mov ah,4c
int 21

r cx
23
w
q
```

GETFUNCY waits for the user to press any one of the function keys F1 through F10. If the user presses a different key, the program beeps and waits for the user to press another key. An ERRORLEVEL is returned to indicate which function key the user selected — from ERRORLEVEL 1 for F1 through ERRORLEVEL 10 for F10.

The following batch file, TESTFUNC.BAT, shows GETFUNCY in action:

```
@echo off
echo Press a Function Key
getfuncy
if errorlevel 10 echo You pressed F10
if errorlevel 9 if not errorlevel 10 echo You pressed F9
if errorlevel 8 if not errorlevel 9 echo You pressed F8
if errorlevel 7 if not errorlevel 8 echo You pressed F7
if errorlevel 6 if not errorlevel 7 echo You pressed F6
if errorlevel 5 if not errorlevel 6 echo You pressed F5
if errorlevel 4 if not errorlevel 5 echo You pressed F4
if errorlevel 3 if not errorlevel 4 echo You pressed F3
if errorlevel 2 if not errorlevel 3 echo You pressed F2
if errorlevel 1 if not errorlevel 2 echo You pressed F1
```

Creating disk and drive utilities

The following paragraphs examine two utilities to help with drive management.

Abort, Retry, Fail? Not!

There are few prompts uglier than an Abort, Retry, Fail? message emanating from a batch file when it is trying to access an empty drive.

The following script, DRIVEAOK.SCR, creates the program DRIVEAOK.COM, which tests whether drive A has a disk installed:

```
n driveaok.com
a 100
mov ax,2524    ; Change interrupt handler for Int. 24
mov dx,0113    ; New handler at address 0113 (see below)
int 21         ; Call Interrupt
mov ah,36      ; Get free space on drive
mov dl,01      ; Drive A is test drive
int 21         ; Call interrupt
mov ax,4c00    ; Got this far drive must be OK — set 0 errorlevel
int 21         ; Call it a day
mov ax,4c01    ; Critical error — drive A not ready — set 1 errorlevel
int 21         ; Call it a day

r cx
18
w
q
```

There is more to this compact script than meets the eye. When an empty drive is accessed, the DOS critical error handler, interrupt 24h, is invoked. The first task is to change the critical error handler to some custom code and bypass the usual Abort, Retry, Fail? message. Interrupt 21h, subfunction 25 instructs DOS to change the interrupt handler for the interrupt specified in register AL. The new interrupt handler is identified in register DX. In this case, DX points to byte 113 of the data segment, which is simply the code to set an ERRORLEVEL of 1 and terminate the program.

The next step is to try to access the drive and thereby provoke a critical error if the drive is not ready. Interrupt 21h, subfunction 36h gets the free space on the drive specified in register DL. If the free space information is returned, the program terminates with a 0 ERRORLEVEL. Otherwise, a critical error occurs, and the custom error handler is invoked.

The program sets an ERRORLEVEL of 1 if the drive is open and 0 if it contains a disk. The following batch fragment file shows how to use DRIVEAOK in a batch file and avoid the standard DOS error message:

```
@echo off
:START
driveaok
if errorlevel 1 goto message
rem Insert A related commands below
echo A is OK
goto quit
:MESSAGE
echo Insert a formatted disk in drive A
pause
goto start
:QUIT
```

You can use the following script, DRIVEBOK.SCR, to create the program DRIVEBOK.COM, which tests whether drive B has a disk installed:

```
n drivebok.com
a 100
mov ax,2524     ; Change interrupt handler for Int. 24
mov dx,0113     ; New handler at address 0113 (see below)
int 21          ; Call Interrupt
mov ah,36       ; Get free space on drive
mov dl,02       ; Drive B is test drive
int 21          ; Call interrupt
mov ax,4c00     ; Got this far drive must be ok—set 0 errorlevel
int 21          ; Call it a day
mov ax,4c01     ; Critical error—drive B not ready—set 1 errorlevel
int 21          ; Call it a day

r cx
18
w
q
```

A script to determine the boot drive

If you are writing a batch file that copies, modifies, or searches the start-up files, you need to determine the boot drive. Don't just assume that the boot drive is C.

The following script, BOOTDRV.SCR, uses interrupt 21h, function 33h to determine the boot drive and creates the file BOOTDRV.COM:

```
n bootdrv.com
a 100
mov ax,3305     ; Get boot drive
int 21          ; Call Interrupt
mov al,dl       ; Move boot drive to AL
mov ah,4c       ; Exit with errorlevel
int 21          ; Call it a day

r cx
B
w
q
```

Register DL is updated with the boot drive, which is then returned as an ERRORLEVEL. Drive A is ERRORLEVEL 1, drive B is ERRORLEVEL 2, and so on.

The following batch file, TESTBOOT.BAT, shows BOOTDRV.COM in action:

```
@echo off
bootdrv
if errorlevel 4 if not errorlevel 5 echo Booted from drive D
if errorlevel 3 if not errorlevel 4 echo Booted from drive C
if errorlevel 2 if not errorlevel 3 echo Booted from drive B
if errorlevel 1 if not errorlevel 2 echo Booted from drive A
```

Summary

This chapter showed how you can use DEBUG for many purposes other than tracking bugs in programs. You examined the following applications for DEBUG:

▶ You can browse program and ASCII files with the D (dump) and S (search) commands. Unlike EDIT, DEBUG displays every byte in the file, including the carriage return and line feed characters.

▶ You can patch programs such as QBASIC.EXE and CHOICE.COM to change their behavior and properties by using the E (edit) command. EXE files, however, must first be renamed with a different extension.

▶ DEBUG is ideal for creating small and compact utilities to extend and enhance batch files.

▶ Programs can be created interactively or by redirecting script files to DEBUG.

▶ The A (assemble) command enables you to enter commands using assembly-language mnemonics.

Part IV of this book contains a complete and thorough command reference for all the DOS 6 programs and device drivers.

Part IV:
The Complete DOS 6
Command Reference

The Complete DOS 6 Command Reference

Introduction

This section is an at-a-glance summary of every DOS command available in DOS 6, including all the popular DOS commands, such as XCOPY and MD, as well as device drivers, such as ANSI.SYS. The section even includes programming commands, such as GOTO, used in batch files. In short, if DOS has a command or program — and DOS 6 contains more commands than ever — you'll find it listed in this reference.

With so many commands to choose from, the task of sorting the more important commands from the least used commands can be difficult. To help you separate the wheat from the chaff, I have *rated* each command on a scale from 1 to 10. The best and most relevant commands receive a score of 10. At the other end of the scale, ratings in the range from 1 to 3 indicate poor or obscure commands.

A *command banner* introduces every command. Each command banner includes the name of the command, the command's rating on *Bob's Scorecard,* and a set of four check boxes that identifies when you use the command. Each check box can appear in one of the following three ways:

- A filled-in, black box indicates the primary use of the command.

- An X in the box indicates less frequent use of the command.

- An open or empty box signifies that the command is not used in that category.

The command banner for the PATH command looks like this:

The check boxes for PATH indicate that it is used primarily in the AUTOEXEC.BAT file, primarily in batch files, occasionally at the DOS prompt, but never in the CONFIG.SYS file.

I give the PATH command a rating of 7 because every respectable DOS user needs to use the PATH command, but it can be improved. The path length has a 127-character limit, for example, and no direct support exists for path sets — batch files must be used to switch between paths. PATH is a good command, but not a great one.

To further assist you in using this reference, all commands appear in alphabetical order, regardless of the command's category. The DOS command HELP precedes the device driver HIMEM.SYS, for example, which is followed by IF, a batch file command.

Command Use Conventions

It is often more difficult to describe a command than it is to use it! This statement is especially true when you can use a command in many different ways and when it has a variety of *options* and *switches*.

Consider the EDIT command you use to edit a text file. In its simplest form, you just enter the command `edit`, the editor runs, and away you go. Alternatively, you can specify the name of the file you want to edit when you enter the command, as shown in the following example:

```
edit c:\autoexec.bat
```

The editor automatically loads the file, ready for editing. Because you can include a drive and a directory path when you enter a filename, you can load files not located in the current directory.

In addition, the EDIT command supports a variety of switches that control some of the editor properties. You can use the /B switch, for example, to force the editor to appear on-screen in black and white rather than color. As with many DOS commands, EDIT clearly has more capability than first meets the eye.

To help you understand all the options and switches available with the DOS commands, a "Usage" section that defines the complete command syntax follows every command "Description." The syntax line includes all optional components and uses special conventions that define command use. The syntax line for the EDIT command, for example, is as follows:

```
edit [[drive:][path]filename.ext] [/b] [/g] [/h] [/nohi]
```

This description can seem daunting at first. With an explanation, however, it provides a convenient and concise way to define each command and its options. The following conventions used in *DOS 6 SECRETS* are similar to the ones used in the DOS 6 on-line help.

You can always display an explanation of the syntax and usage of each command by using the DOS HELP command or by entering a command followed by the /? switch.

Mandatory elements

Any part of a command that is *mandatory,* such as the command name, does *not* appear in square brackets ([ ]). For example, the only part of the syntax line for the EDIT command that appears without square brackets is edit. The syntax line for the DEL command, however, always contains at least two mandatory elements not enclosed in square brackets: the command name del and the name of the file to be deleted.

Optional elements

Any optional components of a command *are enclosed* in square brackets. The /B switch in the EDIT command, for example, is displayed in the use syntax as [/b] to indicate that it is optional (syntax lines appear in lower case).

Most DOS commands support the /? switch to display command help. To avoid unnecessary repetition, the standard /? switch is not repeated for every command.

Entering filenames

Often, commands that accept filenames can accept either a simple filename, a filename that includes the file path, a filename that includes a drive name, or a fully qualified filename that includes drive and path and filename. The following examples show the EDIT command with some of these filename variations:

```
edit 123.bat

edit \batfiles\123.bat

edit d:123.bat

edit d:\batfiles\123.bat.
```

The syntax used to denote this filename flexibility is shown in this example:

[[*drive:*][*path*]*filename.ext*]

The square brackets indicate that each component is optional. The italics indicate that a component is a *variable*.

Because a filename is optional in the EDIT command, the filename components are enclosed in a pair of square brackets. DEVICE, on the other hand, requires a filename to be specified, that is, it is not optional, so it has the following syntax:

[*drive:*][*path*]*filename.ext*

Entering wildcards

Some DOS commands operate on one or more than one file. A good example is the COPY command, which you can use to copy a single file or a collection of files. You can use the DOS wildcard characters * and ? to identify a filename pattern. The syntax for a command that accepts a filename or a wildcard filename is as follows:

[*drive:*][*path*][*wildcard.ext*]

Examples of some filenames that adhere to this command syntax are as follows:

```
*.*

c:\*.sys

d:\batfiles\????it.bat

config.sys

\windows\win.ini
```

Complex commands

Some commands have rarely used switches that can complicate the syntax and the command description. In these cases, you will find an extra section called "Extended use." A good example of this treatment is with the [/A] and [/B] switches in the COPY command. Because you use the COPY command without these switches 99 percent of the time, they are discussed only in the "Extended use" section.

Revisiting EDIT

The syntax for the EDIT command hopefully makes more sense now. You may recall that the syntax for EDIT is described as follows:

```
edit [[drive:][path]filename.ext] [/b] [/g] [/h] [/nohi]
```

To summarize, you can enter the EDIT command with no parameters, or you can optionally accept a single filename with as many as four switches.

Command Summary

There are more than 75 commands and device drivers available in DOS 6. Appendix A provides an alphabetical summary of every command and a brief description of the command.

The appendix also identifies the commands that DOS 5 supports but that have been dropped (thankfully) from DOS 6. DOS 6 users can obtain the DOS 5 versions of these commands on a Supplemental disk from Microsoft Corporation or from DOS resellers.

Description

The ANSI.SYS device driver provides ways to spruce up the DOS display capabilities, control the cursor location, and assign special functions to keys.

Usage

```
device[high]=[drive:][path]ansi.sys [/x] [/k] [/r]
```

Options and switches

```
[drive:][path]
```

This option identifies the directory in which ANSI.SYS is located, if it is not in the boot directory. SETUP places ANSI.SYS in the \DOS directory by default.

```
[/x]
```

On extended keyboards, you can perform some operations by using more than one physical key. Two keys can enter the + character, for example, and you can use two PgUp keys. The /X switch instructs DOS to treat these keys independently. With this switch in effect, you can remap each of a pair of keys differently.

```
[/k]
```

This switch instructs ANSI.SYS to treat an extended keyboard (with 101 keys) like a standard 84-key keyboard. In this state, ANSI.SYS treats an extended key the same as its standard equivalent.

```
[/r]
```

This switch adjusts line scrolling to make ANSI.SYS more compatible with programs designed for the disabled, which read the text from the display.

Remarks

Having installed ANSI.SYS, you can use special escape sequences to manage the display colors, control the cursor location, and assign strings to keys. You can use the DOS commands PROMPT, ECHO, and TYPE to communicate the escape sequences to ANSI.SYS.

ANSI.SYS provides a way to add some spice to the boring DOS display, but Windows it isn't. ANSI.SYS gained its popularity in the days before graphical user interfaces existed, and by today's standards its capabilities are limited.

When ANSI.SYS is installed, you can use the MODE LINES= command to set EGA and VGA systems in condensed display mode with 43 or 50 lines.

Because the /X and /K switches are opposite instructions, you cannot specify both of them at the same time.

Example

You make the following entry in the CONFIG.SYS file to install ANSI.SYS:

```
device=c:\dos\ansi.sys
```

Additional information

Refer to Chapter 6 for a full discussion of ANSI.SYS, and to Appendix C for a summary of the escape codes that ANSI.SYS supports.

See also MODE.

Bob's Shareware Collection disks

An excellent replacement for ANSI.SYS is FANSI-CONSOLE, from Hersey Micro Consulting, Inc. See Chapter 6 for further information about this utility.

Description

APPEND is to data files what PATH is to programs. You use APPEND to tell DOS which drives and directories to search in for data files (such as spreadsheets and word processing documents) when a program doesn't find them in the default directory.

Usage

```
append [[drive:][path1]] [;[drive:][path]] [[/x] or [/x:on] or
[/x:off]] [[/path:on] or [/path:off]] [/e]
```

Options and switches

You can use APPEND with no switches. When APPEND is used in this way, DOS displays the active list of appended directories.

```
[[drive:][path1]] [;[drive:][path]]
```

Semicolons separate the list of directories to be searched for data files. Each directory can optionally include a drive identifier.

```
[[/x] or [/x:on] or [/x:off]]
```

The /X switch instructs DOS whether to search for programs and data files in the appended directories. The /X:OFF switch indicates that DOS should not search the appended directories for programs and batch files. /X and /X:ON have the same meaning, and both switches instruct DOS to search the appended directories for programs and batch files. To activate the /X (or /X:ON) status, you must specify the switch the first time you enter the APPEND command. You can use /X:OFF and /X:ON thereafter to toggle the search status.

```
[[/path:on] or [/path:off]]
```

Typically, when a program prompts you for a filename, you can enter either a basic filename and extension or a fully qualified filename including a path and even a drive letter. You use the /PATH switches to control whether appended directories are searched when you have entered a filename that includes a path. /PATH:ON specifies that appended directories be used even when you have entered a fully qualified filename. /PATH:OFF specifies that appended directories are searched only when you have entered a filename and no path.

```
[/e]
```

This switch instructs DOS to insert an APPEND entry in the environment. APPEND normally stores the list of appended directories internally, and this list is referenced by only low-level DOS functions, which in turn are called by general programs. By adding a copy of the APPEND directories to the environment, the appended directories are directly accessible to all programs and batch files.

You cannot use the /E switch in conjunction with the [[*drive*:][*path*] parameters. If you want to have an APPEND environment entry, you must use the APPEND command twice — first with the /E switch and then by specifying the appended directories. If you use APPEND first without the /E switch, the /E switch cannot be turned on later; therefore, you must reboot the system before executing APPEND with the /E switch.

To cancel the list of appended directories, enter the APPEND command followed by a space and a semicolon (append ;). A programmer must have dreamed up this syntax — why can't we use something as simple as APPEND /OFF?

Remarks

APPEND is not the most important DOS command you will encounter. Because most contemporary programs provide their own ways to find data files, APPEND is really useful with only less sophisticated programs. Generally, good file and path management help you avoid the need for the APPEND command.

If you enter the APPEND command twice, the paths entered with the first command are overwritten by the second command.

DOS ignores any invalid paths entered with APPEND (no error message is generated).

Examples

The following two APPEND commands instruct DOS to keep a copy of the appended directories in the environment and to identify three directories to be included in the appended list:

```
append /e
append c:\batfiles;c:\;c:\wp\docs
```

You can use the /X:OFF switch to instruct DOS to ignore the suspended directories as follows:

```
append /x:off
```

The following command assigns two appended directories and specifies that they should be ignored when a fully qualified filename is entered:

```
append d:\data\ap;c:\123r24 /path:off
```

Additional information

See also PATH and SUBST.

Most programs use DOS services behind the scenes to perform common tasks such as creating, changing, and deleting files. These programs are serviced by calling an interrupt — the program interrupts DOS and asks for some data or service. One of the most common interrupts used by software is Interrupt 21h, which provides many file-related services. DOS searches appended directories for a file for the Open File (subfunction Fh), Open File Handle (subfunction 3Dh), and Get File Size (subfunction 23h) operations, even if the /X:OFF setting is in effect.

When /X:ON is in effect, the operations Find First Entry (subfunction 11h), Find First File (4Eh), and Execute Program (function 4Bh) search the appended directories.

Most users think that, after a command has been entered, DOS determines whether the command is internal. If not, they believe that DOS looks in the current directory for the program or batch file, and, finally, every directory in the environment PATH is searched. In fact, before the PATH is searched, DOS searches the *appended* directories if the /X:ON switch is active. This feature provides a convenient way to use APPEND to add one or more directories temporarily to the search path. If, for example, you enter the following command:

```
append c:\batfiles /x:on
```

DOS searches the BATFILES directory and looks for a program or batch file before searching the environment path. Furthermore, because the BATFILES directory is appended, you do not have to be in the BATFILES directory to edit a BAT file. You can edit a batch file called 123.BAT, for example, from any directory by simply entering the following command:

```
edit 123.bat
```

Because the appended directories are searched for programs and data files, you can then execute the batch file from any directory by entering the command

```
123
```

Microsoft does not recommend using APPEND with Microsoft Windows or the Windows SETUP program.

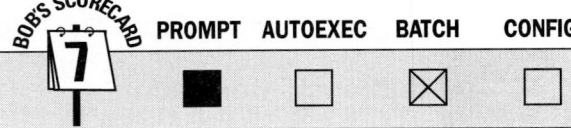

Description

Every file has four standard attributes: read-only, archive, system file, and hidden file. You use the ATTRIB command to set or clear any of these attributes for one or more files. You can also use ATTRIB to view file attributes.

Usage

```
attrib [+r or -r] [+a or -a] [+s or -s] [+h or -h]
[[drive:][path]wildcard.ext] [/s]
```

Options and switches

ATTRIB is the equivalent of entering the following command:

```
attrib *.*
```

ATTRIB can be entered with no parameters or switches; it displays by default the attributes of all the files in the default directory.

```
[+r or -r]
```

This option sets or clears the read-only attribute.

```
[+a or -a]
```

This option sets or clears the archive attribute.

```
[+s or -s]
```

This option sets or clears the system attribute.

```
[+h or -h]
```

This option sets or clears the hidden attribute.

[[*drive:*][*path*]*wildcard.ext*]

This option specifies a filemask that identifies the files whose attributes will be displayed or updated. The filemask must include a filename portion. To change the attributes in the BATFILES directory, for example, use the format c:\batfiles*.* rather than c:\batfiles. If you don't specify a filename portion, ATTRIB addresses the specific directory entry rather than all the files in the directory.

[/s]

This switch instructs DOS to process all matching files in the current directory and all its subdirectories.

Remarks

The most commonly used attributes are archive and read-only. The backup program, including DOS's own MSBACKUP command and all commercial backup utilities, normally clears the archive attribute when a file is backed up (saved to disk or tape). Whenever a file is revised, DOS resets the archive attribute.

You can use the read-only attribute to help prevent a file from being modified or deleted. That is, the file can only be *read,* not *written.* You can set the read-only attributes of the AUTOEXEC.BAT and CONFIG.SYS files to help prevent someone (or something) from modifying the file. The technique is far from foolproof, however. A savvy user (such as yourself) can use the ATTRIB command to remove the read-only attribute and edit and save the file, and then use ATTRIB to reactivate the read-only attribute.

You cannot delete files that have the read-only, system, or hidden attributes set. To delete this type of file, you first must turn off the S, H, and R attributes. If the following message is displayed when you try to delete a file:

Access denied

the file probably has one of these attributes set.

If a file has both the system and hidden attributes set, you can clear just one or the other but must clear them both at the same time.

Examples

You can use the following command to make the AUTOEXEC.BAT file read-only:

attrib +r c:\autoexec.bat

To make sure that all the database files (with a DBF extension) can be deleted from the OLDFILES directory, enter the following command:

```
attrib -r -h -s c:\oldfiles\*.DBF
```

To review the file-attribute settings of all files in the current directory, enter the following command:

```
attrib
```

Bob's Shareware Collection disks

The HotDIR Plus program, from Robert Woeger, displays file attributes when it is used with the /1 and /2 switches. PocketD from Pocketware can list and modify file attributes.

Additional information

DOSSHELL can be used to change file attributes. The MSBACKUP, RESTORE, and XCOPY commands access the archive attribute.

In versions of DOS before 5.0, the DIR command did not display hidden files (files with the hidden attribute on) or search subdirectories for files. If you work on a system with an older version of DOS and you want to list an entire directory, including hidden files, simply use ATTRIB in place of DIR. Hidden files and standard files are listed.-

The /S switch instructs DOS to access all the files in the specified or default directory and all the subdirectories underneath it. This switch provides a quick and easy way to search an entire disk for one or more files, if the version of DOS does not support the DIR /S switch. If you cannot remember the location of the file RESUME.DOC, for example, you can enter the following command:

```
attrib c:\resume.doc /s
```

DOS then displays the attributes of *all* RESUME.DOC files on your hard disk. Along with the file attributes, DOS displays the directory in which each file was found. ◈

BACKUP

The BACKUP command was discontinued with the release of DOS 6. Refer to MSBACKUP for information about the new DOS backup command.

Description

If you ever have executed a command by mistake, such as running CHKDSK on the wrong drive, you probably have tried to abort the command by pressing Ctrl-Break or Ctrl-C. You use the BREAK command to control how frequently DOS checks to see whether you have pressed Ctrl-Break or Ctrl-C while a command or program is executing.

Usage

You can either include the BREAK command in the CONFIG.SYS file or enter it from the command line. The syntax in the CONFIG.SYS file is as follows:

```
break=on or break=off
```

Except in the CONFIG.SYS file, the usage rules are as follows:

```
break [on or off]
```

Options and switches

When you use the BREAK command with no options or switches, DOS displays the current BREAK setting.

As you might expect, the ON switch means that the extra checking for Ctrl-Break is enabled, and the OFF switch is used to disable the extra checking.

Remarks

The BREAK setting is off by default, and DOS checks for Ctrl-C or Ctrl-Break only while getting user input from the keyboard or when writing to the screen or printer. When BREAK is set on, DOS additionally checks for Ctrl-C or Ctrl-Break when reading and writing to disk.

Enabling extended break-checking slows system performance somewhat, but not significantly.

Examples

You can add the following line to the CONFIG.SYS file to activate extended Ctrl-C or Ctrl-Break checking:

```
break=on
```

Alternatively, you can add a line to the AUTOEXEC.BAT file as follows:

```
break on
```

To display the active setting, enter the command with no parameters as follows:

```
break
```

Additional information

Most users think that pressing Ctrl-C is the same as pressing Ctrl-Break, but a DOS Jedi knows better.

Ctrl-Break is more reliable because it uses a special interrupt mechanism. Ctrl-C, on the other hand, is processed through the keyboard buffer like any other key combination. Although DOS's programs have been written to check the keyboard buffer for Ctrl-C, they look at only the first character in the buffer. If you have pressed another key before Ctrl-C, the DOS program does not notice it.

You can use the CHKDSK command to demonstrate this process. Execute CHKDSK and, while it is running, press Ctrl-C. The command terminates before completion. Run CHKDSK a second time, and press the spacebar and then Ctrl-C. CHKDSK notices only the spacebar in the keyboard buffer and therefore completes normally. Ctrl-Break gets the attention of CHKDSK regardless of the other keystrokes already waiting in the keyboard buffer.

	BOB'S SCORECARD	PROMPT	AUTOEXEC	BATCH	CONFIG
BUFFERS	4	☐	☐	☐	■

Description

This command, designed to improve disk performance, controls the number of disk buffers used by DOS when reading files. Buffers are memory blocks designed to store data during disk read and write operations and to improve system performance.

Usage

```
buffers=p[,s]
```

Options and switches

When BUFFERS is not used, DOS assigns a default number of buffers. The value assigned depends on the amount of available memory, as follows:

Memory installed	Default buffers
Less than 128K	3 or less
128K – 255K	5
256K – 511K	10
More than 512K	15

```
=p
```

This parameter specifies the number of (primary) buffers and must be in the range from 1 through 99.

```
[,s]
```

This option specifies the number of secondary or read-ahead buffers and must be in the range from 1 through 8. If S is not specified, the number of secondary buffers defaults to 0.

Remarks

DOS buffers are similar to dumb disk caches. Whenever data is read from disk, it is transferred from the disk to the buffers and then from the buffers to main memory to be accessed by the executing program. If a program requests from disk some data that already is stored in a buffer, DOS transfers the data directory from the buffer to main memory. Memory-to-memory transfers are much faster than disk-to-memory transfers.

The secondary buffer cache is used as a *read-ahead* buffer — when data is read from disk, the sectors that follow are read also, in anticipation that this data also will be needed momentarily. Reading several sectors at a time is more efficient than reading them one at a time as necessary.

Many modern hard drives already do this kind of buffering on their controllers, so you will want to test to see if secondary buffers help or hinder performance in your system. Using the secondary buffer cache is especially useful on older systems. SMARTDRV.EXE doesn't work with the 8086 processor, and older hard drives do not have exotic hardware caches.

The value of BUFFERS has clearly diminished, thanks to superior disk-caching software, such as SMARTDRV. DOS, buffers and disk caches perform a similar function and, in some cases, can compete with each other and adversely affect system performance. If you use a disk cache, you should deliberately use a low buffer setting (2 or 4, for example) with no secondary buffers, to enable the disk cache to work unimpeded. You may want to use a higher BUFFERS setting (10, for example) if the disk-cache software does not support all drives, such as floppies or CD-ROM drives.

If you do not use a disk cache (and clearly you should), you should take advantage of BUFFERS. The default values are conservative, to say the least. Typically, a BUFFERS value of 20 to 40 is appropriate, and the secondary buffer cache should be set to its maximum value of 8. If too many buffers are allocated (more than 60, for example), DOS may spend more time managing the buffers than it would save by going directly to the disk. Also, more buffers mean less memory for your programs.

On a standard system, every buffer consumes approximately 530 bytes of memory; 512 bytes of this amount are used to store a single sector of data, and the remainder is used for buffer management. When DOS is loaded into the high memory area (HMA), the buffers also are loaded there, if room is available. After DOS has been loaded, room is available for 48 buffers. If you exceed 48, *all* the buffers are loaded into base memory. You can find out how much memory DOS is using for buffers by typing mem /d/p.

Examples

Use the following command to allocate 40 standard buffers and no secondary buffers:

```
buffers=40
```

To allocate 20 buffers and 8 secondary buffers, use the following command:

```
buffers=20,8
```

Additional information

See also MEM and SMARTDRV.

	PROMPT	AUTOEXEC	BATCH	CONFIG

CALL

Description

If you use batch files, you will want to understand and use CALL. It enables one batch file program to execute a second batch file, after which control is returned to the first batch file.

Usage

call [*drive:*][*path*]*filename* [*batch–parameters*]

Options and switches

[*drive:*][*path*]*filename*

This option is the name of the batch file to be executed. The BAT extension does not have to be specified. CALL can be used to run COM and EXE files, in fact, but you have no good reason to do so. If you do not specify a file path, DOS searches for the file in the current directory and then in the path in the normal manner.

[*batch–parameters*]

If the batch file being called requires some parameters, you should specify them after the batch filename in the same way as you enter them from the command line.

Remarks

The main value of CALL is that control returns to the calling program after the secondary batch file has finished executing. If you enter just the name of the second batch file (and do not precede the name with CALL), control is passed to the second batch file, and any remaining commands in the original batch file are *not* executed.

Do not use redirection symbols (<, >, <<, >>) and pipes (|) with the CALL command.

CALL enables a batch file to call itself, but you should provide some logical way for the operation to terminate; otherwise, it will loop forever. In fact, because each CALL execution consumes 80 bytes of conventional memory, eventually a looping batch file will terminate with an insufficient memory error.

Note: On older systems, before DOS 3.3, you may encounter a batch file statement beginning with `command /c`. Old Jedis used this trick before CALL was available. It has almost the same effect as CALL, but it uses a secondary copy of COMMAND.COM. Using the `command /c` trick, however, does not allow the second batch file to alter the environment permanently because it's acting on a copy, not the master environment. Unless you are writing batch files to run on pre-DOS 3.3 systems, use the CALL command.

Examples

The following extract from an AUTOEXEC.BAT file shows the CALL command used to execute the batch file SAVEM.BAT:

```
@echo off
path c:\;c:\windows;c:\batfiles;c:\pckwik
call savem
prompt $p$g
```

To execute the batch file DOWNFONT.BAT and pass two parameters, you should add the following command to a batch file:

```
call downfont times helv
```

Additional information

Refer to Chapter 10 for more information about batch file programming.

Bob's Shareware Collection disks

The disk includes a number of tools for enhancing batch file operations: TurboBat, in the ExtraDOS Toolbox, compiles batch files; BATUTIL, from CtrlAlt Associates, provides slick user-interface tools.

BOB'S SCORECARD	PROMPT	AUTOEXEC	BATCH	CONFIG
CD or CHDIR 7	■	■	■	□

Description

This command changes the default (current) directory. Although CD is a basic, no-frills command, you probably use it every day. If it were taken away, you would surely miss it!

Usage

```
cd [[drive:][path] or [..]]
```

Options and switches

When you use CD with no options or switches, DOS displays the current default directory.

[*drive:*][*path*]

This option identifies the drive whose default directory will be changed, along with the new directory or path. You can omit the `drive:` component if you are changing the default directory of the current drive — as is usually the case. If the path does not commence with a backslash, the path is assumed to extend from the current directory.

[..]

Use a pathname of .. to change to the parent directory. You can precede the two dots with a drive letter to change the default directory of another drive to the parent directory.

Remarks

The CD command is one of the most commonly used DOS commands. To master DOS, you must be able to navigate quickly around directories. Remember that you can use the TREE command to display a visual map of a disk's directory structure.

Examples

Assume that your hard disk is configured with the following structure:

```
C:\
  LOTUS
    ├─BUDGET
    └─SAMPLES
  ─WP
  ─GAMES
  ─PARADOX
  ─BATFILES
  ─WINDOWS
      ├─SYSTEM
      ├─NDW
      └─WAVES
          └─WAYNEWLD
  └DOS
```

To change directories from the root directory to the WINDOWS subdirectory called WAVES, you enter the following command:

```
cd\windows\waves
```

To *then* change directories to the subdirectory WAYNEWLD, you can enter one of the following commands:

```
cd waynewld
```

```
cd\windows\waves\waynewld
```

If the default directory is C:\LOTUS\SAMPLES, the following command changes the default directory to C:\LOTUS:

```
cd..
```

If the default directory is C:\LOTUS\SAMPLES, the following command changes the default directory to C:\LOTUS\BUDGET:

```
cd..\budget
```

Additional information

See also PROMPT, RD, MD, and TREE.

Bob's Shareware Collection disks

Because CD has not been enhanced significantly since an early version of DOS, a number of Shareware alternatives are smarter and easier to use than CD. My favorite is Keith Ledbetter's LCD utility. LCD enables you to change directories quickly to any drive on the system by entering a partial directory. If more than one directory matches the partial name, a pop-up dialog box enables you to choose the directory. Great!

Description

The CHCP command is used with international character sets to display or change the active code page.

Usage

```
chcp [nnn]
```

Options and switches

When you use CHCP with no switches, DOS displays the current active code page.

[*nnn*]

This option specifies the number or ID of the code page to be activated.

Remarks

Code-page management is necessary only when you want to change from the default code page to an alternative. It's not a command I use every day!

Unfortunately, changing code pages is not as easy as it seems. You can use CHCP to change code pages only after DOS has been primed with commands such as COUNTRY, NLSFUNC, and MODE.

Code pages are supported on the display, the keyboard, and the printer. Normally, you want all three devices to be on the same (code) page. CHCP sets the code page for all three devices. To change the code page on an individual device, use the MODE SELECT command.

Code pages are not supported on CGA and monochrome systems — the character sets are stored in video ROM and cannot be changed.

Examples

Enter the following command to see the active code page:

```
chcp
```

If your system has been configured for Italian use, you can switch to the secondary Italian code page by entering the following command:

```
chcp 437
```

Additional information

Refer to Chapter 9 of the *MS-DOS User's Guide* for a thorough discussion of international configuration issues.

See also COUNTRY, MODE, NLSFUNC, and KEYB.

BOB'S SCORECARD

	PROMPT	AUTOEXEC	BATCH	CONFIG
CHKDSK 7	■	⊠	⊠	□

Description

The primary function of CHKDSK is to check the integrity of a disk's file structure. CHKDSK reports disk errors and, optionally, corrects them. CHKDSK displays a summary of the disk's use and the system's memory status.

Usage

```
chkdsk [drive:][[path]wildcard.ext] [/f] [/v]
```

Options and switches

When you use CHKDSK with no options or switches, DOS reports the status of the default drive.

[drive:][[path]wildcard.ext]

This option identifies the drive, filemask, or individual file whose integrity will be checked.

[/f]

This switch instructs CHKDSK to try to fix any errors it encounters.

[/v]

This switch specifies that a list of filenames should be generated as each file is checked.

Remarks

The following example shows output generated by CHKDSK:

```
Volume Serial Number is 0000-16F5

    112 lost allocation units found in 9 chains.
    458752 bytes disk space would be freed

 211787776 bytes total disk space
     77824 bytes in 2 hidden files
    946176 bytes in 212 directories
```

```
206786560 bytes in 6432 user files
  3518464 bytes available on disk

     4096 bytes in each allocation unit
    51706 total allocation units on disk
      859 available allocation units on disk

   655360 total bytes memory
   528944 bytes free
```

The /F parameter is used to instruct DOS to correct any anomalies in the FAT. The most common problem encountered is lost allocation units. Although these clusters of the disk are marked as being in use, paradoxically no file claims to own them. In other words, they are not being used, but DOS does not reuse them. These situations may occur when a system crash occurs or when the system is turned off while a file is being saved to disk.

CHKDSK's solution to the problem is to remove the in-use flag for each of the clusters. This action frees up the clusters to be used again and provides more free disk space — something we all yearn for. Before clearing the in-use flag, DOS generates the following prompt:

```
112 lost allocation units found in 9 chains.
Convert the lost chains to files?
```

If you enter Y, the data from these clusters is saved, with a CHK extension, in a set of files in the root directory. You can peruse these files with an editor and see whether any data is worth salvaging. If you respond with N, the data is not saved.

Don't be overly concerned if one of the lines in the CHKDSK output identifies bad sectors. Most hard disks have some bad sectors, which are identified during the disk formatting process.

Previous versions of CHKDSK were a bit too bold about fixing things when the /F parameter was used. When two files each claimed some of the same clusters, CHKDSK /F would automatically arbitrate the dispute over the "cross-linked" clusters, sometimes with less than helpful results. DOS 6 modestly refrains from meddling with cross-linked clusters, even when /F is used. You will need a third-party file repair utility to perform this delicate surgery.

Examples

To check the integrity of the default drive, enter the following command:

```
chkdsk
```

The following command checks for errors on drive C and corrects any errors it encounters:

```
chkdsk c: /f
```

The following command tests the integrity of a floppy disk in drive A:

```
chkdsk a:
```

Additional information

Refer to Chapter 4 for more information on CHKDSK.

See also DEFRAG, MEM, and VOL.

Disk fragmentation can significantly impair the overall performance of a system. If a filename, or filemask, is specified with the CHKDSK command, DOS reports the overall disk status, along with any files (which match the filemask) that are fragmented.

The command chkdsk *.* entered from the WINDOWS directory, for example, generated the following output:

```
Volume Serial Number is 0000-16F5
Errors found, F parameter not specified
Corrections will not be written to disk

    101 lost allocation units found in 8 chains.
    413696 bytes disk space would be freed

211787776 bytes total disk space
    77824 bytes in 2 hidden files
   946176 bytes in 212 directories
206917632 bytes in 6433 user files
  3432448 bytes available on disk

     4096 bytes in each allocation unit
    51706 total allocation units on disk
      838 available allocation units on disk

   655360 total bytes memory
   528944 bytes free

C:\WINDOWS\AMILABEL.INI Contains 3 non-contiguous blocks
C:\WINDOWS\VBRUN100.DLL Contains 2 non-contiguous blocks
```

```
C:\WINDOWS\CONTROL.INI Contains 2 non-contiguous blocks
C:\WINDOWS\WINHELP.EXE Contains 5 non-contiguous blocks
C:\WINDOWS\FAXMNG.EXE Contains 3 non-contiguous blocks
C:\WINDOWS\PREC.EXE Contains 8 non-contiguous blocks
C:\WINDOWS\PREC.DOC Contains 2 non-contiguous blocks
C:\WINDOWS\PMIX.EXE Contains 10 non-contiguous blocks
C:\WINDOWS\MIX.EXE Contains 2 non-contiguous blocks
C:\WINDOWS\LSMTOGL.DLL Contains 2 non-contiguous blocks
C:\WINDOWS\FLW.INI Contains 2 non-contiguous blocks
C:\WINDOWS\WININI.OLD Contains 2 non-contiguous blocks
C:\WINDOWS\WBINXZ.EXE Contains 3 non-contiguous blocks
```

Refer to the DEFRAG command for information about how to defragment a disk.

 CHKDSK expects to be the only program running. You should not run it from within a multitasking environment such as DesqView or Windows. When you run CHKDSK from such an environment, it often incorrectly reports allocation and fragmentation problems.

Also, CHKDSK does not work on drives that have been affected by the ASSIGN, SUBST, or JOIN commands.

Do not use the CHKDSK program from early versions of DOS on systems running DOS 6. Because many internal changes have taken place in DOS's file management, old versions of CHKDSK can corrupt the DOS 6 FAT.

		PROMPT	AUTOEXEC	BATCH	CONFIG
CHOICE	BOB'S SCORECARD 8	☐	■	■	☐

Description

The command enables a batch file to prompt the user to select an option by pressing a key. CHOICE sets the ERRORLEVEL to indicate which key was pressed.

Usage

```
choice [/c[:]keys] [/n] [/s] [/t[:]c,nn] [text]
```

Options and switches

When you use CHOICE with no switches, DOS prompts the user to press Y or N.

[/c[:]*keys*]

This option identifies the list of valid keys the user can press. The colon is optional, but it should be used for clarity. If the /S switch is not specified, the valid keys are not case dependent (/abc and /ABC, for example, have the same meaning). Unfortunately, function keys and key combinations such as Alt-A are not supported.

[/n]

CHOICE displays the valid keys in square brackets by default ([A,B,C], for example). This display is referred to as the CHOICE prompt. Use /N to suppress the prompt display.

[/s]

The /S switch enables case sensitivity and instructs CHOICE to treat upper- and lowercase characters separately. When you do not specify /S, the key case is ignored.

[/t[:]*c*,*nn*]

This option instructs CHOICE to wait a specified number of seconds and then assume that a specific key was pressed. This switch is useful in batch files that occasionally can be run unattended. Again, the colon is optional, but it should be used for clarity. *nn* specifies the number of seconds to wait for the user to make a choice. If a key is not pressed after *nn* seconds, CHOICE continues as though the user has pressed the *c* character. *nn* must be a value in the range from 0 to 99. If a larger number is specified, the digits after the first two are assumed to be the prompt text. An error message is displayed if the character *c* is not one of the valid characters specified with the /C switch.

[*text*]

The remaining text following all the switches is echoed to the display before the character prompt. The text should be enclosed in quotation marks if it includes the / character.

Remarks

You can determine which key the user pressed by checking the ERRORLEVEL returned by CHOICE. If the user pressed Ctrl-Break or Ctrl-C, a 0 error level is returned; if an error is in the command switches and CHOICE fails, a 255 ERRORLEVEL is returned; otherwise, the error level indicates the key the user pressed — an error level of 1 is returned if the first key (specified with /c:keys) was selected, a 2 for the second key, and so on. You can test the

ERRORLEVEL with the IF batch file command to divert execution to the appropriate section of the batch file.

Although you can execute CHOICE from the DOS prompt, you have no sane reason to do so.

The maximum number of characters in a single CHOICE command is 127, which provides a maximum text prompt of 120 characters when no switches are used. When additional switches are specified, the maximum text size is reduced accordingly.

Examples

The following batch file uses all the default switches but specifies a brief message:

```
@echo off
CHOICE Do you want to load the mouse
if errorlevel 2 goto quit
mouse /y
:quit
```

When the batch file is executed, the valid keys default to *y, Y, n,* and *N,* and the following prompt appears:

```
Do you want to load the mouse [Y,N]?
```

The following batch file uses the /C switch to specify the valid keys:

```
@echo off
CHOICE /c:mtn Do you want to load the Mouse, Tablet or Neither
if errorlevel 3 goto end
if errorlevel 2 goto Tablet
mouse /y
goto end
:Tablet
tabk /c:345
:end
```

The valid keys are M, T, or N in upper- or lowercase. When the batch file is executed, the following prompt appears:

```
Do you want to load the Mouse, Tablet or Neither [M,T,N]?
```

The batch file tests the ERRORLEVEL (in reverse order) to ascertain which key the user pressed. A value of 3 indicates that the user pressed N, and a value of 2 indicates that the user pressed T; otherwise, the mouse driver is installed.

You can improve the CHOICE statement in the preceding batch file example by adding a /T switch as follows:

```
choice /c:mtn /t:n,9 Do you want to load the Mouse, Tablet or Neither
```

If the user does not make a choice within nine seconds, CHOICE returns an ERRORLEVEL of 3, as though the user pressed N.

Additional information

CHOICE provides an easy way to build a menu system with a single batch file. Refer to Chapter 10 for more information about this technique and other ways to use CHOICE.

See also ECHO, IF, and PAUSE.

Bob's Shareware Collection disks

Although CHOICE *really* improves the power of batch files, it pales in comparison to STACKEY and BATUTIL. The Turbobat batch file compiler, from Foley Hi-Tech Systems, provides an excellent way to stop users from tampering with batch files and improves batch file performance.

Do not use the pipe and filter characters (|, <, >, >>, <<) in the CHOICE text, even if the text is enclosed in quotation marks. DOS interprets these characters as command switches and causes CHOICE input or output to be suppressed.

Description

The CLS command is used to clear the screen. CLS removes all the displayed characters, sets the color to gray on black, and repositions the cursor to the top left corner of the display.

Usage

```
cls
```

Options and switches

None

Remarks

Although you can use CLS from the DOS prompt, it most often is used in a batch file before executing a command, displaying a message, or drawing a menu.

You can use ANSI.SYS to customize the display colors you may prefer to gray on black.

Example

The following batch file fragment uses CLS to clear the screen and then displays a message:

```
. . . . .
cls
echo Make sure a floppy disk is in drive A.
echo To abort the operation press Ctrl-Break.
pause
. . . . .
```

Additional information

See also ANSI.SYS.

Bob's Shareware Collection disks

The BATUTIL batch enhancer, from CtrlAlt Associates, provides a variety of tools for enhancing your display.

BOB'S SCORECARD	PROMPT	AUTOEXEC	BATCH	CONFIG
COMMAND 5	☒	☒	☒	■

Description

Starts a new copy (or instance) of COMMAND.COM, the command interpreter. As its name suggests, the command interpreter is responsible for accepting user input commands and invoking the appropriate function or external command.

Although the COMMAND.COM file is an essential part of DOS, you rarely need to execute the command directly. You can use COMMAND directly to adjust the environment size, but the preferred technique is to use the SHELL command.

Usage

The syntax for COMMAND is as follows:

```
command [[drive:]path] [device] [/e:nnnnn] [/p [/msg]] [/c text]
[/k filename]
```

When COMMAND is used with the SHELL command, the syntax is as follows:

```
shell=[[drive1:]path1]command.com [[drive:]path] [device] [/e:nnnnn]
[/p [/msg]]
```

Options and switches

Used with no options or switches, COMMAND invokes a secondary copy of COMMAND.COM. You can unload this secondary copy by entering the EXIT command. Although this command seems to be of little value, it provides the opportunity for some clever tricks (see the upcoming SECRET).

```
[[drive1:]path1]command.com
```

This option identifies the location of the command interpreter (COMMAND.COM) when it is not located in the root directory of the boot drive.

```
[[drive:]path]
```

This option specifies where DOS should look for COMMAND.COM during a session. This path is used to update the environment variable COMSPEC.

```
[device]
```

This option identifies a DOS device to be used for default command input and output. Normally, the device is CON (the console or monitor). The following table shows the valid devices.

Device	Description
AUX	The auxiliary device
CON	The console or display
LPT1	The device connected to LPT1
LPT2	The device connected to LPT2
LPT3	The device connected to LPT3
PRN	The printer
COM1	The device connected to COM1
COM2	The device connected to COM2
COM3	The device connected to COM3
COM4	The device connected to COM4

Under normal circumstances, you do not need to use this switch. These capabilities usually are exploited by specialist programs involving remote operations, such as debuggers and file-transfer programs.

Note: CTTY can identify a different input-output device without invoking a secondary copy of COMMAND.COM.

    [/e:*nnnnn*]

This switch is used to specify the size of the environment, which can range from 160 to 32,768 bytes. The switch is commonly used when COMMAND is invoked with the SHELL statement in CONFIG.SYS. If the switch is not used, the environment size defaults to 256 bytes.

    [/p [/msg]]

The /P switch makes the new copy of COMMAND.COM permanent. That is, you cannot EXIT back to the parent command processor. When the /P switch is used, DOS automatically executes AUTOEXEC.BAT. Normally, you should use this switch only when COMMAND is invoked with the SHELL statement in CONFIG.SYS. When the /P switch is used, the /MSG switch can be specified to instruct DOS to keep all DOS messages in memory. The /MSG switch is designed for unfortunate users who are running DOS from floppy disks — messages can be displayed without retrieving them from disk every time.

    [/c *text*]

Before the introduction of the CALL batch command, the /C switch was used in batch files to launch other batch files. The TEXT command identifies the command or program to be executed as soon as the secondary copy of COMMAND.COM is loaded. Note that a space is required between the /C and the command text.

    [/k *filename*]

This switch instructs COMMAND to execute the specified program and leave the user at the DOS prompt when the program has executed. This switch was introduced with DOS 6 primarily to enable Windows users to execute a start-up batch file other than AUTOEXEC.BAT when selecting the DOS Prompt window.

You should not use this command with the SHELL statement.

Remarks

In versions of DOS before 3.3, COMMAND was often used as a way to run secondary batch files; since 3.3, however, the CALL command performs that task. Nowadays, COMMAND is used primarily with the SHELL statement in CONFIG.SYS to adjust the environment size.

To economize on memory use, the DOS command interpreter is loaded into memory in two blocks. The *resident* block is loaded permanently in memory and remains there for the entire session. The code that interprets user input from the DOS prompt, however, is loaded in the top of base memory and can be overwritten by an executing program. After all, the executing program does not need access to this code. This part of COMMAND.COM is referred to as the *transient* block. When the program terminates, DOS reloads the transient block from COMMAND.COM.

Examples

The following line from CONFIG.SYS uses COMMAND with the SHELL statement to increase the environment size to 500 bytes. It also sets the COMSPEC environment variable to C:\DOS6\COMMAND.COM:

```
shell=c:\dos6\command.com c:\dos6 /e:500
```

The following line from a batch file uses the pre-DOS 3.3 trick of using a secondary copy of COMMAND.COM to launch a batch file:

```
command /c saveit.bat
```

Additional information

Refer to Chapter 10 for more information on using the /K switch with COMMAND.

See also CALL, CTTY, EXIT, PATH, and SHELL.

Sometimes I want to change my path statement temporarily so that DOS searches for programs in an alternative set of directories. On my own system, I use PutPath and GetPath batch files; when I work on someone else's system, these files are not always available.

A nifty way to change the path temporarily is to execute COMMAND before changing the path. After I finish experimenting, I return to the original path by entering EXIT. This step terminates the secondary copy of COMMAND.COM along with the modified environment and restores the original environment.

BOB'S SCORECARD	PROMPT	AUTOEXEC	BATCH	CONFIG
COPY 6	■	☒	■	☐

Description

This command copies one or more files to another location or to the same location with a new filename. You can instruct COPY, in its extended form, to treat the files as ASCII or binary.

Usage

copy [*drive:*][*path*]*wildcardS.ext* [*drive:*][*path*][*wildcardT.ext*] [/v]

Options and switches

[*drive:*][*path*]*wildcardS.ext*

This option identifies the source file or files to be copied. When a path is specified with no filename (C:\DOS, for example), DOS assumes the *.* wildcard. You must specify this switch.

[*drive:*][*path*][*wildcardT.ext*]

This option identifies the target location where the files will be copied. If no filename is specified, the files retain their original names. If a wildcard is used, the file copies are renamed by using the wildcard. If a single target file is specified with multiple source files, the source files are concatenated (combined) in a single target file. If no target path or filename is specified, the source files are copied to the current directory.

[/v]

This switch instructs DOS to verify that the data in the target file can be read successfully. It does not check to see whether the target is an accurate copy of the source. Unless you are experiencing unreliable disk access, you do not need to use this switch. COPY operations take about 30 percent longer when this switch is active.

Remarks

The source or target filenames can be devices. You may be familiar with the following statement:

copy con newfile.ext.

This command instructs DOS to copy characters from the console (or keyboard) to the file NEWFILE.TXT. Any characters you type are added directly to the file. This command provides a quick way to create a file when no editor is available. You should enter the end-of-file character Ctrl-Z to close the file and return to the DOS prompt. Similarly, you can print a file by copying it to a printer device (PRN or LPT1, for example).

COPY does not copy zero-length files, although XCOPY does. COPY does not copy hidden or system files, nor does XCOPY. You must use the ATTRIB command first to remove the hidden and system file attributes.

The target file normally is assigned the same date and time stamp as the source, but the archive attribute is set to ON to ensure that the new file is included in the next incremental backup.

The read-only file attribute is not copied to the target file — the target file always has the read-only flag turned off.

Examples

Use the following command to copy AUTOEXEC.BAT to AUTOEXEC.BAK:

```
copy c:\autoexec.bat *.bak
```

To copy all the files with a BAT extension in the BATFILES directory to the OLDSTUFF directory, enter the following command:

```
copy \batfiles\*.bat \oldstuff
```

The following command copies all the files from the root directory to the current directory:

```
copy \
```

The following command prints the file INFO.TXT to the printer connected to LPT1:

```
copy info.txt lpt1
```

Be careful when you are using wildcards in the source and not in the target. The following command copies all the BAT files in the current directory and creates a single large file called BLOB:

```
copy *.BAT BLOB
```

Additional information

Refer to Chapter 2 for more information on COPY.

See also DEL, MOVE, RENAME, REPLACE, VERIFY, and XCOPY.

Bob's Shareware Collection disks

PCOPY, one of the Patriquin Utilities from Patri-Soft, is a superb shareware utility for copying files. PCOPY can copy files based on date or size, "best-fit" files for optimal use of floppy disk free space, synchronize source and target disks, prompt before overwriting files, and process all nested subdirectories. After you use PCOPY, you will wonder how you got along without it.

PocketD from Pocketware also provides excellent file copying utilities.

Extended use

In rare circumstances, you may need to use the + operator and the /A and /B switches with the COPY command.

The + operator is used to combine multiple source files in a single target file. The following command combines three files (FILE.ONE, FILE.TWO, and FILE.TRE) in a single large file, FILE.BIG:

```
copy file.one+file.two+file.tre file.big
```

DOS can use one of two ways to determine how many bytes to copy: by referencing the file's directory entry and noting the size of the file in bytes, or by copying bytes until the Ctrl-Z or end-of-file character is encountered. You can use the /A and /B switches with both the source and target files to control the way DOS manages the COPY operation.

The /A switch is designed for use with ASCII files that contain one Ctrl-Z character. Used with the source file, /A instructs DOS to copy bytes up to the first Ctrl-Z. Used with the target, /A instructs DOS to add a Ctrl-Z to the end of the target file.

The /B switch is used with binary files that may have no Ctrl-Z characters or many of them. /B instructs DOS to ignore Ctrl-Z characters and use the directory entry to determine the total file size.

You can use the COPY command to change the date and time of a file. The trick is to add a plus and two commas (+,,) after the source filename and remember to use /B. To update AUTOEXEC.BAT to the current date and time stamp, for example, change to the boot directory and enter the following command:

```
copy /b autoexec.bat+,,
```

The plus-comma-comma suffix can be used, when you are copying files, to instruct DOS to assign the current date and time to all the new target files. ◈

BOB'S SCORECARD		PROMPT	AUTOEXEC	BATCH	CONFIG
COUNTRY	3	☐	☐	☐	■

Description

The COUNTRY command configures the country language conventions for your system.

Usage

country = *xxx* [,*yyy*] [,[*drive:*][*path*[*filename.ext*]]]

Options and switches

xxx

This code identifies the country whose conventions are used. The code is the same as the standard international dialing directories.

,*yyy*

DOS uses as many as 256 different characters to display information about the screen and to send to the printer. A complete set of 256 characters is referred to as a *code page*. The optional *yyy* parameter identifies the code page DOS will use. Every country DOS supports has a standard code page and an alternative code page. If this option is not specified, DOS uses the standard code page associated with the specified country code.

[,[*drive:*][*path*[*filename.ext*]]]

The syntax for the COUNTRY command is the opposite of most device drivers because the driver filename is specified after the other switches (perhaps in deference to the French). If the COUNTRY.SYS file is not located in the root directory of the boot drive, or if the device driver is not named COUNTRY.SYS, you must specify the fully qualified filename of the device driver. If SETUP was used to install DOS, COUNTRY.SYS is located in the \DOS directory.

Remarks

If you are a U.S. user and you have no international systems-support issues, you don't have to worry about this command. It may come as a shock, but not everybody wants a PC configured for the U.S.A.

The COUNTRY.SYS device driver is used to configure a system in order to use another country's display conventions. Areas affected by COUNTRY.SYS are the date and time display, the characters in the alphabet, the symbol used to denote currency, and the sort order of files. If you do not have a COUNTRY entry in CONFIG.SYS, your system automatically is configured as a U.S.A. system.

To fully configure a system for international use, you should use the KEYB command to control the keyboard properties.

Examples

You can use the following entry in CONFIG.SYS to set the country setting to Spain:

```
country=034
```

To configure the system to Italy when the device driver is located in the \DOS directory, enter the following command (note the two commas):

```
country=039,,c:\dos\country.sys
```

Use the following command to configure the system for Denmark with the alternative code page:

```
country=045,865,c:\drivers\country.sys
```

Additional information

Refer to Chapter 9 of the *MS-DOS User's Guide* for further information about international customization.

See also KEYB, NLSFUNC, DISPLAY.SYS, PRINTER.SYS, and CHCP.

	BOB'S SCORECARD 3	PROMPT	AUTOEXEC	BATCH	CONFIG
CTTY		■	⊠	⊠	☐

Description

This command is an odd one. CTTY enables a different device to be used for keyboard and display I/O.

Usage

```
ctty device
```

Options and switches

device

This option, the alternative device source, can be any one of the following: PRN, LPT1, LPT2, LPT3, CON, AUX, COM1, COM2, COM3, and COM4.

Remarks

CTTY is not your everyday DOS command. You will use it rarely, if ever. Its most common use is to access your computer remotely. It is used with the DOS 6 command INTERSVR, for example, when the /RCOPY switch has been specified to transfer the InterLink files to another computer using a serial port.

To use CTTY with a serial port, the MODE command first must be used to set the communication characteristics (baud rate and parity, for example).

To return control to the default console, specify the device CON.

The default console can also be reassigned by using COMMAND.

Examples

Use the following two commands to prepare a client PC to be controlled by an INTERSVR on the server PC, ready for remote installation of INTERLNK:

```
mode com1:2400,n,8,1,p
ctty com1
```

Additional information

See also COMMAND, INTERSVR, INTERLNK, and MODE.

	BOB'S SCORECARD	PROMPT	AUTOEXEC	BATCH	CONFIG
DATE	5	☒	☒	☒	☐

Description

The DATE command sets the system date.

Usage

```
date [mm-dd-[yy]yy]
```

Options and switches

When DATE is executed without switches, it displays the current system date and prompts for the input of a new date. Just press Enter to return to the DOS prompt.

[*mm-dd-*[*yy*]*yy*]

This option specifies the new system date. The format and order of the days, months, and years depends on the country configuration. In the U.S., the standard format is mm-dd-yy, where the year is in the range from 80 to 99 (1980 to 1999). You can specify the year in 4-digit form to enter years in the range from 1980 to 2099. The days, months, and years separators can be periods (.), hyphens (–), or slashmarks (/).

Remarks

You must keep the system date accurate so that filenames are assigned the correct date. Calendaring software also uses the system date.

Example

The following command sets the date to my 40th birthday:

```
date 02-20-1996
```

Additional information

See also COUNTRY and TIME.

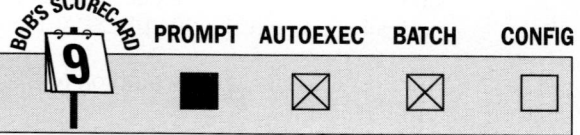

| | BOB'S SCORECARD | PROMPT | AUTOEXEC | BATCH | CONFIG |

Description

The DBLSPACE command creates and manages compressed drives on hard disks and floppies.

Usage

The following syntax lines are all acceptable uses of the DBLSPACE command:

```
dblspace

dblspace /chkdsk [/f] [drive:]

dblspace /compress drive1: [/newdrive=drive2:] [/reserve=size]

dblspace /convstac=stacvol drive1: [/newdrive=drive2:] [/cvf=sss]

dblspace /create drive1: [/newdrive=drive2:] [/size=sz or
/reserve=sz]

dblspace /defragment [drive:]

dblspace /delete drive:

dblspace /format drive:

dblspace [/info] drive:
```

```
dblspace /list

dblspace /mount[=nnn] drive1: [/newdrive=drive2:]

dblspace /ratio[=factor] [drive: or /all]

dblspace /size[=size1 or /reserve=size2] drive:

dblspace /unmount [drive:]
```

Options and switches

When you use DBLSPACE with no switches, DOS displays a full-screen menu. Alternatively, you can execute DBLSPACE with a variety of switches to automatically invoke a specific DBLSPACE command.

The /NEWDRIVE switch, common to many of the DBLSPACE commands, is described as follows:

```
[/newdrive=drive2:]
```

When an entire standard DOS drive is compressed, an extra logical drive is created. The drive letter originally assigned to the uncompressed drive is reassigned to the compressed drive. The portion of the original drive that remains uncompressed is assigned a new drive letter. The next available drive letter is used by default. The /NEWDRIVE switch can optionally be used to instruct DBLSPACE to use a specific drive letter. The switch can be abbreviated to /NEW.

The main DBLSPACE commands and their related switches follow:

```
dblspace /chkdsk [/f] [drive:]
```

In the same way that CHKDSK checks the integrity of a standard DOS drive, the /CHKDSK switch instructs DBLSPACE to check the integrity of a DoubleSpace drive. The /F switch instructs DOS to correct any errors it encounters. If a drive is not specified, DBLSPACE checks the default drive.

```
dblspace /compress drive1: [/newdrive=drive2:] [/reserve=size]
```

This command instructs DBLSPACE to create a compressed DoubleSpace drive from the existing standard DOS drive *drive1:* and compress the files on the drive. Use the /RESERVE (or /RES) switch to control how much of the original drive is left uncompressed. By default, DBLSPACE reserves 2MB on a hard drive.

```
dblspace /convstac=stacvol drive1: [/newdrive=drive2:] [/cvf=sss]
```

This command converts an already compressed Stacker drive, *drive1:*, to a DoubleSpace drive. STACVOL identifies the Stacker volume to be converted. A DoubleSpace drive is a large hidden file with the name `dblspace`.*nnn*; you can use the /CVF switch (short for *compressed volume file*) to specify a filename extension for this hidden file. The extension must be a three-digit number in the range from 000 to 254. By default, DBLSPACE assigns the lowest available (unused) number as the extension.

```
dblspace /create drive1: [/newdrive=drive2:] [/size=sz or
/reserve=sz]
```

This command creates an empty DoubleSpace drive by using the free space on standard DOS drive *drive1:*. Use /SIZE or /RESERVE to control how much space is given to the DoubleSpace drive. The /SIZE switch specifies in megabytes the amount of physical space that should be used to create the DoubleSpace drive. Conversely, /RESERVE specifies in megabytes how much physical space should not be used in creating the DoubleSpace drive (that is, how much free disk space to leave uncompressed). Decimal values are accepted (/SIZE=5.75, for example). If neither switch is specified, DOS assumes a switch of /RESERVE=2.

```
dblspace /defragment [drive:]
```

This command is DBLSPACE's equivalent of DEFRAG for DoubleSpace drives. If the drive is not specified, the default drive is used.

```
dblspace /delete drive:
```

Use this powerful switch with caution. The /DELETE switch deletes a DoubleSpace drive and all the files stored on the compressed drive. Kaboom. See the caution at the end of this command section.

```
dblspace /format drive:
```

Use this destructive command with caution. Like the standard DOS FORMAT command, /FORMAT formats a DoubleSpace drive and destroys every file stored on the drive. Unfortunately, because you cannot unformat a DoubleSpace drive, you have no chance to recover the formatted files. Ouch!

```
dblspace [/info] drive:
```

This switch displays interesting information about a DoubleSpace drive, including compression statistics and the drive label. If you execute the DBLSPACE command and specify only a DoubleSpace drive letter, DOS assumes the /INFO switch.

```
dblspace /list
```

This switch lists all the DoubleSpace drives on the system.

```
dblspace /mount[=nnn] drive1: [/newdrive=drive2:]
```

This command remounts a DoubleSpace drive that was previously disabled using the /UNMOUNT switch. You can use the *nnn* switch to specify the filename extension of the hidden DoubleSpace file. The extensions are three digits in the range from 000 to 254, and DOS tries by default to mount the hidden file DBLSPACE.000.

```
dblspace /ratio[=factor] [drive: or /all]
```

DOS reports the amount of free space available on a DoubleSpace drive by multiplying the physical free space by the compression ratio. The /RATIO switch updates the compression ratio used in this calculation. Any ratio in the range from 1.0 to 16.0 is accepted, but it normally is in the range from 1.5 to 2.5. If /RATIO is specified with no ratio factor, DOS uses the average compression ratio of all the existing files on the drive. You can use /RATIO on a single drive or on all drives.

At boot time, DOS automatically adjusts each DoubleSpace drive's compression ratio based on the compression ratio of each drive's existing files.

```
dblspace /size[=size1 or /reserve=size2] drive:
```

This command changes the size, in megabytes, of a DoubleSpace drive. Behind the scenes, DOS changes the total size of the hidden dblspace.*nnn* file. You can specify the size explicitly with the *=size1* argument, or, conversely, use the /RESERVE switch to tell DOS to leave the specified number of megabytes on the uncompressed (parent) drive.

```
dblspace /unmount [drive:]
```

This command makes a DoubleSpace drive unavailable temporarily and frees the drive letter assigned to it. It can be remounted with the /MOUNT switch.

Remarks

Don't run DBLSPACE from within a multitasking environment such as DOSSHELL or Windows.

Both the /COMPRESS and /CREATE switches create new DoubleSpace drives. Use the /COMPRESS switch to compress all the files on an existing drive, and use /CREATE to create a new empty drive using the free space on an existing drive.

A standard DOS drive must have free space if it is to be compressed. A hard disk requires a minimum of 1MB of free space, and a floppy drive requires 200K.

If DBLSPACE encounters a Windows swap file on a drive that is being compressed, the file automatically is moved to the uncompressed drive.

You can use the /UNMOUNT and /MOUNT switches to assign a DoubleSpace drive a new drive letter. See Chapter 4 for more information.

You can use the file DBLSPACE.INF to control some of the default actions of DBLSPACE.

Examples

Use the following command to start DBLSPACE in interactive mode and prompt you for selections and options:

```
dblspace
```

To create a new drive using 40MB of drive D, use the following command:

```
dblspace /create f: size=40.
```

Use the following command to create a new drive, compress all the files on drive C, and leave the minimum amount of space for the uncompressed drive:

```
dblspace /compress c: /reserve=0
```

To defragment the files stored on DoubleSpace drive F, enter the following command:

```
dblspace /def f:
```

Additional information

Refer to Chapter 4 for a thorough discussion of the DBLSPACE utilities.

See also CHKDSK, DBLSPACE.SYS, DEFRAG, and FORMAT.

The /DELETE and /FORMAT commands are destructive. Any existing files on the DoubleSpace drive are destroyed. Use these switches with caution, and make sure that you do not need the data on the drive.

If you accidentally delete a DoubleSpace drive, you can recover your files if you use UNDELETE immediately to restore the dblspace.*nnn* file.

You cannot recover DoubleSpace files that have been formatted accidentally. Be warned! 🤚

BOB'S SCORECARD **8** | PROMPT □ | AUTOEXEC □ | BATCH □ | CONFIG ■

DBLSPACE.SYS

Description

This command loads the disk-compression driver DBLSPACE.BIN to the bottom of base memory or upper memory.

Usage

You should add the DBLSPACE.SYS statement to CONFIG.SYS and load it either in base memory with a DEVICE= statement or in upper memory with a DEVICEHIGH= statement:

```
device[high]=[drive:][[path]dblspace.sys /move
```

Options and switches

[drive:][[path]

This option identifies the location of the DBLSPACE.SYS file. SETUP puts this file in the \DOS directory by default.

```
/move
```

The /MOVE switch is really a comment. Any switches specified with DBLSPACE.SYS are ignored. The developers of DOS added the /MOVE switch to provide a hint about the purpose of the device driver.

Remarks

DBLSPACE.SYS is not a device driver for DoubleSpace drives — it is a device driver to *move* the DBLSPACE.BIN device driver in memory.

During system boot-up, IO.SYS loads DBLSPACE.BIN at the top of conventional memory and just leaves it there for the duration of the processing of CONFIG.SYS, or until DBLSPACE.SYS is loaded and moves it. If the DBLSPACE.SYS statement is added to the CONFIG.SYS with the DEVICE= statement, DBLSPACE.SYS will move DBLSPACE.BIN to the bottom of conventional memory. If the DBLSPACE.SYS statement specifies DEVICEHIGH, it is DBLSPACE.BIN that will be moved to upper memory.

During system boot-up, IO.SYS loads DBLSPACE.BIN before CONFIG.SYS has even been looked at. It initially is loaded at the top of memory, adjacent to the memory area occupied by IO.SYS. It must be loaded into base memory because no memory management software has been loaded to create the UMBs that early in the booting cycle. If the CONFIG.SYS file does not contain a DBLSPACE.SYS driver, DBLSPACE.BIN is left at the top of conventional memory. This can be a problem if one of your other drivers wants the use of the top of conventional RAM, too! Consequently, DBLSPACE.SYS should be declared early on, just after your memory manager, in your CONFIG.SYS so that it can do its work and free up the potentially disputed real estate at the top of the conventional memory.

Example

Use the following command to instruct DOS to move DBLSPACE.BIN into upper memory with DBLSPACE.SYS:

```
devicehigh=c:\dos\dblspace.sys /move
```

Additional information

Refer to Chapter 4 for a thorough discussion of the DBLSPACE utilities.

See also DBLSPACE.

Description

This command starts the infamous DEBUG program for creating and analyzing program files.

Usage

```
debug [[drive:][path]filename] [parameters]
```

Options and switches

When you enter DEBUG with no switches, the terse hyphen prompt (–) is displayed. In this mode, you can execute debug commands interactively. Enter a ?, for example, to see a list of all the DEBUG commands.

[[*drive:*][*path*]*filename*]

This option identifies the name of the program to be debugged.

[*parameters*]

This option identifies any command-line parameters required by the program being debugged.

Remarks

Enter q at the hyphen prompt to quit from DEBUG.

Example

Use the following command to execute debug and load the file DEMO.EXE:

```
debug demo.exe
```

Additional information

Refer to Chapter 11 for more information about using DEBUG.

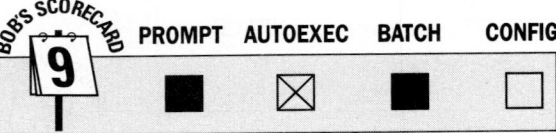

		PROMPT	AUTOEXEC	BATCH	CONFIG
DEFRAG	**9**	■	⊠	■	☐

Description

This command increases disk performance by defragmenting files.

Usage

```
defrag [drive:] [/f or /u] [/s[:]order] [/v] [/b] [/skiphigh]
[/bw] [/lcd] [/g0]
```

Options and switches

When you execute DEFRAG with no switches, a menu of choices appears. You can then press F1 to display DEFRAG's custom on-line help.

[*drive:*]

This option specifies the drive to be defragmented. If a drive is not specified, the default drive is used.

`[/f or /u]`

The /F switch (for *full* optimization) ensures that no empty spaces are between files. This switch helps to reduce future file fragmentation but increases the time taken to perform the defragmentation.

The /U switch instructs DEFRAG to defragment the files and leave any empty spaces (or "holes") that may be created.

`[/s[:]`*order*`]`

This switch instructs DEFRAG to reorganize the files and directories so that they are sorted in a specific order. The following switches are used with /S to identify the sort order:

Switch	*Sort Order*
N	Sorted by filename in ascending order (A first)
−N	Sorted by filename in descending order (Z first)
E	Sorted by extension in ascending order
−E	Sorted by extension in descending order
D	Sorted in date/time order (oldest files first)
−D	Sorted in date/time order (most recent files first)
S	Sorted by file size (smallest first)
−S	Sorted by file size (largest first)

The colon (:) in the /S command is optional but should be used for clarity.

`[/v]`

The /V switch instructs DEFRAG to verify the written data by performing a CRC check. This switch can slow the defragmentation process by as much as 30 percent.

`[/b]`

The /B switch instructs DEFRAG to reboot the computer on completion.

`[/skiphigh]`

This switch forces DEFRAG to load into conventional memory. By default, DEFRAG tries to load itself into UMBs and leave the maximum memory available for the defragmentation operation.

`[/bw]`

The /BW switch forces DEFRAG to use monochrome colors.

`[/lcd]`

Like /BW, the /LCD switch forces DEFRAG to use colors that can be viewed easily on LCD (laptop) displays.

`[/g0]`

DEFRAG uses custom characters by default to give the program a graphical look. Specify /G0 to force DEFRAG to use standard ASCII characters rather than the custom ones.

Remarks

To make sure that no lost allocation units exist, before running DEFRAG, run the following command:

`chkdsk /f`

Run DEFRAG at least once a week to optimize your hard disk performance and to enhance your chances for data recovery.

You should not run DEFRAG inside Windows, DOSSHELL, or any other multitasking environment. DEFRAG can defragment only local drives, not network drives.

Because DEFRAG is licensed from Symantec, some discrepancies exist between the statistics reported by DEFRAG and the "same" statistics reported by CHKDSK. These discrepancies are not serious and reflect different reporting methodologies. DEFRAG includes the root directory in the count of total directories, for example, and CHKDSK does not.

If DEFRAG fails, an error code is set that can be checked by an `if errorlevel` statement in a batch file. The following ERRORLEVELs can be generated:

ERRORLEVEL	Message
0	All is well, DEFRAG completed with no errors.
1	An unexpected internal error occurred.
2	DEFRAG could not run because no free clusters existed. Create some space by deleting unnecessary files, or move some files temporarily to another disk.
3	Ctrl-Break was pressed to abort the operation.
4	A general error occurred (whatever that means).

5	Error reading a cluster.
6	Error writing a cluster.
7	An allocation error occurred.
8	Memory error.
9	Insufficient memory.

Examples

Use the following command to execute DEFRAG in interactive mode:

```
defrag
```

Use the following command to perform a full optimization on drive C, sorting files with the newest files first and forcing a reboot on completion.

```
defrag c: /f /s:-d /b
```

Additional information

Refer to Chapter 4 for a thorough discussion of disk defragmentation.

See also CHKDSK and DBLSPACE /DEF.

BOB'S SCORECARD	PROMPT	AUTOEXEC	BATCH	CONFIG
DEL (ERASE) 6	■	☒	☒	☐

Description

This command deletes one or more files.

Usage

You can execute the command as either DEL or ERASE:

```
del [drive:][path]wildcard.ext [/p]
```

```
erase [drive:][path]wildcard.ext [/p]
```

Options and switches

[*drive:*][*path*]*wildcard.ext*

This option specifies the name of the file or files to be deleted. If a filename is not specified and a drive or path is specified, DOS assumes the wildcard *.*.

```
[/p]
```

This switch instructs DOS to prompt you individually before deleting each file. Even if the /P switch is omitted, DOS prompts for confirmation before deleting all the files in a directory.

Remarks

The information stored in the file is not erased. Behind the scenes, the filename is marked with a special character — ASCII character 229, to be precise, called *sigma*. The clusters the file occupies are marked as available; when a new file is created, these clusters can be used to store the data for the new file. That the file's data is not erased immediately makes file undeletion possible, even when no backup has been made.

A shortcut for deleting every file in the current directory is to use a single period (.) rather than *.*.

If you try to delete a file that has the read-only attribute set, DOS displays a message that access is denied. You can always use the ATTRIB command to remove the read-only flag, but be careful. The file may be marked as read-only for the express purpose of preventing you from deleting it.

Examples

You can use any of the three following commands to delete every file in the TRASH directory:

```
del \trash

del \trash\.

del \trash\*.*
```

Use the following command to delete all BAK files in the current directory:

```
del *.bak
```

To instruct DOS to prompt you before deleting every WK1 file in the 123 directory, enter the following command:

```
del c:\123\*.wk1 /p
```

Additional information

Refer to Chapter 3 for more information about precautions and measures you can take to avoid accidental data loss.

See also MSBACKUP, UNDELETE, and DELTREE.

Bob's Shareware Collection disks

CMFiler, from NoVaSoft, is a full-screen file manager that provides, in addition to many other things, easy ways to tag and delete files.

To delete a classified or sensitive file and ensure that no one (and no program) can undelete it, delete it with RELDEL, from TARDIS DP Consultants. RELDEL overwrites the file's data, shrinks the file to zero bytes, and then deletes it.

BOB'S SCORECARD 5 PROMPT ■ AUTOEXEC ☐ BATCH ☐ CONFIG ☐

DELOLDOS

Description

When you install DOS 6, a copy of your old version of DOS is saved in a special subdirectory. Use DELOLDOS to delete the copy of the old DOS version and free up disk space.

Usage

```
deloldos [/b]
```

Options and switches

```
[/b]
```

This switch instructs DELOLDOS to use monochrome colors. Alternatively, you can press F5 to switch to monochrome while DELOLDOS is running.

Remarks

When you install DOS 6, SETUP makes a backup copy of your old DOS files in a directory named OLD_DOS.1. What's more, if you install DOS 6 more than once, directories OLD_DOS.2 and so on are created. This facility is most valuable to beta testers who install DOS 6 a number of times — as a general user, you normally load DOS 6 only one time.

The OLD_DOS.*n* directory contains all the files from the old DOS directory, along with copies of the system files from the boot directory and copies of AUTOEXEC.BAT and CONFIG.SYS (renamed with a DAT extension).

The uninstall disk (created by SETUP) includes the program UNINSTALL, which deletes the DOS 6 files and restores the old copy of DOS by transferring files from the OLD_DOS.*n* directory to their original locations.

You don't need to keep the OLD_DOS.*n* directory for more than a few weeks while you become confident that DOS 6 is stable on your system. After a few weeks of trouble-free DOS 6 use, run DELOLDOS to remove the old DOS files.

Example

To delete the copy of your old DOS version, just enter the following command:

```
deloldos
```

Additional information

See also UNINSTALL.

If you run DELOLDOS, you cannot run UNINSTALL to restore your old version of DOS. Don't run DELOLDOS until a few weeks after installing DOS 6, when you are confident that you will not need to UNINSTALL it.

If you compress your boot drive with DBLSPACE, you cannot run the UNINSTALL program, and the old version of DOS becomes useless. If you DBLSPACE your drive, you might as well run DELOLDOS to create even more disk space.

Description

This powerful and potentially destructive command removes a directory, all of its subdirectories, and all the files in the directories — just like that.

Usage

```
deltree [/y] [drive:]path
```

Options and switches

[*drive:*]*path*

This option is the name of the directory to be deleted. This directory and all of its subdirectories are removed. You can specify wildcards in the directory name, but you must be careful — if a wildcard matches a filename, the file also is deleted.

```
[/y]
```

This switch suppresses the warning prompt (deletes the files and directories with prompting for confirmation).

Remarks

DELTREE returns a non-0 ERRORLEVEL if the command was aborted or 0 ERRORLEVEL if the specified tree was deleted.

Examples

Use the following command to remove the \TRASH directory and all its files and subdirectories:

```
deltree \trash
```

To delete the \123W\SAMPLE directory and bypass the confirmation prompt, enter the following command:

```
deltree /y \123w\sample
```

To delete all directories beginning with *TR* and their subdirectories, enter the following command:

```
deltree \tr*.
```

Additional information

See Chapter 1 for more information on DELTREE.

See also DEL and RD.

Bob's Shareware Collection disks

The Bob's Shareware Collection disks are packed with tools to aid file deletion chores. CMFiler, the file manager from NoVaSoft, provides visual tools for deleting entire directory trees — I prefer it because I can easily see what is being deleted. PDELETE, from Patri-Soft, and PocketD, from Pocketware, both provide extensive and flexible file deletion options using command-line switches.

Although this command is useful, it is also very powerful. DELTREE will delete all files contained in a directory and its subdirectories regardless of attributes. With one brief command, you can erase all the files on your hard disk. Never use this command while you are distracted — think before you use DELTREE!

DEVICE

Description

This CONFIG.SYS statement loads a device driver into conventional or base memory.

Usage

device=[*drive:*][*path*]*filename.ext* [*device-parameters*]

Options and switches

You can use the device statement only in the CONFIG.SYS file.

[*drive:*][*path*]*filename.ext*

This option is the name of the device driver file. If the file is not located in the root directory of the boot disk, you should specify the full path.

[*device-parameters*]

This option specifies the additional parameters and switches that some device drivers must have when they are loaded.

Remarks

Device driver software is used to provide software links to a hardware device such as a scanner, mouse, or fax card. The device drivers are supplied with hardware and must be installed in CONFIG.SYS before the hardware can be used. DOS 6 includes a variety of device drivers for managing memory, the display, and connected computers.

CONFIG.SYS often includes multiple device statements, and the order can be important. HIMEM.SYS, for example, must be installed before EMM386.EXE. Vendors indicate whenever their device drivers must be loaded in a special order.

Most, but not all, device drivers have a SYS extension. Some programs have dual purposes and can be loaded as devices and executed from the command line. DOS 6's SMARTDRV.EXE is an example.

Example

The following example shows a plain CONFIG.SYS that includes three DEVICE statements:

```
FILES=20
BUFFERS=15
DEVICE=C:\FCONSOLE.DEV
DEVICE=C:\WINDOWS\MOUSE.SYS /Y
DEVICE=C:\DOS\SMARTDRV.EXE
LASTDRIVE=P
```

Additional information

Device drivers installed with DEVICE are normally loaded into base (or conventional) memory. You can use the DEVICEHIGH command to load devices into UMBs.

See Chapter 5 for more information on DEVICE.

See also DEVICEHIGH, INSTALL, and MEMMAKER.

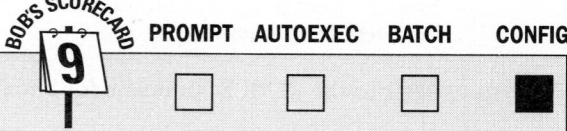

	BOB'S SCORECARD **9**	PROMPT	AUTOEXEC	BATCH	CONFIG
DEVICEHIGH		☐	☐	☐	■

Description

Gotta have it. DEVICEHIGH, the sister to DEVICE, is used to load device drivers into upper memory.

Usage

```
devicehigh=[drive:][path]filename.ext [device-parameters]
```

Options and switches

The DEVICE statement can be used only in CONFIG.SYS.

[*drive:*] [*path*]*filename.ext*

This option specifies the name of the device driver file. If the file is not located in the root directory of the boot disk, you should specify the full path.

[*device parameters*]

This option specifies the additional parameters and switches required by the device driver.

Note: See the "Extended use" section for additional switches.

Remarks

Before device drivers can be installed with DEVICEHIGH, the upper memory area must be configured using the HIMEM.SYS, EMM386.EXE, and DOS=UMB statements.

The order of the DEVICEHIGH statements in CONFIG.SYS has a real impact on the amount of free memory. Tuning the DEVICEHIGH statements to optimize memory use can be a lengthy and time-consuming process. The MEMMAKER command, however, can completely automate this difficult task.

If insufficient memory exists to load a device into upper memory, DEVICEHIGH uses base memory, just as DEVICE does.

You can load programs and device drivers into upper memory by using the LOADHIGH command.

Refer to the DEVICE command for additional remarks regarding device drivers.

Example

The following example shows a simple CONFIG.SYS file that uses DEVICEHIGH to load the MOUSE.SYS device driver into upper memory:

```
DEVICE=C:\DOS\HIMEM.SYS
DEVICE=C:\DOS\EMM386.EXE RAM I=B000-B7FF NOEMS
BUFFERS=15,0
FILES=50
DOS=HIGH,UMB
DEVICEHIGH=C:\WINDOWS\MOUSE.SYS /Y
```

Additional information

Refer to Chapter 5 for a thorough discussion of memory management techniques.

See also DEVICE, EMM386.SYS, HIMEM.SYS, LOADHIGH, and MEMMAKER.

Bob's Shareware Collection disks

DOS 6 supports DEVICEHIGH on only 386 and later systems. UMB_DRV.SYS, Christopher Blum's excellent memory manager, provides advanced memory capabilities to 286 users as well as users of 386 and later systems.

Extended use

Although DEVICEHIGH loads the device driver into the largest free area of upper memory by default, this step is not always efficient. To provide more control over memory use, DEVICEHIGH also supports the /L and /S switches. You normally should leave the responsibility of determining the best settings for these switches to MEMMAKER.

The following example shows the syntax for these two advanced switches:

    [[/l:*region*][,*minsize*][;*region2*][,*minsize2*]]

The /L switch is used to control the region of UMBs in which the device is loaded. (The MEM /F command displays the free regions of upper memory. Device drivers can be too large to fit in one region.) The /L switch enables you to specify a second region. You can use the MINSIZE parameter to ensure that adequate memory is allocated for the device — some device drivers require more memory during operation than they do when they are being initialized.

Thanks to MEMMAKER, the following example configuration uses the /L switch:

```
DEVICEHIGH /L:2,12048 =C:\DOS\SETVER.EXE
DEVICEHIGH /L:2,55168 =C:\WINDOWS\MOUSE.SYS /Y
DEVICE=C:\U\FAX\SATISFAX.SYS IOADDR=0350
DEVICEHIGH /L:2,11712 =C:\PROAUDIO\MVSOUND.SYS D:5 Q:7 J:0
DEVICEHIGH /L:2,33696 =C:\PROAUDIO\TSLCDR.SYS /D:MVCD001 /R /P:3
```

    [/s]

The /S switch (for *shrink*) instructs DEVICEHIGH to reduce the allocated memory after the device driver has been initialized. This switch is used with device drivers that need more memory to load than they do during subsequent operation.

	BOB'S SCORECARD 7	PROMPT	AUTOEXEC	BATCH	CONFIG
DIR		■	⊠	⊠	☐

Description

This command displays information about one or more files, including name, size, and the date and time of last creation.

Usage

```
dir [drive:][path][wildcard.ext] [/p] [/w] [/a[:]attr] [/o[:]order]
[/s] [/b] [/l] [/c]
```

Options and switches

When you use DIR with no switches, the switches specified in the environment variable DIRCMD are used. If DIRCMD is not set, all files, excluding hidden files, are displayed in a single column.

    [*drive:*][*path*][*wildcard.ext*]

This option specifies the file or files whose details are listed. If no filemask is specified, a wildcard of *.* is assumed.

    [/p]

This switch instructs DOS to *p*ause for a keypress after filling the display with file details.

    [/w]

This switch instructs DOS to display the filenames in *w*ide format with five filenames to a row. No file details are displayed when this switch is used.

    [/a[:]*attr*]

This switch displays only files that match the specified attributes. The following codes are used with the /A switch to identify the attributes:

Code	Attribute
H	List hidden files
−H	List files that aren't hidden
S	List system files
−S	List nonsystem files
D	List directories but not files
−D	List files but not directories
A	List files with the archive attribute set
−A	List files that don't have the archive attribute set
R	List read-only files
−R	List files that are not read-only

You can specify multiple codes, but do not separate them with spaces (/A:HS−R, for example). If you specify the /A switch with no codes, all files are listed. If you omit the entire switch, DIR lists all files in the current directory except hidden and system files.

The colon is optional but should be used for clarity.

    [/o[:]*order*]

This switch identifies the order in which files are displayed (sorted, for example). The following codes are used with the /O switch to control the sort order:

Code	*Sort Order*
N	Sorted by filename in ascending order (A first)
−N	Sorted by filename in descending order (Z first)
E	Sorted by extension in ascending order
−E	Sorted by extension in descending order
D	Sorted in date/time order (oldest files first)
−D	Sorted in date/time order (most recent files first)
S	Sorted by file size (smallest first)
−S	Sorted by file size (largest first)
G	Grouped with directories displayed before files
−G	Grouped with files displayed before directories
C	Sorted by DBLSPACE compression ratio (least compressed first)
−C	Sorted by DBLSPACE compression ratio (most compressed first)

You can specify multiple codes, but do not separate them with spaces. If you specify the /O switch with no codes, the switch /O:GN is applied (sorted in ascending filename order with directories grouped first). If you omit the entire switch, DIR lists the files in the unsorted (or FAT table) order.

The colon (:) in the /O command is optional but should be used for clarity.

    [/s]

The /S DOS switch is my favorite switch of all time. It instructs DOS to list the files in the specified directory *and* all subdirectories. It provides a convenient (if not lightning-fast) way to search for a file or files across multiple directories.

    [/b]

This switch displays the filenames in a brief format, with only the filenames and no file details, and suppresses the standard heading and summary information. If you specify both /B and /W, /B is used, and /W is ignored.

```
[/l]
```

By default, all filenames and details are displayed in uppercase. The /L instructs DIR to display all alphabetical characters in lowercase.

```
[/c]
```

This switch displays DBLSPACE file-compression ratios for every file. This switch is ignored when /B or /W also is specified.

Remarks

If you regularly use one or more switches with the DIR command, you can save yourself some keystrokes by using the DIRCMD environment variable. DIR applies any switches associated with the DIRCMD environment variable every time it is executed. To always sort the file list in alphabetical order with directories first and the pause switch in effect, for example, enter the following command:

```
set dircmd=/o:gne/p
```

DIR applies those switches thereafter and any others you specify on the command line. You might consider adding the SET statement to AUTOEXEC.BAT, to apply the defaults automatically. To disable an environment switch temporarily, enter the switch preceded by a minus sign. Having executed the preceding command to set DIRCMD, you can execute DIR without the pause switch by entering the following command:

```
dir /-p
```

To clear the DIRCMD settings, enter the following command:

```
set dircmd=
```

You can simplify the DIR command by using DOSKEY macros. Refer to Chapter 9 for more information.

Examples

Use the following command to display all the files with a DOC extension in the WORD directory and pause the output after every full screen:

```
dir \word\*.doc /p
```

Use the following command to display all hidden files on drive C:

```
dir c:\ /a:h /s
```

To display on drive D all the directories sorted in alphabetical order, use the following command:

```
dir d:\ /a:d /o:n /b /s
```

The following command displays all the files in the current directory sorted by name and then by extension, using lowercase characters:

```
dir /o:ne /l
```

Additional information

See also ATTRIB, DBLSPACE, DOSKEY, SET, and TREE.

Bob's Shareware Collection disks

Robert Woeger's elegant utility HotDIR Plus provides additional capabilities for listing files. The most obvious is the use of colors to differentiate between different file types and directories. (You can even configure these colors.) HOTDIR PLUS also has a six-column display option.

PocketD provides excellent file listing capabilities, including full color support, powerful sorting and selection options, flexible filemask support, and a special Tiny Mode which can show hundreds of files in a single screen.

If you are using DIR to search for files, try Bruce Gavin's superb QFIND program. It is blazingly fast and has a wealth of features, including searching inside zip files, searching multiple drives, optional directory change when a match is found, and much more.

If you cannot remember where a file is located and you don't have a file-finder utility, just use the DIR command with the /S switch. To find the file SECRET.DOC on drive C, for example, enter the following command:

```
dir c:\secret.doc /s
```

This secret shouldn't be a secret, but few people realize that the /A switch (with no codes) displays all files including hidden and system files. Use the following command to display all files in the root directory of drive C:

```
dir c:\ /a
```

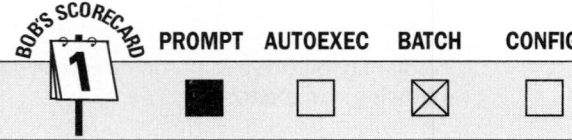

Description

This command compares two floppy disks to see whether they contain identical data.

Usage

```
diskcomp drive1: drive2: [/1] [/8]
```

Options and switches

drive1: drive2:

This option specifies the drive letters that identify the drives containing the disks to be compared. If you have only one drive to compare two disks, use the same letter twice (a: a:, for example), but get ready for some serious floppy swapping.

`[/1]`

This switch instructs DISKCOPY to compare only the first side. Nowadays, all floppies use both the upper and lower surfaces of the disk; in the early days of the PC, however, single-sided floppies were common.

`[/8]`

This switch, inherited from the days of DOS 2.0, is used to compare only the first eight tracks.

Remarks

DISKCOMP compares the disks on a track-by-track basis. Even if the two disks contain the identical files, DISKCOMP reports a discrepancy if the files are stored physically in a different order.

DISKCOMP does not compare two hard drives, nor does it compare floppy disks of different media types.

When you use DISKCOMP in a batch file, the following ERRORLEVELs may be returned:

ERRORLEVEL	Message
0	The disks are identical.
1	The disks are not identical.
2	The user aborted the comparison (Ctrl-Break was pressed).
3	DISKCOMP could not read one of the disks.
4	An unexpected internal error occurred.

I rarely use this cantankerous old command, but it's there if you need it.

Examples

Use the following command to compare the disks in drives A and B:

```
diskcomp a: b:
```

To compare two disks when you only have one floppy disk drive, enter the following command:

```
diskcomp a: a:
```

Additional information

Use the FC command to compare two files.

See also DISKCOPY.

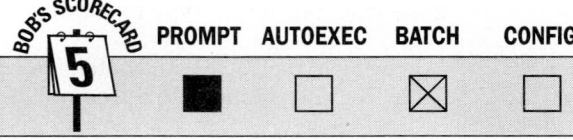

Description

This command duplicates all the data from one floppy disk to another.

Usage

```
diskcopy [sourcedrive:] [targetdrive:] [/1] [/v]
```

Options and switches

[*sourcedrive:*] [*targetdrive:*]

This option specifies the source and target drives. You can specify the same drive for both drives, and DOS prompts you (many times) to switch disks during the copy operation. If you omit the target drive, the current drive is assumed. If you omit both drives, the current drive is used for the source and the target.

```
[/1]
```

This old switch instructs DISKCOPY to copy only the first side; because all disks are now double sided, however, you probably will never use this switch.

```
[/v]
```

This switch instructs DISKCOPY to perform a CRC check to *verify* that the data written to the target can be read successfully. It does not guarantee that the source and target disks are identical — use DISKCOMP for true verification.

Remarks

You can use DISKCOPY to duplicate only floppy disks, not hard disks.

When you use DISKCOPY, any data on the target disk is overwritten.

If the target disk is not formatted, DISKCOPY automatically formats it during the copy procedure.

Because DISKCOPY copies the data on a track-by-track basis, the disk media must be identical. You cannot use DISKCOPY to duplicate, for example, a 1.2MB 5¼-inch disk to a 1.44MB 3½-inch disk. Use XCOPY to copy data on a file-by-file basis from one media type to another.

You can use DISKCOPY in a batch file, and it returns the following ERRORLEVELs to indicate the completion status:

ERRORLEVEL	Message
0	The copy operation was successful.
1	An error occurred in reading or writing data.
2	The user aborted the copy (Ctrl-Break was pressed).
3	A critical (hardware) error occurred.
4	An unexpected internal error occurred.

Examples

Enter the following command to duplicate the disk in drive A to a target disk in drive B:

```
diskcopy a: b:
```

Use the following command to duplicate a disk by using the single drive A:

```
diskcopy a: a:
```

Additional information
See also DISKCOMP and XCOPY.

Bob's Shareware Collection disks
DUPE, from Best Technology, provides a fast and convenient way to duplicate disks, without all the floppy swapping.

BOB'S SCORECARD **3**	PROMPT	AUTOEXEC	BATCH	CONFIG
DISPLAY.SYS	☐	☐	☐	■

Description
This command provides international character support by allowing code-page switching.

Usage
The DISPLAY.SYS device driver must be loaded in CONFIG.SYS with either a DEVICE= or DEVICEHIGH= statement as follows:

```
device[high]=[drive:][path]display.sys con[:]=(type[,[hwcp][,n]])
```

Options and switches
[*drive:*][*path*]

This option identifies the directory in which DISPLAY.SYS is located, if it is not in the boot directory. SETUP places DISPLAY.SYS in the \DOS directory by default.

type

This option identifies the type of installed display adapter. Specify EGA for EGA and VGA systems, or LCD for LCD displays. The types CGA and MONO are allowed also, but because these devices don't support code-page switching, DISPLAY.SYS serves no purpose on such systems.

[*hwcp*]

This option identifies that *hardware code page*, and can have one of the following values:

Code	Value
437	United States
850	Multilingual (known as Latin page I)
852	Slavic (known as Latin page II)
860	Portuguese
863	Canadian-French
865	Nordic

[*n*]

This option informs DISPLAY.SYS of the number of additional code pages supported by the device. The value is hardware dependent; as a rule of thumb, however, use 6 for EGA/VGA, 1 for LCD, and 0 for CGA and MONO.

Remarks

You should use this device driver only if you are configuring your system for international use.

Example

Use the following statement in CONFIG.SYS to configure a VGA system for Portugal with one additional code page:

```
device=c:\dos\display.sys con=(ega,860,1)
```

Additional information

Refer to Chapter 9 of the *MS-DOS User's Guide* for further information about configuring DOS for international use.

See also CHCP, DEVICE, DEVICEHIGH, KEYB, MODE, NLSFUNC, and PRINTER.SYS.

Extended use

DISPLAY.SYS optionally supports code-page subfonts with the following syntax:

```
device[high]=[drive:][path]display.sys con[:]=(type[,[hwcp][,(n,m)]])
```

where *m* specifies the number of subfonts the display hardware provides. Subfonts are normally used for storing different-size characters (the characters used in 43-line mode, for example). The default values are 2 for EGA, 1 for LCD, and 0 for CGA and MONO.

PROMPT   AUTOEXEC   BATCH   CONFIG

Description
Controls whether DOS is loaded in high memory (on 286 systems and higher) and whether DOS should manage the upper memory area (on 386 systems and higher).

Usage
The DOS statement is used in CONFIG.SYS. Two DOS= entries are supported using the following syntax:

```
dos=high or low
dos=umb or noumb
```

Alternatively, you can use one of the following formats to combine the HIGH and UMB identifiers in a single DOS= statement:

```
dos=[high or low][,umb or noumb]
```

Options and switches
```
[high or low]
```

Use the HIGH switch to instruct DOS to load some of its code in high memory (HMA) or LOW to load the entire operating system in base memory. Normally, you do not specify LOW because it is the default.

```
[umb or noumb]
```

Use the UMB switch to instruct DOS to manage the upper memory area or NOUMB to instruct DOS to ignore UMBs. Again, you do not normally specify NOUMB because it is the default.

Remarks
You must load the extended memory manager HIMEM.SYS, or a third-party equivalent, before the DOS=HIGH instruction can be installed. DOS cannot be loaded HIGH on 8086 systems.

Similarly, you must load EMM386.EXE, or a third-party equivalent, and configure it to provide UMBs before the DOS=UMB statement can be processed. UMBs are supported on only 386 or later systems.

Examples

The following CONFIG.SYS file loads DOS into high memory and instructs DOS to manage UMBs:

```
DEVICE=C:\DOS\HIMEM.SYS
DEVICE=C:\DOS\EMM386.EXE RAM
DOS=HIGH,UMB
DEVICEHIGH=C:\WINDOWS\MOUSE.SYS /Y
```

On a 286 system, the CONFIG.SYS has to be adjusted to remove the UMB support as follows:

```
DEVICE=C:\DOS\HIMEM.SYS
DOS=HIGH
DEVICE=C:\WINDOWS\MOUSE.SYS /Y
```

Additional information

Refer to Chapter 5 for a thorough discussion of memory management.

See also DEVICEHIGH, EMM386.EXE, HIMEM.SYS, LOADHIGH, MEM, MEMMAKER, and MSD.

Bob's Shareware Collection disks

UMB_DRV.SYS, from Christopher Blum, provides advanced memory management capabilities for all PC types including 8086 and 80286 systems.

On 386 systems and higher, MEMMAKER.EXE can update CONFIG.SYS automatically and, if necessary, add HIMEM.SYS, EMM386.EXE, and DOS=UMB statements. It doesn't, however, add a DOS=HIGH statement because SETUP adds it when DOS 6 is installed.

DOSHELP

See FASTHELP.

DOSKEY

Description

DOSKEY provides three primary and very useful functions: the ability to recall previous commands to save retyping, command-line editing (no more backspace), and a simple but effective macro utility.

Usage

```
doskey [/insert or /overstrike] [/reinstall] [/bufsize=size]
[/macros] [/history] [macroname=[text]]
```

Options and switches

By running DOSKEY with no switches, you gain command recall and command editing.

```
[/insert or /overstrike]
```

Just like a standard editor, DOSKEY supports insert and overstrike modes for editing the command line. This switch is used to control whether DOSKEY starts in overstrike or insert mode. If you do not specify this switch, DOSKEY starts in overstrike mode. While you are editing, you can switch or toggle the mode by pressing Ins.

```
[/reinstall]
```

The first time you execute DOSKEY in a session, the program is loaded in memory as a TSR and records every DOS command as it is executed. To clear the history of old commands, you can reexecute DOSKEY with the /REINSTALL switch. You must use the switch also if you want to reinstall DOSKEY with a larger buffer.

```
[/bufsize=size]
```

DOSKEY uses a buffer to store the history of executed commands and DOSKEY macros. By default, 512 bytes of memory are reserved for this buffer. You can use the /BUFSIZE switch to allocate a different buffer size, but 256 is the minimum.

```
[/macros]
```

This switch displays a list of all active DOSKEY macros. The /M switch has the same meaning.

```
[/history]
```

This switch displays a list of all the previous DOS commands stored in DOSKEY's buffer. The /H switch has the same meaning.

```
[macroname=[text]]
```

This option defines a macro and assigns it a specific name. Thereafter, whenever the user enters the *macroname* on the command line, DOSKEY executes the *text* associated with the macro. It provides a great way to customize DOS and simplify complex commands. You can delete a macro by specifying MACRONAME= with no *text*.

Remarks

Having installed DOSKEY, you can recall previous commands by pressing the up- and down-arrow keys. PgUp recalls the oldest command, and PgDn the most recent.

The following table shows the keys you can use to edit the command line.

Key	Action
Left arrow	Move left one character
Right arrow	Move right one character
Ctrl-left arrow	Move left one word
Ctrl-right arrow	Move right one word
Home	Move to the beginning of the command line
End	Move to the end of the command line
Esc	Erase the command

If you don't use a third-party alternative, I recommend that you use DOSKEY all the time by adding it to your AUTOEXEC.BAT file. DOSKEY is a TSR and on 386 systems and higher, you can save base memory by installing DOSKEY with LOADHIGH.

Examples

Use the following line from AUTOEXEC.BAT to load DOSKEY into high memory and set it to Insert Mode:

```
loadhigh c:\dos\doskey /insert
```

To create a macro, BAKFIG, for making a backup of CONFIG.SYS, enter the following command:

```
doskey bakfig=copy c:\config.sys c:\config.bak
```

To reload DOSKEY with a buffer size of 800 bytes and clear the command history, enter the following command:

```
doskey /reinstall /bufsize=800
```

Additional information

Refer to Chapter 9 for a thorough explanation of DOSKEY.

See also LOADHIGH.

Bob's Shareware Collection disks

Moderne Software's excellent command-line utility, Anarkey, offers all the features of DOSKEY, and then some. For example, you can load and save command histories to disk.

A little-known feature of DOSKEY is that it enables you to execute multiple commands at one time, much like OS/2 does. Having typed the first command, press Ctrl-T and then type the next command, press Ctrl-T again and enter the third command, and so on. DOS displays the paragraph character (¶) to show you where Ctrl-T was pressed. When you press Enter, every command is executed in turn.

To make the directory DEMO and then change to the directory, for example, you enter the following command:

```
c:\>md demo ¶ cd demo
```

Description

This command starts the DOS Shell program. DOS Shell provides menuing, file-management, and task-switching tools.

Usage

```
dosshell [/t[:res]] [/b]
```

or

```
dosshell [/g[:res]] [/b]
```

Options and switches

The DOSSHELL switches are used only to control the display characteristics. If you run DOSSHELL with no switches, the settings from the last DOSSHELL session are used.

```
[/t]
```

This switch starts the DOSSHELL in Text Mode.

```
[/g]
```

The /G switch starts the DOSSHELL in Graphics Mode.

```
[:res]
```

This option indicates which resolution to use and, optionally, the number of lines. The resolution is coded with one of three letters: *l* for low resolution, *m* for medium resolution, and *h* for high resolution. The supported resolutions are hardware dependent; the following table shows the possible permutations:

Switches		*Number of Display Lines*		
Mode	*Resolution*	*Mono/CGA*	*EGA*	*VGA*
/T:	l	25	25	25
/T:	m,m1,h,h1	N/A	43	43
/T:	m2,h2	N/A	43	50
/G:	l	25	25	25
/G:	m,m1	N/A	43	30
/G:	m2	N/A	43	34
/G:	h,h1	N/A	43	43
/G:	h2	N/A	43	60

```
[/b]
```

This switch instructs DOSSHELL to use monochrome colors.

Remarks

If you cannot be bothered by all these switches, just run DOSSHELL with no switches and choose the display settings you want from the Options Display menu.

The DOSSHELL.INI file contains the detailed initialization settings for DOSSHELL.

If you use Windows, DOSSHELL has limited value; File Manager and Program Manager are clearly superior. Don't load Windows from within the DOSSHELL — quit to DOS first.

Examples

Use the following command to start the DOSSHELL in black-and-white mode:

```
dosshell /b
```

Use the following command to start the DOSSHELL in 34-line graphics mode on a VGA system:

```
dosshell /g:m2
```

Additional information

Chapter 2 has further information about using and customizing the DOS Shell.

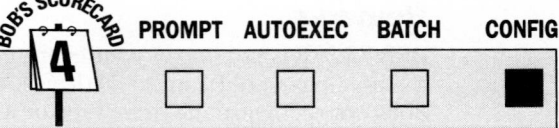

DRIVER.SYS

	PROMPT	AUTOEXEC	BATCH	CONFIG
4	☐	☐	☐	■

Description

This device driver creates logical floppy drives with different characteristics from the physical drive. You can use it also to extend the BIOS on old systems to enable newer drive types to be installed.

Usage

```
device[high]=[drive:][path]driver.sys /d:number [/c] [/f:factor]
```

Options and switches

[*drive:*][*path*]

This option identifies the directory in which DRIVER.SYS is located, if it is not in the boot directory. SETUP places DRIVER.SYS in the \DOS directory by default.

/d:*number*

This switch identifies the drive number of the physical *floppy* drive. Drive A has a value of 0, if present, drive B has a value of 1, and so on.

`[/c]`

Most modern drives have change-line support. That is, they can sense quickly when the drive door is open. If your physical drive supports change-line support (most do), specify /C to speed up floppy disk access.

`[/f:factor]`

This switch identifies the disk drive type. One of the following values is accepted for the *factor*:

Value	Drive Type
0	360K or less 5¼-inch drive
1	1.2MB 5¼-inch drive
2	720K 3½-inch drive
3	1.44MB 3½-inch drive
4	2.88MB 3½-inch drive

If you do not specify this switch, DOS assumes /F:2.

Remarks

DRIVER.SYS is not one of your everyday commands. Its use has diminished with the dominance of 1.2 and 1.44 drives. You should use it only if your system BIOS does not recognize the drive type or if you are adding an external drive (installing a 1.44 drive on an original IBM PC-AT, for example).

You might consider using DRIVER.SYS to create a logical drive that has different characteristics from the physical drive. If you have a 1.2MB drive, for example, you might configure an additional *logical* drive D to be a 360K floppy drive. When you access drive D, you are using drive A, but DOS treats it as though it were a 360K drive. This technique saves you from having to remember FORMAT switches and the like.

The drive letter assigned to the logical drive depends on the number of drives already assigned. At the time the DRIVER.SYS statement is processed, the next available drive letter is used.

Examples

Use the following CONFIG.SYS entry to support an external 1.44MB floppy drive:

```
device=c:\dos\driver.sys /d:2 /f:7
```

Use the following command to create a logical drive D (assuming that you have only one hard drive), which uses drive A as though it were a 360K drive:

```
device=c:\dos\driver.sys /d:0 /f:0
```

Additional information

See also DEVICE, DEVICEHIGH, DRIVPARM, and FORMAT.

Extended use

If the physical drive does not match any of the /F:FACTOR characteristics, you can use the following three switches to define the custom drive type:

[/h:*heads*]

This switch specifies the number of read-write drive heads. The default is 2, but values in the range from 1 to 99 are accepted.

[/s:*sectors*]

This switch specifies the number of sectors per track. Values in the range from 1 to 99 are accepted.

[/t:*tracks*]

This switch specifies the number of tracks per drive. Values in the range from 1 to 999 are accepted.

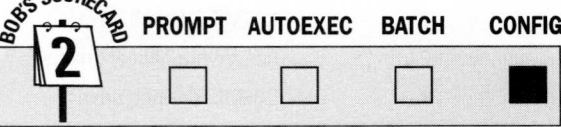

	PROMPT	AUTOEXEC	BATCH	CONFIG
DRIVPARM	☐	☐	☐	■

Description

This command is used to define or redefine the properties of disk and tape drives (block devices).

Usage

You should place the DRIVPARM command in CONFIG.SYS.

```
drivparm=/d:number [/c] [/f:factor] [/h:heads] [/i] [/n]
[/s:sectors] [/t:tracks]
```

Options and switches

/d : *number*

This switch identifies the physical device number of the drive. Drive A is 0, drive B is 1, drive C is 2, and so on. The value must be in the range from 0 to 255.

[/c]

Use this switch when the device can detect that the drive door is open (like DRIVER.SYS).

[/f : *factor*]

This switch identifies the drive type, where *factor* can have one of the following values:

Value	Drive Type
0	360K or less 5¼-inch drive
1	1.2MB 5¼-inch drive
2	720K 3½-inch drive
3	(No longer supported)
4	(No longer supported)
5	Hard disk
6	Tape drive
7	1.44MB 3½-inch drive
8	Read/write optical drive
9	2.88MB 3½-inch drive

If you do not specify this switch, DRIVPARM uses /S:2.

[/h : *heads*]

This switch identifies the number of read/write heads on the drive. The default depends on the drive type, but values in the range from 1 to 99 are accepted.

[/i]

This switch indicates that the drive is a 3½-inch floppy disk. You should use it when the ROM BIOS doesn't support 3½-inch drives.

[/n]

The /N switch indicates that the drive contains nonremovable media (a hard disk, for example).

[/s:*sectors*]

This switch identifies the number of sectors per track that the drive supports. The default depends on the drive type, but values in the range from 1 to 99 are accepted.

[/t:*tracks*]

This switch identifies the number of tracks per side that the drive supports. The default depends on the drive type, but values in the range from 1 to 99 are accepted.

Remarks

DRIVPARM is a highly specialized command you normally use only when instructed to do so by a hardware vendor.

Unlike DRIVER.SYS, DRIVPARM can modify only the properties of an existing drive and cannot be used to create additional logical drives.

If the affected drive is installed through a device driver, the DRIVPARM statement should be located in CONFIG.SYS on the line immediately after the drive's primary device driver.

Additional information

See also DRIVER.SYS.

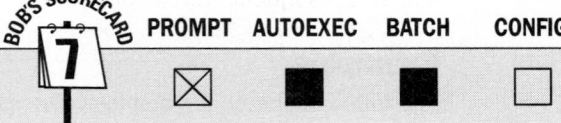

ECHO

Description

This command controls how batch file commands are displayed during execution.

Usage

You can use the ECHO command in one of the following two forms:

```
echo [on or off]
```

```
echo [message]
```

Options and switches

When you use ECHO without switches, it displays the current echoing status (whether echoing is on or off). This feature is not one I use every day.

```
[on or off]
```

DOS displays every command line of a batch file by default as the line is executed. If it encounters the ECHO OFF command, DOS suppresses the command-line displays (or echoes). You can turn command echoing on again with the command ECHO ON.

```
[message]
```

When echoing is turned off, you can use the message switch to display a message.

Remarks

Batch files are often used to simplify complex or repetitive tasks. The ECHO statement is designed to reduce the screen clutter that occurs when these batch files are executed. Think of it as a *clean screen* setting.

Every time a batch file executes, the ECHO status defaults to on.

You can suppress the echoing of *any* single command individually by prefixing the command with the @ character. Standard practice is to start a batch file with the command @ECHO OFF, to suppress the echoing of the first statement and all subsequent statements.

Examples

The following batch file displays a message and waits for user input:

```
@echo off
CHOICE Do you want to load the mouse
if errorlevel 2 goto quit
mouse /y
:quit
```

The following batch file clears the screen and uses ECHO to display a message:

```
@echo off
cls
echo Searching for hidden files....
dir \*.* /a:h /s
echo Search complete
```

Additional information

Refer to Chapter 10 for more information about batch file programming techniques.

See also ANSI.SYS, PAUSE, and CHOICE.

Bob's Shareware Collection disks

BATUTIL, from CtrlAlt Associates, provides some excellent tools for sprucing up batch file output.

ECHO suppresses the display of the line to be executed, but it does not suppress the output generated by the executing command. You can often suppress unwanted output from command-line utilities by using >nul to pipe the output to a nul device. The following batch file, for example, copies CONFIG.SYS but suppresses the output from the COPY command:

```
@echo off
echo Backing up system files
del c:\config.bak > nul
copy c:\config.sys c:\config.bak > nul
if exist c:\config.sys echo Copy successful!
```

To display a blank line (for cosmetic reasons), don't use just the command ECHO with no message. Because DOS assumes that you want to determine the active echo setting, it displays a message that ECHO is on or ECHO is off — not very useful!

To display a blank line, use the ECHO command followed immediately by a period (.) with no spaces. The following batch file, for example, displays a menu item on every other line:

```
@echo off
cls
echo 1) Lotus 1-2-3
```

```
echo.
echo 2) Word 5.5
echo.
echo 3) Windows
echo.
. . . . .
```

ECHO is designed for batch files, but you can use it from the command prompt as well. To suppress the DOS prompt temporarily, enter the command ECHO OFF. Bingo! The DOS prompt has gone. Enter ECHO ON and it comes back.

Description

This command invokes a full-screen editor for viewing and editing ASCII (text) files. This command is ideal for use with BAT and INI files.

Usage

```
edit [[drive:][path]filename.ext] [/b] [/g] [/h] [/nohi]
```

Options and switches

When you use EDIT with no switches, the editor displays a welcoming dialog box.

[[*drive:*][*path*]*filename.ext*]

This option specifies the name of the ASCII file to be edited. If the file does not exist, a new, empty file is created.

[/b]

This switch suppresses colors and uses only black and white. Use this option on monochrome or LCD systems.

[/g]

This switch instructs DOS to use a special screen-writing technique to improve performance on CGA systems.

```
[/h]
```

On EGA systems, the editor switches into 43-line mode; on VGA systems and better, the editor switches to 50-line mode. The editor uses 25 lines by default.

```
[/nohi]
```

This switch instructs DOS to use the eight low-intensity colors.

Remarks

Press F1 at any time to view EDIT's on-line help. If the help doesn't work, select **O**ptions Help **P**ath from the menu and enter the path to the file EDIT.HLP.

EDIT supports block operations such as cut, copy, and paste. To select a block of text, either hold down a Shift key and use the cursor keys, or press the left mouse button down and drag the mouse cursor to select the text. Search, replace, and print operations also are supported.

The editor can edit only one file at a time, and sufficient memory must exist for the entire file to be loaded into memory; no limit exists, however, on the length of each text line.

Please use the edit menu **O**ptions **D**isplay to change the text colors from boring gray on black to something a little more upbeat.

Examples

To edit the CONFIG.SYS file, enter the following command:

```
edit c:\config.sys
```

To edit the WIN.INI file in 50-line mode on a VGA system, enter the following command:

```
edit c:\windows\win.ini /h
```

Additional information

Chapter 10 includes some tips for using EDIT.

Bob's Shareware Collection disks

As useful as EDIT is, it still cannot perform many editing tasks. If you want an easy-to-use but industrial-strength editor, try QEDIT, from SemWare. In addition to all the standard editing features, QEDIT supports editing of multiple files at one time, copying and pasting between files, column-oriented block operations, and a rich macro language, and it is fully customizable.

The DOS file EDIT.COM invokes QBASIC.EXE with a /EDITOR switch. If DOS cannot locate QBASIC (because it is not in the path or because you have deleted it), you cannot use EDIT.

BOB'S SCORECARD	PROMPT	AUTOEXEC	BATCH	CONFIG
EGA.SYS 3	☐	☐	☐	■

Description

This device driver supports DOSSHELL task swapping on EGA systems.

Usage

```
device[high]=[drive:][path]ega.sys
```

Options and switches

```
[drive:][path]
```

This option identifies the directory in which EGA.SYS is located, if it is not in the boot directory. By default, SETUP places EGA.SYS in the \DOS directory.

Remarks

If you use DOSSHELL for task swapping and your computer has an EGA video display, you must load the EGA.SYS device driver in CONFIG.SYS. EGA.SYS has no other uses.

EGA.SYS enables the DOSSHELL to maintain the video modes for every active session.

Example

Use the following command in CONFIG.SYS to load the EGA.SYS device drivers:

```
devicehigh=c:\dos\ega.sys
```

Additional information

See Chapter 2 for a discussion of the DOSSHELL.

See also DEVICE, DEVICEHIGH, and DOSSHELL.

PROMPT   AUTOEXEC   BATCH   CONFIG

EMM386

Description

EMM386 is both a device drive and a command which provides advanced memory management capabilities on 386 systems and higher.

Usage

You can execute EMM386 from the DOS prompt by using the following syntax:

```
emm386 [on or off or auto] [w=on or w=off]
```

When EMM386 is used as a device driver in CONFIG.SYS, it has the following bevy of switches:

```
device=[drive:][path]emm386.exe [on or off or auto] [w=on or
w=off] [memory] [min=size] [mx or frame=address or /pmmmm]
[pn=mmmm] [x=mmmm–nnnn] [i=mmmm–nnnn] [b=mmmm]
[l=minxms] [a=altregs] [h=handles] [d=nnn] [noems] [novcpi]
[highscan] [nohi] [verbose] [ram=mmmm–nnnn] [rom=mmmm–nnnn]
[win=mmmm–nnnn] [nomovexbda] [altboot]
```

So many switches, so little time.

Options and switches

Note: Some switches, such as I= and X=, accept a memory range and have the syntax *mmmm–nnnn. mmmm* is the hexadecimal address of the first segment in the range, and *nnnn* is the hexadecimal address of the last segment in the range I=b000 - b7ff.

```
[drive:][path]emm386.exe
```

This option identifies the directory in which EMM386.EXE is located, if it is not in the boot directory. By default, SETUP places EMM386.EXE in the \DOS directory.

```
[on or off or auto]
```

This option controls whether EMM386 support for expanded memory and UMBs is active or dormant or in Auto Mode. By default, as you might expect,

EMM386 is on. In Auto Mode, EMM386 provides EMS or UMB support only when such memory is requested by a program. You can turn off EMM386 only when the UMBs are not occupied and when no EMS memory is allocated. This switch is rarely used on most systems.

```
[w=on or w=off]
```

The Weitek brand math coprocessor can interfere occasionally with some DOS programs. Use the W= switch on systems equipped with the Weitek coprocessor. By default, support is off. This switch also is rarely used.

```
[memory]
```

This option specifies the maximum amount of extended memory EMM386 converts to expanded memory. The value is in kilobytes and must be in the range from 64K to 32768K. EMM386 uses a memory pool and converts extended memory to expanded memory only when a program requests expanded memory. When the program no longer needs the memory, it is returned to the pool. If the NOEMS switch is used, no expanded memory is supported. By default, EMM386 enables all XMS memory to be converted to EMS.

```
[min=size]
```

This switch sets the minimum amount of memory, in kilobytes, that EMM386 reserves as expanded. By default, EMM386 allocates 256K of memory as EMS memory when EMM386 is loaded without the NOEMS switch. To conserve extended memory, use MIN=0.

```
[mx or frame=address or /pmmmm]
```

You can use any one of these three switches to control where the EMS page frame is located in upper memory. The page frame occupies 64K of memory, which provides four 16K pages. Specify any value in the range from M1 to M14, to use the following memory locations:

Value	Location	Value	Location
1	c000	8	dc00
2	c400	9	e000
3	c800	10	8000
4	cc00	11	8400
5	d000	12	8800
6	d400	13	8c00
7	d800	14	9000

Use switches m10 through m14 only on systems with 512K memory or more.

The FRAME= switch serves precisely the same function as M*X*, but you explicitly specify the memory address. Using M7, for example, is the same as using FRAME=d800. Only use addresses on the 400K boundary, as shown in the preceding table. The /P switch is the same as FRAME=.

[pn=*mmmm*]

Use this switch to set the specific address of each 16K page. LIM EMS 4.0 enables each page to be located in different memory locations (the 64K page frame does not have to occupy contiguous memory). *n* must be a value in the range from 1 to 4 (use p1=, p2=, p3=, and p4=). The p*n* switch supports values in the range from p0 to p255, where p0 to p3 are the standard four pages (you can allocate more than four pages). This switch is rarely used.

[x=*mmmm–nnnn*]

This switch instructs EMM386 not to use a specific area of upper memory (to exclude it). *mmmm* must be lower than *nnnn,* and the values must be in the range from a000h to ffffh. This switch is used when EMM386 does not recognize that an area of upper memory is already occupied.

[i=*mmmm–nnnn*]

This switch instructs EMM386 to *i*nclude an area of upper memory it otherwise would avoid. *mmmm* must be lower than *nnnn,* and the values must be in the range from a000h to ffffh. This switch is commonly used on color video systems to include the unused monochrome video BIOS region (I=b000–b7ff, for example). If a memory area is explicitly excluded with X=, any contradictory attempts to include it with I= are ignored.

[b=*mmmm*]

This switch sets the lowest memory address used for EMS bank switching. Bank switching, standardized in EMS 4.0, enables programs such as DesqView to use expanded memory to manage multiple DOS sessions. The default value is 4000h. This switch is rarely used.

[l=*minxms*]

This switch, the converse of [*memory*], identifies the amount of extended memory to reserve (or not convert to expanded memory). This value is zero by default, which enables all extended memory to be converted to expanded memory.

[a=*altregs*]

Alternative register sets are used by programs, such as DesqView, that manage multiple DOS sessions. By default, EMM386 provides seven alternative register sets. If you run many DOS sessions concurrently, you can improve performance by increasing the number of registers, but you lose more than 200 bytes of base memory for every additional set. Values in the range from 0 to 254 are accepted.

[h=*handles*]

This switch sets the number of available EMS handles. The default is 62, but any value in the range from 2 to 255 is accepted.

[d=*nnn*]

This switch sets the amount of memory, in kilobytes, reserved for DMA buffers. By default, 16K is allocated, but values in the range from 16 to 256 are accepted.

[noems]

This popular switch is used to instruct EMM386 to provide UMB support but not expanded memory. When you use this switch, an additional 64K of upper memory is available as UMBs — this memory otherwise would be used for the EMS page frame.

[novcpi]

If NOEMS is used, you can use the NOVCPI switch to disable VCPI EMS support and save additional extended memory.

[highscan]

This option instructs EMM386 to use a rigorous technique to search all the upper memory for free space; this search can cause a lockup on some systems. Remove HIGHSCAN to stop EMM386 from searching all that upper memory. You can use the I= and X= switches to identify "manually" the memory EMM386 should use.

[nohi]

By default, EMM386 loads some of its code in upper memory. Specify NOHI to force EMM386 to load entirely in base memory.

`[/verbose]`

This switch instructs EMM386 to display detailed progress messages while EMM386 is loading.

`[ram=`*mmmm–nnnn]*

This option instructs EMM386 to only use the specified memory addresses for allocation as UMBs. *mmmm* must be lower than *nnnn,* and the values must be in the range from a000h to ffffh.

`[rom=`*mmmm–nnnn]*

This switch specifies the range of upper memory to be used as shadow RAM. *mmmm* must be lower than *nnnn,* and the values must be in the range from a000h to ffffh.

`[win=`*mmmm–nnnn]*

This switch instructs EMM386 to leave a range of upper memory so that Windows can use it. *mmmm* must be lower than *nnnns,* and the values must be in the range from a000h to ffffh.

`[nomovexbda]`

This switch instructs EMM386 not to move extended BIOS information from base to upper memory.

`[altboot]`

Use this switch if you experience problems rebooting the system using Ctrl-Alt-Del when EMM386 is loaded.

Remarks

HIMEM.SYS must be loaded before EMM386.EXE is loaded.

In the majority of cases, you can use MEMMAKER, the DOS 6 memory optimizer, to fine-tune the EMM386 switches.

 In earlier versions of DOS, the EMM386 default provided only EMS, and the RAM switch was used to explicitly instruct EMM386 to provide EMS *and* UMB support. With DOS 6, EMM386 defaults to provide EMS and UMB support.

Also, EMM386 now automatically includes the region c000:efff.

Examples

The following extract from CONFIG.SYS loads EMM386 and optimizes upper memory by suppressing expanded memory support and utilizing the monochrome video BIOS area.

```
device=himem.sys
device=c:\dos\emm386.exe ram i=b000-b7ff noems
```

The following statement from CONFIG.SYS instructs EMM386 to emulate expanded memory and reserve an area of upper memory for Windows:

```
device=c:\dos\emm386.exe ram i=b000-b7ff win=b300-b7ff
```

Additional information

Memory management issues are discussed thoroughly in Chapter 5.

See also DOS, DEVICE, DEVICEHIGH, HIMEM.SYS, MEM, MEMMAKER, and SMARTDRV.

Bob's Shareware Collection disks

EMM386 can be used on only 386 systems and higher. UMB_DRV.SYS, from Christopher Blum, additionally provides advanced memory management capabilities for 286 systems.

ERASE

See DEL.

BOB'S SCORECARD	PROMPT	AUTOEXEC	BATCH	CONFIG
EXIT 7	■	□	■	□

Description

This command terminates the current COMMAND.COM session and returns to the preceding COMMAND.COM session.

Usage

```
exit
```

Options and switches

None.

Remarks

If you use Windows, you are accustomed to using EXIT to terminate a DOS session and return control to Program Manager. You use this command also when you *drop to DOS* from a DOS program such as 1-2-3 or Turbo Pascal. These programs launch a second copy of the command interpreter. After you execute EXIT, the secondary copy is terminated and you return to the application program.

Example

To return from a Windows DOS box to Program Manager, enter the following command:

```
exit
```

Additional information

See also COMMAND.

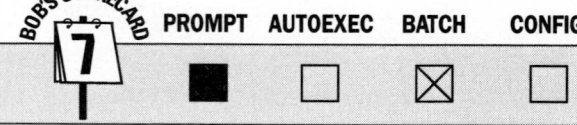

Description

DOS 6 is distributed in compressed files on the DOS disks. You must use EXPAND to transfer files manually from the DOS distribution disks to your system.

Usage

```
expand [drive:][path]filename.ext [,[drive:][path][filename.ext [....]]
destination
```

Options and switches

When you use EXPAND with no switches, it prompts for the source filename and the destination.

    [*drive:*] [*path*]*filename.ext*

This option specifies the name of the source file to be transferred from the DOS 6 master disks. You can specify multiple filenames when they are separated by spaces, but wildcards are not supported.

    destination

This option specifies the drive or path to which the file is copied. If a single source file is specified, you can optionally specify a new filename for the target file. Normally, however, you should retain the original DOS filename.

Remarks

Conceptually, EXPAND is similar to COPY except that EXPAND decompresses the source file before copying it to the destination.

When you first install DOS 6, SETUP transfers all the DOS files to your system. Use EXPAND if one or more of the DOS files is damaged or deleted.

Examples

Use the following command to expand the file and copy it to the DOS subdirectory:

```
expand b:edit.hl_ c:\dos
```

The following command copies three files to the DOS subdirectory:

```
expand a:cga.vi_ a:cga.in_ a:cga.gr_ c:\dos
```

Additional information

 View the file PACKING.LST on the DOS Setup disk 1 to see which DOS 6 disk contains the files you want to restore. All compressed files have an underscore character at the end of the filename. If a file has no underscore, such as QBASIC.EXE, it is not compressed and can be transferred by using COPY or XCOPY.

FASTHELP or DOSHELP

BOB'S SCORECARD 3

PROMPT	AUTOEXEC	BATCH	CONFIG
■	☐	☒	☐

Description

This command provides terse help on nearly all DOS commands but not on device drivers.

Usage

```
fasthelp [command–name]
```

Options and switches

When you execute FASTHELP with no switches, help is displayed for every DOS 6 command, and the display is paused after every screen.

[*command–name*]

This option specifies the name of the DOS command you want help with.

Remarks

The help text that is displayed is stored in the ASCII file DOSHELP.HLP, located in the same directory as the FASTHELP program. You can modify this command to add your own help text for such items as batch files and utilities.

Help is available also by using the help command or by executing DOS utilities with the /? switch.

Examples

To display help for the batch command MEM, enter the following:

```
fasthelp mem
```

To display a list of all DOS commands and a brief description, enter the following command:

```
fasthelp
```

Additional information

Refer to Chapter 2 to learn how to customize the help file.

See also HELP.

You can print a copy of the FASTHELP output by redirecting the output to the printer with the following command:

```
fasthelp > PRN
```

FASTHELP is smart enough not to pause for a keypress when the output is redirected. ◉

BOB'S SCORECARD	4	PROMPT	AUTOEXEC	BATCH	CONFIG
FASTOPEN		⊠	⊠	⊠	⊠

Description

This command improves file performance by speeding access to frequently used files.

Usage

Use the following syntax from a batch file or DOS prompt:

```
fastopen drive:[[=]n] ... [/x]
```

Alternatively, because FASTOPEN is a TSR, you can use INSTALL in CONFIG.SYS as follows:

```
install=[drive:][path] fastopen.exe drive:[=n] ... [/x]
```

Options and switches

drive:

This option specifies the drive to be managed by FASTOPEN. You can specify multiple drives, but you must separate each one with a space.

```
[[=]n]
```

This option specifies the number of files on the drive on which FASTOPEN maintains statistics. Values in the range from 10 to 999 are accepted, and 48 is the default. Note that 48 bytes are allocated for every file.

```
[/x]
```

This switch instructs DOS to use expanded memory rather than base memory.

Remarks

I do not recommend that you use this command. FASTOPEN is a poor person's disk cache. FASTOPEN just records details of where a file is stored when it is opened. If you open the file again later, DOS obtains the file details from memory rather than rereading the FAT. Tangible performance gains are realized only on systems that open and close files frequently (database applications, for example). FASTOPEN works only on local hard drives.

Far more performance gains are realized if you use SMARTDRV or a third-party disk cache — these programs cache the file data and the location details.

Do not load FASTOPEN from within the DOSSHELL or Windows or any other multitasker.

You must reboot your system to change the FASTOPEN configuration.

Example

Use the following command to instruct FASTOPEN to monitor 50 files on drives C and D and store the details in expanded memory:

```
fastopen C:=50 d:=50 /x
```

Additional information

See also INSTALL and SMARTDRV.

Do not use DEFRAG or any other disk defragmenter if FASTOPEN is installed. You can lose valuable data.

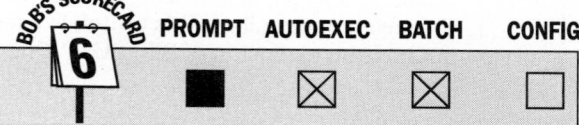

	BOB'S SCORECARD	PROMPT	AUTOEXEC	BATCH	CONFIG
FC	6	■	⊠	⊠	☐

Description

FC, short for *file* compare, compares two files and highlights any differences.

Usage

Use the following syntax when you compare two ASCII files:

```
fc [drive:][path]filename1.ext [drive:][path]filename2.ext [/a] [/c]
[/l] [/lbn] [/n] [/t] [/w] [/nnnn]
```

Use the following syntax when you make a binary comparison of files:

```
fc [drive:][path]filename1.ext [drive:][path]filename2.ext [/b]
```

Options and switches

[drive:][path]filename1.ext

This option specifies the name of the first file to be compared.

[drive:][path]filename2.ext

This option specifies the name of the second file to be compared. FC accepts a wildcard as the second filename, but normally you specify the individual filename.

`[/a]`

This switch specifies that an *a*bbreviated list of differences should be displayed when you are comparing ASCII files. Only the first and last lines in each set of differences will be displayed.

`[/c]`

This switch instructs FC to ignore the case of letters.

`[/l]`

The /L switch instructs FC to use a line-by-line comparison to identify the location of blocks of lines missing from a file, and to try to resynchronize and find the next common line. This switch is used by default when the filename does not have an extension of BIN, COM, EXE, LIB, OBJ, or SYS.

`[/lbn]`

This switch sets the internal line buffer. By default, 100 lines are reserved to store a missing block from one of the files. If FC fails and returns this message:

```
Resync failed. Files are too different
```

try using the /LBN switch to increase the buffer size.

`[/n]`

This switch instructs FC to display line numbers in comparing ASCII files.

`[/t]`

By default, FC treats a tab character as though it were eight spaces during an ASCII compare. This switch instructs FC to use the Tab character for the comparison and not to expand the tabs with spaces.

`[/w]`

This switch instructs FC to treat contiguous white-space characters (spaces and tabs) as a single space. Use this switch when you are comparing two ASCII files and you don't care about differences in the spaces and tabs.

`[/nnnn]`

FC tries to resynchronize ASCII files when one or more lines is encountered in one file and not in the other. This switch specifies how many lines must be identical before FC assumes that the files are resynchronized. By default, the value is 2.

`[/b]`

This switch instructs FC to perform a binary (byte-by-byte) comparison of the files. In this mode, FC does not attempt to resynchronize after a problem occurs. This mode is assumed when you are comparing files with the following extensions: BIN, COM, EXE, LIB, OBJ, or SYS.

Remarks

Use | MORE to pause after each screen.

If you use the /B switch to perform a binary comparison, do not use any other switches (specify only the filenames).

When a difference is found during a binary compare, FC displays, in hexadecimal, the position from the beginning file, the byte value in file 1, and the byte value in file 2.

Examples

Consider the following two ASCII files that detail omelette recipes:

RECIPE.ONE

```
two eggs
dash of milk
half diced tomato
tablespoon cheese
half diced green pepper
```

RECIPE.TWO

```
two eggs
dash of milk
pinch salt
two cups jalapeno
half diced tomato
tablespoon cheese
half diced chile pepper
```

You can use the following command to compare the two files in ASCII mode and display line numbers:

```
fc recipe.one recipe.two /n
```

The following output is generated:

```
Comparing files RECIPE.ONE and RECIPE.TWO
***** RECIPE.ONE
    2:  dash of milk
    3:  half diced tomato
***** RECIPE.TWO
    2:  dash of milk
    3:  pinch salt
    4:  two cups jalapeno
    5:  half diced tomato
*****

***** RECIPE.ONE
    4:  tablespoon cheese
    5:  half diced green pepper
***** RECIPE.TWO
    6:  tablespoon cheese
    7:  half diced chile pepper
*****
```

Additional information

See also DISKCOMP.

BOB'S SCORECARD	PROMPT	AUTOEXEC	BATCH	CONFIG
FCBS 〔3〕	☐	☐	☐	■

Description

This command specifies the maximum number of file control blocks DOS can have open at any time.

Usage

FCBS is used in CONFIG.SYS with the following syntax:

```
fcbs=x
```

Options and switches

x

This option identifies the maximum number of file control blocks. Any value in the range from 1 to 255 is accepted. If CONFIG.SYS has no FCBS entry, DOS assigns 4.

Remarks

FCBS, a hand-me-down from DOS 1, was superseded by the FILES= statement in DOS 2. Few (useful) programs use the outdated FCBS file-management technique.

Example

To save memory, add the following FCBS statement to CONFIG.SYS:

```
fcbs=1
```

Additional information

Refer to Chapter 5 for other memory-saving techniques.

See also FILES.

BOB'S SCORECARD | 7 | PROMPT ■ | AUTOEXEC ☐ | BATCH ☒ | CONFIG ☐

FDISK

Description

This command prepares a new hard disk for formatting and manages logical drive assignments on a partitioned disk.

Usage

```
fdisk [/status]
```

Options and switches

Used with no switches, FDISK presents a full-screen menu for configuring the physical hard disks.

```
[/status]
```

This switch instructs FDISK to display a brief summary of the system's hard drive configuration. The configuration summary cannot be piped to a file or device.

Remarks

FDISK is responsible for storing the disk partition information on the hard disk. This information is stored in the *master partition table,* located in the first sector of the first track on the first platter. When you first boot the computer, the partition table is inspected and attention turns to the boot partition from which the appropriate operating system is loaded. The partition used to boot the computer is referred to as the *active partition.*

DOS recognizes two types of partitions: the *primary* partition and the *extended* partition. Every DOS system must have a primary partition. If you want the entire disk to be a single logical drive (typically drive C), you need only a primary partition. If you want to divide the disk into multiple DOS partitions, however, you must create an extended partition also. The extended partition is used to record as many as 23 additional logical drives. The primary partition should be identified as the active partition if you want your computer to boot up under DOS. The primary partition contains the DOS boot files IO.SYS, MSDOS.SYS, and COMMAND.COM.

To change the size of a logical drive (a partition), you must delete the old partition and create a new one.

Examples

Use the following command to run the FDISK program, which presents you with the main menu:

```
fdisk
```

To see your current partition status, enter the following command:

```
fdisk /status
```

Additional information

MSD provides additional information about your hard disk configuration. Refer to Chapter 4 for a thorough discussion of hard disk management.

See also FORMAT, MSBACKUP, and MSD.

FDISK can damage your health. If you are using FDISK on a system that is already partitioned and that has useful data, be careful. Destroying a partition and losing all the data in the partition is too easy. Make sure that you have a complete, up-to-date backup of your entire system before you make any changes to the partition structure. Unlike most DOS commands, you should not experiment with this one.

BOB'S SCORECARD	7	PROMPT	AUTOEXEC	BATCH	CONFIG
FILES		□	□	□	■

Description

This command specifies the number of files that DOS can have open concurrently.

Usage

```
files=nn
```

Options and switches

nn

This option specifies the maximum number of open files. Any value in the range from 8 to 255 is accepted. When CONFIG.SYS does not include a FILES command, DOS uses 8.

Remarks

You might think that you never will need more than eight files open at a time. That situation may have existed five years ago, but things certainly have changed. If you use Windows, consider setting FILES to 40 or more; otherwise, a value of 20 to 30 is appropriate.

Each additional file handle you specify with FILES consumes 60 bytes.

Most well-behaved programs display a meaningful message if a file cannot be opened because of a shortage of file handles. If you encounter this type of message, increase the FILES setting by 5, and try again. You should not need a FILES allocation larger than 50.

Example

Use the following command in CONFIG.SYS to enable DOS to have 40 open files:

```
files=40
```

Additional information

See also FCBS.

	PROMPT	AUTOEXEC	BATCH	CONFIG
FIND	■	■	⊠	☐

Description

This command searches for text in one or more files.

Usage

find *"string"* [[*drive:*][*path*]*filename.ext* ...] [/v] [/c] [/n] [/i]

Options and switches

"string"

This option specifies the string to search for, enclosed in double quotation marks. If the string you want to search for includes a quote character, specify two quotation-mark characters together so that DOS interprets it as one quotation mark within the string.

[[*drive:*][*path*]*filename.ext* ...]

This option specifies the file in which to search for the text. Wildcards are not supported, but you can specify multiple filenames.

[/v]

This switch instructs FIND to identify all the lines that do *not* include the string.

[/c]

This switch instructs FIND to display the total number of lines where the string was found (the *c*ount).

[/n]

This switch displays a line number with each line.

[/i]

This switch instructs FIND to ignore the character case (a case-insensitive search).

Remarks

FIND is designed for ASCII files, and the search string is noticed only if it is situated on a line (the string cannot extend beyond a line break).

The DOS editor, EDIT, includes a search and a search-and-replace facility.

If you do not specify a filename, FIND interprets all the characters you type on the command line searching for the string. This effectively disables normal command input. Just press Ctrl-Break to return to the DOS prompt.

Examples

Use the following command to search for the text *goto* in AUTOEXEC.BAT and display line numbers on matching lines:

```
find "goto" autoexec.bat /n
```

I generated the following output on my system:

```
———— AUTOEXEC.BAT
[6]goto %CONFIG%
[10]goto QUIT
[15]if errorlevel 3 goto continue
[16]if errorlevel 2 goto single
[18]goto continue
```

Additional information

See the FOR command for an example of using FIND on multiple files.

See also FOR and EDIT.

Bob's Shareware Collection disks

SeakEasy, from Correlation Systems, is an excellent full-screen text-finding utility. It can search multiple files with wildcards, and even search the current directory, all nested subdirectories, or the entire drive.

The versatile PocketD program from Pocketware includes text searching options that you can invoke from the command line by using switches.

You can pipe the output from the DIR command to FIND, which is an easy way to search for filenames that contain a specific character string.

To find all files on drive C that include the characters *read*, for example, enter the following command:

```
dir c:\*.* /s /b | find "read" /i
```

The /B switch improves performance because FIND must search only the filenames and not the file size and date of creation, for example. When the /B switch is omitted, you can use FIND to show all the files created or modified on a certain date. The following command searches for all the files modified on March 31, 1993:

```
dir c:\*.* /s | find "03-31-93"
```

Note: If you ask FIND to look for several words separated by spaces, it will fail to recognize them if the words get split up across two lines. ◈

Description

This command executes a command or statement multiple times and applies a new string or filename with each iteration.

Usage

When FOR is used in a batch file, the syntax is as follows:

```
for %%variable in (set) do command [command-parameters]
```

When you execute FOR from the DOS prompt, the syntax is as follows:

```
for %variable in (set) do command [command-parameters]
```

Note: The difference is the double % symbol in batch files.

Options and switches

%%variable and *%variable*

A single character variable identifier that represents the active value in the *set*. The variable value is updated with the next value in the *set* with each iteration of the FOR loop. The variable is represented by a single character, but the following characters are not allowed:

0 through 9   / | <   >

The same variable identifier often is used in the command or the command parameters.

  (*set*)

This option specifies a list of one or more strings or filenames separated by spaces. With each iteration of the loop, a value from the list is used in place of the *variable* identifier.

  command

This option specifies the command to be executed with each iteration of the loop.

  [*command-parameters*]

This option specifies any parameters or switches the command requires.

Remarks

You can use wildcards when filenames are used in the (*set*).

Examples

The following batch file command lists all the programs in the current directory:

```
@echo off
for %%n in (*.EXE *.COM *.BAT) do echo %%n
```

In the preceding example, the variable name acts as a placeholder, and the name that is used is not important. The same results can be achieved, for example, with the following command (the only difference is the variable identifier name):

```
@echo off
for %%a in (*.EXE *.COM *.BAT) do echo %%a
```

When you combine FOR with FIND, you can use FOR to search for files that contain some specific text. When the following command is executed from the DOS prompt, it searches all TXT and ME files for the string:

```
for %s in (*.txt *.me) do find "help" %s.
```

Only EXEs and COMs work as commands. If you want to repeatedly execute a batch file, be sure to use the CALL command to call the batch file. For example, the following statement will execute all the batch files in the root directory:

```
@echo off
for %b in (\*.bat) do call %b
```

Additional information

Refer to Chapter 10 for some more examples of using FOR in batch files.

Description

This command formats a floppy or hard disk and creates a new file allocation table; optionally marks bad sectors.

Usage

Note: A high-density disk drive is capable of formatting disks with different capacities. The FORMAT command provides several different switches you can use to achieve the same FORMAT results. Consequently, you can use FORMAT in any of the following ways:

```
format drive: [/v[:label]] [/q] [/u] [/s] [/f:size]

format drive: [/v[:label]] [/q] [/u] [/s] [/t:tracks /n:sectors]

format drive: [/v[:label]] [/q] [/u] [/s] [/1] [/4]

format drive: [/q] [/u] [/s] [/1] [/4] [/8]
```

Options and switches

drive:

This option specifies the drive to be formatted.

[/v[:*label*]]

This switch instructs FORMAT to assign a volume label to the newly formatted disk. If you use /V without the new label, FORMAT prompts you to enter the new label after the drive has been formatted. The label can be 11 characters long and is converted automatically to uppercase.

[/q]

This switch instructs FORMAT to perform a quick format. This mode provides a fast way to reformat disks that are in good condition. In Quick Mode, the FAT and root directories are cleared, but the disk sectors are not reformatted — think of it as a fast way to erase all the files and subdirectories on a disk.

[/u]

FORMAT normally records key file information behind the scenes before formatting a disk. UNFORMAT accesses this information when you try to undo an accidental format. The /U command forces an unconditional format, which means that the disk cannot be unformatted. Use the switch only when you are experiencing read or write errors with the disk.

[/s]

This switch makes a disk bootable by copying the operating system files IO.SYS, MSDOS.SYS, COMMAND.COM, and DBLSPACE.BIN.

The remaining switches control the capacity of formatted disks.

[/f:*size*]

I think that this switch provides the easiest way to specify the size of the disk. Use one of the following numbers:

Size Number	Disk size
160	A 160K single-sided double-density 5¼-inch disk
180	A 180K single-sided double-density 5¼-inch disk
320	A 320K double-sided double-density 5¼-inch disk
360	A 360K double-sided double-density 5¼-inch disk
720	A 720K double-sided double-density 3½-inch disk
1200	A 1.2MB double-sided high-density 5¼-inch disk
1440	A 1.44MB double-sided high-density 3½-inch disk
2880	A 2.88MB double-sided super-high-density 3½-inch disk

The *size* number optionally can be followed with K or KB (720, 720K, and 720KB, for example, all have the same meaning).

    [/t:*tracks* /n:*sectors*]

This switch explicitly identifies the number of tracks and the number of sectors to apply during the format.

    [/1]

This old switch is rarely used because it creates single-sided disks.

    [/4]

This switch formats a 360K 5¼-inch disk in a 1.2MB drive.

    [/8]

This old switch is rarely used either because it creates the now obsolete 320K floppies used in DOS 1.1.

Remarks

You can use the UNFORMAT command to undo an accidental disk format if the /U switch was not specified. See the caution later in this section.

The now obsolete /B switch is still supported. /B was required with DOS versions before DOS 4 and was used to reserve space for system files. Thanks to /S, the /B switch no longer is required, but it is preserved for backward compatibility.

A disk volume label can be changed subsequently with the LABEL command.

When FORMAT is used in batch files, it returns one of the following ERRORLEVELs:

ERRORLEVEL	Message
0	The disk was formatted successfully.
3	The user aborted the format by pressing Ctrl-Break.
4	An unexpected error occurred!
5	The user entered N when prompted to confirm the FORMAT operation.

Examples

Use the following command to format a disk in drive A, assuming that the disk and the drive capacities are the same:

```
format a:
```

Use the following command to format a 360K disk in a 1.2MB drive:

```
format b: /s:360
```

Use the following command to create a bootable disk and add the volume label TECHNOJOCK:

```
format a: /v:technojock /s
```

Additional information

See also DELTREE, FDISK, LABEL, and UNFORMAT.

Bob's Shareware Collection disks

The New-Ware program Format Master provides full-screen formatting tools for formatting floppy disks. If you are formatting disks to make copies of other disks, try DUPE, from Best Technology. It can format and copy a disk much faster than DOS, and it's easy to use.

Use the FORMAT command with caution. Although you can use it to undo a format, it is not foolproof, and valuable data may get lost. UNFORMAT cannot recover fragmented files, for example. Always inspect a drive before formatting it to verify that you no longer need the files.

The following three undocumented switches are supported by FORMAT:

```
/backup
```

This switch bypasses the Insert new diskette prompt.

```
/select
```

This switch does not format the disk at all, but creates the UNFORMAT files MIRROR.FIL and MIRRORSAV.FIL.

```
/autotest
```

Use this switch to quickly format a single diskette. The Insert new diskette prompt, the prompt for a volume label, and the prompt Format another (Y/N) are all bypassed.

Description

This command instructs DOS to continue processing batch file commands at a specific location in the batch file.

Usage

goto *label*

Options and switches

label

This option identifies the next location in the batch file where commands should be processed. The label is not case sensitive, and as many as eight characters are supported. The label can include spaces, but not the characters <, >, [,], %, *, −, +, =, \, /, . , ,; ,:, or |.

Remarks

A colon must precede the target location, *label*. If a batch file includes the statement goto quit, for example, another line in the batch file must have the contents :quit.

You can specify batch file parameters %0 through %9 as the GOTO label.

Example

The following batch file uses GOTO in conjunction with IF and ERRORLEVEL to load a device driver:

```
@echo off
CHOICE /c:mtn Do you want to load the Mouse, Tablet or Neither
if errorlevel 3 goto end
if errorlevel 2 goto tablet
mouse /y
goto end
:tablet
tabk /c:345
:end
```

Additional information

Chapter 10 includes numerous examples of batch files using GOTO.

See also CHOICE, ERRORLEVEL, and IF.

Bob's Shareware Collection disks

TurboBat, with the ExtraDOS Toolbox from Foley Hi-Tech Systems, compiles batch files to improve performance and prevent other people from tampering with the code.

BOB'S SCORECARD	PROMPT	AUTOEXEC	BATCH	CONFIG
GRAPHICS 7	■	■	☒	☐

Description

This command enables you to print graphics screens just by pressing PrtScr on CGA, EGA, and VGA systems.

Usage

```
graphics [type] [[drive:][path]filename.ext] [/r] [/b] [/lcd]
[/printbox:std or /printbox:lcd]
```

Options and switches

[*type*]

The instructions used to print graphics vary from printer to printer. You use this switch to identify the printer type.

The following printer types are supported:

COLOR1	IBM PC Color printer with single color ribbon
COLOR4	IBM PC Color printer with a RGB ribbon
COLOR8	IBM PC Color printer with a CMY ribbon
DESKJET	HP Deskjet printer
GRAPHICS	IBM Personal Graphics, Proprinter, or Quietwriter printer
GRAPHICSWIDE	11-inch model of IBM Personal Graphics
HPDEFAULT	All HP PCL printers
LASERJET	Original HP LaserJet printer
LASERJETII	HP LaserJet Series II printer
QUIETJET	HP QuietJet printer
QUIETJETPLUS	HP QuietJet Plus printer
RUGGEDWRITER	HP RuggedWriter printer
RUGGEDWRITERWIDE	HP RuggedWriterwide printer
THERMAL	IBM PC-Convertible Thermal printer
THINKJET	HP ThinkJet Printer

[[*drive:*][*path*]*filename.ext*]

This option specifies the name of a graphics profile file that contains the printer escape codes (see the SECRET later in this section). DOS uses the file GRAPHICS.PRO by default in the DOS directory.

[/r]

This switch instructs DOS to print the image in reverse (black on-screen is black on the printer). By default, DOS prints white (or any other color) as black.

```
[/b]
```

This switch is used on color printers to print the background in color.

```
[/lcd]
```

The /LCD switch instructs DOS to use the same aspect ratio as an LCD display rather than a CGA ratio. This switch is the same as /PRINTBOX:LCD.

```
[/printbox:std or /printbox:lcd]
```

This switch controls the aspect ratio of the printed image. STD is used by default. Use /LCD — it's shorter.

Remarks

You can optionally load the GRAPHICS TSR, which uses about 6K of memory, into upper memory with LOADHIGH.

PostScript printers are not supported.

Example

To use the default settings to install graphics print-screen support, enter the following command:

```
graphics
```

Additional information

See also LOADHIGH and PRINT.

The ASCII file GRAPHICS.PRO contains all the printer control codes and escape sequences for the supported printers. If your printer is not supported, copy the file to CUSTOM.PRO and use the codes in your printer manual to adjust the codes for one of the existing printers. Then install GRAPHICS and specify CUSTOM.PRO as a switch.

Description

This command displays full-screen on-line help for DOS commands and device drivers.

Usage

```
help [topic] [/b] [/g] [/h] [/nohi]
```

Options and switches

When you use HELP with no switches, it displays a full-screen index of all the DOS commands and device drivers.

[*topic*]

This option specifies the name of the command or device driver you want help with. If the switch is not specified, or if the topic is unknown, the main help index is displayed.

[/b]

This switch suppresses colors and uses only black and white. Use this option on monochrome or LCD systems.

[/g]

This switch instructs DOS to use a special screen-writing technique to improve performance on CGA systems.

[/h]

On EGA systems, HELP switches to 43-line mode; on VGA systems and better, it switches to 50-line mode. HELP uses 25 lines by default.

[/nohi]

This switch instructs DOS to use the eight low-intensity colors.

Remarks

I use this great command all the time.

To quit from on-line help and return to the DOS prompt, press Alt-F,X.

In addition to specifying the standard commands and device drivers, you can specify the following additional subtopics or categories:

Command	Help Topic
batch	Batch file commands
config	CONFIG.SYS commands
international	Commands for international configurations
multi-config	Commands for creating a multiboot CONFIG.SYS menu

Many commands also display help when you use the /? switch.

Examples

To display help on HIMEM.SYS, enter the following command:

```
help himem.sys
```

To get help about batch file commands, enter the following command:

```
help batch
```

To display the main help index (or contents), enter the following command:

```
help
```

Additional information

Refer to Chapter 2 for additional information about the DOS help facilities.

See also FASTHELP.

Description

This device driver is responsible for managing extended memory on 286 systems and higher.

Usage

```
device=[drive:][path]himem.sys [/a20control:on or off]
[/cpuclock:on or off] [/eisa] [/hmamin=m] [/int15=xxxx]
[/numhandles=n] [/machine:xxxxx] [/shadowram:on or off]
[/verbose]
```

Options and switches

You usually use HIMEM.SYS with no switches. The majority of the switches are for use on nonstandard hardware.

[*drive:*][*path*]

This option identifies the directory in which HIMEM.SYS is located, if it is not in the boot directory. By default, SETUP places HIMEM.SYS in the \DOS directory.

[/a20control:on **or** off]

The A20 pin on 286 CPUs and higher is used to provide access to the high memory area (HMA); it must be managed by only one program or device driver. By default, HIMEM.SYS takes control of the a20 handler if it is set to OFF when HIMEM.SYS is loaded (it applies the switch /A20CONTROL:ON). To load HIMEM.SYS and instruct it not to handle the a20 pin, use the switch /A20CONTROL:OFF.

[/cpuclock:on **or** off]

On some systems, HIMEM.SYS can slow overall system performance significantly. If this slowdown occurs, use the switch /CPUCLOCK:ON to return the system to its original speed (HIMEM.SYS will function more slowly). By default, HIMEM.SYS uses /CPUCLOCK:OFF.

[/eisa]

Use this switch only on EISA bus systems with more than 16MB of RAM to instruct HIMEM.SYS to manage all extended memory; otherwise, HIMEM.SYS may manage only the first 16MB.

[/hmamin=*m*]

Only one application, usually the DOS kernel, can use the HMA. You can use the /HMAMIN switch to stop a small application from using the HMA. Use this switch to instruct HIMEM.SYS to give HMA control only to applications that request a minimum of *m* kilobytes of memory.

[/int15=*xxxx*]

Some older extended memory applications do not adhere to the XMS specification and use interrupt 15h to allocate extended memory. Use the /INT15 switch to reserve *xxxx* kilobytes of extended memory for servicing interrupt 15h requests. *xxxx* must be a value in the range from 64 to 65535, and it must not be greater than the total amount of installed memory. By default, HIMEM.SYS does not reserve any memory for these outdated programs.

`[/numhandles=`*n*`]`

Extended memory is managed in blocks (EMBs), and HIMEM.SYS by default can manage 32 EMBs. Use the /NUMHANDLES switch to specify a different value in the range from 1 to 128. /NUMHANDLES has no effect when running Windows in 386 enhanced mode.

`[/machine:`*xxxxx*`]`

HIMEM.SYS performs hardware-specific tasks that vary from computer to computer. When HIMEM.SYS is loaded, it checks to determine the computer type. If HIMEM.SYS does not recognize the computer model, it assumes that it is an IBM PC-AT. You can use the /MACHINE switch to explicitly identify the host computer brand. *xxxxx* can be one of the strings or numbers in the following table:

Number	String	Computer model
1	at	IBM PC-AT or 100 percent compatible
2	ps2	IBM PS/2
3	ptlcascade	Phoenix Cascade BIOS
4	hpvectra	HP Vectra (A and A+)
5	att6300plus	AT&T 6300 Plus
6	acer1100	Acer 1100
7	toshiba	Toshiba 1600 and 1200XE
8	wyse	Wyse 12.5 MHz 286
9	tulip	Tulip SX
10	zenith	Zenith ZBIOS
11	at1	IBM PC AT (alternative delay)
12	at2	IBM PC AT (alternative delay)
12	css	CSS Labs
13	at3	IBM PC AT (alternative delay)
13	phillips	Phillips
14	fasthp	HP Vectra
15	ibm7552	IBM 7552 Industrial Computer
16	bullmicral	Bull Micral 60
17	dell	Dell XBIOS

`[/shadowram:on` **or** `off]`

This switch can be used on some systems equipped with shadow RAM (systems that copy ROM code into faster RAM. This switch can save some extended memory (for applications) and is designed for systems with less than 2MB of extended memory. Use the switch /SHADOWRAM:ON to leave shadow RAM active, and /SHADOWRAM:OFF to disable it. By default, HIMEM.SYS attempts to disable shadow RAM on systems with 2MB or less of extended memory; otherwise, it leaves it on.

```
[/verbose]
```

This switch instructs HIMEM.SYS to display additional data as it loads.

Remarks

HIMEM.SYS (or a third-party extended memory manager) must be installed before DOS can be loaded high and before EMM386 can be installed.

MEMMAKER automatically adds a HIMEM.SYS statement to CONFIG.SYS.

Example

On most systems, you install HIMEM.SYS with no switches on the first line of CONFIG.SYS as follows:

```
device=c:\dos\himem.sys
```

Additional information

Refer to Chapter 5 for a thorough discussion of DOS 6 memory management issues.

See also DEVICE, DOS=, EMM386, MEM, and MEMMAKER.

Description

This command provides a conditional branch in a batch file execution.

Usage

You can use IF to compare two strings, test the ERRORLEVEL a program returns, or test whether a file exists by using one of the following three syntax formats:

```
if [not]  string1==string2  command

if [not]  errorlevel  number command

if [not]  exist  [drive:][path]wildcard.ext  command
```

Options and switches

```
[not]
```

The IF statement normally executes *command* when the test condition is true. Use the NOT operand when you want *command* to be executed when the test condition is false.

command

This option specifies any valid DOS or batch command.

string1==string2

This option returns a true value when the two strings are identical. To test for an empty string, use quotation marks to surround both values (see the "Examples" section below). The test is case sensitive.

errorlevel *number*

This option returns a true value when the ERRORLEVEL returned by the last command is equal to or greater than the specified *number*.

exist [*drive:*][*path*]*wildcard.ext*

This option returns a true value when one or more matching files exist.

Remarks

You can use batch file variables (%1 through %9) in place of strings, ERRORLEVEL numbers, or filenames.

Always remember that the ERRORLEVEL test returns true if the *number* is *less than* or equal to the ERRORLEVEL. For example, ERRORLEVEL 0 always returns true because the 0 always is less than or equal to the ERRORLEVEL. You must test for multiple ERRORLEVELs in reverse order (see the second example in the following "Example" section).

Examples

The following batch file adds extensive error checking to improve on the RENAME command and illustrates many uses of the IF statement:

```
@echo off
rem A batch file to test for file before renaming it
if "%1"=="" goto novar
if "%2"=="" goto novar
if "%1"=="%2" goto duplicate
if not exist %1 goto nosource
if exist %2 goto oldtarget
rename %1 %2 > nul
if not exist %2 goto failed
echo File Renamed!
goto quit
:duplicate
echo Source and Target filenames must be different
goto quit
:failed
echo Target file not created
goto quit
:nosource
echo Cannot Find the source file
goto quit
:oldtarget
echo The Target file already exists
goto quit
:novar
echo You must specify a source and target filename
:quit
```

The following batch file illustrates that you must test ERRORLEVEL in reverse order:

```
@echo off
CHOICE /c:mtn Do you want to load the Mouse, Tablet or Neither
if errorlevel 3 goto end
if errorlevel 2 goto Tablet
mouse /y
goto end
:Tablet
tabk /c:345
:end
```

Additional information

Chapter 10 shows many ways you can use an IF statement in batch files.

See also CHOICE and GOTO.

Bob's Shareware Collection disks

TurboBat, with the ExtraDOS Toolbox from Foley Hi-Tech Systems, compiles batch files to improve performance and prevent other people from tampering with the code.

	BOB'S SCORECARD 8	PROMPT	AUTOEXEC	BATCH	CONFIG
INCLUDE		☐	☐	☐	■

Description

This command is used in a multiboot CONFIG.SYS file to instruct DOS to process a specific block of commands.

Usage

    include=*blockname*

Options and switches

blockname

This option specifies the name of the configuration block whose commands are executed.

Remarks

Starting with Version 6, DOS supports multiple configurations in CONFIG.SYS. A set of menu commands is used to define a boot-up menu, and DOS branches to a specific block based on a user's selection.

The INCLUDE statement provides a convenient way for multiple configurations to share a common set of commands without duplicating them.

After processing the commands, DOS returns to the command immediately following the INCLUDE statement.

You can nest INCLUDE blocks as much as ten levels deep (an INCLUDE block can include another block, which in turn can include another block, and so on).

When a block is named [common], it is included automatically in all blocks.

Example

The following CONFIG.SYS file includes the block [basics] in both configuration menu options.

```
[menu]
menuitem=justmouse,Just the Mouse
menuitem=gainers,Big Gainers
menudefault=gainers,5

[basics]
files=30
buffers=15

[justmouse]
include basics
device=c:\windows\mouse.sys /y

[gainers]
include basics
device=c:\dos\himem.sys
device=c:\dos\emm386.exe ram i=b000-b7ff noems
device=c:\dos\smartdrv.exe
dos=high,umb
devicehigh=c:\windows\mouse.sys /y
```

Additional information

Multiple configurations are discussed in depth in Chapter 8.

See also MENUCOLOR, MENUDEFAULT, MENUITEM, and SUBMENU.

Description

This command loads memory-resident programs from CONFIG.SYS and avoids the allocation of unnecessary environment space.

Usage

install=[*drive:*][*path*]programname [*program parameters*]

Options and switches

[*drive:*] [*path*] *programname*

This option specifies the name of the memory-resident program.

[*program parameters*]

This option specifies the program's optional parameters and switches.

Remarks

Not all memory-resident programs function correctly when you load them with INSTALL.

Each INSTALL statement is processed after all the device drivers have been installed, regardless of the location of the INSTALL statement in CONFIG.SYS.

On 386 systems and higher, you should load programs into UMBs with LOADHIGH rather than into base memory with INSTALL.

Example

Use the following statement in CONFIG.SYS to install KEYB (the DOS keyboard manager):

```
install=c:\dos\keyb gr /e
```

Additional information

See also LOADHIGH.

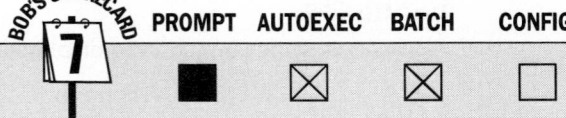

			PROMPT	AUTOEXEC	BATCH	CONFIG
INTERLNK			■	☒	☒	☐

Description

This command changes the drive assignments for two computers connected by way of InterLink.

INTERLNK.EXE is a dual-purpose program: You must first use it as a device driver in CONFIG.SYS, and then you can execute it as a program from the DOS prompt. See the following INTERLNK.EXE section for a description of the syntax when INTERLNK.EXE is used as a device driver.

Usage

```
interlnk [client[:]=[server][:]]
```

Options and switches

When you use INTERLNK without switches, it displays the status of the active InterLink drive assignments.

client[:]=

This option specifies the letter of the drive on the local (or client) system that is to represent a drive on the server. The drive must have been used in the initial configuration when the two computers were first linked. The colon (:) is optional but should be used for clarity.

[*server*][:]

This option specifies the name of the host drive on the InterLink server that is accessed when the client drive letter is used. If you use this switch, you terminate the client drive connection. The colon (:) is optional but should be used for clarity.

Remarks

To connect two computers, the client must load INTERLNK.EXE as a device in CONFIG.SYS, and the server must be running the INTERSVR command.

A LASTDRIVE statement must also be added to the CONFIG.SYS file if you want to assign a drive letter greater than D to one of the remote computer's drives.

Examples

Use the following command to display the status of all connected drives:

```
interlnk
```

To assign the drive letter D to the server's C drive, enter the following command:

```
interlnk d:=c:
```

To disconnect the drive D assignment on the local (client) system, enter the following command:

```
interlnk d:=
```

Additional information

If you're handy with hardware, you can make your own parallel cable for use with InterLink. Just be sure that the pins at one end are connected to the pins at the other as follows:

2–15
3–13
4–12
5–10
6–11
15–2
13–3
12–4
10–5
11–6
25–25

The cable set used with LapLink will also work with InterLink. For slower serial port communication, you can purchase a "null-modem" cable at many computer supply stores or Radio Shack.

 Refer to Appendix D for details about how to connect two computers with InterLink.

See also INTERLNK.EXE and INTERSVR.

INTERLNK.EXE	BOB'S SCORECARD 7	PROMPT	AUTOEXEC	BATCH	CONFIG
		☐	☐	☐	■

Description

This device driver is responsible for connecting two computers by way of serial or parallel ports.

Usage

```
device=[drive:][path]interlnk.exe [/drives:n] [/noprinter]
[/com[:][n or address] [/lpt[:][n or address] [/auto] [/noscan]
[/low] [/baud:rate] [/v]
```

Options and switches

[*drive:*][*path*]

This option identifies the directory in which INTERLNK.EXE is located, if it is not in the boot directory. By default, SETUP places INTERLNK.EXE in the \DOS directory.

[/drives:*n*]

By default, INTERLNK.EXE redirects only three server drives. When the server has drives other than drive C, use this switch to increase the number of supported drives. When you specify a value of zero, only server printers are available.

[/noprinter]

This switch instructs INTERLNK.EXE not to allow access to the server's printer or printers.

[/com[:][*n* or *address*]

By default, INTERLNK.EXE scans all serial and parallel ports looking for a connection to a remote computer. Use the /COM switch to instruct INTERLNK.EXE to scan only serial ports. INTERLNK.EXE uses a port (without scanning) if you specify it by number (COM1, for example) or by address (3F8).

[/lpt[:][*n* or *address*]

Use the /LPT switch to instruct INTERLNK.EXE to scan only parallel ports. INTERLNK.EXE uses a port (without scanning) if you specify it by number (LPT1, for example) or by address (378).

[/auto]

Use this switch to instruct INTERLNK.EXE to install only if it can establish an immediate connection with the server. If a server is not found, the device driver is not loaded, and no memory is wasted.

[/noscan]

This switch instructs INTERLNK.EXE to install without trying to connect to the server.

[/low]

By default, INTERLNK.EXE tries to load into UMBs. Use this switch to instruct INTERLNK.EXE to load into base memory.

```
[/baud:rate]
```

By default, a link is established with a 115200 baud rate. If you experience (intermittent) connection problems, use this switch to slow the data-transmission speed. The following values are accepted: 9600, 19200, 38400, 57600, and 115200.

```
[/v]
```

Use this switch if you experience timer conflicts when two computers are connected by way of COM ports.

Remarks

An active link can be established only when the server computer is running INTERSVR.

Because INTERLNK.EXE by default loads automatically into available UMBs, you do not have to load it by using DEVICEHIGH.

If you know which port the client is connected through (and you should if you wired them together), use the /COM*n* or /LPT*n* switch to prevent INTERLNK.EXE from scanning the ports. The system boots faster, and memory is saved. Use MSD to determine the explicit address for the serial and parallel ports.

If you do not plan to use the server's printer, specify /NOPRINTER to save memory.

If the server computer has more than one hard drive, remember to use the /DRIVES switch to enable links with all the server drives.

You cannot execute the following commands executed on a server drive: CHKDSK, DEFRAG, DISKCOMP, DISKCOPY, FDISK, FORMAT, MIRROR, SYS, UNDELETE, and UNFORMAT.

You can interlink two computers using different versions of DOS, but remember that early versions of DOS cannot access drives larger than 32MB.

Examples

Use the following statement to load INTERLNK.EXE with default settings:

```
device=c:\dos\interlnk.exe
```

Use the following statement in CONFIG.SYS to load the INTERLNK.EXE device driver and establish a link, without printer support, on COM1:

```
device=c:\dos\interlnk.exe /com1 /noprinter
```

Use the following statement to load INTERLNK.EXE and provide access to drives A through E on the server:

```
device=c:\dos\interlnk.exe /drives:5
```

Additional information

Refer to Appendix D for details about how to connect two computers with InterLink.

See also INTERLNK and INTERSVR.

Description

This command establishes a computer as a server in an InterLink session and makes the local drives and printers available to the remote computer.

Usage

```
intersvr [drive:] [/x=drive:] [/com[:][n or address]] [/lpt[:]
[n or address]] [/baud:rate] [/b] [/v]
```

Options and switches

[*drive:*]

By default, INTERSVR redirects all drives. Specify one or more individual drives to identify explicitly which drives should be redirected.

[/x=*drive:*]

This switch enables individual drives to remain private and not be redirected. You can specify multiple /X switches.

[/com[:][n or *address*]]

By default, INTERSVR scans all serial and parallel ports to look for a connection to a remote computer. Use the /COM switch to instruct INTERSVR to scan only serial ports. INTERSVR uses a port (without scanning) if you specify it by number (COM1, for example) or by address (3F8).

`[/lpt[:][n or address]]`

Use the /LPT switch to instruct INTERSVR to scan only parallel ports. INTERSVR uses a port (without scanning) if you specify it by number (LPT1, for example) or by address (378).

`[/baud:rate]`

By default, a link is established with a 115200 baud rate. If you experience (intermittent) connection problems, use this switch to slow the data-transmission speed. The following values are accepted: 9600, 19200, 38400, 57600, and 115200.

`[/b]`

This switch suppresses colors and uses only black and white. Use this option on monochrome or LCD systems.

`[/v]`

Use this switch if you experience timer conflicts when two computers are connected by way of COM ports.

Remarks

The *server computer* is the computer running INTERSVR, and the *client computer* is the connected computer (using INTERLNK.EXE as a device driver).

You can redirect to the client computer only standard removable drives (such as floppies and Bernoullies) and local hard disks. INTERSVR does not support network drives or CD-ROMs.

You can use the [*drive:*] switch to change the drive letter assignments on the client computer. Drives are assigned on the client computer in ascending alphabetical order and in the same sequence as they are specified on the INTERSVR command line.

When INTERSVR is run from within Windows, DOSSHELL, or any other multitasker, you cannot task switch (you must terminate INTERSVR to return to other tasks).

No special device drivers have to be installed on the computer running INTERSVR.

To exit from INTERSVR, press Alt-F4.

Examples

Use the following command to start INTERSVR in Automatic Mode, where all drives are redirected:

```
intersvr
```

Use the following command to establish a link on LPT1 and make drive C available to only the client:

```
intersvr c: /lpt1
```

Use the following command to set up an InterLink server, without enabling the floppy drives to be redirected:

```
intersvr /x=a: /x=b:
```

Use the following command to assign drive D on the server as drive D on the client (assuming that the client has only one hard drive) and to assign drive C on the server as E on the client:

```
intersvr d: c:
```

Additional information

Refer to Appendix D for details about how to connect two computers with InterLink.

See also INTERLNK and INTERLNK.EXE.

Extended use

You can use INTERSVR to install the INTERLNK.EXE file on the client system by using the /RCOPY switch as follows:

```
intersvr /rcopy
```

Description

This command configures the keyboard for international (non-USA) use.

Usage

```
keyb [xx[,[yyy] [,[drive:][path]filename.ext]]] [/e] [/id:nnn]
```

Because KEYB is a memory-resident program, INSTALL can load it in CONFIG.SYS by using the following syntax:

```
install=[drive:][path]keyb.com [xx[,[yyy]
[,[drive:][path]filename.ext]]] [/e] [/id:nnn]
```

Options and switches

When you execute KEYB with no switches, the active keyboard settings are displayed.

```
[xx]
```

This option specifies a two-character code that represents the country setting.

```
[yyy]
```

This option identifies the code page you want to use.

```
[drive:][path]filename.ext
```

This option identifies the keyboard-definition file. KEYB uses KEYBOARD.SYS by default if it is located in the search path.

```
[/e]
```

Use this switch if you have an Enhanced Keyboard installed on an 8086 system.

```
[/id:nnn]
```

This switch is used in countries in which more than one keyboard layout is supported (U.K., France, and Italy). This code specifies which keyboard layout to use.

Remarks

Run HELP KEYB to obtain an up-to-date list of all the supported codes.

KEYB returns the following ERRORLEVELs:

ERRORLEVEL	Message
0	Install successful
1	Invalid code or syntax used
2	Keyboard definition file was bad or could not be found
4	A keyboard or monitor error occurred
5	Unexpected error

Example

Use the following command to configure the keyboard for a French user and to use the alternative character set:

```
keyb fr,437
```

Additional information

Appendix C in *MS-DOS User's Guide* includes layouts for the 20 most common keyboards.

Refer to Chapter 9 in *MS-DOS User's Guide* for a thorough discussion of international configuration issues.

See also CHCP, COUNTRY, DISPLAY.SYS, MODE, and NLSFUNC.

Description

Every disk has a volume label. Use the LABEL command to change the volume label.

Usage

```
label [drive:][label]
```

Options and switches

When you use LABEL with no switches, it displays the current label (and serial number) and prompts for a new label. Press Ctrl-Break to abort.

[*drive:*]

This option specifies the drive whose label is changed. The current drive is selected by default.

[*label*]

This option specifies the new label. The label can be as long as 11 characters and is converted automatically to uppercase.

Remarks

The label is displayed when you list files with DIR or when you enter the VOL command. Also, the label is used as a security mechanism when you format a hard drive.

LABEL cannot be used on a SUBST drive.

Avoid using the following characters in a label:

$$* ? / \backslash | . , ; : + = [ ] \{ \} \& \wedge < > "$$

Examples

Use the following command to change the default drive label to *DRIVE C*:

```
label drive c
```

To change the label for drive D to CADDRIVE, enter the following command:

```
label d:caddrive
```

Additional information

See also DIR, FORMAT, and VOL.

Bob's Shareware Collection disks

CMFiler, from NoVaSoft, is an excellent file manager that provides a myriad of disk- and file-management functions. You can press V to modify a disk volume label.

BOB'S SCORECARD	PROMPT	AUTOEXEC	BATCH	CONFIG
LASTDRIVE 6	☐	☐	☐	■

Description

This command specifies how many logical drives DOS recognizes.

Usage

```
lastdrive=x
```

Options and switches

x

This option specifies a letter in the range from A to Z.

Remarks

You must use the LASTDRIVE statement in CONFIG.SYS. Try to situate LASTDRIVE before device drivers that consume drive letters.

By default, DOS supports one extra drive in addition to the physical drives.

LASTDRIVE typically is used on systems that connect to networks, use RAM disks, or that use InterLink to connect to another computer's drives.

If you specify too many drives, you waste memory at a rate of approximately 80 bytes per drive. Specify only the drives you need.

Example

To make sure that DOS supports drives up to the letter M, enter the following command:

```
lastdrive=M
```

Additional information

Refer to Chapter 5 for a discussion of other memory-saving techniques.

LH

See LOADHIGH.

	BOB'S SCORECARD	PROMPT	AUTOEXEC	BATCH	CONFIG
LOADFIX	5	■	⊠	■	☐

Description

This command corrects the problem of packed file corruption that some programs experience when DOS is loaded HIGH.

Usage

```
loadfix [drive:][path]programname [program parameters]
```

Options and switches

[*drive:*][*path*]*programname*

This option specifies the name of the program that cannot be run when DOS is loaded HIGH.

[*program parameters*]

This option specifies any parameters required by the problem program.

Remarks

Some (older) programs do not run if you load them in the first 64K of base memory, and they display a message that the packed file is corrupt. These programs expect DOS to occupy the first 64K of memory and become confused when they are loaded there.

This problem is not a significant one — I have been unable to find even one well-known package that requires this fix. It's there if you need it, however.

Example

If the program THINGY.EXE displays the message that the packed file is corrupt, try to execute it with LOADFIX:

```
loadfix thingy
```

Additional information

Refer to Chapter 5 for more information about loading DOS HIGH.

See also DOS=.

LOADHIGH   BOB'S SCORECARD **7**   PROMPT ☒   AUTOEXEC ■   BATCH ☒   CONFIG ☐

Description

In the same way you use DEVICEHIGH to load device drivers in upper memory, you use LOADHIGH to load programs in upper memory.

Usage

```
loadhigh [drive:][path]programname [program parameters]
```

Options and switches

[*drive:*][*path*]*programname*

This option specifies the name of the program that is loaded HIGH.

[*program parameters*]

This option specifies any parameters the program requires.

Remarks

DOS supports this command on only 386 systems and higher.

You can use DOS memory management software to load programs only if you include HIMEM.SYS, EMM386, and DOS=HIGH statements in CONFIG.SYS, as shown in the following example:

```
device=c:\dos\himem.sys
device=c:\dos\emm386 ram
dos=umb
```

If insufficient free upper memory exists, the program is loaded into conventional memory. To find out whether a program has been loaded HIGH, use the MEM /M command and specify the program name.

The following DOS programs are TSRs that can be loaded HIGH: APPEND, DOSKEY, GRAPHICS, KEYB, MODE, NLSFUNC, PRINT, and SHARE.

The DOS memory optimizer MEMMAKER automatically sets programs (in AUTOEXEC.BAT) to be loaded HIGH when appropriate.

LOADHIGH can be abbreviated as LH.

Example

Use the following command to load DOSKEY HIGH:

```
loadhigh c:\dos\doskey
```

Additional information

Refer to Chapter 5 for more information about upper memory.

See also DEVICEHIGH, DOS=, EMM386, HIMEM.SYS, and MEM.

Bob's Shareware Collection disks

UMB_DRV.SYS, from Christopher Blum, supports UMBs on 286 systems and provides advanced memory management for the PCs ranging from 8086 to 486.

Extended use

By default, LOADHIGH loads the program in the largest free area of upper memory, but this action is not always efficient. To provide more control over memory use, LOADHIGH supports the /L and /S switches also. You normally should leave to MEMMAKER the responsibility of determining the best settings for these switches.

Use the following syntax for these two advanced switches:

```
[[/l:region][,minsize][;region2][,minsize2]...]
```

You use the /L switch to control the region of UMBs in which the program is loaded. (The MEM /F command displays the free regions of upper memory. Device drivers may be too large to fit in one region.) The /L switch enables additional regions to be specified. You can use the MINSIZE parameter to ensure that adequate memory is allocated for the program — some programs require more memory during operation than when they are being initialized.

The following example configuration, thanks to MEMMAKER, uses the /L switch:

```
lh /l:1,6400 c:\dos\\doskey
lh /l:2,13984 c:\dos\share
```

Note: MEMMAKER uses the abbreviated name LH rather than LOADHIGH.

```
[/s]
```

The /S switch (for *SHRINK*) instructs LOADHIGH to reduce the allocated memory after the program has been initialized. You use this switch with programs that need more memory to load than they do during subsequent operation.

PROMPT **AUTOEXEC** **BATCH** **CONFIG**

Description

This command creates a new directory.

Usage

    md [*drive:*]*path*

or

    mkdir [*drive:*]*path*

Options and switches

    [*drive:*]

This option specifies the drive on which you want the directory to be created. If the drive is omitted, DOS tries to create the directory on the current drive.

    path

This option specifies the name of the new directory. Do not end the path with a backslash character. If the path begins with "dot dot" (..), the directory is created extending from the parent directory; if the path begins with a backslash (\), the new directory is created from the root directory; otherwise, the new directory is created from the current directory.

Remarks

DOS can create only one additional directory level at a time. If the directory \THIS did not exist, for example, MD could not, in a single statement, create the directory \THIS\THAT. You first must create the directory \THIS.

You can use the PROMPT and CD commands to identify the current directory.

Examples

To create the new directory NOTES below the DOS directory, enter the following command:

    md \dos\notes

To create a new directory STUFF on drive A when the default drive is C, enter the following command:

```
md a:\stuff
```

Use the following command to create the directory \123W\BUDGET when the current directory is \123W\SAMPLE:

```
md..\budget
```

Additional information

See also CD, PROMPT, RD, and TREE.

Bob's Shareware Collection disks

CMFiler, from NoVaSoft, provides an easy interface for managing, moving, and creating directories.

Description

This command displays valuable information that shows how your system's memory is utilized and how much free memory is available.

Usage

```
mem [/classify or /debug or /free or /module modulename]
[/page]
```

Options and switches

When you use MEM with no switches, a 15-line summary of the system's memory utilization is displayed.

```
[/classify]
```

This switch shows all the device drivers and programs loaded in memory, and details the base (conventional) and upper memory use by program and a summary of overall memory use. Because the output exceeds 25 lines on most systems, you should use /P to pause the display after each screen.

```
[/debug]
```

This switch provides detailed information about each device driver and program loaded in memory, in ascending memory order from conventional to upper memory. The starting segment of each program is shown in hexadecimal. Again, you should use the /P switch on most systems.

```
[/free]
```

This switch lists available areas of base and upper memory.

```
[/module modulename]
```

This switch provides memory-use statistics about an individual program. Use the /D or /C switch to get the device driver or program name.

```
[/page]
```

You can use this switch with any of the other memory switches to pause after each screen.

Examples

To display information about each program loaded in memory, enter the following command:

```
mem /c /p
```

To determine how much memory is used by the MSCDEX program, enter the following command:

```
mem /m mscdex
```

To see a summary of free memory, enter the following command:

```
mem /f
```

Additional information

Chapter 5 shows how MEM is used to help optimize memory use.

The DOS 6 diagnostic program MSD provides a map of upper memory use.

See also CHKDSK, DOS=, EMM386.EXE, HIMEM.SYS, and MEMMAKER.

To check whether a program is already loaded before executing a second copy, you can use the MEM /M progname command. If the program is not loaded already, MEM displays the string *progname* is not currently in memory. Although this test is useful from the DOS prompt, it does not help in batch files because MEM does not set an ERRORLEVEL.

The FIND command sets an ERRORLEVEL when a string is not found, however. By piping the output from MEM /C to FIND and testing for the string not currently, a batch file easily can test whether a program is loaded in memory.

The following simple batch file uses this technique to test for the DOSKEY, and loads it if it was not found in memory:

```
mem /m doskey | find "not currently"
if errorlevel 1 goto loaded
DOSKEY
goto quit
:loaded
echo DOSKEY was already loaded
:quit
```

You can use this clever trick to test for any program or device driver — yes, even Windows, DesqView, and DOSSHELL. No more need for assembly language programs to determine whether a program is loaded. This technique is explored more fully in Chapter 10.

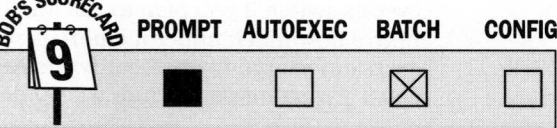

		PROMPT	AUTOEXEC	BATCH	CONFIG
MEMMAKER	BOB'S SCORECARD 9	■	☐	☒	☐

Description

This command assesses your memory configuration and modifies CONFIG.SYS and AUTOEXEC.BAT to make optimum use of memory.

Usage

```
memmaker [/b] [/batch] [/swap:drive] [/t] [/undo] [/w:n,m]
```

Options and switches

```
[/b]
```

The /B switch displays text in black and white. Use this switch on monochrome and LCD systems.

`[/batch]`

This switch runs MEMMAKER unattended. Whereas MEMMAKER normally prompts for confirmation of various actions, in Batch Mode MEMMAKER takes the default action without prompting.

`[/swap:`*drive*`]`

This switch advises MEMMAKER of the boot drive letter so that it optimizes the correct CONFIG.SYS and AUTOEXEC.BAT files. This switch is necessary only on systems that swap the boot drive at start-up. Although disk-compression utilities are the usual drive swappers, you do not need to use this switch with DBLSPACE or Stacker 2.0+.

`[/t]`

If you experience problems with MEMMAKER and are connected to a token-ring network, use the /T switch to disable token-ring detection.

`[/undo]`

Start MEMMAKER with the /UNDO switch to revert to your original system configuration (the configuration before MEMMAKER's last changes).

`[/w:`*n*`,`*m*`]`

Use this switch if you plan to run MEMMAKER in *Express* Mode and want to control how much upper memory is reserved for Windows' translation buffers. The *n* and *m* arguments identify the two buffer sizes in kilobytes. Use a value of /W:0,0 if you don't use Windows. By default, Express Mode uses /W:12,12.

Remarks

You can use this command only on 386 systems and higher.

MEMMAKER reboots the system. To avoid data loss, close all active applications, including Windows, before running MEMMAKER.

MEMMAKER can be executed in *Express* Mode or *Custom* Mode. In Express Mode, MEMMAKER makes all the decisions; in Custom Mode, you can choose from a variety of optimization options.

Examples

To use default switches to run MEMMAKER interactively, enter the following command:

```
memmaker
```

To run MEMMAKER and suppress all confirmation prompts, enter the following command:

```
memmaker /batch
```

To revert to the pre-MEMMAKER configuration, enter the following command:

```
memmaker /undo
```

Additional information

Chapter 5 includes a detailed explanation of how MEMMAKER works and series of tips for how to help MEMMAKER succeed.

See also EMM386, HIMEM.SYS, and MEM.

Bob's Shareware Collection disks

MEMMAKER runs only on 386 systems and higher. For advanced memory support on 286 systems, try UMB_DRV.SYS, from Christopher Blum.

Extended use

MEMMAKER supports the /SESSION switch, but it is used internally during the optimization process. You should not specify this switch when you execute MEMMAKER.

During the optimization process, MEMMAKER records program and device driver statistics in the MEMMAKER.STS file in the DOS directory. This ASCII file is not deleted when you exit from MEMMAKER. The file contains interesting insights and information about how your programs use memory.

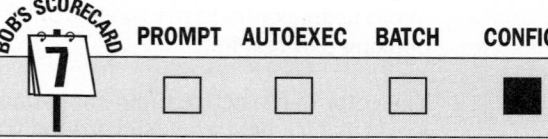

	PROMPT	AUTOEXEC	BATCH	CONFIG
MENUCOLOR	☐	☐	☐	■

Description

This statement enables you to configure the display colors for the multiconfiguration menu.

Usage

```
menucolor=f[,b]
```

Options and switches

f

This option specifies the menu foreground (text) color. Any value in the range from 0 to 15 is accepted. The default value is 7 (light gray).

[, b]

This option specifies the menu background color. Any value in the range from 0 to 15 is accepted. The default value is 0 (black).

Remarks

The MENUCOLOR statement must be placed in the [MENU] or SUBMENU block of CONFIG.SYS.

The following list shows the 16 color codes:

Code	Color	Code	Color
0	black	8	dark gray
1	blue	9	light blue
2	green	10	light green
3	cyan	11	light cyan
4	red	12	light red
5	magenta	13	light magenta
6	brown	14	yellow
7	light gray	15	white

Avoid using colors in the range from 8 to 15 for the background — flashing or blinking text results.

The color of the active topic bar cannot be configured and is always light gray. Avoid using a light gray background (code 7); otherwise, the highlighted bar is not visible.

The color settings apply to the output that AUTOEXEC.BAT commands and other DOS commands generate. Use CLS to clear the display and set the colors back to (boring) light gray on black.

Examples

Use the following CONFIG.SYS extract to set the menu color to yellow on blue:

```
[menu]
menucolor=14,1
menuitem=Plain,Totally Plain
menuitem=Gainers,Big Gainers
```

Use the following statement to set the foreground color to light red:

```
menucolor=12
```

Additional information

Refer to Chapter 8 for a thorough discussion of multiconfiguration options.

See also MENUDEFAULT and MENUITEM.

Description

This statement sets the default item in a multiconfiguration menu and option-ally the number of seconds to wait for user input before applying the default.

Usage

```
menudefault=blockname[,timeout]
```

Options and switches

blockname

This option specifies the name of the default menu block. This block is high-lighted when the menu is first displayed. BLOCKNAME must correspond to a name specified by the MENUITEM statement, but the comparison is not case sensitive.

[, *timeout*]

This option specifies the number of seconds to wait for user input before pro-ceeding with the default block. Any value in the range from 0 to 90 is accepted. A multiconfiguration menu does not have much value if you specify a time-out value of 0: The instant the menu is displayed, the default option is selected, and you have no opportunity to make a selection.

Remarks

If you choose to use it, the MENUDEFAULT statement must be located in the [MENU] block or a SUBMENU block. If MENUDEFAULT is not specified, DOS sets the default to item 1.

I use a time-out value of nine seconds, which gives me enough time to make a choice, even at 7 a.m. If you change selections by using the cursor keys before the timeout has expired, DOS waits indefinitely for a selection.

Example

The following CONFIG.SYS extract sets the default selection to the GAINERS block and waits for nine seconds for user input:

```
[menu]
menucolor=14,1
menuitem=Plain,Totally Plain
menuitem=Gainers,Big Gainers
menudefault=Gainers,9
```

Additional information

Refer to Chapter 8 for a thorough discussion of multiconfiguration options.

See also MENUCOLOR and MENUITEM.

	BOB'S SCORECARD	PROMPT	AUTOEXEC	BATCH	CONFIG
MENUITEM	8	☐	☐	☐	■

Description

This statement identifies a menu option on a multiconfiguration menu.

Usage

```
menuitem=blockname[ ,item description]
```

Options and switches

blockname

This option specifies the name of the block of configuration commands to be executed, if the item is selected. Elsewhere in the file, a unique block heading must have the format [*blockname*]. *blockname* is not case sensitive.

[, *item description*]

By default, the item description is the blockname. You can optionally specify an item description, which can include spaces and is displayed in the same case in which it is entered. The text can contain as many as 70 characters.

Remarks

Do not assign a blockname of *menu* or *common* because these blocknames are reserved for other uses. Blocknames may not include the characters \ / , ; = [ ] or the space character.

Every item in the menu automatically has a number prefix, and you can have up to nine menu items in each menu.

In addition to processing the commands located in the [*blockname*] block, DOS processes commands located in any blocks with the name *[common]*.

If DOS can't find a block with the specific blockname, the item will not appear in your menu.

Examples

The following CONFIG.SYS extract defines a menu on which the blockname is used as the description:

```
[menu]
menucolor=14,1
menuitem=Frugal
menuitem=Everything
menudefault=Everything,9
. . . . .
[frugal]
. . . . .
[everything]
. . . . .
```

A topic description has been added to the following similar menu:

```
[menu]
menucolor=14,1
menuitem=Frugal,Max memory but no CD or network
menuitem=Everything,All optional drivers loaded
menudefault=Everything,9
. . . . .
[frugal]
. . . . .
[everything]
. . . . .
```

Additional information

You should use the SUBMENU command if the item needs to display a secondary configuration menu.

Refer to Chapter 8 for more information on MENUITEM.

See also MENUCOLOR, MENUDEFAULT, and SUBMENU.

Note: MIRROR is not officially part of DOS 6. The DOS 5 version of MIRROR is, however, included on the DOS 6 Supplemental programs disk, available from Microsoft. If you have upgraded from DOS 5, you can use the copy of MIRROR that came with it — it should still be in your DOS directory.

Description

The deletion tracking feature provided by MIRROR (using the /T switch) is now provided by UNDELETE, so is not documented here. However, every DOS 6 user should use MIRROR to save a copy of the FAT and root directory for each hard disk. In addition, MIRROR should be used with the /PARTN switch to save a copy of the hard disk partition table.

Usage

```
mirror [drive:[....]] [/1]
```

or

```
mirror /partn
```

Options and switches

When you use MIRROR without any switches, the FAT and root directory details are saved for the default drive.

    drive:[. . .]

This option identifies one or more drives whose FAT and root directory details will be saved in hidden files.

```
[/1]
```

By default, if MIRROR sees an existing copy of MIRROR.FIL (the hidden file containing all the FAT and root directory data), it will copy the file to MIRROR.BAK, before creating a new MIRROR.FIL file. The /1 switch instructs MIRROR not to keep a backup copy, that is, to keep only one file.

```
/partn
```

This switch instructs MIRROR to make a copy of the hard disk partition table and save it to a diskette.

Remarks

The MIRROR command creates vital data recovery information and should be used in AUTOEXEC.BAT to make copies of the partition table and copies of the FAT and root directory for each hard drive.

If the /1 switch is used, MIRROR will delete the file MIRROR.BAK if it finds one.

You can determine whether a disk contains the hidden MIRROR files by using the UNFORMAT command with the /J switch and pressing Esc when prompted.

Examples

Use the following command to create the hidden MIRROR files that record the FAT and root directory of the default drive:

```
mirror
```

To make a copy of the FAT and root directory for drives C, D, and E, enter the following command:

```
mirror c: d: e:
```

To make a copy of the hard disk partition table, enter the following command:

```
mirror /partn
```

Additional information

Refer to Chapter 3 for a full explanation of how the MIRROR files are used during an UNFORMAT operation.

See also FORMAT, UNDELETE, and UNFORMAT.

MKDIR

See MD.

MODE

Description

For clarity, the MODE command is divided into the following subcommands:

- mode com*n*
- mode *device* CP
- mode *device* /Status
- mode *display*
- mode lpt*n*
- mode con

MODE COM*n*

Description

This command sets the communication settings for a serial port.

Usage

    mode com*n*[:] [*b*,[*p*[,*d*[,*s*[,*r*]]]]]

or (in longhand)

    mode com*n*[:] [baud=*b*] [parity=*p*] [data=*d*] [stop=*s*] [retry=*r*]

Options and switches

```
comn[:]
```

This option specifies the serial port whose settings are adjusted. MODE supports four serial ports (COM1, COM2, COM3, and COM4).

```
[baud=b]
```

This option specifies the port's data-transmission rate, where *b* is the first two digits of the baud rate. The following table lists the supported rates.

Code	Baud rate
11	110
15	150
30	300
60	600
12	1,200
24	2,400
48	4,800
96	9,600
19	19,200

```
[parity=p]
```

This option specifies the method used for parity checking. *p* can be one of the following letters: N (none), E (even), O (odd), M (mark), or S (space). Parity checking is set to *even* by default.

```
[data=d]
```

This option indicates how many bits comprise each character. The value is 7 by default, but a value in the range from 5 to 8 is accepted.

```
[stop=s]
```

This option indicates how many bits define the end of each character. The value is 2 by default (or 1, at the slowest rate of 110 baud), and the values 1, 1.5, and 2 are accepted.

`[retry=r]`

This option specifies how transmission errors should be handled. *r* can be one of the following characters:

Letter	Action
E	Returns an error when the port is busy
B	Returns the busy code when the port is busy
P	Keeps retransmitting until the printer accepts the data
R	Returns the ready code when the port is busy
N	Ignores a busy port and takes no action

Remarks

You can omit parameters by using the abbreviated syntax, but you must use commas as placeholders to indicate which parameters are null.

If any of the parameters are omitted, the preceding setting for the specified serial port is used.

Examples

Use the following command to set the COM2 port communication parameters:

```
mode com2: baud=2400 parity=n data=8 stop=1 retry=p
```

You can execute the same command in abbreviated form as follows:

```
mode com2:2400,n,8,1,p
```

You can later modify the same port to not retry with the following command:

```
mode com2:,,,,n
```

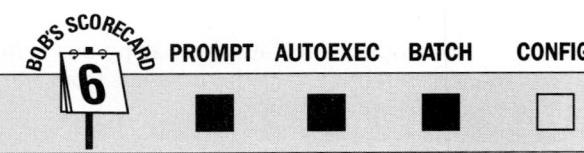

| | PROMPT | AUTOEXEC | BATCH | CONFIG |

MODE CON

Description

This command adjusts the keyboard's typematic rate.

Usage

```
mode con[:] [rate=r delay=d]
```

Options and switches

```
[rate=r]
```

This option specifies how quickly additional characters are entered when a key is held down. The rate approximates to characters per second, and a value in the range from 1 to 32 is accepted. The default is 20.

```
[delay=d]
```

This option sets the amount of time a key must be held down before additional characters are automatically entered. The following values are accepted: 1 (0.25 second), 2 (0.5 second), 3 (0.75 second), and 4 (1 second).

Remarks

Some older systems do not allow the typematic rate to be adjusted.

Example

Use the following command to set the keyboard at full throttle:

```
mode con: rate=32 delay=1
```

BOB'S SCORECARD	PROMPT	AUTOEXEC	BATCH	CONFIG
MODE *device* **CP** 6	■	■	■	☐

Description

This command manages the code pages for the monitor, keyboard, and printer.

Usage

The MODE *DEVICE* CP command has the following four primary formats:

```
mode device cp prepare=((yyy [...]) [drive:][path][filename.ext])
```

```
mode device cp select=yyy
```

```
mode device cp refresh
```

```
mode device cp /status
```

Options and switches

   device

This option specifies the console or printer device. The following devices are supported: CON, LPT1, LPT2, and LPT3.

   prepare ((*yyy* [...]) [*drive:*][*path*][*filename.ext*])

A code page must be prepared before it can be selected. *yyy* identifies the appropriate code page. Execute HELP MODE to display the list of supported code pages. Optionally, specify the name of the code-page information file — these files are installed in the DOS directory and have an extension of CPI.

   select=*yyy*

After a code page is prepared, you can select it with the SELECT switch.

   refresh

This option re-installs a code page after it has been hosed by a rogue program.

   /status

This switch displays information about the installed code pages.

Remarks

In general, use CHCP to change the code page in preference to the MODE command. CHCP changes all devices in one command and ensures that the country and code-page settings match.

The following table details the DOS 6 code-page information files located in the DOS directory.

File	Description
EGA.CPI	For EGA displays on PS/2s
4201.CPI	IBM Proprinter models 4201 and 4202
4208.CPI	IBM Proprinter models 4207 and 4208
5202.CPI	IBM Quietwriter III
LCD.CPI	IBM PC Convertible liquid crystal display

Example

Use the following commands with MODE to prepare the code page and CHCP to activate the code page:

```
mode con cp prepare=((863)c:\dos\ega.cpi)
chcp 863
```

Additional information

See also CHCP and NLSFUNC.

MODE *device* **/STATUS**   BOB'S SCORECARD 5   PROMPT ■ AUTOEXEC ■ BATCH ■ CONFIG □

Description

This command instructs MODE to display information about an individual device or all devices.

Usage

```
mode [device] /status
```

Options and switches

[*device*]

This option specifies the name of a device (COM1, COM2, COM3, COM4, CON, LPT1, LPT2, LPT3, or PRN). If no device is specified, the status of all devices is displayed.

Remarks

Use the I MORE pipe to pause the display after each screen.

Examples

Use the following command to display the status of all devices:

```
mode /status | more
```

Use the following command to display the status of LPT1:

```
mode lpt1 /status
```

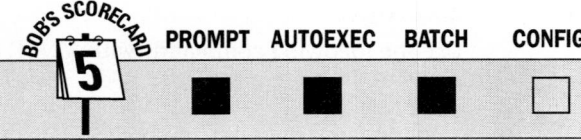

BOB'S SCORECARD 5   PROMPT   AUTOEXEC   BATCH   CONFIG

MODE *display*

Description
This command sets the active display-adapter configuration.

Usage
The MODE DISPLAY subcommand has the following three formats:

```
mode [display] [,shift[,t]]

mode [display] [,n]

mode con[:] [cols=c] [lines=n]
```

Options and switches

```
[display] [,shift[,t]]
```

display can have one of the following values:

Value	Description
40 or 80	Sets the number of characters across the screen (columns)
bw40 or bw80	Sets the number of characters and forces the display mode to black and white
co40 or co80	Sets the number of characters and forces the display mode to color
mono	Sets the number of characters to 80 on a monochrome display adapter

shift shifts the display to the left or right on CGA systems. Accepted values are L (left) and R (right).

```
t
```

This option displays a test pattern on CGA systems.

```
con[:] [cols=c] [lines=n]
```

This option sets the number of characters per line (cols) and lines per screen (lines). *c* can have a value of 40 or 80. *n* can be 25, 43 (on EGA and VGA systems), or 50 (on VGA systems). You can use this MODE command format only on systems on which ANSI.SYS is installed.

Remarks

One of my favorite uses for the MODE co80 command is to restore the cursor when a program has crashed and the cursor has disappeared. You can use the same command to return the system to Text Mode when a graphics program crashes and drops you to DOS in Graphics Mode.

If you have vision problems or have difficulty reading the display, you may benefit from using the MODE co40 command to switch to 40-character mode.

Many contemporary programs (especially full-screen applications) ignore the active mode setting.

Examples

To switch to black-and-white mode with 40 characters per line, enter the following command:

```
mode bw40
```

If ANSI.SYS is installed, you can enter the following command on a VGA system to switch to 50-line mode:

```
mode con: cols=80 lines=50
```

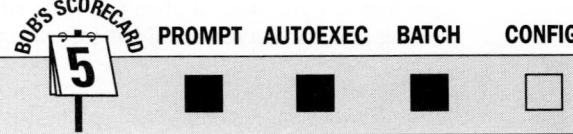

MODE LPT*n*

BOB'S SCORECARD 5 — PROMPT ■ AUTOEXEC ■ BATCH ■ CONFIG □

Description

This command redirects printer output from a parallel port to a serial port or reconfigures a parallel port.

Usage

```
mode lptn[:]=comn[:]
```

Options and switches

```
lptn[:]
```

This option specifies the parallel port whose output is redirected to the serial port. Valid values are LPT1, LPT2, and LPT3.

```
comn[:]
```

This option specifies the serial port that receives the output sent to the parallel port. Valid values are COM1, COM2, COM3, and COM4.

Remarks

In most cases, you must use MODE com*n* to configure the serial port before redirecting an LPT port to it.

Example

Use the following command to set COM2 to 9600 baud with even parity, and then redirect LPT2 output to it:

```
mode com1 96,e,,,p
mode lpt2=com2
```

Extended use

The MODE lpt*n* command also is used, although rarely, to reconfigure a parallel port, by using the following syntax:

```
mode lptn[:] [c][,[l][,r]]
```

or by using the following longhand syntax:

```
mode lptn[:] [cols=c] [lines=l] [retry=r]
```

c specifies the number of characters per line and can be either 80 or 132. *l* specifies the number of lines per inch and can be 6 or 8. *r* specifies the retry setting and can have one of the following values:

Value	Description
e	Returns "error" on a busy port
p	Keeps retrying until the printer accepts the character
r	Returns ready on busy port
n	No retry action (default)

BOB'S SCORECARD   7

	PROMPT	AUTOEXEC	BATCH	CONFIG
MORE	■	⊠	⊠	□

Description

This command pauses the output from a command-line utility after every screen (it stops text from scrolling off the top of the screen).

Usage

command [command–parameters] | more

or (to display a file's contents)

more < [drive:][path]filename.ext

Options and switches

command

This option specifies any command-line program whose output might fill the screen.

[command–parameters]

Optional parameters required by the command-line program.

[drive:][path]filename.ext

This option specifies the name of an ASCII file whose contents you want to view.

Remarks

Any lines longer than the display width (usually 80 but can be 40) are wrapped to the next line.

When the screen has been filled, MORE displays this string:

— MORE —

Press any standard key to see the next screen. MORE does not pause the output for the last partial screen.

The commands DIR and MEM provide the /P switch to pause the display after each screen to avoid the need to use MORE with them.

Examples

To display the status of all devices and pause after each screen, enter the following command:

mode /status | more

To view the contents of the file READ.ME, enter the following command:

more < read.me

Additional information

MORE is used often with the following DOS commands: ATTRIB, MODE /STATUS, TREE, and TYPE.

Bob's Shareware Collection disks

The outstanding LIST program, from Buerg Software, is the champion of file viewers. You can page up *and* page back through a file, search for text, view in hexadecimal, display a ruler, leave, and jump to bookmarks.

CMFILER, the first-class file manager from NoVaSoft, has the capability to view files.

Description

This command moves files from one path to another and renames directories.

Usage

    move [drive:][path]filemask[, [[drive:][path]filemask[...]] target

Options and switches

[*drive:*][*path*]*filemask*

This option identifies the name of the source file to be moved. Wildcards are not supported. This option can also be a directory name if the intent of the MOVE operation is to rename a directory; you must specify this switch.

[, [[*drive:*][*path*]*filemask*[...]]

You can specify additional source files, with each filename being separated by a comma.

target

This option identifies the target location where the files will be copied. The target location can be a drive letter followed by a colon, a directory name, or a combination of the two. If a single source file or directory is specified, to re-name the file or directory you can specify a new filename or directory as the target.

Remarks

Unlike COPY, the MOVE command requires both a source and target to be specified on the command line.

If you're moving a file to a new path on the same drive, MOVE will just modify the file's directory entries to relocate it in the new path; the file's data remains in the same physical location on the disk. This process is much faster than actually moving the file's data.

When using MOVE to rename directories, the source and target directories must both stem from the same parent directory — you cannot use MOVE to restructure the directory hierarchy.

Examples

Use the following command to move all the files with the WK1 extension from the current directory to the directory C:\OLDFILES:

```
move *.wk1 c:\oldfiles
```

To move the files HIGH.DBF and LOW.DBF from the current directory to the D:\DBASE\PLAN directory, enter the following command:

```
move high.dbf,low.dbf d:\dbase\plan
```

Use the following command to move the file WELCOME.DOC from the directory C:\AMIPRO\DOCS to the directory C:\AMIPRO\SEMINAR and rename the file HOWDY.DOC:

```
move c:\amipro\docs\welcome.doc c:\amipro\seminar\howdy.doc
```

To rename the directory D:\DBASE\FILES\BUDGET to D:\DBASE\FILES\FORECAST, enter the following command:

```
move d:\dbase\files\budget d:\dbase\files\forecast
```

Additional Information

Refer to Chapter 2 for a discussion of MOVE.

See also COPY, XCOPY.

Bob's Shareware Collection disks

PocketD, from Pocketware, can move files with far more flexibility than DOS can, and it includes the following features: multiple wildcards are supported;

files can be selected based on file size, date stamp, and even contents; optional prompts before overwriting files, and much more. PCOPY from Patri-Soft and CMFILER from NoVaSoft also provide excellent file moving options.

PROMPT AUTOEXEC BATCH CONFIG

MSAV

Description

This command runs the full-screen utility Microsoft Anti-Virus, which scans drives for viruses and optionally removes them.

Usage

```
msav [drive: or /a or /l] [/s or /c] [/r] [/n or /p [/f]]
[/video] [/videomode]
```

Options and switches

When you run MSAV with no switches, it displays a full-screen menu.

[*drive:*]

This option specifies the drive to scan for viruses. If no drive is specified, the default drive is scanned.

[/a]

Use /A to scan all drives except floppies.

[/l]

Use /L to scan all drives except network drives.

[/s]

The /S switch scans for viruses but does not correct them.

[/c]

The /C switch scans and cleans (removes) viruses.

[/r]

This switch instructs MSAV to create a detailed report in the ASCII file MSAV.RPT in the root directory of the scanned drive.

[/n]

This switch runs MSAV in command-line mode (rather than the default full-screen mode) and automatically creates the MSAV.RPT file in the root directory. The name of the active file is displayed during the scanning procedure.

[/p]

The /P switch runs MSAV in command-line mode also. This switch is similar to /N, but the messages are displayed on-screen rather than written to a report file.

[/f]

You can use this switch in conjunction with /N or /P to suppress the display of filenames during the scanning procedure.

[/video]

This switch instructs MSAV to display a list of all the optional command-line switches used to control the video display characteristics.

[/*videomode*]

This switch sets the display characteristics in full-screen mode. Run MSAV /VIDEO to see a list of valid switches.

Remarks

By default, MSAV creates a checksum file named CHKLIST.MS in every directory of the scanned drive. This file is used to record a unique value for every file. During subsequent virus checks, MSAV recomputes the checksum and compares it to the value stored in CHKLIST.MS; if the checksum value is different, the file has been modified.

The CHKLIST.MS file provides an added level of security. If you don't want hundreds of CHKLIST.MS files scattered throughout your system, however, select Options from the MSAV main menu and uncheck the Create New Checksums option.

If you have installed the Windows version, MWAV, you can delete all the CHKLIST.MS files by selecting the menu option Scan Delete CHKLIST Files. Alternatively, use the PocketD shareware program to delete them in one command.

All the optional MSAV settings are stored in the ASCII file MSAV.INI in the DOS directory. You can instruct MSAV to access the MSAV.INI file in a specific directory by setting the environment variable MSDOSDATA equal to the specific directory in which the active INI file is located (SET MSDOSDATA=D:\VIRUS, for example).

Examples

To start MSAV in interactive full-screen mode, enter the following command:

```
msav
```

Enter the following command to scan but not remove viruses on all drives except floppies:

```
msav /s /a
```

Additional information

Refer to Chapter 3 for a thorough discussion of viruses.

If you have installed the Windows utilities for DOS 6, you may prefer to use MWAV, the Windows version of MSAV. It provides all the same functionality but takes full advantage of Windows' rich graphical environment.

Description

This command runs the full-screen utility Microsoft Backup, which backs up and restores copies of your files.

Usage

```
msbackup [setup filename] [/bw or /lcd or /mda]
```

Options and switches

When MSBACKUP is run with no switches, a full-screen menu is displayed.

[*setup filename*]

This option specifies the name of an MSBACKUP setup file (with the extension SET) that details the files to be backed up and the configuration. If you do not specify a setup file, DEFAULT.SET is used.

[/bw]

This switch instructs MSBACKUP to suppress colors and use black and white.

[/lcd]

This switch instructs MSBACKUP to use a color scheme suitable for LCD laptop displays.

[/mda]

Use this switch on monochrome systems.

Remarks

For the first time in the history of DOS, a useful file-backup utility is included with the operating system. Good-bye, BACKUP — hello, MSBACKUP.

MSBACKUP is a full-screen backup utility for saving *and* restoring files. It can perform full backups, incremental backups, backups based on date, or backups of only selected files.

You control the backup settings with a backup SET file. Use the File menu to save the current configuration in a SET file or to load a configuration from a SET file. MSBACKUP searches for SET files in three locations:

1. The environment, to see whether a path is specified for the MSDOSDATA variable

2. The MSBACKUP directory

3. The default directory

MSBACKUP contains a wealth of on-line help. Press F1 at the menu to browse through the help text.

You can use the old-style RESTORE program to restore files backed up with old versions of BACKUP, but RESTORE is *not* used with MSBACKUP data. MSBACKUP uses a special catalog file when it restores files. One copy of the catalog is stored on the last disk of the backup, and another is stored by default in the DOS directory. Use the Backup Set Catalog list box to select a catalog. If you cannot find the backup catalog, you can instruct MSBACKUP to rebuild the catalog by selecting the Catalo**g** option from the **R**estore menu.

MSBACKUP does not back up to tape, but you can back up to any disk drive, hard disk, or network drive.

On systems on which Windows 3.0 or higher is installed, SETUP adds the file VFINTD.386 to the system directory. This file enables MSBACKUP to be run in a DOS session within Windows in Enhanced Mode. If you are using Windows, however, use MWBACKUP rather than MSBACKUP.

MSBACKUP provides no switches for automating the backup execution — you must run the full-screen application and make menu selections.

MSBACKUP must be started from a hard disk.

Examples

Use the following command to run MSBACKUP and present the main menu:

```
msbackup
```

If you have a backup SET file called BUDGET.SET, you can enter the following command to load the configuration file automatically:

```
msbackup budget.set
```

Additional information

MWBACKUP, the Windows version of MSBACKUP, provides the same features and capabilities. Refer to Chapter 3 for a full discussion of the backup tools.

If MSBACKUP reports the error that the DMA buffer size is too small, use the D=96 switch with EMM386.EXE to increase the DMA buffer size, and try again.

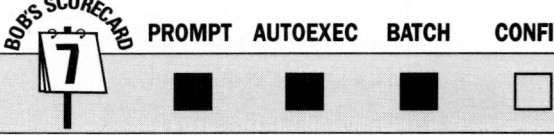

Description

MSCDEX (short for *Microsoft CD-ROM Extensions*) makes a CD-ROM behave like a standard disk device and assigns a logical drive letter to the CD-ROM drive. Most CD-ROM drives can only be accessed after MSCDEX has been installed.

Usage

```
mscdex [/e] [/k] [/s] [/v] [/d:name[...]] [/l:drive]
[/m:buffers]
```

Options and switches

`[/e]`

This switch instructs MSCDEX to store the CD-ROM cache buffers in expanded memory.

`[/k]`

Use this switch when accessing CD-ROM disks that contain files stored using the Japanese Kanji format. It's not a switch I use everyday.

`[/s]`

Short for *share*, /S allows the CD-ROM to be accessed by other network users, provided you are running network software like Windows For Workgroups.

`[/v]`

Short for *verbose*, /V instructs MSCDEX to display memory usage statistics when it loads.

`[/d:`*name*`[...]]`

This switch specifies the name of the CD-ROM device driver loaded in CONFIG.SYS. Normally, you would only specify a single /D switch, but if you have multiple CD-ROM drives, you should specify each device's driver name.

`[/l:`*drive*`]`

This switch specifies the drive letter that will be assigned to the drive. By default, MSCDEX assigns the next available drive letter.

`[/m:`*buffers*`]`

This switch specifies the number of sectors to cache. Each sector consumes a little under 2K of memory, and the default value is 10 sectors. There are only marginal performance advantages in using a higher value.

Remarks

MSCDEX can be loaded high with the LOADHIGH (or LH) command to save base memory.

MSCDEX will only load successfully if a CD-ROM device driver (supplied by the hardware vendor) is also loaded in CONFIG.SYS. Most CD-ROM device drivers support a `/d:`*name* switch to assign the device driver a unique name. The device driver name specified in CONFIG.SYS must correspond exactly with the name specified using MSCDEX's /D switch. If a matching device driver was not successfully loaded, MSCDEX will fail and display the message

```
No valid CD-ROM device driver selected.
```

Note: CONFIG.SYS may include two device drivers that appear related to the CD-ROM. The second device driver provides the sound support.

To conserve memory, configure EMM386 to support expanded memory and specify the /E switch to instruct MSCDEX to install the CD-ROM buffers in expanded memory. Using default settings, MSCDEX will consume 35K of memory (high or base), but when /E is specified, the memory usage drops to 16K.

Examples

If a CD-ROM device driver was installed in CONFIG.SYS using the /D:MSCD001 switch, use the following command to install MSCDEX, using default settings:

```
mscdex /d:mscd001
```

Use the following command to install MSCDEX with 15 expanded memory sector buffers and display verbose installation messages:

```
mscdex /d:mscd001 /m:15 /e /v
```

Use the following command to make the CD-ROM drive accessible from other workstations on the network and install the buffers in expanded memory:

```
mscdex /d:mscd001 /s /e
```

Additional information

*See also DE*VICE, EMM386, LOADHIGH, MEMMAKER.

			PROMPT	AUTOEXEC	BATCH	CONFIG
MSD		9	■	⊠	■	☐

Description

This command analyzes and reports on your detailed system configuration.

Usage

MSD is used interactively with the following syntax:

```
msd [/i] [/b]
```

or MSD can create reports by using the following syntax:

```
msd [/i] [/f[drive:][path]filename.ext] [/p[drive:][path]filename.ext]
[/s[drive:][path][filename.ext]]
```

Options and switches

```
[/i]
```

This switch instructs MSD not to scan the hardware. Use this option when MSD cannot load and hangs while it is examining your system.

```
[/b]
```

This switch instructs MSD to suppress colors and use black and white.

```
[/f [drive:][path]filename.ext]
```

This switch instructs MSD to create an ASCII file that reports your system's details. Before the report is created, MSD prompts for your name, address, and a one-line comment. These details are written at the top of the report.

```
[/p [drive:][path]filename.ext]
```

Like /F, the /P switch instructs MSD to record its findings in a file, but it doesn't prompt for name and address details.

```
[/s [drive:][path][filename.ext]]
```

This switch writes a summary of your system's configuration. The output is written to the display by default, but you can save it in a file by specifying a filename.

Remarks

MSD was first released (but not documented) with Microsoft Word 5.5, and later an enhanced version was released with Windows 3.1. It proved to be such a valuable tool that Microsoft enhanced it still further and included it in DOS 6.

MSD is designed as a diagnostics tool because it provides detailed information about your system's configuration. On one of my systems, it generates more than 40 pages of statistics.

The /F*filename* switch is well suited to those of us involved in telephone technical support — you can instruct a remote user to run MSD with the /F switch, enter details, and then send the file to you. The file contains your clients' details and information about the following topics:

- Computer and BIOS details
- Memory
- Video
- Network
- Operating system
- Environment settings
- Mouse
- Game adapters
- Disk drives
- LPT ports
- COM ports
- IRQ settings
- TSR programs
- Device drivers

It even includes copies of the computer's key configuration files, including CONFIG.SYS, AUTOEXEC.BAT, SYSTEM.INI, WIN.INI, PROTOCOL.INI, and DBLSPACE.INI.

When you run MSD interactively, it first snoops around your hardware to assess the system configuration. On some systems, this process can take as long as a couple of minutes. Be patient.

If MSD does not load, use the /I switch and select each category individually. Eventually, you select the category that is causing the problem, and the system hangs. You then know the area of your system to investigate.

Examples

To run MSD interactively and select information from a menu, enter the following command:

```
msd
```

To prompt for name and address details and then write your computer details to the file MSD.OUT, enter the following command:

```
msd /f msd.out
```

Additional information

Refer to Chapter 2 for more information on MSD.

See also CHKDSK, MODE /STATUS, and MEM.

	BOB'S SCORECARD	PROMPT	AUTOEXEC	BATCH	CONFIG
MWAV	9	☐	☐	☐	☐

Description

This command is the Windows version of MSAV. Refer to the MSAV section for more information.

	BOB'S SCORECARD	PROMPT	AUTOEXEC	BATCH	CONFIG
MWAVTSR	7	☐	☐	☐	☐

Description

This command provides Windows support for messages generated by VSAFE. You should load it from Windows when VSAFE is installed. See VSAFE for more information.

BOB'S SCORECARD 9 | PROMPT | AUTOEXEC | BATCH | CONFIG

MWBACKUP

Description

This command is the Windows version of MSBACKUP.

The first time you run MWBACKUP, it invokes an automatic test procedure. This procedure involves checking the DMA integrity and performs a small backup-and-restore operation to ensure that everything is functioning reliably. Have two disks ready for the small backup — use the disk drive you will select for real backups.

MWBACKUP and MSBACKUP are compatible. See MSBACKUP for more information.

If MWBACKUP reports the error that the DMA buffer size is too small, add a SETDMABUFFERS=96 entry in SYSTEM.INI to increase the DMA buffer size.

BOB'S SCORECARD 9 | PROMPT | AUTOEXEC | BATCH | CONFIG

MWUNDEL

Description

You use this Windows version of UNDELETE to recover accidentally deleted files and directories.

Usage

```
mwundel
```

Options and switches

None.

Remarks

When you select the DOS utilities for Windows during SETUP, a Microsoft Tools group is created automatically. Double-click the Undelete icon to run MWUNDEL.

Both UNDELETE and MWUNDEL can perform three types of file undeletion: sentry, tracker, and DOS. Refer to the UNDELETE section for more details.

In addition to the features described in UNDELETE, MWUNDEL can search an entire drive for a deleted file.

When a directory is selected, MWUNDEL automatically displays a list of all the deleted files and a statement of the files' condition. This condition gives an indication of the chances for successful undeletion and has one of the following values:

Value	*Message*
Perfect	The file can be undeleted automatically.
Excellent	Because all the files clusters are consecutive and none of them have been used, in all likelihood the file can be recovered successfully.
Good	It appears that all the file's clusters are available, although they are not contiguous. You should be able to undelete the file.
Poor	The first file cluster is being used by another file. The chances of recovery are slim to none.
Destroyed	All the file's clusters have been reused.
Recovered	You have undeleted the file in this session.

MWUNDEL cannot undelete files categorized as poor or destroyed. Try the DOS command UNDELETE on these files.

Additional information

Chapter 3 explains a number of ways to guard against data loss.

See also UNDELETE.

	BOB'S SCORECARD	PROMPT	AUTOEXEC	BATCH	CONFIG
NLSFUNC	6	☒	■	☒	☒

Description

This command provides *N*ational *L*anguage *S*upport by enabling code-page switching.

Usage

From the command line, NLSFUNC has the following syntax:

```
nlsfunc [[drive:][path]filename.ext]
```

Because NLSFUNC is a TSR, you can install it from CONFIG.SYS by using the INSTALL command as follows:

```
install=[idrive:][path]nlsfunc.exe [[drive:][path]filename.ext]
```

Options and switches

```
[[drive:][path]filename.ext]
```

This option specifies the name of the country driver. DOS provides the COUNTRY.SYS driver for this function. Alternatively, you can use the COUNTRY= directive before the NLSFUNC entry to identify the location and name of the country driver.

Remarks

You should be concerned about this command only if you are configuring DOS for international use.

On 386 systems and higher, you can use the LOADHIGH directive in AUTOEXEC.BAT to load NLSFUNC into UMBs. NLSFUNC uses about 3K of memory.

Example

Use the following statement from AUTOEXEC.BAT to install national language support:

```
nlsfunc
```

Additional information

Refer to Chapter 9 of the *MS-DOS User's Guide* for a detailed description of how DOS can be configured for international use.

See also CHCP, COUNTRY, DISPLAY.SYS, KEYB, and MODE CP.

NUMLOCK

PROMPT   AUTOEXEC   BATCH   CONFIG

Description

This command controls whether the pesky keyboard Num Lock key is set to On or Off at system boot-up.

Usage

```
numlock=[on or off]
```

Options and switches

```
[on or off]
```

It should come as no surprise that you specify ON to turn Num Lock on and OFF to turn it off.

Remarks

The NUMLOCK statement must be located in the [MENU] section of CONFIG.SYS.

Example

The following CONFIG.SYS extract declares a menu and turns off Num Lock:

```
[menu]
menucolor=14,1
menuitem=Plain,Totally Plain
menuitem=Gainers,Big Gainers
menudefault=Gainers,9
numlock=off
```

Additional information

Chapter 8 explores system-configuration options in detail.

See also MENUCOLOR, MENUDEFAULT, MENUITEM, and SUBMENU.

Description

This command stores a list of directories that DOS searches when it looks for a program or batch file.

Usage

path [[*drive:*][*path*][;...]]

Options and switches

When you execute the PATH command with no switches, the active search path is displayed.

[*drive:*][*path*][;...]

This option specifies a list of directories separated by colons. Normally, you should include the drive so that DOS searches the correct path no matter which drive is current.

Remarks

Every computer with a hard disk should have a PATH statement included in AUTOEXEC.BAT.

The search path is stored in the DOS environment as the PATH variable. Enter the SET command, with no parameters, to see the complete environment.

When you execute a command, DOS determines whether it is an internal DOS command and, if not, searches the current directory. DOS searches every directory specified in the path in the order in which it is specified. As soon as it finds a program, the search terminates and the program is executed.

To improve performance, locate the most frequently accessed directories toward the beginning of the path.

Do not add too many directories to the path — DOS slows down as it searches all the specified directories for a command. Furthermore, avoid putting floppy disk directories in the search path. DOS really slows down as it accesses the floppies to look for a program.

Despite the pleas from users, the PATH is still limited to a maximum of 127 characters. To fit more directory names into the PATH, you need to resort to tricks such as shortening your directory names, using the SUBST command to substitute the shorter logical names for your longer directory names, or using the `append /x:on` command. Chapter 2 explains some other techniques that may alleviate PATH problems.

Examples

Use the following PATH statement to instruct DOS to search four directories for programs:

```
path c:\windows;c:\dos;c:\;c:\batfiles
```

Use the following batch file statement with the environment variable `%path%` to insert a new directory at the beginning of the path:

```
set path=c:\utils;%path%
```

Additional information

You can use the APPEND command to influence the search path.

Refer to Chapter 2 for more information on PATH.

See also APPEND and SET.

	PROMPT	AUTOEXEC	BATCH	CONFIG
PAUSE	☐	☒	■	☐

Description

This command temporarily halts batch file execution and waits for the user to press a key.

Usage

```
pause
```

Options and switches

None.

Remarks

When DOS encounters a PAUSE command, it suspends the batch file and displays a message telling the user to press any key to continue. When a key is pressed, batch file execution resumes at the line following the PAUSE command.

You can terminate the execution of the batch file execution pressing Ctrl-Break.

Use the CHOICE command to pause batch file execution and not display the standard PAUSE message.

Example

The following batch file uses ECHO to display a message and then pauses while the user reads the message:

```
@echo off
cls
echo Preparing to print NOTES.TXT.
echo Make sure the printer is connected and online, and
pause
print notes.txt
```

Additional information

See also CHOICE and ECHO.

Bob's Shareware Collection disks

BATUTIL, from CtrlAlt Associates, provides enhanced messaging and pausing utilities. TurboBat, a batch file compiler in the ExtraDOS Toolbox from Foley Hi-Tech Systems, provides an excellent way to prevent users from tampering with batch files and improves batch file performance.

BOB'S SCORECARD 7	PROMPT	AUTOEXEC	BATCH	CONFIG
POWER	■	■	■	☐

Description

This command reduces power consumption to prolong battery life on portable computers.

Usage

```
power [adv[:max or :reg or :min]]
```

or

```
power [std] or [off]
```

Options and switches

When you execute POWER with no switches, the current power configuration is displayed.

```
[adv:max]
```

This option activates maximum power conservation but can slow down applications.

```
[adv:reg]
```

This option turns on power conservation. This command does not save as much power as the MAX switch does, but it has only a limited impact on application performance. This switch is the default.

```
[adv:min]
```

This option implements modest power savings but has little impact on performance.

```
[adv std]
```

Use this switch on systems with Advanced Power Management (APM) hardware to instruct POWER to use the hardware-specific power-management facilities.

```
[adv off]
```

This option turns off the POWER utility.

Remarks

Before you can use POWER as a command, you must install it as a device driver in CONFIG.SYS (see POWER.EXE). You use POWER from the command line only to change the settings that were set at boot time in CONFIG.SYS.

If you use the STD switch on a computer that doesn't have APM hardware, power conservation is turned off.

Examples

To see the current power settings, enter the following command:

```
power
```

To maximize power savings, enter the following command:

```
power adv:max
```

Additional information

See also POWER.EXE.

BOB'S SCORECARD

POWER.EXE 7   PROMPT   AUTOEXEC   BATCH   CONFIG   ☐   ☐   ☐   ■

Description

This device driver conserves power on battery-powered computers.

Usage

```
device[high]=[drive:][path]power.exe [adv[:max or :reg or :min]
or [adv std] or [adv off] [/low]
```

Options and switches

[*drive:*][*path*]

This option identifies the directory in which POWER.EXE is located, if it is not in the boot directory. SETUP places POWER.EXE in the \DOS directory by default.

[adv:max]

This option activates maximum power conservation but can slow down applications.

```
[adv:reg]
```

This option turns on power conservation. This command does not save as much power as the MAX switch, but it has only a limited impact on application performance. This switch is the default.

```
[adv:min]
```

This option implements modest power savings but has little impact on performance.

```
[adv std]
```

Use this switch on systems with Advanced Power Management (APM) hardware to instruct POWER to use the hardware-specific power-management facilities.

```
[adv off]
```

This option turns off the POWER utility.

```
[/low]
```

This switch forces the device driver to be loaded in base memory.

Remarks

By default, POWER automatically loads into upper memory, so it should be installed using the DEVICE= statement rather than DEVICEHIGH=.

If you use the STD switch on a computer that doesn't have APM hardware, power conservation is turned off.

You can subsequently change power settings by executing POWER from the command line.

Examples

To load POWER by using the default settings, add the following line to CONFIG.SYS:

```
device=c:\dos\power.exe
```

To set power consumption to the maximum but install the device drive in base memory, add the following line to CONFIG.SYS:

```
device=c:\dos\power.exe adv:max /low
```

Additional information

See also DEVICE and POWER.

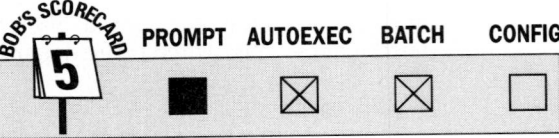

PROMPT AUTOEXEC BATCH CONFIG

Description

This command provides background printing capabilities that enable you to proceed with tasks while one or more files is being printed.

Usage

```
print [/d:device] [/b:size] [/u:ticks1] [/m:ticks2] [/s:ticks3]
[/q:numfiles] [/t] [[drive:][path][filename.ext[ ...]] [/c] [/p]
```

Options and switches

When you use PRINT with no switches, the status of the print queue is displayed. If print has not been executed in this session, it is installed in memory by using default settings.

[/d:*device*]

This switch specifies the device to use for printing (LPT1, LPT2, LPT3, PRN, COM1, COM2, COM3, or COM4).

[/b:*size*]

This switch sets the size of the print buffer in bytes. Any value in the range from 512 to 16384 is accepted, and the default is 512. Increasing the value speeds up print times.

[/u:*ticks1*]

This switch sets the number of clock ticks PRINT waits to get a response from the print device when it begins to print a job. Any value in the range from 1 to 255 is accepted, and the default is 1.

[/m:*ticks2*]

This switch sets the number of clock ticks PRINT tries to print a character. Any value in the range from 1 to 255 is accepted, and the default is 2.

[/ s : *ticks3*]

This switch sets the number of clock ticks the CPU allocates for the print task. Any value in the range from 1 to 255 is accepted, and the default is 8. Increasing the value improves print times but slows down the foreground task.

[/ q : *numfiles*]

This switch specifies the maximum number of files that can be queued while they are waiting to be printed. Any value in the range from 4 to 32 is accepted, and the default is 10.

[/ t]

This switch removes all files from the print queue.

[*drive:*][*path*]*filename.ext* [. . .]

In a list of one or more files to be printed, each filename must be separated by a space, and wildcards are not supported.

[/ c]

This switch indicates that the filename preceding the switch and all filenames following the switch are removed from the print queue.

[/ p]

The /P switch indicates that the filename preceding the switch and all filenames following the switch are added to the print queue. This switch is designed for use at the same time as the /C switch.

Remarks

You should not use PRINT, designed to print only ASCII files, to print binary files such as word processing documents or spreadsheets. PRINT does not support PostScript printers.

There are approximately 18.2 clock ticks per second.

PRINT automatically expands tabs with eight spaces and finishes printing a file when it encounters the end-of-file character (value 26).

You can use the switches /D, /B, /U, /M, /S, and /Q only the first time PRINT is executed in a session.

Do not delete or rename your file while it is printing or in the queue you'll confuse PRINT.

Examples

To print the configuration files, enter the following command:

```
print c:\config.sys c:\autoexec.bat
```

To cancel all pending print jobs, enter the following command:

```
print /t
```

Additional information

The NET USE command can provide access to another computer's printer.

Description

This command customizes the prompt DOS displays when it is ready to receive a command.

Usage

```
prompt [text]
```

Options and switches

[text]

This option specifies the text to be displayed as the command prompt. The text can include special character codes to instruct DOS to substitute some dynamic text or a line feed.

Remarks

Every computer with a hard disk should have a PROMPT statement in AUTOEXEC.BAT.

The following table shows the special character codes supported by PROMPT.

Code	Example	Description
$b	|	The | character
$d	Sun 03-21-1993	The current day and date
$e		The Esc character (used when ANSI.SYS loaded)
$g	>	The > character
$h		Erases the preceding character; like Backspace
$l	<	The < character
$n	D	The default drive
$p	C:\DOS	The default drive and directory
$q	=	The = character
$t	10:58:15.73	The time in hours:minutes:second:hundredths
$v	MS-DOS Version 6.00	The DOS version number
$$	$	The $ character
$_		Moves to the beginning of the next line

The prompt is stored in the DOS environment by using the name PROMPT.

If you change to an empty floppy drive and have the path ($p) set in the PROMPT, DOS generates the following message:

```
Abort, Retry, Fail?
```

because it cannot ascertain the default directory on the floppy disk drive. Just enter F, for fail.

Examples

You establish the most popular prompt, which shows the default drive followed by the > character, by executing the following command:

```
prompt $p$g
```

Use the following prompt statement to generate a two-line prompt that shows the DOS version number on the first line and the text Enter a command ===> on the second line:

```
prompt $v$_Enter a command ===$g
```

Use the following prompt with the Backspace facility to prune off the year from a date prompt:

```
prompt $d$h$h$h$h$h$p
```

Additional information

You can enhance PROMPT by using the ANSI.SYS device driver. Refer to Chapter 6 for more details.

BOB'S SCORECARD | PROMPT | AUTOEXEC | BATCH | CONFIG

QBASIC | 7 | ■ | ⊠ | ⊠ | ☐

Description

This command invokes the full-screen development environment for creating and running basic BASIC language programs.

Usage

```
qbasic [/b] [/g] [/h] [/mbf] [/nohi] [[/run]
[drive:][path]filename.ext]
```

Options and switches

```
[/b]
```

This switch suppresses colors and uses black and white.

```
[/g]
```

Use this switch on CGA systems to improve screen-display speeds.

```
[/h]
```

This switch sets the display to 43- or 50-line mode on EGA and VGA systems, respectively.

```
[/mbf]
```

This switch instructs QBASIC to use the function names MKDMBF$, CVSMBF, and CVDMBF rather than MKD$, CVS, and CVD.

```
[/nohi]
```

This switch forces the use of the low-intensity colors.

```
[/run]
```

This switch loads and executes the specified program.

> [*drive:*][*path*]*filename.ext*

This option specifies the name of the program source file to load. If an extension is not specified, QBASIC assumes that the file has a BAS extension.

Remarks

In addition to providing the QBASIC interpreter, the QBASIC.EXE program provides two important DOS services. The program EDIT.COM calls QBASIC by using the /EDITOR switch, which instructs QBASIC to behave as an editor with no programming facilities. Also, QBASIC is called on by HELP to provide the full-screen on-line DOS help. Behind the scenes, HELP.COM calls QBASIC with the /QHELP switch (must be uppercase).

 Don't delete the QBASIC.EXE file, even if you never intend to program in BASIC. Without QBASIC, EDIT and HELP are useless.

Examples

To start QBASIC, enter the following command:

```
qbasic
```

To run the program GORILLA.BAS, enter the following command:

```
qbasic /run gorilla
```

	BOB'S SCORECARD	PROMPT	AUTOEXEC	BATCH	CONFIG
RAMDRIVE.SYS	5	☐	☐	☐	■

Description

This command creates a RAM disk (a virtual disk in memory) to improve performance.

Usage

```
device[high]=[drive:][path]ramdrive.sys [disksize sectorsize
[numentries]] [/e] [/a]
```

Options and switches

[*drive:*][*path*]

This option identifies the directory in which RAMDRIVE.SYS is located, if it is not in the boot directory. SETUP places RAMDRIVE.SYS in the \DOS directory by default.

[*disksize*]

This option specifies the size of the RAM disk in kilobytes. Any value in the range from 4 to 32767 is accepted, and the default is 64.

[*sectorsize*]

This option specifies the size, in bytes, of each sector. Three sizes are supported: 128, 256, and the default 512.

[*numentries*]

This option specifies the maximum number of files and directories the RAM drive can support. Any value in the range from 2 to 1024 is accepted, and the default is a modest 64.

[/e]

This switch creates the disk in extended memory.

[/a]

This switch creates the disk in expanded memory.

Remarks

RAM disks were most popular when very few applications could take advantage of extended memory. By using extended memory for a RAM disk, you could not only find a use for the expensive memory but also speed up disk-intensive applications.

The popularity of RAM disks has waned with the emergence of high-performance disk caches. They, too, use memory to improve the performance of disk-related tasks, but they work automatically with all files, without the need to copy files to the RAM disk or the need to remember to save changed information to your real hard drive before powering down.

If you do not specify /E or /A, the RAM disk is created by using base memory.

Example

Use the following line in CONFIG.SYS to create a RAM disk of 1.45 megabytes, using extended memory:

```
device=c:\dos\ramdrive.sys 1450 /e
```

Additional information

See also DEVICE, DEVICEHIGH, EMM386.EXE, and HIMEM.SYS.

	BOB'S SCORECARD	PROMPT	AUTOEXEC	BATCH	CONFIG
RD (RMDIR)	6	■	☐	☒	☐

Description

This command removes (that is, deletes) an empty directory.

Usage

RD [*drive:*]*path*

Options and switches

[*drive:*]*path*

This option specifies the name of the directory to be removed.

Remarks

RD deletes only directories that are completely empty (that do not contain any files or directories). Use DELTREE to delete a directory and all the files and directories contained in it.

If the path begins with .. (dot dot), the directory extending from the parent directory is removed; if the path begins with a \ (backslash), the directory is deleted from the root directory; otherwise, the directory extending from the current directory is deleted.

You cannot remove the current directory — you must change first to a different directory. You cannot remove the root directory.

DOS also supports the long name of the command, RMDIR.

Examples

To remove the OLDSTUFF directory, enter the following command:

```
rd oldstuff
```

To remove the SAMPLES directory from drive A, enter the following command:

```
rd a:\samples
```

Additional information

You can manage directories more visually by using the DOSSHELL.

See also CD, DELTREE, and MD.

Bob's Shareware Collection disks

CMFILER, from NoVaSoft, includes advanced directory-management tools, including the capability to prune part of a directory tree and graft it to a new parent directory.

	BOB'S SCORECARD	PROMPT	AUTOEXEC	BATCH	CONFIG
REM	7	☐	■	■	■

Description

This command provides a way to add comments to any batch file and CONFIG.SYS.

Usage

```
REM [text]
```

Options and switches

[*text*]

This option specifies any comment or string, but it must not include the characters >, <, or |.

Remarks

REM is short for *rem*ark.

Any text or commands on a line that start with REM are ignored.

Examples

The following batch file starts with some comments that describe the purpose of the file:

```
rem XYZ.BAT by R D Ainsbury
rem Description: turns on the external lights at night!
....
```

In the following CONFIG.SYS example, REM is used to temporarily disable the mouse command:

```
FILES=20
BUFFERS=15
rem DEVICE=C:\WINDOWS\MOUSE.SYS /Y
```

Additional information

See also ECHO.

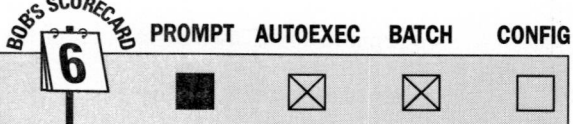

RENAME (REN)	BOB'S SCORECARD 6	PROMPT	AUTOEXEC	BATCH	CONFIG
		■	☒	☒	☐

Description

This command changes the name of one or more files.

Usage

```
rename [drive:][path]wildcards.ext  wildcardt.ext
```

or

```
ren [drive:][path]wildcards.ext  wildcardt.ext
```

Options and switches

[*drive:*][*path*]*wildcards.ext*

This option specifies the name of the source file or files to be renamed. Wildcards are supported.

wildcardt.ext

The new name for the file or files. Wildcards are supported, but every new name must be unique (no other file in the same directory can have the same name).

Remarks

Renamed files are created in the same directory as the source (you cannot use RENAME to move a file — use MOVE).

You cannot use RENAME to rename a directory — use the DOSSHELL.

Examples

Use the following command to rename the file THISWEEK.TXT to LASTWEEK.TXT:

```
rename thisweek.txt lastweek.txt
```

To rename all ME files to TXT, enter the following command:

```
rename *.me *.txt
```

Additional information

See also COPY, DOSSHELL, LABEL, and MOVE.

Bob's Shareware Collection disks

The file manager CMFILER, from NoVaSoft, includes file-renaming facilities and a whole lot more.

 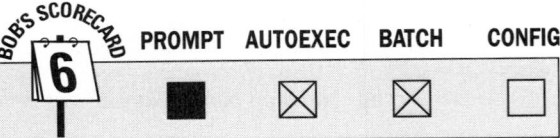

	PROMPT	AUTOEXEC	BATCH	CONFIG
REPLACE	■	⊠	⊠	☐

Description

This special form of the COPY command is designed to synchronize the contents of two directories.

Usage

```
replace [drive1:][path1]wildcard.ext [drive2:][path2] [/a] [/p] [/r]
[/w] [/s] [/u]
```

Options and switches

    [drive1:] [path1] wildcard.ext

This option specifies the source directory and the file or files to be copied.

    [drive2:] [path2]

This option specifies the target directory.

    `[/a]`

This switch instructs REPLACE to add (copy) files from the source that don't exist in the target. You cannot use this switch with /S or /U.

    `[/p]`

Use this switch to force a confirmation prompt before overwriting files or creating new files.

    `[/r]`

This switch instructs REPLACE to overwrite read-only files.

    `[/w]`

When you specify this switch, REPLACE pauses and waits for you to press a key before commencing.

    `[/s]`

Use this switch to make REPLACE search all subdirectories of the target path for matching files.

    `[/u]`

This popular switch instructs REPLACE to update only the files in the target path that are older than the same-named files in the source directory.

Remarks

REPLACE sets the ERRORLEVELs covered in the following table.

ERRORLEVEL	Description
0	Successful operation
1	Invalid DOS version
2	No matching source files
3	Either the source or destination path did not exist
5	The target files cannot be replaced — they might be read-only
8	Insufficient memory to run REPLACE
11	Syntax (command format) error

Examples

Use the following command to update all the older common files in the directory C:\HOMEWORK with files from drive A:

```
replace a:\*.* c:\homework /u
```

Use the following command to copy all the new font files from drive B to C:\FONTS:

```
replace a:\*.fnt c:\fonts /a
```

Additional information

See also ATTRIB, COPY, MOVE, and XCOPY.

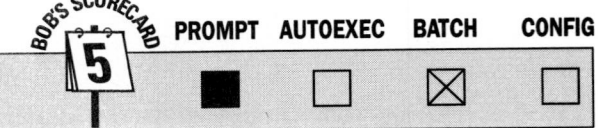

	PROMPT	AUTOEXEC	BATCH	CONFIG
RESTORE	■	☐	☒	☐

Description

RESTORE is included in DOS 6 to enable you to restore files that were stored on floppy disks by using the original DOS BACKUP utility. BACKUP is no longer included with DOS because it has been replaced by the superior utilities MSBACKUP and MWBACKUP.

Usage

```
restore drive1: drive2:[path[wildcard.ext]] [/s] [/p] [/b:date]
[/a:date] [/e:time] [/l:time] [/m] [/n] [/d]
```

Options and switches

drive1:

This option specifies the drive that identifies where the backup files are located.

drive2:[path[wildcard.ext]]

This option specifies the name of the drive in which the files will be restored. Files can be restored selectively by using wildcards, but the path must be the same as the path from which the files were originally backed up.

[/s]

This switch restores all the matching files in the backup subdirectories and the parent directory.

[/p]

This switch instructs RESTORE to prompt for verification before replacing read-only files.

[/b:*date*]

This switch restores files modified on or before the specified date. The format of the DATE is dependent on the country configuration — use the DATE command to see the correct format for your system.

[/a:*date*]

This switch restores files modified on or after the specified date.

[/e:*time*]

This switch restores files modified at or earlier than the specified time. The format of *time* is dependent on the country configuration — use the TIME command to see the correct format for your system.

[/l:*time*]

This switch restores files modified at or later than the specified time.

[/m]

This switch restores only files that have been modified since they were backed up.

[/n]

This switch restores only files that have been deleted, moved, or renamed since the backup.

[/d]

This switch performs a dry run by displaying all the files it would RESTORE based on the specified flags and switches.

Remarks

Unlike earlier versions of RESTORE, the DOS 6 version can restore files from backups created with any version of DOS ranging from DOS 2.0 to DOS 5.0.

RESTORE returns the ERRORLEVELs listed in the following table.

ERRORLEVEL	Description
0	Successful operation
1	No matching files were found on the backup disk
3	The user aborted the restoration by pressing Ctrl-Break
4	An unexpected error occurred

Do not use RESTORE on drives affected by ASSIGN, JOIN, or SUBST.

Examples

Use the following command to restore the file BUDGET86.WK1 from drive A to C:\123\PLANS:

```
restore a: c:\123\plans\budget86.wk1
```

Use the following command to restore all changed files in the directory D:\GOALS:

```
restore b: d:\goals\*.* /m
```

Additional information

See also MSBACKUP and MWBACKUP.

RMDIR

See RD.

SET

Description

This command enables you to create, modify, delete, and view environment variable settings.

Usage

    set [varname=[string]]

Options and switches

When you use SET without switches, the entire environment is displayed.

[varname=]

This option specifies the name of the environment variable. Spaces are allowed, but do not use the following characters: <, >, |, :, ", (,), =, or .

[string]

This option specifies the new string to assign to the variable. If no string is specified, the variable is removed from the environment. Avoid the same characters shown for the variable name in the preceding paragraph.

Remarks

Make sure that you do not include a space before the = character; otherwise, the space forms part of the variable name.

If you get a message that environment space has run out, there is insufficient room to add the specified string. Use the SHELL and COMMAND statements to increase the environment size.

Variable names are not case sensitive, but the strings are stored in the same case in which they are entered.

Batch files can substitute environment strings in commands by specifying the variable name inside two percent characters (%TEMP%, for example).

If you execute COMMAND, a secondary copy of the environment is created. When you use EXIT to return to the original command processor, the original environment is restored.

Examples

To see the entire environment, enter the following command:

```
set
```

Use the following command to set the TEMP environment variable to E:\TRASH:

```
set temp=e:\trash
```

Use the following command to remove the environment variable TEMP:

```
set temp=
```

Additional information

See also COMMAND, DIR, PATH, PROMPT, and SHELL.

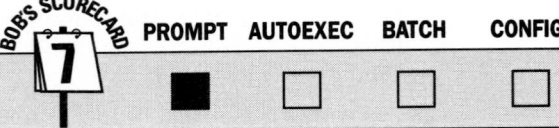

BOB'S SCORECARD   **PROMPT**   **AUTOEXEC**   **BATCH**   **CONFIG**

SETUP

Description

This command runs the DOS 6 installation and setup program.

Usage

```
setup [/m] [/q] [/e] [/f] [/i] [/b] [/u]
```

Options and switches

```
[/m]
```

This switch instructs SETUP to run a minimal installation. SETUP installs only the main startup files (IO.SYS, MSDOS.SYS, COMMAND.COM, and DBLSPACE.BIN).

```
[/q]
```

Use the /Q switch to install all the DOS files after you have used the minimal INSTALL switch.

[/e]

This switch instructs SETUP to install the optional DOS utilities Anti-Virus, Backup, and Undelete.

[/f]

This switch installs DOS 6 on floppy disks.

[/i]

This switch skips hardware detection when SETUP is loaded.

[/b]

This switch instructs SETUP to display text in black and white.

[/u]

This switch forces SETUP to proceed with the installation even when it detects a disk partitioning scheme that may be incompatible with DOS 6.

Remarks

Unfortunately, SETUP tries to force you to install all DOS files on the boot drive. To create a DOS directory on a different drive, you must first run a minimal installation. You can subsequently use the /Q switch and specify any drive as the target for the external DOS files.

During installation, SETUP requires one (or maybe two) floppy disks to create an UNINSTAL disk.

Example

To install DOS 6, insert the setup disk in drive A and enter the following command:

```
a:setup
```

Additional information

Refer to Appendix A for more information on SETUP.

See also UNINSTAL.

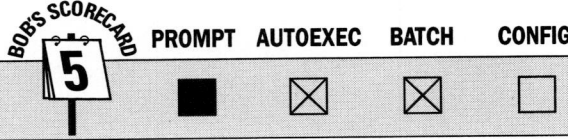

Description

Use SETVER if you have programs that expect a specific version of DOS to be installed and that won't run with DOS 6. SETVER displays and modifies the version table in which programs and fake version numbers are stored.

Usage

```
setver [drive:path] [filename.exe n.nn]
```

or

```
setver [drive:path] [filename.ext [/delete [/quiet]]]
```

Options and switches

When you use SETVER with no parameters or switches, the current contents of the version table appears, showing the program name and the fake DOS version that DOS 6 reports to the program.

[*drive:path*]

This option specifies the location of the SETVER.EXE program (*not* the location of the program). By default, SETUP places the file in the \DOS directory.

[*filename.exe*]

This option specifies the name of the program (including the extension) DOS should "trick" into believing that a different version of DOS is running.

[*n.nn*]

This option specifies the fake DOS version number (5.00, for example). The program name and version number are added to the version table.

[/delete]

This switch instructs SETVER to remove the program from the version table. The switch can be abbreviated as /D.

```
 [/quiet]
```

This switch suppresses the deletion status message.

Remarks

The version table is effective only when SETVER.EXE (discussed in the next section) is loaded as a device driver in CONFIG.SYS.

Changes to the version table are implemented only the next time the system is booted.

Examples

Use the following command to display the version table entries:

```
setver | more
```

Use the following command to fool the DUMBCHCK.EXE program into thinking that it is being executed on a DOS 4.01 system:

```
setver dumbchck.exe 4.01
```

Use the following command to remove the METRO.EXE entry from the version table:

```
setver metro.exe /d
```

Additional information

See also SETVER.EXE.

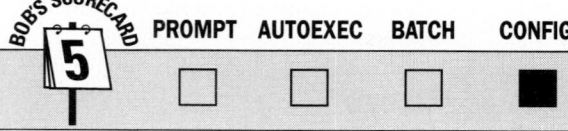

		PROMPT	AUTOEXEC	BATCH	CONFIG
SETVER.EXE	5	☐	☐	☐	■

Description

This command loads the version table into memory so that DOS can fool specific programs into thinking that they are being run on a different version of DOS.

Usage

```
device[high]=[drive:][path]setver.exe
```

Options and switches

`[`*drive:*`][`*path*`]setver.exe`

This option identifies the directory in which SETVER.EXE is located, if it is not in the boot directory. By default, SETUP places SETVER.EXE in the \DOS directory.

Remarks

SETVER.EXE is both a device driver and an executable DOS command.

You can modify entries in the version table by running SETVER.

Example

Use the following statement in CONFIG.SYS to load SETVER.EXE as a device driver:

```
device=c:\dos\setver.exe
```

Additional information

See also SETVER.

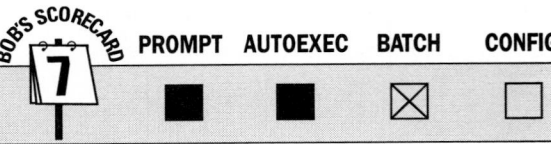

BOB'S SCORECARD 7	PROMPT	AUTOEXEC	BATCH	CONFIG
SHARE	■	■	⊠	☐

Description

This command allows file sharing and locking for multi-user or multi-application access.

Usage

`share [/f:`*space*`] [/l:`*locks*`]`

Options and switches

`[/f:`*space*`]`

This switch specifies the amount of memory, in bytes, to be reserved for temporarily storing the file-locking details. By default, 2048 bytes are allocated.

[/ l : *locks*]

This switch specifies the maximum number of files that can be simultaneously locked. By default, 20 files can be locked at any time.

Remarks

Because the defaults usually are appropriate, SHARE is typically loaded with no switches.

Use SHARE if you use a network or multitasking software, such as the DOSSHELL, Windows, or DesqView.

You can load SHARE from CONFIG.SYS by using the INSTALL command. Alternatively, on 386 systems and higher, you can conserve base memory by using LOADHIGH to load SHARE into UMBs.

Example

Use the following command to load SHARE into UMBs:

```
loadhigh c:\dos\share
```

Additional information

See also INSTALL, LOADHIGH, and MEMMAKER.

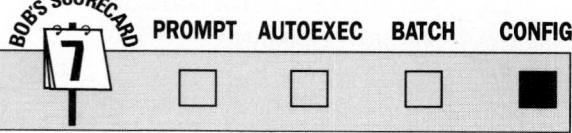

Description

This command sets the options for COMMAND.COM or enables a different command processor to be loaded.

Usage

shell=[[*drive:*]*path*]*filename.ext* [*parameters*]

Options and switches

[[*drive:*]*path*]*filename.ext*

This option specifies the location and name of the command interpreter (COMMAND.COM, for example).

[*parameters*]

This option specifies optional parameters to specify the characteristics and settings of the command interpreter.

Remarks

SHELL is used most often in conjunction with COMMAND.COM to change one or more command processor settings (the environment size, for example).

A number of third-party command interpreters, such as 4DOS and NDOS, provide more features than COMMAND.COM. You usually load these interpreters by using the SHELL statement.

MEMMAKER is suspicious of shells other than COMMAND.COM and will disable them by remarking out the SHELL statement containing them. If you're using a third-party command interpreter and run MEMMAKER, you will need to manually edit your CONFIG.SYS file to restore it.

Example

Use the following statement in CONFIG.SYS to set a larger environment size for COMMAND.COM:

```
shell=c:\dos\command.com c:\dos /e:800
```

Additional information

See also COMMAND.

	BOB'S SCORECARD	PROMPT	AUTOEXEC	BATCH	CONFIG
SHIFT	6	☐	☐	■	☐

Description

This command allows access from a batch file to more than nine passed parameters by dropping the first passed parameter (%1) and shifting all other parameters left one position.

Usage

```
shift
```

Options and switches

None.

Remarks

Before the first SHIFT operation, the %0 parameter identifies the name of the batch file. After the first SHIFT operation, the tenth passed parameter is moved to the %9 variable, the ninth passed parameter is moved to the %8 variable, and so on, until the first passed parameter is moved to the %0 position and the previous %0 value is lost.

You use SHIFT also in batch files in which a single command has to be executed against each passed parameter — SHIFT provides a convenient looping tool (see the following COPYBAK example).

Example

The following batch file, COPYBAK, uses SHIFT to process multiple filenames passed to the batch file and to copy the specified files to the C:\BAK directory:

```
@echo off
:start
if "%1"=="" goto finish
copy %1 c:\bak
shift
goto start
:finish
```

Additional information

Refer to Chapter 10 for a discussion of advanced batch file techniques.

Bob's Shareware Collection disks

TurboBat, in the Extra DOS Toolbox from Foley Hi-Tech Systems, can compile batch files to make them secure and improve execution speed.

SIZER

MEMMAKER uses this command during the optimization process; it is not intended for general use.

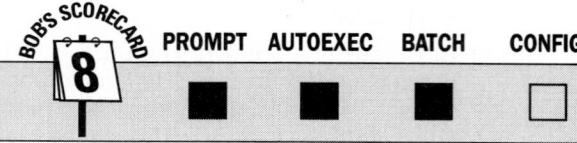

Description

This command installs or configures the extended memory disk cache.

Usage

smartdrv [[*drive*[+ or -] ...] [/e:*elementsize*] [*initcachesize*]
[*wincachesize*] [/b:*buffersize*] [/c] [/r] [/l] [/q] [/s]

Options and switches

[*drive*[+ or -] ...

This option specifies the letter of one or more drives. Every drive specified with a plus sign (+) is read cached and write cached; every drive specified with a minus sign (–) has caching disabled; if neither plus nor minus is specified, the drive has read caching but not write caching. If no drive is specified, floppy disks are read cached, and hard drives are read cached and write cached.

[/e:*elementsize*]

This switch specifies the amount of cache memory, in bytes, that is managed in each block transfer. The following values are supported: 1024, 2048, 4096, and the default 8192.

[*initcachesize*]

This option sets the size of the cache, in kilobytes, that is used when Windows is not running.

[*wincachesize*]

This option sets the amount of memory, in kilobytes, that SMARTDRV.EXE relinquishes when Windows is running.

[/b:*buffersize*]

This switch sets the size of the read-ahead buffer in kilobytes. The *buffersize* must be an exact multiple of the *elementsize,* and defaults to 16K (16,384 bytes).

```
[/c]
```

This switch forces cache data to be written immediately to disk. By default, SMARTDRV.EXE uses delayed writes to improve performance, but it can result in data loss if the power shuts off unexpectedly.

```
[/r]
```

This switch clears the data from the disk cache and restarts SMARTDRV.EXE.

```
[/l]
```

This switch forces SMARTDRV.EXE to install in base (low) memory. By default, SMARTDRV.EXE tries to load into UMBs when they are available.

```
[/q]
```

This switch suppresses installation messages when SMARTDRV.EXE is loaded.

```
[/s]
```

This switch displays a status report.

Remarks

The following table shows the default values for *initcachesize* and *wincachesize* are based on the total amount of installed extended memory, as follows:

Extended memory	initcachesize	wincachesize
1MB (or less)	All extended memory	0K
2MB (or less)	1MB	256K
4MB (or less)	1MB	512K
Less than 6MB	2MB	1MB
More than 6MB	2MB	2MB

SMARTDRV.EXE does not support network or CD-ROM drives, but INTERLNK drives can be read cached.

After SMARTDRV.EXE has been installed, you can execute it additional times, but only the DRIVE+/–, /C, and /R switches are valid.

SMARTDRV.EXE uses extended memory for the cache, but only when HIMEM.SYS (or a similar utility) is installed in CONFIG.SYS.

If you have DoubleSpace volumes, use SMARTDRV.EXE to cache the physical drive (the drive that contains the hidden file DBLSPACE.*nnn*). If you cache both the physical drive and the compressed volume, cache performance is impaired.

Examples

Use the following statement in AUTOEXEC.BAT with the default values to install SMARTDRV.EXE; SMARTDRV.EXE displays additional status information when it has been loaded:

```
c:\dos\smartdrv /s
```

Use the following statement to install a 4MB cache and specify that 2MB should be relinquished when Windows is running:

```
c:\dos\smartdrv 4096 2048
```

Additional information

Chapter 4 provides more insights into using SMARTDRV.EXE and suggests additional performance-enhancing techniques.

See also BUFFERS, EMM386.EXE, FASTOPEN, HIMEM.SYS, and RAMDRIVE.SYS.

Extended use

In addition to being an executable program, SMARTDRV.EXE can be loaded as a device driver in CONFIG.SYS. The only purpose for using SMARTDRV.EXE as a device driver is to install double buffering by using the following syntax:

```
device=c:\dos\smartdrv.exe /double_buffer
```

Double buffering involves moving data first from the disk cache to a conventional memory buffer and then off to disk. This technique is needed on systems that use a bus-mastering disk controller, such as the ones used for SCSI devices.

If you do not know whether your system has to use double buffering, you can find out easily. Install SMARTDRV.EXE in CONFIG.SYS with the /DOUBLE_BUFFER switch and also in AUTOEXEC.BAT. Use your system for a while, and then execute SMARTDRV with no switches to see a summary of the cache statistics. If every drive includes a no in the buffering column, double buffering is not necessary, and you can remove the SMARTDRV.EXE statement from CONFIG.SYS.

By default, SMARTDRV.EXE uses write caching on hard drives. In this mode, SMARTDRV.EXE does not immediately write the data to disk but does so within a few seconds when disk activity slows down. This action provides tangible performance improvement but increases the potential for data loss. If your system power is switched off (or if the reset button is pressed, a program hangs, or the system loses power), the data may not have been written to disk. Do not switch your system off immediately after performing an operation that involves saving data.

You can disable the write cache by using the *drive-* switch.

Description
This command sorts input data and directs the sorted output to a device or file.

Usage
sort [/r] [/+n] [<] [*drive1:*][*path1*]*filename1.ext*
[> [*drive2:*][*path2*]*filename2.ext*]

or

[*command* |] sort [/r] [/+n] [> [*drive2:*][*path2*]*filename2.ext*]

Options and switches
[/r]

This switch forces a descending-order sort (from 9 to 0 and from Z to A).

[/+n]

This switch instructs SORT to base the sort on a specific column (the character located *n* characters from the left margin, for example).

[*drive1:*][*path1*]*filename1.ext*

This option specifies the file containing the base text that has to be sorted.

[*drive2:*][*path2*]*filename2.ext*

This option specifies the new file in which the sorted data is saved.

The > and < characters are pipes that pass the output from one element as the input to the other. You use the | filter to pass the output from a command as input to SORT.

Remarks

SORT is not case sensitive and should be used on only ASCII files and data.

SORT was often used to sort directory listings, but the DIR /O switch has made that old DOS Jedi trick redundant.

SORT can handle input of only 64K or less.

Examples

Use the following command to sort the records in the ASCII file NAMES.TXT and place the sorted list in the file ADDRESS.TXT:

```
sort < names.txt > address.txt
```

If the last name begins in column ten, you can sort the data by last name with the following command:

```
sort /+10 < names.txt > address.txt
```

Use the following command to display the sorted list on-screen:

```
sort < names.txt
```

Additional information

See also DIR, MORE.

		PROMPT	AUTOEXEC	BATCH	CONFIG
BOB'S SCORECARD 5	STACKS	☐	☐	☐	■

Description

This command allocates memory to manage hardware interrupts.

Usage

```
stacks=n,s
```

Options and switches

n

This option specifies the number of stack frames. Accepted values are 0 or any number in the range from 8 to 64.

s

This option specifies the size, in bytes, of each frame. Accepted values are 0 or any number in the range from 32 through 512.

Remarks

On XTs, original PCs, and IBM PC-portables, the default STACKS setting is 0,0; on all later models, the default is 9,128.

If you encounter stack error messages, such as `Internal Stack Overflow`, you may need to add a STACKS statement to CONFIG.SYS or increase the number and size of the stack frames.

To conserve memory, you may want to experiment with a STACKS setting of 0,0. This setting can save more than 2,000 bytes of base memory.

Examples

Use the following statement in CONFIG.SYS to eliminate any memory allocation for STACKS:

```
stacks=0,0
```

Use the following statement to implement nine stack frames, each of which is 256 bytes:

```
stacks=9,256
```

Additional information

Refer to Chapter 5 for other memory-saving techniques.

PROMPT   AUTOEXEC   BATCH   CONFIG

SUBMENU

Description

This command provides a way to branch to a secondary menu in a multiconfiguration system.

Usage

    submenu=*blockname*[, *itemtext*]

Options and switches

blockname

This option specifies the name of another menu block in CONFIG.SYS that defines a secondary menu. Elsewhere in the file, a unique block heading must have the format [*blockname*]. *blockname* is not case sensitive.

[, *itemtext*]

The blockname is displayed by default as the item description in the menu. Optionally, you can specify a different item description by using the *itemtext* parameter. This description can include spaces and is displayed in the same case in which it is entered. The text can contain as many as 70 characters.

Remarks

Do not assign a blockname of *menu* or *common* because these blocknames are reserved.

Every item in the menu topic is automatically prefixed with a number.

Example

The following extract from CONFIG.SYS defines a two-menu configuration file:

    [menu]
    menucolor=14,1
    menuitem=Plain,Totally Plain
    menuitem=Gainers,Big Gainers
    submenu=Support,Load Peripheral Drivers
    menudefault=Gainers,9

```
[support]
menuitem=Tablet, Tablet Only
menuitem=Cdrom, CD-ROM Only
menuitem=Tplusc, Tablet and CD-ROM
```

. . . .

Additional information

Refer to Chapter 8 for a thorough description of the multiconfiguration commands.

See also MENUCOLOR, MENUDEFAULT, and MENUITEM.

Description

This command assigns a drive letter alias to a specific directory.

Usage

        subst [*drive1:* [*drive2:*[*path*]]]

or

        subst *drive1:* /d

Options and switches

When you use SUBST with no switches, a list of substituted drives is displayed.

   drive1:

This option specifies the drive letter that will be an alias to the real path.

   drive2:[*path*]

This option specifies the path that will be assigned to the drive letter alias.

   /d

This switch removes the drive substitution for the specified drive.

Remarks

The drive letter assigned to the substituted path must be less than or equal to the LASTDRIVE.

Do not create SUBST drives from within Windows.

To change the path assigned to a SUBST drive, you must first delete the drive with the /D switch and then reassign the drive with a new SUBST command.

Examples

Use the following command to substitute drive letter D for the path C:\COMPILER\C700\BIN:

```
subst d: c:\compiler\c700\bin
```

Use the following command to remove the substituted drive D:

```
subst d: /d
```

Additional information

See also LASTDRIVE.

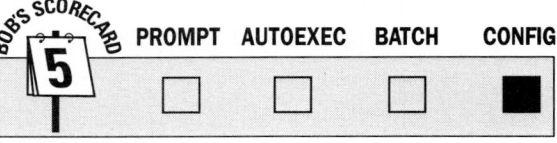

	PROMPT	AUTOEXEC	BATCH	CONFIG
SWITCHES 5	☐	☐	☐	■

Description

SWITCHES is a miscellaneous collection of four configuration switches for customizing the behavior of the operating system.

Usage

```
switches=[/w] [/k] [/n] [/f]
```

Options and switches

```
[/w]
```

Use this switch if you are running Windows 3.0 and want to move the file WINA20.SYS from the root directory of the boot drive.

`[/k]`

This switch instructs DOS to treat an Enhanced Keyboard as a standard keyboard. Use this switch only if a program cannot run with an Enhanced Keyboard.

`[/n]`

This switch prevents you from using the F5 and F8 keys at start-up. Use this switch to prevent users from bypassing your CONFIG.SYS and AUTOEXEC.BAT commands.

`[/f]`

This switch instructs DOS not to wait two seconds after displaying the message that MS-DOS is starting. You normally use this switch in conjunction with /N.

Remarks

If you use the /W switch, you must add the following statement in the [386enh] block of SYSTEM.INI to tell Windows 3.0 where the file is located:

If you use the /K switch with SWITCHES and you want to load ANSI.SYS, you must also use the /K switch with ANSI.SYS.

The SWITCHES statement does not have to be located at the beginning of CONFIG.SYS. DOS scans the file for a SWITCHES statement before displaying the message that MS-DOS is starting.

Example

To disable the F5 and F8 keys and suppress the two-second delay, enter the following line in CONFIG.SYS:

```
switches=/f /n
```

Additional information

Refer to Chapter 8 for more information on SWITCHES.

See also ANSI.SYS.

BOB'S SCORECARD

7

	PROMPT	AUTOEXEC	BATCH	CONFIG
SYS	■	☐	☒	☐

Description

This command makes a formatted drive bootable or updates the DOS version by transferring the primary DOS files IO.SYS, MSDOS.SYS, COMMAND.COM, and DBLSPACE.BIN to the root directory of a drive.

Usage

```
sys [drive1:][path] drive2:
```

Options and switches

```
[drive1:][path]
```

This option specifies the drive from which the new versions of the DOS files are to be copied. If no drive is specified, SYS looks in the root directory of the default drive.

```
drive2:
```

This option specifies the drive in which the files will be copied.

Remarks

SYS transfers files to only local drives (not to network drives) and not to drives affected by ASSIGN, JOIN, or SUBST.

The system files also are transferred to a drive when it is formatted with the /S switch.

Examples

To transfer the primary DOS files from the disk in drive A to drive C, enter the following command:

```
sys a: c:
```

To transfer the system files from the current drive to the disk in drive B, enter the following command:

```
sys b:
```

Additional information

See also FORMAT.

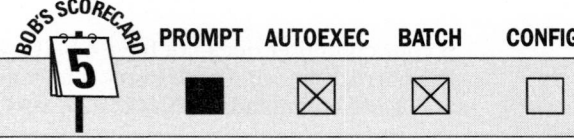

	PROMPT	AUTOEXEC	BATCH	CONFIG

TIME

Description

This command displays and sets the system time.

Usage

`time [hours[:minutes[:seconds[.hundredths]]]] [a or p]]`

Options and switches

When you execute TIME with no parameters, the current time is displayed and you are prompted to enter a new time. Press Ctrl-Break or Esc and then Enter to return to the DOS prompt.

[*hours*]

This option specifies the current hour, in the range from 0 to 23.

[*minutes*]

This option specifies the current minute, in the range from 0 to 59.

[*seconds*]

This option specifies the current second, in the range from 0 to 59.

[*hundredths*]

This option specifies the current hundredths of a second, in the range from 0 through 99.

[a or p]

This option indicates whether the time entered is a.m. or p.m. The hour must be less than 13 to use an *a*. By default, DOS assumes a.m. for all values less than 12.

Remarks

The TIME format is dictated by the active country setting in CONFIG.SYS.

You do not have to specify the complete time. I usually enter only the hour and minute. I am not too concerned if the system clock (or any clock, for that matter) is accurate to the second.

If your computer does not have a battery-supported clock, you have to enter the correct date and time every time you boot your computer. If so, add DATE and TIME commands to AUTOEXEC.BAT.

Examples

You can use one of the following two statements to set the time to 3:18 p.m.:

```
time 15:18

time 3:18p
```

I always get confused about how to enter the time between 12 noon and 1 p.m. The following command sets the clock to 25 minutes past noon:

```
time 12:25p
```

The following two commands show how the time can be set to 25 minutes past midnight:

```
time 12:25a

time 0:25
```

Additional information

See also DATE.

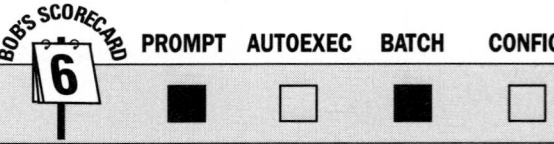

	PROMPT	AUTOEXEC	BATCH	CONFIG
TREE	■	□	■	□

Description

This command displays the directory structure of an entire drive or for a specific directory and its subdirectories.

Usage

```
tree [drive:][path] [/f] [/a]
```

Options and switches

[*drive:*][*path*]

This option specifies the drive or path whose directory structure you want displayed. By default, TREE uses the current directory.

[/f]

This switch lists all the files located in each directory.

[/a]

This switch instructs TREE to use standard ASCII characters rather than line-drawing characters to draw the directory structure diagram. This switch is normally used when you are redirecting output to the printer, and the printer prints foreign characters rather than lines and corners.

Remarks

Use the | MORE pipe to pause the display after each screen.

Examples

Use the following statement to produce a directory tree diagram of the directory C:\WP:

```
tree c:\wp
```

To view the entire directory structure of drive C, enter the following command:

```
tree c:\ |more
```

To print the entire directory structure of drive C to a printer that doesn't support line-drawing characters, enter the following command:

```
tree c:\ /a> prn
```

Additional information

See also CD, DELTREE, DIR, and MORE.

Bob's Shareware Collection disks

You can switch the CMFILER file manager, from NoVaSoft, into Tree Mode by pressing Shift-T. In this mode, you can traverse the entire drive by using the tree and still use all the tagging and file-management facilities. You can even highlight directories that contain files whose names match a specified wildcard.

LCD, from McAfee Associates, provides an easy way to change directories.

TYPE	BOB'S SCORECARD 5	PROMPT	AUTOEXEC	BATCH	CONFIG
		■	⊠	■	☐

Description
This command displays the contents of an ASCII file.

Usage
        type [*drive:*][*path*]*filename.ext*

Options and switches
        [*drive:*][*path*]*filename.ext*

This option specifies the name of the file whose contents will be displayed. If you do not specify a path, the file is assumed to be in the current directory.

Remarks
If the file is too large to display on one screen, use | MORE to pause the display after each screen.

Unfortunately, TYPE is limited in its capabilities: you cannot search for text, you can only scroll forward through the file, and it doesn't handle binary files very well, for example.

You may prefer to use EDIT to browse larger files or preferably use one of the shareware utilities (see the following "Bob's Shareware Collection disks" section).

Example
To display the contents of CONFIG.SYS, enter the following command:

        type c:\config.sys | more

Additional information
See also EDIT, PRINT, and MORE.

Bob's Shareware Collection disks

If you want to view files, you have only one choice: LIST, from Buerg Software, is the champion file browser. You can page up *and* page back through a file, search for text, view in hexadecimal, display a ruler, leave, and jump to bookmarks.

CMFILER, the first-class file manager from NoVaSoft, has the capability to view files.

BOB'S SCORECARD | 8 | **UNDELETE** | PROMPT ■ | AUTOEXEC ■ | BATCH ■ | CONFIG ☐

Description

This command provides mechanisms for enhancing the chances of recovering deleted files and tries to undelete files that have been deleted.

Usage

To install the UNDELETE memory-resident tools or review the status of deleted files, use the following syntax:

```
undelete /list or /all or /purge [drive:] or /status or /load or
/u or /s[drive] or /t[drive[-entries]
```

To undelete one or more files, use the following syntax:

```
undelete [[drive:][path]wildcard.ext] [/dt or /ds or /dos]
```

Options and switches

When you use UNDELETE with no switches or parameters, UNDELETE attempts to restore all deleted files in the current directory but prompts for confirmation before trying to undelete each file it finds.

```
/list
```

This switch displays a list of all the deleted files.

```
/all
```

This switch tries to recover all deleted files without prompting for confirmation or prompting for the first character of the filename. A number-sign (#) character is used automatically as the first character. If a file with this name already exists, UNDELETE keeps substituting alternative characters until a unique filename is found.

/purge [*drive:*]

This switch deletes the backup files stored in the sentry directory.

/status

This switch shows the type of delete protection currently in force.

/load

This switch installs the memory-resident delete-protection portion of UNDELETE by using the setting defined in the DELETE.INI file, which is located in the same directory as UNDELETE.EXE.

/u

This switch unloads, and therefore disables, the memory-resident delete-protection facility.

/s[*drive*]

This switch installs the memory-resident delete-protection portion of UNDELETE by using the Delete Sentry protection method. If a drive is not specified, the drives defined in DELETE.INI are used; if DELETE.INI does not exist, the current drive is protected.

/t[*drive*[-*entries*]]

This switch installs the memory-resident delete-protection portion of UNDELETE by using the Delete Tracker protection method. You can optionally specify the maximum number of entries in the tracker file PCTRACKR.DEL. The default value is dependent on the hard disk size and ranges from 25 on 360K floppies to 303 on hard drives greater than 32MB.

You use the following switches to undelete files:

[[*drive:*][*path*]*wildcard.ext*]

This option specifies the name of the file or files to be undeleted.

```
[/ds]
```

This switch instructs UNDELETE to try to recover only files that have been protected by using the Delete Sentry method.

```
[/dt]
```

This switch instructs UNDELETE to try to recover only files that have been protected using the Delete Tracker method.

```
[/dos]
```

This switch instructs UNDELETE to try to recover files by using only standard DOS techniques. Use this flag to instruct UNDELETE to ignore the Delete Sentry or Delete Tracker records.

Remarks

DOS provides the following three levels of deletion protection:

Delete Sentry. A hidden directory named \SENTRY is used to store copies of deleted files. The TSR portion of UNDELETE monitors all file-deletion activity and substitutes a command to move the file in place of the file deletion. This form of protection provides the most security because you can undelete the file just by moving it from the deleted directory back to the original directory. On the down side, you don't recover any disk space when you delete a file because it isn't really deleted.

Delete Tracker. A hidden file named PCTRACKR.DEL is created in the root directory of the monitored drive. This file contains the name of the deleted file and a list of all the clusters in which the file's data was stored. This method doesn't offer as much protection as the sentry method because other files can still overwrite the clusters. It consumes much less disk space, however, and the chances of recovery are good if there has been limited activity since the file was deleted.

DOS. No records are maintained about deleted files, and UNDELETE tries to recover a file's data by using the FAT. When this technique is used, you must identify the filename's first letter because it is modified when the file is deleted. The chances of recovery are greatly reduced by using this method. The odds are improved, however, if the file has recently been deleted, if the file is small, or if the disk is regularly defragmented (so that the file is stored in contiguous clusters). This method does not require that you load UNDELETE as a TSR.

You cannot recover deleted directories with UNDELETE.

Always keep regular file backups as insurance against file loss.

When you install UNDELETE as a TSR (using the /S, /T, or /LOAD switches), you can load it in upper memory with LOADHIGH.

Examples

You should add the following command to AUTOEXEC.BAT to install Sentry Delete protection for drive C:

```
undelete /sc
```

Use the following command with the sentry method to undelete the file RESIGN.DOC:

```
undelete resign.doc /ds
```

Use the following command to try to undelete all files in the current directory and be prompted to confirm each file:

```
undelete
```

Use the following command to clear (delete, really) all the copies of deleted files stored on drive D:

```
undelete /purge d:
```

Additional information

Windows users may prefer to use MWUNDEL for general undeletion tasks. Refer to Chapter 3 for a detailed description of UNDELETE.INI and other data-protection and -recovery techniques.

See also DEFRAG, DEL, DELTREE, MWUNDEL, and UNFORMAT.

Bob's Shareware Collection disks

CMFILER, from NoVaSoft, implements a facility similar to Delete Sentry whereby copies of deleted files are retained in a special directory, if the files are deleted by using CMFILER.

To delete a confidential or private file and make sure that nobody UNDELETEs it, use RELDEL, from Tardis DP Consultants. But remember, after it's gone, it's gone!

UNINSTAL

Description

This command removes DOS 6 and restores the previous version of the operating system.

Usage

```
uninstal
```

Options and switches

UNINSTAL does not support the /? switch. When you enter the UNINSTAL command with the /? switch, the switch will be ignored and UNINSTAL will proceed with the removal of DOS 6. (You can abort the program by pressing F3 twice.)

Remarks

The UNINSTAL program is copied to the UNINSTAL disk by SETUP when DOS 6 is installed.

To restore the previous version of the operating system, insert the UNINSTAL disk in the boot drive and press Ctrl-Alt-Del.

UNINSTAL uses the files stored in the highest numbered OLD_DOS directory along with the files on the UNINSTAL disk to restore the previous version of the operating system.

You cannot use UNINSTAL to restore the previous version of the operating system if you have done any of the following:

- Run the DELOLDOS command
- Deleted any files in the OLD_DOS directory
- Installed DoubleSpace or any other disk compression program
- Repartitioned the hard drive
- Reformatted the boot drive

You can temporarily boot your system using the previous version of the operating system by inserting the UNINSTAL disk in the boot drive and rebooting. The system will boot from the floppy (using the previous version of the operating system) and automatically start the UNINSTAL program. When UNINSTAL prompts for confirmation, press F3 twice to terminate the UNINSTAL operation. You will be left at the A prompt, having booted with the previous version of the operating system.

Additional information

See also SETUP.

Description

This command recovers files and directories destroyed by an accidental FORMAT.

Usage

```
unformat drive: [/l] [/test] [/p]
```

Options and switches

drive:

This option specifies the drive to be unformatted.

```
[/l]
```

This switch instructs UNFORMAT to list every file and subdirectory as they are processed. By default, UNFORMAT displays only fragmented files and subdirectories. Normally, the list scrolls off the screen at a rate of knots. Press Ctrl-S to suspend scrolling, and then press any key to resume.

```
[/test]
```

This switch performs a dry run that indicates how the disk would be unformatted, but no unformatting is performed.

```
[/p]
```

This switch directs UNFORMAT output to LPT1.

Remarks

UNFORMAT cannot unformat a formatted DoubleSpace volume.

UNFORMAT cannot reverse a FORMAT that was performed by using the /U switch. When FORMAT is used *without* the /U switch, a mirror file is created that stores critical UNFORMAT information.

UNFORMAT cannot recover files that are fragmented. You should keep your disk unfragmented by running DEFRAG regularly.

If you have used your disk after using FORMAT, you should consider enhancing your chances for data recovery by using a third-party data-recovery tool such as the Norton Utilities, PC Tools, or the Mace Utilities.

Always keep regular backups of your data for added protection.

Examples

Use the following command to try to unformat a disk in drive B:

```
unformat b:
```

Use the following command to evaluate the unformat situation for drive D:

```
unformat d: /test
```

Additional information

Chapter 3 provides more information about data protection and recovery.

See also FORMAT, MWUNDEL, and UNDELETE.

BOB'S SCORECARD 5   PROMPT AUTOEXEC BATCH CONFIG

VER

Description

This command displays the DOS version number.

Usage

```
ver
```

Options and switches

None.

Remarks

The MSD diagnostic utility displays the version number.

Example

To see the DOS version number, enter the following command:

```
ver
```

Additional information

See also MSD.

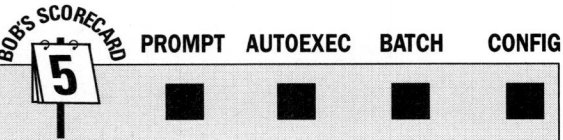

Description

This command instructs DOS to verify that data just written to disk can be read back into memory.

Usage

VERIFY is one of those rare commands that has the same syntax whether it is used in CONFIG.SYS or a batch file or is executed from the DOS prompt.

```
verify [on or off]
```

Options and switches

When you use VERIFY without a switch, the current VERIFY setting is displayed.

```
on or off
```

Specify ON to instruct DOS to verify all written data or OFF to turn off data verification.

Remarks

The verification process involves checking to see that the CRC value stored on disk in the sector header is the same as the CRC value of the data written to disk. This process is by no means a thorough verification that the data can be reread from the disk.

I usually leave verification off because it slows down disk throughput and provides only limited safeguards.

Examples

To see the current verification status, enter the following command:

```
verify
```

To turn on data verification, enter the following command:

```
verify on
```

Additional information

See also CHKDSK and COPY.

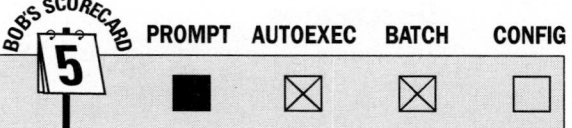

	PROMPT	AUTOEXEC	BATCH	CONFIG
VOL	■	⊠	⊠	☐

Description

This command displays a disk's volume label and serial number.

Usage

```
vol [drive:]
```

Options and switches

```
[drive:]
```

This option specifies the drive letter of the disk. By default, the current disk is used.

Remarks

A serial number exists for all disks formatted with DOS Version 4.0 or later.

The same data is printed at the beginning of standard DIR lists.

Example

Enter the following command to see the volume label and serial number of the default drive:

```
vol
```

Additional information

Use LABEL to change the volume label. The serial number is assigned automatically when the drive is formatted.

See also DIR, FORMAT, and LABEL.

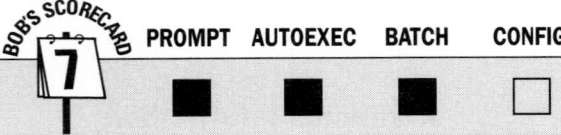

Description

This command loads the anti-virus TSR to monitor disk activity and protect against virus infection.

Usage

```
vsafe [/option[+ or -] ...] [/ne] [/nx] [/ax or /cx] [/n] [/d]
[/u]
```

Options and switches

When you execute VSAFE with no switches, it is installed with default settings.

```
[/option[+ or -] ...]
```

This switch specifies a number in the range from 1 to 8 that identifies the VSAFE option you want (see the "Remarks" section) followed by the plus sign (+) to enable the option or a minus sign (–) to disable it. You can subsequently modify all eight options from the VSAFE pop-up menu.

```
[/ne]
```

This switch instructs VSAFE *not* to load into expanded memory. When expanded memory is used, VSAFE uses 7K of base memory and 64K of expanded memory.

```
[/nx]
```

This switch instructs VSAFE *not* to load into extended memory. When extended memory is used, VSAFE uses 23K of base memory and 23K of extended memory.

`[/ax or /cx]`

By default, the VSAFE menu can be popped up by pressing Alt-V. Use either the /AX or /CX switch to instruct VSAFE to pop up on a specific Alt- or Ctrl-key combination, respectively. X represents the key you want (/CN for Ctrl-N, for example).

`[/n]`

This switch instructs VSAFE to monitor network drives.

`[/d]`

This switch turns off the checksum option.

`[/u]`

This switch uninstalls VSAFE from memory if no other memory-resident program has been installed since VSAFE. You can uninstall VSAFE by pressing Alt-U when the pop-up menu is displayed.

Remarks

If no memory options are specified, VSAFE tries to use expanded memory; if no expanded memory is available, VSAFE tries to use extended memory; otherwise, it loads into base memory and uses about 44K.

The following table lists the valid option codes in addition to the default setting and a brief description.

Option	Default	Description
1	On	Warns before allowing a hard disk format
2	Off	Warns that a program is trying to load as a TSR
3	Off	Intercepts all hard disk writes and then prompts for approval before proceeding
4	On	Checks all program files for viruses as they are opened
5	On	Monitors all disk boot sectors for viruses
6	On	Intercepts all attempts to write to a hard disk boot sector or partition table
7	Off	Intercepts all attempts to write to a floppy disk boot sector
8	On	Intercepts all attempts to change the contents of a program file

A number of options force VSAFE to pop up a dialog box that asks for approval before another program can make changes to the disk. If you use Windows with VSAFE installed, you must load the DOS 6 program MSAVTSR.EXE — this program enables VSAFE to pop up a Windows-style dialog box to ask for approval. Ideally, you add the statement LOAD=C:\DOS\MSAVTSR.EXE in WIN.INI to load the program automatically every time you start Windows. Always disable option 3 when you use Windows.

VSAFE does not check for specific brands of viruses. It protects the areas usually infected by viruses and provides a generic protection against all viruses.

If VSAFE suspects that a virus is active and it cannot inform you, it beeps (or, more accurately, tweeps) the PC speaker and reboots the system. If this process occurs, do not log on to a network — run MSAV immediately.

Do not start up VSAFE from Windows.

Examples

To install VSAFE by using the default settings, enter the following command:

```
vsafe
```

To install VSAFE and disable options 4 and 8 but enable option 7, enter the following command:

```
vsafe /4- /8- /7+
```

Additional information

Use the program MSAV or MWAV to scan memory and files for known viruses and to remove them.

 Refer to Chapter 3 for more information on VSAFE.

See also BACKUP, MSAV, MWAV, and MWAVTSR.

		PROMPT	AUTOEXEC	BATCH	CONFIG
XCOPY	BOB'S SCORECARD 8	■	⊠	■	☐

Description

An enhanced version of COPY that can copy files and directories and that loads multiple files in memory to improve performance.

Usage

```
xcopy [drive:][path]wildcardS.ext [drive:][path][wildcardT.ext]
[/a or /m] [/d:date] [/p] [/s] [/e] [/v] [/w]
```

Options and switches

[*drive:*][*path*]*wildcardS.ext*

This option identifies the source file or files to be copied. When you specify a path without a filename (c:\dos, for example), the *.* wildcard is assumed. This switch must be specified.

[*drive:*][*path*][*wildcardT.ext*]

This option identifies the target location where the files will be copied. If you don't specify a filename, the files retain their original names. If you use a wildcard, the file copies are renamed using the wildcard. If you don't specify a target path or filename, the source files are copied to the current directory.

[/a]

This switch copies only matching files that have the archive bit set.

[/m]

Like /A, /M copies only matching files that have the archive bit set, but XCOPY also turns the archive bit off after the file is copied.

[/d:*date*]

This switch copies only matching files that have a date stamp equal to or later than the specified date. The format of the date is dependent on the country setting — run the DATE command to see the current format for your system.

[/p]

This switch instructs XCOPY to prompt you before creating any directories on the target drive.

[/s]

This switch copies all files in all subdirectories from the source path.

`[/e]`

Use this switch with /S to instruct XCOPY to create even empty subdirectories on the target path if they exist on the source path.

`[/v]`

This switch instructs DOS to verify that the data in the target file can be read successfully. It does not, however, determine whether the target is an accurate copy of the source.

`[/w]`

This switch prompts for a key to be pressed before starting the XCOPY.

Remarks

XCOPY is much faster than COPY because it reads multiple files into memory at one time and then writes them to the target path.

Sometimes an XCOPY command is ambiguous and XCOPY doesn't know whether the target name represents a file or a directory. In these cases, XCOPY asks you to confirm the meaning of the target name.

Unlike COPY, XCOPY does not concatenate multiple files in a single target file — it just copies each file in turn to the target file.

XCOPY returns the following ERRORLEVELs:

ERRORLEVEL	Message
0	Copy completed successfully.
1	No matching source files.
2	The user aborted the copy operation by pressing Ctrl-Break.
4	A file-reading error occurred.
5	A file-writing error occurred.

Examples

Use the following command to copy all files and directories from the disk in drive A and reproduce the directory structure on drive B:

```
xcopy a:\*.* b: /s /e
```

Use the following command to copy all the files in C:\123W\BUDGET to drive I:

```
xcopy c:\123w\budget i:
```

Use the following command to copy all the files that have the file attribute set from the D:\WP\NOTES directory to drive A:

```
xcopy d:\wp\notes a: /m
```

Additional information

Refer to Chapter 2 for more information on XCOPY.

See also ATTRIB, DATE, DISKCOPY, and MOVE.

Bob's Shareware Collection disks

PCOPY, on of the Patriquin Hard Disk Utilities from Patri-Soft, can do everything XCOPY can, and much more. PCOPY can copy files based on date or size, "best-fit" files to optimally use floppy free space, synchronize source and target disks, prompt before overwriting files, and process all nested subdirectories.

PocketD, the general-purpose utility from Pocketware, provides extensive file copying options.

CMFILER, the file manager from NoVaSoft, makes it easy to tag and copy multiple files.

Part V:
Bob's Better-Than-DOS
Shareware Collection

Part V:
Bob's Better-Than-DOS
Shareware Collection

Introduction

The disks accompanying this book contain some world-class *shareware* programs. Refer to the last page of the book for complete installation instructions.

Nearly all of these programs include text files documenting how to get the most from the software, and these documentation files will be automatically installed to your hard disk along with the executable programs.

Call me old-fashioned, but I much prefer reading printed documentation to browsing text on-screen. This part of the book, therefore, contains information about every shareware program supplied with the book. Unfortunately, there wasn't room to include the complete documentation for every program, so, in most cases, you will find condensed versions of the documentation available on disk.

If you don't find answers to your questions in this part of the book, try looking at the documentation files on disk. Better still, try pressing F1 while the application is running; many of the full-screen programs include comprehensive on-line help.

Shareware

Shareware programs provide the opportunity for you to receive a fully functional, free version of a program to try out for (usually) a period of about 30 days. At the end of the trial period, you can decide whether you want to keep the program.

If you like the program, register it with the author. With registration, you receive added benefits. To register, fill out an order form (copies are included with each program in this Part) and send your payment to the shareware author. The registration fee for shareware programs depends on the product (usually from $20 to $50) but is usually a nominal sum when you consider the quality of the software.

If you decide not to register the program, remove it from your hard disk and owe nothing. This "honor system" (of paying only if you use the software) is very important if the concept of shareware is going to survive. Shareware authors must be supported if they are going to be able to continue to provide quality software at a minimal cost.

Benefits of Registration _____

When you register a shareware program, you usually receive most of the following benefits:

- **A registered version of the software**

    Many registered copies of shareware programs are slightly better than the unregistered versions. For example, with TurboBat (one of the ExtraDOS utilities), the unregistered version has a copyright screen that appears when you first run the program. This screen boldly proclaims that the version being run is an evaluation version only; the registered version replaces this screen with a registered copy designation. Some registered copies of shareware actually contain more features and functionality than their unregistered counterparts.

- **Technical support**

    Most registrations come with telephone, fax, and/or computer bulletin board support.

- **Professionally printed manuals**

    With many shareware programs, you receive a printed manual when you register. This manual, which is more detailed than the on-line printed documentation, often provides illustrations.

- **Free upgrades**

    In most cases, registration gives you the benefit of free upgrades to a future version of the program, with features that may enhance the version you have.

- **Added programs**

    In a few cases, you receive with your registration a disk that contains a registered version of the program, along with other _bonus_ shareware programs.

■ **License and money-back guarantee**

Some shareware authors offer you a money-back guarantee with registration. Most registered shareware also offers you a permanent license to use the program on your PC.

■ **Source code or custom programming options**

Some authors give you source code when you register; others offer custom programming options instead. You may have to pay extra for these benefits.

The biggest overall benefit of registering is that the registration of shareware encourages the development of new shareware programs.

Where to Get Shareware

Shareware is usually distributed by electronic information services, such as CompuServe, GEnie, and many others, as well as electronic bulletin board services (BBSs). See Appendix E for further information on these electronic services.

The Association of Shareware Professionals (ASP)

The Association of Shareware Professionals (ASP) was formed in 1987 to "strengthen the future of *shareware* (user-supported software) as an alternative to software distributed under normal retail marketing methods."

Note that the ASP members subscribe to a code of ethics and are committed to the concept of shareware. The ASP certifies programs that meet their criteria for shareware and sponsors events at computer industry events, such as COMDEX and PC EXPO and many others. If you are a software author, the ASP may help you find distribution channels for your program.

The ASP demands professionalism from its members. For example, each ASP author must acknowledge every registration to the purchaser and must provide at least three months of technical support for their products. ASP members must also stand behind any benefits they offer.

Membership dues in the ASP are very reasonable. For more information, write the Executive Director, Association of Shareware Professionals, 545 Grover Road, Muskegon, MI 49442-9427, or send a message to CompuServe 72050,1433.

The ASP Ombudsman Program _____

To resolve any questions about the role of shareware, registrations, licenses, and so on, the ASP established an Ombudsman to hear all parties. Not all of the shareware authors who have programs on the *DOS 6 SECRETS* disks (*Bob's Better-Than-DOS Shareware Collection*) are members of the ASP. But if you have a support problem with an author who is an ASP member, and you cannot settle it directly with the author, the Ombudsman may help you find a remedy. Remember that you cannot expect technical support for any program unless you are a registered user of that program.

Assume that the following ASP statement applies to each of the programs on the *DOS 6 SECRETS* disks: "These programs are produced by members of the Association of Shareware Professionals (ASP). ASP wants to make sure that the shareware concept works for you. If you are unable to resolve a shareware-related problem with an ASP member by contacting the member directly, ASP may be able to help. The ASP Ombudsman can help you resolve a dispute or problem with an ASP member, but does not provide technical support for members' products. Please write to the ASP Ombudsman at P.O. Box 5786, Bellevue, WA 98006, or send a CompuServe message to ASP Ombudsman, 70007,3536."

General Shareware License Agreement _____

Each of the shareware programs on the *DOS 6SECRETS* disks has its own license agreement and terms. These are printed in the section describing each program, or in a text file enclosed with the program on the disk. Most programs are copyrighted (and assume "All Rights Reserved" even where not explicitly stated). In general, you should assume that any shareware program adheres to at least the following license terms suggested by the ASP, where Program is the specific shareware program, and Company is the program's author or publisher:

The Program is supplied as is. The author disclaims all warranties, expressed or implied, including, without limitation, the warranties of merchantability and of fitness for any purpose. The author assumes no liability for damages, direct or consequential, which may result from the use of the Program.

The Program is a *shareware* program, and is provided at no charge to the user for evaluation. Feel free to share it with your friends, but please do not give it away altered or as part of another system. The essence of *user-supported* software is to provide personal computer users with quality software without high prices, and yet to provide incentives for programmers to continue to develop new products. If you find this program useful, and find that you continue to use the Program after a reasonable trial period, you must make a registration payment to the Company. The registration fee will license one copy for one use on any one computer at any one time. You must treat this software just like a copyrighted book. An example is that this software may be used by any number of people and may be freely moved from one computer location to another, as long as there is no possibility of it being used at one location while it's being used at another — just as a book cannot be read by two different persons at the same time.

Commercial users of the Program must register and pay for their copies of the Program within 30 days of first use or their license is withdrawn. Site-license arrangements may be made by contacting the Company.

Anyone distributing the Program for any kind of remuneration must first contact the Company at the address provided for authorization. This authorization will be automatically granted to distributors recognized by the ASP as adhering to its guidelines for shareware distributors, and such distributors may begin offering the Program immediately. (However, the Company must still be advised so that the distributor can be kept up-to-date with the latest version of the Program.)

You are encouraged to pass a copy of the Program along to your friends for evaluation. Please encourage them to register their copy, if they find that they can use it. All registered users will receive a copy of the latest version of the Program. You are also encouraged to give feedback to the shareware authors by sending in comments about the existing programs and what you would like to see in the future.

Each of the programs and documentation thereto are published and distributed with this book with the written permission of the authors of each. The programs herein are supplied as is. Robert D. Ainsbury and IDG Books Worldwide Inc. individually and together disclaim all warranties, expressed or implied, including, without limitation, the warranties of merchantability and of fitness for any particular purpose; and assume no liability for damages, direct or consequential, which may result from the use of the programs or reliance on the documentation.

Software Installation _____

Complete installation instructions for the DOS SECRETS disks are printed on the last page of this book.

Disk Contents _____

The following programs are included on the *DOS 6 SECRETS* disks (*Bob's Better-Than-DOS Shareware Collection*).

Bob's Better-Than-Shareware Collection Disks: Contents at a Glance

Program	Description	Disk Space Required
ANARKEY	Command Line Enhancer	326K
ARJ	File Compression Tools	395K
BATUTIL	Batch File Enhancer	539K
CMFILER	File Manager	377K
DOG	Disk Defragmenter	119K
DUPE	Disk Duplicator	81K
EXTRADOS		346K
ALARMCLK	Alarm Clock	
ALLSUB	Subdirectory Processor	
CALENDAR	Calendar Lister	
CLEANUP	Hard Disk Cleanser	
DISKINFO	Disk Information Utility	
NO	File Exclusion Utility	
TURBOBAT	Batch File Compiler	
TURBOTXT	Text File Compiler	
FANSI	ANSI.SYS Replacement	879K
FORMAT MASTER	Disk Formatter	300K
HOTDIR PLUS	Directory Lister	102K
LCD	Directory Changer	74K
LIST	File Browser	257K
PATRI-SOFT		414K
PCOPY	File Copying Utility	
PDAILY	Executes Once-a-Day	
PDEL	File Deleting Utility	
POCKETD	Directory/Copy/Search+	231K
QFIND	File Finder	83K
QEDIT	Full-screen Editor	356K

RELDEL	Permanent File Eraser	31K
SECRETS	Batch Files etc. from Book	20K
SEEKEASY	Text Search Utility	131K
SPINTOOL	Disk Analysis Software	33K
STACKEY	Keyboard Manager	295K
UMBDRV	Memory Manager	98K
VIRUSCAN	McAfee Virus Scanner	367K

ANARKEY

Version 4.0
Copyright © 1988–1991 by Steven Calwas, Moderne Software

Introduction

Anarkey is an intelligent command-line editor for DOS. With Anarkey, complete input lines can be entered with two or three keystrokes. Anarkey is intelligent because there is no need to tell it what you want to enter on the command line; simply press the <Tab> key and Anarkey figures out what you want and does it for you.

Program and Documentation Files

By default, the install program for the *DOS 6 SECRETS* diskettes will install all of the Anarkey files in the directory \SECRETS\ANARKEY. This directory has not been added to the search path. You can execute the program from its home directory, add the directory to the search path, or copy the Anarkey files to a directory that is included in the search path.

The complete Anarkey distribution includes the following files:

ANARKEY.COM	Anarkey Program
ANARKEY.DOC	Anarkey User Manual
ANARKEY.SUM	Summary list of Anarkey key assignments
101-KEYS.COM	Support for Enhanced 101/102-Key Keyboards
ANARKED.EXE	The Anarkey Keystroke Editor
ANARKMD.EXE	The Anarkey Command-Line Utility
CONVERT.EXE	The Anarkey AKA-Conversion Utility
LOAD.EXE	The Anarkey Loader
CREDIT.CRD	Information on registering by credit card
ORDERFRM	Registration form
READ.ME	Read this file first

Note: Only Chapters 1, 2, and 9 are reprinted here. For full documentation, please read the file ANARKEY.DOC.

Chapter 1: Tutorial

Here is a list of the main operations Anarkey provides:

- Line-edit features comparable to those found in word processors.
- Ability to save input lines for later retrieval.
- Three methods to retrieve saved command lines:
    1. Sequentially walk through the list of saved commands.
    2. Line completion where you enter a portion of the line and Anarkey completes the remainder for you.
    3. Pop-up window which lists all saved commands. Supports a mouse.
- A text substitution capability called an AKA (also referred to as an *alias* or *synonym*). The Convert program is included in the Anarkey package to translate the alias and synonym definitions of other editors to Anarkey's format. AKAs can even be executed from a batch file.
- Enter multiple commands on a single input line.
- A 255-character input line.
- Comprehensive filename completion.
- Environment variable editing.
- Use expanded memory.
- Display a non-blinking cursor.
- Pop-up windows with built-in mouse support to retrieve saved commands and complete filenames as well as to edit environment variables.
- Configurable key assignments.
- A MegaKey which analyzes the input line, determines the type of Anarkey operation you want, and does it for you automatically. The MegaKey is what makes Anarkey an intelligent command-line editor.

- Write the list of saved commands and AKAs to a disk file for future restoration.
- Comprehensive UNIX switchar support.
- Pop-up help window with configurable help text.
- Full support for enhanced 101/102-key keyboards.
- Pop-up windows offer you a choice between two mouse interfaces.
- Special support for the 386 Enhanced Mode of Microsoft Windows 3.0.
- And much more!

Anarkey is written entirely in assembly language for maximum efficiency in memory usage and execution speed. When installed in its default configuration, Anarkey uses about 11K of memory. If expanded memory is available, Anarkey requires only 1K of conventional memory.

Installation

Anarkey makes significant use of the Anarkmd program. To guarantee that Anarkey works properly at all times, place the ANARKMD.EXE file in a directory specified in the PATH environment variable.

To run Anarkey, execute the ANARKEY.COM program from either the DOS prompt or from your AUTOEXEC.BAT file. Since you will probably want Anarkey active whenever you are using your computer, executing Anarkey from the AUTOEXEC.BAT file makes the most sense.

When run, Anarkey installs itself into the DOS environment and terminates but stays resident. A default configuration is used but can be modified via command-line options. Anarkey options are described in Chapter 11 of the complete online manual. For the remainder of this tutorial, we assume the default configuration is in effect.

Once resident, Anarkey handles all input requests for the following situations:

- The DOS command line
- Redirected input
- DEBUG, SYMDEB, EDLIN, and several third-party programs
- All DOS sessions running under Windows 3.0 in 386 enhanced mode

Notice that Anarkey does not process lines executed from a batch file. However, the Anarkmd program described in Chapter 16 provides an indirect method to support batch files.

Note: Please read the ANARKEY.DOC FILE for the "Quick-Start Tutorial" section omitted here if you need help getting started with Anarkey.

Install Anarkey by executing the ANARKEY.COM program.

Anarkey lets you place the cursor anywhere within the input line and enter or delete characters. Once a line has been saved, it can be retrieved so you won't have to retype it. Pressing the <Up> and <Down> arrow keys "walks" you through the list of saved lines. Once retrieved, a line can be edited using the line-edit functions.

You can display a full-screen window containing the list of the saved commands by pressing <Alt-F4>. (Make sure ANARKMD.EXE is stored somewhere along your PATH variable before doing this.) If you want to enter something on the input line, press the <Tab> key and Anarkey figures out what you want and does it automatically.

Chapter 2: The Pop-Up Help Window

The help window can be popped up by pressing <Alt-F1> or <Alt-H> whenever Anarkey is active, for example, at the DOS command prompt. Before you pop up the window, make sure the Anarkmd program (in the file ANARKMD.EXE) is in either the current directory or a directory specified in the PATH environment variable. After pressing the help key, a full-screen window will be displayed containing a list of Anarkey functions and their current key assignments.

Note: Anarkmd must be in the current directory or along the PATH because it actually performs the entire pop-up window operation. Anarkey simply executes Anarkmd, telling it to display the help window. But all this is performed automatically in the background, and you do not need to worry about it.

The information displayed in the window is actually read from a standard text file just before the window pops up. By reading and displaying a separate text file, Anarkey saves precious DOS memory by not keeping the help information resident. It also provides great flexibility in the content and format of the displayed help information. In other words, you can modify the help text file to your heart's desire, even include help information about other programs if you wish. Only two restrictions apply: (1) the file cannot exceed 65,000 characters in size and (2) the file may not contain more than 1,000 lines of text.

Since a text file must be loaded to gather the help information, Anarkey must be informed of the help file's name. Anarkey first looks for the file name in an environment variable called **HELP@**. If **HELP@** is defined, it should specify the drive, directory, and filename of the helpfile. For example,

```
SET HELP@=c:\anarkey\anarkey.hlp
```

If HELP@ is not defined, Anarkey assumes the help file's name is ANARKEY.SUM and will attempt to locate a file with that name. ANARKEY.SUM is a text file distributed with Anarkey which contains a list of Anarkey functions and their default key assignments. ANARKEY.SUM can also be updated by Anarked, the Anarkey Keystroke Editor, if you modify any of the default key assignments. Anarked is explained in Chapter 13.

Depending upon which version of DOS you are running, Anarkey will search for the ANARKEY.SUM file in two locations. First, if running under DOS version 3.0 or later, Anarkey searches for ANARKEY.SUM in the same directory in which Anarkmd is located, also called the home directory. Under versions of DOS prior to 3.0, Anarkey does not check this location.

If the ANARKEY.SUM file is still not found, Anarkey looks for it in the current directory.

These search steps and the order in which they are performed are outlined below:

1) File specified in HELP@ environment variable
2) ANARKEY.SUM in Anarkmd home directory (DOS 3.0+ only)
3) ANARKEY.SUM in current directory

If all attempts to locate the help file fail, Anarkey displays an error message (Help file

not found) and ends the help operation. Otherwise, the help file is loaded and displayed in the pop-up window.

With the help window displayed, the following keystrokes are recognized and acted upon:

<F1>	Display help for pop-up window
<Esc>	Exit the help window
<Enter>	Same as <Esc> key
<Up>	Scroll the window contents up one line
<Down>	Scroll the window contents down one line
<PgUp>	Scroll the window contents up one page
<PgDn>	Scroll the window contents down one page
<Home>	View top of help file
<End>	View bottom of help file

In addition to keystroke input, if a mouse is installed on the computer, it can be used to scroll through the help window. Anarkey supports the Microsoft and any Microsoft-compatible mouse. With the mouse installed, a separate mouse cursor is displayed in the middle of the window in the form of a solid block character. By moving the mouse, the mouse cursor can be moved anywhere on the screen.

Scrolling operations are performed with the mouse by moving the mouse cursor to specific locations in the window and clicking (pressing and releasing) the left mouse button. For example, you can position the mouse cursor anywhere over the

```
Press F1 for help
```

message in the upper right corner of the window and click the left mouse button. This will have the same effect as pressing <F1> in that it will display an additional help screen. Pressing either mouse button will clear this secondary help window.

On the far right edge of the help window is a scroll bar. The scroll bar is actually composed of four separate sections. At the very top of the bar is a single-character up-arrow. To scroll the window contents up one line, position the mouse cursor on this arrow and click the mouse button. A down-arrow is located at the very bottom of the scroll bar. Click on it to scroll the window contents down one line. The remainder of the scroll bar is divided into two equal halves. Click on the top half to scroll the window up one page; click on the bottom half to scroll down one page. You can also press and hold the mouse button with the mouse cursor positioned at any of these locations. Doing so is the same as repeatedly clicking on the item.

Note: To clear the help window, click the right mouse button.

After exiting the help screen, you will be returned to the DOS command prompt. Any characters entered at the prompt when the help window was popped up will still exist.

The mouse movements described in this chapter are also applicable to the other pop-up windows that Anarkey supports. These other windows are discussed in future chapters.

Anarkey also supports an alternative mouse interface (in case you don't like the interface described in this chapter). The alternative mouse interface is described in Appendix I.

Note: See the ANARKEY.DOC file for Chapters 3–8 omitted here.

Chapter 9: The MegaKey and MenuKey

The MegaKey and MenuKey are two of Anarkey's most potent strengths. With these two simple keys, you gain access to all of Anarkey's completion, line-retrieval, and window functions.

The MegaKey

In the previous chapters, you learned about several separate Anarkey functions which retrieve and complete items on input lines. Each of those functions and their assigned keystrokes are listed:

<F5>, <Ctrl-K>	Retrieve line from history buffer
<F7>, <Ctrl-D>	Complete directory name
<F8>, <Ctrl-F>	Complete filename
<F9>, <Ctrl-E>	Retrieve environment variable

Rather than force you to remember all those keystrokes and have to think about which one to press at a given time, Anarkey combines them all into a single MegaKey. By default, the MegaKey is assigned to <Tab>. When you press <Tab>, Anarkey determines on its own the type of completion or retrieval operation you desire and does it for you. Of course, you can still press any of the keys listed above, but in most instances, it will be easier to just press <Tab> and let Anarkey do all the work.

Like all the other retrieval and completion functions, the MegaKey can be pressed repeatedly to cycle through the list of possibilities. The MegaKey will correctly determine the desired type of operation an amazingly high percentage of the time. However, you may occasionally have to cycle through some unwanted completions before getting to the one you want.

The MenuKey

The MenuKey is a close cousin of the MegaKey. Like the MegaKey, it combines several operations to a single key. The MenuKey can be thought of as a front-end to all of Anarkey's pop-up window functions listed below.

<Alt-F1>, <Alt-H>	Pop-up help window
<Alt-F5>, <Alt-K>	Pop-up line retrieval window
<Alt-F8>, <Alt-F>	Pop-up filename completion window
<Alt-F9>, <Alt-E>	Pop-up environment window

The MenuKey is assigned to the <Alt-Tab> and <Shift-Tab> keys. However, be aware that the <Alt-Tab> key is not normally recognized on DOS systems. If your system has an enhanced, 101-key keyboard (i.e., a keyboard with <F11> and <F12> keys), you can use the 101-Keys program to allow DOS to recognize <Alt-Tab> and many other keystrokes. 101-Keys is discussed in Chapter 15.

Like all the other Anarkey window functions, be sure the Anarkmd program is located in either the current directory or a directory along the PATH before pressing the MenuKey.

The MenuKey displays a pop-up menu. Each of the above operations is listed in the menu. In addition, the item *Return to Command Line* is included in the menu. Using the selection techniques discussed for windows in previous chapters, you select a menu item via the keyboard or a mouse. The operation you select is then executed.

For example, if the help window menu item is selected, the pop-up help window is displayed on-screen. The effect is the same as if you had pressed the <Alt-F1> key to display the window, but now you only have to remember a single key, the MenuKey, to display any of the supported Anarkey windows.

Summary

Despite its brief length, this chapter described Anarkey's most powerful functions, the MegaKey and MenuKey. These two functions are great leaps toward a state of total Anarkey, a state without keystrokes. Learn them and your life at the command prompt will become a pleasure.

<Tab>	MegaKey
<Alt-Tab>	MenuKey
<Shift-Tab>	Same as <Alt-Tab>

ANARKEY Function Summary

Help Window

Help window   <Alt-F1> or <Alt-H>

Line Editing Functions

Cursor movement:
To start of line .... <Home>
To end of line .... <End>
Right one character .... <Right>
Right one word .... <Ctrl-Right>
Left one character .... <Left>
Left one word .... <Ctrl-Left>

Character deletion:
Character left .... <Backspace>
Current character .... <Del>
Word right .... <Ctrl-T>

To end of line .... <Ctrl-End> or <Ctrl-Y>
Delete line .... <Esc>

Character retrieval:
Single char from previous line .... <F1>
Remainder of previous line .... <F3>
Remainder of prev line
and execute .... <Alt-F3>

Miscellaneous:
Accept line .... <Enter>
Toggle input mode .... <Ins>
Accept next keystroke
unmodified .... <Ctrl-U>

MegaKey and MenuKey

MegaKey .... <Tab>
MenuKey .... <Alt-Tab> or <Shift-Tab>

History Buffer Functions

Retrieve previous buffer line .... <Up>
Retrieve next buffer line .... <Down>
Complete line .... <F5> or <Ctrl-K>
Complete line and
accept .... <F6> or <Ctrl-L>
History-buffer
window .... <Alt-F5> or <Alt-K>
Restore CBL, get next line .... <PgDn>
Display buffer contents .... <F4>
Display buffer contents
from bottom .... <Ctrl-F4>
Write buffer to
\ANARKEY.LOG .... <Ctrl-W>
Save line in buffer, do not
execute .... <Ctrl-J>
Remove current buffer line .... <Ctrl-Z>
Clear buffer .... <Ctrl-X>

AKA Functions

Display AKAs .... <Alt-F4>
Undefine all AKAs .... <Alt-X>

Directory, Program, and File Name Completion Functions

Complete directory
name .... <F7> or <Ctrl-D>
Complete file/program
name .... <F8> or <Ctrl-F>

Filename-completion
window .... <Alt-F8> or <Alt-F>

Environment Variable Retrieval

Retrieve environment
variable .... <F9> or <Ctrl-E>

Environment-variable
window .... <Alt-F9> or <Alt-E>

UNIX Switchar Programs

Display UNIX programs .... <Shift-F4>

Miscellaneous Functions

Check command lengths .... <F2>

Repress multiple commands
per line .... <F10> or <Ctrl-R>

ANARKEY 4.0 Registration Form

Name: _____

Company: _____

Address: _____

City: _____

State: _____ Country: _____

Zip: _____ Phone: _____

Remit to:
Steven Calwas
Moderne Software
P.O. Box 3638
Santa Clara, CA 95055-3638
(408)247-0509

(3434 Warburton Avenue, Suite 10, 95051)

Please send me a registered Anarkey disk and printed manual.

❏ Anarkey includes disk and printed manual
$29.95 each $ _____

❏ Network License, includes one disk and manual
Note: Although one physical copy of the software is delivered, each network user must obtain a license.
First user .... $29.95 $ _____
Subsequent users .... x $10.00 each $ _____
CA residents, add sales tax .... $ _____
Shipping and Handling
U.S.: .... $4.00 $ _____
Outside U.S.: .... $8.00 $ _____
Total .... $ _____
Specify Disk Size: ❏ 5.25" ❏ 3.5"
Payment by:
❏ Check   ❏ Money Order
❏ Credit Card (be sure to attach CREDIT.CRD form)

ARJ

Version 2.30
Copyright © 1990–92 by Robert K. Jung

Introduction

ARJ version 2.30 is a full-featured shareware release. The use of ARJ in a business, commercial, government, or institutional environment requires a license. This software as originally released by the author came in an ARJ self-extracting archive with an ARJ-SECURITY envelope to prevent tampering. Re-archival of this software will lose this security feature.

ARJ is the result of my desire to use my interest in compression technology to produce an archiver for personal use on my PC and on minicomputers that provides power and excellent flexibility. I expect ARJ will continually be improved both in speed, compression, and features. There are plans to port versions of ARJ to other platforms in the future pending sufficient time and funding.

Important: Users of ARJ should read the WHATSNEW.DOC and UPDATE.DOC files which contain information about the latest improvements to ARJ.

Major Features of ARJ

- ARJ is currently the trendsetter in PC file archivers in terms of features and compression.
- ARJ 2.30 currently provides excellent file compression in terms of resulting archive size and speed.
- ARJ includes an option to create multiple volume archives with one command making ARJ useful for making backups to multiple floppies or archiving a very large file to several floppies without SLICEing.
- ARJ includes a myriad of commands and options to provide outstanding flexibility in archiver usage.

Program and Documentation Files

By default, the install program for the *DOS 6 SECRETS* diskettes will install all of the ARJ files in the directory \SECRETS\ARJ. This directory has not been added to the search path. You can execute the program from its home directory, add the directory to the search path, or copy the ARJ files to a directory that is included in the search path. For instance, to install the ARJ software, you may simply copy ARJ.EXE, REARJ.EXE, REARJ.CFG, and ARJSORT.COM to one of the directories named in your DOS PATH statement found in your AUTOEXEC.BAT.

File Contents

ARJ230.EXE	An ARJ-SECURED self-extracting archive containing the following files:

ARJ.DOC	ARJ user manual
ARJ.EXE	Version 2.30
ARJ_BBS.DOC	List of ARJ support BBSes
ARJSORT.BAT	Sort archive by various parameters
ARJSORT.COM	Compiled ARJSORT.BAT file
ARJSORT.DOC	ARJSORT user manual
CREDIT.CRD	Form for handling credit card orders
LICENSE.DOC	License policy for ARJ
ORDERFRM.DOC	Order form for ARJ
README.DOC	Read this file first

REARJ.CFG	Default REARJ configuration file
REARJ.DOC	REARJ user manual
REARJ.EXE	Archive conversion utility
REGISTER.EXE	Program to register ARJ programs
SYSOP.DOC	SYSOP registration special offer
TECHNOTE.DOC	ARJ technical information
UPDATE.DOC	Update to ARJ user manual
WHATSNEW.DOC	Changes to ARJ from 1.00 to now
WHY_ARJ.DOC	ARJ commercial
ARJBACK.BAT	Batch file to fully back up C: to A:
ARJREST.BAT	Batch file to restore to C: from A:
ARJUPDAT.BAT	Batch file to incrementally back up C:
REARJALL.BAT	Batch file to REARJ ZIP, LZH to ARJ

Terminology

The following terms are used throughout this manual.

ARCHIVE — This is a file containing one or more files in a compressed or noncompressed state and containing file-related information such as filename and date-time last modified, etc.

ARJ FILE — This is an archive created by ARJ (sometimes called an *arjive* in slang terminology).

BACKUP TYPE ARCHIVE — This is an ARJ archive which has the internal backup flag turned on. This causes all current and future updates to the archive to *not* overwrite internal files in the archive when adding files with the same names as ones already in the archive. The older duplicate files in the archive will be marked as backups.

COMPRESSION — The process of encoding redundant information into data requiring less storage space.

COMPRESSION PERCENTAGE/RATIO — The percentage compression reported by ARJ is a variation of one of the TWO standard methods of expressing compression ratio in the technical literature. ARJ uses the compressed size/original size ratio. The other method is the inverse ratio. When ARJ reports 96 percent as the compression ratio, that means that the compressed file is 96 percent of the original size (very little compression). Other archivers use their own methods. LHARC uses the same ratio as ARJ.

EXTRACTION or UNCOMPRESSION — The processing of re-creating the exact information that was previously compressed.

SELF-EXTRACTION MODULE (SFX) — This is an archive that is an executable file that is capable of extracting self-contained files.

TEXT MODE — In text mode, ARJ inputs the file using the C library text mode which translates the carriage return, linefeed control characters of MS-DOS to a single linefeed character. This saves space and provides the option for cross platform file extraction. On another platform, the host C library would change the single linefeed to the host text newline separator sequence. In addition, for platforms such as PRIMOS which set bit 8 in ASCII text characters, ARJ sets/resets bit 8 according to the platform extracted to. When extracting a text mode file to the same type of platform archived from, ARJ will *not* strip the 8-bit text to 7-bit text.

VOLUMES — These are ARJ archives that are in sequence and have been created by a single ARJ command. Files in the volumes may span volumes in a split format. These volumes are usable archives.

Features of ARJ

- Currently ranks as one of the best in compression in terms of size reduction of the currently available archivers including PKZIP 1.10, PAK 2.51, ARC 7.0 (ARC PLUS), LHARC 1.13c, LHA 2.13, and the new ZOO 2.10. ARJ is particularly effective with database files, graphics files, and large documents. With the **–jm or –jm1** option, ARJ usually compresses even smaller at a cost of time.
- Archive and individual file comments with option of inputting comments from a file.
- ARJ has MS-DOS 3.x international language support for the proper casing of filenames and text.

- 32 bit CRC file integrity check.
- DOS volume label support.
- Empty directory support.
- File-generation archive support where ARJ will allow the user to keep several versions of the same file in an archive.
- Test new archive before overwriting the original archive option.
- Multiple volume archives with one ARJ command. This allows the user to back up a full hard disk drive to multiple floppies. Recovery of individual files is convenient because each volume is an individual archive except for split files. No need to use SLICE with ARJ.
- Archive file reordering facility with the option of sorting by file size, file extension, CRC value, date-time modified, filename, pathname, compression ratio, file attribute, and more.
- String searching with context display within archive files.
- Built-in facility to recover files from broken archives.
- Self-extraction feature that is internal to the ARJ runfile. The SFX module is full-featured with a built-in help screen.
- Internal string data integrity check in ARJ to resist hacking à la LHARC to ICE.
- Archive security envelope feature to resist tampering with secured archives. This feature disallows ANY changes to a secured archive. Not even comments can be changed.
- Password option to encrypt archived files.
- Text mode data-compression option to enable movement of text files from one host machine to another. Text mode also results in slightly greater file size reduction on MS-DOS machines.
- File extraction to screen in a paged mode to permit browsing through an archive.
- Specification of the files to be added to an archive via one or more list files. In addition, ARJ can generate a list file.
- Specification of files to be excluded from processing by ARJ.
- Subdirectory recursion during compression and extraction.

Release Notes

The only difference between the registered version and the shareware version is the version/copyright message. Registered users receive a registration code to change the version message.

The use of ARJ in a business, commercial, institutional, or government environment requires a license. However, business, commercial, institutional, and government users may use ARJ for evaluation purposes for a period of 30 days. See the file LICENSE.DOC for full details.

While evaluating ARJ, you should use the **–jt** (test archive) option to verify new ARJ archives of your data.

This version has been tested under DOS 2.11, 3.3, 4.01, and DOS 5.0 (and under 6.0 by Bob).

Here is a suggested command that will test ARJ on all of your files:

```
ARJ a -r -jt -y "-vasdel a:\vol.*"
    a:\vol c:\*.*
```

ARJR, DEARJ, and REARJ Programs

The new programs ARJR and DEARJ are available to registered and licensed users of ARJ. ARJR is the ARJ program minus the help screen and SFX modules. DEARJ is the ARJR program minus the archive creation/modification functions.

There are two versions of REARJ, the shareware version and the registered version. The registered version contains a number of additional enhancements including environment variable usage, !listfile capability, and selection by date-time.

See the LICENSE.DOC and ORDERFRM.DOC files for more information.

UNARJ and DEARJ are *not* the same program.

Quick Start to Using ARJ

Please note that switch options may be placed anywhere in the command line.

To create an ARJ archive containing all of the files in the current directory:

```
ARJ a archive
```

To create an ARJ archive containing all files with the **.DOC** extension in the current directory:

```
ARJ a archive *.DOC
```

To create an ARJ archive containing all of the files in the named directory and all files in subdirectories of the named directory:

```
ARJ a -r archive
    named_directory\*.*
```

To create an archive containing files without path specs:

```
ARJ a -e archive
    named_directory\*.*
```

For maximum compression, use the **–jm** or **–jm1** options. For better speed, use the **–m2** option:

```
ARJ a -r -jm archive
    named_directory\*.*

ARJ a -r -m2 archive
    named_directory\*.*
```

To create an ARJ archive containing the full specified pathnames of the stored files including any drive and root specs:

```
ARJ a -r -jf archive
    C:\top_directory\*.*
```

To back up your hard disk to multiple volume archives on drive A with archive testing and archive bit resetting:

```
ARJ a -r -jf -jt -a1 -b2 -vvas
    A:backup C:\*.*
```

To extract all of the files in an archive to the current directory:

```
ARJ e archive
```

To extract all of the files in an archive to a named directory:

```
ARJ e archive named_directory\
```

To extract all files with the **.DOC** extension to the current directory:

```
ARJ e archive *.DOC
```

To extract all of the files in an archive re-creating the original directory structure:

```
ARJ x archive
    original_directory_name\
```

The ending \ character is optional if the original_directory_name already exists.

To extract all of the files in an archive containing absolute pathnames to the original paths:

```
ARJ x -jf archive
```

To list all of the files in an archive:

```
ARJ l archive
```

How to Create an Executable Self-Extracting ARJ Archive

The command

```
ARJ y -je archive
```

will create a full featured self-extracting archive from an already built archive.

The command

```
ARJ y -jel archive
```

will create a smaller self-extracting archive.

Syntax: `ARJ y -je archive` produces archive.exe.

Under DOS systems other than 2.11, 3.2, 3.3, 4.0, and 5.0 you may have to rename the self-extract module to ARJSFX.EXE to do the extraction.

See the **–je** option for more information.

Converting Other Archive Files to ARJ Format

Included with this software is the program REARJ. This program can be used to individually or collectively convert archive files from other formats to the ARJ format.

```
REARJ *.ZIP *.ARC *.LZH
```

will convert all ZIP, ARC, and LZH archives in the current directory to the ARJ format. See the REARJ.DOC for more information about REARJ.

How to Use ARJ

If you type `ARJ [return]`, you will see a simple help screen.

If you type `ARJ -? [return]`, you will see more detailed help information.

ARJ Limitations

ARJ will accept up to

64 filenames/wildnames on command line

16,000 filenames resulting from wildnames

8,000 filenames/wildnames to exclude

8,000 ARJ filenames resulting from wildnames

2,048 character comments

(up to 25 lines or 1 file)

For compressing, ARJ requires approximately 290,000 bytes plus the memory necessary to store all of the pathnames to be archived when using the default compression method (**–m1**).

For extracting, ARJ requires approximately 166,000 bytes plus. The program DEARJ (available to registered users) requires approximately 123,000 bytes plus.

There is no limitation on the number of files that can be stored in one archive. However, each add command can only add a maximum of 16,000 files at a time depending upon memory availability. I expect that a normal maximum of 5,000 to 8,000 filenames can be handled without running out of memory during the compress phase.

If you do not have enough memory, you should use the **–l** switch to dump the filenames to a list file. You can then break the list file into smaller files and use multiple ARJ commands to archive all of the files.

Example:

```
ARJ a -r -lname.lst archive \*.*
```

If the above command fails due to lack of memory, split the name.lst file into smaller pieces named name1.lst, name2.lst, etc. Then execute:

```
ARJ a archive !name1.lst
ARJ a archive !name2.lst
    .
    .
```

ARJ currently does not see that wildnames like C:*.* and C:*.* can actually represent the same thing. ARJ would expand each of those two wildnames into a list that could be up to twice as long as necessary.

When updating an archive, ARJ creates a temporary file named ARJTEMP.$nn in the current directory or work directory. While ARJ is scanning a wildcard filespec, ARJ will change the name of the target archive to ARJTEMP.$nn while the scan is proceeding to avoid including the archive itself in an add or move command. Also, as a result, you cannot add a file named ARJTEMP.$nn to an ARJ archive. Please note that the name of this temporary file may change at a future revision of ARJ.

Important Differences Between ARJ and LHARC

ARJ by default stores the full specified pathname of files archived minus any drive letter and root symbol. The **e** and **x** commands will by default extract all of the files in the archive without using date-time stamps to select files. You should specify **–u –y** to duplicate LHARC functionality.

The **f** command in ARJ requires the **–r** switch to be identical to the LHARC **f** command if the original archive was created using the **–r** switch.

Important Notes

When using the **–w** working directory switch, ARJ does not check on space availability before overwriting the original archive if it exists. Be sure that you have enough disk space for the new archive before using the **–w** switch. If ARJ aborts in this situation because of disk space, ARJ will keep the temporary archive.

By default, ARJ does not see hidden or system files. ARJ will process system and hidden files when you specify the **–a** switch.

Like LHARC and PKZIP, ARJ requires extra disk space to UPDATE an archive file. ARJ will back up the original archive while it creates the new archive, so enough room must be available for both archives at the same time.

Currently, ARJ will not extract overwriting a read only file.

Tips to Using ARJ Efficiently

When archiving to diskettes, you should use the **–w** option to set a working directory on your RAMDRIVE or hard disk drive to speed up building the archive. You should use the **–jt** option when archiving to diskettes or when you really want to be sure that ARJ will be able to extract what you have archived. There are cases where your hardware or memory-resident software will corrupt your work, so the **–jt** option is excellent insurance.

Using the **–js** option saves time by not compressing archives.

You should use the **–e** option whenever you do not need to store pathnames in an archive that you are creating. This will save space.

Convert an ARJ archive into a self-extracting archive with a command like the following:

```
ARJ y archive -je
```

To capture a comment from an ARJ archive, use the following command:

```
ARJ e archive ... -zcomment.txt
```

ARJ has several compression methods that provide size/time tradeoffs. Method 4 **–m4** is about twice as fast as method 1. The **–jm1** and **–jm** options modify the **–m1** and **–m2** options to provide even greater compression at a cost in time.

Using ARJ Within Other Programs

Since ARJ uses over 280,000 bytes of memory during compression, it is difficult to use ARJ in a large application program unless that program swaps itself out of memory when it executes DOS commands like ARJ. However, there is at least one shareware program available that will automatically swap your large application program out of memory whenever it shells out to DOS to execute a command. The program SHROOM by Davis Augustine should be able to solve this memory problem for you. The latest version is named SHROM18J.ZIP on Channel One BBS. According to the SHROOM documentation, you can reach the author at:

CompuServe id 72230,3053
Davis Augustine, P.O. Box 390178,
Cambridge, MA 02139

This is not an endorsement of the product SHROOM.

The easiest way I have found to use this product is to type

```
SHROOM COMMAND
```

SHROOM **–v** COMMAND will let you see SHROOM in action when you shell out to execute a DOS command.

ARJMENU Program

A new program called ARJMENU by Michael McCombs will be released shortly. As far as I know, it is the only menu-driven interface program that supports ALL of the features of ARJ. This program is aimed at users who hate command-line interfaces. ARJMENU allows the user to pick and choose ARJ options. The user does not have to remember the ARJ switch syntax. The newest version of the program supports ARJ version 2.30. You can reach the author at:

Internet/ARPANet:
mccombs@sumax.seattleu.edu
Michael McCombs, 517 Ninth Ave. #310,
Seattle, WA. 98104

Using ARJ as a Backup Program

ARJ can be used as a substitute for a backup program. However, it does not have the diskette critical-error handling or data recovery facilities of a FASTBACK, etc. So you should be sure of the reliability of your diskettes.

The following partial command lines illustrate a full backup command, an incremental update command, and a restore command. The only parts missing are the names of the files to backup/restore.

```
ARJ a A:backup -r -vvas -a1 -b2 -i1
  -js -jt -jiC:\backup.inx -wC:\ -m4

ARJ a A:backup -r -vvas -a1 -b1 -i1
  -js -jt -jiC:\backup.inx -wC:\ -m4

ARJ x A:backup -vv -jycn
```

You should familiarize yourself with the above switches so that you can modify the above command lines as needed.

If you have a RAMDRIVE large enough, you should change the **–w** option to point to the RAMDRIVE.

If you have enough free hard disk space, you can build all of the diskette volumes on the hard disk for later copying to diskette. In this case, you will need to change the name of the archive to **C:backup** or similar. The **–vvas** option should be changed to **–v360**, **–v720**, or whatever is appropriate for your diskette size.

Please note that 360, 720, 1200, and 1440 are abbreviations for the standard diskette sizes. Other sizes will require your entering the entire number. Another change is to add the option **–y**

which will turn off the Ok to proceed ... prompt. Lastly, if the **–w** option is pointing to the hard disk, you should remove the **–w** option entirely.

```
ARJ a C:backup -r -v360 <other
  options> -m4 -y
```

Important: Only a maximum of 100 volumes can be built on a disk at one time because of the volume suffix rolling over at *.A99 to *.A00 when using default archive naming. However, if you specify the starting archive name with a suffix of **.000** or **.001**, ARJ will create 1,000 or 999 uniquely named volumes.

```
ARJ a C:backup.000 -r ..........
```

Both backup commands will pause for a system command. You can execute DOS commands at this point. This is a suitable place to do a **dir a:** to make sure that your disk is formatted and has enough free space on it. You may need to execute **format a:** or **del a:**. A very useful command might be **QDR A:**. QDR is a utility from Vern Buerg. You will need to type **exit** to allow ARJ to continue.

If the backup fails after completing one or more diskettes, you can restart at the next archive after the last successful volume. You will need to examine the information in the BACKUP.INX file to find the name of the file that is to start this archive. It will usually be the same as the last filename in the previous volume. You will also need the byte position to start in this same file. That can be determined from the information in BACKUP.INX. You can then retype the exact same backup command as before with a few changes. You will append the right **.Ann** suffix to the archive name, and you will add the options **–jx** and **–jn** with the proper arguments.

For example, if the above full backup command failed during diskette two on filename DOS\MODE.COM which was started at byte 125, this would be the correct command:

```
ARJ a A:backup.A01 -r -vvas -a1
  <other> -m4 -jx125 -jnDOS\MODE.COM
```

The most error prone step is determining the correct **–jn** option. Be sure to spell the filename exactly the same as it appears in the BACKUP.INX file. A common error concerns the use of the root directory symbol \ with the **–jn** option. Verify the presence or absence of the root symbol \ in the backup index file.

If the restore fails after one or more diskettes, simply retype the same command as before but add the right **.Ann** suffix to the archive name. If ARJ has aborted because of a disk full on a file split between volumes, you will have to restart at the first volume that contains that file.

Backup-Type Archives and Backup Files

New to ARJ 2.30 and ARJ archives is the concept of backup-type archives. Normally, when adding duplicate files to an ARJ archive, ARJ will overwrite the existing file. However, at ARJ 2.30 with a backup-type archive, ARJ will keep the existing file by marking it as a backup and inserting the new file. This will make ARJ archives larger than normal. It is possible to have more than one duplicate backup file. You can make an archive a backup type by using the **–jb** option during the add or by typing

```
ARJ y archive -jb
```

Any further additions of already existing files will result in more files marked as backups. You may reset that backup flag by specifying the **–jb1** option as in

```
ARJ y archive -jb1
```

This feature is useful when backing up frequently modified files. One archive can have several days worth of backups. The existence of backup files or the backup archive flag is indicated when executing the **l** or **v** commands. There will be a message at the end of the display. The backup files themselves can be displayed by using the **–jg** or **–jg1** options with the **l** or **v** commands.

To extract a specific backup file, you have several options. You can execute

```
ARJ e archive filename -jg -q
```

and enter **yes** on the specific instance that you wanted extracted. You can specify the exact modification date-time that you want as in

```
ARJ e archive filename -jg -
  o910101120000 -ob910101130000
```

You can specify the sequence number of the file in the archive. To extract the fifth file in the archive, type

```
ARJ e archive 5 -jg -#
```

The sequence number is available in the **v** command display. Or you can extract all occurrences of the file with

```
ARJ e archive filename -jg -jo
```

Duplicates will be renamed with numeric file extensions (.000).

The **ARJ k archive *.*** command can be used to purge an archive of all backup files.

You can unmark backup files with **ARJ y archive –jb2**. You can unmark specific files such as the fifth file in the archive with

```
ARJ y archive -# -jb2 5
```

You should not use the **–e** option when adding files to a backup-type archive because ARJ will not have the ability to distinguish between files with the same filespec and different pathspecs. You could end up with duplicate files in the archive as opposed to one recent file and several backup files.

The Filespec "..."

Several times in this document and the UPDATE.DOC file, there is mention of the filespec "...". This filespec is chosen so as to not match any existing filename. ARJ will *not* generate an error or warning for not matching "..." specifically.

ARJ Error Situations

The following is a description of how ARJ will respond in various error situations.

Add:

If a user-specified file is not found during an add, ARJ will continue processing and will keep the archive and terminate with an error condition. In a disk full condition or any other file i/o error, ARJ will promptly terminate with an error condition and delete the temporary archive file unless the user has specified the **–jk** switch.

Move:

ARJ will only delete files that have been successfully added to the archive. If you have specified the **–jt** (test) switch, ARJ will abort on any error. If you specify the **–jk** switch, ARJ will not delete the temporary archive upon an abort.

Extract:

In a disk full condition or any other file i/o error, ARJ will promptly terminate with an error condition and delete the current output file.

CRC errors or bad file data:

In the case where an ARJ archive has been corrupted, ARJ will report a CRC error or a Bad file data error. These corruptions can be the result of an unreliable diskette, a computer memory problem, a file transfer glitch, or incompatible CACHING software. Most of these errors are the result of file transfer glitches and bad diskettes. A few are the result of an incompatible interaction with SUPER PCKWIK 3.3 advanced diskette support or Windows 3.0.

ARJ DOS errorlevels and their meanings:

0   success

1   warning (specified file to add to archive not found, specified file to list, extract, etc., not found, or answering negatively to OK to proceed to next volume... prompt)

2   fatal error

3   CRC error (header or file CRC error)

4   ARJ-SECURITY error or attempt to update an ARJ-SECURED archive

5   disk full or write error

6   can't open archive or file

7   simple user error (bad parameters)

8   not enough memory

ARJ User Action Prompts

ARJ prompts the user for action at certain times. There are several types of prompts. One is for yes/no permission, another is for a new filename, another is for archive comments, and one other is for search strings. The yes/no prompts will also accept **quit** for program termination and **always** to bypass further user prompts. Since ARJ uses STDIN for user input,

be careful about typing ahead, anticipating prompts. ARJ may prompt you for an unexpected action and use your earlier input. The **–jy** option lets you change the prompting modes to single character query mode. See the section on **–jy** for more information.

ARJ Environment Variable

ARJ will first look for an environment variable named ARJ_SW and use its value as switch options for ARJ. If ARJ finds such an environment variable, it will display a message to that effect.

You can inhibit ARJ from using this environment variable by using the **–+** option. You can also set the name of the environment variable with the **–+** option. For example, to instruct ARJ to use the switches set in the environment variable ARJ_SW2, you might use a command such as the following:

```
ARJ a -+ARJ_SW2 archive
```

Specifying environment switches

Use the following syntax to individually specify default ARJ switches:

```
SET ARJ_SW=<switches>
```

Example:

```
SET ARJ_SW=-w\temp -k -e
```

Do *not* add any blanks after the variable name ARJ_SW. As in LHARC, command-line switches can be selected to override ARJ_SW settings. ARJ will allow you to use a different switch character – or / in ARJ_SW and in the command line except when using the **–ju** (unix) option.

Specifying switches in a configuration file

If the ARJ_SW environment variable specifies a filename (text not beginning with a switch character), ARJ will open that filename and scan it looking for a line of text that begins in column 1 with the same letter as the ARJ command being executed. The following text is processed as the ARJ_SW switches. This allows each ARJ command to have its own switch settings. In addition, ARJ will also look for the + (plus) symbol in column 1 to use as a miscellaneous switch string. This string will be added to any command switch string found (if any). If no command switch string is found, ARJ will use the miscellaneous switch string as the ARJ_SW switch settings. Note that the + switch settings will *not* be used if the + string occurs below the command switch string.

For example, to instruct ARJ to use the switches in the file ARJ.CFG, you can use the following command:

```
SET ARJ_SW=C:\ARJ\ARJ.CFG
```

where C:\ARJ\ARJ.CFG contains

```
a -jm1 -jt -i1
c -zcomment.txt
+ -jv
l -jp
e -i1
```

AND is equivalent to

```
a -jm1 -jt -i1
c -zcomment.txt
l -jp -jv
e -i1 -jv
f -jv
v -jv
all other commands
    .
    .
    .
```

In the above example, any ARJ **a** commands will use **–jm1 –jt –i1** as the ARJ_SW switch options.

The ARJ_SW variable or the ARJ_SW configuration file switch settings may *not* have quoted switches such as **–vasformat a:**.

ARJ Command-Line Syntax

```
ARJ <command> [-<switch>[-|+|
    <option>]...]
    <archive_name>[.ARJ]
    [<base_directory_name>\]
    [<!list_name>|<path_name>|<wild_name>...]
```

Commands and switches can be entered in upper- or lowercase. Switches can be placed anywhere after the command ARJ.

ARJ supports the use of either – or / as the switch option character. The first occurrence of either – or / that ARJ encounters in the ARJ_SW variable will determine the switch symbol for processing ARJ_SW. The first occurrence of either – or / that ARJ encounters in the command line will determine the switch symbol for processing the command line except when the **–ju** (unix) option has been specified in ARJ_SW. You may *not* mix and match switch symbols.

Throughout this document, the symbol / may be substituted for – in switch usage.

Examples:

```
ARJ a A:archive *.* /va /r
    is correct.
ARJ a A:archive *.* /va -r
    IS INCORRECT USAGE!
```

Switches specified on the command line will either toggle or override switches specified with the ARJ_SW environment variable. Switch usage is identical to that of LHARC.

-s+	turns on switch **s**.
-s-	turns off switch **s**.
-s	toggles the state of switch **s**.
-sname	provides the name argument for switch **–s**.
--	skip processing of any more switch options.

Switch options CAN be combined to save command-line length. However, some switch options take optional string arguments and, therefore, must be the last option in a combined argument token string because ARJ accepts the rest of the argument token as the optional argument. You can combine **–r** and **–i** to make **–ri**. You can combine **–wd:** and **–i** with **–iwd:** because the switch option taking the string argument is last. Please note that switches that *only* accept the +, –, **0, 1, 2** modifiers can be combined in any order. The following switches must be last in a combined switch argument: **–g, –l, –m, –o, –t, –v, –w, –x, –z, –!, –$, –jc, –jd, –jh, –ji, –jn, –jp, –js, –jw, –jx, –jy, –jz.**

Warning: The **j** in **–jX** option switches is a SHIFT symbol. Therefore, a combined **–jatv** is a combination of **–ja, –jt,** and **–jv,** since the **j** shifts the meaning of subsequent symbols in the argument token string. The use of more than one **j** shift symbol per argument token string is *not* supported for future versions.

Examples:

```
-rijvta <=> -r -i -jv -jt -ja
-i1kwd:\ <=> -i1 -k -wd:\
```

ARJ will accept an ending – on most switches such as **–w–**. The **–x** switch option is one exception. The one caveat is that for switches that support an optional argument string such as **–wd:**, that switch option must *not* be followed by a concatenated switch option such as **–w–r**. An argument token string such is **–rikw–** is acceptable because the **–w** option is the last one. One special switch combination is the **–jyyr** combination. You can turn off the **y** and **r** modifiers with **–jyyr–**.

The switch option -- tells ARJ that there are no more switch options to process in the current command line. This is useful when you need to enter filenames beginning with **–**.

Example:

```
ARJ a archive-----testfile
```

The standard ARJ file suffix is **.ARJ**. Subsequent multiple volume archives end in **.A01, .A02**, etc, up to .A99, .A00, .A01. It is possible to have multiple volumes start at **.001** and go up to **.999**.

The ARJ command must be the first nonswitch argument after **ARJ**. The ARJ archive name must be the first filename on the command line. The base directory, if any, must be the second filename argument. The switches and other filenames can be in any order. The base directory name should end with \ (backslash) or : (colon). However, ARJ will still accept directory names without the \ character if the directory already exists. This feature is limited to the add-type and extract-type commands.

You can specify a wildcard for the archive name such as ***.ARJ** for all ARJ commands except for the add commands (a, f, j, m, u). If you also specify the **–r** switch, ARJ will search subdirectories for ARJ archives (*.ARJ) also.

Examples:

```
ARJ l –r *
```
will list all of your *.ARJ files.

```
ARJ c *.arj –zbbs.cmt
```
will comment all of your archives.

Wild_names follow MS-DOS convention. ***.*** means all files. ***.DOC** means all files with an extension of .DOC. **?B*.*** means all files with a second character of **B**.

The default for <wild_name> for all commands except for **d** is ***.***.

For the add, move, freshen, and update commands, filename matching in the archive requires an exact path match depending upon the **–e** option. For non-update commands, specified filenames with paths will force a full pathname match.

You can supply one or more filenames for files containing lists of files to be added to an archive. The filenames must be listed one per line with no leading or trailing blanks. The list filename(s) must be prefixed with **!**. If you want to archive a filename beginning with **!**, you must use the **–!** option to set a new list file character.

You can exclude filenames/wildnames from the list of filenames to be processed by ARJ.

Example:

```
ARJ a software *.* -x*.exe -x*.obj
```

adds all files in the current directory except .EXE and .OBJ files.

Note: See the ARJ.DOC file for the detailed command reference omitted here.

Sample ARJ Commands

a Add files to archive

ARJ a archive
ARJ a archive –n
ARJ a archive –f
ARJ a archive –jt
ARJ a archive –jt1
ARJ a archive –jt2
ARJ a archive –q
ARJ a archive –r
ARJ a archive dir\ –o
ARJ a archive dir\
ARJ a archive dir\ *.doc *.exe
ARJ a archive !names.lst
ARJ a archive --name–.txt
ARJ a archive name1 name2 name3
ARJ a a:archive –we:\ –vas c:\ –r –b2
ARJ a a:archive.001 –we:\ –vvw360 c:\ –r –b1
ARJ a archive –vw360 c:\ –r –y
ARJ a archive c:\ *.* –r –jt1 –jf

b execute Batch or DOS command

ARJ b archive name.txt
ARJ b archive –jwOUT.NAM
ARJ b archive SHEZ.EXE –jwSHEZ.EXE
ARJ b archive *.exe –jwTEMP.EXE "–jq TEMP –help"

c Comment archive files

ARJ c archive
ARJ c archive –z
ARJ c archive –zcomment.txt
ARJ c archive –zNUL
ARJ c archive file1 –jzcomment.txt
ARJ c archive *.doc –jzNUL

d Delete files from archive

ARJ d archive *.doc
ARJ d archive *.* –jg
ARJ d archive *.* –n
ARJ d archive *.* –y
ARJ d archive !names.lst

e Extract files from archive

ARJ e archive *.doc
ARJ e archive *.doc –d
ARJ e archive –jd50000
ARJ e archive –jo
ARJ e archive –c
ARJ e archive dir\ *.doc –jt
ARJ e archive *.doc –y
ARJ e archive –# 10 15 20–40

f Freshen files in archive

ARJ f archive
ARJ f archive –r
ARJ f archive dir\ –r
ARJ f archive dir\ *.doc –r
ARJ f archive dir\ –r –jt2

g Garble files in archive

ARJ g archive –gpassword
ARJ g archive *.doc –gpassword
ARJ g archive –g?

i check Integrity of ARJ.EXE

ARJ i
ARJ i c:\bin\arj.exe

j Join archives to archive

ARJ j archive name1.arj name2.arj name3.arj
ARJ j archive *.arj
ARJ j archive arjsfx.exe
ARJ j archive *.arj –o911201
ARJ j archive *.arj –r

k pacK bacKup files in archive

ARJ k archive *.*
ARJ k archive *.* –y
ARJ k archive *.doc –n

l List contents of archive

ARJ l archive
ARJ l archive *.doc
ARJ l archive –o911201
ARJ l archive –o911201 –ob911231
ARJ l archive –n
ARJ l archive –jg
ARJ l archive –jp

m Move files to archive

ARJ m archive
ARJ m archive *.doc
ARJ m archive dir\ *.doc
ARJ m archive dir\ *.doc –o
ARJ m a:archive.001 dir\ –r –vvwas –jt2

n reName files in archive

ARJ n archive
ARJ n archive *.doc
ARJ n archive !names.lst
ARJ n archive –o911201

o Order files in archive

ARJ o archive !names.lst
ARJ o archive *.bat *.exe *.doc
ARJ o archive file1 file2 file3

p Print files to standard output

ARJ p archive
ARJ p archive –jp
ARJ p archive *.doc
ARJ p archive –o911201
ARJ p archive name.txt > PRN

r Remove paths from filenames

ARJ r archive
ARJ r archive *.doc
ARJ r archive –o911201 –ob911231

s Sample files to screen with pause

ARJ s archive
ARJ s archive *.doc –y
ARJ s *.arj –y –r

t Test integrity of archive

ARJ t archive
ARJ t archive *.exe
ARJ t archive !names.lst
ARJ t archive –jt1

u Update files to archive

ARJ u archive *.doc
ARJ u archive *.doc –jo

v Verbosely list contents of archive

ARJ v archive
ARJ v archive *.doc
ARJ v archive –jv
ARJ v archive –jv1
ARJ v archive –jp
ARJ v archive –jg

w Where are text strings in archive

ARJ w archive
ARJ w archive –jp
ARJ w *.arj –jp
ARJ w *.arj *.doc
ARJ w *.arj *.txt –jq+5+string
ARJ w archive "–jq–3–to be or not"

x eXtract files with full pathname

ARJ x archive *.doc
ARJ x archive *.doc –d
ARJ x archive –jd50000
ARJ x archive –jo
ARJ x archive –c
ARJ x archive dir\ *.doc
ARJ x archive –jf
ARJ x archive *.doc –jyc

y copY archive with new options

ARJ y archive –je
ARJ y archive –je1
ARJ y archive –jb
ARJ y archive –jb1
ARJ y archive –jb2
ARJ y archive *.bat –jb2

Known ARJ Issues/Problems

Due to the inner workings of Turbo C++, ARJ may run out of memory if your computer is configured with thousands of bytes of environment variables. A workaround is to spawn another COMMAND.COM as in

```
command /e:200 /c arj x archive
. . . . . . . .
```

When using a working directory, ARJ does not check for disk space before overwriting the original archive. Be sure you have enough space before updating an archive using the **–w** switch.

Because of a bug with extended archive header processing, you should convert to ARJ 2.10 and above as soon as it is practical to do so. This bug is *not* a current problem because no version of ARJ supports the use of the extended header.

TSRs that activate via *hot keys* may be inhibited by ARJ during user keyboard input. This is a "feature" of the Turbo C++ getc( ) function. A partial workaround is to use the ARJ **–jyry** option to go to single key query mode.

A similar problem occurs with HYPERDISK and staged writes. HYPERDISK's timer delay appears to be inhibited during ARJ user keyboard input such as during Ok to ... volume/ diskette?. This causes an error when you swap to the next diskette. The workaround is to use the ARJ **–jyry** option to go to single key query mode.

There is a reported problem using ARJ and floppy disk drives when using the disk cache program SUPER PCKWIK 3.30 with advanced diskette support (/D+). The system may occasionally hang when ARJ attempts to read/write the diskette. You may also get CRC or Bad file data errors. Disabling the SUPER PCKWIK option with /D– appears to remove this problem. Other programs have similar problems with this feature of SUPER PCKWIK.

Note: Please see the ARJ.DOC file for information on technical support, acknowledgments, ARJ availability, distributors, etc.

ARJ Registration Form (rev 7):

Name: _____

Company: _____

Address: _____

City: _____

State: _____ Country: _____

Zip: _____ Phone: _____

Remit to:

Robert K. Jung
2606 Village Road West
Norwood, Massachusetts 02062 USA

Prices subject to change without notice.

INDIVIDUAL REGISTRATION for the use of ARJ,
REARJ, ARJSFX, and ARJSFXJR for MS-DOS:
each registration is $35 .... $ _____

ARJ-SECURITY ENVELOPE
serial number(s) $50 each .... $ _____

Please note that this is a separately charged item.
List the exact name(s) that you want displayed by
ARJ security envelope. The display will look like the
following line:

ARJ archive created by (this is where your name is
placed) R#nnnn

_____

(Exact name, MAX of 60 characters, add more
sheets if necessary)

TERMS:

When ordering software diskettes, licensees and
registrations get the REARJ, ARJR, and DEARJ
programs in addition to the normal ARJ software.

Current software & documentation
diskette(s) ....$5 each $ _____

Next ARJ release software &
docs diskette(s) ....$5 each $ _____

TOTAL PRODUCT .... $ _____

Massachusetts residents add
MASS sales tax ....5% $ _____

For orders outside the USA, add
shipping and handling ....$5.00 $ _____

TOTAL ORDER .... $ _____

For payment by non-USA BANK CHECK,
add (see TERMS below) ....$40.00 $ _____

TOTAL ENCLOSED .... $ _____

Specify Disk Size: ❏ 5.25" ❏ 3.5"

Payment: ❏ Check ❏ Cash ❏ Money order
❏ Credit card - See instructions in file
CREDIT.CRD

Authorized Signature:

_____

TITLE: _____

DATE: _____

Payment must be made by check, US POSTAL Money Order, or International Money Order in USA funds drawn
on a USA bank made out to Robert K. Jung. Corporate purchase orders (net 30) for orders over $200 will be
accepted from FORTUNE 500 corporations within the USA and Canada. All orders outside of the United States
and Canada must be prepaid. Checks may require two weeks to clear. Please allow a few weeks for delivery.
Credit card orders for ARJ software are handled by arrangement with Public Software Library. See the file
CREDIT.CRD for more information. If necessary, CHECKS drawn on a non-USA bank for amounts over $100
(USA) or its equivalent will be accepted. Please add a $40 (USA) surcharge to cover handling, currency ex-
change, and bank transfer costs. This surcharge does NOT apply to bank checks which are written for USA
funds with a USA bank named on the check. Please allow several weeks for the check to clear and for delivery.

BATUTIL

Version 4.0
Copyright © 1988–1991 by Barry Simon and Richard Wilson
CTRLALT Associates (R)

Chapter I: Overview

Introduction

BATUTIL is a program included in the STACKEY package by CTRLALT Associates. It can only be registered as part of STACKEY.

Note: The documentation for BATUTIL is quite extensive. Only a small portion of it is duplicated here (in *DOS 6 SECRETS*). Please see the BATUTIL.DOC file (and the other files included on the diskettes) for more detail on how to use BATUTIL.

I.2 What BATUTIL Does

BATUTIL is a program with two purposes: to give you power inside your batch files and to give you more control over the DOS environment. To get a feel for the program, please run BUDEMO.BAT which is included with the distribution files.

Included in the information that you can get returned in either the DOS errorlevel, stored in BATUTIL's internal variables, or an environmental variable are

- Current time, date, day of the week.
- Total amount and amount free of disk space, memory, and EMS.
- CPU type and type of coprocessor if present.
- Whether a file exists not only in the current directory but also on the DOS path. If it exists on the DOS path, the actual directory can be returned in another environmental variable.
- Whether a file has today's date or not.
- Whether one of two files is older than another.
- You can parse a filespec into individual components.
- You can do arithmetic on integers and dates.

- You can manipulate strings including case change and centering.
- Whether Desqview or Carousel is running and, if so, which partition you are in; whether Windows is running underneath you.

Some of these options may not seem so useful at first sight, but, for example, whether a file has today's date or not can be used to make a routine that will only get run once per day. Chapter VII will explain sample uses of BATUTIL.

Central to the design of BATUTIL is the notion of "high level" language. There are much more sophisticated batch languages available, and with them one can write menus at least as involved as are available in BATUTIL's MENU command. But doing so requires you to write a little program in the batch language while MENU is a built-in command of BATUTIL; if you want to, BATUTIL comes with a full-featured language dubbed BUSIC. It includes IF..THEN..ELSE, CASE, WHILE, REPEAT, and GOTO, all of which can be used in the style of DOS batch languages.

In addition to getting information from the operating system, you can pass information to and get information from the user. BATUTIL gives you considerable control over displaying information including the possibility of turning the cursor on and off and displaying messages in various colors. And BATUTIL understands the metastrings that STACKEY does, so you can easily display data such as today's date in English.

User input can be obtained in various forms. A getkey routine lets you list a set of keys using STACKEY syntax and get which key in the list the user has hit:

- Whether a lock key is currently pressed.
- With some simple commands, you can pop up an elegant menu for the user to pick from and have the choice returned in the errorlevel.

- You can have the user input a string and get it stored in the environment.
- You can have the user type in a user name or password and see whether it matches a predetermined list and have which item is matched reported in the errorlevel.
- You can pop up a filename list for the user to choose from and have the answer stored in the environment.

BATUTIL also gives you considerable control over the DOS environment. It is able to do this by using undocumented features of the operating system. As always, such features should be used with care.

Important: Please read carefully the warning at the start of Chapter V concerning using undocumented features to access the DOS environment.

BATUTIL's environmental control has been tested with PC DOS Version 2.0, 2.1, 3.0, 3.1, 3.2, 3.3, 4.0, 5.0, and some flavors of MS-DOS. Besides being able to place information into the environment via user input, BATUTIL will

- Display more information about the environment than the SET command.
- Allow you to put strings in the environment up to a length of 255 characters rather than the 127 character maximum that DOS allows. In particular, with BATUTIL your PATH string can be up to 250 characters rather than the 122 characters that you can enter with DOS. (While DOS doesn't care about long paths, you may have an application program that does and crashes if it finds a path over 127 bytes.)
- Allow simple commands to add a directory to your PATH without inadvertently adding one already there and allow deletion of a directory from your PATH.
- Allow full screen editing of your environment and PATH.
- Allow you to save the environment to a file, to load or merge a file into the environment, and to kill the environment (use with care).

Program and Documentation Files

By default, the install program for the *DOS 6 SECRETS* diskettes will install all of the BATUTIL files in the directory \SECRETS\BATUTILS. This directory has not been added to the search path. You can execute the program from its home directory, add the directory to the search path, or copy the BATUTIL files to a directory that is included in the search path.

The files in the BATUTIL package are as follows:

BATUTIL.EXE	The basic program. The only file required to use BATUTIL.
BATUTIL.HLP	Online help called by BATUTIL, if you use BATUTIL ? or BATUTIL !.
BATUTIL.DOC	Documentation in electronic form.
BUDEMO.BAT	Sample batch file which will call the other sample batch files.
COLORDEM.BAT	Sample batch file showing color capability.
EQUIP.BAT	Sample batch file showing ability to read hardware.
INPUTDEM.BAT	Sample batch file showing ability to get input from the user.
MENUDEMO.BAT	Sample batch file showing BATUTIL's menu-making capability.
SHOWDEMO.BAT	Sample batch file showing display options including big characters and metastrings.
SOUNDEMO.BAT	Sample batch file with BATUTIL's 20 sounds/tunes.
LANGDEMO.BAT	Sample batch file demonstrating the new language features of BATUTIL 4.0.

WHATEL.EXE Program described in Section II.7 to determine errorlevel and timing for some commands.

Because of our desire to keep the basic files on a single disk and to keep download time low, we are encouraging distribution of a small shareware version without the BATUTIL.HLP file. If you have a version without this file and want it for evaluation, it can be downloaded from our support section of CompuServe as BUHELP.EXE (Section 12 of PCVENA), or you can get it from many disk vendors including PBS (1-800-426-3475). If you upload this program to a BBS, please keep BATUTIL.HLP as a separate file.

Important: Users of 4DOS Version 2.x, please read Section V.1 before calling for technical support. See Section I.4 for items in Version 1 not carried over to Version 4.x.

I.3 Help, Verbose Modes, and European Dates

You can obtain interactive help for BATUTIL by typing in

```
batutil ?
```
or
```
batutil !
```

at the DOS prompt. To obtain help, the binary file BATUTIL.HLP must be available in the current directory, the directory where BATUTIL is loaded, or in your path. BATUTIL looks for the first two nonblank characters following the ? (or !), and if they are a valid BATUTIL command, you will be immediately sent to the help for that command. Otherwise, the main help menu will be displayed. For example

```
batutil ? SE
```

would display help for BATUTIL's SET command as would

```
batutil ?see the beautiful program
```

BATUTIL ? displays the menu-oriented help with various special effects. If these effects and the slightly longer time they take bother you,

batutil ! will display help without the special fades for displaying material.

The help program uses color attributes on a graphics monitor. If you have a two-color graphics monitor (such as on a laptop) or the colors are hard to see, the help program will use monochrome attributes if you use **SET BU!=bw** in your AUTOEXEC.BAT file or at the DOS command line before running BATUTIL. Note that on a true monochrome adapter (IBM MDA or Hercules monographics card), the help program will not use color attributes whether you use that set command or not.

Normally, BATUTIL exits when there is an error and sets the errorlevel between 200 and 253. There are three levels of visual error reporting that you can have turned on. For debugging purposes, the default is a verbose mode where BATUTIL will explain why it is exiting. For batch files you distribute, you may want to have verbose mode turned off and instead use a Quiet mode where no messages are displayed. To turn on this quiet mode, just make the first nonblank character in the command line the letter Q. Thus,

```
batutil {}
```

would display an error message, while

```
batutil Q {}
```

would exit without any message. For distributed batch files made with BATUTIL, you may want to turn on quiet mode using an environmental variable as described in Section I.5. Command-line mode takes precedence over any mode set in the environment and, in particular, you can override the mode set in the environment and restore to the default Verbose mode by making V the first letter on the command line after BATUTIL.

Chapter IX of the BATUTIL.DOC file has a complete list of error codes with an explanation of each. The on-line help main menu has an option to list all error numbers and their meaning.

In batch files, the error message may disappear too fast for you to see. In addition to Verbose mode, BATUTIL has a Pause mode which shows the error message and waits for a key before exiting. Pause mode is set with the letter P.

To see the information which BATUTIL is placing in the environment while testing out what a command will do, the following one line batch file (or an equivalent CED synonym), is useful:

```
batutil %1 %2 %3 %4 %5 %6 %7 %8 %9
   {EC $x(rc)}
```

The final command echoes the current value of the environmental variable RC to the screen.

There is an additional special parameter you can use at the start of the command line: E for European. It will change to European date conventions; so, while

```
batutil {ec $E}
```

would echo

```
December 19, 1991
```

the command

```
batutil E {ec $E}
```

would echo

```
19 December 1991
```

The E command affects the following: the meaning of $d, $E, and the translation used for dates. For example

```
batutil {ec $E(1/2/91)}
```

returns

```
January 2, 1991
```

while

```
batutil E {ec $E(1/2/91)}
```

returns

```
1 February 1991
```

since 1/2/91 is also translated using European conventions.

I.4 New in Version 4.0

Version 1.0 was released bundled with Stackey 3.0 and this numbering caused some confusion; so, with this upgrade, we have upped the version number of BATUTIL all the way to 4.0 to make the numbers the same.

The most significant difference in this new version is the addition of a built-in language described further in Sections I.9, I.10, and Chapter VI. For this language to work effectively, we needed to remove the restriction of a single 127-character command line, and it is now possible to read commands in from a file as described in Section I.7. As a bonus, you need not load BATUTIL many times and that increases the speed of command processing by a considerable amount.

This may mean that you'd like to use BATUTIL's RUn command to run a program from a BATUTIL batch file without exiting BATUTIL. In Version 1.0, BATUTIL took over 200K when you used RUn, limiting it for these purposes. With this version, BATUTIL will swap itself to the hard disk or EMS memory leaving a core of about 11K in conventional RAM. About 300K of disk space or EMS is required. By default, EMS is used if available, but you can tell BATUTIL to use the disk. This swapping mechanism RUn command will not work on systems with floppy drives only and no EMS; so, you'll have to use the non-swapping mode (set up by placing **BUSWAP=!** in your environment).

Included in the language support are the following:

- Labels and Goto
- Calling subroutines
- IF..THEN..ELSE and CASE
- WHILE and REPEAT
- 32 internal variables as well as the use of the DOS environment for storing information
- FOR loops using an internal loop variable
- FOR loops using a list
- FOR loops using file wildcards like DOS batch files
- FOR loops varying through a directory tree
- An interactive trace mode
- String manipulation including change of case, length, formatting, searching, and word count
- Integer arithmetic with four functions, mod, and power
- Date manipulation including date arithmetic
- Reading and writing to files with optional metastring translation
- Reading from the screen
- Memory peeks and pokes
- I/O port peeks and pokes

Other new features include the following:

- Reading the number of file handles and DOS buffers
- Determining if BATUTIL is running in a Windows DOS box
- Determining if Norton's NDOS is running
- Determining if SHARE is loaded
- Determining the value of last drive
- A command to display text boxes with choice of frame characters and shadows
- Mouse support in the $F routines
- A $N metastring like $Q but with input restricted to numbers and a test to see if a string is a number between allowed maximum and minimum values
- The #I command which now identifies 486 CPUs
- Super metastrings to force commands that do not do metastring translation on their parameters to do such translation after all
- Menu which can now be set to timeout after a fixed time
- Support for European dates
- A password mode for entry of strings which are masked

Note: Please see the BATUTIL.DOC file for a list of changes from Version 1.0.

I.5 Basic Syntax

Command: REmark

You give BATUTIL a series of commands on the command line or read them in from a file. There are about 130 different commands. Lest that overwhelm you, we note that many commands are just giving different pieces of hardware information which you'll rarely want. Even the most complex idea (menus) is controlled by one basic command and by fewer than ten commands which effect options (like whether the menu explodes). Chapter VIII is a detailed alphabetical command reference. When you invoke BATUTIL's help, one option is an alphabetical list of commands which will give you a panel with syntax and parameters for each.

The basic syntax is

```
batutil {command1} {command2} ...
```

Each command is placed inside braces {} (or square brackets []). On the command lines, the braces are critical. It doesn't matter whether you have spaces between } and the next { or not. For reading commands from a file, braces are not needed if commands are on distinct lines, see Section I.7.

Commands are broken into two classes: normal commands and BUSIC language commands. All normal commands have a two-element minimal truncation. That is, all normal commands are distinguished already in the first two symbols, and any substring of the command that has at least two letters will work. For example, the basic command to get a report on the environment is

```
batutil {envrep}
```

The minimal truncation for that is EN. We'll often write ENvrep to emphasize this. Thus

```
batutil {en}
```

or

```
batutil {envr}
```

would work just as well as the full name. The basic commands are not case sensitive; so, {EN} or {En} or even {eNvRe} would do the same thing as {envrep}.

While to emphasize minimal truncation, we'll write ENvrep, please bear in mind that BATUTIL commands are NOT case sensitive although $ metastrings ARE.

The BUSIC language commands IF, WHILE, CALL, FOR, FORDIR, REPEAT, CASE, END, RET, ENDCASE, UNTIL, and BEGIN cannot be abbreviated although they are not case sensitive. To avoid accidents, the HACKER + command cannot be abbreviated but must be used in full.

In addition, much of the metastring translation acts as if it were commands. There is little difference between the HOur command which sets the errorlevel to the current hour and $H which returns the current hour in a string; therefore, {HO} and {ER $H} are equivalent.

Roughly fifty of the commands return to the user (i.e., you as a batch file writer) a number from 0 to 199. If the command in question appears inside {}, then that number is stored in the environmental variable RC (short for "return code"). Environmental variables are discussed at the start of Chapter V. If the command appears in [], then BATUTIL will exit without running the rest of the command line. It will also place this integer in the DOS errorlevel where you can test it with commands like

```
if errorlevel ....
```

(see Chapter VII). IF THE LAST COMMAND ON THE LINE RETURNS AN INTEGER AND IT IS PLACED IN {}, THEN the integer is both placed in the real environment and placed in the error level. For example, DRive reports the current drive with 0=A, 1=B, etc. If the current drive is D, then

```
batutil .... [DR]
```

will set the errorlevel to 3, while

```
batutil .....{DR} {echo hi there!}
```

would set an environmental variable RC to 3 and then echo `hi there!`. Thus, if you ran the SET command after BATUTIL, you'd find the line RC=3 on your screen.

Every time a command would set the environmental variable RC, it also would set the internal variable $r accessible via metastring translation. If you wish to run BATUTIL in a mode where it doesn't use the user's environment, the {RC $} command will tell BATUTIL to only use $r and not set an environmental RC variable.

Some commands will take optional parameters which also appear inside the braces for that command. Thus, **@Disk** gives the free disk space. If no parameter is specified, the current default drive will be used. Otherwise, you can specify a drive as in

```
batutil {@D C}.
```

BATUTIL will object to incorrect syntax, so if you tried

```
batutil {@D 3}
```

then BATUTIL will exit (with an appropriate message if Verbose mode is on). You can separate the command from the first parameter by any of the following:

```
<space> <comma> = or :
```

Rules of separation of multiple parameters for those few commands which accept multiple parameters depend on the commands.

Some commands do explicit metastring translation of their parameters and others do not. For any non-BUSIC command, if you place the parameters inside $!(...), then metastring translation will take place before the parameters are passed on. Thus, even though NUmberfiles does not normally do metastring translation, the command {NU $!(...)} would first do metastring translation on ... and then process the command

```
{NU —}
```

where --- is the metastring translation of ... This supermetastring translation even allows $Q, $N, and $F file input.

Before doing anything, BATUTIL scans the command line and makes sure that every command is a proper one for this version of BATUTIL. If not, it will exit. Otherwise, it will execute the commands one at a time. It does not check for parameter syntax until that command is reached. Thus, {@D 3} will halt BATUTIL when reached, but earlier commands will have already run.

You may place remarks in the BATUTIL command line by enclosing them inside {} with the REmark command as in

```
batutil {AT 4F}{CL}{REM clears the
screen in red!}
```

I.6 Setting BATUTIL Options from the Environment

You can effect BATUTIL's behavior with five environmental variables: BU@, BU^, B4$, CUR, and BUSWAP. These are set with the DOS SET command or BATUTIL's SEt command.

When BATUTIL loads, before reading the rest of its command line, it looks for an environmental string of the form

```
BU@=string
```

and it first reads that string as if it were a command line and places the commands in it to be processed first. This is intended primarily to allow you to change the built-in default options to some other value. For example, to turn off beeps and change the default on GEtkey from flushing the keyboard to not, you'd use

    BU@={NB}{NF}

This option is useful if you want to permanently turn on pause mode or European date mode. You'd use

    BU@=P E {NB}

if you wanted to also turn beeps off.

Since BATUTIL looks in the environment, you place the information that you want there using the DOS SET command (or BATUTIL's SET command if you want!). For example, you might place a line

    set BU@=P E {NB}

in your AUTOEXEC.BAT file. It is important to place NO spaces between BU@ and the =. Spaces after the = are unimportant.

There are four other environmental variables of interest. One is the variable B4$. At the end of the commands to edit your path and the environment ({PAthedit} and {EDitenv}) and after using help, a screen will appear reminding you of the fact that BATUTIL is shareware, limited to a 30-day trial period. You can suppress this screen by placing

    B4$=I paid

in your environment. Obviously, having told you the secret, you can do it even if you haven't paid — let your conscience be your guide. The variable BU^ can be used to turn off ^Break handling; see Section I.11.

BATUTIL's RUn command swaps to hard disk or EMS. You can control where swapping takes place with the BUSWAP variable. This is discussed in Section II.7.

The final environmental string that BATUTIL pays attention to is CUR (for CURSOR). It looks for two possibilities:

    CUR=on

Normally, BATUTIL restores the cursor when exiting, even if you have turned it off with the {CU –} command of Section III.7. If this string is present, the cursor is not turned back on, but its state is not changed.

    CUR=off

When starting or exiting the program, BATUTIL will turn the cursor off if this string is found at that point. All other values of CUR are ignored.

I.7 Reading Commands from a File

Commands: FCommand, INclude

Four commands are able to read information in from a file. The FCommand command, which is equivalent to the INclude command, reads new commands from a file. The ECho command displays text on the screen in colors you set before the echo command; PRetty displays text in colors that you can adjust as part of the string displayed; and MEnu displays a user-defined menu. The analogous file-reading commands are FEcho, FPretty, and FMenu. Each command takes two parameters: the first is a filename and is required; the second, a label name which is optional. If the filename is given without a drive or directory, then it is searched for first in the current directory. If not found by BATUTIL, BATUTIL will attempt to add an extension of BAT and look again. Then the same search is made in the directory that BATUTIL was loaded from (under DOS 3.0 and later) and finally in the DOS path. If still not found, BATUTIL exits and an error message is issued.

If no label name is given, then BATUTIL will start reading and processing the file from its beginning. If a label is given, BATUTIL reads the file from the beginning but searches until it finds a line beginning with

    :label

(leading spaces before the : are ignored and labels are NOT case sensitive). For example

    batutil {FE foobar.txt hi}

would look for a file named foobar.txt and then search for a line starting with

    :hi

If the label is not found, then BATUTIL exits with an error message. Otherwise, the file is processed one line at a time until the next line beginning with a : is located. Lines whose first symbol is a ; are ignored (i.e., treated as remarks).

You can combine batch file labels and BATUTIL's labels to keep the extra lines to display in the batch file itself. For example, the following could be at the start of a batch file:

```
goto codestart :echostart
This line will be echoed
and this will appear on the next
    line
;but this line is a remark
The last line doesn't have an
    explicit CR added
:codestart
batutil {FEcho %0 echostart}
```

Because BATUTIL will add .BAT to a filename if it cannot find the file without that, the %0 will be properly interpreted (unless you happen to have a file with the same name as the batch file and no extension).

FEcho, FMenu, and FPretty are limited to reading in 25 or fewer lines. FCommand/INclude will read in up to 1,023 commands. You can nest INclude commands to get around the 1,023 command limitation, but BATUTIL is an interpreted language and such large projects should normally not be done using such a language.

You can place multiple commands on a single FCommand line by separating them with one or more of the four characters [ ] { }.

Please look closely at the demonstration batch files for an introduction of how to use the file commands effectively. A typical batch file that only calls BATUTIL commands including the RU command could have the form:

```
@echo off
batutil {INc %0 code}
quitbat
:code
BATUTIL commands
```

To make this work, you'd need a zero-byte batch file called QUITBAT.BAT in your path. You can make such a file at the DOS command line by typing

```
rem > quitbat.bat
```

FEcho and FPretty are discussed in Section III.7 and FMenu in Section IV.2.

BATUTIL stores the name of the last file you have asked to read commands, echo, pretty, or menu from and will reuse it if you use the

filename %0 in one of these commands. See the sample batch files.

I.8 BATUTIL's Line Editor

Four of BATUTIL's commands allow editing of line input: the EDenv and PAthedit commands, which allow you to edit any environmental variable; your path; the USername command which prompts for a string to be matched; and the $Q/$?/$N subcommands of BATUTIL's SEt, which place information in the environment. When such input is asked for, the following edit keys are active:

<Enter>	accepts the current string and exits
<Esc>	restores the original value of the string; if that original value is empty, <Esc> blanks the line except, in that case, <Esc> with a blank line exits and returns an empty string
<Left>, <Right>	move the cursor by a character
<^Left>, <^Right>	move the cursor by a word
<Home>, <End>	to the beginning or end of the line
<Ins>	toggles insert mode which starts as overwrite mode; the cursor shape indicates what the current mode is
<Del> and <Bks>	do their usual single character functions
<^X> or <^Y>	blanks the entire line
<^End>	blanks to the end of the line
<^Home>	blanks from the start of the line to the current position
<^T>	blanks from the cursor position through the next blank space

In addition, WordStar commands are accepted for most of these functions; for example, ^S is the same as <Left>, and the two letter ^QS (or ^Q^S) is the same as <Home>.

In situations where the quantity being edited has a prior value, that value is displayed when the line editor starts up and the cursor is at the end of line. Hitting an alphanumeric key (as opposed to a cursor key) as the first key will blank the original value which can be restored with <Esc>. The $N input must be an integer, and only integer input is accepted.

In each case, the input string has a maximum length which may be larger than the edit window on-screen. If it is larger, the line editor will scroll horizontally if the cursor moves to the start or end of the edit window.

The point is that the editor is quite intuitive and most users will have no trouble using it without explicit directions.

I.9 BUSIC — A First Look

BATUTIL includes a full-featured language which goes way beyond the DOS batch language. We dub it *BUSIC* for **B**atUtil's **S**tandard **I**nstructions and **C**ommands. Despite the name, it is closer to Pascal or C than BASIC. While it can be used at the command line, the use of {}'s gets tedious, and we recommend limiting BUSIC to INclude sets of commands. Chapter VI is devoted to this language, but we'll make a few general remarks here.

There are 32 internal variables. Two are special: $r is like the RC environmental variable, and $% tracks the last fileIO error when IOerrors are trapped. These two variables cannot be set with the set command but can be ECHOed with metastring translation or used in other places, for example, inside a comparison after an IF, where they are read.

You will most often use the internal variables $1,...,$0, ten in all. In addition, while they are more awkward to use, there are an additional 20 variables which are indicated by $ followed by one of the ASCII codes 130–149, that is $é, $â, ..., $ò. These can be set with commands like

    SEt $1=....

The set is actually optional for these 30 variables, that is

    $1=$Q

is the same as

    SEt $1=$Q

and would place up an edit box whose value is stored in $1.

The commands:

    ++ $1

and

    -- $1

(where $1 is any of the 30 internal variables that you can set) will check to see if $1 is number (if $1 is not, then there will be an error exit!) and if so increase or decrease it by one. If the variable is empty, it is treated as if it were 0 for purposes of these commands.

The keywords in the language cannot be abbreviated. We'll usually capitalize them for emphasis, but they are not case sensitive. After THEN or ELSE in an IF clause, after FOR, after a CASE option, and after a WHILE or REPEAT, you need to place a legitimate BATUTIL command, for example

    IF $1>6 THEN ECho it is greater
       than 6.

In all of these cases, you can replace the command by the single keyword BEGIN and then place several commands each on a separate line (or separated by {}[]) with an END to indicate that you finished the set of commands started with a BEGIN. For example, to count the files in a directory starting with b, echoing their names to the screen, you could use

    $1=0
    FOR $2 in (b*.*) DO BEGIN
    ++ $1
    ECho $1:$2$_
    END

Our sample will indent commands between BEGIN/END pairs for readability, but leading spaces are ignored by BUSIC.

$R is a special metastring. It will read from a text file (see Section VI.5 for discussion of reading from files and writing to them). If the file you read from is **con**, then special handling is done and you read from the screen. You can read from absolute screen positions or positions relative to the current one.

BATUTIL's TRace command is discussed in Section VI.12. There is a powerful but dangerous option that allows you to directly read and write from/to memory and or a processor IO port. Because we'd not want you to do this by accident, you must turn this mode on within EACH running of BATUTIL with a {HACKER +} command. We discuss this in Section VI.13.

I.10 String Manipulation, Arithmetic, and Date Arithmetic

BATUTIL includes special metastrings to handle string manipulation and arithmetic. $s (to be distinguished from $S=space) when translated manipulates a string. The syntax is

```
$s(X,string,Y)
```

where S is a single letter key and Y specifies parameters which are special to each value of X. For example,

```
$s(W,string,4)
```

would become the fourth word in the string and

```
$s(U,string)
```

would make the string Uppercase. Section VI.2 describes this metastring in full details.

$V (to be distinguished from $v=DOS version) does arithmetic. The syntax is to put an arithmetic string inside parentheses following $V. For example,

```
$V(1+4)
```

would translate to 5. Only integer arithmetic is done. Operations are summarized in Section VI.3. Multiple parentheses are handled, and there is metastring translation inside the (..) so that you can use $1, etc. and environmental variables. For example internally, BATUTIL translates ++$1 to

```
SEt $1=$V($1+1)
```

In Version 1.0, $E, $M, $D, $Y, $W referred to today in English, the month, day of month, year, and weekday. That remains true IF these are not followed by a (. If they are, BATUTIL will attempt to translate the argument into one of three formats:

1. Sees if it is number between 1 and 7305 and interprets it as a date between 1/1/80 and 12/31/99
2. Sees if it has the format MM-DD-YY or MM/DD/YY and interprets it in that format as an American style date

3. Looks for a filename with that name and interprets it as the date of that file

So, for example, if the file C:\dos\command.com has a date of 12/19/88, then all three of $E(12/19/88), $E(C:\dos\command.com), and $E(3276) would become December 19, 1988 after metastring translation. If the European date switch is turned on, then the date is interpreted as DD/MM/YY in place of MM/DD/YY.

The use of number of days after 1/1/80 wouldn't be useful if you had to count the days yourself. So, there is a metastring $J which counts that number of days. With no parameters, it is today and for example $J(12/19/88)=3276. Thus, for example, you could do date arithmetic with

```
batutil {EC the date 200 days from
today is $E($V(200+$J))}
```

I.11 Control Break Handling

BATUTIL looks especially for the user to press ^Break. If this is pressed during the running of BATUTIL, then the message

```
Quit BATUTIL(Y/N)?
```

pops up. If you answer yes, then BATUTIL pops up a message:

```
Halt Batch file too(Y/N)?|
```

With either response to this question, BATUTIL is then halted. If you've also answered yes to the second question, then BATUTIL will turn DOS Break on and place a ^C buffer so the batch file should offer you the chance to terminate it. If you prefer running with Break off, you'll need to do that by hand if you use this emergency exit. This response is to ^Break only and NOT also to Ctrl-C.

If you answer N to the initial QUIT BATUTIL question, then BATUTIL will ask

```
Turn TRACE On(Y/N)?
```

Either way BATUTIL will continue, but if you answer yes to the TRACE ON question, then BATUTIL's single step debug mode is turned on, but not until the currently executing command is finished.

If you quit BATUTIL with ^Break but elect not to halt the batch file, BATUTIL exits with the errorlevel set to 255.

For third-party batch files, you may want to turn off ^Break to prevent the user from breaking at an inconvenient point. When BATUTIL loads, it checks to see if **BU^=no** is in the environment. If it is, then the ^–Break handler is not installed. So, just include set BU^=no in the batch file to avoid this premature exit.

Please see the BATUTIL.DOC file for Chapter 2 omitted here.

Chapter III: Display Tools

Note: Please see BATUTIL.DOC for sections III.1–III.9 omitted here. (Be sure to read about Bigecho in III.6; it's a fun command.)

III.10 Sounds

Command: SOund, NSound

Parameter: SOund takes a single required number from 1 to 20 and an optional second number. NSound takes a -- or an optional +.

BATUTIL comes with ten brief sounds and ten tunes. The ten tunes were made with PIANOMAN. Each has a number.

The ten sounds are as follows:

    1: ping
    2: wolf whistle
    3: random electronic sound
    4: short buzz
    5: tweet
    6: alarm clock ring
    7: buzzer
    8: electronic sound 1
    9: electronic sound 2
    10: train with Doppler effect

The tunes are fragments from the following pieces:

    11: Dance of the Clowns
    12: Habana from Carmen
    13: Sailor's Hornpipe
    14: Mapleleaf Rag
    15: Land of Hope and Glory (Pomp and Circumstance)
    16: Porky Pig Theme ("That's All Folks")
    17: Pop Goes the Weasel

    18: William Tell Overture (Lone Ranger's Theme), Part I
    19: William Tell Overture, Part II
    20: Yellow Rose of Texas

You invoke a sound with BATUTIL by using the sound command which takes one or two parameters. The first parameter must be an integer from 1 to 20 and indicates the sound from the above list. The second parameter indicates the number of times to repeat the sound; if the second parameter is absent, the sound is issued once. For most sounds you won't want any repeats, but for sound 3 you'll want a repeat count of 15 or more, and sound 4 will do with a few repeats. The repeat count must lie between 1 and 60.

Thus

```
batutil {SO 3 30}
```

will repeat sound 3 thirty times. The William Tell Overture is broken into two parts, to allow you to take an action in the middle as in

```
batutil {EC CTRLALT Associates}{SO
18}{EC $Spresents}{SO 19}
```

If you don't want the SOund command issued, you can use the NSound command. This is intended primarily for use in the options set in the environment as in

```
set @BU={NS}
```

which would be useful if you normally had sounds in your batch files but were working late at night and didn't want to disturb others. The {NS –} command would turn sound back on even if there is a previous {NS}.

Chapter VII: Tips and Examples

VII.1 General Tips

After a BATUTIL menu, you will typically need to branch on a number of different possibilities. The commands

```
IF $r=6 GOto menu6
IF $r=5 GOto menu5
IF $r=4 GOto menu4
IF $r=3 GOto menu3
IF $r=2 GOto menu2
IF $r=1 GOto menu1
```

followed by choice 0 code will work, but the following is more elegant. If there are six menu choices, have labels menu0,..., menu6. Use

```
GOto menu$r
```

For an example of this, see the sample batch file BUDEMO.BAT.

It is most convenient to place the fmenu and fecho lines in the batch file itself. If the batch file is foobar.bat, you could use

```
{FEcho foobar.bat label}
```

but that will fail if the user renames the batch file, so use

```
{FEcho %0 label}
```

instead. To handle this possibility, BATUTIL looks first for the filename specified with a {fecho ....} command by name and if that fails it tries the extension BAT.

VII.2 Returning to Your Initial Directory

You can arrange to return to your initial directory in a batch file, say one that changes to C:\123 and runs Lotus with

```
batutil {SEt dr=$n di=$p}
C:
cd \123
lotus
%dr%:
cd %di%
```

This uses DOS's environmental substitution.

You could arrange to save a set of your earlier directories and return to them with two batch files: PUSHDIR and POPDIR. PUSHDIR.BAT would read

```
batutil {SEt dr3=$x(dr2)
   di3=$x(di2) dr2=$x(dr1)
   di2=$x(di1)
   dr1=$n di1=$p}
```

all on one line. POPDIR.BAT would read

```
%dr1%
cd %dr1%
batutil {SEt dr2=$x(dr3)
di2=$x(di3) dr1=$x(dr2) di1=$x(di2)
dr3= di3= }
```

In terms of directory manipulation, suppose you not only want to return to the original

directory, but you have a program named silly in \foo which insists that its directory be in the path even if it is the default directory. You want to add it to the path but later remove it. Use

```
batutil {SEt dr=$n di=$p}{ad
C:\foo}
C:
cd \foo
silly
batutil {DE C:\foo}
%dr%:
cd %di%
```

VII.3 Using BATUTIL in Your AUTOEXEC.BAT

A number of actions (special to an AUTOEXEC.BAT) make BATUTIL valuable. Your AUTOEXEC.BAT may take a long time to run because you run a defragmenting utility or use a FAT/root dir saver like DOS's mirror or you might copy a lot of files to a RAM disk. You might care to branch at the end of the batch file, say to run Software Carousel or not. Of course, you can ask a question, but what if you don't want to always stand around and would like to default to running Carousel if you aren't there? You could use (as a fragment of your AUTOEXEC.BAT)

```
batutil {EC Run Carousel (Y/N)?}{GE
   wa6 y n}
if errorlevel 2 goto nocar
carousel
:nocar
```

You could even have the time counted down by replacing the first line with

```
batutil {EC Run Carousel (Y/N)? $L
   secs left}{GE wa6 y n}
```

So, you've solved the problem of waiting around if you do want to run Carousel. But, what if you don't want to? With the above fragment, you'd need to wait around. Here is where the test of the lock keys comes in. Immediately before the first line of the above fragment, you could put

```
batutil {QL C-}
```

```
if errorlevel 1 goto nocar
```

Then, if you hit Capslock before you go off, Carousel wouldn't run. Actually, you could avoid an extra running of BATUTIL and two lines of the file by using:

```
batutil {QL C-}{IF $r=1 THEN GOto
    halt2}
{EC Run Carousel (Y/N)?}{GE wa6 y
    n}
```

as the first line of the fragment. For then if Caps was set, the GOto halt2 command causes BATUTIL to exit with an errorlevel of 2 just as if you answered no!

Another problem that you'll often want to cope with in a batch file is some operation like defragmentation that you only want to run once a day. Here is a fragment to do that:

```
batutil {TO newday.tst}
if not errorlevel 1 goto already
echo a >newday.tst
STUFF TO DO ONCE
:already
```

What this does is, if the errorlevel is exactly 0, then one skips to the label already. Otherwise, the file newday.tst is given today's date so that the next time it is run, **batutil {to newday.tst}** will return errorlevel 0. But what if you sometimes work past midnight and don't want the newday stuff done until morning? Replace

```
batutil {TO newday.tst}
```

with

```
batutil {TO 5 newday.tst}
```

which will make the changeover at 5AM rather than midnight.

VII.4 A Clean Sweep

Here is a simple BATUTIL code fragment that will delete all *.BAK files anywhere on disk.

```
SEt buswap=!
FORDIR $1 IN () DO BEGIN
$2=$A($1\)
NU $!($2*.bak)
IF $r > 0 THEN BEGIN
RUn command /cdel $2*.bak
ECho $1:$r files erased
END
END
```

Note the use of $2=$A($1\) to place a single trailing backslash as explained in Section VI.10.

Note also that the supermetastring **$!** in the **nu** command is necessary because metastring translation is not done on that command.

VII.5 Directory Lister with Smart Wildcards

You may want to know how to get a name listing of all files whose names includes a string anywhere in the filename; see, for example v10, n16, pg 424. Here's a way to do it with BUSIC:

```
@echo off
if '%1'=='' goto error
batutil {$1=%1}{IN %0 code}
for %%a in (%foo##%) do echo %%a
set foo##=
goto end
:code
$2=$s(S,$1) $5=$1*.* $4=?
FOR $3=8 TO 2 DO BEGIN
IF $2=$3 THEN GO next
$5=$5$S$4$1*.*
$4=?$4
END
LA next
CASE $2 OF
1: $5=$5$S*.$1*$S*.?$1*$S*.??$1
2: $5=$5$S*.$1*$S*.?$1
3: $5=$5$S*.$1
ENDCASE
SET foo##=$5
:error
echo a parameter is required
:end
```

VII.6 A Two-Year Old's Delight

Here is a simple batch file which delighted Barry's two-year-old daughter:

```
for %%a in (1 2 3 4 5 6 7 8 9) do
    batutil
{GE IN}{SO 1%%a}
```

This will wait for the insert key and then play 9 tunes. The INsert key was especially picked for two reasons: it is large and easy for little hands to reach. It is not a repeating key so that it is less likely that several keystrokes will get through and abort the tunes.

VII.7 Sample Batch Files

You will learn a lot about how to use BATUTIL by studying the sample batch files provided. We'll make some comments about them here.

The complicated contortions in the BATUTIL 1.0 manual are no longer needed because we can use internal variables on the whole. Notice that we use the **{RC $}** command to prevent RC from being placed in the environment.

BUDEMO {FEcho %0} and a variant on the goto fmenu$r tricks are discussed in Section 1 (we use CALL in place of GOto). It turns the cursor off with the

```
set cur=off
```

command.

Most of the separate batch demos are called with a simple use of FCommand. Notice that this use allows the same code to be used to call the subsidiary batch files from within BUDEMO.BAT as well as stand alone.

Notice how BUDEMO.BAT sees if BATUTIL.HLP is in the current directory or on the path and

stores the information in $Å. It then calls the appropriate menu with a

```
FM $!(%0 fmain$Å)
```

The supermetastring **$!(...)** is needed because FM does not normally do metastring translation.

Because calling help requires a separate running of BATUTIL, we need some fancy footwork with DOS batch files to call help from the ninth menu choice.

SOUNDMEMO.BAT is also straightforward. Note the way the fpretty command is used to produce the second screen with its special box.

SHOWDEMO.BAT's most interesting feature may be the last panel that illustrates how to use the fpretty command for a display of different columns in different colors. Note the use of the $$.

Note INPUTDEM.BAT's use of **$L** with spaces after it.

Note that EQUIP.BAT gets all its information and saves it in internal variables and then displays it all at once.

The study of these samples should give you an idea of how to use BATUTIL.

CMFiler

Version 5.35
Copyright © 1991–92 Charles F. Martin, NoVaSoft

Introduction

CMFiler provides a quick, simple, one-touch operating environment for your IBM-compatible 80x86-based computer running under DOS Version 2 or later. While its name implies it is a file manager, it is much, much more. Once you have used CMFiler for a few sessions, you will not want to struggle with the DOS COMMAND.COM command processor or your other file managers ever again! CMFiler was painstakingly written in Assembly language over a three-year period, carefully factoring in the suggestions of a dozen of the world's pickiest software critics. It is compact and lightning fast.

Note: See the file CMFILER.DOC on diskette for complete documentation. The Overview section and Chapter 1 of the tutorial are printed here along with a command summary and some information on the CMFiler editor (CMeditor).

Program and Documentation Files

By default, the install program for the *DOS 6 SECRETS* diskettes will install all of the CMFILER files in the directory \SECRETS\CMFILER. This directory has not been added to the search path. You can execute the program from its home directory, add the directory to the search path, or copy the CMFILER files to a directory that is included in the search path.

File Contents

There are ten files in the CMFiler package.

CMFILER.COM	The kernel of the CMFiler program
CMFILER.OVY	Its supporting program overlay
CMFILER.DOC	The full documentation
CMFILER.BRF	A brief summary of features for quick reference
CMFILER.REG	A file containing the registration form
DESC2NAR.COM	A program for 4DOS/NDOS users for converting the DESCRIPT.ION files containing file and directory notes into the CMFiler NARATIVE.CF file format
DESC2NAR.DOC	The documentation for DESC2NAR.COM. DESC2NAR is provided as a freeware adjunct to the CMFiler shareware disk/file manager for 4DOS/NDOS users
CHANGES	A brief compilation of the changes and bug fixes since Version 5.22
READ.ME	A file with installation instructions
FILE_ID.DIZ	A description file used by BBS system operators

CMFiler is capable of doing everything your DOS COMMAND.COM processor or other file manager can do and more but with EASE! — displaying two directories side-by-side, copying one or more files from one directory to another, backing up files in the same directory, deleting and renaming files and directories, setting file and directory attributes, concatenating (stringing together) multiple files, viewing and editing files, making and removing subdirectories, printing files in the background while you perform other tasks, setting disk volume labels, printing directory listings, keeping notes, displaying two disk structures side-by-side as "trees," and performing a full set of operations on their structures and executing child pro-

cesses — all with a minimum number of keystrokes and maximum "transparency."

Operations are keyed to single-letter mnemonics, making CMFiler intuitive and easy to learn. For example, the letter C means *copy*, the letter D *delete*, and so forth. Almost everything you need to know about CMFiler is contained in a two-line prompt at the bottom of the screen or can be summoned instantly with a single keystroke (surprise! H for "help"), with no delay for external file reading, since the help is embedded in the program code. There are only a few things for which you will need to refer to this manual once you begin using CMFiler.

CMFiler employs the BIOS (Basic Input/Output System) and DOS disk service routines which are embedded in ROM or loaded into RAM when your computer boots, and the DOS file operation safeguards and error flags are employed, such as denying access to remove non-void subdirectories. I have added a few of my own, such as protection of files against being overwritten by zero-length files of the same name (resulting from an occasional DOS read-write failure).

CMFiler performs most operations immediately and does not ask for confirmation as other file managers do, unless file destruction is involved. You must confirm with a separate keystroke, for example, that you really *do* want to delete files, or that you really *do* want to overwrite a more recent version of a file during a copy operation. Otherwise, CMFiler takes for granted that you are doing exactly what you had in mind on the basis that a mistake can be recovered from with just a few more keystrokes. The mass operations, like copying large numbers of tagged files, all have an Esc bailout.

Program Logical and Physical Organization

The CMFiler program code is organized logically (in the programmer's sense) into three sections or modules. These will be referred to variously as the *main module* or *main screen*, the *editor module* or *editor*, and the *tree module* or *tree functions*. Each module performs some major function or group of functions which is fundamentally different from the rest, discussed further below. On the other hand, the program is broken physically into two main pieces; in this case two files, namely the file CMFILER.COM, sometimes referred to herein as the *kernel*, and the file CMFILER.OVY or the *overlay*. The kernel contains the most vital part of the main module, the starter, and the overlay, which the kernel loads contiguous to itself in memory, contains the rest of the main module, plus all of the editor and tree modules. A memory map is included in this manual for those interested.

The main module displays one directory on the left side of the screen or two directories in side-by-side panels. The subdirectories of each directory are always shown at the top of the listing in alphabetical order followed by the files in one of seven user-specified ordering schemes. Commands operate on a subdirectory or one or more files in one panel (the source panel). Some commands, like Copy, write to the directory in the other panel (the target panel). The main module gives a somewhat myopic or microscopic view of your disk, one directory at a time, but does so with the most complete set of file and directory services available in the file manager. The other two modules (editor and tree) are accessed from the main, and the editor may also be accessed from the tree.

The editor is called to create, edit, or view a file. To view or edit an existing file in the main module, just put the cursor on it and press E or Enter. To create a file, press F and type in a name for the new file.

The tree module is called from the main module with Shift-T. It displays the entire directory tree structure of one disk in the left panel, or two trees for the same or different disks in side-by-side panels. Whole structures (branches) of a tree — or if you wish just the files in one directory — may be copied, moved, or deleted in their entirety. Some file manager documentation calls this kind of capability *prune-and-graft*. This capability is macroscopic in scope compared to the main modules as it deals with the big picture of your disk organization. But CMFiler does much more than most file managers. In addition to the macroscopic prune-and-graft-type operators, you may do some microscopic things as well, like display

the files in each subdirectory as you navigate through the tree, find a specific file anywhere on the disk, search for a text string in all or some of the files on the disk — even view or edit a file, and delete it without having to return to the main file services module. This latter feature, in particular, makes disk cleanup a breeze!

Security Features

CMFiler incorporates security features which support its use on systems containing sensitive information.

- You may specify a password and change it at any time during a session which must be given back to reenter CMFiler once it has gone to screen-saver mode (about 1½ minutes after last keystroke from main screen display). This password is the bottommost field in the data entry screen presented by the key combination Shift-F10 (discussed in further detail in Chapter 4).

- You may force CMFiler into screen-saver mode with the key combination Ctrl-S. This is so that if you want to secure access to your computer immediately you don't have to wait the 1½ minutes for the screen saver and password to automatically be invoked.

- If you set the option **Clear I/O buffers if located?** in the Shift-O Options screen, CMFiler will attempt to locate and overwrite all the DOS input/output buffers with the continuous string CFCFCFCF... before starting any file writing operations. This operation ensures that the file being written does not contain any stray data in the "slack space" of the last sector written that was hanging around from a previous I/O operation. (***DR DOS USERS:*** The option to clear I/O buffers should NOT be invoked if you are operating under DR DOS. This operating system responds very ungracefully to the buffer clearing feature. For this reason, I have set the default option to NOT clear I/O buffers.)

CMFiler also employs a rudimentary check-summing routine to check the .COM and .OVY files each time they are loaded. This routine will sense any changes in the execution code and fixed data areas of either file and warn the user of the corruption. Files may become corrupted as a result of an operating system error during data transmission, a sector going bad on a disk, or external tampering by a person or a virus. This check-summing feature can detect (and has detected) the presence of some older file infecting viruses but may be foiled by modern stealth viruses. DO NOT count on it for virus protection. There is no substitute for good antivirus software. I use and strongly recommend Wolfgang Stiller's Integrity Master. He is President of Stiller Research and a member of the ASP's Virus Information Panel, and a recognized expert in the anti-virus community.

Monitor Options

CMFiler should work with all reasonably current IBM-compatible CGA/EGA/VGA and monochrome monitors. Although, I have heard of some problems with machines under very early BIOS versions.

You may specify a type of monitor one of two ways:

- When first run, if CMFiler cannot find a .CFG file containing previously specified user option data and does not sense a monochrome monitor installed (which only supports one color set), it knows it cannot tell for sure what you have installed; then it will ask you to specify a monitor type by pressing C, L, T, or M. Your choice is immediately recorded by CMFiler, creating a .CFG file. If you have an LCD monitor other than Tandy, you may invoke a generic LCD color set with the letter L. For Tandy LCDs, use T. (Tandy, for some unfathomable reason, inverts the function of the high-intensity bit in the color attribute.) If you have a monochrome monitor being driven by a color card, CMFiler senses the color card's presence, not the monitor's. Press M for this case to force the monochrome color set.

- You may also put one of these four letters in the command line, preceded by the character @, and bypass the initial question.

Precautions and Limitations

There are a few precautions and limitations to be aware of:

- Terminate-and-Stay-Resident programs should NOT be launched from CMFiler. At best you will end up with a fragmented memory when you exit CMFiler, and at worst you will have a SYSTEM CRASH.

- CMFiler requires a minimum of 197K of free memory to run. This permits generous memory allocations for the directory listings, a print spooler buffer, and a large copy buffer. During application launching, however, the resident portion of CMFiler can be made to occupy as little as 19K using the Small footprint option of the Kernel command (letter K pressed from the main screen — discussed more in Chapters 1 and 4).

- Maximum directory size recognized by the main module varies from 300 to 1,200 entries, depending on free memory available. If the directory size limit is reached, an informational note is given. The rest of the directory is inaccessible, as though it were hidden. This is a benign, non-damaging limitation.

- The algorithms used by the editor module place certain limitations on it in edit mode which do not apply in view mode. If you attempt to edit a file which exceeds these limitations, the editor reverts to view mode automatically:

   Files too large to fit in available memory in one shot.
   Files with more than 16,380 lines.
   Files with lines longer than 8,190 characters if editing in NoWrap mode.

- The tree module limits the number of entries in a directory tree structure to 505 total subdirectories and the total files to 3,488.

- The main and tree modules both limit the depth of directory nesting to eight levels (e.g., **C:\1\2\3\4\5\6\7\8** is an example of the most deeply nested path allowed) and the length of path specifications to 66 characters (this is a DOS limitation).

- A limitation of DOS itself, which users frequently run into and are puzzled by because of the cryptic error message DOS returns, is the maximum number of entries permitted in the root directory. This number is 112 for 5.25" disks formatted at 360K and 3.5" @ 720K, and 224 for 5.25" @ 1.2MB and 3.5" @ 1.44MB. The error message returned is `Access denied creating file`. Be aware that the volume label and each subdirectory is an "entry," as well as each file.

- Finally, CMFiler does not yet support mouse or 43/50 line EGA/VGA display capability. If there is overwhelming request for addition of mouse support or 43/50 line display, I will consider adding it.

Additional Note for Windows Users

Though not designed as a Windows application, CMFiler appears to be operating satisfactorily as a DOS program in the Windows environment. One nuisance feature will probably need to be corrected if you are running it under Windows, however. The default assumption on return from screen-saver mode is that the disk directories have not been altered while CMFiler has been idling. Under Windows, this is not necessarily a valid assumption since another foreground application may have operated on the directories CMFiler was selected to when it went into the background. Therefore, for Windows users there is a switch which may be set using the command Shift-O (where O is for Options) telling CMFiler to refresh the directory listings on return from the screen saver.

Tutorial — Chapter 1: File Handling

Getting Started, or the kernel and the overlay

As mentioned above, I refer to the 19K CMFILER.COM file as the *kernel* or the vital part of the main module and the 82K CMFILER.OVY file as the *overlay*, which contains the rest of the main module and the editor

and tree modules. Physically breaking the program into two files served two purposes — it got around an arcane 64K limit on .COM files imposed by DOS, and it let me give you two options for how much of the program to leave resident in memory when launching applications from CMFiler (more in Chapter 4).

For now, copy CMFILER.COM and CMFILER.OVY into the root directory of your hard disk or a working floppy using your good ol' DOS COMMAND.COM processor and save a write-protected copy for your library. With the DOS system prompt showing the drive these two files are now on, run the kernel CMFILER.COM by entering cmfiler or CMFILER. The DOS command processor will load and execute CMFILER.COM, which in turn will find and load the overlay CMFILER.OVY. The whole 101K (19+82) is now residing in memory ready to respond to commands.

The first thing you will likely see is a request for monitor information. CMFiler cannot distinguish between a color monitor and an LCD monitor, and the default color set for the color monitor is a poor choice for LCD monitors. When you see the message press C, M, L, or T (some Tandy LCDs employ a backward convention on the high-intensity attribute, and thus a separate color set has been dedicated to them). As soon as you press one of these letters, you will see disk activity. CMFiler is creating a file of user configuration data (called CMFILER.CFG) in the same directory the .COM file is in. It will update this file as you select other setup options.

Rename CMFILER to spare my fingers

Now, feel free to rename CMFILER.COM to CF.COM for short and the overlay and configuration files from CMFILER.OVY and CMFILER.CFG to CF.OVY and CF.CFG. (It is important to keep all of these files named THE SAME, by the way.) In fact I will refer to them simply as CF from here on, since that results in fewer keystrokes for me! Put the cursor on the line reading CMFILER COM and press the letter R (for *rename*).

A window will open up at the bottom that says:

```
Rename CMFILER.COM
    to >CMFILER.COM<
```

with the cursor blinking on the first position in the data entry field denoted by the > < pair. (CMFiler is assuming that you want to rename just the CMFILER.COM file since the most frequent use of the rename facility is renaming single files. CMFiler is offering you the same name as the default entry in the new name field since often when you rename a file you may be only changing a few characters.)

In this case, we want to rename all the files that start with CMFILER; that is, we would really like to use the DOS wildcard convention *. If we were renaming this family of files from the DOS prompt, we would type in the command **ren cmfiler.* cf.***. In the CMFiler rename facility, the upper line is the first parameter of the DOS rename command and the lower line the second. We therefore want the upper line to read CMFILER.*. To do this press either the up arrow or PgUp, and press Tab to move over to the C in COM. Type * and press Enter or down arrow. Now the window reads

```
Rename CMFILER.*
to >CMFILER.* <
```

Simply type **CF.*** and press Enter. The files are now renamed.

This quick exercise sounds complicated when you read it, but won't be when you try it. And it illustrates a few nice touches I have tried to build in to minimize your keystrokes.

From here on the explanations are not so detailed. I recommend you fiddle with scratch disks until you are familiar with all of CF's capabilities. If you are running DOS Version 2, put CF, both the .COM and .OVY files, on one of the paths defined in a DOS path command so that it can find itself after running other applications. This is not necessary under DOS Version 3 and later.

The screen

You should by now have noted an economy of screen usage. The left panel shows the contents of the root directory on the default drive. Line 1 of this active panel shows the disk volume name if any and a prompt area for four display enhancement features: the key combination Ctrl-O (denoted by ^O to save space) allows selection of one of seven file Ordering schemes, ^H toggles the Hide mode switch, ^C toggles the

Compare mode switch, and ^M allows specifying a file Mask. Line 2 shows the path to the current directory, whose first 20 entries are displayed in lines 3–22. Line 23 gives vital information about the disk, such as room left, and lines 24–25 contain an abbreviated help screen.

The thick versus thin sections of the vertical line to the left of the file list denote the relative position and size of the current screen display within the full directory listing.

If you do not press a key within about 1½ minutes, the screen goes into screen-saver mode. Just press any key to return to the main display. You may force the screen-Saver mode with Ctrl-S.

The help area

The two-line help area at the bottom of the screen contains a set of abbreviated cues to assist with the recollection of the mnemonic single-key commands. With no modifier keys pressed [i.e., the Shift-, Alt-, and Ctrl- keys all up], the help area shows the operations available with the unmodified keys with the mnemonic code highlighted. These are typically the most frequently used operations; the letter C for *Copy file(s)*, E for *Edit file*, D for *Delete file or directory*, T for *Tag file*, the number 1 for *toggle the file Read-only attribute*, and so forth.

Additional commands are available which use similar mnemonic devices, but with the keyboard modified by Shift-, Alt-, or Ctrl-. Press one of the Shift- keys, and notice the change in the bottom lines. These are the commands enabled by the letters shown in highlight and modified by the key you are holding down. Press Ctrl- and Alt- in turn. Just be aware that the visual cues for the modifier keys are there when you want them.

More on the modifier keys

Incidentally, there is some rationale for which of the Shift-, Alt-, or Ctrl- keys was used as the modifier for a particular modified operation, and there are some devices which may help you remember the modified keys as well as the more straightforward mnemonic devices of the unmodified keys:

- The modifier Shift- is often used for operations involving transfers of control or data to or from the other panel. For example, pressing Shift-Enter when the cursor is on a subdirectory entry causes this subdirectory in the other panel to be displayed and moves you across to it. Other commands which follow this convention and which you will encounter in more detail are Shift-Left/Rt Arrow, Shift-P, Shift-*, Shift-\, and Shift-F.

■ The modifier Ctrl- is most often used to toggle the state of a switch or tags — that is, to invert something. For example, Ctrl-H toggles the state of the hide switch , i.e., if Y (yes or on) it goes to N (no or off), if N it goes to Y. Other examples include Ctrl-O, Ctrl-M, Ctrl-C, Ctrl-A, and Ctrl-L.

■ The modifier Alt- is most often used just to indicate an operation associated with a mnemonic alphabet key, but for which the unmodified key was already in use as a mnemonic for a more frequent operation. For example, C means *Copy* and is one of the most frequent operations; Alt-C means *add file spec to Command tail* and is used far less frequently. (In the editor, Alt-modified keys are used a LOT, since the unmodified keys are used for typing text!)

Two panels

Each of two panels corresponds to a path to files in the DOS vernacular. Open the right panel by pressing the right arrow. You will be prompted at the bottom of the screen to specify a drive letter. (Lines 24–25 become the dialog area for information to you about what CF is doing or what it is waiting for you to do.) Just press the letter corresponding to a valid drive; don't press Enter, just a letter key. The root directory of that drive will be shown in the right panel in the same format as the left panel. The bright yellow color of the path specification on line 2 and the blinking cursor now identify the right panel as the source path. The left panel has become the target or destination path for copy and append operations.

Whenever CF is in compare mode and the cursor is on the name of a file in the source panel that also happens to exist anywhere in the target path, the target panel display is adjusted so that the file appears in the panel, and its date/time signature is put in high-intensity to catch your eye and show you the duplication. If the date, time, and size of the two files are not

the same, the date/time signature of the NEWER file will blink. You can toggle compare mode off and on with the key combination Ctrl-C (the mnemonic is compare).

Color palette

For display in CGA/EGA/VGA systems, CF has four choices of color palettes. The command Ctrl-P (for Palette) lets you cycle through the choices with the spacebar and select a different color scheme with Enter or return to the original one with Esc. The choice is permanently recorded in the .CFG file (discussed in more detail later).

Alphabetic case options

CF also has four options for the alphabetic cases used in the panel displays. The command Ctrl-E (for casE) lets you cycle through the choices with the spacebar as in the Palette above which are 1) files and directories all uppercase, 2) directories in uppercase, file in lower, 3) all in lowercase, and 4) all in modified-Tauck convention where all letters are lowercase except the first and any that follows a non-alphabetic character (e.g., Cmfiler.Com or Read-Me.1St). I have found this last convention by far the easiest to read.

Cursor movement

Shift back and forth with the left and right arrow keys. You are in effect switching source and target paths. Use the up/down arrows, PgUp/PgDn, Home, and End keys to move the cursor within a panel. PgUp moves the cursor to the top of the panel if it was not already there, and then moves up 19 lines in the directory. PgDn is similar for the opposite direction. Home goes to the first line of the directory; End, to the last.

The command G (for *Go to...*) lets you type in a file name to move the cursor to within the directory listing. As you type, the cursor is repositioned to the first file described by the character string you are building. When you have come to the file you want, press Enter or Esc. Alt-G is the equivalent Go to. . . for subdirectories.

In Compare mode whenever there is a duplicate filename highlighted in the opposite panel, you may jump directly across to it with the move Shift-Lf/Rt Arr, vice the unmodified arrows.

Switching drives or disks

CF cannot tell when you have changed disks in the drive whose contents are shown on one of the screen panels. You have to tell it by putting the cursor in that panel and pressing Shift-R (for *Refresh*) or N (for *New drive*) and the letter designator for that drive at the ensuing prompt. If you want to switch drives, say from A to B for the right-hand panel, put the cursor to the right and press N and B.

Sometimes when you are doing single-panel operations like constructing a note set or editing files, it is a distraction to have both screen panels open at once. To close the right-hand panel and return to single left-hand panel display, put the cursor in the right-hand panel and press N and Enter.

Subdirectories

Make a new subdirectory in the source path by pressing M (for the DOS command *Mkdir*) and entering a name. Find it in the display in alphabetical order, move the cursor to it, and press Enter. Note the new path on line 2 of the screen display and only the <Parent> entry in the file listing. Go back to the parent directory by pressing Enter with the cursor on the <Parent> entry or P with the cursor anywhere in the panel. You can navigate down and back up through the directory levels in a path this way, one level at a time. If you are several levels deep, there is another quicker way back to the root directory than by hitting P repeatedly, and that is the backslash key \. It works like the DOS command cd \.

To put a subdirectory from the current source panel list into the target panel, put the cursor on its name and press Shift-Enter. The subdirectory is listed in the opposite panel, and the cursor shifts over to it. In similar fashion, Shift-P puts the source panel's parent directory into the opposite panel, and Shift-\ puts the source's root into the opposite panel. Finally, Shift-* puts the source directory itself into the target. This is handy for quickly setting up the same panels side-by-side for ZIPping/unZIPping, discussed in Chapter 4.

Remove a subdirectory by placing the cursor on it and pressing D (for *Delete*, which I use interchangeably for file deletion and subdirectory removal). Note that the subdirectory has to be empty first — a DOS safeguard.

Copy some files, then do it with tags

Put the cursor on a filename and press the letter C. This copies the file from the source to the target path. Tag several files with the letter T or the spacebar. Now press C to copy this group from source to target. Clear all the tags with A (tag/untag All). Press A again, and see that all the files are now tagged. Untag an individual file with T. (T actually toggles the state of an internal tag bit assigned to each file and used for temporary marking purposes only. A clears all the tags if any were set or sets all the tags if all were clear. No information is changed on the disk itself. These are volatile tags maintained only until the directory is reread for some reason, such as a file deletion or a copy operation into the directory.)

CF looks first at the space available on the target path before it starts to copy. If it doesn't see enough room free, it doesn't start the operation and alerts you to this limitation. This prevents write errors, messed up file allocation tables, and incomplete files that can result when space runs out during a copy operation.

CF has several special features in the copy operation:

- If an identical file exists in the target path — same name, extension, date, time, AND size — CF does not normally copy the source to the target as this would be wasted motion on the assumption that the files are identical. This no overcopy feature is controlled by one of seven switches which may be toggled in the user setup menu brought up with the command Shift-O (for user Options). It is sometimes useful to change its state.

- If a file by the same name but newer date/time is found on the target, CF will ask you specifically to verify that you really do want the newer file overwritten.

- If the source file has length 0 bytes or if the source and target files have the same date/time but the source is smaller, CF will ask for overwrite confirmation. This provides some protection against overwriting a good file with one which has become corrupted by a previous copy error.

■ If a file by the same name but with the read-only attribute set is found on the target, CF will ask you to verify that you want it overwritten. (Likewise, if the target file is hidden and the hide switch is on.)

Tagging, backing up

With a couple of files tagged, look at the line just below the last line of the directory listing. You will see the space in use in the current directory (KB Used), the amount of disk space occupied by any tagged files (Tagd), and the space still free (Free). Also, the current number of files tagged in the line below will appear after each tagging operation. Disk space is expressed in kilobytes, in integer multiples of the disk media cluster size, so what you see is the amount of space ACTUALLY tied up on the disk. (If your disk is a 5.25" DSDD floppy, its clusters are probably one K each. Every file takes up at least one cluster so a 1-byte file takes up one K of disk space, the same as a 1,024-byte file.)

Assuming the amount of space represented by tagged files is less than or equal to space available, press B to back up all the tagged files. CF's convention for assigning backup filenames in this operation is to reuse the first two letters of the extension (filling blanks with exclamation points), and then make the last letter of the extension a tilde character (~). Thus, the backup should always immediately follow the primary file in any alphabetical listing.

Moving files

With the panels selected to different subdirectories on the same disk, one or more files may be moved from one subdirectory to the other. This operation does not read and write the file data clusters but only changes the subdirectory table entries so large files may be moved around quickly. Tag files if desired as with Copy and press the move command Shift-C (instead of C, think of moving as just another kind of copying, but you are shifting files to a different directory instead).

If the conditions are not satisfied for moving the files (e.g., the directories are not on the same disk), CF will copy the files to the target path but will not delete the tagged files in the source. You may delete the tagged files with two more keystrokes if you wish, but CMFiler does not assume this is what you meant. This encum-brance is deliberate. Because CMFiler is so fast, I have made it require confirmation whenever any file destruction is requested.

Deleting a file

With the cursor on a file and no files tagged, pressing D results in deleting the file under the cursor after confirmation. If one or more files are tagged, they will be deleted after confirmation, not the file under the cursor. Alt-Tags discussed below are treated the same as normal tags as far as the delete operation is concerned. On hard disks, the default configuration of CF actually performs what I will call a soft delete for this operation. The files are not deleted using the DOS delete function but rather are redated to the current date and time, and moved into a directory created by CF called CF_TRASH.CAN. If you delete files from your hard disk by mistake, they are RELIABLY recoverable just by switching to the CF_TRASH.CAN directory and moving them back to the directories they came from using Shift-C.

If you delete a second file by the same name as a file already collected in the CF_TRASH.CAN directory by a previous soft delete operation, CF tries to rename this second file by replacing the last character in the extension with a 1. If this name is already in use, it tries to rename with a 2 instead, then a 3, and so on through 9. Thus, you are assured under all reasonable circumstances of not losing any deleted files, even duplicates. The only problem is that you may have trouble telling which duplicate is the original, as CF redates each of them during the soft delete.

Each time you select a new drive in the main module, CF looks to see if it is a hard drive (A and B are always taken to be floppies), creates the directory CF_TRASH.CAN if it is not already present, and then looks in CF_TRASH.CAN for the presence of files with any date earlier than the current date. If it finds any, it will ask you if you want to purge them — that is, perform the hard DOS file delete on yesterday's trash. You have the options **yes**, **no**, or **Enter to view** to see what is in the trash can. You probably want to keep the CF_TRASH.CAN as uncluttered as possible just to avoid tying up disk space need-lessly. If you prefer to "empty the trash" less often than daily, be prepared to be pestered with the same question the first time you select that disk each day! (The D command always performs a hard delete in the CF_TRASH.CAN directory; this is the one exception.)

This soft delete facility is NOT intended as a means of backing up files, but rather is built in SOLELY for the purpose of RELIABLE recovery from inadvertent file deletion.

An additional delete option is available, Ctrl-D or hard delete. This operation performs the DOS delete, always regardless of the type disk selected. Use it when you KNOW you will not want to recover the deleted files.

And if you are REALLY sure of yourself, you can turn D from soft delete to hard delete. There is a switch available for this purpose in the Shift-O user Options menu mentioned above.

The tagging convention expounded on

For all the above commands (copy, delete, move, back up), the operation is performed on ALL THE TAGGED FILES in the source panel if ANY are tagged and only on the file at the cursor if NONE are tagged. Some file managers offer different commands for copy tagged and copy file at cursor, and so forth. I have always found this unnecessarily complicated. For the FEW occasions in which you have a bunch of files tagged to do one of these operations (say you want to copy them), and you discover just before you start that you really wanted to do some other operation on just one of them first (say you realize one of them is out-of-date and you want to delete it), you will have to either untag them all with A, do the operation on the one file and then retag and do the original operation, OR just postpone the one-file operation. For this example, it is easier just to toggle the tag on the one out-of-date file off with T, copy the other bunch, clear the tags, and delete the one. It becomes just a matter of a little thought about the order in which you do things.

The view operation (discussed in Chapter 2) does NOT clear existing tags. So, suppose you are cleaning up a disk, tagging files that you recognize by name as no longer needed in preparation for a single, massive delete, and you come to one you aren't sure about. Put the cursor on it, press Enter (the view command),

browse through it and decide if it's a keeper, and Esc from view mode. Note the previously placed tags are still there, and the cursor is still on the mystery file waiting for you to decide whether or not to tag it.

Renaming a file OR a directory

Since we've already done this, I'll just briefly say that it works for directories, too. A word about the wild card character *: In the earlier exercise, we used it in the first window to declare that we wanted to rename all the files with CMFILER as the name, and any extension, to CF with the same extension. You may use the * in the name field of the first window instead of the extension but not in both. Used in the name field, it means change this extension, wherever it appears, to this other extension. This option is less useful.

If used in the first data window, the * MUST also be used in the second window in the same position. CF always senses the use of * in the first window and seeds the second window with this character in the right position.

The * may be used in the second window, even if not in the first, as a shorthand for *keep the same name (extension)*. For example, if you wanted to rename just CMFILER.DOC to CF.DOC, put the cursor on CMFILER DOC in the source panel, press R, type **CF.*** in the lower window, and Enter. Saves some keystrokes. This is a wildcard convention taken from DOS. (Sorry to you DOS heavies: For simplicity, I chose not to complicate things by including ? in the wildcard library for this facility!)

Some additional tagging options

In addition to T (which toggles the state of an individual file's normal Tag) and A (which clears or sets All tags), there are some more tagging operations. Alt-T applies an *append tag* discussed later. Alt-M tags all the files in the panel with the same naMe as the file under the cursor; Alt-E, same Extension. Alt-D tags all files in the panel with the same Date as the file at the cursor, Alt-N tags all files Newer, and Alt-O, Older. Alt-P tags in the oPposite panel all the files with the same names as files tagged in the source panel. (This is good for updating to a floppy only the files which were already on it.) And finally, Ctrl-A toggles the state of All tags in the panel.

If, for example, you wanted to copy all .COM files, you would put the cursor on any .COM file, press Alt-E, and C. Or suppose that at the end of the day you wanted to copy/update all the files written or revised today. Just put the cursor on any file with today's date and press Alt-D and C. Then suppose you wanted to delete all the earlier files. Press A to clear the tags, Ctrl-O and D, and confirm the deletion as requested after a final check of the screen.

Copy with rename

You may copy a file and rename it in one operation. Only one file at a time may be copied in this way. The command is Alt-R (copy with Rename). It operates only on the file at the cursor.

The file freshener

Suppose you have a floppy disk with backups for some of the files in a hard disk directory, and you want to freshen them periodically. With either panel set up with the primary directory whose files you are backing up, put the backup floppy in a floppy drive, arrow across to the other panel and press N and the drive letter to bring up its root directory (now in the source panel), and then just press Shift-F (for Freshen). CF tags all the backup files in the source panel if none were already tagged or leaves existing tags as is if some were tagged. Then CF tags all the files in the opposite panel with the same name as tagged files in the source but which are NEWER, then copies these to the source, and finally updates the source panel display leaving the primary directory in the target panel display tagged to show you what was copied. Just four keystrokes! No excuses ever again for not backing up files.

Different ways to show the files

Ctrl-O (for *Order*) sets a screen which gives seven choices for file ordering with the cursor blinking on the current selection. Press a number key 1 through 9. The files will now be reordered in the new scheme. The options for ordering by date/time are particularly useful in the visual sense when backing up just the files revised today as in the example above.

The data entry window

The data entry window you encountered in the renaming exercise responds to most of the usual line-editing keypresses.

■ Insert toggles the mode between Typeover and Insert. The mode stays set for each subsequent entry. In Typeover mode, any default entry is cleared if the first keystroke is an alphanumeric character.

■ Ctrl-Lf/Rt Arrow and Tab/Shift-Tab go right or left to the space following the next blank or punctuation mark. Shift-Lf/Rt Arrow go to beginning or end of data field. Home goes to the beginning of the field.

■ Lf/Rt Arr, Bksp, and Del perform the usual functions.

■ End goes to the blank after the last non-blank character.

■ Alt-Keypad permits entry of any ASCII code as a decimal number. Hold down the Alt- key while you type in a number from 1 to 255 on the numeric keypad. When you lift the Alt- key, the IBM symbol for that ASCII code will appear in the window and the cursor will advance a space.

■ Ctrl-D deletes to the end of the line.

■ Esc aborts the operation.

■ Down Arrow is equivalent to Enter. In some cases, Up Arrow moves up a line. (The rename facility in the main module and the replace string facility in the editor use this convention.)

■ For entering filenames and subdirectories, all letter keys are registered as uppercase, regardless of Caps Lock or Shift-key positions, just for the sake of uniformity and ease of alphabetizing. For command-line parameters, which may be case-sensitive, both cases are enabled.

Disk Space Occupied versus Actual File Size

Now take a look at the file listing. You see the name of the file, date, time and size in K. As with the disk space information just below the file list display, size is in integer multiples of clusters occupied. If you want to see exactly how big a file is in bytes, press + to expand the size field. (I had to give away the file time to do this and still keep the two panels readable.) Shift back to the contracted kilobyte form of file size with -.

File attributes

Also in the file list, to the far right in each panel, you will probably see A's. This means that the

DOS Archive attribute bit is set in the file attribute byte. DOS sets this bit every time it operates on a file. CF lets you operate on this bit and the other bits in the DOS file attribute byte — Read-only, Hidden, and System. Before doing this exercise, look at the top line of the display. If you see *Hide=N*, that means that files with the DOS Hidden attribute set will be displayed anyway — i. e., the CF Hide switch is off. Chances are you will see Y instead of N, meaning that the Hide switch is on the default setting. In this setting, files will disappear from view as you set the DOS hidden attribute, so we need to toggle the hide switch to N. Press Ctrl-H to toggle the hide switch off.

Either tag one or more files, or position the cursor on the file whose attribute(s) you want to set, and press 1 to toggle the state of the Read Only attribute, 2 to toggle the Hidden attribute, 3 to toggle the System file attribute, 4 to toggle the Archive attribute, or 0 (zero) to clear all attributes. You may also toggle the hide attribute (with 2) of a subdirectory, but this must be done one subdirectory at a time. Note that hiding a file makes it invisible to CF only when the hide switch is set on, as shown in the top line. Toggle this hide mode off and on with the combination Ctrl-H (discussed further below). Decide for yourself which mode you prefer. Some people like to hide the overhead files and directories on their disks and leave the hide switch on as the default setting to clean up the display.

Changing the date/time stamp of a file

You may change the date and/or time of a file by putting the cursor on it and pressing Alt-F. A data window opens for you to first enter the new date, using the current date in the file's date/time stamp as the default, and then the time. This operation is not permitted on Read-only files.

Alt-Tagging and appending

Suppose you have two files that you want to stick together as one heel-to-toe. Tag them with append tags with the key combination Alt-T or Alt-Space in the order in which you want them to be concatenated, and press C. CF will offer you a filename for the new concatenated file consisting of the name of the first file Alt-Tagged plus the extension .APF (for APpended

File). You may edit or accept that name as given. Then it creates this file in the target path and appends into this file each of the Alt-Tagged source files in order. You may concatenate up to 35 files at a time this way. The order in which the file was Alt-Tagged is shown in the character that appears to the left of the filename as it is tagged (1–9, then a–z). If you had pressed B instead of C after affixing the Alt-Tags, the concatenated file would have been written as a backup into the source path instead of the target.

Printing a file

You can print a file to the parallel printer just by putting the cursor on the file and pressing L (print fiLe). The file will be put into a special print queue for printing to line printer 1 on the parallel port as a background process while you are doing other things, like editing another file, updating disks, etc. Up to five files may be put in the print queue, which may be viewed with Shift-L.

At times the printer may halt momentarily during disk operations. CF gives preference to disk operations over printing to avoid any conflict in time-critical operations. You may terminate printing with Ctrl-L. This actually clears the entire print queue. To force a form feed at the end of the file you have just queued, press Ctrl-F before you queue the next file. CF sets an internal flag to check that the last character sent to the printer from that file is a form feed. If it is not, then it sends one. (Ctrl-F is active when no file is printing, also, as a way of form-feeding the printer from the keyboard.)

CMFiler 5.35 at a Glance

The following is an overview of CMFiler's commands in various modules.

Disk/directory operations in Main Module:

Alt-Q or Esc+other key	Quit CMFiler
N	New drive or disk in source panel
V	specify Volume label
Shf/Ctl-N	view/edit Notes

\	display root directory in source
Enter	display dir in source panel
Shf-Enter	display dir in targ panel
P	display Parent in source panel
Shf-P	display Parent in target panel
M	Make directory in source panel
D	Delete directory (must be empty)
Alt-L	print directory Listing
R	Rename directory
H	Help
Shf-T	go to Tree module
Shf-O	setup Options
Shf-S	Save option switches

File operations in Main Module:

1234	toggle file attrs RHSA
T or Space	normal file Tag
Alt-T or Alt-Space	Alt Tag
A	set/reset All tags
Ctl-A	toggle All tags
Alt-E	tag all files with same Ext
Alt-P	replicate tags in oPposite pnl
Alt-F	change File date/time
Alt-N/O/D	tag all Newer/Older/same Date
C	Copy/append file(s) to target
Shf-C	move files within disk
B	copy/append file(s) as Backup in source panel with extension "._xx"
R	Rename file
Alt-R	copy file with Rename
D	"soft" Delete file(s) in source
Ctl-D	"hard" Delete file(s)
F	create new File
Shf-F	Freshen source from target
E	Edit existing file
Enter	view existing file, no edit
L	print fiLe with spooler
Shf-L	look at fiLe print queue
Ctl-L	clear fiLe print queue

Ctl-F	Form feed line printer
G/Alt-G+ltrs	Go to file/dir
Shf-L/R Arr	go across to match file

Display enhancements in Main Module:

Ctl-E	select alphabetic casE
Ctl-P	select color Palette
Ctl-C	toggle Compare mode Ctl-
H	toggle Hide mode
Ctl-O	select file Order scheme
Ctl-S	force screen-Saver
Ctl-M	set file Mask
+/– :	long/short form of file size
5	toggle system date/time display

Directory operations in Tree Module:

N	New drive or disk in source panel
P	move cursor to Parent directory
M	Make directory under cursor
R	Rename directory at cursor
2	hide directory
Ctl-H	toggle Hide switch
Ctl-O	Toggle file Overcopy switch
Ctl-C	toggle Compare switch
Shf-L/R Arr	go across to path match
Shf-U/D Arr	go to next dir in level
C	Copy source under target
Shf-C	move source under target
Alt-C	Copy just directory array
I	copy source Into target
Shf-I	move source Into target
J	copy Just files in directory
Shf-J	move Just files
D	"soft" Delete source structure
Ctl-D	"hard" Delete source struct
Alt-D	"hard" delete just files
Alt-L	Lprint tree structure
S	Show files
Alt-R	Refresh tree from disk
G/Alt-G	Goto file/directory

Shift-F	Find text
Esc	return to main, old paths
Enter	return to main, new paths
H/F1	Help
Alt-Q	Quit CMFiler

File viewing/editing

F1	Help

Alt- - modified keys:

S	Switch from view to edit
F	Find string
R	search and Replace string
G	Global search and replace string
X	find/replace neXt matching string
M	Mark beginning or end of block
C	Copy marked block
V	moVe marked block
Y	delete block
P	Print marked block
O	Output marked block to a file
Keypad number	ASCII code entry direct from keypad
N	type Null character
+/– :	enable/disable delimiter markers
W	toggle line Wrap mode
H	Help

Ctrl- - modified keys:

T	delete word
D	delete to end of line
Y	delete line
F	Form feed line printer
Enter	select delimiter type (CR,LF,CR+LF,LF+CR) (in edit mode)

Cursor moves:

Esc	exit
Enter in view mode	exit
Unmod Arrows	move one character or line
Ctl-Lf/RtArr	move to first character of next word, left or right
Shf-Lf/RtArr	move to beginning/ end of line

Home/End	move to beginning/ end of line
PgUp/PgDn	move one video page (20 lines)
Ctl-PgUp/PgDn	move 10 video pages (200 lines) up or down
Alt- B/E	move to Beginning/ End of file

Child process operations in Main Module:

S	Shell to DOS
K	set resident Kernel size (L or S)
Q	Quick execute as child process
Ctl-Enter	set comm tail delimiter
Alt-C	add file spec to Comm tail
Alt-T	Tag for addition to comm tail
X	ready file spec for eXecution — follow with Alt-/Shf-/Ctl-X:
Alt-X	add Alt-Tagged files to comm tail, edit comm tail, eXecute on Enter
Shf-X	add Alt-Tagged files to comm tail, no edit, immediate eXecute
Ctl-X	add file at cursor to comm tail, no Alt-Tagged files, no edit, immediate eXecute
Shf-F10	add/edit custom F-keys
F10	view/select F-keys
F1-F9	ready application assigned to custom F-key for execution, add default offering to comm tail — follow with Alt-/Shf-/Ctl-X
Shf-F1-F9	ready F-key, add default comm tail offering and Alt-Tagged files to comm tail, immediate execute
Ctl-F1-F9	ready F-key, add default comm tail offering and filename at cursor to comm tail, no Alt-Tagged files, immediate execute
Z	ZIP Alt-Tagged files in source to Alt-Tagged target, with comm tail edit
Shf-Z	Same, without comm tail edit
U	UNZIP file at cursor to target, with comm tail edit
Shf-U	Same, without comm tail edit

CMFiler 5.35 Registration Form

Name: _____

Company: _____

Address: _____

City: _____

State: _____ Country: _____

Zip: _____ Phone: _____

Make checks payable to Charles F. Martin or NoVaSoft and

Remit to:
3239 Riverview Dr.
Triangle, VA 22172-1421 USA
Phone (703) 221-1471/1833 CompuServe 72130,1400
Internet 72130.1400@compuserve.com

Enclosed is $30 to register as a user of CMFiler. I understand I will receive by mail a copy of the latest registered version of CMFiler and a hard copy of the user's manual. I will also receive a free copy of a future major upgrade, as well as user support by mail for at least one year. CompuServe subscribers may receive their user support by CIS E-mail, and periodic free upgardes for as long as they wish.

In extension of the single-user license conferred to my company by this registration, also enclosed is $_____ for _____ additional complete copies of CMFiler at $15 per copy, and/or $_____ for _____ unsupported additional users at $7.50 per additional users ($5 per additional student user at schools), based on a good-faith estimate of the total number of users afforded access to CMFiler as a workplace resource. I will inform users that the license extensions thus granted do not authorize their private use

of CMFiler outside my company's workplace environment.

Send my upgrades on ❏ 5.25" ❏ 3.5" floppy disk.

Also send me upgrades by E-mail.

My CIS ID is _____

I also understand I will receive a $10 commission every time a new registrant refers to me as the source of his/her evaluation copy of CMFiler. The registered user who gave me my shareware copy of CMFiler, and who will be sent a $10 commission is

_____

Name of Registered User/Street/City/State/Zip
Other ways to register:

* With Master Card, Visa, American Express, or Discover from the Public (software) Library (PsL), by voice to 1-800-2424-PsL or 713-524- 6394, by FAX to 713-524-6398, or by CompuServe Email to 71355,470. Order CMFiler, part number 10657. These phone numbers are for orders only. To ensure that you get the latest version, PsL will notify us the day of your order, and we will ship the product directly to you. Any questions about the status of shipment of the order, refunds, registration options, volume discounts, dealer pricing, site licenses, etc., must be directed to NoVaSoft at 703-221-1471 or the address above, and not the PsL order numbers. You may also mail credit card orders to PsL at P. O. Box 35705, Houston, TX 77235-5705.

* With major credit card through the CompuServe Shareware Registry. Just GO CIS:SWREG and order entry #15.

Disk OrGanizer

Version 3.17
Copyright © 1991 by Soft GAM's Software

Introduction

A disk that has been in use a while will usually become slower accessing the data and programs that have been stored on it. This is due to two problems:

- The disk has become fragmented.
- There are deleted entries in directories.

Disk OrGanizer will solve these problems and make your disk run like new. If the size of a directory decreases enough after removing the deleted entries, Disk OrGanizer can also recover some disk space.

Disk OrGanizer has been tested with MS-DOS 2.10, 3.01, 3.10, 3.30, 4.01, and 5.0 (and by Bob on 6.0) on logical drives as large as 600 megabytes. It is believed that Disk OrGanizer will operate on any MS/PC-DOS disk.

Disk OrGanizer performs extensive tests before it starts to move data to make sure that the File Allocation Table (FAT) and directories are in good repair.

Program and documentation files

By default, the install program for the *DOS 6 SECRETS* diskettes will install all of the DOG files in the directory \SECRETS\DOG. This directory has not been added to the search path. You can execute the program from its home directory, add the directory to the search path, or copy the DOG files to a directory that is included in the search path.

Installation

To install Disk OrGanizer, you need only copy it to a directory on your PATH.

Important: Please back up your hard disks before you run Disk OrGanizer.

You can test Disk OrGanizer by typing the following command:

```
DOG [d:] /TEST
```

d: is an optional drive specifier. (The brackets mean optional and should not be typed.) If no drive is specified, the current drive will be used.

If Disk OrGanizer reports errors and you have not run Disk OrGanizer before, you should run CHKDSK with the /F switch and repair the disk. If you have not backed up your disk, Disk OrGanizer will warn you as to how many files may need to be backed up.

Disk OrGanizer will also list any files that are open on the disk that you are organizing. Disk OrGanizer will not be able to move these files nor pack the directories that they are in. If you have used other disk defragment programs before and have had no problem, it should be safe to run Disk OrGanizer. Disk OrGanizer will move HIDDEN files; most other disk defragmenters don't move these files. If you have not run any disk defragment programs before, you should read the rest of this chapter.

Background programs

Disk OrGanizer reads and writes to the disk directly. If a program tries to write to the disk while Disk OrGanizer is operating, data may be lost. You should not run Disk OrGanizer on a disk that you know will be written to. Programs that are likely to write to the disk are printer spoolers, multitasking programs like Windows or DesqView, switching programs, and network programs.

If you have FASTOPEN installed on your computer, you will need to reboot your computer after you run Disk OrGanizer. Some background programs leave files open all of the time. Disk OrGanizer will not move files that are open, and it will not pack a directory that has open files in it. If you do not know if you have these programs on your computer, I would suggest that you run Disk OrGanizer from a floppy disk as described in the "Quick Start"section.

Copy-protected programs

Disk OrGanizer may make some copy-protected software unusable. It is recommended that you remove any copy-protected software from your disk before you run Disk OrGanizer if you can't determine its compatibility with Disk OrGanizer.

Power failure

Disk OrGanizer can recover from a power failure or reboot. If a power failure or inadvertent reboot occurs while Disk OrGanizer is running, you should run Disk OrGanizer again as soon as possible. Disk OrGanizer will report any errors that it finds on the disk and ask you if you would like to repair them. If you answer yes to all of the questions, Disk OrGanizer will repair the disk and then continue operation as normal. You should not use any third-party CHKDSK-type programs that recover lost clusters. If you use CHKDSK, you should NOT make the lost cluster chains into files.

Quick start

If you would like to defragment your disk and get back to work without having to read the rest of this manual, the simplest and safest way to run Disk OrGanizer is described here. The first thing to do is to find an old or unused floppy disk. Then format this disk with a copy of the system:

```
FORMAT A: /sys
```

Copy DOG.EXE to the floppy disk:

```
COPY DOG.EXE A:
```

You may need to create or copy CONFIG.SYS on the new disk if you have disk drivers or an EMS memory driver that needs to be installed.

Reboot your computer **(Ctrl-Alt-Delete)** with the new disk installed in the A: drive.

DOS will ask you for the date and time. This is because there is no AUTOEXEC.BAT file. Enter the correct date and time.

Run Disk OrGanizer on your hard disk.

```
DOG C: /AUTO /CRC /TRUNCATE
```

Disk OrGanizer will test the disk (like CHKDSK), give you a report, and analyze the disk to determine the best place to have the directories and files on the disk. Disk OrGanizer will tell you how many directories need to have deleted files removed (packed), tell you how many directories can be made shorter (truncated), and tell you the number of clusters that it will have to move to defragment the files and directories on the disk.

You will then be asked if it is OK to write to the disk. If you answer no to this question, Disk OrGanizer will quit without ever having written to the disk. If you answer yes, DiskOrGanizer will pack the directories, truncate the directories, and then start moving clusters.

While Disk OrGanizer is moving clusters, you will see the following message:

```
X nnnnn - elapsed time 0:00:00
    estimated 0:00:00
```

X is either R)eading, S)orting, C)omputing CRC, W)riting, T)esting CRC, L)inking new clusters, or U)pdating FAT and directories. *nnnnn* is the number of clusters that have been moved. *Elapsed time* is the amount of time Disk OrGanizer has been moving clusters, and *estimated* is the approximate amount of time it will take to organize the disk.

You can quit from Disk OrGanizer at any time by pressing the escape (Esc) key or a ^C. Stopping Disk OrGanizer while it is moving clusters may cause extreme fragmentation. Rerun Disk OrGanizer as soon as possible if you abort while it is moving clusters. If you think that Disk OrGanizer has stopped running, press the spacebar. You should then hear a beep within a few seconds. When it is done it will check the disk once again, give you a new report, and then exit.

You should then remove the floppy disk from the A: drive and reboot your computer. You should notice that the programs on your disk load a little faster. If Disk OrGanizer truncated some directories, you will also have more free disk space.

Using Disk OrGanizer

The purpose of Disk OrGanizer is to speed up the access of files on your disks. There are two things that slow down access of data: deleted files in directories and fragmented files. The actual placement of files on a disk has very little to do with the amount of time it takes to load a file. Most disk defragment programs take a long time to run, and this keeps people from running them often.

Disk OrGanizer has complex algorithms that allow it to defragment all of the files on a disk while moving very few clusters. Although Disk OrGanizer can control the placement of files and directories on the disk, I would suggest that you refrain from using this feature as it can greatly increase the number of clusters that Disk OrGanizer will need to move and give you very little benefit. The exceptions are directories that are read often, such as the directories on the PATH which you may want to move near the File Allocation Table (see the AUTO command.)

Modes

The mode determines how Disk OrGanizer will organize a disk:

FILL	Defragments files and puts them as close to the FAT as possible. FILL will not leave any free space between files. FILL may leave files fragmented around BAD disk sectors and unmovable files. This mode gives you all of the benefits that you get from other disk defragmenters but only takes a fraction of the time to run.
FAST	Defragments all files and attempts to put them in one area of disk space. FAST may leave gaps of free space between files.
QUICK	Like FAST mode but does not try as hard.

DEFRAG   Defragments the files on the drive without concern for their placement.

The following modes will more than likely cause all of the files and subdirectories on a disk to be moved.

DATE   Puts the files on the disk, oldest files first (closest to the FAT). Using this mode once in a while, it can take a long time to run, may decrease the number of clusters that Disk OrGanizer will need to move with the FAST or FILL mode.

DIRECTORY   Puts the files on the disk in the order it finds them in the directories. That is, the first file or subdirectory in the root directory will be closest to the FAT (also referred to as LOW), followed by the second file in the root, etc.

The following modes are for compatibility to older versions. They are of little use.

FRAGMENTED   Puts all of the files that are not fragmented on the disk first, and then puts the fragmented files on the disk. Using this function will slowly put all of the files that change size away from the FAT. This mode does not work well if you have BAD clusters or system files other than DOS on the disk.

PACKED   Leaves the files in the same order as it finds them on the disk, by cluster.

Switches

CRC   Causes Disk OrGanizer to read data after it is written to the disk, and tests to make sure that it was written correctly.

BATCH   Tells Disk OrGanizer to suppress all prompts. This is useful for running Disk OrGanizer from

a batch file. If this switch is set, any error will cause Disk OrGanizer to terminate.

NOVERIFY   Tells DOS not to verify data written to the disk (see VERIFY in your DOS manual). This will increase the speed of Disk OrGanizer, but will allow data to be lost. This switch should not be used on a floppy disk, but it may be used on a hard disk at your own risk. This is for people to whom speed is more important than data integrity. If you have set the CRC switch, then Disk Organizer will verify the data, and you can include this switch to improve performance.

Command-line syntax

The command-line syntax to run Disk OrGanizer from the DOS prompt is as follows:

```
DOG [d:] [orderfile] [/commands]
    [/mode] [/switches]
```

(The []'s mean optional and should not be typed.)

d: is an optional drive specifier. If no drive is specified, the current drive will be organized.

Orderfile is the path and filename of the order file. If this is not included, Disk OrGanizer will look for a file called ORDER.DOG in the root directory of the drive being organized, and if it does not find that, it will look in the environment for DOG=d:\path\filename and use that file. If no orderfile is found, the DOS NUL device is used. If you have an orderfile and don't wish to use it, you can tell Disk OrGanizer to use the NUL file as an orderfile (i.e., DOG NUL /AUTO).

Commands consist of AUTO and TRUNCATE.

Mode tells Disk OrGanizer where to place the files on the drive. You must supply a mode to suppress the shareware sign-on message. The mode can be set on the command line or in an orderfile.

Switches allow you to control several options as to how Disk OrGanizer will test the data that is moved and interact with the operator. Switches can be set on the command line or in an orderfile.

Command-line commands

TRUNCATE   Tells Disk OrGanizer to truncate all subdirectories.

AUTO   Tells Disk OrGanizer to put the directories defined in the PATH environment variable first, followed by the file defined by the COMSPEC environment variable, and then all of the other directories. If no other mode has been specified, it will then order the rest of the files as if the /FILL mode was set.

Orderfile syntax

The orderfile can be used as a simple configuration file or can be used to tell DOG the exact order that you would like to have your files on a disk.

Modes and switches that are given on the command line will override those in the orderfile.

You may find it more convenient to run Disk OrGanizer from a batch file than to use the orderfile feature. Again, I would like to point out that the placement of files has little effect on the speed at which they can be read.

If you use the AUTO command-line command, you may not end up with what you expected. (See listing 2.1.)

Setting the mode

To give a mode in the order file, enclose it in square brackets ([]). A mode must be given on the command line or in the order file for Disk OrGanizer to run. A mode given on the command line will override the mode in the ORDER file.

Setting switches

Listing 2-1: A very simple ORDER.DOG file

```
                  ; The []s must be
                  ; included.
[FILL]            ; set the mode
                  ; Truncate all of
                  ; the directories
[TRUNCATE ALL]    ; Directories that
                  ; that have already
                  ; been specified,
```

```
                  ; will not be
                  ; truncated. The
                  ; AUTO command line
                  ; command appends
[PATH]            ; these three
                  ; orderfile commands
[COMSPEC]         ; to the end of the
                  ; orderfile.
[ALLDIR]          ;
;
```

Setting switches

Switches can be specified in the orderfile by enclosing them in square brackets ([]). (See the section on switches above.)

Order file commands

The area of the disk close to the FAT is called the LOW area and the area away from the FAT is called the HIGH area. Any file that is not named anywhere in the ORDER.DOG file is said to FLOAT.

In making this file, you should name as few files as possible.

The following three commands are a shorthand for file and directory names:

PATH   The same as listing all of the directories in the PATH environment variable that are on the drive being organized.

COMSPEC   The filename given in the COMSPEC environment variable is used if it points to the drive being organized.

ALLDIRECTORIES   The same as listing all of the directories on the drive.

The following commands tell where to place named files:

LOW   Tells Disk OrGanizer to place the files described by following filenames close to the FAT. This also affects the FREE command.

HIGH   Tells Disk OrGanizer to place files described by following filenames away from the FAT. This also affects the FREE command.

Listing 2-2: Sample ORDER.DOG file

```
;
[DEFRAGMENT]    ; if no mode is
                ; given on the
                ; command line use
                ; DEFRAGMENT
[FORCE]         ;
\COPYPRO.SYS    ; I don't want this
                ; file to move
[FLOAT]
[TRUNCATE]      ;
\DIR_A\         ; Truncate sub-
                ; directory DIR_A,
                ; but let it FLOAT.

;
[LOW]           ; Set move files
                ; LOW.
\DOS\           ; Truncate sub-
                ; directory DOS, and
                ; put it
                ; next to the FAT.
[ENDTRUNCATE]
\COMMAND.COM    ; COMMAND.COM will
                ; be placed after
                ; \\DOS.
[FREE 500]      ; leave some room
;
[HIGH]          ; set move files
                ; HIGH.
\AUTOEXEC.BAT   ; As this file is
                ; used only once, on
                ; reboot, we can
                ; move it away from
                ; the FAT.
\CONFIG.SYS     ; another seldom
                ; used file.
\ORDER.DOG      ; This file will be
                ; placed just in
                ; front of
                ; CONFIG.SYS
```

FORCE   Tells Disk OrGanizer not to move the files that follow. If you are going to FORCE files, you should do it before you place files LOW or HIGH.

FLOAT   Tells Disk OrGanizer to ignore the files that follow. This is used if you wish to TRUNCATE a subdirectory but don't want to put it LOW, HIGH, or FORCE. *Note:* In future releases this may be used to allow SYSTEM files to be moved.

These commands control whether named directories will be truncated.

TRUNCATE ALL   Truncates all directories on the disk.

TRUNCATE   Subdirectories named between TRUNCATE and ENDTRUNCATE will have their size changed so that they will use as little space as possible.

ENDTRUNCATE   See TRUNCATE above.

System directories and directories that have already been placed LOW, HIGH, or FORCED will not be truncated.

The following command will force clusters to be left free.

FREE nnnn   Tells Disk OrGanizer to leave *nnnn* (a number) clusters of free space after the last file named in the order file if files are being placed LOW or before the file if files are being placed HIGH. Disk OrGanizer ignores this command if there isn't enough free disk space. The *nnnn* may be replaced with an asterisk (*) if you want all available free clusters in a location.

File identifiers

A file identifier is a string that starts with a backslash (\), has zero or more subdirectory names separated by backslashes (the Path), and ends with a filename or subdirectory name. A file identifier ending with a subdirectory name can be followed by an optional backslash.

It is important to understand that a subdirectory is a file with a special format and that Disk OrGanizer treats subdirectories just like files in the orderfile except that subdirectories can be TRUNCATED. You must always include the full path of a file or subdirectory. Wildcards may be used in filenames. But please note that including a large number of files in the ORDER file can greatly increase the amount of time it takes Disk OrGanizer to organize a disk.

Comments

A comment starts with a semicolon and ends with a carriage return.

Registration, Copyright, and Technical Support

This document and the program files DOG.EXE ("the software") are copyrighted by the author. The copyright owner hereby licenses you to use the software, given these restrictions:

- The program shall be supplied in its original, unmodified form which includes this documentation.
- For-profit use without a license is prohibited.
- The program may not be included or bundled with other goods or services. Exceptions may be granted upon written request only.

- No fee is charged; an exception is granted to not-for-profit user's groups, which are permitted to charge a small fee (not to exceed $5) for materials, handling, postage, and general overhead. No other organization is permitted to charge any amount for distribution of copies of the software or documentation, or to include copies of the software or documentation with sales of their own products.

Technical support is available by phone, by mail, CompusSrve, and E-mail to registered and licensed users. Limited support is also available to help you to get Disk OrGanizer to operate on a computer so that you can evaluate it.

CompuServe: PPN# 73210,3374

the Bit Boutique BBS 707-778-8944, 2400 baud

Leave E-Mail to ALLEN MORRIS

DOG Registration Form

Name: _____

Company: _____

Address: _____

City: _____

State: _____ Country: _____

Zip: _____ Phone: _____

Remit to:
G. Allen Morris III
Soft GAM's Software
P.O. Box 1311
Mendocino, CA 95460
SSN# 559-29-3621

(707) 961-1632 (10 a.m. to 6 p.m. Pacific Time)

No license is required to run Disk OrGanizer on a computer that is not used for business. The fee for a license depends on the estimated number of copies of the program that you will use. For local area networks, one copy must be licensed for each computer that will be using the program on the network. A license is not transferable.

Quantity	Price	Update
1	$30.00	$6.00
2 to 9	$25.00	$5.00
10 to 49	$20.00	$4.00
50 to 99	$15.00	$3.00
100 to 199	$10.00	$2.00
Unlimited at one sight	$2,000.00	$400.00
Additional sites unlimited at each sight	$1,000.00	$200.00

The price to update to a new version applies only to the quantity previously registered. Regardless of the quantity purchased you will receive only one disk and one printed manual. Additional manuals are available for $6 each. You may make as many copies as are licensed and one archive copy. Orders of $50 or less must be prepaid. Orders over $50 — NET 30 days.

DUPE

Version 1.23
Copyright © 1992, BEST TECHNOLOGY

Introduction

DUPE is a shareware utility that allows you to copy disks faster and easier than MS-DOS's DISKCOPY program.

DUPE's advanced features:

1. Copies an entire floppy disk, any size, in a single drive with *no disk swapping*.
2. Can write multiple copies of a disk while reading the original only *once*.
3. Copies only the *used* portion of a disk.
4. Beeps after each task.
5. Formats disks up to 50 percent faster than DISKCOPY.

Program and Documentation Files

By default, the install program for the *DOS 6 SECRETS* diskettes will install all of the DUPE files in the directory \SECRETS\DUPE. This directory has not been added to the search path. You can execute the program from its home directory, add the directory to the search path, or copy the DUPE files to a directory that is included in the search path.

Command Format

The program should be invoked as follows:

    DUPE [drive]: {Options}

[drive] is a mandatory argument specifying the disk drive to use for the copy operation. *Options* are as follows:

/W	copy Whole disk
/U	copy Used portion of disk only
/FN	Format destination only when Necessary
/FA	Format destination Always
/WO	Warn before Overwriting
/NW	overwrite with No Warning
/S	Sound on
/Q	Quiet—no sound
/C	Clone options to EXE

Registration

To register, perform a <Print-Screen> of the on-line order form, fill it out, and sent it to BEST TECHNOLOGY.

DUPE 1.23 Registration Form

Name: _____

Company: _____

Address: _____

City: _____

State: _____ Country: _____

Zip: _____ Phone: _____

Remit to:
BEST TECHNOLOGY
915 Sherwood Forest Lane
Saugus, MA 01906, U.S.A.

Specify Disk Size: ❏ 5.25" ❏ 3.5"

Payment must be made in checks drawn on U.S. Banks in U.S. Dollars, or CASH.

DUPE Single User version. Payment must be enclosed. Single user version must be PREPAID.
each ....$12.95 $ _____
DUPE Corporate User version
each ....$29.95 $ _____
DUPE Site License version
each ....$99.95 $ _____
Corporate and Site License orders are billed if Purchase Order is enclosed.
MASS Sales/Use tax (MASS residents only)
....5% $ _____
Surcharge for Foreign Orders ....$10.00 $ _____
Shipping and Handling ....$3.00 $ _____
TOTAL .... $ _____

ExtraDOS Toolbox Professional

Copyright © 1985–1992 by Foley Hi-Tech Systems

Overview

ExtraDOS Toolbox Professional is a compilation of powerful and sophisticated tools for MS-DOS users. The programs offer functionality. Some enhance programs already found in MS-DOS; other tools were familiar to the Unix world and are now available in MS-DOS. ExtraDOS also compliments PC Tools and Norton utilities by offering many features not found in these packages. The quality of our tools will allow you to work faster, smarter, and better.

Program and Documentation Files

By default, the install program for the *DOS 6 SECRETS* diskettes will install all of the ExtraDOS files in the directory \SECRETS\EXTRADOS. This directory has not been added to the search path. You can execute the program from its home directory, add the directory to the search path, or copy the ExtraDOS files to a directory that is included in the search path.

Features Of ExtraDOS Toolbox

The following documents that appear bold are included on the enclosed diskettes. All other documents are available from Foley Hi-Tech Systems.

ADDCOMM	Allows you to define the actual address of your communications ports in the DOS lower memory segment, allowing older machines to support COM3 and COM4.
ALARMCLK	**Provides a simple alarm clock for MS-DOS machines. Used with SETALARM.EXE.**
ALLSUB	**Allows any command or program to be run on the current directory as well as all on subdirectories of the current directory. This is useful for deleting groups of files or performing tasks with programs that don't normally allow for subdirectories.**
AREACODE	AREACODE is a utility that will help you locate the region to which an area code applies or to locate the area code for a specific region.
BANNER	Create a large banner using a standard ASCII printer.
BOOT	Reboot PC from within a batch file or from the DOS command line.
BOOTCTL	Boot system on hard drive even with a non-system floppy disk in the A: drive.
BOOTLOCK	Locks out the [CTRL]C, [CTRL][BREAK], and [CTRL][ALT][DEL] keystroke functions. Disable one or any combination of these functions.
BRKBOX	Software version of a breakout box. Displays the status of the Serial or Parallel ports on the screen. This is a very handy tool when trying to debug communications or printing problems.
CALENDAR	**Display monthly or yearly calendar.**
CAT	UNIX-like CAT utility for displaying, printing, and combining files.
CHIMES	Quarterly hour clock chimes. Westminster, Saint Michael, or Whittington chimes.
CLEANFL	Makes the task of cleaning floppy drive heads much easier and more thorough. Moves the head of the floppy drive to travel the entire span of the cleaning floppy rather than just using a small portion of the cleaning diskette.

CLEANUP   **Cleanup allows you to recover valuable space that is eaten up by unused or duplicate files on your hard and floppy drives. Quickly isolates unused and duplicate files and removes them.**

COUNT   Counts the number of characters, words, and lines in a file.

CREDITS   A listing of those responsible for ExtraDOS Toolbox Professional.

CURLOCK   CURLOCK locks the cursor shape (optionally set with CURSOR) so that no matter what software you use the cursor will not be changed.

CURSOR   Lets you change the size and shape of the DOS cursor.

CUT   UNIX-like utility for displaying and printing text files in different formats by eliminating columns and other formatting options.

CUTPASTE   Small clipboard utility for MS-DOS. CUTPASTE allows you to pop up over any DOS application and copy a portion of the information displayed on the screen and paste it into another application, to the printer, or to a file.

DELAY   Sets a user-defined delay in batch files or CONFIG.SYS.

DETAB   Strips any tab characters from an ASCII text file and converts them into spaces. This is especially useful when working with old formatted files that you would like to work with in an editor which treats fixed tabs differently.

DISKINFO   **Reads the boot sector of a disk and then makes a DOS call to find out the information that DOS has for that disk. It will then list out the information in a side-by-side format so that you may compare the reports from DOS and the boot record.**

EDIT   SuperEdit full-screen editor. Many features including multiple windows, text-formatting options, and pull-down menus.

EVAL   DOS command-line calculator that evaluates mathematical expressions input on the command line.

FILEATTR   Allows you to set or change the attributes of a group of files.

FILEINFO   Alleviates the problem that DOS has created by only allowing 8 characters to describe a file. FILEINFO provides a way of adding comments to files in any directory.

FILESIZE   Displays a list of files and their respective sizes with summary that gives total sizes, number of files, total space on disk, and space available both in bytes and percentage.

FILETREE   Scans the directory structure of a disk and gives a top-down tree listing of the entire disk's directory structure.

FINDFILE   Will locate files by searching the entire disk for a specified file. Also searches within compressed files to search for filenames. When it finds a matching file, it will display the directory the file was found in, the complete filename, the file size, creation date and time, and any attributes associated with the file.

HELP   HELP prints out help messages on some of the more useful and popular DOS commands.

HEXDUMP   Provides you a quick dump of the contents of any file. The advantage of HEXDUMP is that you can quickly dump the contents of any file to the screen without having to

	load the overhead of a shell program.
HUSH	A utility that can eliminate a majority of the sounds generated by the PC's internal speaker.
KILLDIR	Makes eliminating a directory and all of its contents a lot easier. It displays information about the directory that includes the number of files and their sizes as well as any subdirectory information.
LASER	Helps you set your laser printer's mode and also makes it easy for you to send control codes to it.
LICENSE	**License information.**
LS	UNIX-like file-listing utility. It has many advanced features beyond that of the DIR command found in DOS.
MONITOR	MONITOR displays an adjustment pattern for your monitor. It is useful when trying to align and adjust monitors. Support HERCULES through VGA cards.
MOVE	Move files to different locations on the hard disk without having to copy and delete manually. Supports multiple hard drives including network drives.
NAMEDIR	Renames directories without emptying or modifying their contents.
NO	**File exclusion utility. Lets you run a command on all files except specified groups.**
ORDERFRM	**Order form.**
PATHFIND	Allows you to search the file path for any files. Will display the files that it finds in order of appearance within the path. This is handy when you are trying to locate a

	similar program or file that could exist in multiple places in your path statement.
PSPRINT	Allows you to print DOS ASCII Text files on a PostScript device without the usual conversion.
SCRNATTR	Sets the foreground, background, and border colors at the DOS prompt.
SPEEDRAM	Increases the speed of your system CPU by changing the refresh rate of your system's 8253 timer chip. SpeedRam should increase your CPU's performance from 2 percent to 10 percent.
TEXTSRCH	Searches for all occurrences of a given string inside of a specified text file.
TIDY	Scans drives for any .BAK and 0 length files and deletes them automatically.
TOUCH	A UNIX-like utility used to stamp a file's attributes with the current system date and time.
TURBOBAT	**Compiles batch files into .COM binary programs. This will greatly increase the speed of large batch files by allowing them to run in machine code rather than interpreted DOS commands.**
TURBOTXT.TXT	Text Filer Compiler.
USEMEM	Program allows you to use up memory for testing programs and applications with a minimal memory setting.
USEMOUSE	Gives any DOS application the ability to use the mouse.
VIDMODE	Set the current video mode from the DOS prompt. Allows switching to any of the supported text modes.
VOLLABEL	Allows you to view and modify the volume label on any disk.
WARRANTY.TXT	**Warranty information.**

ALARMCLK

DOS Alarm Clock
Version 2.00

Introduction

ALARMCLK provides a simple alarm clock for MS-DOS machines. ALARMCLK is split into two programs. You may install as many alarms as you wish per session. ALARMCLK is the alarm clock TSR that loads into memory and keeps track of the alarms that you specify. Once ALARMCLK is loaded, use SETALARM to set as many alarms as you like.

Command Format

```
ALARMCLK [/D] [/U] [/Inn]
SETALARM [time] [PM] [/D] [/U]
    [/Inn]
```

TIME Time in HH:mm format. 12-hour or 24-hour clocks are both accepted for the time format.

PM ALARMCLK will assume AM with 12 hour format unless PM is defined.

/D Deactivates all alarms

/U Removes ALARMCLK.COM from memory

/Inn Specify a new ID number

ALLSUB

Perform a Task in All Subdirectories
Version 2.05

Introduction

ALLSUB allows you to run any command or program in the current directory as well as in all subdirectories of the current directory. This is useful for deleting groups of files or performing tasks with programs that don't normally allow for subdirectories. As the command is performed in each subdirectory, ALLSUB will display the directory of execution.

Command Format

```
ALLSUB [command]
```

[command] is any valid DOS command or program.

CALENDAR

Display monthly or yearly calendar
Version 1.33

Introduction

CALENDAR displays a calendar from DOS in one of two formats, either one month or 12 months of one year.

Command Format

```
CALENDAR [mm] yyyy [/C#] [/L##]
    [/T##]
```

mm month [1..12]

yyyy year [0..9999]. If 2 digits are used, the year will be 19yy.

C# display in # columns [2..3(default)]

L## shifts display left by ## chars [0(default)..80]

T## shifts display down by ## lines [0(default)..40]

Example

    CALENDAR 66 /C2

will display a calendar in 2 columns for the year 1966

Note: If you want to pause the display of a full year, press [CTRL]S to pause the screen and then any key to continue the display.

CLEANUP

Disk Drive Cleanup & Space Recovery Version 2.06

Introduction

With the ever increasing size and lowering cost of disk space, it isn't uncommon to find PCs with an average of 80MB. Having larger disk drives has also made managing them become more complex. It is no longer feasible to remember the name and location and purpose of every file on your system. Often files and programs will be installed on a temporary basis only to be forgotten and either outdated or left behind. You can quickly devote as much as 25 percent of your hard disk to unused or duplicate files. Cleanup provides a comprehensive way of dealing with this problem by quickly isolating unused and duplicate files and removing them, freeing up valuable hard disk space. Cleanup displays the name of each file as it is deleted and a summary showing the total amount of disk space that has been recovered.

Warning: The main function of Cleanup is to recover lost disk space by removing duplicate and unused files. You have total control over which files will and will not be deleted, but with large hard disks it is easy to overlook single file names and accidently delete a desired file. It is suggested that you back up your disk before running Cleanup. This will ensure that you have a means of recovering files that you delete by accident. The other alternative is to have a copy of Norton Utilities UnErase or a similar type product.

Command Format

    CLEANUP [/L50]

/L50 Force into 43/50 Line mode on EGA/VGA monitors

Using Cleanup

Cleanup is a menu-driven program. After initializing the program, you are prompted with a list of disk drives in your system. In this list you are allowed to toggle the search amongst any installed drives in your system. Drives that are allowed but not attached are "grayed" out, and you cannot select these drives. When you select a drive, a check mark will note when a drive is selected. You may select any combination of all available drives. All of the drives selected will be treated as one large volume across which all duplicates and file marking will take place. This is particularly handy if you have more than one hard drive on which you keep files, and you might end up with duplicate files across the drives. Once you have selected the drives to scan, press the [F10] key to start scanning.

After all of the directories have been scanned, you will be located at the main menu of Cleanup. In the upper right hand corner of the screen, is the Current Status window. This window will always display information about the program's status. The number of directories, files, and duplicate files is calculated after selecting the drives and will not change until you exit the program and run again. The number of tagged files and bytes will show you the current statistics for the files that have been tagged for deletion.

These numbers will be updated as you tag or untag files for deletion.

There are two methods for tagging files for deletion. The first method is to use the Auto Tag and Auto Untag menus. These menus are identical in options, and perform exactly the opposite tasks. The Auto function allows you to tag groups of files all at one time. Once tagged, you may then go in and manually untag individual files using the manual tag option.

The following are the options available from the Auto Tag and Auto Untag menus:

ALL — All allows you to tag/untag all of the files scanned. This is generally only useful for untagging files. Be careful as if you use this to tag files, you will tag all of the files on the selected drives for deletion.

SMALLER DUPLICATES — This will look at the list of duplicate files and whenever there is a difference in size, the smaller file will be marked for duplication.

OLDER DUPLICATES — This is quite handy and will compare all of the duplicate files and mark the oldest files. This is useful when you wish to keep only the most recent version of a file on your system.

BACKUP FILES — This option will mark all files ending in .BAK. This was the original function of the TIDY program from which Cleanup evolved. Many programs and editors create a backup of a file when updating it. After a while these backups can clutter up your system.

TEMP FILES — There are many programs that make use of temporary files while processing work. Sometimes, if these programs are interrupted or crash, the temporary files will be left on your drive. Most software uses the convention of naming temporary files with a .$$$ extension. This option will mark all files ending in .$$$.

EXT xxx — This allows you to tag a group of files with a particular extension that you know should be removed. With this option you can specify any group of files by giving the extension name. All files ending in the extension that you provide will be tagged. Be careful that you wish to delete all files ending in the extension before running the Erase option.

ZERO LENGTH — This was the other option available on the TIDY program. Another type of temporary file that can often be created is one that was opened but never properly closed. This will often result in a file entry in your directory with a file size of 0 bytes. The zero length is misleading. Every file entry requires at least one cluster; thus ,the minimum disk space used by a 0 byte file is the cluster size (512 bytes or more). Having a lot of 0 byte files can actually take away space from your drive. Choosing this option will mark all files with a size of 0 bytes for deletion.

LENGTH n — Like the Zero length files above, there may be instances where you create a lot of small files that you wish to tag for deletion. This option allows you to input a specific file size. All files matching this file size will be tagged for deletion.

The MANUAL TAG option from the Main Menu allows you to view the list of files and to manually tag or untag files. When you first enter this screen, you will be presented with the list of duplicate files. To view all of the files in the system, press the [F6] key. Then to switch back to the list of only duplicate files, again press the [F6] key. Tagged files will be marked with a check mark next to the name, and will appear in red on color monitors. To view the list, use the up and down arrow keys. To tag a particular file, press the [ENTER] key. Pressing it a second time will untag the file. To untag a tagged file, highlight the file and press the [ENTER] key. Once again, the [ENTER] key will continue to toggle the tag on and off. When you are done viewing the manual tag list, press the [F10] key.

Once you are happy with the list of tagged files, choose the ERASE TAGGED option from the main menu. This will erase all files that were previously tagged. There is no UNDO feature on

this program, so once they are deleted you will have to use an unerase program such as Norton Utilities Quick Unerase to recover any erased files. If you have accidentally deleted a file, do not use the disk drive until the file has been unerased. Changing data anywhere on the disk could result in permanently losing the information in the file.

Warning: There have been some reports of problems when using Cleanup in a machine that is running both FASTOPEN and SMARTDRIVE. The best solution is to remove the usage of FASTOPEN as it can cause sorting problems with the file list on large disk drives.

DISKINFO

**Disk Drive Information Display
Version 1.4**

Introduction

DISKINFO is a utility that will read the boot sector of a disk and then make a DOS call to find out the information that DOS has for that disk. It will then list out the information in a side-by-side format so that you may compare the reports from DOS and the boot record. Most items reported are self-explanatory. Every disk is divided up into tracks, sectors, and clusters.

track	is a single ring around a disk.
sector	a pie-shaped wedge of a track.
cluster	is the smallest unit to which DOS can interact with the disk drive, and it is a group of Clusters.

System ID	is the 8 byte record that is put on the disk when it is formatted.
Media Descriptor	is a byte value that describes what type of media the disk is.

Command Format

```
DISKINFO [d:][/?][/NOH]
```

d:	is the drive to view; if no drive is specified, information on the current drive will be displayed.
/?	Displays help information.
/NOH	Suppress Header Display.

NO

**DOS File Exclusion Utility
Version 2.00**

Introduction

NO is a utility that gives many DOS commands and external utilities the ability to exclude certain groups of files from the effects of the program called.

Command Format

```
NO [filespec] [command parameters]
```

filespec	is any valid DOS file specification including wildcards
command	is any DOS command, or external program
parameters	normal parameters passed to the command or program

Notes

NO hides files in the current directory from most programs and utilities by putting the

HIDDEN file attribute on. It then calls the command or program with the specified parameters. Once the command is complete, NO will remove the HIDDEN file attribute from the specified files.

NO is very useful when using commands such as DEL *.* when you want the action to take effect on all but a certain group of files.

NO is recursive, which means you can stack groups of excluded files together by stacking NO commands.

Examples

```
NO *.EXE DIR
```

will display all files in the current directory with the exception of files ending in .EXE.

```
NO FILE.* DEL *.*
```

will delete all files in the current directory except those beginning named FILE with any extension.

```
NO *.EXE NO *.COM DEL *.*
```

will delete all files in the current directory except .EXE and .COM files.

TURBOBAT

Turbo Batch File Compiler

Introduction

TurboBAT allows you to compile standard DOS batch files into .COM binary programs. This will greatly enhance the speed of large batch files by allowing them to run in native code rather than interpreted DOS commands. The resulting .COM files may call nested batch files without losing the parent since the parent calling program is now no longer a batch file.

Command Format

```
TURBOBAT [/1][/4][/A][/Dname][/I]
   [/L][/T][/X] file[.ext]
```

/1   Insert single-stepping code. This creates a version of the output that is useful when debugging a batch file. When the output .COM program is run, it will single-step through each line of the original program.

/4   Supress 4DOS warning messages. Don't report any warning messages generated by the use of 4DOS-specific commands.

/A   Supress all warning messages (same as /4/I/L/X). Don't display any warning messages, only error messages.

/Dname   Include full symbolic tracing information. If NAME is specified, the information will be sent to the named file; otherwise is displayed via the standard error device. There must not be any spaces between /D and NAME.

/I   Ignore nonstandard labels. DOS supports labels up to 8 characters long for use with the goto statement. Many people use the label as a comment field rather than a label, and this can cause problems when a label that is used in a non-standard fashion shows up during the compile stage of the batch file. DOS will normally just ignore this error.

/L   Relaxed label-length checking. The normal label size recognized by DOS is 8 characters. In many cases, people use the : as a placeholder for the program without ever referencing the label. The problem is that if you have more than one long label name where the first 8 digits match another label, the file won't compile because it will look as though you have duplicate labels. This switch relaxes that limit.

/T   Compile with line-number TRACE information. The line-number information is displayed via the standard error device. When running the output program compiled with this option on, you will get a display of each line number as the program is running. This is useful when trying to determine where a program is failing.

/X   Suppress extension warning messages. Normally during compilation, TurboBAT will warn you about any lines that make use of commands that are supported by the compiler but are not supported by DOS. Using the /X will tell TurboBAT not to warn you about any BATCH files that will not function under normal DOS conditions.

/B-   Use ANSI escape sequences instead of the BIOS. The default screen I/O is now handled by making calls to the video BIOS. This ensures that the compiled batch file will work on any machine with or without ANSI.SYS installed. The drawback to this is that BIOS calls are much slower than ANSI calls. If you know that the machine that will be running the compiled program and then using the /B- command will speed up the video calls.

Notes

TurboBAT is a multipass batch file compiler. It takes interpreted DOS batch files and turns them into binary programs that can execute up to as much as 4 times faster than normal batch files. While supporting all of the normal DOS functions that can be called from within a batch file, TurboBAT also provides many additional features including support for many 4DOS/ NDOS commands.

Extended Batch Commands

TurboBAT supports many commands beyond those supported in normal batch files. Some of these commands are in support of J.P. Softwares 4DOS Batch Enhancements, and others are to replace small external DOS utilities.

Internally Supported Commands

DOS Commands and batch file commands that are directly supported by TurboBAT and require no external programs are as follows:

%?   "Internal" environment variable. Expands to the error level of the last executed program as a string. Example: SET LASTERROR=%?

BEEP   BEEP [frequency duration ...] Sounds a tone of the specified frequency for the duration in clock ticks. The defaults are 440Hz (A below middle C) for 2 clock ticks (about ¼ second).

The list of tones and durations can be repeated on a single line. The table is identical to the 4DOS tone table.

Note: Please see the file TURBOBAT.TXT for table omitted here.

BOOT   BOOT [WARM | COLD] Boots the computer. If no options are specified or if WARM is specified, a WARM boot will occur. If COLD is specified, the computer will go through the entire cold boot process. Under Desqview, a warm boot will only close the window.

CDD   CDD drive:path Changes subdirectories and drives. This command will change the current directory and drive to the one specified in [drive:path] and make the current DOS drive equal to the value in [drive]. Normally within DOS the CD command will change directories on any drive that you specify but will keep the current drive the same. CDD allows you to switch to that drive rather than stay on the current drive.

CHDIR/CD   CD path
CD drive:path
Changes the current directory

CLS
:   as specified in path. If a drive is specified, changes the current directory of that drive to the directory specified in path.

CLS
:   `CLS [[bright] [blink] fg on bg]`

    Clears the screen and optionally sets the screen color. When setting the colors, the syntax is identical to the COLOR command.

COLOR
:   `COLOR [bright] [blink] fg ON bg`

    Uses ANSI escape sequences to set the screen color. Only the first three letters of each command word are actually significant. The following colors are allowed:

    BLACK   BLUE GREen RED
    MAGenta CYAn YELlow WHIte

    Example: COLOR BRIGHT WHITE ON BLUE

DELAY
:   `DELAY [seconds]`

    Pauses for the specified interval in seconds. If no duration is given, it will pause for 1 second.

ECHO
:   `ECHO [message]`

    If the /D switch was used at compile time, you can enable or disable command-echoing with ECHO OFF and ECHO ON. ECHO without any text will indicate if the /D switch was used when the file was compiled, not the current status of command echoing. To display a blank line, use "ECHO:" or "ECHO.".

ECHOS
:   `ECHOS [message]`

    Displays the message without appending a cr/lf to the end of the message like ECHO does. (Used to be ECHONLN but was updated to match the 4DOS command.)

ELSE
:   If the IFF condition was false, the lines from ELSE to ENDIFF will be executed. See Also IFF.

ELSEIFF
:   `ELSEIFF condition [THEN]`

    Similar structure to the IFF command. If the previous IFF was false and the current condi-

tion is true, the code following will be executed to the next ELSE, ELSEIFF, or ENDIFF statement. Each use of ELSEIFF counts as a nesting level. The compiler actually converts this command into logical ELSE^IFF^ENDIFF statements. See Also IFF.

ENDIFF
:   Terminates an IFF statement. See Also IFF.

EXIT
:   EXIT is used when at the DOS level if you are running within a shelled version of the command interpreter and you wish to exit the shelled session. The EXIT command is ignored by TurboBAT. See also QUIT.

FOR
:   `FOR %%var IN (file list) [DO] command`

    Allows more than a single letter as the loop variable. Can be nested. The loop variable can be tested from other lines by treating it as a normal environment variable. The word "DO" is required by DOS but is optional under 4DOS and Turbobat.

GOTO
:   `GOTO label`

    Will jump control to the label. Labels are marked as a line beginning with a :.

GOSUB
:   `GOSUB label`

    Calls a label in the current batch file as a subroutine. Must have a matching RETURN statement. The end of the batch file does *not* act as a RETURN.

IF
:   `IF [NOT] first (== | EQ | NE | LT | LE | GT | GE) second command`

    `IF [NOT] ERRORLEVEL [== | EQ | NE | LT |LE | GT | GE] value command`

    `IF [NOT] ENVFREE [== | EQ | NE | LT |LE | GT | GE] value command`

    `IF [NOT] EXIST filename command.`

    `IF [NOT] ISDIR path command`

EQ (equal), also '==' and '='

NE (not equal),

LT (less than),

LE (less or equal),

GT (greater than),

GE (greater or equal).

If no compare command is used for ERRORLEVEL or ENVFREE, the default of GE will be used.

EXIST tests for the existence of a file.

```
IF EXIST my.cfg GOTO
  continue
ECHO Configuration file
  is missing
QUIT 99
:continue
```

ISDIR tests if the given path specification is an existing subdirectory.

```
IF NOT ISDIR \work MD
  \work
```

ENVFREE tests the available environment space.

IF ENVFREE LT 123 ECHO Insufficient environment space

IFF `IFF condition [THEN]`

If the condition is true, the lines up to ELSE, ELSEIFF, or ENDIFF (whichever appears first) will be executed. IFF statements may be nested up to 15 levels deep. See also IF.

```
IFF %? EQ O THEN
GOTO CONTINUE
ELSEIFF %? EQ 99
THEN GOTO CRITICAL
ELSE
GOTO ERROR
ENDIFF
```

INKEY `INKEY [/Wn] [message]`
`%%var`

Gets a single keystroke and places it in the environment. %%var is the environment variable that will be assigned the keystroke. If /W is specified, the command will wait up to

that many seconds, (e.g., /W10). It will also optionally display a message. If a wait of zero is used (/W0), the command will return immediately if no keystrokes are pending. The wait period can be specified in the environment, but the /W must be present on the line at compile time, for example:

```
inkey /w%delay Press
  any key: %%key
```

Displayable keystrokes (characters above the space) are stored as their corresponding character. Keystrokes that do not have a corresponding character are displayed as a number, (e.g., the carriage return as "13"). Extended keystrokes such as F1 are stored with a preceding '@', (@59 for F1).

INPUT `INPUT [/Wn] [message]`
`%%var`

Gets a string and places it in the environment. %%var is the environment variable that will be assigned the string. The string is terminated by a carriage return or end of file mark (^Z). Extended keystrokes are ignored. /Wn is the optional maximum time in seconds to wait for the first keystroke. Once a keystroke is entered, this command will not time out.

MKDIR `MKDIR [pathname]`
MD `MD [pathname]`

Will create a new directory of PATHNAME.

PATH Displays or Sets the Path.

PAUSE `PAUSE [message]`

Displays an optional message. If no message is specified, the default of "Press a key when ready..." is used. In addition, a CR/LF is not output until after the key is pressed.

PROMPT Displays or Sets the DOS Prompt.

QUIT `QUIT [exitcode]`

Unconditionally halts the compiled batch file. If no exitcode is specified, zero will be used. The exit code can refer to an environment variable. If the variable is not a number or does not exist, zero will be used. Examples:

```
SET var=1
QUIT %var
```
Exits with 1.
```
SET var=test
QUIT %var
```
Exits with 0 because %var is not a number.

REM REM is the standard DOS Remark field. REM lines are ignored by the TurboBAT Compiler.

REPEAT/ UNTIL Similar to the Pascal structure. May be nested up to 15 deep. Redirection is not allowed on a line containing REPEAT or UNTIL.
```
REPEAT
ECHO %1
SHIFT
UNTIL "%1" EQ ""
```

RETURN Return from a subroutine call. If no subroutines are pending, it will terminate the batch file with an exit code of 255.

RD/RMDIR Remove Directory. This will remove the directory specified as long as there are no files in it.

SCREEN SCREEN row column [message]

Positions the cursor using ANSI sequences and displays an (optional) message. The cursor coordinates are 0 based, the normal range being 0–24 rows and 0–79 columns.

SCRPUT SCRPUT row col [bright] [blink] fg ON bg message

Writes the message at the specified screen coordinates using the specified colors. The cursor position is restored to the position before the command. ANSI escape sequences are used throughout.

SET Alone, SET will display the current environment variables, or followed by an environment variable, SET will set the environment variable to the given value.

SHIFT Same as standard DOS. I will be expanding this command for 4DOS compatibility to accept a shift factor, with support for a negative number which will get back previously shifted parameters.

SINGLESTEP SINGLESTEP ON | OFF

Enables or disables single-stepping. The /1 compiler switch must be used for this command to have any effect. The options are resolved at compile time so you cannot use an environment variable or command-line parameter to set the status.

TEXT/ ENDTEXT The text that follows, up to ENDIFF, will be displayed as if each line was preceded by an ECHO. Output redirection is more efficient using this command instead of individually redirected ECHO commands since the file will only be opened and closed once, while the file will be opened and closed for each ECHO command.
```
TEXT
This could be a menu or
it could be help
information
ENDTEXT

TEXT >dummy
This text will be sent to
the redirection file.
Up to, but not including
the ENDTEXT command.
ENDTEXT
```

UNSET Deletes the environment variable from the master environment.
```
UNSET RESULT
```

WHILE/ WEND Similar to the Pascal structure. May be nested up to 15 deep. Redirection is not allowed on a line containing WHILE or WEND.

```
WHILE "%1" NE ""
    ECHO %1
    SHIFT
WEND
```

Commands Handled by Calling the Comspec

These commands are supported by calling COMMAND.COM:

CALL, DIR, DEL, REN, VER, VOL, CTTY, CHCP, TYPE, COPY, DATE, TIME, ERASE, BREAK, RENAME, DELETE, VERIFY, COMMAND

These commands will only work if 4DOS is the active COMSPEC:

FREE, DRAWBOX, DRAWHLINE, DRAWVLINE, MEMORY COMPILER ERROR MESSAGES

TurboBat contains a library of internal error messages and will display the error number and message when an error or warning is found. Files with just warnings will compile, files with errors will not compile.

Note: Please see the file TURBOBAT.TXT for a section on warnings and error messages omitted here.

TURBOTXT

Text File Compiler
Version 1.11

Introduction

TurboTxt will convert a standard text file into a self-displaying COM program, containing both text and the necessary code to display the text.

Command Format

```
TURBOTXT [/Axx] [/Fxx] source
    [destination]
```

/Axx	Sets the video attributes for the text being displayed. xx is the attribute value. Use the chart below to calculate the attribute value you wish to use.
/Fxx	Sets the video attributes for the help line at the bottom of the screen being displayed. xx is the attribute value. Use the chart below to calculate the attribute value you wish to use.
source	The source text file to be compiled. Can be any standard DOS text file up to 63k bytes.
destination	Can be any valid DOS filename. If no destination is entered, the file created will be called README.COM.

Colors

TurboTXT allows you to choose the video attributes that will be used to display the text in the compiled README.COM program. The number used to set the attribute is calculated by choosing the background color and then the nearground color. The formula to use to get this number is:

A = BACKGROUND COLOR x 16

B = NEARGROUND COLOR

xx = A + B;

BACKGROUND COLORS		*NEARGROUND COLORS*	
BLACK	0	BLACK	0
BLUE	1	BLUE	1
GREEN	2	GREEN	2
CYAN	3	CYAN	3
RED	4	RED	4
MAGENTA	5	MAGENTA	5
BROWN	6	BROWN	6
LIGHTGRAY	7	LIGHTGRAY	7
		DARKGRAY	8
		LIGHTBLUE	9
		LIGHTGREEN	10
		LIGHTCYAN	11
		LIGHTRED	12
		LIGHTMAGENTA	13
		YELLOW	14
		WHITE	15

So to display LIGHTRED text on a BLUE background you would use the following calculation:

A = 1 x 16 = 16

B = 12

xx = 16 + 12 = 28

TURBOTXT /A28 README.TXT

Notes

The code overhead is slightly more than 1k bytes. When this program is executed, the displayed text can be scrolled with the cursor keys. Direct screen writing is used so the display is extremely fast. Snow suppression will occur if a CGA monitor is detected. The text file must be less than 63K in size, and any lines exceeding the width of the screen will be truncated. It is possible for the resultant COM program to be smaller than the original text file. Most text files use a two-byte sequence of a carriage return and line feed (0Ch and 0Ah) to terminate each line. When the text is converted, the two bytes are replaced by a single null byte (00h). Needless to say, the larger the text file, the better the chance of a size savings.

If the output file is not specified, README.COM will be used. If the extension is omitted from the output filename, COM will be used.

The following keys are available when the created program is executed:

Up Arrow	Scroll up one line
Down Arrow	Scroll down one line
Page Up	Scroll up one page
Page Down	Scroll down one page
Left Arrow	Scroll Left one character
Right Arrow	Scroll Right one character
Home	Go to start of text
End	Go to end of text
ESC	Exit program
Alt-X	Exit program

The .COM program produced automatically supports screen sizes other than 80x25. As long as the proper screen values are in the BIOS data area and the screen width is at least 80 columns and no greater than 255 columns, it will work with the detected mode automatically.

Example

```
TurboTxt help.txt help
```

The text in HELP.TXT is used to create HELP.COM.

ExtraDOS Toolbox Professional Registration Form

Name: _____

Company: _____

Address: _____

City: _____

State: _____ Country: _____

Zip: _____ Phone: _____

Fax orders: Country Code and number: _____

Remit to:
Foley Hi-Tech Systems
185 Berry Street
San Francisco, CA 94107

VOICE:(415) 882-1730, Mon.–Fri., 9:00 a.m. - 5:00 p.m. Pacific.
FAX: (415) 882-1733
BBS: (415) 882-1735, 8N1, 12-9600 BPS, V22.bis, V.32.bis, V.42.bis, HST 14.4K
CIS: 70262,1642

We offer discounts on quantity orders, multiple-user licenses, and dealer pricing. Please call for details. We accept Visa, MasterCard, company or personal checks. You can order the entire toolbox or individual utilities by listing them.

FHTS, please send:
ExtraDOS Toolbox License Registration w/ manual, (all 52 FHTS Shareware Utilities)
each ....$59.95 $ _____
Copies of _____ Single Utility
each ....$19.00 $ _____
Copies of _____ Single Utility
each ....$19.00 $ _____
Copies of _____ Single Utility
each ....$19.00 $ _____
CA residents, add sales tax ....8.25% $ _____
Shipping and Handling
U.S.: ....$2.95 $ _____
Canada ....$5.00 $ _____
Other International Locations: ....$9.00 $ _____
TOTAL (U.S. Funds drawn on U.S. Bank) .. $ _____

Specify Disk Size: ❏ 5.25" 360K ❏ 3.5" 720K
Payment by:
❏ Check (Mail only) ❏ MasterCard ❏ Visa
Call for Corporate P.O. Approval
Credit Card #: _____
Exp. Date: _____
Authorized Signature: _____

Prices and terms subject to change without notice.

FANSI-CONSOLE

Fast, Powerful ANSI.SYS Replacement
Version 3.00
Copyright © 1984–1991, Hersey Micro Consulting, Inc.

What Is FANSI-CONSOLE?

Technically, FANSI-CONSOLE is a complete replacement for the IBM or compatible MS(PC)-DOS console driver as well as the screen and keyboard parts of the ROM BIOS. More importantly to you, it has many features that make the use of nearly every IBM-PC application program more convenient. It does so many things, we also call it "The Integrated Console Utility."

What Does FANSI-CONSOLE Do for Me?

- Speeds up all screen writing done through MS(PC)-DOS or ROM BIOS calls from 1.2 to 3.0+ times, or from 1.4 to 8.0+ times with optional quick mode hardware scrolling! Includes the screen writing of ALL the standard MS(PC)-DOS commands such as TYPE, DIR, ECHO, and MORE. Speedup amount depends on computer, display adapter type, and application program.

- Provides a scroll recall facility which allows reviewing lines which have scrolled off the screen which you would otherwise lose forever! You can save up to about 800 screenfuls using Expanded Memory managed by any other device driver which meets the Lotus/Intel/Microsoft Specification. Or you can save fewer lines using some regular MS(PC)-DOS memory. You may save the scrolled line buffer to a file or cut & paste into nearly any program, such as word processors. If not automatically saved, you can take a snapshot of a screen. You can save the lines in full color, or you can conserve memory and just save the characters.

- Adds zip to your cursor keys and other keys, up to 5 times typically!

- Adds a much larger typeahead buffer (255 characters)!

- Optional automatic single or dual screen display dimming (both screens in a two-screen computer) after specifiable period of inactivity! Prevents burning patterns into your screen phosphors.

- Frees your eyes from CGA scroll blinking!

- Provides many more ANSI X3.64 standard escape sequences than IBM's ANSI.SYS program! Space prevents us from listing them all here; ask about any you are specifically interested in. It supports nearly all the VT100 series escape sequences and many more! Has at least 50 extra private RM/SM mode settings and at least 15 extra private multivalue mode settings, giving full control over a multitude of screen and keyboard features.

- A DEC VT100/VT52 emulation toggle which provides VT100 emulation when used with our MODEM86 or many other communication programs! Programming support for separately scrolled windows via ANSI X3.64 escape sequences (SSR)! You can use the escape sequences with any programming language. Your program thinks it is writing to an ANSI or VT100 style terminal!

- Optional ANSI X3.64 sequences processed during BIOS TTY calls!

- Optional one finger pausing!

- Optional controls to change the behavior of shifting and locking keys! Rearrange keys like switching Left-Shift and BackSlash! Optional Dvorak keyboard arrangement!

- Keyboard induced debugging breakpoints for assembly language programmers!

- Keyboard macros just like those in ANSI.SYS, with option to have them expanded all the time instead of just for DOS calls! More memory for ANSI-compatible keyboard macro strings than standard IBM-PC ANSI.SYS device driver allows! You can specify how much memory to use.

- Shorten bell time length!
- Add a key click!
- Extends IBM-PC screen and keyboard ROM BIOS to be IBM-PC AT compatible!
- Extends EGA ROM BIOS to be more VGA compatible!
- Control over colors used by many programs!
- Software support for 50 line CGA displays with interlace, or doubled scan lines with interlace for those screen adapters that have interlace hardware capability!
- Support for 43 line displays with Enhanced Graphics Adapters (EGA) and Enhanced Graphics Displays (EGD)!
- Software support for differing (larger) screen text dimensions for those compatible display adapters that have that hardware capability!
- So many other little features, they just don't fit here! Nearly every feature is optional and easily changeable using a menu-driven program!
- Easy installation, just like MS(PC)-DOS ANSI.SYS. Place one line in the CONFIG.SYS file and MS(PC)-DOS automatically loads FANSI-CONSOLE every time you start MS(PC)-DOS.

Is FANSI-CONSOLE Compatible with My Hardware and Software?

FANSI-CONSOLE is compatible with thousands of existing programs. It supports all IBM compatible modes of operation on most IBM-PC compatible computers and adapters, including AT, 386, 486, PS/2, EGAs, and VGAs. It may not yet support some extended functions unique to specific compatibles.

Program and Documentation Files

By default, the install program for the *DOS 6 SECRETS* diskettes will install all of the FANSI-CONSOLE files in the directory \SECRETS\FANSI. This directory has not been added to the search path. You can execute the program from its home directory, add the directory to the search path, or copy the FANSI-CONSOLE files to a directory that is included in the search path.

Note: The documentation for FANSI-CONSOLE is quite lengthy, and therefore, it is not reprinted in its entirety here. Please see the on-line documentation for complete details. Of particular interest are Chapter 2, entitled "Starting Quickly" (especially Section 2.2 "How Do I Quickly Install FANSI-CONSOLE?"), and Chapter 3, entitled "Detailed Installation." Sections 2.1 and 2.3 are included here for your convenience.

Do I Need to Read the Whole FANSI-CONSOLE User Manual?

NO! You do not need to read the whole manual from cover to cover to take advantage of FANSI-CONSOLE. You only need to know the information in this chapter to get started. If you want really brief instructions, just read the description of this chapter in the table of contents! It really tells you what to do! We know how much you hate to read the manual before trying out a program. Unfortunately, the nature of FANSI-CONSOLE prevents us from making it menu driven.

The manual has an extensive index at the end to help you when you run into problems finding what you want to know. It also has a glossary at the end to help you find the meaning of technical terms and abbreviations. Please use them, especially if you do not read the manual from cover to cover. For example, you can look up the keyword "problem" in the index to find solutions to many common problems. This includes those you may run into when you install FANSI-CONSOLE.

If you cannot find something where you first looked in the index, let us know! We think the index should be comprehensive. That minimizes the number of calls we get asking about things the manual fully explains but you cannot find.

The chapter entitled "Compatibilities and Limitations" describes how to solve compatibility problems with FANSI-CONSOLE. You should read that if you experience problems.

If you can not find what you want to know in the abbreviated user manual found on the distribution diskettes, then it is probably time to order a complete, printed User Manual. You can tell this when you find yourself looking for a page number mentioned in the index or table of contents which the abbreviated user manual does not include. The index and the table of contents are complete, but the rest of the abbreviated user manual is not! The abbreviated user manual is only complete enough to install FANSI-CONSOLE and test it for compatibility with your hardware and software. It should convince you that FANSI-CONSOLE really is fast and professional, and that you really need the complete printed manual!

Lastly, even though you can use FANSI-CONSOLE without reading the chapter on its distribution, please read it, too. It has important information about what we expect in return from you for your being able to use FANSI-CONSOLE.

How Do I Use FANSI-CONSOLE?

Now that you have installed FANSI-CONSOLE, you just proceed as you always do and mostly ignore that you installed FANSI-CONSOLE. When the FANSI-CONSOLE banner appears on your screen when you start MS-DOS, many programs magically write to the screen faster without your further intervention.

As noted before, you may want to use the typeahead buffer more than before. We made the extended typeahead buffer a non-optional part of FANSI-CONSOLE since FANSI-CONSOLE only uses the extended buffer when the normal buffer fills! So you do not need to use any FANSI-CONSOLE options to extend the typeahead buffer. You may also want to take advantage of the new special keys described here.

This section describes some keys that you can use that give extra functionality that they did not give without FANSI-CONSOLE. We occasionally refer to the *DarkPlus* and *DarkMinus* keys. These are just the slightly darker colored plus and minus keys on the right-hand edge of the keyboard. We do this to distinguish them from

the lighter colored *LightPlus* and *LightMinus* keys just to the left of the BackSpace key at the top of the keyboard.

Using the Ctrl-F key

Press the Ctrl-F key to simply flush (empty) the typeahead buffer. FANSI-CONSOLE leaves the Ctrl-F in the buffer, but many programs ignore it or do something harmless. If you use an application that does something dangerous with the Ctrl-F key, you may want to try the Ctrl-S key instead.

Using the Ctrl-S key

Press the Ctrl-S key to flush the typeahead buffer and, if the current program uses Ctrl-S as a pause key, cause the current program to pause. Most programs pay attention to this key and pause; otherwise, they probably ignore it. The standard IBM-PC console software processes the Ctrl-S slightly differently. It does not flush the typeahead buffer when you press a Ctrl-S. This means that the standard IBM-PC console software ignores the Ctrl-S character if you already typed some characters into the typeahead buffer.

Using the Ctrl-Num-Lock key

Press the Ctrl-Num-Lock key to cause the display to pause without flushing the typeahead buffer. With FANSI-CONSOLE, this key combination works similarly to the way it works with the standard IBM-PC console software. One advantage, however, is that unlike the standard IBM-PC console software, FANSI-CONSOLE prevents the appearance of duplicate lines during a pause. Press any other different key combination to unlock the pause. Unless the second key combination is a Ctrl-Break or a Ctrl-C, FANSI-CONSOLE ignores it other than for clearing the pause. Any program that works with FANSI-CONSOLE pauses with Ctrl-Num-Lock. For other ways to pause, see the descriptions of Ctrl-S in the previous paragraph, of Pause in the next paragraph, and of the /L option in the chapter entitled "Detailed Installation."

Using the Pause key

For enhanced keyboards, the Pause key always remains a one-finger pause key. To use the one-finger pause key, press the Pause key to cause the display to pause without flushing the typeahead buffer. The Pause combination works differently than the Ctrl-Num-Lock combination. Unlike Ctrl-Num-Lock, Pause acts as a toggle. When you disable the scroll recall feature and you pause, you may use other keys to typeahead without affecting the pause. If you enabled the scroll recall feature, then you may do scroll recall when paused. Pressing Pause a second time clears the pause. Usually Pause is more convenient than Ctrl-Num-Lock mostly because it is a one-finger FANSI-CONSOLE pause key. Any program that works with FANSI-CONSOLE pauses with Pause. For other ways to pause, see the descriptions of Ctrl-S and Ctrl-Num-Lock in the previous paragraphs in this section.

Using the Ctrl-C or Ctrl-Break keys

Press the Ctrl-C key to cancel most programs. FANSI-CONSOLE treats it the same way as the Ctrl-Break key for programs using MS-DOS input. It treats both keys the same way that the standard IBM-PC console software treats the Ctrl-Break key. It flushes the typeahead buffer before placing a Ctrl-C in it. The standard IBM-PC console software processes the Ctrl-C slightly differently. It does not flush the typeahead buffer when you press a Ctrl-C. This means that the standard IBM-PC console software ignores the standard MS-DOS Ctrl-C cancel character when you already typed some characters into the typeahead buffer. Pressing Ctrl-C does not cancel any program that Ctrl-Break does not cancel when using the standard IBM-PC console software.

Using the Ctrl-Alt-Enter key

Press the Ctrl-Alt-Enter key to exit from many programs with infinite loops. It brings you back to the MS-DOS command prompt. If you used the MS-DOS CONFIG.SYS STACKS= command, then using the Ctrl-Alt-Enter key leaves MS-DOS considering one of these stacks permanently in use. MS-DOS remains OK when you do this once, but not if you do this repeatedly. You run out of stacks one at a time, and MS-DOS eventually fails. If you do not use the MS-DOS CONFIG.SYS STACKS= command, then using the Ctrl-Alt-Enter key does not cause this problem. If you press the Ctrl-Alt-Enter key when in the

middle of an MS-DOS or other system software call, it may leave MS-DOS in an unstable state. So the best use consists of neatly saving your RAM-disk or other work files before restarting MS-DOS. Like all others, this key combination only works when keyboard interrupts remain enabled!

What to do when key combinations do not work

Some computers have some special non-IBM standard keyboard functions when you do not install FANSI-CONSOLE. The key combinations for these functions frequently include Ctrl-Alt. This includes key combinations for such things as: configuration setup, CPU clock speed change, and screen intensity controls. For example, some computers change hardware clock speeds when you press a certain key combination, such as Ctrl-Alt-Backslash, or Ctrl-Alt-DarkPlus and Ctrl-Alt-DarkMinus. When you install FANSI-CONSOLE, these key combinations do not work the same way, unless FANSI-CONSOLE itself supports that function.

Instead, when you install FANSI-CONSOLE, you must press the Ctrl-Alt-Grave key combination once before each such key combination you want to use. The Grave character is the backward-pointing accent. You use the same key as for the Tilde (the squiggly line!) character. Make sure you press the Grave key last and release it before the Ctrl and Alt keys.

Pressing the Ctrl-Alt-Grave key combination tells FANSI-CONSOLE that you wish to use the original BIOS keyboard interrupt processor. So remember, Ctrl-Alt-Grave "brings the original keyboard BIOS back from the grave." It only affects the next key combination. It does not remain permanently in effect. However, you can do that too, if you do not mind losing most FANSI-CONSOLE keyboard features. See the description of the FANSI-ORIGKEY mode in the chapter entitled "Changing options at run-time." Note that the abbreviated user manual found on the diskettes does not include this chapter, but the complete printed user manual does.

If the special function associated with the key combination when you do not install FANSI-CONSOLE affects the keyboard or the screen processing, it usually does not work with FANSI-CONSOLE even if you press the Ctrl-Alt-Grave key combination first. This is because most such functions require continued support after completing the key combination function, and nothing can give that support because FANSI-CONSOLE has replaced the keyboard and screen handling. However, in these cases FANSI-CONSOLE usually has a similar function which you can do using a different key or some type of control sequence.

The Ctrl-Alt-Grave key combination is NOT a way to momentarily turn off keyboard macros! Although it happens to work for macros expanded at the BIOS level, FANSI-CONSOLE still expands DOS-level macros for any keycodes placed into the typeahead buffer with the help of the Ctrl-Alt-Grave key combination.

Unless FANSI-CONSOLE has the same control functions, no way exists to use macros or the FANSI-CONSOLE SEND command to duplicate the functions of those key combinations which you must precede with Ctrl-Alt-Grave. The original BIOS keyboard handler must process the scan codes directly from the hardware registers for those key combinations. No way exists for any program such as FANSI-CONSOLE to put things into these hardware registers for other programs such as the original BIOS keyboard handler. FANSI-CONSOLE CANNOT duplicate these functions this way. Unfortunately, you CANNOT make ANY shortcut way to do them without knowing how to do the functions and writing your own program to them. Specifically, you CANNOT use FANSI-CONSOLE keyboard macros or keyboard description files to do this. Instead, you ABSOLUTELY MUST press Ctrl-Alt-Grave and then really press those key combinations to do the functions.

Special Key Table

In summary, FANSI-CONSOLE defines the following keys. It treats them differently than the standard IBM BIOS. These keys function this way within nearly all programs. This is a partial list. It just has the keys already described more completely in this chapter. The chapter entitled "Keyboard Arrangement" describes more special FANSI-CONSOLE keys and also has a more complete list at the end. Note that the abbreviated user manual found on the diskettes does not include this chapter, but the complete printed user manual does.

Ctrl-Alt-Enter	Exits the currently running MS-DOS program.
Ctrl-Alt-Grave	Passes the next key combination to original BIOS keyboard interrupt handler.
Ctrl-Break	Call Ctrl-Break interrupt. Usually exits current program or stops process.
Ctrl-C	Flushes the typeahead buffer and adds Ctrl-C. Similar to normal Ctrl-Break.
Ctrl-F	Flushes the typeahead buffer and adds Ctrl-F.
Ctrl-Num-Lock	Pause without flushing typeahead buffer. Must press another, different key combination to unlock!
Ctrl-Prtsc	Converted to Ctrl-P. The MS-DOS command editor treats this as console printer echo toggle.
Ctrl-P	FANSI-CONSOLE does not change the way this key works. The MS-DOS command editor treats this as printer echo toggle.
Ctrl-S	Flushes the typeahead buffer and adds Ctrl-S. Many programs treat this as a pause.
Pause	Causes the display to pause without flushing the typeahead buffer. Must press the same key to unlock!
Others	If your computer has special non-IBM compatible key sequences, refer to the description of Ctrl-Alt-Grave.

Testing for FANSI-CONSOLE

You may want to write programs with capabilities which depend on having FANSI-CONSOLE installed. Any program may test whether you installed FANSI-CONSOLE. FANSI-CONSOLE has another device name besides CON:. You may also open it as FCON:. So, to allow your FANSI-CONSOLE program to test whether you installed FANSI-CONSOLE, simply make the program attempt to open the device FCON: for reading. If the open attempt succeeds, then you installed FANSI-CONSOLE. If the open FANSI-CONSOLE attempt fails, then you did not install FANSI-CONSOLE. If you did not install FANSI-CONSOLE, you may want your program to print an error message, or just use a slightly different mechanism for screen writing.

You can make a batch file do different things depending on whether you installed FANSI-CONSOLE. Just use the following example as an outline:

```
IF EXIST FCON ECHO FC HERE!

IF NOT EXIST FCON ECHO *NO* FC
HERE!
```

MS-DOS only checks the first part of a filename — the characters before the extension — when it determines whether the filename is a device name. It ignores the filename extension when it does this. Thus, when you install FANSI-CONSOLE, you cannot read or write files with

names like FCON.???. This includes directories! If you try, you really use FCON: (FANSI-CONSOLE) instead. If you write to FCON:, then FANSI-CONSOLE writes data to the console. If you read from FCON:, then FANSI-CONSOLE reads data from the keyboard.

For more information about detecting FANSI-CONSOLE, see the section entitled "How does my program detect whether I installed FANSI-CONSOLE?" in the chapter entitled "Programming Background" in the FANSI-CONSOLE Technical Manual.

Usually, if you uninstall FANSI-CONSOLE, you should install the standard MS-DOS ANSI.SYS console device driver instead. If you uninstall FANSI-CONSOLE, but you use programs, batch files, or a prompt that uses ANSI X3.64 control sequences codes, you need to replace the "DEVICE=FCONSOLE.DEV" line in the CONFIG.SYS file with a line containing "DEVICE=ANSI.SYS".

FANSI-CONSOLE Registration Form

Name: _____

Company: _____

Address: _____

City: _____

State: _____ Country: _____

Zip: _____ Phone: _____

Remit to:
Hersey Micro Consulting, Inc.
P.O. Box 8276
Ann Arbor, Michigan 48107-8276
(313) 994-3259

Specify Disk Size: ❏ 5.25" ❏ 3.5"
Specify Operating System: ❏ DOS ❏ OS/2

Payment by:
  ❏ Check ❏ Credit Card
    Make checks payable to:
    Hersey Micro Consulting, Inc.

Authorized Signature: _____
Card number: _____
Expires: _____

FPN FANSI-CONSOLE Complete Package New
(includes both software & both manuals)
    each ....$119.95 $_____
FMN FANSI-CONSOLE User Manual New
(includes software & user manual)
    each ....$75.00 $_____
FDN FANSI-CONSOLE Diskettes Only New
(includes software only)
    each ....$49.95 $_____
FSN FANSI-CONSOLE Master Serializer New
(includes software master & serializer)
    each ....$44.95 $_____
Shipping (see below) .... $_____
Michigan residents add sales tax ....4% $_____
TOTAL .... $_____

We accept Visa, Master Card, and American Express with no surcharge. Add shipping and handling (for 1 copy): UPS Ground to continental USA $4, UPS 2nd Day to continental USA $6, UPS 2nd Day Alaska/Hawaii $8, UPS Next Day $15, Fed Ex Priority 1 $30, Fed Ex Std Air $15.

FormatMaster

Version 4.6
A Menu Driven Floppy Disk Formatter
Copyright © 1987–92 by New-Ware

Getting Up And Running

Operation of FormatMaster is relatively simple and straightforward. Almost all operations are accomplished through selection of a menu item, either via the cursor bar and hitting ENTER or by pressing the key of the first letter of a menu item. However, some initialization steps should be taken before attempting to format any disks.

Program and Documentation Files

By default, the install program for the *DOS 6 SECRETS* diskettes will install all of the FormatMaster files in the directory \SECRETS\FORMASTR. This directory has not been added to the search path. You can execute the program from its home directory, add the directory to the search path, or copy the FormatMaster files to a directory that is included in the search path.

Program Initialization

Here are the two things you should do to get the program to a fully functional state.

1. Select SET DRIVE TABLE from the main menu. FM will normally detect and use the correct parameters for the type of drives in your system, but if the actual drive information differs, use the drive table menu to make the appropriate changes.

2. Make sure that the DOS utility SYS.COM is in a directory that is listed in your path string and that this directory is on the system boot drive if you intend to transfer system files to a newly formatted diskette. See the file PATHINFO.TXT for more information on the DOS PATH command.

FormatMaster Operation

FormatMaster is menu driven and therefore quite easy to use. The main menu contains the following selections:

```
Simultaneous Format/Verify
Format/Verify via DOS
Format/Verify via BIOS
Rapid Format
Only Verify
Define Drive Table
Enter DOS
Check Disk
Transfer System      OFF
Add Vol Label        OFF
cYclic Format        OFF
Beeps     ON
Verify    OFF
Quit to DOS
Print Registration
@ Configure FM
```

Menu items are selected either by moving the cursor bar to the desired item and pressing return (MOUSE LEFT BUTTON) or by pressing the key corresponding the highlighted character. Two of the items above are toggles, i.e., they are either on or off and each time you select one, it is toggled to the opposite setting. If TRANSFER SYSTEM ON is set, then FormatMaster will invoke SYS.COM to transfer system files to the freshly formatted disk. Make sure that COMMAND.COM is not a hidden file. If ADD VOLUME LABEL ON, then you will be prompted to enter a disk label prior to formatting any disks.

The main menu may be skipped by executing FormatMaster with the drive letter and a colon on the command line as follows:

```
FM a:
```

In this case, the main format routine window will appear and FormatMaster will be ready to format the drive whose letter was placed on the command line. It is suggested that some users might desire to configure different copies of FM.EXE in different ways and then load the desired copy with the drive letter on the command line to speed up operation and to minimize keystrokes.

All menu items are augmented by a help line that is written between the top two double lines of the screen.

Formatting Options

The first three menu items on the main menu access different formatting techniques. The first of these is the SIMULATANEOUS FORMAT/ VERIFY option. This will format and verify a diskette in the same manner that DOS accomplishes that feat. This option will be the slowest but safest method of formatting.

The second technique, FORMAT/VERIFY VIA DOS, is really only a variant of the above option. Here the disk is formatted using DOS first and then, if the Verify switch is set, a full verification is performed. Separating the two functions permits formatting without verifying. If you are using high quality diskettes, you can save a lot of formatting time by skipping the verification.

The third technique, FORMAT/VERIFY VIA BIOS, uses direct BIOS calls instead of DOS calls and is included for those who might still be using a DOS version less than 3.1 or those who have difficulty formatting add-on floppy drives via DOS.

Please note that if you are running a version of DOS that is earlier than 3.1, the first two menu items will be disabled.

Formatting a Disk

Selection of one of the first three menu items brings up a menu of available system floppy drives. If this menu does not accurately reflect the actual drives in your system, then use the DEFINE DRIVE TABLE option on the main menu to properly configure FM for your system.

If the disk you have placed in the designated drive is already formatted, it may contain valuable data and FormatMaster will warn you of this condition and give you four options in a pop-up menu. Options on this menu are

OK — Continue
Abort
View
Check Disk
Quit To DOS

Use Abort to discontinue the formatting operation. The View option will display an abbreviated directory listing of the target drive so that you may decide if you really want to format the disk or not. The Continue option will proceed with formatting. Since the target disk is already formatted, you may desire to save some time by doing a Quick Format. The Quick Format option simply re-initializes the FAT and ROOT DIRECTORY areas of the diskette instead of doing a complete track-by-track format. Verification will proceed normally if that switch is ON. The View option will clear the screen and display the files on the target drive. The Check Disk option displays information similar to the DOS CHKDSK utility.

If the disk is not formatted, FormatMaster will check the capacity entry in the drive table and if the drive is a high capacity drive, you will be asked whether you desire to format a high capacity diskette. If the disk contains data, FormatMaster will automatically adjust to the proper format mode. After this query, FormatMaster will format the disk, updating the track counter as it formats each track. When the formatting is complete, if the TRANSFER SYSTEM toggle is ON, the system files will be transferred and if the ADD VOLUME LABEL toggle is on, the volume label entered from the main menu will be added to the target disk. A disk counter is incremented and displayed during cyclic formatting to help you keep track of the number of disks formatted.

If Cyclic formatting is not in progress, a YOUR CHOICE submenu is presented at the completion of each disk format/verify operation. Options on this menu are

Format Another
Main Menu
Check Disk
Quit To DOS

These options are self-explanatory.

Rapid Format

RAPID FORMAT provides a way to very quickly reformat disks that are already formatted. If you have a batch of formatted disks that you desire to re-initialize, use this option. Instead of formatting the disk track-by-track, as is necessary in the case of a fresh, unformatted diskette, FormatMaster will skip the track formatting and re-initialize the FAT and directory sectors. The disk will then be just as if you did a full track-by-track format. If you use this feature in conjunction with CYCLIC = ONE (OR TWO), things tend to go rather rapidly, so there is a pause for a key press to allow time for swapping disks. THE VERIFY option may be used in conjunction with this feature.

A previously formatted disk may have bad sectors that were marked by DOS or FormatMaster when it was formatted. FormatMaster will detect this situation and automatically verify and update the disk FAT following the rapid format.

Note that it is NOT possible to rapid format an unformatted disk.

Only Verify

ONLY VERIFY = ON turns on diskette verification but will not format the target disk. This feature is to be used ONLY with formatted disks and is useful in verifying the integrity of a data diskette. The diskette FAT will NOT be updated following the verification check. If FormatMaster discovers bad sectors on the disk, it is strongly advised to attempt to copy all the data from the diskette to a freshly formatted and verified diskette and then reformat and re-verify the diskette.

Define Drive Table

FormatMaster will attempt to detect how the floppy disk drives in your system are configured at runtime. Specifically, it is important to know the size (3½" or 5¼") of each drive and whether or not that drive is high capacity. Because there are so many configuration variants among PCs and ATs (and clones), it may not necessarily be true that floppy drives are sequentially designated from A to D. In fact, there are some systems with add-on 3½" drives (and attendant drivers) that are addressed as a letter that is higher than the hard drive letters in the system. For this reason, you may need to use the FM drive table setup feature to assure proper performance.

At runtime FormatMaster will automatically set the drive table according to information de-

rived from the ROM BIOS or DOS (version 3.2 or later). In most cases this information will accurately reflect the status of the drives in your system, and it will be unnecessary to alter the drive table. There may be some cases, however, where the table is not set properly by FormatMaster, particularly in the case of add-on 3½" drives that use a DOS logical drive designator (i.e., B:,C:,D:) that is not in the usual sequence. The first time you run FormatMaster you should check the drive table settings to determine if they match the way your system is configured. If so, you need do nothing more (although it is okay to save the drive table, if you wish). Otherwise, use the menu to set the table properly and be sure to save the table before attempting to format any disks.

Floppy disk controllers can address at most up to four drives and access the available drives through numeric codes that range from 0 to 3. For example, just about every PC-type machine in the world will have a DOS drive A that is accessed by the BIOS as drive 0. Normally, DOS drive B will be accessed as drive 1, and so on. It should be clear by now that there are two ways of addressing system drives. You communicate with DOS about system drives using *logical* drive designators, which are alphabetic letters ranging from A to Z. DOS in turn calls the machine ROM BIOS to perform low level disk operations (read, write, format, etc.) and uses *physical* drive designators that are numbers. FormatMaster uses a user-defined drive table that keeps track of four important items — the DOS logical drive designator, the BIOS physical drive number, the size of the drive, and whether the drive is a normal or high capacity drive. A high capacity drive is one that supports both normal and high density diskettes. For example, the AT comes with a high capacity 5¼" drive as DOS drive A. It will format either normal (360K) or high-density (1.2MB) floppies. Many systems now have high capacity 3½" drives which format either 720K or 1.4MB diskettes.

Configuring the FM drive table is relatively simple. You select one of the four drives from the menu and then use the drive table parameter entry dialog window. This window will display the drive letter, drive size, and drive capacity edit fields to you. Use the mouse, Tab key, or Enter key to move through the fields. You can set the drive letter by pressing any letter key. The drive size and density fields are toggled by pressing the spacebar, + key, or – key. To accept and store your changes press the F10 key; otherwise, press the Esc key.

Once you have made the settings appropriate for your system, you can save them permanently to disk via the @ CONFIGURE FM main menu function. If in doubt about which logical drive matches which physical drive, you can experiment. FM contains numerous checks to determine if a hard drive is selected for formatting and will abort if this is the case. In addition, FM makes no calls to any DOS or BIOS function that writes to or formats a hard disk. One way to ensure that the drive table is properly configured and only floppy drives will be accessed is to perform an FM Check Disk operation with a formatted disk in each of the available system drives.

Enter DOS

ENTER DOS provides the means to *shell out* to the DOS level to perform whatever operations desired. Entering the command EXIT from the DOS level will return you to the FormatMaster main menu.

Check Disk

Selection of this item will bring up the drive selection submenu. Upon selection of a drive, FormatMaster will display a window that contains nearly the same information as the DOS CHKDSK utility provides. The Check Disk function is also available from the choice menu that is displayed during format/verify operations.

Transfer System

System diskettes differ from data diskettes in that they contain a slightly different boot sector and they must contain the two DOS system files as well as a compatible copy of COMMAND.COM (or 4DOS.COM/NDOS.COM). FormatMaster will transfer system files to a freshly formatted disk, but you must ensure that it can access the DOS utility SYS.COM. You do this by ensuring that the file SYS.COM is in a directory whose name appears in your DOS path statement. For example, if your DOS files are in a directory named C:\DOS, then the directory pathname C:\DOS *must* appear in

your path command. Please read the file PATHINFO.TXT for a more detailed explanation of the DOS PATH command feature. FormatMaster invokes SYS.COM to transfer system files to the newly formatted disk.

FormatMaster will attempt to locate SYS.COM, the DOS system files, and COMMAND.COM at runtime. If these files cannot be located, the Transfer System option on the main menu will be disabled.

4DOS and NDOS users should note that you have a choice of which command interpreter you wish copied to a floppy diskette when creating a system disk. If FM finds a copy of DOS COMMAND.COM anywhere in your DOS path, it will copy that file to the system disk. Otherwise, it will copy the file specified by the DOS environment variable COMSPEC=.

Add Vol Label

ADD VOLUME LABEL provides a means for the entry of a diskette volume label prior to formatting any disks. Selecting this item results in the presentation of a window which will prompt for the desired volume label. Any valid DOS label name may be entered. If the entered label name contains a number as the LAST portion of the name, that number can be used to add sequential serial numbers to each formatted diskette. For example, if the entered name is SER-0001, FormatMaster will use SER-0001 for the first disk, SER-0002 for the second disk, SER-0022 for the 22nd disk, and so on. Any sequence of numeric digits ('0' to '9') may be used, but they must comprise the LAST portion of the label name. SER-0022X would not be used for sequential disk numbering. If an acceptable sequential number is entered, you will be asked if you wish to use the entered label for serializing disks. If the response is Y(es), then disks formatted using the Cycle Format option will be automatically sequentially serialized using the entered digit series as a base. The last serial number used can be saved via the "" menu item. When saving the current configuration to disk, FormatMaster will ask if you wish to save the current serial number. If the response is Y(es), then the current label name and sequence number is saved to disk. The next time FormatMaster is run it will use the next number in the sequence for cyclically formatting and adding the volume label. To turn off the addition of a volume label, simply press ESC or enter an empty string when prompted for the label. Entry of a label name that does not contain a proper sequence of digits at the end of the name will stop the sequential updating of the serial number.

If the toggle is ON, it may be set to OFF by selecting the menu item, deleting the current volume label, and returning to the main menu.

Cyclic Format

CYCLIC FORMAT, when set to ONE or TWO, provides a means to rapidly format disks in TWO of your system floppy drives. Selecting this item will bring up a submenu from which ONE drive or TWO drive cyclic formatting may be selected. When entering the main format display, you will be prompted to enter two items for each drive. The first is the DOS drive letter designator. Make sure that this is a drive letter that you have set up in the SET DRIVE TABLE option. If your drive table setting indicates that the selected drive is a high capacity drive, you will be asked if you are going to be formatting high capacity diskettes in the drive. In this manner, any two drives in your system may be used for the cyclic formatting. After entering the pertinent information, you will be instructed to ready the selected drives for formatting. As soon as you press any key, the formatting of the two drives will start. You may terminate the formatting cycle by pressing the ESC key at any time. The formatting operation will continue to completion on whichever drive is active at the time the key is pressed, and a message will appear that informs you that the formatting will be terminated following the formatting of the current drive. If the Esc key is pressed a second time, the formatting will terminate immediately.

Beeps

FormatMaster signals a number of operation completions with an audible beep. The beeps may be suppressed by toggling the Beeps toggle to OFF.

Verify

VERIFY = ON switches the verification feature on and off. If set to ON, disk verification will be performed using the BIOS CRC verification routine. Every sector on the disk is checked, and all bad sectors are marked. FormatMaster will report bad sectors as cluster groups in the Advisory Message box. At the end of the verification, if there were any bad sectors found, FormatMaster will update the File Allocation Table (FAT) to lock out those sectors. Note that turning verification to ON will slow down the total formatting process. In some cases, FormatMaster may be more stringent than DOS and mark more sectors unusable. That will result in less total disk space available on a damaged disk, but is preferable to the opposite approach.

Quit to DOS

QUIT TO DOS terminates FormatMaster and returns you to the DOS level. Alt-X will also terminate the program. Pressing the Esc key can also be used to exit FM but a confirmation window is presented first.

Print Registration

PRINT REGISTRATION FORM brings up a window that will prompt you for the entry of registration information and then will create a registration form on your printer that can be mailed to New-Ware.

@ Configure FM

To semi-permanently configure FormatMaster, use the @ CONFIGURE FM.EXE option. All the current toggle settings will be saved to disk so that each time you execute the program, it will start up with the toggles as set when you invoked this option. In addition, if you have started FormatMaster with an M (or m) on the command line, the monochrome (composite) monitor color settings will also be saved so that it will not be necessary to use the M on the command line.

Configuration settings are saved to a file named FMTMAS.CFG. The save configuration screen will indicate where FM intends to save this file and gives you a chance to save it to a specific location of your choice. When FM loads, it will look first in the current directory for FMTMAS.CFG. If it finds it, it will load it and proceed. If not, it will then search all the directories found in the DOS path for the file. It will load the first copy of FMTMAS.CFG it finds.

The Escape Key

The ESC key can be used to exit from just about any menu or operation. It will also abort formatting with an advisory message. If the cyclic toggle is in effect, FormatMaster will terminate the operation after completing the format operation on the current disk. If the Esc key is pressed a second time, formatting will be aborted immediately.

Error Handling

All detected errors are reported in the Error Message box, and error messages are accompanied by an audible beep. Bad disk clusters detected during verification are reported in the Advisory Message box.

Terminate-and-Stay-Resident (TSR) Version

A special version of FormatMaster that installs as a memory-resident TSR is available directly from New-Ware. This version permits users to pop up FormatMaster from within a non-graphics application program and format floppy disks. POPFM requires only 6K of normal RAM and utilizes EMS, XMS, or hard disk to swap code/data in and out of memory. The activation key combination (hot key) is user-configurable. Users who order POPFM will receive the full FormatMaster package plus the special TSR utility for $30.

Technical Notes

FormatMaster is written in a combination of Turbo Pascal 6.0 and assembly language and makes generous use of TurboPower Software's excellent Turbo Professional 5.23 package. Formatting is accomplished via INT 13h ROM BIOS service calls based upon parameters in the drive table or via the DOS block device control (IOCTL) function.

Disk verification during format does not perform a rigorous sector read/write type of verification and can be skipped if one is using decent quality diskettes. Note that the DOS device control function also utilizes the BIOS disk sector verification function. New-Ware has formatted and distributed thousands of low cost bulk-purchased diskettes that were formatted by FM without verification. The disk return rate to date has been practically nil.

The program was developed on an AST 20 Mhz Premium/386 equipped with one dual capacity 5¼" disk drive, one dual capacity 3½" disk, and a VGA monitor running MS-DOS 5.0 and QEMM 6.1. It has been thoroughly tested on the 386, an AST Premium/286, AST Bravo 286, and a 386 SX clone. MS-DOS 3.2, 3.3, and 4.01 were used on standard 360K/720K and dual capacity 1.2M/1.4M disk drives.

Monitor Problems

Many laptop portables and those machines with a *composite* monitor can trick programs like FormatMaster into thinking that there is a fully functional Color Graphics Adaptor (CGA) on board. If you load the program and the cursor bar is not visible or the display looks strange, quit the program using Alt-X and reload it with an M (either case) on the command line.

Example:

```
FM m
```

This will force FormatMaster to use a set of monochrome attributes that should work fine on LapTop and composite monitors. Using the main menu Config command will save the current color configuration so that using the m on the command line will no longer be necessary the next time FormatMaster is loaded.

Mouse Support

FormatMaster supports all the popular Mouse systems. The left button is used to enter a carriage return and the right button serves as an ESC key.

BBS Access

The New-Ware Shareware Products BBS operates 24 hours per day, 7 days per week. Node #1 is dedicated to registered users only. Node #2 is open to all callers. Users registering via the BBS receive access to latest registered version within one day after leaving their credit card data. Users who register by mail or phone may also access the registered version by BBS, but you MUST log on and leave a comment to the sysop to the effect that you are a registered user and desire access. The author can also be contacted on CIS via PPN 71535,665 (please use EMAIL).

FormatMaster Registration Form

Name: _____

Company: _____

Address: _____

City: _____

State: _____ Country: _____

Zip: _____ Phone: _____

Remit to:
New-Ware
8050 Camino Kiosco
San Diego, CA 92122-1820

Registering FormatMaster may be accomplished in one of the following ways:

1. Mail a check or money order in the amount of $20 payable to New-Ware. California residents please add 7.75% sales tax ($21.55 total). (Please send $30 for the TSR version).

2. Mail your Visa or Master Card number, expiration date, name, address, and phone number. No other credit cards can be accepted.

3. Call (619) 455-6225 and leave your Visa or MasterCard number, expiration date, name, address, and your phone number. If you call the voice number to register, you may get an answering machine. Have your card or the form printed by FormatMaster ready so you can leave your registration information quickly and accurately.

4. Call the Shareware Products BBS and register on line. The number is (619) 455-5226, N/8/1, 1200/2400 baud. Your credit card can usually be validated within one day, and this is the quickest way to get a copy of the registered version.

FormatMaster will be shipped first class mail within two days of receipt of a registration.

HotDIR Plus

Version 7.2
Copyright © 1992 by Robert Woeger

Introduction

HotDIR was the first and in my opinion is the best color-sorted directory utility. I originally released version 1.0 back in early 1987, followed by the "famous" HotDIR 2.1. Due to the change with hard disks larger than 33MB in DOS 4 and DOS 5, I rewrote HotDIR from scratch and released the HotDIR Plus 7.0 series. HotDIR Plus 7.0 and 7.1 were only released to a few people, and 7.2 is the first MAJOR release of HotDIR Plus.

Scope of HotDIR

HotDIR Plus is a color-sorted directory utility. HotDIR Plus is unique in that it was the first to display files by color (based on what extension they were). It has options to sort your files in many different ways, and list them left to right or up and down, plus in 1, 2, 4, or 6 column format. I believe that once you've tried HotDIR you'll be hooked. Your files will *pop out* at you, and that is how the "Hot" in HotDIR came about. I originally wrote HotDIR for a friend of mine, Dr.

John German, to help him see the different files by type (extensions) easier. He said, "that's Hot"! and I soon released the original HotDIR 1.0 to the world. I got such an enthusiastic response from HotDIR that I wrote HotDIR Plus.

Program and Documentation Files

By default, the install program for the *DOS 6 SECRETS* diskettes will install all of the HotDIR Plus files in the directory \SECRETS\HDIRPLUS. This directory has not been added to the search path. You can execute the program from its home directory, add the directory to the search path, or copy the HotDIR Plus files to a directory that is included in the search path.

Using the Program

Type **HDIRPLUS /h** to get the help screen.

All commands are described on the help screen and appear as a forward slash followed by a letter of the option. You may use multiple commands when you invoke HDIRPLUS:

```
Format: HDIRPLUS [path] [filespec]
        [/option] [/option] ...
```

Examples:

```
HDIRPLUS \os2\system /c /2
```

This will display a 2-column directory format and clear the screen first. It will display all files in directory \os2\system.

```
HDIRPLUS
```

This will display all files in the default drive/ directory and use the predefined options. Default or those modified through HDIRCNFG.EXE. HDIRPLUS /r Information about registering your copy of HotDIR Plus.

```
HDIRPLUS /h
```

List of all commands available for HotDIR Plus.

```
HDIRPLUS a: /p
```

Display directory of A: drive and toggle Pause at end of screen mode.

```
HDIRPLUS /p >prn
```

Sends HotDIR Plus's output to the printer without page pauses. You can send output to a file by placing >filename instead of >prn.

Summary

Here is a summary of command switches used by HotDIR Plus:

/H   displays on-line help screen

/R   displays information on how to register your copy

/N   No sort (unsorted raw file directory)

/F   Filename sort (factory default)

/E   Sort by extension

/D   Sort by date (oldest to newest files)

/S   sort by file size

/1   1-column display format

/2   2-column display format

/4   4-column display format (factory default)

/6   6-column display format

/C   toggles Clear screen at beginning of directory display

/P   Pause at end of screen toggle

/U   Up/Down file sort/display toggle — alternate is left-to-right display

The HDIRCNFG.EXE file

A program named HDIRCNFG.EXE is included to give you greater flexibility and control over the permanent HotDIR Plus settings. The above commands are great for overriding the default settings, but when you want to permanently change the colors used by HotDIR Plus, sort options, column displayed, etc., use HDIRCNFG to change HDIRPLUS.EXE. HDIRCNFG.EXE modifies the HDIRPLUS.EXE program itself and writes the changes inside the HotDIR Plus program. This was done to keep from having a separate configuration file for HotDIR Plus floating around. Due to a programming error on my part, HotDIR Plus 7.1 was clobbered whenever the HDIRCNFG program was run and the options saved. This has now been fixed, but I encourage you to make a backup copy of HDIRPLUS.EXE before running the HDIRCNFG utility.

Simply run HDIRCNFG and it will prompt you to change each setting. If you make a mistake, just do not save the changes, exit HDIRCNFG, and rerun.

If you want to remove an extension name and color, simply overwrite the extension name with another extension and color. If you want to just disable one extension, make sure you use blanks for the extension name. Make sure you move the other extensions forward and make the blank extension the last in the list. Otherwise, the blank extension will cause HotDIR Plus to stop searching for other colors and extensions that are after a blank entry.

HDIRCNFG is very versatile and powerful, but I recommend you get familiar with HDIRPLUS first before you change options. Most every option is able to be changed through HDIRCNFG.EXE. If you want to temporarily override an option, use a command switch when invoking HotDIR Plus. Also, you can change the number of lines to display per screen with HDIRCNFG. This is very useful for EGA & VGA monitors when in 43 or 50 line per screen mode.

HDIRCNFG uses standard BASIC COLOR command color numbers. It is recommended that you use colors between 0 and 15. 16–31 are blinking versions of the lower 0–15 colors. The most common colors numbers are

0   Black

1   Blue

2   Green

3 Cyan
4 Red
5 Magenta
6 Yellow
7 White
8 Gray
9 Light blue
10 Light green
11 Light cyan
12 Light red
13 Light magenta
14 Hi intensity yellow
15 Hi intensity white

File Number and Size Limits for HotDIR Plus

There are some self-imposed limits with HotDIR Plus which are

- No more than 1,000 files per subdirectory. This is a reasonable number of files, and it helps keep HotDIR's sort and data areas to a reasonable size.
- File sizes up to 9,999,999 may be displayed without breaking HotDIR Plus's formatting on the screen. I chose this number as most files are less than 10 megabytes in size each. Note that the disk size may be over 1.6 gigabytes and HotDIR Plus should report the total disk free correctly. Only each file is limited to a maximum of 10 megabytes. If a file is greater than 10 megs, the file size should be displayed properly, but you will notice that since it takes extra digits to display, your 2-, 4-, or 6-column HotDIR Plus display may "wrap around" on the line where that huge file is. One-column displays will work best if you have a lot of huge 10 meg+ files in a directory.

HotDIR Plus 7.2 Registration Form

Name: _____
Company: _____
Address: _____
City: _____
State: _____ Country: _____
Zip: _____ Phone: _____

Remit to:
Robert Woeger
2423 Hagerman St.
Colorado Springs, CO 80904-3228 U.S.A.
(719) 471-8306

Payment by:
❑ Check ❑ Money Order ❑ Purchase Order

Specify Disk Size: ❑ 5.25" ❑ 3.5"

Upon registering, you will receive a registered version of HotDIR Plus, discounts/notice of software upgrades in the future, and full legal rights to use HotDIR Plus on your machine(s). Please read the terms of the software license and restrictions in the file HOTDIR.DOC. For information on quantity discounts, site licenses, and distribution of HotDIR Plus with your software, contact the author.

Regular HotDIR registration is $20 and includes a disk with the latest registered version of HotDIR Plus for DOS, software license, technical support, and news on updates. You may also register for $20 via CompuServe's Shareware Registration service (GO SWREG) and use Registration ID #364 to register your copy of HotDIR Plus. You will receive all the above including a disk with the registered version. Your CompuServe account will be billed the $20 and they will forward your name to us. For $15 you get all the above less the disk with the registered version of HotDIR Plus.

HotDIR Plus for DOS w/ disk
  each .... $20.00 $ _____
HotDIR Plus for DOS no disk
  each .... $15.00 $ _____
HotDIR Plus for DOS & OS/2 disk
  each .... $25.00 $ _____
Colorado residents add sales tax .... $ _____
TOTAL .... $ _____

Please send U.S. funds only.

Thank you for your business. Orders normally sent U.S. Mail 2nd day priority mail. All shipping & handling fees included in purchase price.

Led's Change Directory

A PC-DOS / MS-DOS Intelligent Directory Changer
Version 4.0
Copyright © 1991 by Keith Ledbetter.

Note from the Author: McAfee Associates (the makers of SCAN and other anti-virus tools) are now distributing LCD. At press time, a new version of LCD, called MCD, is in the final stages of development. Contact McAfee Associates at (408) 988-3832 for further information about the LCD and MCD utilities.

Introduction

LCD is a program designed to make changing directories much easier, especially when you have a large hard drive with lots of different partitions.

LCD is a work-alike to Peter Norton's NCD command, but with one significant difference. LCD works *across all drives* by maintaining the directory database of all drives on drive C:, instead of one database on each individual drive like NCD does. This means that you don't have to specify a drive letter when changing to a directory on a different drive.

Program and Documentation Files

By default, the install program for the *DOS 6 SECRETS* diskettes will install all of the LCD files in the directory \SECRETS\LCDFILES. This directory has not been added to the search path. You can execute the program from its home directory, add the directory to the search path, or copy the LCD files to a directory that is included in the search path.

Changing Directories

LCD is used to quickly switch between directories across any of your hard drives.

Syntax:

`LCD partial_` `directory_name`	change to a directory
`LCD md directory_` `name`	create directory; update database now

`LCD rd directory_` `name`	delete directory; update database now
`LCD /scan` `[drivelist]`	scan drives and build directory database
`LCD /qscan` `[drivelist]`	scan drives (ignore dirs with extensions)
`LCD *`	bring up handy speed search and browse window

You simply invoke LCD and give it the full or partial name of the directory you wish to change to. For example, if you have a directory named C:\PROCOMM\DOWNLOADS, you could switch to this directory with the command:

    C:> LCD down

LCD will first try to do an immediate change to the directory name that you specify. If that change works, LCD simply exits immediately. If it fails, then LCD looks into your directory database and tries to figure out the directory name that you wanted by doing fuzzy comparisons. If more than one directory existed with the same partial name that you gave to LCD, it will display a scrollable dialog box on the screen containing all of the matches found. Simply use the arrow keys to highlight the path that you want to change to, then press <Enter>.

Scanning Directories

The first time you execute LCD, you must specify the /SCAN parameter

    LCD /scan

which instructs LCD to scan all of your hard drives and build a file called LCD.IDX in the root directory of drive C. You will need to periodically rescan all of your drives to add to the table any new directories that you have created.

If you only want LCD to know about certain specific drives (i.e., only non-network drives), you can specify a drive list after the /SCAN keyword. To have LCD only scan drives C, E, F, and G, you'd do this:

```
C:> LCD /SCAN CEFG
```

If you are sure that you don't have subdirectories which have an extension in their name (for example, C:\PROGRAMS.OLD\), you can specify /QSCAN instead of /SCAN. This causes LCD to scan almost 50 percent quicker than normal.

Direct Database Updating

You can also use LCD to create and remove directories with immediate database updating. This means that you don't have to continually scan your drives to update the directory database. LCD will create or delete the directory specified and then update the LCD.IDX database at the same time. For example, to create a directory on drive F: and put that directory in the database, you would do:

```
C:> LCD md f:\test
```

This ability comes in especially handy for users of command shells that allow aliasing, such as CED and 4DOS. With these utilities, you can change the standard MD and RD commands to invoke LCD instead. With 4DOS, you would set up the aliases like this:

```
C:> alias md 'lcd md %1'
C:> alias rd 'lcd rd %1'
C:> alias cd 'lcd %1'
```

The LCD Environment Variable

If you would rather have LCD keep its LCD.IDX database somewhere other than the root directory of drive C:, you can specify the filename you want used in the LCD environment variable. For example, if you'd like to keep the LCD.IDX file on drive D: in your UTILS directory, you would put

```
SET LCD=D:\UTILS\LCD.IDX
```

in your AUTOEXEC.BAT file.

Note: Be sure to read the HISTORY.DOC file for changes that were made in this version.

LCD Version 4.0x Registration Form

Name: _____

Company: _____

Address: _____

City: _____

State: _____ Country: _____

Zip: _____ Phone: _____

Remit to:
Keith Ledbetter
4240 Ketcham Drive
Chesterfield, VA 23832
(804) 674-0780 (6:00 p.m. - 10:00 p.m. Eastern Time)

Disk with branding utility
   each ....$15.00 $ _____
TOTAL .... $ _____

Payment by: ❑ Check ❑ Money Order
   Please make payment (in US funds) payable
   to "Keith Ledbetter."

Specify Disk Size: ❑ 5.25" 1.2MB ❑ 3.5" 1.44MB
   ❑ 5.25" 360K ❑ 3.5" 720K

Site, corporate, network, and reseller licenses are available for LCD.

LIST

A File Viewing and Browsing Utility
Version 7.7
Copyright © by Vernon D. Buerg 1983–92.

Introduction

LIST is a user-supported program. It is not public domain. You may use LIST and give it to your friends, but you may not sell it or use it in business without obtaining a license. See the last page for information about licensing.

You use LIST to display files on your monitor, line by line with the aid of scrolling, positioning, and filtering commands.

LIST PLUS has many new commands which go beyond usual file viewing and browsing. We will explain how LIST is used, and then how the new file management commands are used.

Program and Documentation Files

By default, the install program for the *DOS 6 SECRETS* diskettes will install all of the LIST files in the directory \SECRETS\LIST. This directory has not been added to the search path. You can execute the program from its home directory, add the directory to the search path, or copy the LIST files to a directory that is included in the search path.

LICENSE	Licensing information and sample licensing agreement.
LIST DOC	Documentation file for LIST (may be PRINTed).
LIST HST	Version history, summary of changes to LIST.
LIST COM	LIST command, Plus version, all commands and features.
LISTR COM	LIST regular version.
LISTS COM	Small version of COM file without help screen.
DRLIST COM	Special CTTY/ANSI version of LIST.
DRLIST DOC	Documentation for DRLIST to be PRINTed.
COLOR PAT	Example DEBUG input to change colors.
-READ.ME	Registration information.
WHATSNEW	New command-line switches.
MAILER	Registration form.
LIST.ICO	Windows icon for LIST.
DIALER PAT	Example DEBUG input to change dialer COM port.
LISTMOD DOC	Documentation for customizing LIST.
PROGRAMS	List of other programs.

Varieties of LIST.COM

Before going into all of the ways in which LIST can be used to display files, let's look at the three different varieties of LIST so that you understand the capabilities of each. Then, we'll go on and define certain terms like redirection, piping, and filtering. In this way, you will better understand how you can use these things with LIST.

LISTS.COM — small version

- Runs in about 30K.
- Limited to smaller files (around 600K).
- Excludes the Alt-X (screen-saving) function.
- Excludes the Alt-G (goto DOS) function.
- The Help screen is minimal.

LISTR.COM — regular version

- Runs in about 80K.
- Handles files up to 16MB.
- Excludes the Alt-V (file selection) function.
- Excludes the Alt-I (insert filename) function.
- The Alt-W (windowing function) is minimal. That is, you get two equal-sized windows; there is no ability to change window dimensions.

LIST.COM — PLUS version

- Plus Alt-V file selection menu
- Plus file management functions like copy and delete

- Plus Alt-I hypertext-like file selection
- Plus a help screen for the file selection Alt-V functions
- Plus a second help screen for regular functions
- Plus the Ctrl-T telephone dialer

There is also a commercial version of LIST called LIST Enhanced. The main differences between LIST Plus and LIST Enhanced are

The File Selection menu has

- File tagging, including tag all, untag, retag, etc.
- Archive file extract and add/update commands
- A sweep command to execute a specified program with all of the tagged files
- A hardcopy (print) command for printing files with a user program
- Commands to change screen colors for all displayable items
- Shell to DOS
- Change video modes
- A directory tree display command
- The rename command that can rename directories
- A command to create new directories

The viewer part has

- The Alt-E command presents a menu offering up to 6 video modes including 132x25, 132x43, 80x43, etc., if the video adapter supports that text mode.
- Viewing of EBCDIC and ASCII files.
- Handling of fixed-length record files like database files at two or more times the usual speed.
- Optional number (on the left side) of each record.
- Command-line parameters to position to a given record number or to the end of file.
- Handling of files up to 32MB in size, larger upon request.
- The wrap option splits the line at a word boundary.

In general the commercial version

- Allocates memory more efficiently; can run in as little as 100K with all functions.

- Supports UltraVision video utility.
- Has options to use regular DOS input routines that take advantage of PCED, DOSKEY, or other keyboard utilities; or, to use an internal input routine which allows command-line editing.
- Has a customization program that can be used to set any of the LIST options or toggle and save them to a file or read the options saved in a file; the customization program can define other printer names, can define all the names of archive programs used.
- Has a 170-page spiral bound manual.
- Has a 6-panel Quick Reference card of all commands.
- Has one year of free updates.
- Has telephone, FAX, and BBS support.

LIST Enhanced may be purchased at computer stores or ordered directly from Buerg Software. Registered users of LIST receive a $20 discount.

The documentation file is marked with | before new and changed lines. It is marked with a double asterisk ** for LIST PLUS only features.

Warning: LIST PLUS (LIST.COM) has the ability to DELETE files from your system!!

If you elect to use USE LIST PLUS, please read the section on the file selection menu found later in this manual.

Note: Please see the file LIST.DOC for the sections omitted here on DOS terms and command lines.

Starting LIST

To start LIST, type the command LIST at the DOS prompt followed by the name(s) of the files that you want to see. For example

```
C:>LIST CONFIG.SYS    (displays file
                       CONFIG.SYS)

C:>LIST *.DOC          (displays all DOC
                       files in current
                       directory)
```

The *filename* is optional. If omitted, LIST PLUS will bring up a display of *all* files and subdirectories in the current directory. You may use the cursor keys to highlight the file that you would like to work on and press ENTER. Or, you may highlight any sub-directory entry and press ENTER to change to that subdirectory. You may also use LIST to display piped or redirected files.

To display a redirected file, use a < (less-than symbol) before the name of the file that was redirected and add the /S parameter to the LIST command.

For example, the output of the DIR command can be written to a file called XYZ, and then LIST can be instructed to read that file.

```
dir a: >xyz
list <xyz /s
```

To see a piped file, omit the filename, but supply the /S.

```
dir a: | list /s
```

Or, to LIST a file within an ARC archive:

```
ARC /p arcname.arc filename.ext |
    list /s
```

or

```
ARCE arcname filename.ext /p | list
    /S
```

Here, the ARC or ARCE program is invoked to extract the FILENAME.EXT file. The /P switch for these programs sends the output to the standard output device, and this output is piped to LIST. Once the file is displayed on your screen, you may use the cursor positioning keys to move around and see different parts of the file. There are also commands to search for text, print, split the screen, display other files, change colors, change the way the data is displayed, and many other operations.

Exiting LIST

There are several ways to exit LIST depending on how you want the screen to look.

The F10 command returns you to DOS with the DOS prompt on the bottom line. The last page that was displayed by LIST is left on the screen.

The ESCape key also returns you to DOS without changing the screen. In LIST PLUS, the ESCape key is also used to cancel an operation or to exit the file selection menu.

The X command returns you to DOS and clears the screen. The DOS prompt is on the top line of the screen.

The Alt-X command uses the screen-saving feature. It returns you to DOS and displays the screen that you had before LIST was run.

Entering Commands

You enter commands by pressing a single key or a combination of keys. There are often several ways to perform the same function with different keys. For example, D and PgDn both perform a scroll down one page function. This lets you pick the keys that you are most accustomed to.

When you press keys, they are entered into a keyboard buffer. Holding down a key can put many copies of that key into the buffer. This means that when you let up on a key, the program can still be processing input from the keyboard buffer. For example, by holding down the PgDn key, LIST scrolls down one page for each time the PgDn key is placed in the keyboard buffer. When you let up on the key, the buffer may not yet be empty and LIST will continue to page down. To make LIST stop when you let up on a key, you use the Alt-K key-ahead toggle.

Keyboard enhancement utilities, such as PCED, may also change the way that LIST reads the keyboard. With PCED, for example, pressing the ESCape key at a prompt is different. You do not see the / that DOS normally sends when you cancel an input line.

Display Format

The monitor display is defined in terms of lines and columns. A typical monitor can display 25 lines of 80 columns each. LIST attempts to use the number of lines and columns for the monitor mode in use. For example, if the monitor is in 132 column mode, LIST displays 132 characters per line. If the monitor is set for other than 25 lines, such as 35, 43, or 50 lines, LIST displays that many lines per screen.

If you use the Alt-E command to change EGA/VGA modes, the EGA palette, cursor, and other settings are set to the DOS default values. LIST does not preserve fonts or palettes. The top line of the display is called the Status line. The bottom line is called the Command line. The remaining lines are called the primary display window and are usually lines two through 24.

Status Line Format

The Status line has two formats. The default format is

```
|LIST lllll nnnnnnn +sss mm/dd/yy
  hh:mm - filename |
```

where,

LIST	is the name of this program.
lllll	is the line number of the first line in the primary display window (under the status line).
nnnnnnn	is the line number of the last record of the file; if the last record of the file has not been read, this field shows the percentage of the file that has been read.
+sss	if displayed, this is the Scroll amount, in multiples of 10, corresponding to the number of columns that the display has been shifted to the right to view records longer than 80.
mm/dd/yy	is the file's creation date (not today's date); or
dd-mm-yy	is the file's date in European format.
hh:mm	is the file's creation time (not today's time).
filename	is the name of the file you are currently viewing.

Note: The date and time shown on the top line is not the current date. It is the date and time when the file was created.

Note: See the file LIST.DOC for the visual example omitted here.

Command-Line Format

The Command line has two formats. The default format is

```
|Command Keys: ^v->< PgUp PgDn
  F10=exit F1=Help |
```

and the optional format after using the Alt-Z toggle is

```
|Command Toggles: h8kMpswTclJ
  F10=exit F1=Help |
```

where,

command indicates the current process:

Command	function prompt; you are being asked to enter a command; enter the letter, or press the keys for the action to be performed.
Reading	the file data is being read.
Filter	the file data is being formatted for display.
Looking	the Scan/Find text is being searched for.
Scan '	you are being asked to enter text to locate.
Find '	in the file, up to 31 characters may be entered.
# lines?	you are being asked to enter a 1- to 5-digit number that is the amount of lines to skip.
Line #?	you are being asked to enter a 1- to 5-digit line number to which the display is to be positioned.

message may be one of:

```
'*** Text not found ***'
the Scan/Text was not found in the
  file

' *** Top of file ***'
the first line of the file is being
  displayed

'*** End-of-file ***'
the last line of the file is being
  displayed
```

Toggles: Indicates status of toggles: lowercase means OFF, uppercase means the option is ON.

H	indicates that the hex Dump display option is in use.
b	the 'b' is replaced by a 7, 8, or * depending on which of those options is in effect.
K	indicates that the Keyboard flush option is in use.
M	indicates that tests for monitor retrace are not made.

P   indicates that Print is in use.

S   indicates file sharing option is in use.

W   indicates that the Wrap mode is in effect.

T   indicates that TAB characters are expanded.

C   toggles continuous scrolling.

L   indicates that the pre-loading option is on.

J   indicates that line feeds are added to lone carriage return control characters, and backspaces are handled.

A sample Command Line might look like this, after looking for a word that was not found:

```
|Command *** Text not found ***
   Toggles: h*kMpswTclJ F10=exit
   F1=Help|
```

Scrolling

You view different parts of the file by scrolling. That is, you use the cursor positioning keys up, down, left, and right to move the display one increment in that direction. For example, press the down-arrow key to move the display one line in the file (i.e., display the next line in the file).

The PgDn and PgUp cursor keys move the display one full screen in either direction.

Rather than press the up and down keys once for each line, you may use continuous scrolling. Use the C key to toggle continuous scrolling on or off. The default is off. When toggled on, pressing the up- or down-arrow keys results in a moving display. For example, when you press the down arrow, the next line of the file is displayed automatically every second or so. It is like holding down the arrow key. To stop the continuous scroll, press the spacebar.

The speed of the continuous scroll can be adjusted by pressing the + (plus) or – (minus) key while the display is moving. The plus key makes the display move faster, and the minus key makes it move slower. You can save the speed value by using the cloning command (see "Configuring LIST, Cloning," later on in this documentation). The speed is independent of the computer speed and can be adjusted from approximately 50 lines per minute to 1,000 lines per minute.

Summary of scrolling commands:

right arrow	Move display right 10 columns.
left arrow	Move display left 10 columns.
down arrow	Display next line of file.
up arrow	Display previous line of file.
PgUp key	Display previous "page," 23 (or 41) lines back.
PgDn key	Display next "page," 23 (or 41) lines ahead.
C key	Turns continuous scrolling on or off spacebar — or any key, interrupts continuous scrolling.
+ (plus)	Makes continuous scroll incrementally faster.
– (minus)	Makes continuous scroll slower.

Positioning to Lines

Each displayable line of the file is assigned a line number. The first line is assigned line number 1. The highest allowable line number is 16 million. In order to determine the last line number of a file, the entire file must be read. For this reason, the first time that the END (bottom) command is issued, it will take longer to process. This is not necessary if the file has been completely read (see the Alt-L preloading option). If the Wrap option is in effect, there is one line number required for each 80 bytes of the file's records. Thus, the line number does not represent the actual number of lines in the file. If the hex dump option is in effect, there is one line number required for each 16 bytes of the file. For example, an 80-byte line will be displayed as 5 lines.

You may position to a specific line number by using the Ctrl-Home or the # key. When Ctrl-Home is entered, you are prompted for the line number. Enter the line number. The display will now begin with that line number at the top of the screen. To position forward or backward, you may use the + (plus) or – (minus) keys. You are prompted to enter the number of lines to be skipped. The display resumes at the line number shown on the top (status) line plus or minus the number of lines that you specified.

When you change a filter option, such as Wrap, the line numbering changes. An attempt is made to retain the same file position, but the file may be repositioned at the top.

You may also reposition to the last *active* line by using the Alt-Y bookmark command. The last active line is one displayed after a Scan or Find command, or marked using the Alt-M or Alt-B commands, or the line set by the Ctrl-Y bookmark command. Up to ten bookmark lines may be saved by Ctrl-Y and recalled by Alt-Y.

Summary of positioning commands:

Ctrl-HOME, or #	Prompts for exact line number to display
+ (plus)	Prompts for the number of lines to skip for positioning further ahead in the file
– (minus)	Prompts for the number of lines to skip for positioning to an earlier line
Alt-Y	Reposition to the last bookmark
Ctrl-Y	Set new bookmark line number

Scanning for Text

There are three ways to initiate a search for text.

- First is the Find (\ or F) command. Use this command to search for text without regard to the case (upper or lower) of the letters.

- Second is the Scan (/ or S) command. Use this command to search an exact match. That is, the search is case sensitive.

- The third way to initiate a search for text is with the /F command-line switch. With it, you supply the text to search for, and LIST begins the search before displaying the file, and before asking for commands. The search continues through all selected files until a match is found, or the last file has been searched. This search is case insensitive.

Each search begins at the line displayed on the top of the screen and proceeds in a forward direction until the end of file. You may start a search that goes backward rather than forward by using the ' (left quote) key instead of Find (\), or by using ' (right quote) instead of Scan (/).

To enter the Scan search text, type a slash (/) followed by up to 31 characters. The Scan text is displayed on the command line. The Scan is case sensitive. That is, lowercase Scan text will only match lowercase file text.

While the program is searching for the text, the bottom display line is changed to say Looking. Pressing ANY key while the search is in progress will terminate the search and display the message Text not found on the bottom line.

If the text is found, the line containing it is displayed as a high-intensity line (bright color) in the middle of the screen. The search text is displayed in reverse video colors on the highlighted line. The line where the found text is displayed depends on the setting of the "Find Row" (see "Configuration" section).

The display is scrolled left or right, as needed, so that the found text is visible.

If the text is NOT found, the command line is changed to say '*** Text not found ***', and the rest of the display remains unchanged.

To find the next occurrence of the same text, use the A)gain command, or press the F3 key. If you wish to continue the search through all of the remaining files, use the Alt-A command. To find the previous occurrence, press the F9 key.

If the a keyboard enhancement program, such as PCED, is installed, the up/down cursor keys may be used to recall and edit previously entered Scan/Find text.

In a shared file environment, if the file changes while being listed, the file position may become invalid. Use the HOME command to ensure proper file synchronization, or use the Alt-S (share files) command again.

Summary of scanning commands:

/ or S	Scan for text with exact match
v or '	Scan for text going backward
\ or F	Find text with case-insensitive search
^ or '	Find case-insensitive text going backward
F3 or A	Find next occurrence of text
F9	Find previous occurrence of text

Alt-A Scan for next occurrence of the text, and continue on to the next file until the text is found. See the file LIST.DOC for sections omitted here on Marking and Extracting Lines, Printing, and Telephone dialer.

Displaying Multiple Files

You can display more than one file at a time. LIST keeps track of up to 32 files at a time. You supply the filenames in the command line, through the Alt-F (get new filespec) command, through the Alt-I (insert filespec) command, and through the Alt-V file selection menu. The Alt-F command is disabled when viewing a piped file.

You can specify up to 16 filespecs on the command line. Each filespec can contain wildcards. Thus, several files can be selected via the command line. For example,

```
LIST *.DOC *.TXT
```

will display all files with an extension of DOC and TXT.

To display the next file, you use the Q or Ctrl-PgDn command. When the last file has been displayed, you can exit LIST by using the X, F10, ESCape, or Alt-X commands depending on how you want the screen to look when LIST ends.

To display the previous file, you use the Z or Ctrl-PgUp (control and PgUp keys together). The 1 command restarts the displaying of files with the first file.

The Alt-F asks you for a new filename, and you may enter a simple filename, or one that includes wildcards. These new filenames are added to the table of filenames that LIST keeps. Thus, you can use Alt-F for several different filenames, and use the Ctrl-PgDn and Ctrl-PgUp commands to move among them.

The Alt-I command allows you to select a filespec that is in the file you are viewing. You position the cursor to the filespec on the screen, and press enter to add it to the list of files to display.

The Alt-V command displays a list of files in the current directory. You move the cursor to a file that you want to display, and press enter to add that file to the list.

Summary of file review commands:

Q	display next file, if any
Z	display previous file
1	display first selected file
Ctrl-PgUp	display previous file
Ctrl-PgDn	display next file
1	restart displaying with first file
Alt-F	prompt for new filename or filespec to display
Alt-I	Insert a filespec that is displayed
Alt-V	select a file from a menu

Windows

LIST can display data in one or two parts of the screen called windows. The Alt-W command toggles this split screen mode. Entering Alt-W while the screen is split restores the display to a single, full-sized display.

In the regular version, the screen is split in the middle. The top half of the screen remains the same, and the bottom half becomes the part of the screen where files are displayed. Thus, the top window becomes a scratch pad.

In the LIST PLUS version, you are allowed to split the screen at any point. After entering Alt-W, you are asked to position the cursor to the spot where the screen will be split. By placing the cursor in column 1, you can adjust how many lines will be used by the top and bottom windows. This would be a vertical, or one window above the other, split.

By positioning the cursor to the top line with the HOME key, you can then use the left- and right-arrow keys to adjust how wide each of the windows is to be. This would be a horizontal, or side-by-side, split.

You may display a different file in each window, and move between them. You use the Ctrl-V command to switch from one window to the other. You may also use the Review commands to display a different file in the second window. The Ctrl-V command has no effect unless you are viewing two or more files (i.e., a different file in each window).

Each window uses different colors. You can use the color commands to set the colors that you like, and then use the Alt-C command to save them.

Note: Please see the file LIST.DOC for sections omitted here.

Command Key Summary

Cursor keys:

Cursor key	Function
left arrow	scroll left 10 columns
right arrow	scroll right 10 columns
up arrow	up one (previous) line
down arrow	down one (next) line
Enter	continue to next page
END	position to end of file (bottom)
ESCape	Exit program unconditionally
HOME	restart from first line (top)
PgUp	scroll up one page, 23 lines
PgDn	scroll down one page, 23 lines

Function keys:

Function key	Function
F1	Displays the HELP screen.
F3	Find NEXT occurrence of text after Scan or Find.
F9	Find the PREVIOUS occurrence of text.
F10	Exit to DOS.

For changing display colors:

F2	Change background color for Find/Scan text
F4	Change foreground color for Find/Scan text
F5	Change background color for main body of display
F6	Change foreground color for main body of display
F7	Change background color for top and bottom lines
F8	Change foreground color for top and bottom lines

Letter Keys

The Letter key commands are mnemonic. That is, the letter in some way indicates what the command does.

Letter(s)	Function
A	Find next occurrence of 'text' (Again)
B	Skip to end of file (Bottom)
C	Toggles continuous scrolling
D	Scroll down one page
F	Find 'text' regardless of case
G	Get new filename/filespec (also Alt-F)
H	Display the Help screen
K	Toggles keyboard key-ahead
L	Scroll Left 10 columns
M	Toggles Monitor retrace testing to eliminate snow
N	Down one (Next) line
P	Toggles the printing of displayed lines
Q	Quits current file and displays next file, if any
R	Scroll Right 10 columns command
S	Scan for exact text match, case dependent
T	Restart from first line (Top)
U	Scroll Up one page (23 lines)
W	Toggles the Wrap option for displaying long lines
X	Terminate, clear screen, and eXit to DOS
Z	Display the previous file
7	Toggles the 7-bit filter
8	Toggles the 8-bit filter
*	Toggles the star filter
+	Position a given number of lines forward
-	Position a given number of lines backward
?	Displays the Help screen
space	Scrolls down one page
\	text Find any case 'text' going forward
/	text Scan exact case 'text' going forward
' or ^	Find any case 'text' going backward
' or v	Find exact case 'text' going backward

Control- keys:

The Ctrl- key commands are entered by pressing the Ctrl key at the same time as you press one of the following letter keys:

Ctrl- key	Function
Ctrl-HOME	Position to a specific line by number
Ctrl-PgDn	Display next file
Ctrl-PgUp	Display previous file
Ctrl-left	Reset display to column 1 (i.e., scroll full left)
Ctrl-right	Scroll full right (to the end of the current line)
Ctrl-A	Scroll full left
Ctrl-C	Display next page, scroll down
Ctrl-D	Scroll right 10 columns
Ctrl-E	Display previous line, scroll up 1 line
Ctrl-F	Send a form feed control character to the printer
Ctrl-H **	Hang up the telephone
Ctrl-N	Display previous file
Ctrl-P	Print the entire file
Ctrl-R	Display previous page, scroll up
Ctrl-S	Scroll left 10 columns
Ctrl-T **	Dial a telephone number
Ctrl-U	Display previous file
Ctrl-V **	Switch display windows
Ctrl-W	Display previous line, scroll up one line
Ctrl-Y **	Save current line number as bookmark line for a–Y
Ctrl-X	Display next line, scroll down one line

Alt- keys:

The Alt- key commands are entered by pressing the Alt key at the same time as you press one of the following letter keys:

Alt- key	Function
Alt-A	Search for next occurrence of text, continue to next file until found.
Alt-B	Mark bottom line of display.
Alt-C	Copy options and setting to LIST.COM.
Alt-D	Write marked lines, or found line, to a file.
Alt-E	Toggle 25 or 43/50 line display with EGA or VGA.
Alt-F	Enter additional filenames to display.
Alt-G	Goto DOS temporarily to enter DOS commands.
Alt-I **	Insert a filespec from the screen display.
Alt-H	Toggle Hex display mode.
Alt-J	Toggle the "junk" filter.
Alt-L	Toggle preloading of files.
Alt-M	Mark the line at the top of the display.
Alt-N	Toggle the Alt-X screen-saving feature.
Alt-O	Write marked lines, or found line, to the same file. Used by Alt-D.
Alt-R	Toggle the display of a ruler line on top line.
Alt-S	Toggle the file Sharing option.
Alt-T	Toggle the TAB control character filer.
Alt-U	Unmark lines marked by Alt-M and Alt-B.
Alt-V **	Invoke the File Selection Menu.
Alt-W	Toggle split screen.
Alt-X	Exit to DOS and display the original screen.
Alt-Y	Reposition to the last *active* line (bookmark).
Alt-Z	Toggles the command line in the bottom line. The default is to display the cursor key usage. Using Alt-Z changes the bottom line to show the option switches "Toggles:" settings.

Limitations

- The LIST.COM program requires about 64K of memory. If more memory is available, it is used to store more of the file in memory. At least 80K is required to use the DOS Shell, and 9K more is required if the screen-saving option (on by default) is enabled.

- The line number is currently limited to 16 million.
- The file size is limited to 16 million bytes for ASCII files, and 4 million bytes for hex-dump files. Versions for larger files are available to licensed users.

- The review limit is 32 files for the regular and Plus versions. The bookmark limit is 10 entries.
- PC DOS Version 2.0 or later is required. DOS version 3.0 or later is required for file sharing.
- ANSI.SYS is *not* required.

THE BUERG UTILITIES Registration Form

Name: _____

Company: _____

Address: _____

City: _____

State: _____ Country: _____

Zip: _____ Phone: _____

Remit to:
Buerg Software
139 White Oak Circle
Petaluma, CA 94952

(707) 778-1811 from 10a.m. to 7p.m. Pacific time, M-F.

CompuServe: 70007,1212 Forums: IBMAPP, IBMCOM, IBMHW, IBMNEW, IBMPRO, IBMSYS, and HAMNET

Data/BBS: (707) 778-8944, -or- (707) 778-8841, 24-hour bulletin board systems FAX: (707) 778-8728

The registered version of LIST Plus is $37 plus appropriate postage. You receive a disk with the latest version, notification of updates, and a printed manual.

The commercial (retail) program LIST Enhanced is $99 plus shipping and may NOT be copied or distributed.

Copies of the "Buerg Utilities" disk set for personal use may be obtained on 5.25"/1.2MB or 3.5"/1.44MB diskettes for $60 plus shipping.

The above products may be ordered by sending check, money, or credit card information with the "Mailer" included with this file. Or you may order with a credit card by phone.

Please send me the following:

LIST Plus, Version 7, registration (disk, manual, notification of major updates)
   each .... $37.00 $ _____
     Shipping and Handling each:
     U.S. & Canada .... $3.00 $ _____
     Other .... $5.00 $ _____
LIST Enhanced, Version 1.8, commercial package (dual media, 160-page manual in slipcase, quick reference card)
   each .... $99.00 $ _____
     Shipping and Handling each:
     U.S. .... $6.00 $ _____
     Canada .... $12.00 $ _____
     Other .... $24.00 $ _____
Complete Buerg Utilities (includes registered LIST Plus, 1.2MB/1.44MB disks only)
   each .... $60.00 $ _____
     Shipping and Handling each:
     U.S. & Canada .... $3.00 $ _____
     Other .... $5.00 $ _____
California sales tax .... 7.5% $ _____
TOTAL .... $ _____

Specify Disk Size: ❑ 5.25" 360K ❑ 3.5" 720K
❑ 5.25" 1.2MB ❑ 3.5" 1.44MB

Payment by:
  ❑ Check ❑ Money Order
  ❑ Visa ❑ Master Card ❑ Discover
  Check or Money Order payable to Buerg
  Software in U.S. funds.

Authorized Signature: _____

Expiration Date: _____

Card Number: _____

Patriquin's Hard Disk Utilities

Copyright © 1987–1992 by Norm Patriquin, Patri-Soft

Overview

The Patri-Soft Utilities were developed out of my own need for enhancements to commands that are provided with DOS. I found that DOS commands did not provide me with functions I commonly needed or options I felt were obviously necessary for normal system maintenance. For example, the DOS COPY command fails to warn you before overlaying a file with the same name. I was hurt by this flaw once too many times and decided to develop my own alternative.

Basically, the Patri-Soft Utilities all function in a way you would expect them to. For instance, PCOPY works just like DOS COPY. Without any additional parameters, it will copy files like DOS, except some safeguards are implemented. To override the safeguards, or to use an addi-

tional feature, specify additional parameter switches.

Note: The following utilities are included with this book: PCOPY, PDAILY, and PDELETE. Others are mentioned on the order form. Contact Patri-Soft for additional information on the utilities not included here.

Program and Documentation Files

By default, the install program for the *DOS 6 SECRETS* diskettes will install all of the Patriquin files in the directory \SECRETS \PATRUTIL. This directory has not been added to the search path. You can execute the program from its home directory, add the directory to the search path, or copy the Patriquin files to a directory that is included in the search path.

PCOPY

Copyright © 1987–1992 by Patri-Soft

Introduction

PCOPY is an advanced replacement for the DOS COPY command — one of the most used of the DOS commands. Unfortunately, the DOS COPY abilities are very limited and are not sufficient for many disk maintenance chores. PCOPY is similar to the DOS COPY command in that it copies file data between disks and hard disk directories. In addition, PCOPY provides intelligent file selection and processing options. PCOPY options allow you to use a single PCOPY command to perform a function that would require many complex DOS COPY commands.

PCOPY also provides a safer way to copy files than that provided by the DOS COPY command. It allows you to copy only newer files or update a directory with the contents of another. PCOPY will never allow you to overlay a file unknowingly.

PCOPY allows you to specify standard DOS wildcard pathnames in the source file specifications, and standard pathnames for the target directory specification.

PCOPY attempts to anticipate your needs and then help you accomplish your intent. For instance, if PCOPY determines that the target directory name does not exist, it will ask you if it is to be created. If you respond <YES>, PCOPY will create the directory. With the /SAve option, if you are about to overlay a file with another file with the same name, you will be asked if the older duplicate file is to be renamed with a version number.

The PCOPY.DOC file contains a section outlining all changes for all releases of PCOPY. If you already have a current release, this file will let you identify the changes since the version you have.

This archive should contain the following files:

PCOPY.EXE	PCOPY execution file.
PMOVE.BAT	A batch file to be used with PCOPY. Causes files to be deleted from the source location after they have been copied.
PCOPY.DOC	PCOPY documentation file. Use the following command to print PCOPY documentation.
	`COPY PCOPY.DOC PRN:`
PCREADME	A file to explain the contents of PCOPY system.
ORDER.FRM	Text form for ordering PCOPY. Use the following command to print this file.
	`COPY ORDER.FRM PRN:`

The PMOVE Option of PCOPY

PMOVE is an option of the PCOPY command you can use to move files between disks and directories on disks. PMOVE combines the functions of DOS COPY and DELETE commands to simplify the moving of files. In addition to just moving files, PMOVE also allows you to specify selection criteria to better qualify the files to be moved.

PMOVE automatically determines the environment in which the move is requested and determines if the data must be physically moved or if it can be moved by simply renaming it. The file will be moved by renaming it if the move is to another directory on the same disk device. This is much faster than physically moving the file. In addition, it reduces free space fragmentation, and allows you to move very large files between directories when they could not otherwise be moved with DOS COPY because of insufficient space.

The only difference between PCOPY and PMOVE is that PMOVE removes the file from the source location after it has been successfully copied to the target location.

PMOVE is implemented as a .BAT file that invokes PCOPY with the /X parameter.

PCOPY Features

- Copies files to and from any disk or directory.
- Allows you to save older versions of files with new names before replacing them.
- Moves files by copying them or renaming them to the new location.
- Deletes the original file if /X is specified.
- Creates target directories if needed.
- Makes sure the DOS archive flag is set correctly for each file as it is moved.
- Preserves the DOS date and time for each file moved.
- Allows you to pause processing at any time by pressing any keyboard key. Once stopped, the program can be terminated by pressing <ESC>.
- Provides file selection and processing control options to tailor the move process to your own needs.
- Allows commands to be tested so you may be sure that commands are specified as you desire.
- Copies updated files to a special disk or directory.
- If there is not sufficient space on the current target disk, PCOPY allows you to place another disk in the drive and continue processing. This lets you copy groups of files larger than disk size to other computers.
- Start with a specific file in a directory.
- End with a specific file in a directory.
- Process files based on the date stored in the directory entry.
- Warns you before overlaying a file unless specific parameters indicating otherwise are specified.
- Checks target disk for available space before starting to copy files. This saves time when the copy will not be able to be completed.
- Gives you constant status of the progress of the command.
- Runs with windows or using standard DOS screen output.

- Format new floppy disks as they are needed by pressing <F3> at any prompt.
- Process one directory, a single directory subtree, or all directories on a disk (/S).
- Allows you to indicate that multiple input disks are to be used and prompts for the next one after each disk is processed.
- Create a series of output disks filled efficiently with files from the source location. DOS ERRORLEVEL set to indicate error conditions. PCOPY may be used in .BAT files to copy files, and you may confirm results are good.
- Special wildcard matching allows you to select all files with specific text in filename.

PCOPY Command and Parameters

PCOPY lets you specify command parameters to qualify the copy criteria. These parameters are optional. If no parameters are specified, PCOPY performs in a manner similar to the DOS COPY command, except that it prompts you before overlaying files. The command format and parameters are described as follows.

```
PCOPY from_file [to_file]
    [(/ parameters)]
```

[from]   Enter the DOS file specification for the directory and filenames to be moved. The filename portion of the file specification may contain wildcard characters documented by DOS (* and ?).

You may also specify special pattern selection for text. For example, *DISK*.* would select all files that have the characters **DISK** anywhere in the first portion of the filename. *DI*S*K*.* type specification also works.

You may optionally supply a file containing a list of input filenames. Create a file containing a filename or complete pathname on each line. Specify the name of this file as the source filename to PCOPY and add the @ character before the name. The list of files will be processed as if they were all specified on the input command line.

For file list processing, PCOPY understands the output of the DOS DIR command. You may use the DOS redirection feature to direct DIR output to a file, edit the file to add or remove entries, and then provide this to PCOPY as input. For example:

```
DIR A: >DIRLIST
(edit dirlist)
PCOPY @DIRLIST B:
```

[to]   Enter the DOS file specification for the directory and filename to be copied to. If the *to* specification is not entered, files will be moved to the current directory.

If a single level name is supplied as the last part of the target file specification, PCOPY will search for a directory that matches the specified name. If it does not exist, PCOPY will prompt you to determine if the name is a filename or a directory name. To avoid this prompt, append the name with a \ if it is a directory name, or a . to indicate it is a filename. For example:

```
PCOPY *.* C:\DIRNAME\ PCOPY
    *.* C:\FILENAME.
```

/4   4DOS support. PCOPY will copy and insert the appropriate 4DOS descriptions when copying files.

/A   Archive. Selects only files that have been marked updated by DOS. This flag is updated by DOS whenever a file is processed with an intent to change or create new data.

/AF   Assume that the target specified is a File. This will suppress PCOPY's prompt if the target does not exist.

/AD   As above, except Assume Directory.

/AP   APpend. All source files selected will be concatenated and placed together in a single output file. The output file will be given the name of the first or only selected input file, or the target filename specified.

If a target filename already exists when append is specified, all source files copied will be appended to the target file. To cause an already existing target file to be replaced by the copied files, also specify the /R parameter.

To combine 3 files into one with /AP, use a command like the following:

```
PCOPY FILE1,FILE2,FILE3
      NEWFILE /AP/R
```

/AZ   Append text files removing Ctrl-Z characters. Like /AP except Ctrl-Z characters will be removed from the end of all but the last file copied.

/B   Backup. When specified, the DOS ARCHIVE attribute is reset after a file has been copied.

/BA   BAtch processing. Normally, PCOPY will pause if you press any key during processing. This can interfere with programs that store keystrokes in the keyboard buffer for subsequent activity. The /BA parameter sets "no-windows" mode and disables the "key press" check to leave stored keystrokes undisturbed.

/BW   Black and white. Forces PCOPY to use monochrome colors even when it detects a color display environment.

/CD:xxx   This parameter allows PCOPY to invoke any command of your choice for each file PCOPY selects. With this parameter, PCOPY will not copy your data. It simply becomes a file selection utility.

To use this parameter you must supply the command PCOPY is to execute. To be compatible with DOS command-line option specifications, you must use special substitution characters to build a command to your specifications.

The following special characters are used:

\#   Is replaced with the full pathname of the file to be processed.

\$ Is replaced with the filename of the file selected.

@   Is replaced with the target filename PCOPY would have copied the file to, if the COPY operation was active.

[Is replaced with a single space character.

]   Is replaced with a backslash character (\).

}   Is replaced with a slash (/) character. This must be used to allow a command to include / parameters, since PCOPY will interpret a slash as one of its own parameters.

PCOPY can be used to drive an EDIT command with variable parameters. The following is an example:

```
PCOPY *.c/d:)1jan89
/cd:EDIT[#[}F[}pf:]log
```

Assuming file C:\COMP\TEST.C was selected, the following command would result.

```
EDIT C:\COMP\TEST.C /F
/PF:\LOG
```

To execute the command, PCOPY invokes a second copy of the DOS command processor. When the /CD parameter is used, PCOPY forces operation without windows to eliminate screen flashing between commands.

/CF:path   This parameter alters the meaning of the /CD parameter. When specified with a full DOS pathname (including the filename), it causes PCOPY to write all generated commands to the specified file. The commands will not be executed by PCOPY. This allows you to generate a .BAT file that can be modified and executed at a later time.

For example, to generate commands and place them in batch file DOIT.BAT:

```
PCOPY *.c/d:)1jan89
    /cd:EDIT[#[}F[}pf:]log
    /CF:DOIT.BAT
```

/C2 /C3 Specify /C2 or /C3 to use different colors when PCOPY is used with windows operation. To make this color change permanent, specify the parameter in the DOS environment variable.

/D:[(]xxx date Select files based on their last update date. This parameter may include a date or a number of days value, and optionally a condition modifier that changes the use of the date or number of days specified.

When xxx contains a valid date, the date is compared to the last update date of the file, contained in its directory entry. The file is selected if the condition specified by the condition modifier is met. The condition modifier meanings are

(File date is older than that specified.

)   File date is newer than that specified.

=   File date is equal to that specified.

If the condition modifier is not specified,) is assumed. Date values may be specified in any of the following formats:

MM/DD/YY   12/31/80
MM-DD-YY   12-31-80
DDMMMYY   31DEC80

If xxx contains a numeric value instead of a valid date, that positive number is used to calculate a date value. The new date value

becomes the current date minus the number of days specified by the numeric value in xxx. Then that date is used as in the calculation above.

The /D: parameter may be specified twice to select files between two dates (date ranges). /D:(1FEB90/D:)1MAR90

When two dates are specified, a file's date must qualify selection based on both date parameters. Specify the /DO parameter to indicate an OR condition between the dates. This will allow any file meeting either date parameter to be selected for processing.

/D- Delete all files on target drive before starting copy.

/D2 Add files to those already on the first output disk. Then delete all files from subsequent disks provided before copying to them. Use /D2 when you want to append files to a set of already existing disks. This parameter allows you to continue backing up to a partially used disk and then reuse disks containing old unwanted backup files.

/DC & DCA Directory Copy. PCOPY will create a duplicate directory on the output disk for every directory processed on the source disk. Directories are only created when files are to be copied to them. See also the /S option. This is useful for copying all files and directories from one disk to another.

Specify /DCA (Directory Copy-All) to copy all directories from source to target drive, even when no files will be moved to the new directory.

/DL Same as /DC except that only the last node of the source directory is copied to the target pathname specified.

/DO   Specify when two /D: date parameters are used. Indicates either date parameter may be met to qualify a file for processing. See also the /D: parameter.

/DR:xxx   Drive. Use to process multiple disk drives. /DR assumes the presence of the /S parameter, which indicates to process all directories on the source disks. If you are using PCOPY for backup, this lets you process all disk drives with a single command.

          The following command will copy all modified files from hard drives C:, D:, and E: to the floppy disk in drive A:. The /D2 parameter will ensure each new output disk is cleared of all files before it is written to.<shift right 44> <alt T><alt C><tab 3><down 6>t<enter>

```
PCOPY *.* A: /DR:CDE/A/D2
```

/DS   Same as /DC except that only the current directory level and all its subordinate levels are copied to the target directory. The target directory may contain a pathname with multiple directory levels, so you can copy one directory structure below another directory structure.

/DX   When target names are single level names with no extensions, PCOPY will ask you if the name refers to a directory or to a new file to be created. If you specify this parameter, PCOPY assumes names without extensions are new directory names.

/DY   Synchronize source and target directory files. Before copying the first file to any directory, PCOPY will determine if any files exist in the target directory but not on the source directory. If so, PCOPY will remove those files from the target directory. Use this parameter when you want to update one directory or disk to be exactly like another.

IMPORTANT!!

PCOPY has the ability to synchronize an entire drive by traversing the directories, deleting directory trees and files that are on the target but not the source. This feature is utilized by a careful combination of switches. Relevant switches are /S, /DC, and /U. Situations vary, so we have forced the /TF (Test First) on PCOPY when you use /DY. To override this Test, use the /TO parameter. BE SURE THE TEST PRODUCES THE DESIRED RESULTS BEFORE DOING IT FOR REAL! If you have any questions, or need a customized command line, feel free to call the Patri-Soft technical support line, (714) 352-2820.

To synchronize two drives:

```
PCOPY C:\ D:\ /DY/S/DC
```

To synchronize two directories:

```
PCOPY C:\UT D:\UT /DY
```

To synchronize a drive and a target dir tree:

```
PCOPY C:\ D:\BACKUP /S/DC/DY
```

/E   Select and move only files that exist in both the source and target directories. This allows you to replace all duplicate named files.

/EQ   Designed for batch file operation. Use this parameter to prevent PCOPY from requiring you to press a key to terminate processing (Exit Quick).

          Note: Previous versions of PCOPY supported this option using the /EX. Parameter.

/EX   Exclude files. The exclude facility allows you to provide a list of pathname and filename specifications that are to be excluded from PCOPY processing. Since searching through data on your hard disk requires extensive processing and disk read time, excluding files from the process will save you time, and will reduce the number of false matches displayed for your requests.

          The exclude facility is implemented with two actions. First, you will need to create an exclude specification file and place it in the same directory where PCOPY is installed on your hard disk. This file will contain the names of all the files and paths to be excluded. Name the file PCOPY.EXC.

You may specify DOS pattern names to exclude groups of files with a single specification. Like DOS, use the '*' to indicate the last part of a filename or filename extension may be any set of characters. Also like DOS, use the '?' to indicate that any single position of a filename may be any character.

In addition to DOS, two additional pattern features are available. You may place an '*' anywhere in the filename to indicate any set of characters may exist in this point in the name. For pathnames, you may place an '**' at the end of a directory path specification to indicate the specification applies to the specified directory and all subordinate directories. Using '**', you can exclude an entire path with a single specification.

Following are examples:

1. *.EXE
2. *.COM
3. TEST*.*
4. *TEST*.*
5. DO?FIX.*
6. PC*XX.*
7. C:\DOS*.*
8. \TEST*.*
9. D:\GAMES***.*

Explanations for the above examples:

1. Excludes all filenames with the extension .EXE from processing.
2. Excludes all filenames ending with extension .COM.
3. Excludes all filenames beginning with the letters "TEST" from processing.
4. Excludes all filenames having the characters "TEST" anywhere in the first portion of the filename.
5. Exclude files having 'DO' as the first 2 characters of the filename, and 'FIX' as the 4th, 5th, and 6th filename characters. The 3rd character of the filename may be any character.
6. Exclude files having a name beginning with the 2 characters PC and where the first portion of the filename ends with the characters 'XX.' Any 0 to 4 characters may exist between the 'PC' and 'XX' in the first portion of the filename.
7. Exclude all files from the DOS directory on drive C:.
8. Exclude all files from the TEST directory existing on any drive searched.
9. Exclude all files from the D:\GAMES\ directory and also exclude all files and directories subordinate to the GAMES directory.

Activating exclude —

Exclude will only be functional when the /EX command parameter is specified. When /EX is specified, you must have a valid exclude file. PCOPY will not continue without one. If you wish exclude to be active during all executions, specify /EX as part of the PCOPY= DOS environment variable. See later in the documentation for a description of this feature.

/F:file

First. Do not start processing until the specified filename is encountered in the source directory. This parameter is useful for restarting a move or copy that has been terminated. You may specify DOS pattern name characters * and ? to identify the file to begin processing.

/FI Fill.

Fill output disks as efficiently as possible. Normally, files are copied in the sequence in which they are found in the source directory. If a large file cannot be copied onto the output disk, a new disk is requested even though there may be enough space left on the output disk to hold other smaller files. The /FI parameter causes files to be copied in descending size sequence. When the next file will not fit on the output disk, PCOPY searches for another file that will fit on the disk before requesting a new output disk. When a new disk is placed in the drive, PCOPY begins processing the larger files again. Eventually, all files requested will be copied.

/FL

PCOPY's automatic disk formatting senses the drive type and will format the disk, if necessary, accordingly. If you want to format a low density disk in a high density drive, use this parameter.

/FO

Format Off. This turns off PCOPY's automatic disk formatting/checking.

/IFA: pathname

Check to determine that the source file does not already exist in an alternate directory before processing it. If it does not exist, processing will continue. Use just like IFP specified as follows.

/IFP: pathname

Determine if the source file to be copied already exists in the pathname specified by IFP. If it does exist, process the file. If it does not exist, skip the file. For example,

```
PCOPY *.BAT \newdir
        /IFP:\testdir
```

copies files from the current directory to \NEWDIR only if each file already exists in \TESTDIR.

/L:file

Last. Stop processing after the specified filename is encountered in the scan of the directory. The file specified will be processed if it matches selection criteria. You may specify DOS pattern name characters * and ? to identify the file to begin processing.

/LG

LoG activities. PCOPY will create a disk log of all actions it takes. This is useful if you are using PCOPY as a backup system. The log will help you locate the disk on which a file has been backed up.

The log file will be named PCOPY.LOG. For DOS versions 3.0 or later, the log will be created in the same directory from which PCOPY is executed. Other DOS versions will put the log in the current directory.

If the log does not exist, PCOPY will create it. If the log does exist, PCOPY will add to it. To begin a new log, delete PCOPY.LOG before running PCOPY.

/M

More. Stop the screen from scrolling past the end without user intervention.

/ME

MErge. Works like using /U and /X parameters to move the most current files from one directory into another. In addition, it deletes all the files that are not moved. This effectively merges the most current files from two directories into a single directory.

/MU

MUltiple. Process multiple input disks. After the first input disk is processed, PCOPY will prompt you for additional disks. Indicate <Y> to process more disks or <N> to terminate processing.

/N

New files. Only move files that do not already exist on the target directory. If the file already exists, do not move it.

/NA   No Archive. Only process files that do not have the DOS ARCHIVE attribute set in the directory entry. With this parameter specified, PCOPY will only process those files that have already been backed up. Files not backed up will not be processed.

/NP   No Pause. Use when you have made the /P parameter the default action with the SET PCOPY=/P command in the DOS environment, and want to override it.

/NW   No Windows. PCOPY will not use windows during processing. All screen output will be done through standard DOS facilities.

/O: Omit. Specify a list of filename
filename-   patterns that are to be omitted
list   (excluded) from PCOPY processing. If multiple filename patterns are specified, separate them with commas. For example:

          /O:*.BAK,*.EXE,TEST*.*

/P   Pause before each file is moved and ask for approval to process it.

/QA:x   Quit After process x number of files. This can be useful if you only want to process a certain number of files.

/R   Replace any duplicate files on the target disk or directory. PCOPY will replace files regardless of file dates and times.

/RD   Reset Date. Normally, PCOPY retains the original date and time of a file when copying it. With /RD specified, the copied file will have the current date.

/RE   REgister the program. Use this option to register your copy of the PCOPY utility. You will need to have the registration number and code that is sent to you after you request registration.

When you specify this parameter, part of the registration screen also allows you to modify the

windows option permanently. If you do not want windows during processing, use this option to change the windows program option. You do not need to be registered to change this information.

/RO   Read Only. PCOPY is just like DOS COPY when it enounters RO files. PCOPY will copy the file, but does not copy the Read Only attribute. Using /RO places the Read Only attribute on the target file.

/S   System. If a source directory is supplied, that directory and all subordinate directories will be processed. If no source directory is specified, all directories on the disk will be processed.

/SA   SAve. Instead of overlaying already existing files with duplicate names, PCOPY renames the file in the target directory with a version number before the new file is copied. This ensures that no data is lost. This facility can be used to save successive versions of a file in a directory.

If the file has an extension name, the last two characters of the extension are replaced with a number from 01 to 99, depending on the next available number. PCOPY determines the next available number by looking in the directory for other files with similar names. /SF System Files. Normally, PCOPY skips files marked with the DOS SYSTEM attribute. Using /SF causes SYSTEM files to be selected for processing.

/SHx   File sharing options.

/SHA Ignore file sharing and copy all files.

/SHR Allow files opened for read to be copied.

/SHN Disallow all file sharing.

/SP   Split files. /SP indicates PCOPY is to split a file onto another disk if there is insufficient room on the first disk.

/SP:nnn Split a file nnn characters into the file. If disk space permits, both parts of the split file will remain in the target directory.

/SPL:nnn Split a file at line number nnn. This can be useful for breaking a file into parts for editing.

Split File Parameters:

You may split a file into two or more parts with PCOPY. This is useful for copying files larger than a diskette will hold, or for dividing files into smaller parts for editing. PCOPY identifies the file parts by replacing the second character of the file's extension with a number. For example, PCOPY.EXE could be split into PCOPY.E1E and PCOPY.E2E.

The time field of the first part of a split file holds the replaced extension character. For this reason, PCOPY can only automatically rejoin an unmodified split file. Just reference the first part of the split file, and the rest will be copied. You may also rejoin files using DOS COPY or PCOPY explicit commands on each part of a split file, as follows:

Rejoining Split File with DOS COPY:

```
COPY /B FILENM.E1E+
    FILENM+E2EFILENM.EXE
```

Rejoining Split File with PCOPY:

```
PCOPY A:\FILENM.E1E,A:
    \FILENM.E2E
    FILENM.EXE/SP
```

IMPORTANT! PCOPY cannot split files into more than NINE parts.

/SS:nnn Terminate processing when the source drive's freespace reaches the value specified by the /SS parameter. Use when moving files from one drive to another using the /X parameter. The command

PCOPY C:*.* D: /X/SS:1000000 will cause PCOPY to move files from drive C: to drive D: until the freespace on source drive C: is greater than or equal to 1,000,000 characters.

/ST:nnn Terminate processing when the target drive's freespace becomes less than or equal to the value specified by the /ST: parameter. The command PCOPY C:*.* d: /ST:500000 will cause PCOPY to copy files to target drive D: until drive D: has less than or equal to 500,000 characters freespace.

/SZ: [(] [)] nnn Select a file based on its size. The (indicates that files less than the indicated size are to be selected. The) indicates to select files greater than the size. If neither is specified, (is assumed.

/T Test. Test the command without actually updating any files. Issue messages to indicate what will happen if the command is executed without the /T parameter.

/TO When using the /DY parameter, PCOPY forces /TF. Use this to override the test.

/T:[(][)] [=]xxx Time. Select files based on the relationship between their last update time and the time specified in the command. The /T: parameter may also contain an operator that reverses or modifies the meaning of the time specified, just like the date parameter.

Examples of /T:xxx Parameter

1. Process files updated before 11:20 a.m.

   /T:(11:20a or /T:(11:20

2. Process files updated before 11:20 p.m.

   /T:(11:20p or /T:(23:20
   —> military time

3. Process files updated after 11:20 p.m.

   /T:)11:20p

4. Process files updated within 60 seconds after 11:21 p.m.

`/T:=11:21p`

5. Leading zeros in hour may be omitted.

`/T:)1:20`

/TF   Test First. Works similar to the /T parameter, but after test processing is complete, PCOPY will ask you if you want to execute the command as if the /T parameter were not present. If you respond <Y>, the command will be executed and files will actually be processed.

/U   Update files. Only copy files that do not exist on the target directory or duplicate filenames that are newer than their counterparts on the target directory or disk. Specifying this option results in the most current version of each selected file being in the target directory.

/V   Verify. Use the DOS VERIFY option while copying data. This causes all data to be reread after it is written to disk to ensure it was written properly.

/WH   WHy. Indicate why files are not selected for processing. Normally, PCOPY will not show filenames that are not selected for processing. Specifying /WH will cause PCOPY to display a message indicating why any file was not selected for processing.

/WT   Wait. Wait for disk to be mounted before beginning processing. This parameter is intended primarily for systems with floppy disks. Before beginning the copy process, PCOPY will ask you to place the proper disks in the drives. This allows you to have PCOPY on a different disk than the disks being processed.

/X   Move files. This parameter changes PCOPY's function to move files instead of copying them. After the file is copied, it will be deleted from the source location. If the file is moved to another directory on the same disk, the directory entry for the file is updated, but the actual data is not moved. This provides for the fastest move possible.

PCOPY Menu Operation

When you start PCOPY without command-line specifications, it displays a menu for entering copy specifications. Three menus are available for specification of options. You proceed forward and backward through the menus by pressing the <PgUp> and <PgDn> keys. Once you are completed specifying options, press <F10> to start processing. Press <ESCape> at any time to exit from PCOPY. If you need PCOPY help for batch operation, press <F1>.

You may save a particular combination of menu specifications for use at a later time by assigning copy profile names to them. PCOPY saves up to four different copy profiles. To use these in a subsequent execution of PCOPY, simply select one of the saved names from the menu. All options on the menus will be set to reflect the contents of the saved profile options.

Menu options are specified in one of two ways. First, you may be asked to key specific parameter information into parameter fields. Second, you select toggle options by positioning the highlight bars over options specified and pressing the <Enter> key. PCOPY will only allow compatible options to be specified, so turning on some options may automatically deactivate others. You see this happen when watching highlighted options.

Use the up- and down-arrow keys or the tab keys to move from option to option. A short help line is provided at the bottom of the display to assist you in understanding each option. It changes as you move the cursor from option to option on the display.

First menu of PCOPY

■ Copy Profile

An area is provided for you to provide an optional copy profile name to be associated with these parameters. Provide a 1–8 character name. The parameters specified for this process will be saved and associated with this profile name.

To the right of the name field are names for up to four copy profiles previously saved. To use the parameters of any one of these profiles, press <1>, <2>, <3>, or <4>. The menu will automatically change to reflect the saved specifications.

■ From Path

Enter the file specification for files to be copied. The same rules apply as for command-line specifications. See that section of this document for details. Following are examples:

```
C:\DIRNAME\*.EXE
\DIRNAME\*.EXE
\DIRname
*.exe
```

■ Drives

Enter additional drives to be searched for the path specification in From Path above.

■ To Path

Specify the target location where files are to be copied. Following are examples:

```
C:
C:\DIRNAME
C:\DIRNAME\FILENAME
```

■ Process Options

COPY MOVE TEST VERIFY WRITES

Highlight the MOVE or COPY action to take. TEST mode causes PCOPY to execute without really copying data. Use TEST to check that your parameters are correct (/TF ,/X, /V).

■ Multiple Directories?

ENTIRE DISK ALL SUBORDINATE DIRECTORIES

Indicate what directories are to be read to find files to be processed. SUBORDINATE DIRECTORIES indicates to read the current directory and all of its subordinate directories to find files to process (/S, /DS).

■ Directory Actions?

CREATE NEW CREATE ALL CREATE/ADD LASTNODE MERGE SYNCHRONIZE

Specify actions to be taken at the directory level.

CREATE NEW — Automatically create directories needed on the output disk (/DC).

CREATE ALL — Automatically create directories for every directory read on the source disk (/DCA).

LASTNODE — Use the last directory level from the source disk, and append it to the directory name on the target disk. This creates a new directory structure under the target directory specification (/DL).

MERGE — Merge files from the source specification into the target directory. Delete old or exact duplicate files from the source location. Replace newer duplicate files on the target location (/ME).

■ File Filtering?

NEW & MORE RECENT FILES ONLY NEW FILES PAUSE/ASK FOR EACH FILE MARKED FOR BACKUP READONLY HIDDEN SYSTEM

Indicate selection criteria for files to be processed:

NEW — Copy files that do not exist on the target directory and files that exist but are newer.

ONLY NEW — Process files that do not already exist on the target directory (/N).

PAUSE/ASK — Stop and prompt for approval before processing each file (/P).

MARKED BK — Process files that have been modified since they were previously backed up (/A).

READONLY — Process files that have their readonly attribute set (/RO).

HIDDEN — Process files that have their hidden attribute set (/SF).

SYSTEM — Process files that have their system attribute set (/SF).

The second PCOPY menu. Access this menu by pressing <PgDn> from the first PCOPY menu.

The Second Menu of PCOPY Options

■ LIST FILES NOT PROCESSED

Show filenames matching the filename criteria but were not processed for other reasons. Indicates filename and the criteria that caused it to be skipped (/WH).

■ SET DOS FILE CHANGED INDICATOR AFTER COPY

After copying the file, reset the DOS attribute indicating the file needs backup (/BA).

■ SET DOS FILE DATE TO TODAY AFTER COPY

After copying the file, set the date and time on the file to the current date (/RD).

■ FILL OUTPUT DISKS EFFICIENTLY WITH BEST FIT

Process files in a sequence that will allow them to efficiently fit on output diskettes. PCOPY will find files to completely fill a disk before going on to additional disks (/FI).

■ ERASE OUTPUT DISKS BEFORE USING ERASE ON ALL BUT FIRST

Erase all files on target disks before copying files to them. 'ALL BUT FIRST' is normally used during backup to add files to the first backup disk used (the last one used for the previous backup run), and then erase all subsequent disks before copying to them (/D- , /D2).

■ APPEND COPIED FILES TOGETHER IN ONE OUTPUT FILE

All files being copied are to be merged into one output file. The output file is the filename specified on the target specification (/AP).

■ FILES MAY BE DIVIDED INTO PARTS ACROSS DISKS

Split files onto multiple disks if there is not enough room on the target diskette for the entire file to fit. See the /SP command-line parameter.

■ ASK FOR MULTIPLE INPUT DISKETTES

Causes PCOPY to ask for more input diskettes after the first diskette is processed.

Great when reading from a series of diskettes (/MU).

■ DISABLE SOUNDS DURING PROCESSING

Disables speaker beeps normally sounded to inform the user some action is needed (/SO).

The Third and Last PCOPY Menu

■ Select files by size

If a numeric value is specified, only files larger than (>) or smaller than (<) the value are processed. The numeric value must be preceded by < or > (/SZ:).

■ Select by date From Date: to Date:

If one or more dates are specified, only files having a date less than or greater than the dates specified will be selected for processing (/D:).

■ Stop when Source Drives freespace >

If a numeric value is specified, PCOPY will check the source drive's freespace before copying each file. If the drive's freespace is greater than the value specified, processing will stop. Use with MOVE option to empty a disk up to a specified level of freespace (/SS:).

■ Stop when Target Drives freespace <

If a numeric value is specified, PCOPY will check the target drive's freespace before copying each file. If the freespace is less than the value specified, processing will stop. Use to copy files to a disk until it has less than n characters free (/ST:).

■ Duplicate Files: REPLACE SAVE OLD COPY ONLY DUPLICATES

Indicate how to process files that already exist on the target directory.

REPLACE — Overlay files regardless of date/time (/R).

SAVE OLD — Rename the target file and then copy the source file to the directory. The new name will have a number placed in the file extension to indicate the version of the file (/SA).

ONLY DUPs — Select duplicate filenames for processing. Ignore all other files (/E).

■ Networks: NO FILE SHARING COPY
FILE BEING READ COPY ALL IN USE

When using PCOPY in network environments, indicate how PCOPY is to proceed when files are found to be in use by other tasks in progress.

NO SHARE   Skip files in use (/SHN).

READ   Process files being read by
            another task (/SHR).

ALL   Continue to process any file
            already in use (/SHA).

■ Process files in date sequence:
ADCENDING DESCENDING

Process files in date sequence. Use to copy the most recent files, or the oldest files to a target location (/SN, /SO).

Ways to Use PCOPY

1. Copy files from floppy disk to hard disk

   PCOPY is safer than DOS COPY when copying files to your system. It prevents you from accidently replacing a file with another of the same name.

   When PCOPY encounters a duplicate file, it will stop and ask if the file is to overlay the already existing one. You can tell PCOPY to REPLACE or UPDATE files with /R and /U command-line parameters.

   Following are samples of the simplest copy commands using PCOPY:

   If you are copying to the current directory on the hard disk:

       PCOPY A:*.*

   To copy to a specific directory:

       PCOPY A:*.* \SPECDIR

2. Taking changed files from work to home

   It is common to need to take files from home to work or vise versa. Since it is difficult to keep track of all the files you may have updated, it is convenient to let PCOPY find the updated files by copying all files updated within the last *n* days to a diskette. You reduce copy time by not copying an entire directory and are sure to get all newly changed files.

       PCOPY *.* A:/d:3 <== updated last
           3 days

       PCOPY *.* A:/D:)1DEC90 <== After
           date

3. Copy files modified before/after a time

   Sometimes the only way to identify recently changed files is by using the time they were updated. PCOPY can select files by time of day. You might use this option to determine what files were updated after 5:00 p.m. Remember, with the /T TEST option, PCOPY serves as a unique facility to locate and list files matching your selection criteria. PCOPY's unique selection facilities can be used to locate and list files. The /T option indicates to scan disks and simulate processing but do not actually move or change any data.

4. Quick move files to a new directory on the same hard disk

   Moving files with DOS requires two commands: COPY the data and then DEL the files from their original location. In addition to requiring two commands, it forces DOS to copy the data. If the file is larger than the available freespace on the hard disk, a copy of the data is not possible.

   PCOPY moves files to new directories on the same disk without having to physically copy the data. It simply moves the file reference to a new directory. Even huge files move in an instant!

       PCOPY \OLDDIR*.DAT \NEWDIR /X

5. Copy only duplicate files

   To update a directory with duplicate files from another directory or disk:

       PCOPY \FROMDIR1 A:*.* /E

6. Copy multiple groups of files by extension names

   Use PCOPY to process multiple file selection specifications with a single copy command. Separate each with a comma.

       PCOPY *.BAT,*.EXE,*.COM \EXEDIR

7. Copy files excluding files of one or more extension names

   The OMIT feature lets you exclude files from processing using command-line specifications. It is commonly used to exclude program files when copying to diskettes.

```
PCOPY *.* A: /O:*.EXE,*.BAT,*.COM
```

8. Copy files containing specific characters in their name

When you need to select or find files having a specific word in their names, but the filenames do not begin with the word, PCOPY can locate them.

Copy all files having names containing the 3 consecutive characters **ZIP**.

```
PCOPY *ZIP*.* \ZIPFILES
```

9. Display files having specific name

Use PCOPY to find all occurrences of files by name on a disk. PCOPY can scan a disk and display or process files from multiple directories. The /S (SCAN) parameter causes PCOPY to search all directories.

```
PCOPY *.DOC \TEST /S/T
```

10. Copy only newer files between disks and directories

One of the most common uses of PCOPY is to copy data between diskettes and hard disks. Use the update (/U) parameter to make sure only newer files are updated. Add the "WHY" (/WH) parameter to cause PCOPY to show any files that were not processed. Note that you can specify the target directory name without trailing \.

```
PCOPY A:*.* C:\NEWDIR /U/WH
```

11. Copy a disk including all directories to a new disk

PCOPY copies directories too. Simply specify the Directory Copy parameter (/DC). The file will be copied to the same directory name on the target drive. If the directory does not exist, it will automatically be created for you. Adding the Scan (/S) parameter causes PCOPY to scan all disks on the source drive. Using a combination of /S/DC, you can copy all files and directories from one disk to another.

Note: /DC only copies directories when files are to be copied into them. This ensures that unneeded directories are not also copied. To copy every directory even if no files are

copied, specify the All Directory Copy (/DCA) parameter instead of /DC.

```
PCOPY A:*.* F: /DC/S
```

12. Copy a directory and all subordinate directories

To copy or move files from a directory and all its subordinate directories use PCOPY's /DS parameter. The following example scans the directory C:\WP and any subordinate directories to copy all files having the extension name .TOM to a diskette.

```
PCOPY \WP\*.TOM A: /DS
```

13. Fill one or more diskettes from hard disk files

DOS COPY and XCOPY are unable to copy a set of files to multiple diskettes. When the first diskette is full, they stop.

PCOPY is not limited to copying to a single diskette. It detects when a disk is full and asks if the copy is to continue on to additional output diskettes. PCOPY also makes maximum use of diskette space.

When you are attempting to copy many files to diskettes for backup or transporting, you want to use as few diskettes as possible. The PCOPY Fill (/FI) parameter causes PCOPY to fill output diskettes without wasting space. With the /FI parameter, when PCOPY is unable to fit a file on an output diskette, it saves that filename for later processing and searches for another file that will fit on the disk. This results in significant savings in diskettes and time to process them.

```
PCOPY C:\WP\*.* A: /FI
```

14. Copy files larger than a floppy disk to multiple diskettes

Unlike DOS COPY and XCOPY, PCOPY can copy files larger than a diskette to multiple diskettes. This is accomplished by splitting large files into multiple parts. PCOPY only splits files when there is insufficient space on the output disk and when the split parameter is specified. The Split (/SP) parameter tells PCOPY it is OK to split large files. Following is an example:

```
PCOPY C:\WP\*.* A: /SP/FI
```

To restore split files, simply use PCOPY to copy the files back to a disk large enough to contain the entire file. PCOPY will find the split files and automatically recombine them.

```
PCOPY A:*.* C:\WP /MU
```

15. Backup from hard disk to floppy disks

PCOPY is not a full backup system, but its features allow it to be used for backup processing. It is very effective for backing up one hard disk to another. Following is a basic explanation of backup procedures.

The most common backup technique is referred to as Incremental Backup. This technique uses two different backup commands to implement initial full backup and daily incremental backup.

Incremental backup lets you avoid repeatedly backing up your entire system each time you want to back up. Instead, the first time you backup copy your entire system to disks. Then, each subsequent day (or other backup period) you only back up the files that have changed since the previous back up. If you are like most users, your "daily" backups will require only a couple of minutes because you only modified a small portion of your files since you last backed up.

A special DOS maintained file archive attribute supports incremental backup. The flag is an indicator field that is kept by DOS in each file's directory entry. It is stored along with file date, time, and size information. Whenever DOS, or an application, creates or changes a file, this archive attribute flag is set to indicate the file needs to be backed up. Programs that support backup use this flag to distinguish between files that need backup and those that have already been backed up.

Whenever a program backs up a file, it should reset the flag to indicate backup has been done. Then, incremental backup processing will know to skip the file and not back it up again until it has changed.

Full backup

Following is an example of using PCOPY to backup hard disk C: to diskettes in drive A:.

First, we will show the PCOPY command to make the first backup.

```
PCOPY C:*.* A: /DC/S/D-/A/LG/FI
```

The above command causes PCOPY to copy all files on drive C: to drive A:. /DC and /S cause directory names to be copied to the target drive and make PCOPY back up from all directories. Since this is the first backup, /D- is included to force all files on drive A: to be deleted prior to the copy. /A causes PCOPY to reset the DOS archive flag on each processed file to show the files were backed up. The /LG parameter asks PCOPY to write a log record to PCOPY.LOG for each file written. The log file can be used to locate the diskette containing a file to be restored. /FI causes PCOPY to fill all disks efficiently and make optimum use of diskette space.

This command should only be run for the first backup.

```
INCREMENTAL BACKUP (Daily backup)
```

The following command causes PCOPY to scan your disk to find files that have changed since your previous backup, and add them to your already started set of backup diskettes.

```
PCOPY C:*.* A: /DC/S/D2/A/LG/FI/B
```

The incremental backup command is almost the same as the full backup except for two parameters. The /B parameter causes PCOPY to only process files that have the archive (backup) attribute set. Processing will be confined to changed files. /D2 is used in place of /D-. /D2 indicates that PCOPY is to append files to the first backup disk and then to erase all files before reusing any additional diskettes.

After running your full backup, keep track of the last diskette written to. This will be the first disk provided for the next Incremental Backup. Label a set of backup disks and number them sequentially. Use a specially marked diskette sleeve for storing the last disk used. This will make it easy to identify when running backup again.

Restoring files from backup disks

Use PCOPY to restore any file from the backup disks. The PCOPY.LOG file contains a complete list of all backups done. You can examine this file to determine if and when a file was backed up. Then use the following PCOPY command to restore any files.

```
PCOPY A:filename.ext C: /MU/DC/S
```

16. Combine one or more files to a single new file

Use PCOPY to combine two DOS text files into a single output file. The following command copies two files to a single file, DOS.TXT. The append parameter causes them to be concatenated together.

```
PCOPY DOC.TX1,DOS.TX2 DOS.TXT /AP
```

17. Copy and save duplicate files with a new generated name

Use PCOPY when you need to copy updated files to diskettes that already contain previous versions of the same files. The /SA parameter indicates PCOPY is to save old versions of files by renaming them with version numbers in their extension names. PCOPY.C would be renamed to PCOPY.C01 before a new PCOPY.C is copied to the same diskette.

```
PCOPY \UPDATES \CSOURCE /R/SA
```

18. Merge two directories

Use PCOPY to move all files from one directory to another making sure the most current version of files in both directories are kept.

Merging files from one directory into another involves three actions. First, PCOPY moves files from the source directory that do not already exist on the target directory. Second, it moves newer duplicate files to the target directory. Third, it deletes files from the source directory that were not copied to the target directory.

```
PCOPY \fromdir \todir /ME
```

19. Execute any command with selected files as parameters

Since PCOPY has file selection capabilities not available in other programs, it can be used to select files to be processed by other commands and applications. For example, the following command will start an EDIT command for all P*.C files found by PCOPY. With the /CD parameter, PCOPY only starts

other commands. It does not copy or move data.

```
PCOPY P*.C /CD:EDIT[#
```

20. Search multiple directories for files to copy

Use PCOPY to scan a set of directories and copy files to a new location. This is useful if you are not sure of exactly what directory a filename exists in or if files from multiple directories are to be copied. Use the /S or /DS parameter.

Here is a sample command:

```
PCOPY LOOKFOR.ZIP A: /S/DR:CDE
```

21. Delete files on target disk and copy files to it

You may keep a work diskette handy by your machine to use to transport files between home and office. Use the /D-command with PCOPY to erase any old files on the disk before copying new files to it. This saves you from having to use a delete command and press Y to delete all files. The following command will erase the disk in drive A: and then copy files to it.

```
PCOPY PW*.C A:/D-
```

22. Restarting a previously incomplete copy

Sometimes it is necessary to stop a copy and start again at a later time. Even with a single diskette, the DOS COPY command is unable to resume processing from a specific filename. The PCOPY /F:filename.ext parameter provides PCOPY with a starting filename. The following command copies all files from PCOPY.C in a directory to diskette drive A:

```
PCOPY *.* A: /F:PCOPY.C
```

If you are referring to a hard disk, you do not need the /F command to resume processing. Simply specify the /U parameter. PCOPY will skip all files previously copied and start when the first uncopied file is reached.

23. Freeing disk space by copying files to archive disks

When your hard disk becomes full, you can use PCOPY to locate old files and move them to diskettes for archival storage. The following command finds files in the ARCHIVE directory that are older than a specified date and move them to diskette. Include the /SS:nnn command to stop processing when sufficient freespace is available on the hard disk.

```
PCOPY \ARCHIVE A: /X /D:(1jan89
  /ss:1000000
```

24. Transporting an entire disk to another computer

Copying one disk and all its subdirectories to another disk is easy. The first command copies all files to diskettes. The second command copies the files and directories from the diskettes back to any hard disk.

```
PCOPY C:*.* A: /DC /S /FI
PCOPY A:*.* C: /DC /S
```

25. Determine differences between files in two disks

One of the most useful functions of PCOPY does not copy files at all. To compare and report the differences between files on a diskette and the files on a hard disk directory, use the PCOPY command in test mode.

```
PCOPY A:*.* \DIRNAME /U/WH/T
```

The /T parameter indicates test mode no copy or move is to be done. The /U indicates to update any newer files. The /WH indicates to show why any files would not be copied. The resulting display shows the new files, which are newer versions, and what files are already on the drive as duplicates. It will also indicate what files are older copies of the same filenames.

26. Keeping files on two computers in synchronization

The /DY synchronization parameter indicates PCOPY is to make the target directory contain the same files as the source specification. It saves time by only copying files needed. An important feature is its ability to remove any files from the target drive that are not on the source drive being copied from.

This command is especially useful for transporting files from work to home and home to work using diskettes. A quick command at the end of each day will copy the files and remove deleted ones.

```
PCOPY \WORDPROC\*.* A: /DY
  Work to diskette
PCOPY A:*.* C:\WORDPROC /DY
  disk to home
```

27. Saving generation backup copies of files

Products that back up files before changing them often do not consider situations when a user stops and starts an application many times between backups. Unless multiple backup files are maintained, good versions of a file can be lost when good backup versions are replaced with bad versions.

Since PCOPY can create backup files with consecutively numbered names, you never lose a backup version. Just use PCOPY to make a copy of the file(s) to a backup directory before starting your application.

```
PCOPY %1 \BACKUP/SA/NW/U
  Make backup

123 %1 <=== Start application
```

After you next back up your system, delete the PCOPY backup versions to free space on your hard disk. Use the PDEL delete utility to delete all files in the BACKUP directory without being prompted to confirm the delete request.

After Backup:

PDEL \BACKUP*.*/NC Erase backup directory

28. Quickly copying files from one diskette to another

Since multiple floppy drives on a system cannot be accessed at the same time, it is very inefficient to copy files from one floppy disk to another. Instead, create a temporary directory on your hard disk, and first copy the files to the hard disk directory. Then move them from the hard disk directory to the output diskette. This greatly reduces copy time by avoiding multiple stopping and starting of floppy drives. If you can use a RAM disk as an intermediate drive, the copy will be very fast.

```
MD C:\TEMP
PCOPY A:*.*/NW
PCOPY C:\TEMP B:/X/NW
RD C:\TEMP
```

PDAILY

Copyright © 1986 by Norm Patriquin
Version 1.0

What Is PDAILY?

PDAILY allows the user to execute a set of DOS commands on a once per day basis. It is most useful for customizing your daily system startup procedure to perform some selected functions the first time the system is started each day and to bypass them if the system is started again the same day.

The system was developed to remind me of my daily planning tasks once each day. PDAILY works in conjunction with the DOS ERRORLEVEL batch command facility. The following statements show how selected commands are executed once per day.

Example:

```
ECHO OFF
PDAILY
IF NOT ERRORLEVEL GOTO NOTNOW
PLANNER
DEL *.BAK
BACKUP *.* A:/A
:NOTNOW
MENU
```

Command Parameters

PDAILY allows several command parameter switches to be specified to customize the process. All of these parameters are optional. The command format and switch parameters are described below. A quick review of command

parameters is always available by entering the PDAILY command with the /H parameter.

Command Format: PDAILY [logfilename] (/ switches)

logfilename	You may optionally specify the alternate name of a log file PDAILY is to use. This is a zero-length file that is used to keep the current PDAILY status. This feature is useful to keep PDAILY status for more than one event or activity. Use a different logfilename for each PDAILY event controlled. If not specified, PDAILY.DAT is used.
/H	Display help about PDAILY.
/N	Return the proper ERRORLEVEL command, but do not change it. Running PDAILY again will produce the same ERRORLEVEL the next time it is run, even the same day.
/R	Reset PDAILY status from ALREADY DONE TODAY to NOT YET DONE TODAY. The next time PDAILY is run, it will indicate the commands are to be executed again.
/T	Print status messages to indicate what ERRORLEVEL PDAILY has set.

PDELETE

Version 4.4
Copyright © 1992 by Norm Patriquin

What Is PDELETE?

PDELETE is an advanced Delete command to be used in DOS operating systems. It may be used in place of the DOS Erase and Delete command or instead of it. Like other Patriquin utilities, PDELETE gives you more control of command processing and provides a much safer way to

process files. PDELETE also provides several features not found with the standard DOS command.

Unlike other delete utilities, PDELETE does support DOS paths and wildcards. It keeps you aware of what files are being processed and provides an emergency stop feature just in case you have started something you feel is wrong.

PDELETE's file selection parameters provide you with numerous options for specifying the files to be deleted. You may select by directory, file, date, attribute, size, and even starting and ending filename.

The PDEL.DOC file contains a section outlining all changes for all releases of PDEL. If you already have a current release, this file will let you identify the changes since the version you have.

This archive should contain the following files:

PDEL.EXE	PDELETE execution file.
PDEL.DOC	PDEL documentation file. Use the following command to print PDEL documentation.
	`COPY PDEL.DOC PRN:`
PDREADME.TXT	A file to explain the contents of PDEL system.
WHATSNEW.DEL	Enhancement notes for this release.
ORDERFRM.TXT	Text form for ordering PDEL. Use the following command to print this file.
	`COPY ORDERFRM.DOC PRN:`
PDEL.1	A one-line description of PDELETE.
PDEL.DES	A multi-line description of PDELETE. May be used when uploading PDELETE to BBS systems.

Features

- Advanced file selection.
- Emergency STOP by pressing any key.
- Delete entire directories and remove them from disk.
- Optionally wipe file data from disk during delete to prevent it from being recovered by unauthorized person.
- Optional verify feature lets you approve each file before it is deleted.
- Optionally deletes HIDDEN / SYSTEM / READONLY files.
- Delete files until specified freespace is available.

- Advanced DOS Pattern capability. *TEST*.*
- Test feature allows you to try a command before actually deleting any files.
- Deletes from multiple disk drives with a single command.
- Accepts a list of files to be deleted.
- Exclusion capability allows files to be protected from deletion.

Command Parameters

PDELETE allows several command parameter switches to be specified to customize the process. All these parameters are optional. The command format and switch parameters are described below. A quick review of command parameters is always available by entering the PDEL command with no parameters.

Command Format:

PDEL	filespec,filespec,filespec [(/ switches)]
filespec	Enter a DOS file specification. Pathnames and standard DOS wildcard characters are allowed.

Multiple file specifications may be provided as shown in the above example. Separate each filename pattern with a single comma. For example:

`PDEL *.BAK,*.BK!,*.TMP`

Special pattern selection like *DISK*.* may be specified. *DISK*.* would select all files that have the chars 'DISK' anywhere in the first portion of the filename. *DI*S*K*.* type specification also works.

As an alternative, a file containing a list of input files may be supplied. Create a file containing lines with a filename or complete pathname on each line. Provide this filename as the source filename to PDEL and add an @ character before the name. The list of files will be processed as if they were all specified on the input command line. When the /S parameter is specified, an input file list may only contain file names. It may not contain directory names.

For file list processing, PDEL understands the output of the DOS DIR command. You may use the DOS redirection feature to direct DIR output to a file, edit the file to add or remove entries, and then provide this to PCOPY as input. For example:

DIR A: >DIRLIST

(edit dirlist)

PDEL @DIRLIST B:

/A   Archive — Selects only files that have been marked updated by DOS. This flag is updated by DOS whenever a file is processed with an intent to change or create new data.

/BA   Batch file processing. PDEL always checks to determine if the user has pressed a key to pause processing. This check can interfere with programs that store keystrokes in the keyboard buffer for subsequent processing. The /BA parameter sets no-windows mode and disables the key press check to leave stored keystrokes undisturbed.

/BW   Forces PDEL to use monochrome colors even when it detects color display environment. (Black & White)

/C   Overrides /NC when /NC is placed in the DOS environment variable. /C indicates to ask before deleting any files if a file pattern of *.* is specified.

/C2 /C3   Specify /C2 or /C3 to display the window processing screen in an alternative color scheme. To make this color change permanent, specify the parameter in the DOS environment variable.

/CE   Clean Empty directories. Usage: PDEL <path> /DE. PDEL will scan the entire disk and remove all empty directories in the specified tree. To process an entire drive,

specify the root directory. Ex. PDEL C:\ /DE. *Note:* Only /T can be used with this parameter. No files will be deleted at any time.

/DE   Delete Empty directories. Using this parameter, PDEL will remove all directories in which all files have been deleted from. For example, if PDEL deletes all files from the directory C:\WORK, it will then remove the directory.

/D:[(]xxx Date.   Select files based on the relationship between [)] their last update date and the date specified. This [=] parameter includes a date or number of days value. It may also contain a modifier that reverses or modifies the use of the date specified.

When xxx contains a date, the date is compared to the last update date of the file. The last update date of the file is the date contained in its directory entry. The file is selected if the condition specified by the condition modifier is met. The condition modifier meanings are

'(' = Select files whose date is older than the date specified.

')' = Select files whose date is newer than the date specified.

'=' = Select files whose date is equal to the date specified. If the condition modifier is not specified, ')' is assumed.

Date values may be specified in any of the following formats:

MM/DD/YY   12/31/80

MM-DD-YY   12-31-80

DDMMMYY   31DEC80

If xxx contains a numeric value, that positive number is used to calculate a date value a number of days prior to the current date. Then that date is used as in the calculation above.

Example:

/D:(1JAN86	Process files updated before 1JAN86
/D:)1JAN86	Process files updated after 1JAN86
/D:=1JAN86	Process files updated 1JAN86
/D:(5	Process files modified prior to 5 days ago
/D:)5	Process files modified within the last 5 days
/D:=5	Process files modified 5 days ago

/DI   Delete the disk DIrectory specified in the command. This will remove the directory, all files within it, and all the directories and files subordinate to it.

Only use this as a stand-alone parameter. Use a command like the following one to remove a directory from your disk:

```
PDEL \OLDDIR /DI
PDEL *.*/DI
— or —
PDEL \OLDDIR\*.* /DI
```

/DR:xxx   Use to process multiple disk drives. Processing will attempt to delete the specified files from all drive letters provided with the /DR:xx parameter.

For example, the following command will delete *.BAK files from hard disks C:, D:, and E:.

PDEL *.BAK/DR:CDE

/EQ   Exit PDEL without user intervention. Before PDEL exits window operation, it requests you to press any key. This parameter bypasses this request so you can use PDEL in DOS batch files.

/EX   Exclude files. The exclude facility allows you to provide a list of pathname and filename specifications that are to be excluded from processing.

The exclude facility is implemented with two actions. First, you will need to create an exclude specification file and place it in the same directory where PPDEL.EXE is installed on your hard disk. This file will contain the names of all the files and paths to be excluded. Name the file PDEL.EXC.

You may specify DOS pattern names to exclude groups of files with a single specification. Like DOS, use the '*' to indicate the last part of a filename or filename extension may be any set of characters. Also like DOS, use the '?' to indicate that any single position of a filename may be any character.

In addition to DOS, two additional pattern features are available. You may place an '*' anywhere in the filename to indicate any set of characters may exist in this point in the name. For pathnames, you may place an '**' at the end of a directory path specification to indicate the specification applies to the specified directory and all subordinate directories. Using '**', you can exclude an entire path with a single specification.

Following are examples:

1. *.EXE
2. *.COM
3. TEST*.*
4. *TEST*.*
5. DO?FIX.*
6. PC*XX.*
7. C:\DOS*.*
8. \TEST*.*
9. D:\GAMES***.*

Explanations for the previous examples:

1. Excludes all filenames with the extension .EXE from processing.

2. Excludes all filenames ending with extension .COM.

3. Excludes all filenames beginning with the letters "TEST" from processing.

4. Excludes all filenames having the characters "TEST" anywhere in the first portion of the filename.

5. Exclude files having 'DO' as the first 2 characters of the filename, and 'FIX' as the 4th, 5th, and 6th filename characters. The 3rd character of the filename may be any character.

6. Exclude files having a name beginning with the 2 characters PC and where the first portion of the filename ends with the characters 'XX.' Any 0 to 4 characters may exist between the 'PC' and 'XX' in the first portion of the filename.

7. Exclude all files from the DOS directory on drive C:.

8. Exclude all files from the TEST directory existing on any drive searched.

9. Exclude all files from the D:\GAMES\ directory and also exclude all files and directories subordinate to the GAMES directory.

Activating exclude —

Exclude will only be functional when the /EX command parameter is specified. When /EX is specified, you must have a valid exclude file. PDEL will not continue without one. If you wish exclude to be active during all execution, specify /EX as part of the PDEL= DOS environment variable. See later in the documentation for a description of this feature.

/F:file   First. Indicates that processing is not to start until the specified full filename is encountered in the scan of the directory.

/FS:nnnn   Freespace. PDELETE will delete files as long as there is less than nnnn thousand (nnnn * 000) of free space available on the disk. This is very helpful for cleaning up disks but retaining as many files as possible.

/L:file   Last. Indicates that processing is to stop after the specified full filename is encountered in the scan of the directory. The file specified will be processed if it matches selection criteria.

/M   Stop screen from scrolling from scrolling past the end without user intervention (MORE).

/NC   PDELETE asks "Are you Sure?" when you request files to be deleted with "*.*" patterns. To ignore this question, specify /NC. Place this in the DOS environment variable with SET PDEL=/NC to prevent PDEL from ever asking if you are sure.

/NT   Prevent ending statistics about freespace and files deleting from printing.

/NS   Sets all sounds generated to the speaker OFF. (No Sound)

/NW   No Windows — Do not use windows during processing. All screen output will be done through standard DOS facilities.

/O: filename-list   Specify a list of filename patterns that are to be Omitted (excluded) from PDEL processing. If multiple filename patterns are specified, separate them with commas.

For example:

/O:*.BAK,*.EXE,TEST*.*

An alternate form of the /O parameter allows all files but the original filename pattern to be deleted. Specify /O without any filename. For example, to delete all files except *.EXE files ===> PDEL *.EXE /O

/P   Pause before each file is updated to allow user to approve or reject the action for each file.

/RE   Use the /RE parameter to indicate any file with special attributes is also to be removed from the disk. Files with HIDDEN, SYSTEM, or READONLY attributes will be processed.

/RO   Include files marked with DOS readonly attribute.

/S   System — If a source directory is supplied, that directory and all subordinate directories will be searched for files to delete. If no source directory is specified, all directories on the disk will be searched for the specified filename pattern to delete.

/SH   Include files marked with DOS Hidden attribute. Normally, PDELETE will bypass these files.

/SF   Include files marked with DOS System attribute.

/SO   Process files from oldest to newest.

/SN   Process files from newest to oldest.

/SZ: [(] [)] nnn   Select a file based on its size. The left paren indicates that files less than the indicated size are to be selected. The right paren indicates to select files greater than the size. If right or left paren is not specified, a left paren is assumed. Following are examples.

> /SZ:100   Select files less than 100 characters
>
> /SZ:(100   Select files less than 100 characters
>
> /SZ:)100   Select files greater than 100 characters

/T   Test the command. Use this switch when you would like to test the command entered without actually updating any files. This is one of the best features of PDEL. Since PDEL is so powerful, the /T parameter is provided to allow you try any command in a simulate mode before actually deleting any files from your disk. Provide the /T parameter with any PDEL command to get a trial run without having any files deleted.

For example: PDEL *.BAK/T/S will search all directories in the current disk for *.BAK filers and will show what files would be deleted if this same command was run without the /T parameter.

/TF   Like test, but after test operation is complete, you will be asked if delete is actually to be done. (Test First) The test first allows you to try a command and then immediately execute the command again without the test option. It is a way to perform the test and live runs using a single command.

/W   Forces window operation. Since PDEL defaults to window operation, this parameter is only useful when you have previously deactivated window operation by placing /NW in the PDEL= DOS environment variable.

/WI   For data security, erase all disk areas that contain the file when it is deleted. This will prevent unauthorized users from recovering the file or examining its data by using special disk utilities.

/WH   PDELETE will indicate to you WHy files did not get processed. If a file is bypassed, normally PDELETE will not tell you why or when.

Use /WH when you want to determine why PDEL has not deleted a file you felt it should. /WH causes DEL to show why it bypassed processing for any files.

Setting of default parameters (DOS Environment) Default parameters are parameters that do not need to be specified each time PDEL is started. Any PCOPY parameter may be specified as a default parameter.

Use the DOS SET command to specify the parameter name and contents to be used by PDEL each time it is started. The following example indicates that PDEL is always to assume /NC and /NW are specified:

```
SET PDEL=/NC/NW
```

Once this DOS command is issued, each subsequent use of PDEL will operate as if these parameters have been specified on the command line. The SET command is most commonly placed in the AUTOEXEC.BAT file so it may be in effect every time your machine is started.

Examples:

Delete all *.BAK files on current default drive

```
PDEL *.BAK /S
```

Delete all *.BAK files over 30 days old

```
PDEL *.BAK /S/D:(30
```

Remove directory \ACCTING1 from drive A:

```
PDEL A:\ACCTING1 /DI
```

Patriquin's Hard Disk Utilities Registration Form

Name: _____

Company: _____

Address: _____

City: _____

State: _____ Country: _____

Zip: _____ Phone: _____

Remit to:
Patri-Soft
5225 Canyon Crest Dr, Suite 71-358
Riverside CA, 92507

(714) 352-2820 (Voice)
(714) 352-2825 (Data)
(714) 352-1527 (Fax)

Visa/Master Card orders are also accepted through telephone orders. Call Public Software Library: 800-242-4775 or 713-665-7017 to order.

Specify Disk Size: ❑ 5.25" ❑ 3.5"

Payment by:
  ❑ Check or ❑ Money Order
  (made out to Patri-Soft)
  ❑ Visa ❑ Master Card

Authorized Signature: _____
Expiration Date: _____
Card Number: _____

❑ Registration of all Patriquin Utilities with program disk and User's Guide.
  each ....$45.00 $ _____
❑ Update Service — in addition to above, send the next version automatically when it is available.
  each ....$25.00 $ _____
❑ PCOPY — File Copy, Move, Backup, Update, more!
  each .... $20.00 $ _____
❑ PSEARCH — Locate files on your disk.
  each ....$20.00 $ _____
❑ PDELETE — Save space with automatic disk cleanup
  each ....$20.00 $ _____
❑ PPRINT — Advanced file print w/special formats
  each ....$20.00 $ _____
❑ PALERT — Warns you of low disk space
  each ....$15.00 $ _____
❑ PATTR — Manage attributes of DOS files
  each ....$10.00 $ _____
❑ PDAILY — Automatically execute commands once/day
  each ....$10.00 $ _____
❑ Update a registered set with new disk and manual — show proof of previous registration
  SER=_____
  each ....$15.00 $ _____
SHIPPING/HANDLING FOR ALL ORDERS
  ADD ....$5.00 $ _____
California residents, add state sales tax
  ....7.75% $ _____
TOTAL .... $ _____

PocketD

(D.EXE) Directory Listing File & Management Program
Version 1.67c
Copyright © By Jeff Rollason, PocketWare 1990–1992

Introduction

PocketD is a small, flexible, powerful color directory listing program and exceptionally powerful DOS utility. Its highly generalized design and range of built-in features allows it to be used for almost any purpose, including for example: virus checking, disk cataloging, disk backup reminder, reversing unintended copies, DOS menu system, programmer's MAKE system, and much, much more.... PocketD is the one program most likely to fulfill all of your file management needs and probably the nearest you will get to the DOS user's equivalent of the Swiss Army knife.

Features

PocketD is 25K in size and supports over 120 options, including the following key features (expanded and detailed in the file FEATURE.CMP):

- Full ON-LINE HELP giving direct access to help on each option
- Optimized file COPYing to multiple disks
- Safe file/dir COPY/MOVE/RENAME selected by any criteria
- Fast MOVE by copying directory entry, rather than COPY+DELETE
- SEARCH for files across multiple drives and subdirs
- Search or view contents of ZIP, ZOO, LZH, ARC, PAK, PKA, & ARJ archives
- Advanced wildcard system, allowing multiple filespecs such as "*TMP*F*" or "*=D*" (match any name containing a digit 0-9) etc.
- Highly programmable execution and display TEMPLATE(s), providing a viable alternative to a command-line programming language, allowing the creation of powerful interactive utilities and the emulation of programs such as WHICH, NCD, & MAKE
- Detection of, and testing for, PKLITE, DIET, and LZEXE compression
- TOUCH and full ATTRIB for modifying file and dir dates/attributes

- On-line BROWSE of file lists for VIEWING, DELETION, RUNNING, etc.
- A user-defined color MENU system for use in BAT files
- Analysis of ENVIRONMENT variables (e.g., PATH LIB, INCLUDE, etc.), STRING SEARCH in binary or text files for presence or absence of literal or "typed" strings (e.g., alphabetic, non-numeric, etc.)
- Automatic BEST-FIT directory listing format option
- RECURSED SUMMARY of subdir contents within directory listing
- BAR-CHART display of relative file/subdir sizes
- Display of EXECUTION SIZE of programs
- SORT by 6 keys (e.g., type, size, date) and by row or column
- Full COLOR options, allowing assignment for specified filespecs
- Automatic support for 80x43, 132x60, and any other screen sizes
- 37 user-defined parameters

Overview

PocketD is good for both the occasional and the advanced user. It provides the usual day-to-day file operations, such as file copying, in a safe and easy-to-use format. It also bends over backwards to accommodate each user's particular tastes by offering vast numbers of tailoring options.

PocketD's multiple features can be combined to provide a powerful and highly generalized DOS tool. The following gives a couple of examples:

```
D /WTc A:
```

This compact example will search the whole disk (W) for files modified today (T) and copy them (c) to A:. This also gives the user the opportunity to view each file before copying it. Extra conditions can also be added:

```
D /WTc A: /E{20k!'Microsoft'
```

which will only include executable files (E) less than or equal to 20 kilobytes (20K) and excluding those that contain the string 'Microsoft' ("!" specifies "NOT").

```
D /WR .GIF [GIFVIEW $w] [COPY $w A:
// PKZIP SAVE $w]
```

This example searches the whole disk for graphic *.GIF files. The user can then browse these and optionally choose to view particular files using the program GIFVIEW and/or optionally copy them to drive A: and add them to the ZIP file SAVE.ZIP. The user can process any file in any order and any number of times.

Doubts

Q1.   Why use a program like PocketD when there are so many attractive alternatives, such as PCTOOLS or NORTON Commander which provide menu-driven interfaces to file management?

A1.   The reason is that these menu-oriented packages provide very good point-and-shoot interfaces to file VIEW, COPY, MOVE, and DELETE, but do not allow the user to construct automated file management procedures, such as:

"Take all the ZIP files on drive A: and unpack each into its own subdirectory on drive C:"

This is not possible with these programs without repetitive keywork. Such operations require the use of packages such as MKS Shell or Command Plus and custom written routines to automate such operations.

PocketD can perform operations of this type conveniently and efficiently from a single command line, allowing the user to preview the operation before running it (e.g., from drive C:)

```
D A:.ZIP [MD $n//PKUNZIP $w
    $n\]? Preview and..
```

```
D A:.ZIP [MD $n//PKUNZIP $w
    $n\]R Run
```

Q2.   Why should I use PocketD when there are other existing rivals?

A2.   The only obvious rival is the much larger DX program by Econo-soft. DX has specialized features that PocketD does not support, such as "U.S. Defense standard"

file deletion, file compare, and the ability to touch or rename files inside archives.

Despite its smaller size, PocketD still has more options, including advanced string searching inside files, a built-in file viewer, and full on-line help, not supported by DX. It also has a much more powerful template facility and much more flexible directory display (see the file FEATURE.CMP).

Q3.   Why use PocketD when I do not require complex file management?

A3.   PocketD is an attractive full-color directory listing program with many handy features such as automatic display format selection, which chooses a listing format for you. It also has a much more agreeable and powerful COPY facility than DOS's COPY, providing the user protection against common errors and giving informative feedback about the copy/move operation being completed.

PocketD makes day-to-day operations more pleasant and less error-prone (e.g., backing up of the day's files to disk). It allows the user to discard many utilities that are already used. PocketD saves disk space and provides all of these facilities with a single common range of command options.

Program and Documentation Files

By default, the install program for the *DOS 6 SECRETS* diskettes will install all of the PocketD files in the directory \SECRETS\POCKETD. This directory has not been added to the search path. You can execute the program from its home directory, add the directory to the search path, or copy the PocketD files to a directory that is included in the search path.

The following is a description of the contents for each file included with PocketD.

Main files

README.D	Read this file first.
D.EXE	The program PocketD (26K) help files that follow are optional.
D.HLP	The one page help (2K) view by **D** /?

D.MAN	On-line option manual (55K) view by **D /?x**
D.GDE	On-line User Guide (39K) view by **D /??**
D.DOC	On-line General Doc (23K) view by **D /?doc**
EPSON2A.COM	A program to convert the file FEATURE.CMP containing IBM graphic codes to ordinary text, allowing printing to printers other than IBM/Proprinter/BJ10E. This program can also be used to strip out Epson codes from other files.
CHANGES.D	Details the changes between different versions of PocketD.
FEATURE.CMP	This comprehensively compares PocketD's features with other programs such as PCOPY, DX, RIR, etc. This file can be viewed by typing: D /q FEATURE.CMP followed by "L" (list).
REGISTER.DOC	This provides details of how to register.
VENDOR.DOC	Application for Shareware vendors.
INSTALL.BAT	An installation program for PocketD.
DEMO.BAT	A demonstration and tutorial for PocketD.
*.BAT	Various examples of how PocketD can be used to emulate other utilities such as NCD, WHICH and WHEREIS, etc. (See below.)

Additional BAT files

The following BAT files will give usage help if used with the single parameter /?. For example

```
DELBUT /?
```

Most can accept additional options. For example

```
FD /T
```
will select the 1st subdirectory found that was created today.

The BAT files provided include:

"f1 f2 .." below indicates multiple filespecs as parameters.

PsL_UNPK d1 d2	This will unpack a PsL disk of self-unpacking programs. See D /?? for details.
ATTRIB flags f1 f2..	A full ATTRIB command allowing setting and clearing of all flags.
DELBUT f1 f2 ..	Delete all but filespecs f1 f2 ..
DELDIR f1	Recursively delete specified subdirectory.
FD f1 f2 ..	Search for and select a subdirectory matching f1 (or f2, etc.).
TOUCH f1 f2..	Touch the matching files to give the current date and time.
VDEL f1 f2 ..	Delete all matching files, prompting before each.
WHEREIS f1 f2 ..	Search for files/dirs matching filespecs
WHICH f1	Will show from which subdirectory DOS would run the program *f1* (See D /??).

10 Nifty Things You Can Do With PocketD

1. Use it instead of DOS's DIR for viewing your directories.

   Just typing *D* gives you a sorted double column display that pauses when the screen is full. In addition to this, you can add configurable color-coding of filenames and more tailoring and display options than any other directory listing program (as of June '92).

2. Use it to back up your disks.
   ```
   D /WTccu A:
   ```
   would search the whole drive for files modified or created today and copy them to drive A:, providing that either the file does not already exist on A: or is older. (PocketD provides 19 copy sub-options).

3. Look for hard-to-find files.
   ```
   D *ASP* /W!E'Shareware' /c
   ```
   would search the whole drive for files with names containing the string "ASP", where the file is nonexecutable and contains the string "Shareware" inside the file. Any files

found can then be optionally viewed and/or copied to the current directory. You can make this search more specific by adding size and date ranges and multiple include/exclude filespecs.

4. Create a BAT file that could rebuild the subdirectory structure of your hard disk.

   ```
   D /WDu[md $w//] > RESTDIR.BAT
   ```

5. Uncompress each ZIP file on A: into its own subdirectory on the current drive.

   ```
   D a:*.ZIP [MD $n//PKUNZIP $w $n\]R
   ```

6. Take a PROCOMM log file and rename it to give a unique name based on its date.

   ```
   D PCPLUS.LOG [D $f $d.* [REN $f
     $d.$$F]R.u]R/.m
   ```

   giving names of the form 92Feb03.1, 92Feb03.2, 92Feb12.1, etc.

7. Search for files in any subdirectory or ZIP, ARC, PAK, LZH, ZOO, or ARJ archive.

   ```
   D *.TXT *=D=D* /WZ
   ```

   would search the current drive scanning all subdirectories, including any archives

found, for any files with the extension .TXT or a consecutive double digit in its name (e.g., DIET14.EXE but not PRO1V2.COM).

8. Analyze your hard disk to find out the relative sizes of each subdirectory

   ```
   D /r%gss
   ```

   This example also gives the relative percentage usage of each subdirectory and plots a bar chart to show the relative sizes, sorting the output by subdirectory size.

9. To remind you when you haven't backed up your hard disk recently.

   ```
   D BACK.TAG /!:-7 [You have not
     backed-up your disk since $d//]
   ```

10. Ask multi-option questions from within BAT files (e.g., AUTOEXEC.BAT).

    ```
    D /Ywbd /'Choose (W)indows,
      (B)ackup hard disk or (D)os
      prompt ?'
    IF ERRORLEVEL 3 GOTO DOS
    IF ERRORLEVEL 2 GOTO BACKUP
    IF ERRORLEVEL 1 GOTO WINDOWS
    ```

PocketD Registration Form

Name: _____

Company: _____

Address: _____

City: _____

State: _____ Country: _____

Zip: _____ Phone: _____

U.K. address for information
and orders in Sterling: U.S. Orders:

PocketWare   PsL

Box 2369, Hendon   P.O. Box 35705

London, NW4 1NR, England   Houston, TX 77235-5705

You can order in the following ways:

* U.S. dollars with your MC, Visa, AmEx, or Discover card by calling 800-2424-PsL or 713-524-6394 or by FAX to 713-524-6398 or by CIS to 71355,470 or by mail to the PsL address. Quote PsL item #10474. These numbers are for ordering only. For product information, technical support, site licences, etc., write to the U.K. address or contact via CIS 100031,3537.

* Via CompuServe. Type "GO SWREG" and select Reg ID 126(private) and 127(commercial).

* Pounds Sterling by cheque, banker's draft, or money order against any U.K. bank to the U.K. address.

Inquiries are welcomed for bundling with other software (already bundled with PC-ACCESS).

PsL item #10474   Private/Educational   Commercial

Price per copy   £19.00, $35.00   £29.00, $54.00

Prices include a pocket-sized 110-page manual with each registered copy. See the file REGISTER.DOC for details on multiple-copy orders and site licenses. See the file D.DOC for registration benefits.

Quantity: _____ (or Site) UK or US

Total : ....£ _____ $ _____

Basic S&H : ....£   2.00 $ 4.00

Overseas S&H: ....£ _____ $ _____

Total cost: ....£ _____ $ _____

Overseas Shipping: If ordering multiple copies from outside the U.K. (excluding Site Licence purchase)

   add for each additional ....£   1.70 $ 3.00

   Covers cost of shipping multiple manual copies.

Specify Disk Size: ❏ 5.25" ❏ 3.5"

Payment by: ❏ Check ❏ Other

       ❏ MC ❏ VISA ❏ AmEx ❏ Discover

MC/Visa/AmEx/Discover for US $ to PsL only! (valid for UK Sterling only) Cheq/Draft/MO for UK £ to PocketWare only!

Authorized Signature _____

Expiration Date _____

Card Number _____

QEdit(R) Advanced

The "Quick Editor"
Version 2.1
Copyright © 1985–1991 Applied Systems Technologies, Inc.
SemWare and QEdit are registered trademarks of Applied Systems Technologies, Inc.

Introduction

"You can never be too rich, too thin, or have too much RAM and Disk storage." Ancient American proverb, ca. 1980.

This manual describes the use and operation of QEdit, a full-screen text editor for the IBM PC and compatible computers. The manual includes installation instructions, a user's guide, and a reference section which explains all of QEdit's commands.

QEdit is a text editor as opposed to a word processor. This means that most of its features are geared toward creating and maintaining program source code and other text files. However, QEdit can also be used like a word processor to write documents or letters since it includes word-wrapping and paragraph reformatting capabilities.

QEdit was developed with these goals in mind:
FAST OPERATION — More than anything else, QEdit was designed to operate quickly, especially in these areas:

- Initially loading a file for editing.
- Displaying/Updating the screen.
- Moving through the editing window.
- Searching for text.
- Saving a file back to disk.

EASE OF USE — This version of QEdit includes:

- Optional *Pop-Down* menus.
- Customizable Help Screen.
- Complete execution from a single file (Q.EXE).
- Pop-up file directory and picker.

COMPACT PROGRAM SIZE — Every effort was made to keep the program size as compact as possible. Even though memory is getting cheaper all the time, we didn't want QEdit to require any more memory than absolutely necessary.

Features

These are just some of the many features you will enjoy while using QEdit:

- It is very fast!
- It is customizable. QEdit can be easily configured the way you like it. This includes the meaning of ALL special keys on the keyboard (Alt, Ctrl, and function keys; <Home>, <PgUp>, etc.), colors, screen appearance, and many other options.
- It utilizes all available memory. With QEdit you can edit files as large as your computer's memory will allow.
- It allows true multi-file editing. The number of files you can edit is limited only by available memory.
- It enables you to view files through up to eight *windows*. You can have multiple views of the same file or view a different file in each window.
- It provides up to 99 scratch buffers for cut-and-paste or template operations.
- It allows you to exit to DOS (or a DOS shell) temporarily and use DOS commands from within the editor.
- It is easy to use. You can use the optional Pop-Down menus to access QEdit's commands, and there is a Help Screen which you can customize for your own needs.
- It supports Character, Line, and Column Blocks.
- It allows you to create macros which will execute a series of commands and keystrokes by pressing a single key.
- It provides wordwrap and paragraph reformat capabilities.
- It saves deleted words, lines, and Blocks in a deletion buffer for later recall.
- It provides *C mode*, which utilizes automatic indentation for C language programming.

- It locates matching braces and parentheses, a useful feature for programming.
- It will load multiple files from the DOS command line, with or without wildcard characters.
- It allows you to specify up to six default file extensions for use when loading files and determining tab settings.
- It allows you to execute command-line compilers from within QEdit, using its macro capability.
- It provides line drawing to create diagrams and tables.
- It supports enhanced (101 key) keyboards.
- It supports up to 200-column and 100-line screens.
- It supports EGA 43-line mode and VGA 50-line mode.
- It is compact. Even with all these features, QEdit requires less than 50K of disk space.

Program and Documentation Files

By default, the install program for the *DOS 6 SECRETS* diskettes will install all of the QEDIT files in the directory \SECRETS\QEDIT. This directory has not been added to the search path. You can execute the program from its home directory, add the directory to the search path, or copy the QEDIT files to a directory that is included in the search path.

The following files are included on the distribution diskette.

File	Description
Q.EXE	The editor program. This is the only file required to run QEdit Advanced.
QCONFIG.EXE	The configuration program. This program allows you to customize QEdit.
QCONFIG.DAT	The default Keyboard Definition File.
QHELP.TXT	The default Help text.
QEDIT.DOC	The documentation for the shareware version of

	QEdit, including LICENSE and WARRANTY information.
ORDERFRM.DOC	Handy order form.
READ.ME	Read this file first.
QEDITTSR.DOC	Release notes about the new TSR version of QEdit.
VENDOR.DOC	Restrictions/Authorizations for Disk Vendor distribution.

Chapter 1: User's Guide for QEDIT

Quick start

With QEdit you can edit any text file with a few simple commands. The next three sections briefly describe the quickest way possible to load, edit, and save a file.

Getting started

Using QEdit is simple and straightforward.

To initiate QEdit, type **Q <Enter>**. The Editor will respond with a prompt for the name of the file to be edited.

```
File(s) to edit: <Esc = abort>
```

Enter the filename. The filename may include full path designation.

QEdit Tip: At any FILE TO EDIT prompt, you may use wildcard characters (* or ?) to obtain a list of matching files in the directory.

You may optionally include the filename on the DOS command line in order to bypass this prompt. For example, from the DOS command line, type

```
Q filename <Enter>
```

In the editor

Once you are in QEdit, the cursor movement keys (Left, Right, Up, Down, Home, End, ...) allow you to move around in the text. To obtain a help screen, simply press <F1>. Pressing <F1> again returns you to the text.

To obtain a menu of QEdit commands, press <Esc>. You may then use the cursor movement keys to position the cursor bar over the desired command. Pressing <Enter> will execute the command.

QEdit Tip: Pressing <Esc> will abort any editor prompt.

Getting out

The easiest way to get out of QEdit and save all the work you have done is to enter <Alt F> <G>.

Menus

QEdit provides an easy-to-use Pop-Down style menu system. The menu system is very helpful while learning to use the editor. It is also handy for executing seldom-used commands.

To access the menus and execute a command:

1. Press <Esc>. The main menu will be displayed at the top of the screen. The main menu consists of a list of sub-menu items.
2. Select a sub-menu item. You may do this by moving the cursor bar to the desired item and pressing <Enter> or by typing the capital letter of the desired item.
3. Execute a command. This is done in the same manner as selecting the sub-menu items.

Note: See the file QEDIT.DOC for visual example omitted here.

You can execute many QEdit commands using the menus. As you become more familiar with the editor, you may wish to use the <Ctrl>, <Alt>, and function keys, instead of the menus, to execute commands more quickly. A cross reference of all QEdit commands can be found in Appendix A.

The status line

At the top of the editing screen is the Status Line. The Status Line constantly displays information regarding the file you are currently editing.

Note: Please see the file QEDIT.DOC for visual example omitted here. It shows the Status Line with a description of the information displayed.

For more information on Insert, AutoIndent, WordWrap, and Box Drawing, refer to the "Modes" section in this chapter. For more information on macro recording, refer to the "Macros" section in this chapter.

QEdit Tip: The Status Line may be configured to appear at the bottom of the screen. Refer to the "Colors/Screen Options" section of Chapter 2 for more information.

Files

Creating new files

There are three different ways to create new files, ready for editing:

1. From the DOS command line, enter <Q> followed by one or more new filenames. Each filename must be separated by a space. For example, typing

   `Q file1 b:file2 \dir1\file3 <Enter>`

   will create **file1** in the current directory, **file2** on disk drive B, and **file3** in the directory **dir1**.

QEdit Tip: When specifying file names to QEdit, you may use full path designations if desired.

2. From the DOS command line, type **Q <Enter>**. QEdit will respond with the prompt:

   `File(s) to edit: <Esc = abort>`

   Enter one or more new filenames, each separated by a space.

3. From within the editor, enter the EditFile <Alt E> command. The above prompt will appear. Again, you may enter one or more new filenames, each separated by a space.

Loading existing files

Loading existing files works exactly like creating new files (in the previous section) with two exceptions

- The filename(s) specified must exist on disk.
- The filename(s) may contain wildcard characters (*, ?).

QEdit can be configured to respond to wildcarded filename entries in one of two ways:

1. Load all matching files into the editor.
2. Show all the matching filenames in a *pick* listing. You can then use the cursor keys to find the file you want and press <Enter> to load it into the editor.

QEdit can also be configured to use default file extensions, such as DOC and PAS when entering filenames. For more information on configuring these options, refer to the "General Options" section of Chapter 2.

Multiple files: the ring

QEdit is a true multi-file editor. It allows as many files as will fit into memory to be loaded at the same time. All of these files can then be edited by simply switching back and forth between them without having to save and load each file individually. Switching between files is accomplished very quickly and easily.

A simple explanation of how QEdit handles multiple files will help you in manipulating and editing multiple files.

QEdit maintains all loaded files in a *ring*.

Note: See the file QEDIT.DOC for visual example omitted here.

In the ring we see that six files have been loaded into the editor. You can, of course, load many more files — as many as your computer's memory will allow.

Assume the file currently being edited is file *B*. You may then move from one file to another in any of the following ways:

- Enter the NextFile <Alt N> command. You will now be editing the next file in the ring, file *C*.
- Enter the PrevFile <Ctrl KP> command. You will now be editing the previous file in the ring, file *A*.
- Enter the EditFile <Alt E> command. The editor will prompt for a filename. You may enter the name of any file in the ring. The editor will make the entered file the current one for editing.

You may, at any time, add files to the ring or discard files from the ring. If you add a new file to the ring using the EditFile command, it will become the current file and the old current file will become the previous file. If you delete a file from the ring, the previous file will become the current file.

QEdit Tip: When loading files, be aware that QEdit will not load two copies of the same file. If you issue the EditFile command for a file already loaded, that file will become the new current file.

Saving files and exiting

QEdit provides several different ways to save files, discard files, and exit the editor. A set of five basic commands provides assorted combinations of saving, discarding, and exiting in order to suit individual preferences.

We recommend selecting one or two methods with which you feel most comfortable and using them consistently.

Note: Please see the file QEDIT.DOC for table omitted here. It summarizes these commands and their effects.

Viewing and getting around in the text

QEdit is quite versatile in allowing you to move around in the text. With simple keystrokes you can either move a few characters or lines at a time or move from one end of the file to another. You can go to specific lines in the file or go to each occurrence of a particular string of characters. And with QEdit's windows, you can view up to eight files at a time or have multiple views of the same file.

As you will see, there are quite a few commands in QEdit for moving around in your text. If you are not already familiar with these types of commands, try them out. You will probably find some new commands that will be useful for your applications of QEdit.

Cursor movement
Moving through a file

QEdit provides several commands which enable you to move about in a file.

BegFile <Ctrl PgUp> and EndFile <Ctrl PgDn>

As their names imply, these commands move the cursor to the beginning or end of the current file. BegFile positions the cursor at column one on the first line of the file. EndFile positions the cursor after the last nonblank character on the last line of the file.

PageUp <PgUp> and PageDown <PgDn>

PageUp scrolls the text toward the top of the file, one page-full, less one line, at a time. PageDown scrolls the text toward the end of the file, one page-full, less one line, at a time.

HalfPgUp and HalfPgDn

These commands work exactly like the PageUp and PageDown commands, except that they scroll only one-half page at a time.

QEdit Tip: All QEdit commands, including those without default key assignments, can be assigned as the user desires, to almost any key. Refer to the "Keyboard Configuration" section of Chapter 2 for more information.

ScrollUp <Ctrl W> and LineUp

These commands scroll the text one line at a time toward the beginning of the file. The ScrollUp command will cause the cursor to remain on the same line of text until it reaches the bottom of the screen, while the LineUp command will cause the cursor to remain stationary on the screen.

ScrollDown <Ctrl Z> and LineDown

These commands scroll the text one line at a time toward the end of the file. The ScrollDown command will cause the cursor to remain on the same line of text until it reaches the top of the screen, while the LineDown command will cause the cursor to remain stationary on the screen.

GotoLine <Ctrl J>

Upon entering the GotoLine command, QEdit will prompt with:

```
line number: <Esc = abort>
```

By typing a line number and <Enter>, QEdit will *jump* the cursor to the specified line number. An easy way to move about quickly in your text is to keep track of critical positions by noting their line number, which is displayed on the Status Line, and then using this command to jump to those positions.

GotoBlockBeg <Ctrl QB> and GotoBlockEnd <Ctrl QK>

These commands move the cursor to the beginning or to the end of the currently marked Block. If the marked Block is in another file, QEdit will make that file the current file and then move you to the beginning or end of the Block. For more information on using marked Blocks, refer to the "Block Commands" section in this chapter.

PrevPosition <Ctrl QP>

This command can come in very handy. It moves you to the cursor's previous position. Although it would not be of much use if you had only moved a character or two, it can be useful for larger jumps of the cursor.

For example, perhaps you are in the middle of a file and want to check something at the very beginning of the file. To get to the beginning, you would simply enter BegFile <Ctrl PageUp>. After you look at the beginning, you want to get back to where you were previously. You could use PageDown, but that could be tedious, especially if your file is large. The easiest way would be to enter PrevPosition, and with a single keystroke, you are immediately back where you started.

Note: PrevPosition can only take you back to the cursor's immediately previous position.

If there are intervening keystrokes that move the cursor, PrevPosition will move you back to the most recent location of the cursor.

Find <Ctrl QF> and RepeatFind <Ctrl L>

These commands will search for a specific string of characters in the file. Upon entering the Find command, QEdit will prompt for the string of characters for which to search. Search for

```
<Esc = Abort>
```

Enter the desired string of characters and press <Enter>.

QEdit will then prompt for the search options to use.

```
Options [BGLIW] (Back Global Local
    Ignore-case Whole-words):
I
```

Enter the letter(s) corresponding to the option(s) you want and press <Enter>. The available options are (see Appendix E for additional options):

[B] = Search backward from the current cursor position. When you choose *B*, QEdit will search backward from the cursor position toward the beginning of the file. Otherwise, it will search from the cursor position toward the end of the file.

[I] = Ignore the case (capital or lowercase) of the search string. For example, "Hello" would match "hello" if this option is chosen. This option is set ON by default.

[W] = Search for whole words only. For example, when this option is chosen, the word "sent" will match only the actual word "sent". Otherwise, any other words that contain the string (such as "sentence" or "absent") would also match.

Once the Find command is executed, the cursor will be placed at the first occurrence of the search string found in the text. To locate subsequent occurrences of the search string, simply enter the RepeatFind command.

If you want to search for a string and replace it with another string, refer to the "Replacing Text" section in this chapter.

Match <Alt F3>

This is a specialized search command. It acts only on the characters ( ), { }, and [ ]. With the cursor placed on one of these characters, enter the Match command. QEdit will locate the logical matching character of the pair. This command can be useful for programming in languages where complicated expressions are grouped using these characters.

Moving around on the screen

These commands affect the cursor position within the current screen of displayed text.

BegScreen <Ctrl Home> and EndScreen <Ctrl End>

These commands move you to the first or last line of the screen (or current window if you have windows open). The cursor's column position does not change.

BegLine <Home> and EndLine <End>

You are probably already familiar with these commands. BegLine moves the cursor to the beginning, or column one, of the current cursor line. EndLine moves the cursor to the last nonblank character of the current cursor line.

ScreenLeft <Alt F5> and ScreenRight <Alt F6>

These commands scroll the entire text to the left or right one column at a time. You can change the number of columns which are shifted each time using the QEdit configuration program. Refer to the "Colors/Screen Options" section of Chapter 2 for more information.

WordLeft <Ctrl Cursor Left> and WordRight <Ctrl Cursor Right>

These commands move the cursor to the first character of the previous or following word in the text.

MakeCtrofScreen <Shift F5>, MakeTopofScreen <F5>, MakeBotofScreen

These three commands change the position of the cursor line on the screen (or window, if you have windows open). They can be useful if you prefer to work at the bottom or top of the screen or if you want to keep the text surrounding your cursor line in view.

The MakeCtrofScreen command scrolls the text on the screen (either up or down) until the cursor line is the center line of the screen.

The MakeTopofScreen command scrolls the text upward until the cursor line is the top line of the screen.

The MakeBotofScreen command scrolls the text downward until the cursor line is the last line of the screen.

Moving by lines and characters

These commands enable you to move in short increments through the text.

CursorLeft <Cursor Left> and CursorRight <Cursor Right>

These commands move the cursor one column to the right or left on the cursor line.

When you use CursorLeft, the cursor will stop when it reaches the left edge of the screen, unless the text has been scrolled to the left. In that case it scrolls the text to the right one column at a time until it reaches column one.

When you use CursorRight and the cursor reaches the right edge of the screen, it will begin to scroll the text to the left. It will stop scrolling when it reaches the maximum line length.

CursorUp <Cursor Up> and CursorDown <Cursor Down>

These commands move the cursor up or down in the file one line at a time. The cursor's column position does not change.

Using windows

QEdit provides the ability to view different areas of files (either multiple files or the same file) at the same time, through the use of windows. A window is a portion of the screen that allows you to view text. You can divide your screen into as many as eight horizontal windows. You can then view as many as eight different files through these windows or have multiple views of a single file. This capability can be quite helpful for comparing text, copying text, and moving text.

Note: Please see the file QEDIT.DOC for split-window example omitted here.

Creating windows

To create a window, use the HorizontalWindow <Ctrl OH> command. The screen will be split into two halves, or windows, each window having its own Status Line. The cursor will reside in the newly created window, making it the current window.

If only one file is being edited, the newly created window will simply be an additional view of the same file. QEdit will not load more than one copy of the same file.

If multiple files are being edited, the newly created window will be a view of the next file in the ring. (Refer to the "Multiple Files" section in this chapter.) If desired, you can configure QEdit to prompt for the name of the file to be viewed in the new window instead of the editor automatically selecting the next file in the ring. Refer to the "General Options" section of Chapter 2 for more information.

Once the screen has been split into windows, entering the HorizontalWindow command again will affect the current window. All other windows will remain unchanged.

Switching windows

When multiple windows are opened, editing will only take place in the current window (the window containing the cursor). For editing text in other windows, two commands are provided to switch from one window to another.

- The PrevWindow <Ctrl OP> command will move the cursor to the window above the current window. If the current window is at the top of the screen, the cursor will move to the last window on the screen.
- The NextWindow <Ctrl ON> command will move the cursor to the window below the current window. If the current window is at the bottom of the screen, the cursor will move to the first window on the screen.

Changing window size

You can change the size of any of the windows on the screen with the commands below.

- The GrowWindow <Ctrl OG>, ShrinkWindow <Ctrl OS>, and ResizeWindow <Esc><W><R> commands allow you to change the size of the current window. Upon entering any of these commands, QEdit will prompt you to change the size of the window by using the cursor up and cursor down keys.
- The ZoomWindow <Ctrl OZ> command will cause the current window to fill the entire screen as all other windows disappear. To restore the screen with all windows, simply press <Ctrl OZ> again. Be careful not to confuse this command with the OneWindow command (see below). OneWindow fills the screen with the current window (like ZoomWindow does), but it also closes all windows except the current one. ZoomWindow leaves the other windows intact, even though they are hidden from view.

Closing windows

There are two commands to close windows.

- The CloseWindow <Ctrl OC> command closes the current window. The current window will disappear and the cursor will be placed in the window above the closed window, making it the new current window. When the closed window is at the top of the screen, the window below the closed window will become the new current window.
- The OneWindow <Ctrl OO> command closes all windows except the current window. The current window will fill the entire screen. Note that closing a window does not discard files from the editor.

Copying, moving, replacing, and deleting text

Block commands

In this section, we will see how to mark and manipulate Blocks. A Block is some portion of the text file which has been specifically delineated using QEdit's Block marking commands. We will see how to manipulate Blocks both directly and through the use of intermediate storage areas known as buffers.

QEdit contains a rich set of Block commands. There are commands to mark Blocks by lines, columns, and characters. There are commands to copy, move, shift, and delete Blocks. These commands are very useful for transferring text from one file to another. There are also cut-and-paste commands, as well as commands to move Blocks to and from named Scratch Buffers.

Marking and unmarking a block

Before you can manipulate a Block, you must first *mark* or outline a Block. There are four ways of marking a Block in QEdit. The one you choose will depend on the editing situation and what you find most comfortable to use.

MarkLine <Alt L>

This command allows you to mark a Block in whole line increments. In other words, the Block will contain complete lines only and no portions of lines. To use this command, place the cursor anywhere on the first line of the text you wish to mark and press <Alt L>. (Notice that the line is immediately marked.) Now, move the cursor (the Block will *follow* the cursor) to the last line of text to be marked and press <Alt L> again. You now have a marked Block, ready for manipulation.

DropAnchor <Alt A>

This command allows you to mark a Block one character at a time. In other words, the Block will contain a stream of characters (which can span over multiple lines). To use this command, place the cursor over the first character of the text you wish to mark and press <Alt A>. Then begin moving the cursor toward the end of the text to be marked. Notice that the Block follows the cursor position. Once the cursor is placed

over the last character to be marked, press <Alt A> again. You now have a marked Block, ready for manipulation.

MarkCharacter

This command works just like DropAnchor except that while marking the Block, the cursor is not included within the Block.

MarkCharacter is provided as a replacement for the DropAnchor command. If you want the cursor position included in character Blocks, then continue to use DropAnchor; otherwise, replace the DropAnchor command with this command in the QCONFIG.DAT file. Refer to the "Keyboard Configuration" section of Chapter 2 for more information on changing QEdit command assignments.

MarkColumn <Alt K>

This command allows you to mark one or more columns of text. To use this command, place the cursor over the upper left-hand character of the text you wish to mark and press <Alt K>. Then begin moving the cursor to the right and/or downward. Notice that the Block follows the cursor position. Once the cursor is placed over the lower right-hand character of the Block, press <Alt K> again. You now have a marked Block, ready for manipulation.

QEdit Tip: When using the MarkLine, MarkCharacter, MarkColumn, and DropAnchor commands, it is not necessary to mark the end of the Block. QEdit will assume the end of the Block to be the current cursor position for DropAnchor, MarkCharacter, and MarkColumn and the current cursor line for MarkLine. Marking the end of the Block is only necessary when moving or copying text within the same file.

MarkBlockBegin <Ctrl KB> and MarkBlockEnd <Ctrl KK>

This is another method of marking a Block one character at a time. To mark a Block with this command, place the cursor over the first character of the text you wish to mark and press <Ctrl KB>. Then position the cursor one character past the end of the text that is to be marked and press <Ctrl KK>. The Block is now marked and ready for manipulation.

UnmarkBlock <Alt U>

Entering the UnmarkBlock command causes the currently marked Block to be unmarked.

QEdit allows you to mark one Block at a time. If you mark a Block and then go elsewhere in the file and attempt to mark another Block, QEdit will simply extend the first Block by including all the text between the original Block and the current cursor position. If you mark a Block in one file and then go to another file and mark a Block, QEdit will automatically unmark the Block in the first file.

Also, if you mix types of Block marking, by entering MarkLine followed by DropAnchor or vice-versa, QEdit will mark the Block according to the last command entered.

Manipulating blocks directly

QEdit provides several ways to manipulate a marked Block. The following commands act directly on a marked Block.

QEdit Tip: When Copying or Moving Blocks, blocks marked using the DropAnchor, MarkCharacter, MarkColumn, and MarkBlockBegin/End commands will always be inserted beginning at the current cursor position. Blocks marked using the MarkLine command will be inserted at either the line before or the line after the current cursor line. Refer to the "General Options" section of Chapter 2 for more information.

CopyBlock <Alt C>

This command makes a copy of the marked Block and inserts it where you decide. You can insert this copy of the Block at some other place in the same file or in another file. The original Block of text, from which you made the copy, is not affected.

To use this command, first mark the Block as described above. Next, move the cursor to the position in the file where you wish to insert the marked text. (Or, if you have multiple files loaded and wish to copy text from one file to another, use the NextFile, PrevFile, or EditFile commands to get a new current file and likewise position the cursor). Now enter the CopyBlock <Alt C> command. The Block will be inserted at the new position. You may notice, after you use CopyBlock, that the newly inserted Block of text

is now marked and the original Block is unmarked. To unmark the copied Block, enter the UnmarkBlock command.

QEdit provides an easy method for copying the same Block repeatedly. Refer to the Copy and Paste commands in the following section for more information.

CopyOverBlock <Alt Z>

This command is for use with column Blocks only. It works just like CopyBlock except the Block is copied to the current cursor position by overlaying existing text and without shifting text to the right.

MoveBlock <Alt M>

This command works exactly like CopyBlock with one exception: Upon entering the MoveBlock <Alt M> command, the originally marked Block is deleted from the file.

As with the CopyBlock command, you can move a Block to another part of the same file or from one file to another.

QEdit provides an easy method for deleting a Block from its original position and inserting it repeatedly at other positions.

Refer to the Cut and Paste commands in the following section for more information.

DeleteBlock <Alt G>.

This command simply deletes a marked Block of text from the file. To use this command, first mark a Block of text to be deleted, then enter the DeleteBlock command. The marked text will be deleted from the file. (Deleted Blocks will be placed in the Kill buffer. Refer to "The Kill Buffer" section in this chapter for more information.)

ShiftLeft <Shift F7> and ShiftRight <Shift F8>

These commands allow the User to shift text contained in a Block to the left or right. To use these commands, first mark a Block. Now enter ShiftLeft or ShiftRight. The entire marked Block of text will be shifted one column to the left or right respectively. If there is no marked Block of text or the cursor is outside of the marked Block, the current cursor line will be shifted. This command is very useful for changing indentation for portions of text or source code.

Manipulating blocks using scrap buffers

QEdit provides an extremely helpful device for quickly manipulating Blocks of text. This device consists of a Scrap Buffer and four QEdit commands which act on the Scrap Buffer.

The Scrap Buffer is a temporary holding area for marked Blocks of text. The commands Cut, Copy, Paste, and PasteOver are solely responsible for placing text into the Scrap Buffer and copying text from the Scrap Buffer.

When you issue a Copy or Cut command (we will discuss how to use these in the following section), the marked Block is placed into the Scrap Buffer. The next time you Copy or Cut a Block into the Scrap Buffer, the previous contents of the Scrap Buffer are deleted and replaced with the new Block.

You can repeatedly use the Paste and PasteOver commands as many times as needed to insert a copy of the Block held in the Scrap Buffer at multiple positions in your file or files. The Paste and PasteOver commands do not purge the contents of the Scrap Buffer.

Copy <grey +> and Paste <grey *> or PasteOver <Ctrl PrtSc>

To copy a section of text from its present position and insert it somewhere else:

1. Mark the text using the Block marking commands.

2. Enter Copy <grey +>. This places a copy of the marked text into the Scrap Buffer.

3. If you want to insert the text somewhere else within the same file, use the cursor movement commands to place the cursor where you wish to insert the text.

4. If you want to insert the text in another file, switch to that file using the NextFile, PrevFile, or EditFile command to access that file. Then, likewise place the cursor at the desired position.

5. Enter Paste <grey *> to insert the text. If you have copied a column Block into the Scrap Buffer and wish to insert it by overlaying existing text then use PasteOver <Ctrl PrtSc> instead of Paste.

Since Paste and PasteOver leave the contents of the Scrap Buffer intact, you can make multiple insertions in the same or different files. Simply move the cursor to the file and position where you wish to make additional insertions and enter Paste <grey *> or PasteOver <Ctrl PrtSc>. Please note that the next time you issue a Cut or Copy command, the previous contents of the Scrap Buffer will be discarded.

Cut <grey -> and Paste <grey *> or PasteOver <Ctrl PrtSc>

Cut and Paste/PasteOver work exactly like Copy and Paste/PasteOver except that Cut will delete the marked Block from the file. You can still make multiple insertions of the text using the Paste or PasteOver Commands.

QEdit Tip: QEdit can be configured to have the Cut and Copy commands act on the current cursor line if no Block is marked. Refer to the "Advanced Options" section of Chapter 2 for more information.

Manipulating blocks using scratch buffers

A Scratch Buffer is a special type of buffer to which you assign a name. QEdit allows you to create and name up to 99 Scratch Buffers for each editing session. These can be useful if you have several different Blocks of text that you want to insert in multiple locations. The commands StoreScrbuff <Ctrl BS>, AppendScrbuff<Ctrl BA>, and GetScrbuff <Ctrl BL> are used to place text in, and retrieve text from, a Scratch Buffer. Whenever you issue one of these commands, QEdit will ask you for the name of the Scratch Buffer. The contents of all Scratch Buffers are discarded when the editor is terminated.

StoreScrbuff <Ctrl BS> and AppendScrbuff <Ctrl BA>

To place a Block of text into a named buffer:

1. Mark the Block.

2. If you want to create a new Scratch Buffer containing the marked Block, enter StoreScrbuff <Ctrl BS>. (This command is also used if you wish to replace the current contents of a Scratch Buffer with the marked Block). If you want to append the marked Block to the current contents of the Scratch Buffer, enter AppendScrbuff <Ctrl BA>.

3. QEdit will prompt for the name of the Scratch Buffer.

```
Store (Append) to buffer: <Esc = abort>
```

4. Enter a name. It is best to use a name which reflects the contents of the buffer and is easily remembered.

The Block is now stored in a Scratch Buffer under the assigned name.

GetScrbuff <Ctrl BL>

To retrieve the contents of a named Scratch Buffer and insert it at the current cursor position:

1. Position the cursor where you wish the contents of the named Scratch Buffer to be inserted.
2. Enter GetScrbuff <Ctrl BL>. QEdit will prompt for the name of the Scratch Buffer to be retrieved.

```
Get from buffer: <Esc = abort>
```

3. Enter the name of the desired Scratch Buffer.
4. Repeat the above steps whenever you want to insert the contents of a Scratch Buffer into your text.

Examples of block commands

This section contains examples of commonly used Block Commands.

Copying or moving a Block within the same file.

1. Position the cursor at the beginning of the Block to be copied or moved.
2. Enter DropAnchor <Alt A> to mark a stream of characters, or MarkLine <Alt L> to mark whole lines, or MarkColumn <Alt K> to mark a column of text.
3. Position the cursor at the end of the Block to be copied or moved.
4. Enter DropAnchor, MarkLine, or MarkColumn again to mark the end of the Block.
5. Move the cursor to the location in the file where you want to insert the marked Block.

6. Enter CopyBlock <Alt C>, CopyOverBlock <Alt Z> (column Blocks only), or MoveBlock <Alt M>.
7. Enter UnmarkBlock <Alt U> to unmark the Block.

The Block has now been copied or moved.

Copying or moving a Block to another file.

1. Position the cursor at the beginning of the Block to be copied or moved.
2. Enter DropAnchor <Alt A> to mark a stream of characters, or MarkLine <Alt L> to mark whole lines, or MarkColumn <Alt K> to mark a column of text.
3. Position the cursor at the end of the Block to be copied or moved.
4. Switch to the *target* file using the file commands EditFile, NextFile, or PrevFile.
5. Move the cursor to the location in the file where you want to insert the marked Block.
6. Enter CopyBlock <Alt C>, CopyOverBlock <Alt Z> (column Blocks only), or MoveBlock <Alt M>.
7. Enter UnmarkBlock <Alt U> to unmark the Block.

The Block has now been copied or moved.

Copying or moving a Block for multiple insertions in the same file.

If you want to insert the same Block at several positions within a file, follow these steps:

1. Position the cursor at the beginning of the Block to be copied or moved.
2. Enter DropAnchor <Alt A> to mark a stream of characters, or MarkLine <Alt L> to mark whole lines, or MarkColumn <Alt K> to mark a column of text.
3. Position the cursor at the end of the Block to be copied or moved.
4. If you want to leave the Block in its original position and insert copies of it at other locations, then enter Copy <grey +>.

If you want to delete the Block from its original position and insert copies of it at other locations, then enter Cut <grey ->.

The Block is now stored in the Scrap Buffer.

5. Move the cursor to the location in the file where you want to insert the Block.

6. Enter Paste <grey *> or PasteOver <Ctrl PrtSc> (column Blocks only).

The Block is now inserted. Repeat steps 5 and 6 for each additional insertion.

Copying or moving a Block for multiple insertions in more than one file.

If you want to insert the same Block at several positions in more than one file, follow these steps:

1. Position the cursor at the beginning of the Block to be copied or moved.

2. Enter DropAnchor <Alt A> to mark a stream of characters, or MarkLine <Alt L> to mark whole lines, or MarkColumn <Alt K> to mark a column of text.

3. Position the cursor at the end of the Block to be copied or moved.

4. If you want to leave the Block in its original position and insert copies of it at other locations, then enter Copy <grey +>.

If you want to delete the Block from its original position and insert copies of it at other locations, then enter Cut <grey ->.

The Block is now stored in the Scrap Buffer.

5. Switch to the target file using the file commands EditFile, NextFile, or PrevFile.

6. Move the cursor to the location in the file where you want to insert the Block.

7. Enter Paste <grey *> or PasteOver <Ctrl PrtSc> (column Blocks only).

The Block is now inserted. Repeat steps 5-7 for each additional insertion.

Copying multiple Blocks for insertion in one or more files.

If you have several Blocks that you want to insert in several different files, follow these steps:

1. Position the cursor at the beginning of the first Block.

2. Enter DropAnchor <Alt A> to mark a stream of characters, or MarkLine <Alt L> to mark whole lines, or MarkColumn <Alt K> to mark a column of text.

3. Position the cursor at the end of the first Block.

4. Enter AppendScrbuff <Ctrl BA> if you want to append to an existing Scratch Buffer. Otherwise, enter StoreScrbuff <Ctrl BS> to create or overwrite an existing Scratch Buffer.

5. QEdit will prompt for the name of the buffer. Enter a name. (It is best to use a name which reflects the contents of the buffer and is easily remembered).

The Block is now stored in a Scratch Buffer under the assigned name. Repeat steps 1-5 for each additional Block you want to store.

6. Switch to the target file using the file commands EditFile, NextFile, or PrevFile.

7. Move the cursor to the location in the file where you want to insert a Block.

8. Enter GetScrbuff <Ctrl BL>. QEdit will prompt for the name of the Scratch Buffer. Enter the name of the desired Scratch Buffer for insertion.

Repeat steps 6 through 8 for each insertion of a stored Block.

Note: Please see QEDIT.DOC for more information on the following topics omitted here: non-block commands, copying text, moving text, deleting and undeleting text, kill buffers, macros, printing, modes, etc.

One interesting command to make note of is ToggleBoxDraw:

ToggleBoxDraw <Shift F1>

This is a specialized command which is really a mode of operation that can be switched ON or OFF. If switched ON, the cursor movement keys (up, down, right, left) can be used to *draw* lines in the text. This can be very useful for creating graphs and tables. To switch Box Drawing mode ON, enter <Shift F1>. To switch OFF, enter <Shift F1> again.

Word processing commands

QEdit has all the features you need to do basic word processing. In addition to the commands which enable you to view and edit your text (discussed in previous sections), QEdit provides word-wrapping and paragraph reformatting capabilities. Also, Appendix E contains information on QEdit commands for changing case, centering a line (or block of lines), and filling a block.

The right margin

To benefit from the word-wrap and paragraph reformatting features of QEdit, an appropriate right margin must first be set. The default setting is column 60. This may be changed using the configuration program. (Refer to the "General Options" section of Chapter 2 for instructions on how to change the right margin setting.) This value of the right margin will be used each time the editor is initiated.

QEdit provides the ability to change the right margin setting temporarily while the editor is running without affecting the permanent setting. To change the right margin setting temporarily, enter the SetRmargin <Ctrl OR> command. QEdit will prompt with:

```
right margin [1..300]:
   <Esc = abort>
60
```

Enter the desired column number for the right margin. The new setting will be in effect until the SetRmargin command is entered again or the next time the editor is initiated. WordWrap mode is automatically switched ON whenever the right margin is set using this command.

WordWrap

WordWrap is a QEdit mode which can be switched ON and OFF using the ToggleWordwrap <Ctrl OW> command. When switched ON, this mode will cause the cursor to advance automatically to the next line when text is being entered.

The cursor will advance to the next line based on the right margin, which is set using the SetRmargin <Ctrl OR> command. Once the cursor reaches the right margin and a nonblank character is typed, the cursor, along with the word (i.e., any continuous string of nonblank characters) currently being typed, will be advanced to the next line.

The cursor will not advance to the next line if the current line does not contain at least one space.

Paragraph Reformatting

The WrapPara <Alt B> command will reformat text from the current cursor position to the next blank line or the end of the file.

The right-hand side of the text will be reformatted based on the right margin. The right margin is set using the SetRmargin <Ctrl OR> command.

The left-hand side of the text will be reformatted based on AutoIndent mode. If AutoIndent mode is switched OFF, the left margin will be column one. If AutoIndent mode is switched ON, the first nonblank character on the line immediately AFTER the cursor line will be used for the left margin. Using the line AFTER the cursor line allows for special indentation for the first line of a paragraph.

Note: See the file QEDIT.DOC for Chapters 2 and 3 omitted here. Chapter 3 includes a more detailed command reference than the one from Appendix A included here.

APPENDIX A. List Of Commands

By function

Menu (Esc) Default Customized
Command Sequence Keystroke Keystroke

Cursor Movement

BegFile	Ctrl PgUp
BegLine	Home
BegScreen	Ctrl Home
CursorDown	Cursor Down
CursorLeft	Cursor Left
CursorRight	Cursor Right
CursorUp	Cursor Up
EndFile	Ctrl PgDn
EndLine	End
EndScreen	Ctrl End
GotoBlockBeg	Ctrl QB
GotoBlockEnd	Ctrl QK
GotoLine	Ctrl J
HalfPgDn	
HalfPgUp	
LineDown	
LineUp	
MakeBotofScreen	
MakeCtrofScreen	Shift F5
MakeTopofScreen	F5

PageDown	PgDn	
PageUp	PgUp	
PrevPosition	Ctrl QP	
ScreenLeft	Alt F5	
ScreenRight	Alt F6	
ScrollDown	Ctrl Z	
ScrollUp	Ctrl W	
WordLeft Ctrl	Cursor Left	
WordRight Ctrl	Cursor Right	

Editing

AddLine	EA	F2
Align		
Backspace		Backspace
DelCh		Del
DelLine		ED Alt D
DelLtWord		Ctrl Backspace
DelRtWord		Ctrl T
DelToEol	EE	F6
DupLine	F4	
GetPrev	Ctrl — (dash)	
InsertLine	EI	Alt F2
JoinLine	EJ	Alt J
Literal		Ctrl P
Return		Enter
SplitLine	ES	Alt S
UnKill	EU	Ctrl U

Block/Scratch Buffer

AppendScrbuff		CtrlBA
Copy		grey +
CopyBlock	BC	Alt C
CopyOverBlock		Alt Z
Cut		grey -
DeleteBlock	BD	Alt G
DropAnchor		Alt A
GetScrbuff		Ctrl BL
MarkBlockBegin	BB	Ctrl KB or F7
MarkBlockEnd	BE	Ctrl KK or F8
MarkCharacter		
MarkColumn		Alt K
MarkLine		BL Alt L
MoveBlock		BM Alt M
Paste		grey *
PasteOver		Ctrl PrtSc
ShiftLeft		Shift F7
ShiftRight		Shift F8
StoreScrbuff		Ctrl BS
UnmarkBlock	BU	Alt U

File

ChangeFilename	FC	Alt O or Alt F,C
EditFile	FL	Alt E or Alt F,L
Exit		Ctrl KD
File	FF	Ctrl KX or Alt F,F
GExit	QX	Alt X or Alt Q,X
GFile	F	Alt F,G
GPQuit	QQ	F3 or Alt Q,Q
GSave		Alt Y
KillFile		Ctrl KZ
NextFile	FN	Alt N or Alt F,N
PQuit	FQ	Ctrl KQ or Alt F,Q
PrevFile FP Ctrl KP or Alt F,P		
Quit		
ReadBlock	FR	Alt R or Alt F,R
SaveFile	FS	Ctrl KS or Alt F,S
WriteBlock	FW	Alt W or Alt F,W

Window

CloseWindow	WC	Ctrl OC
GrowWindow	WG	Ctrl OG
HorizontalWindow	WS	Ctrl OH
NextWindow	WN	Ctrl ON
OneWindow	WO	Ctrl OO
PrevWindow	WP	Ctrl OP
ShrinkWindow	WR	Ctrl OS
ZoomWindow	WZ	Ctrl OZ

Macro

CurrentFilename		
ExecuteScrap		Ctrl Enter
MacroRead	MR	
MacroRecord	MM	Ctrl M
MacroWrite	MW	

Printing

PrintAll	PA	Alt P,A
PrintBlock	PB	Alt P,B
PrintEject	PF	Alt P,F
SetPrintLeftMargin	PL	Alt P,L
SetPrintPageSize	PP	Alt P,P

Tab

SetCtabwidth	OC	
SetPtabwidth	OP	
TabLt Shift		Tab
TabRt		Tab

Find/Replace

Find	SF	Ctrl QF
FindReplace	SR	Ctrl QA
RepeatFind	SA	Ctrl L

Toggles

ToggleBackups	OB	
ToggleBoxDraw		Shift F1
ToggleEnterMatching	OE	
ToggleIndent	OA	Ctrl QI
ToggleInsert	OI	Ins
ToggleSmartTabs		Ctrl QT
ToggleTabsExpand		Alt V
ToggleTabsOut		AltI
ToggleWordwrap	OW	Ctrl OW

Other

Dos		Alt F9
Escape		Escape
InsertDate		
InsertTime		
MainMenu		Escape

Match		Alt F3
QuickHelp		Alt H or F1
SetEGA25		
SetEGA43		
SetRmargin	OR	Ctrl OR
Shell	FO	F9 or Alt F,O
ShowEntryScreen		Alt F10
ToggleEGA43		Ctrl F1
UndoCursorline		Ctrl QL
WrapPara		Alt B

See the file QEDIT.DOC for an alphabetical listing of commands and for Appendices B–E omitted here.

QEDIT Advanced 2.15 Registration Form

Name: _____

Company: _____

Address: _____

City: _____

State: _____ Country: _____

Zip: _____ Phone: _____

Remit to:

SemWare Order Form #9108-OF04
4343 Shallowford Rd, Suite C3A
Marietta, GA 30062-5022 USA

We take Visa, Master Card, American Express, Diners Club, Carte Blanche, and Discover. You can use this handy order form to order by MAIL, or by:

PHONE: (404) 641-9002 (Mon-Fri, 9 a.m.-5 p.m. ET)
FAX: (404) 640-6213
BBS: (404) 641-8968 (1200/2400/9600 HST, <N81>)
COMPUSERVE: 75300,2710

NOTE: We offer quantity discounts and multiple-user licenses. We also offer student/educational discounts, discounts to BBS sysops, US and Georgia govt. agencies, and approved User Groups. Call for details.

SemWare, send me:

QEdit Advanced with Printed Manual — includes single-user licensed copy of software (Version 2.15) with 90-day limited warranty, spiral-bound indexed manual, reference card, low-cost upgrades.
  each .... $54.95 $ _____
SHIPPING, each copy
  US/Canada/Mexico .... $3.00 $ _____
  Overseas .... $10.00 $ _____
Purchase Orders under $100.00, add Billing Fee. (DOES NOT APPLY to PREPAID Check or Charge Card orders.)
  Billing Fee .... $6.00 $ _____
Georgia Residents please add Sales Tax
  GA Sales Tax .... 5% $ _____
TOTAL (U.S. funds drawn on U.S. bank) ... $ _____

Payment by:
  ❑ Check ❑ Visa ❑ MC ❑ AmEx ❑ DC
  ❑ CB ❑ Discover ❑ Purchase order # _____
Authorized Signature: _____
Expiration Date: _____
Card Number: _____

PRICES SUBJECT TO CHANGE WITHOUT NOTICE. Call to confirm current prices. TSR and OS/2 VERSIONS AVAILABLE!

QFIND

Version 2.22
Copyright © 1992 by Online Reference Software

Introduction

QFIND is an ultra high-speed file finding program. It searches the disk drive(s) for the specified files using the standard DOS drive, filename and wildcard structure.

Program and Documentation Files

By default, the install program for the *DOS 6 SECRETS* diskettes will install all of the QFIND files in the directory \SECRETS\QFIND. This directory has not been added to the search path. You can execute the program from its home directory, add the directory to the search path, or copy the QFIND files to a directory that is included in the search path.

The registered version will optionally search ZIP files. The unregistered version contains the following files:

Filename	*Contents*
README	Shareware distribution instructions
README.PRN	Document printing instructions
QFIND.DOC	This file
QFIND.EXE	Uses intelligent output display
QFIND.HST	History file QFIND versions
QFIND.HDR	CompuServe file description header
QFIND.KEY	CompuServe file description keyboards
QINST.EXE	Installation and customization program
SNAPSHOT.EXE	Capture disk sectors for bug reports
ORDER.FRM	Ordering and registration form

Enhancements

QFIND has the following enhancements:

ZIP file search
Fuzzy name search
Installation program
Speed
Color
Single or multiple drive search
Elapsed time
Exclusive hidden file search
Standard DOS display format
Intelligent output display
Support 80x43 and 132x43 screen sizes
EMS memory used when available
DOS 5 extended disk partition support
Dynamic data segment allocation
Debugging aid
DesqView aware

Features

Standard features include the following:

Install program
Speed
Automatic search of multiple drives
Automatic wildcard names
Colors
Elapsed Time
Display uses DOS directory format
Intelligent I/O
Long screen support
Dynamic memory allocation
EMS memory support
Extended disk partitions
SNAPSHOT debugging aid
DesqView aware

Registered features include the following:
 Fuzzy search for embedded name characters
 Search single drive only
 Hidden-only file search
 Pause when screen is full
 Verbose path display
 Goto first match
 Scroll buffer
 CGA snow check control
 ZIP file search

Colors

The user may configure the text and inverse video colors used by QFIND during operation. The banner colors are fixed and cannot be changed. The default value is to accept whatever colors are found at the cursor location when QFIND loads. Invoke QINST and choose the Customize Colors option from the main menu. The Normal Text and Inverse Video data are displayed in the colors currently installed in QFIND. The uninstalled version of QFIND defaults to whatever colors are present at the cursor when the program is invoked. QINST provides an option on the Colors Menu to restore the defaults. QINST displays the default colors in black and white until they are changed. The demo strings are displayed in the new color after each selection. The colors are not installed in QFIND until the user exits QINST. The user is prompted to enter the hexadecimal values for the text or inverse video option. The number is always entered as a 2-digit number. Results are unpredictable if a single digit is entered. The left number is the Background color. The right number is the Foreground color.

Following are the color option settings:

 07 = White text on black
 17 = White text on blue
 70 = Black text on white (inverse)

The user may enter any value up to FF if the blink is desired. The color banners are fixed colors and may not be changed by the user. TEXT colors are for the filename matches displayed when QFIND executes. A file that matches the input argument will be displayed as a TEXT color even if it is a ZIP file. INVERSE colors are for the subdirectory names and/or ZIP filenames that are displayed. A ZIP file holding a member file that matches the input argument is displayed in INVERSE color. The member will be displayed in TEXT color.

Drive range

The user may configure QFIND to stop searching after a specified drive letter. This will be useful to those who have a network drive and don't wish to search all logical drives. Floppy drives that have been ASSIGNED to a higher letter may also be bypassed using this configuration option. The default is for drive 'Z.' Invoke QINST and choose the Drive Search Range option from the main menu. The current highest drive will display as a drive letter. The default value in QFIND is 'Z.' The default value for the starting drive is the first hard drive. QFIND begins its search with the first hard drive unless the command-line filename contains a drive letter or the first starting drive is set with QINST. In either case, the search will automatically increment the drive number until no more drives are left to search. Any drive that appears as a valid DOS disk will be searched. If the user has ASSIGNED a floppy drive as a different drive with a letter higher than the last hard disk, it too will be searched. QFIND will pause for a moment if the floppy is empty and then it will quit. Installing the highest search drive option will stop QFIND from searching assigned drives. Another use is on a very large drive that goes from C to W or even higher. In spite of QFIND's tremendous speed, it will still slow down on a very large drive, particularly so, if that drive contains many ZIP files. The user can limit the search range by using the Highest Search option.

Switches

The user may configure QFIND for any of the command-line switches. These switches are actually toggles, and may be overridden on the command line. If the /Z switch is set by QINST, using it on the command line will toggle it to OFF for a one-time run of QFIND.

CGA snow checking

QINST is invoked without a command-line name. An optional command line argument [/OFF] will bypass CGA snow checking for machines that have problems with it or don't need it.

Example: QINST /OFF

This switch will force QINST to run with snow checking disabled. The user may install this option into QFIND by selecting the SWITCHES entry on the first menu.

Performance

QFIND is significantly faster than other file finders.

The following times were derived from the OLR BBS server. Files=32, Buffers=25, No cache, Defragged disk.

827 - normal files
712 - zip files
7259 - zip members

16 MHz 80286
82MB C:
DOS 5.0

Zip Search

QFIND222	:39	1107%
PKFIND10	7:12	100%
SST 53a	7:12	100%

Normal Search

QFIND222	1.65	276%
PKFIND10	4.56	100%
SST 53a	5.47	83%

Other file finders were tested but not included. They were unable to read the ZIP files or crashed under the large disk partition.

DOS automatic wildcards

QFIND uses the DOS wildcard system for command-line arguments.

FILENAME.	= FILENAME.
FILENAME	= FILENAME.???
FILE	= FILE????.???
FILE.	= FILE .???
.EXE	= ????????.EXE

*123.*45	= ????????.???
.	= ????????.
.*	= ????????.???
.	= ????????.???
*	= ????????.???
*.	= ????????.
.X	= ????????.X??

Elapsed time

QFIND displays the total amount of time required to search all drive(s).

Totals are displayed for number of files matching the input argument, total number of files, and number of directories.

DOS directory format

QFIND displays all file data in the DOS directory format. All file data exactly matches the DOS location and format conventions.

The file attributes are appended to the standard DOS display as both a hex number and their associated name(s).

Intelligent output display

QFIND determines if DOS I/O redirection to a disk file or printer is active.

When redirection is active, all output is displayed a second time using DOS. All screen output except the author banners are then output to the redirected device or file. For the screen, the color attribute found at the starting cursor location is used.

QFIND automatically uses whichever video page number is active at start-up. The user video configuration remains unchanged.

Long screen support

QFIND uses the screen mode that is active at start-up. The 80x43 and 132x43 text screens are supported. 40 column mode is not supported.

Dynamic memory allocation

Internal data segment sizes are allocated on the fly for each logical drive that is searched. Memory is allocated in the exact amount required for each drive.

Assume no EMS memory, extended disk partitions and options enabled for a worst-case memory map:

    13K code and stack space
    128K FAT table
    64K path table
    64K scroll buffer
    64K minimum directory data
    <u>16K floating zip segment</u>

    349K memory requirements

EMS memory support

QFIND will utilize up to 12 pages of EMS memory for the path table and scroll buffer. This increases the directory data space by 132K, and reduces a potential out-of-memory error when searching large subdirectories.

QFIND identifies the EMMXXXX0 device drive signature and then allocates EMS memory via DOS interrupt 67h with LIM 3.2 or higher. The current context mapping is saved at entry and is then restored when QFIND terminates.

QFIND currently supports 512 directories and an unlimited amount of files.

QFIND can execute as a child process of a parent that uses EMS memory without interfering with the parents' data.

Extended disk partition support

QFIND supports DOS disk partitions greater than 32MB. Note that QFIND will not work on some non-DOS partitions. A valid DOS boot sector is required on each drive that is searched. Use the DOS FDISK command to DISPLAY the partition table information when a non-DOS partition is suspected.

Multiple drive search

QFIND will search multiple drives in ascending order starting with the drive specified by the user. If none is specified, then the first hard disk is assumed. Note that systems without a hard drive or RAM disk must ALWAYS specify the drive letter. QFIND defaults to the first drive after the last installed floppy disk.

SNAPSHOT disk dump

The SNAPSHOT utility captures only the Boot sector, the FAT tables, and the ROOT directory.

No user data is dumped. The captured data is then written to SNAPSHOT.DAT on the default drive. The utility does not dump SUBST, JOINed, NETWORK, or OS/2 drives. It utilizes Undocumented DOS Function 52h to determine the drive type and location of user data. DOS versions 3.1 and higher are supported. In debugging mode, QFIND operates on this disk image the same as it would on a real disk. The program can be single cycled to determine the exact nature of the problem.

Fuzzy search

QFIND will support the following command-line arguments for embedded characters. Bracketing a string of characters with '*' tells the parser to match that sequence of characters anywhere in the filename and/or extension.

Rules:

1. A fuzzy search field must begin with the asterisk (*) in the first position of the name or file extension.
2. At least one valid DOS character must be between the two asterisk brackets. The '?' wildcard is valid. Two consecutive asterisks will return an error.
3. The fuzzy character count can be no more than 8 for the name field, or 3 for the extension field. This count does not include the brackets (*). An over length name or extension returns an error.

A full length field of fuzzy bytes will be interpreted as a non-fuzzy search, and no error will be returned.

IB*AB*	= IB??????	.???
IB.COM	= <<IB>>	.COM
IB	= <<IB>>	.???
IB.i*	= <<IB>>	.i??
IB.*i*	= <<IB>>	. <<i>>
I?M.COM	= <<I?M>>	.COM
1234567.*12*	= <<1234567>>	. <<12>>
12345678	= 12345678	.???; Legal but useless
LOTUS.*123*	= LOTUS	.123; Legal but useless

123456789	= ERROR	; Over length name
**.Exe	= ERROR	; Double splats together
LOTUS.*1234*	= ERROR	; Over length
extent*A*B *C.EXE	= ERROR	; More than 2 '*' wildcards

Command-Line Switches

See Registered Documentation for more information.

Implementation

Screen performance has been improved by utilizing direct screen writes. Snow prevention is implemented only when the CGA card is detected. Snow checking is disabled when DesqView is active. QFIND uses IOCTL function 4408h to check each drive to determine if it is removable or fixed media. Removable media drives are read with BIOS, and fixed drives are read with DOS. This bypasses the DOS error message that is generated when the drive door is open. QFIND uses the DOS direct read interrupt Int25h. DOS 4 and higher versions deviate from earlier versions in the manner that this interrupt is implemented. QFIND automatically uses the extended partition calling convention for DOS 4 and up. QFIND operates correctly under MS-DOS 5.0 and the extended size disk partitions it supports. QFIND takes over one interrupt vector, Int23h (Control Break). The control break allows the user to quit QFIND at any point during the execution. The vector is restored upon any exit from the program. A user-entered ^C causes the program to terminate and restore the ^C vector at exit. QFIND performs direct reads of the disk and cannot damage the integrity of the disk. No writes are done to the disk. QFIND is written entirely in Turbo Assembler v3.2.

PIF

QFIND is "ill behaved" in screen management functions as direct screen writes are used.

QFIND is "ill behaved" for vectors as it takes over Int 23h, the Control-Break vector.

DOS Errorlevel

0 - No errors

1 - Parsing error

2 - Insufficient Memory

3 - DOS read error

4 - Invalid boot sector

5 - User ^C

6 - Network was found

CGA snow checking

CGA snow checking will be implemented when a successful test of the retrace hardware has been completed. Some oddball monographics cards do not correctly support the horizontal retrace bit in CGA status port 3DAh. The result is QFIND hanging forever, waiting for the bit to change state. The test first waits for the retrace bit to become clear, then waits for it to set again. If either test fails, then the retrace hardware is assumed defective and snow checking is disabled. It is also disabled when DesqView is active. Non-standard use of this port can cause unpredictable results. If this is suspected, the user may enable or disable CGA snow checking from the SET SWITCHES panel of QINST. This will override the start-up tests and force the CGA snow testing into the mode selected by the user. The suggested method is to set CGA snow checking to OFF which will bypass any potential hang condition. If no screen snow is encountered, leave the switch off. Performance is significantly improved with snow checking turned off.

Error messages

Unable to locate or read header for.

The ZIP file is damaged or corrupted.

Logic error locating central directory for

Internal error in QFIND

Insufficient memory to search this subdirectory

A subdirectory greater than 64K is being searched and not enough memory is available to load it.

/L switch has requested a scroll buffer and no EMS memory is available. Scroll buffer removes 64K of DOS memory that is available for directory loads.

QFIND is trying to run in 384K or less.

QFIND is running from another program which has SHELL'd out to DOS.

`Insufficient memory to search xxx.ZIP`

Not enough free memory available to load the ZIP file central directory for searching.

`Invalid boot sector for drive x:`

Non-standard DOS boot sector was detected. Bytes per sector is zero or not contained in the set of 64,128,256,512,1024,2048,4096,8192.

Boot sector has returned Zero bytes per sector. Specialized RAM disks such as some AST products do not utilize a standard DOS boot sector.

Usage

Valid switches are /G /H /L /P /S /V /Z

/G Goto Match

The default drive and directory are changed to that of the first matching file.

/H Hidden file(s)

Only file attributes that match either the system or hidden bits will be displayed. This switch disables the /Z switch.

/L List scroll buffer

The first 819 lines of output are saved in a scrollable buffer. This switch disables the /P switch. I/O redirection cancels this switch.

/P Pause mode

The program will pause when the screen is full.

/S Single drive

Only a single drive will be searched.

If not specified, the default drive is assumed. Otherwise, the first file specified by the user is the only drive searched.

/V Verbose path display

Every path searched will be displayed. Useful to build a complete path table of the specified drive(s) by searching for a nonexistent file.

/Z search zip files

All PKZIP files will be searched for member(s) matching the input argument. Corrupted ZIP files will be identified with an error message. Empty ZIP files are not reported.

Command-line examples

`QFIND file.`

Start with the default hard drive.
No dot defaults to all file extensions.
Match all occurrences of 'file????.???'

`QFIND file`

Start with the default hard drive.
The dot specifies no file extension.
Confine match to 'file'.

`QFIND *`

Start with the default hard drive.
Find all files.

`QFIND *.*`

Start with the default hard drive.
Find all files.

`QFIND *.* /H`

Start with the default hard drive.
Find hidden files only.

`QFIND *.* /V`

Start with the default hard drive.
Display all paths as they are scanned.

`QFIND *.* /H /S`

Start with the default drive.
Find hidden files only.
Check only the default drive.

`QFIND A:*.*`

Start with the A: drive.
Find all files.

`QFIND G:*.* /S`

Start with the G: drive.

Find all files.

Check only the G: drive.

```
QFIND *.* /H /S > PRN
```

Start with the default hard drive.

Find hidden files only.

Check only the first hard drive.

Redirect output to printer.

```
QFIND *.* /H /S > C:\Temp\Dir.Lst
```

Start with the default hard drive.

Find hidden files only.

Check only the first hard drive.

Redirect output to disk file on drive C:

```
QFIND *IBM*
```

Find any occurrence of the letters 'IBM' in the file name field. The file extent field defaults to .???

```
QFIND *IB??IO*
```

Find any occurrence of the letters 'IB??IO' in the filename field. The file extent field defaults to '.???'.

This example would find IBMBIO.COM.

```
QFIND *.*A*
```

Find any occurrence of the letter 'A' in the file extension field. The letter can be in position 1, 2, or 3. The filename field defaults to '????????'.

```
QFIND E:Command.Com /G
```

Find COMMAND.COM starting with the E: drive and change to the drive:directory where it was found.

SUBST drives

DOS allows disk subdirectories to appear as a different drive letter. This is done by using the SUBST command.

```
SUBST E: C:\UTIL
```

will cause the C:\UTIL subdirectory to appear as Drive E:.

QFIND and many DOS commands will ignore a SUBST drive. Under DOS 5.0, the following commands will not work, or are not recommended with a SUBST drive:

Assign	Diskcopy	Mirror
Backup	FDisk	Recover
Chkdsk	Format	Restore
Diskcomp	Label	Sys

Networks and OS/2

The current version QFIND does not support network drives or OS/2. It will complain and exit if either is detected. OS/2 is identified by checking the DOS version. A major value of 10 (OS/2 v1.0) or higher is returned by OS/2.

DesqView

QFIND is DesqView aware. It will make a call to DesqView to determine the location of the DV Alternate Screen Buffer. This display buffer will be used for all screen writes.

Cursor control and keyboard routines are done entirely with BIOS. This enables QFIND to run in the background in a small window. No polling is done during scroll buffer viewing. This allows DesqView to swap out QFIND when it is waiting for user input.

The video display routines are coded as 'DesqView Critical.' The message display routine cannot be swapped out until it has completed its function. Other than the color banners, a message display is a single line of text. QFIND crashes with old versions of QEMM (v5.00).

BUG Reports

Bug reports are welcome.

1. Make/Version of DOS
2. Copy of AUTOEXEC.BAT and CONFIG.SYS
3. Names of TSRs if any, that are loaded
4. Redirected copy of QFIND in verbose mode, e.g., QFIND<nonexistent.file> /V > DUMP.FIL. This provides a list of all subdirectories.
5. Use SNAPSHOT to take a dump of the suspect disk.
6. Run CHKDSK against the failing drive.

Attempt to diagnose any bugs by unloading all TSRs and start with as simple a system as possible.

QFIND v2.22 Registration Form

Name: _____

Company: _____

Address: _____

City: _____

State: _____ Country: _____

Zip: _____ Phone: _____

Your EMAIL: _____

QFIND found on: _____

OLR Password: _____ 3 to 8 chars

Remit to:
Bruce Gavin
9341 Ridgeside Lane
Orangevale, CA 95662

CompuServe: 70137,3244
Online Reference BBS:
(916) 988-7551 (voice)
(916) 988-0920 (data) 9600 v.42bis / 8N1

Diskette deliveries come with additional Online
Reference shareware files.

Specify Disk Size: ❏ 5.25" ❏ 3.5"

Total Copies x Unit Price .... $ _____

Total enclosed .... $ _____

Terms:
Check or Money Order drawn on a USA bank in U.S.
funds.

Upgrade Fees for Registered Owners:
Diskette Upgrade $5
Overseas Diskette Upgrade $7
Unlimited Upgrades via BBS No Charge

Registration Fees:
BBS delivery $20
Diskette delivery $25
Overseas diskette delivery $27

Please see the file ORDER.FRM for multiple-copy
discounts.

Site license provides one diskette to create multiple
copies. Please include your EMAIL address on the
order form.

This allows you to be easily notified for updates.

RELDEL

Version 1.37s
The Real File Deleter
Copyright © 1990–1993 by TARDIS DP Consultants

Introduction

RELDEL was born out of safety and security
concerns with the standard DOS DELETE command. The DOS command has two potential
problems which we needed to work around.
First is safety. The DOS DELETE command
automatically deletes all the files matching the
file specification without prompting. If you
accidentally type in DEL *.BAS instead of *.BAK,
you have deleted your Basic source code instead of backup files. Second, even if you delete
a file, many common utilities and the DOS
UNDELETE command can restore the file to
predeleted condition. If you are deleting sensitive information, and you don't want anyone
coming behind you and resurrecting your file,
the DOS DELETE command is not for you.

RELDEL, on the other hand, automatically
prompts you to delete each file. You must respond **Y** before the file is deleted. Note that
there are command-line parameters which will
delete files without prompting. RELDEL also
destroys the contents of any file (even read-
only, system, or hidden files) before deleting
them. After writing random ASCII garbage,
RELDEL writes out all ASCII 0 and then truncates the file to 0 bytes. Finally, the file is
deleted. It is impossible for any utility to resurrect the file in usable condition.

Program and Documentation Files

By default, the install program for the *DOS 6 SECRETS* diskettes will install all of the RELDEL files in the directory \SECRETS\RELDEL. This directory has not been added to the search path. You can execute the program from its home directory, add the directory to the search path, or copy the RELDEL files to a directory that is included in the search path.

Using RELDEL

RELDEL is incredibly easy to use. You have three options for its use:

1) Display each file on the screen and prompt for its deletion.
2) Display each file on the screen and automatically delete it. No prompting is performed.
3) Display nothing on the screen and don't prompt for anything.

Options

Here is a description of each option and its parameters.

Display each file on the screen and prompt for its deletion.

The command syntax is simply RELDEL <filespec>. For example, if you type

```
RELDEL *.TXT
```

all files with the TXT extension are permanently deleted. No command-line options should be entered.

Display each file on the screen and automatically delete it. No prompting is performed.

The command syntax is similar to the above example except that you add a space and /P to the end of the command. For example,

```
RELDEL F*.* /P
```

will delete all files which start with the letter F, but will not prompt you for permission to delete them. Each file still displays as it is deleted.

Display nothing on the screen and don't prompt for anything.

The command syntax is similar to the above example except that you add /D to the end of the command. For example,

```
RELDEL *.DBF /P/D
```

will delete all files with the extension DBF but will not prompt you for permission to delete them. Absolutely nothing is displayed on the screen during the process. This option is very handy in batch files or as called from another program.

As you can see, RELDEL is both powerful and easy to use. If you ever need help with the command syntax, you may simply enter RELDEL with no file specification. Help information automatically displays.

Note: As a safety precaution, RELDEL should only be used to delete files in the current directory.

RELDEL 1.37s Registration Form

Name: _____

Company: _____

Address: _____

City: _____

State: _____ Country: _____

Zip: _____ Phone: _____

Remit to:
TARDIS DP Consultants
Department 3
6 Sedely Ct.
Greensboro, NC 27455
To register RELDEL, send a check or money order for $7 (payable to Charles L. Cranford, the author).

SeekEasy

Version 7.07
Copyright © 1992 by Correlation Systems

Overview

SeekEasy is an easy-to-use *fuzzy-logic* text-finding program. It scans your disk files, finding text that even approximately matches what you asked for and displays what it finds in *best-matches-shown-first* order. It neatly solves those "I *know* it's in here *somewhere!*..." situations.

With SeekEasy, you don't have to remember the exact wording or spelling of the text in the file you're trying to find. If your requested text is even *close*, SeekEasy will find the file! For example, if a file somewhere on your disk holds the text "...THE TRUNK OF THE ELEPHANT IS...", SeekEasy can find it even if your request is for "EPHALANT'S TRUNQ."

Typical applications: finding all your source code files — perhaps created over many years — that reference a function name you now wish to change; finding the filename of a year-old letter to your Uncle Mort when you don't remember exactly the name you used in the letter, etc.

SeekEasy can search through one file or up to all the files on an entire drive. Matched text is displayed along with its filename. The *probable match* words are highlighted and twelve lines of the file around the matched words shown for context. The display window may be scrolled forward and backward through the file to show more surrounding text.

SeekEasy will scan *all* file types — word processor, database, even **.COM** and **.EXE** files if desired. It can be told which filenames or file types to ignore and/or to always include in the search. It has many default settings of this type that are user-customizable through simple menus.

Note: SeekEasy will *find* text, but it won't *alter* it — you must use the appropriate word processor, database program, etc., for that.

Some Detailed Features Of SeekEasy

■ It will handle files of any length. It displays 12 lines of a file on the screen at once, and you can scroll the 12-line window through the entire file if you wish one line or a screen at a time.

■ If so instructed, it will search one file or all the files in a directory, a directory and all its *child* directories, or a whole drive's worth of files. It will also search through specific files on a list and/or skip files on another list you can set up within SeekEasy.

For example, SeekEasy can be set to automatically search, say, REFERENC.TXT, plus all *.LST files, while skipping over a particular file named BIGFILE.LST. And these choices can be saved as the *default* mode of operation.

■ SeekEasy will search floppy disks, hard disks, Bernoulli-Box drives, etc.

■ At the end of a search, SeekEasy shows you the items it found in *best-matches-first* order — the highest scoring (as evaluated by its fuzzy-logic matching algorithms) block of text is shown first, then the next-highest scoring, etc.

■ You can mark blocks of text that SeekEasy has found, then send the blocks of text out to a printer or a disk file for reviewing later.

■ SeekEasy is highly customizable. Defaults can be set specifying the files to search, search mode, turning beeps on or off, printer port to use, screen colors, etc. — all through simple menu choices.

■ SeekEasy does not use up valuable disk space with index files, as do cross-referencing programs.

■ Wherever it makes sense, each screen in SeekEasy has one or more pages of Help Screens behind it, available at the press of the F1 key.

System Requirements

SeekEasy will run fine on just about any IBM PC or compatible computer. The minimum system requirements are

PC-DOS or MS-DOS, version 2.0 or higher.

If running under Windows, Windows 3.0, or higher.

256K or more of RAM.

One or more disk drives.

Monochrome or color monitor.

Parallel- or serial-interface printer for printouts.

Installing SeekEasy

General issues:

There are two things you should probably do before you install and use SeekEasy. Neither is required, but each may make using SeekEasy easier and more productive:

A) Run the DOS TREE command and direct the output to your printer, for later study. This will show you how your disk is divided up. To do this at the DOS prompt, type **TREE > PRN** and then press Enter. This assumes your PRN device is on, and if it is a serial printer, it has been set to the proper baud rate.

B) If it's not already part of your AUTOEXEC.BAT file, issue the following command at the DOS prompt: **PROMPT PG** and press Enter. This changes the standard DOS prompt to show your current location in the directory tree. It would be best to place this command into your AUTOEXEC.BAT file, so it will be invoked each time you turn on your system.

SeekEasy will run under Windows 3.0 and above. It operates the same as under DOS, except that under Windows it can perform searches in the background (in 386 Enhanced Mode).

Program and Documentation Files

By default, the install program for the *DOS 6 SECRETS* diskettes will install all of the SEEKEASY

files in the directory \SECRETS\SEEKEASY. This directory has not been added to the search path. You can execute the program from its home directory, add the directory to the search path, or copy the SEEKEASY files to a directory that is included in the search path.

For best performance, copy both the SEEKEASY.EXE and the SEEKEASY.PIF files from our disk to your \WINDOWS directory. An alternate choice would be to copy the two files to any directory on your DOS *Path* list.

Running SeekEasy

Running SeekEasy under MS-DOS

To run SeekEasy once it's installed per the above instructions, just type **SEEKEASY** and then press Enter. If the program does not run, it is probably because it is not in a directory on your DOS Path.

If you wish to run SeekEasy under the DOS 5.0 DOSSHELL program-switcher, we refer you to your DOS manual. See Chapter 3 (MS-DOS Shell Basics) and Chapter 8 (Customizing MS-DOS Shell). They explain it better than we could.

Running SeekEasy under Windows

Since it's basically a DOS application, SeekEasy runs best in the full-screen mode. It will do searches in the background, if Windows is running in the 386 Enhanced mode.

In the preferred full-screen mode, you may use the standard Windows program switching keys: Alt-Enter toggles SeekEasy between a window and full-screen display mode. Alt-spacebar brings up the "switch to another program" menu, and Alt-Esc toggles between SeekEasy and any other open program windows.

The SEEKEASY.PIF file is a Program Information File that tells Windows about the program and its capabilities. SeekEasy will run under Windows just using the default PIF Windows assigns to unknown programs, but it will run better if Windows can use the customized SeekEasy .PIF file.

Problems to watch for when running under Windows 3.0

To search files in a CD-ROM under Windows using SeekEasy or any other program, two things have to be verified or done:

A) If it isn't there already, add the following statement to your SYSTEM.INI file in the [386Enh] section:

```
DEVICE=LANMAN10.386
```

Yes, you may not be on a LAN (Local Area Network), but you still have to do this, say the Windows folks, in their README.TXT file. Believe it. If you don't do this, you WILL eventually see crashes while searching your CD-ROM with SeekEasy!

B) If it isn't already there, expand/copy the LANMAN10.386 file from the Windows source disk to your C:\Windows directory. Note that you have to *Expand* this file while copying it. It is delivered in compressed form on the Windows source (floppy) disk. For Windows 3.0, the compressed version is 1548 bytes long and the expanded version is 8786 bytes. To expand the LANMAN10.386 file, first find the EXPAND.EXE program file on the Windows source disks, and copy it into your hard disk's \Windows directory. Then insert the Windows source disk that has the LANMAN10.386 file on it, and from your Windows directory on your hard disk issue the command:

```
EXPAND A:LANMAN10.386 C:\WINDOWS
```

You should then see the LANMAN10.386 file on your hard disk, and it should be larger than the copy on your Windows source (floppy) disk was.

Screens

SeekEasy uses a variety of screens.

Main search screen

To perform a search, you need to specify two things:

A) The text you'd like to find matches to
B) Which file or files you want the program to search

Pressing the Enter key toggles you between the two fields that specify these items.

You specify the text to be matched in the blank screen area to the right of the **Search for:** prompt.

Specifying which file or files to search is a bit more involved. The basic file specification is the file-spec indicated in the blank screen area to the right of the **File Spec:** prompt. This basic specification can be added to, subtracted from, or overridden by settings made on the **Search Spec** screen which can be reached by pressing F2. See the discussion in the following section regarding the Search Specification Screen for a more complete description of how this all works.

Note that when you press Enter to select the **File Spec:** area, a box pops up showing **Search Specification** information. This is just a summary of the major settings from the Search Specification Screen, shown for your verification prior to your starting a search. To actually change the settings, you must press F2 to go the Search Specification Screen.

The file specification may include the DOS wildcards **?** and *****. **?** means *any single character matches this*, while the ***** means *any one or more characters matches this, from here to the end of the filename prefix or suffix*. See your DOS manual for a more thorough description of wildcards. The file specification most people use is just ***.***.

When you're viewing the results of a search, you may occasionally notice that the same line of information appears in two different items. This is normal. In *Stream* mode, to ensure the text you are looking for is not split — partially in one item and partially in another — the items overlap by one line. Thus, if a search found an item with high-scoring text in the last line of the item, it would also see that the next item (with its one line of overlap) STARTED with that line, and give it a high match score also.

In *Formatted* mode, the program logic tries to break *items* at the ends of sentences. If it cannot find what it believes is the end of a sentence within the last three lines of a screen's worth of text, it will arbitrarily force the end of the item, and set a one line duplication/overlap as is done by the Stream mode. Except for this case, *Formatted* mode does NOT overlap item boundaries.

If you have set the settings on the Search Specification screen to perform a search that includes the files listed on the *Scan List* as well as the one you specify on the Main Search Screen, then the instructions to the right of the *Search Spec:* prompt will change to indicate that putting an entry there is optional. The program will start a search without any specified file(s) here since the Scan List entries on the Search Specification Screen will satisfy the requirement that *some* file specification must exist before a search can be done.

Due to memory limitations, SeekEasy will display only the 200 best matches to the text you told it to search for. If what you ask for isn't within the best 200 matches, you need a clearer search specification!

SeekEasy DOES "evaluate" all of the matches it finds while searching. The 200 items you see after a search operation are the BEST 200 it could find, not just the first 200!

When you press F10 to begin a Search operation, SeekEasy may occasionally warn you that it appears you are performing the same search you just did, and ask for verification. The purpose for this is if you had just completed a LONG search of a big hard disk or CD-ROM, you DON'T want to accidentally press F10 again, throw away all the search results, and start the search all over again! SeekEasy therefore requests confirmation before it starts the search, to ensure that you really *do* want it to "forget" all the search results but repeat the identical search again.

Starting a Search Operation erases all records of the previous Search Operation, so be sure you are done with the results of one search before beginning another.

Strange looking characters on the screen, unusual data display, etc.: SeekEasy attempts to work with the widest possible range of data formats. One of the ways it does this is to clip off the high bit (bit 7, counting from 0) of the file data it reads. This allows files in WordStar and similar formats to be read without confusion. This bit is normally 0 for standard ASCII so removing it creates no problems. However, for graphics characters, clipping off this bit sometimes converts the graphics character into a printable character, which will be displayed on the screen. This is normal and just a function of SeekEasy's efforts to convert everything it sees into human readable format.

Also note that while Formatted mode tries to display data in a more normal manner — expanding tabs, recognizing carriage-return/line-feeds, etc. — it also clips the high bit and will also generate the same strange looking characters.

Down near the bottom right corner of the screen you'll see two status items displayed — **MODE:** and **BEEP:**. These are information-only displays of settings made in the Utilities Settings screen, reachable by the F3 key. To change these, you have to go to the Utility Settings screen. These status items are shown here just for your information, as it is often useful to know what they are prior to starting a search. The **BEEP:** setting can also be changed DURING a search.

Search specification screen

Any changes you make to the settings on this screen only apply for the current SeekEasy session, unless you save them as your new default setting. See the F10 discussion below.

The discussion that follows assumes you are familiar with DOS's directory structure. If not, please review the information in your DOS manual regarding directories, paths, and so on.

Once SeekEasy is running, it ignores any DOS path settings. SeekEasy's search area is controlled only by the path information you specify on the Search Specification screen.

Starting at the top of this screen, and working down:

The *current location* shown just below the screen title refers to the drive and disk path/directory that you were in when you started the SeekEasy program. Once SeekEasy has been started, this cannot be changed. These settings are the ones used in the F2 operation discussed below, if no explicit settings are shown there.

F2 — START SEARCH AT: This specifies where SeekEasy BEGINS its search. It may also be where the search ends, depending on other settings on this screen.

A typical entry in this section would be **C:\TEST**. In this, the DRIVE (or disk) is specified as **C:** and the STARTING DIRECTORY is specified as **\TEST**.

This area is left blank in the "as shipped" configuration of SeekEasy. With this blank, when you start SeekEasy from a given directory, the search automatically starts in that directory, on that drive. This was deemed the most general-purpose setting possible.

Note that one common mistake is to put an entry in this spot of **C:**. This specifies the DRIVE (**C:**) but NOT the **root directory** (\).

F3 — SEARCH AREA: This specifies HOW FAR the search goes once it is started in the drive/directory set by the F2 setting above. The options are **this directory**, **this plus child directories**, and **the entire drive**.

The first choice — *just the selected directory* — says to search all the files in this directory that meet the file spec criteria.

The second choice — *child directories* — says to include all subdirectories in the search.

The third choice — *the whole disk option* — says only to use the drive information ("C:") in the F2 setting. Any directory/path information is ignored, since the search will always start at the root directory of the specified drive and cover ALL directories in the drive.

Example:

Suppose you had a disk directory structure (simplified for this discussion) as follows:

```
C:\
| |—DOS
| |—UTIL
| |—TEST
        | |—HARDWARE
        | |—SOFTWARE
```

Further, suppose your *starting directory* was **C:\TEST**.

- If you chose **just the selected directory**, your search would only cover the files in the C:\TEST directory.

- If you chose **selected directory plus its child directories**, then your search operation would cover the files in THREE directories:

    C:\TEST
    C:\TEST\HARDWARE
    C:\TEST\SOFTWARE

- And, if you chose the **whole disk option**, search would cover ALL SIX directories — the three above, plus:

    C:\ (the root directory)
    C:\DOS
    C:\UTIL

F4 — SEARCH FILE: While the F2 and F3 keys above specify the area(s) on the disk to be searched, this specifies which files within those areas will be opened and examined.

SeekEasy builds a *file specification* — or file spec for short — from up to three sources:

A) The **File Spec:** you entered on the Main Search Screen.

B) The Scan List file specifications.

C) The Skip List file specifications.

This entry controls which of the above three sources are active during a search.

There are four choices:

- **The Specified File Only**: This tells SeekEasy to JUST search the file(s) specified in the **File Spec:** entry the user typed in on the Main Search Screen. You may have specified a specific file (**MYFILE.DOC**) or a group of files, using wildcard characters (**MYFILE.***).

- **The Specified File Blocked By The Skip List Names**: This is the default configuration as shipped. This tells SeekEasy to operate the same as in the above mode, EXCEPT to ignore any file whose name is covered by the filenames (or specifications using wildcards) shown in the Skip

List. This is normally used to speed searches by having SeekEasy skip **.EXE** and **.COM** files, etc.

There are two things to know about priorities here:

First, the Skip List can block a file specified by the **File Spec:** entry. In other words, if a user specified a file spec of **HELP.***, and had a Skip List entry of ***.EXE**, SeekEasy would search a file called HELP.DOC, but would NOT search a file named HELP.EXE, if it existed.

Second, the Skip List will NOT block a user-entered **File Spec:** entry if that entry is SPECIFIC — if it has no wildcards in it. Thus, if in the above example the user had specified a file spec — not of **HELP.*** but of **HELP.EXE** — then SeekEasy WOULD search the HELP.EXE file, even though it was on the Skip List.

- **The Specified File, Blocked By The Skip List Names Plus The Scan List Names**: This acts just like the option above, except IN ADDITION TO the user-entered **File Spec:** name, the program also uses all of the entries, if any, in the Scan List.

As before, the Skip List can block Scan List or user-entered **File Spec:** entries, unless they are specific filenames (without wildcards).

If this option is chosen, the user does not have to actually enter a **File Spec:** entry on the Main Search Screen to start a search, as long as the Scan List has at least one entry.

- **The Specified File, Plus The Scan List Names**: This acts just like the option above would act if the Skip List were empty: it searches **File Spec:** plus Scan List files.

As an example: If you wished to search, say, all **.DOC** and **.TXT** files, you could specify this any number of ways, all equivalent. Here are two:

A) Enter ***.DOC** for the **File Spec:** info on the Main Search Screen, and put ***.TXT** in

the Scan List, then choose the Search Files choice of Specified File Plus Scan List Names.

B) Or, you could leave the **File Spec:** entry on the Main Search Screen blank, and put ***.DOC** and ***.TXT** both into the Scan List, and enable that.

F5 — SKIP LIST: This is used per the above instructions. Entries must be separated by spaces. They can be uppercase or lowercase, or any mixture. Note that if you specified a file specification of ***.*** here, it would block ALL files from being searched when this list is activated, except for any file specified on the Main Search Screen without any wildcards at all. You normally should NOT use a file specification of ***.*** here.

The normal use for the Skip List is to ignore files you don't want to waste time searching through. Users normally customize this list to block the scanning of large files on their systems that have nothing of interest in them. The settings shipped as the factory defaults are only a first approximation of the files most users want to skip. You should change these settings to suit your preferences, then save the settings as the new default settings.

F6 — SCAN LIST: Same formatting, etc., as the above. You MAY use ***.*** here if you wish, without any danger of missing files.

F10 — SAVE AS NEW DEFAULTS: This takes ALL of the settings on this screen, plus those on the **UTILITY SETTINGS** screen, and saves them to disk as the new default values. The next time SeekEasy is run from disk it will come up with the settings as they were when you saved them as your new defaults.

Note that the defaults settings are stored inside the SEEKEASY.EXE program disk file. There are no separate configuration files to worry about. This will become apparent by the status messages issued during this operation, as the program finds the SEEKEASY.EXE file, then finds the proper spot to insert the information, then successfully saves it. However, you will NOT cause any problems if you rename SeekEasy to something shorter such as SE.EXE, etc. It "knows" what name it's run as.

Utility settings screen

As in the Search Specification screen, any changes you make here only hold for the current SeekEasy session, until you save them as your new default settings, see the F10 discussion below.

Going down the functions, from the top of the screen on down:

F2 — BEEP AT END OF A SEARCH: This one's pretty clear. Try the three choices and see which one you like. Note that this item can also be changed DURING a search operation itself — see the bottom of the *Search In Progress* screen for what key to use. A change made then is just like a change made here. It will remain as you set it, but will not become the new default setting until you save it to the disk as such.

F3 — BEEP ON ERRORS: This either enables or not a single beep whenever an error occurs such as disk-read error, trying to send a marked block out to a printing device that doesn't exist, etc. Set it to match your preference.

F4 — EXPAND TABS: The program help screen says it all.

F5 — PRINTER LOCATION: Used to select the destination of marked blocks sent to the printer. The factory default setting is LPT1. *Note:* If you select a non-existent printer, or if you have a printer problem while printing marked blocks, don't panic. Even if everything appears locked up, be patient. At the most, in about 90 seconds SeekEasy will unlock things and recover, giving you an error message explaining the problem.

If you're using a serial printer and it doesn't respond, suspect baud rate settings, or that the printer or its cable is not wired to hold both the CTS and DSR signals high when it's ready to accept data.

F6 — PRINTER LEFT-MARGIN OFFSET: The program help screen says it all. Experiment with this to see what your printer is most happy with, then save it as the new default setting.

F7 — SEARCH AND DISPLAY MODE: The program's help screen pretty much covers this. *Note:* If you do any *block mark* operations, then change this mode from Formatted to Stream or

Stream to Formatted. The blocks you marked may now have their start/finish points in error by one line or so.

F8 — FLAGGING MATCHED TEXT IN REVERSE VIDEO: This applies to the results of Search operations. Words that the SeekEasy algorithm thinks are significant are normally flagged in reverse video to make the probable matches easier to find on the screen. How the displaying is done does not change how items are evaluated or scored, only which words are flagged in reverse video.

The choices are

- **Flag All Matches**: SeekEasy flags any word fragment that it thinks is even a little bit significant. This gives you the most information, but results in a very cluttered display.

- **Flag Medium And Strong Matches**: This raises the threshold of what should be shown in reverse-video slightly, to get rid of some of the clutter. This is the factory default setting.

- **Flag Only Strong Matches**: This only reverse-video flags good, solid matches but may cause you to miss something "sorta similar" to what you asked for because it wasn't flagged.

- **Flag No Matches At All**: If you don't like the reverse-video flagging of probable matches, choose this — it doesn't flag anything in search results, just shows you what it found in the standard best-matches-first order.

Note: This setting can be changed at any time without affecting the search results. You can look at the search results, go to this screen, and change this setting, then return to the Main Search Screen and see how the data looks at the new setting.

F9 — TEXT/BACKGROUND COLOR SELECT: The factory default setting for this is #3, yellow/blue. When it's started, SeekEasy checks the hardware configuration and either allows color choices or allows only black and white choices. You can change the choices, and even save them as the new defaults, but SeekEasy will still allow only what it thinks are the proper range of choices the next time it is run. You can force it to think it is running on a color or black-and-white system by invoking SeekEasy with an extra parameter, as

```
SEEKEASY C <Enter>
SEEKEASY M <Enter>
```

SEEKEASY C forces the program to ignore the hardware configuration it detects and allow color choices.

SEEKEASY M tells it to act as if it detects a black-and-white (monochrome) system and allow only B/W color combinations.

F10 — SAVE DEFAULTS: See the description of the similar key in the description of the Search Specifications screen. Note that if you do this, it saves both the settings on this screen AND the settings on the Search Specifications screen, as the new defaults.

Block mark/print screen

The same scrolling keys work essentially the same way here as they did in the Main Search Screen.

Follow the screen instructions to mark the block. The text shown in reverse-video is what will be sent to the printer or disk file you specify.

Be sure to move the cursor to the line PAST the last line you want included in your block.

If you choose to send the block to a disk file, SeekEasy may tell you that the file that you specify already exists. If so, it will give you the option of overwriting the file or appending the block onto the end of the file. Overwriting erases the old file and replaces it with a new one holding just the block you've marked, while Appending simply adds the content of the block onto the end of the existing file.

When the marked block is being sent to the printer or a disk file, the display will position the text such that the top line in the display area is the one currently being sent to the printer or disk file. Thus you can monitor the progress of the operation by watching the display and seeing what data is currently going out. At the end of the operation, the last line of the marked block will be shown at the top line of the display area.

Searching screen

You may end the search operation at any time by pressing the ESC key. SeekEasy will use whatever it has managed to find in its search up till that time.

Each *progress indicator dot* indicates 10% of the file has been read.

F3 : During a search (but not after), if you realize you wish to change how or if the computer beeps at the end of a search, just press F3 to skip through all the possible *beep after* settings. Just press the key once, then wait — it may take a second or so for the program to break into its search at a convenient spot to act on your keypress. You'll see the new status reflected at the top of the screen.

F9 : If you see that the program has started scanning through a large file, and you know that the file doesn't have any information in it you want, you can skip the rest of it by pressing this key. SeekEasy will go on to the next file and continue its search.

If the file (or file type — .PIC, whatever) you skipped is a file or file type you regularly have to skip over, you should consider adding it to the Skip List and saving that as your new default setting.

Performance Tips

See the full manual supplied to registered users for information regarding how to maximize the speed of your Search operations. There are many (sometimes interacting) choices in this area.

The full manual also contains information describing how the SeekEasy algorithm "sees" your search request. This will help you perform more accurate searches, increasing the odds that the item you want will be the first one or two SeekEasy shows you after a search.

Technical Support

Correlation Systems offers unlimited telephone and by-mail support of SeekEasy to registered users. We'll answer simple questions about getting SeekEasy up and running from anyone, but we can handle more complicated issues only for registered users.

SeekEasy 7.07 Registration Form

Name: _____

Company: _____

Address: _____

City: _____

State: _____ Country: _____

Zip: _____ Phone: _____

Remit to:
Correlation Systems
P.O. Box 39
Lomita, CA 90717
(310) 833-3462,

Send cash, check, or money-order (no credit card orders).

SeekEasy is distributed as SHAREWARE. The full registration fee is just $39.95. For this you receive a disk with the latest SeekEasy program version, a full user's manual — including many "performance optimizing" tips available nowhere else, and unlimited telephone support for SeekEasy-related questions. Also, as a registered user you are notified about upgrades and receive special low pricing.

TO ORDER: Please fill out the form, and include $39.95 (California residents also add sales tax; for orders from outside the USA, add $10). All payment must be in U.S. funds, payable on a U.S. bank. Prices already include postage and handling. If you have any questions, call 10 a.m.-6 a.m., California time.

Amount each .... $39.95 $ _____
Sales tax (Calif. residents only) .... $ _____
Orders from outside USA add .... $10.00 $ _____
Total enclosed .... $ _____

Payment by: ❏ Check ❏ Cash ❏ Money Order

Specify Disk Size: ❏ 5.25" ❏ 3.5"

Lot # 0007

SPINTEST & SPINTIME

by Steven Gibson

Introduction

Please see "A GUIDE TO HARD DISK SECTOR INTERLEAVING" included in the file INTLEAVE.DOC. A few excerpts are included here. The guide carefully shows how to use the two included programs to determine whether your own IBM PC or compatible's hard disk drives have their sector interleave set correctly. The too often neglected SECTOR INTERLEAVING factor of a hard disk has a dramatic impact on data transfer rates. So many computers are so badly interleaved that it's quite likely that you could increase your own hard disk's performance by four to seven times just by optimally setting your disk's interleave factor!

Included with this INTLEAVE.DOC file are two small programs: SPINTEST.COM and SPINTIME.COM. The main program, SPINTEST.COM, determines how many disk revolutions your IBM compatible personal computer requires to read an entire 17 sector track from its hard disk. (SPINTEST is also fully compatible with the 25 or 26 sector tracks used with the high-density RLL controllers.) Running SPINTEST on the many computers at Gibson Research, and in many local computer dealerships, we discovered something quite surprising: Most computers being sold today are horribly interleaved. We turned up many machines which required more than 17 entire revolutions just to read or write one full track! These same machines flew along at 4:1 but not at 3:1. Any way you look at it, the issue of sector interleaving involves the complex interactions among the disk drive, the controller make and model (even the revision level), the processor, and system clock rate.

Program and Documentation Files

By default, the install program for the *DOS 6 SECRETS* diskettes will install all of the "SPIN" files in the directory \SECRETS\SPINTOOL. This directory has not been added to the search path. You can execute the program from its home directory, add the directory to the search path, or copy the "SPIN" files to a directory that is included in the search path.

Overview of the Interleave Diagnostic Programs

The issues involving hard disk sector interleaving have gone unnoticed for so long because there has never been a clear way to see what's really going on deep inside a hard disk. After seeing the importance of this issue, we decided to change this. The two programs SPINTEST and SPINTIME determine exactly how many revolutions the disk requires to transfer one entire track of data for any standard MFM or RLL controller. The programs were hand-written in 100 percent machine language (as is everything Steve Gibson writes and Gibson Research publishes) to give them the required measuring resolution speed.

The Spintest Program

SPINTEST determines exactly how many revolutions your hard disk currently requires to perform a full track transfer. DOS transfers a full track whenever programs or files larger than 9K are read or written, which is most of the time. SPINTEST does NOT directly read your drive's interleave, but the drive's interleaving performance can be easily inferred from SPINTEST's full track transfer revolution count.

SPINTEST averages the time required for each of over two hundred full track reads in order to accurately determine the revolution count per read. Then, the number of revolutions required to read just one track and the controller's full-track data transfer rate are computed. SPINTEST only reads data from your drive so data is NEVER altered.

Over two hundred track reads were used because of the inconsistent disk transfer behavior of AT&T's 6300 machines. These exhibit a maddening inconsistency in their ability to transfer disk data. Sometimes they get the next sector and often not. This means that a much looser than normal interleave generates MUCH BETTER overall disk throughput for AT&Ts. For this reason, and to guarantee correct results on any machines which may behave similarly, SPINTEST performs many track reads and averages the results.

Since SPINTEST measures track read time, it must assume a given ratio between elapsed time and disk rotation rate. Some "weirdo" clone computers have a clock which runs faster than normal when in their "turbo" (8 MHz) mode, and some lap computers have tiny hard disks spinning at weird speeds. If these do not sound like your situation, SPINTEST will deliver correct readings and you'll not need SPINTIME's confirming measurements.

But if EITHER of these cases might be you (if you have a weirdo clone computer or hard disk sporting laptop), SPINTIME will tell you for sure. SPINTEST is only usable when SPINTIME gives standard readings. The single (not surprising) exception to this is for the AT&T 6300 and 6300 Plus machines. Due to the overall problems they experience with disk transfers, SPINTIME may show a reading lower than 3600 RPM. For 6300's this is normal. SPINTIME is interesting regardless since it determines EXACTLY how fast your hard disk is really spinning!

Running SPINTEST

To run SPINTEST, simply type its name at the DOS prompt.

Important!: Read the section IMPORTANT SPINTEST AND SPINTIME NOTES, before you begin!

Since SPINTEST takes the average of over 200 track reads, the time required to run this test will vary between approximately 14 seconds for a fast 2:1 interleaved machine to 98 seconds for an incorrectly interleaved 26-sector RLL encoded hard disk. So simply type **SPINTEST** at the DOS prompt and wait a minute or two.

Running SPINTIME

SPINTIME has two purposes: To determine the speed of your system's clock (if you suspect that it might be weird), and to verify that your system's hard disk is spinning at close to the 3600 RPM standard. Your system's clock is checked by measuring SPINTIME's exact execution time. It should require EXACTLY 60 SECONDS to run, no matter what. During that time, it is busy watching your hard disk spin, counting every revolution. After EXACTLY 60 seconds, it displays your drive's exact RPM (within its measuring resolution.) IF SPINTIME's total execution time is NOT EXACTLY 60 seconds or the displayed RPM is not close to 3600, SPINTEST's reported revolution count won't mean anything either. SPINTIME's real value is to assure you that SPINTEST is delivering worthwhile answers.

Important SPINTEST and SPINTIME Notes!

Both programs assume and require DOS 2.0 or higher. They operate on your system's FIRST hard disk only (drive C). The hard disk must be bootable, and have its controller plugged into a slot that does not require special CONFIG.SYS device drivers for operation. SPINTEST and SPINTIME will never disturb your hard disk data, but if your disk is some kind of odd-ball, they may not function correctly.

The tests will be more accurate if your normal collection of memory-resident programs (if any) are not in memory at the time. Many resident programs "steal" so much time from the computer that a delicate timing analysis could be upset. It would be wise to boot your machine from a plain DOS diskette when running these tests for maximum reliability. Also, turn off (or better yet remove) any disk caching software you might be using. Disk caching intercepts the disk reading performed by the programs and renders their measurements invalid (and rather humorous). By the way, disk caching program

performance is significantly improved through proper disk interleaving.

What It All Means

So now you're wondering: What do the numbers mean? How do they compare with industry norms and everyone else's? Should I be dancing on roof tops or wringing my dealer's neck?

A hard disk spins at 3600 revolutions per minute, or 60 revolutions per second. A track has 17 sectors of 512 bytes per sector. This means that data passes under your drive's head at a rate of 522,240 bytes per second. (This number is 768,000 for RLL controllers with 25-sector tracks.) Your system will achieve some fraction of this maximum possible rate as determined by the number of rotations required to read or write each track. The number 522,240 (or 768,000) is divided by the number of revs per track (as SPINTEST does) to calculate your drive's data transfer rate.

Since your system's performance is meaningful only when compared to other properly and improperly interleaved systems, see the table (included with the on-line documentation file INTLEAVE.DOC) to get a feeling for where the industry stands.

We have seen that WD controllers which miss at 3:1 will do beautifully at 4:1. Several InfoWorld readers have independently confirmed that AT&T machines (with WD controllers) perform best at the very loose interleave of 6:1. Even the old true blue IBM controller which runs at 6:1 can always do 5:1 and even 4:1 in a faster than 4.77 MHz machine.

Determining Factors

So what system factors influence and determine the optimal interleave setting for a given set of equipment? After a sector of data has been read it must be moved from the controller's on-board buffer into the computer. This is done with a process known as DMA (Direct Memory Access). The time required to transfer the sector determines how soon the controller will be ready to read the next sector. For this reason add-in Accelerator "Turbo" Cards do not generally change a machine's optimum interleave since the main system clock speed, which continues to control DMA memory accesses, is not changed. The less expensive "Speed Booster" products which alter the basic system clock timing DO have a tremendous impact on optimal interleave by running the DMA faster and thus moving the data in and out faster.

Gibson Research and Interleaving

When we began these experiments, we had no idea that so many personal computers were so poorly interleaved. Without the aid of SPINRITE, changing a hard disk's sector interleave manually requires first backing up all hard disk data onto some secure medium. Then a low-level reformatting is performed. This messy task was never designed for the casual computer user since it requires unpublished knowledge of the internal details of your controller, using the DOS DEBUG command to poke hexadecimal values into the 8088's machine registers and starting the low-level format. After this, the FDISK and FORMAT commands are used to create a partition table and lay down the high-level formatting information. After all this, the backed-up data must be copied back onto the drive.

Then, if the experimentally chosen interleave was not correct, most of the process would have to be repeated with a different trial interleave factor. Responding to the clear need for a better solution to the task of hard disk sector interleaving optimization, we developed the

now-famous SPINRITE product to automate and streamline this "re-interleaving" process.

SPINRITE quickly determines the optimal interleave setting for any disk of any size in any system with any clock rate. Once determined, the existing interleave of the disk can be RESET automatically and in just a few minutes, leaving all your disk data intact and in place! It also performs several other useful hard disk utility functions which have never before been available.

Get Your Disk Spinning Right!!

Even if SPINTEST turned in excellent results of 3 or 4 revs, you should still check out Gibson Research's new product for the other surprising (never before offered) hard disk capabilities it brings. If you received results like 10, 12, or even 17, 18, or 19 revolutions, there is no doubt that your system could be running four to five times faster in minutes!

To receive all the details about SPINRITE simply phone or send your name and address either through our 24-hour BBS or through the US Mail. Ask for our completely descriptive SPINRITE literature.

GIBSON RESEARCH CORPORATION
22991 La Cadena
Laguna Hills, CA 92653
Phone: (714) 830-2200
Tech Support: 830-2500
Fax: 830-0300 24-hour
BBS: 830-3300

STACKEY

Version 4.0
CTRLALT Associates (R)
Copyright © 1986–1992 by Barry Simon & Richard M. Wilson

Introduction

STACKEY, a utility from the makers of CTRLALT, will automatically place keystrokes in your keyboard buffer. It is intended for use in connection with batch files. Here is a typical example of a batch file "lot.bat" for use with 1-2-3 using STACKEY:

```
stackey W18 CR"/FR%1.wk1" CR
123
```

Entering "lot mysht" at the DOS command line starts the batch file with mysht as %1. STACKEY has the command line passed to it by the batch processor with %1 already replaced by mysht. Thus STACKEY places in the keyboard buffer the text: **/FRmysht.wk1** followed by a carriage return. The initial W18 tells STACKEY to pause about 1 second to allow 1-2-3 to load. If it weren't there 1-2-3 would happily remove the keystrokes from the buffer before allowing any input. These characters wait in the buffer until a program requests keyboard input. The batch file then loads 1-2-3 which requests input and gets it from STACKEY. /FR calls up a dialog to retrieve a worksheet and %1.wk1 followed by a CR loads that worksheet. The CR after the W18 will banish the opening logo screen in those versions with an opening logo.

And this example hardly uses the power of STACKEY: you can stack any function key or legal Alt-key combination; you can even stack today's date or the current directory name. You can stack commands to turn the Num Lock state on and off. You can stack commands to set colors on the CGA and remap colors on the EGA or VGA.

You can stack a PrtSc. You can stack commands to call up SIDEKICK, SIDEKICK PLUS, or any other program that pops up on pairs of shifts. You can invoke CTRLALT PLUS, CAROUSEL, or DESQVIEW. STACKEY has numerous methods for controlling the flow of a STACKEY

"script." You can put delays in or have STACKEY delay its playback until a given message appears on the screen or you can have script playback pause until you hit a key. You can pause playback and later restart it with appropriate hotkeys and even flush STACKEY's buffer that way. STACKEY scripts can even branch depending on what hotkey is hit or what message appears on the screen.

Despite its power, ease of use is an important part of STACKEY. Rather than cryptic codes for keys like F1, you need only use F1. There is even a recorder which you can use to make batch file fragments with the keystrokes you want.

STACKEY also has a utilities mode allowing you to use it to replace lots of little utilities that switch monitors or ports, restore or change the cursor, or even reboot your machine. STACKEY comes with a second program BATUTIL, described in a separate manual with which you can manipulate your environment or get input in batch files.

Finally STACKEY has a special mode of interest to programmers giving you access to STACKEY's insides, allowing you to place inline code in the middle of a STACKEY script.

And STACKEY does its magic with only about 1.7K of resident code (with the default buffer size).

For a quick summary of what STACKEY can do, you can call up help any time you are at the DOS command line with the command

```
stackey ?
```

(see the HELP!! Section I.8 below) or you can consult the quick summary at the end of the documentation.

For the New User

STACKEY is a powerful package which has many features that you won't want to use too often. For that reason the manual is long, but many parts can be skipped when you first start using the program. For the basic stacking commands, you'll want to read the first three sections of Chapter II after reading the next section.

After that, you can be off and running. If you want to use utilities mode, you'll need to read Chapter V; if you want to set colors with STACKEY, you'll need Chapter IV. This latter chapter is long because of the EGA color tutorial which is included. If you have a CGA, you should only read the first four sections. If you've been confused when hearing about int 16H and int 9, you might look at the keyboard basics parts of Chapter VI.

While STACKEY has numerous options to change the way it works, typically set and changed with /../ instructions on the command line, we have set the defaults to be the most reasonable. Thus, you need not worry about these questions unless you find yourself in a situation where you wished STACKEY worked differently in order to properly interface some particular application program. You may be able to tell it to act in an appropriate way.

New in Version 4.0

Here are the major new features in this version:

- There is a script recorder. This is a separate resident program you only need to load when you want to record a script. A companion program takes the script recorded in memory and writes it to a file either in a format suitable for inclusion in batch files using STACKEY or in a FILEKEY format.
- The string that a scan command searches for can now be enclosed in ".." as an alternate to (..). This allows scans to include the characters ()<> and |.
- There is now a wildcard character for scan string (ASCII 168, the ¿ character).
- The SC and SS scan commands have been supplemented by SJ (Scan Jump) and SU (Scan jump qUietly) commands which will scan for several strings on the screen and

jump to a label in the script depending on which string is found.

- The WS wait for a specific key command has been supplemented by a WJ (Wait Jump) command which waits for one of several different keys and jumps to a label in the script depending on which key is hit.
- There is now a resident version of the UNtil command. That is a command which will pause a STACKEY script until a fixed time.
- There is now a flag to track whether $E and $d use the American or European convention on dates.

Program and Documentation Files

By default, the install program for the *DOS 6 SECRETS* diskettes will install all of the Stackey files in the directory \SECRETS\STACKEY. This directory has not been added to the search path. You can execute the program from its home directory, add the directory to the search path, or copy the Stackey files to a directory that is included in the search path.

There are eight executable programs

STACKEY.COM	The basic program
SKRES.COM	Version for special loading; see Section III.11
EGAPAL.COM	Program to allow STACKEY to control permanent palettes on the EGA
VGAPAL.COM	Program to allow STACKEY to control permanent palettes on the VGA
BOXES.COMS	mall program for the demonstration batch file CGACOLOR.BAT
SKREC.COM	Program to record STACKEY scripts in memory
SKGET.COM	Program to take a macro recorded by SKREC and store in a file in STACKEY or FILEKEY format

Four demonstration batch files

CGACOLOR.BAT	Demonstrates STACKEY's color commands for the CGA
COLOR.BAT	Demonstrates STACKEY's color commands for the EGA by displaying all 64 colors; use a parameter to indicate the time between color changes in half second units (e.g., "color 3" would give 1.5 second change times)
SEECOLOR.BAT	Allows you to see any color or colors supported on the EGA by typing in their numbers or color patterns (e.g., "seecolor 14" or "seecolor RrGgB" or "seecolor 23 42")
SOUNDS.BAT	Illustrates the {BEEP} command

The help files

*STACKEY.HLP	Basic Help file

Note from the Author: The shareware disks (in *DOS 6 SECRETS*) do not contain all of the files available in the shareware version of Stackey. The omitted files relate to Stackey external interfaces and are mainly of value to programmers. See the Stackey documentation files included on the diskette for source information for the complete set of files].

Because of our desire to keep the basic files on a single disk and to keep download time low, we are encouraging distribution of a 'small' shareware version without the starred files. If you got a version without this file and want it for evaluation, it can be downloaded from our support section of CompuServe as SKREST.EXE (section 12 of PCVENA) or it can be gotten from many disk vendors including PBS (1-800-426-3475). They will send you a disk with the STACKEY and BATUTIL help files for $5 including S&H. If you upload this program to a BBS, please keep STACKEY.HLP as a separate file.

In addition, there are the files associated with BATUTIL discussed in the BATUTIL documentation.

While these programs are the package and may be distributed as such, the original disks from CTRLALT Associates come with the files in compressed format. The file README.COM on the distribution disk will explain how to install the programs. You cannot just use the copy command. If you got them from another source, that source may have used another packing method.

Loading and Using STACKEY

The first time that STACKEY is invoked, it loads a small resident portion which becomes permanently resident taking about 1.5 kilobytes of RAM for code plus whatever buffer size you choose. By default, the buffer size is 128 'keystrokes' or 256 bytes. This can be changed; see Chapter III — indeed many of the new features takes 3–10 keystrokes of buffer space and some considerably more, so you may want a larger buffer. It displays the message

```
Resident part of STACKEY now in
    place.
```

and proceeds to read its command line. At later times, STACKEY will find itself in memory and only read its command line. If you are using a hardware or software protocol that allows loading in high memory (MAXIT board, 386max, or QEMM), you'll want to use SKRES rather than STACKEY as you will if you want a buffer with over 10,000 keystrokes (see Section III.11).

STACKEY will place keystrokes in its stack according to the rules of syntax described below. If there is a syntax error, it will exit with no keyboard stacking and give an error message. For example, saying

```
stackey "hello "CRthere
```

will result in the error message

```
Oops! There is an error on the
    STACKEY command line.
"hello "CRthere
^
Unrecognized command.
```

The arrow (shown as a caret here) will point to the first place on the line that STACKEY was unable to interpret. The command line to send hello on one line and there on the next should have said

```
stackey "hello "CR"there"
```

The arrow will indicate other errors; for example, if you ask STACKEY to swap printer ports but you only have one printer port, STACKEY will exit with

```
Oops! There is an error on the
    STACKEY command line.
{PRN}
^
Hardware or software environment
    does not appear to support this
    command.
```

The syntax is fine but there is an error none the less. Similarly, if you try to swap Carousel partitions but STACKEY finds that Carousel isn't loaded, you will get an error message.

The command line is parsed into parts consisting of text between quotes, two character special codes, hex and decimal input, delays, and special commands. Some of the two character special commands allow an integer for the second "character" which may be more than one numeral. The special commands include EGA/VGA color settings between square [] brackets and utilities commands inside pointed braces {}. Certain features like SCan and SHift take parameter inside (). If only a utility is called up and the final } is left off, the resident part of STACKEY will not load. Spaces between the parts are optional so that

```
stackey F1"hello"^r@E
```

is the same as

```
stackey F1 "hello" ^r @E
```

or even

```
stackey F1   "hello" ^r@E
```

but

```
stackey F 1"hello"^r@E
```

which splits the two character code. F1 will result in an error message.

Help!!

Eighteen screens of help are available if you type

```
stackey ?
```

To get help, the file STACKEY.HLP distributed with STACKEY must be available either in the default directory or in your path. This STACKEY.HLP file is different from the files of the same name distributed with STACKEY 2.0 and 3.0. If that old STACKEY.HLP is found, STACKEY will exit with the error message:

```
The file STACKEY.HLP has wrong
    format or version number.
```

The first help screen is a table of contents and the last one an index. You can search by hitting S or goto a given page with Goto. The help is a useful summary but not really a replacement for reading the manual!

On a true monochrome monitor like the original MDA or Hercules card, STACKEY ? will show up in the proper two color attributes. But on a color adapter with monochrome screen (for example, most laptops), the "colors" may make the help invisible or ugly. On such a screen call for help with

```
STACKEY ?m
```

When you exit the help, a screen appears reminding you to register. You can suppress this screen by placing

```
B4$=I paid
```

in your environment. Obviously, having told you the secret, you can do it even if you haven't paid — let your conscience be your guide.

Errorlevel

If STACKEY can interpret its command line and does not find the buffer full, it exits with an error level of 0. If there is an error in the command line, the ERRORLEVEL is set to 1; if there is a buffer overflow, the ERRORLEVEL is 2 and if there is any kind of DOS file error whether due to an invalid path or an open drive door in the {dumpf} utility, the ERRORLEVEL is set to 3. You can test the ERRORLEVEL in batch files with the **if ERRORLEVEL..** DOS command. All error messages are directed to standard output so you can redirect them to NUL and suppress them if you will handle errors with ERRORLEVEL. An example of this can be found in the demonstration batch file COLOR.BAT. If you enter an illegal parameter value, say **color a**, the batch file responds by suppressing an error message from STACKEY and giving you one appropriate to the batch file. How STACKEY responds to an error is controlled by the /t/ and /c/ commands discussed in Chapter III. By default, STACKEY will flush its and BIOS's buffers when there is an error, but the batch file will continue.

If STACKEY finds that the version number of the resident part does not agree with the version number of the file that you have invoked, it will exit with an ERRORLEVEL of 4.

Chapter II: Placing Keystrokes in the Buffer

Stacking Text

Most often, you will want to stack ordinary alphanumeric data, that is the white letters in the center of the keyboard including the numbers, punctuation, braces, etc. You do this by placing the text within quotes on the command line as in

```
stackey "hello there"
```

or

```
stackey 'hello there'
```

Either single or double quotes can be used. Once a quote occurs on the line, every letter counts until a matching quote OF THE SAME TYPE occurs. So to place

```
"Hi!", he said
```

in the stack, you can use

```
stackey '"Hi!", he said'
```

You cannot stack both types of quotes within one string but you can stack strings with both types of quotes by using more than one string. For example, to stack

```
"I can't come", he said
```

use

```
stackey '"I can' "'" 't come", he
    said'
```

Later, we will describe the command codes SQ and DQ for placing quotes. You could also use:

```
stackey DQ"I can't come"DQ", he
    said"
```

to stack the above string.

While you will mainly stack ASCII characters corresponding to the white keys between quotes, you can also stack an ASCII character such as the graphics characters. STACKEY will simulate the hitting of the A key if you use stackey "A"; it will simulate entering an ASCII code above 128 as if it were entered from the Alt-numeric keypad.

Two-Character Codes

Many keys on the keyboard do not correspond to any ASCII character. For these and also for a few ASCII characters, STACKEY recognizes special two-character codes. The first of these can be a special symbol such as ^, @ or, #. Because some programs like CED give special meaning to some of these codes, we have given them alternatives. That is, as the FIRST character in these codes:

~ means the same as ^
(means the same as @
) means the same as #
* means the same as $

This replacement is only effective for the first character, so that you cannot replace ^^ by ~~ but only by ~^. If you need to stack a control-^ and ^ has a special meaning, you will have to use another method like hex codes. These alternatives are not applicable in the color setting commands (i.e., you cannot use [)3 1=4] in place of [#3 1=4]).

You stack function keys using one of F,S,C,A (for function, shifted function, control function, and alt function) followed by a single digit; 0 stands for 10; on an enhanced keyboard – stands for 11; and = for 12 (note the – and = keys are on the numeric row in the eleventh and twelfth place). Thus Ctrl-F10 is stacked with C0 and

```
stackey C2 A3 S5 F0 A-
```

would stack the sequence Ctrl-F2, Alt-F3, Shift-F5, F10, Alt-F11. You may use either uppercase or lowercase for the key letter f,s,c,a. Do not confuse ^1 (for Control-End) and C1 or @1 (for Alt-1) and A1. You can stack the numbers on the numeric keypad with N0,..., N9, the numeric decimal point (Shift Del) with N, and the grey +, – and * with N+, N– and N*.

The BIOS also makes codes for certain Alt key combinations: legal possibilities are Alt- followed by any letter or number (top row numbers) or the following special symbols: – =. These can be stacked by preceding the key with @, for example

```
stackey @a @2 @-
```

will stack Alt-A followed by Alt-2 followed by Alt-minus. It does not matter if you use upper- or lowercase letters or if you use @! rather than @1 or @_ rather than @–.

Similarly, available control combinations are the letters A-Z, [,\,],^,_,`,@ left arrow, right arrow, home, end, PgUp, PgDn, PrtSc. These are entered using the ^ (or ~) as the first key. ^A through ^Z will enter those control codes as will ^[, ^\,.... The six keys, on the numeric keypad corresponding to ^Home, etc. can be entered with the corresponding numbers 1,3,4,6,7,9. Thus

```
stackey ^z ^Z ^[ ^6
```

will stack two Ctrl-z's, an escape, and then Ctrl-Right Arrow (but the "escape" here is entered as if you depressed the control key and then struck [; to enter an escape as if you hit the Escape key, use $e or ES as described below). For the letters, ^ may be followed by an upper- or lowercase letter. For the remaining combinations, only one possibility is allowed. For example, do not confuse ^^ and ^6.

In the next chapter, we will discuss the PH two character code which stacks a PHony keystroke and the WR two character code which stacks a "Wait for Request."

Next, there are two-character mnemonics for special key combinations as follows:

LA	Left Arrow
RA	Right Arrow
UA	Up Arrow
DA	Down Arrow

PU	Page Up
PD	Page Down
HM	Home
EN	End
IN	Insert
DE	Delete
G+	Grey plus ("+" will send the top row +; also N+)
G–	Grey minus ("–" will send the top row –; also N–)
G*	Grey star ("*" will send the top row *; also N*)
CP	Control PrtSc
PS	PrtSc
TA or TB	Tab
ST or BT	Shift Tab (=Back Tab)
ES	Escape (also $e)
BS	Backspace (also $h)
SP	Spacebar (also " ")
CR	Enter (carriage return)
LF	Ctrl-Enter (line feed)
FF	Form Feed (^L)
DQ	The double quote "
SQ	The single quote '
CB	Ctrl-Backspace

These codes can be entered in upper- or lowercase. It is a little known fact that Ctrl-Backspace is a legitimate keystroke that even enters a valid code: ASCII 127.

PS for PrtSc will simulate the pressing of the Shift-PrtSc key. If some other program, for example PIZAZZ PLUS, has taken over that key, it will be called up with PS.

^! will simulate the Ctrl-Break key; for techies, it places an ASCII 0 word in the keyboard buffer and then calls int 1BH.

STACKEY provides support for combinations understood by the enhanced keyboard or by the BIOS that comes with machines supporting the enhanced keyboard. First, the following Alt-key combinations are allowed: Alt-[Alt-] Alt-; Alt-' Alt-` Alt-\ Alt-, Alt-. Alt-/. These are entered with the combinations A[ A] A; A' A` A\ A, A. A/. In addition we have the following codes for the enhanced keyboard:

Alt-Bksp	AB
Alt-Enter	AC
Alt-Esc	AE
Alt-Tab	AT
Ctrl-Tab	CT

The Alt-keypad cursor keys (i.e., everything but the 5 key but including Ins and Del) are allowed keys with an enhanced keyboard. You enter them with K followed by the number, (e.g., Alt-Left is K4 and Alt-Del is K, and the center key [unshifted 5 when numlock isn't on] is K5). In addition we have

Alt-Numpad K /	K/
Alt-Numpad K *	K*
Alt-Numpad K –	K–
Alt-Numpad K +	K+
Alt-Numpad K Enter	KC
Ctrl- K /	^/
Ctrl- K *	^*
Ctrl- K –	^–
Ctrl- K +	^+
Ctrl- K Up [8]	^8
Ctrl- K 5 [5]	^5
Ctrl- K Dn [2]	^2
Ctrl- K Ins[0]	^0
Ctrl- K Del[.]	^.
Grey Enter	GE or GC

While most programs do not distinguish them, the enhanced BIOS will distinguish the cursor pad keys and the numeric pad keys. The cursor pad keys are given by

Cursor pad End	G1
Cursor pad DA	G2
Cursor pad PD	G3
Cursor pad LA	G4
Cursor pad RA	G6
Cursor pad Hm	G7
Cursor pad UA	G8
Cursor pad PU	G9
Cursor pad Ins	G0
Cursor pad Del	G.

The logic behind the codes is a little stretched. The G is because the keys are grey; the 1, 2, 3 correspond to the numbers the keys correspond to on the keypad (not the cursor pad!).

An appendix to this chapter summarizes all the two-character codes in alphabetic order.

Status Toggles

You can turn NumLock, etc., on or off from the STACKEY command line. The syntax is

+N	Turn NumLock on
–N	Turn NumLock off
+C	Turn CapsLock on
–C	Turn CapsLock off
+S	Turn ScrollLock on
–S	Turn ScrollLock off
+I	Turn BIOS insert mode indicator on
–I	Turn BIOS insert mode indicator off

Strictly speaking, the discussion of status toggles does not belong in this chapter since they are handled in real time. That is, rather than placing a command in the resident buffer, a command like +N is interpreted and acted on by the non-resident part of STACKEY as soon as it reaches the interpretation of that part of the command line. In this sense, the lock toggles are like utilities and, indeed, they are included also in utilities mode. They continue to be available in two-code form for compatibility with earlier versions of STACKEY. BATUTIL will let you read the state of the lock keys from a batch file; see Section IV.9 of the BATUTIL documentation.

Prompt Metastrings

STACKEY supports the full set of metastrings allowed in the DOS PROMPT command as well as the added strings supported by the program SEND.COM of Howard Rumsey and Barry Simon. Specifically:

$$	The character "$"
$t	The time in HH:MM:SS.hh format
$d	The date in DAY MM-DD-YYYY format (e.g., Tue 9-30-1986)
$p	The current path in full (e.g., C:\BIN\FOO)
$v	The current DOS version

$n	The current default drive
$g	The character ">"
$l	The character "<"
$b	The character "|"
$q	The character "="
$h	The backspace
$e	The ESCape
$_	CR/LF (i.e., <Enter> followed by Ctrl-<Enter>)
$P	Same as $p in the root dir and as $p\ elsewhere
$T	Time in HHMM format
$M	Month in MM format (e.g., 09)
$D	Day in DD format (e.g., 03)
$Y	Year in YY format (e.g., 86 in 1986 and 01 in 2001)
$W	Day of the week in English (e.g., Sunday)
$E	The date in English (e.g., February 18, 1988)
$H	Hour from 00 to 23
$m	Minute from 00 to 59

There is a difference between uppercase and lowercase after the $. Because of STACKEY's send mode (see Section II.10), you need no longer use the SEND program but can use STACKEY instead. That is, you can use STACKEY to send these codes to standard output.

STACKEY keeps an internal flag that affects the meaning of $E. When the flag is American (the default but it can be set with /a/), $E will be, for example, February 18, 1988 and $d is, for example, Thu 2-18-1988. When the flag is European (set with /e/), $E would be, for example, 18 February 1988 and $d Thu 18/2/1988. If you want the European effect all the time, load STACKEY with

```
stackey /e/
```

Decimal and Hex Codes

This section deals with advanced features not needed by most users. See Chapter VI for a tutorial on keyboard basics used in this section.

You may enter various ASCII key combinations from the keyboard by pressing Alt (or by pressing Alt-Left Shift) and tapping one to three digits on the keypad and then releasing Alt. To stack keystrokes as if entered in this way, use \ followed by a decimal number, so

```
stackey \104\101\108\108\111
```

at the DOS command line will cause **hello** to appear on your screen.

Keystrokes are stored in the buffer as a set of two hex bytes: a scan code and an ASCII code. You can enter such a combination by typing an X followed by four hex digits. The first two are the scan code and the second pair the ASCII code. For example

```
stackey X2368 X1265 X266C X266C
       X186F
```

at the DOS command line will cause **hello** to appear on your screen. The hex digits a–f and the letter x can be either upper- or lowercase.

Because they are used internally by STACKEY, the scan codes E0 through FF (which are not legal anyway) are allowed but take the place of two keystrokes in STACKEY's buffer. STACKEY will place in the keyboard buffer whatever combination you tell it to, even if it is an illegal combination. DOS will only pay attention to the ASCII half of such combination as will many programs. Some keyboard macro programs will allow such possibilities. For example, KEYWORKS associates Ctrl-Up Arrow (a keystroke not supported by an old style BIOS) with 8448. Stackey X8448 will call up the KEYWORKS macro assigned to Ctrl-Up if one is defined. Some combinations are filtered out by the so-called enhanced keyboard.

Invoking Special Programs and Keystrokes

Most TSRs will not pop up by responding to strokes in the keyboard buffer and, as a result, STACKEY cannot invoke them by its usual method. However, when we have special information about a program, we can provide a special routine for that program in particular. We'll discuss those commands, all new in Version 3.0 here. For programs that pop up on depression of several shift keys, like SIDEKICK, we can simulate depressing shift keys as discussed in the next section. Here are the special invocation routines:

CTRLALT PLUS: CA will invoke the main menu of CTRLALT PLUS so, for example

```
stackey CA"MAP"
```

will print the entire screen even if you are in 43 or 50 line mode. If CTRLALT PLUS is not loaded, you'll get an error message from STACKEY.

DESQVIEW: Quarterdeck provides two methods for macros to simulate the Desq key which work on different keyboards or BIOS. We have assigned them to D1 and D2. So for example

```
stackey D1"Z"
```

would zoom the current window to full screen. The combination DL is the same as the Desqview learn key. Finally {boot=d} as a utility will invoke a Desqview specific reboot command.

CAROUSEL: You can tell Carousel to switch to partition n with Qn where n=1,2,...,9,0 (0 is for partition 10); with Carousel 3.0 or later, you can also use Q– and Q= to switch to partitions 11 and 12. Thus you might have a sequence of batch files that successively loads partitions 1,2,.... If you want to load program "foobar" in partition 6, issue the string "hello" followed by F1 to the program and then switch to partition 7, you'd end the batch file for partition 6 with

```
stackey "hello" F1 W36 Q7
foobar
```

The wait command W36 which is discussed in the next chapter (and pauses for 2 seconds) gives the program time to react to the keystrokes before the swap. You may need to adjust the W command for particular applications.

TESSERACT PROGRAMS: Tesseract is a library of TSR routines provided by Innovative Data Concepts as a shareware product. If a TSR is written with these routines, you can invoke it with the TE command:

```
stackey TE(idstring)
```

will call up the tesseract TSR with the given idstring name. You'll need to consult the

documentation that came with your program to find the required idstring, but here is an example. Suppose you have SWAPSP and want to dial the third entry in your phone book under M. Use

```
stackey TE(SWAPSP15)"PM"DNDNCR
```

The idstring must be exactly eight characters in length. For Tesseract programs that allow multiple hotkeys, each hotkey has a number. TE(idstring) will call the program with hotkey 0. For other hotkeys, place a /NN after the idstring. Thus, for example

```
stackey TE(idstring/23)
```

would invoke the program in question via hotkey 23.

CLONE SPEEDUP/SLOWDOWN: Many clones have two speeds adjusted with ^@G+/–. You can simulate this with

```
stackey Z+
```

to speedup and

```
stackey Z-
```

for slowdown. This will not work with all clones.

You might object to some of these additions to STACKEY by saying that you don't use CAROUSEL and object to resident memory being taken by the CAROUSEL command. In fact, most of these commands take NO additional memory — they use the inline feature discussed in Section VI.7.

Simulating Depression of Shift Keys

Some popups come up when you depress a pair of shift keys. You can simulate the depression of any subset of the four shifts with the command SH which takes two parameters in the form

```
SH(XXX,YY)
```

where XXX is some subset of the letter C,A,L,R for the Control, Alt, Left shift, and Right shift respectively and YY is a number from 1 to 65,535. This command simulates depressing the shift keys in question for YY clock ticks. You'll need to experiment with the value of YY depending on the program. We added that parameter because different programs seem to require different values. For example, with a default SIDEKICK Ctrl+Alt, you can invoke the SIDEKICK main menu from within a STACKEY script with

```
stackey SH(CA,1)
```

but invocation of SIDEKICK PLUS requires

```
stackey SH(CA,n)
```

where n is at least 7 or 8 while PRIMETIME (with say C+L as hotkey) seems to require

```
stackey SH(CL,10)
```

You'll need to adjust the shift mask to whatever combination you've chosen for your application. For example, if you've changed the SIDEKICK popup to C+L, use SH(CL,1) rather than SH(CA,1).

Stacking Real Time Beeps

STACKEY scripts can include real time BIOS beeps with the special two key code BE. Beeps are especially useful combined with loops and waits and with jumps (see Section III.2). II.9

Pop-up Messages

STACKEY scripts can include pop-up messages that are displayed and take over the machine until the user hits a key. There are two versions depending on whether you want the key hit passed to the underlying application.

```
STACKEY MP(hi there)
```

will display the message **hi there** in a box and pass the keystroke on while

```
STACKEY ME(hi there)
```

would eat the keystroke. These messages are implemented as inline code to avoid having to permanently use resident memory but as a result they take a lot of buffer space. A message takes 156 bytes plus 7 times the length of the message. The default buffer has only 256 bytes so that long messages will require you to load STACKEY with the command (see Sections III.11 and III.12) to take a larger buffer.

Sending to Standard Output

STACKEY places keystrokes in the keyboard buffer. However, you can tell STACKEY to instead send the interpreted material to standard output. You could then redirect this output to a file or the printer. Thus STACKEY provides a replacement for the SEND program of Rumsey and Simon. With their permission, a modified version of the documentation for SEND is provided as an appendix to this chapter.

To send output to the standard output, include the special symbol underscore in the STACKEY command line so that STACKEY _"hello"$_ will have the same effect as

```
echo hello
```

Following the character _ (underscore) the ONLY allowed codes are

- character strings in quotes
- control codes of the form ^x with x=a,...,z,[,\,],^ or _ (but not ^1, or ^@ etc)
- prompt metastrings in extended form as discussed above
- upper ASCII codes in the form \xxx
- the following two character codes: TA, TB, ES, BS, SP, CR, LF, FF, SQ, BQ, CB

Any other codes, even ones normally legitimate in STACKEY (e.g., LA which doesn't have an ASCII equivalent) will produce an error message but only AFTER the codes prior to it on the command line are already sent to standard output.

The special command _ is only in effect for the line it is issued on; you must include it on each line which you wish to send to standard output. It need not be the first command on the line and a second _ will toggle back to real mode.

If you have CED or a similar command-line processor that allows synonyms or aliases, we suggest that you use CED SYN send 'stackey _&a'

Appendix to Chapter VIII

Here is a quick summary of the STACKEY command-line syntax:

- ? will give help
- _ will send the remainder of the line to standard output
- Place text inside single or double quotes
- F1-F0,F–,F=; S1-S0,S–,S=; A1-A0,A–,A=; C1-C0,C–,C= for function keys
- @x or (x for Alt-x where x=letter or number
- ^x or ~x for Ctrl-x where x=letter or number

(***Note:*** @number for top row numbers; ^number for keypad)

- LA,RA,UA,DA for arrow keys
- PU,PD,HM,EN for Page Up/Dn, Home, End
- IN,DE for Insert/Delete
- N0,...,N9,N. for numeric keypad numbers and decimal point
- G+,G–,G* or N+,N–,N* for Grey keys
- PS for PrtSc
- CP for Ctrl-PrtSc, CB for Ctrl-Backspace
- TA or TB for Tab; ST or BT for Shift Tab
- ES,BS,SP,CR for Escape, Backspace, Space, Enter
- FF, LF for form feed (^L) and Ctrl-Enter
- DQ,SQ for " and '
- PH and WR for two kinds of "phony keystroke"
- +/–N,+/–S,+/–C,+/–I to turn On/Off Num, Scroll, Caps Lock, Insert
- SH(X,nnn) with X a subset of CALR simulates shifts for nnn ticks
- CA invokes CTRLALT PLUS
- Qn switches to Carousel partition n
- Dn with n=1 or 2 invokes Desqview main menu
- TE(idstring,keyid) for Tesseract programs
- Z+/– clone speedup/slowdown
- P–/+ to disable, reenable Shift-PrtScrn
- BE for BIOS beeps
- MP(msg), ME(msg) for pop-up messages
- $x or *x for prompt metastrings with SEND extensions (see following)

- \nnn with nnn=decimal number for Alt-keypad entry
- Xhhhh with hhhh=hex word for direct hex entry
- #nnn or)nnn to repeat the next keystroke nnn times
- :nnn label (nnn=0 to 255)
- Jnnn jump to label nnnn
- Wnnn to insert a delay of nnn ticks (18.2 ticks = 1 sec)
- Mnnn to insert a delay of nnn minutes
- Jnnn jump to label nnnn
- Wnnn to insert a delay of nnn ticks (18.2 ticks = 1 sec)
- Mnnn to insert a delay of nnn minutes
- UNhh:mm resident until command
- SC(string) to scan at cursor position
- SCn,m(string) to scan at absolute position
- SS(string) and SSn,m(string) to scan silently
- SJ(string1; string2;....; string n) to scan multiple strings
- SU(string1; string2;....; string n) to scan multiple strings silently
- WB pause script until buffer is empty
- WH pause script for restart hotkey
- WK pause script for any key Convention: X=subset of CALR; Y=single keystroke like "a" or F1
- WS(X,Y) pause for specific key
- WJ(X1,Y1;X2,Y2;...Xn,Yn) pause for multiple hotkeys
- H!(X,Y) resets flush buffer hotkey (default=AL,!)
- H*(X,Y) resets flush scan hotkey (default=AL,G*)
- H–(X,Y) resets stop hotkey (default=AL, G–)
- H+(X,Y) resets restart hotkey (default=AL,G+)
- CL,NL,SL,SR CapsL, NumL, ScrollL, SysReq for hotkey only
- ! to flush buffer

- ; to stop reading command line (for comments)
- /Bnnnn/ to change buffer size on initial loading
- /Rnnnn/ to force extra loading with new buffer size
- /i/ /s/ and /p/ for impatient, patient, smart processing
- /t/ and /n/ to turn test mode on and off
- /c/ and /d/ to turn continue mode on and off
- /u/ and /o/ to push and pop the s,t,c flags
- /a/ and /e/ to set American vs European dates for $E & $d
- /?/ to query the s,t,c flags
- Ln to set coLors on the CGA (n=0,...,15)
- Pn to set palette on the CGA in mode 4 (n=0,1)
- [c=nn] to map color number nn to slot c on the EGA
- [#m;c=nn] to do the map in the permanent table for mode m
  - #A:All palettes
  - #T:Ultravision, text modes only
  - #U:Ultravision
- +/–B to turn blinking on/off on the EGA or VGA
- IL(xx/xx/xx/xx) InLine command (USE WITH CAUTION!)
- EX(filename) External inline (USE WITH CAUTION!)

In summarizing utilities mode, minimal truncations are capitalized. Only use the leading capitol letter for x.

- {BOOT} or {REBOOT} for a warm reboot
- {BOOT=C} or {REBOOT=C} for a cold reboot
- {MONitor=x} x=Color,Mono,Switch
- {Prn} to switch LPT1 and LPT2
- {COmm} to switch COM1 and COM2
- {CUrsor=x} x=+/– to turn standard cursor on/off
- {CUrsor=n,m} to put cursor on scan lines n through m
- {CPosition=n,m} to move the cursor to row n, column m
- {MODe=n} switch to allowed video mode

- {LInes=n} n=25,43(50) to shift modes on the EGA (VGA)
- {LO=xy} where x is + or – and y=N,S,C or I to toggle lock keys
- {Wait=nnn} Real time pause of nnn clock ticks; n between 1 and 32K
- {Until=HH:MM} Real time pause until time HH:MM
- {DUMPP} to do a screen dump to printer
- {DUMPF=x}, {DUMPL=x} to append screen to file with filespec "x"
- {DUMPOF=x}, {DUMPOL=x} to overwrite screen to file
- {HALT} stops batch file with ^C
- {Keywait}, {Enterwait} pause for input
- {Abortwait}, {~abortwait} pause for input to abort
- {BEep=nn,mm} nn = inverse pitch, mm = duration PROMPT metastrings and extensions:
- $v = DOS version
- $n = current drive
- $p = current path
- $P = current path with \
- $$ = the character $
- $g = the character >
- $l = the character <
- $q = the character =
- $h = the character bks
- $b = the character |
- $e = the character esc
- $_ = CR/LF-
- $t = time in HH:MM:SS.hh format
- $T = time in HHMM format
- $H = hour from 0 to 23
- $d = date in DAY MM-DD-YYYY
- $M = month in MM format
- $D = day in DD format
- $Y = year in YY format
- $W = day of the week
- $E = date in English

FILEKEY has the following conventions:

- default interprets as pure text
- $$ toggles between pure text and STACKEY command mode
- $; in text mode suppresses CR and remainder of line

STACKEY & BATUTIL Registration Form

Name: _____

Company: _____

Address: _____

City: _____

State: _____ Country: _____

Zip: _____ Phone: _____

Remit to:
Advanced Support Group
11900 Grant Place
Des Peres, MO 63131
1(800)872-4768
1(314)965-5630
FAX 1(314) 966-1833

You may register by phoning or writing (9 a.m.-5 p.m. Eastern time).

Registration fees are as follows:

License to STACKEY & BATUTIL with printed docs $49

Upgrade to version 3.0 registered users $25

All registrations will get you the printed documentation and the latest version on disk. The printed documentation is essentially identical to the documentation on disk. In addition, there is a $4 shipping and handling fee for registrations in the US and Canada and $13 outside the US/Canada (the package is sent via Air Freight). These are the fees for our US registration point. Please see on-line documentation for additional details on licensing.

Visa, Mastercard, and American Express are accepted. Registrations may also be sent to Advanced Support Group via their CompuServe mailbox Advanced Support Group 70304,3642.

Registration gives you the right to use any version of STACKEY and BATUTIL with a major version number of 4. If there is a version 5, an update fee may be required.

Registered users may obtain support in several ways. Please see on-line documentation for details about support and about multiple-copy discounts. BATUTIL and STACKEY are not normally sold unbundled but only together. Some exceptions apply.

UMB_DRVR.SYS & UMB_EMS4.SYS Device Drivers

UMB_DRVR.SYS and UMB_EMS4.SYS are device drivers for memory management on DOS-based systems. Please carefully read the documentation for each of these programs prior to installation. It is important to have thorough understanding of memory management before making changes on your system.

UMB_DRVR.SYS Device Driver

UMB provider for 286/386/486 systems
Version 5.22
Copyright © 1991, 1992 by Christopher Blum

Program and Documentation Files

By default, the install program for the *DOS 6 SECRETS* diskettes will install all of the UMB files in the directory \SECRETS\UMBDRV. This directory has not been added to the search path. You can execute the program from its home directory, add the directory to the search path, or copy the UMB files to a directory that is included in the search path.

Introduction
UMB_DRVR.SYS is a device driver that will use the *shadow RAM* capability of the memory

controller portion of many chip sets to A) force all ROMs not specifically excluded to be shadowed, and B) expand DOS base memory beyond 640K if possible, and C) provide UMBs (Upper Memory Blocks) to DOS for loading programs and device drivers into upper memory while *not* using any memory below 640K and remaining in *real* mode.

One advantage of this driver is that many if not all other device drivers and TSR programs may be loaded *high* including HIMEM.SYS (even though the DOS documentation says not!).

A second advantage of using UMB_DRVR is that some device drivers that cannot be loaded high when a software EMS emulator is providing the Upper Memory Area because of their use of DMA I/O (this includes some CD-ROM drivers, for example) will work with UMB_DRVR.SYS. This has to do with the characteristics of virtual-86 mode, 386+ memory management facilities, and DMA hardware interactions. See MISCELLANEOUS NOTES — DMA ACCESS TO UPPER MEMORY for more information and possible restrictions.

In addition, remaining in real mode allows programs that must be able to use protected or virtual-86 mode themselves, such as Borland's Turbo Debugger (TD386.EXE / TDH386.SYS), to operate as intended (and yes, TDH386.SYS can be loaded high with no problems).

Definitions

Hex addresses are given in full hex notation as opposed to Intel segment:offset form (i.e., A0000 in full hex is the same as A000:0 in seg:off form). The memory sizes are referred to in Kilobytes (1,024 decimal), Megabytes (1,048,576 decimal), and Gigabytes (1,073,741,824 decimal).

BASE MEMORY — RAM available to DOS and programs from location 0 to 640K-1 (9FFFF hex). All programs have access to this area.

UPPER MEMORY — The area between 640K (A0000) and 1M-1 (FFFFF). This is the area where ROMs on expansion cards reside (usually), where the EMS base area (the *window* into EMS memory) is (usually), and where Upper Memory Blocks (UMBs) are created for loading device drivers, programs, etc., high with the DOS 5 DEVICEHIGH and LOADHIGH commands.

DOS does not create UMBs itself, but rather relies on a program called a *UMB provider* to supply them. DOS then manages the upper memory area as an extension of base memory with special characteristics when you use the DOS=xxxx,UMB command. Programs like UMB_DRVR, QEMM, 386^MAX, and others are UMB providers.

HIGH MEMORY AREA (HMA) — The HMA is memory from 1M (100000) to 1M+64K-16 (10FFF0) (i.e., the first 64K-16 bytes of extended memory). It can be accessed on 286 and up CPUs in real mode because the address calculation logic does not wrap to location 0 from FFFFF, allowing a program to use the segment *FFFF* to access memory up to 10FFF0. On the earlier 8088 and 8086 processors, the wrap to location 0 was used by some software. To maintain compatibility, system designers have included a way to make the newer CPUs act like the older ones. It is a *gate* that can allow the CPU's address line 20 (A20) to be held to 0 (emulating the behavior of the older CPUs), or to be passed through. With DOS 5, use of the HMA must be through a program which controls access to it by opening this gate for times the HMA must be accessed and closing it so that other programs cannot accidently get at the HMA. The DOS 5 program which performs this function is the device driver *HIMEM.SYS*. Other programs such as QEMM, 386^MAX et.al. also provide this function. The HMA is managed as a total unit (i.e., only one program "owns" it, and "owns" it all). This is where most of DOS is placed when you use HIMEM.SYS and the DOS=HIGH command. As stated before, when DOS is loaded high, no other program can use this portion of memory. The definition of this area and its use is standardized in the Extended Memory Specification (XMS) issued by Microsoft / Lotus / Intel / AST Research, although there is question as to where the credit for the discovery of the area and its first usage in real mode should go.

EXTENDED MEMORY — Memory starting at 1M (100000) that is accessible by the CPU in protected mode. On a 286, this range extends up to 16M-1 (FFFFFF), and on 386 and above CPUs up to 16M-1 (FFFFFF) in 16-bit mode and up to 4G-1 (FFFFFFFF) in 32-bit mode (not used by vanilla DOS, but possibly by some DOS extenders). Under DOS, this memory is accessed in several ways:

1. BIOS INT 15H functions — This method is the oldest and least standardized, but requires no special drivers. Programs directly access the BIOS functions to utilize the memory, and must take great pains to avoid "stepping on" other users — many different methods of *marking* used memory exist, even not marking at all.

2. DOS EXTENDERS — These facilities are supplied by several vendors including Phar-Lap and others. They are included within a program and allow that program access to extended memory using the extender's own techniques (usually in protected mode).

3. XMS functions — This method is defined in the XMS standard that was mentioned earlier. It offers a way for many different programs to concurrently use extended memory easily without worrying about the underlying memory management problems. This method is the one used by all of the DOS 5 utilities that use extended memory to provide their services. A device driver is required to provide the XMS services. The DOS 5 driver is HIMEM.SYS. QEMM and other programs also provide XMS access. Most XMS servers including HIMEM.SYS will allow some portion of extended memory to be left outside their control so that programs using the BIOS INT 15H method can still work. Note that DOS 5 *requires* XMS services to access the HMA to load the major part of itself high.

EXPANDED MEMORY — This is memory that conforms to the Expanded Memory Specification put out by Lotus / Intel / Microsoft. It is sometimes referred to as EMS, LIM 3.2, or LIM 4.0 memory. This type of memory is not directly addressable by the CPU, but requires use of additional facilities to be accessed. This memory is available via multiple 16K *pages* in a (usually) 64K window called the EMS base page area within the Upper Memory Area, starting somewhere between C0000 and E0000 on a 16K boundary. The CPU can access this window in real mode and uses the support facilities to map different pages into the window. Although the CPU can only access EMS memory totalling the window size at any one time, it can *move*

the window to access all of the expanded memory available.

Expanded (EMS) memory can be implemented in several ways:

1. HARDWARE — Hardware support outside the CPU (usually within the support chip set on the motherboard, or on an expansion slot card) handles the mapping of the memory, controlled by a software driver which merely flips hardware *switches*, and the system runs under DOS in real mode with very little EMS management CPU overhead.

2. SIMULATED — This approach uses extended memory to simulate expanded memory by moving 16K pages back and forth between extended memory and the window (usually *below* 640K, which reduces the base memory area by the window size). Although it has the disadvantages of (usually) reducing base memory and increasing the EMS management CPU overhead, it runs in real mode on any 286 or higher processor without requiring anything more than a software driver. This is the only software option available for many 286 systems. An example of this type of driver is UMB_EMS4, distributed with this package (which, by the way, does *not* reduce your DOS base memory because it uses a 64K window in the upper memory area!).

3. EMULATED — This technique is a sort of cross between 1 and 2. It uses the paging hardware built into 386 and newer processors in conjunction with virtual-86 mode to do the mapping tasks required to provide EMS memory. It is similar to 1 in that the mapping is really done by the hardware, and to 2 in that it also involves nontrivial software to provide the virtual-86 mode environment necessary for it to work. Its advantages are that it works on any 386 or newer CPU without any other special hardware and does not reduce the base memory like 2, but it also has the drawback of restrictions, additional overhead, and complexity introduced by virtual-86 mode. There are several packages that support this type of EMS, including EMM386.EXE supplied with DOS

5, and programs like QEMM, 386^MAX, NETROOM, and Memory Commander. Additionally, these EMS emulators can provide the Upper Memory Area using the same techniques, and generally are good at providing enhanced system functionality for a relatively modest impact on system processor overhead if you have the proper CPU.

With respect to performance of UMB_DRVR.SYS versus the software EMS emulator EMM386.EXE supplied with DOS 5, here are some benchmark results supplied by a (happy) user:

"System: 386SX 20MHz, VLSI TOPCAT chip set, 4MB RAM, no math processor. DOS version: MS/DOS 5.0 UMB_DRVR.SYS version: 5.09 Benchmark: CHECKIT 3.0 main system benchmark.

CONFIG.SYS	Dhry-stones	Whet-stones
None	3767	76.7K
DEVICE=C:\ UMB_DRVR.SYS /C=13 DEVICEHIGH=C:\DOS\ HIMEM.SYS DEVICEHIGH=C:\DOS\ ANSI.SYS	4042	77.1K
DEVICE=C:\DOS\ HIMEM.SYS DEVICE=C:\DOS\ EMM386.SYS NOEMS DEVICEHIGH=C:\DOS\ ANSI.SYS	3683	45.7K

As you can see, there is a significant difference when using UMB_DRVR, not to mention the extra memory saved below 640K. The benchmarks ran faster with UMB_DRVR than they did with no CONFIG.SYS at all. "

Important: The driver must be installed *before* HIMEM.SYS is installed.

It is an XMS 2.0 server providing UMBs to DOS via that standard. The chip set parameter is processed and the proper routine called to remap the unused shadow RAM to DOS-usable memory. Available memory starting at A0000 is used to expand DOS base memory beyond 640K,

and other available memory (i.e., above the video memory) is used for UMBs (the areas DOS uses for DEVICEHIGH or LOADHIGH commands).

The driver by default will not use any areas used for video memory. It also forces all ROMs including the system BIOS (F0000-FFFFF) to be shadowed unless forced to be excluded (refer to MISCELLANEOUS NOTES for considerations concerning disk controllers and network cards). If the BIOS has a *boot page* at F0000-F7FFF that the driver can recognize (containing system/CMOS setup code — AMI is one brand that has this), that area will be mapped in as available upper memory since it is not needed after boot time.

The driver should be loaded as the first driver if possible. This allows following drivers and resident programs to be loaded high — even HIMEM.SYS and EMM386.SYS (DOS documentation says they can't, but it works; see MISCELLANEOUS NOTES — WINDOWS and EMS DRIVERS, however). It will initialize, supply UMBs, and terminate leaving a small stub above 640K. To ensure proper chip set function, all warm boots (CTL+ALT+DEL) will be forced to be cold boots after UMB_DRVR is installed. Appropriate status and error messages are issued during processing and a map of the driver's action is displayed.

One of my systems is a 386SX with the Chips and Technologies NEATsx chip set and an AMI (American Megatrend) BIOS dated 04/09/90. It has 4MB of RAM and a Hercules Monochrome Graphics card. I load DOS into the HMA using HIMEM.SYS, supply simulated EMS from the XMS memory pool using UMB_EMS4, and load Borland's Turbo Debugger device driver TDH386.SYS for 386 virtual debugging (TD386.EXE). Using UMB_DRVR defaults and loading all drivers (except SETVER) high gives me 704K base memory for DOS, a maximum executable program size of almost 689K, and 224K in one UMB located at C0000-F7FFF with over 143K still free in that upper memory block for any other TSRs or drivers I may want to load. The following information is extracted from that system (Note: 1K = 1024 decimal).

UMB_DRVR.SYS initializes showing:

```
Chip-controlled RAM at:
              AAAABBBBCCCCDDDDEEEEFFFF
              048C048C048C048C048C048C
has been
configured
as:           DDDDvvvvUUUUUUUUUUUUUUss

DOS base memory expansion = 64K
Upper memory block (UMB) area = 224K

[D]OS base memory,
[e]ms base page area,
[s]hadowed ROM,
[U]pper memory area,
[v]ideo, [-]excluded
```

The command **MEM /C** (in DOS 5) displays the following:

Conventional Memory:

Name	Size in Decimal		Size in Hex
MSDOS	12304	(12.0K)	3010
SETVER	400	(0.4K)	190
COMMAND	2624	(2.6K)	A40
FREE	64	(0.1K)	40
FREE	705328	(688.8K)	AC330
Total FREE:	705392	(688.9K)	

Upper Memory:

Name	Size in Decimal		Size in Hex
SYSTEM	65712	(64.2K)	100B0
HIMEM	1072	(1.0K)	430
UMB_EMS4	73136	(71.4K)	11DB0
TDH386	7920	(7.7K)	1EF0
FREE	146976	(143.5K)	23E20
Total FREE:	146976	(143.5K)	

Total bytes available to programs

```
(Conventional+Upper):
                      852368 (832.4K)
Largest executable
program size:         705184 (688.7K)
Largest available
upper memory block:   146976 (143.5K)
   3080192 bytes total EMS memory
   3080192 bytes free EMS memory
```

```
3145728 bytes total contiguous
extended memory
   0 bytes available contiguous
   extended memory
3080192 bytes available XMS memory
   MS-DOS resident in High Memory
   Area
```

Note: If the video card were a CGA, the DOS base RAM expansion would be 96K(!) with executable program size a whopping 721K(!) — a pretty good cure for *RAM cram*! These same results can (and have been repeatedly) achieved on 286 machines!

Miscellaneous notes
Boot page
If UMB_DRVR.SYS uses the boot page area (see INTRODUCTION for definition) by default and your system crashes, you need to use the /M= parameter to force it to be part of the BIOS (use ## or —). If no boot page is recognized, you may still try the /M= parameter (with ++ for F0000-F7FFF) if you are brave enough. Heed the warning about having a bootable diskette, however — you may need it.

EMS DRIVERS (EMM386, QEMM, 386^MAX, NETROOM, MEMORY COMMANDER, ETC)

If you run EMS, it is most efficient in terms of contiguous memory to have your EMS base address immediately following your video RAM and any adjacent ROM (e.g., C0000-CFFFF for CGA or monochrome, C8000-D7FFF for VGA) or at the top of the usable area (e.g., E8000-F7FFF with a boot page, E0000-EFFFF without). It is also more efficient in terms of CPU usage over-head to use the hardware EMS driver for your chip set or your EMS memory card instead of a software emulation; see "Introduction" (virtual-86 mode, benchmark).

If you use an EMS driver (hardware or software emulation), you should use the /M= parameter to force UMB_DRVR to exclude the EMS base area. Make sure you *do not* have your driver try to map in the upper memory (640K – 1M) area (other than the EMS base area) — UMB_DRVR has done that already (refer to your driver's documentation). You should be able to use DEVICEHIGH/LOADHIGH to put your driver into upper memory in most cases. If you do not have an EMS driver, try UMB_EMS4 (please refer to UMB_EMS4.DOC). There have been some problems reported running EMM386 with UMB_DRVR — I recommend against it. UMB_EMS4 should provide the services you need.

ROMS that cannot be shadowed (disk controllers, network cards)

Some ROMs cannot be shadowed by normal means because they have some RAM or a memory-mapped I/O port they must use included in their address space (e.g., some RLL, ESDI, and SCSI disk controllers, and also some network cards) and shadowing is done using protected RAM. These ROMs will sometimes work when shadowed by this driver if they are within a protection block also containing UMBs. Try letting UMB_DRVR shadow the ROM and see if it works. If your system hangs up or you have problems with disk or network access with the ROM shadowed, you must use the /M= parameter to exclude it from UMB_DRVR.SYS control. Refer to CHIP-SET-SPECIFIC NOTES for any special considerations.

DMA access upper memory

DMA (Direct Memory Access) is a method of data transfer between main memory (RAM) and I/O devices without requiring CPU intervention. Standard AT-compatible floppy disk controllers use it, as do some other devices, such as CD-ROMs and data acquisition hardware. It is supported through the Intel 8237A DMA controller chip, or by compatible integrated devices like the 82C206, or even by compatible components within the motherboard chip set. These devices control the data / address busses in the system to do the transfer while the CPU does other work. They do not have access to the internal 386+ CPU memory management facilities during their operation, and so are unaware of remapping of memory done there. Most of the time this is not a concern, as software that handles the remapping also handles DMA setup by intercepting accesses to the DMA controller registers and trying to keep things straight for DMA I/O. This can become a concern if the DMA transfer spans a page boundary that in virtual memory is to an adjacent page, but in real memory is not. Most of the 386-type

mappers either automatically or through parameters try to avoid this situation by causing the area to be mapped (as much as possible) into contiguous memory.

UMB_DRVR, on the other hand, uses hardware external to the CPU that maps in the upper memory area contiguously such that DMA access to the upper memory area is no different than to the base 640K. The DMA mapping requirements that the device drivers are aware of for a standard AT system do not change when UMB_DRVR provides the upper memory area. Note that some drivers still cannot load high because they are "confused" by being at a higher address in memory than the program that is using them, but this is becoming much less common as drivers are rewritten to be able to take advantage of the DOS 5 high memory capabilities.

One consideration remains, however: *very* few chip sets that are supported by UMB_DRVR are designed such that the RAM that is mapped into the upper memory area can only be accessed by the CPU. UMB_DRVR performs a test for proper DMA function at initialization and issues a warning message if DMA is not possible to the upper memory area. If (and *only* if) this is the case, any DMA accesses attempted to an area above 640K and below 1M will not work, and the following restrictions will apply:

1. If you boot from a floppy disk or try to load any driver or TSR high reading it from a floppy, do not load UMB_DRVR.SYS — if you do, your system will probably hang up immediately upon trying to load anything into upper memory.

2. Almost no hard disk controllers use DMA, but if you have one that does, you will probably have problems with loading any driver or TSR into upper memory, and you may not be able to use UMB_DRVR at all.

3. Device drivers that use DMA for access to buffers within the driver itself, or allocated immediately after the driver when it initializes, cannot be loaded high on your system.

4. No DOS base memory expansion from unused video memory should be used (all DOS base RAM should be capable of DMA access).

Note: These restrictions apply *only* if DMA access to upper memory is *not* available (i.e., if UMB_DRVR issues the warning message).

Microsoft Windows

Windows 3.0 and 3.0A have been tested as follows:

386 Enhanced mode:

Windows will run in 386 enhanced mode with UMB_DRVR if the line

```
EMMExclude=A000-FFFF
```

is added to the SYSTEM.INI file, [386Enh] section. Note that a practical minimum of 4MB of RAM on your system is suggested to run in this mode. Also note that SETVER.EXE must be loaded LOW, and ANSI.SYS (if used) must be loaded LOW. There may be other drivers like this . . . experiment. Refer to UMB_EMS4.DOC for considerations regarding UMB_EMS4 and Windows.

Standard mode:

Windows in standard mode works with UMB_DRVR and HIMEM.SYS, with or without an EMS driver (hardware or software) loaded high or low. Note you must have a minimum of something like 512K or more extended memory to run in standard mode (i.e., do not have a software EMS driver remap ALL of your extended memory to expanded).

Program access to upper memory with DOS 5 managing UMBs

1. Record current status of memory system so you can restore it.

    int 21H/ax=5800h - returns al=strategy (see below)

    int 21h/ax=5802h - returns al=UMB link state (see below)

2. Set up for memory allocation / deallocation.

    int 21h/ax=5801h/bh=0/bl=strategy

    int 21h/ax=5803h/bh=0/bl=UMB status

00h	first fit, low memory	00h = remove UMBs from mem chain
01h	best fit, low memory	01h = add UMBs UMBs to mem chain

02h	last fit, low memory	(UMBs must be chained for access)
40h	first fit, high memory	
41h	best fit, high memory	
42h	last fit, high memory	
80h	first fit, try high and then low memory	
81h	best fit, try high and then low memory	
82h	last fit, try high and then low memory	

3. Do normal int 21h/ah=48h, int 21h/ah=49h, int 21h/ah=4Ah as desired.

4. Restore values saved in step 1 above.

The system defaults to first-fit-low with UMBs not chained. If you chain the UMBs, strategies 00/01/02 affect the entire chain. For example, with the UMBs chained and strategy 00, you will get memory from the UMB area if the request cannot be satisfied from low memory.

Determining your chip set

If your system documentation or CMOS setup screen does not tell you what chip set you have, the best way to find out is to open the cover on your system and look at the motherboard.

Warning: MAKE SURE THE SYSTEM IS OFF AND UNPLUGGED WHEN YOU OPEN IT TO LOOK AT THE MOTHERBOARD!

The chip you will be looking for may not be one of the larger in size, but it will have many (usually 80+, sometimes up to 200 or more) pins. The number that identifies the key chip in the set is listed in CHIP-SET-SPECIFIC NOTES for each chip set supported. If you find a matching number on one of the chips on your motherboard, use the /C= value shown for that set. If you don't see a match, refer to the sections BAD NEWS, MAYBE?, and COMING ATTRACTIONS. Note that some chips only contain peripheral support and *do not* indicate what chip set you have. These include, but are not limited to

> 82C206 (many brands)
>
> 82C601, 82C710, 82C711 (Chips and Technologies)
>
> VL82C100, VL82C106, VL82C107, VL86C050, VL16C45x, VL16C55x
>
> (VLSI Technology)
>
> 82C452, 85C206 (Silicon Integrated Systems)
>
> TACT82206 (Texas Instruments)

Again, these chip numbers *do not* indicate what chip set you have. If you find one of these on your motherboard, you should keep looking!

Chip note specific notes
User-specified available memory mode

/C=00 - Chip ID(s): None (286, 386SX, 386DX, 486)

This selection causes UMB_DRVR to map the areas specified in the /M= parameter, using the + (plus) character, as upper memory. Please note the following points when using this mode:

1. This mode *cannot be used* unless you have a way to actually map read-write RAM into the area between 640K (A0000) and 1M (100000) through your CMOS setup or some other program provided by your system or chip-set manufacturer, or a memory expansion card that maps RAM into that area on the AT bus. *Note:* The system BIOS brand MRBIOS from Microid Research will include the capability to set up your memory this way if your chip set supports it.

2. No verification or manipulation of any chip set is done.

3. ROM shadowing is totally controlled by your system BIOS and CMOS setup parameters.

4. No checking is performed other than the memory read-write and DMA tests.

5. Warm boots are *not* forced to be cold boots.

6. It is *your responsibility* to properly determine and specify which areas can be used.

Chips & Technologies: CS8221 NEAT, CS8281 NEATsx, CS8223 LeAPset, CS8283 LeAPset-sx, Texas Instruments TACT82S411 Single Chip AT, United Microelectronics (UMC): UM82C210 286/386SX AT

/C=01 - Chip ID(s): (C & T) 82C212, 82C241 (286) 82C812, 82C841 (386SX); (TI) TACT82S411 (286, 386SX); (UMC) UM82C212 (286, 386SX)

These chip sets allow the 384K of motherboard RAM at A0000-FFFFF to relocate to extended memory at 100000-15FFFF on systems with only 1MB of RAM. If this remapping is enabled when UMB_DRVR.SYS enables this area, the remapping is removed and the size of your extended memory is reduced by 384K (i.e., it disappears). Note that this applies only to systems with *exactly* 1MB of memory. These chip sets map in 16K segments, but write protection for the area C0000-FFFFF is in 64K segments. To allow maximum memory utilization the driver marks any segment containing UMBs as read/write. If the 64K segment also contains a ROM shadow, it is not protected. Although it should not be necessary, if you wish to have a ROM be shadowed and protected, exclude any non-ROM areas within the 64K segment (e.g., for a VGA ROM at C0000-C7FFF, exclude C8000-CFFFF). If you must force a ROM to be unshadowed, you need only exclude the 16K segment(s) it occupies (e.g., for a disk ROM at C8000-CBFFF, exclude C8000-CBFFF). UMB_DRVR.SYS will recognize the EMS setup for these chip sets and will exclude the EMS base segment if the EMS hardware is enabled when UMB_DRVR initializes. Use of the /M= parm is not required in this case.

VLSI Technology VL82C200

/C=02 - Chip ID(s): VL82C201,VL82C202,VL82C203,VL82C204 (286, 386SX) (all 4 chips required)

This chip set uses a jumper or switch to enable shadow RAM ability. This does not actually cause shadowing, but must be in proper position for UMB_DRVR.SYS to work. Check your system documentation. This chip set maps and protects in 64K segments. To allow maximum memory utilization, 64K segments containing UMBs are set to read/write. If the 64K segment also contains a ROM shadow, it is not protected. Although it should not be necessary, if you wish to have a ROM be shadowed and protected, exclude any non-ROM areas within the 64K segment (e.g., for a VGA ROM at C0000-C7FFF, exclude C8000-CFFFF). If you must force a ROM to be unshadowed, exclude the entire 64K segment on a 64K boundary (e.g., for a disk ROM at C8000-CBFFF, exclude C0000-CFFFF).

FOREX FRX36C300

/C=03 - Chip ID(s): FRX36C300 (386DX)

This chip set maps in 32K segments from C0000 to EFFFF, and one 64K segment for the system BIOS (F0000-FFFFF). RAM at A0000-BFFFF is always remapped to the highest area and cannot be used by the driver. Protection is set globally, meaning that all used RAM (shadow or UMBs) is marked read/write. The chip set also remaps D0000-EFFFF to the highest area if there is nothing shadowed in that area. When UMB_DRVR.SYS enables this area, the remapping is removed and the size of your extended memory is reduced by 128K. If you must force a ROM to be unshadowed, exclude the entire 32K segment on a 32K boundary (e.g., for a disk ROM at C8000-CBFFF, exclude C8000-CFFFF).

Chips & Technologies: CS8230 386/AT, CS8231 Turbo Cache 386/AT, CS8233 PEAKset/386, CS82310 PEAKset DM/386

/C=04 - Chip ID(s): 82C302, 82C307, 82C311, 82C351 (386DX)

These chip sets maps in 16K segments, but write protection for the area C0000-FFFFF is in 64K segments. To allow maximum memory utilization, the driver marks any segment containing UMBs as read/write. If the 64K segment also contains a ROM shadow, it is not protected. Although it should not be necessary, if you wish to have a ROM be shadowed and protected, exclude any non-ROM areas within the 64K segment (e.g., for a VGA ROM at C0000-C7FFF, exclude C8000-CFFFF). If you must force a ROM to be unshadowed, you need only exclude the 16kK segment(s) it occupies (e.g., for a disk ROM at C8000-CBFFF, exclude C8000-CBFFF).

Chips & Technologies: 82C235 SCAT, 82C836 SCATsx, CB8291 ELEAT, CB8295 ELEATsx, CS8285 PEAKset-sx, CS8227 CHIPSlite, CS8288 CHIPSlite-sx

/C=05 - Chip ID(s): 82C235 (286), 82C836 (386SX)

These chip sets allow the 384K of motherboard RAM at A0000-FFFFF to relocate to extended memory at 100000-15FFFF on systems with only 1MB of RAM. If this remapping is enabled when UMB_DRVR.SYS enables this area, the remapping is removed and the size of your extended memory is reduced by 384K (i.e., it disappears). Note that this applies only to systems with *exactly* 1MB of memory. These chip sets map in 16K segments, but write protection for the area C0000-FFFFF is in 32K segments. To allow maximum memory utilization, the driver marks any segment containing UMBs as read/write. If the 32K segment also contains a ROM shadow, it is not protected. Although it should not be necessary, if you wish to have a ROM be shadowed and protected, exclude any non-ROM areas within the 32K segment (e.g., for a ROM at C8000-CBFFF, exclude CC000-CFFFF). If you must force a ROM to be unshadowed, you need only exclude the 16K segment(s) it occupies (e.g., for a disk ROM at C8000-CBFFF, exclude C8000-CBFFF).

ETEQ Micro COUGAR II

/C=06 - Chip ID(s): 82C491 (386DX, 486)

This chip set maps in 16K segments from C0000 to EFFFF, and one 64K segment for the system BIOS (F0000-FFFFF). Memory protection is done in 64K segments from C0000 to EFFFF. The hardware does not allow read/write access to the area F0000-FFFFF (i.e., the ROM can be shadowed and protected, but the driver cannot use the boot page). The driver also cannot use the RAM at A0000-BFFFF. The chip set can remap A0000-BFFFF and D0000-EFFFF to the highest area if no shadowing is done in that area. If this remapping is enabled and UMB_DRVR.SYS enables the area D0000-EFFFF, the remapping is removed and the size of your extended memory is reduced by 256K. Although it should not be necessary, if you wish to have a ROM be shadowed and protected, exclude non-ROM areas within the 64K segment: e.g., for a ROM at C8000-CBFFF, exclude C0000-C7FFF and

CC000-CFFFF. If you have a VGA ROM at C0000-C7FFF, you only need exclude CC000-CFFFF. If you must force a ROM to be unshadowed, you need only exclude the 16K segment(s) it occupies (e.g., for a disk ROM at C8000-CBFFF, exclude C8000-CBFFF).

OPTi Sx/AT, Sx/AT Cache

/C=07 - Chip ID(s): 82C281, 82C282, 82C283 (386SX)

These chip sets maps in 16K segments from C0000 to EFFFF, and one 64K segment for the system BIOS (F0000-FFFFF). Memory protection is in 64K segments from C0000 to EFFFF. The hardware does not allow read/write access to the area F0000-FFFFF (i.e., the ROM can be shadowed and protected, but the driver cannot use the boot page). The driver also cannot use the RAM at A0000-BFFFF. These chip sets can remap A0000-BFFFF and D0000-EFFFF to the high end of extended memory if no shadowing is done in either area. If this remapping is enabled and UMB_DRVR.SYS enables the area D0000-EFFFF, the remapping is removed and the size of your extended memory is reduced by 256K. Although it should not be necessary, if you wish to have a ROM be shadowed and protected, exclude non-ROM areas within the 64K segment: e.g., for a ROM at C8000-CBFFF, exclude C0000-C7FFF and CC000-CFFFF. If you have a VGA ROM at C0000-C7FFF, you only need exclude CC000-CFFFF. If you must force a ROM to be unshadowed, you need only exclude the 16K segment(s) it occupies (e.g., for a disk ROM at C8000-CBFFF, exclude C8000-CBFFF).

OPTi DX/BB PC/AT

/C=08 - Chip ID(s): 82C496 (386DX, 486)

This chip set maps in 16K segments from C0000 to EFFFF, and one 64K segment for the system BIOS (F0000-FFFFF). Memory protection is done in 64K segments from C0000 to EFFFF. The hardware does not allow read/write access to the area F0000-FFFFF (i.e., the ROM can be shadowed and protected, but the driver cannot use the boot page). The driver also cannot use the RAM at A0000-BFFFF. The chip set can remap A0000-BFFFF and D0000-EFFFF to the highest area if no shadowing is done in that area. If this remapping is enabled and UMB_DRVR.SYS enables the area D0000-EFFFF,

the remapping is removed and the size of your extended memory is reduced by 256K. Although it should not be necessary, if you wish to have a ROM be shadowed and protected, exclude non-ROM areas within the 64K segment: e.g., for a ROM at C8000-CBFFF, exclude C0000-C7FFF and CC000-CFFFF. If you have a VGA ROM at C0000-C7FFF, you only need exclude CC000-CFFFF. If you must force a ROM to be unshadowed, you need only exclude the 16K segment(s) it occupies (e.g., for a disk ROM at C8000-CBFFF, exclude C8000-CBFFF).

OPTi 386WB PC/AT, 486SXWB PC/AT

/C=09 - Chip ID(s): 82C391 (386DX), 82C493 (486)

These chip sets maps in 16K segments from C0000 to EFFFF, and one 64K segment for the system BIOS (F0000-FFFFF). Memory protection is done in 64K segments from C0000 to EFFFF. The hardware does not allow read/write access to RAM at F0000-FFFFF (i.e., the ROM can be shadowed and protected, but the driver cannot use the boot page). The driver also cannot use the RAM at A0000-BFFFF. Although it should not be necessary, if you wish to have a ROM be shadowed and protected, exclude non-ROM areas within the 64K segment: (e.g., for a ROM at C8000-CBFFF, exclude C0000-C7FFF and CC000-CFFFF). If you have a VGA ROM at C0000-C7FFF, you only need exclude CC000-CFFFF. If you must force a ROM to be unshadowed, you need only exclude the 16K segment(s) it occupies (e.g., for a disk ROM at C8000-CBFFF, exclude C8000-CBFFF).

OPTi 386/486WB EISA

/C=10 - Chip ID(s): 82C682 (386DX, 486)

This chip set maps and protects in 16K segments at C0000-DFFFF, one 64K segment at E0000 and one 64K segment for the system BIOS at F0000. The driver cannot use the RAM at A0000-BFFFF. If one of the 64K segments contains both shadowed ROM and UMB area, it is marked read/write. All ROMs in the C0000-DFFFF area are protected. If you must force a ROM to be unshadowed, you need only exclude the 16K segment(s) it occupies (e.g., for a disk ROM at C8000-CBFFF, exclude C8000-CBFFF) unless it is in the E0000 block or you wish to force the BIOS (F0000-FFFFF) to be unshadowed. Then you must exclude the entire 64K block (E0000-EFFFF and/or F0000-FFFFF).

Elite Microelectronics Eagle, Falcon

/C=11 - Chip ID(s): e88C311 (386DX), e88C411 (486)

These chip sets map and protect in 16K segments for the entire area C0000-FFFFF. All shadowed ROMs are write-protected. UMB_DRVR cannot use the RAM at A0000-BFFFF. These sets always remap A0000-BFFFF to the highest memory area, and can selectively remap C0000-FFFFF in 64K blocks if no shadowing is done within the 64K block. If this remapping is active and UMB_DRVR enables shadow memory within one of the remapped 64K blocks, the remapping is removed and the size of your extended memory is reduced. If you must force a ROM to be unshadowed, you need only exclude the 16K segment(s) it occupies (e.g., for a disk ROM at C8000-CBFFF, exclude C8000-CBFFF).

VLSI Technology SCAMP

/C=12 - Chip ID(s): VL82C310, VL82C311 (286, 386SX), VL82C311L (286)

These chip sets map and protect in 32K segments for A0000-BFFFF, 16K segments for C0000-DFFFF, and 32K segments for E0000-FFFFF. If a ROM shadow shares a 32K segment from E0000 to FFFFF with a UMB area, it is marked read/write. Any shadowed ROM from C0000-DFFFF is protected, as is any 32K segment from E0000 to FFFFF that is all shadowed ROM. These sets can remap A0000-FFFFF to the highest memory area if no shadowing is done and system memory is 1MB, 2MB, 3MB, or 4MB. If remap is active and UMB_DRVR enables any shadow memory, the remapping is removed and the size of your extended memory is reduced. Note that this applies only to systems with *exactly* 1MB, 2MB, 3MB or 4MB installed. If you must force a ROM to be unshadowed, you need only exclude the 16K segment(s) it occupies if it is between C0000 and DFFFF (e.g., for a disk ROM at C8000-CBFFF, exclude C8000-CBFFF). If it is between E0000 and FFFFF, exclude all areas in the 32K segment (e.g., for a disk ROM at E0000-E3FFF, exclude E0000-E7FFF).

VLSI Technology: VL82C286, VL82C386 TOPCAT, Intel 82340SX, 82340DX, (These sets are all made by VLSI Technology)

/C=13 - Chip ID(s): (VLSI) VL82C320 (286, 386SX), VL82C330 (386DX)

VL82C320A (286, 386SX, 486)

(Intel) 82343, 82346 (286, 386SX)

82343A (286, 386SX, 486)

These chip sets map in 16K segments for the entire area from A0000 to FFFFF and protect in 16K segments from C0000 to FFFFF. All shadowed ROM areas are protected. The video area (A0000-BFFFF) and the boot page (F0000-F7FFF) can only be utilized on the VL82C320 / 82343 "A" revisions (this implementation was chosen to avoid the DMA limitation; see MISCELLANEOUS NOTES — DMA ACCESS TO UPPER MEMORY). UMB_DRVR will recognize the various chips and enforce these restrictions accordingly. These sets can remap A0000-FFFFF to the high end of extended memory if no shadowing is done and system memory is exactly 1MB or 2MB. If this remapping is active and UMB_DRVR enables shadow memory, the remapping is removed and the size of your extended memory is reduced. Note that this applies only if the system memory size is exactly 1MB or 2MB. If you must force a ROM to be unshadowed, you need only exclude the 16K segment(s) it occupies (e.g., for a disk ROM at C8000-CBFFF, exclude C8000-CBFFF).

OPTi HiD/386 AT, HiB/486 AT

/C=14 - Chip ID(s): 82C382 (386DX), 82C482 (486)

These chip sets map in 16K segments from C0000 to EFFFF and one 64K segment for the system BIOS (F0000-FFFFF). Memory protection is done in 64K segments from C0000 to EFFFF. The hardware does not allow read/write access to the area F0000-FFFFF (i.e., the ROM can be shadowed and protected, but the driver cannot use the boot page). The driver also cannot use the RAM at A0000-BFFFF. The chip sets can remap A0000-BFFFF and D0000-EFFFF to the highest area if no shadowing is done in that area. If this remapping is enabled and UMB_DRVR.SYS enables the area D0000-EFFFF, the remapping is removed and the size of your extended memory is reduced by 256K. Although it should not be necessary, if you wish to have a ROM be shadowed and protected, exclude non-ROM areas within the 64K segment: e.g., for a ROM at C8000-CBFFF, exclude C0000-C7FFF and CC000-CFFFF. If you have a VGA ROM at C0000-C7FFF, you only need exclude CC000-CFFFF. If you must force a ROM to be unshadowed, you need only exclude the 16K segment(s) it occupies (e.g., for a disk ROM at C8000-CBFFF, exclude C8000-CBFFF).

Sun Electronics SUNTAC ST62CS24, ST62CS25

/C=15 - Chip ID(s): ST62C241 (286), ST62C251 (286, 386SX)

These chip sets have two memory-mapping modes: one for extended memory and one for expanded (EMS) memory. You must have your system configured for extended memory only for UMB_DRVR to recognize the chip set. Also, some BIOSs (e.g., newer AMI) relocate the video ROM before shadowing it. This can cause fragmentation of your upper memory. If this is the case, turn off video shadowing in your CMOS / extended setup. The driver will shadow your video ROM when it sets up the upper memory area. See your CMOS setup or system documentation. These chip sets map and protect in 16K segments from C0000 to DFFFF and in 32K segments from E0000 to FFFFF. The driver cannot use the RAM at A0000-BFFFF. All shadowed ROMs from C0000 to DFFFF and the system BIOS are protected. The chip sets always remap A0000-DFFFF to the highest area, and remap E0000-FFFFF there if no shadowing is done. UMB_DRVR must remove the remapping for E0000-FFFFF if active, and must use some extended memory to supply the upper memory area. Your extended memory size will be adjusted accordingly. If you must force a ROM to be unshadowed, you need only exclude the 16K segment(s) it occupies (e.g., for a disk ROM at C8000-CBFFF, exclude C8000-CBFFF).

Texas Instruments TACT83000

/C=16 - Chip ID(s): TACT83442 (386SX, 386DX, 486)

This chip set maps in 16K segments from A0000 to FFFFF, and memory protection is done in 16K segments from C0000 to FFFFF. All shadowed ROMs are protected. The chip set can remap any 64K segment from A0000 to FFFFF not used for shadowing to the upper end of extended memory. If this remapping is active and UMB_DRVR.SYS uses any of the remapped area, the remapping is removed and the size of your

extended memory is reduced. If you must force a ROM to be unshadowed, you need only exclude the 16K segment(s) it occupies (e.g., for a disk ROM at C8000-CBFFF, exclude C8000-CBFFF).

Silicon Integrated Systems High Performance 80386

/C=17 - Chip ID(s): 85C310 (386DX)

This chip set maps in 16K segments from C0000 to DFFFF, and two 64K segments for E0000 and F0000. Memory protection is global, so no shadow areas are protected. The driver cannot use the area from A0000 to BFFFF. The chip set, depending on memory configuration, can remap either 256K or 384K of unused shadow area to the upper end of extended memory. If this remapping is active and UMB_DRVR uses any of the remapped area, the remapping is removed and your extended memory size is reduced. If you must force a ROM to be unshadowed, you need only exclude the 16K segment(s) it occupies (e.g., for a disk ROM at C8000-CBFFF, exclude C8000-CBFFF).

Silicon Integrated Systems High Performance ISA486

/C=18 - Chip ID(s): 85C401 (486)

This chip set maps in 32K segments from C0000 to EFFFF, and one 64K segment for F0000. Memory protection is global, so no shadowed areas are protected. The driver cannot use the area from A0000 to BFFFF. If you must force a ROM to be unshadowed, you must exclude the 32K segment(s) it occupies (e.g., for a disk ROM at C8000-CBFFF, exclude C8000-CFFFF).

Installation

Warning: Please be sure you have reviewed the miscellaneous and chip-set-specific notes prior to installing. Also, make sure you have backed up your system and that you have a diskette you can boot from in case you have problems with your CONFIG.SYS settings.

Installation (preferably as the first driver) is via the lines:

```
DEVICE=UMB_DRVR.SYS /C=nn
    [/M=sssssssssssssssssssssss]
DOS=[HIGH|LOW],UMB (Required -
    turn on DOS 5 UMB support)
```

in your CONFIG.SYS file. The /C= parameter is required — nn is the chip set from "CHIP-SET-SPECIFIC NOTES." The /M= parameter is optional and is used to override defaults.

Error messages

DMA NOT SUPPORTED (WARNING)

See MISCELLANEOUS NOTES — DMA ACCESS TO UPPER MEMORY.

SHADOW RAM TEST FAILURE

This message is issued when the shadow RAM read/write test fails. It is usually an indication that you are trying to use memory that is not available, or (possibly) you do not have the chip set you have specified. Check your CMOS setup and any jumpers or switches per your hardware documentation. Also review CHIP-SET-SPECIFIC NOTES earlier in this document for any requirements. This can also occur if you are trying the example listed in the INSTALLA-TION section using a portion of the video RAM area on a VGA system in CGA mode and your VGA hardware will not allow it.

CHIP SET NOT RECOGNIZED

As much as possible, UMB_DRVR.SYS tries to verify that you have the chip set you indicated in the /C= parameter. If you are sure you have the chip set and have correctly specified it, contact me (see TECHNICAL SUPPORT) and I will try to straighten things out. This message can also occur if a program (e.g., CMOS setup from DOS, disk defragger) reboots the system in a certain way. In this case, it can be cleared with the reset button or by power down / power up.

XMS ALREADY INSTALLED

You have not installed UMB_DRVR.SYS before HIMEM.SYS (UMB_DRVR.SYS issues message), or you have omitted or incorrectly specified the line **DOS=xxxx,UMB** in your CONFIG.SYS (HIMEM.SYS issues message). Correct your CONFIG.SYS file and reboot.

INCORRECT DOS VERSION

UMB_DRVR.SYS requires MS/DOS 5.0 (or higher) for proper operation.

INVALID PARAMETER(S)

On the DEVICE= statement for UMB_DRVR.SYS you have: 1) omitted or incorrectly specified the /C= parameter, 2) incorrectly specified the /M= parameter, or 3) included extra parameter(s). Check that you have entered the proper 2-digit number for your chip set, that (if specified) the /M= parameter contains 24 characters from the set "." (period), '–' (minus), '+' (plus), and '#' (pound sign), and that nothing else is specified. Correct your CONFIG.SYS file and reboot.

Please see the file UMB_DRVR.DOC for details on the following topics which have been omitted here:

1. BAD NEWS (CHIPS THAT WILL NOT BE SUPPORTED)
2. MAYBE? (NEED TECHNICAL DATA TO SUPPORT)
3. COMING ATTRACTIONS (SUPPORT PLANNED OR UNDER DEVELOPMENT)

If your chip set is not listed, have your system vendor or the chip set manufacturer contact me and I will try to support it.

A newer, more flexible (read as less Neander-thal, approaching the Bronze Age) user interface is coming as soon as I get the time.

Also in the works are features to save even more precious memory below 640K by:

— loading the primary shell (COMMAND.COM) into upper memory
— relocating all DOS areas possible to upper memory, including FCBS=, FILES=, BUFFERS=, STACKS=, and LASTDRIVE=
— allowing the lower portion of the video RAM area to be switched in and out to expand DOS base RAM beyond 640K but not inhibit graphics modes (only for chip sets with video area support)

I have (I think) found a way to *reliably* test for and list the chip set in a machine. I will be including a separate program to do this in the package soon. Of course, it will only recognize the chip sets it supports, so a negative result will not necessarily mean you have a chip set that will not be supported later.

If there is enough interest, I will also write device-specific EMS drivers for the hardware facilities in the EMS-capable chip sets. Please Emily or surface mail your thoughts (no phone calls on this, please — save those for support questions).

Technical Support

Technical support, including preregistration questions or install assistance, is available by phone at your expense. Please be aware that I am in the Eastern US time zone (GMT-4 or GMT-5 depending on season) and try to call at a reasonable hour: that is, 9 a.m. to Noon, 1 p.m. to 5 p.m., or 7 p.m. to 10 p.m. Saturday is OK, but _please_ avoid Sundays. I can also be contacted via Emily on CompuServe, BIX, and INTERNET — I monitor my mail almost every day. It is not necessarily a good idea to leave me messages on CompuServe in the forum sections unless your question or discussion is of general interest. The Postal Service may also be used.

UMB_EMS4.SYS Device Driver

Version 5.22
EMS simulator for 286 / 386 / 486 systems
Copyright © 1991, 1992 by Christopher Blum

Introduction

UMB_EMS4.SYS is a device driver providing EMS simulation from XMS (HIMEM.SYS) extended memory. It is a software implementation of the LIM 4.0 standard, implementing all features of the specification except page aliasing, which requires actual hardware support.

All XMS extended memory is considered to be available also as EMS. The XMS memory is dynamically configured to EMS and back as programs open and close EMS handles. You should see, when you do a MEM display, that the EMS available and XMS available track with each other.

**Important:** The driver must be installed _after_ UMB_DRVR.SYS and HIMEM.SYS have been installed, preferably using the DEVICEHIGH command to load into upper memory. It requires about 72K of memory to initialize, and takes no parameters.

Requirements and Restrictions

UMB_EMS4 has been run on 286, 386, and 486 systems with excellent results. It will run on any system supported by UMB_DRVR.SYS, DOS 5.0, and the HIMEM.SYS XMS server.

Do _not_ use simulated EMS provided by UMB_EMS4 for disk cache programs such as PC-Quick, HyperDisk, SMARTDRV.SYS, etc. They will work better with extended memory than simulated EMS (see also following).

The driver is Windows-386-enhanced-mode-aware, but you need to start Windows in enhanced mode using **WIN /3** (UMB_EMS4 will back itself out at Win init and reinstall at Win exit, but you must force enhanced mode) if you want it. The driver will not allow Windows to start in enhanced mode if any simulated EMS users are active. This is to allow Windows full use of extended memory, and further explains why you can't have any cache programs use EMS if they need to run while Windows is active. This can also affect shell programs or COMMAND.COM replacement programs such as 4DOS. If you have a choice, select to use extended memory for any such applications.

I _strongly_ suggest that you set your XMS handle count to 64 by using /NUMHANDLES=64 for HIMEM.SYS, because the driver uses XMS handles and the EMS 4.0 specification says you should have a minimum of 64. It will work with the HIMEM.SYS default of 32, but there is some chance that programs which normally would run might not in that environment.

Miscellaneous Notes

If you're interested, here are some benchmark figures, run on a 16 MHz 386sx with Chips & Technologies NEATsx chip set with 4MB memory. The hardware figures below reflect the NEATsx EMS facilities using Chips and Technologies NEAT EMS driver version 2.0 and 2MB EMS.

PC Magazine Labs Benchmark 6.0

	Hardware	UMB_EMS4
EMS read	527.83	12.80 (K/sec)
EMS write	527.83	12.80

MOVETEST (PC Labs EMS Move test, 256KB move timing in seconds)

— 64 byte records — 128K records —

In the following table, **Conv** means **Conventional**.

	Hardware	UMB_EMS4
EMS => Conv	1.81	1.42
Conv => Conv	0.71	0.65
Conv => EMS	1.86	1.42
EMS => EMS	1.86	1.64
	Hardware	UMB_EMS4
EMS => Conv	.05	.05
Conv => Conv	.05	.05
Conv => EMS	.05	.05
EMS => EMS	.05	.05

Disk defragmentation program

(100MB drive, 80MB data. Program run two times, organizing data in two different orders. Identical initial data for all runs. Program used 2MB of EMS or Extended memory for buffers)

	Run #1	Run #2	Avg
	(times in min:sec)		
EMS (Hardware)	7:03	7:15	7:09
EMS (EMM386)	7:15	7:32	7:24
Extended (XMS)	8:53	9:14	9:04
EMS (UMB_EMS4)	11:50	11:05	11:28

Don't let these figures scare you — most programs tested run very well with UMB_EMS4 and show little performance difference. The above figures are *worst case* and do not reflect the average program. Many programs such as Quattro Pro 3.0, Lotus, dBASE, Paradox, a selection of games, several TSRs including a print spooler, and various others have been tested with no problems.

Installation

Important: Please be sure you have reviewed this documentation prior to installing. Also, make sure you have backed up your system and that you have a diskette you can boot from in case you have problems with your CONFIG.SYS settings.

Installation is via the lines

```
DEVICE=UMB_DRVR.SYS ...
DOS=HIGH,UMB
DEVICEHIGH=HIMEM.SYS /NUMHANDLES=64
DEVICEHIGH=UMB_EMS4.SYS
```

The driver will print a status report at initialization, and self-explanatory error messages if installation fails.

If you do not have enough upper memory to load UMB_EMS4 high, you may use DEVICE= to load into conventional memory, but it is much better to load it high if possible. Rearranging your CONFIG.SYS to do so is highly suggested.

Again, as with any new software, *make sure that your system is backed up,* and verify the operation of your programs. It is impossible for me to test all configurations and programs. If you have problems, let me know and I will try to straighten them out.

Known Incompatibilities

WordPerfect version 5.1 crashes if you use its default EMS 4.0 support. This can be avoided by either using the execute command

```
WP /32
```

when running it, or the command

```
SET WPC=/32
```

in the AUTOEXEC.BAT file at bootup. Either of these actions tells WordPerfect to use LIM 3.2 calls only. I am in contact with WordPerfect Corporation and am working on the problem.

UMB_DRVR.SYS, Version 5.22 Registration Form

Name: _____

Company: _____

Address: _____

City: _____

State: _____ Country: _____

Zip: _____ Phone: _____

Remit to:
Christopher Blum
1022 East Wayne Avenue
Wooster, Ohio 44691

(216) 262-3786
CompuServe: 76625,1041
INTERNET: 76625.1041@compuserve.com
BIX: cblum

* Email system / routing / ID _____
Computer description, configuration, chip set, etc.

_____

_____

_____

_____

Comments _____

_____

_____

_____

_____

Cost (U.S. Funds) $25 (no credit cards).

VIRUSCAN

Version 9.13V101
Copyright © 1989–1993 by McAfee Associates

System Requirements

SCAN requires 320K of RAM and DOS 2.0 or above (some features require DOS 3.1 or above).

SCAN is designed to check stand-alone and networked PCs for viruses. For network file servers please use NETSCAN instead.

SCAN displays messages in English (default); foreign language support is available as well.

Program and Documentation Files

By default, the install program for the *DOS 6 SECRETS* diskettes will install all of the VIRUSCAN files in the directory \SECRETS\SCAN. This directory has not been added to the search path. You can execute the program from its home directory, add the directory to the search path, or copy the VIRUSCAN files to a directory that is included in the search path.

Important: Write-protect the floppy disk containing the VIRUSCAN (SCAN.EXE) program before scanning to prevent VIRUSCAN from becoming infected by a computer virus.

Overview: (Known Virus Detection)

VIRUSCAN Version 9.13V101 (filename SCAN.EXE) identifies all 1,134 known computer viruses and their variants. Some viruses have been modified so that more than one "strain" exists. Counting such modifications, 1,830 viruses exist.

All known viruses infect one or more of the following areas: the hard disk partition table (alias Master Boot Record); the DOS Boot Sector of disks; or one or more executable files on the system. Executable files include operating system files, .COM files, .EXE files, overlay files, or any other files containing program code. A virus that infects more than one area, such as a boot sector and an executable file is called a multipartite virus.

SCAN checks files, subdirectories, diskettes, or entire systems for pre-existing computer virus infections. It will identify the virus infecting the system and the area where it was found, giving the name of the virus as well as the I.D. code used with CLEAN-UP to remove it.

Infected files can be removed using the /D switch in SCAN to erase the file, or with the CLEAN-UP universal virus removal (disinfection) program. CLEAN-UP is recommended because in most cases it will eliminate the virus and fully restore infected programs or system areas to normal operation.

The VIRLIST.TXT file describes all viruses identified by SCAN and their associated I.D. codes for removal by CLEAN-UP.

Overview: (Unknown and New Virus Detection)

SCAN has three separate methods of detecting unknown and new viruses:

- Validation codes which can be periodically checked against to look for the changes made by a virus to files or system areas.
- Generic and Family virus detectors to look for new viruses which are derivatives of older viruses.
- External virus signatures to insert new virus signature strings on a temporary basis to SCAN.

Synopsis: (Technical Description of Known Virus Detection)

SCAN detects known viruses by searching the system for strings (sequences of bytes) unique to each computer virus and reporting their presence if found. For viruses which encrypt or cipher their code so that every infection of the virus is different, SCAN uses detection algorithms (programs) that work by statistical analysis, heuristics, or code disassembly.

Synopsis (Technical Description of New/ Unknown Virus Detection)

SCAN checks for new or unknown viruses by comparing files against previously recorded validation (checksum) data. SCAN has two levels of validation which are stored in three separate ways:

- A simple 10-byte long validation checksum may be appended to .COM and .EXE files. If a file has been modified, it no longer matches the checksum and SCAN will report the file may have become infected. (/AV, /CV, /RV switches)
- An enhanced 52-byte validation and recovery data checksum can also be created. This can be appended to the end of files like the 10-byte checksum, or stored in a separate log file which can be offline (e.g., on floppies) for recovery purposes. CLEAN-UP can restore infected files, partition tables, or boot sectors using this information. (/AG, /CG, /RG switches and /AF, /CF, /RF switches)

Note: If validation codes are attached to files, SCAN will NOT add codes to the partition table, boot sector, or system files. Instead, a separate hidden file will be created in the root directory named SCANVAL.VAL containing data for these areas.

Note: Files which are self-checking (e.g., Lotus 1-2-3) should not be validated with the /AV (Add Validation) or /AG (Add Generic) switches which modify files. Instead, use the /AF (Add File) switch.

- SCAN also checks for new or unknown viruses by searching for Generic or Family virus strings. These are strings that have been found repeatedly in different viruses. Since virus writers may use the older pieces of code for new viruses, this allows SCAN to detect viruses which have not been written yet.

VIRUSCAN can be updated to search for new viruses by an External Virus Data File, which allows the user to input new search strings for viruses. (/EXT switch)

Authenticity

Before using SCAN for the first time, verify that it has not been tampered with or infected by a virus by using the enclosed VALIDATE program. For instructions on using VALIDATE, please read the VALIDATE.DOC file.

The validation results for Version 9.13V101 should be

```
FILE NAME: SCAN.EXE
SIZE: 111,681
DATE: 02-11-1993
File Authentication
Check Method 1: B9BD
Check Method 2: 19EE
```

If your copy of SCAN differs, it may have been damaged or have options stored in it with the /SAVE switch. Run SCAN with only the /SAVE option to remove any stored options and then re-run VALIDATE. Always obtain your copy of VIRUSCAN from a known source. The latest version of VIRUSCAN and validation data for SCAN.EXE can be obtained from McAfee Associates' bulletin board system at (408) 988-4004 or from the McAfee Virus Help Forum on CompuServe (GO MCAFEE), or the mcafee.COM anonymous ftp site on the Internet.

VIRUSCAN performs a self-check when run. If SCAN has been modified in any way, a warning will be displayed and the user will be prompted to either continue or quit. SCAN can still check for viruses; however, if SCAN reports that it has been damaged, it is recommended that a clean copy be obtained.

Beginning with Version 72, all of McAfee Associates' VIRUSCAN series are archived with PKWare's PKZIP Authentic File Verification. If you do not see an -AV after every file is unzipped and receive the `Authentic Files Verified! # NWN405 Zip Source: McAFEE ASSOCIATES` message when you unzip the files, then do not use them. If your version of PKUNZIP does not have verification ability, then this message may not be displayed. Please contact us if you believe tampering has occurred to the .ZIP file.

Command Summary

VIRUSCAN checks files and other areas of the system that can contain a computer virus. When a virus is found, SCAN identifies the virus and the file or system area where it was found.

SCAN examines files based on their extension. The default extensions supported by SCAN are .APP, .BIN, .COM, .EXE, .OV?, .PGM, .PIF, .PRG, .SWP, .SYS, and .XTP. Additional extensions can be added with the /E option, or use the /A to check all files.

Command Format:

```
SCAN {drive(s)} {options}
```

{drive(s)} — Indicates a drive or drives to be scanned

Options are

\	Scan root directory and boot area only
/? /H or /HELP	Displays help screen
/A	Scan all files, including data, for viruses
/AD	Scan all local drives for viruses
/AF {filename}	Store recovery & validation data to {filename}
/AG {filename}	Add recovery & validation data to files EXCEPT for those listed in {filename}
/AV {filename}	Add validation codes to files EXCEPT for those listed in {filename}
/BELL	Beep whenever a virus is found
/CERTIFY	List files that do not have a validation code
/CF {filename}	Check for viruses using recovery & validation data stored in {filename}
/CHKHI	Check memory from 0K to 1,088K
/CG	Check recovery & validation data on files
/CV	Check validation codes on files
/D	Overwrite and delete infected files
/DATE	Save the date and time SCAN was last run (use /SHOWDATE to display)
/E .xxx .yyy	Scan overlay extensions .XXX and .YYY
/EXT {filename}	Scan using external virus data from {filename}

/FAST	Speed up VIRUSCAN's output (see below for specifics)
/HISTORY {fname}	Create infection log {fname} appending to old log
/M	Scan memory for all viruses (see below for specifics)
/MAINT	Scan "invalid media" error (damaged) disk
/MANY	Scan multiple disks
/NLZ	Skip internal scan of LZEXE-compressed files
/NOBREAK	Disable Ctrl-C and Ctrl-Brk during scanning
/NOEXPIRE	Do not display expiration notice
/NOMEM	Disable memory check
/NOPAUSE	Disable screen pause when scanning
/NPKL	Skip internal scan of PKLITE-compressed files
/REPORT {fname}t	Create infection log {fname} deleting the old log
/RF filename	Remove recovery & validation data stored
/RG	Remove recovery & validation data from files
/RV	Remove validation codes from specified files
/SAVE	Save specified options as new default options
/SHOWDATE	Display the date and time SCAN was last run (use /DATE to save date and time)
/SUB	Scan all subdirectories inside a subdirectory
/UNATTEND	Scan using DOS critical error handler (required if used within Windows or OS/2)

@{filename}	Scan using options from {filename}

Please see the file SCAN101.DOC for details on Options.

Examples

The following examples show different option settings:

```
SCAN C:
```

To scan drive C:

```
SCAN A:R-HOOPER.EXE
```

Scans file "R-HOOPER.EXE" on drive A:

```
SCAN A: /A /CV
```

Scans all files and checks validation codes for unknown viruses on drive A:.

```
SCAN B: /D /A
```

Scans all files on drive B: and prompts for erasure of any infected files, if found.

```
SCAN C: D: E: /AV /NOMEM
```

Scan for viruses, add validation codes to files on drives C:, D:, and E:, and skip memory checking.

```
SCAN C: D: /M /A
```

Scan memory for all viruses, all files on drives C: and D: for viruses.

```
SCAN C: D: /E .WPM .COD
```

Scans drives C: and D:, including .WPM and .COD files

```
SCAN C: /EXT A:SAMPLE.ASC /BELL
```

To scan drive C: for known computer viruses and also for viruses added by the user via the external virus data file option, and beep whenever a virus is found.

```
SCAN C: /M /NOPAUSE /REPORT
A:INFECTN.RPT
```

To scan for all viruses in memory and drive C: without stopping, and create a log file INFECTN.RPT on drive A:

```
SCAN E:\DOWNLOADS /SUB
```

To scan all subdirectories under the directory DOWNLOADS on drive E:

```
SCAN C: D: E: /FAST /CERTIFY
```

To perform a fast scan of drives C:, D:, and E: and check for any files that do not have validation codes.

```
SCAN @C:\SCANOPTN.LST
```

To run SCAN using configuration file SCANOPTN.LST located in the root directory of drive C:.

```
SCAN /AD /M
```

Scan all hard drive partitions and memory for viruses.

Exit Codes

After VIRUSCAN has finished running, it will set the DOS ERRORLEVEL. ERRORLEVELs are used in batch files to pass the results of a program's actions. The ERRORLEVELs returned by SCAN are:

Errorlevel	Description
0	No viruses found
1	One or more viruses found
2	Abnormal termination (program error)
3	One or more uncertified files found
4	Ctrl-C or Ctrl-Break aborted scan

If a user stops the scanning process, SCAN will set the ERRORLEVEL to 4. If you wish to prevent users from stopping the scanning process, then run SCAN with the /NOBREAK option.

Virus Removal

What do you do if a virus is found? You can contact McAfee Associates for help, their authorized agents, or use the CLEAN-UP program.

McAfee Associates can be reached by BBS, CompuServe, FAX, Internet, or Telephone and there is no charge for support calls to McAfee Associates (Authorized agents may charge normal McAfee Associates consulting rates).

The CLEAN-UP universal virus disinfection program can disinfect virtually all reported computer viruses. It is updated with each release of the SCAN program to remove new viruses. CLEAN-UP can be downloaded from McAfee Associates' BBS, the McAfee Virus Help Forum on CompuServe, and the mcafee.COM

and WSMR-SIMTEL20.Army.Mil sites on the Internet, or from any of the agents' BBSes listed in the enclosed AGENTS.TXT text file.

It is strongly recommended that you get experienced help in dealing with viruses if you are unfamiliar with anti-virus software and methods. This is especially true for *critical* viruses and partition table/boot sector-infecting viruses as improper removal of these viruses can result in the loss of all data and the use of the infected disk(s). (For a listing of critical viruses, see the /M switch listed under OPTIONS above).

Before removing a boot sector or partition table-infecting virus, it is recommended that you cold boot the infected PC from a clean DOS disk and back up any critical data.

For qualified assistance in removing a virus, contact McAfee Associates directly or any of the Authorized Agents in your area. Agents may charge McAfee Associates' normal consult rates for their services.

If you wish to remove a file-infecting virus manually, cold boot the PC from a clean (virus-free) DOS system disk and run SCAN with the /A and /D switches to erase all infected files. Any files removed in this manner cannot be recovered.

Tech Support

McAfee Associates can be contacted by BBS, CompuServe, FAX, or InterNet 24 hours a day, or by telephone at (408) 988-3832, Monday through Friday, 7:00 a.m. to 5:30 p.m. Pacific Time.

BBS Access

Our 25-line BBS is accessible 24 hours a day, 365 days a year, except for scheduled downtime and maintenance. All lines run US Robotics Courier HST Dual Standard ASL modems operating from 1,200 bps to 16,800 bps with line settings of 8 data bits, no parity, and one stop bit.

The McAfee Virus Help Forum On CompuServe

We are now sponsoring the McAfee Virus Help Forum on CompuServe. To reach the McAfee

Virus Help Forum, type GO MCAFEE at any CompuServe prompt. A free introductory membership is available. For more information, please read the enclosed COMPUSER.NOT file.

Internet Access to McAfee Asociates Software

The latest versions of McAfee Associates' anti-viral software is now available by anonymous ftp (file transfer protocol) over the Internet from the site mcafee.COM. If your domain resolver does not support names, use the IP# 192.187.128.1. Enter "anonymous" for your user I.D. and your own email address for the password. Programs are located in the pub/antivirus directory. If you have any questions, please send email to support@mcafee.COM

McAfee Associates' anti-viral software may also be found at the Simtel20 archive site WSMR-SIMTEL20.Army.MIL in the

PD1:<MSDOS.TROJAN-PRO> directory and its associated mirror sites WUARCHIVE.WUSTL.EDU (US), NIC.SWITCH.CH (Swiss), NIC.FUNET.FI (Finland), SRC.DOC.IC.AC (UK), and RANA.CC.DEAK.OZ.AU (Australia).

Please see the file SCAN101.DOC for Appendixes A, B, and C.

Important Notice — Please Read!

Due to the nature of anti-virus software, the slight chance exists that a virus may be reported in a file that is not infected by that virus.

If you receive a report of a virus infection which you believe may be in error, please contact McAfee Associates by telephone at (408) 988-3832, by fax at (408) 970-9727, or upload the file to our BBS at (408) 988-4004 along with your name, address, daytime telephone number, and electronic mail address, if any.

VirusScan Registration Form

Name: _____

Company: _____

Address: _____

City: _____

State: _____ Country: _____

Zip: _____ Phone: _____

Remit to:
McAfee Associates, Inc.
3350 Scott Blvd. Bldg. 14
Santa Clara, CA 95054-3107

(408) 988-3832 office
(408) 970-9727 fax
(408) 988-4004 BBS (25 lines)
U.S.A. USR HST/v.32/v.42bis/MNP1-5
CompuServe GO MCAFEE
InterNet support@mcafee.COM

A registration fee of US $25 is required for the use of VIRUSCAN by individual home users. Registration entitles the holder to unlimited free upgrades from McAfee Associates' BBS, the Internet, and the McAfee Virus Help Forum on CompuServe as well as technical support for one year. When registering, a diskette containing the latest version may be requested for an additional US $9. Only one diskette mailing will be made.

Registration is for home users only and does not apply to businesses, corporations, organizations, government agencies, or schools, which must obtain a license for use. Contact McAfee Associates directly or an Authorized Agent for more information.

Part VI:
Appendixes

Page 809 ◇ **Appendix A**
Installing DOS 6

Page 815 ◇ **Appendix B**
DOS Command Quick Reference

Page 825 ◇ **Appendix C**
ANSI.SYS Quick Reference

Page 831 ◇ **Appendix D**
Interacting with Workgroups and Networks

Page 879 ◇ **Appendix E**
Additional DOS Information Sources

Appendix A

Installing DOS 6

Upgrading to DOS 6

Upgrading to DOS 6 couldn't be easier, but before you execute the SETUP program from disk 1 of DOS 6, you need to make the following preparations:

- During the installation procedure, you will be prompted to insert an Uninstall disk. (SETUP will transfer old DOS files to this disk to enable a subsequent UNINSTAL, if it becomes necessary.) Have ready a disk that is the same media type as the DOS 6 disks and label the disk *Uninstall*. The disk does not need to be formatted, but if the disk is formatted and contains files, the files will be overwritten. If you are installing DOS from 360K disks, you will need two Uninstall disks.

- DOS 6 uses considerable more disk space than its predecessors, especially if you install the optional Windows utilities. Make sure that you have enough free space — between 5 and 10 megabytes on your boot drive. SETUP will check your available space and report an error if there is insufficient room on the boot drive.

- If you are running on a network, suppress mail and print notifications or log off the network. SETUP sometimes aborts when a memory-resident utility pops up a message during installation.

- Disable any third-party disk cache software.

- Disable any delete-protection software such as MIRROR.

- Disable any anti-virus TSRs that monitor disk writes.

Having made the necessary preparations, just insert disk 1 of the DOS 6 set into a disk drive (assumed to be drive A in this appendix's examples) and enter the following command:

```
a:setup
```

If you find that the display is difficult to read or even illegible, press F5. If this action doesn't help, press F3 twice to exit SETUP and then reenter the command using the /I switch to instruct SETUP not to perform any hardware checks:

```
a:setup /i
```

SETUP will then guide you through the DOS 6 installation process.

If you experience any other problems during installation, refer to Chapter 9, "Diagnosing and Solving Problems," of the *Microsoft MS-DOS User's Guide*.

Having installed DOS 6, you should consider running DBLSPACE to increase your disk storage capacity and MEMMAKER (if you own a 386+ system) to optimize memory usage. Refer to Chapters 4 and 5, respectively, for further details on these programs.

 SETUP moves the files from the old version of DOS into a directory called OLD_DOS.1. If the directory already exists, SETUP will create a new OLD_DOS directory using the lowest available extension number — OLD_DOS.2 or OLD_DOS.3. After you have been using DOS 6 for a few days without any problems, use DELOLDOS to erase all the OLD_DOS directories. After running DELOLDOS, you will not be able to UNINSTAL DOS 6.

Installing to Floppies

To create a bootable DOS 6 floppy without installing DOS 6 on the hard disk, use the /F switch as follows:

```
a:setup /f
```

Have ready a disk that is the same size as the DOS 6 disks (3 ½-inch or 5 ¼-inch) and label it *Start-up*. The disk does not need to be formatted. Be prepared for a lot of floppy swapping as SETUP transfers files from the DOS 6 disks to the start-up disk. When the installation is complete, SETUP will reboot the system.

Gone are the days when DOS would fit on a single disk. Because of space limitations, SETUP installs the following files on the start-up disk:

IO.SYS

MSDOS.SYS

COMMAND.COM

DBLSPACE.BIN

ATTRIB.EXE

DEBUG.EXE

EXPAND.EXE

FDISK.EXE

FORMAT.COM

RESTORE.EXE

SYS.COM

CHKDSK.EXE

EDIT.COM

QBASIC.EXE

XCOPY.EXE

MSD.EXE

MSAV.EXE

DBLSPACE.EXE

Installing a Minimum Configuration

If you want to upgrade to DOS 6 but only want to install the minimum number of DOS 6 files needed to upgrade (because you are short on disk space, for example), use the /M switch as follows:

```
a:setup /m
```

SETUP will simply transfer the DOS 6 start-up files to the root directory of the boot drive. You will, however, still need to supply an Uninstall disk, which will be used to store the old DOS start-up files.

After the system is rebooted, you may be surprised to find that you no longer have the CONFIG.SYS and AUTOEXEC.BAT files. I sure was. Presumably, SETUP removes these files because there is a remote chance that some of the commands in these start-up files may conflict with the new version of DOS.

 Copies of the original CONFIG.SYS and AUTOEXEC.BAT files are stored on the Uninstall disk with a DAT extension. Copies of these files can also be found in the root directory of the boot drive, with the extension NEW. SETUP may have made modifications to the NEW files, however, such as adding a call to SMARTDRV.EXE in AUTOEXEC.NEW.

 Most of the DOS 6 files are stored in compressed form on the installation disks. All the compressed files have an underscore (_) as the third character in the filename extension. You cannot simply copy these files to the hard disk and use them. You must selectively install individual files using the EXPAND program. Copy the EXPAND.EXE file from disk 1 of DOS 6 to a directory on the path. The full syntax for EXPAND is detailed in Part IV, "The Complete DOS 6 Command Reference." But, as an example, the following command copies three files to the DOS subdirectory:

```
expand a:cga.vi_ a:cga.in_ a:cga.gr_ c:\dos
```

View the file PACKING.LST on disk 1 of DOS 6 to see which DOS 6 disk contains the files you want to transfer to the hard disk.

Installing the Windows Components of DOS 6

If you install DOS 6 and specify that you do not want to install the Windows utilities, you can install them later by running SETUP with the /E switch as follows:

```
a:setup /e
```

SETUP will transfer the Windows utilities MWBACKUP, MWUNDEL, and MWAV, which occupy just less than 3MB of disk space, to the hard drive. SETUP will also add a WINTOOLS group to Program Manager and add a Tools menu to File Manager.

You can also use the /E switch with SETUP to install the DOS versions of Backup, Anti-Virus, and Undelete, if you elected not to install them when you first upgraded to DOS 6.

Installing DOS 6 Manually

If you want to transfer all the DOS 6 files to your hard drive but do not want your system files upgraded, use the /Q switch with SETUP as follows:

```
a:setup /q
```

In most cases, you use the /Q switch only after previously installing the DOS 6 start-up files using /M (the minimum configuration switch discussed earlier).

The Windows files are not installed when SETUP is used with the /M switch. The DOS files consume approximately 4.2MB of disk space.

Installing to a Nonboot Drive

SETUP provides no convenient way for you to install the external DOS files on a drive other than the boot drive. By running SETUP multiple times using different switches, however, you can get the desired results. The following steps outline the procedure:

1. Execute SETUP with the /M switch to perform a minimal install, which only updates the start-up files.

2. Resurrect your AUTOEXEC.BAT and CONFIG.SYS files using the NEW files in the root directory or the DAT files on the Uninstall disk.

3. Execute SETUP with the /Q switch to perform a manual installation and, when prompted, specify the appropriate drive and directory where SETUP will place the DOS 6 files.

4. Execute SETUP with the /E switch to install the Windows utilities.

Uninstalling DOS 6

If you have not run DBLSPACE or DELOLDOS since installing DOS 6, you can revert back to your previous operating system by using the Uninstall disk that was used during the DOS 6 installation. Just insert the Uninstall disk into the drive and execute the following command:

```
a:uninstal
```

Appendix B

DOS Command Quick Reference

This appendix provides a summary of all the commands, device drivers, and ancillary files provided with DOS 6. The programs and files are listed in alphabetical order within the following categories:

- Standard DOS 6 files
- Files installed only when an older version of the file is present on the system
- Files used by SETUP but not installed
- Old files available on the DOS 6 Supplemental disk

Standard DOS 6 Files

ANSI.SYS	Provides ways to spruce up the DOS display capabilities, control the cursor location, and assign special functions to keys.
APPEND.EXE	Tells DOS which drives and directories to search in for data files (such as spreadsheets and word processing documents) when a program doesn't find them in the default directory.
APPNOTES.TXT	Contains information about running specific programs with DOS 6.
ATTRIB.EXE	Sets or clears attributes for one or more files. You can also use ATTRIB to view file attributes.
BREAK	Controls how frequently DOS checks to see whether you have pressed Ctrl-Break or Ctrl-C while a command or program is executing.

BUFFERS	Controls the number of disk buffers used by DOS when reading files. *Buffers* are memory blocks designed to store data during disk read and write operations and to improve system performance.
CALL	Enables one batch file program to execute a second batch file, after which control is returned to the first batch file.
CD	Changes the default (current) directory.
CHCP	Used with international character sets to display or change the active code page.
CHKDSK.EXE	Checks the integrity of a disk's file structure, reports disk errors, and, optionally, corrects them. CHKDSK displays a summary of the disk's use and the system's memory status.
CHOICE.COM	Enables a batch file to prompt the user to select an option by pressing a key. CHOICE sets the ERRORLEVEL to indicate which key was pressed.
CLS	Removes all the displayed characters, sets the color to gray on black, and repositions the cursor to the top left corner of the display.
COMMAND	Starts a new copy (or instance) of COMMAND.COM, the command interpreter.
COMMAND.COM	Displays the command prompt, interprets typed commands, and contains internal MS-DOS commands.
COPY	Copies one or more files to another location or to the same location with a new filename. You can instruct COPY, in its extended form, to treat the files as ASCII or binary.
COUNTRY.SYS	Configures the country language conventions for your system.
CTTY	Enables a different device to be used for keyboard and display I/O.
DATE	Sets the system date.
DBLSPACE.BIN	Compression kernel — handles all file compression and decompression.
DBLSPACE.EXE	Creates and manages compressed drives on hard disks and floppies.
DBLSPACE.SYS	Relocates the compression kernel (DBLSPACE.BIN) to low conventional memory or to upper memory.

DEBUG.EXE	Creates and analyzes program files.
DEFRAG.EXE	Increases disk performance and enhances data recovery chances by defragmenting files.
DEL	Deletes one or more files.
DELOLDOS.EXE	Deletes all OLD_DOS directories from a disk.
DELTREE.EXE	Removes a directory, all its subdirectories, and all the files in the directories — just like that.
DEVICE	Loads a device driver into conventional or base memory.
DEVICEHIGH	Loads device drivers into upper memory if it's available or base memory if there is no room in upper memory.
DIR	Displays information about one or more files, including the name, size, and date and time of last creation.
DISKCOMP.COM	Compares two floppy disks to see whether they contain identical data.
DISKCOPY.COM	Duplicates all the data from one floppy disk to another.
DISPLAY.SYS	Provides international character support by allowing code-page switching.
DOS=	Controls whether DOS is loaded in high memory (on 286 systems and higher) and whether DOS should manage the upper memory area (on 386 systems and higher).
DOSHELP.EXE	See FASTHELP.
DOSKEY.COM	Provides three primary and very useful functions: the ability to recall previous commands to save from re-typing, command-line editing (no more backspace), and a simple but effective macro utility.
DOSSHELL.COM	Provides menuing, file-management, and task-switching tools.
DRIVER.SYS	Creates logical floppy drives with different characteristics from the physical drive.
DRIVPARM	Defines or redefines the properties of disk and tape drives (block devices).
ECHO	Controls how batch file commands are displayed during execution.
EDIT.COM	Starts the full-screen editor for viewing and editing ASCII (text) files.
EGA.CPI	Contains code-page information for EGA monitors.

EGA.SYS	Supports DOSSHELL task swapping on EGA systems.
EMM386.EXE	Provides advanced memory-management capabilities on 386 systems and higher.
ERASE	See DEL.
EXIT	Terminates the current COMMAND.COM session and returns to the preceding one.
EXPAND.EXE	Transfers and decompresses files from the DOS distribution disks to your system.
FASTHELP.EXE	Provides terse help on nearly all DOS commands but not on device drivers. You can also use DOSHELP.
FASTOPEN.EXE	Improves file performance by speeding access to frequently used files.
FC.EXE	Compares two files and highlights any differences.
FCBS	Specifies the maximum number of file control blocks DOS can have open at any time.
FDISK.EXE	Prepares a new hard disk for formatting and manages logical drive assignments on a partitioned disk.
FILES	Specifies the number of files that DOS can have open concurrently.
FIND.EXE	Searches for specific text in a file or files.
FOR	Executes a command or statement multiple times and applies a new string or filename with each iteration.
FORMAT.COM	Formats a floppy or hard disk and creates a new file allocation table; optionally marks bad sectors.
GOTO	Instructs DOS to continue processing batch file commands at a specific location in the batch file.
GRAPHICS.COM	Enables you to print graphics screens just by pressing PrtScr on CGA, EGA, and VGA systems.
HELP.COM	Displays full-screen on-line help for DOS commands and device drivers.
HIMEM.SYS	Manages extended memory on 286 systems and higher.
IF	Provides a conditional branch in a batch file execution.
INCLUDE	Instructs DOS to process a specific block of commands when used in a multiboot CONFIG.SYS file.
INTERLNK.EXE	Changes the drive assignments for two computers connected by way of InterLink.

INTERSVR.EXE	Parallel or serial file-transfer server.
IO.SYS	The DOS basic input/output system (BIOS) that prepares the system at start-up and contains resident device drivers.
KEYB.COM	Configures the keyboard for international (non-USA) use.
KEYBOARD.SYS	A device driver that supports different keyboard layouts.
LABEL.EXE	Creates, changes, or deletes a disk volume label.
LASTDRIVE	Specifies how many logical drives DOS recognizes.
LH	See LOADHIGH.
LOADFIX.COM	Fills the first 64K of conventional memory so that no programs load there.
LOADHIGH	Loads programs in upper memory.
MD	Creates a new directory.
MEM.EXE	Displays valuable information that shows how your system's memory is utilized and how much free memory is available.
MEMMAKER.EXE	Assesses your memory configuration and modifies CONFIG.SYS and AUTOEXEC.BAT to make optimum use of memory (for 386 and higher systems).
MENUCOLOR	Configures the display colors for a multiconfiguration menu.
MENUDEFAULT	Sets the default item in a multiconfiguration menu and optionally the number of seconds to wait for user input before applying the default.
MENUITEM	Identifies a menu option in a multiconfiguration menu.
MODE.COM	Configures devices such as printers, monitors, keyboards, and communication ports.
MORE.COM	Pauses the output from a command-line utility after every screen.
MOVE.EXE	Moves files from one path to another and renames directories.
MSAV.EXE	Runs the full-screen utility Microsoft Anti-Virus, which scans drives for viruses and optionally removes them. Installed when non-Windows tools are selected from SETUP.
MSBACKUP.EXE	Runs the full-screen utility Microsoft Backup, which backs up and restores copies of your files. Installed when non-Windows tools are selected from SETUP.

MSCDEX.EXE	Makes a CD-ROM behave like a standard disk device and assigns a logical drive letter to the CD-ROM drive.
MSD.EXE	Analyzes and reports on your detailed system configuration.
MSDOS.SYS	The DOS kernel — manages files, directories, memory, and environments.
MSTOOLS.DLL	Windows 3.x File Manager extensions. Installed when Windows tools are selected from SETUP.
MWAV.EXE	Windows program that scans drives for viruses and optionally removes them. Installed when Windows tools are selected from SETUP.
MWAVTSR.EXE	Provides Windows support for messages generated by VSAFE.
MWBACKUP.EXE	Backup for Windows. Installed when Windows tools are selected from SETUP.
MWUNDEL.EXE	Windows version of UNDELETE to recover accidentally deleted files and directories. Installed when Windows tools are selected from SETUP.
NLSFUNC.EXE	Provides National Language Support by enabling code-page switching.
NUMLOCK	Controls whether the keyboard Num Lock key is set to On or Off at system boot.
PACKING.LST	Lists the files located on each DOS 6 disk.
PATH	Stores a list of directories that DOS searches when it looks for a program or batch file.
PAUSE	Temporarily halts batch file execution and waits for the user to press a key.
POWER.EXE	Reduces power consumption to prolong battery life on systems compliant with APM (Advanced Power Management).
PRINT.EXE	Provides background printing capabilities that enable you to proceed with tasks while one or more files are being printed.
PROMPT	Customizes the prompt DOS displays when it is ready to receive a command.
QBASIC.EXE	Invokes the full-screen development environment for creating and running BASIC language programs.
RAMDRIVE.SYS	Creates a RAM disk (a virtual disk in memory) to improve performance.

RD	Removes (that is, deletes) an empty directory.
README.TXT	Contains information that is hardware specific or was available too late to be printed in the manuals.
REM	Provides a way to add comments to any batch file and CONFIG.SYS.
REN	See RENAME.
RENAME	Changes the name of one or more files.
REPLACE.EXE	Synchronizes the contents of two directories.
RESTORE.EXE	Restores files that were stored on floppy disks by using the original DOS BACKUP utility.
RMDIR	See RD.
SETUP.EXE	Runs the DOS 6 installation and setup program.
SETVER.EXE	Displays and modifies the version table in which programs and fake version numbers are stored. This enables programs that expect a specific version of DOS to be installed to run with DOS 6.
SHARE.EXE	Allows file sharing and locking for multiuser or multiapplication access.
SHELL	Sets the options for COMMAND.COM or enables a different command processor to be loaded.
SHIFT	Used in batch files to drop the first passed parameter (%1) and shift all other parameters left one position.
SIZER.EXE	Used by MEMMAKER during the optimization process; it is not intended for general use.
SMARTDRV.EXE	Creates a disk cache in expanded or extended memory.
SMARTMON.EXE	Monitors SMARTDRV cache performance under Windows.
SORT.EXE	Sorts input data and directs the sorted output to a device or file.
STACKS	Allocates memory to manage hardware interrupts.
SUBMENU	Provides a way to branch to a secondary menu in a multiconfiguration system.
SUBST.EXE	Assigns a drive letter alias to a specific directory.
SWITCHES	A miscellaneous collection of four configuration switches for customizing the behavior of the operating system.
SYS.COM	Makes a formatted drive bootable or updates the DOS version by transferring the primary DOS files IO.SYS, MSDOS.SYS, COMMAND.COM, and DBLSPACE.BIN to the root directory of a drive.

TIME	Displays and sets the system time.
TREE.COM	Displays the directory structure of an entire drive or for a specific directory and its subdirectories.
TYPE	Displays the contents of an ASCII file.
UNDELETE.EXE	Provides mechanisms for enhancing the chances of recovering deleted files and tries to undelete files that have been deleted.
UNFORMAT.COM	Recovers files and directories destroyed by an accidental FORMAT.
UNINSTAL.EXE	Restores the previous version of DOS after installing the DOS 6 Upgrade. (Created on the Uninstall disk.)
VER	Displays the DOS version number.
VERIFY	Instructs DOS to verify that data just written to disk can be read back into memory.
VOL	Displays a disk's volume label and serial number.
VSAFE.COM	Monitors disk activity and protects against virus infection.
WINA20.386	Enables DOS 6 to run with Microsoft Windows 3.0 in 386 Enhanced Mode.
WNTOOLS.GRP	Windows Tools program group. Installed when Windows tools are selected from SETUP.
XCOPY.EXE	An enhanced version of COPY that can copy files and directories and that loads multiple files in memory to improve performance.

Files Installed Only When an Older Version of the File Is Present on the System

DMDRVR.BIN	A device driver for the Disk Manager disk partitioning program
MOUSE.COM	Microsoft Mouse driver
MSCDEX.EXE	Microsoft CD-ROM extensions
SSTOR.SYS	A device driver for the SpeedStor disk partitioning program

Files Used by SETUP but Not Installed _____

SETUP.EXE	DOS 6 Upgrade installation program
AV.GRP	Renamed as WNTOOLS.GRP during setup
CONFIG.SYS	Base configuration
AUTOEXEC.BAT	Base configuration

Old Files Available on the DOS 6 Supplemental Disk _____

4201.CPI	Code-page information for IBM Proprinters II and III, Models 4201 and 4202
4208.CPI	Code-page information for IBM Proprinters X24E Model 4207, XL24E Model 4208, and compatibles
5202.CPI	Code-page information for IBM Quietwriter III Printer Model 5202 and compatibles
ASSIGN.COM	Redirects requests for disk operations on one drive to a different drive
BACKUP.EXE	The old MS-DOS backup program; replaced by MSBACKUP.EXE
COMP.EXE	Compares the contents of two files or two sets of files byte by byte
CV.COM	Update for older versions of the CodeView debugging program
EDLIN.EXE	A line-oriented text editor
EXE2BIN.EXE	Converts executable files to binary format
GORILLA.BAS	A sample QBasic program
GRAFTABL.COM	Enables the display of extended characters of a specified code page in Graphics Mode
JOIN.EXE	Joins a disk drive with a directory on another disk drive
LCD.CPI	Contains code-page information for certain liquid crystal displays
MIRROR.COM	Tracks deleted file information

MONEY.BAS	A sample QBasic program
MSHERC.COM	Provides support for a Hercules monitor running with EDIT or QBASIC
NIBBLES.BAS	A sample QBasic program
PRINTER.SYS	Supports code-page switching for parallel port printers
PRINTFIX.COM	Disables verification of a printer's status line
RECOVER.EXE	Recovers readable information from a defective disk
REMLINE.BAS	A sample QBasic program

Appendix C
ANSI.SYS
Quick Reference

This appendix provides a summary of all the ANSI.SYS commands for controlling the display, controlling cursor movement, and reassigning keys.

 All ANSI.SYS commands are prefixed by two special characters: the Esc character, which has the ASCII value 027, and the left square-bracket character ([), which has the ASCII value 019. In EDIT, you can enter the Esc code by pressing Ctrl-P and then pressing the Esc key. EDIT displays the Esc character as a left-pointing arrow (←).

The ANSI.SYS commands are summarized in the following categories:

- Color display codes used with Esc[*code*m
- Display attribute codes used with Esc[*code*m
- Text erasing codes
- Cursor-control codes
- Display mode control codes
- Keyboard control codes

Color Display Codes Used with Esc[*code*m

Color	Foreground Code	Background Code
Black	30	40
Red	31	41
Green	32	42
Brown	33	43
Blue	34	44

Color	Foreground Code	Background Code (continued)
Magenta	35	45
Cyan	36	46
Light gray	37	47

Display Attribute Codes Used with Esc[*code*m

Code	Attribute
0	All attributes off
1	Bright intensity
4	Underline (monochrome systems only)
5	Blinking text
7	Reverse video
8	Hidden or invisible

Text Erasing Codes

Code	Description
Esc[2J	Clears the screen
Esc[K	Erases line from cursor position to end of line

Cursor-Control Codes

Escape Sequence	Action
Esc[*row*;*col*H	Moves the cursor to the specific row and column. If only one value is specified (without a semicolon), it is assumed to represent the column, and the row defaults to 1.
Esc[s	Saves the active cursor position.
Esc[u	Repositions the cursor to the position it occupied when the last s (save) command was issued.
Esc[*pos*A	Moves the cursor up the number of rows specified by the *pos* variable. The cursor stops when it reaches the first row.

(continued)

Escape Sequence	Action (continued)
Esc[posB	Moves the cursor down pos rows. The cursor stops when it reaches the last row.
Esc[posC	Moves the cursor to the right pos columns. The cursor stops when it reaches the last column.
Esc[posD	Moves the cursor left pos columns. The cursor stops when it reaches the first column.

Display Mode Control Codes

Escape Sequence	Description
Esc[=0h	Text — monochrome, 40 columns by 25 lines
Esc[=1h	Text — color, 40 columns by 25 lines
Esc[=2h	Text — monochrome, 80 columns by 25 lines
Esc[=3h	Text — color, 80 columns by 25 lines
Esc[=4h	Graphics — 4-color, 320 by 200 pixels
Esc[=5h	Graphics — monochrome, 320 by 200 pixels
Esc[=6h	Graphics — monochrome, 640 by 200 pixels
Esc[=7h	Enables line wrapping
Esc[=13h	Graphics — color, 320 by 200 pixels
Esc[=14h	Graphics — 16-color, 640 by 200 pixels
Esc[=15h	Graphics — monochrome, 640 by 350 pixels
Esc[=16h	Graphics — 16-color, 640 by 350 pixels
Esc[=17h	Graphics — monochrome, 640 by 480 pixels
Esc[=18h	Graphics — 16-color, 640 by 480 pixels
Esc[=19h	Graphics — 256-color, 320 by 200 pixels

Keyboard Control Codes

Key	Standard	With Shift	With Ctrl	With Alt
A	97	65	1	0;30
B	98	66	2	0;48
C	99	67	3	0;46
D	100	68	4	0;32
E	101	69	5	0;18
F	102	70	6	0;33
G	103	71	7	0;34
H	104	72	8	0;35
I	105	73	9	0;23
J	106	74	10	0;36
K	107	75	11	0;37
L	108	76	12	0;38
M	109	77	13	0;50
N	110	78	14	0;49
O	111	79	15	0;24
P	112	80	16	0;25
Q	113	81	17	0;16
R	114	82	18	0;19
S	115	83	19	0;31
T	116	84	20	0;20
U	117	85	21	0;22
V	118	86	22	0;47
W	119	87	23	0;17
X	120	88	24	0;45
Y	121	89	25	0;21
Z	122	90	26	0;44
1	49	33	N/A	0;120
2	50	64	0	0;121
3	51	35	N/A	0;122
4	52	36	N/A	0;123
5	53	37	N/A	0;124
6	54	94	30	0;125

(continued)

Key	Standard	With Shift	With Ctrl	With Alt (continued)
7	55	38	N/A	0;126
8	56	42	N/A	0;126
9	57	40	N/A	0;127
0	48	41	N/A	0;129
-	45	95	31	0;130
=	61	43	N/A	0;131
[	91	123	27	0;26
]	93	125	29	0;27
Spacebar	92	124	28	0;43
;	59	58	N/A	0;39
'	39	34	N/A	0;40
,	44	60	N/A	0;51
.	46	62	N/A	0;52
/	47	63	N/A	0;53
`	96	126	N/A	0;41
Enter (keypad)	13	N/A	10	0;166
/ (keypad)	47	47	0;142	0;74
* (keypad)	42	0;144	0;78	N/A
- (keypad)	45	45	0;149	0;164
+ (keypad)	43	43	0;150	0;55
5 (keypad)	0;76	53	0;143	N/A
F1	0;59	0;84	0;94	0;104
F2	0;60	0;85	0;95	0;105
F3	0;61	0;86	0;96	0;106
F4	0;62	0;87	0;97	0;107
F5	0;63	0;88	0;98	0;108
F6	0;64	0;89	0;99	0;109
F7	0;65	0;90	0;100	0;110
F8	0;66	0;91	0;101	0;111
F9	0;67	0;92	0;102	0;112
F10	0;68	0;93	0;103	0;113
F11	0;133	0;135	0;137	0;139
F12	0;134	0;136	0;138	0;140

(continued)

Key	Standard	With Shift	With Ctrl	With Alt (continued)
Home	0;71	55	0;119	N/A
Up arrow	0;72	56	0;141	N/A
PgUp	0;73	57	0;132	N/A
Left arrow	0;75	52	0;115	N/A
Right arrow	0;77	54	0;116	N/A
End	0;79	49	0;117	N/A
Down arrow	0;80	50	0;145	N/A
PgDn	0;81	51	0;118	N/A
Insert	0;82	48	0;146	N/A
Delete	0;83	46	0;147	N/A
Print Screen	N/A	N/A	0;114	N/A
Pause	N/A	N/A	0;0	N/A
Backspace	8	8	127	0
Enter	13	N/A	10	0
Tab	9	0;5	0;148	0;165
Home (gray key)	224;71	224;71	224;119	224;151
Up arrow (gray key)	224;72	224;72	224;141	224;152
PgUp (gray key)	224;73	224;73	224;132	224;153
Left arrow (gray key)	224;75	224;75	224;115	224;155
Right arrow (gray key)	224;77	224;77	224;116	224;157
End (gray key)	224;79	224;79	224;117	224;159
Down arrow (gray key)	224;80	224;80	224;145	224;154
PgDn (gray key)	224;81	224;81	224;118	224;161
Ins (gray key)	224;82	224;82	224;146	224;162
Del (gray key)	224;83	224;83	224;147	224;163

Appendix D

Interacting with Workgroups and Networks

The InterLink Connection

If you just want to connect two PCs together occasionally to transfer files or share a printer, you don't need to invest in a network. DOS 6 offers InterLink commands for providing these basic services. InterLink is primarily designed to connect a laptop PC to a desktop PC, but you can use it to connect any two PCs that can be wired together using serial or parallel ports.

Wiring the two computers together

You can use three different types of cable to connect two computers: a bi-directional parallel cable, a three-wire serial cable, or a seven-wire null modem serial cable. When choosing cables, consider the following pros and cons:

■ Because parallel cables use several lines simultaneously, parallel connections are inherently faster than serial connections. The cable, however, is bulkier and must be connected to the parallel printer port — that is, a female DB25 connector. Many older desktop systems have only one parallel port, and if the port is being used for InterLink, it cannot also be connected to a printer.

■ File transfer speeds are significantly slower when you use serial connections because data is transferred along only one "wire." Most PCs have a spare serial port. If no spare is available, you usually can temporarily disconnect an external modem or mouse to free a serial port. If you use a serial connection, the InterLink software can be remotely installed on one PC.

■ Each computer can use a different port number, but both computers must use the same port type. For example, you can connect a serial cable to COM1 on one computer and COM3 on the other.

Because I don't perform large file transfers very often, I use the three-wire serial cable option. Three-wire serial cable comprises a length of standard telephone cable with a nine-pin (DB9) serial connection at each end. It's not the fastest configuration, but the cable is thin enough to carry around in my notebook PC carrying case.

Establishing an InterLink connection

The InterLink tools are provided in the form of two programs: INTERLNK.EXE and INTERSVR.EXE. When you use InterLink to connect two computers, you run INTERLNK on one computer and INTERSVR on the other.

MS-DOS documentation refers to the PC running INTERSVR as the *server* and to the computer running INTERLNK as the *client*.

How to install INTERLNK

INTERLNK.EXE is both a device driver and an executable program. Install INTERLNK.EXE in CONFIG.SYS in the computer that will be fully functional and will have access to the drives and printers attached to the remote computer. By default, INTERLNK.EXE automatically loads high into available UMBs, so you do not need to load it using DEVICEHIGH.

INTERLNK.EXE supports a variety of switches, all of which are documented in Part IV, "The Complete DOS 6 Command Reference." One frequently used switch is /DRIVES. By default, INTERLNK.EXE only provides access to three drives on the remote (server) computer. Use the /DRIVES switch to access drives beyond drive C. The following statement in CONFIG.SYS provides access to drives A through E on the remote printer:

```
device=c:\dos\interlnk.exe /drives:5
```

You may also need to add or modify the LASTDRIVE= statement in the CONFIG.SYS file to ensure that the client system can accommodate these additional drive letters.

You can use a variety of switches to reduce the memory requirements of INTERLNK.EXE. By default, INTERLNK.EXE scans the installed serial and parallel ports, looking for a connection to a server computer. To save memory, you can instruct the device driver to use an explicit port instead of scanning for a connection. Use the /LPT*n* or /COM*n* switch, replacing *n* with the actual port number — for example, /LPT1. Also, if you do not plan to use the server's printer, specify /NOPRINTER to save memory.

Install INTERLNK.EXE only when you intend to connect one computer to another. Don't waste valuable memory on the device driver if you don't plan to use it. Use the /AUTO switch to instruct INTERLNK.EXE to install only if it can establish an immediate connection with a server. If a server is not found, the device driver is not loaded, and no memory is wasted. If you use the /AUTO switch, make sure that the server machine is actively running the INTERSVR.EXE program before you boot the client computer.

The following statement from CONFIG.SYS installs INTERLNK.EXE (when the server is active) via COM2 and provides access to drives A through E on the remote computer. It does not provide printer support.

```
device=c:\dos\interlnk.exe /drives:5 /com2 /auto /noprinter
```

How to install INTERSVR

The server computer needs no special device drivers. To establish a connection, the server computer simply executes the INTERSVR command. INTERSVR supports a variety of switches (see the Command Reference for details) but is most often executed with no switches, as follows:

```
intersvr
```

By default, INTERSVR redirects all drives to make them available to the client computer. You can use the *drive*: and /X=*drive*: switches to control which drives are available to the client. To explicitly identify which drives should be redirected, use the *drive*: switch and specify one or more individual drives; to exclude certain drives, use the /X=*drive*: switch, specifying one or more drives.

When a successful connection is established, the server computer drives are assigned to additional drive letters on the client computer. The server computer displays the status of the connection and a list of the drive connections. The list shows the server drive letter and printer ports along with the corresponding drive letter and port assignments on the client.

 If INTERLNK.EXE is not installed on the remote computer, you can transfer the INTERLNK.EXE file by using INTERSVR with the /RCOPY switch (for remote copy).

Three easy steps to successful linking

To recap, you should take the following steps to connect two computers with InterLink:

1. Wire the two computers using a bidirectional parallel cable, a three-wire serial cable, or a seven-wire null modem cable.

2. Execute the INTERSVR.EXE program on the computer that is to act as the server.

3. Boot the client computer with INTERLNK.EXE installed as a device driver. Remember to use the /DRIVES switch if the server has more than one hard drive.

You can boot the client computer before the server computer starts running INTERSVR if the /AUTO switch was not used with the device driver. After INTERSVR is started, the client computer should execute INTERLNK.EXE to establish the connection.

Using server resources

To check the drive and port assignments, just enter the INTERLNK command on the client computer. When you issue the command, INTERLNK displays the active settings. The following is an example display:

```
Port=COM1

    This Computer         Other Computer
      (Client)              (Server)
    - - - - - - - - - - - - - - - - - - - - - - - - - - - - - - - -
      E:    equals      A:
      F:    equals      B:
      G:    equals      C: (211Mb)  UPSTAIRS-C
      H:    equals      D: (173Mb)  UPSTAIRS-D
      I:    equals      E: (167Mb)  UPSTAIRS-E
    LPT2:   equals    LPT1:
```

To access the server drives, use the drive and port aliases listed in the first (client) column. You have full read and write access to the remote drives.

If, for example, the settings are as shown in the sample display, you can edit the AUTOEXEC.BAT file on the server computer by entering the following command:

```
edit g:\autoexec.bat
```

Similarly, you can access the server's printer by outputting data to the LPT2 port.

One of my old computers (Bessie) does not have a 3½-inch drive. I can still install software from 3½-inch floppies by using InterLink to link my notebook computer (Ralph) to Bessie. Because InterLink provides access to the floppies on the server, I can install software to my old computer using the notebook's drive A.

Understanding InterLink limitations

Only local hard disks and standard removable drives (such as floppies and Bernoullies) can be redirected to the client computer. InterLink does not support network drives, CD-ROMs, or devices such as modems, fax cards, and scanners.

Unlike some third-party products, such as LapLink Pro, InterLink does not support a dial-up file transfer facility. In other words, the client cannot dial up the server and establish a connection via a modem. In addition, InterLink is slower than similar third-party products.

When you run INTERSVR from within Windows, DOS Shell, or any multitasker, you cannot switch tasks. You must terminate INTERSVR to return to other tasks.

You cannot execute the following commands on a server drive: CHKDSK, DEFRAG, DISKCOMP, DISKCOPY, FDISK, FORMAT, MIRROR, SYS, UNDELETE, and UNFORMAT.

But, hey, the price is right.

Workgroup Wizardry _____

To provide DOS 6 with rudimentary networking capabilities, Microsoft offers a separate product called *Workgroup Connection*. This product allows any DOS 6 computer to connect to a Windows for Workgroups, Windows NT, Microsoft LAN Manager, or compatible network. The remainder of this appendix explains how to use the Workgroup Connection software and includes a supplementary Command Reference detailing the complete syntax for all the Workgroup Connection commands.

To gain access to a network, all your system needs is a network card (or plug-on network adapter) and the appropriate wiring to connect into the network (coaxial, twisted pair, or fiber optic cable).

A DOS 6 system using Workgroup Connection can access disk drives, CD-ROMs, and printers connected to other computers in the network (if these other computers are running full network software), but not tape drives, scanners, and modems. Such a system, however, cannot share its local disk drives and printers with other users. In other words, you can access devices on other computers that are running full network software, but those other systems cannot access your devices. If you need to share your system's local devices with other users, you must install additional network software that is compatible with the network software used by your workgroup — for example, Windows for Workgroups.

In addition to the basic network software needed to communicate with other *nodes* (systems on the network) and access their devices, DOS 6 includes a copy of Microsoft Mail 3.0. If your workgroup uses Microsoft Mail, you can participate fully in workgroup electronic mail.

Installing the network software

 DOS 6 Workgroup Connection files cannot be installed on a Vertisoft System DoubleDisk drive. Also, you should not install the Workgroup Connection on a machine that already has LAN Manager or Windows for Workgroups installed.

Before you install the Workgroup Connection software on your system, install the network card and cabling. The software drivers that you will install are dependent on the specific brand of network card in use, and the setup program will try to detect the type of network card. If the program cannot determine the card type, you are prompted to select one from a list, as shown in Figure D-1.

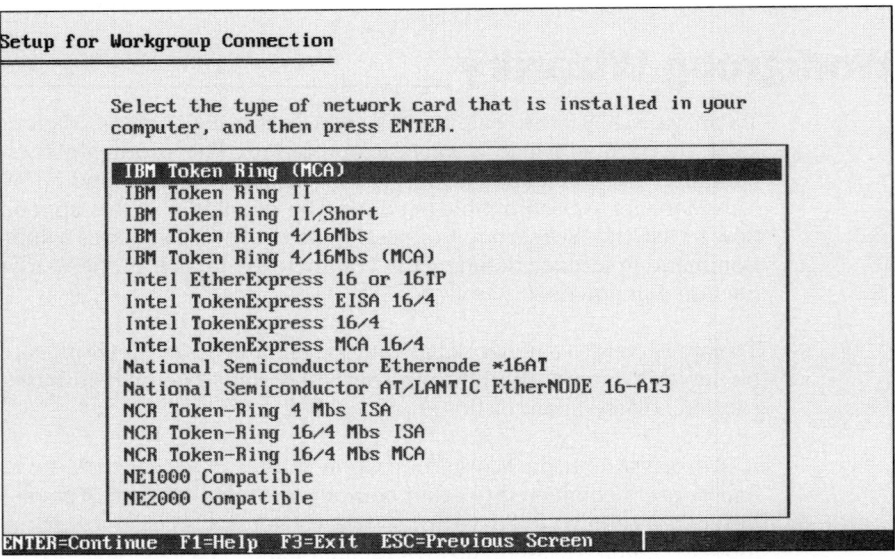

Figure D-1: SETUP displays a list of supported network cards.

On lower power systems, such as 8086-based PCs and XTs, SETUP can take as long as five minutes to check system configurations.

During the installation procedure, you are prompted to supply the name of the workgroup you want to join. If you do not know the workgroup name, ask the network administrator or a colleague for the correct name. Don't just make up a name; if you do, the installation will not be successful. A colleague using Windows for Workgroups or Windows NT can verify the workgroup name by selecting the Connect <u>N</u>etwork Drive option from the <u>D</u>isk menu in File Manager.

In addition to the workgroup name, you need to specify two additional unique names: your user name and your computer name. In most (organized) workgroups, user names are assigned according to some standard, such as the first five characters of the user's last name plus the first two initials. The computer name often reflects the location of the computer; for example, the room number might be used as the computer name. Check with the network administrator to determine appropriate user and computer names.

The workgroup name, computer name, and user name can each be up to 15 characters long. Names can include letters, numbers, or the following characters:

! # $ % & ( ) ^ _ ' { } and ~

Sometimes, the first eight characters of the user name are used by a network program to create files; use a naming convention that ensures that the first eight characters of each user name are unique.

Armed with this information, you can install the Workgroup Connection software. Insert the Workgroup Connection setup disk and execute the SETUP program from it.

If SETUP aborts, displaying a message indicating that it cannot update or edit the file PROTOCOL.INI, you may have insufficient memory available. Make more memory available and try again.

Figure D-2 shows the settings screen that SETUP displays after it assesses your system configuration and prompts you for the computer and workgroup names. Notice that the program assumes that the computer name and user name are the same. To change any option, use the cursor keys to highlight the option and press Enter.

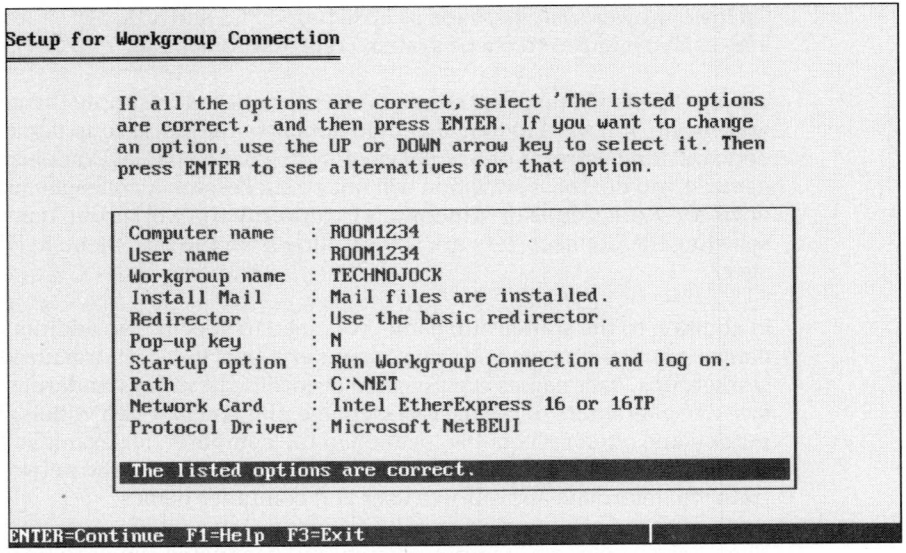

```
Setup for Workgroup Connection

        If all the options are correct, select 'The listed options
        are correct,' and then press ENTER. If you want to change
        an option, use the UP or DOWN arrow key to select it. Then
        press ENTER to see alternatives for that option.

        ┌─────────────────────────────────────────────────────────┐
        │ Computer name    : ROOM1234                             │
        │ User name        : ROOM1234                             │
        │ Workgroup name   : TECHNOJOCK                           │
        │ Install Mail     : Mail files are installed.           │
        │ Redirector       : Use the basic redirector.          │
        │ Pop-up key       : N                                   │
        │ Startup option   : Run Workgroup Connection and log on. │
        │ Path             : C:\NET                              │
        │ Network Card     : Intel EtherExpress 16 or 16TP       │
        │ Protocol Driver  : Microsoft NetBEUI                   │
        │                                                         │
        │ The listed options are correct.                        │
        └─────────────────────────────────────────────────────────┘

ENTER=Continue   F1=Help   F3=Exit
```

Figure D-2: SETUP displays the Workgroup Connection settings.

Reviewing network commands

The main command for managing workgroups is appropriately named NET. The NET command supports a whole family of subcommands, which are summarized in Table D-1.

The Pop-Up program provides an easy way to control network settings by using menus and dialog boxes rather than command switches. Pop-Up is discussed in detail later in this chapter.

Connecting to a network

During the Workgroup Connection setup, SETUP makes modifications to CONFIG.SYS and AUTOEXEC.BAT. These modifications are to load network drivers and automate the network log-on procedure.

Before modifying CONFIG.SYS and AUTOEXEC.BAT, SETUP makes backup copies, assigning an extension of 001 (or the next available number).

Table D-1	Net Command Summary
Command	*Description*
NET CONFIG	Shows the active workgroup settings, including the computer name, user name, software version, workstation directory, and workgroup.
NET LOGOFF	Disconnects the computer from the workgroup and displays all connections to disk drives and printers that are being disconnected.
NET LOGON	Connects your workstation to a workgroup. If a password is not specified on the command line, you are prompted to enter it.
NET PASSWORD	Changes the log-on password. A password is not case sensitive.
NET PRINT	Manages shared printers in the workgroup and the print jobs for your workstations.
NET START	Establishes a workgroup connection and optionally loads the Pop-Up utility to simplify creating drive and printer connections.
NET STOP	Disconnects a workstation and optionally unloads the Pop-Up TSR.
NET TIME	Synchronizes your computer's date and time with the network. This command only works on a network using LAN Manager, which has a designated time server.
NET USE	Connects or disconnects network drives and printers.
NET VER	Displays the version number of the network redirector.
NET VIEW	Provides an easy way to determine the computer names of the other computers in the workgroup, along with names of the shared directories and printers.

Network entries in CONFIG.SYS

The following is an example of the network commands added to CONFIG.SYS:

```
device=C:\NET\protman.dos /i:C:\NET
device=C:\NET\workgrp.sys
device=C:\NET\exp16.dos
LASTDRIVE=Z
```

In most circumstances, you can load all three device drivers into UMBs using DEVICEHIGH. Use the network for a few days with the device drivers loaded low to ensure that no other network problems exist and then use MEMMAKER to optimize your configuration. If you experience problems with the device drivers loaded high, change the DEVICEHIGH statements back to DEVICE. Then add the three device driver names to MEMMAKER.INF, placing an asterisk before each device driver name, and run MEMMAKER again. (Refer to Chapter 5 for more information on MEMMAKER.)

The PROTMAN.DOS device driver examines the settings in the file PROTOCOL.INI (located in the directory specified with the /I switch) and then binds the appropriate network protocols with the network adapter card device driver (in the example, EXP16.DOS). The PROTMAN.DOS device driver must be located before other network drivers in CONFIG.SYS.

The following is a typical PROTOCOL.INI file:

```
[network.setup]
version=0x3100
netcard=ms$ee16,1,MS$EE16
transport=ms$netbeui,MS$NETBEUI
lana0=ms$ee16,1,ms$netbeui

[MS$EE16]
IOCHRDY=Late
IOADDRESS=0x300
DriverName=EXP16$
IRQ=3
TRANSCEIVER=Thin Net (BNC/COAX)

[protman]
DriverName=PROTMAN$
PRIORITY=MS$NETBEUI

[MS$NETBEUI]
DriverName=netbeui$
SESSIONS=6
NCBS=12
BINDINGS=MS$EE16
LANABASE=0
```

You can easily view PROTOCOL.INI from the File menu of MSD.

All PROTOCOL.INI files contain [NETWORK.SETUP] and [PROTMAN] sections. There are additional sections specific to the network adapter card and the network protocol — in the example, the sections are named [MS$EE16] and [MS$NETBEUI].

You should not directly edit PROTOCOL.INI. Instead, run SETUP to modify the settings. If you want to change the IRQ setting for the network adapter card, for example, run SETUP and press Enter to select the Network Card option. Then select the Edit Settings option to modify the detailed card settings (see Figure D-3).

```
Setup for Workgroup Connection

        The settings for your network card are listed below. If all
        the settings are correct, select 'The listed options are
        correct'. Then press ENTER. If you want to change a setting,
        use the UP or DOWN arrow key to select it. Then press ENTER
        to see alternatives for that setting.

        Network Card : Intel EtherExpress 16 or 16TP

         Drivername=EXP16$
         IOADDRESS=0x300
         IRQ=3
         I/O Channel Ready=Late
         Transceiver Type=Thin Net (BNC/COAX)

         The listed options are correct


F1=Help  F3=Exit  ESC=Previous Screen
```

Figure D-3: Use SETUP to modify network adapter card settings in PROTOCOL.INI.

How to log on to the network

If you accept the default SETUP Startup option, which is Run Workgroup Connection and log on, the following line is added at the beginning of AUTOEXEC.BAT:

```
c:\net\net start
```

NET START is the primary command for connecting to the network. When you execute NET START without any switches, the settings located in the

Network Protocols

The network protocol defines how data and applications messages are packaged and routed around the network. Two standard protocols are NETBIOS and NETBEUI.

NETBIOS stands for *Network Basic Input/Output System*. This system is supported by most network operating systems and by most networked applications. NETBEUI stands for

NETBIOS Extended User Interface. Introduced in 1985 by IBM, it is a compact network protocol designed for small networks with 20 to 200 workstations.

NETBEUI is the only protocol directly supported by DOS 6. However, third-party (OEM) protocols can be installed using SETUP.

SYSTEM.INI file in the NET directory (not \WINDOWS) are used. The following list is a typical SYSTEM.INI file, which details the workstation's network settings:

```
[network]
computername=ROOM1234
lanroot=C:\NET
autostart=basic
dospophotkey=N
username=ROOM1234
workgroup=TECHNOJOCK
reconnect=yes

[Password Lists]
ROOM1234=C:\NET\ROOM1234.PWL
```

NET START has two functions: it establishes a network connection, and it performs a log-on. If the NET LOGON command is executed before NET START, Workgroup Connection automatically calls NET START before logging on.

NET START does not allow you to enter a password as a parameter, whereas NET LOGON does. If you use the NET LOGON command, specifying the password along with a /YES switch, you can automatically invoke NET START and NET LOGON without being prompted for a password. For example, change the command

```
c:\net\net start
```

to

```
c:\net\net logon room1234 abracadabra /yes
```

If you want to log on as a different user, just enter the NET LOGON command, and Workgroup Connection automatically issues a NET LOGOFF command before executing the NET LOGON command.

Password management

The first time you log on to the network, Workgroup Connection asks you to confirm your password. The password is stored in encrypted form in the network directory, in a file with a PWL extension. The first eight characters of the filename identify the user name. A full list of PWL files and their corresponding user names is maintained in the [PASSWORD LISTS] section of SYSTEM.INI. This allows many different users to access the network from one workstation.

Use the NET PASSWORD command to change the log-on password for the active user name. You must be connected to the network to execute this command. Passwords are not case sensitive and can be up to 14 characters long.

If you forget your password, delete the *username*.PWL file (where *username* represents your network user name) and log on. Workgroup Connection assumes that you are a new user and prompts you to enter a new password.

Using network resources

The Workgroup Connection utilities allow your workstation to access shared directories and printers attached to other computers that are running full network software, such as Windows for Workgroups.

Don't assume, however, that because you have access to the network, you automatically are able to use network resources. Every resource, such as a printer or directory, must be explicitly shared and assigned a resource name. The resource name is known as the *sharename*. In addition, some resources can only be shared when a password is entered.

Using the Pop-Up utility

You can either use the Pop-Up program or the NET subcommand utilities to access shared resources. But the Pop-Up utility provides the easiest and most interactive way to access shared directories and printers.

Loading and running Pop-Up

To execute the Pop-Up program, just log on and then enter the following command:

```
net
```

You also can install the Pop-Up program as a TSR. To do so, enter the following command:

```
net start popup
```

The TSR consumes about 30K of memory. You can pop it up over Text Mode applications and at the DOS prompt by pressing Alt-N. You also can use SETUP to configure Pop-Up to use a different Alt-letter combination (see Figure D-2).

The Pop-Up utility is not designed to handle monochrome display systems. If you want to use Pop-Up on a monochrome system, use the MODE command to set the display mode to mono before you execute the NET command. The following two statements launch Pop-Up on a monochrome system:

```
mode mono
net
```

You can remove the Pop-Up TSR from memory, provided that no other TSRs were loaded after it, by entering the following command:

```
net stop popup
```

Pop-Up has two main screens: one for managing remote directory connections and another for managing remote printers. Figure D-4 shows the main Disk Connections display. You can toggle between the Disk Connections and Printer Connections by pressing Alt-S (the SHOW command).

Notice that the computer names are prefixed by double backslash characters. Workgroup Connection always uses the double backslash convention to indicate a computer or workgroup name.

```
 Disk Connections                      [ how Printers]
 Drive: F:                             [ Connect  ]
 Path:
 [X] Reconnect at startup              [  Browse  ]

         Current connections          [Disconnect]

   D: is \\UPSTAIRS\UPSTAIRS           [  Exit    ]
   E: is \\DOWNSTAIRS\DOWN
                                       [  Help    ]



 ESC=Exit  TAB=Next Field  ↑ or ↓=Select Item   F1=Help
```

Figure D-4: Pop-Up's Disk Connections display.

In this example, drive D is mapped to the directory with the sharename *Upstairs* on the \\UPSTAIRS computer. Drive E is mapped to the directory with the sharename *Down* on the \\DOWNSTAIRS computer. There is no way to determine precisely what directory or drive is represented by a sharename. For example, *Down* might actually be mapped to C:\THIS\THAT\THEOTHER or D:\.

Connecting to directories

To connect to a remote drive, you can enter an explicit path in the **Path** field, using the convention *ComputerName**Sharename.* But the easiest method is to use the **B**rowse option. To invoke this option, press Alt-B. Pop-Up displays a list of all workstations currently connected to the network. If a particular computer name is not listed as you expected, the computer is probably turned off or not logged in to the network.

In the Browse window, use the cursor keys to highlight a workstation. A list of shared drives is displayed in the lower window. Press Tab (or Alt-D) to shift to the sharenames and select one by using the cursor keys and pressing Enter. Figure D-5 shows the list of sharenames for the shared directories on the \\UPSTAIRS computer.

By default, Pop-Up assigns the next available drive letter, but you can select any unused drive letter by pressing Alt-V before making the connection. If you want

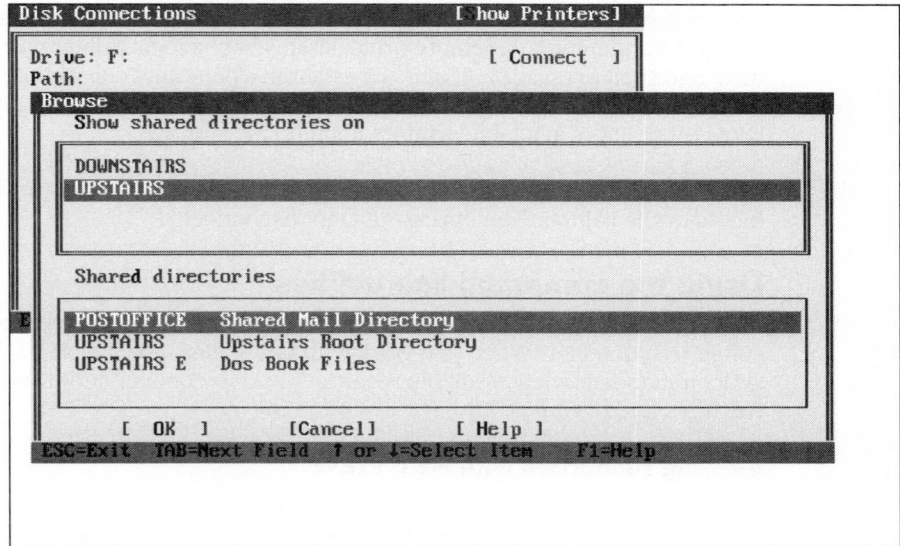

Figure D-5: Using the Browse option.

to assign a drive letter that is already in use to a new path, you must first disconnect the existing path.

If you want to connect to a remote directory every time you log on to the network, press Alt-R and then press the spacebar to toggle the check mark in the Reconnect at Startup field before you select the Browse option. Paths that are reconnected at start-up are referred to as *persistent connections*.

Persistent connections are recorded in the binary file CONNECT.DAT, which is located in the NET directory. A quick way to remove all persistent connections is to delete the file CONNECT.DAT. Alternatively, enter the following command at the DOS prompt:

```
net use /persistent:clear
```

Connecting to shared printers

You can assign different shared printers to different local printer ports. When you try to print to the redirected printer port, the output is automatically sent to the network printer.

To use a remote printer, you must assign it to a local parallel port (LPT1 through LPT3). Use Pop-Up to establish connections to shared printers as well as to pause, resume, and delete your queued print jobs.

Press Alt-S to switch from Pop-Up's Disk Connections dialog box to the Form Connections dialog box. The process of attaching to a remote printer is very similar to attaching to a remote drive. First, select a local printer port by pressing Alt-T and then pressing 1, 2, or 3. To establish a persistent connection, press Alt-R and press the spacebar to insert a check in the Startup field. Then press Alt-B to browse the list of available printers and choose a printer.

To disconnect from a shared printer, press Alt-N and use the cursor keys to highlight the printer. Then press Alt-D to disconnect.

Using the command-line utilities

Although the Pop-Up utility is easy to use, its interactive nature is not well suited to batch files. When you work with batch files, use the NET subcommands to view available resources and to connect and disconnect directories and printers.

Viewing resources with NET VIEW

You can use the NET VIEW command to display a list of shared resources to which you may have access. If you execute the NET VIEW command with no parameters, a list of workstations connected to your workgroup is displayed. Here is an example:

```
Server Name                Remark
-------------------------------------------------------------------------
\\MCCARTP                  Room 1231
\\STARRR                   Desktop system
\\LENNONJ                  Room 1236
\\HARRISG                  What sort of remark
\\AINSBUB                  Mr Big Disk
The command completed successfully.
```

If your network has more than one workgroup, you can display a list of workstations connected to a selected workgroup. To do this, specify the workgroup name as a parameter with NET VIEW. Here is an example:

```
net view \\sales
```

To ascertain what shared resources are available at a specific workstation, enter the NET VIEW command with the name of the workstation as a parameter. If I enter the command net view \\ainsbub, for example, the following output is displayed:

```
Shared resources at \\AINSBUB
Sharename    Type         Comment
-------------------------------------------------------------------------
POSTOFFICE   Disk         Shared Mail Directory
ROOTC        Disk         Drive C Root Directory
SWAPE        Disk         Directory E:\SWAP
QMS-PS       Print        Postscript printer
The command completed successfully.
```

Accessing remote directories and printers

You can use the NET USE subcommand to connect and disconnect remote directories and printers.

If you enter NET USE with no switches, a completed list of the active connections is displayed. Here is an example:

```
Status        Local name        Remote name
-------------------------------------------------------------------------
OK            D:                \\STARRR\LYRICS
OK            F:                \\HARRISG\SONGS
OK            LPT1              \\AINSBUB\QMS-PS
The command completed successfully.
```

 Workgroup Connection can assign remote directories to local drive letters that were allocated with Quarterdeck's QEMM Lastdrive command. These drives, however, do not show up in the NET USE list.

Refer to the Command Reference at the end of this appendix for a complete description of each of the NET USE switches and parameters. The following paragraphs provide some common examples of how you can employ the NET USE and NET PRINT commands to perform different tasks.

Reviewing directory examples

The basic syntax for connecting with remote drives using NET USE is

```
net use drive: \\computer\path [/p:yes or no]
```

where *drive* is the drive letter that will be used to reference the directory specified in *computer**path*. The optional /P switch can be used to control whether the connection is persistent — that is, whether the connection is to be reestablished each time you log on to the network.

To connect to a directory with sharename ROOTC on the \\AINSBUB computer as drive D, you would enter the following command:

```
net use d: \\ainsbub\rootc
```

If you want to make the drive assignment persistent (so the connection is reestablished every time you log on), you can add the /P switch. Here is an example:

```
net use d: \\ainsbub\rootc /p
```

 To access a printer or directory on a computer whose name includes one or more spaces, enter the entire device name in quotes. Here is an example:

```
net use e: "\\silly name\rootc"
```

To disconnect drive D, enter the following command:

```
net use d: /delete
```

 You do not have to connect to a remote directory to access its files if the directory was made shareable without a password. You can explicitly access an individual file using the following syntax:

*computername**drivename**path**filename*.*ext*

For example, to edit the contents of the SAYWHAT.HEY file from the computer named ROOM2554, on the drive named CDRIVE, you would enter the following command:

```
edit \\room2554\cdrive\saywhat.hey
```

Reviewing printer examples

The basic syntax for connecting with remote printers using NET USE is

```
net use lptn \\computer\queue [/p:yes or no]
```

where lptn is the local printer port that will be used to direct output to the printer specified in \\computer\queue. The optional /P switch can be used to control whether the connection is persistent.

The following command redirects all LPT1 output to the shared printer called HPIII on the computer named \\MCCARTP:

```
net use lpt1: \\mccartp\hpiii
```

To disconnect from the remote printer assigned to LPT1, enter the following command:

```
net use lpt1: /delete
```

You can use the command NET PRINT to manage print queues after a connection with a printer is established. After you send a job to the printer, you must determine the job number before you can pause, resume, or delete the job. To see the print jobs assigned to one of your ports, enter the print command in the following format:

```
net print lptn
```

For example, to list all the print jobs queued at the printer assigned to LPT1, enter

```
net print lpt1
```

The following command pauses job 234 queued at the LPT1 printer:

```
net print lpt1 234 /pause
```

To resume printing the job, you would enter the following command:

```
net print lpt1 234 /resume
```

To delete job 667 from the LPT3 print queue, you would enter the following command:

```
net print lpt3 667 /delete
```

Accessing CD-ROMs

You can access a remote CD-ROM drive (provided that it is shared by the owner) just as you can any other directory. The owner of the CD-ROM system must be using MSCDEX.EXE version 2.2 or later, and MSCDEX must be installed with the /S switch. Here is an example:

```
c:\dos\mscdex /s /d:mvcd001 /m:10 /v
```

You do not need to install MSCDEX on your own computer to access a remote CD-ROM drive. However, if you need MSCDEX to access a local CD-ROM drive, do not install it with an /S switch.

 If a network problem occurs, Workgroup Connection displays a brief error message and an error number. To obtain a longer description of the error and suggestions about how to correct the problem, use the NET HELP command and specify the error number. For example, to obtain a full description of network error 64, you would enter the following command:

```
net help 64
```

Mail Secrets

To use Microsoft Mail, your computer must have a network card and be connected to the network. At least one other computer in the network must be running a network operating system or a peer-to-peer network, such as Windows for Workgroups. In other words, you cannot simply connect two or more computers by using Workgroup Connection and use the Mail facility.

Using the Workgroup Connection MAIL command, you can join other Microsoft Mail users in your network and participate fully in workgroup electronic mail.

Installing Mail

Before running Microsoft Mail for the first time, log on to the network by issuing the NET START or NET LOGON command. Then enter the following command:

```
mail
```

MAIL launches into Setup Mode and prompts you for the name of the workgroup post office. The workgroup post office actually is a directory located on one of the computers in your workgroup. You must enter the post office directory name in the following format:

   *computername**sharename*

If you do not know the post office name, ask a network administrator or do some snooping with the NET VIEW command — by default, a Windows for Workgroups or Windows NT post office directory has the sharename (not surprisingly) *postoffice*.

During setup, MAIL prompts you to enter your name, password, telephone number, alternate telephone number, office location, and an optional note. Be aware that other network mail users are able to view these details (except for the password) when they compose mail. Figure D-6 shows the confirmation list that MAIL setup presents before creating your mailbox.

Be sure to make a note of the mailbox name. You must specify this name every time you start the Mail program. By default, your mailbox name is the same as your network user name.

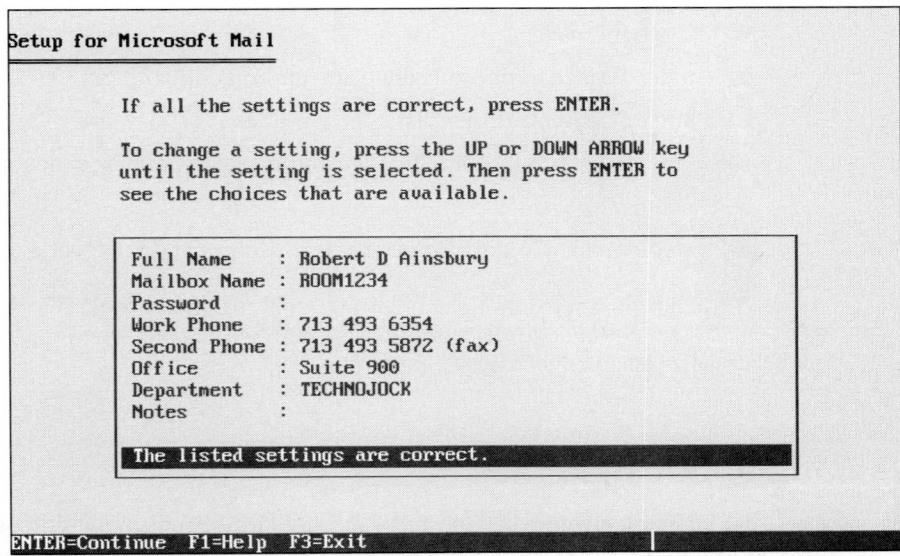

Figure D-6: The MAIL setup confirmation list.

Running Microsoft Mail

To run Microsoft Mail, just log on to the network and enter the MAIL command. You are then prompted for your mailbox name and your password. Alternatively, you can specify the mailbox and password (using the -P switch) as command-line parameters. For example, to use mailbox CLINTOW with the password PEROT, you can go directly to the Mail main menu by using the following command:

```
mail clintow -pperot
```

During setup, MAIL creates a persistent connection. By default, it assigns drive M to the workgroup post office directory. If you connect to the post office directory using another drive, you must use the -D switch when you execute MAIL. The switch informs Workgroup Connection of the post office drive. For example, if the post office is assigned to drive F, you use the following command to start Mail:

```
mail clintow -pperot -df
```

Microsoft Mail is a full-featured electronic mail program that enables you to perform the following tasks:

- Send, receive, and print messages
- Reply to messages
- Send a message to one colleague and carbon copy others
- Create a personal address list
- Create mail groups to simplify distribution to common recipients
- Attach a file to a message
- Store old mail in folders for easy categorization and retrieval

The Mail program is intuitive and straightforward. Refer to the *Workgroup Connection User's Guide* for a general description of the Mail program. A useful tutorial is also provided.

Locating your mail files

All of your electronic mail messages, file folders, groups, and address lists are stored in the workgroup post office, not on a local hard disk. If you are not logged on to the network and connected to the main post office directory, you are not able to use MAIL. You are not even able to read old messages or prepare new messages for distribution.

All mail files are stored in encrypted form. Their contents cannot be readily deciphered.

Receiving new mail

By default, MAIL constantly checks for new incoming messages whenever the program is running. You can use the -X switch to instruct MAIL to use a polling method instead. When you use this switch, MAIL defaults to checking for new messages every 30 seconds, but you can specify any polling period from 0 to 199 seconds by including the -N switch. You can only use the -N switch when -X is also specified.

The following command starts MAIL, instructs it to use the polling method, and specifies a polling period of 60 seconds:

```
mail -x -n60
```

Remember, MAIL only checks for messages when it is running. It is not a TSR. You should install the Workgroup Connection program MICRO if you want to be informed of incoming mail while you are running another application, such as a word processor or spreadsheet program.

When you execute MICRO, you must specify your mailbox name. To instruct MICRO to monitor all mail sent to mailbox ROOM1234, for example, you would enter the following command:

```
micro room1234
```

MICRO can notify you of incoming mail in one of three ways. It can display a discrete character in the top right corner of the screen, display a brief pop-up message, or display a detailed pop-up message that includes the name of the sender and the mail subject. You can establish your preferred notification method by using one of the following switches:

-f*minutes*   Instructs MICRO to display a nonintrusive character in the top right corner of the screen. The *minutes* parameter indicates the desired display time. The character is removed after the specified number of minutes.

-n*minutes*   Instructs MICRO to display a window notifying you that mail has arrived. You must press Esc to proceed with your application. The window is removed after the specified number of *minutes*.

If you will be running graphics applications, such as Windows or the graphics version of DOS Shell, use the -F switch. In other words, instruct MICRO to display the special notification character rather than a pop-up window. MICRO is unable to successfully display pop-up messages when your system is in Graphics Mode.

If neither switch is specified when MICRO is installed, a setting of -N1 is used. If the -N switch is in effect, you can also use the -P switch, instructing MICRO to provide information about the message (the name of the sender and the subject of the message). If your mailbox is password protected, you must specify your password. The following command installs MICRO, instructing it to poll the mailbox ROOM1234 once every two minutes and display a detailed message when mail is received:

```
micro room1234 -n2 -pabrcadabra
```

In Figure D-7, you see a message from MICRO in the lower left corner of the screen. MICRO indicates that BOB sent a mail message about Tuesday's staff meeting.

If you use the -F switch, which tells MICRO to use a nonintrusive character to alert you to incoming mail, you can remove the indicator by pressing Alt-F1.

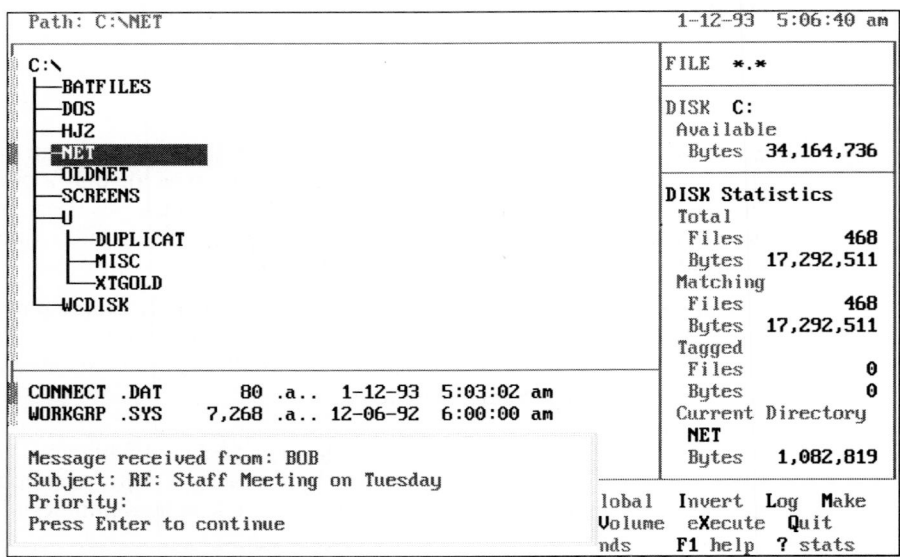

Figure D-7: A sample MICRO message.

MICRO consumes about 13K of RAM. You can unload MICRO from memory (provided that no other TSRs were loaded after it) by specifying the -U switch as follows:

```
micro -u
```

Refer to Part IV, "The Complete DOS 6 Command Reference," for a complete description of all MICRO switches.

If you execute MAIL while MICRO is installed, specify the -M switch. MAIL leaves it up to MICRO to inform you about incoming messages. Here's an example:

```
mail clintow -pperot -df -m
```

Forgetting your password or mailbox name

Every workgroup post office has a designated mail administrator — someone responsible for managing the system. If you forget your password, the administrator can come to your rescue. The administrator cannot tell you the old password but can overwrite your old password with a new one.

The administrator can also tell you your mailbox name and optionally modify your mailbox settings (such as phone numbers, office location, and so on).

Workgroup Connection Command Reference __

This section is a summary of the following Workgroup Connection programs:

MAIL	NET PRINT
MICRO	NET START
NET	NET STOP
NET CONFIG	NET TIME
NET LOGOFF	NET USE
NET LOGON	NET VER
NET PASSWORD	NET VIEW

Refer to the beginning of Part IV for a thorough description of the formatand syntax conventions used in this Command Reference.

PROMPT   AUTOEXEC   BATCH   CONFIG

MAIL

Description

This command installs Microsoft Mail, the DOS 6 electronic-mail program.

Usage

```
mail [mailboxname] [-lines] [-c] [-dn] [-h] [-m] [-nseconds] [-
ppassword] [-sdisplay] [-v] [-wcolor] [-x]
```

Options and switches

Note: The first time you try to run the MAIL program, DOS invokes the MAIL setup program.

When you execute MAIL with no switches, you are prompted for a mailbox name (assumed to be on drive M), and — if all is well — the main menu appears.

   [*mailboxname*]

This option specifies your personal mailbox name. Every mail user in the workgroup has a mailbox (in a dedicated directory). If the mailbox is not specified, MAIL prompts you for it. If you do not use the –D switch, MAIL assumes that the mailbox is located on drive M.

   [*-lines*]

This option specifies the number of display lines to use. EGA systems support 43 lines, and VGA systems support 43 and 50 lines. By default, 25 lines are used.

   [-c]

On some (obscure) color systems, because MAIL thinks that it is running on a monochrome system, it uses only black and white. Use the –C switch to instruct MAIL to use colors.

[-d*n*]

n specifies the drive that contains the workgroup mailbox. Any letter (from A to Z) is accepted, and M is the default.

[-h]

This switch displays the command-line help; it has the same effect as /?.

[-m]

This switch informs MAIL that, because MICRO (the mail notifier) is loaded, MAIL does not need to signal when new mail is received.

[-n*seconds*]

Used with the –X switch, –N specifies the polling frequency, in seconds, to check for new mail. MAIL checks for new messages every 30 seconds by default, but any value in the range from 0 to 199 is accepted. A value of 0 disables polling altogether.

[-p*password*]

This switch identifies the mailbox password. If the switch is not specified, MAIL prompts for the password. If your mail is confidential in any way, do not record the password in a batch file.

[-s*display*]

Use this switch when MAIL cannot detect the video system. Valid values for display are MONO, HERC, CGA, EGA, and VGA.

[-v]

This switch suppresses screen flicker on CGA systems.

[-w*color*]

This switch specifies the border color. Any value in the range from 0 (black) to 15 (white) is supported.

[-x]

This switch instructs MAIL to poll for new messages rather than continually check for new mail.

Remarks

To use Microsoft Mail, your computer must have a network card and be connected to the network. At least one other computer in the network must be running a network operating system or a peer-to-peer network, such as Windows for Workgroups. In other words, you cannot simply connect two or more computers using DOS 6 and use the MAIL program.

Each user has an individual mailbox in a *postoffice* located on one of the computers running the network software. If you are unsure of the mailbox name, contact your network administrator.

Examples

To start MAIL by using the mailbox BOBBY when the postoffice is located on drive F, enter the following command:

```
mail bobby /df
```

To start MAIL and poll for messages every 60 seconds, enter the following command:

```
mail -x -n60
```

Additional information

See also MICRO and NET.

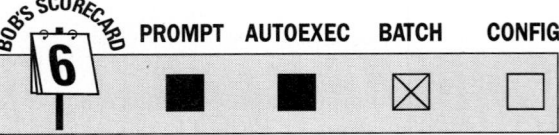

			PROMPT	AUTOEXEC	BATCH	CONFIG
MICRO	BOB'S SCORECARD	6	■	■	⊠	☐

Description

This command is a small TSR that checks your mailbox and notifies you when new mail is received.

Usage

micro *mailboxname* [-c] [-d*n*] [-f*minutes*] [-n*minutes*] [-p*password*] [-u] [-x*seconds*]

Options and switches

mailboxname

This option is the name of your mailbox.

[-c]

This switch forces MICRO to use colored text, even when it thinks it is running on a monochrome system.

[-d*n*]

n specifies the drive that contains the workgroup mailbox. Any letter (from A to Z) is accepted, and M is the default.

[-f*minutes*]

This switch instructs MICRO to display a (nonintrusive) character in the top right corner of the display. It makes you aware that mail has arrived but enables you to proceed with your application. The character is removed after the specified number of *minutes*.

[-n*minutes*]

This switch instructs MICRO to pop up a window to notify you that mail has arrived. You must press Esc to proceed with your application. The window is removed after the specified number of *minutes*. If neither the –F or –N parameter is specified, a setting of –N1 is applied.

[-p*password*]

This switch instructs MICRO to provide information about the mail (who sent the mail and the subject). If your mailbox is password protected, you must specify your password.

[-u]

This switch unloads MICRO from memory, assuming that no other TSRs were loaded after MICRO.

[-x*seconds*]

This switch instructs MICRO to poll for new messages one time every specified number of *seconds* rather than constantly check for new mail. The value of *seconds* can be any number in the range from 1 to 3600.

Remarks

You must create a mailbox with MAIL before you can run MICRO.

You can remove the mail notifier before the expiration time by pressing Alt-F1.

If you are running graphics applications, such as Windows or the graphics version of DOSSHELL, use the /F switch.

Examples

To install MICRO to monitor Buster's mail and instruct MICRO to display the discrete mail notifier for five minutes, use the following command:

```
micro buster -f5
```

To install MICRO to monitor BClinton's mail when the mailbox is situated on the J drive, enter the following command:

```
micro bclinton -dj
```

Additional information

See also MAIL.

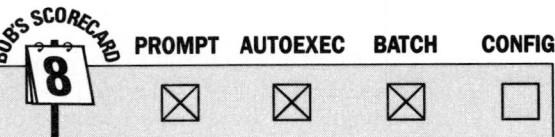

Description

Provides DOS with workgroup (network) capabilities. The NET family of commands can be used only on systems that have a network card installed and that are connected to a Windows for Workgroups or Microsoft LAN Manager (or compatible) network.

When you execute NET with no switches, the network pop-up utility is displayed for configuring drives and printers.

For clarity, the NET command has been divided into the following subcommands:

NET CONFIG
NET LOGOFF
NET LOGON
NET PASSWORD
NET PRINT
NET START
NET STOP
NET TIME

NET USE
NET VER
NET VIEW

To take advantage of any of the NET commands, you should have the network device drivers installed in CONFIG.SYS, as shown in the following examples:

```
device=c:\net\protocol.sys /i:c:\net
device=c:\net\workgrp.sys
device=c:\net\exp16.dos
```

Note: The last device driver is a network card driver. The Workgroup Connection program SETUP installs the appropriate driver after determining the type and brand of network card.

On most systems, you then establish a network connection by entering the command NET START or adding it to AUTOEXEC.BAT. If the following message appears:

```
Error 3653: The protocol manager could not be found
```

check CONFIG.SYS to make sure that the network drivers are installed.

After you enter your username and password, any persistent connections are established. Bingo, you're connected.

The HELP switch for the NET command has the same effect as /?. Optionally, you can specify an error message or subcommand (NET HELP LOGOFF or NET HELP 3653, for example).

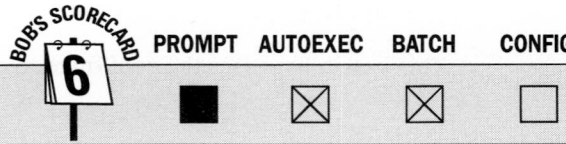

	PROMPT	AUTOEXEC	BATCH	CONFIG
NET CONFIG	■	⊠	⊠	☐

Description

This command shows the active workgroup settings.

Usage

```
net config [/yes]
```

Options and switches

```
[/yes]
```

This optional switch suppresses any prompts for confirmation. Normally, however, there are no prompts.

Remarks

The settings displayed include the computer name, username, software version, workstation directory, and workgroup.

The computer name always has a prefix of two backslashes (\\BUSTER, for example). This convention is used when you want to access a remote drive or printer.

Example

To display the workgroup settings, enter the following command:

```
net config
```

	BOB'S SCORECARD	PROMPT	AUTOEXEC	BATCH	CONFIG
NET LOGOFF	6	■	☒	☒	☐

Description

This command disconnects your computer from the workgroup.

Usage

```
net logoff [/yes]
```

Options and switches

```
[/yes]
```

This switch bypasses the confirmation prompt.

Remarks

During the log-off operation, NET displays all the connections to disk drives and printers that are being disconnected.

Logging off does not unload network device drivers from memory.

Use this command to disconnect from the workgroup and log on as a different user.

Example

Enter the following command to disconnect your workstation from the workgroup:

```
net logoff
```

		PROMPT	AUTOEXEC	BATCH	CONFIG
NET LOGON	BOB'S SCORECARD 6	■	■	■	☐

Description

This command connects your workstation to a workgroup.

Usage

```
net logon [username [password or ?]] [/yes]
```

Options and switches

If you execute NET LOGON with no other parameters, you are prompted to enter your username and password.

[*username*]

This option specifies the username you want to use to log on.

[*password* or ?]

This option specifies the password for the username ID. If you use ? as the password, NET prompts for the password even if you use the /YES switch.

[/yes]

This switch instructs NET to bypass any confirmation prompts.

Remarks

If you never have logged on as *username,* NET asks you to confirm your password.

The NET START command automatically invokes NET LOGON after the redirector has been loaded. If you try to run NET LOGON before NET START, NET automatically invokes NET START first.

If you are already logged on when you enter the NET LOGON command, NET executes a LOGOFF command.

When you first connect to a drive or printer with NET USE you can optionally specify that the connection be *persistent*. This option saves you from having to connect to remote drives and printers every time you log on. When you log on, any persistent connections are automatically reestablished.

Examples

To log on to the workgroup as SUGAR, enter the following command:

```
net logon sugar
```

To log on as SPIKE by using the password SESAME, enter the following command:

```
net logon spike sesame
```

 Each username password is stored in a special encrypted file. The file is named with the convention *username*.PWL and is located in the NET directory.

If you forget your password, delete the *username*.PWL file and log on. NET thinks that you are a new user and prompts for a new password. Voilà, you are back in business.

 The NET START command does not enable you to enter a password as a parameter. If you use the NET LOGON command and specify the password and a /YES switch, you can automatically invoke NET START and log on without being prompted for a password. For example, change the following command:

```
net start
```

to

```
net logon buster abracadabra /yes
```

 ## Additional information

See also NET START and NET LOGOFF.

NET PASSWORD

Description

This command changes the log-on password for the active username.

Usage

```
net password [oldpassword [newpassword]]
```

Options and switches

[*oldpassword*]

This option specifies the existing password.

[*newpassword*]

This option specifies the new password, which can be as long as 14 characters.

Remarks

The password is stored in a special encrypted file in the NET directory. The filename begins with the first eight characters of the username and has a PWL extension. If you forget your password, simply delete this file.

The password is not case sensitive.

Examples

To be prompted through the password-changing process, enter the following command:

```
net password
```

To change the password from SUPERCALI to FRAGILISTIC, enter the following command:

```
net password supercali fragilistic
```

Extended use

You can use the NET PASSWORD command also to change the password on a Microsoft LAN Manager server or domain. Enter the command HELP NET PASSWORD for more information.

Description

This command manages shared printers in the workgroup and the workstation's print jobs.

Usage

```
net print \\computername[\queue] or lptn [/yes]
```

or

```
net print \\computername or lptn [job# [/pause or /resume or
/delete]] [/yes]
```

Options and switches

\\computername

This option specifies the workgroup computer name whose print queues are polled.

[\queue]

This option specifies the name of the printer queue.

lptn

This option specifies the name of the local parallel port whose data is redirected to the network printer.

[job#]

This option specifies the number of a specific print job.

```
[/pause]
```

This switch pauses a job that is being printed.

```
[/resume]
```

This switch resumes the printing of a job that was suspended.

```
[/delete]
```

This switch stops a job from being printed.

```
[/yes]
```

This switch bypasses any NET PRINT confirmation prompts.

Remarks

All workgroup computers and shared printers are assigned an alias or name. Use the NET USE command to establish a connection to a shared workgroup printer.

You can assign different shared printers to different local printer ports. When you try to print anything to the redirected printer port, the output automatically is sent to the network printer.

After you have sent a job to the printer, you must determine the job number before you can pause, resume, or delete the job. To see the print jobs assigned to one of your ports, enter the print command in the following format:

```
net print lptn
```

You cannot share your printer or printers with other computers in the workgroup, unless, of course, you install a network program, such as Windows for Workgroups.

Other users in the workgroup who are running Windows for Workgroups can make their printers available by using the Printer Share option in Print Manager.

Examples

If you are connected to two laser printers on the workstation named ROOM2332, you can see which printer has the least number of outstanding jobs by entering the following command:

```
net print \\room2332
```

To see how many jobs you have waiting when you have connected the LPT1 port to a shared printer, enter the following command:

```
net print lpt1
```

To cancel job number 445, enter the following command:

```
net print \\room2332 445 /delete
```

Additional information

The NET USE command establishes a connection with a shared printer.

BOB'S SCORECARD 7	PROMPT	AUTOEXEC	BATCH	CONFIG
NET START	■	■	■	☐

Description

This command establishes a workgroup connection and optionally loads the pop-up utility to simplify the creation of drive and printer connections.

Usage

```
net start [popup or basic or full or workstation or netbind
or netbeui] [/list] [/yes]
```

Options and switches

When you execute NET START with no switches, the settings located in the SYSTEM.INI file in the NET directory are used. This file was created by WCSETUP.

```
[popup]
```

This option loads the pop-up utility as a TSR.

```
[basic]
```

This option starts the basic redirector.

```
[full]
```

This option starts the full redirector.

```
[workstation]
```

This option starts whichever redirector was specified when WCSETUP was first run.

```
[netbind]
```

This option binds network protocols and drivers.

```
[netbeui]
```

This option starts the generic NetBEUI interface.

```
[/list]
```

This switch displays the active network settings.

```
[/yes]
```

This switch bypasses the standard confirmation prompts.

Remarks

Don't run NET START from within a multitasking session, such as DOSSHELL or Windows.

NetBIOS, or *Net*work *B*asic *I*nput/*O*utput *S*ystem, is supported by most network operating systems and most networked applications.

NetBEUI, or *NetB*IOS *E*xtended *U*ser *I*nterface, is a compact network protocol designed for small networks with between 20 and 200 workstations.

NetBIOS and NetBEUI are supported by Windows for Workgroups.

NetBEUI generally is faster and more efficient than NetBIOS, but it is not as widely adopted. WCSETUP configures NET START to default to the appropriate interface.

Examples

To use the defaults from SYSTEM.INI to start the workgroup connection, enter the following command:

```
net start
```

To install the pop-up TSR, enter the following command:

```
net start popup
```

Additional information

See also NET LOGON and NET STOP.

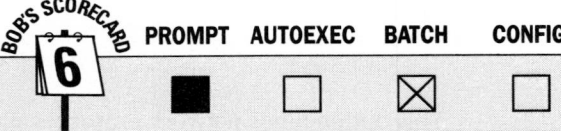

	PROMPT	AUTOEXEC	BATCH	CONFIG
NET STOP	■	☐	☒	☐

Description

This command disconnects a workstation and optionally unloads the pop-up TSR.

Usage

```
net stop [popup or basic or full or workstation or netbeui]
[/yes]
```

Options and switches

```
[popup]
```

This option unloads the pop-up utility but leaves the workgroup connection intact.

```
[basic]
```

This option stops the basic redirector.

```
[full]
```

This option stops the full redirector.

```
[workstation]
```

This option stops whichever redirector is named in SYSTEM.INI.

```
[netbeui]
```

This option stops the NetBEUI interface.

```
[/yes]
```

This option bypasses the standard confirmation prompts.

Remarks

The most common use of NET STOP is to unload the pop-up utility.

Although you can use NET STOP before you reexecute NET START with new parameters, you rarely will want to do so.

Examples

To unload the pop-up utility, enter the following command:

```
net stop popup
```

Enter the following command to log off and disconnect from the workgroup:

```
net stop
```

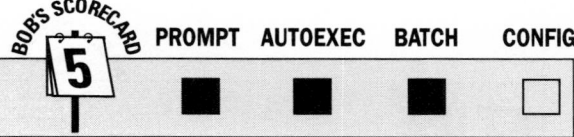

BOB'S SCORECARD **5** PROMPT AUTOEXEC BATCH CONFIG

NET TIME

Description

This command synchronizes your computer's date and time with the network's.

Usage

```
net time [\\computer or /workgroup:wgname] [/set] [/yes]
```

Options and switches

```
[\\computer]
```

This option specifies the name of the time server computer with which you want to synchronize your date and time.

```
[/workgroup:wgname]
```

This option specifies that you want to synchronize with a time server computer on another workgroup.

```
[/set]
```

This switch automatically synchronizes your computer.

```
[/yes]
```

This switch bypasses the standard confirmation prompts.

Remarks

This command works only on networks that use Microsoft LAN Manager and that have a designated time server. It does not function with Windows for Workgroups.

Example

The following command synchronizes the local system time with the time on the workstation BIGBEN:

```
net time \\bigben /set
```

Description

This command connects or disconnects network drives and printers.

Usage

NET USE supports the following uses:

net use [*drive:* or *] [*computer**path* [*password* or ?]]
[/persistent:yes or no] [/savepw:no] [/yes]

net use [lpt*n*] [*computer**queue* [*password* or ?]]
[/persistent:yes or no] [/savepw:no] [/yes]

net use drive: or *computer**path* or * /delete [/yes]

net use lpt*n* or *computer**queue* /delete [/yes]

net use /persistent:yes or no or list or save or clear
[/yes]

Options and switches

[*drive:*]

This option specifies the drive letter of the shared drive.

*

When you use * to create a link with a remote directory, * indicates that the
next available drive letter should be used. When * is used with the /DELETE
switch, however, all printer and drive connections are removed.

lpt*n*

This option specifies the name of the local printer port (LPT1, LPT2, or LPT3).

computer

This option specifies the name of the computer sharing the printer or drive.

path

This option specifies the path on the remote computer accessed by way of a
local drive letter.

queue

This option specifies the name of the printer attached to the remote computer.

password or ?

If the owner of the shared resource (printer or drive) has password-protected
it, you can specify the password or be prompted for it by adding using the ?
character.

/delete

This switch disconnects the specified drive or drives or the specified printer or
printers.

/persistent:yes

This switch instructs NET to store the connections in the network INI file so
that the connections are established automatically every time you log on from
this workstation. All subsequent connections in the same session also are persistent until another persistent switch is used.

/persistent:no

This switch specifies that the current connection and all subsequent connections are effective for only the current session.

```
/persistent:save
```

This switch makes all active connections persistent.

```
/persistent:list
```

This switch displays a list of all persistent connections.

```
/persistent:clear
```

This switch clears all persistent connections and deactivates them.

```
/savepw:no
```

This switch instructs NET USE not to record the password. This switch ensures that persistent connections to password-protected resources always prompt for the password.

```
[/yes]
```

This switch bypasses the standard confirmation prompts.

Remarks

NET USE is much easier to use than it is to define.

By using the /PERSISTENT switch, you can automate the drive- and printer-connection procedure so that the same connections are established every time you log on. All connections are persistent by default. After you have established your standard connections and made them persistent, you can turn off the persistent setting by using the command NET USE /PERSISTENT:NO.

Thankfully, the /PERSISTENT switch can be abbreviated as /P.

If an annoying colleague has assigned a computer a name that includes a space, the drive or print queue name must be included in quotes (`"\\silly name\root"`, for example).

Use the NET VIEW command to determine computer names, shared drive names, and shared printer names.

Examples

To connect the local drive G with the shared directory COMMON on the computer named BUSTER, enter the following command:

```
net use g: \\buster\common
```

To redirect all LPT1 output to the shared printer and call POSTSCRIPT on the computer named BOSS, enter the following command:

```
net use lpt1: \\boss\postscript
```

To disconnect drive Z from a remote computer, enter the following command:

```
net use Z: /delete
```

To see a list of all active connections, enter the following command:

```
net use
```

To make all the active connections persistent, enter the following command:

```
net use /p:save
```

To see a list of all persistent connections, enter this command:

```
net use /p:list
```

To erase all persistent connections permanently, enter the following command:

```
net use /p:clear
```

Additional information

You can use the Pop-Up network utility to manage shared resources.

You do not have to connect to a drive to access files on another workgroup computer. If the specified path has been made shareable without a password, you can explicitly access an individual file by using the following syntax:

*computername**drivename**path**filename.ext*

To list the contents, for example, of the CONFIG.SYS file from the computer named ROOM2554 on the drive named CDRIVE, enter the following command:

```
type \\room2554\cdrive\config.sys
```

NET VER

BOB'S SCORECARD **5**

PROMPT	AUTOEXEC	BATCH	CONFIG
■	☒	☒	☐

Description

This command displays the version number of the network redirector.

Usage

```
net ver
```

Options and switches

None.

Remarks

Enough said.

NET VIEW

BOB'S SCORECARD **5**

PROMPT	AUTOEXEC	BATCH	CONFIG
■	☒	☒	☐

Description

This command provides an easy way to determine the computer names of other computers in the workgroup and the directories and printers they made shareable.

Usage

```
net view [\\computername] [/yes]
```

or

```
net view [/workgroup:wgname] [/yes]
```

Options and switches

When you execute NET VIEW with no switches, a list of all the computer names actively connected in the workgroup is displayed.

[*computername*]

When the name of a specific computer is specified, a list of all shared resources is displayed.

[/workgroup:*wgname*]

This switch instructs NET VIEW to display the computer names for a different workgroup.

[/yes]

This switch bypasses the standard confirmation prompts.

Remarks

Only computers connected to the network at the time you issue the NET VIEW command are listed.

Examples

To see a list of all computers connected to your workgroup, enter the following command:

```
net view
```

To see a list of all the resources that can be shared on the computer named BUSTER, enter the following command:

```
net view \\buster
```

Appendix E

Additional DOS Information Sources

Brilliant though this book may be (!), you can use many other valuable sources of information to keep you primed as a bona fide DOS Jedi. This appendix includes some excellent information sources. It is organized into the following categories:

- Microsoft telephone support
- Magazines and periodicals
- PC user groups
- On-line sources
- Information for users with disabilities

Microsoft Telephone Support

If you can't find the answers to your questions in this book, in the *MS-DOS User's Guide*, or in the TXT files located in the DOS directory, you can call Microsoft at 1-206-646-5104. Be aware that 90 days after your first call, however, you will only be able to get voice support on DOS 6 directly from Microsoft by using the 900 service at 1-900-555-2000, at a cost of $2 per minute. Rather than call the 900 service, you can pay a flat rate of $25 per call (!) by calling 1-206-646-5108.

Magazines and Periodicals

The DOS Resource Guide, an IDG publication, is a quarterly gem that is packed with contemporary information about DOS and general PC utilities. I first discovered it in my grocery store and have been a regular reader ever since.

For all the latest scoop on the PC scene, I recommend that you subscribe to *PC World,* published by PC World Communications Inc. The pace in the PC market-place is too fast to rely on books alone.

PC User Groups

Over the years, the single most important source of my PC information and knowledge comes from PC user groups. To steal a phrase from Tony the Tiger, *they're grrreat!*

If you aren't active in a PC user group, you really ought to give it a try. If you don't know how to find your nearest user group, look at Appendix I of *PC SECRETS,* published by IDG Books Worldwide, or contact the Association of PC User Groups (APCUG) for a list of user groups by writing them at 1730 M Street N. W., Suite 700, Washington D.C. 20036.

On-Line Sources

If you have a modem, you can enjoy a wide variety of on-line information ser-vices that will extend and improve your DOS knowledge. Unless otherwise stated, you should set your communications software to no parity bits, 8 data bits, and 1 stop bit to access these services by modem.

To update the virus signatures to improve DOS 6's virus protection, call the Microsoft-sponsored BBS system at 1-503-531-8100. Appendix D of the *Microsoft MS-DOS User's Guide* explains the full procedure.

Microsoft also provides a general product-support BBS, known as the *Microsoft Product Support Download Service,* which contains text files that discuss DOS issues, as well as provides miscellaneous program updates. To access this BBS, call 1-206-936-6735.

Microsoft also runs a forum on CompuServe. To gain general access to the Mi-crosoft forum, type `go microsoft` at a ! prompt. Alternatively, you can enter `go msdos6` to go directly to the DOS 6 section. CompuServe also provides a wealth of independent DOS information sources. Most major software vendors have their own forums that you can access by typing `go borland,` `go lotus,` and `go aldus,` for example. For more information on computer viruses, you can type `go virusforum` and for more information on the Association of Shareware Professionals, type `go shareware`.

If you are not currently a member of CompuServe and are interested in joining, you can call Microsoft to provide you with an introductory membership kit. To obtain the kit, call 1-800-848-8199 and, when prompted, press 1 and ask for operator 230.

A wealth of excellent BBSs are scattered all over the globe. If you do not know any BBS numbers, I suggest that you look at Appendix H of *PC SECRETS* or contact the Association of Shareware Professionals (ASP) for a list of ASP-approved bulletin boards. You can write to ASP at 545 Grover Rd., Muskegon, MI 40442.

Information for Users with Disabilities

Microsoft is leading the way among the major software companies in providing additional support and services for users with disabilities. I hope that the other major vendors will follow Microsoft's lead.

For general information on Microsoft's options for users with disabilities, call 1-800-426-9400. If you use a TT or TDD compatible text telephone, call 1-206-635-4948.

AccessDOS extends DOS 6 to make it more useful to users with restricted dexterity by providing, for example, sticky Ctrl/Alt/Shift keys and mouse use via keyboard. The ADOS.COM program is available on the DOS 6 Supplemental disk; the program was developed by the Trace R&D Center at the University of Wisconsin-Madison.

For more information on AccessDOS and other products for PC users with disabilities, call Trace R&D Center using the voice line 1-608-263-2309 or the text telephone line at 1-608-263-5408, or write to them at the following address:

Trace R&D Center
S-151 Waisman Center
1500 Highland Avenue
Madison, WI 53705-2280

Index

00n files, in backup, 83
4DOS, 42–43
486 microprocessor, 181
8086 microprocessor, 169, 174
   IRQ assignments for, 244
   memory management and, 186–187
80286 microprocessor, 178
   IRQ assignments for, 245
   memory management and, 186
   Protected Mode, 178, 179
   Real Mode, 178, 179
80386 microprocessor, 180
   features, 180
   memory management and, 186
   running in Virtual 8086 Mode, 180
? switch, 14, 17, 229
   UNINSTAL command and, 591
   using, 44–45
/? switch, 229
/A switch, 2
   DIR command with, 426–427
   for displaying files, 53
   for filemasks, 53
   for listing subdirectories, 53
   MSAV command with, 528
/B switch
   DEFRAG command with, 415
   EDIT command with, 371
   FC command with, 463
   FIND command with, 470
   FORMAT command with, 474
   MEMMAKER command with, 507–508
/BUFSIZE switch, 287
/BW switch, 416
/C switch
   CHOICE command with, 309, 323
   MEM command with, 187, 506
      output from, 188–189
   MSAV command with, 528

/D switch, 20
   MEM command with, 187, 506
   MSCDEX command with, 533
   SETVER command with, 566
   XCOPY and, 47
/DS switch, 94
/DT switch, 94
/E switch, 318
   SETUP with, 812
   XCOPY command with, 600
/EDITOR switch, 312
/F switch, 16
   CHKDSK command with, 123
   FORMAT command with, 473
   MEM command with, 187
   MSD command with, 61, 535, 536
   SWITCHES command with, 265
/FREE switch, 20
/H switch, DOSKEY with, 438
/I switch
   FIND command with, 322
   MIRROR command with, 515
/INSERT switch, 287
/K switch, 218
   for COMMAND.COM, 334, 400
   SWITCHES command with, 581
/L switch, 20
   DEVICEHIGH command with, 425
   DIR command with, 428
   FC command with, 462
   LOADHIGH command with, 503
   MSAV command with, 528
/LIST switch, 145
   DEVICEHIGH and LOADHIGH commands
      with, 194
/M switch, 47
   DOSKEY command with, 438
   MEM command with, 187, 222, 330–331
   SETUP with, 812
/MOVE switch, 195
/N switch, 16

CHOICE command with, 323
DEFRAG command with, 415
DRIVPARM command with, 445
MSAV command with, 529
SWITCHES command with, 265
/O switch, DIR command with, 427
/O-D switch, 56
/P switch, 2
    COMMAND command with, 399
    EMM386 command with, 453
    MEM command with, 188, 505–506
    MSAV command with, 529
    MSD command with, 535
    PRINT command with, 549
    XCOPY command with, 47
/PARTIN switch, 71, 97
/Q switch, SETUP command with, 564, 565, 813
/QHELP switch, 19
/R switch, 104
    INTERSVR command with, 833
/REINSTALL switch, 287
/S switch, 2
    DEVICEHIGH command with, 425
    DIR command with, 427
    LOADHIGH command with, 503
    MSAV command with, 528
    MSCDEX command with, 533
    for shrinking memory allocation, 20
    with UNDELETE loaded, 91
    XCOPY command with, 47, 599
/T switch
    CHOICE command with, 309, 323
    MEMMAKER command with, 508
    with UNDELETE loaded, 91
/TEST switch, 97
/U switch
    DEFRAG command with, 141, 415
    FORMAT command with, 473
    for unloading UNDELETE, 91
/V switch, 291
    FORMAT command with, 473
    MSCDEX command with, 533
/W switch, 2
    SWITCHES command with, 580, 581
/X switch, 218
    INTERSVR command with, 494

—A—

A (DEBUG) command, 340–341
addressing
    of HMA, 182
    memory, 167–171
    Protected-Mode, 180
Advanced SCSI Programming Interface
    (ASPI), 256
ALARMCLK utility, 670
ALLSUB utility, 670
ANARKEY, 299–303, 613–618
    buffer management, 302
    command-line editing, 299–300
    for completing directory name, 299
    environmental editing, 300–301
    filenames and directories list, 300
    history lists, 301–302
        illustrated, 301
    macros, 302
    MegaKey shortcut, 302–303
    MenuKey shortcut, 303
    pop-up environment window, 301
    registration form, 618
    See also DOSKEY
ANSI.SYS, 218–223
    for changing keystrokes, 237
    color display codes, 825–826
    cursor control codes, 227, 826–827
    description, 373
    determining if loaded, 222–223
    display attribute codes, 225, 826
    display codes, 224
    display mode control codes, 231, 827
    escape codes, 230
    escape sequences, 219
        multiple, 221–222
        special, 220
    example, 374
    going beyond, 239
    H command, 226

keyboard control codes, 234–236,
    828–830
for line wrapping, 232
options and switches, 373–374
p command, 237
quick reference, 825–830
S command, 226
sending instructions to, 218–222
    multiple escape sequences, 221–222
    using batch files, 219–220
    using PROMPT command, 220–221
    using TYPE command, 220
switches supported by, 218
text erasing codes, 826
use of, 373
ANSISET.BAT, 227–229
help screen, 229
APPEND command, 375–378
examples, 376–377
/PATH switches, 375, 377
switches, 375–376
usage, 375
Windows and, 378
applications, help, 46
arenas, 200
ARJ, 618–631
registration form, 631
Association of Shareware Professionals
    (ASP), 607
members, 607
ombudsman program, 608
support, 608
ATTRIB command, 378–380
archive attribute, 379
examples, 379–380
options, 378–379
read-only attribute, 379
to remove read-only flag, 418
for removing hidden/system file
    attributes, 401
switches, 379
usage, 378
AUTOEXEC.BAT, 14
checking, 281
clean boot and, 262

color codes and, 269
commands, 281
CONFIG environment variable and,
    276–277
configuring, 276–278
examples, 22, 23
interactive boot and, 263–264
interrupting, 16
MIRROR command and, 37
synchronizing, with CONFIG.SYS, 15–16
using MEMMAKER and, 197
    additional modifications, 203
    calling other programs and, 205
    IF statements and, 205
    optimization process modification, 202
See also batch files; CONFIG.SYS

— B —

backup
age of, 87
convenience of making, 88
copies of, 87
differential, 79
on DoubleSpace drives, 86
file selection, 75–78
    using include/exclude clauses, 76–78
    using point and click, 76
files created and used by, 81–83
floppies, 83
    location of, 87
full, 79
incremental, 79
making good, 80
restoring files from, 84–85
size limitation, 86
speed optimization of, 81
strategy for, 86–88
tips, 73
type selection, 78–79
BACKUP program, 74
floppy disks and, 83
backup programs, 29–31
operation limits, 86
using, 74–86

weaknesses of, 31
See also backup programs
bank switching, 176
base memory, 160
    ANSICODE.BAT, improving, 223
    BUFFERS statement, tuning, 209
    environment size, minimizing, 208
    FCBS allocation, minimizing, 210
    FILES statement, tuning, 209
    LASTDRIVE, minimizing, 210
    MSCDEX consumption, minimizing, 210
    saving, 207–210
    STACKS command, optimizing, 209–210
    trading, for extended memory, 211
    See also memory
batch files
    adding efficiency and power to, 335–336
    ANSIATTR.BAT, 225
    ANSICODE.BAT, 219
    ANSIOK.BAT, 222
    ANSISET.BAT, 227–229
    avoiding message prompts in, 314
    BATUTIL and, 335–336
    checking ERRORLEVELs in, 325
    CHKFRAG.BAT, 316–317
    command summary, 306–307
    creating, 311
    dates, times and, 323–328
    for directory existence, 328–329
    for DOS version check, 330
    DOSKEY, 294
        macros and, 294–295
    editing, 311
    explained, 306
    function of, 306
    ISDOS6.BAT, 330
    moving beyond, 305–336
    navigating around, 312–313
    NEWPATH.BAT, 318–319
    non-standard ASCII characters in,
        311–312
    OLDPATH.BAT, 318–319
    ONLYONCE.BAT, 328
    redirection and piping characters in,
        313–317

routines, 328–332
    running, once per day, 327–328
    SAVEENV.BAT, 320
    for saving current directory, 331–332
    for sending instructions to ANSI.SYS,
        219–220
    SETDATE.BAT, 327
    TCD.BAT, 331–332
    TESTBOOT.BAT, 365
    TESTFUNC.BAT, 362
    TESTWILD.BAT, 329
    TODAYIS.BAT, 324
    tools for, 307
    for TSR check, 330–331
    TURBOBAT and, 336
    WAITFOR.BAT, 326
    for wildcard checking, 329–330
    with Windows 3.1, 332–334
    WINSTART.BAT, 333
    See also AUTOEXEC.BAT; DOS, batch
        facility
BATFILES directory, 377
BATUTIL utility, 335–336, 386, 397, 632–645
    character commands, 335–336
    for cleaning up output, 447
    for pausing utilities, 544
    See also TURBOBAT utility
binary files, 338
    editing, 338–339
BIOS, compression, 184
    See also ROM-BIOS
Bob's Better-Than-DOS Shareware Collec-
        tion, 6–7, 610–611
    ALARMCLK utility, 670
    ALLSUB utility, 670
    ANARKEY program, 299–303, 613–618
    ANSISET.BAT batch file, 229
    ARJ program, 618–631
    BATUTIL utility, 335–336, 386, 397, 447,
        544, 632–645
    CALENDAR utility, 670–671
    CLEANUP utility, 671–673
    CMFiler utility, 66, 419, 421, 499, 585, 601,
        645–659
    contents list, 610–611

DEBUG utility, 324
Disk OrGanizer, 32, 141–142, 659–665
DISKINFO utility, 673
DUPE program, 433, 475, 666
FANSI-Console, 239, 681–686
FormatMaster, 475, 687–693
HotDIR Plus, 57, 380, 429, 693–695
LCD utility, 60, 388, 586
Led's Change Directory, 696–697
LIST program, 64, 526, 587, 698–707
NO utility, 673–674
Patriquin's Hard Disk Utilities, 708–732
PCOPY utility, 48, 402, 601, 708–725
PDAILY utility, 726
PDEL program, 51
PDELETE program, 97–98, 421, 726–732
PocketD program, 48–49, 403, 421, 527,
    601, 733–736
PREFIX.EXE utility, 320–321
QEDIT utility, 449, 737–751
QFIND utility, 54, 172, 429, 752–759
RELDEL utility, 51, 97–98, 419, 590,
    759–760
SCAN utility, 25
SeekEasy utility, 469, 761–769
SpinTest program, 127, 769–772
SpinTime program, 127, 769–772
STACKEY utility, 31, 41–42, 773–785
TURBOBAT utility, 46, 336, 386, 396, 477,
    544, 571
TURBOTXT utility, 679–680
UMB_DRV_SYS, 19–20, 424, 436, 456, 509,
    785–800
VIRUSCAN, 800–805
boot, system, 261
    determining, drive, 365
    initial, phase, 262
    interrupting and controlling, 261–265
        forcing [Y/N] prompt, 264
        SWITCHES command and, 264–265
        using clean-start key, 262–263
        using interactive start key, 263–264
    rebooting and, 361
BREAK command, 381–382
    Ctrl-Break and, 382
    examples, 381–382
    options, 381
    switches, 381
    usage, 381
buffer
    ANARKEY, 302
    command, 288
    DOSKEY, 286
    read-ahead, 383
buffering
    double, 131–132
        identifying, 574
    track, 130
    write, 130
BUFFERS command, 209, 382–384
    examples, 384
    options and switches, 383
    usage, 382
bulletin board services (BBSs), 607, 880–881
bus, 248
    address, 249
    AT, 251
    data, 249
    design, 248
    EISA, 252–255
    future of, 257
    innovations, 255–257
    ISA, 249–251
    local, 255–256
    mastering, 252
    MCA, 251–252
    role of, 249
    SCSI and, 256
    types, 249
        MSD option showing, 250
    VL, standard, 256

— C —

C (DEBUG) command, 341
caches. *See also* disk caches
CALENDAR utility, 670–671
CALL command, 307, 385–386
    examples, 386
    options and switches, 385
    usage, 385
    value of, 385

CAT files
    accessing, 84
    in backup, 83
    unable to find, 85
Catalog files, 82
CD command, 59, 386–388
    examples, 387–388
    options and switches, 387
    usage, 386
CD-ROMs
    accessing, 850
    MSCDEX, 210
    SMARTDRV and, 134
    See also MSCDEX command
CHCP command, 388–389
    examples, 389
    options and switches, 389
    usage, 388
CHDIR command, 59, 386–388
    examples, 387–388
    options and switches, 387
    usage, 386
checksum, 102
    getting rid of, files, 102
    scanning, 102
CHKDSK command, 123, 137, 390–393
    ., 392
    earlier versions of, 393
    examples, 391–392
    /F parameter and, 391
    options and switches, 390
    output generated by, 390–391
    running, 393
    usage, 390
CHKDSK tool, 28
    for determining file fragmentation
        on DoubleSpace drive, 126
    error messages, 124–126
    with /F switch, 123
    function of, 123–126
    using, 92
CHKLIST.CPS files, 101–102
CHOICE command, 35, 292, 393–396
    in batch files, 307
        example, 308

with /C switch, 309, 323
changing, 350–352
disadvantages of, 308
ERRORLEVEL and, 394–395
examples, 395–396
features, 308
for fixed-period delay, 323
for menu systems, 310
    illustrated, 211
    output, 310–311
with /N switch, 323
options and switches, 393–394
pipe and filter characters and, 396
slash mark and, 310
with /T switch, 309, 323
usage, 393
valid keys display, 394
clean boot, 262
    DoubleSpace and, 263
    STACKER and, 263
    See also boot, system
clean-start key, 262–263
CLEANUP utility, 671–673
clock cycles, 167
clockspeed, 166
CLS command, 396–397
    for clearing screen and displaying
        message, 397
    example, 397
    options and switches, 396
    usage, 396
clusters, 115–116
    chains of, 120
    problems with SMARTDRV and, 134
    status of, 117
    See also sectors
CMFiler, 66, 419, 421, 499, 505, 590, 601,
        645–659
    for advanced directory management
        tools, 556
    illustrated display, 66
    registration form, 659
    Tree Mode, 585–586
    for viewing files, 526

CMOS chip, 165–166
code-page management, 388–389
    CHCP command and, 389
    information files, 520
    MODE device CP command and, 520
    MODE SELECT command and, 389
codes
    ANSI.SYS, 825–830
    break, 233
    cursor control, 227
    display, 224
    display attribute, 225
    display mode control, 231
    keyboard control, 234–236
    make, 233
    PROMPT character, 551
    scan, 232–233
        understanding, 233
    VSAFE option, 597
colors
    background, 224
        code, 269
    changing display, 218
        See also ANSI.SYS
    codes for MENUCOLOR command, 269,
        510
    EDIT, 312
    foreground, 224
        code, 269
    low-intensity, 480
        forcing, 552
    suppressing, 480
    for system prompt, 230
COMMAND.COM, 334
    resident block, 400
    transient block, 400
COMMAND command, 318, 397–400
    for changing path temporarily, 400
    description of, 397
    examples, 400
    /K switch with, 400
    options and switches, 398–399
    usage, 398
command-line, 287
    accessing, switches, 291–292

editing, 287–288
    ANARKEY, 299–300
utilities, 846–849
    NET USE, 847–848
    NET VIEW, 846–847
    reviewing directory examples and, 848
    reviewing printer examples and, 849
commands
    ANSI, 223
    assigning to keys, 237–239
    AUTOEXEC.BAT, 281
    batch file, 307
    complex, 372
    CONFIG.SYS, 279–280
    configuration, 15
    DEBUG, 339–346
        entering, 346–349
    directory navigation, 59–61
    disabling, 296–297
    discontinued DOS, 36
    displaying syntax and usage of, 371
    DOSKEY, 288–290
        executing multiple, 290
        saving, without executing, 289–290
        selecting, by number, 288–289
        using characters to select, 289
    enhancing, 296–297
    explanation of in *DOS 6 SECRETS*, 9
    filenames and, 371–372
    help sections of, 17
    mandatory elements of, 371
    menu, 15
    network, 838
    optional elements of, 371
    with options and switches, 9
    quick reference, 815–824
    replacing, 296–297
    startup, 16
        combining, 269–272
    submenu, 40
    supplemental disk, 36
    syntax for, 9
    use conventions, 370–373
    wildcards and, 372
    Windows DOS session, to avoid, 334

commands, list of
  4HELP, 43
  @, 307
  ALIAS, 43
  ALLSUB, 51
  APPEND, 375–378
  ATTRIB, 378–380
  BACKUP, 380
  [BLOCKNAME], 15
  BREAK, 381–382
  BUFFERS, 382–384
  CALL, 307, 385–386
  CD, 59, 386–388
  CHCP, 388–389
  CHDIR, 59, 386–388
  CHKDSK, 123, 137, 390–393
  CHOICE, 35, 292, 307–310, 350–352,
      393–396
  CHOICEAZ, 352
  CHOOSE, 278
  CLEANUP, 51
  CLS, 396–397
  COMMAND, 318, 397–400
  COPY, 47, 372, 400–403
  COPYTO, 298
  COUNTRY, 403–405
  CTTY, 405–406
  DATE, 406–407
  DBLSPACE, 27–28, 46, 145, 407–411
  DEBUG, 413–414
  DEFRAG, 31–32, 46, 292, 414–417
  DEL, 50, 153, 298, 417–419
  DELALL, 298
  DELOLDOS, 419–420
  DELTREE, 36, 52, 153, 420–421
  DEVICE, 422–423
  DEVICEHIGH, 20, 191, 194, 198, 423–425
  DHELP, 43
  DIR, 53–59, 208, 425–429
  DISKCOMP, 430–431
  DISKCOPY, 431–433
  DOS, 435–436
  DOSHELP, 45
  DOSKEY, 437–439
  DOSSHELL, 46, 380, 439–441

DRIVPARM, 443–445
ECHO, 218, 307, 314, 445–448
EDIT, 46, 370–372, 373, 448–450
EMM386, 451–456
ERASE, 50
EXIT, 456–457
EXPAND, 457–458
FASTHELP, 17, 45–46, 459–460
FASTOPEN, 460–461
FC, 461–464
FCBS, 464–465
FDISK, 465–467
FILES, 467–468
FIND, 54, 55, 322, 330, 468–470
FOR, 307, 329, 470–472
FORMAT, 290, 472–476
GOTO, 307, 476–477
GRAPHICS, 477–479
HELP, 17, 40, 371, 479–481
IF, 307, 328–329, 484–487
INCLUDE, 15, 487–488
INSTALL, 488–489
INTERLNK, 489–491
INTERSVR, 494–496
KEYB, 496–498
LABEL, 307, 498–499
LASTDRIVE, 210, 499–500
LOADFIX, 500–501
LOADHIGH, 20, 191, 194, 198, 501–503
MD, 504–505
MEM, 20, 187–189, 222, 505–507
MEMMAKER, 46, 507–509
[MENU], 15
MENUCOLOR, 15, 268, 509–511
MENUDEFAULT, 15, 268, 511–512
MENUITEM, 512–514
MIRROR, 32, 37, 92, 514–515
MODE command, 230–231, 516–524
  MODE COMn, 516–518
  MODE CON, 518–519
  MODE device CP, 519–521
  MODE device /STATUS, 521
  MODE display, 522–523
  MODE LPTn, 523–524
MODE SELECT, 389

MORE, 524–526
MOVE, 36, 49–50, 526–528
MSAV, 46, 528–530
MSBACKUP, 29–30, 46, 530–532
MSCDEX, 532–534
MSD, 36, 54, 61–62, 172, 534–537
MWAV, 537
MWAVTSR, 537
MWBACKUP, 538
MWUNDEL, 46, 538–539
NHELP, 43
NLSFUNC, 539–540
NO, 52
NUMLOCK, 541
PATH, 318, 369–370, 542–543
PAUSE, 307, 543–544
PCOPY, 48
POWER, 544–546
PRINT, 548–550
PROMPT, 218, 220–221, 550–552
QBASIC, 46, 552–553
RD, 555–556
REM, 307, 556–557
RENAME, 315, 557–558
REPLACE, 558–560
RESTORE, 560–562
SET, 208, 318, 563–564
SETUP, 36, 564–565
SETVER, 566–567
SHARE, 568–569
SHELL, 208, 569–570
SHIFT, 307, 570–571
SIZER, 571
SMARTMON, 46
SORT, 575–576
STACKS, 209, 576–577
SUBMENU, 15, 272, 578–579
SUBST, 579–580
SWITCH, 580–581
SWITCHES, 16, 264–265
SYS, 582–583
TIME, 324–326, 583–584
TREE, 584–586
TYPE, 218, 220, 586–587
UNDELETE, 31, 32–33, 587–590

UNFORMAT, 31, 95–97, 592–593
UNINSTAL, 147, 591–592
VC, 291
VER, 330, 593–594
VERIFY, 594–595
VOL, 595–596
VSAFE, 596–598
XCOPY, 17, 47–48, 598–601
See also Workgroup Connection com-
    mands
Common Access Method Committee (CAM),
    256
compression
    BIOS, 184
    data, 30, 143
    disk, 25–26
    of entire drive, 144–146
    floppy data, 156–157
    ratios, 155–156
        modifying, 155–156
    SMARTDRV and, 156
    See also DoubleSpace
CONFIG.SYS, 14
    boot menu file, 14–15
    BUFFERS statement, 209
    checking, 278–281
    clean boot and, 262
    configuration commands, 279–280
    confirmation before execution in, 17
    DBLSPACE.BIN and, 26–27
    DoubleSpace and, 148–149
    enhancements, 14
    entries to include in, 280
    examples, 22–23
    FCBS allocation in, 210
    FILES statement, 209
    increasing memory with, 189–192
    interactive boot and, 263–264
    interrupting, 16
    LASTDRIVE command in, 210, 500
    for loading ANSI.SYS, 218
    loading DBLSPACE.BIN high and, 195
    loading DOS high with, 189
    for loading INTERLNK.EXE, 493–494
    loading specific command in, 264

MEMMAKER, 21
    additional modifications, 203
    MENU of options and, 204
    optimization process modification, 202
    menu with commands in COMMON
        section, 277–278
    menu with two options, 275–276
    with multiple configurations, 23
        startup, 265
    network entries in, 839–840
    STACKS command, 209–210
    for start-up menus, 266–267
        blockname, 267
        combining commands, 269–272
        command combination example,
            271–278
        commands, 265–266
        commands, adding to beginning, 271
        defining, 266–267
        including [MEMSTUFF], 271
        simplifying, 270
    SWITCHES command and, 16
    synchronizing, with AUTOEXEC.BAT,
        15–16
    for two-menu system, 273–274
    using MEMMAKER and, 197
    for utilizing UMBs, 191
    See also AUTOEXEC.BAT
configurations, 14–17
    AUTOEXEC.BAT, 276–278
    commands for, 15
    device driver switch and, 17
    installing minimum, 811–812
    interruption keys, 16
    IRQ, displaying, 246
    keeping track of, changes, 207
    locking up system with, 213–214
    MEMMAKER and, 204–205
    menus for, 14–16
        boot, 14
    multiboot, 265–278
    multimenu, 272–276
    multiple, 23
    power system, 261–282

controllers, 242
    interrupt, connecting two, 245
    SCSI, 112, 256
    twin-interrupt, 248
COPY command, 47, 372, 400–403
    /A switch, 372, 403
    /B switch, 372, 403
    for changing file date/time, 403
    examples, 402
    extended use, 403
    options and switches, 401
    usage, 401
COUNTRY command, 403–405
    examples, 404–405
    options and switches, 404
    usage, 404
creating
    ANARKEY macro, 302
    ASCII script files, 349
    batch files, 311
    directory, 306
    filemasks, 54–55
    multiboot configurations, 265–278
    prompts, 230
    utilities with DEBUG, 355–365
Ctrl-Alt-Del, system doesn't respond to, 214
Ctrl-Break, 382
CTTY command, 405–406
    examples, 406
    options and switches, 405
    with serial port, 406
    usage, 405
CURSFAT.COM program, 347
    listing, 347
    steps for creating, 348
CURSNORM.SCR, 349
cursor
    in batch files, 312–313
    control codes, 227
    positioning, 226
CVF (compressed volume) files, 144
    in full drive compression, 144–146
cylinder, 114
    breaking 1,024 barrier, 114
    See also tracks

— D —

D (DEBUG) command, 341–342
data
  bus, 249
  compression, 143
    floppy, 156–157
  destruction, 97–98
  encoding schemes, 113
  recovering, 93–97
    hard disk partition, 97
data protection
  precautions, 88–91
    accidental file deletion, 88–89
    installing deletion protection, 89
    UNDELETE.INI and, 90–91
  tools, 71–72
  See also data
data storage, 113
  areas, 113
  clusters, 115–116
  file allocation table, 117
  sectors, 114–115
  tracks, 114
  zone bit recording and, 115, 116
  See also hard disks
DATE command, 406–407
  example, 407
  options and switches, 406
  usage, 406
DBLSPACE.BIN, 26–27, 143, 148
  CONFIG.SYS and, 27
  loading, high, 195
DBLSPACE command, 27–28, 407–411
  /CHKDSK switch, 408
  /COMPRESS switch, 410
  for compression ratio modification,
      155–156
  /CREATE switch, 410
  Custom Mode, 27
  /CVF switch, 409
  /DELETE switch, 409
  examples, 411
  Express Mode, 27
  /FORMAT switch, 409

/INFO switch, 409–410
INI file, 411
/LIST switch with, 145
menu, 152
/MOUNT switch, 410
/NEWDRIVE switch, 408
/RATIO switch, 410
/RESERVE switch, 408
for resizing drive, 151
running, 410
/SIZE switch, 409
for summary of drives, 27–28
switches, 153
/UNMOUNT switch, 410
usage, 407–408
See also DoubleSpace
DBLSPACE.SYS, 195, 412–413
  example, 413
  options and switches, 412
  usage, 412
DEBUG, 324, 337–366
  ASCII script files with, 349
  Assemble Mode, 349
  changing cursor to block, 347
  command reference, 339
  commands, 339–346
    ?, 339–340
    A, 340–341
    C, 341
    D, 338, 341–342
    E, 342
    F, 342
    G, 342
    H, 342–343
    I, 343
    L, 343
    M, 343
    N, 344
    O, 344
    P, 344
    Q, 339, 344
    R, 344
    S, 345
    T, 345
    U, 345

W, 345
XA, 346
XD, 346
XM, 346
XS, 346
commands, entering, 346–349
CURSFAT.COM, 347–348
date routines, 356–358
editing with, 338–339
    files with EXE extension, 353
features, 337
help command, 340
hex calculator, 354
for looking for YN references, 351
patching default EDIT filemask, 352–355
patching programs with, 350–355
    changing CHOICE command, 350–352
    default EDIT filemask, 352–355
segment alias support, 347
utilities, creating, 355–365
    disk and drive, 363–365
    keyboard management, 358–362
    returning to DOS/setting
        ERRORLEVEL, 355–356
    working with dates, 356–358
for viewing ASCII files, 339
DEBUG command, 413–414
    examples, 414
    options and switches, 413–414
    usage, 413–414
DEFRAG command, 31–32, 46, 292, 414–417
    /B switch, 415
    /BW switch, 416
    ERRORLEVELs from, 416–417
    examples, 417
    failure, 416
    /N switch, 415
    options and switches, 414–416
    /U switch, 415
    usage, 414
DEFRAG tool, 28, 31–32
    disk map, 32
    forcing into conventional memory, 292
    for keeping files unfragmented, 91
    memory problems, 139–142

running, interactively, 138
    with /U switch, 141
    using, 137–139
defragmentation, 91
    benefits of, 136–142
    defined, 137
    of DoubleSpace volumes, 150–151
    of hidden files, 140
    methods, 138
        Files Only, 138, 140
        Full Optimization, 138, 139
    using DEFRAG for, 137–139
DEL command, 50, 153, 298, 417–419
    examples, 418
    options and switches, 417–418
    usage, 417
delete sentry, 88
    installing, 89
    using, 89
delete tracker, 88
    installing, 89
    using, 89
deleting, files, 50–52, 119–120
    See also undeleting
DELOLDOS command, 419–420
    example, 420
    options and switches, 419
    UNINSTALL and, 420
    usage, 419
DELTREE command, 36, 52, 153, 420–421
    ERRORLEVELs and, 421
    examples, 421
    options and switches, 420–421
    usage, 420
DEVICE command, 422–423
    example, 423
    options and switches, 422
    usage, 422
device drivers, 257
    .SYS extension, 472
    attributes table, 259
    block, 259
    categories of, 259
    character, 259
    CHKSTATE.SYS, 21

COUNTRY.SYS, 404
DBLSPACE.BIN, 26–27, 143, 148, 195
DBLSPACE.SYS, 195, 412–413
DEVICEHIGH installation, 424
disk, 257
DISPLAY.SYS, 433–434
displaying, 258
DoubleSpace, 152
    removing, 152–153
DRIVER.SYS, 441–443
EGA.SYS, 450
EMM386, 451–456
explained, 257–259
help sections, 17
HIMEM.SYS, 481–484
installed with DEVICE, 423
INTERLNK.EXE, 489, 491–494
loading, 259
POWER.EXE, 35, 546–548
RAMDRIVE.SYS, 553–555
routines, 257
SETVER.EXE, 567–568
SMARTDRV.EXE, 572–575
switch for, 17
See also ANSI.SYS
DEVICEHIGH command, 20, 191, 423–425
    example, 424
    extended use, 425
    /L switch, 425
    MEMMAKER and, 198
    options and switches, 423–424
    /S switch, 425
    usage, 423
    using, 194
dialog boxes
    Backup (from MSBACKUP), 74
    Backup (from MWBACKUP), 75
    Change Size, 151
    Edit Include/Exclude List, 76
        from MSBACKUP, 77
        from MWBACKUP, 78
    HELP Find, 41
    Select Backup Files, 76
    Select Catalog, 84
    Special Selections, 79
        from MWBACKUP, 80

DIR command, 53–59, 208, 425–429
    /A switch, 426
    displaying files, 53
        size of, 208
    examples, 428–429
    filemask creation and, 54–55
    /L switch, 428
    listing subdirectories and, 53
    /O switch, 427
    options and switches, 426–428
    /S switch, 427
    searching
        for directory name and, 55–56
        for files and, 54
    setting default, switches, 56–57
    Shareware alternatives to, 57–59
    usage, 425
DIRCMD variable, 5
    disabling, 56
directories, 118–119
    appended, 377
    batch file
        for existence of, 328–329
        for saving, 331–332
    changing, 298
    creating, 306
    file information in, 118
    moving up tree, 60
    navigation commands for, 59–61
    network examples, 848
    PATH command and, 542
    recovering, 96
    remote—accessing, 847–848
    renaming, 558
    in search paths, 318
    special file in, 119
    specifying, 76–77
disabled user information, 881
disk
    fragmentation, 31–32
    intercepting, changes, 297
    interweave, 126–128
        defined, 127
        illustrated, 127
        setting, 127–128

partitioning, 121–123
platter, 110
  illustrated, 111
  servoplatter and, 123
read/write head, 110
  illustrated, 111
See also disk caches; disk utilities; hard
  disks
disk caches, 129
  assigning memory to, 129, 131
  bit rate, 129
  delayed write caching and, 132–133
  double buffering and, 131–132
  file mirroring and, 130
  functioning of, 130
  improving throughput with, 129–134
  performance, 33
  RAM drives and, 136
  status display, 132
  track buffering and, 130
  write buffering and, 130
  See also SMARTDRV program
Disk OrGanizer (DOG), 32, 659–665
  defragmentation methods, 142
  functions of, 141
  registration form, 665
  sample output from, 142
  switches, 141
disk utilities, 25–33
  disk fragmentation and, 31–32
  DoubleSpace disk compression, 25–26
  See also disk
DISKCOMP command, 430–431
  in batch files, 430
  ERRORLEVELs, 431
  examples, 431
  function of, 430
  options and switches, 430
  usage, 430
DISKCOPY command, 431–433
  ERRORLEVELs, 432
  examples, 432–433
  options and switches, 431–432
  usage, 431
  using, 432

DISKINFO utility, 673
display
  attribute codes, 225
  changing color, 218
  changing, lines, 230–232
  changing, modes, 230–232
  codes, 224
  jazzing up, 223–224
  mode control codes, 231
  setting, attributes, 225
DISPLAY.SYS, 433–434
  example, 434
  extended use, 434
  options and switches, 433–434
  usage, 433
DMA (direct memory access), 247
  backup speeds, 248
  concurrent read/write, 248
  dual, 248
  understanding, 247–248
DOS 6 SECRETS, 1–2
  audience for, 2
  commands explanation, 9
  conventions used in, 78
  disks, 6–7
  feedback on, 10
  organization of, 3–6
DOS 6, 1
  data protection tools, 71–72
  disadvantages, 13
  disk space required for, 809
  improvements from DOS 5, 2, 13
  installing, 809–813
  memory management tools, 185
  uninstalling, 813
  upgrading to, 1, 36–37, 809–810
DOS command, 435–436
  examples, 436
  HIMEM.SYS and, 435
  options and switches, 435
  usage, 435
DOS Resource Guide, 879
DOS Shell program, 62–68
  configuration details, 67
  file manager, 65

File menu, 66, 68
file selection/management, 64–66
file viewing with, 64
    for mouse users, 65
Options menu, 64, 65, 66, 67
primary interface of, 63
task switching with, 67–68
uses, 64
View menu, 64, 65
DOS
    batch facility, 305
    command interpreter, 400
    extenders, 183–184
    loading high, 189–190
DOSHELP command. *See* FASTHELP
DOSHELP.HLP, 45
    custom version of, 45
DOSKEY
    identifier, 292
    buffer size, setting, 286
    changing default mode, 286
    command history, 288
        erasing, 290
        listing, 289
    as command-line manager, 287–290
    commands, 288–290
        characters to select, 289
        entering multiple, 293
        executing multiple, 290
        saving, without executing, 289–290
        selecting, by number, 288–289
    functions, 285
    going beyond, 299–303
    Insert Mode, 286
    installing, 285–286
        in Insert Mode, 286
    keys for command-line editing, 438
    keys, most often used, 288
    macros, 290–294
        accessing command-line switches and,
            291–292
        batch file comparison, 294–295
        common task, 298
        extending search path, 298
        installed, 293
        intercepting drive changes, 297

question-mark help, 295
reinstalling, 291
removing, 291
replacing/disabling DOS commands,
    296–297
reviewing, settings, 293
supporting multiple file names,
    297–298
tricks, 295–298
Overtype Mode, 286
piping with, 292–293
redirection with, 292–293
reinstalling, 287
See also ANARKEY
DOSKEY command, 437–439
    /BUFSIZE switch, 437
    examples, 438–439
    for executing simultaneous multiple
        commands, 439
    /H switch, 438
    /M switch, 438
    options and switches, 437–438
    /REINSTALL switch, 437
    usage, 437
    See also DOSKEY
DOSSHELL command, 46, 380, 439–441
    to change file attributes, 380
    examples, 441
    Graphics Mode, 440
    options and switches, 440
    for renaming directories, 558
    Text Mode, 440
    usage, 439–440
DOSSHELL.INI, 67
DoubleSpace, 25–26
    algorithms, 143
    booting process, 148–149
    CHKDSK and, 126
    clean boot technique and, 263
    compressing floppies with, 156–157
    defragmenting, volumes, 150–151
    device driver, 26, 27
    disadvantages of, 28
    drives, 144–146
        compression ratios, 155–156
        custom setup, 146–147

express option, 146
host letter, 154
installing, 146–151
letter assignments, 153–155
removing, 152
resizing, 151–152
size limitations, 147
Stacker and, 147
error messages, 150
features, 142
files, 148
INI, 148
full-screen illustrated, 29
function of, 142–143
mechanics, 143–146
with SMARTDRV, 133, 134
swap files and, 149–150
using, 142–157
See also DBLSPACE command
DOUBLESPACE.SYS, 27
DPMI (DOS Protected Mode Interface), 183
DR DOS, 1
DRAM chip, 163–164
illustrated, 163
parity value and, 163
See also SRAM chip: RAM
DRIVER.SYS, 441–443
examples, 442–443
extended use, 443
factor values, 442
options and switches, 441–442
usage, 441
using, 442
DRIVPARM, 443–445
factor values, 444
/N switch, 445
options and switches, 444–445
usage, 443
DUPE program, 433, 475, 666
registration form, 666

— E —

E (DEBUG) command, 342
ECHO command, 218, 307, 314, 445–448
in date/time batch files, 323–328
for displaying blank line, 447–448

examples, 446–447
functioning of, 447
options and switches, 446
usage, 445–446
uses of, 446
EDIT, 311
colors, 312
for creating ASCII file, 349
/EDITOR switch and, 312
features not supported by, 313
filemask, default, 352–355
launching, 298
QBASIC rather than, 312
EDIT command, 370, 448–450
/B switch in, 371
for CGA systems, 448
on EGA systems, 449
examples, 449
with filename variations, 371–372
functions of, 449
for LCD systems, 448
options and switches, 448–449
syntax, 373
usage, 448
editing
ANARKEY
command-line, 299–300
environmental, 300–301
batch files, 311
command-line, 287–288
DOSKEY, 438
with DEBUG, 338–339
DOSKEY keys, 287–288
EEMS (Enhanced Expanded Memory
Specification), 175
EGA.SYS, 450
example, 450
options and switches, 450
usage, 450
EISA bus, 252–255
illustrated, 253, 254
ISA bus comparison, 253, 255
MCA bus comparison, 253
EMM386, 23, 451–456
286 systems and, 186
Auto Mode, 452

D switch, 248
enhancements, 23
examples, 456
FRAME= switch, 453
function of, 192
HIGHSCAN option, 454
MEMMAKER and, 455
NOEMS switch, 452
  added to, 214
  using, 454
NOHI option, 454
options and switches, 451–455
/P switch, 453
usage, 451
Weitek coprocessor and, 452
EMS (expanded memory specification), 176
  history of, 175
  page frame, 176
  See also expanded memory
environment, DOS, 208
  assigning new data to, variable, 318
  changing search path and, 318–319
  increasing, 318
  innovations, 317–322
  minimizing size of, 208
  PROMPT variable, 318
  restoring, 320–321
  saving, 320–321
  storing date in, variable, 327
  TEMP variable, 320
  uppercasing input in, 321–322
ERASE command. *See* DEL command
Error Correction Code (ECC), 81
error messages
  CHKDSK, 124–126
  DoubleSpace, 150
ERRORLEVELs, 320
  batch files, checking, 325
  from DEFRAG failure, 416–417
  DISKCOMP, 431
  DISKCOPY, 432
  FORMAT, 474
  IF command, 485, 486
  for indicating if search was found, 330
  KEYB, 497–498

REPLACE, 559–560
RESTORE, 562
set by KEYSTATE.COM, 359
setting, 355–356
support, 322
WEEKDAY.COM and, 324
WHATYEAR.COM and, 324
XCOPY, 600
ESDI (Enhanced Small Device Interface), 112
EXIT command, 456–457
  example, 457
  options and switches, 457
  usage, 457
EXPAND command, 457–458
  examples, 458
  options and switches, 458
  usage, 457
expanded memory, 23, 160
  defined, 176
  managing, 211–212
  See also EMS (expanded memory specification)
Extended Industry Standard Architecture.
    See EISA bus
extended memory, 160, 176–182
  defined, 178
  explained, 178–179
  from free base memory, 211
  illustrated, 177
  maximizing, 210–211
  See also memory
ExtraDOS Toolbox Professional, 51, 667–680
  ALARMCLK, 670
  ALLSUB, 670
  CALENDAR, 670–671
  CLEANUP, 671–673
  DISKINFO, 673
  NO, 673–674
  registration form, 680
  tools list, 51–52
  TURBOBAT, 46, 336, 386, 396, 477, 487,
    571, 674–679
  TURBOTXT, 679–680

—F—

F (DEBUG) command, 342
FANSI-Console, 239, 681–686
  features, 239
  registration form, 686
Fastdisk, 135
  using, 135
FASTHELP command, 17, 459–460
  customizing, 46
  examples, 459
  options and switches, 459
  output printout, 460
  usage, 459
  using, 45–46
FASTOPEN command, 460–461
  disadvantages, 461
  example, 461
  options and switches, 460
  usage, 460
FASTOPEN utility, 136
FC command, 461–464
  /B switch, 463
  examples, 463–464
  /L switch, 462
  options and switches, 462–463
  usage, 461–462
FCBS command, 464–465
  example, 465
  options and switches, 465
  usage, 465
FDISK command, 465–467
  examples, 466
  options and switches, 465–466
  usage, 465
  warning, 467
FDISK program, 122
FHELP batch file, 42
file allocation table (FAT), 117
  12-bit, 118
  16-bit, 118
  cluster status, 117
  in deleting files, 119
  partitioning and, 122
  in reading files, 119

  in writing files, 120
  See also files
filemasks
  /A switch for, 53
  creating, 54–55
  EDIT, default, 352–355
  multiple, commands for, 297–298
  specifying, 76–77
  See also Files
filenames
  entering, 371–372
  supporting multiple, 297–298
files
  ASCII script, 349
  backup selection of, 75–78
    options for, 79
    using include/exclude clauses, 76
    using point and click, 76
  batch, 219–220
  compressed volume, 144
  compression of, 143–144
  configuration, 14
  created and used by backup, 81–83
    00n, 83
    CAT, 83
    Catalog, 82
    INI, 83
    LOG, 83
    SET, 82
    SLT, 82
  decompression of, 143–144
  DEFRAG for unfragmenting, 91
  defragmenting, 137–142
    hidden, 140
  deleting, 50–52, 119–120
    all, 51
  deletion of, accidental, 88–89
  displaying, 53
  DoubleSpace, 86, 148
  erasing, 97–98
  fragmented, 31, 136–137
    determining, 137
    ialso defragmentation
  reading, 119
  recovering, 32–33

lost, 93–97
    with UNFORMAT, 97
restoring, from backup, 84–85
searching for, 54
selected, identification of, 76
selection/management of, 64–66
swap, 149–150
undeleting, 93–95
viewing in DOS Shell, 64
writing, 120
See also file allocation table (FAT);
    filemasks; filenames
FILES command, 209, 467–468
    example, 467
    options and switches, 467
    usage, 467
FIND command, 54, 55, 468–470
    /B switch, 470
    enhancements, 322
    ERRORLEVELs and, 330
    examples, 469
    /I switch with, 322
    no filename specification, 469
    options and switches, 468
    usage, 468
FINDDIR.BAT, 55
    contents of, 55
    example of using, 56
FLEXDIR.BAT, 55
FOR command, 307, 329, 470–472
    examples, 471–472
    options and switches, 470–471
    usage, 470
FORMAT command, 290, 472–476
    /B switch, 474
    ERRORLEVELs, 474
    examples, 475
    /F switch, 473
    options and switches, 472–474
    /U switch, 473
    undocumented switches, 475–476
    usage, 472
    /V switch, 473
FormatMaster program, 475, 687–693
    registration form, 693

formatting
    high-level, 120, 121
    low-level, 120–121
        destructive, 128
    See also unformatting

— G —

G (DEBUG) command, 342
GOTO command, 307, 476–477
    example, 476–477
    options and switches, 476
    usage, 476
GRAPHICS command, 477–479
    example, 479
    /LCD switch, 479
    options and switches, 477–479
    supported printer types, 478
    usage, 477

— H —

H (DEBUG) command, 342–343
hard disks, 109
    alignment problems, 128
    checking characteristics of, 116
    components, 110
    controllers, 112
        explained, 112–113
    DoubleSpace letter assignments, 153–155
    illustrated, 111
    inside, 110–111
    mechanics of, 110–113
    MSD program and, 116–117
    partitioning, 121–123
        reasons for, 122
    preparing new, 120–123
        disk partitioning, 121–123
        low-level formatting, 120–121
    saving onto, 113
    speeding up, 126–142
    surface deterioration, 128
    See also data storage

Help
    applications, 46
    index, 19
    invoking, system, 43
    irritations of, 19
    menu, 18
    notes example, 18
    on-line, 17–19
    question-mark, 295
    searches, 40–42
    tricks for Microsoft C programmers, 43
HELP command, 17, 479–481
    4DOS/NDOS and, 42–43
    examples, 481
    Find dialog box, 41
    help text for, 43
    options and switches, 480
    submenu commands, 40
    subtopics, 481
    suppressing colors with, 480
    for syntax and usage, 371
    usage, 480
HELP.HLP, 19, 43
hexadecimal numbers, 167–169
high memory. *See* upper memory
HIMEM.SYS, 189, 481–484
    effects of using, 190
    example, 484
    host computer table, 483
    installation of, 484
    /INT15 switch, 482
    /MACHINE switch, 483
    /NUMHANDLES switch, 483
    options and switches, 482–484
    /SHADOWRAM switches, 484
    slowing of performance, 482
    usage, 481
HMA (high memory area), 182
    addressing of, 182
    using, 482
    See also upper memory
HotDIR Plus, 57, 380, 429, 693–695
    display, 57
    registration form, 693–695

—I—

I (DEBUG) command, 343
IDE (Integrated Drive Electronics)
    controller, 112
IF command, 307, 328–329, 484–487
    ERRORLEVELs, 485, 486
    examples, 486
    NOT operand, 485
    options and switches, 485
    usage, 484–485
INCLUDE command, 15, 487–488
    example, 488
    options and switches, 487
    usage, 487
    using, 487–488
include/exclude clauses, 76–78
Industry Standard Architecture. *See* ISA bus
INI files
    in backup, 83
    Windows data protection utilities and, 73
    See also DOSSHELL.INI files
INSTALL command, 488–489
    example, 489
    memory-resident programs and, 489
    options and switches, 489
    usage, 488
installing
    DOS 6 SECRETS disks, 609
    DOS 6, 809–813
        manually, 812
    DOSKEY, 285–286
    to floppies, 810–811
    INTERLNK, 832–833
    INTERSVR, 833
    Microsoft Mail, 850–851
    minimum configuration, 811–812
    network software, 836–838
    to nonboot drive, 812–813
    uninstalling DOS 6 and, 813
    Windows components, 812
InterLink, 831–835
    establishing, connection, 832–834
    limitations, 835

speed of, 835
steps to successful linking, 833–834
using server resources and, 834
wiring computers together and, 831–832
INTERLNK command, 489–491
description of, 489
examples, 490
functions of, 489
options and switches, 490
parallel cable for use with, 491
usage, 490
INTERLNK.EXE, 489, 491–494, 832–833
/COM switch, 492
defaults, 492–493
/DRIVES switch, 832
examples, 493–494
loading, 493–494
UMBs and, 492
/LPT switch, 492
options and switches, 492–493
usage, 491
INTERLNK program, 35, 835
installing, 832–833
interrupt
controllers, connecting two, 245
handler, 243
request lines, 244–245
See also IRQs
service routine (ISR), 243
vector table, 243–244
vectors, 243–244
See also interrupts
interruption keys, 16
interrupts, 242
categories of, 242
hardware, 242
software, 242
See also interrupt, vectors
INTERSVR command, 494–496
/COM switch, 494
examples, 496
extended use, 496
/LPT switch, 495
multitasking and, 495
options and switches, 494–495

/R switch, 833
usage, 494
/X switch, 494
INTERSVR program, 835
installing, 833
interweaving
disk, 126–128
memory, 167
IRQs, 244
assignments
for 8086/8088-based systems, 244
for 80286-based systems and higher, 245
reviewing, 246–247
displaying configuration, 246
hardware devices and, 247
ISA bus, 249–251
EISA bus comparison, 253, 255
illustrated, 254
MCA bus comparison, 252

—K—

KEYB command, 496–498
for Enhanced Keyboard, 497
ERRORLEVELs, 497–498
example, 498
options and switches, 497
usage, 497
keyboard
control codes, 234–236
customizing, 232–239
management utilities, 358–362
changing state of special keys, 358–360
rebooting PC, 361
waiting for function key, 361–362
scan codes and, 233
keys
assigning commands/strings to, 237–239
checking/changing state of, 358–360
clean-start, 262–263
codes for, 232–237
DOSKEY, 288
command-line editing, 438

editing, DOSKEY, 287–288
interactive start, 263–264
interruption, 16
remapping, 237
start, controlling, 264–265
KEYSTATE.COM, 358
ERRORLEVELs set by, 359

— L —

L (DEBUG) command, 343
LABEL command, 307, 498–499
examples, 499
options and switches, 498–499
on SUBST drive, 499
usage, 498
laptop tools, 35
LASTDRIVE command, 210, 499–500
example, 500
options and switches, 500
usage, 500
LCD utility, 60–61, 388, 586
illustrated display, 60
Led's Change Directory, 696–697
registration form, 697
LH command. *See* LASTDRIVE command
line wrapping, 232
LIST program, 64, 526, 587, 698–707
registration form, 707
LOADFIX command, 500–501
example, 501
options and switches, 501
usage, 501
LOADHIGH command, 20, 191, 501–503
example, 502
extended use, 503
/L switch, 503
MEMMAKER and, 198
options and switches, 502
programs available to use, 502
/S switch, 503
system lockup and, 214
usage, 502
using, 194

local bus, 255–256
connectors, 256
lockup, system
with new configuration, 213–214
program causes, 214
while running MEMMAKER, 212
LOG files, in backup, 83

— M —

M (DEBUG) command, 343
macros
ANARKEY, 302
DOSKEY, 290–294
magazines and periodicals, 879–880
MAIL command, 850, 856–858
-C switch, 856
-D switch, 856
examples, 858
-N switch, 857
options and switches, 856–857
setup confirmation list, 851
usage, 856
-X switch, 857
See also Microsoft Mail
master partition table, 122, 466
active partition, 466
function of, 123
See also partitioning, disk; partitions
MCA bus, 248, 251–252
EISA bus comparison, 253
illustrated, 255
ISA compared to, 252
MD command, 504–505
examples, 504–505
options and switches, 504
usage, 504
MEM commands, 20, 187–189, 505–507
/C switch, 506
/D command, 257, 506
output listing, 258
example output, 187
examples, 506
/M switch, 187, 222, 330–331
options and switches, 505–506

/P switch, 505–506
switches used with, 187–188
UMBs and, 191–192
usage, 505
MEMMAKER command, 46, 507–509
/B switch, 507–508
examples, 508–509
extended use, 509
options and switches, 507–508
for suppressing confirmation prompts,
509
/T switch, 508
/UNDO switch, 508
usage, 507
MEMMAKER program, 20–23
advance options, 21
AUTOEXEC.BAT modification, 202
additional, 203
calling programs and, 205
IF statements and, 205
CHKSTATE.SYS utility, 21, 201
CONFIG.SYS modification, 202
additional, 203
MENU of options and, 204
Custom Mode, 198, 199, 508
configuration options, 200
DOS= statements, 191
DOS=HIGH statement, 198
example of using, 196–197
excluding programs from analysis, 206
explained, 201–204
Express Mode, 198, 199, 508
function of, 195
INI file, 206
locking up of system with, 212
main option screen, 198, 199
modes of running, 20–21
multiple configurations and, 205
NOEMS switch, 199
running, 198–201
SHELL command and, 570
SIZER.EXE utility, 21, 201, 571
success of, 204–206
memory
addressing, 167–171

hexadecimal numbers, 167–169
multiple, 170
segments and offsets, 169–171
assigning to cache, 129, 131
base, 160
saving, 207–210
cache, 165
checking, 171–172
conflicts, solving, 212–214
conventional, 160
DEFRAG problems, 139–142
EMM386 enhancements and, 23
expanded, 23, 160, 175–176
managing, 211–212
extended, 160, 176–182
maximizing, 210–211
hardware, 162–167
CMOS chip, 165–166
DRAM chip, 163–164
SIMMs, 165
speed issues, 166–167
SRAM chip, 164–165
high, 182
interleaved, 167
management, 19–23
for 8086 users, 186–187
for 80286 users, 186
for 80386 users, 186
tools, 185
managers, 183
maximizing, 159–215
optimization tools, 20–23
optimizing, 167
paging, 176
parity errors, 164
random-access (RAM), 161
read-only (ROM), 161
removing DoubleSpace device driver
from, 152–153
ROM-BIOS (read-only memory-basic
input/output system), 162
speed issues, 166–167
clock cycles and, 167
clock speed and, 167
precharge time and, 167
wait state and, 167

terms, 161
types, 171–182
upper, 131–132, 172–175, 189–190, 193, 195, 200–201, 204
blocks, *See* UMBs (upper memory blocks)
video, 174
virtual, 184–185
warehouse, 174–175
illustrated, 174
MENUCOLOR command, 15, 268, 509–511
color codes, 510
color codes for, 269
examples, 510–511
options and switches, 510
placement of, 510
usage, 509
MENUDEFAULT command, 15, 268, 511–512
example, 512
options and switches, 511
specifications, 512
usage, 511
MENUITEM command, 512–514
blocknames, 513
examples, 513
options and switches, 512–513
usage, 512
menus
adding programs to, 67–68
configuration, 14–16
Help, 18
multimenu configurations and, 272–276
escape option, 274
user confirmation prompting, 275–276
new commands for, 15
See also start-up menus
messages, suppressing, 314–316
See also error messages
MFM (modified frequency modulation), 113
Micro Channel Architecture. *See* MCA bus
MICRO command, 853, 858–860
examples, 860
mailbox creating before running, 859
options and switches, 858–859

sample, message, 854
switches, 853
usage, 858
microprocessors, 242
486, 181
80286, 178–179
80386, 180–181
DX/DX2, 181
interrupting, 242
SX, 181
See also Environment and Tools manual, 43
Microsoft Mail, 850
features, 852
files, locating, 852–853
installing, 850–852
mailbox name, 855
password, 855
postoffice, 858
receiving new mail with, 853–855
running, 852
-X switch, 853
See also MAIL command
Microsoft telephone support, 879
MIRROR command, 32, 37, 92, 514–515
description of, 514
examples, 515
/I switch, 515
options and switches, 514–515
usage, 514
MIRROR program, 71
features missed by, 92
UNFORMAT and, 96–97
MKDIR command. *See* MD command
MODE command, 230
control codes, 231
for setting number of characters per line, 231
syntax, 230
See also MODE subcommands
MODE COMn command, 516–518
examples, 518
options and switches, 517–518
supported transmission rates, 517
transmission errors and, 518
usage, 516

MODE CON command, 518–519
    example, 519
    options and switches, 519
    usage, 518
MODE device CP command, 519–521
    code-page information files, 520
    example, 521
    options and switches, 520
    SELECT switch, 520
    supported devices, 520
    usage, 519
MODE device /STATUS command, 521
    examples, 521
    options and switches, 521
    usage, 521
MODE display command, 522–523
    display values, 522
    examples, 523
    formats, 522
    options and switches, 522
    for restoring cursor, 523
    usage, 522
MODE LPTn command, 523–524
    example, 524
    extended use, 524
    options and switches, 523
    retry setting values, 524
    usage, 523
MODE SELECT command, 389
MORE command, 524–526
    examples, 525
    options and switches, 525
    usage, 525
MOVE command, 36, 49–50, 526–528
    COPY command differences, 50
    examples, 527
    options and switches, 526
    source/target requirement, 527
    syntax, 49
    usage, 526
    using, 49–50
MOVE'EM, 186
MSAV command, 528–530
    /A switch, 528
    /C switch, 528

CHKLIST.MS and, 529–530
    examples, 530
    /L switch, 528
    /N switch, 529
    optional settings, 530
    options and switches, 528–529
    /P switch, 529
    /S switch, 528
    usage, 528
MSAV program, 24–25, 71
    illustrated, 24
    INI file, 102
    MWAV comparison, 104
    updating signature lists, 101
    uses, 98
MSBACKUP command, 29–30, 46, 530–532
    backup settings, 531
    examples, 532
    options and switches, 530–531
    SET file searches, 531
    usage, 530
MSBACKUP program, 29, 46, 71
    backup speed, 248
    catalog menu options, 85
    Compare option, 80
    dialog box, 30
    ECC system, 81
    features, 29–30
    MWBACKUP comparison, 74–75
    STACKEY utility and, 31
MSCDEX command, 532–534
    /D switch, 533
    examples, 534
    loading, 533–534
    options and switches, 533
    /S switch, 533
    usage, 532
    /V switch, 533
    See also CD-ROMs
MSCDEX utility, 210
MSD command, 36, 54, 61–62, 172, 534–537
    examples, 537
    /F switch, 535, 536
    /filename switch, 536
    options and switches, 535

/P switch, 535
  usage, 535
MSD program, 36, 54, 61–62
  for checking memory, 171–172
  for determining UART type, 133
  Disk Drives window, 117
  for displaying device drivers, 258
  for displaying IRQ configuration, 246
  file finding/browsing tool, 62
  for hard disk info, 116
  illustrated display, 62
  for loaded locations in upper memory,
    204
  memory/computer displays for, 173
  for showing bus type, 250
MSDOSDATA variable, 73
multimenu configurations, 272–276
  escape option, 274
  user confirmation, 275–276
  See also start-up menus
MWAV command. i MSAV command
MWAV utility, 33–34, 46, 72
  illustrated, 100
  INI file, 102
  MSAV comparison, 104
  updating signature lists, 101
  uses, 98
  See also MSAV command; MSAV program
MWAVTSR command, 537
MWBACKUP command, 538
  See also MSBACKUP command
MWBACKUP program, 29, 33–34, 46, 72
  backup speed, 248
  Compare option, 80
  ECC system, 81
  features, 29–30
  MSBACKUP comparison, 74–75
  for recovering files, 33
  running, 81
  See also MSBACKUP program
MWUNDEL command, 46, 538–539
  options and switches, 538
  undeletion success value, 539
  usage, 538

MWUNDEL utility, 33–34, 46, 72
  deleted files displayed by, 94
  using, 93

—N—

N (DEBUG) command, 344
NDOS, 42–43
NET command, 838, 860–861
  description, 860–861
  subcommands, 860–861
  summary, 839
NET CONFIG command, 861–862
  example, 862
  options and switches, 861
  usage, 861
NET LOGOFF command, 862–863
  example, 863
  options and switches, 862
  usage, 862
NET LOGON command, 842, 863–864
  examples, 864
  options and switches, 863
  usage, 863
  username.PWL file, 864
  /YES switch, 863
NET PASSWORD command, 843, 865–866
  examples, 865
  extended use, 866
  options and switches, 865
  usage, 865
NET PRINT command, 849, 866–868
  examples, 867–868
  functions of, 867
  options and switches, 866–867
  usage, 866
NET START command, 841, 868–870
  examples, 869
  functions, 842
  NetBEUL and, 869
  NetBIOS and, 869
  options and switches, 868–869
  usage, 868
NET STOP command, 870–871
  common use of, 871
  examples, 871

options and switches, 870
usage, 870
NET TIME command, 871–872
example, 872
options and switches, 871–872
usage, 871
NET USE command, 847, 872–875
? character and, 873
/DELETE switch, 873
examples, 874–875
options and switches, 872–874
/PERSISTENT switch, 874
syntax, 848
usage, 872
NET VER command, 876
options and switches, 876
usage, 876
NET VIEW command, 846–847, 876–877
examples, 877
options and switches, 876–877
usage, 876
NETBEUI protocol, 841
description of, 869
NETBIOS protocol, 841
description of, 869
network
commands, 838
CONFIG.SYS entries, 839–840
connecting to, 838–843
how to log on, 841–842
protocols, 841
resources, using, 843–850
CD-ROM access, 850
command-line utilities, 846–849
Pop-Up utility, 843–846
software, 836
installing, 836–838
NLSFUNC command, 539–540
example, 540
options and switches, 540
usage, 540
NO utility, 673–674
Norton
Desktop for Windows (NDW), 72
Disk doctor, 92

NUMLOCK command, 541
example, 541
options and switches, 541
usage, 541

— O —

O (DEBUG) command, 344
on-line
help, 17–19
sources, 880–881

— P —

P (DEBUG) command, 344
parity
checks, 164
errors, 164
value, 163
partitioning, disk, 121–123
active partition and, 123
FDISK program for, 122
master partition table and, 122
reasons for, 122
partitions, 466
active, 466
types of, 466
password
management, 842–843
Microsoft Mail, 855
PATH command, 318, 369–370, 542–543
character limits, 543
examples, 543
improving performance and, 542
options and switches, 542
usage, 542
paths
changing, temporarily, 318–319, 400
searching, 61
Patriquin's Hard Disk Utilities, 708–732
PCOPY utility, 708–725
PDAILY utility, 726
PDELETE utility, 726–732
registration form, 732

PAUSE command, 307, 543–544
  CHOICE command and, 544
  example, 544
  options and switches, 543
  usage, 543
  PC user groups, 880
  PCI (Peripheral Component Interconnect), 256
PCOPY utility, 48, 402, 601, 708–725
  advantages of, 73
  illustrated, 48
  /X switch to, 50
PDAILY utility, 726
PDEL program, 51
PDELETE utility, 97, 421, 726–732
  using, 98
PIC (programmable interrupt controller), 244
pipe characters, 292, 313
  substitutions for, 293
piping
  for avoiding message prompts, 314
  command output to FIND, 317
  DIR command output to FIND, 469
  with DOSKEY, 292–293
  ECHO output to command, 314
  examples, 314–315
  See also redirection
PKZIP program, 143, 144
PocketD program, 48–49, 403, 421, 469, 527–528, 601, 733–736
  deleting files with, 51
  as DIR alternative, 58
  file size analysis, 58
  file size analyzation, illustrated, 59
  flexible wildcards and, 58
  registration form, 736
  using Tiny Mode, 58
Pop-Up program, 838
  Browse option, 845–846
  connecting to directories, 845–846
  connecting to shared printers, 846
  Disk Connections display, 844
  Form Connections dialog box, 846

  loading and running, 843–845
  in monochrome systems, 844
  removing TSR, 844
  using, 843–846
POWER command, 544–546
  APM hardware systems and, 545
  examples, 546
  MAX switch, 545
  options and switches, 545
  STD switch, 546
  usage, 545
POWER.EXE, 35, 546–548
  APM hardware systems and, 547
  examples, 547
  loading, 547
  location of, 546
  MAX switch, 547
  options and switches, 546–547
  STD switch, 547
  usage, 546
POWER program, 35
PREFIX.EXE utility, 320–321
PRINT command, 548–550
  examples, 550
  first time switches, 549
  options and switches, 548–549
  /P switch, 549
  PostScript printers and, 549
  for specifying printing device, 548
  usage, 548
printers
  connecting to shared, 846
  network examples, 849
  remote, accessing, 847–848
processor type, finding, 172
programs
  adding, to menu, 67–68
  BOOTDRV.COM, 365
  CAPSOFF.COM, 360
  CAPSON.COM, 360
  CHOICE.COM, 350–352
  CHOICEAZ.COM, 352
  CURSFAT.COM, 347
    creating, 348

CURSNORM.COM, 349
DRIVEAOK.COM, 363–364
GETFUNCY.COM, 361–362
KEYSTATE.COM, 358–359
    ERRORLEVELs set by, 359
loading, 68
REBOOT.COM, 361
starting, 68
swapping between, 68
terminating, 68
WEEKDAY.COM, 356
WHATDAY.COM, 357
WHATMON.COM, 357
WHATYEAR.COM, 357
PROMPT command, 218, 550–552
    character codes, 551
    examples, 551–552
    options and switches, 550
    usage, 550
    using, 220–221
prompts, forcing [Y/N], 264
Protected-Mode, 178
    addressing scheme, 180
    applications, 183
PROTOCOL.INI file, 840
    contents of, 840
    SETUP for modifications of, 841

— Q —

Q (DEBUG) command, 344
QBASIC, 312
    features, 312
QBASIC command, 46, 552–553
    /EDITOR switch, 553
    examples, 553
    options and switches, 552–553
    /QHELP switch, 553
    usage, 552
QBASIC.EXE file, 19, 312
    changing default wildcard, 355
QEDIT(R) Advanced, 313, 449, 737–751
    registration form, 751
QFIND, 54, 172, 429, 752–759
    registration form, 759

QRAM, 186
Qualitas' 386MAX, 183
Quarterdeck's Expanded Memory Manager,
    183
question-mark (?)
    (DEBUG) command, 340
    confirmation prompt, 17
    for forcing [Y/N] prompt, 264
    help, 295
    SWITCHES command and, 264
    See also /? switch; ? switch
qz switch, 51

— R —

R (DEBUG) command, 344
RAM, 161
    cram, 192
    drives, 135–136
    ROM vs., 161–162
    shadow, 184
    See also DRAM chip; SRAM chip
RAMDRIVE.SYS, 553–555
    example, 555
    options and switches, 554
    usage, 553
RD command, 555–556
    examples, 556
    functions of, 555
    options and switches, 555
    usage, 555
rebooting, 361
redirection
    to a NUL device, 315–316
    with DOSKEY, 292–293
    example, 315–316
    See also piping
redirection characters, 292, 313
    substitutions for, 293
RELDEL utility, 51, 419, 590, 759–760
    registration form, 760
    using, 98
REM command, 307, 556–557
    examples, 557
    options and switches, 556
    usage, 556

RENAME command, 315, 557–558
    examples, 558
    options and switches, 557–558
    renaming directory and, 558
    usage, 557
REPLACE command, 558–560
    ERRORLEVELs, 559–560
    examples, 560
    options and switches, 559
    usage, 558
RESTORE command, 560–562
    date/time variables, format of, 561
    ERRORLEVELs, 562
    examples, 562
    options and switches, 561–562
    usage, 560
RESTORE program, 74
RMDIR command. *See* RD command
ROM, 161
    RAM vs., 161–162
ROM-BIOS, 162
    location of, 192
    shadow RAM and, 184

—S—

S (DEBUG) command, 345
scan codes, 232–233
    understanding, 233
SCAN utility, 25
script files
    ASCII, 349
    BOOTDRV.SCR, 365
    CAPSOFF.SCR, 360
    CAPSON.SCR, 360
    CURSNORM.SCR, 349
    DRIVEOAK.SCR, 363–364
    GETFUNCY.SCR, 361–362
    KEYSTATE.SCR, 358
    REBOOT.SCR, 361
    WEEKDAY.SCR, 356
    WHATDAY.SCR, 357
    WHATMON.SCR, 357
    WHATYEAR.SCR, 357–358

SCSI (Small Computer System Interface),
    112, 256
    controller, 112
Search menu, 40
searching
    for files, 54
    for partial directory name, 55–56
    paths, 61
sectors, 114–115
    clusters, 115–116
    dividing disk into, 121
    illustrated, 115
    soft sectoring and, 121
    See also tracks
SeekEasy utility, 469, 761–769
    registration form, 769
SET command, 208, 318, 563–564
    examples, 564
    options and switches, 563
    unallowed varname characters, 563
    usage, 563
SET files, in backup, 82
SETUP, 72
    backup file selection from, 75
    /E switch, 812
    /M switch, 812
    for PROTOCOL.INI modifications, 841
    /Q switch, 813
    supported network cards display, 836
    Workgroup Connection settings display,
        838
SETUP command, 36, 564–565
    example, 565
    options and switches, 564–565
    /Q switch, 564, 565
    usage, 564
SETVER command, 566–567
    /D switch, 566
    examples, 567
    options and switches, 566–567
    usage, 566
SETVER.EXE command, 567–568
    example, 568
    options and switches, 568
    usage, 567

SHARE command, 568–569
   example, 569
   loading, 569
   options and switches, 568–569
   usage, 568
   uses, 569
Shareware programs, 6–7, 605–606
   ASP and, 607
     members, 607
     ombudsman program, 608
     support, 608
   DIR alternatives, 57–59
   license agreement, 608–609
   registration of, 7
     benefits, 606–607
   where to get, 607
   See also Bob's Better-Than-DOS
     Shareware Collection
SHELL command, 208, 569–570
   COMMAND.COM and, 570
   example, 570
   MEMMAKER and, 570
   options and switches, 569–570
   usage, 569
SHIFT command, 307, 570–571
   in batch files, 571
   example, 571
   options and switches, 570
   usage, 570
sidebars, 8
signature characters, 218
SIMMs (single in-line memory modules), 165
   illustrated, 166
SIZER command, 571
SLT files, in backup, 82
SMARTDRV.EXE, 572–575
   buffersize variable, 572
   as device driver, 574
   DoubleSpace volumes and, 574
   elementsize variable, 572
   examples, 574
   extended use, 574–575
   for identifying double buffering, 574
   initcachesize/wincachesize default
     values, 573

installing in low memory, 573
   options and switches, 572–573
   usage, 572
   write caching, 575
SMARTDRV program, 33, 129
   caching compressed drives with, 15
   cluster problems with, 134
   default cache sizes, 131
   with DoubleSpace
     installed, 133
     using, 134
   FASTOPEN and, 136
   memory allocation, 129
   resolving communications problems
     with, 133
   using, 129–133
     with CD-ROMs, 134
     with DoubleSpace drives, 134
   See also disk caches
SMARTMON utility, 34, 46
soft sectoring, 121
SORT command, 575–576
   > and < characters, 576
   examples, 576
   options and switches, 575–576
   usage, 575
SpinRite program, 128
SpinTest program, 127, 769–772
SpinTime program, 127, 769–772
SRAM chip, 164–165
   See also DRAM chip; RAM
STACKER
   clean boot and, 263
   DoubleSpace drives and, 147
STACKEY utility, 31, 41–42, 773–785
   ECHO comparison, 314–315
   registration form, 785
STACKS command, 576–577
   examples, 577
   options and switches, 577
   stack error messages and, 577
   usage, 577
start-up menus, 265
   changing colors for, 268–269
   changing headings for, 269

commands for, 266
CONFIG.SYS file for, 266–267
defining, 266–269
entries per menu, 267
setting defaults for, 268
See also multimenu configurations
Stealth, 184
strings, assigning to keys, 237–239
subdirectories, listing, 53
SUBMENU command, 15, 578–579
blockname variable, 578
example, 578–579
options and switches, 578
syntax, 272
usage, 578
SUBST command, 579–580
examples, 580
options and switches, 579
usage, 579
Windows and, 580
swap files, 149
problems with, 149–150
SWITCH command, 580–581
example, 581
/K switch, 581
options and switches, 580–581
usage, 580
/W switch, 580, 581
switches, 9
ANSI.SYS, 373–374
APPEND command, 375–376
ATTRIB command, 378–379
BREAK command, 381
BUFFERS command, 383
CALL command, 385
CD command, 387
CHCP command, 389
CHKDSK command, 390
CHOICE command, 393–394
CLS command, 396
COMMAND command, 398–399
command-line, 291–292
COPY command, 401
COUNTRY command, 404
CTTY command, 405

DATE command, 406
DBLSPACE command, 408–410
DBLSPACE command line, 153
DBLSPACE.SYS, 412
DEBUG command, 413–414
DEFRAG command, 414–416
DEL command, 417–418
DELOLDOS command, 419
DELTREE command, 420–421
DEVICE command, 422
for device drivers, 17
DEVICEHIGH command, 423–424
DIR command, 56–57, 426–428
DISKCOMP command, 430
DISKCOPY command, 431–432
DISPLAY.SYS, 433–434
DOS command, 435
DOSKEY command, 437–438
DOSSHELL command, 440
DRIVER.SYS, 441–442
DRIVPARM command, 444–445
ECHO command, 446
EDIT command, 448–449
EGA.SYS, 450
EMM386 command, 451–455
EXIT command, 457
FASTHELP command, 17, 459
FASTOPEN command, 460
FC command, 462–463
FCBS command, 465
FDISK command, 465–466
FILES command, 467
FIND command, 468
FOR command, 470–471
FORMAT command, 472–474
GOTO command, 476
GRAPHICS command, 477–479
HELP command, 480
HIMEM.SYS, 482–484
IF command, 485
INCLUDE command, 487
INSTALL command, 489
INTERLNK command, 490
INTERLNK.EXE, 492–493
INTERSVR command, 494–495

KEYB command, 497
LABEL command, 498–499
LASTDRIVE command, 500
LOADFIX command, 501
LOADHIGH command, 502
MAIL command, 856–857
MD command, 504
MEM command, 505–506
MEMMAKER command, 507–508
MENUCOLOR command, 510
MENUDEFAULT command, 511
MENUITEM command, 512–513
MICRO command, 853, 858–859
MIRROR command, 514–515
MODE COMn command, 517–518
MODE CON command, 519
MODE device CP command, 520
MODE device /STATUS command, 521
MODE display command, 522
MODE LPTn command, 523
MORE command, 525
MOVE command, 526
MSAV command, 528–529
MSBACKUP command, 530–531
MSCDEX command, 533
MSD command, 535
MWUNDEL command, 538
NET CONFIG command, 861
NET LOGOFF command, 862
NET LOGON command, 863
NET PASSWORD command, 865
NET PRINT command, 866–867
NET START command, 868–689
NET STOP command, 870
NET TIME command, 871–872
NET USE command, 872–874
NET VER command, 876
NET VIEW command, 876–877
NLSFUNC command, 540
NUMLOCK command, 541
PATH command, 542
PAUSE command, 543
POWER command, 545
POWER.EXE, 546–547

PRINT command, 548–549
PROMPT command, 550
QBASIC command, 552–553
RAMDRIVE.SYS, 554
RD command, 555
REM command, 556
RENAME command, 557–558
REPLACE command, 559
RESTORE command, 561–562
SET command, 563
SETUP command, 564–565
SETVER command, 566–567
SETVER.EXE, 568
SHARE command, 568–569
SHELL command, 569–570
SHIFT command, 570
SMARTDRV.EXE, 572–573
SORT command, 575–576
STACKS command, 577
SUBMENU command, 578
SUBST command, 579
SWITCHES command, 580–581
SYS command, 582
TIME command, 583
TREE command, 585
TYPE command, 586
UNDELETE command, 587–589
UNFORMAT command, 592
UNINSTAL command, 591
VER command, 594
VERIFY command, 594
VOL command, 595
VSAFE command, 596–597
XCOPY command, 599–600
  See also DOS switches
SWITCHES command, 16, 264
  ? character and, 264
  controlling start keys with, 264–265
  switches, 265
SYS command, 582–583
  examples, 582
  options and switches, 582
  usage, 582

—T—

T (DEBUG) command, 345
task switching, 67–68
    performing, operations, 67–68
TIME command, 583–584
    CONFIG.SYS country setting and, 583
    examples, 584
    feeding Enter to, 324
    FIND command and, 325, 326
    no battery-supported clock and, 584
    options and switches, 583
    for pausing batch file until time is
        reached, 325–326
    usage, 583
tracks, 114
    illustrated, 115
    See also sectors
TREE command, 584–586
    examples, 585
    options and switches, 585
    usage, 584
    | MORE pipe, 585
TSRs, 88–89
    checking for, 330–331
    Windows required, 333
TURBOBAT utility, 46, 336, 386, 396, 477,
        487, 571
    batch file tampering prevention, 544
    See also BATUTIL utility
TURBOTXT utility, 679–680
TYPE command, 218, 586–587
    example, 586
    limitations, 586
    options and switches, 586
    usage, 586
    using, 220

—U—

U (DEBUG) command, 345
UART chip, 133
    history of, 133
UMB_DRV_SYS, 424, 436, 456, 503, 785–799
    for advanced memory support, 509
    registration form, 800

UMBs (upper memory blocks), 184
    CONFIG.SYS file for using, 191
    controlling load order and location,
        193–194
    cram, 192
    creating, 190
    identifying, space, 192–193
    INTERLNK.EXE and, 492
    loading programs into, 191
    memory allocation, 194–195
    regions, 193–194
    using, 190–192
    See also upper memory
UNDELETE command, 31, 32–33, 587–590
    Delete Sentry and, 589
    Delete Tracker and, 589
    deleted directories and, 589
    DOS and, 589
    examples, 590
    options and switches, 587–589
    switches for undeleting files, 588
    usage, 587
UNDELETE.INI file, 90–91, 588
    example of, 90
    sections of, 90
UNDELETE utility, 31, 32–33, 72
    delete sentry method, 89
    delete tracker method, 89
    deleted file list with, 94
    file protection methods, 33
    loading, 88
    TSR, 88–89
undeleting, 95
    files, 93–94
UNFORMAT command, 31, 95–97, 592–593
    examples, 593
    limitations, 593
    options and switches, 592
    usage, 592
UNFORMAT utility, 72, 95–97
    limitations, 97
    MIRROR files and, 96–97
    recovering directories with, 96
    recovering files with, 97

unformatting, 95–97
    process of, 96
UNINSTAL command, 147, 591–592
    ? switch and, 591
    limitations, 591
    options and switches, 591
    usage, 591
UNINSTALL program, 419, 420
    DBLSPACE and, 420
uninstalling DOS 6, 813
upper memory, 131–132
    address space, 172
    B area of, 201
    defined, 172
    loading DBLSPACE.BIN into, 195
    loading DOS into, 189–190
    monochrome region of, 201
    optimizing, for use with Windows,
        200–201
    showing loaded locations in, 204
    utilization of, 193
    See also UMBs (upper memory blocks)
utilities. *See* disk utilities; windows-hosted
        utilities

— V —

VCPI (Virtual Control Program Interface),
        184
VER command, 330, 593–594
    example, 594
    options and switches, 594
    usage, 593
VERIFY command, 594–595
    examples, 595
    options and switches, 594
    usage, 594
VESA (Video Electronics Standards
        Association), 256
    VL bus standard, 256
virtual memory, 184–185
virus(es)
    classification types of, 99–100
    cleaning, 103
    defined, 98
    functioning of, 99–100

guarding against, 102–103
identifying, 101–103
measures, 98–100
on-line info, 104
phenomenon, 98–99
potential damage caused by, 100
protection, 24–25, 72
removing, 103–104
scanning for, 101
signatures, 24
    updating, 25
VIRUSCAN utility, 800–805
    registration form, 805
VOL command, 595–596
    example, 596
    options and switches, 595
    usage, 595
VSAFE command, 596–598
    /AX switch, 597
    /CX switch, 597
    examples, 598
    option codes, 597
    options and switches, 596–597
    uninstalling, 597
    usage, 596
VSAFE program, 24, 72, 102–103
    function of, 25, 98, 598
    with Windows, 103

— W —

W (DEBUG) command, 345
wait state, 167
    zero, 167
wildcards
    changing default in QBASIC.EXE, 355
    checking for, 329–330
    entering, 372
Windows 3.1, Microsoft, 332–334
    adding WINPMT variable, 333
    batch files with, 332–334
    checking for, 334
    commands not good with, 334
    DOS session settings and, 333
    /K switch and, 334
    lowercase variable, 334

suppressing default message, 332
windir variable, 334
WINSTART.BAT, 333
See also Windows, Microsoft
Windows for Workgroups, 836, 837
Windows, Microsoft
    Anti-Virus, 72, 73
    APPEND command and, 378
    Backup option, 72, 73
    Enhanced mode performance
        improvement, 135
    Fastdisk, using with, 135
    installing
        applications, 72
        components of DOS 6, 812
    optimizing upper memory for, 200–201
    Undelete option, 72–73
    utilities, 33–34
    VSAFE with, 103
    See also Windows 3.1, Microsoft
windows-hosted utilities, 33–34
Workgroup Connection, 835
    command reference, 855–877
    settings, 838
    software, 838
        installing, 837
    using, 835–836
    See also Workgroup Connection
        commands
Workgroup Connection commands, 855–877
    MAIL, 850, 856–858
    MICRO, 853–855, 858–860
    NET, 838–839, 860–861
    NET CONFIG, 861–862
    NET LOGOFF, 862–863

    NET LOGON, 842, 863–864
    NET PASSWORD, 865–866
    NET PRINT, 849, 866–868
    NET START, 841–842, 868–870
    NET STOP, 870–871
    NET TIME, 871–872
    NET USE, 847–848, 872–875
    NET VER, 876
    NET VIEW, 846–847, 876–877
write buffering, 33
    See also buffering

— X —

XA (DEBUG) command, 346
XCOPY command, 17, 47–48, 598–601
    /E switch, 600
    ERRORLEVELs, 600
    examples, 600–601
    options and switches, 599–600
    reasons to use, 47
    /S switch, 599
    switches supported by, 47
    usage, 599
    See also COPY command; PCOPY utility
XD (DEBUG) command, 346
XM (DEBUG) command, 346
XMS (extended memory specification), 179
XS (DEBUG) command, 346

— Z —

zone bit recording, 115
    explained, 116

Notes

Notes

Notes

Notes

Notes

Notes

Notes

Notes

Notes

Notes

Notes

Notes

Notes

Notes

Notes

Notes

Notes

COMPUTER BOOK SERIES FROM IDG

...For Dummies Computer Book Series™

The #1 Computer Books Series For Beginners — over 2,000,000 books in print!. These books end the frustrations of beginning computer users who know they aren't dumb, but find that PC hardware, software, and computer jargon make them feel helpless. Lighthearted, down-to-earth, and packed with valuable information ...*For Dummies* Books are the perfect survival guides for anyone forced to use a computer.

DOS For Dummies,™ 2nd Edition
by Dan Gookin

Learn DOS the fun and easy way with Dan Gookin's humorous reference for the rest of us – covers DOS ver. 2-6.

$16.95 USA/$21.95 Canada/£15.45 UK & EIRE, ISBN: 1-878058-75-4

PCs For Dummies™
by Dan Gookin and Andy Rathbone

The non-nerd's guide to PC configuration, upgrading, and repair – for the computer phobic!

$16.95 USA/$21.95 Canada/£15.45 UK & EIRE, ISBN: 1-878058-51-7

WordPerfect 6 For Dummies™
by Dan Gookin

The sequel to the international bestseller *Word Perfect For Dummies,* now completely revised for WordPerfect 6.0.

$16.95 USA/$21.95 Canada/£15.45 UK & EIRE, ISBN: 1-878058-77-0 — Available Aug. 1993

OS/2 For Dummies™
by Andy Rathbone

Bestselling *PCs For Dummies* author Andy Rathbone offers a fun and easy survival guide to beginning and intermediate users who need to co-exist with OS/2.

$19.95 USA/$26.95 Canada/£18.45 UK & EIRE, ISBN: 1-878058-76-2

1-2-3 For Dummies™
by Greg Harvey

Simplifies Lotus 1-2-3, the perfect introduction for the spreadsheet averse.

$16.95 USA/$21.95 Canada/£15.45 UK & EIRE, ISBN: 1-878058-60-6

Windows For Dummies™
by Andy Rathbone, coauthor of the bestselling PCs For Dummies

Teaches new Windows users the essentials of Windows with humor and style!

$16.95 USA/$21.95 Canada/£15.45 UK & EIRE, ISBN: 1-878058-61-4

Macs For Dummies™
by David Pogue

Finally, a friendly guide to plugging in and learning how to use your Mac!

$16.95 USA/$21.95 Canada/£15.45 UK & EIRE, ISBN: 1-878058-53-3

Word for Windows For Dummies™
by Dan Gookin

Bestselling author Dan Gookin brings his lighthearted ...*For Dummies* approach to Word for Windows— today's fastest growing word processing program.

$16.95 USA/$21.95 Canada/£15.45 UK & EIRE, ISBN: 1-878058-86-X — Available June 1993

UNIX For Dummies™
by John Levine

The fun and friendly guide that takes the mystery out of UNIX.

$19.95 USA/$26.95 Canada/£18.45 UK & EIRE, ISBN: 1-878058-58-4

Excel For Dummies™
by Greg Harvey

The best beginner's guide to Excel 4 for Windows —today's fastest growing spreadsheet program.

$16.95 USA/$21.95 Canada/£15.45 UK & EIRE, ISBN: 1-878058-63-0

C Programming For Dummies™
by Dan Gookin, author of the #1 Bestseller DOS For Dummies

A painless primer – unique, entertaining style to teach the essentials of C Programming. Guaranteed to appeal to even the most cautious C novice. Never stuffy, this hands-on tutorial is loaded with easy and entertaining examples.

$19.95 USA/$26.95 Canada/£18.45 UK & EIRE, ISBN: 1-878058-78-9 — Available June 1993

For More Information Call 1-800-762-2974

Macworld Authorized Editions

Designed specifically for the Macintosh user, Macworld Books are written by leading *Macworld* magazine columnists, technology champions, and Mac gurus who provide expert advice and insightful tips and techniques not found anywhere else. Macworld Books are the only Macintosh books authorized by *Macworld*, the world's leading Macintosh magazine.

Macworld Guide To Microsoft System 7.1, 2nd Edition
by Lon Poole, Macworld *magazine's "Quick Tips" columnist*

The most recommended guide to System 7, updated and expanded!

$24.95 USA/$33.95 Canada/£22.92 UK & EIRE, ISBN: 1-878058-65-7

Macworld Networking Handbook
by David Kosiur, Ph.D.

The ultimate insider's guide to Mac network management.

$29.95 USA/$39.95 Canada/£27.45 UK & EIRE, ISBN: 1-878058-31-2

Macworld Guide To Microsoft Word 5
by Jim Heid, Macworld *magazine's "Getting Started" columnist*

Learn Word the easy way with this *Macworld* Authorized Edition. Now updated for Word 5.1.

$22.95 USA/$29.95 Canada/£20.95 UK & EIRE, ISBN: 1-878058-39-8

Macworld Guide To Microsoft Excel 4
by David Maguiness

Build powerful spreadsheets quickly with this *Macworld* Authorized Edition to Excel 4.

$22.95 USA/$29.95 Canada/£20.95 UK & EIRE, ISBN: 1-878058-40-1

Macworld Guide To Microsoft Works 3
by Barrie A. Sosinsky

Get inside the new Works so you can work more productively—the perfect blend of reference and tutorial.

$22.95 USA/$29.95 Canada/£20.95 UK & EIRE, ISBN: 1-878058-42-8

Macworld Music & Sound Bible
by Christopher Yavelow

Finally, the definitive guide to music, sound, and multimedia on the Mac.

$37.95 USA/$47.95 Canada/£34.95 UK & EIRE, ISBN: 1-878058-18-5

Macworld Complete Mac Handbook
by Jim Heid

The most complete guide to getting started, mastering, and expanding your Mac.

$26.95 USA/$35.95 Canada/£24.95 UK & EIRE, ISBN: 1-878058-17-7

Macworld QuarkXPress Designer Handbook
by Barbara Assadi and Galen Gruman

Macworld magazine's DTP experts help you master advanced features fast with this definitive tutorial, reference and designer tips resource on QuarkXPress.

$29.95 USA/$39.95 Canada/£27.45 UK & EIRE, ISBN: 1-878058-85-1 — Available July 1993

Macworld PageMaker Bible
by Jo Ann Villalobos

The ultimate insiders' guide to PageMaker 5, combining an authoritative and easy-to-use reference with tips and techniques. Includes 3 1/2" disk of templates.

$39.95 USA/$52.95 Canada/£37.60 UK & EIRE, ISBN: 1-878058-84-3 — Available July 1993

For More Information Call 1-800-762-2974

PC World Handbook

Expert information at your fingertips. Perfect for readers who need a complete tutorial of features as well as a reference to software applications and operating systems. All PC World Handbooks include bonus disks with software featuring useful templates, examples, and utilities that provide real value to the reader.

PC World DOS 6 Handbook, 2nd Edition
by John Socha, Clint Hicks, and Devra Hall

Completely revised and updated! Includes extended features of DOS and the 250 page command reference that Microsoft excludes. A complete tutorial and reference PLUS Special Edition of Norton Commander software.

$34.95 USA/$44.95 Canada/£32.95 UK & EIRE, ISBN: 1-878058-79-7

PC World Excel 4 for Windows Handbook
by John Walkenbach and David Maguiness

Complete tutorial and reference by PC World's spreadsheet experts, with a FREE 32-page Function Reference booklet.

$29.95 USA/$39.95 Canada/£27.45 UK & EIRE, ISBN: 1-878058-46-0

PC World Microsoft Access Bible
by Cary Prague and Michael Irwin

This authoritative tutorial and reference on Microsoft's new Windows database is the perfect companion for every Microsoft Access user.

$39.95 USA/$52.95 Canada/£37.60 UK & EIRE, ISBN: 1-878058-81-9

PC World WordPerfect 6 Handbook
by Greg Harvey

Bestselling author and WordPerfect guru Greg Harvey brings you the ultimate tutorial and reference – complete with valuable software containing document templates, macros, and other handy WordPerfect tools.

$34.95 USA/$44.95 Canada/£32.95 UK & EIRE, ISBN: 1-878058-80-0 — Available July 1993

Official XTree MS-DOS, Windows, and Hard Disk Management Companion, 3rd Edition
by Beth Slick

The only authorized guide to all versions of XTree, the most popular PC hard disk utility.

$19.95 USA/$26.95 Canada/£18.45 UK & EIRE, ISBN: 1-878058-57-6

PC World Q&A Bible, Version 4
by Thomas J. Marcellus, Technical Editor of The Quick Answer

The only thorough guide with a disk of databases for mastering Q&A Version 4.

$39.95 USA/$52.95 Canada/£37.60 UK & EIRE, ISBN: 1-878058-03-7

QuarkXPress for Windows Designer Handbook
by Barbara Assadi and Galen Gruman

Make the move to QuarkXPress for Windows, the new professional desktop publishing powerhouse, with this expert reference and tutorial.

$29.95 USA/$39.95 Canada/£27.45 UK & EIRE, ISBN: 1-878058-45-2

PC World You Can Do It With DOS
by Christopher Van Buren

The best way to learn DOS quickly and easily.

$19.95 USA/$26.95 Canada/£18.45 VAT UK EIRE, ISBN: 1-878058-38-X

PC World You Can Do It With Windows
by Christopher Van Buren

The best way to learn Window 3.1!

$19.95 USA/$26.95 Canada/£18.45 VAT UK EIRE, ISBN: 1-878058-37-1

For More Information Call 1-800-762-2974

Order Form

Order Center: (800) 762-2974 (8 a.m.-5 p.m., PST, weekdays) or (415) 312-0600

For Fastest Service: Photocopy This Order Form and FAX it to : (415) 358-1260

Quantity	ISBN	Title	Price	Total

Shipping & Handling Charges

Subtotal	U.S.	Canada & International	International Air Mail
Up to $20.00	Add $3.00	Add $4.00	Add $10.00
$20.01-40.00	$4.00	$5.00	$20.00
$40.01-60.00	$5.00	$6.00	$25.00
$60.01-80.00	$6.00	$8.00	$35.00
Over $80.00	$7.00	$10.00	$50.00

In U.S. and Canada, shipping is UPS ground or equivalent.
For Rush shipping call (800) 762-2974.

Subtotal _____

CA residents add applicable sales tax _____

IN residents add 5% sales tax _____

Canadian residents add 7% GST tax _____

Shipping _____

TOTAL _____

Ship to:

Name _____

Company _____

Address _____

City/State/Zip _____

Daytime Phone _____

Payment: ❑ Check to IDG Books (US Funds Only) ❑ Visa ❑ MasterCard ❑ American Express

Card # _____ Exp. _____ Signature _____

Please send this order form to: IDG Books, 155 Bovet Road, San Mateo, CA 94402.
Allow up to 3 weeks for delivery. Thank you!

BOBS93

Disclaimer and Copyright Notice _____

Note

IDG Books Worldwide, Inc., warrants that the disks that accompany this book are free from defects in materials and workmanship for a period of 60 days from the date of purchase of this book. If IDG Books receives notification within the warranty period of defects in material or workmanship, IDG Books will replace the defective disks. The remedy for the breach of this warranty will be limited to replacement and will not encompass any other damages, including but not limited to loss of profit, and special, incidental, consequential, or other claims.

5 ¼" Format Available. The enclosed disks are in 3 ½-inch, 1.44MB format. If you don't have a drive that size or format, and cannot arrange to transfer the data to the disk size you need, you can obtain the programs on 5 ¼ 1.2MB disks by writing: IDG Books Worldwide, Attn: *DOS 6 SECRETS* Disks, IDG Books Worldwide, 155 Bovet Rd., Suite 310, San Mateo, CA 94402, or call 800-762-2974. Please allow 3–4 weeks for delivery.

IDG Books Worldwide, InfoWorld Publishing Inc., and the author specifically disclaim all other warranties, express or implied, including but not limited to implied warranties of merchantability and fitness for a particular purpose with respect to defects in the disks, the programs, and source code contained therein, and/or the techniques described in the book, and in no event shall IDG Books Worldwide, InfoWorld, and/or the author be liable for any loss of profit or any other commercial damage, including but not limited to special, incidental, consequential, or other damages.

Licensing Agreement

Do not open the accompanying disk package until you have read and unless you agree with the terms of this licensing agreement. If you disagree and do not want to be bound by the terms of this licensing agreement, return the book for refund to the source from which you purchased it.

The contents of these disks are copyrighted and protected by both U.S. copyright law and international copyright treaty provisions. The individual programs on these disks are copyrighted by the authors of each program respectively. Each program has its own use permissions and limitations. You may copy any or all of these utilities to your computer system. To use each program, you must follow the individual requirements and restrictions detailed for each in the documentation contained in Part V of this book. Do not use a program if you do not want to follow its licensing agreement. Absolutely none of the material on these disks or listed in this book may ever be distributed, in original or modified form, for commercial purposes.

Installation Bob's Better-Than-DOS Shareware Collection Disks _____

Attention: Before installing any of the programs from the distribution disks, read the Disclaimer and Copyright Notice on the previous page.

The programs included on the *DOS 6 SECRETS* disks are stored in compressed form. To transfer these programs to your hard drive, you *must* use the INSTALL program from Disk #1. You cannot install the software by using the DOS COPY command.

The INSTALL program allows you to specify the target drive and a parent directory (beneath which all the selected programs will be installed in individual subdirectories). Approximately 6MB of disk space is required to install all the programs. The space requirements for individual programs are listed in Part V.

The following steps detail the installation procedure:

> **Step 1. Insert Disk #1.** Put the disk labeled *Disk 1* in either drive A or B, depending on the correct floppy drive size for your computer.
>
> **Step 2. Run the INSTALL program.** From the DOS prompt, enter the command
>
>> `a:install or b:install`
>
> **Step 3. Enter the target drive and directory.** Following a welcome screen, INSTALL prompts you to enter a drive and directory. Unless you specify otherwise, the drive C:\SECRETS is used by default.
>
> **Step 4. Select the programs you want to try.** INSTALL will display a list of all the programs available on the disks. By default, every program is selected and marked with a check mark in the leftmost column. Use the up- and down-arrow keys to navigate through the list and use the spacebar to toggle the selection status of each individual program. After you have selected the desired programs, press the Enter key.
>
> Each program is installed into a unique directory. Following is a list of all the directories created by the INSTALL program:

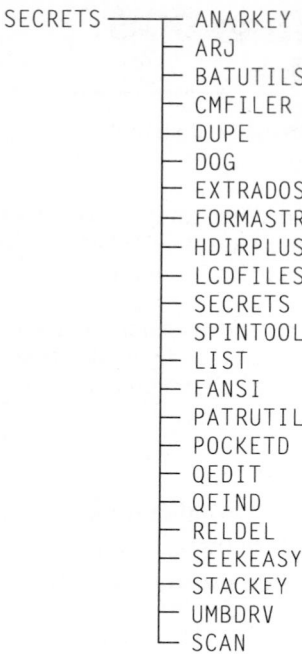

```
SECRETS ——————— ANARKEY
              ├── ARJ
              ├── BATUTILS
              ├── CMFILER
              ├── DUPE
              ├── DOG
              ├── EXTRADOS
              ├── FORMASTR
              ├── HDIRPLUS
              ├── LCDFILES
              ├── SECRETS
              ├── SPINTOOL
              ├── LIST
              ├── FANSI
              ├── PATRUTIL
              ├── POCKETD
              ├── QEDIT
              ├── QFIND
              ├── RELDEL
              ├── SEEKEASY
              ├── STACKEY
              ├── UMBDRV
              └── SCAN
```

Step 5. Try out the software. INSTALL does not make any modifications to your AUTOEXEC.BAT file, so none of the new directories will be added to the search path. The easiest way to evaluate a program is to change directories to the specific program's directory and then execute the program. Refer to Part V for further details about each program.

Step 6. Register the programs you use. If you like a program and continue to use it, register your copy. A copy of a registration form for each program is included in Part V.

IDG BOOKS WORLDWIDE REGISTRATION CARD

**IDG
BOOKS**

THE WORLD OF
COMPUTER
KNOWLEDGE

Title of this book: _____

My overall rating of this book: ❑ Very good [1] ❑ Good [2] ❑ Satisfactory [3] ❑ Fair [4] ❑ Poor [5]

How I first heard about this book:

❑ Found in bookstore; name: [6] _____ ❑ Book review: [7]

❑ Advertisement: [8] _____ ❑ Catalog: [9]

❑ Word of mouth; heard about book from friend, co-worker, etc.: [10] ❑ Other: [11]

What I liked most about this book:

_____

_____

What I would change, add, delete, etc., in future editions of this book:

_____

_____

Other comments:

_____

Number of computer books I purchase in a year: ❑ 1 [12] ❑ 2-5 [13] ❑ 6-10 [14] ❑ More than 10 [15]

I would characterize my computer skills as: ❑ Beginner [16] ❑ Intermediate [17] ❑ Advanced [18] ❑ Professional [19]

I use ❑ DOS [20] ❑ Windows [21] ❑ OS/2 [22] ❑ Unix [23] ❑ Macintosh [24] ❑ Other: [25]_____
(please specify)

I would be interested in new books on the following subjects:
(please check all that apply, and use the spaces provided to identify specific software)

❑ Word processing: [26] _____ ❑ Spreadsheets: [27] _____

❑ Data bases: [28] _____ ❑ Desktop publishing: [29] _____

❑ File Utilities: [30] _____ ❑ Money management: [31] _____

❑ Networking: [32] _____ ❑ Programming languages: [33] _____

❑ Other: [34]

I use a PC at (please check all that apply): ❑ home [35] ❑ work [36] ❑ school [37] ❑ other: [38] _____

The disks I prefer to use are ❑ 5.25 [39] ❑ 3.5 [40] ❑ other: [41]_____

I have a CD ROM: ❑ yes [42] ❑ no [43]

I plan to buy or upgrade computer hardware this year: ❑ yes [44] ❑ no [45]

I plan to buy or upgrade computer software this year: ❑ yes [46] ❑ no [47]

Name: _____ Business title: [48] _____ Type of Business: [49] _____

Address (❑ home [50] ❑ work [51]/Company name: _____)

Street/Suite# _____

City [52]/State [53]/Zipcode [54]: _____

❑ **I liked this book!** You may quote me by name in future
IDG Books Worldwide promotional materials.
My daytime phone number is _____

RETURN THIS
REGISTRATION CARD
FOR FREE CATALOG

❏ YES!

Please keep me informed about IDG's World of Computer Knowledge.
Send me the latest IDG Books catalog.

Fold Here

_____

_____

_____

PLACE
STAMP
HERE

IDG Books Worldwide, Inc.
155 Bovet Road
Suite 310
San Mateo, CA 94402

Attn: Reader Response

Fire and Emergency Services Instructor
Seventh Edition

Frederick M. Stowell
Project Manager/Writer

Barbara Adams
Senior Editor

Validated by the International Fire
Service Training Association

Published by
Fire Protection Publications
Oklahoma State University

Note: At the suggestion of our customers, this printing of **Fire and Emergency Services Instructor**, 7th edition, contains several changed photographs, including the cover photo, which did not appear in the first printing. These changes were made in order to show photographs that represented the safest procedures or behaviors for both instructors and students. Other than these photos, no significant content changes were made to the manual.

RECYCLABLE

The International Fire Service Training Association

The International Fire Service Training Association (IFSTA) was established in 1934 as a "nonprofit educational association of fire fighting personnel who are dedicated to upgrading fire fighting techniques and safety through training." To carry out the mission of IFSTA, Fire Protection Publications was established as an entity of Oklahoma State University. Fire Protection Publications' primary function is to publish and disseminate training texts as proposed and validated by IFSTA. As a secondary function, Fire Protection Publications researches, acquires, produces, and markets high-quality learning and teaching aids as consistent with IFSTA's mission.

The IFSTA Validation Conference is held the second full week in July. Committees of technical experts meet and work at the conference addressing the current standards of the National Fire Protection Association and other standard-making groups as applicable. The Validation Conference brings together individuals from several related and allied fields, such as:

- Key fire department executives and training officers
- Educators from colleges and universities
- Representatives from governmental agencies
- Delegates of firefighter associations and industrial organizations

Committee members are not paid nor are they reimbursed for their expenses by IFSTA or Fire Protection Publications. They participate because of commitment to the fire service and its future through training. Being on a committee is prestigious in the fire service community, and committee members are acknowledged leaders in their fields. This unique feature provides a close relationship between the International Fire Service Training Association and fire protection agencies, which helps to correlate the efforts of all concerned.

IFSTA manuals are now the official teaching texts of most of the states and provinces of North America. Additionally, numerous U.S. and Canadian government agencies as well as other English-speaking countries have officially accepted the IFSTA manuals.

ISBN 0-87939-271-1   *Library of Congress Control Number: 2006921219*

Seventh Edition, First Printing, April 2006   *Printed in the United States of America*

10   9   8   7   6   5   4   3

If you need additional information concerning the International Fire Service Training Association (IFSTA) or Fire Protection Publications, contact:

Customer Service, Fire Protection Publications, Oklahoma State University
930 North Willis, Stillwater, OK 74078-8045
800-654-4055   Fax: 405-744-8204

For assistance with training materials, to recommend material for inclusion in an IFSTA manual, or to ask questions or comment on manual content, contact:

Editorial Department, Fire Protection Publications, Oklahoma State University
930 North Willis, Stillwater, OK 74078-8045
405-744-4111   Fax: 405-744-4112   E-mail: editors@osufpp.org

Table of Contents

Preface..xii
Introduction.................................. 1
Purpose and Scope................................. 1
Fire and Emergency Services Training History.... 1
Book Organization.................................... 2
Overview of Instructor Functions...................... 3
Importance of Instruction and Training........... 4
Key Information.. 4

Part A General Knowledge and Skills

1 Challenges of Fire and Emergency Services Instruction.......................... 9
Instructor Obligations.......................... 10
To Students... 10
To the Organization............................... 12
To the Profession.................................. 13
To Themselves..................................... 13
Instructor as Role Model.......................... 14
Effective Instructor Characteristics.................. 16
Leadership Abilities................................ 16
Strong Interpersonal Skills...................... 17
Subject and Teaching Competencies.............. 18
Desire to Teach.................................... 18
Enthusiasm.. 18
Motivation... 19
Preparation and Organization.................... 19
Ingenuity, Creativity, and Flexibility............. 20
Empathy... 20
Conflict-Resolution Skills....................... 20
Fairness... 20
Personal Integrity................................. 20
Teaching Traits to Emphasize.......................... 20
Honesty Versus Bluffing........................... 20
Sincerity Versus Sarcasm......................... 21
Solutions Versus Complaints...................... 21
Inspiration Versus Intimidation.................. 22
Positive Humor Versus Offensive Humor....... 22
Instructor Challenges.......................... 22
Multiple Priorities................................ 23
Diverse Students.................................. 23
Organizational Apathy........................... 23
Multiple Changes................................. 24
Cooperative Relationships....................... 24
Organizational Promotion........................ 24

Management Directives............................24
Safe Training Environments.......................24
Professional Development........................25
Course Schedules................................25
Funds and Resources............................25
Qualified Instructor Recruitment..................26
Instructor Reference Checklist...................... 27
Analyses..27
Instructional Facilities, Props, and Acquired Structures.........................27
Diversity Issues..................................28
Legal Requirements and Accommodations....29
Audience Recognition...........................29
Summary...................................... 30

2 Safety and the Training Function....... 35
The Safety Challenge.......................... 35
Training Casualties..............................36
Casualty Prevention............................37
The Instructor's Role.......................... 39
Safe Training Environment......................40
Planning Safe Training Scenarios.............. 41
Inspecting and Repairing Facilities and Props........................ 42
Monitoring Training Activities.................. 43
Safety-Related Teaching Topics.................44
Instructor Incident Safety Officer Duties........44
Instructor as Safety Role Model.................45
Reinforcing Safety............................46
Implementing Safety Plans...................46
Accident Prevention and Management........... 47
Prevention..47
Management......................................48
Factors..48
Investigations.................................50
Analyses.......................................50
Mitigation Activities...........................52
Resources: Safety Guidelines, Regulations, and Information.......................... 53
Federal Government Agencies....................53
State/Provincial and Local Safety and Health Agencies...........................54
Standards Writing Organizations...............55
National Fire Protection Association...........55
American Society for Testing and Materials...56

American National Standards Institute 56
Underwriters Laboratories Inc. 56
Professional Organizations and Associations 57
Summary **57**

3 Legal and Ethical Considerations 61
Law and the Instructor **61**
Legal Terminology 62
Types of Laws 64
Legislative (Statutory) Law 64
Administrative Law 67
Judiciary Law 67
Law Applications **67**
Records Management 68
Training and Attendance Records 68
Legal Requirements 68
Legal Liability 70
Vicarious Liability 71
Foreseeability 72
Liability Reduction 72
Copyright Laws and Permissions 73
Students' Rights 75
Environmental Issues 76
Water 76
Atmosphere 76
Soil 77
General Considerations 77
Ethical Conduct **77**
Components of Ethics 78
Personal Ethics Origins 78
Unethical Conduct Causes 78
Personal Justifications 79
Ethics Program 79
Elements 79
Code of Ethics 79
Ethical Issues 80
Summary **82**

4 Effective Interpersonal Communication 85
Interpersonal Communication Basics **85**
Sender 87
Message 87
Medium or Channel 87
Receiver 87
Feedback to the Sender 88
Interference 88
Interpersonal Communication Purposes **89**
Verbal Component **90**

Cultural Concept of Words 90
Verbal Skills Improvement 91
Nonverbal Component **92**
Kinesics 92
Nonverbal Communication Improvement 93
Listening Skills **94**
Attending 95
Understanding 95
Remembering 95
Evaluating 96
Responding 96
Improving Listening Skills 96
Summary **97**

5 Instructional Facilities and Props 101
Instructional Facilities **101**
Infrastructure Requirements 102
Permanent Facilities 104
Mobile Training Facilities 106
Training Props **108**
Permanent Structures 108
Rescue/Extrication Training Area 108
Flammable/Combustible Liquids and
    Hazardous Materials Training Area 109
Live-Fire Training Area 110
Portable Training Props 111
Acquired Structures **112**
Environmental Conditions 113
Structural Conditions 113
Training Possibilities 114
Instructor Responsibilities 114
Fuel Usage 115
Water Supply Requirements 115
Summary **115**

6 Report Writing and Record Keeping 119
Report Writing **119**
General Considerations 120
Report Writing Criteria 121
Organization 121
Report Development 123
Writing Style 123
Executive Summary 123
General Record-System Components **125**
Record Categories 126
Training 126
Budget 128
Inventory 128

Maintenance.................................... 129

Personnel...................................... 130

Record-Keeping System Development.......... 130

Requirement Definitions...................... 130

System Plan.................................... 131

System Implementation 131

Project Completion........................... 133

Evaluation 133

Revision... 133

Data Interpretation 133

Legal Requirements 133

Summary **134**

7 Principles of Learning 137

Development of Learning Principles 137

Pedagogy.. 137

Androgogy...................................... 138

Other Learning Theories...................... 138

Terminology 139

Domains of Learning 141

Cognitive (Knowledge)........................ 141

Psychomotor (Skills) 143

Affective (Attitude) 144

Styles and Methods of Learning.................. 145

Styles 145

Methods 145

Laws of Learning 146

Readiness 146

Exercise 146

Effect... 147

Disuse.. 147

Association...................................... 147

Recency.. 147

Primacy 147

Intensity 148

Motivation 148

Motivation Techniques for Adult Students.... 148

Motivation — Relationship to Learning........ 148

Theories of Learning and Remembering 149

Memory.. 151

Sensory... 151

Short-Term (Working)......................... 153

Long-Term 153

Factors that Affect Learning 153

Learning Obstacles............................. 153

Learning Plateaus.............................. 154

Approaches to Teaching 155

Traditional...................................... 156

Mastery 156

Advantages.................................... 157

Disadvantages 157

Approaches to Student Assessment................ 157

Norm-Referenced Assessments 158

Criterion-Referenced Assessments............... 158

Summary 159

8 Student Attributes and Behaviors.....163

Student Characteristics 163

Life Experiences 164

Motivation 164

Adult Responsibilities 165

Confidence...................................... 165

Learning Style Variations 165

Demographic Factors........................... 165

Age.. 166

Gender.. 167

Culture and Ethnicity........................ 168

Educational Background...................... 169

Students as Individuals 169

Individuals With Low Literacy Levels 170

Individuals With Learning Disabilities 171

Gifted Students 172

Slow Learners or Slow Students 172

Nondisruptive, Nonparticipating Students... 173

Shy or Timid.................................. 173

Quiet or Bored................................ 174

Uninterested................................. 174

Disruptive, Nonparticipating Students 174

Talkative and Aggressive 174

Show-Off..................................... 175

Nondisruptive, Participating, Successful

Students...................................... 175

Student Behavioral Management................... 175

Reviewing Policies............................. 176

Counseling...................................... 177

Learning Issues............................... 177

Behavioral Issues............................. 177

Coaching.. 178

Process....................................... 180

Techniques................................... 181

Providing Peer Assistance 182

Mentoring...................................... 182

Controlling Disruptive Behavior...................183
    Instructor-Caused....................184
    Student-Caused.....................184
Summary.....................................**186**

Part B Instructor I Requirements

9 Preparation for Instruction...............189
Lesson Plans **189**
Definition...190
Components.......................................190
Four-Step Method of Instruction 193
    Preparation....................................193
    Presentation...................................195
    Application 195
    Evaluation 196
Instructor Preparation.....................**196**
Attitude for Learning.............................196
Advance Organization 197
Session Preparation 197
Session Logistics.................................199
Course Continuity and Consistency.............**200**
Continuity..201
    Instructor Changes 201
    Weather Variations......................202
    Equipment and Material Variations 203
    Instructional Resource Variations 203
    Appropriate Testing Location Variations ...203
    Differences in Learning Styles 203
Consistency 205
    Safety Factors 205
    Types of Training Material...............205
    Resource Materials 205
    Approaches to Teaching 205
    Skill Performances........................206
Physical Setting................................**206**
Classroom Environment.........................207
    Seating 207
    Lighting.......................................209
    Temperature.................................209
    Noise Level 210
    Audiovisual Equipment..................211
    Other Classroom Considerations..............212
Outside Environment 213
Summary.....................................**215**

10 Instructional Delivery......................219
Instructional Delivery Methods....................**219**
Instructor-Led Presentation Types 220
    Lecture..221
    Illustrated Lecture 222
    Discussion....................................223
    Demonstration 224
    Multiple Instructors........................225
Technology-Based Training 227
    Types..227
    Advantages and Disadvantages 228
    Security.......................................228
Other Instructional Methods.....................230
    Self-Directed Learning 230
    Individualized Instruction................231
Presentation Techniques **232**
Characteristics of Effective Speakers 232
Nonverbal Elements 234
Presentation Preparation.........................234
Attitudes/Values Display 236
Presentation Organization Format 236
Methods of Sequencing 236
Instructional Methods for Active Learning **237**
Strategies..238
Advantages 239
Motivational Techniques 240
Encouragement for Success 241
Reinforcement of Learning.......................241
    Repetition.....................................241
    Behavioral Reinforcement 242
Techniques for Questioning 242
    Purposes 242
    Effective Guidelines 243
    Question Types..............................244
    Instructor Responses......................245
Summary **245**

11 Audiovisual Technology **249**
Audiovisual Training Aid Benefits **250**
Audiovisual Training Aid Selection..............**250**
Learning Objectives and Lesson Content 251
Required Student Performance...................251
Class Size and Interaction 251
Pace of Learning..................................252
Practice Factors...................................252
Evaluative Factors 252
Budget Limitations................................253

Audiovisual Training Aids Use and
  Development.................................... 253
Transitions in Presentations........................ 255
  Purposes..255
  Timing..255
  Types and Development.........................256
    Verbal Transitions *256*
    Nonverbal Transitions.......................*257*
    Media Transitions and Animations...........*257*
Audiovisual Training Aid Types..................... 258
  Nonprojected Training Aids 258
    Marker Board Illustrations *258*
    Illustration or Diagram Displays *261*
    Duplicated Materials *261*
    Models *262*
    Audiotapes and Compact Discs................*263*
    Casualty Simulation Training Aids............*263*
  Projected Training Aids 264
    Video and Multimedia Projectors/Large-
      Screen Images *265*
    Visual Presenters/Displays *266*
    Television/Programs and Video
      Presentations *267*
    Slide Projectors/Slides *268*
    Overhead Projectors/Transparencies..........*268*
  Simulators......................................269
    Electronic Simulators *270*
    Display Boards *270*
    Smoke Simulators...........................*270*
    Computer Simulations.......................*270*
    Virtual Reality Simulations *271*
    Anatomical/Physiological Mannequins.....*271*
  Ancillary Equipment.............................271
    Television Monitors *271*
    Projection Screens..........................*272*
Cleaning, Care, and Maintenance................. 272
  Cleaning..273
  Care 273
  Maintenance....................................273
Summary 274

12 Structured Exercises,
    Demonstrations, and Practical
    Training Evolutions 277
Structured Exercises 277
  Case Studies....................................277
  Role-Plays 279
  Brainstorming Sessions 280

  Simulations.....................................281
  Field and Laboratory Experiences 282
Psychomotor Skills Demonstrations............. 282
Practical Training Evolutions 283
  Training Locations 284
  Evolution Planning..............................284
  Safety and Health Considerations 288
  Evolution Control 290
    Simple Training Evolutions *290*
    Complex Training Evolutions.................*291*
  Fire-Suppression Training Evolutions 292
    Small Fires *293*
    Interior Structural Fires......................*294*
    Exterior Fires...............................*294*
  Technical Training Evolutions 295
  Instructor Preparation 298
Summary 298

13 Student Progress Evaluation
    and Testing 303
Formal Evaluations Through Testing 304
  Test Types......................................304
    Interpretation Classification...................*305*
    Purpose Classification.......................*305*
    Administration Classification *306*
  Test Administration.............................308
    Written Tests................................*308*
    Performance Tests...........................*308*
  Test Scoring....................................310
    Oral Tests..................................*310*
    Written Tests................................*310*
    Performance Tests...........................*311*
  Grade Reporting................................314
  Test Security...................................314
Feedback.. 315
  Positive Feedback...............................316
  Negative Feedback..............................316
  Feedback Applications..........................316
Summary 317

Part C Instructor II Requirements

14 Lesson Plan Development.............321
The Lesson Plan and Its Components 321
  Purposes and Benefits 322
  Parts and Components 323
Learning Objectives 329
  Development 330
  Action Verbs 331

Lesson Plan Types and Formats......................**331**
    Types 332
        Cognitive Lesson Plans...........................*332*
        Psychomotor Lesson Plans *333*
    Formats 333
Lesson Plan Creation **338**
Lesson Plan Modification or Adaptation **339**
Ancillary Components **339**
    Information Sheet 339
    Skills Sheet 341
    Worksheet 341
    Study Sheet 346
    Assignment Sheet 346
Audiovisual Components...........................**349**
    Development Guidelines.............................349
    Equipment 350
        Cameras *350*
        Scanners *351*
        Video Capture Devices............................*351*
        Video Editing Devices *351*
Lesson Plan Evaluation and Revision............**352**
    Evaluation 352
    Revision 353
Summary **353**

15   Instructor and Course
     Evaluations **357**
Instructor Evaluations **357**
    Supervisor Evaluations 358
    Advantages...358
    Characteristics....................................358
    Performance Evaluation Processes...................359
    Evaluation Uses 361
        Strengths *361*
        Weaknesses *361*
    Evaluation Instruments 361
    Student Evaluations of Instructors 361
Course/Lesson Evaluations.......................**363**
    Considerations for Planning 363
    Formative Evaluations 363
        Field Test *364*
        Observation *364*
    Summative Evaluations 364
        Supervisory Personnel Surveys *365*
        Student Learning Surveys *368*
    Evaluation Results 368
Summary **371**

16   Student Testing Instruments.........**375**
Test Planning Steps **376**
    Determine Test Purpose and Type 376
    Identify and Define Learning Objectives 377
    Prepare Test Specifications.........................380
        Table of Specification *380*
        Time Requirements.................................*381*
        Test Planning Sheet *382*
    Construct Appropriate Test Items.................383
        Match Test Items to Learning
          Objectives......................................*383*
        Eliminate Testing Language and
          Comprehension Barriers *383*
        Avoid Giving Clues to Test Answers *383*
        Select Proper Level of Test Item
          Difficulty *384*
        Determine Appropriate Number of
          Test Items *384*
        Ensure Test Usability *385*
        Ensure Validity and Reliability *386*
Test Instruments **387**
    Common Considerations for All Tests 387
        Format..*387*
        Test Item Arrangement *387*
        Test Item Difficulty *388*
        Instructions.....................................*389*
    Written Test Types 390
        Multiple-Choice..................................*390*
        True-False *393*
        Matching...*396*
        Short-Answer/Completion *398*
        Essay..*399*
        Interpretative Exercises *401*
    Oral Tests...401
        Advantages.......................................*402*
        Disadvantages *402*
    Performance (Skills) Tests.........................402
        Advantages.......................................*405*
        Disadvantages *405*
Test Data Collection **405**
    Criterion-Referenced Grading System 406
    Scoring Methods 407
        Composite Scoring and Point Systems *407*
        Class Participation Rating Scale *407*
Test Item and Result Analyses....................**408**
    Validity and Reliability Components............408
    Statistical Test Result Analysis...................408

Test Item Analysis......................409
   Difficulty Index......................409
   Discrimination Index......................410
   Distracter Analysis......................410
Corrective Techniques 411
Summary **411**

17 Course and Evolution Management **415**
Transition Usage......................**415**
Discussion Management......................**417**
Discussion Format 418
Preparation Planning......................419
Large Group Discussions......................419
Small Group Discussions......................419
Techniques 420
Leadership Skills......................421
Training Evolution Management......................**421**
Incident Command System Duties and Functions 422
Incident Command System Components......................424
Evolution Planning 425
Multiagency Training Evolutions 426
Implementation 426
Supervision 426
Evaluation 427
Summary **428**

18 Administrative Duties......................**431**
Research Process **431**
Data Collection......................431
Information Sources 433
   Internet......................434
   Government Agencies......................436
   Libraries......................436
   Educational Institutions......................436
   Professional Organizations......................437
   Testing and Standards Organizations 438
   Vendors/Manufacturers 438
   Nonprofit Organizations 438
Validity 439
Reference Material Citations 439
Analysis Process **439**
Types 440
   Cost/Benefit......................440
   Process......................440
   Policy......................440
   Program......................440

   Needs 441
   Task 441
   Risk 441
Steps 441
Application 442
Budget Preparation and Development **442**
Budget Types......................443
   Capital 444
   Operating 444
Sources of Funds 444
   Grants/Gifts 445
   Fundraising 445
Budget Development Process 446
   Plan 446
   Prepare 446
   Implement 448
   Monitor 448
   Evaluate 449
   Revise 449
Purchasing Process **450**
Determine Needs 450
Conduct Research 451
   Survey Other Jurisdictions 452
   Review Manufacturers' Business Histories......................452
   Request References 452
   Review Standards and Regulations 452
   Review Industry Trends 452
   Compare Various Products......................456
   Determine Equipment Compatibility 453
   Review Purchasing Ordinances and Laws 453
   Develop Request for Proposal 453
Evaluate Equipment......................454
Review Product Data......................455
Conduct Purchasing Process......................455
   Determine Funding Sources 456
   Create Bid Specifications......................456
   Evaluate and Score Proposals......................457
   Award Purchase Contract 458
Evaluate and Revise the Process 458
Summary **458**

19 Supervision and Management **461**
Methods and Styles of Supervision......................**461**
Challenges 462
   Anticipating Problems 462
   Establishing and Communicating Goals and Objectives......................463

    Involving Employees in the Process 464
    Creating an Effective Team 464
    Creating Job Interest Within a Team 466
  Responsibilities 467
    Completing Tasks 467
    Building Teamwork and Cooperation 468
    Developing Skills 468
    Maintaining Positive Examples/Attitudes 469
    Maintaining Records and Reports 469
  Leadership Elements 469
Methods and Styles of Management **469**
  Functions 470
  Skills 470
Resource Scheduling **471**
  Determine Needs 472
  Determine Requirements 473
  Determine Availability 473
  Coordinate Training 474
  Create a Schedule 474
  Publish the Schedule 475
  Revise the Schedule 476
Summary **476**

Part D Instructor III Requirements

20 Administration: Records, Policies,
    and Personnel **479**
Records Management **480**
  System Types 481
  System Components 481
  Training Records 481
  Forms Development 484
Development of Training Policies **484**
  Policies 485
  Procedures and Guidelines 485
  Need for New Policy, Procedure,
    or Guideline 486
  Revision Process 487
  Adoption Process 488
    Identify Need 488
    Develop Draft Document 489
    Submit Draft for Review 489
    Adopt Document 490
    Publish Document 490
    Implement Document's Contents 490
    Evaluate Effectiveness 491
  Standards 491

Human Resources Management **493**
  Supervision 493
    Challenges 493
    Responsibilities 494
  Staff Selection 494
    Qualifications 495
    Position Advertising 496
    Internal/External Sources 496
    Recruitment and Training 496
    Applications and Interviews 496
    Employee Orientation 497
  Personnel Evaluations 497
    Characteristics 498
    Process 498
    Periodic Job-Performance Evaluations 499
    Feedback Evaluations: 360-Degree
      Concept 500
    Legal Considerations 500
Summary **500**

21 Analysis and Evaluation **503**
Analysis Process **503**
  Types 504
    Cost/Benefit 504
    Process 504
    Policy 504
    Program 505
    Need 505
    Task 505
    Risk 506
  Process Steps 507
  Application 507
Evaluation Process **508**
  General Methodology 508
    Evaluation Types 509
    Evaluation Methods 509
  Application Skills 510
    Organizations 510
    Programs 511
  Evaluation Plans 512
  Course and Instructional Design
    Evaluations 513
    Considerations for Planning 513
    Formative Evaluations 514
    Summative Evaluations
      (Reaction Surveys) 515
    Evaluation Results 516
Summary **517**

22 Program and Curriculum Development 521
Sample Planning Model 522
Training Program and Curriculum Design 523
    Identify Needs.......................................524
        Needs Analysis *524*
        Job Performance Requirements *525*
        Hierarchy of Work *526*
        Task Analysis.............................*527*
        Cost/Benefit Analysis *528*
    Select Goals, Objectives, and Resources........528
        Goals....................................*528*
        Objectives...............................*529*
        Resources................................*533*
    Design Curriculum/Course.......................533
        Group Similar Objectives *534*
        Develop Lesson Plans *534*
        Sequence Lessons into Courses *534*
        Sequence Courses into Curriculum *534*
        Create Evaluation Instruments............*537*
    Implement Curriculum/Course....................538
        Select Qualified Instructors.............*539*
        Create or Select Appropriate
          Training Aids *539*
        Present a Pilot of the Course *539*
    Evaluate Curriculum/Course 539
        Evaluate Course Materials................*540*
        Evaluate Instructor Performances.........*540*
Curriculum/Course Revision........................ 540
Summary 542

Appendices

A NFPA Job Performance Requirements (JPRs) with Chapter and Page References 545
B Leadership Styles 547
Leadership Traits...................................... 547
Behavioral Leadership 548
    Basic Leadership Style 548
    Two-Dimensional Leadership Style...............548
    Comtemporary Leadership Category............549

Situational Leadership................................ 550
    Leadership Continuum Model.....................550
    Situational Leadership Model 551
Principled Leadership................................. 552
C Instructor Resources 555
D Emergency Incident Casualty Statistics 557
E NIOSH Training Fatality Report: 2003 559
F Risk-Management Formulas 571
G Incident Command System Forms 573
H OSHA State-Plan States and Non-State-Plan States 589
I Training Organization Code of Ethics 591
J Structural Live-Fire Training Forms 593
K NIOSH Firefighter Fatality Report: 2005 601
L NIOSH/CDC Workplace Solutions Live-Fire Training Report............... 609
M NIOSH Training Fatality Report: 2002 613
N Sample Request for Proposal 623
O Equipment Evaluation Form........... 625
Glossary 631
Suggested Readings 649
Index 655

Preface

The seventh edition of the IFSTA **Fire and Emergency Services Instructor** manual is written to assist fire and emergency services personnel in meeting the job performance requirements (JPRs) of National Fire Protection Association (NFPA) 1041, *Standard for Fire Service Instructor Professional Qualifications* (2007). It provides the basic level of knowledge that is required for NFPA Level I, Level II, and Level III Fire and Emergency Services Instructors and instructor candidates.

It should be understood that this manual is the foundation for the education and certification of each instructor level and as professional development for personnel currently in those positions. Additional reading and course work are highly recommended for those instructors who aspire to the position of training division manager in the fire and emergency services organization.

Acknowledgement and special thanks are extended to the members of the IFSTA validation committee. The following members contributed their time, wisdom, and knowledge to the development of this manual:

IFSTA Fire and Emergency Services Instructor
7th Edition
Validation Committee

Chair
Randal E. Novak
Iowa Fire Service Training Bureau
Ames, Iowa

Secretary
Jeremy F. Donovan,
Central Florida Fire Academy
Orlando, Florida

Vice Chair
Gary Wilson,
Fire Rescue Training Institute
University of Missouri
Columbia, Missouri

Committee Members

Julie Coffman
Alabama Fire College
Tuscaloosa, Alabama

Dave Coombs
St. Helens, Oregon

Steven W. Edwards
Oklahoma State University
Stillwater, Oklahoma

Russell W. Emons
Connecticut Fire Academy
Windsor Locks, Connecticut

Stan Gibson
Coos Bay Fire and Rescue
Coos Bay, Oregon

George A. Jamieson
Oregon Department of Public Safety Standards and Training
Pendleton, Oregon

A. Byron Johnson, Ed.D.
Alexandria Fire Department
Alexandria, Louisiana

Wendy Johnson
Department of Defense Fire Academy
San Angelo, Texas

Lawrence P. McAndrews
Virginia Department of Fire Programs
Glen Allen, Virginia

Lawrence L. Preston
Maryland Fire and Rescue Institute
University of Maryland
College Park, Maryland

R. Peter Sells, SBStJ, BSc
Toronto Fire Services
Toronto, Ontario Canada

Scott Somers
Phoenix Fire Department
Phoenix, Arizona

The following individuals contributed their assistance and comments as reviewers for this manual:

Laura Agostini
City of Madison Fire Department
Madison, Wisconsin

Gloria Bizjak
Maryland Fire and Rescue Institute
University of Maryland
College Park, Maryland

Scott W. Carrigan
New Hampshire Fire Academy
Nashua, New Hampshire

Jim Eastman
Sacramento Metropolitan Fire District
Roseville, California

Darren Olquin
San Ramon Valley Fire Protection District
San Ramon, California

Chuck Tuggle
City of Orange Fire Department
Orange, California

Bill Vandevort
Northtree Fire International
Marina, California

The following individuals and organizations contributed information, photographs, and other assistance that made completion of this manual possible:

Alabama Fire College

Austin (TX) Fire Department

Dawn Beisner

Chris Browning

Jerry Burch

Central Florida Fire Academy

Cherry Hill (NJ) Fire Department

Ken Cochane, Oklahoma State University

Tim Cooper

Lubna Culbert

Wil Dane

U.S. Department of Defense

Karen Doerr

Bob Esposito

U.S. Federal Emergency Management Agency,
Photographers: Jocelyn Augustino, Michael
Rieger, Jason Parks, and Mark Wolf

Michael Graves

Andrew Haag

James Harrison

Iowa Fire Service Training Bureau

Elaine Johns, Oklahoma State University

Ed Kirtley, Oklahoma Fire Service Training

Kenneth Krulish, Jr.

Bill Lefkowitz

Louisiana State University, Fire and Emergency Training Institute

Mike Mallory

Maryland Fire and Rescue Institute

Skip Mason

Mesa (AZ) Fire Department

Chris Mickal

Rick Montemorra

Montgomery (AL) Fire Department

Oklahoma State University, Fire Service Training

Michael Regenhard

Jeff Sexton, Oklahoma State University

Stillwater (OK) Fire Department

City of Stillwater, Oklahoma

Dr. Jessica Stowell

Elias Tomlinson, Florida Bureau of Fire Standards and Training

Tulsa (OK) Fire Department

Virginia Department of Fire Programs

Additionally, gratitude is extended to the following members of the Fire Protection Publications **Fire and Emergency Services Instructor Project Team** whose contributions made the final publication of this manual possible:

Project Manager/Staff Liaison/Writer
Fred Stowell, Senior Technical Editor

Editor
Barbara Adams, Senior Editor

Technical Reviewers
Rachel Hutchinson, FPP Projects Coordinator
Jeff Fortney, Senior Technical Editor

Proofreaders
Cindy Brakhage, Senior Editor
Lynne Murnane, Senior Editor

Curriculum Development
Bill Robinson, Curriculum Coordinator
Beth Ann Fulgenzi, Curriculum Developer

FPP Photographer
Jeff Fortney, Senior Technical Editor

Production Manager
Don Davis

Illustrators and Layout Designers
Ann Moffat, Production Coordinator
Lee Shortridge, Senior Graphic Designer

IFSTA Projects
Craig Hannan, IFSTA Project Coordinator

Library Researchers
Susan F. Walker, Librarian
Shelly Magee, Assistant Librarian
Jenny Brock, Cataloger

Editorial Assistant
Tara Gladden

Introduction

Fire and emergency services instructors have traditionally provided vocational-type training for their organizations. Training subjects include basic skills taught to entry-level personnel as well as specialist-level and in-service training for current personnel. The authority having jurisdiction (AHJ), which may be local, state/provincial, or national, usually mandates the level and type of skills-based training that is required.

As fire and emergency services organizations have acquired additional duties and responsibilities and personnel have increased educational requirements, instructors have become increasingly responsible for providing academic knowledge. Instructors today provide both vocational skills training and adult education for personnel of their organizations as well as a larger audience that may include personnel from other organizations and citizens from the community.

The professional nature of a fire and emergency services instructor's function has been established not only by tradition but also by the development of a National Fire Protection Association (NFPA) professional qualifications standard, NFPA 1041, *Standard for Fire Service Instructor Professional Qualifications* (2007). This standard establishes the job performance requirements (JPRs) for all personnel of the fire service who are assigned to the training function. It also supports the company-level training requirements of Fire Officer Level I in NFPA 1021, *Standard for Fire Officer Professional Qualifications* (2003).

The 7th edition of the IFSTA **Fire and Emergency Services Instructor** manual contains learning objectives for each chapter that are related to the JPRs in NFPA 1041. A correlation between the learning objectives and the JPRs is contained in **Appendix A**, which also includes the page numbers in the manual that contain the information to meet the JPR.

Purpose and Scope

The *purpose* of **Fire and Emergency Services Instructor,** 7th Edition, is to provide personnel with basic information necessary to meet the JPRs of NFPA 1041 for Instructor Levels I, II, and III. In addition, company officer candidates who wish to meet the JPRs of NFPA 1021 Level I must also certify to Level I Instructor requirements.

The *scope* of the manual is to provide current fire and emergency services instructors and instructor candidates with basic instructional knowledge. This knowledge is necessary to develop skills for preparing and presenting training for personnel of fire and emergency services organizations through a variety of methods.

Fire and Emergency Services Training History

The history of the fire and emergency services in North America dates to the earliest colonial period. Then, as now, the majority of fire service personnel were volunteers who provided fire protection for the population in their communities. Career organizations emerged in the 1860s as communities attempted to respond to the growing threat of fires in highly congested areas that had multiple types of occupancies, which were constructed of or contained a variety of flammable materials.

In the early years, training was provided for new recruits by current personnel and sometimes took the form of *on-the-job* training where new recruits with little or no formal training responded to fires. By 1889, some large communities such as Boston, Massachusetts, established drill schools to provide basic training and company drills. Systematic training at fire colleges and state and provincial fire academies began in 1914 and continue to the present day.

The trend toward providing increasing levels of knowledge led to the establishment of the U.S. National Fire Academy (NFA) in Emmitsburg, Maryland, and numerous university-level degree programs in fire science and administration throughout North America. These degree programs include two-year associate degrees, four-year bachelor degrees, and postgraduate degree programs.

The NFPA professional qualification standard for instructors (1041) was originally written in the mid-1960s when minimum criteria for fire service instructor qualifications were established. The actual standard was adopted in 1976 and revised periodically until its most recent edition in 2007.

As part of the growth of fire and emergency services instruction, the International Fire Service Training Association (IFSTA) has worked to provide accurate and current training materials for firefighters and emergency responders. Beginning in 1934, IFSTA has held annual conferences of fire service representatives to determine training needs and create manuals and curriculum materials to satisfy those needs.

IFSTA manuals are based on the requirements set forth in the NFPA professional qualifications standards and other applicable standards. The manuals are validated by professionals in the appropriate field, representing management, emergency response, training, and prevention as well as associated government agencies and the private manufacturing sector of the profession.

Book Organization

This 7th edition of the IFSTA **Fire and Emergency Services Instructor** manual is divided into four parts to present information in a logical manner, starting with the basics and building on them. Part A (General Knowledge and Skills) provides information in the following areas that is essential to all three instructor levels:

- Challenges of fire and emergency services instruction
- Safety and the training function
- Legal and ethical considerations
- Effective interpersonal communication
- Instructional facilities and props
- Report writing and record keeping
- Principles of learning
- Student attributes and behaviors

Part B (Instructor I Requirements) provides instructor and officer candidates with the knowledge necessary to satisfy the requirements for Level I Instructors as defined in NFPA 1041 and includes basic information in the following areas:

- Preparation for instruction
- Instructional delivery
- Audiovisual technology
- Structured exercises, demonstrations, and practical training evolutions
- Student progress evaluation and testing

Current Level I Instructors will also find information in Part C (Instructor II Requirements) that satisfies the JPRs for Level II Instructors such as the following:

- Lesson plan development
- Instructor and course evaluations
- Student testing instruments
- Course and evolution management
- Administrative duties
- Supervision and management

Finally, Level III Instructor requirements may be satisfied by studying the information provided in Part D (Instructor III Requirements) that focuses on the following topics:

- Records, policies, and personnel
- Analysis and evaluation
- Program and curriculum development

Besides learning objectives, a chapter table of contents is included at the beginning of each chapter to assist the student in navigating the chapter and achieving the intended learning outcomes. Appendices contain additional examples of training documents and other valuable information.

A list of pertinent books and articles that provide additional information is found in the Suggested Readings at the end of the manual. A glossary of terms will also assist the student in the learning process.

The terms *Incident Command System (ICS)* and *Incident Management System (IMS)* have been and continue to be used interchangeably in the fire and emergency services in North America. In the U.S., the National Incident Management System (NIMS) uses the ICS term while the National Fire Service Incident Management System Consortium Model Procedures Committee uses the IMS term. For all practical purposes, ICS and IMS mean the same thing in terms of command and control of an emergency incident. The IFSTA **Instructor** manual validation committee chose to use the ICS terminology because of its inclusion in the NIMS model.

Overview of Instructor Functions

While it is acknowledged that the majority of fire and emergency services personnel will only be interested in the information provided for Level I Instructor JPRs (Parts A and B), all instructor candidates and current instructors are encouraged to read the information in Parts C and D also. These parts provide information that will be useful to them in their day-to-day training activities. Each level has distinct duties and responsibilities as defined by NFPA 1041, including the following:

- *Level I Instructor* — Fire service instructor who delivers instruction from a prepared lesson plan. *Other responsibilities:*
  — Assembles course materials
  — Uses instructional aids and evaluation tools
  — Reviews and adapts lesson plans to meet the needs of individual students, groups, and the AHJ

— Organizes the teaching environment to maximize the learning experience and provide a safe learning environment
— Presents a lesson from a prepared lesson plan, adjusting the presentation as required to ensure that objectives are attained
— Prepares and maintains training records in accordance with the requirements of the jurisdiction

- *Level II Instructor* — Fire service instructor who has satisfied the Instructor I professional qualifications and has the knowledge and ability to develop individual lesson plans for a specific topic, learning objectives, instructional aids, and evaluation instruments. *Other responsibilities:*
  — Manages instructional resources, including facilities, personnel, time, funds, and records
  — Schedules training sessions based on overall training plans of the AHJ
  — Supervises and coordinates the activities of other instructors
  — Evaluates subordinate instructors
  — Develops instructional materials, including the creation of lesson plans and modification of existing lesson plans
  — Develops student, course, and instructor evaluation instruments
  — Analyzes the results of student evaluations to determine test validity

- *Level III Instructor* — Fire service instructor who has satisfied the Instructor II professional qualifications and has demonstrated the knowledge and ability to develop comprehensive training programs, curriculums, and courses for use by single or multiple organizations. *Other responsibilities:*
  — Administers organizational/agency policy and procedures
  — Administers training records system
  — Selects training staff
  — Creates instructor evaluation plan
  — Conducts organizational needs analyses

— Develops training goals and implementation strategies

— Creates or modifies programs, curriculums, and courses required to fulfill the organization's training needs

— Creates a program evaluation plan

Importance of Instruction and Training

Officers and personnel of fire and emergency services organizations often face potentially life-threatening conditions and must react to those conditions quickly, effectively, and safely. The safety of these personnel and citizens who rely on them depends on the quality of training and instruction that they receive through their organizations.

Providing high-quality training and instruction is critical for successfully meeting the mission of all fire and emergency services organizations: protecting the community from hazards that create risks to life and property. Success lies in the ability of personnel to meet citizens' needs in an effective, efficient, and safe manner. Personnel must be proficient in all the skills required to meet these needs.

The fire and emergency services instructor's job is to prepare personnel to provide the services required by citizens of the community or service area. The instructor candidate and the current instructor will find the necessary information to fulfill these requirements in this manual. Effective training is accomplished when instructors take the following actions:

• Ensure the safety of personnel who must meet the requirements and demands of the organization.

• Educate personnel so that their activities can provide effective services to external customers (citizens), the community, and the service area.

• Motivate personnel to achieve their best performance while engaged in the mission of the organization.

• Provide challenges for personnel in training activities by teaching them how to select the right people with the right tools and equipment for given situations and perform the organization's requirements.

• Reduce organizational and personal liability through well-planned training programs that follow accepted standards and develop skilled personnel.

• Promote the creation and maintenance of training programs by developing policy recommendations to support new and ongoing training programs.

• Provide the organization's administrators with unbiased reports and well-supported evaluations, conclusions, and recommendations for training programs.

• Encourage organizational self-assessment by developing evaluation plans that measure training objectives and meet organizational policies.

• Create evaluation plans for course improvement that include student input for evaluating instructors, course components, and facilities.

• Provide training to meet the requirements found in federal, state/provincial, and local mandates based on hazards, risks, and threats.

• Continue personal training and education to ensure that the most accurate and current information is delivered.

Key Information

Various types of information in this book are given in shaded boxes marked by symbols or icons. See the following examples:

Sidebar: Obsolete Terms and Their Replacements

Fireman ⟶ Firefighter

Manpower ⟶ Personnel or Staffing

To Man ⟶ To Staff

Nozzleman ⟶ Nozzle Operator

Ladderman ⟶ Firefighter

Information: Executive Summary Example

Because of the increasing demand on the training division to provide recertification courses, mandated specialized training, and entry-level training, it is necessary to implement changes in the training system. Our plan involves performing the following procedures:

- Adding two full-time instructors
- Altering training schedules

Implementing these recommendations will allow the training division to meet the increased demand for training.

Case Study: Instructor Behaviors, Personality, and Effectiveness

You can recall instructors who were *good,* whose classes you enjoyed, and who made you feel like you learned something. You can also likely recall instructors whose classes or teaching techniques were so boring you dreaded attending, but you had to because it was a certification or promotion requirement.

List and discuss characteristics that you think instructors should practice and exhibit that help in presenting instruction effectively. Listing characteristics is easy. Now, discuss ways in which instructors can achieve effectiveness.

Case History: Career Lieutenant and Firefighter Die In a Flashover During a Live-Fire Training Evolution

On July 30, 2002, a 32-year-old male career lieutenant (Victim No. 1) and a 20-year-old male career firefighter (Victim No. 2) died while participating in a live-fire training evolution. A flashover occurred several minutes after the fire had been lit in the vacant acquired structure while both of the victims were performing a simulated search and rescue exercise.

Key Information or Tip: Effective Versus Efficient

Although the terms *effective* and *efficient* are sometimes used interchangeably, they have two separate and distinct meanings as follows:

- **Effective** — Something produces the desired result or meets its intended purpose, which could be considered *doing the right thing*.
- **Efficient** — Results are produced with a minimum of effort, waste, or expense; that is, the minimum cost for the maximum effect.

Three key signal words are found in the text: **WARNING, CAUTION,** and **NOTE.** Definitions and examples of each are as follows:

- **WARNING** indicates information that could result in death or serious injury to fire and emergency services personnel. See the following example:

WARNING!
Live-fire training must adhere to the requirements set forth in NFPA 1403, *Standard on Live Fire Training Evolutions* (2002).

- **CAUTION** indicates important information or data that fire and emergency services responders need to be aware of in order to perform their duties safely. See the following example:

CAUTION
Fire and emergency service responders must be familiar with the physiological, emotional, and technological limitations caused by the use of respiratory protection equipment to prevent injury or death.

- **NOTE** indicates important operational information that helps explain why a particular recommendation is given or describes optional methods for certain procedures. See the following example:

NOTE: This information is based on research performed by the International City/County Managers Association, Inc.

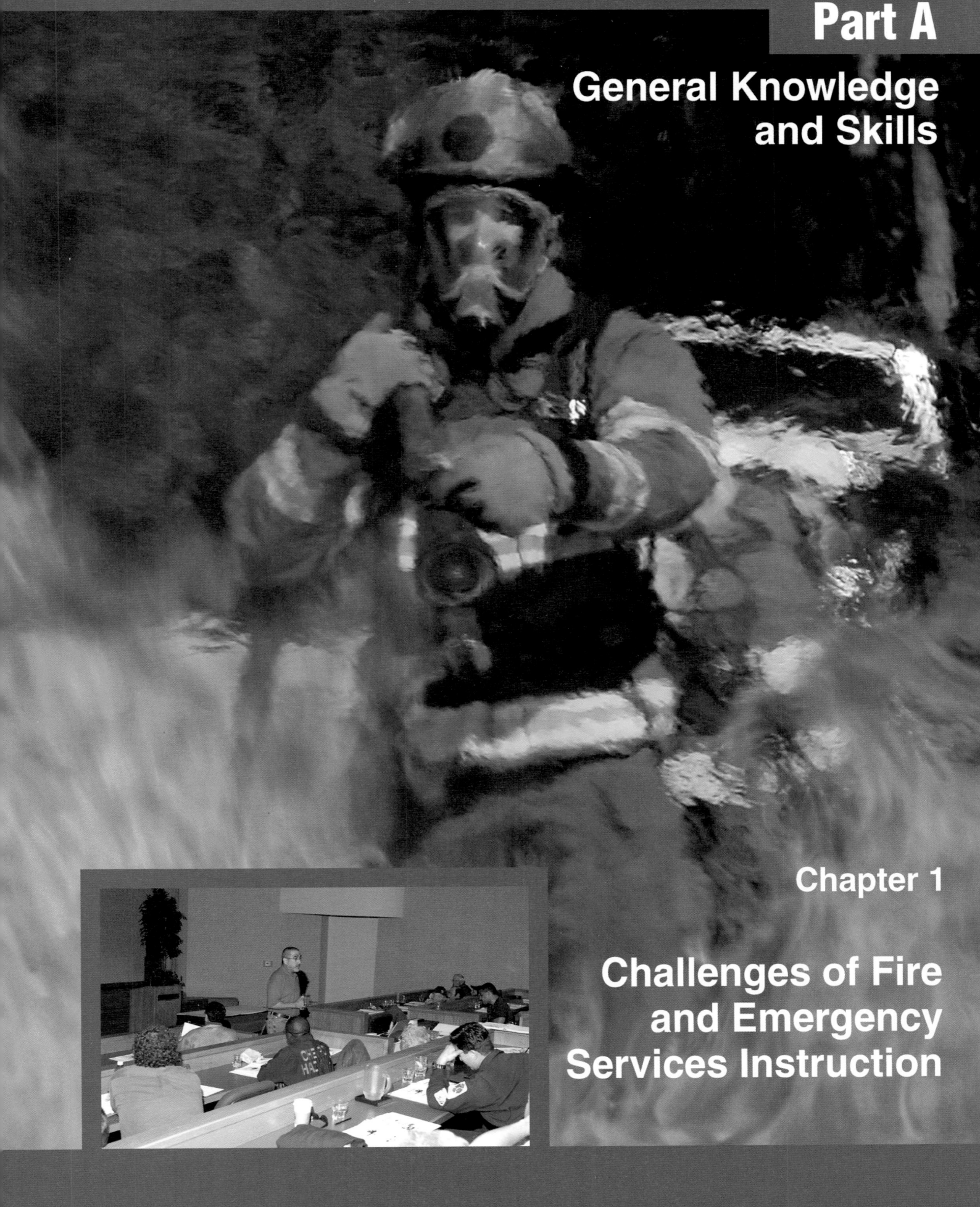

Part A

General Knowledge and Skills

Chapter 1

Challenges of Fire and Emergency Services Instruction

After reading this chapter, students will be able to —

1. Identify obligations of fire and emergency services instructors to students, the organization, the profession, and themselves.

2. Identify accurate statements about ways that the instructor serves as a role model for students.

3. List characteristics of effective instructors.

4. Compare positive and negative teaching traits that can affect student impressions of instructors.

5. Identify solutions to challenges that instructors must meet.

6. Distinguish between the dos and don'ts involved in performing analyses, evaluating instructional facilities and props, managing diversity issues, identifying legal requirements and accommodations, and recognizing audience characteristics.

Chapter Contents

Instructor Obligations
    To Students
    To the Organization
    To the Profession
    To Themselves

Instructor as Role Model

Effective Instructor Characteristics

Teaching Traits to Emphasize
    Honesty Versus Bluffing
    Sincerity Versus Sarcasm

    Solutions Versus Complaints
    Postive Humor Versus Offensive Humor

Instructor Challenges

Instructor Reference Checklist
    Analyses
    Instructional Facilities, Props, and
      Acquired Structures
    Diversity Issues
    Legal Requirements and Accommodations
    Audience Recognition

Summary

Chapter 1
Challenges of Fire and Emergency Services Instruction

The training function is basic to all fire and emergency services organizations. It ensures that all organizational personnel conduct emergency and nonemergency operations in a safe, effective, efficient, and consistent manner. Ensuring that personnel attain the proper level of proficiency requires that they receive both education and training in their professions.

The terms *education* and *training* are often used interchangeably in fire and emergency services organizations; however, they have different meanings. *Education* is generally accepted as meaning the acquisition of knowledge, usually through academic means such as college or university courses. *Training* is primarily the transfer of knowledge regarding vocational or technical skills. Training is usually provided by one of the following entities:

- Fire and emergency services organizations' training divisions

- State/provincial, regional, or national training academies

- Vocational/technical schools

Generally, the organization's training division is the responsibility of a chief officer (Level III certification described in NFPA 1021, *Standard for Fire Officer Professional Qualifications*), although a company officer (Level II) may be assigned the duty. The officer in charge of the training division, especially in a newly formed organization, must perform the following tasks:

- Evaluate training requirements.

- Develop a training program.

- Determine funding sources.

- Determine alternative training sources.

- Evaluate training program results.

Training Function

No single term is universally used to describe the training function within fire and emergency services organizations. Some of the more popular ones are as follows:

- Training office
- Training bureau
- Training division
- Training branch
- Training section
- Training unit
- Training agency
- Training

For the purpose of clarity, this manual refers to the unit that provides training internally as the *training division*. State/provincial, regional, and national training units are referred to by their official title or as the *training agency*.

Curriculum and lesson plan development and course content delivery to recruits and organizational personnel are responsibilities of training officers or instructors under the supervision of the officer in charge of the training division. In jurisdictions that have adopted National Fire Protection Association (NFPA) standards, the instructors must meet the job performance requirements (JPRs) established in NFPA 1041, *Standard for Fire Service Instructor Professional Qualifications* (2007). Non-NFPA compliant organizations should consider meeting these requirements as accepted industry practices.

As indicated in the Introduction, this manual provides information that guides instructor candidates toward becoming effective Level I certified instructors. It also provides the basic knowledge that allows current Level I instructors to advance through Level II and Level III certification criteria. Part A of this manual, which consists of eight chapters, focuses on knowledge that is essential to all instructor levels.

All fire and emergency services instructors have a variety of obligations, including obligations to students, the fire and emergency services organization, the fire and emergency services profession, and themselves. This chapter discusses those obligations as well as the following topics:

- Instructor as role model
- Effective instructor characteristics
- Teaching traits to emphasize
- Instructor challenges
- Instructor reference checklist

Instructor Obligations

Unlike some professions, fire and emergency services instructors are actually professionals in two areas: First, they are teachers for students in both internal and external classes. Internally they are providers of *adult education,* a specialized area of the teaching profession. Externally, they are providers of a variety of topics that constitute *public education.* These topics are as varied as the audiences being taught. Second, instructors are members of the fire and emergency services profession. They must be able to apply the same knowledge and skills that they teach to their students at emergency incidents on a daily basis. This knowledge has been developed over years of experience in the profession.

Thus instructors carry twice the burden of being both teacher and practitioner. However, this situation is also a benefit because it increases the base knowledge that they teach from and their credibility with their students.

Instructors are professionals who meet a standard that is *not* based on working for pay or volunteering time but rather on a high level of personal performance. They are individuals who have developed knowledge and skills as well as practical experience in a variety of subjects related to fire and emergency services operations **(Figure 1.1)**.

Figure 1.1 Fire and emergency services instructors must have the knowledge and experience that qualifies them to teach both new recruits and experienced personnel. *Courtesy of Alabama Fire College.*

As professionals in these two areas, instructors need to possess characteristics that are associated with those professions. They must understand the meaning of the term *profession:* calling or vocation that requires specialized knowledge and long, intense preparation that includes (1) learning scientific, historical, or scholarly principles that apply to specific skills, processes, and methods; (2) maintaining high standards of personal achievement and conduct; and (3) committing to continued study and educational advancement—all with the prime purpose of providing a public service.

Fire and emergency services instructors certainly meet these criteria for members of a profession. Along with the requirements inherent with the teaching profession, there are also obligations for instructors to students, the organization, the profession, and themselves.

To Students

The instructor's primary obligation is to the student. This obligation requires the instructor to focus on the needs and abilities of students at all times. To satisfy this obligation, the instructor must provide information that is current, accurate, and specific to students' needs. Information that satisfies students' needs is easier to learn and retain.

The instructor must also plan, develop, and deliver training that is appropriate for students. Appropriate training ensures that students are able to meet the adopted performance standards established by the authority having jurisdiction (AHJ). The instructor must also measure the student's knowledge and skills based on valid criteria and consistency both before and after training occurs. Included in this instructor obligation are the following responsibilities:

- Perform job-related task analyses.

- Evaluate training programs effectiveness based on student feedback and performance.

- Provide feedback to students on their accomplishments and to supervisors and management on training program results.

Student feedback on course and program results and student performance is important for future curriculum planning and development as well as procedural changes and equipment purchases. Formal, informational feedback to students in the form of grades, assessments, or performance evaluations is important because the information will be used by students as guides for altering study habits, improving testing skills, preparing for lessons, and, most importantly, transferring learning to job performance (**Figures 1.2 a and b**).

In addition to planning, developing, and delivering student-appropriate courses, an instructor must meet the expectations of students in the following ways:

- Be an effective communicator and a good listener.

- Present new knowledge and skills in a positive manner.

- Be a role model, mentor, and counselor.

These multiple challenges are not always easy to manage; yet the instructor must be able to perform effectively in all of these areas in order to meet student expectations. A detailed discussion of communication skills may be found in Chapter 4, Effective Interpersonal Communication.

Finally, safety is the most important obligation that an instructor has to the student. The instructor emphasizes safety in the following ways:

- Provide a safe training environment.

- Teach safe operational practices and safety-related topics.

- Fulfill the duties of an incident safety officer (ISO) during training evolutions (**Figure 1.3, p. 12**).

- Provide a role model by personally adhering to the safety policies and practices of the organization.

Each of these important safety topics is discussed in Chapter 2, Safety and the Training Function. Instructors should remember that safety

Figures 1.2 a and b Skills that are learned and perfected during training must be transferable to the emergency scene. (a) Students learn vehicle extrication skills under the supervision of qualified instructors. (b) At an emergency incident, the skills are applied to remove a trapped victim. *Courtesy of Bob Esposito.*

Figure 1.3 Instructors often perform incident safety officer duties during live-fire and high-risk training exercises.

must always be emphasized to students in such a way that they will continually apply safe practices throughout their careers.

To the Organization

Because the fire and emergency services field is a dynamic, powerful, and constantly changing profession, instructors must monitor changes and apply them to the needs of the organization. Change may be caused by the following factors:

- Revisions in standards and laws

- Improvements in equipment

- Updates in protocols and procedures

- Constant turnover of personnel due to retirements, transfers, or promotions

Change requires constant reevaluation of training programs and personnel performance requirements. Instructors have multiple roles in this changing environment. They research, observe, and participate in the planning, development, and implementation of training programs and curriculums by their organizations and other organizations in similar fields. An instructor may be in a position to contribute in the following ways:

- Plan interorganizational programs and training sessions that broaden knowledge and skills for many levels of fire and emergency services personnel.

- Enhance cooperation and understanding through interagency training.

- Ensure that current professional standards are adopted and applied.

- Teach to meet organizational goals.

In addition, an instructor is also obligated to provide the organization with the best-trained personnel possible. This obligation begins with the recruit or entry-level training courses. An instructor may be responsible for providing only one skill or lesson or the entire training curriculum. At the same time, the audience may consist of just one student or an entire class of students from a variety of organizations from across the state/province, region, or nation. Students may be learning a new topic, taking a course for certification, or developing mastery.

To satisfy this obligation, an instructor must provide high-quality information and then evaluate the student's ability to understand, retain, and apply the knowledge. The result is a well-trained workforce for the organization.

Finally, an instructor is obligated to act in an ethical manner at all times. An instructor provides an example of the quality of personal integrity that an organization expects from every member. This example is displayed not only to the organization's internal students but also to the community when an instructor provides training to residents of the service area. Ethical conduct and decision-making skills are based on strong personal morals and values and the ability to apply logic.

Many organizations have written codes of ethical conduct, including the International Association of Fire Chiefs (IAFC) and individual fire and emergency services organizations. An example of a code of ethics that is applicable to instructors is located in Chapter 3, Legal and Ethical Considerations.

To the Profession

The fire and emergency services have a long history of dedicated service to society. The image of a firefighter or emergency responder *going in harm's way* to rescue or aid a fellow human is deeply ingrained into the minds of most people in North America. Whether that image is based on a Currier and Ives print of firefighters racing on foot to a raging fire in the 1800s or the photo of three firefighters raising the U.S. flag in the ruins of the World Trade Center in New York City, fire and emergency responders and their profession are symbols of heroism and self-sacrifice.

As a member of the fire and emergency services, an instructor has an obligation to sustain that image and more. An instructor is the link to the heritage and tradition of the emergency services and provides a new recruit with an example of that heritage and tradition at work. Thus, an instructor is obligated to maintain a higher standard of professionalism than most members of the emergency services. Instructors must always maintain that high level in the following ways:

- Use sound judgment and logic in the decision-making process.

- Apply ethical and moral principles to their actions.

- Adhere to all laws, standards, protocols, and rules that apply to them and their profession.

This image must be present not only during training but also in everyday life. Citizens of the community or service area judge the organization and the fire and emergency services profession by the actions of each member both on and off duty. It is essential that instructors present positive and professional images to the public.

To Themselves

As is the case with any profession, instructors have personal and internal obligations to themselves, which include the obligation to live by a set of ethical and moral standards that are accepted by society. In addition, instructors have an obligation to continue professional development through the acquisition of knowledge and improvement of skills. Because the fire and emergency services profession is constantly changing, instructors must always

be aware of new improvements or developments. Competent instructors look for opportunities to learn and improve their professional, technical, and instructional skills (**Figures 1.4 a and b**).

Continuing education contributes to learning and expands an instructor's professional abilities and credibility in the following ways:

Figures 1.4 a and b Instructors must remain current on changes, trends, and advances in their profession. This requirement may be accomplished through (a) self-study and (b) attendance at workshops and conferences. *(a) Courtesy of Maryland Fire and Rescue Institute (MFRI).*

- Maintain instructor skills by teaching classes and seminars or facilitating discussion groups and workshops.

- Belong to professional organizations.

- Maintain a network with other instructors through local, state/provincial, or national/international instructor associations.

- Earn professional certification at the appropriate instructor level.

- Maintain management skills such as those used in fire command and supervision by attending professional development seminars and reading professional journals.

- Maintain technical skills such as those used in emergency management, fireground operations, hazardous materials incidents, rescue situations, and emergency medical services (EMS) operations through drills, workshops, and other continuing-education programs.

- Develop the ability to use constructive criticism as a learning tool rather than personal indictment of a student's abilities or personality.

- Develop an open-minded willingness to listen to and consider the ideas of others before coming to a conclusion.

The fire and emergency services organization may have adopted certification standards that require instructors to pursue a minimum number of hours of continuing education. It is a responsibility of instructors to fulfill those requirements. Instructors who apply these methods of personal growth are valuable assets to the organizations that hire them and students who learn from them **(Figure 1.5)**.

Instructor Tip: Broaden Instructional Background

For a broader instructional background, ask to observe or volunteer to serve on planning and development committees. These experiences provide insight into training program needs and requirements, planning and budget processes, and decision-making methods.

Figure 1.5 Instructors must be actively involved in the learning process, take pride in their professional achievements, and take an interest in the accomplishments of their students.

Instructor as Role Model

Fire and emergency service instructors have opportunities to positively influence the actions and ideas of personnel, beginning with new entry-level personnel or recruits and continuing through all the ranks and levels of the organization. By their leadership abilities, knowledge, attitudes, actions, and examples, instructors influence student performance. This influence goes beyond the classroom by providing students with a role model after whom they can pattern their own lives.

As fire and emergency services personnel practice what they learn, they reflect the level of their instructors' knowledge, experience, positive values, interest, influence, and motivation. An important part of being an instructor is to be a role model that influences students in a positive way **(Figure 1.6)**.

Figure 1.6 By following and enforcing safety policies, the instructor provides a positive and influential role model for students.

An instructor is the first official representative of the fire and emergency services organization with whom a new recruit has an extended relationship. This instructor is a role model for new students and influences their learning experiences. Instructors are highly visible to the students who observe them to determine whether they actually do what they are telling others to do. Therefore, an instructor must always act as a positive role model for students. Instructors' actions must always reflect professionalism and demonstrate their attitudes towards students, training, the organization, and the fire and emergency services profession.

An instructor communicates the performance expectations of the organization to the student through training situations and learning experiences. Training that meets the mission statement of the organization is essential. The organization cannot meet its mission without well-trained personnel who are products of effective, committed, and professional instructors.

Instructor Tip: Observe Other Instructors

At every opportunity, observe other instructors in their roles of planning, developing, teaching, and working with others. Ask questions of other instructors to discover why they use certain methods. Determine what methods of organization, persuasion, and teaching seem most effective after observing, questioning, and comparing many instructors and then begin to adapt to those methods.

In this unique position of role model, it is essential that instructors are effective communicators. Basic communication skills include the application of knowledge through interpersonal, oral, and written communications. *Interpersonal* skills are those used to interact with other people on an individual and small-group basis. It requires an understanding of how people communicate, how they develop communication skills, and how they listen and respond to other people. Listening is a key part of interpersonal communication. An instructor's interest and skill in listening and transmitting ideas among all levels of personnel are important assets to the communication process.

Oral communication involves much more than simply speaking in the classroom. It includes developing a central idea, preparing, practicing, and delivering a speech or presentation. Oral communication includes creating dialogue with and among students so that they may learn and share their needs, experiences, ideas, issues, debates, arguments, attitudes, and beliefs. Finally, the instructor must be effective in *written* communication that involves the writing of letters, memos, electronic mail (e-mail), reports, and lesson plans.

Effective communication skills support the development of the instructor as a role model plus provide the communication examples that students may follow. Chapter 4, Effective Interpersonal Communication, discusses the basics of the communication model as it pertains to interpersonal skills. Oral and written communication skills are beyond the scope of this manual but may be obtained in the appropriate college-level courses.

Effective Instructor Characteristics

Generally, role models have certain characteristics that inspire people to follow their examples. Most people can remember role models who had profound influences on their lives or educational experiences. Certainly, fire and emergency services instructors themselves are no exception. They have had teachers or instructors who influenced them by stimulating interest and creating motivation.

By recognizing the characteristics of the teachers or instructors who were most effective in stimulating and facilitating the learning experience, new instructors can adopt those same qualities to develop or improve their own teaching skills. Some characteristics that effective instructors possess include the following:

- Leadership abilities
- Strong interpersonal skills **(Figure 1.7)**
- Subject and teaching competencies
- Desire to teach
- Enthusiasm
- Motivation
- Preparation and organization
- Ingenuity, creativity, and flexibility
- Empathy
- Conflict-resolution skills
- Fairness
- Personal integrity

Leadership Abilities

Effective instructors must be effective leaders. An effective instructor leads or guides students through the requirements, knowledge, and skills of a class while ensuring that the needs of each student are met. This instructor provides appropriate learning opportunities, examples, and ideas and encourages students to discuss, think, and come to an appropriate conclusion. An instructor who is a good leader enables students to take the lead in appropriate learning situations.

Figure 1.7 One of the characteristics of an effective instructor is the ability to apply interpersonal communication skills. *Courtesy of Jocelyn Augustino, photographer, U. S. Federal Emergency Management Agency.*

An effective instructor also knows when to follow. Instructors are followers within the organization. Although they may *not* have a direct influence on guiding policy-making decisions, instructors always follow and promote the organization's goals, objectives, and administrative policies and procedures.

Instructors should study the various leadership models that have been developed over the past century and determine the most appropriate model or style for them, the instructional situation, and the students. Three leadership styles that have been defined through research — *autocratic*, *democratic*, and *laissez-faire* — can be placed on a continuum or line between two extremes (see key information box).

Balanced Leader Continuum

Autocratic	Democratic	Laissez-Faire
Controlling	Minimal control	No control
Makes all decisions	Involves students	Makes no decisions
Work-oriented	Balanced concerns	People-oriented

The extremes of the leadership continuum line are autocratic on one end and laissez-faire on the other. Instructors will find themselves at various points along this line throughout their careers and even on any given work day in their lives. To be a *balanced leader* means to approach leadership from a moderate or centered point on the line.

The balanced leader is concerned with getting the work accomplished while considering the needs, safety, and concerns of students. Therefore, the leader involves students in the decision-making process and allows them to work with minimum supervision when it is appropriate. This type of leadership fosters respect and trust within the student group.

Democratic leadership also implies that a situational-leadership model can be a valuable tool that permits an instructor to vary the amount of leadership required based on the situation and ability of students. See **Appendix B,** Leadership Styles.

Instructors lead by example; therefore, instructors *never* ask students to do anything that they themselves have not done or would not do. This example also means that instructors follow the rules, regulations, policies, and procedures of the organization and apply them fairly and evenly to all students and other members of the organization. Decisions must be based on accurate information and able to withstand the application and scrutiny of logic.

Finally, the examples set by instructors must be ethical and based on the values, beliefs, and morals of the individual, the organization, and society. Additional leadership qualities of an effective instructor include the following:

- *Self-confidence* — People's self-images contribute to the images others have of them. Self-confidence is developed thorough self-examination and having a clear appraisal of oneself.

- *Trustworthiness* — Subordinates must be able to trust the decisions made by the leader. This trust is based on the leader's experience and the experience subordinates have had with the leader.

- *Consistency* — Leaders must be consistent in decisions, actions, and relationships.

- *Responsibility* — Leaders must accept responsibility for the outcome of decisions and actions. Ultimate responsibility cannot be delegated.

- *Acceptance* — Leaders must accept limitations (whether personal, situational, or political) that cannot be overcome. Accepting that a solution may *not* be available and then working with the next best alternative requires flexibility on the leader's part.

- *Expertise* — Skills and abilities that are based on knowledge and experience are essential to command presence. Attempting to bluff through a situation can result in unacceptable loss of credibility.

Strong Interpersonal Skills

Instructors must have strong interpersonal skills that include clarity, sensitivity, and fairness. *Clarity* involves the ability to precisely and clearly explain concepts and processes through a systematic presentation of material. An instructor presents the material in such a way that students can easily understand. Summarization often adds clarity to a presentation. Information is summarized at the end of each section. When students do *not* understand the material, the instructor must be able to restate the concept in a style that students will understand.

Sensitivity is the ability to view the learning environment from the student perspective and recognize the barriers to learning and communication. Sensitivity involves having a personal interest in students.

Instructors must be *fair and impartial* to all students, open-minded, and willing to hear, consider, and discuss ideas with them (**Figure 1.8, p. 18**). In particular, instructors must be able to listen to and understand the needs of students.

Instructors must also be able to apply interpersonal skills when dealing with other instructors, staff members, supervisors, and the public. These skills enable instructors to work well with other people. They must be able to develop relationships that are built on mutual respect, rapport, and confidence.

Figure 1.8 The instructor must have a desire to understand the needs of students and the ability to work with them individually. *Courtesy of Iowa Fire Service Training Bureau.*

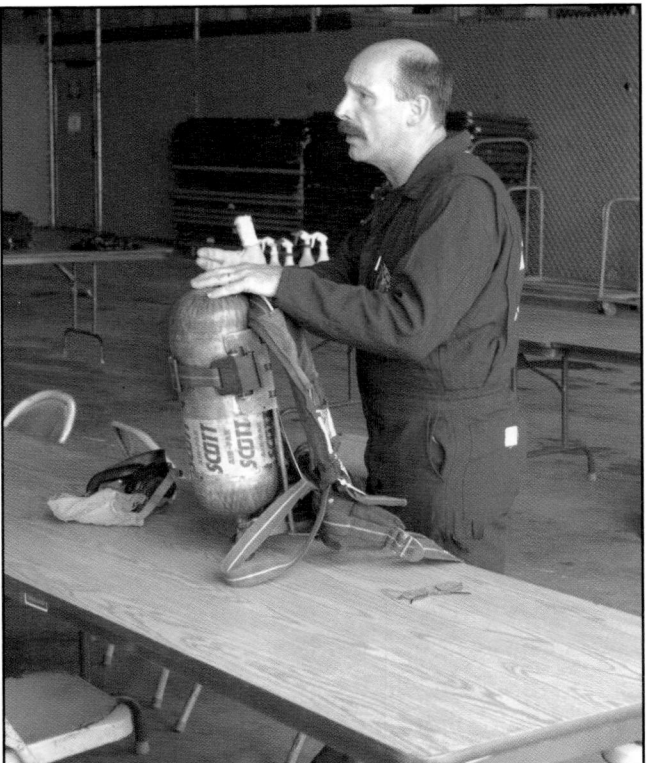

Figure 1.9 An effective instructor must have the ability to present technical information that all students will understand. This ability requires strong communication skills and an understanding of the learning process.

Subject and Teaching Competencies

Instructors must have the background knowledge and experience to teach a subject and its skills, and they must have the ability to transfer that knowledge and experience to others. Because learning is a lifelong process, it does *not* stop with the end of a class or completion of a degree program. Instructors must continually seek to increase their knowledge and skills in technical subject matter and educational methodology. They must be open-minded and attempt to learn and understand alternative methods and ideas. It is important to maintain and add to skill ability and knowledge so that these concepts may be transmitted to students.

Instructors cannot effectively or convincingly teach new skills or policies when they themselves have *not* learned them or remained current with changes. Instructors can renew professional and career abilities, maintain skills, and improve instructional methods through continuing education and professional development so they may continue to interest and motivate students and coworkers. A responsible instructor seeks opportunities to continually improve and maintain certification requirements **(Figure 1.9)**.

Desire to Teach

Instructors can improve teaching skills only through experience, study, and professional development. Unless they have a desire to teach, no amount of knowledge and experience can make them effective instructors. Possessing a desire to teach affects performance and motivation, which contribute to success in the classroom and on the job.

Enthusiasm

Enthusiasm is contagious! Instructors can generate enthusiasm in both students and administrators alike when they show a high degree of interest in a subject and teaching it, in students and the outcomes of their progress, and in the success of the training course. Enthusiasm is created through the following expressions:

- Lively and varied vocal delivery
- High energy levels
- Obvious love of teaching and the subject matter

When the educational experience becomes fun and exciting, students' willingness to participate increases. As a result, administrators will be more supportive of instructor and curriculum needs.

Motivation

Instructors must have the motivation, desire, and determination to achieve goals and stimulate that desire in their students. Instructors must show students that they are motivated to help each individual learn by giving each of them every opportunity to do so. Some of the ways instructors can motivate others are as follows:

- Clearly communicate what must be performed and how it must be performed.
- Show students the importance of the presented information.
- Make the knowledge and skills easy to understand and learn.
- Allow for mistakes as students practice and improve.
- Encourage students as they attempt to learn.
- Reward successful attempts.
- Correct unsuccessful attempts without criticism.

Effective instructors are also motivators who communicate instructional concepts and are enthusiastic about the mission of the organization. Effective instructors strive to create this same level of vision and enthusiasm within the organization. When an instructor has succeeded in creating this type of environment, then that individual will be a successful leader. The environment created by this approach to leading people has positive effects on individuals, students, training programs, and the collective results achieved by the organization.

Preparation and Organization

Like the time-honored Boy Scouts' motto, instructors must *be prepared*. Preparation involves being *organized*. Together these two elements are accomplished through detailed course outlines, established course objectives, defined evaluation procedures, and preparation for each class session. Before a class session, instructors prepare in the following ways:

- Assemble all materials, handouts, audio or visual materials, props, and equipment in the classroom or training area.
- Test equipment for proper operation, ensure that replacement parts (as needed) are available, and prepare alternative plans.
- Eliminate learning barriers such as audible and visual distractions, uncomfortable environmental temperatures, and poor lighting.
- Arrive at least 30 minutes before the start of any training course and probably 45 minutes to an hour when it is the first time teaching in a particular classroom or location.

Instructors must also practice their presentations to determine whether sufficient time and materials have been allocated for the topic. A well-organized and prepared instructor is also one who can manage time efficiently. This requirement is particularly important when it is necessary to develop lesson plans for a new course or topic **(Figure 1.10)**.

Figure 1.10 Effective instructors take the time to prepare for every lecture and presentation. Preparation includes becoming familiar with a variety of audiovisual equipment.

Ingenuity, Creativity, and Flexibility

An effective instructor understands that a teaching or learning technique suitable for one student or group of students may *not* be suitable for another. Instructors can demonstrate *ingenuity* and *creativity* by developing or using various training aids and supplemental materials and discovering and using innovative means of presenting information to meet the needs of every student. They must also be *flexible* and able to alter the training process quickly when there are changes in the environment, props, equipment, or size of the class.

Empathy

Empathy is the ability to understand the feelings and attitudes of another person. Instructors must be able to put themselves *in the shoes* of others and understand the students' points of view, opinions, problems, or challenges. Empathetic instructors have a sincere desire to help individuals learn, are *not* condescending or punitive, and do *not* act superior or threatening. Having empathy is especially important when working with students who have learning difficulties.

Conflict-Resolution Skills

There are occasions when an instructor must act to resolve conflict between students and the organization and between students themselves. Instructors may have to resolve disputes in the following situations:

- In the class
- On evaluations and tests
- With many types of personalities and responsibilities
- On a variety of other issues that may arise during the course

In these situations, an instructor listens to both sides and suggests solutions and may have to assist both sides in formulating a solution without showing preference for a particular side of the issue. An instructor must work to create win-win situations and relationships between all parties.

Fairness

Adults have often told their children that *life is not fair*. That concept, however, does *not* relieve people, and especially instructors, from applying fairness in their duties and relationships with others. *Being fair* means treating all students equally, providing the same learning opportunities, and evaluating the performance against an established objective standard and *not* against a subjective set of results. When students perceive that an instructor is biased against them or favors another student, the instructor's credibility will be damaged. Instructors must always be fair and open in their dealings with students.

Personal Integrity

Personal integrity is based on the values and morals of the individual. It can be stated as a personal code of ethics that provides the instructor with specific guidelines for action and decisions. Personal integrity must also be consistently applied to all situations and people. Students will respect instructors who consistently follow their personal ethical codes. Student respect is easy to maintain when an instructor adheres to personal integrity but difficult to gain when that integrity is compromised or questioned.

Teaching Traits to Emphasize

Instructors are constantly observed and evaluated by their students. The impressions that students form of their instructors affect student participation, responses, enthusiasm, and motivation. When students develop a negative attitude based on their perceptions of the instructor, the learning experience may be inhibited. The sections that follow compare some positive and negative teaching traits that can affect students' impressions of instructors. As instructors develop instructional skills, they need to be aware of these traits and avoid the negative ones while emphasizing the positive ones (**Figure 1.11**).

Honesty Versus Bluffing

Instructors must always be truthful and honest. Students realize that an instructor may *not* know all the answers. Students want and expect honesty and prefer instructors who are willing to admit

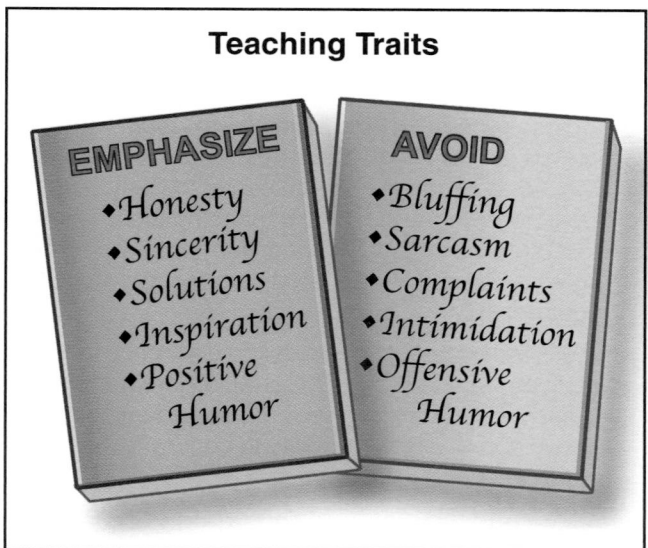

Teaching Traits

EMPHASIZE
- Honesty
- Sincerity
- Solutions
- Inspiration
- Positive Humor

AVOID
- Bluffing
- Sarcasm
- Complaints
- Intimidation
- Offensive Humor

Figure 1.11 Instructors must learn to recognize teaching traits, emphasize the positive ones, and avoid the negative ones.

that they do *not* know but are willing to find the answers to questions. Instructors do *not* need to be embarrassed when they cannot answer a question during class. Instructors should be prepared to say, *I don't know the answer to that question, but I'll find out for you* or *Does someone in the class know the answer?* Instructors should *not* attempt to bluff their way through a question quickly because that can cost them their credibility with students. Following are some guidelines for effectively handling this type of situation:

- When a question is appropriate to the lesson, promise to find the answer and do so promptly.

- When a question is of interest to only the student asking, tell the individual where to find the information.

- When there is no exact answer to a question, refer the student to related information.

- When a question refers to material that is in a later lesson, answer briefly and explain that it will be discussed later. Make a note to refer to the question when the material is presented.

- When a question is pertinent to the lesson and of interest to the class, initiate a discussion and ask students for their opinions.

Sincerity Versus Sarcasm

Sincerity is the personal quality of being open and truthful. Sincere attitudes and responses that show an interest in helping students to learn are important traits for instructors to possess. Students react, respond, and cooperate more positively and willingly with instructors who demonstrate a concern for them.

Sarcasm, however, is the use of language that may be insulting, demeaning, or scornful of others. Sarcasm may take the form of verbal or nonverbal language. Because nonverbal language constitutes 55 to 93 percent of a message, instructors must be aware of how they appear and sound to students. Communication specialists maintain that a message is 7 percent verbal, 38 percent vocal quality, and 55 percent body language.

An instructor who uses sarcasm toward a student, situation, or group places the entire class on the defensive. The emotional reactions of the student and the class block effective communication. Instructors must *not* use sarcasm even when students are sarcastic toward them. The instructor should evaluate the situation, consider the circumstances, and manage it in a mature and reasonable manner. Whenever it is necessary to correct this type of inappropriate behavior, the instructor should do it in private and *not* in front of the class or other students.

Solutions Versus Complaints

Few instructors work under ideal conditions, but complaining about the situation, especially to students, accomplishes nothing and creates a negative impression. Students have greater respect for instructors who present interesting material with enthusiasm and optimism than for those who chronically complain. An instructor may have little control over the learning environment, so apologizing or making excuses for a situation should *not* take class time. The following actions can minimize potential problems:

- Prepare lesson plans in advance.

- Inspect equipment and gather supplies before class.

- Arrange for appropriate assistance and props before class.

- Have alternate backup plans prepared.

In the event that something goes wrong, instructors should be prepared to use other resources, creativity, imagination, or alternate plans. They should make the best of a difficult situation with a positive attitude and then resolve the problem before the next session. An instructor provides a more positive role model for students by implementing a solution rather than complaining about the situation.

Inspiration Versus Intimidation

An instructor who attempts to use intimidation to get results will *not* stimulate students to reach their full potentials. An instructor who inspires students to learn, participate, ask questions, and keep trying by using patient, positive, and reasonable methods of guidance and reinforcement will get the best results. Students cannot learn in an environment of fear, stress, and intimidation. Intimidating tactics (or bullying) is usually an expression of fear, frustration, or insecurity on the part of the one who intimidates. People react to intimidators with fear, contempt, and rebellion.

Positive Humor Versus Offensive Humor

Humor can add emphasis to and create interest in a subject. It can also make learning enjoyable and memorable and release tension in the classroom. Instructors should use humor appropriately but cautiously. Humor can lighten a difficult subject and make it easier to learn.

Instructors should also permit students to express their personalities, but they must monitor the expressions to ensure that they do *not* offend others. Offensive or inappropriate humor, jokes, language, and stories that belittle or degrade a person or group of persons have no place in any training session.

In addition, constant humor can make learning ineffective by appearing to de-emphasize the seriousness of some topics. However, *not* using humor can make any learning situation dull. Instructors should find the appropriate balance between humor and the serious aspects of fire and emergency services training.

Case Study: Instructor Behaviors, Personality, and Effectiveness

You can recall instructors who were *good,* whose classes you enjoyed, and who made you feel like you learned something. You can also likely recall instructors whose classes or teaching techniques were so boring you dreaded attending, but you had to because it was a certification or promotion requirement.

What characteristics made the difference in the two types of instructors? Certain characteristics — such as attitude, behavior, and personality as well as knowledge and ability to convey it — contribute to effective instruction.

List and discuss characteristics that you think instructors should practice and exhibit that help in presenting instruction effectively. Listing characteristics is easy. Now, discuss ways in which instructors can achieve effectiveness. For example:

- When instructors must be good listeners, how can they perform good listening techniques?
- When instructors must be knowledgeable, how should they gain and maintain knowledge or remain current in their fields?

Instructor Challenges

Besides the obligations that instructors have (to students, the organization, the profession, and themselves), the characteristics they must possess, and the traits they must exhibit in class, they must also be able to manage other elements of the teaching environment that they may perceive to be challenges. To meet these challenges, they must be able to apply leadership, interpersonal skills, and the other characteristics mentioned previously.

Many of these challenges are no different from those found in other professions or in life in general. Therefore, an instructor should apply knowledge gained from previous experiences and adapt to them. If some of these challenges are new, then the inexperienced instructor may need to seek the advice of peers, supervisors, or other members of the teaching profession. Challenges include dealing with the following issues:

- Multiple priorities
- Diverse students

- Organizational apathy
- Multiple changes
- Cooperative relationships
- Organizational promotion
- Management directives
- Safe training environments
- Professional development
- Course schedules
- Funds and resources
- Qualified instructor recruitment

Multiple Priorities

With the potential for having fewer personnel and increased duties in an organization, instructors may find that they are assigned tasks above and beyond curriculum planning, curriculum development, and course delivery. Additional responsibilities may include administrative duties, logistics duties, or health and safety officer duties.

These responsibilities require the instructor to establish priorities and set goals and objectives to determine completion of projects. Instructors must be effective problem solvers, organizers, time managers, and decision makers. Along with increased duties comes increased personal stress, which an instructor must be able to recognize and manage by identifying, balancing, and establishing priorities (**Figure 1.12**).

Diverse Students

The fire and emergency services in North America generally reflect the diversity of the population as a whole. Instructors must recognize, appreciate, and respect the differences in their students, their peers, and citizens. Instructors should broaden their knowledge and understanding through diversity training, education, and association with diverse people. Instructors should *not* expect all students to act, think, respond, or learn in the same way or at the same rate.

Students are products of their ethnic, racial, family, and cultural backgrounds. Along with gender and age factors, students respond and learn based on that heritage. It is important for instruc-

Figure 1.12 To avoid personal stress, instructors must balance professional and personal obligations by prioritizing each one.

tors to treat each student as a unique human being and provide each with the opportunity to learn and master course content.

Organizational Apathy

An organization's personnel and management may take an apathetic view and *not* always appear supportive of training. They may appear to have a lack of interest or concern for training. Some managers may believe that funds designated for training might be better used for other programs or services. An instructor may have to justify and strive for enough money to support and conduct training programs. Instructors may find that it is necessary to manage adversities through commitment and by finding workable solutions.

Many times instructors can overcome apathy and replace it with respect by providing effective, high-quality instruction. This high-quality instruction results in challenging and credible training programs from which the organization receives excellent evaluations from students and recognition from the community and other fire and emergency services organizations.

Multiple Changes

The only thing constant is change is a phrase that has become popular in the last 50 years. The fire and emergency services in North America are certainly *not* immune to change. As change occurs (for example in standards, protocols, operating procedures, and organization policies), it is the responsibility of instructors as responsible personnel and professionals to accept them, adapt to them, and promote them.

An instructor is in a position to be an advocate of change, a change-agent or champion of needed changes, and a leader who is willing to create progress through organizational change. Part of teaching a course is to bring information and explanation about changes to students and teach them to be careful consumers of information through education, research, and development. Through these methods, instructors can guide students to think critically and make informed decisions for their own organizations.

Cooperative Relationships

Instructors must develop cooperative relationships, which may include participating in the following ways:

- Hire or contract with instructors from other organizations and colleges.

- Work with personnel from other organizations and agencies on planning and implementing joint training programs.

- Provide consulting services and training to other organizations.

Even in the fire and emergency services profession, mergers and consolidations take place, and a history of prior cooperation can benefit instructors. Cooperation with others includes people outside the fire and emergency services profession. Instructors must learn to cooperate with officials from other agencies and levels of government along with leaders in the private sector in both business and education **(Figure 1.13)**.

Organizational Promotion

Instructors must promote the benefits and assets of the organization and its training program to the public and other organizations and agencies

Figure 1.13 Instructors are increasingly required to work with representatives of multiple agencies at all levels of government.

that may send students as external customers. Instructors must ensure that external customers are provided with the same high-quality training that internal customers (organizational personnel) receive, motivating them to return for additional training and causing them to promote their learning experiences. Instructors are responsible for maximizing the value of the organization by ensuring that training courses provide knowledge and skills based on current standards and courses are taught with appropriate instructional methods designed to meet student needs.

Management Directives

As subordinates, instructors must adhere to the management directives and mandates of the organization and its leaders. Instructors may find that organization directives may conflict with personal goals or beliefs and face the challenge of fulfilling job requirements or providing training under conditions that may be disagreeable. Instructors must be flexible and adaptable, accept the challenge, and strive to understand and cooperate or work for a compromise.

Safe Training Environments

Instructors must be familiar with local, state/provincial, and federal safety regulations as they apply to training, especially for live-fire evolutions, hazardous materials training, and confined-space drills. Students must be assured that safety is the primary concern of the organization. When students are confident that training is being provided with the greatest level of safety, they will then be able to practice the technical skills of their professions (some of which involve risk) without distraction. See Chapter 2, Safety and the Training Function, for additional information on safety and training issues.

Professional Development

An effective instructor continues to learn by taking advantage of continuing education and professional development opportunities. Topics for the instructor vary from adult education methodology to fire and emergency services courses and even personal improvement topics such as time and stress management.

Sources include the human resources department of the local jurisdiction, state/provincial, regional, and national training agencies or academies, and seminars sponsored by vendors or manufacturers. When individual states/provinces or organizations do *not* offer resources, instructors should check with local vocational/technical schools, community colleges, universities, and libraries.

Self-directed study can be based on information in professional journals and books that report the latest research, providing resources for further study and offering excellent articles written by experienced professionals. Many colleges, universities, and professional organizations also offer continuing education programs by correspondence and through distance learning technology based on Internet and instructional/interactive television (ITV). See **Appendix C,** Instructor Resources.

Course Schedules

Fire and emergency services organizations have a unique challenge in scheduling training courses and curriculums. This challenge is the result of a variety of pressures that include the following:

- Increase in state/provincial and federally mandated training

- Increase in the complexity of topics that must be taught

- Addition of more courses provided to the public

- Increase in emergency responses that reduces available training times

- Decrease in active duty personnel in career organizations

- Decrease in participation in volunteer organizations

- Increased competition for available time in the lives of volunteers

As organizations become busier, there is often less time for training. Unfortunately it may then become a low priority, but organizations must maintain required training as well as attempt to fulfill additional training requirements (**Figure 1.14, p. 26**).

Organizations must have a mission statement that describes goals and includes training as an integral part of successful operations. Instructors must take an active role in guiding management in planning and scheduling appropriate and required training sessions. It may become necessary to create approaches to providing training such as the use of closed-circuit television to connect remote sites with the training facility.

Funds and Resources

It is sometimes the case that when federal, state/provincial, and local funds are low, training programs are the first to lose their funding. At the same time, government mandates requiring training continue.

Reduction in revenues may have an effect on the resources available for training programs, requiring instructors to create new ways to achieve training goals. Some creative methods of meeting goals and maintaining training programs include (but are not limited to) the following:

- Develop cooperative relationships with other training organizations, business/industry, and educational institutions.

- Seek funding from new sources such as grants, business and industrial sponsors/partnerships, and donations.

- Raise funds by providing training to other agencies and the private sector.

Training Division Planning Calendar

Planning Calendar for July

Sun	Mon	Tue	Wed	Thu	Fri	Sat
	June 1 2 3 4 5 6 7 8 9 10 11 12 13 14 15 16 17 18 19 20 21 22 23 24 25 26 27 28 29 30	**August** 1 2 3 4 5 6 7 8 9 10 11 12 13 14 15 16 17 18 19 20 21 22 23 24 25 26 27 28 29 30 31	**1** SCBA Certification Class (1) A Shift	**2** SCBA Certification Class (1) B Shift	**3** SCBA Certification Class (1) C Shift	**4** Exterior station cleaning and lawn maintenance A Shift
5 B Shift	**6** Station and Apparatus Cleaning and Maintenance; Company Drills C Shift	**7** Home Inspections (9-12 AM) Hydrant Inspections (1-5 PM) A Shift	**8** SCBA Certification Class (2) B Shift	**9** SCBA Certification Class (2)	**10** SCBA Certification Class (2) A Shift	**11** Exterior station cleaning and lawn maintenance B Shift
12 C Shift	**13** Station and Apparatus Cleaning and Maintenance; Company Drills A Shift	**14** Home Inspections (9-12 AM) Hydrant Inspections (1-5 PM) B Shift	**15** SCBA Certification Class (3) C Shift	**16** SCBA Certification Class (3) A Shift	**17** SCBA Certification Class (3) B Shift	**18** Exterior station cleaning and lawn maintenance C Shift
19 A Shift	**20** Station and Apparatus Cleaning and Maintenance; Company Drills B Shift	**21** Home Inspections (9-12 AM) Hydrant Inspections (1-5 PM) C Shift	**22** SCBA Certification Class (4) A Shift	**23** SCBA Certification Class (4) B Shift	**24** SCBA Certification Class (4) C Shift	**25** Exterior station cleaning and lawn maintenance A Shift
26 B Shift	**27** Station and Apparatus Cleaning and Maintenance; Company Drills C Shift	**28** Home Inspections (9-12 AM) Hydrant Inspections (1-5 PM) A Shift	**29** SCBA Certification Class (5) B Shift	**30** SCBA Certification Class (5) C Shift	**31** SCBA Certification Class (5) A Shift	

Figure 1.14 Training schedules often must compete with other needs of the emergency services organization. Volunteer organizations have an even greater challenge because personal obligations of members must be considered.

Qualified Instructor Recruitment

All fire and emergency services organizations experience turnovers in personnel. The training division is *not* immune to this movement of personnel in and out of the division or organization. It is important that instructors assist in locating and recruiting talented and knowledgeable applicants to fill training division vacancies.

The primary source of applicants is internal to the organization. Instructors are familiar with the skills, abilities, and knowledge of the person-nel they have contact with on a daily basis. The organization's fire officers, both emergency and nonemergency personnel, may provide a trained and accessible pool of applicants.

Another source (external to the organization), especially in volunteer/combination organizations, are professional educators from the community. Organizations that seek external applicants may wish to consider instructors and firefighters/emergency responders who have retired from other fire and emergency services organizations, in particular the military.

In an organization, each individual has a position that relates to others. Everyone works with someone at his or her own level, someone superior, and possibly someone who is subordinate on an organizational chart. Each position has responsibilities with multiple demands from the following groups:

- Administration or superiors
- Other organizations and jurisdictions
- Peers and coworkers
- Subordinates and trainees

Outside the organization, individuals also have personal responsibilities to themselves, their families, and their communities. With the added responsibilities of *instructor,* individuals may find it difficult to balance or fairly meet all commitments and responsibilities both within and outside the organization.

Organizational charts show the positions of major personnel categories: administrators, middle managers, and support staff. As an instructor, where is your position on the chart? List the roles and responsibilities of the instructor position in your organization. Share your ideas with others to find other or overlapping areas of responsibility. Answer the following questions:

1. As an instructor, how many individuals above you are you responsible to? How many below you are you responsible for? Is the number manageable?

2. What are your main responsibilities toward each level on the organizational chart, including peers or coworkers on your own level?

3. Do you believe that your responsibilities are manageable? Why or why not? What can you do to ensure that you can fulfill your responsibilities?

Share your conclusions. Was there a common thread among peers, supervisors, and subordinates? Was it positive or negative? How can instructors promote the positive aspects? How can they revise the negative aspects if any?

Instructor Reference Checklist

Effective instructors, regardless of certification level, must be able to recognize situations and determine the proper course of action based on available information. The sections that follow list *dos* and *don'ts* that give instructors quick references regarding analyses, instructional facilities (including props and acquired structures), diversity issues, legal requirements, and audience recognition. The comments are expanded in later chapters of this manual.

Analyses

Instructors must be able to analyze situations, equipment, courses, and information and then determine their value to students, the training program, and the organization. While learning how to properly perform an analysis is detailed and complicated, there are a few general concepts to keep in mind.

Do	Don't
Collect as much information from as many sources as possible before doing an analysis.	Depend on one source for information, especially a product vendor or manufacturer.
Ensure that information is accurate, reliable, credible, and current.	Make a recommendation without first performing a thorough analysis.

Instructional Facilities, Props, and Acquired Structures

Instructional facilities, props, and acquired structures are essential to effective fire and emergency services training programs. They can also be the source of both injuries and fatalities if they are *not* used safely and properly. Chapter 5, Instructional Facilities and Props, discusses these items in depth.

Do	Don't
Adhere to all the appropriate safety requirements for live-fire training such as NFPA 1403, *Standard on Live Fire Training Evolutions* (2002).	Violate the safety requirements of appropriate laws and standards such as NFPA 1403.
Inspect all facilities and props on a regular basis **(Figure 1.15)**.	Modify any commercially produced prop such as a fire behavior simulator without the manufacturer's permission and assistance.
Repair and replace props or facilities as required.	Use a donated prop without first inspecting, cleaning, and repairing it (if necessary).
Have a designated ISO present during all high-hazard training activities.	Use an acquired structure without first ensuring that it meets the requirements outlined in NFPA 1403.
Require the use of all approved personal protective equipment (PPE), including the appropriate respiratory protection equipment and personal alert safety system (PASS) devices, by all personnel involved in the training evolution.	Perform training in inclement weather that may create an additional hazard or risk.
Use the adopted accountability system and the Incident Command System (ICS) at all training sessions.	
Provide adequate breathing air, air cylinders, cartridges, canisters, and filter masks as necessary for all personnel involved in the training evolution.	
Emphasize safe operating procedures during all training evolutions.	
Keep visitors and spectators at a safe distance from training exercises.	
Have EMS personnel available during live-fire and technical-rescue training exercises.	

Diversity Issues

All groups are diverse in one sense or another. Diversity may be the result of differences in ethnic or racial backgrounds, age, gender, religion, sexual orientation, rank, or experience. Within the normal emergency response company (such as an engine company), the diversity may consist of many or all of these categories. The fire and emergency services instructor must be able to recognize that

Figure 1.15 Before all practical training exercises, the instructor must inspect training facilities and props for damage and operation. *Courtesy of Maryland Fire and Rescue Institute (MFRI).*

diversity exists within the training class or audience and build on the benefits of diversity while reducing the potential for inappropriate comments or bias.

Do	Don't
Show respect for all members of the audience.	Tell inappropriate jokes, anecdotes, or stories that may be hurtful or prejudiced.
Adapt teaching methods to the members of the audience.	Use profanity or inappropriate language.
Encourage all personnel to participate and provide their opinions and experiences.	Permit audience members to use inappropriate language, jokes, anecdotes, or stories.
Use language and examples that are relevant to all members of the audience.	Show favoritism to a single student or group.
	Openly criticize a student in the presence of others.

Legal Requirements and Accommodations

Laws that apply to fire and emergency services training and instructors are discussed in Chapter 3, Legal and Ethical Considerations. This short section of dos and don'ts (bottom of page) is focused mainly on the requirements of the Americans with Disabilities Act (ADA) and the Canadian Charter of Rights and Freedoms as well as other laws that specify access or accommodations for students.

Audience Recognition

Instructors must constantly be aware of the audience, its composition, its attitude, and its changing mood. Audience awareness is an essential

Figure 1.16a The instructor should be familiar with accessibility requirements for classrooms and training areas and ensure that they exist and are properly marked. Automatic door controls are placed near the accessible doors and located at wheelchair height.

Do	Don't
Ensure that accessibility is provided for instructional classrooms and facilities. See **Figures 1.16 a and b (p. 30)**.	Assume that all students are physically, mentally, and emotionally similar and able to learn in the same environment.
Provide a teaching environment that ensures the best possible learning experience for all students.	Patronize students who have physical, mental, or emotional disabilities.
Provide appropriate handouts or training aids for students who may be visually or audibly impaired. For example, these aids could include graphics that may be difficult to interpret by people who have colorblindness (estimated to be 8 to 10 percent of the male population).	

Do	Don't
Remain focused on the audience at all times.	Attempt to present all of the material in one session without rest breaks.
Watch for visual and audible indications that the audience may *not* understand and adapt the presentation accordingly.	Attempt to provide extremely detailed information that may be difficult to comprehend without providing supplemental handouts that contain the same information.
Ask questions of audience members to ensure that they understand.	Patronize or talk down to the audience.
Permit questions from the audience either during or at the end of presentations.	Use job-specific jargon unless the entire audience is familiar with it and its use is essential to understanding the topic.
Provide a comfortable learning environment with appropriate breaks at specified intervals.	
Provide interactive projects to keep the audience engaged with the topic.	
Collect as much information (such as age, profession, culture, learning environment, and organizational structure) as possible before preparing for an unfamiliar audience.	

component in the communication and delivery processes. Both of these areas are discussed in later chapters.

Summary

Fire and emergency services personnel who decide to become instructors must understand the obligations that they have to students, the organization, the profession, and themselves. They must have or be able to develop the characteristics normally associated with effective educators, the most important of which is the desire to teach. Instructor candidates must develop traits that provide a positive impression for students and create a professional image for the organization and the fire and emergency services profession in general.

Figure 1.16b Universally accepted symbols (such as the one shown) indicate doors that meet Americans with Disabilities Act requirements. *Courtesy of Maryland Fire and Rescue Institute (MFRI).*

Instructor candidates must have the knowledge and ability to accept the challenges that teaching affords and select the positive traits rather than the negative ones that some situations may create. Finally, they must be able to manage delicate situations that are created by diversity, legal requirements, and various training situations. Once instructor candidates have achieved these objectives, they will be equipped to join the ranks of a small but proud group that call themselves *fire and emergency services instructors*.

I didn't know what to do!

In the fire and emergency services profession, this is *not* an acceptable answer following an emergency incident or accident involving responders. The responsibility of knowing what action to take falls into two areas: the individual responder in the situation and the training staff that trained that individual.

Responders, regardless of rank, position, or authority, must be capable and confident in their ability to handle any situation in which they are placed. Simply being a *firefighter* or *paramedic* does *not* qualify an individual to effectively respond in an emergency situation. An individual must have the knowledge to meet the established certification criteria, practice the skills until they are *second nature,* and be flexible enough to modify the skills quickly as the situation changes.

The training staff that provides knowledge also bears responsibility for an individual's actions. Whether it is a national, state/provincial, or local training organization, it must provide the required level of training that has been established by the jurisdiction.

When it comes to training, leave nothing to chance. Assuming that students will learn critical information on their own is not an acceptable alternative to providing the information and then testing to see whether it has been learned and can be applied.

The importance of training in the emergency services cannot be overemphasized. It provides basic knowledge required to perform the assigned tasks safely and efficiently, ensures (through testing) that knowledge has been learned, and reinforces knowledge through refresher training or periodic practical training evolutions or scenarios.

Finally, instructors are also responsible for learning the skills necessary to train fire and emergency services personnel. They must be able to present information in a manner that all students will understand.

Instructors must be flexible and able to alter or modify lessons to meet the changing needs of students or the learning environment. And they must be able to create and administer qualification exams that will ensure that students have gained the knowledge that is critical to their safety and success in a high-risk profession.

Chapter 2

Safety and the Training Function

After reading this chapter, students will be able to —

1. Define accident.

2. List places where injuries and fatalities can occur.

3. List recommendations for casualty prevention.

4. List responsibilities of an organization's administration in preventing casualties.

5. List methods by which jurisdictions can reduce risk.

6. List areas in which the instructor has a role in creating and ensuring a safe work environment.

7. Identify facts about the instructor's role in providing a safe training environment.

8. List conditions under which the instructor may be responsible for teaching safety-related topics.

9. Identify facts about the instructor fulfilling the duties of the incident safety officer (ISO).

10. Identify facts about providing students with a positive, proactive safety role model.

11. List information that students need to know in case of an accident.

12. Identify facts about accident prevention and management.

13. List the factors that contribute to accidents.

14. Identify the purposes of an accident investigation.

15. Describe the instructor's role in an accident investigation.

16. Identify facts about accident analyses and mitigation activities.

17. Identify responsibilities of public and private agencies and organizations in the area of safety.

Chapter Contents

The Safety Challenge
Training Casualties
Casualty Prevention

The Instructor's Role
Safe Training Environment
Safety-Related Teaching Topics
Instructor Incident Safety Officer Duties
Instructor as Safety Role Model
Reinforcing Safety
Implementing Safety Plans

Accident Prevention and Management
Prevention
Management

Resources: Safety Guidelines, Regulations, and Information
Federal Government Agencies
State/Provincial and Local Safety and
Health Agencies
Standards Writing Organizations
Professional Organizations and Associations

Summary

Chapter 2
Safety and the Training Function

Fire and emergency services instructors have a responsibility to understand the safety concerns and challenges that fire and emergency services personnel face. This responsibility means having an understanding of the injuries and fatalities that can occur during training as well as at emergency incidents. This understanding helps instructors to comprehend their roles in providing safe training experiences.

Instructors must also be role models for their students and peers by advocating and adhering to safe practices. Instructors must have a basic understanding of *accidents* (defined as sequences of unplanned or uncontrolled events that produce unintended injuries, deaths, or property damage) and how they can be prevented, managed, investigated, and analyzed. This chapter provides information on these topics as well as providing sources for safety-related information and courses.

Instructors are faced with a challenge in providing training that reduces the potential for injuries or fatalities at emergency incidents while still providing a safe training environment, which is *not* an easy task. Injuries and fatalities can occur during the following situations:

- When responding to and returning from incidents
- At the incident scene (**Figure 2.1**)
- During training
- During work shifts at the station

Instructors must be aware of statistics that show that fire fighting is a dangerous profession. Knowing these statistics and the causes of the injuries and fatalities they represent assists instructors in

Figure 2.1 Interior structural fire fighting can be one of the most hazardous tasks firefighters perform in the line of duty. *Courtesy of Alabama Fire College.*

planning and providing safe training that reduces and perhaps eliminates firefighter injuries and fatalities.

The Safety Challenge

Casualties (injuries and fatalities) may occur anytime emergency services personnel are engaged in any activity. The challenge for the instructor is to provide realistic training that creates situations that are similar to actual emergencies while still providing the maximum level of safety during the training exercise. To meet this challenge, an instructor must be aware of the types and numbers of injuries and fatalities that may occur.

Statistics on casualties that occur during emergency operations are provided in **Appendix D**. The sections that follow discuss the injuries and fatalities that may occur during training and how they may be prevented. The most recent figures may be obtained from the following organizations or agencies:

- National Fire Protection Association (NFPA)
- U.S. Fire Administration (USFA)
- International Association of Fire Chiefs (IAFC)
- International Association of Fire Fighters (IAFF)
- Other U.S. and Canadian government agencies

Training Casualties

Between 1987 and 2003, statistics show that training-related injuries increased by nearly 21 percent. In 2001, approximately 7,000 injuries occurring during training exercises were reported. The leading type of injury was strain/sprain (51 percent) followed by wound/cut/bleeding/bruise (20 percent). Heart attacks and strokes only constituted 1 percent of the injuries reported in May 2003 by the USFA.

Statistics show that training-related fatalities, which are about 10 percent of all annual firefighter line-of-duty-deaths, have also risen in recent years. The training-related fatalities annual average between 1978 and 2001 has been 10, with a low of 3 in some years, and a high of 15 in 1987. The leading cause of training-related fatalities has been heart attacks followed by traumatic injuries. These statistics are even more tragic when one considers that they occurred at situations over which the instructor had full control, including the location, fire load, personnel, equipment, and tactics in use.

Strategic Initiatives

In March 2004, the National Fallen Firefighters Foundation in cooperation with the U.S. Fire Administration (USFA) hosted a summit involving approximately 200 leaders from throughout the nation's fire and emergency services. The *Summit Initial Report* identified and provided additional background for the following 16 initiatives that were formulated by summit participants:

1. Define and advocate the need for a cultural change within the fire service relating to safety, incorporating leadership, management, supervision, accountability, and personal responsibility.

2. Enhance the personal and organizational accountability for health and safety throughout the fire service.

3. Focus greater attention on the integration of risk management with incident management at all levels, including strategic, tactical, and planning responsibilities.

4. Empower all firefighters to stop unsafe practices.

5. Develop and implement national standards for training, qualifications, and certification (including regular recertification) that are equally applicable to all firefighters, based on the duties they are expected to perform.

6. Develop and implement national medical and physical fitness standards that are equally applicable to all firefighters, based on the duties they are expected to perform.

7. Create a national research agenda and data collection system that relates to the initiatives.

8. Utilize available technology wherever it can produce higher levels of health and safety.

9. Thoroughly investigate all firefighter fatalities, injuries, and near misses.

10. Ensure grant programs support the implementation of safe practices and/or mandate safe practices as an eligibility requirement.

11. Develop and champion national standards for emergency response policies and procedures.

12. Develop and champion national protocols for response to violent incidents.

13. Provide access to counseling and psychological support for firefighters and their families.

14. Provide more resources for public education and champion it as a critical fire and life safety program.

15. Strengthen advocacy for the enforcement of codes and the installation of home fire sprinklers.

16. Make safety a primary consideration in the design of apparatus and equipment.

Casualty Prevention

As sobering as these casualty figures are, they can be reduced. Changes in policies and procedures by the organization's administration as well as instructors incorporating safety into the training curriculum can cause a major reduction in these figures. Some of the recommendations provided in the USFA report, *Trends and Hazards in Firefighter Training*, Special Report-0 May 2003 (TR-100) include the following:

- Follow established guidelines and currently accepted procedures and standards for training.

- Ensure that training and safety standards and procedures are followed at all times.

- Include the use of live-burn evolutions in a variety of structure types to provide realistic fire-fighting experiences for students.

- Train firefighters or emergency responders to recognize the visual and physical clues to impending danger (such as changes in smoke conditions) and anticipate fire behavior in a variety of building types **(Figure 2.2, p. 38)**.

An essential element for preventing training-related casualties during live-fire training is NFPA 1403, *Standard on Live Fire Training Evolutions*. Instructors must be familiar with the requirements of this standard for all live-fire training in purpose-built burn buildings, acquired structures, and burn props. Safety requirements must be enforced by the instructor in charge of the training evolution, the designated incident safety officer, (ISO) and the organization's administration.

To reduce the potential risks to personnel, all fire and emergency services organizations regulated by legally adopted NFPA standards are required to have a risk-management plan. After plan implementation, it must be monitored for effectiveness. This plan is designed to accomplish the following objectives:

- Identify risks.

- Evaluate the potential based on frequency and severity of the risk.

- Establish appropriate controls to minimize or eliminate the risk.

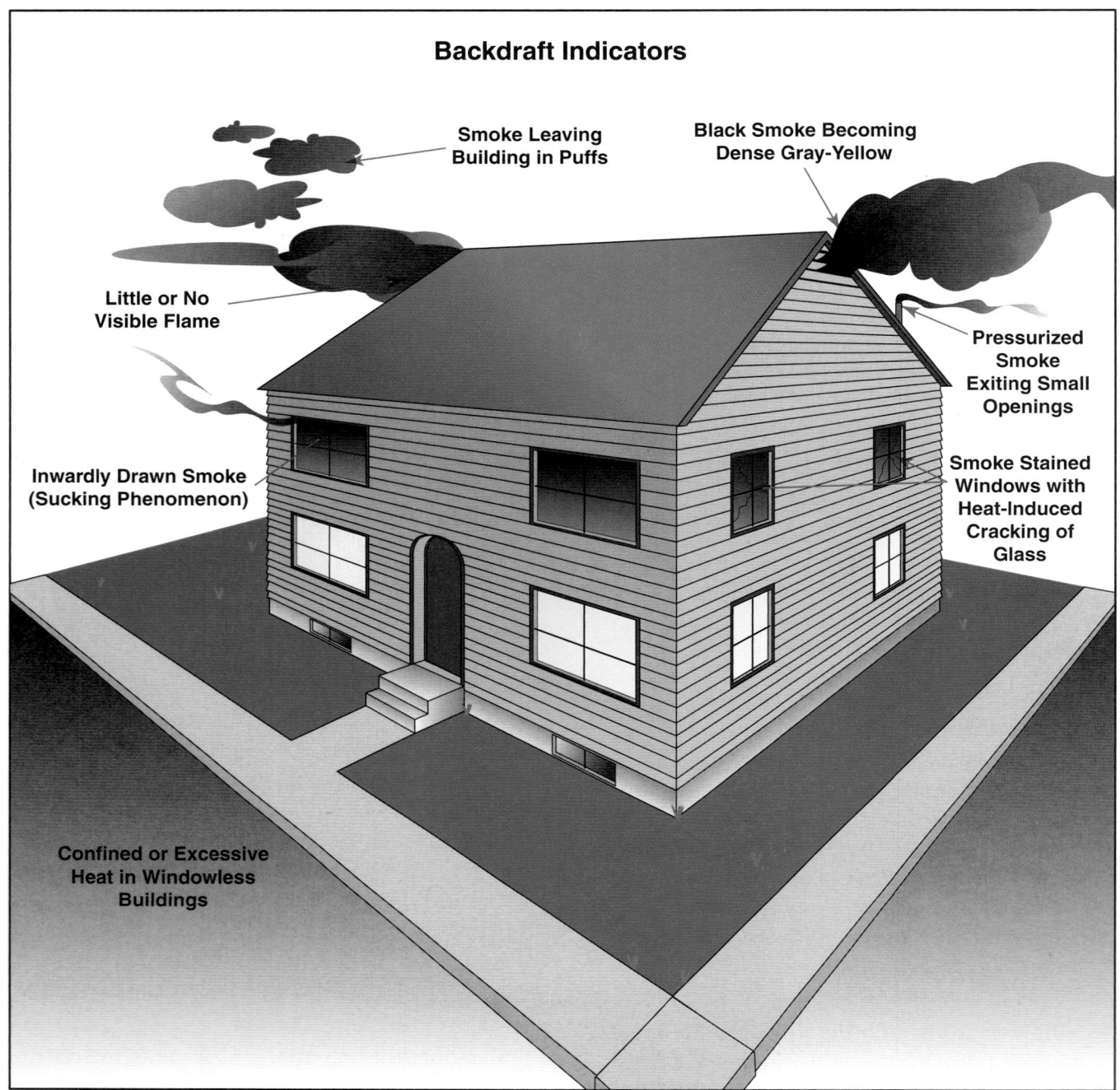

Backdraft Indicators

Smoke Leaving Building in Puffs

Black Smoke Becoming Dense Gray-Yellow

Little or No Visible Flame

Pressurized Smoke Exiting Small Openings

Inwardly Drawn Smoke (Sucking Phenomenon)

Smoke Stained Windows with Heat-Induced Cracking of Glass

Confined or Excessive Heat in Windowless Buildings

Figure 2.2 To reduce the potential for fatalities and injuries at structural fires, firefighters must be trained to recognize backdraft indicators.

The risk-management plan includes all job-related activities in which fire and emergency services personnel (emergency and nonemergency) normally participate, including emergency, nonemergency, training, and support activities. See the information box for a detailed outline of the process.

Instructors can play a significant role in preventing injuries and fatalities during training evolutions. However, it is imperative that the organization's administration support and enforce safety, fitness, and health and wellness programs in all aspects of the organization's operations. The administration should commit to taking the following responsibilities:

Risk-Management Plan Development Steps

1. *Risk identification* — List potential problems for every aspect of fire and emergency services training. Examples of sources of information that may be useful in the process are as follows:

- Lists of risks to which members are or may be exposed

- Records of previous accidents, illnesses, and injuries (both locally and nationally)

- Facility and apparatus survey/inspection results

2. *Risk evaluation* — Evaluate each item listed in the risk-identification process by asking the following two questions:

- What is the potential frequency of occurrence?

- What is the potential severity and expense of its occurrence?

Use this information to set priorities in the control plan (needs assessment). Some sources of information include the following:

- Safety audits and inspection reports

- Prior accident, illness, and injury statistics

- Application of national data to local circumstances

- Professional judgment in evaluating risks unique to the jurisdiction

3. *Risk control* — Determine which control should be implemented and documented once risks are identified and evaluated. Two primary methods of controlling risk, in order of preference, are as follows:

- Totally eliminate/avoid the risk or activity that presents the risk wherever possible. For example, when the risk is falling on ice, then do *not* allow members to perform training evolutions outside when icy conditions are present.

- Take steps to control the risk when it is not possible or practical to avoid or eliminate it. Also consider developing specific safety programs, standard operating procedures (SOPs), training, and inspections as control methods. In the previous example, methods of control would be applying sand/salt or wearing footwear with ice cleats attached.

4. *Risk-management monitoring and follow-up* — Periodically evaluate the selected controls to determine whether they are working satisfactorily. If they are not, identify and implement new control measures.

Reprinted with permission from NFPA 1500, *Standard on Fire Department Occupational Safety and Health Program*, Copyright© 2002, National Fire Protection Association, Quincy, MA 02269. This reprinted material is not the complete and official position of the National Fire Protection Association on the referenced subject, which is represented only by the standard in its entirety.

- Provide adequate personal protective equipment (PPE).

- Ensure that all apparatus and equipment are maintained.

- Ensure that all safety equipment is properly installed and operating.

- Provide policies and procedures for the safe use of the apparatus and equipment.

- Address the fitness, health, and wellness of personnel through the following elements:
  — Job-related physical fitness testing
  — Annual medical evaluations and periodic examinations
  — Health and wellness related information and training
  — Employee assistance programs

The Instructor's Role

It should be apparent that fire and emergency services personnel work in high-risk environments that are inherently unsafe. Although it is impossible to remove the risks completely to create a totally safe work environment, it is possible to reduce the risk and increase the safety level. Through the efforts of fire and emergency services organizations and instructors, jurisdictions can reduce risks through a variety of the following methods:

- Provide and require the use of approved PPE.

- Provide training in safety topics and practices.

- Teach the safest methods for accomplishing skills and tasks.

- Adhere to safety regulations and standards both in training and at emergency incidents.

- Establish and adhere to the National Incident Management System (NIMS) Incident Command System (ICS).

- Use a personnel accountability system.

- Investigate, analyze, and correct unsafe activities and behaviors.

- Establish safety policies and procedures for use in all work-related activities.

- Establish and use appropriate rehabilitation based on NFPA 1584, *Recommended Practice on the Rehabilitation of Members Operating at Incident Scene Operations and Training Exercises* (2003).

- Conduct a brief safety critique at the end of every training drill.

The fire and emergency services instructor is actively involved with each of these methods. The instructor's role in creating and ensuring a safe work environment can be divided into four broad training-related categories:

- Provide a safe training environment.

- Teach safety-related topics.

- Fulfill the duties of the health and safety officer (HSO) or ISO when assigned.

- Provide students with a positive, proactive safety role model.

The methods for ensuring a safe work environment are used in each of these categories and help to reinforce the commitment of the organization to employee safety. This section provides information that guides the instructor through these four categories. The information meets or in some cases exceeds the job performance requirements (JPRs) of NFPA 1041, *Standard for Fire Service Instructor Professional Qualifications,* for Instructor Levels I and II. It also proves valuable for Instructor III personnel who must be able to evaluate the training practices of their subordinate instructors.

In addition, Fire Officer I personnel will find the information applicable to company-level training performed at the station and other sites remote from the training facility (see NFPA 1021, *Standard for Fire Officer Professional Qualifications*). Additional information on the duties of the HSO and ISO is found in NFPA 1521, *Standard*

for Fire Department Safety Officer, and the IFSTA **Fire Department Safety Officer**, 2nd Edition, manual.

The most important thing to remember is that safety must be taught and practiced during training. By requiring safety training and applying the use of safe practices, fire and emergency services personnel will automatically apply the safe practices during emergency incidents. Safety must be a permanent behavioral trait that becomes automatic to the firefighter or emergency responder during daily activities.

Safe Training Environment

The training division is responsible for providing a safe training environment for all instructors and training students. The requirements for providing this level of safety are found in national laws, state/provincial laws, local ordinances, government rules and regulations, international consensus standards, organizational policies and procedures, and even case law. The instructor must ensure that requirements are implemented before, during, and after training is provided to students. The training environment includes the following facilities:

- Classrooms

- Props

- Permanent and mobile facilities

- Remote sites

- Acquired structures and facilities

A detailed description of each of these types of training facilities is provided in Chapter 5, Instructional Facilities and Props. The training environment is supplemented by the use of PPE approved by the authority having jurisdiction (AHJ), adequate rehabilitation, and sufficient student supervision based on an accepted student-instructor ratio.

Fire and emergency services training attempts to duplicate as closely as possible the hazards, risks, and situations found during emergency responses. As training becomes more realistic, the benefit to the student increases while the potential risk also increases. This balancing of realism and safety creates a challenge for training instructors

Figure 2.3 Safety must be the first concern of instructors when conducting high-hazard training such as high-angle rescue. *Courtesy of Central Florida Fire Academy.*

and administrators. To ensure a safe training environment, instructors must plan scenarios to meet safety requirements, inspect and repair facilities and props, and monitor training activities (**Figure 2.3**).

Planning Safe Training Scenarios

Planning for safety in training scenarios involves two analysis processes: First is performing an initial *task analysis* that determines the tasks emergency responders perform at emergency scenes. Second is creating a *hazard/risk analysis* that determines the potential safety threats that may be encountered during training and emergency operations. Each of these processes should be completed before initial training in any skill or activity.

Taken together, the task analysis and the hazard/risk analysis cause the instructor and training administrator to focus on potential safety concerns and eliminate or minimize them before an accident occurs. The implementation of the analyses results occurs in the incident action plan (IAP) that is used during each training scenario.

Task analysis. A task analysis consists of a detailed review of each physical task or job that is performed by emergency personnel. Each task is divided into steps that are required to complete the task. For example, the task of lifting a 14-foot (4.3 m) single or roof ladder may consist of the following steps:

Step 1: Kneel beside the ladder, facing the tip.

Step 2: Grasp the middle rung with the near hand.

Step 3: Lift the ladder.

Step 4: Pivot into the ladder as it rises.

Step 5: Place the free arm between two rungs so that the upper beam comes to rest on the shoulder.

The task analysis should also list the type of safety equipment that is worn or used to perform the task. In the ladder-lift example, full protective clothing including helmet, bunker (turnout) coat and trousers, boots, and gloves may be required. Each step should also take into consideration the safety requirements involved in the step. In this example, lifting with the legs rather than with the back is a major consideration. The task analysis not only provides a basis for skills training but also for developing a job-related skills test for hiring new personnel (**Figure 2.4**).

Hazard/risk analysis. A hazard/risk analysis identifies potential problem areas and is the foundation for a risk-management plan. As part of the organization's hazard/risk analysis, the training

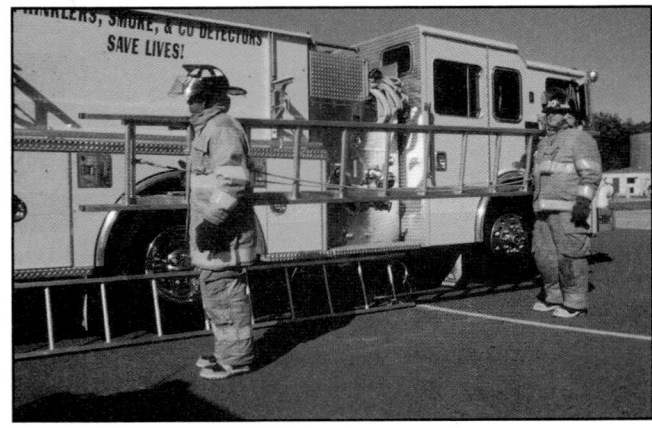

Figure 2.4 A task analysis must be performed on each task that firefighters perform as part of their assigned duties such as the two-person ladder carry shown here.

division reviews all activities that may result in a risk to personnel. For example, driver/operator training may require novice or inexperienced personnel to drive apparatus on public streets or highways. This situation creates a potential risk to both personnel and the public. The results of the hazard/risk analysis are then used to develop training procedures that contain safe practices and instill the desired safe behavior traits in the student.

Hazards and Risks

In everyday conversation, the terms *hazard* and *risk* are often used interchangeably; however, technically, they describe two different things. The term *hazard* usually refers to the source of a risk. A *risk*, on the other hand, is the likelihood of suffering harm from a hazard. Risk can also be thought of as the potential for failure or loss. In other words, *risk* is the exposure to a hazard. A *hazard* is a condition, substance, or device that can directly cause an injury or loss.

Incident action plan. Safety during both emergency operations and training scenarios depends on the implementation of the NIMS ICS of which the IAP is an important element. A specific IAP is unique to the incident or scenario, although all IAPs have common elements. The IAP establishes the strategic goals and tactical objectives of the operation or scenario for a specific time period. The primary strategic goal of all IAPs is life safety. During training scenarios where the instructor has control over most of the situation, safety should be guaranteed. Unfortunately, the statistics provided earlier show that this situation is *not* always the case.

Therefore, it is essential that instructors and training directors develop consistent and thorough IAPs for each type of training scenario in which students engage. Consider the following requirements for each IAP and scenario:

- Reevaluate each IAP and scenario for potential safety violations.

- Correct or eliminate any violations found.

- Communicate the IAP to all training scenario participants so that they are aware of the desired goals and objectives.

- Provide students with examples of proper operating procedures for future emergency operations while still emphasizing that flexibility in the IAP is important.

Inspecting and Repairing Facilities and Props

It is a tradition of the fire and emergency services that personnel inspect, maintain, and repair tools, apparatus, facilities, and personal equipment on a regular basis. Depending on the item, the inspection may occur at the beginning of a work period, weekly, monthly, semiannually, or annually. The organization's personnel perform some of the inspections, while others must be performed by a third-party certification organization. Internal personnel or external vendors or maintenance companies may also perform maintenance and repairs.

To ensure a safe training environment, instructors must also inspect, maintain, and repair training facilities, props, tools, and equipment. The AHJ should establish an inspection time schedule based on industry practice, manufacturer's recommendations, and local needs. Generally, inspections by emergency response personnel of tools, facilities, apparatus, and equipment should occur on the same schedule in the stations **(Figure 2.5)**.

Figure 2.5 Training props and sites should be inspected for condition and operation periodically and before use in a training exercise. This inspection is especially important in sites designed to replicate structural collapse. *Courtesy of Louisiana State University.*

Safety on the Training Ground

Instructors are gathering and inspecting the property and the equipment they will use for a combined training exercise with law enforcement, fire, and rescue personnel. The scenario describes a partial collapse of a seven-story building under construction in a busy downtown area that is being renovated. Inclement weather had weakened poured concrete supports, and the top floor collapsed, blowing out lower supporting structures, bricks and blocks, and wooden framework. There are multiple casualties, including construction workers, bystanders and passersby, and occupants of nearby vehicles and shops.

To simulate a collapsed building and a disaster scene (and to have space to gather personnel and units), instructors are using an abandoned and decomposing warehouse in an old, little-used industrial section of town near the riverfront. The training organization has permission from the city and the site owners to use the property. Answer the following questions about hazards:

1. Think of similar areas in your jurisdiction or in cities you may have visited. List and discuss some hazards that instructors may expect to find in the described location.

2. What types of injuries could occur to participants if these hazards are not removed?

3. Regarding some of the hazards you may think of, such as waste product containers or used tires, what special arrangements must instructors or their organizations make to dispose of these items? What agencies in your jurisdiction would you contact?

4. If you were to plan a similar exercise in your jurisdiction, what possible alternative locations could you use? Are these locations safer? Are they more convenient? In what ways are they convenient or safer?

5. Does your organization have safety guidelines for selecting training sites? Have you had the opportunity to use them? After reading this chapter, do you think the guidelines are reasonable? Why or why not?

Inspections should also occur before any training course or scenario. Not only does periodic inspection ensure a safe training environment, but it also ensures that all equipment and tools are in working condition before training courses begin.

During entry-level recruit classes, inspection, maintenance, and repair (within limits) may be assigned to class members and used as a training activity. Maintenance and repairs that are beyond the capabilities of students or instructors should be delegated to certified or authorized repair personnel, which is the case with respiratory breathing equipment.

Repair, maintenance, and replacement records should be kept on all tools, apparatus, and equipment used by the training division. The records provide a basis for developing an accurate operating budget, justifying repair or replacement, and determining the value of a particular type of equipment. See Chapter 6, Report Writing and Record Keeping, for additional information.

Monitoring Training Activities

Because conditions during training can change rapidly and unexpectedly, instructors must continually monitor training activities. NFPA 1500, *Standard on Fire Department Occupational Safety and Health Program*, requires the presence of a designated ISO during high-hazard training evolutions. However, the presence of an ISO does not relieve all instructors who are present of the obligation to monitor the training with safety in mind **(Figure 2.6, p. 44)**. Instructors should be aware of and watch for the following safety concerns:

- Symptoms of physical and psychological stress in students, instructors, or other participants

- Changes in weather conditions, including wind direction, velocity, humidity, and temperature

- Unusual fire behavior in or around a training prop or burn building

- Failure of PPE or respiratory protection equipment

- Audible alarms from personal alert safety system (PASS) devices or low-pressure alarms on respiratory protection equipment

- Loss of water pressure or volume from supply hoses or hydrants

When a potential safety problem becomes apparent, the instructor should notify the designated incident commander (IC) and ISO for the

Figure 2.6 Instructors must monitor student training to ensure that proper safety behavior is performed.

training evolution. Steps should then be taken to rapidly decrease the risk and protect sudents from further risks.

Safety-Related Teaching Topics

Generally, the responsibility for teaching safety-related topics is assigned to the HSO of the organization. This delegation of duty exists in organizations that have adopted NFPA 1521. However, it may become the duty of an Instructor I under one of the following conditions:

- There is no HSO in the organization.
- The instructor also performs the function of the HSO in the organization.
- The organization can only meet its safety training obligations by spreading the responsibility between both the HSO and the training staff.

Therefore, instructors should assist the HSO in the development of lesson plans for safety-related topics. Knowledge of safety-related material benefits and prepares the instructor for the possibility of teaching the material in the future. Safety-related curriculums are available from sources such as the Home Safety Council (HSC), American and Canadian Red Cross societies, and other educational and awareness organizations. A detailed discussion of the duties and responsibilities of the HSO may be found in the IFSTA **Fire Department Safety Officer**, 2nd Edition, manual.

Instructor Incident Safety Officer Duties

The duties assigned to the HSO and ISO are outlined in NFPA 1521 and mandated in NFPA 1500. This section provides a brief overview of the ISO duties as they relate to fire and emergency services instructors. Detailed explanations may be found in the IFSTA **Fire Department Safety Officer**, 2nd Edition, manual.

All instructors should meet the JPRs of NFPA 1521 for ISO. Meeting this standard not only provides the instructor with the necessary knowledge and skills to fill this function during training evolutions but also during large-scale emergency operations. NFPA 1521 requires that the ISO position be filled with a fire organization officer who meets the requirements of Fire Officer Level I. The ISO must have the knowledge, skills, and ability necessary to manage an incident scene safely. In addition, the knowledge of safety and health hazards involved in emergency operations is required. Other knowledge requirements basic to the Level I Instructor include the following:

- Fire behavior (dynamics)
- Building construction
- Organization's personnel accountability system
- Emergency scene rehabilitation section operation

During either an emergency incident or training scenario, the IC has the ultimate responsibility for safety-related issues. At a large incident or training scenario, the safety function may be given to another chief officer, a trained company officer, the HSO, another member of the safety office, a staff officer trained to perform this function such as an instructor, or a combination of these individuals. In small organizations, the IC may find it necessary to perform this function along with other duties. Regardless of the type of incident or training scenario, the role of ISO must be defined in the fire and emergency services organization's written standard operating procedures (SOPs), based on the requirements in NFPA 1521.

At either an emergency incident or training scenario where activities are judged by the ISO to be unsafe or involve an imminent hazard, the ISO has the authority to alter, suspend, or terminate those activities. The ISO immediately informs the IC of any actions taken to correct imminent hazards. At an emergency incident or training scenario where the ISO identifies hazards that do *not* pose an imminent danger, the ISO takes appropriate action through the IC to mitigate or eliminate the hazard. When the incident or training scenario is large enough to warrant more than one ISO, assistants are appointed with the necessary authority to perform the same functions.

Statistics published by RAND® Worldwide in a March 2004 report, *Analysis of Emergency Responder Injuries and Fatalities,* indicate that more firefighters are killed and injured at emergency incident scenes during fire attack operations than during any other activity. Using an ISO provides a means of focusing specifically on safety while monitoring conditions, activities, and operations to determine whether appropriate risk-management procedures are being followed.

Through continual risk assessment, an ISO evaluates and suggests effective tactics that provide a successful outcome of an incident or training scenario while ensuring the safety of personnel operating at the incident or scenario. As outlined in NFPA 1521*, other ISO duties that apply to both emergency and training situations include the following:

- Ensure that incident scene rehabilitation is established.

- Monitor the scene and report the status of conditions, hazards, and risks to the IC.

- Ensure that a personnel accountability system is used.

- Ensure that all personnel understand the IAP.

- Provide the IC with a risk assessment of the IAP.

- Designate safety zones, collapse zones, danger or hot zones, and other hazard areas.

- Evaluate motor vehicle traffic hazards.

- Monitor radio transmissions to ensure proper and effective communications.

- Identify the need for additional assistant ISOs.

- Evaluate hazards associated with helicopter landings.

The assignment of a qualified instructor to act as ISO during all potentially hazardous training scenarios not only increases the level of safety but also provides an additional level of reality to scenarios. During training involving company personnel, company officers may be assigned the ISO duties while under the supervision of a training officer.

---

* Reprinted with permission from NFPA 1521, *Standard for Fire Department Safety Officer,* Copyright © 2002, National Fire Protection Association, Quincy, MA 02269. This reprinted material is not the complete and official position of the National Fire Protection Association on the referenced subject, which is represented only by the standard in its entirety.

Instructor as Safety Role Model

When safety is emphasized and learned in training, it tends to be remembered and practiced during emergency response operations. The instructor is the primary role model for safety and must take that role seriously. Instructors cannot just mention safety guidelines and expect students to follow them. Instructors must demonstrate and reinforce these guidelines.

Following safety guidelines or plans developed or adopted by the training division has a significant effect on reducing injuries and fatalities of fire and emergency services personnel in training and at emergency incidents. Fire and emergency services organizations conduct emergency operations under the NIMS ICS, which provides an organized structure for operational coordination and effectiveness as well as safety aspects of emergency situations. Instructors must be familiar with the locally adopted, established NIMS ICS and safety procedures and then integrate them into training exercises.

Instructor Tip: Know Safety Policies and Guidelines

Be sure you are aware of your organization's safety policies and guidelines for each emergency services training course that you teach. If you don't have a copy, get one. If you are *not* sure how to implement these policies and guidelines, talk with other instructors. If a policy is in place and you, as an instructor, do *not* follow its guidelines, you may be held liable for injuries to students.

Reinforcing Safety

Safety is an issue that must be continually emphasized. Instructors must plan and devote appropriate time in every session to cover all areas of safety such as the following:

- Requirements or procedures for ensuring safety
- Safeguards and equipment used for preventing accidents
- Procedures for managing and investigating accidents

An instructor is in a position to influence students and other personnel in using proper safety procedures. Because instructors constantly interact with personnel in planning and presenting courses, they set the stage and provide role models for implementing, enforcing, and following safety requirements.

Safety awareness and practice begin in training sessions. In classroom lessons, instructors increase awareness in the following ways:

- Describe possible hazards and explain the necessary precautions.
- Describe the proper equipment to use.
- Reinforce the appropriate safety rules before the participants begin to practice a skill.

When *planning* practical training evolutions, instructors look for potential hazards in the sessions and then eliminate them. Instructors must also plan to address the precautions to take to prevent injury while training, train students to recognize job hazards, and teach them how to control or eliminate these hazards. These steps help ensure an acceptable level of risk in a risky profession and prevent injuries.

When *conducting* practical training evolutions, instructors must either act as ISO or appoint a safety officer who acts as ISO or monitor. This training assignment can be particularly useful during company drills by permitting company officers to perform as ISO. Another important step to take before starting any practical training evolution is to review the safety rules and equipment-use guidelines (**Figure 2.7**).

To ensure that all students understand these rules and guidelines, provide them in writing. Read the written rules and guidelines aloud as the

Figure 2.7 Instructors should familiarize students with the organization's safety policy that applies to an exercise before any training exercises are conducted. *Courtesy of Louisiana State University, Fire and Emergency Training Institute.*

students read them silently. Some organizations require that participants in a training course sign a statement that they have read and understood these rules and guidelines.

Fire and emergency services programs often train nonemergency services employees. Although these students may *not* be required to perform all aspects of the curriculum on their jobs, instructors must enforce all safety procedures as these employees participate in the course. It is still important that they follow safety guidelines even though all training procedures may *not* pertain to or affect them.

Safety must be stressed and made a high priority from the beginning of the course. In the position of role model, instructors will demonstrate safe procedures that students will imitate and incorporate into their skills so that they become habits.

Implementing Safety Plans

As part of the risk-management plan, all organizations must establish safety policies and procedures to follow in the event of an accident during classroom and drill ground exercises. As instructors begin all courses and practical training evolutions, they should first discuss and explain the organization's safety plan, program, and policies. In some organizations, the training administrator presents the safety policies to entry-level personnel to emphasize management's support and demonstrate that instructors are authorized to enforce the policies.

Parts of the safety plan include the names of contact personnel, duties to perform or assign, and types of documentation to complete and maintain. In case of an accident, instructors must know the procedures to follow and explain them to students. Students need to know the following information:

- What signals are given when an accident occurs
- What to do when the signal is given
- What steps to take to help the injured person
- Whether training stops or proceeds

Accident Prevention and Management

The first step to safe training programs is *preventing accidents,* which means preventing the loss of personnel, property, money, and time. The learning environment, whether inside or outside the organization, must meet safety codes and be free of structural problems and natural or human-caused hazards that can potentially cause injury. The time required for the completion of paperwork to report an incident for review, evaluation, and determination of methods for preventing a recurrence in a similar incident should also be a consideration.

Managing accidents is the next step for creating a safe training environment, which includes identifying accident factors, investigating accidents that do occur, and analyzing those accidents to look for causes and trends. Recommendations are then made for accident prevention.

Prevention

Accidents are usually the result of unsafe acts by persons who are unaware or uninformed of potential hazards, are ignorant of the safety policies, or fail to follow safety procedures. Accidents may also be caused by conditions in the physical environment that were *not* examined or considered as potential hazards. The majority of accidents are predictable and preventable.

Instructor Tip: Check Class and Training Environments

Interior Precautions:

Before starting class sessions, check the environment for safety hazards and alleviate them. Look for the following hazards at inside training sites:

- Unstable or broken chairs, tables, and desks
- Loose carpeting and cords that can trip individuals
- Frayed wires, overloaded sockets, and plugs without grounds

Ensure that exits are properly marked and lighted and *not* blocked by tables, chairs, or other items. If the classroom does *not* have windows, does the room have auxiliary lighting? If *not,* what alternate means of lighting is available? What other hazards might be present in this environment?

Exterior Precautions:

Look for the following hazards at outside training sites and props:

- Debris, rocks, holes, or uneven areas that could cause falls and injuries
- Unstable building parts such as walls, chimneys, and flooring that could collapse
- Sharp edges, protrusions, or other types of physical damage on training props that might result in an injury

Ensure that overhead electrical transmission lines will *not* interfere with ladder raises or aerial operations. Also, when training is being done along roadways, ensure that emergency vehicles display all appropriate visual markings. What other hazards might be present in this environment?

The occurrence of an accident indicates that someone failed to plan, someone performed in an unsafe manner, or an unsafe condition existed. Instructors can reduce the potential for accidents by planning for safety and maintaining control over the training situation. Accident-prevention steps include the following:

- Plan carefully for training scenarios.
- Ensure that appropriately trained personnel assist in supervising scenarios.
- Inform students of safety policies and potential hazards.

- Inspect and repair tools, equipment, props, and apparatus before starting training sessions.
- Assign an ISO to each training scenario.
- Model and reinforce safety policies and procedures by personally adhering to them.

Management

When an accident does occur, instructors must be able to manage the situation. Managing accidents requires advanced preparation, and instructors must be aware of the factors that may result in an accident. Instructors must be trained in the techniques of accident investigation and analysis, and they must be able to generate recommendations for future accident prevention (mitigation) based on the analysis results.

Factors

After an accident occurs, it is often easy to see the cause and wonder why anyone would create or tolerate unsafe mechanical or physical conditions or take a risk and perform an unsafe act. Many factors cause individuals to disregard risks, all of which can be controlled (**Figure 2.8**). Some accident factors include the following:

- *Management* — Oversight, omission, or mismanagement that affects other factors
- *Situation* — Facilities, tools, equipment, or vehicles unavailable, in disrepair, or not used or used improperly
- *Environment* — Noise, vibration, temperature extremes, poor lighting, and moisture that affects concentration or ability to function

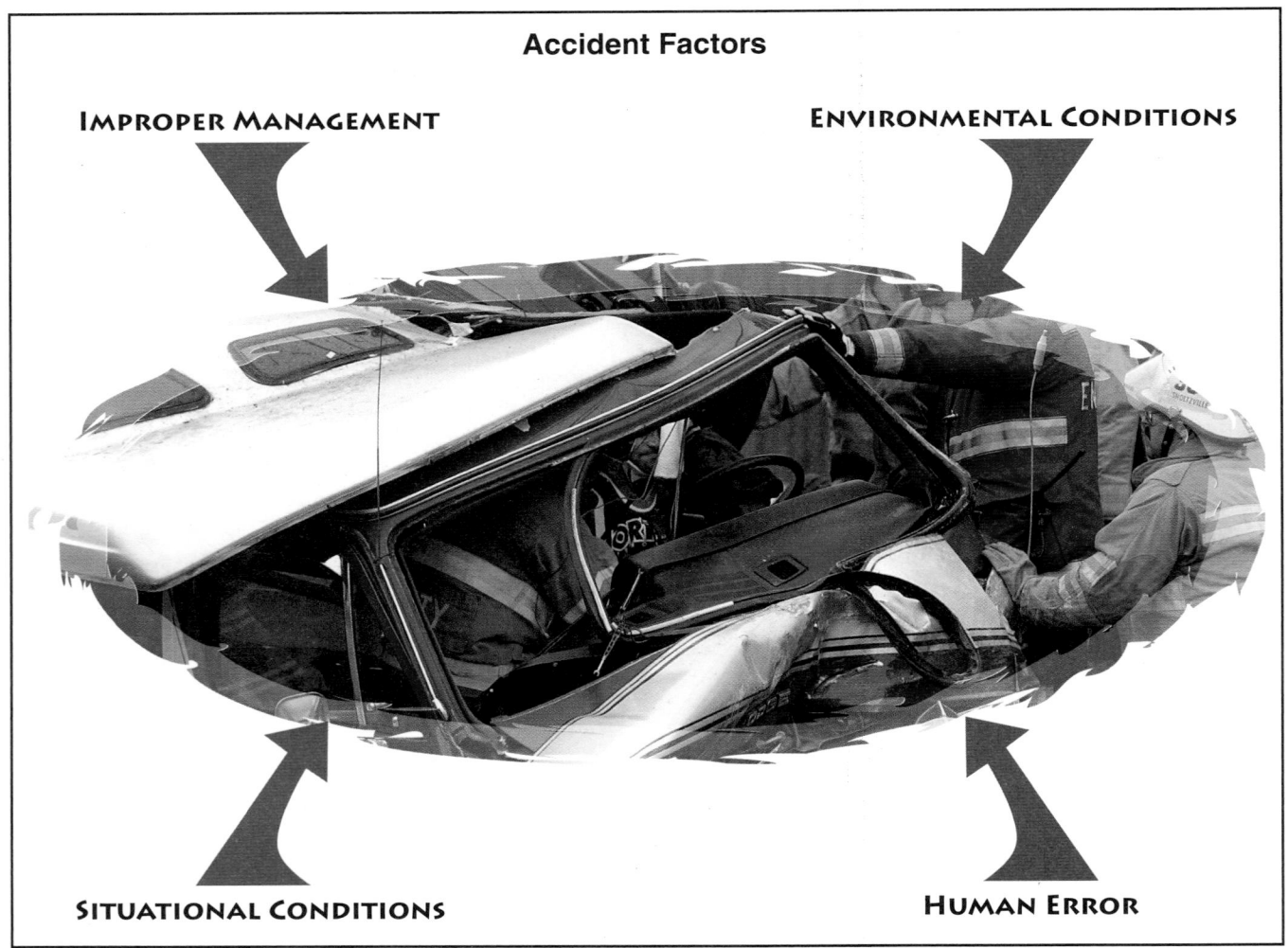

Figure 2.8 Illustration of the factors that contribute to accidents. *Photo courtesy of Bob Esposito.*

- *Human* — Individuals and their experiences, ignorance or innocence, and self-assurance

While all factors are significant and may contribute to other factors, the human factor plays a major part in accidents. Analyses of industrial accidents indicate that accidents do *not* distribute themselves by chance but happen frequently to some people and infrequently to others. A reason for this occurrence is the *human factor:* Some individuals fail to learn from experience or instruction on how to control known hazards, causing that person to become involved in accidents more frequently.

Three human factors contribute to accidents. Before allowing participation in a training scenario, an instructor should determine whether any of the following factors apply to an individual student:

- *Improper attitude* — Readjust faulty attitudes or behaviors so that the individual does *not* create or become involved in an accident. *Is the individual:*
  — Irresponsible or reckless?
  — Inconsiderate or uncooperative?
  — Fearful of or phobic about the situation?
  — Egotistical or jealous?
  — Intolerant or impatient?
  — Excitable or oversensitive?
  — Obsessive or absentminded?

- *Lack of knowledge or skill* — Correct these defects by providing proper training and an appropriate opportunity to practice under supervision. *Is the individual:*
  — Sufficiently informed about the training?
  — Capable of interpreting the training and convinced of its need?
  — Experienced in requisite knowledge and skills and capable of decisive actions?
  — Properly trained and able to recognize potential hazards/risks?

- *Physical limitations* — Guide individuals to seek professional assistance if the instructor is unable to help students overcome all physical constraints. In many cases, an instructor can work with individuals to improve their confidence and abilities. Before doing any physical activity, an instructor can lead participants through some simple warm-up activities that include muscle stretching and strengthening exercises. An instructor who is *not* familiar with how to properly and safely perform these exercises should consult the organization's health unit, HSO, or physician for guidance. *Is the individual:*

— Able to see and hear well enough for the situation?
— Able to safely perform a task based on physical characteristics?
— Limited by aerobic capacity or strength?
— Affected by a medical condition, allergy, or illness?
— Limited by a physical or mental condition?
— Affected by substance abuse, causing reduced reaction times?
— Affected by legally prescribed medication, causing reduced reaction times?

Especially important to instructors is any condition or factor that could lead to the injury or death of a participant. Undoubtedly, good training plays an important role in enhancing safety while responding to, acting on, and returning from any fire or emergency incident. The twofold concern of safety on the fire or emergency scene and safety on the training ground both depend on teaching, enforcing, and reinforcing behaviors that participants must learn, adapt, and practice at all times.

Instructor Tip: Check Records for Injury Trends

Check available training records and reports belonging to the organization to see whether any injury trends occurred during training over the past 5 to 10 years. Also, check the training accident reports of neighboring emergency organizations and reports available from the USFA, NFPA, or other U.S. or Canadian government agency. Answer the following questions:

- From the information given, can you determine whether an injury was due to faulty equipment or to improper behavior?
- Based on the information or conclusions found in the reports, were new safety guidelines implemented?
- What steps (that you may have been unaware of before) will you now take to teach students appropriate safety behaviors?

Investigations

Accidents usually occur through a logical and predictable sequence of events. Investigate all accidents to determine their cause and sequence and then decide what steps to take to prevent their reoccurrence. Investigations are *fact-finding* but not *faultfinding* procedures; that is, the sole purpose of an investigation is to determine what factors resulted in the accident and *not* who to blame for the accident.

Accident investigations must be conducted with objective determination and free of personal feelings toward management or those involved in the accident. The purposes of accident investigation include the following:

- Avoid loss of human resources and equipment.

- Ensure cost-effectiveness in the use of personnel and equipment.

- Improve the morale of both the organization's personnel and the public.

- Determine the change or deviation that caused the accident.

- Determine hazardous conditions to which fire and emergency services personnel may be exposed.

- Direct the attention of the administration to the causes of accidents.

- Examine facts as though they have a legal bearing on accident cases.

Instructors usually work with the HSO or ISO in conducting investigations of accidents that occur during training **(Figure 2.9)**. Both the instructor and ISO will likely be present when the accident occurs and are most able to provide detailed information. The ISO is generally responsible for the accident investigation as required in NFPA 1521. In some cases, external organizations have the responsibility for making an investigation of the accident. In those cases, the instructor must be prepared to provide assistance to those organizations and coordinate investigative activities with them.

Instructors must also make students aware that the intent of investigation procedures is *not* to cast blame but rather to determine why an accident occurred. The investigation determines

Figure 2.9 Instructors who are assigned incident safety officer duties for training exercises may be required to perform accident investigations if an accident occurs. *Courtesy of Alabama Fire College.*

and analyzes the events that caused the accident so future accidents can be prevented and training procedures can be reevaluated and revised for safety effectiveness.

Often, instructors and students who are involved in or witness an accident are afraid to provide information, thinking that they may *get someone in trouble*. The situation cannot be resolved and future situations cannot be prevented when valuable information is withheld. The instructor's role is then as follows:

- Explain all points of the organization's safety policies.

- Ensure that all safety precautions are followed.

- Describe all steps that must be taken in the event of an accident.

- Emphasize the positive purpose of an investigation.

Analyses

Once accident data has been collected, the ISO reviews and analyzes it to determine causes and makes recommendations for prevention. Included in the process of accident review and analysis is the examination of current and past records for significant areas that may have been overlooked during the hazard/risk analysis. Keeping records of activities becomes an important responsibility of the HSO, safety office, instructors, and training division administrators.

Careful record keeping often reveals minor situations and trends that indicate the need for corrective action. For example, a scratch is *not* disabling, but when it is received from a piece of equipment that was placed or used in an awkward position or without protective equipment, the incident points to a need for corrective action. Investigators reviewing records note the number of scratches reported in similar situations and follow the record review with research, interviews, and discussions that lead to recommendations for appropriate changes.

While reviewing records for types and frequency of injuries, investigators can list and categorize injuries in order to prioritize hazards and take appropriate corrective action. Consider the following two factors when prioritizing hazards (**Figure 2.10**):

- Performance frequency of the hazardous activity and how it directly relates to the accident or injury frequency
- Relative severity of the potential loss

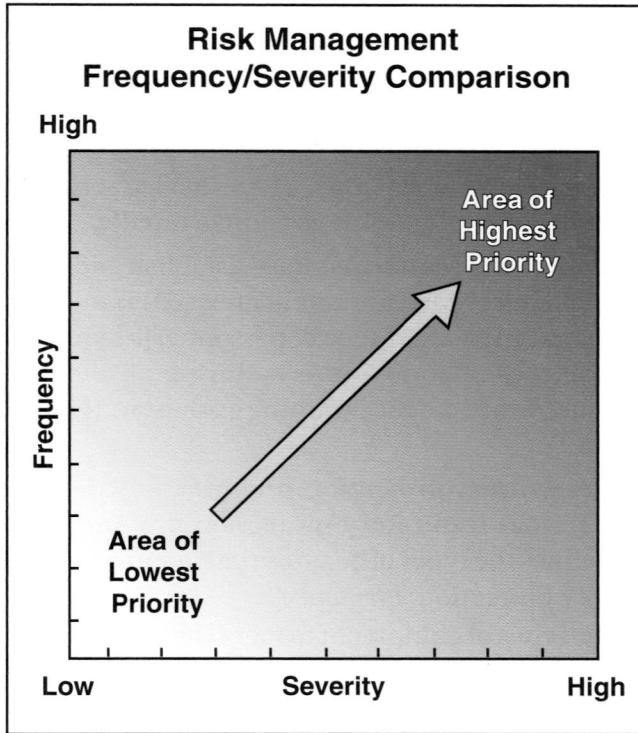

Figure 2.10 When prioritizing hazards, an instructor must consider the severity and frequency of the hazard. Top-rated hazards are those that are both the most severe and most likely to occur.

For example, a frequently performed task may have the risk of causing a minor hand injury when the task is *not* performed correctly. It may be a higher priority to address this hand-injury hazard than to address an infrequently performed task that has the potential for a more serious injury. Ideally, all hazards are addressed as high priorities for training, but hazard prioritization is often a reality and necessity imposed by limited training resources and a common-sense approach to eliminating injuries. See **Appendix F,** Risk-Management Formulas, for the frequency/severity table and calculation formulas.

Performing the following actions enables investigators to analyze circumstances or conditions surrounding accidents:

- Identify and locate principal sources of accidents by determining the materials, machines, equipment, or tools most frequently involved with accidents and job-producing injuries.
- Disclose the nature and size of the accident problem in different operations.
- Indicate the need for engineering revisions by identifying the unsafe conditions of various types of equipment.
- Identify problems in operating procedures and processes contributing to accidents.
- Disclose unsafe practices that might suggest or direct additional training.
- Identify personnel placement where lack of ability or physical handicap contributes to accidents.
- Enable supervisors to use time, personnel, and resources more effectively by providing information about hazards and unsafe practices in their operations.
- Permit an objective evaluation of the safety program's progress.

Accident analyses can also reveal the need for additional training in specific procedures. Individuals may act with good intentions yet *not* understand the consequences of their actions. In many cases, individuals who perform unsafe acts are *not* aware of the safety factor until an accident occurs. Under these conditions, individuals can become involved in accidents that result in injuries, fatalities, or property damage.

Figure 2.11 The incident safety officer must be prepared to stop any training exercise when an unsafe act occurs and correct the behavior that resulted in that act. *Courtesy of U.S. Department of Defense.*

The instructor's role is to ensure that all training is conducted under the safest possible conditions **(Figure 2.11)**. The instructor looks at all training exercises with safety in mind from the beginning to end and also makes students aware of the need to look for accident potentials.

Mitigation Activities

Activities that prevent or minimize the effects of a hazard are referred to as *mitigation* or prevention activities. Because training involves behavioral changes, the instructor is responsible for developing and presenting training that will cause these changes or improvements. Improvements in human behavior must come from behavior changes. Some critical areas need ongoing attention and enforcement. For example, the following topics are critical to fire and emergency services training organizations and must be emphasized in their programs:

- *Driver/operator education* — Educate fire and emergency services responders to pay attention to and practice safe driving habits, including controlling speed, observing traffic rules, and ensuring that everyone on the apparatus or in the vehicle is seated and wearing a seatbelt. The proper operation of pumps and aerial devices is also an essential topic to ensure safe operation.

- *Health and fitness* — Encourage better health and fitness, which can result in additional reductions in fatalities and serious injuries of fire and emergency services personnel. *Procedures:*
  — Screen applicants and current personnel based on the criteria in NFPA 1582, *Standard on Comprehensive Occupational Medical Program for Fire Departments.*
  — Continue to monitor personnel by requiring them to meet fitness requirements throughout their careers.
  — Provide annual medical evaluations and annual occupational fitness evaluations for all personnel.

- *PASS devices* — Train all fire and emergency services personnel in the use of PASS devices. Properly maintain and test PASS devices on the same schedule that all PPE is tested.

- *Incident action plan* — Establish and use IAPs during all types of emergency incidents and high-hazard training evolutions. See **Appendix G** for copies of ICS Forms 201 through 206 and 215 that are used for developing written IAPs.

- *Personnel accountability* — Include use of a personnel accountability system in the IAP to track personnel by location and function. This system allows the IC to know where personnel are operating and what they are doing so they can be located rapidly if a PASS device activates or hazardous conditions change rapidly.

- *Rapid intervention teams* — Establish and train rapid intervention teams or crews (RITs or RICs) for use in case a rescue of personnel is required. Use these teams or crews during all live-fire and confined-space training evolutions **(Figure 2.12)**.

- *Respiratory protection program* — Establish a formal respiratory protection program that defines the types of hazards that require respiratory protection. *Elements:*
  — Types of equipment to meet the specific hazards
  — Care, maintenance, and use of respiratory protection equipment
  — Fit testing and training required before using the equipment

Figure 2.12 Rapid intervention teams (RITs) should be established during all types of high-hazard training exercises. *Courtesy of District Chief Chris Mickal.*

Training and education programs can reduce the potential for fatalities and injuries among fire and emergency responders. Driver/operator training can address many pertinent and current concerns. Health and safety courses specifically targeting critical issues are already available. More research and course development are needed to continue the downward trends of fatalities and injury rates. Instructors can contribute to affect these trends by being aware of the importance of stressing and enforcing safety in every training course, especially when conducting live-fire or other practical-training evolutions (see Chapter 12, Structured Exercises, Demonstrations, and Practical Training Evolutions).

Resources: Safety Guidelines, Regulations, and Information

Instructors may find it difficult to be current with revisions to existing regulations and the creation of new safety regulations and guidelines by government agencies and other organizations. In addition, when instructors develop safety programs or lesson plans, they must find reliable, accurate, and current information. Many resources and references are available from the following entities:

- Federal government agencies
- State/provincial and local governmental occupational safety and health agencies
- Standards-writing organizations
- Professional organizations and associations

These organizations or agencies can ensure that instructors receive information from credible sources. Knowing the resources and how to contact them (or being on their mailing lists) are valuable assets for any instructor.

Federal Government Agencies

Numerous federal government agencies in North America are responsible for developing, regulating, and ensuring safe workplace policies. In the U.S., the two primary agencies concerned with safety in the workplace are NIOSH and the Occupational Safety and Health Administration (OSHA). The Occupational Safety and Health Act of 1970 created both agencies.

The responsibilities of NIOSH include investigating, researching, and evaluating safety and health hazards in the workplace. The responsibilities of OSHA include setting and enforcing workplace safety and health standards. OSHA also has the authority to issue citations and fines to enforce safety and health standards.

Both federal and state OSHA regulatory agencies enforce worker protection standards for employees. In some states (called *federal OSHA states*) the federal government enforces OSHA regulations that apply to private and federal firefighters in non-state-plan states. Many states have their own occupational safety regulations that are enforced by a state agency. State plans must equal or exceed federal requirements. See **Appendix H** for a list of state-plan states and non-state-plan states. Regulations that apply to volunteer firefighters vary from state to state.

It is important for instructors to know which regulatory organization has jurisdiction over their operations. Occupational safety and health regulations significantly influence fire and emergency services training. These regulations vary among jurisdictions; therefore, instructors must know and use the applicable regulations to ensure safety. Instructors are encouraged to contact their appropriate state/provincial agency to determine the legal requirements and authority.

Other U.S. federal government agencies that can provide training and safety-related information and programs are USFA, Department of Homeland Security-Federal Emergency Management Agency (DHS-FEMA), and the Centers for Disease Control and Prevention (CDC). These organizations can provide information on weapons of mass destruction (WMD), PPE for high-threat incidents, and bioterrorism training.

In Canada, information is available from the Canadian Centre for Occupational Health and Safety (CCOHC). Agencies in both Canada and the U.S. share information and materials. Some Canadian safety regulations are based on or modeled after NFPA standards and U.S. OSHA regulations.

State/Provincial and Local Safety and Health Agencies

States/provinces and local governmental occupational safety and health agencies often have review and enforcement functions. For example, states/provinces may fall under the guidelines of an enforcement organization whose rules and regulations must be observed during a training evolution or exercise. In Canada and the U.S., states/provinces or local agencies may have to fol-low regulations that may differ from, expand upon, or exceed national rules. They may also have to follow additional regulations that are *not* addressed at the federal level.

Instructors and safety officers must know the regulations of all federal, state/provincial, and local agencies — how they differ or contradict each other and which ones must be followed to what extent. Instructors and training administrators must obtain copies and follow all applicable regulations.

Instructors should *not* limit their inquiries to regulations for fire and emergency services. State/provincial and local agencies may have safety regulations written for other industries or organizations that apply to fire and emergency services training. For example, regulations for construction workers on a roof may be applicable to firefighters training for vertical ventilation scenarios. Fire and emergency services trench-rescue operations may be governed by regulations for shoring and cribbing that apply to private contractors that lay underground cables and pipelines (**Figure 2.13**).

Figure 2.13 Trench-rescue training must adhere to all safety regulations that apply to below-grade type work. *Courtesy of Maryland Fire and Rescue Institute (MFRI).*

In addition to enforcement inspectors, many regulatory agencies have consultants or educators who can review pertinent safety regulations with instructors who are planning a training curriculum or course. State/provincial and local health departments or agencies can also provide statistical data and safety programs as well as information on diseases and their prevention.

Standards-Writing Organizations

Standards-writing organizations develop and issue operating procedures and design requirements for various industries, including the fire and emergency services profession. Consensus committees composed of industry representatives develop most of these standards. These standards do *not* become law until adopted by a government authority. The American National Standards Institute (ANSI) does *not* develop standards but facilitates their development through the consensus process. Among the primary standards-writing organizations involved with the fire service are the following:

- National Fire Protection Association (NFPA)
- American Society for Testing and Materials (ASTM)
- Underwriters Laboratories Inc. (UL)
- Underwriters' Laboratories of Canada (ULC)

National Fire Protection Association

NFPA is an organization that develops minimum safety standards and guidelines that many training organizations adopt. Government and other agencies can adopt NFPA standards as their guidelines for safety compliance. Instructors must be aware of and familiar with NFPA standards that relate to safety and guide the performance of live-fire training evolutions and other high-hazard training.

Sample List of NFPA Standards

- **NFPA 1041, *Standard for Fire Service Instructor Professional Qualifications*** — Identifies the professional levels of competence required of fire service instructors; includes requirements for conducting high-hazard training using applicable safety standards and practices

- **NFPA 1402, *Guide to Building Fire Service Training Centers*** — Lists guidelines to follow when building training facilities (including burn buildings, smoke buildings, and combination buildings) and when conducting outside drill ground activities

- **NFPA 1403, *Standard on Live Fire Training Evolutions*** — Lists guidelines to follow during live-fire training evolutions, including information on structures, fuel materials, safety, instructors, and reports and records; also provides guidelines for conducting outside evolutions (not in structures), including information on site preparation, safety, instructor-to-student ratio, and postburn activities

- **NFPA 1410, *Standard on Training for Initial Emergency Scene Operations*** — Contains minimum requirements for evaluating training for initial fire suppression and rescue procedures used by fire department personnel engaged in emergency scene operations

- **NFPA 1500, *Standard on Fire Department Occupational Safety and Health Program*** — Contains information on the guidelines for fire departments to follow in order to ensure the health and safety of firefighters and help prevent accidents and health problems

- **NFPA 1521, *Standard for Fire Department Safety Officer*** — Contains minimum requirements for the assignment, duties, and responsibilities of a health and safety officer and an incident safety officer for a fire department or other fire service organization

- **NFPA 1561, *Standard on Emergency Services Incident Management System*** — Contains the minimum requirements for an incident management system to manage all emergency incidents

- **NFPA 1583, *Standard on Health-Related Fitness Programs for Fire Fighters*** — Outlines a complete health-related fitness program designed for fire departments including job descriptions, rehabilitation, nutrition, and wellness components

- **NFPA 1584, *Recommended Practice on the Rehabilitation of Members Operating at Incident Scene Operations and Training Exercises*** — Contains recommended practices and criteria for developing and implementing an incident scene and training exercise rehabilitation program

Standards are reviewed and revised periodically, and new standards are often created from existing ones. Some of these standards are briefly described in the sidebar (p. 55), but instructors must check with their organizations for the most current standards and to see which ones apply to their organizations, personnel, and instructional responsibilities.

American Society for Testing and Materials

ASTM is another organization that has developed and published numerous technical standards that are used by fire and emergency services organizations. It also develops and conducts training in the performance, use, and application of ASTM standards, many of which apply to equipment used by fire and emergency services personnel. Product safety has been a major factor in the reduction of training injuries, but this result is only possible when training programs emphasize and follow all safety guidelines **(Figure 2.14)**. ASTM technical committees research and develop standards to address areas such as the following:

- Hazardous materials
- Protective equipment
- Footwear
- Occupational health and safety
- Building materials
- Search and rescue
- Other areas that affect personnel in fire-fighting and rescue operations

American National Standards Institute

ANSI is a private, nonprofit membership organization that has the mission of making the U.S. economy more competitive in the world market. To accomplish this mission, ANSI coordinates the private-sector voluntary standardization system through ANSI-accredited member organizations. ANSI does *not* develop standards but facilitates their development through the consensus process. ANSI-approved standards include the following:

- Respiratory protection practices
- Physical qualifications for using respiratory protection equipment
- Fit-testing methods

Figure 2.14 Personnel protective equipment must meet very strict production, care, and use requirements established by various testing and certification organizations. *Photo courtesy of Austin (TX) Fire Department.*

Underwriters Laboratories Inc.

UL in the U.S. and ULC in Canada are active in testing and certifying fire-extinguishing agents and equipment. Agents and equipment that meet these requirements are said to be *UL/ULC listed.* Certification tests and UL/ULC acceptance provide consumers with independent documentation on product-performance characteristics. These independent tests provide ongoing, unbiased assurance that fire-fighting products will perform as advertised.

Information contained in the UL/ULC *Fire Protection Equipment Directory* is often used by progressive fire organizations for prepurchase comparisons. It can also be used to compose purchasing specifications that ensure minimum performance and suitability for a product's intended use.

Professional Organizations and Associations

Fire and emergency services professional organizations such as the IAFC, Canadian Association of Fire Chiefs/Association canadienne des chef de pompiers (CAFC/ACCP), IAFF, and National Volunteer Fire Council (NVFC) are important sources of safety information and model programs.

Fire and emergency services instructor associations and safety organizations also provide information on safety and networking opportunities. These organizations often provide information and sources at the request of instructors who are not members but who need information for their programs. Some of these organizations include the following:

- Fire Department Safety Officer Association (FDSOA)
- International Society of Fire Service Instructors (ISFSI)
- American Society of Safety Engineers (ASSE)

Summary

There is no denying that working in the fire and emergency services is a hazardous occupation — that fact will *not* change. Through education and training, some of the hazards and risks can be reduced or eliminated. Fire and emergency services instructors are keys to the success of this process. They must provide a safe training environment, teach safety-related topics, function as the ISO when assigned, and provide students and peers with a positive safety role model. They must also be capable of performing accident investigations and analyses for accidents that occur during training and at emergency scene incidents.

Instructors will find safety-related information, programs, and guidelines from multiple sources at all levels of government, from standards-writing organizations, and from professional associations. Armed with this information, instructors can provide their students with a foundation of knowledge and skills that will increase safety awareness and produce safe behavioral traits.

Emphasize Safe Training

On June 21, 2005, the fire and emergency services in the United States held a National Safety Stand Down day to emphasize the need for safety at emergency incidents and the need for increased physical fitness of all personnel. The International Association of Fire Chiefs (IAFC) and 19 partnering organizations sponsored the Stand Down as a means of calling attention to the increasing number of line-of-duty deaths (LODD) and injuries.

Training divisions and agencies are not only responsible for providing safety training but also for providing safe training. Numerous personnel, as mentioned in the chapter, have been killed or injured during training evolutions.

To alter this trend, training organizations must institute their own training safety initiatives. Training organizations must be proactive in safety — both in implementing safety procedures and ensuring that personnel are physically capable of performing tasks required during training and on the job.

Safety must be at the forefront of organizational issues. One suggestion is to include safety as an issue at every training staff meeting. A safety topic could be placed on the meeting agenda, discussed, and emphasized. It could even focus on a particular safety-related topic such as the procedure for safely backing an apparatus. The topic could be expanded to determine whether the policy is adequate or needs to be thoroughly reviewed and altered.

Another approach is to establish a monthly or annual Safety Stand Down day within the training organization. Specialists in the safety and health fields could address safety-related topics as well as health and wellness topics. For instance, a daylong seminar in properly performing physical fitness exercises or implementing proper nutrition could be expanded into a train-the-trainer class for company officers.

Finally, in an effort to address heart attacks, the major cause of LODD, a training policy that requires warm-up and cool-down exercises before all practical training evolutions could be developed and required. Rehabilitation facilities should be available during training exercises.

Instructors should be trained to recognize symptoms of heat stress, overexertion, and heart attack in their early stages. *Never* ignore symptoms that may be indicators of serious medical problems. A procedure for providing immediate care should be in place for medical problems that may occur at anytime — in or out of the classroom.

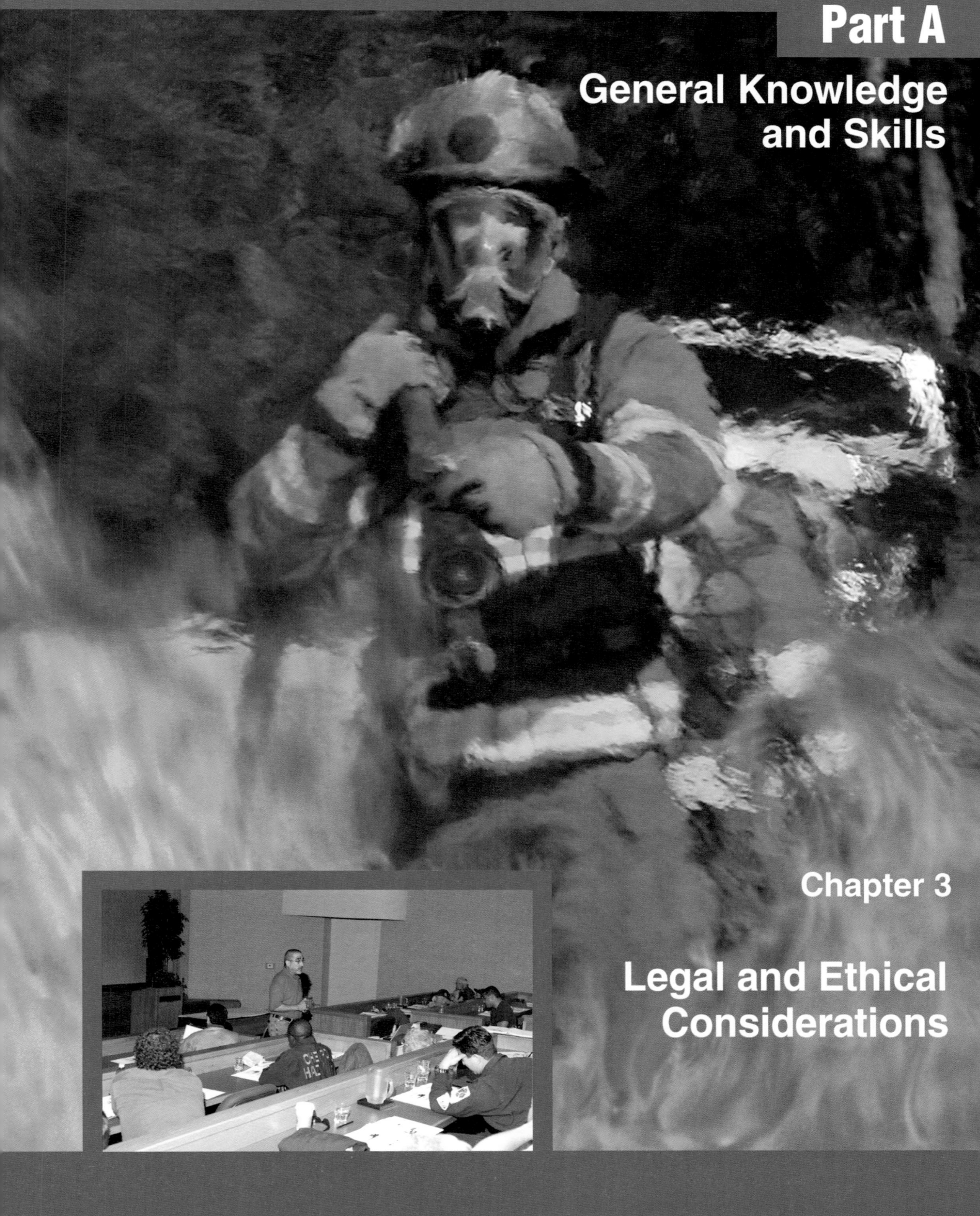

Part A

General Knowledge and Skills

Chapter 3

Legal and Ethical Considerations

After reading this chapter, students will be able to —

1. Identify facts about how legal considerations affect the instructor.

2. Identify legal terms.

3. Distinguish among the types of laws.

4. Identify U.S. legislative laws.

5. Discuss why state/provincial governments and local governments create their own laws and regulations.

6. Describe information contained in training records and attendance records.

7. Identify facts about legal requirements for record keeping.

8. Identify facts about legal liability.

9. List precautions instructors can take to reduce liability.

10. List steps to prevent or minimize personal liability in the event an accident or potentially liable incident occurs.

11. Identify facts about copyright laws and permissions.

12. Describe factors to consider when using photographs, films, or videos.

13. List students' rights.

14. Identify facts about environmental issues.

15. Discuss the basic components of ethics.

16. List characteristics of a written code of ethics.

17. Describe steps to take when resolving an ethical dilemma.

Chapter Contents

Law and the Instructor
Legal Terminology
Types of Laws

Law Applications
Records Management
Legal Liability
Copyright Laws and Permissions
Students' Rights
Environmental Issues

Ethical Conduct
Components of Ethics
Personal Ethics Origins
Unethical Conduct Causes
Personal Justifications
Ethics Program
Elements
Code of Ethics
Ethical Issues

Summary

Chapter 3
Legal and Ethical Considerations

Humans depend on laws to protect and control members of society. Some laws, such as those based on the Bill of Rights of the United States (U.S.) Constitution or the Canadian Charter of Rights and Freedoms, are intended to protect the freedoms or property of the individual. Other laws control society by establishing limits on what people can do. An example is the law that establishes the speed limit on federally funded interstate highways in the U.S. In summary, laws provide social controls for a society.

As members of society, instructors (as well as all members of a fire and emergency services organization) are bound by laws and similar legal restrictions. To effectively perform their duties, instructors must know the laws, regulations, ordinances, codes, standards, and policies that apply to them and their functions. This chapter provides instructors with basic information on the types of laws and legal documents that apply to them, legal issues that may affect their job performance, and how to apply the laws and legal documents along with precautions that should be taken when there is doubt about a legal situation.

At the same time, ethics control the actions of individuals in another way. *Ethics* (sometimes called *moral philosophies*) are the philosophical principles that are used to determine correct and proper behavior by the members of a society. From the viewpoint of the ancient Greek philosophers, a set of ethics (or *ethos*) is the glue that holds a civilization together. Without ethics, there would be chaos, and civilization (or society) would dissolve. Ethics played a large role in early Greek society

and, therefore, the civilization of North America, which is strongly based on the writings of the Greek philosophers.

Unfortunately, the ethical examples that tend to appear in the news media today are predominately examples of the *lack* of ethical conduct more than anything else. The following examples are just some of the ethically questionable activities that appear to be commonplace in society:

- Insider stock trading
- Pork-barrel political programs
- Sexual harassment
- Racial, ethnic, or gender discrimination

Because fire and emergency services organizations are *not* immune to similar situations, it is essential that instructors understand the importance of ethical conduct and how to adhere to it. The last section of this chapter gives the following information:

- Individual and organizational ethical conduct and issues in the fire and emergency services
- Need for and creation of an ethics program
- Overview of how to write a code of ethics for an organization
- Some organizations that have examples of codes of ethics

Law and the Instructor

Instructors and the organizations they work for can be held legally responsible for either their actions or lack of actions. Therefore, instructors must be knowledgeable about the laws, regulations, ordinances, codes, standards, and policies that affect them while performing their duties. National Fire Protection Association (NFPA) 1041, *Standard for Fire Service Instructor Professional Qualifications* (2007), requires the Level I Instructor to have knowledge about the following items:

- Agency policies
- Laws that require record keeping and maintenance
- Laws that permit and restrict the disclosure of personal training information

Level II Instructors have the same requirements plus the knowledge about safety-related rules and regulations. Finally, Level III Instructors, in addition to meeting the requirements of the previous two levels, must have knowledge of all laws that influence the acquisition, storage, and dissemination of test and evaluation results for student performance. A detailed discussion of the record-keeping process is in Chapter 6, Report Writing and Record Keeping.

If all the laws mentioned addressed all of the legal requirements that instructors must know, it would be fairly simple to learn them and apply the information. Unfortunately, keeping records, disseminating student test results, and restricting public access to private information are only small portions of the laws that affect fire and emergency services training activities. Applicable laws include (but are not limited to) the following:

- Federal requirements for teaching specific topics
- Restrictions on discrimination and harassment
- Environmental restrictions
- Definition of student rights

State/provincial and local laws and ordinances include restrictions on open burning at live-fire exercises, adherence to fire and life safety codes, and specific requirements for the transfer of ownership of acquired structures for use in training. When legally adopted, consensus standards establish minimum criteria for student performance and evaluation during training. The sections that follow provide an overview of legal terminology plus an explanation of the various types of legal documents

and a discussion of some of the specific laws that apply to the training function.

Legal Terminology

Understanding the differences between codes, regulations, standards, guides, and laws and how they are enacted are extremely important elements for fire and emergency services personnel. Two general procedures are used in the establishment of laws: First is through statutes promulgated (adopted) by legislative action. Second is through codes, regulations, and standards promulgated into law by agencies with rule-making authority. The latter procedure is the most common one by far and more readily responsive to the need for change.

Promulgation through either course of action has the same force and effect of law. Codes, regulations, guides, standards, and laws that are applied to the fire and emergency services are designed with safety in mind. By following them, liability to responders and the responding agency is managed more easily. Brief explanations of the various terms are as follows:

- ***Code***— Body of law established either by legislative or administrative agencies with rule-making authority; designed to regulate (within its scope) the topic to which it relates. Some codes that apply to the fire and emergency services are as follows:
  - Model building and fire and life safety codes developed by standards-making organizations and adopted as law by the local jurisdiction
  - Examples: *National Building Code of Canada* and NFPA 101, *Life Safety Code®*

- ***Regulation*** — Authoritative rule dealing with details of procedures or a rule or order having the force of law that is issued by an executive authority of government; usually provides specific application to legislative laws or acts. Example: U.S. *Code of Federal Regulations (CFR)* Title 29 (Labor) 1910.120, *Hazardous Waste Operations and Emergency Response* (**Figure 3.1**).

- ***Standard*** — Any rule, principle, or measure established by authority. The terms *occupational safety and health standard* under the U.S. Occupational Safety and Health Act of

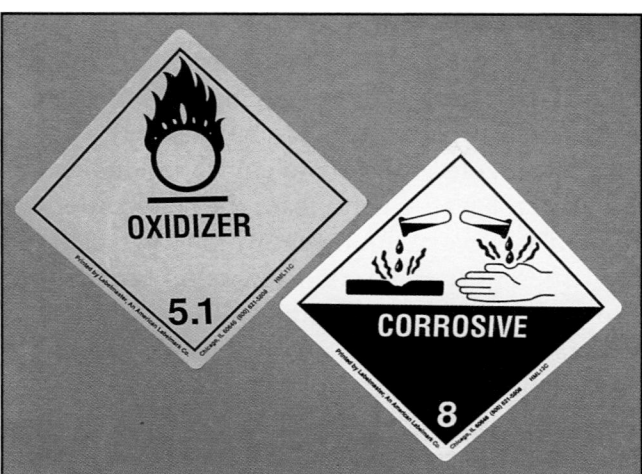

Figure 3.1 U. S. federal laws require the use of various warning signs and symbols to notify the public of the presence of hazardous materials.

1970 mean *a standard that requires conditions or adoption or use of one or more practices, means, methods, operations, or processes reasonably necessary or appropriate to provide safe or healthful employment and places of employment. Details:*

— Most commonly known standards in the fire and emergency services are the consensus standards developed by NFPA of which NFPA 1041 is one.

— Standards have the force of law when they are specifically adopted by a jurisdiction or referenced as mandatory by a regulation of a governing body.

— Standards require only a minimum level of performance or protection; it may be advisable for a jurisdiction to provide requirements based on a higher level.

● *Guide* — Instrument that provides direction or guiding information; does not have the force of law, but may be considered part of what is *reasonable* in a negligence case when determining the standard of care; considered *good industry practice.* Example: NFPA 1402, *Guide to Building Fire Service Training Centers* (2002).

● *Law* — Description of a legal document that sets forth rules that govern a particular type of activity such as the establishment of speed limits on highways; also used to mean a rule or body of rules of conduct inherent in human nature

and essential to the operation of society; used broadly and commonly to address many legal concepts. *Law types:*

— Legislative (statutory)

— Administrative

— Judiciary

These legal documents, codes, regulations, standards, laws, and sometimes guides are created and enforced by governing bodies. The term generally accepted to describe these bodies, regardless of level of government, is *authority having jurisdiction (AHJ).* The AHJ is the entity with responsibilities for approving equipment and enacting policies and procedures of the jurisdiction. The term refers to a broad range of entities because jurisdiction and approval agencies (along with their responsibilities) vary.

When standards (such as those developed by NFPA) are adopted by ordinance, the AHJ has discretion in interpreting and enforcing the standards and can provide equivalent codes as long as the intent of the standard is met or exceeded. Failure to adopt standards or codes can make the AHJ liable for court action. In civil cases, organizations are *not* immune from liability because they did *not* adopt a consensus standard.

In cases of public safety, the AHJ may be an agency or an individual. In many circumstances, a property owner or designated agent may assume the role of AHJ. In government installations, the commanding officer or department official may be the AHJ. Some examples include the following:

● Federal department or agency

● State/provincial department or agency

● Tribal governing council

● Local, municipal, or county department or agency

● Regional department or agency

● Chief executive fire officer

● Fire marshal

● Chief of the training division or agency

● Board of fire commissioners/engineers

● Board of directors

● Labor department chief

- Health department chief
- Building official
- Other government bodies having statutory authority

Instructors have to know and apply legal restrictions and requirements that are the work of AHJs at all levels of government. The challenge is even greater when it is necessary to develop and provide training for multiagency and multijurisdictional scenarios.

Types of Laws

The three types of laws — *legislative (statutory)*, *administrative*, and *judiciary* — apply to the three different jurisdictions that create the laws. Instructors must be aware that all three types apply to the fire and emergency services and the training function. Specific laws are described under each type. It is essential that instructors know and understand which laws apply and be aware of alterations in those laws and the creation of new laws.

Legislative (Statutory) Law

Legislative or *statutory laws* are made by federal, state/provincial, local (county/parish and municipal) legislative bodies and pertain to civil and criminal matters. Due to the nature of these laws, they may not have effect for many years. Legislative bodies have broad power to enact any statute as long as it has some reasonable relationship to protecting the health or general welfare of the public. This broad power is often called *police power*, and the authority to regulate comes with it.

When state/province and local jurisdictions make their own laws, it is for the purpose of ensuring compliance to issues or situations that are specific to their particular needs. A local law-making rule requires that the law meet or exceed the federal law; it *cannot* require less than the federal law unless the state/province or jurisdiction is willing to forgo federal funding for that specific funded project. For example, there are both federal and state clean-air acts in the U.S. When states create regulations to control the pollution output of local industries, the requirements must equal or exceed the federal clean-air standards.

Laws in each state/province, county/parish of that state/province, and local jurisdiction of that county/parish are different. The laws at each of these government levels are based on the needs of local citizens and general environments. State/provincial laws are generic for the state/province, but city laws vary somewhat from city to city and are different from rural or township laws within the state/province. Examples of legislative laws generated at each level of government are in the paragraphs that follow.

Federal government. Instructors must become familiar with the federally created laws that apply to the training function in their states/provinces and jurisdictions. Some examples of U.S. legislative laws are as follows:

- ***Civil Rights Act*** — Amends statutes passed during reconstruction following the American Civil War; passed in 1964. Its purpose is to provide stronger protection for rights guaranteed by the U.S. Constitution such as nondiscrimination in public accommodations.

- ***Title VII of the Civil Rights Act*** — Outlaws employment practices that discriminate based on race, color, religion, sex, or national origin; created the equal employment opportunity (EEO) law. The law also protects female employees from sexual harassment, but recent lawsuits on discrimination on the basis of gender have been expanded to apply to both men and women and include both verbal and physical harassment. This act created the Equal Employment Opportunity Commission (EEOC). *Details:*

  — *Harassment* occurs when a superior purposely exercises authority in a manner that is unnecessarily oppressive and implies malicious and discriminatory actions. The initial intent to protect women from sexual harassment was due to the fact that women held few (if any) positions of workplace authority over men. The act is currently applied to any situation in which an employee, regardless of gender, believes that the workplace is a hostile environment because of perceived harassment.

  — Employees can take classes to enhance job opportunities, and they have certain rights as employees. Regardless of their race, color, nationality, origin, sex, physical disability, or age, both job applicants and employees have specific rights and privileges that are protected by law.

— EEO laws apply to protected groups of individuals who have experienced past workplace discrimination. **Table 3.1** summarizes major federal EEO laws.

- *Americans with Disabilities Act (ADA)* — Prohibits discrimination against a qualified individual with a disability in application, hiring, advancement, discharge, compensation, job training, and other terms, conditions, and privileges of employment; prohibits certain questions of job applicants, including those of medical history, workers' compensation or health insurance claims, absenteeism due to illness, mental illness, and past treatment for alcoholism. Employers must provide reasonable accommodations for disabled workers, and training organizations must provide them for disabled students. *Definitions:*

  — *Disabled person:* One who has a physical or mental impairment that limits one or more *life activities,* has a record of such impairment, and is regarded as having the impairment.

  — *Qualified individual with disability:* Person with a disability who, with or without reasonable accommodations, can perform the essential functions of the position.

  — *Reasonable accommodations:* Facilities (such as restrooms, telephones, parking spaces, and drinking fountains) remodeled and made readily accessible to and usable by individuals with disabilities **(Figure 3.2, p. 66)**. Includes the following:

    ○ Acquiring or modifying equipment or devices

    ○ Adjusting or modifying examinations or training materials or policies appropriately

    ○ Providing qualified readers or interpreters

    ○ Adjusting work schedules

    ○ Providing other reasonable accommodations for disabled individuals

Table 3.1
Summary of Major Federal Equal Employment
Opportunity (EEO) Laws

EEO Law	Description
Equal Pay Act of 1993	Requires equal pay for men and women doing the same job.
Titles VI and VII of the 1964 Civil Rights Act as amended by the 1972 Equal Employment Act	Prohibits discrimination in all employment practices (recruiting, selecting, compensating, classifying, assigning, promoting, disciplining, terminating, and setting eligibility for union membership) based on race, color, sex, religion, or national origin.
1975 Amendment to the Age Discrimination in Employment Act (1967)	Prohibits hiring or employment discrimination of workers over 40 years of age, unless a bona fide occupational qualification (BFOQ) can be established.
Americans with Disabilities Act of 1990	Prohibits job discrimination against disabled people. Requires businesses with 25 or more employees to provide reasonable accommodations for qualified disabled job applicants and employees.

Figure 3.2 Readily accessible and visible parking spaces must be provided for all public buildings.

- ***Privacy Act or Buckley Amendment*** — Prohibits invasion of a person's right to privacy or unwanted publicity, restricts access to personal information such as personnel files and student grades, guarantees access to records only by the covered student or eligible parent or guardian, and prohibits disclosure of personal information without consent. *Details:*

  — Many U.S. state privacy laws have been nationalized by congressional legislation known as the Family Educational Rights and Privacy Act of 1974, which affects federal aid to education and governs educational records — those records directly related to students.

  — Instructors should seek a legal interpretation of the application of federal and state privacy acts on their organizations. The restrictions imposed by these acts may or may *not* apply to fire and emergency services training divisions based on that interpretation.

- ***Affirmative action policies*** — Establish employment programs required by federal statutes and regulations designed to correct past and current discriminatory practices in hiring members of underutilized and minority groups. *Purposes:*

  — Eliminate existing and continuing discrimination.

  — Remedy lingering effects of past discrimination.

  — Create systems and procedures to prevent future discrimination.

State/provincial government. States/provinces create statutes that become *statutory (legislative) laws* that regulate matters ranging from simple to complex such as state/provincial revenue structures, industry, commerce, and professions. Examples:

- Laws for fire and emergency services vehicle operation

- Protection policies such as worker's compensation acts and Good Samaritan laws

- Professional certification requirements such as those for physicians, nurses, paramedics, and firefighters

Local government. Municipal corporations, such as those formed by counties/parishes, cities, or townships, often have their own local needs and create laws (called *ordinances*) that address matters beyond federal or state/provincial laws. *Ordinance* is a local law that applies to persons, things, and activities in a jurisdiction and has the same force and effect as statutory law. Jurisdictions enact ordinances to regulate local needs such as the following:

- Zoning

- Occupancy use

- Speed limits on streets and roads

- Parking

- Trash disposal

- Other community issues (**Figure 3.3**)

Local government departments and organizations. Departments and organizations in cities and towns create their own regulations to guide management and employee actions as they perform

Figure 3.3 Local ordinances may require the posting of traffic warning signs (such as this one) near fire stations.

duties that must also comply with state/provincial and other regulations. Many state/provincial and local laws are based on federal laws and include laws involving hiring and firing policies, affirmative action policies, and workers' compensation insurance requirements. Departments and organizations create their own regulations to address these and additional areas such as the following:

- Liability and personal insurance requirements
- Professional development and certification requirements
- Substance abuse testing
- Driver testing and record policies
- Criminal record policies

Administrative Law

Administrative or regulatory agencies, such as the Occupational Safety and Health Administration (OSHA), create *administrative laws* or *regulations*.

A *regulation* is a rule or similar directive issued by an administrative agency. These agencies have authorization to issue and enforce their directives. Agencies that are authorized to issue regulations follow certain steps such as giving prior notification of the action in a public record and providing an invitation and opportunity for public comment. Regulatory agencies work for the executive branches of government and create laws that regulate areas such as safe operations of certain machinery (for example, breathing apparatus, oxygen-delivery systems, and forklifts) in the workplace.

Judiciary Law

Judiciary law (also known as *judicial legislation* or *case law*) is usually the result of a legal precedent or a judicial decision. These decisions serve as rules for future determinations in similar cases, and these decisions may affect emergency responders almost immediately because there is usually no implementation period. Judiciary law, if heard at the federal level, can have nationwide effect. Some case-law decisions can affect fire and emergency responders even though the original individual case did *not* involve emergency response personnel.

An example is the case of *Whirlpool Corporation vs. Marshall* that determined that an employer could *not* terminate the employment of a worker who refused to perform a task that the individual considered unacceptably risky. Case law is always subject to change and can provide precedents to both sides of an issue.

Law Applications

Knowledge of the concepts of law only provides the foundation for an instructor. An instructor must also be able to apply the concepts to daily practice. This section introduces and develops these practices as they apply to the training function. Specifically, an instructor must be aware of the following issues:

- Legal requirements for record keeping and management
- Liability that accompanies an instructor's actions

- Restrictions that copyright and privacy issues have on classroom preparation

- Importance of students' rights

- Restrictions that environmental protection laws may place on training evolutions and scenarios

Records Management

All levels of fire and emergency services instructors must know the current legal requirements for record keeping. Chapter 6, Report Writing and Record Keeping, provides a detailed look at the types of records normally retained by the organization, the components of the record keeping system, and how to establish a record keeping system. The sections that follow provide a brief overview of the legal requirements for that system.

Training and Attendance Records

While instructors may come in contact with all types of records, two types are of greater interest to them: training records and attendance records. When combined with training records, attendance records are the bases for reports that may be required by the AHJ or other government agency.

Training records. Training records are essential components of a successful training program. Accurate records not only give long-term informational inventories of an organization's training activities, they may also be important and necessary in legal proceedings and management reviews and accreditation programs such as those conducted or administered by the following organizations:

- Insurance Services Office, Inc. (ISO)

- International Fire Service Accreditation Congress (IFSAC)

- National Board on Fire Service Professional Qualifications (ProBoard)

- International Association of Fire Chiefs and International City/County Managers Association (IAFC/ICMA)

The type and format of training records may vary widely, depending upon the specific needs of the organization. NFPA 1401, *Recommended Practice for Fire Service Training Reports and Records,* provides examples of different training forms as well as other helpful information on the design and procedures for effective management of training records. Training records also provide the basis for required federal government reports on legally mandated training. Records document permanent facts, while reports summarize facts contained in the records. Report preparation will be discussed later in this manual. See Chapter 6, Report Writing and Record Keeping.

Attendance records. The daily attendance records for all personnel are primarily maintained to provide data for the distribution of payrolls and benefits. Depending on the classification of the employee, a formal timecard may be required as evidence of actual hours on duty. Other attendance records may be included in the company or unit logbook or timesheet. Overtime pay, annual leave, and sick leave benefits are based on the information that is included in daily attendance records. Attendance records are also used to verify that personnel participated in required training. These records are used as evidence that an individual or unit has completed a specified number of hours of training in a specific topic such as respiratory protection or hazardous materials incident response.

Legal Requirements

State/provincial and federal governments generally have specific laws that direct record keeping and (in some cases) the type of information that is gathered and stored in these records. The requirements for record keeping include record types, retention length, privacy, and public access to the records. However, there are exemptions to public access of some records.

Record types. Examples of the types of records that may be required by various levels of government, agencies, and jurisdictions are as follows:

- *Hiring records* — Applications, test results, medical evaluations, and acceptance/rejection criteria

- *Promotional examinations* — Test materials and test results

- *Medical examinations/evaluations* — Personnel medical records collected throughout employment

- *Exposure reports* — Any actual or perceived exposures to chemical or biological hazards
- *Training records* — Individual and unit training, especially training involving respiratory protection or hazardous materials certification
- *Incident reports* — All emergency response reports (required to be submitted to the federal government as part of the National Fire Incident Reporting System [NFIRS] in states/provinces that participate in the NFIRS program)

Retention length. The length of time that records must be retained by the organization depends on state/provincial and local laws and the specific type of record. For instance, in some states personnel application forms must be retained for 7 years, while exposure report forms and documentation must be retained for 40 years following the retirement or termination of the employee. Instructors should consult the jurisdiction's human resources or legal departments for guidelines on all types of records and the length of retention.

Privacy. Records that must be confidential include personnel files, individual training records, and medical files. Other personal information that is regulated to ensure privacy includes Social Security numbers and test scores. Specific information regarding privacy requirements are as follows:

- *Social Security number* — Many organizations no longer use an employee's Social Security number for records identification. The practice of using other identification methods reduces the opportunity for improper use or potential for identity theft.

- *Personnel files* — Training records may be considered part of an individual's personal, private employment file — a fact that requires an organization to limit access to them. Even when local laws do *not* require this practice, organizations should develop and adopt policies that limit access to training records only to those personnel with a legal need to know.

- *Test scores* — Scores and personal data are considered privileged information and are available only to management and a few other designated personnel with authorization and a specific need to know. *Examples:*

  - In the U.S., the Family Education and Privacy Act prohibits the release of this type of information (state and local restrictions may vary).

  - Similarly, the Canadian province of Ontario has the Municipal Freedom of Information and Protection of Privacy Act (MFIPPA) that places the responsibility on instructors to know their duties and responsibilities under the applicable legislation within their jurisdictions.

Public access. While individual personnel records are confidential, other organization records are *not*. Official meeting minutes and any other notes that are made as part of a meeting are part of public records. Care should always be taken in the recording of any information that might potentially become public. Some records such as incident reports or fire investigations are available to the individuals who own an involved property or are involved in an incident, unless specifically indicated to the contrary by statutory law. Records of responses to emergency medical incidents present restricted access issues due to confidentiality requirements.

Instructors and training administrators must be aware of the state/provincial and local open meetings and open records laws that apply in their jurisdictions. Open meetings and open records acts of the state/province give the exact definition and list of records that are available to the public and media. An example of the definition by one state is as follows:

Public record includes any writing containing information relating to the conduct of government or the performance of any governmental or proprietary function prepared, owned, used, or retained by any state or local agency regardless of physical form or characteristics: all budget and financial records; personnel leave, travel and payroll records; records of legislative sessions; reports submitted to the legislature; and any other record designated a public record by the Senate or the House of Representatives.

Public records include virtually all records created and maintained by state/provincial agencies and jurisdictions within the state/province. Records created or held by a government organization include the following:

- Documents
- Maps
- Photographs
- Videotapes
- Handwritten notes and letters
- Computer data, including electronic mail (e-mail) messages
- All other records

Open records act exemptions. Exemptions exist in many states, but they are limited and have been interpreted very narrowly by the courts. The laws presume that all records are open and place the burden on the jurisdiction to demonstrate that any requested materials are exempt. When a public record contains both exempt and nonexempt material, the exempt portion must be removed and the remaining nonexempt material disclosed. U.S. federal employees must be aware of the application of the Freedom of Information Act on U.S. government agencies. Examples of exemptions are as follows:

- Medical records and other materials involving matters of personal privacy
- Records relating to pending investigations
- Records required by the federal government to be kept confidential such as training, promotional, and educational records
- Trade secrets and certain information of a proprietary nature
- Research data, records, or information that have *not* been published, patented, or otherwise publicly disseminated
- Confidential evaluations submitted to a public agency in connection with the hiring of a public employee

Legal Liability

Liability is a broad, comprehensive term that describes legal responsibility. It implies that when a wrongful act is performed, the individual or or-ganization that committed the act is responsible for correcting it. Instructors and/or organizations may be considered negligent for performing in the following ways:

- Providing incorrect information or instruction
- Failing to instruct in a topic they are responsible for teaching
- Teaching a topic they are unqualified to teach

Instructors can reduce the potential for liability and legal action against themselves and their organizations in the following ways:

- Be aware of standard expectations.
- Teach to the standards.
- Teach only topics they are qualified to teach.
- Provide a safe learning environment.

Instructors are expected to foresee (predict) potential injury events and prevent injuries while training personnel for appropriate performance on the job. The task analysis, hazard/risk analysis, and incident action plan (IAP) discussed in Chapter 2, Safety and the Training Function, provide predictability and opportunity to prevent such injuries.

Training program administrators must remember that training programs require students to learn how to perform high-hazard activities that they are initially *not* fully competent to perform. Administrators and instructors must foresee instructional problems and ensure that all instructors can appropriately perform and demonstrate the skills in a thorough step-by-step introduction and then properly supervise the practice of those skills. Students are trained in a nonemergency environment for skills that will take place in an emergency environment.

Although it is a benefit to make the training activity *realistic,* training activities must be controlled. The inability to manage risk during training activities can lead to injuries and create a liability for the instructor or organization. Injuries that result from emergency scene situations have special legal defenses that do *not* apply to training environment situations. Exposing students to hazardous training environments without having adequate controlling elements could be perceived as negligence in court if an injury occurs (**Figure 3.4**).

Figure 3.4 Adequate control and safety measures must be used for all live-fire and high-hazard training exercises.

Each training session possesses potential variables that affect the safety of the program for students, instructors, tools and equipment, scenarios and evolutions, and the environment. When planning a training session, instructors must make every effort to maintain control and foresee potential dangers or injury situations and reduce (if *not* eliminate) risks to students and personnel.

Even when every precaution has been taken to reduce risks, students may still be injured. Injuries may *not* be due to the fault of instructor oversight but the fault of students who do *not* follow safety guidelines. When planning training evolutions or scenarios, instructors should consider the answers to the following questions:

- Can instructors be held liable for actions of students who irresponsibly act on their own?

- Can individuals be held personally liable for contributing to their own injuries and the injuries of others?

- To what extent are employers liable for injuries caused by their employees?

The sections that follow explain the concepts of vicarious liability, discuss foreseeability, and list criteria to help prevent employer liability. Along with the criteria for preventing employer liability, steps are given that can reduce the possibility of personal liability.

Vicarious Liability

Vicarious liability means that the blame for the actions of one person can be placed on another. It is the liability that is placed on the employer for the acts and omissions of employees during the normal course of their employment. Employers are responsible for the actions of employees. Individuals are responsible for their own negligent actions that cause injury to themselves or others.

The most obvious condition in which vicarious blame occurs is in cases of sexual harassment. When an instructor is aware of harassment between students and fails to act, the instructor may then be liable. When the instructor has *not* been properly trained in recognizing and resolving sexual harassment issues, the organization may then be equally liable.

Foreseeability

Foreseeability is based on the legal concept that reasonable people should be able to foresee the consequences of their actions and, therefore, take reasonable precautions.

Based on the knowledge of the hazard/risk analysis, instructors can predict that certain hazardous conditions will be present during training. The instructor should be able to foresee potential problems with those conditions and then take action to reduce the risks. Foreseeability must also extend to the conditions that instructors anticipate students to meet once they are on the job as well.

Practicing foreseeability requires training administrators and instructors to regularly conduct a task analysis that identifies contemporary duties and tasks that are used by personnel at emergency incidents. An effective instructor remains current with changing trends, policies and protocols, and new technology and research that affect job performance in all areas of fire and emergency services.

The classic example of foreseeability involves a private swimming pool in a neighborhood with children. The argument says that if the owners are *reasonable people,* they will *foresee* that neighborhood children will be tempted to swim in the pool without adult supervision (which is dangerous). What would a reasonable person do? A reasonable person would put a fence around the pool or yard to prevent children from sneaking into the pool and possibly drowning.

Liability Reduction

The hazard/risk analysis should be reviewed and revised to acknowledge changes in the training and operational environments. Instructors should also review litigation involving vocational instructors. Reviews have shown that courts expect reasonable and prudent instructors to perform the following steps:

Step 1: Develop a safety plan or formally developed strategy to prevent injuries.

Step 2: Follow the safety plan.

Step 3: Provide for health and safety of students and participants.

Step 4: Give proper instructions.

Instructors can take precautions to minimize the chances of becoming involved in a liability case. Some of these actions are as follows:

- Ensure that all assisting instructors meet the organization's qualifications and requirements.
- Check equipment regularly for safe operating conditions.
- Maintain written objectives, and document each training session.
- Provide students with a written course description so they can understand all requirements.
- Ensure that students are physically fit and prepared for the tasks.
- Instruct and test all students in the safe operation of equipment.
- Do *not* leave students unattended while they are practicing potentially dangerous skills.
- Do *not* exceed individual skill level when training students or working with other instructors.
- Do *not* ignore, shortcut, or exceed protocols or policies.
- Ensure in as many ways possible (verbal, written, and graphically) that both students and instructors understand the intent and outcome of all directives or instructions as well as the consequences when procedures are *not* followed. Do *not* presume anything.
- Do *not* joke about serious situations or belittle the actions of others in any learning or service situation.
- Respect student privacy. *Never* disclose personal information (except to appropriate authorities) about students, other personnel, or any victim or patient who required emergency services.
- Follow the organization's policy on disclosing information to insurance companies, hospital personnel, legal representatives, news reporters, or other persons who want information on issues that are going through litigation.

In the event an accident or potentially liable incident occurs, the instructor should take the following steps to prevent or minimize personal liability:

Step 1: Always appear professional in appearance on the job and in the training situation. Generally, appearance gives a good impression and implies respect for the responsibilities of the profession.

Step 2: Maintain skill level. Instructors are held accountable for skills. Maintaining current certifications through appropriate and credible refresher courses is critical. The defense of *I didn't know* is unacceptable.

Step 3: Treat other instructors and coworkers, all students, and any community members in all situations with courtesy and respect. Attitude is a major factor in how others judge people and their abilities.

Step 4: Seek advice and guidance from a higher authority when in doubt. Do *not* attempt to make decisions beyond individual knowledge or authority.

Step 5: Document all issues of discrepancy, complaint, and injury accurately and give details on dates, times, conversations, suggested resolutions, outcomes, and follow-up plans.

Step 6: Verify liability insurance coverage provided by the AHJ. Evaluate individual liability and determine additional sources for adequate financial coverage.

Copyright Laws and Permissions

Copyright laws protect the works of artists, photographers, and authors and give them exclusive rights to publish their works or determine who may publish or reproduce them. Since the Copyright Act of 1976 was passed, the majority of U.S. copyright laws are governed by federal statute and include the following provisions:

- All works published in the U.S. before 1923 are considered public domain (subject to appropriation by anyone).
- Works published between 1922 and 1978 are protected for 95 years from the date of publication.

- When the work was created but *not* published before 1978, the copyright lasts for the life of the artist, photographer, or author plus 70 years.
- For works published after 1977, the copyright lasts for the life of the artist, photographer, or author plus 70 years.

Unauthorized use of copyrighted materials is considered infringement on the rights of artists, photographers, or authors. Infringement gives them a right to recover damages or gain profits from the use of their works (**Figure 3.5**).

Instructors and students often copy materials from texts, journals, periodicals, and the Internet for use in class. Whether this copying is copyright infringement depends on how the material is used. The fair use doctrine of the Copyright Act grants the privilege of copying materials to persons other than the owner of the copyright without consent when the material is used in a reasonable manner. Section 107 of the Copyright Act lists the privileges or factors to consider when determining whether the use of copyright materials is *fair use*. A few of the copyright guidelines are as follows:

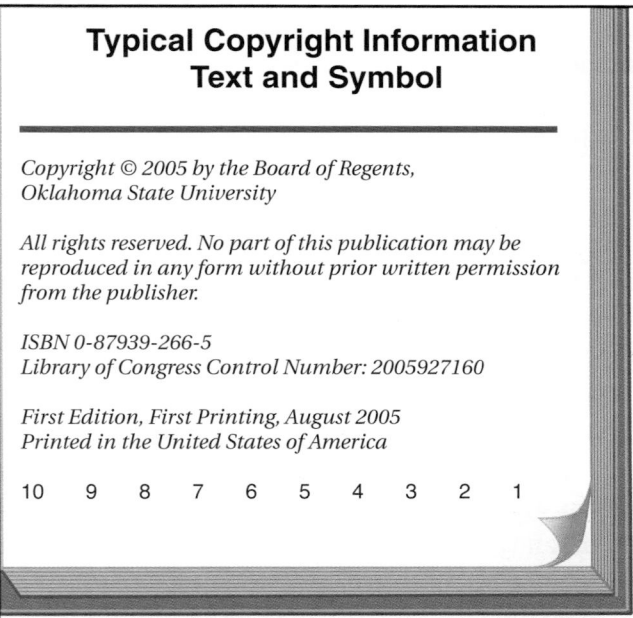

Typical Copyright Information Text and Symbol

Figure 3.5 Typical copyright information text and symbol.

- Teachers may make single copies of the following for scholarly research or when preparing to teach a class:
  — Chapter from a book
  — Article from a periodical, newspaper, or Internet
  — Short story, essay, or poem
  — Chart, graph, diagram, drawing, cartoon, or picture from a book, periodical, or newspaper
  — Videotape copies of television broadcasts
- Teachers may make multiple copies of items for classroom use and discussion by their students provided that the copied material is brief and the idea to copy an item is spontaneous because it is currently appropriate to the day's lesson. Copying must be for the particular class being taught at the time and *not cumulative* or copied repeatedly for subsequent classes.
- Copying shall *not* substitute for buying books, publisher's reprints, or periodicals.
- Students *cannot* be charged for copied materials beyond the cost of photocopying.

Instructors must use proper citations when copying, downloading electronically, or using any materials, regardless of copyright. It is recommended that instructors familiarize themselves with the applicable copyright laws regarding copying print, audio, video, or electronic materials for use in class. Because copyright laws that apply to the Internet or digitally reproduced material are constantly evolving, instructors must monitor those changes. In some cases, digital media may have its own laws that are separate from copyright laws that apply to traditional print media.

Instructors depend on photographic images to provide a sense of reality in their instructional methods by using photographs and film/videos taken at emergency incidents. When fire and emergency services personnel take photographs or shoot motion picture films/videos at a scene, they may be invading the privacy of the individuals or victims involved in the incident. *Invasion of privacy* is the wrongful intrusion into a person's private activities by the government or other individuals.

Individuals have the right to control the use of pictures of themselves and their property. An instructor or organization that uses these pictures or films may be sued for invasion of privacy or libel if permission is *not* obtained. The legality and success of lawsuits to protect the right of privacy depend on several factors such as the following:

- ***Where and who*** — One factor is where the photograph or film/video was made and who was photographed or filmed/taped. Events that are newsworthy and photographed or filmed/taped for the public interest take precedence over the right of privacy. *Details:*
  — Using photographs or films/videos a month after an incident has lost its public appeal and is no longer newsworthy steps over the line of privacy.
  — Images that are retained as *file photos* and used in conjunction with a story of continuing interest may *not* be subject to the privacy requirements.
  — Taking photographs or films/videos is allowed when the setting is a public place rather than an individual's private home.
  — The law allows for photographing and filming/taping publicly famous individuals who are seen in public.
  — It may still be considered an invasion of privacy when any individual, ordinary citizen, celebrity, or criminal is photographed or filmed on a public highway stripped of clothing and dignity and having emergency procedures performed while being rescued from a serious accident.
  — Extreme care must be taken when images are made of severely injured victims or fatalities to *not* infringe on the rights of victims or their families.
- ***Permissions*** — Because of potentially serious legal and professional consequences, organizations must always make arrangements in advance to obtain permissions in writing (called *model releases*) from individuals to take photographs or films/videos of events and use them after events **(Figure 3.6)**.

Photo/Imaging Permission Form

I, _____, hereby grant permission
to the _____ Fire Department for the use of all
photographs, negatives, slides, still, or video digital
images, taken of me today. These images may be used
for educational or instructional purposes as long as
the images remain the property of the _____
Fire Department. This permission is given without any
compensation or remuneration.

Signature_____
Address_____
City_____ State_____
Zip Code_____ Phone_____
Signature of Parent or Guardian (if subject is a minor)

_____

Signature of Witness_____
Date_____

Figure 3.6 Sample model release form used when making photographs or videos of individuals.

- *Restrictions* — Organizations must also explain the purpose of intended use so that individuals can make an informed decision or restrict use to a specific form only such as training. Photographic images, audio recordings, and films/videos of students participating in training classes require written permission before the material is published or used by the organization in the following situations:

  — In training sessions

  — On departmental/organizational web sites

  — On closed circuit or public broadcasts of organizational-sponsored television programs

  Additional limitations are placed on the length of time that a copy of an on-air broadcast can be retained and used. Permission to record a broadcast should be obtained from the producer of the material, and the proper length of time that it may be used should be determined.

- *Rights of individuals* — Individuals must be given the opportunity to preview pictures or films/videos and make a decision before they are used. Individuals may also require that an organization maintain their anonymity while showing the photograph or film/video, which is usually accomplished by blocking faces with graphic overlays or showing them in shadows and altering voices on films/videos by audio distortions.

Students' Rights

Everyone, including students, has *substantive rights,* which include a right to equal enjoyment of fundamental rights, privileges, and immunities. A right to privacy of student records and grades and free speech and expression are also included. Reasonable regulations that are necessary to protect students during training activities can be justified even though they may be perceived as infringing on student rights. However, regulations that limit or eliminate students' substantive rights are *not* legal. Students tend to ignore such unreasonable regulations, and instructors are reluctant to enforce them.

For example, requiring hard hats on a construction site and requiring full turnout gear on the drill ground are safety regulations. A prohibition on eating in the classroom is a safety regulation appropriate for a biology or chemistry lab but may be inappropriate for adults who come directly from work to an evening classroom lecture session. Student expectations of substantive rights may include the following:

- Privacy of records and test scores
- Freedom to hold and express an opinion that may be in opposition to the organization or instructor
- Fair and equal treatment in class
- Nonhostile learning environment free of discrimination or harassment
- Safe work or learning environment
- Equal access to the learning environment and the material being taught

Laws such as the ADA and Civil Rights Act also protect many of these rights. Any rules or regulations that may be perceived as infringing on students' substantive rights should be reviewed, validated, and communicated to students at the beginning of the training session or course. These rules and regulations must be consistently applied to all situations and students throughout the program.

Environmental Issues

The U.S. Environmental Protection Agency (EPA) regulates and controls activities that may have a negative affect on the nation's water, atmosphere, and soil. In each of the states, similar agencies enforce their own rules and regulations that may have an effect on training evolutions. It is essential that training administrators and instructors be familiar with general considerations and environmental regulations and make application for the necessary permits before performing any training activity that may release harmful agents into the environment.

Water

Rivers, streams, lakes, ponds, and other bodies of water can be contaminated by runoff water from training evolutions. Training facilities should have systems that trap, contain, and clean contaminated water from training props, especially when using flammable liquids **(Figure 3.7)**. Some municipal fire and emergency services organizations may have storm drains that are equipped with filtration systems. However, the vast majority of training divisions do *not* have the ability to clean contaminated materials from runoff water before it reaches streams, rivers, or lakes.

Training administrators and instructors should contact the local EPA office or state water resources board to determine the specific requirements that must be met. The quantity of contaminant may be small enough that it will be diluted sufficiently to *not* pose a problem. In any case, permits will probably be required for the training evolution.

Atmosphere

The intentional release of hydrocarbons into the atmosphere from a live-fire exercise may be prohibited or controlled by local *open-burning* ordinances. These ordinances may require acquiring a permit before a live-fire exercise and displaying it at the site. Steps that instructors should take to comply with atmospheric regulations include the following:

Figure 3.7 Typical water purification system used to remove contaminates from water used in training exercises.

Step 1: Adhere to all environmental rules and regulations imposed by all levels of government.

Step 2: Use accelerants that meet EPA guidelines for Class B (flammable/combustible) liquids.

Step 3: Ensure that existing weather conditions do *not* contribute to the spread of contaminants into populated areas.

Step 4: Provide spark and cinder control for adjacent areas.

Soil

Soil becomes contaminated from water runoff that contains byproducts of combustion, fuels, and nonbiodegradable extinguishing agents. These materials (considered hazardous waste when in sufficient quantities) have to be removed along with the soil they contaminate. This process can be costly and could result in litigation. To prevent such a situation, the training administrator and instructor should consult with the EPA office to determine the minimum acceptable level of contamination.

When it is *not* possible to meet the EPA requirements, training should be performed on a nonporous (concrete) surface that can be cleaned with inert materials. Training-type foam extinguishing agents that are nontoxic and biodegradable may also be used.

General Considerations

When possible, fuels that emit the minimum amount of contaminants should be used for live-fire training exercises. Under controlled conditions, the best choices are purpose-built training structures and props that are equipped with natural or propane gas simulators. When these structures and props are *not* available, consider Class A (solid) combustibles such as hay or untreated wood pallets for live-fire exercises. Finally, weather conditions should be monitored during the training evolution to prevent the spread of contaminants by the wind.

Ethical Conduct

The bases for ethics are the socially accepted beliefs, morals, and values of a community or society. Ethical standards express the level of conduct that all members of society are expected to follow. In brief, they are statements of what is right and proper conduct for an individual in all relationships and activities. This conduct may involve relationships with others, the decision-making process, or simply choosing between *right* and *wrong*. Few decisions are as clear, and most involve many choices that fall into the *gray* range between the two extremes of right and wrong.

For example, in a closed society such as a military academy, a requirement for reporting a known infraction of the rules (like cheating) can be enforced. All cadets know that they can be expelled for cheating or for *not* reporting another cadet for cheating. However, military academies are periodically wracked with cheating scandals even with such a strict code. Classic examples abound of situations that challenge basic ethical standards such as lying. In education, ethical situations include the following:

- Sharing of exam papers between successive classes
- Plagiarizing material produced by others
- Cheating on exams

The fire and emergency services are *not* immune to the need for ethical standards of conduct. Because of the position of respect and honor that the services and their members have in North America and other regions of the world, it is important that all members attempt to act in accordance to an ethical code of conduct. It may be argued that members of the fire and emergency services should maintain a higher standard than the average citizen. To accomplish this objective, fire and emergency services personnel must respond in the following ways:

- Understand personal ethics.
- Establish an organizational ethics code.
- Recognize ethical issues that exist in the fire and emergency services.

Components of Ethics

Before an instructor can impose an ethical code of conduct upon entry-level personnel or students, it is necessary to understand three basic components of ethics: origin of personal ethics of individuals, causes of unethical conduct, and how people justify unethical conduct in themselves and an organization. These three elements are important *not* only in recognizing unethical conduct in others but also internally within the individual.

Personal Ethics Origins

Ethics and ethical behavior are learned traits. They are transmitted to an individual from many sources. The primary source is the family, which instills personal values and morals. Other sources are organized religions, educational institutions, society, and peers. The values that are instilled by these sources remain with the individual for life unless the person consciously alters them. Examples of ethical values include the following:

- Honesty
- Integrity
- Impartiality
- Fairness
- Loyalty
- Dedication
- Responsibility
- Accountability
- Perseverance
- Frugality
- Faithfulness
- Heroism
- Patriotism

These values are generally accepted by most cultures and societies of the world to be important to the existence of a civilized society. As the ancient Greek philosophers asserted, a society without ethics would dissolve into chaos. The same is true of organizations that lack values or a commitment to ethics.

Unethical Conduct Causes

In order to create a culture based on ethical behavior, fire and emergency services instructors must understand what contributes to unethical behavior. The potential for unethical conduct on the part of individuals and organizations, including the fire and emergency services, is limitless and too often realized, especially in profit-driven private enterprises. Researchers in private industry have documented the causes of unethical behavior in organizations. Some of these causes are summarized as follows:

- **Behaviors that violate ethical standards** — The use of bribery or payoffs to ensure that an organization is awarded a lucrative contract is rewarded in the form of promotions or bonuses. The unethical conduct is *not* only on the part of the business representative who makes the bribe or payoff but also on the part of the organization's employee who accepts it. Example: Individuals may attempt to influence instructors in the hiring process to certify a relative who may *not* meet the hiring criteria.

- **Bottom-line mentality** — Financial success is all that matters to a company, and any action (ethical or otherwise) is justified when a profit is made for the organization. Thus, ethical standards simply become obstacles that must be overcome in the name of profits. Although making a profit does *not* motivate the fire and emergency services, staying within the constraints of budgets does motivate them. *Examples:*
  - Making the organization *look good on paper* to the political authority can create situations where unethical conduct may occur.
  - In the political public arena, the *political bottom line* is a similar cause where decisions are made to influence the electorate in favor of a politician at the eventual expense of the same voters.
  - *Pork-barrel projects* are government expenditures that may have little or no real value other than to enhance the image of a politician and gain more votes. In the end, citizens may have to pay higher taxes or lose other benefits to support the project.

- **Exploitive mentality** — An attitude in some private and public organizations encourages people to use others in order to succeed. It tends to promote negative stereotyping, undermine compassion, and create a selfish attitude. This attitude may take the following forms:
  - Telling lies about people
  - Starting and spreading rumors
  - Taking credit for the labors of another person

Personal Justifications

When the culture of an organization or society rewards unethical conduct, it is easy to understand how individuals can engage in these types of activities. The individual accepts the benefits of such actions and then justifies them internally. Justification also occurs when a person is trying to make a decision (whether ethical or unethical). Common justifications for unethical conduct include the following:

- Pretending that the action is legal or ethical
- Believing that the action is really in the best interest of the organization or individual
- Believing that the action is okay because no one will ever discover it
- Expecting that the organization will support the action if it is ever discovered
- Believing that the action is acceptable because everyone else is doing it
- Believing that the end (result) justifies the means (method) even when the means are unethical

When the individual has justified the unethical action internally, then it becomes easier to commit the initial action and any similar subsequent actions. To overcome these attitudes, an organization must create a culture that encourages and rewards ethical conduct and disciplines unethical conduct.

Ethics Program

The first step toward creating an ethical culture is the creation of an ethics program that includes an organizational and individual code of ethics. Surveys of the business community have determined that organizations that have a formal ethics program have a strong ethical culture. Employees of these organizations have a positive opinion of the ethical performance of the organization and senior managers.

An ethics program is essential to any fire and emergency services organization and justifies any reasonable expense in resources. A code of ethics and other elements contained in an ethics program are discussed in the sections that follow.

Elements

An ethics program contains certain elements that make it effective. To ensure that the organization maintains an ethical culture, the ethics program needs to include a written code of ethics or ethics policy. Like the organization's mission statement, this code is a brief, one- or two-page statement of the values that govern the organization and the expectations desired in the actions of the management and membership.

Code of Ethics

An essential part of the ethics program is the written code of ethics. Codes of ethical conduct have been established by the IAFC, the American Society for Public Administration (ASPA), and the U.S. House of Representatives (to name a very few). In addition, some states have an ethics commission (such as the Oregon Ethics Commission) that is responsible for establishing guidelines and overseeing issues involving ethics within the state. See the information box, p. 80, for a personal code of ethics example and **Appendix I** for a training organization code of ethics.

Expressing the organization's code of ethics in written form provides the administration, members/employees, and the public with a visible standard to follow. The importance of a written code of ethics cannot be overemphasized because it has the following characteristics:

- Defines acceptable and unacceptable behaviors
- Promotes high standards of practice and fosters a strong ethical climate
- Provides a standard for individuals to judge themselves
- Establishes a framework for professional behavior and strengthens the organization's ethical climate
- Helps to enhance or establish an occupational identity
- Provides a mark of occupational maturity for the department, organization, or profession
- Establishes an environment in which open communication is expected, accepted, and protected

- Provides a clear and concise statement of the type of behavior that is expected from both management and members of the organization
- Establishes the basis for public opinion of the organization, its leaders, and its members

Ethical Issues

The existence of a code of ethics strengthens the ethical culture of the organization but does *not* guarantee that ethical questions will *not* occur to challenge the organization or its employees. Training employees in the importance of making ethical decisions, how to make those decisions, and how to recognize and respond to unethical actions on the part of others provides valuable tools for resolving such issues.

However, instructors must be able to manage issues when they arise during training sessions. The use of logic and reasoning must be supplemented by the use of ethical decision-making. Use the following steps when confronted with an ethical dilemma:

Step 1: *Recognize and define the situation* — Determine the answers to the following questions:

— What is it?

— What has caused it?

— Who is involved?

— What are the potential results?

Step 2: *Obtain all the facts surrounding the situation* — Conduct an objective investigation to gather the details of the event.

Step 3: *List all possible options necessary to respond to the situation* — Develop this list by brainstorming with other members of the organization when time allows. In emergency situations, an instructor may have to rely on personal experience to develop such a list.

Step 4: *Compare each option to established criteria* — Use benchmarks such as legality, morality, benefit, and justification as criteria.

Step 5: *Select the best option that meets the criteria* — Make the decision.

Step 6: *Double-check the decision* — Ask more subjective questions such as the following:

— How would I feel if my family/spouse/friends discovered this?

— How would I feel if this decision were reported in the local/national media?

Step 7: *Take action and implement the decision* — Ensure the factual foundation is firm, criteria are met, and potential for exposure is minimized. The correct decision is the result.

Instructors are role models for their students and lead primarily by example. The most important example they can provide to their students, organization, and community is ethical decision-making and action. An organization's culture is only as sound as the example set by the officers of the organization. This example means that instructors and administrators must establish and adhere to goals that are ethical. Those goals must be based on sound factual evidence and reasoning.

Officers must be honest in the presentation of their decisions when communicating both the decision and results of the decision. Honesty generates acceptance for the decision and builds trust in the officer who made that decision.

It is important for all individuals to be guided by a strong set of beliefs, values, and morals. They must be able to recognize and use ethical behavior in relationships, in decision-making, and as leaders. Of all the axioms for guiding people ethically, the most applicable is the one spoken by Confucius (K'ung Ch'iu) in the sixth century B.C.E. (Before the Common Era) **(Figure 3.8, p. 82)**. When asked by a student, *Is there one expression that can be acted upon until the end of one's days?* Confucius answered: *There is* shu: *Do not impose on others what you yourself do not want.*

Case Study: Making an Ethical Decision

Throughout our lives we face tough choices. As fire and emergency services instructors, we are entrusted to educate current and future firefighters so that our departments or organizations can continue to provide the highest level of service to our customers. Professional codes call for us to establish and maintain a clear set of standards for behavior. Consider the following scenario and discuss how to resolve this situation:

Ryan is a graduating high school senior who has been coming to fire stations with his father, the department's Battalion Chief, since he was a little boy. He enjoys a good reputation around the firehouse and is well liked by fellow firefighters. He has always wanted to become a firefighter and has been working hard toward this goal, and you have always been happy to help. He has come to consider you a confidant and mentor.

Recently, Ryan took an important step toward achieving his goal of becoming a firefighter by obtaining his Firefighter I and Firefighter II certifications.

In a few days, Ryan will take the firefighter recruit entrance exam (a test the department offers only every 2 to 3 years). Certifications for Firefighter I and Firefighter II are required to take the exam.

Today, Ryan comes to you a bit anxious. He tells you that a friend of his in his Firefighter I and Firefighter II courses illegally acquired the answer key for the certification exam. This friend used a copy to pass his exam. Ryan has now begun to feel bad and comes to you for advice.

Questions for Discussion

Imagine you and Ryan are sitting across from each other. The two of you are alone. As a friend and confidant, what would you say to him?

As a certified instructor, you are obligated to inform the course instructor that the certification exam has been compromised. However, in doing so you may jeopardize Ryan's certification, thereby making him ineligible to take the fire department entrance exam. What do you do?

What if you discover that Ryan was the *friend* who used the illegal answer key to pass the exam? Does this change the situation?

Figure 3.8 Confucius: Sixth Century B.C.E. (Before the Common Era) philosopher.

In Western civilization that same ethical axiom is known as the Golden Rule: *Do unto others as you want them to do unto you.* In any civilization, culture, or society, this axiom is a valid ethical strategy to follow.

Summary

Laws directly or indirectly affect the majority of training functions performed by instructors. Some laws mandate the subjects to be taught while others restrict the method in which they are taught. A fire and emergency services instructor must be aware of all the laws that control the training process and how to avoid breaking any of them while teaching the courses. At the same time, an instructor must conform to an ethical code of conduct. The instructor who adheres to a solid ethical code of behavior *not* only provides students with a valuable role model but also finds it easier to remain within the legal constraints established by law.

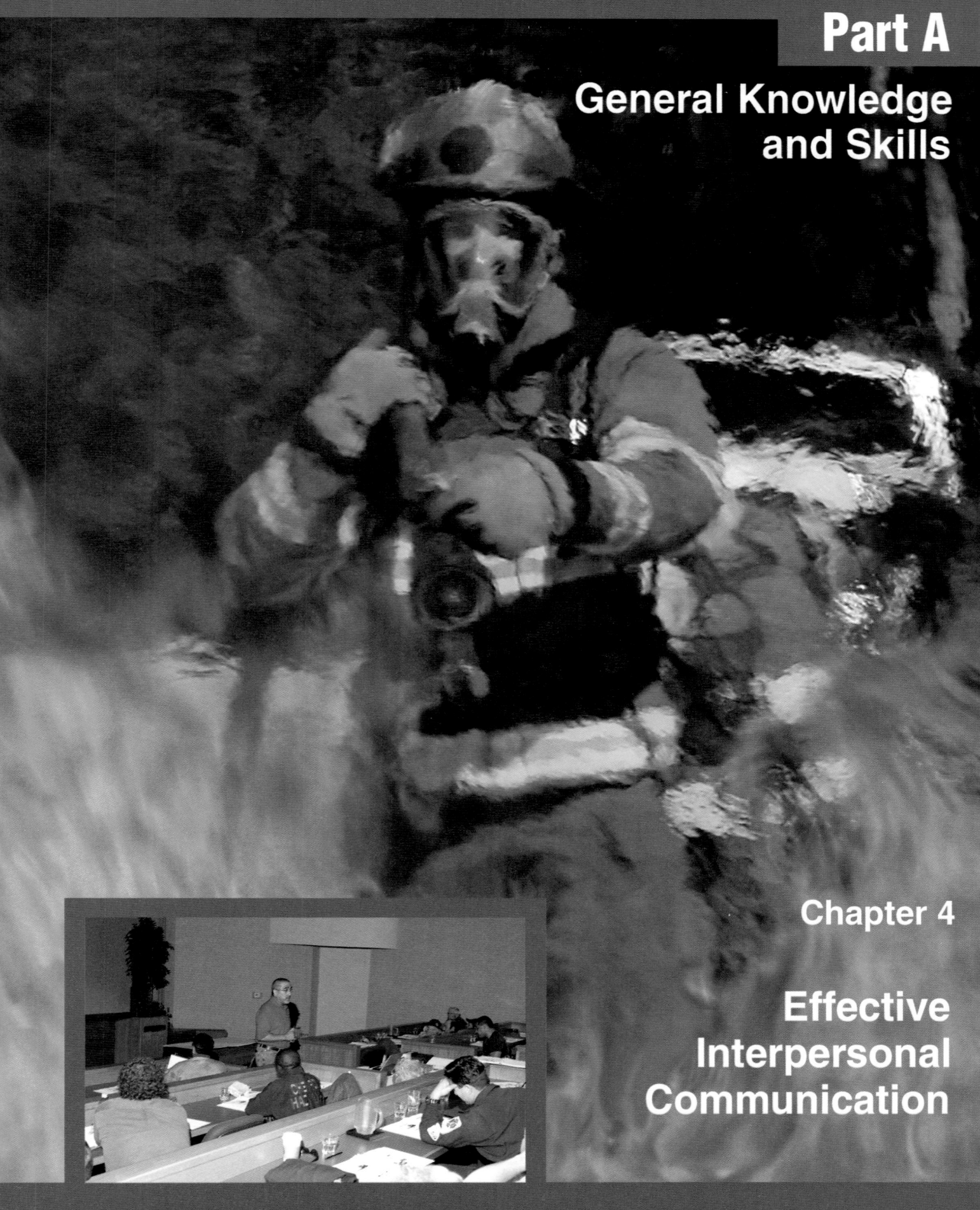

Chapter 4

Effective
Interpersonal
Communication

After reading this chapter, students will be able to —

1. Identify facts about the elements of interpersonal communication.

2. List the purposes of interpersonal communication.

3. Identify facts about the verbal component of interpersonal communication.

4. List verbal skills improvement guidelines.

5. Describe the main elements of kinesics.

6. Identify guidelines for improving nonverbal communication.

7. Identify components of the listening process.

8. Identify ways to improve listening skills.

Chapter Contents

Interpersonal Communication Basics
Sender
Message
Medium or Channel
Receiver
Feedback to the Sender
Interference

Interpersonal Communication Purposes

Verbal Component

Nonverbal Component

Listening Skills
Attending
Understanding
Remembering
Evaluating
Responding
Improving Listening Skills

Summary

Chapter 4
Effective Interpersonal Communication

To be effective, an instructor must be able to communicate with others. Surveys of private sector employers indicate that communication skills rank directly below leadership ability in the skills most employers want new employees to have. Communication skills can be divided into the following three categories:

- Interpersonal communication
- Speech communication
- Written communication

Each of these categories is the subject of hundreds of books, thousands of articles, and numerous college-level degree programs. The concepts found in interpersonal communication are basic to these three categories. This chapter provides a brief overview of these concepts, but remember it is only an overview. It is the instructor's responsibility to further explore the topic through self-directed reading of the books and articles found in the Suggested Readings section at the end of the book or through continuing education courses provided by local colleges or universities. Practicing the skills through application also helps to integrate them into the instructor's personal abilities.

Dr. Rhoberta Shaler has said that *you cannot **not** communicate*. Communication is essential to all societies, professions, and relationships. Effective interpersonal communication skills are the foundations for everything that an instructor does. To be successful, provide a safe training environment. To provide knowledge to students, master the skills of interpersonal communication.

To understand the dynamics of interpersonal communication, it is best to participate in a college-level course on the subject. Such a course involves not only reading and learning the concepts but also practicing them through role-play situations. This chapter explains the basic elements of interpersonal communication, purposes of interpersonal communication, and verbal and nonverbal components of the process. It also discusses listening and emphatic response skills.

Interpersonal Communication Basics

Interpersonal communication is the communication that takes place between two people who have established a relationship, and it occurs on a daily basis in the lives of all people who live in groups. The relationship may be between parent and child, employer and employee, husband and wife, instructor and student, friends, or even two people over the telephone (**Figure 4.1, p. 86**). Unlike formal speech communication (public speaking), interpersonal communication has the following characteristics:

- Casual language
- Casual nonverbal clues
- Frequent changes of the speaker and listener roles
- Spontaneity

The tone of the conversation can change based on the perceptions of the two parties and move across the spectrum of emotions from congenial to angry. Therefore, it is important that all individuals understand and master the skills involved in interpersonal communication. Interpersonal communication consists of the following six basic elements:

Figure 4.1 Interpersonal communication can take place between two or more people in any informal situation including training sessions.

1. Sender
2. Message
3. Medium or channel
4. Receiver
5. Feedback to the sender
6. Interference

Five of the elements of the process are essential for effective interpersonal communication to occur. Understanding the remaining element, *interference,* allows the participant to recognize and overcome this potential barrier to effective communication. The sections that follow discuss the elements as they apply to interpersonal communication (**Figure 4.2**).

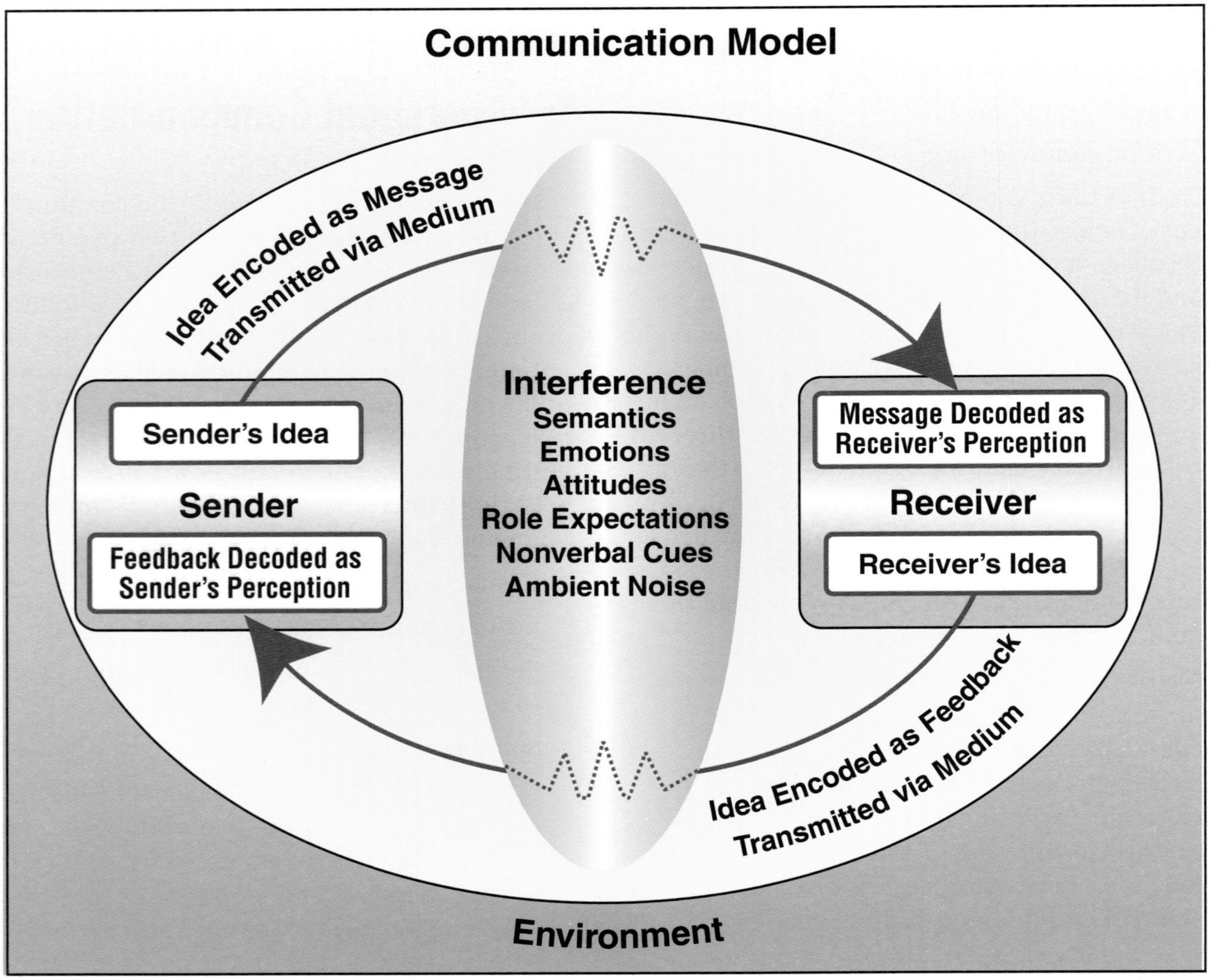

Communication Model

Idea Encoded as Message Transmitted via Medium

Interference
Semantics
Emotions
Attitudes
Role Expectations
Nonverbal Cues
Ambient Noise

Sender's Idea

Sender

Feedback Decoded as Sender's Perception

Message Decoded as Receiver's Perception

Receiver

Receiver's Idea

Idea Encoded as Feedback Transmitted via Medium

Environment

Figure 4.2 Components of the communication model are best represented visually by an oval depicting the relationship among the six elements.

Sender

The *sender* (referred to in some speech communication texts as the *speaker*) originates a message by encoding or turning thoughts and mental images into words. The words are selected based on the perceived ability of the *receiver* (also known as the *listener*) to understand the message. For example, a parent speaking to a child will use words that are simple and easy to understand. On the other hand, an incident commander on the fireground will use brief, specific commands in jargon to which firefighters can quickly react **(Figure 4.3)**.

Message

Most people think of the *message* as the spoken word, but actually, it consists of nonverbal factors or clues as well. The elements of the message may be auditory (spoken or heard), visual (seen), tactile (felt), olfactory (smelled), gustatory (tasted), gestural (a motion), or any combination of these

Figure 4.3 During training, instructors use brief, specific instructions for students. *Courtesy of Central Florida Fire Academy.*

elements. An effective message includes a combination of these elements that conveys the same idea to the receiver or listener.

Medium or Channel

The *medium* or *channel* is the path that the message takes between the sender and receiver. In most interpersonal communication situations, the channel is usually face-to-face. Both the sender and the receiver can take advantage of the various means by which messages are conveyed, leading to better understanding.

In the fire service, messages are often conveyed by other means such as telephone or radio. When radio communication was first introduced into the fire service, simplified *10-signals* were used to ensure that orders were fully understood. The 10-signals were locally developed and agreed upon. As departments began to communicate with neighboring organizations, it became apparent that the signals were *not* the same.

Clear-text (plain English) radio transmissions were originally instituted as part of the Incident Command System (ICS) to replace the confusing 10-signals. The use of clear-text has been included as a mandatory part of the National Incident Management System (NIMS).

Although some fire and emergency services organizations may still use these coded signals, the preferred choice is the clear-text approach to radio communication **(Figure 4.4, p. 88)**. Still, radio and telephone communications are only auditory and can result in miscommunication because the sender and the receiver are apart, out of visual contact, and lack the advantage of nonverbal communication.

Receiver

The *receiver* receives the message and decodes or interprets it. Education, cultural background, perception, attitude, and context all provide the receiver's frame of reference for interpretation of the message, which affects how the receiver understands it. All too often, it is misinterpretation by the receiver, based on these frames of reference, that leads to misunderstandings and arguments. Good listening skills (discussed later in the chapter) are essential for overcoming misunderstandings.

Figure 4.4 Because misunderstandings can occur when radio communication is used, the speaker must be very accurate and use clear text messages.

Feedback to the Sender

The response (called *feedback)* is important to the continuation of the conversation. The message's effect will be obvious to the sender by the auditory, visual, gestural, or tactile response of the receiver. When feedback is positive, then the desired result will be achieved. When it is negative, then confrontation or misinterpretation may result. The sender will have to regroup and alter the wording of the message to ensure that it is properly understood.

Interference

Interference consists of those factors that prevent the receiver from fully receiving a message. Interference may be created by either *internal* or *external* sources. Messages may be misunderstood because the receiver has a hearing impairment (internal barrier) or excessive noise is in the area (external barrier).

Figure 4.5 The SCBA facepiece can be a barrier to both direct conversation and radio communication.

A common occurrence in the fire and emergency services is the use of handheld radios while wearing full facepiece self-contained breathing apparatus (SCBA). Understanding and being understood in this situation is very difficult (**Figure 4.5).**

Misunderstandings also occur when the receiver receives mixed messages based on what is heard and what is seen. For instance, saying *yes* while shaking the head from side to side leads to obvious confusion because in most cultures the nonverbal movement of the head indicates *no.* In this example, the verbal message is inconsistent with the nonverbal or visual message.

Overcoming internal and external interference is challenging for the receiver. To overcome an internal barrier, the receiver must perform the following actions:

- Focus on what the sender is saying.
- Listen carefully.
- Provide feedback immediately.
- Use nonverbal factors or clues to emphasize and acknowledge understanding of the message.

In the case of a hearing impairment, a person should either use hearing aids or increase the volume on radio or telephone equipment. Controlling external interference in a nonemergency situation may include turning off an air conditioner, closing a window or door, or moving the conversation to a quieter location.

At an emergency incident or external training scenario, it may be very difficult (if not impossible) to control the interference. Some alternative actions are as follows:

- Turn off audible warning devices at the incident.
- Use communication headsets or earpieces.
- Rely on agreed-upon hand signals.
- Increase the volume of communication equipment.

However, some situations may involve so much interference that face-to-face communication is the only solution. In these cases, messengers can be used to communicate with units that are located remotely from the command post. Each situation has to be approached as a special situation requiring special solutions.

Interpersonal Communication Purposes

There are five general purposes for interpersonal communication: to learn, to relate, to influence, to play, and to help. Brief descriptions of these purposes are as follows:

1. *Learning* — Acquire knowledge or skills. When a member of a fire and emergency services organization needs to know how to accomplish a task, for instance, an instructor can provide the necessary knowledge.

2. *Relating* — Establish a new relationship or maintain an existing one. When new personnel are hired, they must be welcomed into the organization. Establishing a personal relationship, whether in a career, combination, or volunteer organization, is important to giving a new employee a feeling of belonging, which increases loyalty to the group.

3. *Influencing* — Control, direct, or manipulate behavior. Instructors influence others in situations that involve giving commands during training evolutions, counseling students, or conducting annual fitness reviews for subordinate instructors (to mention a few).

4. *Playing* — Create a diversion and gain pleasure or gratification. In the context of using verbal humor to reduce stress, most emergency re-

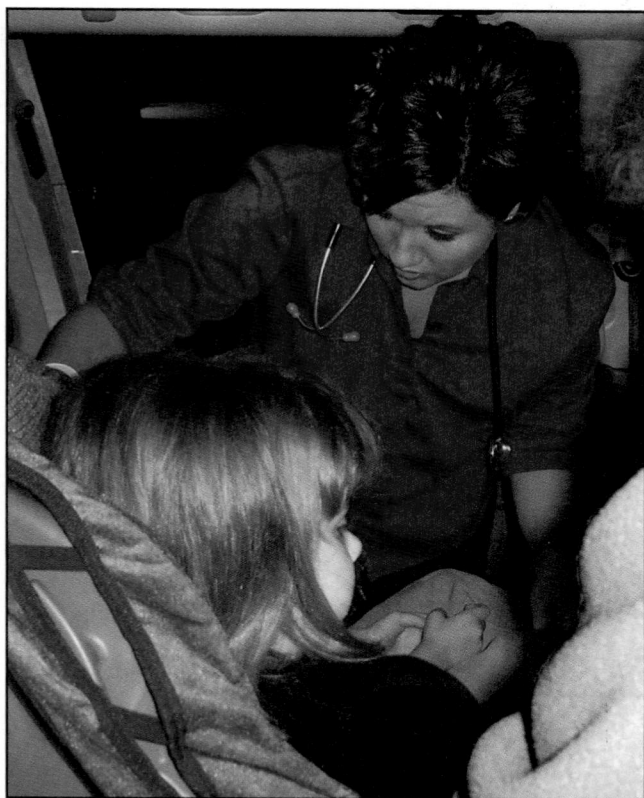

Figure 4.6 A part of the act of rendering medical assistance is consoling and comforting the victim. This assistance is essential when dealing with children. *Courtesy of Alabama Fire College.*

sponders are accustomed to using interpersonal communications in a playful manner during their daily work schedules.

5. *Helping* — Minister to the needs of another person or console someone in the time of tragedy or loss. Consoling victims, relatives, or other emergency responders in situations that involve injuries, fatalities, or losses is part of the duties of fire and emergency services responders **(Figure 4.6)**.

For a conversation to work properly, both the sender and receiver must agree on its purpose. Agreement is usually implied by the shared situation such as the classroom environment in which the instructor and student agree that the purpose of the relationship is for the student to learn. In some cases, the purpose must be stated to ensure that both parties understand it fully. A situation that involves influencing the actions of a subordinate would require that the subordinate understand that the purpose of the conversation involves a change of attitude or behavior.

Verbal Component

Many people think of communication as consisting of only the words they speak. Research by communication professionals, however, indicates that words (the verbal component) only provide the receiver with 7 percent of the message. Nonverbal actions provide the remaining 93 percent. This fact does *not* mean that words are *not* important because they are. Without them, it would be impossible to accurately and effectively convey the total message. Therefore, instructors must understand both the power and weakness of words as part of a message.

Words are abstract. The meanings are generalizations rather than concrete or tangible meanings. Consider the tool used by firefighters to force open doors or windows. Moving from the abstract to the more specific, they are *tools, forcible entry tools, door openers,* or *pry bars.* Depending on the number and variety of tool types carried on an apparatus, the number and type of tool that the listener may respond with can vary when the sender's request is too general. Thus the use of the abstract word *tool* would be avoided and a more specific term such as *pry bar* would be substituted (**Figure 4.7**).

To be effective communicators, instructors must select and use words that accurately symbolize the image that they are trying to convey. This word selection is particularly important when speaking to people who do *not* have a shared experience with the speaker. Explaining how a smoke detector works to someone who does *not* have a background in fire science requires less technical terms than explaining the concept to another emergency responder.

Instructors should always be aware of their audience or listener. The terms that are common to the fire and emergency services may have another meaning or *no* meaning at all to the general public. Avoid technical language and fire service jargon when speaking with the public, elected officials, the media, and others from outside the profession.

As the cultural and ethnic diversity of the fire and emergency services increase, instructors must be aware that words have different meanings to different people. Words once thought to be correct in common usage are now considered improper,

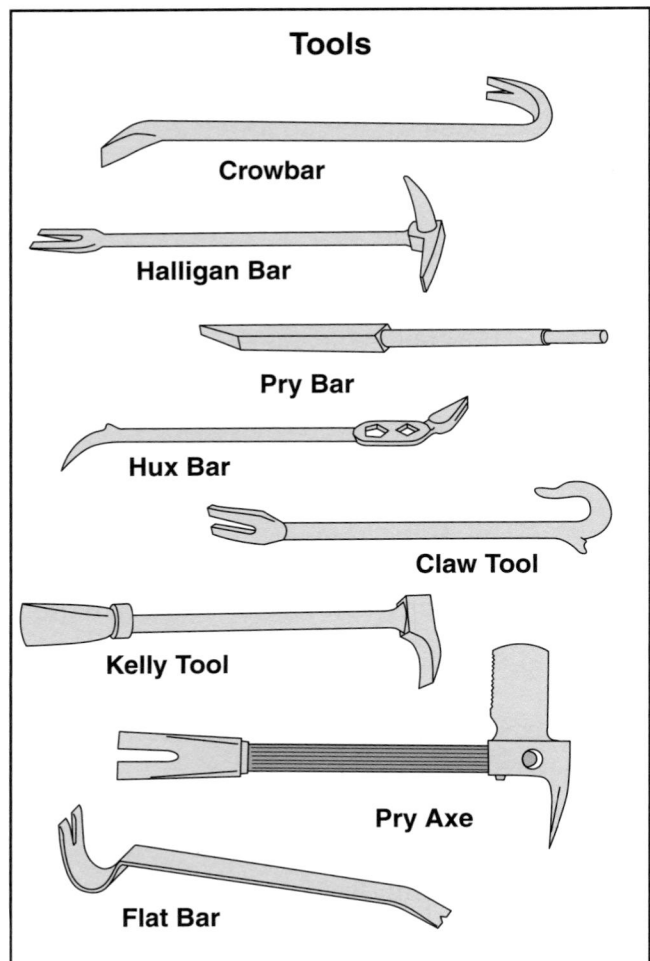

Figure 4.7 The word *tool* generally describes all the items in this illustration. More specifically, each item in the illustration may be described as a *pry bar, crowbar, Halligan bar,* etc.

impolite, or politically incorrect. The sections that follow provide a brief overview of the cultural concept of words and how the instructor can improve verbal skills by focusing on the listener.

Cultural Concept of Words

The meaning or symbolism that people place on words depends on the cultural background of people. Generally, the meanings of words used in North American English are based on a Eurocentric culture (European-based worldview). Therefore, words have been used to compare other people with this traditionally dominant group. The result has been the common use of terms that place these *others* at subordinate positions in society by stereotyping or generalizing certain characteristics or traits of a group of people.

Obsolete Terms and Their Replacements

Fireman ⟶ Firefighter

Manpower ⟶ Personnel or Staffing

To Man ⟶ To Staff

Nozzleman ⟶ Nozzle Operator

Ladderman ⟶ Firefighter

Gender, ethnicity, age, religion, political association, education, and regional background are several ways that people are stereotyped by language. Avoid words that draw attention to these classifications in a negative context in all types of communication. To demean, put down, or degrade people based on the words they use only builds barriers to real communication. It is more productive to attempt to understand other people and show respect for their cultural backgrounds.

It is vitally important for an instructor to understand the symbolism of language and the effect that it can have when speaking to and about members of specific groups. As a leader who provides an example for students of the organization, an instructor must *not* use language that stereotypes people or groups. At the same time, instructors must *not* tolerate the use of this type of language by students or other members of the organization.

The use of stereotypes creates the perception of a hostile work environment that is a major impediment to successful leadership. Slurs, innuendos, name calling, and inappropriate jokes and comments are no longer accepted or tolerated. It is unprofessional, unacceptable, and illegal.

As mentioned in the previous chapter, laws exist at all levels of government that prohibit statements that can be construed as being discriminatory, salacious, or hostile or creating a hostile environment. As a leader and role model, instructors need to avoid making such statements.

Verbal Skills Improvement

To ensure strong interpersonal relationships at work, at home, and in the community, an instructor must develop verbal skills that build understanding. Learning to communicate using generally accepted guidelines helps everyone develop relationships and increase organizational effectiveness and efficiency. To accomplish this skill, it is necessary to practice the following guidelines:

- ***Engage in dual perspective*** — Be aware of the receiver's frame of reference. Recognize the listener as having a different culture and attempt to relate to it rather than diminish it or make fun of it.

- ***Take responsibility for personal feelings and thoughts*** — Do *not* blame someone else for personal feelings and thoughts. Use language that is *I*-based such as *I believe . . .* or *I think . . . .* Avoid phrases such as *You hurt me* or *You disappoint me,* and focus instead on ownership of the feelings and the cause of those feelings such as *I am disappointed by your actions.*

- ***Show respect for the feelings and thoughts of the other person*** — Avoid trying to apply personal feelings to another person such as saying, *I know how you feel.* Because people have feelings based on their personal life experiences, it is almost impossible for anyone to know how another person feels. Understand and respect their positions and build upon those concepts to create strong relationships. A better way of responding in this type of situation is to say *I'm sorry you have to go through this.*

- ***Try to gain accuracy and clarity in speaking*** — Avoid the abstract language that can cause misunderstandings. Avoid generalizations that result in stereotypes such as *All lawyers are crooks.* Generalizations are in themselves false. Be clear and accurate in all types of communication.

- ***Be aware of any special needs of the receiver*** — Be sure to speak slowly and clearly while facing a person when the person is deaf or hard of hearing for example. This procedure makes it easier for the person to read lips. Do *not* exaggerate lip or mouth movements because this action is *not* helpful and may even make the words more difficult to understand.

- ***Avoid speaking or addressing a problem while angry or emotional*** — Pause and place the conversation on hold until emotions are under control. Emotions can cause a speaker to say things that are untrue or hurtful, using words as weapons. This *time-out* allows both parties to get a better perspective of the situation.

Nonverbal Component

Speech communication research indicates that nonverbal communication transmits from 55 to 93 percent of the message. The nonverbal elements are 55 percent of the message, while the vocal tones and inflections are 38 percent (**Figure 4.8**). This research would suggest that nonverbal clues are more important than the verbal message, which is only 7 percent of the total message, and the nonverbal message may overpower the verbal message. Nonverbal clues consist of the following elements:

- *Kinesics* — Use of body motion and position

- *Paralanguage or vocalics* — Vowel sounds or tones used to create the verbal message

- *Self-presentation* — Clothing, touch, use of time, and control of the speaker's environment

An understanding of the importance of each of the elements of nonverbal communication assists the instructor in recognizing and interpreting

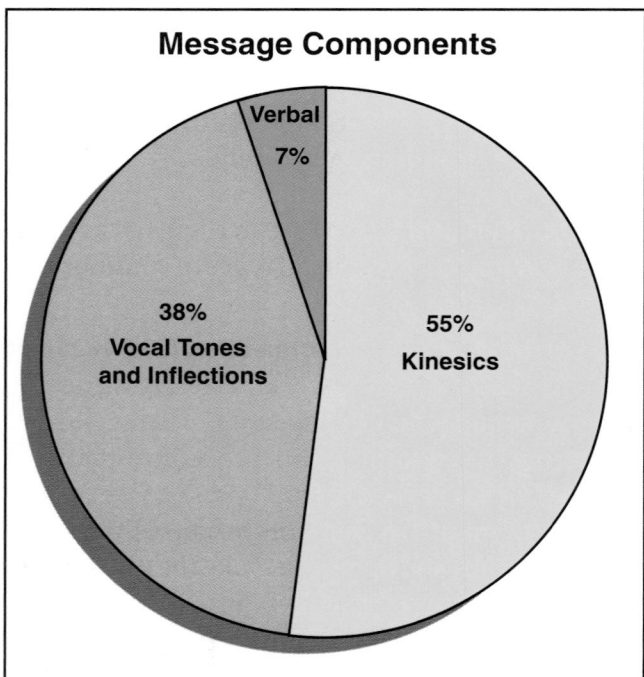

Figure 4.8 As indicated in this illustration, the nonverbal component of most messages provides the listener with the greatest percentage of the message.

those signals, therefore, improving nonverbal communication. While it is important for the instructor to understand each of the elements of nonverbal communication, paralanguage and self-presentation are beyond the scope of this manual. Information on these topics may be found in speech communication textbooks or on the Internet.

Kinesics

The main elements of kinesics include eye contact, facial expression, gestures, posture, and poise. Kinesics can project a person's self-perception, emotional state, approachability, or cultural background. Descriptions are as follows:

- *Eye contact* — The eyes are said to be the *windows of the soul,* giving others access to the most personal emotions of the person to whom they are talking. In Eurocentric cultures, good eye contact can convey self-confidence, honesty, trust, and credibility. Averting one's gaze can indicate deceit, lying, insecurity, or anxiety. However, eye contact is also a function of cultural background. Therefore, the use of eye contact must be appropriate to the situation, the relationship, and the culture. *Examples:*

  — The term *shifty eyed* has been coined to describe someone who *cannot* be trusted because of a lack of eye contact.

  — Many Native American or Asian societies believe that it is disrespectful to make direct eye contact with a person who is *not* of the same status.

  — In the wrong context, too much eye contact can be as damaging as too little. Staring into the eyes of a member of the opposite sex can be considered too personal and intimidating.

- *Facial expression* — The face can show the six basic emotions: happiness, sadness, surprise, fear, anger, and disgust. To effectively communicate the correct message in a relationship, the facial expression must match the verbal message. Because people learn to manipulate their words but *not* their nonverbal clues, the listener will often believe these clues over the words.

- *Gestures* — Many people *talk with their hands.* It is even considered a cultural stereotype for Italians and other Mediterranean cultures. In situations where noise prevents verbal communication, gestures are effectively used to send messages such as *come here* and *stop.* It is important to understand the types of gestures and the parts they play in communication because they allow the listener to understand the speaker more clearly **(Figure 4.9)**. *Details:*

  — This knowledge allows the speaker to identify the gestures used by the listener and adapt to them.

  — People can then learn how to control the unconscious gestures that might offend or distract from the message.

- *Posture* — Sitting or standing erect can create the impression of a person with a great deal of self-confidence and authority. Slouching or standing with stooped shoulders makes a person appear insecure, disinterested, or intimidated.

- *Poise* — Poise is the accumulation of all the other nonverbal elements into one image of self-confidence and authority. Poise is gained by mastering the skills of interpersonal and speech communications. Mastery of these skills helps to overcome the nervousness that some people experience when they are put into situations that involve speaking in public or meeting strangers.

Figure 4.9 Hand gestures can be used to strengthen the meaning of the verbal message, especially in situations where hearing is difficult. *Courtesy of Maryland Fire and Rescue Institute (MFRI).*

Nonverbal Communication Improvement

Improving nonverbal interpersonal communication skills begins with self-reflection. Instructors need to apply the following general concepts:

- *Eye contact* — Learn to maintain eye contact while speaking to people. Also recognize that some cultures find direct eye contact to be disrespectful. Learn to modify the use of eye contact when it is appropriate.

- *Facial expression* — Learn to match the facial expression to the message.

- *Gestures* — Identify and control gestures that are annoying or distracting to others. Learn to use gestures to emphasize and illustrate the message.

- *Poise* — Create poise by building self-confidence and overcoming any fear associated with public speaking or dealing with strangers. Accomplish poise through practice and a command of the information or topic in the message.

- *Vocal characteristics* — Learn to use vocal characteristics appropriately, depending on the message and the situation. Accomplish this skill by practicing speaking slowly (using variation in pitch to provide emphasis), using volume appropriate to the situation, and using proper diction to ensure that the words are clearly understood.

- *Vocal interferences* — Learn to recognize and eliminate filler words from the communication process.

- *Personal appearance* — Maintain a professional appearance at all times, set an example for subordinates, and require the same level of professionalism from the members of the organization.

- *Touch* — Become conscious of the effect that touch can have on others, both positive and negative.

- *Proximity* — Be aware of the cultural differences that determine the use of space, and apply it appropriately.

- *Use of time* — Adjust the application of time based on the individuals or groups who are being dealt with. Explain the requirements to all who are concerned when it is necessary to maintain strict control over time.

Listening Skills

Of all the communication skills discussed in this manual, listening is probably the most important. According to speech communication professionals, listening constitutes approximately 42 to 53 percent of a person's average day (**Figure 4.10**). In the classroom, it is estimated that students spend 50 to 75 percent of class time listening to the instructor, other students, or audio media presentations. Therefore, improving listening skills is essential to effective communication. As role models for their students, instructors must practice good listening skills.

Good listening skills also affect how well people remember what they hear. Recent research indicates that as much as 75 percent of oral communication is ignored, misunderstood, or quickly forgotten by the listener. Researchers also determined that most people remember only 50 percent of a message immediately after they hear it and only 25 percent after 48 hours. Therefore, the more attentive people are, the better they will listen and the more they will retain (**Figure 4.11**).

Many people confuse hearing and listening. Although both activities involve the use of the auditory senses through the use of the ears, they are *not* the same. *Hearing* is a physiological process that involves sound waves striking the eardrums. The majority of the sound waves that enter the ear consist of noise. People hear all sounds around them such as the music playing in an elevator, sound of air passing through the building air-conditioning system, or sounds of traffic on the street. Most of these sounds are ignored and create only a dull background noise to the sounds on which the listener is actually focused.

Figure 4.10 The average person spends 60 to 70 percent of the day in some form of communication. Of that time, 45 to 53 percent is spent listening. Students in class may spend as much as 75 percent of the period listening.

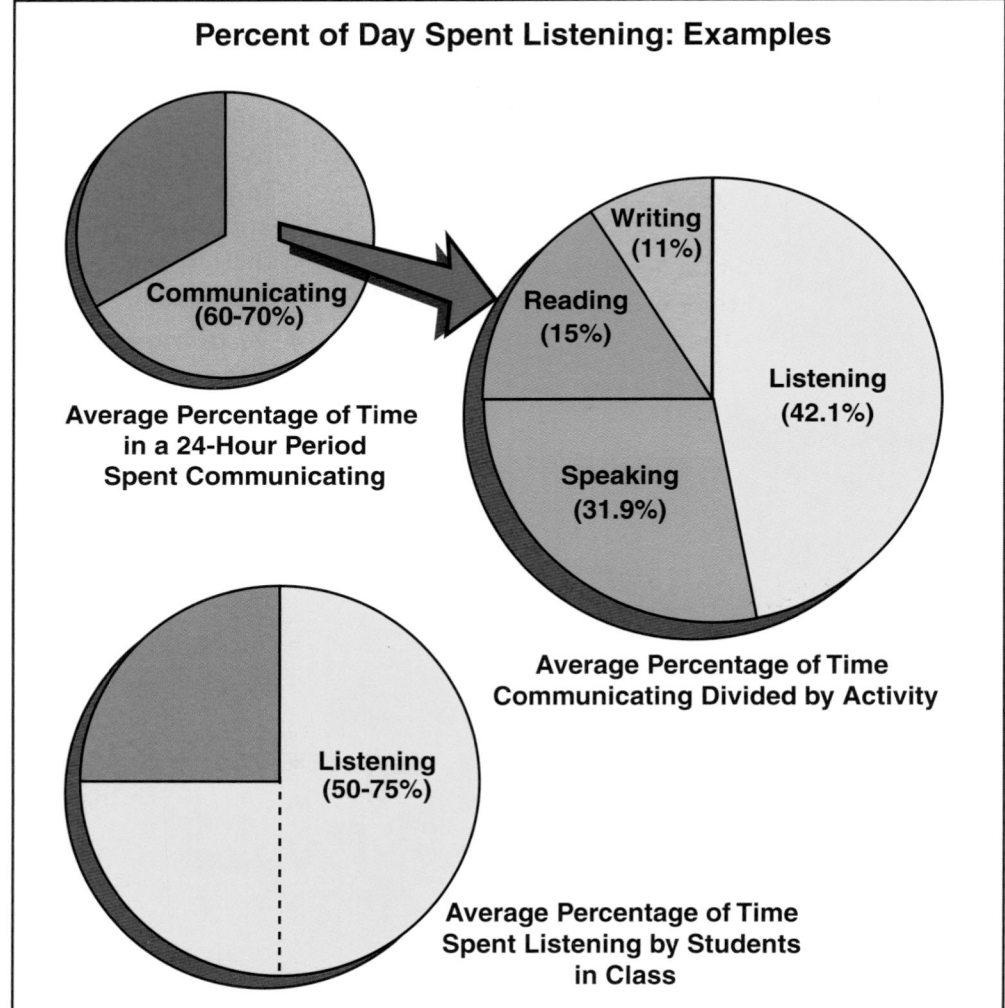

Percent of Day Spent Listening: Examples

Communicating (60-70%)

Average Percentage of Time in a 24-Hour Period Spent Communicating

Writing (11%)
Reading (15%)
Listening (42.1%)
Speaking (31.9%)

Average Percentage of Time Communicating Divided by Activity

Listening (50-75%)

Average Percentage of Time Spent Listening by Students in Class

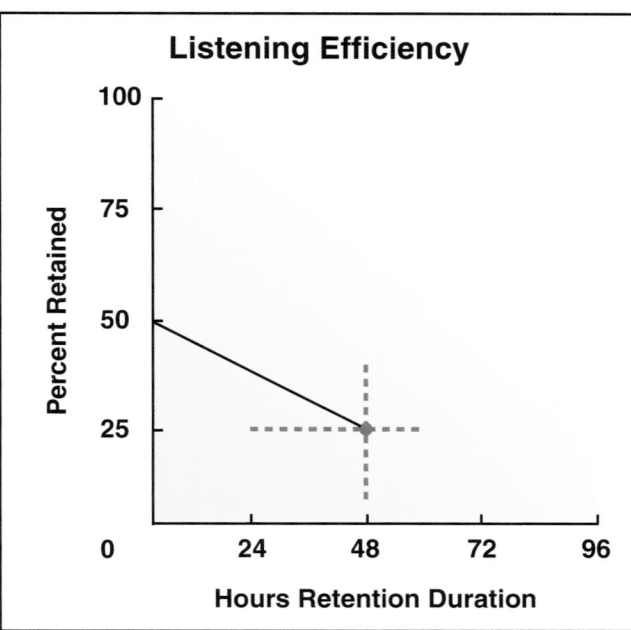

Figure 4.11 Research by Ralph Nichols on listening indicates that immediately after listening to a 10-minute oral presentation, the average listener has heard, understood, and retained 50 percent of what was said. The amount of information retained 48 hours later drops to 25 percent.

Listening, on the other hand, is an active process (the receiving part of the communication process) that includes attending, understanding, remembering, evaluating, and responding to the speaker. Once the instructor has learned the various parts of the listening process, it will be possible to apply them to improve existing listening skills.

Attending

Attending is basically paying attention to the message. It means focusing on the speaker and ignoring other distractions. In a controlled environment such as an interview in an office setting, focus may be easy to accomplish. For example, closing a window or door can reduce traffic noise or turning off a radio and lowering the volume of dispatch speakers during the interview can eliminate distractions. Visual distractions such as clutter on a desk or memorabilia in an office can be removed before the interview.

Controlling the environment of an emergency scene or during a training scenario is much more difficult, causing the listener to concentrate much harder on the speaker. This concentration is particularly important when the com-

munication is occurring over the radio. Some suggestions for improving the attending step are as follows:

- *Be ready to listen* — Look at the speaker when possible. Think about the speaker and what is being said. Visualize the situation or event that the speaker is talking about.
- *Listen to the complete message* — Wait until the speaker has finished delivering the message before responding.
- *Maintain eye contact* — Listen to both the verbal and nonverbal messages.

Understanding

Understanding consists of decoding the message and assigning meaning to it. It involves the following actions:

- Organizing the message into a logical pattern
- Observing the nonverbal clues to help with the meaning of the message
- Asking questions to clarify the meaning of the message

When a message is important or the receiver is unsure of the importance of the message, the receiver can respond by repeating the message word for word or paraphrasing it. *Paraphrasing* is restating the message in different words but keeping the same meaning. Paraphrasing the message back to the speaker to see whether there is agreement can also increase understanding.

Remembering

Remembering what has been said is critical for the message to have the correct effect. To assist in remembering, repeat the information. When possible, take notes, which is an effective and important way to retain the message. Note taking is particularly important during interviews or performance evaluations. Always keep a small notepad available for recording information, whether in the office, in the classroom, or on the training ground.

Another method for remembering specific information is the use of *mnemonics*, a system or technique for improving memory. One useful mnemonic device consists of reducing a phrase to the first letters of each word of the phrase. An example that is familiar to most fire officers is *RECEO*, the basic steps of fire scene operations: Rescue, Exposure, Confinement, Extinguishment, and Overhaul.

Evaluating

Evaluating the message involves critically analyzing it to determine how factual it really is. To evaluate a message, the listener must be able to separate facts from opinions. *Facts* are verifiable data that can support the decision-making process. A radio report that an engine company has reached the seat of a fire and is applying water to it can be verified by the observation that the smoke has changed from black to gray.

An *opinion,* however, is a generalization that may *not* be verifiable without additional data. The report from a witness that everyone has exited a structure *cannot* be verified without a thorough search of the building. Analysis of the message depends on the following factors:

- Personal experience of the listener
- Other available information
- Interpretation of the nonverbal clues from the speaker
- Credibility of the speaker

Responding

Responding to the speaker completes the communication process and means an exchange of roles has occurred (the listener becomes the speaker and vice versa). Without any response, the speaker does *not* know whether the message was received, understood, or will be acted upon. The response needs to be both verbal and nonverbal to indicate that the message was understood. A response may also occur during the understanding step of the process when a question is asked or the message is paraphrased or during the remembering step to help retain the message.

Improving Listening Skills

Practicing good listening skills is the best way to improve them. Listen to speeches or stories on audiotape, and try to repeat the key elements. To improve listening and note-taking skills, the in-structor should practice taking notes at meetings or in classes presented by other instructors. These exercises help overcome the barrier created by information overload and pinpoint the essential elements of the message.

When listening to a speaker, try to focus on the speaker and the message. The greatest distraction is the listener's internal *voice.* This voice may be responding to something that was said earlier or something the listener would like to say. It could just be daydreaming. While this internal monologue is underway, the words of the speaker are being ignored. To overcome this barrier, first identify it. Try responding to the speaker by asking questions or paraphrasing what has been said. When responding is inappropriate such as it would be with a formal speech, take notes of the key points.

Before classes, small group meetings, or individual counseling sessions, remove barriers to listening in the rooms where the meetings will take place. These barriers may include noise-producing equipment or visual distractions such as posters on the walls. Wall decorations in classrooms should supplement the course material and *not* distract from it. During training exercises, try to identify barriers to communication, both over the radio and at the command post.

Training exercises that re-create fireground conditions help to identify potential barriers and provide an opportunity to identify solutions. As part of the postincident evaluation, determine ways to improve listening skills for those involved in the incident. The instructor who is assigned as the incident safety officer and/or critique officer is responsible for identifying communication problems, reporting them, and suggesting ways to overcome them during postincident analyses.

An instructor should work to overcome psychological barriers such as prejudice by accepting others as they are. Prejudice based on preconceived concepts of dress, voice, or attitude can be major barriers to hearing what a speaker has to say.

Barriers to Listening

- **Information overload** — Identify the essential elements of the message.

- **Personal concerns** — Focus on the speaker and the message rather than personal concerns or thoughts.

- **Outside distractions** — Take control of the environment and remove as many distractions as possible.

- **Prejudice** — Focus on the message and *not* the messenger.

Summary

As a foundation to other types of communication, an understanding of effective interpersonal communication is important to all instructors. The concepts can be applied to classroom teaching situations, counseling and mentoring both students and subordinates, and improving relations with external customers of the organization. All fire and emergency services instructors must master the basic interpersonal communication skills in order to be effective teachers. In addition, instructors will find these skills appropriate in all areas of their lives and gain the benefits that good communication skills bring to all relationships.

Tips for Effective Communication

Ed Kirtley, Officer/Instructor Coordinator, Oklahoma Fire Service Training, has written Eleven Keys to Engaging Adult Students, a series of tips for instructors. Some that relate to effective communication skills include the following:

- ***Ask them what they want*** — What better way to find out what students want to learn! It's really quite simple; yet we, as instructors, seldom do it. We assume that they want to know about our chosen topic. It's true that you have to have some agenda and learning objectives when you plan your topic, but you should be willing to modify your plan when the student's needs are somewhat different from what you planned. *What to do:*

  — The best way is to spend time with students before you get to the presentation.

  — Take the time necessary to find out exactly what they want you to address during your presentation.

  — Don't let them get away with simply asking for *something about putting out fire.*

  — When there is a pertinent topic, don't hesitate to recommend it and see whether they have an interest.

- ***See, hear, do*** — Students must receive information through a combination of all three modalities. While it is true that each of us has a modality that is stronger than the other two, learning is optimized when all three are used during a presentation. *Examples:*

  — Let them hear you.

  — Let them see the information presented through audiovisuals.

  — Let them experience it by doing something with the new information such as application, problem solving, etc.

- ***Say thank you*** — This is pretty simple. When you are finished, thank students for their time and giving you the chance to make their lives a little safer. Let them know you appreciate their attention and the opportunity to speak to them. Remember, you are there for them — to meet their needs.

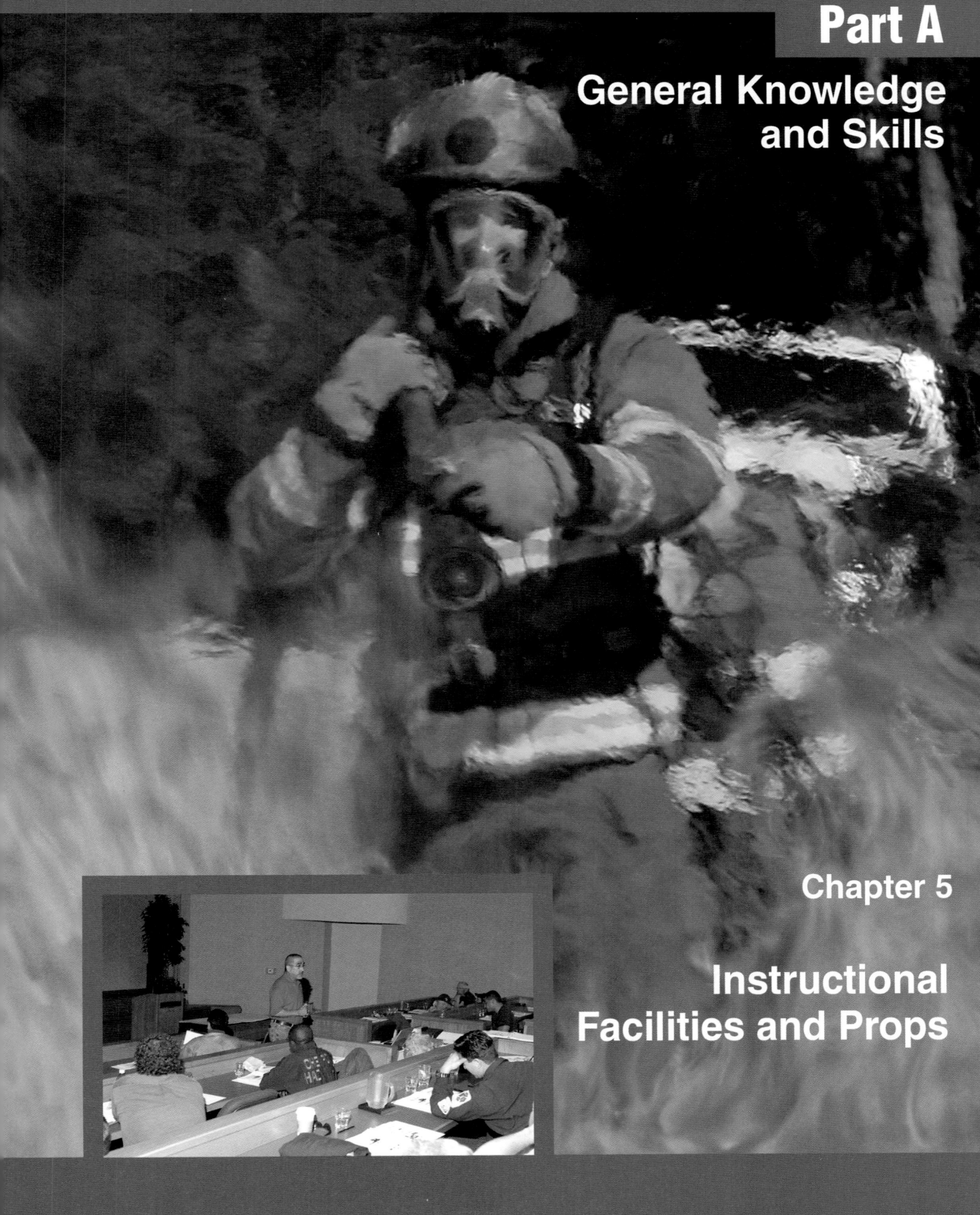

Part A
General Knowledge and Skills

Chapter 5

Instructional Facilities and Props

After reading this chapter, students will be able to —

1. Identify infrastructure requirements.

2. Identify site requirements for permanent facilities.

3. Identify accurate statements about mobile training facilities.

4. Describe rescue/extrication training areas.

5. Identify facts about flammable/combustible liquids and hazardous materials training areas.

6. List live-fire training area characteristics.

7. Discuss portable training props.

8. Identify facts about using acquired structures for live-fire training.

9. Discuss instructor responsibilities when using an acquired structure.

10. Identify accurate statements about safety requirements for using fuels in live-fire training.

Chapter Contents

Instructional Facilities
  Infrastructure Requirements
  Permanent Facilities
  Mobile Training Facilities

Training Props
  Permanent Structures
  Portable Training Props

Acquired Structures
  Environmental Conditions
  Structural Conditions
  Training Possibilities
  Instructor Responsibilities
  Fuel Usage
  Water Supply Requirements

Summary

Chapter 5
Instructional Facilities and Props

Most fire and emergency services organizations have access to some type of instructional facility and several training props. Some organizations may operate state-of-the-art training centers with administrative offices, classroom buildings, elaborate burn buildings, exterior props, and support facilities. Others may only have a small classroom building, portable props, and an area large enough to provide basic entry-level training (**Figure 5.1**).

Some organizations may have access to instructional facilities that are provided by nearby universities, vocational schools, state/provincial or regional training agencies, or other metropolitan fire and emergency services organizations. At a minimum, the instructional facility used by an organization should have structures and props that provide a variety of training scenarios and the opportunity for live-fire exercises.

This chapter gives an overview of instructional facilities, training props, and acquired structures that can be used to provide the level of training required by the organization. Information on infrastructure requirements is also discussed. NFPA 1402, *Guide to Building Fire Service Training Centers* (2002), is an excellent source for information on training facilities. The U.S. Federal Aviation Administration (FAA) also provides information in its publications on the design of aircraft rescue and fire-fighting training simulators.

NFPA 1041, *Standard for Fire Service Instructor Professional Qualifications* (2007), does not address instructional facilities and training props directly, but it does imply that instructors should have knowledge of them. This knowledge is basic to evaluating facilities and props and their usefulness for providing training. Therefore, the instructor and training administrator must know the types of

Figure 5.1 Portable or manufactured buildings can provide excellent temporary and low-cost classroom facilities for training organizations of any size. *Courtesy of Central Florida Fire Academy.*

permanent facilities and props that are available, their uses, the safety requirements of each, and the importance of safety in the use of acquired structures and props.

Instructional Facilities

Instructional facilities cover a wide range of designs and types from the elaborate to the simple. They may be permanent, fixed facilities, mobile units, or acquired structures, each designed and used for a variety of training evolutions. Instructors and training administrators should consult both NFPA 1402 and NFPA 1403, *Standard on Live Fire Training Evolutions* (2002), which establishes the requirements for live-fire or burn training in permanent and acquired structures. In addition to the instructional facilities, a minimum infrastructure to support the facilities, props, and training evolutions is required.

Infrastructure Requirements

To properly support an organization's training program, a permanent instructional facility should provide an infrastructure that consists of the following components:

- *Location*— Site that provides adequate space for the various types of training that are required to meet the organization's needs. *Other considerations:*

  — Easily accessible from all areas of the organization's coverage

  — Remote from other occupancies such as airports, health-care facilities, or schools that may be affected by live burns

  — Large enough for any potential expansion of training requirements based on the organization's strategic plan

- *Adequate water supply*— Volume and pressure required by NFPA 1142, *Standard on Water Supplies for Suburban and Rural Fire Fighting* (2001), to support training operations based on the following factors:

  — Number of attack and backup hoselines used

  — Need for potable (suitable for drinking) water

  — Need to supply sprinkler and water spray systems with necessary volume and pressure

  — Need to supply water for other types of exercises that may take place at the site

- *Fuel source*— Flammable or combustible liquid, liquefied petroleum gas (LPG), or natural gas piped to the burn building or props from a main supply (**Figures 5.2 a and b**).

- *Breathing air supply* — Items supporting respiratory protection equipment, including the following:

Figures 5.2 a and b Storage for flammable and combustible liquids and liquefied petroleum gas (LPG) must be provided in accordance with local hazardous materials storage regulations. (a) Containment pits, highly visible signs, and impact barriers are examples of safety requirements for flammable liquids storage in some jurisdictions. (b) LPG storage tanks in an isolated area surrounded by impact barriers meet local codes. *Courtesy of Central Florida Fire Academy.*

  — Spare replacement breathing-air cylinders

  — Portable breathing-air compressor

  — Piped breathing-air distribution system from a centrally located compressor

  — Fixed or portable cascade system

  — Supplied-air system (**Figures 5.3 a and b**)

- *Apparatus staging, approach, and operational area* — Parking for units *not* involved in the training. *Factors considered:*

Figures 5.3 a and b Students and instructors must have an adequate supply of breathing air during training. Examples: (a) Spare SCBA units. (b) Piped supplied-air systems connected to remote fill stations.

— Short travel routes to the designated training prop

— Space to park the apparatus as though it is at an emergency incident

— Concrete surfaces capable of supporting the weight of apparatus

— Exit routes for apparatus to respond in the event that a unit is dispatched for an emergency call

- *Communications system* — Radio frequency dedicated for the training function or two-way communication devices with limited range. *Elements required:*

  — All personnel engaged in the training exercise must have contact with one another.

  — Communication loop must include incident safety officer and the individual assigned to the fuel shutoff valve control.

- *Weather (wind direction and air speed) monitoring equipment* — Equipment installed at the highest point of a facility to allow personnel to determine the wind effect on burning materials and foam streams and plan attack tactics to take advantage of it.

- *Environmental controls* — Controls (besides the water-decontamination system) that are less obvious, including the following:

  — Use of natural gas or environmentally friendly fuels

  — Use of nonporous concrete surfaces to prevent soil contamination

  — Protocols to determine the effect of weather (temperature extremes, humidity, wind direction, and the like) on training exercises

  — Noise pollution controls such as mandatory hearing protection

- *Equipment decontamination area* — Area designated for the washing and cleaning of personal protective clothing, hoses, nozzles, and other equipment. Contaminated wastewater is piped to the water-decontamination system.

- *Water-decontamination system* — System that accomplishes separation and removal of water contaminants by one or more methods and returns decontaminated water to the system for further use in training exercises **(Figure 5.4, p. 104)**. Separation and removal methods include the following:

  — Use oil separators.

  — Contain contaminated water in a pond that separates oil from water through natural processes (ponding).

  — Add hydrocarbon-eating bacteria to water to destroy oil (bacterial breakdown).

Figure 5.4 Water decontamination systems are used to remove contaminates from water following fire-suppression training exercises.

Water decontamination is particularly important where large quantities of flammable/combustible liquids and foam extinguishing agents are used for training. The local Environmental Protection Agency (EPA) office or state/provincial water resources board can provide assistance in determining the specific requirements for water decontamination.

- *Security* — Methods used to secure the area from public access and prevent vandalism and injury to the public such as the following:

  — Fencing

  — Controlled access gates, guards, and lighting

  — Evacuation signaling system

  — Automatic fire detection and alarm system

Permanent Facilities

Permanent facilities should provide the variety of training scenarios that are required to meet the training needs of an organization. Because state-of-the-art instructional facilities can be extremely expensive, it may be necessary to develop the site in stages, beginning with acquiring sufficient space for expansion. An organization should include the potential for expansion of the facility in its strategic plan. This planning could result in the following actions:

- Purchasing adjacent undeveloped land
- Creating structural designs that permit future expansions
- Locating additional funding sources for future construction and continuing maintenance

Basic training site requirements may include classrooms, administrative offices, parking areas, driving courses, drill towers, burn buildings and props, smoke buildings, and space for transportation incident props and extrication props (**Figure 5.5**). Legislated requirements for handicap parking and access must also be taken into consideration. Specialized sites for aircraft, marine, and petrochemical training and wildland burn areas may be required if those hazards are identified in the service area. Site requirements may include the following items:

- *Classrooms* — Classrooms need to provide a comfortable learning atmosphere with minimal distractions. Audiovisual equipment, computer systems, and Internet access may be included in the rooms as well as chalkboards, dry-erase boards, and easels/pads. Classroom buildings must meet the required accessibility codes. *Examples:*

  — Classrooms may be part of a larger structure that includes demonstration rooms, restroom facilities, and administrative offices.

  — A single classroom in a portable building or trailer may be used.

  — A classroom equipped as a laboratory for fire behavior or sprinkler-system component training could be provided.

- *Administrative offices* — Space requirements for offices depend on the size of the training division. Generally, the structure could include individual offices, conference rooms, restroom facilities, kitchen and eating area, demonstration room or auditorium, library/resource area, storage space, and physical fitness workout space (**Figure 5.6**).

- *Parking areas* — Basic parking requirements for access and the number of parking spaces are generally based on the local building code; however, this requirement is only a minimum for automobiles. Include parking space and easy access for apparatus in the requirements.

Figure 5.5 Permanent training facilities such as this U.S. Department of Defense training center include buildings, props, classrooms, and maintenance shops necessary to support the training function. *Courtesy of U.S. Department of Defense.*

Figure 5.6 Administrative offices are usually located in light-office type structures that contain offices, reception areas, conference rooms, and resource libraries (among other functions).

- *Maintenance and storage structures* — Support structures provide storage for tools, hose, portable props, personal protective equipment (PPE), and materials. These structures may also provide areas for tool and equipment maintenance as well as cleaning and decontamination of clothing and equipment.

- *Driving courses* — Simulated streets, alleys, parking lots, cul-de-sacs, and dead-end driveways provide space for driver/operator training. These courses may be included with the burn and collapse structures for added incident realism. Parked vehicles, overhead wires, and other obstacles may be included to simulate actual driving situations. Off-road driving areas may also be included as part of the driving course.

- *Drill towers* — A multistory, multipurpose tower is a traditional component of training-center facilities **(Figure 5.7)**. It may be open or enclosed and should be optimally six stories in height. In an enclosed structure, a portion can be dedicated for use as a smoke building. *Tower uses:*

  — Sprinkler and standpipe training

  — Ground and aerial ladder training

  — High-angle technical rescue training

  — High-rise structure training

Figure 5.7 A traditional element of training facilities is the multistory drill tower. It is used for multiple purposes including high-angle rescue training, ground and aerial ladder training, and high-rise operations training. *Courtesy of Alabama Fire College.*

- *Live-fire buildings* — Structures that are specifically designed for use in live-fire burn exercises must have characteristics that provide a safe yet realistic training experience for students **(Figure 5.8)**. The structure must be able to withstand the high temperatures created by either fueled props (LPG or natural gas) or Class A fuel loads (excelsior or noncontaminated or treated wood, hay, or straw). *Details:*

  — Local environmental laws or ordinances may regulate the type of fuel used.

  — The building may also be equipped with sprinkler systems and thermal detection devices that activate when the internal temperature reaches a predetermined setting.

- *Smoke buildings* — Enclosed structures are designed to acquaint students with the skills required to function safely in smoke-obscured atmospheres. Nontoxic or artificial smoke is recommended according to NFPA 1500, *Standard on Fire Department Occupational Safety and Health Program,* and NFPA 1402. *Building components:*

  — Monitoring equipment, including closed-circuit television or thermal imaging equipment, for tracking and locating students in the structure

  — Adjustable interior walls to create a variety of floor plans within the space

- *Wildland training areas* — Fire and emergency services organizations that have primary responsibilities for protecting rural, suburban, and urban-interface areas from wildland fires need to develop training areas specific to those needs. NFPA 1402 does *not* address this type of facility, but some options are available as follows:

  — Include live-fire exercises with controlled burns (with proper precautions) in federal or state/provincial forests or parks.

  — Dedicate areas that could be used for this type of training such as the following:

    ☐ Unused military bases

    ☐ National and state/provincial parks

    ☐ Industrial parks

    ☐ Other large open spaces

Figure 5.8 Live-fire burn structures are designed to withstand repeated exposures to fire and heat that is created by either solid or natural-gas fuels.

- *Water rescue training areas* — Water rescue training can be performed in local ponds or lakes, rivers and streams, protected coastal areas, and swimming pools. A permanent training facility may include a swimming pool for both training and physical fitness functions.

- *Specialized props* — Permanent props may include simulated fuel storage tanks, transportation equipment, or collapsed buildings. See Training Props section for detailed descriptions.

Mobile Training Facilities

Fire and emergency services organizations that serve a large geographic area may find that portable or mobile training facilities are more economical and flexible than a permanent facility. Mobile training facilities consist of trailer- or vehicle-mounted classrooms, computer-controlled simulators, smoke trailers, and fire behavior or live-fire simulators **(Figures 5.9 a and b)**. Mobile facilities may supplement or replace a permanent facility or be used as a temporary facility before a permanent structure is built. Benefits of mobile training facilities include the following:

- Provides a means of meeting the training needs of a dispersed student audience

- Creates flexibility in meeting training schedules

Figures 5.9 a and b Portable training units are available in many configurations. They may be designed to (a) provide interior fire attack training or (b) multistory high-rise training. *(a) Courtesy of Dawn Beisner. (b) Courtesy of Central Florida Fire College.*

- Supplements training provided at the permanent facility
- Reduces the cost and lost time that occur when students must be transported to a central location
- Increases public visibility of the organization's training activities
- Uses the mobile facility as a mobile fire and life safety billboard
- Provides a temporary training space until a permanent facility is approved, funded, or constructed

Fire or incident simulators that are designed for teaching tactics, strategy, and incident command to fire officers may be part of the permanent facility or constructed as a mobile unit. Although some fire and emergency services organizations may own simulators, these units may be the property of the state/provincial training organization or a university or vocational school within the region because of their high costs.

Live-fire training or fire behavior simulators (flashover units) as well as mobile smoke rooms may also be used to provide remote site training **(Figure 5.10)**. Instructors and training administrators must *not* alter a commercially constructed

Figure 5.10 Commercially available live-fire training simulators provide the instructor with training aids that can closely simulate actual interior fire conditions in a space. *Courtesy of Central Florida Fire Academy.*

live-fire training or fire behavior simulator without the manufacturer's permission. It is also recommended that only commercially manufactured units be used in training.

Another approach to remote site training is to construct portable training props that can be disassembled and transported in a light truck or van. These props can be used in fire stations or school classrooms at locations distant from the permanent facility. Small portable props can be used to simulate a maze, door or wall section for forcible entry, or small propane-fired kitchen stove to simulate cooking fires.

Training Props

Training props (sometimes referred to as *training aids*) may be permanent structures or portable devices that are used to simulate specific types of situations and teach subjects such as the following:

- Technical rescue
- Vehicle extrication
- Flammable/combustible liquids spill and fire control
- Transportation incident response and control

These props, structures, and devices are located outside and (in some cases) remote from the classroom facilities. They may consist of trenches or collapsed structures, motor vehicles, railcars, ships, aircraft, and flammable liquids processing and storage facilities. They may be used for a variety of training scenarios including rescue, property conservation, and fire suppression. Descriptions of each prop type in the two categories (permanent structure and portable device) are in the sections that follow.

Permanent Structures

Permanent instructional facilities usually include training props that are permanent in nature and may be used for a variety of activities. These props can be used for training for topics such as rescue or extrication, flammable/combustible liquids and hazardous materials spill and fire control, and live-fire training.

Rescue/Extrication Training Area

Depending on the level of rescue training required and tools available to personnel, extrication training props may include simulated trenches, collapsed structures, confined spaces, drill towers, or wrecked or overturned vehicles or machinery. Descriptions are as follows:

- *Trench rescue* — Trench props normally consist of an earthen berm with a trench cut into it. It is used for shoring and cribbing training. The prop itself must be designed in such a way that it simulates a situation that requires shoring but does *not* create a potential for actual collapse of the trench walls.

- *Structural collapse* — Slabs of concrete and construction debris are assembled to represent a collapsed structure creating voids that allow for search and rescue activities. These props must be reinforced to prevent *real* collapses. Space should be provided for heavy lifting equipment (such as cranes) to operate. Elaborate props such as those found in the *Disaster City* area of the Texas A & M training facility may be equipped with hydraulic controls to vary the degrees of collapse **(Figure 5.11)**.

- *Confined space* — This prop may represent any type of confined-space situation including trench or structural collapse. Some props are simply grain silos mounted in steel support frames or storage tanks with limited access. They may be incorporated into a drill tower, smoke building, or live-fire burn building.

Figure 5.11 Some training facilities have purpose-build structures that can simulate structural collapse through the use of hydraulic controls. These props are used for confined-space, rescue, and recovery training.

- **High-angle rescue** — An open or enclosed drill tower can be used to simulate high-angle rescue situations. Students can ascend or descend the exterior of the structure, hoist equipment or lower victims, and practice various rope skills.

- **Vehicle and machinery extrications** — Generally, vehicle and machinery extrications involve portable props (see Portable Training Props section) because a vehicle, for example, can be relocated to various locations and is usually disposed of following the training. However, the permanent portion of the prop can be a nonporous concrete slab (containment pit) capable of controlling the residue from any fire-extinguishment activities that may take place during the evolution. *Details:*

  — The slab should have a curb around the perimeter and slope to drain basins.

  — Contaminated runoff water should then be channeled to the water-decontamination system.

Flammable/Combustible Liquids and Hazardous Materials Training Area

Areas used for flammable/combustible liquids and hazardous materials training simulate incidents involving both spills and fires. The base for the prop is the same type of containment pit constructed of concrete with curbing on all sides mentioned in the vehicle and machinery extrications bullet in the previous section. Besides the vehicle and machinery extrication prop, various types of props may be located in the pit to simulate spill and fire incidents. Descriptions of incidents and props are as follows:

- **Transportation (vehicle) incident** — Because transportation and vehicle accidents are the most common types of incidents encountered by fire and emergency services personnel, training facilities should have some props representing these types of incidents. When fuel lines are permanently attached to the prop, natural gas, diesel, or other combustible material can be used to simulate a fire. All transportation props require the same safety and environmental requirements of other live-fire training props. Unignited spills can be simulated with nonflammable materials. Permanent-type props may include the following:

  — Tank truck or railcar to simulate a vehicle fire

  — Tank truck and automobile collision that requires controlling a fuel spill and a rescue

  — Overturned tank truck creating either a spill or contributing to a fire (**Figure 5.12**)

- **Transportation (aircraft) incident** — Most airport fire-fighting organizations have a simulated aircraft made of heavy gauge steel located in a containment pit (**Figure 5.13, p. 110**). Simulated aircraft structures, permanently fixed to the containment pit, include landing gear assemblies, engine nacelles, wing and engine

Figure 5.12 Props such as this tank truck may be used for fire or spill-control training.

Figure 5.13 Simulated aircraft structures, constructed of heavy steel and located in containment pits, are used for aircraft fire-attack training for both airport and structural fire companies.

components, and fuselage sections. These props are used for fire-suppression training but *not* for extrication training.

- ***Transportation (maritime) incident*** — Major universities and seaboard jurisdictions have access to simulators for training in maritime fire fighting. NFPA 1405, *Guide for Land-Based Fire Fighters Who Respond to Marine Vessel Fires*, contains suggestions for the types of props that should be used for shipboard firefighter training such as the following:
  — Engine room
  — Cargo holds
  — Cargo containers (**Figure 5.14**)
  — Accommodation (living) spaces
  — Fuel tanker piping and valve assemblies (**Figure 5.15**)

Figure 5.14 Maritime shipping containers may be used to simulate container fires on ships or at dock facilities. Interior conditions may be very similar to those created in live-fire simulators.

- ***Flammable and combustible liquids and gas storage and processing incident*** — Props designated for spill-control and fire-fighting training of incidents involving flammable and combustible liquids and gases include the following:
  — Pits to simulate unignited and ignited fuel spills
  — Aboveground storage tanks:
    ○ Vertical
    ○ Horizontal
    ○ Cone top
    ○ Internal floating roof
    ○ External floating roof
  — Overhead flanges
  — LPG facilities
  — Loading docks (**Figure 5.16**)
  — Pump islands
  — Pump stations

- ***Hazardous materials incident*** — Props used for hazardous materials incident training may include some of those described in the previous bullet on flammable and combustible liquids and gas storage and processing incident. Although only a simulated hazardous material is involved in the training and training foam concentrate is used in the exercises, runoff water must still be contained and decontaminated. All training areas must be within a levee system to contain runoff. Props may also include the following:
  — Chemical processing facilities
  — Chemical storage tanks
  — Chemical stage areas (small containers and drums)
  — Chemical spill pits

Live-Fire Training Area

Although any training activity that involves a simulated fire-suppression activity may be considered a *live fire,* the term is generally associated with structure fires. As such, the term can be applied to the live-fire building mentioned in the Permanent Facilities section, the portable live-fire training or fire behavior simulator mentioned in the Mo-

Figure 5.15 Maritime props, such as this simulated tanker, provide training opportunities for engine room, living quarter, and piping and valve assembly fires.

Figure 5.16 Railroad and truck loading docks may be constructed for simulated spill and fire conditions.

Figure 5.17 Thermal sensing devices are located throughout commercially constructed live-fire training simulators to determine the actual temperature within the unit.

bile Training Facilities section, or to the acquired structures mentioned in the Acquired Structures section. Live-fire burn buildings and portable fire behavior or live-fire simulators built specifically for live-fire training purposes have the following characteristics:

- Constructed to meet the guidelines set forth in NFPA 1402 and used to fulfill the requirements of NFPA 1403

- Located remotely from other facilities or occupancies that may be affected by the smoke and heat of a fire

- Located to protect the soil from contaminated runoff water

- Equipped with thermal sensing devices to determine actual temperature within the structure **(Figure 5.17)**

- Equipped with a fuel shutoff or automatic fire-suppression system in the event of an accident

Portable Training Props

Portable training props come in a variety of types. They may be commercially created devices or simple firefighter-inspired creations made from materials at hand. Since the devices are portable, they can be moved from one area of the training facility to another, used as part of a mobile training facility, and stored when not in use. Portable devices may include (but are not limited to) the following:

- **Christmas trees (piping networks, equipped with shutoff valves, that resemble Christmas trees)** — Used to simulate gas pressure fires **(Figure 5.18)**

- **Portable wall and door assemblies** — Used to create spaces for search and rescue training

- **Portable mazes** — Created with ground ladders and salvage covers that can be assembled in a variety of configurations in apparatus or demonstration rooms; used for self-contained breathing apparatus (SCBA) training

- **LPG props** — Designed to create small fires; used for fire-extinguisher training

- **Commercially constructed burn pans** — Designed for fire-extinguisher training with LPG, natural gas, or liquid fuels **(Figure 5.19)**

Figure 5.19 Small commercially constructed burn pans are available for use in fire-extinguisher training.

WARNING!

All training props must meet safety standards, which is especially true of props that are made by members of the organization. Materials must be able to withstand flame impingement, high temperatures, and sudden temperature changes. Fuel shutoff valves must be placed safe distances from the burn area.

Acquired Structures

Firefighter injuries and fatalities during live-fire training in acquired structures have contributed to many of the training-related casualty statistics in recent years. Instructors and training administrators must exercise great diligence in the management of live-fire training in acquired structures. Structures that are acquired for live-fire training (such as vacant houses or retail buildings) present unique challenges to instructors and training administrators **(Figure 5.20)**.

Acquired structures are usually in deteriorating conditions and scheduled for demolition. Sometimes fire and emergency services organizations are invited to burn these structures because burning may be the least expensive way for a property owner to eliminate a building that has outlived its usefulness.

Figure 5.18 A common training prop that is used to simulate gas fires is referred to as a *Christmas tree.*

Figure 5.20 Instructors must inspect all acquired structures to ensure that they meet the requirements of NFPA 1403. The property must be in a safe condition before accepting it for use in live-fire training.

Acquired structures that are used for live-fire training must meet the safety requirements of NFPA 1403. Any building or structure that *cannot* be made safe may *not* be used for interior structural fire-fighting training. An instructor should also consider the cost of making the acquired structure safe enough for the proposed type of training. When the cost exceeds the training benefit, it may be best to locate another structure or postpone the training exercise.

Once a site has been selected and the structure acquired, inspected, and repaired, an instructor then considers the type of training best suited for the specific structure. There will always be a tendency to overreach and set goals and learning objectives that *cannot* be achieved given the limits imposed by the particular structure. The following factors establish those limits:

- Number of instructors available
- Total number of students
- Safety considerations
- Equipment available
- Location and access
- Type of training

Advance planning is critical to the success of any practical training evolution involving acquired structures. When planning for a live-fire exercise in an acquired structure, instructors must consider a variety of issues or factors that can have an ef-

fect on the training evolution. *No* live-fire training should be attempted until the following issues are considered and plans made to address them:

- Environmental conditions
- Structural condition
- Training possibilities
- Instructor responsibilities
- Fuel usage
- Water supply requirements

Environmental Conditions

While climate conditions affect every training evolution, the effect on acquired structures can be extreme. Wind speed and direction, humidity, temperature, and time of day all affect the training environment. Weather extremes are common in many locations, whether it is harsh below-freezing cold or debilitating high temperatures with high humidity. Hazards such as lightning, hail, and high winds may also present additional dangers when severe storms approach.

Equipment noise, light levels, and even the types of vegetation at or near the training ground are important factors that can affect the outcome of a training exercise. When these factors combine with climate conditions to create environments that are detrimental to learning or are inherently unsafe, instructors may have to limit the training exercises or *not* allow the training to occur.

Structural Conditions

Acquired structures must be in compliance with the requirements of NFPA 1403 before they can be used for any live-fire exercises. The training administrator delegates the responsibility for ensuring that the requirements of NFPA 1403 are met to the organization's safety officer or an instructor who is trained as an incident safety officer. The acquired structure is inspected and repairs are made before any training is conducted. Specific requirements are located in Section 4.5.4 of NFPA 1403.

When the presence of asbestos or other hazardous materials is confirmed, the building owner is required to use certified personnel to remove and dispose of the materials. Safety officers and instructors should be familiar with federal, state/

provincial, and local asbestos abatement and hazardous waste disposal regulations. This familiarity ensures compliance with the law and may relieve instructors and organizations from any liability created by the removal of asbestos or hazardous materials.

Training Possibilities

An instructor must first determine whether it is even possible to use a structure for live-fire training. Environmental laws, for example, may prohibit the burning of a structure because of its location. The structure may also have been designated as a historical landmark. When live-fire training is *not* possible, perhaps the structure might be suitable for forcible-entry training, ladder evolutions, search and rescue operations, or a class on building construction. In any event, the building must undergo a complete and thorough inspection.

Instructor Responsibilities

The training administrator or instructor must have written permission from the rightful owner of the property in order to burn a structure. The training administrator or instructor must apply for and receive the appropriate permits from the local jurisdiction. Permits may be required from the fire and life safety division, the building inspections office, state/provincial environmental authority, or the local residential code enforcement office. Having these permits on display is an important part of public relations, demonstrating to citizens that the fire and emergency services organization adheres to the same restrictions that the rest of the community do.

When using an acquired structure, instructors conducting live-fire or other training evolutions must consider the effect on the surrounding neighborhood. Refer to **Appendix J,** Structural Live-Fire Training Forms, for sample forms that may help instructors prepare letters and public announcements. Sample checklists for live-fire training situations are also provided.

An instructor's responsibilities include the following:

• Distribute a notice (letter or brochure) to each resident living within a reasonable distance of the structure, informing them of the date and

time of the training event, a description of the training activity, and its effect (such as street closures) on the surrounding area.

• Plan the placement of hoselines and apparatus carefully, and consider how they may least restrict access to the neighborhood.

• Notify the water department when hydrants are involved.

• Flush water mains so that rust and sediment do *not* cause problems for pumping operations or surrounding households when an acquired structure is located in an area where there has been little flow recently through the water distribution system.

• Prepare water supply and flow analyses. Instructors must know the required fire flow for the structure, including safety margins.

• Videotape or photograph surrounding structures, vehicles, and grounds **(Figure 5.21)**. If neighboring property is damaged by the training evolution, these videotapes and photographs help document the conditions present before the training activity began. Videotape documentation may be important if legal claims arise later.

• Hold a briefing with all participants to explain the training evolutions. Take all participants on a familiarization walk-through inspection of the structure to identify the layout of the building and exits.

Figure 5.21 An instructor should photographically record the existing conditions surrounding an acquired structure before live-fire training evolutions. This record will provide evidence in the event of an accident or damage to an adjacent exposed property.

Fuel Usage

A contributing factor in many live-fire training accidents is the misuse of fuels. Although all live fires in acquired structures are dangerous, following the requirements that are set forth in NFPA 1403 regarding fuel will lessen the possibility that students or instructors will be injured. Safety is always the primary concern during live-fire training exercises. It is generally safe to use propane torches or fireplace lighters to ignite the fuel and then remove the igniting device from the structure once the fire has started. Instructors must adhere to the following NFPA 1403 requirements:*

- Fuels that are used in live-fire training evolutions shall have known burning characteristics that are as controllable as possible.

- Unidentified materials such as debris found in or around the structure that could burn in unanticipated ways, react violently, or create environmental or health hazards shall not be used.

- Pressure-treated wood, rubber, plastic, and straw or hay treated with pesticides or harmful chemicals shall not be used.

- Fuel materials shall be used only in the amounts necessary to create the desired fire size.

- The fuel load shall be limited to avoid conditions that could cause an uncontrolled flashover or backdraft.

- Flammable or combustible liquids (as defined in NFPA 30, *Flammable and Combustible Liquids Code*) shall not be used in live-fire training evolutions in acquired structures.

- The instructor in charge shall assess the selected fire room environment for factors that can affect the growth, development, and spread of fire.

- The instructor in charge shall document fuel loading including all of the following:

  — Furnishings

  — Wall and floor coverings and ceiling materials

  — Type of construction of the structure (type of roof and combustible void spaces)

  — Dimensions of the room

- The fire shall be ignited by an ignition officer in the presence of and under the direct supervision of the safety officer.

---

* Reprinted with permission from NFPA 1403, *Standard on Live Fire Training Evolutions*, 2002 edition. Copyright © 2002, National Fire Protection Association, Quincy, MA 02269. This reprinted material is not the complete and official position of the National Fire Protection Association on the referenced subject, which is represented only by the standard in its entirety.

Water Supply Requirements

Water supply requirements for fire-fighting purposes in rural and suburban areas are provided in NFPA 1142. These requirements should be applied to fire attack during live-fire training evolutions. There must be reliable water sources for the entire duration of any live-fire evolution. In this sense, water supply operations during a live-fire exercise become the *real thing*.

Additional training involving water sources may also be performed in remote locations. Many acquired structures are in locations that are *not* convenient to hydrants or other water sources. These locations provide an excellent opportunity for training evolutions on water shuttle, portable dump tank, large-diameter hose deployment, drafting, and relay pumping operations. However, such training should be completed before a live-fire evolution begins.

Summary

Instructional facilities and props may be found in a wide variety of types, locations, and uses. They provide the training division with the best possible means to train entry-level and current personnel in the skills required to perform their duties. Fire and emergency services instructors must have an understanding of the types of facilities and props that they are expected to use in order to develop the appropriate lesson plans and curriculums required by the jurisdiction while ensuring a safe training environment.

Security Bars on Doors and Windows

Security bars on doors and windows can be found in all urban and rural areas of North America. They may be found in many different designs and styles and are primarily intended to prevent illegal or unauthorized entry into a structure.

At the same time, security bars can also prevent escape, resulting in occupant fatalities and injuries. They have also been responsible for firefighter deaths by blocking an emergency escape route for personnel who have become trapped.

Fire and emergency services personnel should be trained in the recognition of the types of security bars used in their response area, proper operation of the locking or securing devices, and forcible entry methods and tools used for opening bars from outside a structure. Recognition and operation training may be conducted on site or in cooperation with local retailers/wholesalers or manufacturers of the bars. Forcible entry training has to occur at acquired structures that are equipped with bars or on training props especially designed to simulate a secured door or window.

Equally important is training personnel in the emergency egress procedures used by the organization. Barred windows can be simulated during interior search training as well as respiratory protection training involving self-contained breathing apparatus (SCBA) or supplier-air respirator (SAR) units. Rapid intervention team (RIT) training should also include rescues through barred windows or openings.

Practical training evolutions and live-fire training should include situations that involve both open and barred windows and doors. The purpose of all training scenarios, facilities, and props is to provide a realistic learning environment. Therefore, opening or forcing security bars should be an essential part of that training.

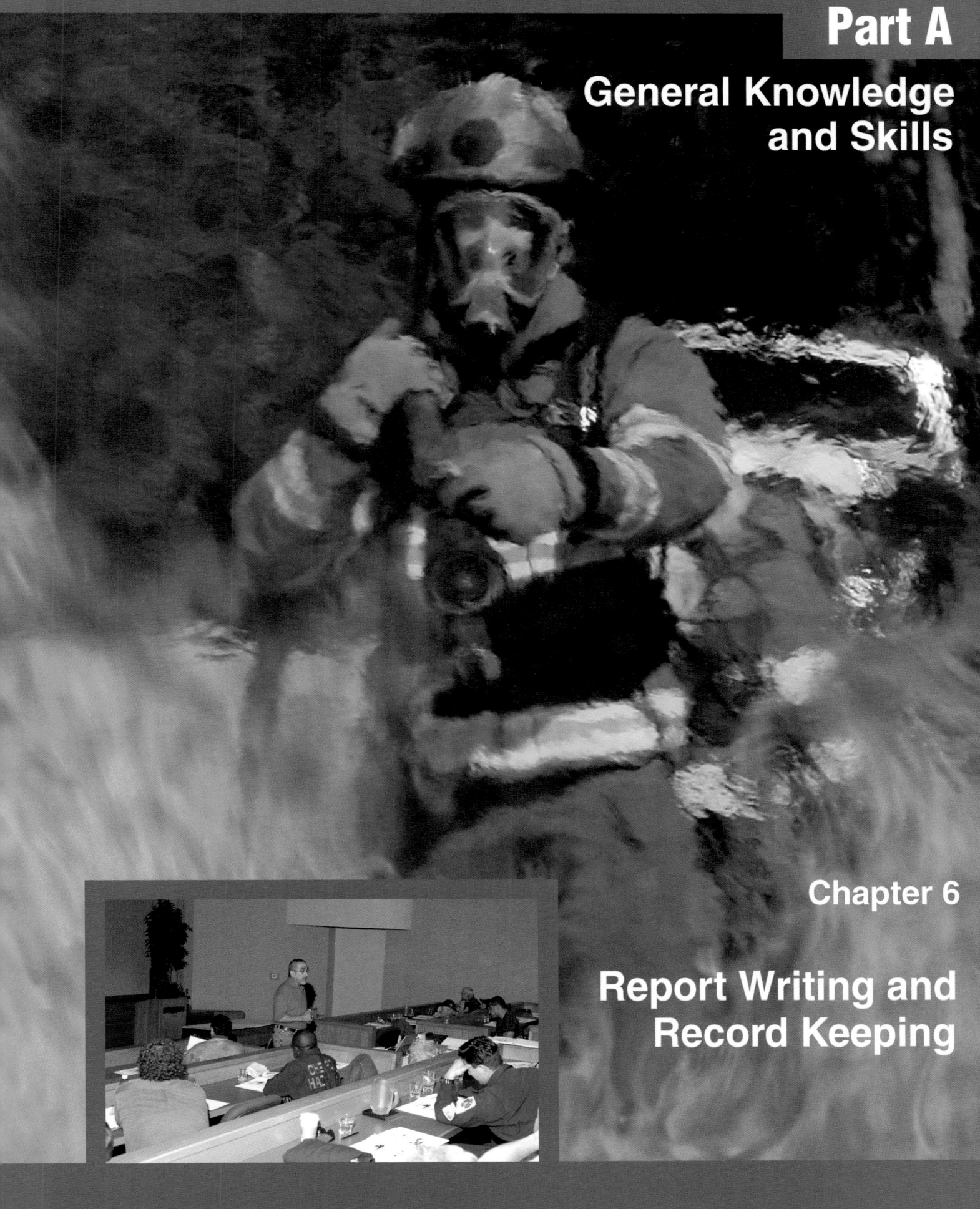

Part A
General Knowledge and Skills

Chapter 6

Report Writing and Record Keeping

After reading this chapter, students will be able to —

1. List fire and emergency services activities that are documented by reports.

2. Explain the two functions of reports generated by instructors.

3. Identify general considerations in report writing.

4. Describe the four parts of a report.

5. Identify guidelines for report development and writing style.

6. Describe the purpose of an executive summary.

7. List the components of an executive summary.

8. List uses of information stored in a record-keeping system.

9. List general categories of records kept in fire and emergency services organizations.

10. List types of training records.

11. Identify facts about considerations for training records.

12. Identify benefits of keeping accurate training records.

13. List information to be gathered for a training records system.

14. Identify questions to answer for an audit of the record-keeping system.

15. Identify facts about budget records.

16. Describe what is included in inventory records.

17. Describe the two categories of maintenance records.

18. Identify facts about personnel records.

19. List steps in the record-keeping system development process.

20. Describe steps in determining the record-keeping requirements of an organization.

21. Identify steps in the system planning phase.

22. Identify accurate statements about system implementation.

23. Identify accurate statements about maintaining a record-keeping system.

Chapter Contents

Report Writing
General Considerations
Report Writing Criteria

General Record-System Components
Record Categories
Record-Keeping System Development
Requirement Definitions
System Plan

System Implemetation
Project Completion
Evaluation
Revision
Data Interpretation
Legal Requirements

Summary

Chapter 6
Report Writing and Record Keeping

Instructors spend part of their on-duty time writing reports and keeping records. *Reports* are the written or verbal accounting of events based on the facts surrounding an incident or response. A company officer, chief officer, or other personnel who are responsible for report writing may provide successive units with a verbal report of a situation, including all visible indicators observed such as status of victims, structural conditions, and tactics that are being employed. Following an incident, a written report is compiled, detailing all pertinent activities required to control the incident.

Records are permanent accounts of known or recorded facts that are used to recall or relate past events or actions taken by an individual, unit, or organization. For example, training records consist of the types and hours of training provided, names of personnel in attendance, learning outcomes achieved, and training resources expended during a specific period of time (to name a few content items). From these records, raw data are then gathered and used to develop reports and show results on the effectiveness of the training performed by the division or agency.

The formats for records may include forms, essays, or simply lists of names. Records may be handwritten, typed, or computer-generated. Reports are generally in essay format and typed or computer-generated. Both reports and records must be stored in a secure format and location with easy access to those who need to use or refer to them.

Record keeping, or information management, is the storage of records and reports accumulated by an organization. Generally, records and reports may be stored as printed hardcopies in filing cabi-

nets or file storage boxes or in electronic formats on magnetic and optical media devices installed on today's computers. This chapter discusses the general concepts of report writing and the process for record keeping within the training division and organization.

Report Writing

As previously stated, records and reports are necessary to document the results and findings of an organization's activities, which include the following:

- Training sessions
- Administrative activities
- Emergency responses
- Fire and life safety programs
- Fire investigations
- Data on injuries, fatalities, and exposures to civilians and emergency responders

To ensure that these activities are performed in accordance with the mission and goals of the organization, the administration of an organization depends on the accuracy and timeliness of these reports. Instructors must be able to write clear, concise, and accurate reports based on the records that are available to them. They must also ensure that all written records are accurately completed, properly filed, and securely stored.

To provide the organization with accurate and well-written reports, instructors should understand some general considerations for reports and follow accepted report-writing criteria. All personnel with report-writing responsibilities should also understand the importance of executive summaries and how to prepare them. Properly written executive summaries are very helpful in decision-making and appreciated by the managers who read them.

General Considerations

Accurate reporting accomplishes the following two important functions:

• Reports keep an administration informed of the accomplishments, problems, and daily training activities of the divisions within an organization.

• Reports provide data on which an administration can base decisions concerning the operations of the various divisions and the organization as a whole for future strategic planning.

Many of these reports become part of a larger report or database on which the administration bases short- and long-term planning decisions. Reports also include data for the annual operating budget.

Instructors should remember that every report they produce is a reflection on themselves, the training division, the organization, and the fire and emergency services. It is also important to remember that the vast majority of the reports they write are public records and as such may be read by people outside the organization or even used as evidence in a court of law.

Information within a report should be structured in a manner that is logical and easily understood. Run-on or incomplete sentences make reports difficult to understand. Correct grammar and punctuation are also extremely important. Fire and emergency services personnel can improve their writing skills through training provided in vocational and college-level technical and report-writing courses.

Report-Writing Responsibilities

NFPA 1041, *Standard for Fire Service Instructor Professional Qualifications,* assigns report-writing responsibilities to instructors at each classification level. Because these responsibilities may vary between organizations, all instructors should be familiar with the types of reports for which each level is responsible. Examples of various types of reports that instructors at each level may be required to complete include the following:

Instructor Level I	Instructor Level II	Instructor Level III
• Course attendance reports	• Budget requests	• Division annual report
• Injury reports	• Budget administration	• Training activity report
• Training activity reports	• Purchase requests	• Accident investigation report
• Lesson outcome (grade) reports	• Specifications	• Executive summary
	• Training activities	• Budget justification
	• Facility and equipment usage	• Disciplinary report
	• Facility and equipment repair requests	
	• Course outcome (grade) reports	
	• Staff attendance reports	
	• Postincident critique	
	• Personnel evaluations	

Instructors should have another person proofread their reports before they are submitted. A proofreader can catch misspelled or improperly used words and poor grammar. Although all computer-based word processing programs have both spell-check and grammar-correcting functions, they are not 100-percent foolproof. Misspelled words reflect poorly on a writer and may cause a reader to question the accuracy and credibility of the report's contents.

Any doubt about the spelling or use of a particular word should be settled by consulting a dictionary. Many good, easy-to-use style guides are available for verifying correct word usage and punctuation. Examples of various style guides may be found in the list of Suggested Readings at the end of this manual.

At the same time that the report is proofread for correct spelling and grammar, it should also be checked for technical accuracy. Incorrect data or inappropriate examples reflect badly on both the writer and training division. A simple mistake in recording the cost of training, for example, can result in a budget crisis if it is allowed to become part of the organization's official budget request. A technical mistake also places the administration, organization, and instructor in the position of having to submit an amended document. This situation could result in a loss of credibility for all involved.

Finally, a report that is correctly written and technically accurate is worthless when it is *not* submitted on time. An instructor must verify the deadline for the report and include sufficient time for data collection, writing, proofing, and revising **(Figure 6.1)**.

Report Writing Criteria

Regardless of the topic of a report, all reports share some general characteristics: organization, development, and writing style. An executive summary is included at the beginning of all reports that exceed five pages. It is usually provided to supervisors or administrative bodies by the author of the original report and attached to the front of the report or paper.

Figure 6.1 Instructors, like other fire and emergency services personnel, are responsible for writing reports that accurately describe events, situations, statuses, conditions, and results of training.

Organization

To keep reports simple and concise, organize them into the following four parts:

- *Heading* — Contains basic information similar to the heading of a memo or electronic mail (e-mail) communication. It includes the date, name of the recipient(s), name of the sender or author, and subject of the report. Some organizations have a formal template or format that provides a space for all of this information.

- *Introduction* — Provides a brief overview of the report in a single paragraph. General contents include the purpose of the report, time period covered by the report, and name or names of the people involved in writing the report.

- *Body* — Contains all information relating to the report, including the following:
  - Reason for the report
  - Statistics
  - Research, program, or project results
  - Problems that were uncovered

  Some graphs and tables may be included if they are visually effective. Otherwise, detailed tables, charts, illustrations, graphs, and process descriptions should be placed in appendices.

- *Conclusion/summary* — Restates the results of the project briefly in the final paragraph or two and recommends changes or other actions **(Figure 6.2, p. 122)**.

Parts of a Report

Heading →

Rinkerville Fire Department
Rinkerville, Nebraska

Office of Training and Education

Introduction →

Date: October 17, 2006
To: All Company Officers
From: James Cassidy, Chief of Training
Subject: Company Drills During Cold Weather

With winter fast approaching, it is important to remember that your primary concern is personnel safety. Company drills are essential to the efficiency of this department, but the need for the drills must be balanced with the risks that are present when training takes place during the winter months. The following precautions have been compiled by the training division and will be in effect for all outdoor company training drills held during the months of December through March or as long as winter weather conditions exist.

Body →

Training evolutions will not be held when:
- Wind velocity exceeds 20 mph.
- Snow has accumulated to a depth of 3 inches.
- Horizontal surfaces are ice-coated.
- Temperatures are at or below freezing.
- Lightening, hail, or tornadoes have been predicted within the next 4 hours.

Training may be held:
- During light to medium rain conditions.
- When temperatures are above freezing.
- When snow is less than 3 inches in depth.
- During sunny conditions with temperature above freezing.

Precautions that must be taken for all winter weather company drills:
- Full personal protective clothing must be worn.
- Rehabilitation must be provided at 30-minute intervals.
- Traction devices (chains) must be applied to all apparatus in snow conditions.
- Ground ladders and aerial devices must be clean and free of ice or mud during training.

The training division believes that these guidelines will provide company officers with a practical approach to winter weather training. Training during winter weather conditions will provide personnel with near-realistic conditions and still reduce the risk inherent during these conditions.

Conclusion →

Figure 6.2 The typical report is organized into four parts: heading, introduction, body, and conclusion/summary.

Report Development

Developing a report depends on providing answers to the five questions that start with the following words: *who, what, when, where,* and *why.* This information is contained in the body of the text and includes specific and concrete facts based on accurate figures and data (**Figure 6.3, p. 124**).

Writing Style

Writing a report or any business-type communication is different from writing an essay in school. While an essay generally contains descriptive language that helps the reader *see* what the author is describing, the style used in reports is concise and simple. Writing *concisely* means eliminating excess words. Writing *simply* means avoiding old-fashioned or excessively technical words. Examples of both concise and simple writing are included in the information box.

Examples: Concise and Simple Writing Styles

Replace	With
Take into consideration	Consider
At the present time	Now or currently
Utilize	Use
Initiate	Begin
Carry out	Perform
Gives off	Discharges or emits
Cover	Discuss
Manmade	Artificial or manufactured
To man	To staff
Impact	Effect or affect
Made up	Composed
Pass on	Transmit or send
Keep up	Maintain
Due to the fact that	Because
Prior to	Before
Employ	Use

Besides writing in a simple and concise style, instructors can highlight complicated information by presenting it in tables or graphs instead of leaving it in the body of the text. For example, the paragraph in the information box is improved by placing the figures into a table. When space on a page becomes an issue, the use of **bold** or *italic* type can also convey the message as well.

Information Included in Paragraph and Table

In comparison, the initial cost of the custom-designed Altera Computer Training Module (CTM) at $30,000 is greater than the generic commercial All-Go CTM that lists at $19,000. Accessories would add $4,000 to the cost of each system, as would the purchase of a full parts inventory of $5,000 and $3,000, respectively.

Comparison of Costs: Custom-Designed and Commercial Computer Training Modules (CTMs) (Dollars)

Manufacturer	Base	Accessories	Parts	Total*
Custom-designed Altera CTM	30,000	4,000	5,000	39,000
Commercial All-Go CTM	19,000	4,000	3,000	26,000

*Difference in total costs = $13,000

Executive Summary

An *executive summary* (also called an *abstract*) is a brief review of the key points in a report, a technical paper, specifications, or an analysis. It is basically the main topic statement of the report followed by bullets denoting the main points. It provides the following benefits:

- Ensures that the essential information contained in the report is read

- Acts as an attention-getter that may spur the audience to read the full report

- Provides senior management with the main points necessary when justifying a report to the media, public, or legislative body

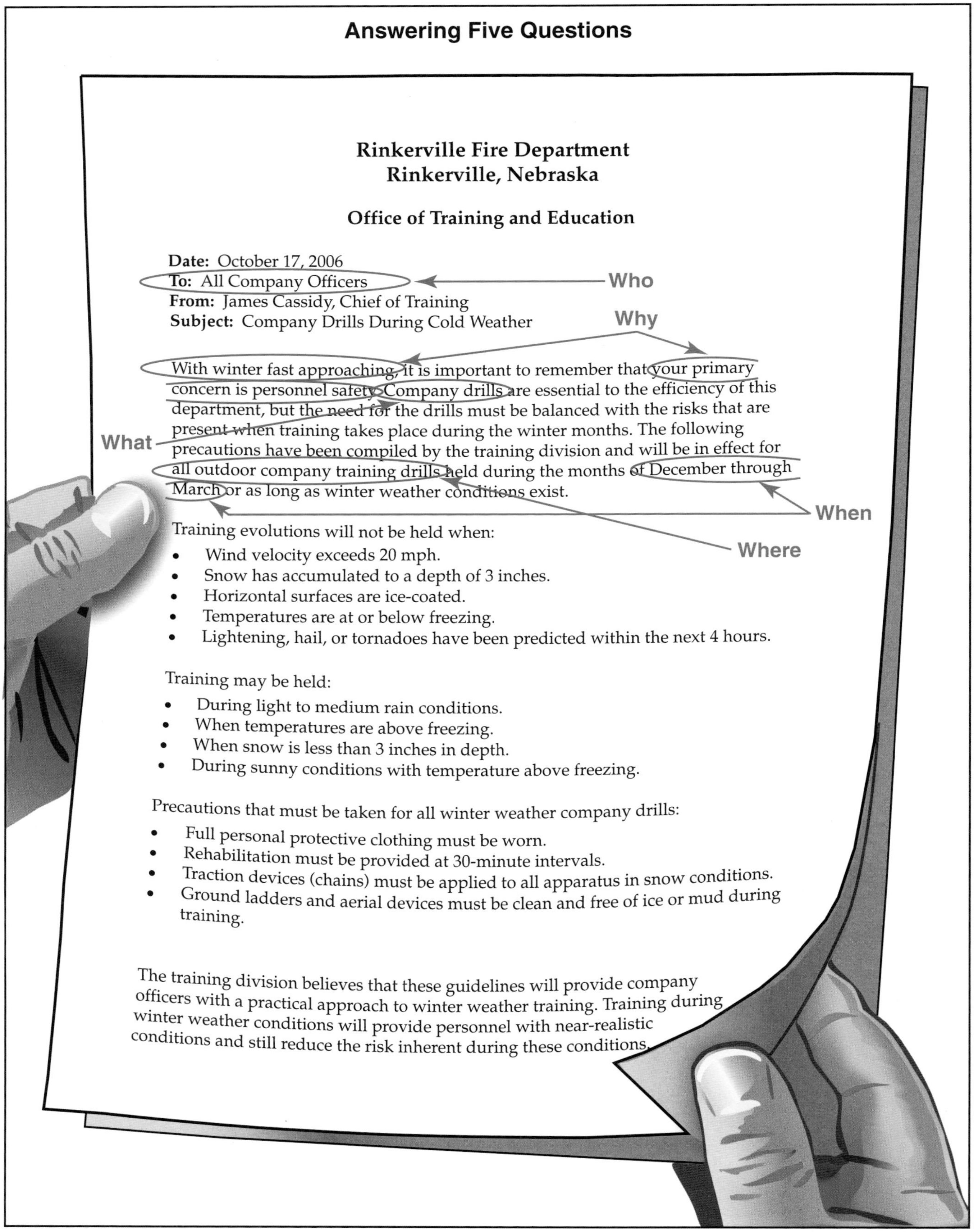

Answering Five Questions

Rinkerville Fire Department
Rinkerville, Nebraska

Office of Training and Education

Date: October 17, 2006
To: All Company Officers ⟵ **Who**
From: James Cassidy, Chief of Training
Subject: Company Drills During Cold Weather   **Why**

With winter fast approaching, it is important to remember that your primary concern is personnel safety. Company drills are essential to the efficiency of this department, but the need for the drills must be balanced with the risks that are present when training takes place during the winter months. The following **What** precautions have been compiled by the training division and will be in effect for all outdoor company training drills held during the months of December through March or as long as winter weather conditions exist.

When

Where

Training evolutions will not be held when:

- Wind velocity exceeds 20 mph.
- Snow has accumulated to a depth of 3 inches.
- Horizontal surfaces are ice-coated.
- Temperatures are at or below freezing.
- Lightening, hail, or tornadoes have been predicted within the next 4 hours.

Training may be held:

- During light to medium rain conditions.
- When temperatures are above freezing.
- When snow is less than 3 inches in depth.
- During sunny conditions with temperature above freezing.

Precautions that must be taken for all winter weather company drills:

- Full personal protective clothing must be worn.
- Rehabilitation must be provided at 30-minute intervals.
- Traction devices (chains) must be applied to all apparatus in snow conditions.
- Ground ladders and aerial devices must be clean and free of ice or mud during training.

The training division believes that these guidelines will provide company officers with a practical approach to winter weather training. Training during winter weather conditions will provide personnel with near-realistic conditions and still reduce the risk inherent during these conditions.

Figure 6.3 A report should answer five questions: *who, what when, where,* and *why.*

If an executive summary were compared to an outline, the main points would be the capital letters of the outline. An executive summary needs to be brief (no longer than two pages), easy to read, and focused on the facts rather than the opinions expressed in the paper. An executive summary includes the following items:

- Statement of the problem
- Recommended solution
- Benefits that will result by following the recommendation
- Recommended or suggested action found in the paper or report (conclusion)

Executive Summary Example

Because of the increasing demand on the training division to provide recertification courses, mandated specialized training, and entry-level training, it is necessary to implement changes in the training system. Our plan involves performing the following procedures:

- Adding two full-time instructors
- Adding five part-time instructors
- Altering training schedules
- Providing training at the stations

Implementing these recommendations will allow the training division to meet the increased demand for training.

General Record-System Components

The information that is stored in the information management or record-keeping system of an organization is essential and has a variety of basic uses. All of these uses apply directly to the records maintained by the training division as well as the organization as a whole. Information uses include the following:

- Justify budget requests or program development.
- Validate or certify that legally mandated programs and training have been provided.

- Project future needs based on current and past requirements.
- Substantiate the results of courses and evaluations of students and programs.

The maintenance of training-related records is so important that NFPA 1041, *Standard for Fire Service Instructor Professional Qualifications*, requires that all three instructor levels have knowledge of the organization's record-keeping system. While both Level I and Level II Instructors are required to manage and coordinate the record-keeping function, the Level III Instructor must be able to administer the system.

This section provides an overview of the information management requirements and practices of fire and emergency service organizations and relates them to the training division's record-keeping requirements. Further details are included in subsequent chapters of this manual.

Record keeping is just one element of the information management system or information technology (IT) system that most public and private organizations depend on today. Information management includes the acquiring, analyzing, organizing, distributing, interpreting, and storing of data and information that provides managers with timely and useful information. The record-keeping function is the storing function of the information that is generated by the information management system.

A wide variety of record types are maintained by fire and emergency services organizations. Records are kept on the following items:

- Personnel
- Facilities
- Vehicles
- Equipment
- Incidents
- Functions
- Maintenance
- Activities

Instructors should be aware of the types of records that are maintained by their organization. All instructors should know the categories of records, the method for developing, evaluating, and revising a record-keeping system, data interpretation, and legal requirements. In addition, knowledge of data collection and analysis methods, system maintenance procedures, and additional legal requirements is essential for Level III Instructors and training administrators. Chapter 20, Records, Policies, and Personnel, contains additional information specific to the Level III Instructor.

Record Categories

The general categories of records kept in fire and emergency service organizations are training, budget, inventory, maintenance, and personnel. Personnel records are *not* explained in detail in this text because they are normally *not* in the realm of responsibility for the fire and emergency services instructor.

Training

Training records are maintained at the company, district/battalion, and administrative levels of the fire and emergency services organization. Each level supplies the next level above with an accumulation of information until the records become part of the organization's information management section. Training administrators and instructors may collect information for some of the following types of training:

- Daily training delivered to individuals or units by the designated instructor such as entry-level or recruit training. *Details:*

  — These records confirm the hours of training received by each member or unit of the organization.

  — In the U.S., these records are mandated by Occupational Safety and Health Administration (OSHA) and must be available upon request by the U.S. Department of Labor at either the federal or state level.

- Company training delivered by a company officer or a member of the company such as basic skills refresher training in proper hose loading **(Figure 6.4)**

- Organizational training delivered to all members of an organization such as time-management or cultural-sensitivity training

- Self-study by an individual such as preparation required to develop a new training course

- Individual training provided by an organization such as courses in public information or media events for the public information officer

- Special training provided by a source outside the organization such as courses attended at the National Fire Academy or the state/provincial fire academy

- Degrees, certificates, or levels of training attained by members of the organization

NFPA 1401, *Recommended Practice for Fire Service Training Reports and Records,* provides examples of different types and formats of training records required to meet the needs of the organization as well as other helpful information on the design and procedures for effective training records management. The format of records may also depend on the type of training for which information is being gathered. Other items of consideration for training records management include privacy requirements, software programs, legal requirements, benefits, record contents, and audits.

Figure 6.4 Company-level training must be well documented to meet local, state, and national requirements. *Courtesy of Dave Coombs.*

Privacy requirements. As mentioned in Chapter 3, Legal and Ethical Considerations, there are privacy considerations and requirements for most records that are maintained by fire and emergency services organizations. Instructors and training administrators must remember that federal and state/provincial laws protect information about an individual's evaluation/testing scores. Instructors in the U.S. and Canada are advised to contact their respective legal counsels for accurate information on current privacy laws. The U.S. and Canada have similar protections:

- ***United States*** — The Family Education and Privacy Act prohibits the release of student testing and evaluation information, which means that the old practice of posting test scores and other personal information on bulletin boards is no longer allowed. Scores and personal data are considered privileged information and are available only to management and a few other designated personnel with authorization and a specific need to know.

- ***Canada*** — At the federal level, the Office of Privacy Commissioner of Canada manages privacy laws. Additionally, all provinces have enacted privacy legislation of their own.

Software programs. While many organizations develop their own training record systems, there are many commercial software programs available for keeping training records. Computer software programs improve the efficiency of record management and make it easy to record, access, and process training information. While the cost of such software may limit its availability to small organizations, they can still develop an effective records system by using organized files. Regardless of the system that an organization uses, appropriate personnel must be able to easily retrieve the information contained in the records and protect it from general access.

Legal requirements. Laws may require organizations to maintain training records for a specified period. In addition, OSHA requires that original hardcopy records such as course sign-in attendance sheets be maintained intact. Training administrators, instructors, or clerical personnel responsible for maintaining training records must be aware of and follow local and state or provincial requirements.

Benefits. The benefits of keeping accurate training records include the following:

- Provides documents for review by appropriate or authorized parties when necessary
- Identifies training areas that are emphasized as well as areas that require more attention
- Provides documentation of required training completion
- Provides information for planning and scheduling future training programs
- Provides evidence that federal and state/provincial training mandates are being met
- Provides a layer of legal protection against lawsuits

Record contents. In developing or improving a records system for a training program, instructors and training administrators must consider what information to gather for the records. Important information to be gathered for any training records system includes (but is *not* limited to) the following:

- Course name
- Dates and hours of each training session
- Names of instructors for each training session
- Any other information deemed appropriate by the organization such as employee identification numbers and locations of training sessions
- Student attendance rosters
- Topics taught at each session
- Lesson plans, workbooks and texts, tests, videotapes, and other course, curriculum, and program event documentation and processes
- Evaluation/testing scores of students when applicable as well as practical skills sheets used as evaluation criteria
- Course evaluations provided by students

Audits. NFPA recommends that the record-keeping system be audited on an annual basis. The completed audit should identify deficiencies and determine the best way to correct them. Additionally, audits help keep the system free of continual mistakes and allow the addition of new ideas and data. To determine the effectiveness of the system, it is suggested that the answers to the following questions be considered:

- What is the purpose of the record?
- Who uses the information in the record?
- How is the information in the record used?
- Does the record provide the necessary information? If not, why?
- Are there other records that provide the same information? If so, which ones?
- How long should/must the records be retained? (**Figure 6.5**)
- What trends in training can be determined from the records?
- Is there a simpler or more efficient way to record the information? If so, describe it.
- How accessible is the information?
- How secure is the information?

Budget

Budget records include all the information that is used to create a budget along with budget status reports, past budgets, and unfunded budget requests. Purchasing records, contracts, surplus sales reports, and other records with this information should also be retained.

At the training-division level, this information includes both the actual and projected costs associated with providing the amount and level of training required by the organization. Knowledge of these costs can assist not only in preparing the budget but also in establishing fees for teaching external customers. Actual costs for providing training include the following:

- Personnel costs (wages and benefits)
- Materials costs
- Instructor certification and training costs
- Prorated cost of the facility designated for training

Inventory

Inventory and fixed assets records are maintained for everything that is assigned to, consumed by, or owned by the organization. These records should

City of Rinkerville Fire Department

Record Identification: ___ Daily Attendance Records, Company Personnel ___

Record Date Range: ___ January 1, 1990 to December 31, 1999 ___
Date Received: ___ February 1, 2000 ___
Discard and Shred after Date: ___ January 1, 2010 ___

Authorization: ___ James Campbell, Administrative Chief ___

Records maintained in accordance with state records retention laws.

Figure 6.5 Archived records should have the date the records can be destroyed clearly marked on them.

Figure 6.6 Records are maintained on all equipment, materials, facilities, and apparatus that is owned and/or leased by the organization.

be accurate and include all the materials, equipment, facilities, land, and apparatus in the possession of the organization (**Figure 6.6**). The training division should maintain a copy listing the equipment and materials assigned to it as well as the location of the equipment and materials. This copy is especially important when equipment assigned to the training division is used to supplement operational equipment during a major incident.

Maintenance

Fire and emergency services organizations keep maintenance records for facilities, vehicles, and equipment. Maintenance records are usually kept in two distinct but closely related categories: preventive maintenance and corrective maintenance. The records are usually maintained and analyzed by the logistics chief, although this duty may be assigned to an instructor or other staff officer in small organizations.

Preventive. As the name implies, *preventive maintenance* is performed to prevent damage from occurring and extend the useful life of an item, vehicle, or facility by reducing wear.

Corrective. Although preventive maintenance helps to increase the useful life of an item, *corrective maintenance* is always possible due to an unforeseen event. Damage may occur because of an accident, overuse, operator error, or even abuse. When a piece of equipment is damaged or ceases to function, it must be repaired or replaced as soon as possible (**Figure 6.7, p. 130**).

Figure 6.7 To accurately track the status of damaged equipment, items should be tagged with the type of damage, date sent for repairs, and name of submitting unit.

Personnel

Instructors should be aware that generally personnel records are confidential. Training records that become part of the employee's personnel record, which is normally maintained by the administrative office, should be safeguarded with privacy in mind. Instructors must be careful to protect that confidentiality by securing all personnel records in their possession. Examples are as follows:

- *Job performance records* — Personal job performance evaluations are part of the individual's personnel file maintained by the organization for each employee. A supervisor may also retain a copy for future job performance evaluations and performance counseling. These records, like the individual's medical records, are confidential.

- *Attendance records* — Daily attendance records for all personnel are maintained to provide data for the distribution of payrolls and benefits. Depending on the classification of the employee, a formal timecard may be required as evidence of actual hours on duty. Other attendance records may be included in the company or unit logbook or time sheet.

Record-Keeping System Development

Because the record-keeping system is part of the management information system, its development should be part of the overall system. Professionals trained in the information management process usually develop information management systems. Some organizations, however, may develop, oper-

ate, and manage a record-keeping system without having an information management system. In this case, the record-keeping system may be developed under contract with an information management professional or internally using the project management team approach.

When an organization creates an internal team, it should follow an established development process. The process includes defining the requirements, planning the system, implementing the system, and completing the project.

Requirement Definitions

The project manager and team members use the following steps to determine the record-keeping requirements of the organization:

Step 1: *Identify research requirements* — Actions:

- Determine the legal requirements for a record-keeping system.
- Determine the type of records that must be maintained.
- Locate the resources (storage systems, storage models, software) for maintaining the records.
- Determine the financial requirements and resources.

Step 2: *Define the project* — Write a preliminary definition of the project. For example: *to develop an integrated record-keeping system for the training division.*

Step 3: *Establish objectives* — Determine project objectives, which may include the following:

- Defining types of records
- Determining interrelationships of the records
- Providing access to records
- Ensuring security of records
- Outlining the final disposal of records

Step 4: *List outcomes* — List in priority order the required (essential) objectives and the desired (nonessential) objectives. The objective may be to create a system that provides accurate information upon request.

Step 5: *Select alternatives* — Generate alternate solutions through brainstorming sessions.

Step 6: *Evaluate choices* — Evaluate the various alternative solutions based on the project definition and objectives.

Step 7: *Select the best solution* — Select the best possible solution based on the requirements of a record-keeping system. Determine a contingency solution also. Establish some form of duplication or redundancy in the event the primary record storage system is lost.

System Plan

During the planning phase, the team lists in detail what will be required for the development of the record-keeping system. Computer-based Gantt and Program Evaluation and Review Technique (PERT) charts can be used in the planning process and for monitoring the implementation phase of the project. Descriptions are as follows:

- *PERT chart* — Plots the project and evaluates the success of each step. It also depicts the individual tasks, time required for each task, and interrelationship or dependency of the various steps with each other.

- *Gantt chart* — Consists of a matrix that lists all the tasks to be performed on the vertical axis. Each row contains a single task identification that usually consists of a number and name. The horizontal axis is headed by columns indicating estimated task duration, resources, and the name of the person assigned to the task followed by a column for each period in the project's duration.

System planning steps include the following:

Step 1: Establish the final project objectives.

Step 2: Establish the strategy required to meet those objectives.

Step 3: Divide the project into logical subunits or steps.

Step 4: Establish performance standards or criteria for each subunit or step.

Step 5: Develop a timeline for each subunit or step.

Step 6: Create a project schedule based on the timelines of the subunits or steps.

Step 7: Determine the cost of each subunit or step and the entire project.

Step 8: Determine the resources necessary for the project.

Step 9: Assign positions, duties, responsibilities, access, and authority to personnel.

Step 10: Determine the required training for implementing the project.

Step 11: Write the necessary specifications for the project.

Step 12: Determine and create the necessary policies and procedures to support the project.

Step 13: Establish processes for monitoring and revising the project.

System Implementation

Once resources are available, the record-keeping system can be officially implemented. Some files and documents that already exist will have to be entered into the system or assigned to a hardcopy file or archive (repository for records that may have historical value but are *not* required for daily decision-making or report writing). Old files will have to be organized by topic such as training, personnel, or incident and placed into the archives.

When a non-computer-based manual system is developed, current records should be sorted by topic and filed accordingly. Copies should be made of all records and kept at remote sites in case an incident destroys the original records. The jurisdiction may have a central file storage space that is available for the organization's use **(Figure 6.8, p. 132)**.

Computer-based systems should have their data storage copied (backed up) on disk, tape, or alternate servers or converted to hardcopy files. All backup files are then stored in a secure area remote from the main system. File storage boxes should be clearly marked with the contents, date filed, security access, and disposal date.

The record-keeping system requires training for all personnel involved in the collection of data. They need to know how to perform the following functions:

- Complete forms.
- Determine what information to keep and/or discard.
- Categorize the various documents.
- Cross-reference the information.
- Use computers to enter records into the database correctly.

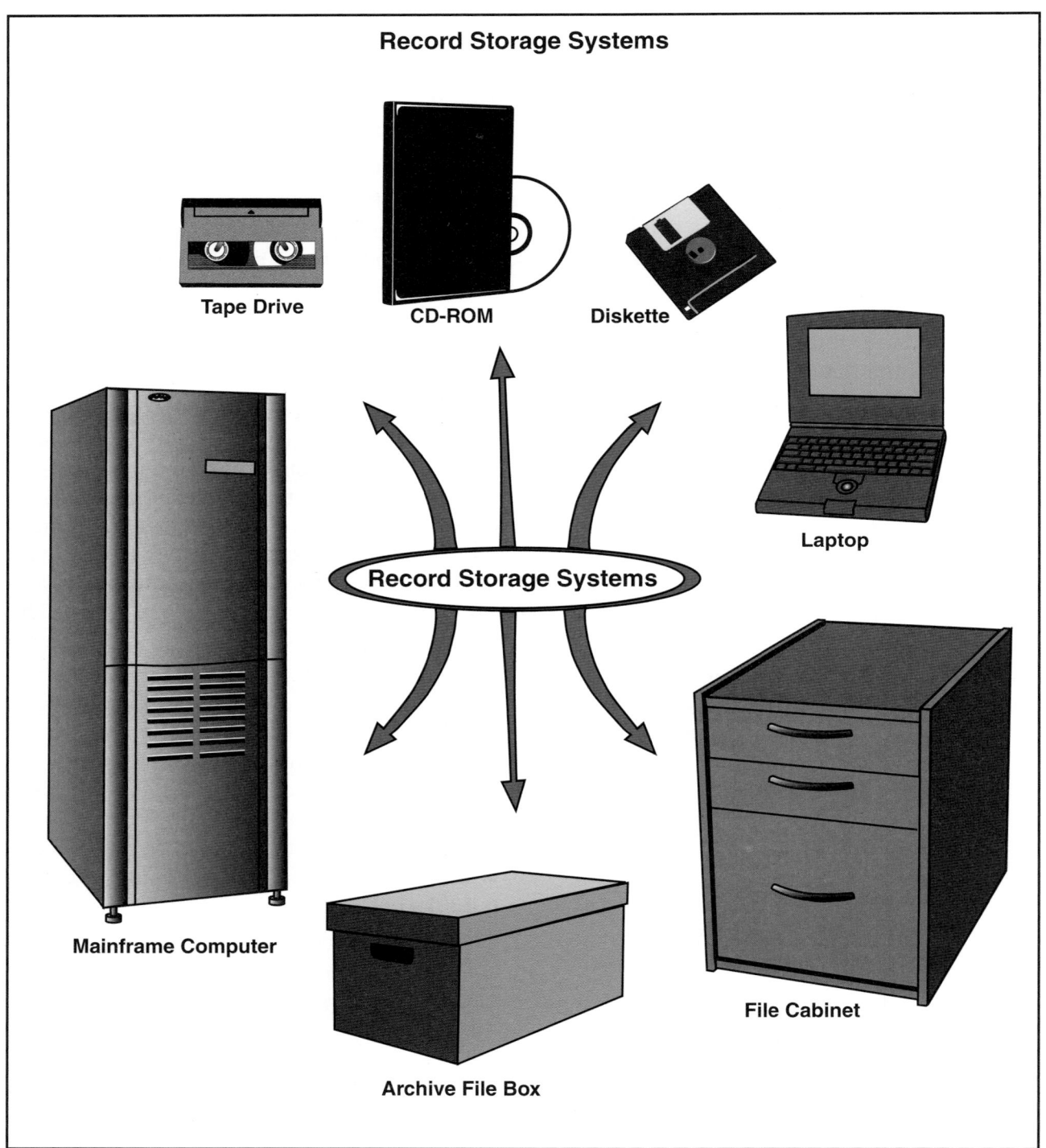

Figure 6.8 Records may be stored in a variety of mediums.

Project Completion

When the record-keeping system is in operation, the project management team should review the process for developing it and make any recommendations to the chief or manager of the organization. Further, they should establish the model for evaluating the system based on goals, processes, or desired outcomes.

Evaluation

The project management team or officer assigned to manage the record-keeping function should evaluate the effectiveness of the system periodically. During the first year of operation, the project manager should evaluate the system by performing frequent spot-checks of random types of records for accuracy. When the information is integrated with other similar information, a sample file should then be compared to determine whether the information is identical in each of the subfiles.

Annual checks of the system can be made following the first year to ensure its effectiveness. Revisions can be recommended based on the outcome of the evaluations.

Revision

A revision may be required when there is evidence of inaccuracies in the data-collection process, a change in data requirements, or the lack of adequate information on which to base decisions. In all cases, legal requirements should be reviewed when the record-keeping system is developed and revised. When revisions are indicated, they should be developed and implemented as soon as possible. Revision situations and correction procedures are as follows:

- *Inaccuracies* — When inaccurate data is entering the system, then training in the recognition and collection of the data may be required. For instance, if instructors are incorrectly estimating the cost of training per student or hour, then it may be necessary to provide additional training to correct the errors.

- *Information type change* — There may be a change in the type of information that is required. For example, the types of data being gathered may need to be expanded to include specific types of training-related injuries in order to collect the appropriate data. A change in the collection form and training in the use of the new form could correct this situation.

- *Additional information needed* — Forms may need to be altered to gather additional information that will aid in decision-making.

Data Interpretation

Data are the raw material from which information is derived. Raw data are collected on forms, in records, on timesheets, and in other formats. For instance, the data that are contained on the average incident report includes the time of the incident, type of incident, and amount of loss.

The *analysis,* which can be performed by a computer program or manual calculation, looks at the relationship between the key elements of the data and between similar information that is gathered from other incident reports.

Depending on the type of information that is desired, the final analysis may include a chart that relates the types of incidents to time of day, the loss based on types of incidents, or the loss based on estimated response time. The resulting information is then used to justify changes in operational strategy, relocation of an existing station, or a change in the building code to require passive fire-suppression systems in existing structures similar to those identified in the raw data.

Legal Requirements

State/provincial and federal governments generally have specific laws that direct record maintenance and (in some cases) the type of information that is gathered and stored in these records. The requirements for record keeping were discussed in detail in Chapter 3, Legal and Ethical Considerations, and include the following:

- Types of records maintained
- Length of retention
- Privacy concerns
- Public access to some records

Summary

The records compiled and maintained by the training division become part of the organization's overall information management effort. The responsibility for administering the record-keeping function may be assigned to the training administrator or a Level III Instructor. This officer must be aware of the types of records that must be retained, the laws that mandate record keeping, the requirements for privacy, and how to use the records.

Regardless of the type of training a member completes, the training division and the organization must keep an accurate training record. Record keeping can range from a simple handmade sheet kept by the instructor to computer records and data files. The training administrator and instructors must have knowledge of the basics of record keeping as well as the legal mandates that require the types of records to be retained.

Instructors and training administrators must also have the ability to convert the data provided by the records into accurate and timely reports. Reports are necessary to keep the administration informed and to verify legally mandated training.

Part A

General Knowledge and Skills

Chapter 7

Principles of Learning

After reading this chapter, students will be able to —

1. Identify characteristics of pedagogy and andragogy.

2. Identify terms associated with the learning process.

3. Describe the three domains of learning

4. Identify the levels of learning in the cognitive domain.

5. Identify steps in the psychomotor domain.

6. Identify accurate statements about the affective domain.

7. List the three basic categories of learning styles.

8. Distinguish among types of learning methods.

9. Identify characteristics of the laws of learning.

10. List techniques that can be used to help motivate students.

11. Identify steps that instructors can take to increase the relationship between motivation and learning.

12. Describe positive actions instructors can take to motivate students.

13. Explain the cone of learning model.

14. Identify memory components and how they affect learning.

15. Identify accurate statements about how student frustrations and learning plateaus affect learning.

16. Identify characteristics of the traditional approach to teaching.

17. Identify characteristics of the mastery approach to teaching.

18. Identify accurate statements about the mastery approach and criterion-referenced teaching, learning, and assessment.

19. Distinguish between the advantages and disadvantages of the mastery approach to teaching.

20. Explain norm-referenced and criterion-referenced assessments.

Chapter Contents

Development of Learning Principles
Pedagogy
Andragogy
Other Learning Theories

Terminology

Domains of Learning
Cognitive (Knowledge)
Psychomotor (Skills)
Affective (Attitude)

Styles and Methods of Learning

Laws of Learning

Motivation

Theories of Learning and Remembering

Memory
Sensory
Short-Term (Working)
Long-Term

Factors that Affect Learning
Learning Obstacles
Learning Plateaus

Approaches to Teaching
Traditional
Mastery

Approaches to Student Assessment
Norm-Referenced
Criterion-Referenced

Summary

Chapter 7
Principles of Learning

Instructor candidates have skills and knowledge based on their own training and experience and a desire to teach, which are excellent foundations for teaching. However, in order to become successful teachers, instructor candidates must also have an understanding of teaching methodology and the basic principles of learning. These principles and concepts are discussed in this chapter and include the following:

- Development of learning principles
- Terminology
- Domains of learning
- Styles and methods of learning
- Laws of learning
- Motivation
- Theories of learning and remembering
- Memory
- Factors that affect learning
- Approaches to learning

Instructor candidates should supplement the information in this manual with additional reading. Educational theories and methodology continue to evolve, and new information frequently becomes available. A Suggested Readings list is at the end of this manual.

In addition, instructors may wish to participate in university-level courses in adult education and teaching methods. Other resources are available through the U.S. Fire Administration's National Fire Academy (NFA), state/provincial training agencies, libraries, and the Internet.

Development of Learning Principles

The formulation of learning principles began in the 5th Century B.C.E. (Before the Common Era). Throughout the ancient world in China, Greece, and the Middle East, philosophers began to develop the theories that have become the foundation of modern educational concepts.

Two principal philosophers, Socrates in Greece and Confucius in China, are responsible for many ancient principles. The Socratic method of finding the truth through asking questions is one of the many learning methods that is popular today. Confucius believed that education was universal and all people have the ability to learn, regardless of class distinction.

Further refinements occurred as education became formalized in the 1800s. When it became apparent during this period that industrialized societies of Europe and North America needed an educated workforce, the basic principles of learning that are in use in the 21st century were developed. Among these principles are the theories of teaching as they apply to children (pedagogy) and adults (andragogy), student behavior, and even the basic classroom environment. Other learning theories were also developed.

Pedagogy

*Pedagogy (ped-a-**go**-je)* is the profession (including principles and methods) for teaching children and youth. It is the principle of learning most often associated with children. Pedagogy is also used generically to describe the methods used to deliver instruction. For many years, these theories were used to deliver learning to adults. Some pedagogical methods are still applied to adult education.

Andragogy

One of the first breaks from the traditional teaching methods came in the 1970s. Dr. Malcolm Knowles, professor, researcher, and author, was among the first theorists to use the term *andragogy (an-dra-go-je)*, which refers to the art of teaching adults. It describes the characteristics of adult students and provides a set of assumptions for most effectively teaching adults. The theory of andragogy is now widely accepted and includes the following assumptions:

- *Self-concept* — Because children lack experience, they depend on others for knowledge and must be directed. The accepted role of children in society is that of student. Once individuals reach the established age of adulthood, their self-concept then changes. Rather than being dependent, newly defined adults become self-sufficient for their own learning needs. Adults, then, have a need to be self-directed while still relying on an instructor or training course to provide the knowledge they desire.

- *Experience* — Adults have accumulated extensive and varied quantities of experiences that serve as resources for them and to which they can relate new information. They also have more personal experiences to contribute to the learning process than children (**Figure 7.1**).

Figure 7.1 Fire and emergency services classes are composed of adults who have experiences that they can contribute to class discussions. *Courtesy of Alabama Fire College.*

- *Readiness to learn* — Children learn those skills that allow them to move from one developmental phase to the next. Each skill must be based on successfully accomplishing the previous one. According to Knowles, this same concept applies to adults. Adults are ready to learn whatever they need to know or do in order to meet job requirements or social roles. Within the fire and emergency services, this type of learning had the following results:

  — Development of requirements found in the NFPA professional qualifications standards

  — Continued development of new and more advanced emergency mitigation skills and demands

- *Learning orientation* — The knowledge and skills that children learn prepare them for future learning. This preparation results in delayed application of the knowledge and skills learned. *Examples:*

  — Children's orientation to learning is *subject-centered* in order to be promoted to successive grade levels.

  — Adults' orientation is *problem-centered* because they have specific purposes for learning and want skills or knowledge that can be applied to real-life problems or situations.

- *Motivation* — Adults have internal incentives or motivators. They are motivated to learn by such factors as increased self-esteem resulting from the successful completion of the learning process and the desire to attain a goal.

Through observation and study, many researchers have found that children sometimes learn better with andragogical methods, while pedagogical methods are sometimes appropriate for adults in certain learning situations. Knowles' research indicated that children have as much need for life-, task-, and problem-centered learning as adults do.

Other Learning Theories

Charles Arnold contributed to the theories of learning during World War I when the U.S. had to train women to work in heavy industry and men to wage war. World War II also provided motivation for the creation of another teaching theory. The *four-step process* was developed to train massive numbers of people to perform tasks in both the military and industrial arenas during the war **(Figure 7.2)**. The training had to be quick, thorough, and effective to prepare either soldiers for battle or workers for the production line.

The four-step process, which will be discussed in detail in later chapters, includes preparation, presentation, application, and evaluation. The process has continued to find success in many areas of adult education.

In addition to Knowles, other educational experts in the 1970s developed theories and suggested practices that have found success in adult education. Dr. Benjamin Bloom proposed the *mastery learning theory* that states: If instructors gave students the appropriate time and opportunity, they could learn anything (see Mastery section under Approaches to Learning).

Figure 7.2 The classic symbol of women in the workforce is the World War II recruiting poster of Rosie the Riveter. *Commissioned by the U.S. War Production Commission, Coordinating Committee.*

Most adults come to class interested in the subject and eager to learn about it. Unfortunately, time limitations imposed by a rigid schedule may prevent students from having the opportunity to master course requirements. As a result, both students and instructors feel unsuccessful and discouraged. Students may feel frustrated by *not* having learned all that is needed or desired from the material. Instructors may feel that the experience has been unsuccessful because valuable material had to be eliminated to meet time constraints.

These theories, ranging from Socrates and Confucius to Arnold, Knowles, and Bloom, have established the basis for adult education today. According to Dr. Robert Mager, it should be the universal goal of instruction to *send students away from instruction with at least as favorable an attitude toward the subjects taught as they had when they first arrived.* When fire and emergency services instructors can succeed in reaching this goal, then they have succeeded in providing students with knowledge they can use.

Terminology

Learning is an active process in which students progress through a series of mental steps to bring about a change in behavior. To assist students in navigating the learning process, instructors strive to make each step clear and concise by presenting the information in a familiar format and style that is easy to understand. Instructors must understand the learning processes and principles and know how to use teaching methods that create interest, stimulate motivation, and ensure successful learning.

To understand the learning process, it is important to understand some of the common terms used to describe it. The following terms are applied throughout this manual in the development and presentation of lesson plans and curriculums:

- *Learning* — Relatively permanent and observable change in a person's behavior that is the result of interaction with the environment. *Learning types:*

    — *Formal learning:* Involves the acquisition of knowledge and skills provided by teachers or instructors in a classroom or other similar controlled setting. Formal learning is enhanced when it is reinforced through frequent and intense practice that promotes understanding and ability.

— *Informal learning:* Occurs through the various experiences that people have in life. Informal learning may be the result of accidentally touching a hot burner on a stove or making an inappropriate statement and being embarrassed in public.

- *Learning outcomes* — Statements that specify what students will know or be able to do once learning is complete. Learning outcomes are usually expressed in terms of the three learning domains: knowledge, skills, or attitudes (see Domains of Learning section). Learning outcomes are based on the needs assessment that defines the duties, jobs, and tasks that a student will be required to perform as a member of an organization.

- *Learning objectives* — Specific statements that describe desired learning results (competencies). Written learning objectives represent the learning outcomes; therefore, they are directly related. Learning outcomes are generally broader, while objectives may be more specific. Learning objectives should always have a very clear measurement/evaluation method. Because both terms (*outcomes* and *objectives*) refer to what students should be able to do, there is often very little to distinguish between them.

- *Teaching/instruction* — Method of transferring knowledge by giving information through various forms of communication in a systematic manner. When teaching/instruction is successful, an observable change occurs in a student's behavior (learning). Effective teaching/instruction includes activities and opportunities for students to demonstrate knowledge and skill and receive instructor feedback on progress toward the specified learning outcome.

- *Education* — Instruction that emphasizes knowledge-based learning objectives that are *not* tied to a specific job as opposed to *training* where learning objectives are tied to a specific job.

- *Training* — Instruction that emphasizes job-specific learning objectives and traditional skills-based instruction as opposed to only knowledge-based education.

- *Motivation* — Internal state or condition that activates and directs behavior toward a goal. Motivation occurs when a person is interested in achieving a specific goal. Although motivation is internal within the student, external influences may also play a role in the educational process. *Examples:*

— An instructor may provide external motivation through the design and delivery of instructional materials that stimulate a student's interests.

— Mandated training or promotional requirements may also create external motivations for students.

- *Needs assessment* — Survey of the types of services required or desired by the community or service area. A needs assessment determines the following items:

— Types of services that an organization will provide

— Resources (personnel, materials, and funds) required to provide those services

— Types of personnel training that will be required to provide the services

- *Task/job analysis* — Detailed survey of the duties, jobs, and tasks that an individual is expected to perform as a member of an organization. Each duty is composed of jobs that must be completed, and each job is composed of a series of tasks. The survey may be illustrated as a pyramid or flow chart with the organization's mission statement at the top and each level of service listed in increasing detail. The type and variety of services performed by an organization (based on the needs assessment) determine the duties and training needs for members of the organization (**Figure 7.3**).

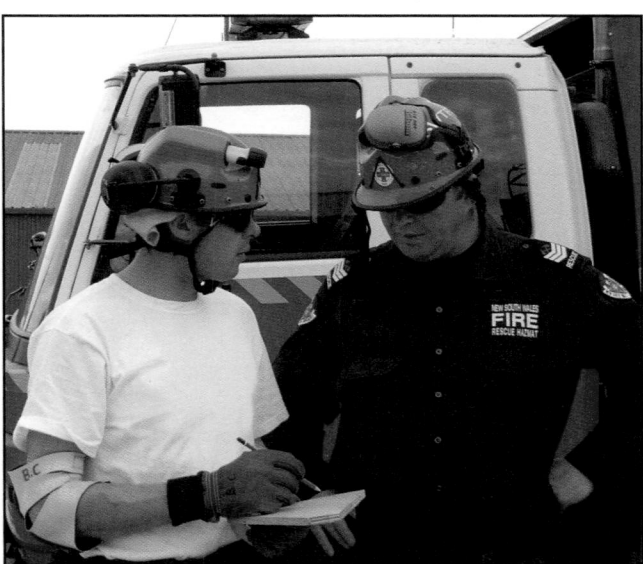

Figure 7.3 Instructors perform task/job analyses to determine the type of training that will be required to prepare fire and emergency services personnel to do their jobs. *Courtesy of Andrew Haag, Senior Rescue Instructor, New South Wales Fire Brigade.*

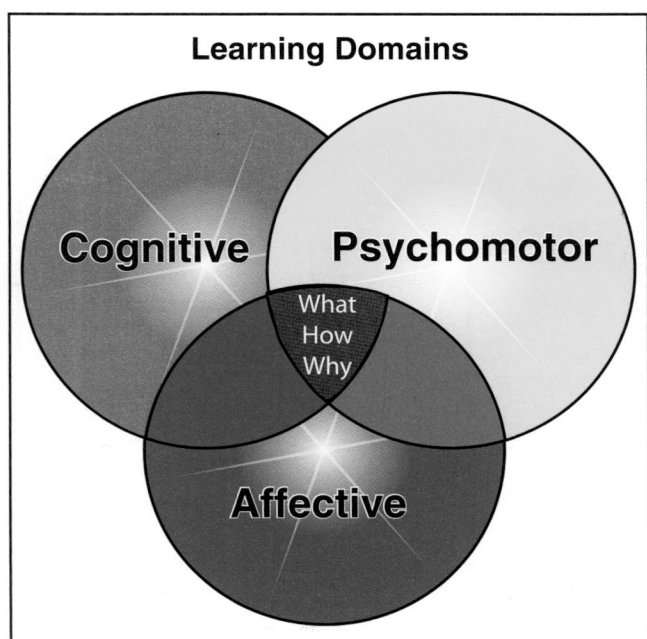

Figure 7.4 Effective learning results from the interrelationship of the three domains — cognitive, psychomotor, and affective — to explain the What, How, and Why of the knowledge to be acquired.

Instructor Tip: Don't Get Confused by Terminology

Learning objectives, instructional objectives, performance objectives, behavioral objectives, specific objectives, enabling objectives, terminal objectives, course objectives, course outcomes, learning outcomes — all these different terms are bound to confuse instructors! While some education professionals may argue that there are differences between these terms, the terms ultimately indicate *desired student performance.* Although understanding terminology is important, an instructor should focus on what is ultimately most important — the desired student performance.

Domains of Learning

In the 1960s, a committee of college professors, chaired by Dr. Benjamin Bloom, identified three types or domains of learning: cognitive (knowledge), psychomotor (skills), and affective (attitude). These domains are interrelated areas in which learning occurs rather than being independent areas of learning. When targeted by instructional methods, learning within the domains enables students to understand a concept, perform a task, or alter a behavior.

Having an understanding of these domains and how they interact will assist the instructor in presenting effective instruction. Through the *cognitive* domain, students gain understanding about a concept or topic. Through the *psychomotor* domain, students perform the skills associated with that concept or topic. Through the *affective* domain, students develop a willingness to perform the behavior correctly and safely. The cognitive, psychomotor, and affective domains are the *what, how,* and *why* of the learning process **(Figure 7.4)**.

Each of the learning domains is divided into several levels of learning **(Figure 7.5, p. 142)**. The levels start from the simple at the bottom to the complex at the top. The student passes through each level on the learning ladder before progressing to the next level. This progression is explained further in the sections that follow.

Cognitive (Knowledge)

The most commonly understood learning domain is the cognitive or knowledge domain. *Cognition* is a general concept that refers to all forms of knowing, including perceiving, imagining, reasoning, and judging. It is the foundation for the other two

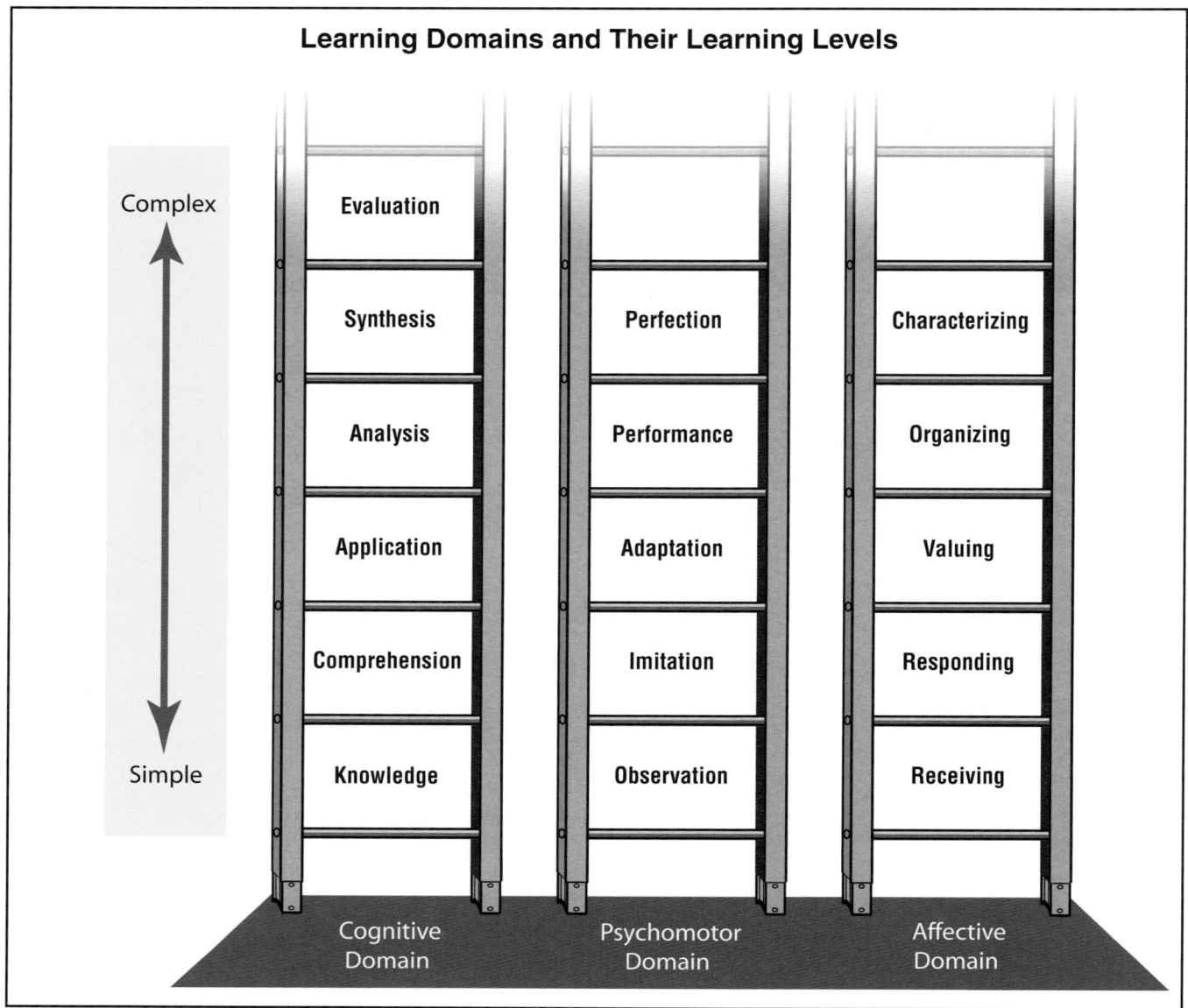

Figure 7.5 Each of the learning domains consists of progressive levels of learning. Like a ladder, the completion of one level leads the student to the next higher level of understanding.

domains. Cognition enables a person to apply knowledge *(what)* to perform a task or skill *(how)* and understand and accept the reasoning *(why)* behind the basic concept.

Cognitive information is usually presented in a *technical* or factual presentation, usually in lecture and discussion form. With various techniques, instructors can prepare students to apply knowledge to skills (psychomotor domain) and understand and accept new ideas and methods (affective domain). To describe and illustrate cognitive material and make it interesting and dynamic, instructors may use the following techniques:

- Use audiovisual and visual aids.
- Show models and other displays.
- Perform demonstrations.
- Involve students in application activities.

The levels of learning in the cognitive domain follow an ordered progression or hierarchy of instructional outcomes. Each level builds upon the previous level and is progressive in its format. The levels of learning in the cognitive domain are as follows:

- *Knowledge* — Students remember, recall, and recognize previously learned facts and theories. They can describe, define, label, list, and match terms and items. *Example:* Define the combustion elements of the fire tetrahedron.

- *Comprehension* — Students understand the meaning of information, compare and contrast information, interpret material, and estimate future trends. They give examples, make explanations, give predictions, and summarize information and ideas. *Example:* Explain how the fire tetrahedron combustion elements interact to create or sustain combustion.

- *Application* — Students use information learned in new and specific situations, apply rules, and apply concepts. They compute, demonstrate abilities, solve problems, modify ideas and actions, and operate equipment. *Example:* Demonstrate how fire extinguishment can occur when one of the combustion elements of the fire tetrahedron is eliminated.

- *Analysis* — Students divide information into its component parts to understand the relationship between the parts and understand the whole. They diagram, identify, and select parts of a whole. *Example:* Analyze the relationship between the combustion elements of the fire tetrahedron.

- *Synthesis* — Students put parts together to form a new whole. They categorize, create, design, organize, revise, and integrate parts to invent new procedures. *Example:* Show how combining various chemical compounds in the absence of oxygen can result in combustion.

- *Evaluation* — Students judge the value of materials or actions based on defined criteria using elements from all other levels. They compare, conclude, contrast, discriminate, and justify decisions based on standards and criteria. *Example:* Justify the use of various extinguishing agents to disrupt the combustion elements of the fire tetrahedron.

Understanding the levels of the cognitive domain enables instructors to create effective lesson plans. They can divide large units of instruction into smaller portions that may be spread over multiple sessions or divided by periodic breaks.

Learning begins with the low levels of cognition and builds to higher levels until the entire unit is learned.

Psychomotor (Skills)

In fire and emergency services training, the most commonly used form of learning is the psychomotor (skills) domain, typically referred to as *hands-on* learning. *Psychomotor* refers to skills involving knowledge learned through the senses that is applied to physical movement. Learning is developed through repeated practice of the skill. Successful completion of the skill is measured in speed, precision, distance, techniques, or sequence of execution.

Like the cognitive domain, the levels of learning in the psychomotor domain progress through successive steps from simple to complex. The student progresses through the following steps:

Step 1: *Observation* — Witness the motor activity as it is demonstrated by the instructor.

Step 2: *Imitation* — Replicate or imitate the demonstrated motor activity in a step-by-step process.

Step 3: *Adaptation* — Modify and personalize the motor activity.

Step 4: *Performance* — Perfect the activity through repeated practice until the steps become habit.

Step 5: *Perfection* — Improve the performance until it is flawless and artful.

Instructors first demonstrate the skill correctly as students watch. Students develop a sense for performing the motions and mentally prepare themselves to take action. As students begin to practice, they imitate the instructor's motions. Instructors guide the students, correct their mistakes, and reinforce correct performance.

Through positive reinforcement (feedback) and continued practice, students develop correct techniques and become proficient so the skill becomes a habit that is performed automatically. With practice and experience, students modify actions or create new formats to fit other situations.

Instructors must be aware that students learn at different rates of speed and levels of ability. Students must be comfortable in one psychomotor level before advancing to the next. Some students may want to observe longer than others before they begin to practice. Others may want more guidance and coaching before feeling confident to work on their own.

Instructors must watch for and understand student abilities at each level and provide appropriate time and opportunity for learning. Studies of vocational training have indicated that providing an adequate amount of time to master each level is critical for the success of most students.

Affective (Attitude)

The least understood domain is the affective (attitude) domain. *Affective learning* involves how individuals deal with issues emotionally and includes the following traits:

- Individual awareness
- Attitudes
- Interests
- Appreciations
- Motivations
- Enthusiasm
- Values

Instructors encourage the development of attitudes and values in subtle and indirect ways, usually by providing students with a positive role model. Instructors, by their own attitudes, *affect* those they teach and may have powerful influences on them. Instructors influence students by providing positive attitudes toward authority, respect, responsibility, and safety (among other values). This attitude instills in students the same values that are demonstrated by instructors. At the same time, negative attitudes can result in students having a low regard for these values.

The affective domain is approached through the preparation step of the lesson plan. Desired changes in behavior must be determined in advance and planned in the lesson. Instructors then emphasize the correct behavior that the student must learn and exhibit.

Learning outcomes of the affective domain take time to achieve and are *not* as readily observable as the results of the cognitive and psychomotor domains. While learning new cognitive information and performing new psychomotor skills, students may alter old attitudes, values, and beliefs.

For example, fire and emergency services personnel once fought fires without the use of respiratory protection and placed great value on the amount of smoke they could *eat*. With new information on the long-term effects to firefighter health and safety, emergency personnel slowly altered their attitudes toward the use of respiratory protection equipment. The use of complete personal protective equipment is now considered common practice that improves personal safety as well as increasing operational effectiveness **(Figure 7.6)**.

As a value system develops over time, it influences personal behavior, develops a characteristic personality, and guides a lifestyle. It is *not* easy for instructors to change a person's character that has long been influenced by a personal value system. While knowledge and skills can be seen and measured, affective changes are *not* immediately seen and are difficult to measure.

However, an affective change can be inferred from other behaviors. For example, a trainee may value safety and demonstrate this by reporting hazards, wearing safety equipment, or following safety rules without being reminded. Instructors should reinforce correct affective behaviors with positive feedback and *not* overlook the indicators of behavioral change.

Figure 7.6 Instructors are responsible for ensuring the safety of their students by requiring the use of full personal protective equipment during high-hazard training.

Instructors' efforts in reinforcing correct affective behaviors will be most effective when students receive a consistent message from their supervisors and leaders. Instructors are often the first agents of affective behavioral change within an organization. Their efforts must be supported by consistent application of the organization's policies, procedures, and practices in the field.

Styles and Methods of Learning

Individuals gather information, process it, and use it in many different ways. These ways are referred to as learning styles and learning methods. Instructors must be flexible (and sometimes very creative) to satisfy the learning styles and methods that are represented in a group of students.

Styles

A *learning style* is the consistent way a person gathers and processes information. People constantly gather information through the five senses: seeing, hearing, touching, tasting, and smelling. Students in the classroom most often use the first three of these senses to gather information. Instructors usually present information that is gathered by students in the following ways:

- *Heard (audio)* — Through lectures or audio-tapes

- *Seen (visual)* — Through videos, photographs, illustrations, charts, graphs, maps, and demonstrations

- *Touched, handled, and performed (kinesthetic)* — Through participation in activities, skills, and projects

By using these senses and various thought-processing methods, students develop a method of participating in the learning process. Students may *not* be aware that they use any particular style to participate in learning nor that they may use different learning styles for different tasks or circumstances. But instructors can recognize different learning styles by making the following observations:

- How individuals perceive, remember, and think about information and solve problems

- How individuals see and make sense of their world and attend to their environment

Figure 7.7 Successful students take notes during class and actively participate in discussions and activities.

- How individuals attend to instruction and participate in activities

Instructors may notice that some students like to read assignments and take notes during lectures **(Figure 7.7)**. Other students may prefer to watch videos and demonstrations of skills. Instructors may also be able to identify those students who actively participate in discussions and physical activities. Instructors will notice that students show different degrees of attention, participation, and interest during presentations and class activities.

These differences are all representative of differing styles of learning based on which sense (or group of senses) provides students with the most accurate amount of information that is acceptable to them. To meet these different learning styles, instructors should plan a variety of teaching methods in their lessons. Using a variety of methods helps instructors reach the many individual learning styles so that all students can participate in a style that enables them to learn.

Methods

A *learning method* is the way an individual thinks or processes information. Thought-processing methods develop as students apply cognitive information to scenarios or practice situations. Students may have a preference for one or more thought-processing methods. As students work through exercises and activities, instructors should note which thought-processing methods they use.

Instructors can then stimulate thinking processes by using a variety of activities that require students to select a performance, determine the logic of a procedure, draw conclusions, and determine outcomes. Generally accepted learning methods include the following:

- **Sequential or linear** — Using a step-by-step, orderly thinking process that has both a beginning and an end and includes the following processes:
  - Analyzing
  - Classifying
  - Reasoning
  - Tracking of times, dates, and events

- **Abstract or symbolic** — Recognizing common qualities in similar but different experiences. Students use written and spoken words and numbers to represent ideas or objects and use equations to express ideas. They also use gestures, postures, and facial expressions to represent feelings, ideas, or actions.

- **Concrete or real objects or items** — Preferring to manage items and work with facts instead of imagining outcomes or the feel of something. Students prefer seeing true-to-life visuals and demonstrations, hearing actual sounds, and touching textures and shapes.

- **Global or holistic** — Seeing the whole picture and forming relationships between concepts, events, or things. Students have an ability to gain insight from an overview or a picture and combine parts into a whole, form associations, make generalizations, and form theories from facts. They are also intuitive.

Instructors must be aware that students may use many methods and styles for learning. Everyone does *not* learn in the same way, and differences are generally a result of individual characteristics, cultures, and experiences. Unfortunately, many of the styles that students use to learn are *not* productive and can contribute to their own failure. Often, students are *not* aware that the way they are studying and trying to learn is *not* working for them.

Instructors can influence students and stimulate learning through teaching methods that are interesting, exciting, and vivid. To give all students an opportunity to learn, instructors must use a variety of teaching methods in order to accomplish the following goals:

- Expose students to different learning techniques.
- Enable students to practice different learning styles.
- Allow students to expand on the learning methods they use so that learning becomes easier.

Laws of Learning

Learning is a basic process of life and based upon certain recognized laws. Successful instructors understand and apply the laws that govern the learning process. During the early part of the 20th century, educational researchers developed certain learning laws that are fundamental to educational theory. These laws may have different effects on each individual student.

Instructors need to understand how the laws affect students and be aware of the many personal characteristics that students, particularly adults, bring to the learning environment. The laws of learning — readiness, exercise, effect, disuse, association, recency, primacy, and intensity — are discussed in the sections that follow.

Readiness

Readiness means a person is prepared to learn — not just ready and willing but also mentally and physically able to learn new knowledge or skills. Prerequisite abilities may depend on prior learning as well as the maturity level of the individual. This readiness to learn is evident in a class where students have high interest in and anticipation of the activities in a lesson.

Exercise

The law of *exercise* stresses the idea that the more an act is practiced, the faster and surer the learning becomes. Repetition is basic to developing adequate responses because no one ever becomes proficient at a skill without performing the operation over and over. The amount of repetition required varies from person to person. Learning is always based on activity, which requires some kind of exercise involving both mind and body **(Figure 7.8)**.

Figure 7.8 Practicing basic skills helps students retain and perfect those skills. *Courtesy of Alabama Fire College.*

Remember that practice does *not* always *make perfect*. Mere repetition may be dull and meaningless if the student *cannot* see and appreciate the reason for it. Repetition is next to useless without the essential elements of interest, meaning, and goal fulfillment. Practice must be accompanied by reward and feedback on results. Punishment or humiliation for poor or incorrect performance while practicing does *not* stimulate learning. The effects of reward, feedback, and punishment have ties with the law of effect.

Effect

Learning is always more *effective* when a satisfaction, pleasantness, or reward accompanies or is a result of the learning process. When the learning situation is annoying or dissatisfying, students will *not* learn or will only learn slowly. However, this statement is *not* saying that learning can always take place in pleasant circumstances or ideal conditions. People often learn worthwhile lessons by *suffering the consequences* of their actions. However, if the goal is desirable and satisfies a need, individuals are usually willing to suffer setbacks while working toward success.

Another factor influencing the effects of learning is the use of either praise or blame (punishment) as a learning tool. Research shows that praise is more effective than blame or punishment in motivating students.

Disuse

This law assumes that habits and memories used repeatedly are strengthened and habits *not* used are weakened through *disuse*. This assumption may be true as students are learning new skills and have *not* yet developed habitual responses, but once ingrained, the skills usually return with little prompting.

Compare this idea with riding a bike, skating, typing, performing cardiopulmonary resuscitation (CPR), or using certain rescue tools infrequently. Once the skill is learned well, the process usually returns once the steps are begun because the knowledge was stored in long-term memory and the motor skill became a habit.

Association

When the mind compares a new idea with something already known, it is using *association*, which means that it is easier to learn by relating new information to similar information from past experiences. Making associations is a great aid to learning. Instructors should provide examples of associations between new (unknown) and known material to help students make connections with previously learned materials.

Recency

The principle of *recency* simply means that the most recent items or experiences are remembered best. Reviews and warm-up exercises are based on the principle that the more recent the exercise, the more effective the performance. Practicing a skill just before using it ensures a more effective performance. The law of recency is closely associated with the law of exercise and with the idea that practice and repetition are aids to learning.

Primacy

The law of *primacy* states the principle that the first of a series of learned acts would be remembered better than others. This law appears to conflict with the law of recency, but consider that each individual learns differently. Some students remember what they heard and saw first — that initial exposure has the greatest effect — while others remember what they heard and saw last because the most recent exposure is still fresh in their minds. The two laws of recency and primacy are the reasons why instructors include an overview and a strong introduction plus a summary and a strong review in their instruction.

Intensity
The principle of *intensity* states that if a stimulus (experience) is vivid and real, it will more likely change or have an effect on the behavior (learning). For example, an instructor who demonstrates how to use a certain rescue tool and involves students in the demonstration is providing an experience that is more likely to be remembered than a lecture on how to use that tool.

This law can be expanded to include the use of the rescue tool in an actual practical training evolution that involves all aspects of a rescue using the tool. David Freedman's book, *CORP Business, The 30 Management Principles of the U.S. Marines,* explains this concept in Management Principle No. 10, Employ Extreme Training: *Situations faced on the job shouldn't seem more daunting than those faced in training.*

Motivation
Knowledge of the basic principles and laws of learning is a foundation for the instructor. A greater challenge can be providing external motivation to the student to learn. Motivating students to achieve their best should be a priority. At the same time, instructors also need to be motivated. Certain job characteristics motivate instructors to participate as expected, and certain internal desires cause them to perform beyond the expected. Various motivation techniques and motivation's relationship to learning are discussed in the sections that follow.

Motivation Techniques for Adult Students
When there is a barrier or deficiency that prevents a student from attaining course goals, student reaction is to either *fight and drive through* the barrier or *give up and withdraw.* Some students need the attention and positive reinforcement from instructors.

By modeling certain behaviors and attitudes, instructors can provide the incentives that influence and motivate reluctant students. By using various instructional methods and relevant learning activities, instructors can stimulate individuals to fight and drive through learning barriers.

Over time and after exposure to a variety of students, instructors will be able to develop an ability to recognize *motivational triggers* and use them to encourage and enhance learning. Instructors play a key role in motivating adult students and can use the following techniques:

- Provide opportunities for students to be creative and develop thinking methods.
- Share ideas and receive positive comments or participate in reasonable debates.
- Promote working together in peer groups to share and learn other methods.
- Show that classroom knowledge and skills can be applied to real-life situations.
- Use visual aids and demonstrations that relate to job requirements.

Motivation — Relationship to Learning
Research indicates that at least half of the adult students who take some form of training or education do so for job-related reasons. Adult students see training and education as a direct benefit to their life situations and apply their new knowledge to solve work- or home-related problem situations. While these examples represent internal motivations for students, instructors can provide external motivation as well. The relationship between motivation and learning is illustrated in the following series of progressive steps that instructors can take:

- Gain interest and ensure success by using a variety of teaching styles that match learning styles, abilities, and needs.
- Use activities that include discussions and expressing opinions to develop thinking skills and generate interest.
- Generate interest and confidence by coaching and guiding skills and offering encouragement and positive reinforcement. Increased confidence stimulates desire to learn and participate.
- Provide opportunities for participation in activities that hold attention and interest, stimulate thinking, develop thinking skills, and develop

relationships with others. Interests, thinking skills, and relationships are then carried into work and life situations **(Figure 7.9)**.

- Provide external motivations such as rewards, recognition, and certificates that cause students to feel successful. Recognizing successful completion of tasks, lessons, and courses with external motivators stimulates internal growth desires and positive changes in values, attitudes, and beliefs.

Instructors can stimulate motivation in students through certain attitudes and ideals that demonstrate their own internalized growth needs. By following a few simple procedures, instructors will see their actions aid students in progressing through learning domain levels and mastering skills. Consider the following actions and how they can motivate students who are exposed to positive attitudes and ideals:

- *Demonstrate enthusiasm* — Show as much interest in the course as that expected of students.

- *Expect success* — Convince students that they are capable of mastering course goals. Instructor expectations are powerful student motivators.

- *Require outstanding performance* — Encourage outstanding performance by guiding and coaching students to that level. Instructors who expect good performance will have students who perform well.

Figure 7.9 Successfully mastering basic skills, such as the operation of a pump panel, depends on the ability of the instructor to stimulate student interest and attention. *Courtesy of Central Florida Fire Academy.*

- *Encourage achievement* — Set goals and motivate students to achieve their best.

- *Stimulate motivation* — Make a conscious effort to determine student motivators.

- *Provide relevancy* — Tell students why the knowledge or skills they are learning is important; students need to understand them.

- *Provide positive reinforcement where deserved* — Praise student achievements and progress publicly.

Theories of Learning and Remembering

Many educational psychologists have done extensive research on how humans learn and remember information. Their theories, research, and conclusions fill many textbooks. This section discusses a few areas of research that explain how instructional methods can affect or influence learning and remembering.

An educational theory promoted by the Greek philosopher Aristotle and later popularized by English philosopher John Locke is that an infant's mind is like a blank slate that is without content until exposed to experiences. Learning begins the moment new life responds to the influence of the outside world. Sound, light, touch, taste, and smell all create responses in a newborn child.

Many messages stimulate the senses, and some of those messages are important enough to work their way through the memory system to be stored. The mind looks at the world through the five senses, and each sense gathers a certain amount of information that is then transmitted to the brain **(Figure 7.10, p. 150)**.

Dugan Laird, an author and consultant in the training and development field, developed the *sensory-stimulation theory*. This theory says simply that *for people to change, they must invest their senses in the process*. Instructors manage this process by stimulating what students see, hear, touch, smell, and taste during a learning session. Laird states that students pay *more attention to sensory experiences than to mental processes or emotional involvement*.

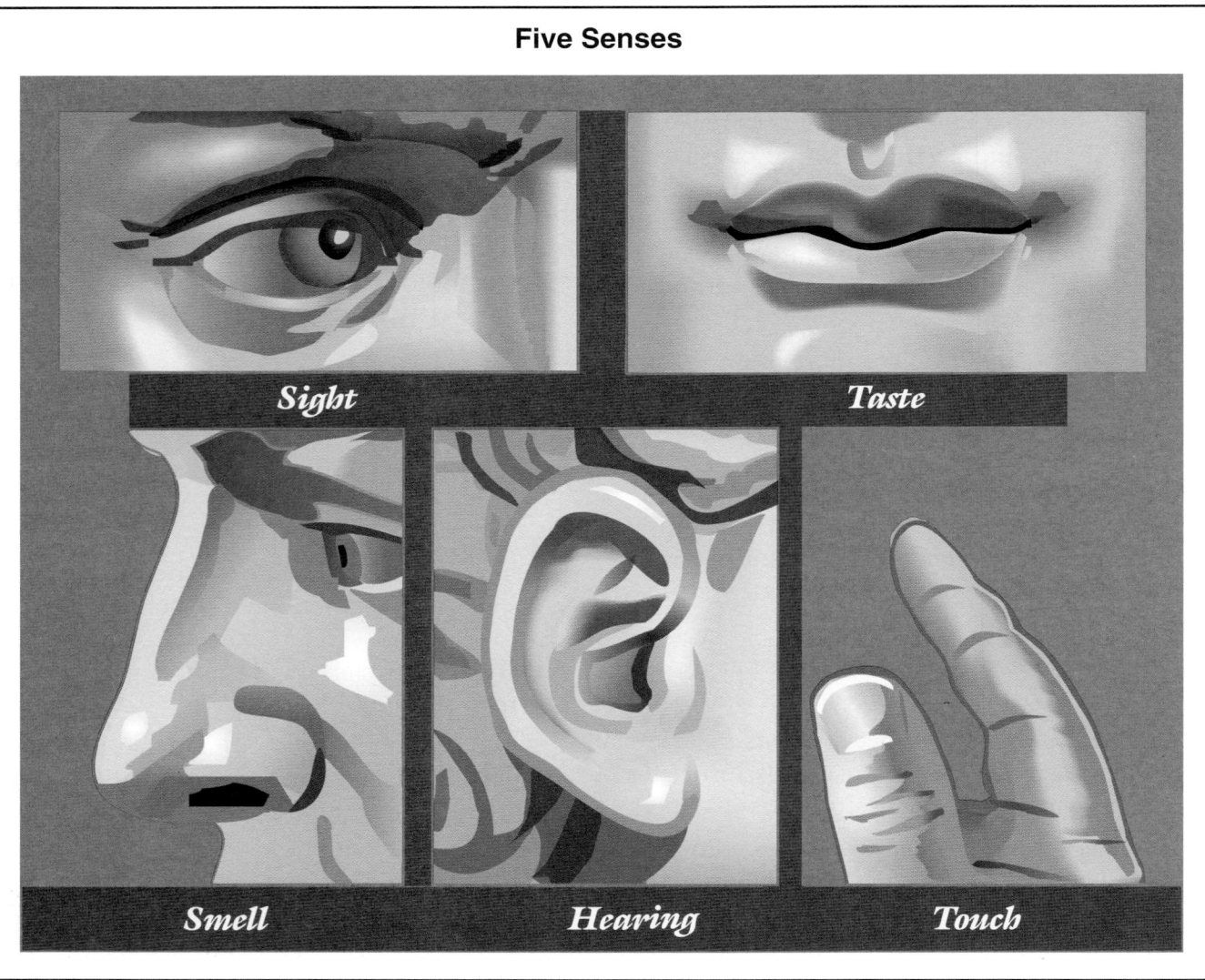

Five Senses

Sight

Taste

Smell

Hearing

Touch

Figure 7.10 The five senses provide individuals with a variety of information and can create a total learning experience.

Those who promote the sensory-stimulus approach to learning emphasize that the sense of sight takes in the most information with hearing next. People learn very little through the remaining three senses, although those senses often stimulate memories **(Figure 7.11)**.

When combined with other theories, a model was developed that is referred to as the *cone of learning* **(Figure 7.12, p. 152)**. The cone of learning model has been used in fire and emergency services training for many years. This cone illustrates that individuals retain approximately the following amounts of information:

- 10 percent of what they read
- 20 percent of what they hear

- 30 percent of what they see
- 50 percent of what they see and hear together
- 70 percent of what they say or repeat
- 90 percent of what they say while doing what they are talking about

In addition, because people learn more as active participants than as passive ones, it becomes obvious that the most effective mode of learning is the one that includes receiving or learning a new idea by a combination of methods that causes individuals to be active or to participate while learning.

As illustrated by the cone of learning, the highest level of remembering occurs when an individual performs a task while saying or describing that task. On the other hand, the cone illustrates that

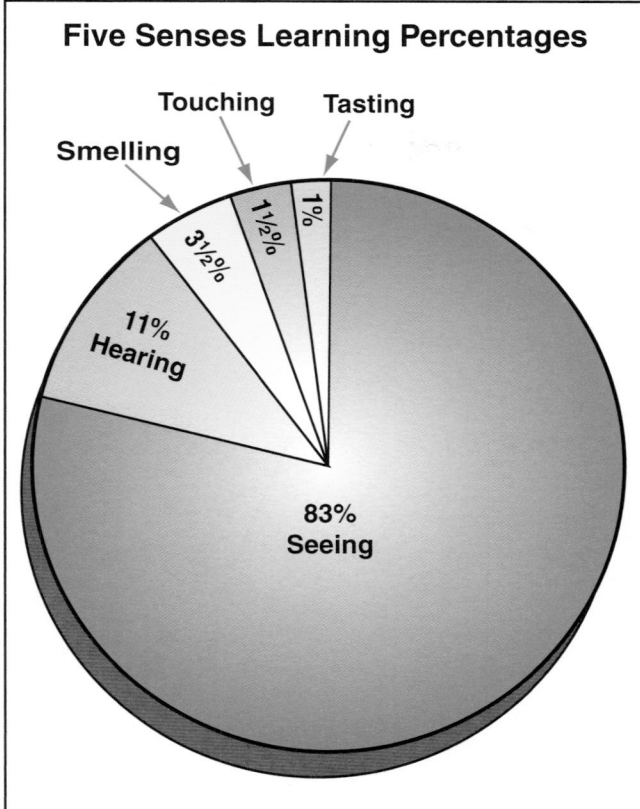

Five Senses Learning Percentages

Smelling

Touching   Tasting

3½%

1½%

1%

11%
Hearing

83%
Seeing

Figure 7.11 The five senses provide individuals with information about their environment. Seeing and hearing provide the greatest amount of information to the brain. Some of this information is acted upon immediately, some of it is ignored, and some of it is remembered.

individuals recall very little from passive methods such as reading an assignment or listening to a lecture. The conclusion appears to be that the more senses used in the learning process, the more information that is remembered for later recall.

Memory

What students store in their memory depends on how instructors gain attention, stimulate the senses, and ensure attention to *stimuli* (any agents, actions, or activities that cause physiological or psychological activity or response). To make learning memorable, instructors must make learning vivid and interactive. Action and color that seize attention and embed into the memory are easy to recall and relate to the time, place, and context in which they were learned. Students must relate new information to what they know so that it fits into their mental *schema* — the mind map that organizes knowledge.

Each individual organizes information differently in a schema that is based on the knowledge stored in different memory areas. Some students have an extensive schema of knowledge, while the schema of other students is limited. When instructors provide new information, students take that information and try to link or relate it to what they already know. When there is some similar concept in their schema or knowledge network, they can remember the information more easily. When the concept is entirely new or unfamiliar, students must take more time to rehearse and store that memory so they can recall it later.

Remembering, or placing information in memory for later recall, is an amazing process. Knowing the process of remembering and recalling helps guide instructors in planning and presenting information. The sections that follow describe the memory components: sensory, short-term or working, and long-term. These components are major factors in learning, and they affect how students learn.

Sensory

The mental storage system for attention-getting sensory stimuli or input (such as odors, sights, sounds, and sensations) is *sensory memory*. A sensory stimulus is either important enough to remember, so commonplace it is disregarded, or unimportant enough that it is forgotten. It is difficult to attend to more than one stimulus at a time and remember it well. In order to remember information, students must give an appropriate amount of attention time to the sensory stimuli they are receiving on the current information before they can attend to other stimuli on new information.

To aid memory, new information must relate to some other known and understood information. Most people have developed a preference for learning through a particular sense, and everyone tends to learn and remember more easily when information is presented to them in their preferred learning style.

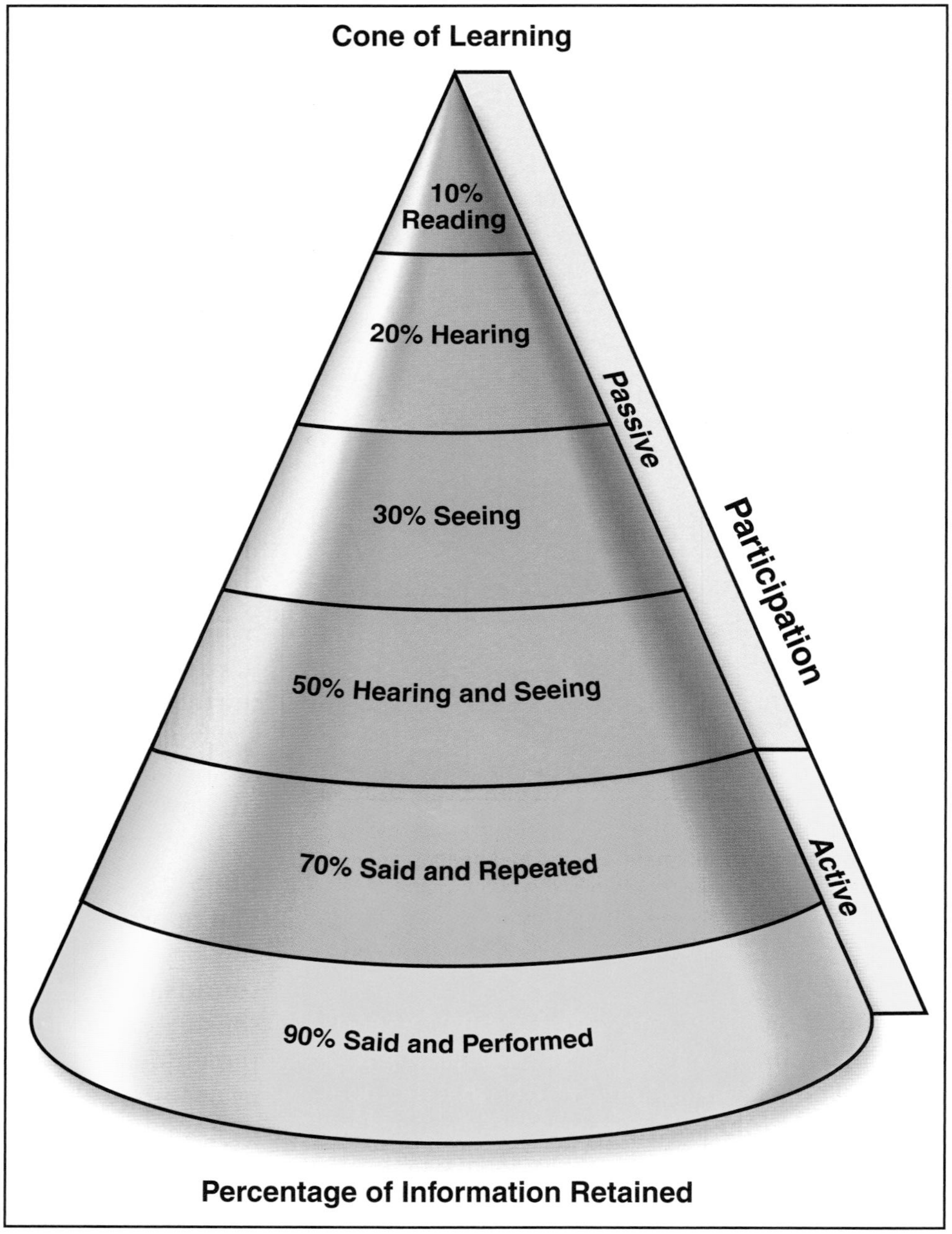

Figure 7.12 The cone of learning illustrates the percentage of information that a person remembers through various passive and active learning experiences. While seeing and hearing may provide the greatest amount of information through a passive manner, only an active learning method will cause the individual to remember the information. That factor is why it is important for students to perform skills rather than just watch them being performed.

Cone of Learning

10% Reading

20% Hearing

30% Seeing

50% Hearing and Seeing

70% Said and Repeated

90% Said and Performed

Passive

Active

Participation

Percentage of Information Retained

Relating New Information to Known Information

The term *hypoxia* is *not* difficult but may be confusing to new emergency care students. The *hypo* part means low — opposite of *hyper*, which means high. The term *hyperactive* should be a familiar one that is used to describe someone who is highly active. The *oxia* part is familiar enough — it comes from oxygen. Taken together, *hypoxia* becomes *low oxygen*.

Once explained, a seemingly difficult or confusing new term suddenly makes sense. Instructors can illustrate the word parts by using different color marking pens as they write on an easel pad or marker board.

Have members of the group hold their breaths as long as possible, tell them as they take that first gasp that they were *hypoxic*, and ask how they felt. The students were actively participating in hearing, seeing, and doing an activity that involved at least three senses. The example was vivid and memorable and likely sent to other memory components and through numerous memory links so that the information will be easy to recall.

Short-Term (Working)

The memory component that holds information for about 20 seconds or so and is limited to about seven items or *chunks* of information is called *short-term (working) memory*. Short-term memory deals with a tiny slice of several sensory events occurring in the present and therefore limits what we receive, process, and remember at the moment. Remembering requires *work* to process information if it is to be stored in long-term memory for later recall.

Memory needs about 20 seconds per item for the short-term memory process to decide whether to save or forget the information. Converting short-term memory to long-term memory requires some rehearsal time (repetition) and time to find a link or relationship with a similar experience or piece of information in memory. Also, when new information is introduced, it can replace the previously learned information.

Instructors must give students some time for conscious thinking, rehearsal, and linking of each piece of information. This teaching method helps maintain information in short-term memory and transfer it to long-term memory.

Long-Term

The memory component that holds information for a long time and is considered permanent storage is *long-term memory*. This memory component uses past information to understand events in the present. Researchers tend to agree that its capacity is limitless. Instructors should relate knowledge that students possess in their long-term memory to new information and concepts. This relationship assists in the transfer of the new information from short-term memory to long-term memory and ensures that students retain the information.

Factors that Affect Learning

Students who are trying to learn and understand but are *not* having success often become frustrated. Instead of learning, they are busy trying to cope with frustration. Instructors must realize that there may be an underlying problem with students who are *not* having success in class and look for these underlying causes. Once instructors discover the obstacles to learning, they may be able to help students resolve some of the frustrations either personally or by directing students to appropriate assistance.

The emotional attitude of students is vital to the learning process. Individuals have difficulty learning when they are concerned with *real* problems such as a death in the family or *imaginary* problems such as feeling that the group does not accept them. Successful students can overcome negative emotional attitudes by focusing on their needs or desires to learn.

Some students need assistance from the instructor to overcome or resolve their problems. Until then, these students may reach *leveling-off* points or *plateaus* in their learning processes.

Learning Obstacles

For the student, the learning process itself can be very frustrating. Generally, though, obstacles to learning consist of external pressures and concerns that make the ability to focus on learning difficult and cause frustration. Frustrations that come from fear and worry include the fear of *not* knowing how to study appropriately, fear of ridicule by the instructor or classmates, or fear of failure if they cannot perform as expected. Many students come to class with personal worries such as leaving someone at home who is sick or trying to resolve financial problems.

Many frustrations arise from the discomfort of the physical environment or class setting. Learning situations where students must stand or sit too long make it difficult to concentrate and learn. Poor lighting and ventilation also have negative effects on learning. Students are also distracted from learning if they must train in dangerous conditions on a poorly organized training ground. They will be more concerned about their safety than about learning.

Other frustrations stem from anxiety or boredom, which may be the result of poor instruction. Students will become anxious if they perceive that they are *not* prepared for the class or do *not* see the relevance to their jobs. When the individual is *not* interested in the subject and the instructor does *not* gain that student's attention through motivational tactics and relevance, boredom will then be high.

Lectures that are too long and instruction that provides little, if any, opportunity to practice quickly lose student interest. Lack of training aids and improper teaching methods quickly bore students and reduce learning. **Table 7.1** lists some areas of student frustrations.

Learning Plateaus

Instructors must recognize and remove negative learning influences in order to improve instruction and promote learning. Like a chain reaction, a student's emotional attitude, caused by external pressures, can cause the student to remain at one level or plateau of learning. Becoming stagnant on this plateau then causes the student to become discouraged, which in turn adds to a negative emotional attitude.

A plateau can be compared to the landing in a flight of stairs — it is a break in upward progress **(Figure 7.13)**. Some students stay there briefly, while others become stuck because they are discouraged or become discouraged because they feel they are stuck. Students sometimes create their own learning plateaus from emotional responses such as fear of failure and boredom. These emotions occupy their minds and interfere with their concentration and progress.

After students master the procedural steps of a skill, they need to practice until they meet a desired skill level. Once they reach this level, they will be exposed to more information and skills and expected to progress to the next skill level.

Individuals may become discouraged if they have *not* been able to practice a task enough to feel proficient at a certain level, or they may find it more difficult to reach a particular skill level. At this point, further progress seems impossible, and an individual may feel like quitting. Athletes often experience plateaus in developing skills. Students, like athletes, must be coached and receive positive feedback as they practice.

Instructors must let students know that these learning plateaus are normal, help them recognize signs of frustration, and work with them to overcome problems. One solution to the problem is to continue practicing until the skill is thoroughly understood and the procedures become automatic. Another solution is to take a break, direct students to review and think about the task for awhile, and then have the students return to it after a period away from it.

When students cannot get past plateaus, it may be that they have formed improper habits or tried to learn something beyond their abilities. Instruc-

Table 7.1
Areas of Student Frustrations

Fear or Worry	Discomfort	Poor Instruction
• Fitting in, acceptance	• Personal strength and stamina	• Class too advanced
• The class situation	• Eyestrain	• Class too simple
• Failure	• Difficulty hearing	• Instructor unprepared
• Ridicule	• Classroom too hot or too cold	• No opportunity for participation
• Keeping up with requirements	• Uncomfortable seats or poor seating arrangements	• No variety in presentation
• Personal Problems	• Dangerous training conditions	• Class too large
• Family		• No direction
• Health		• Relevance not explained
• Money		

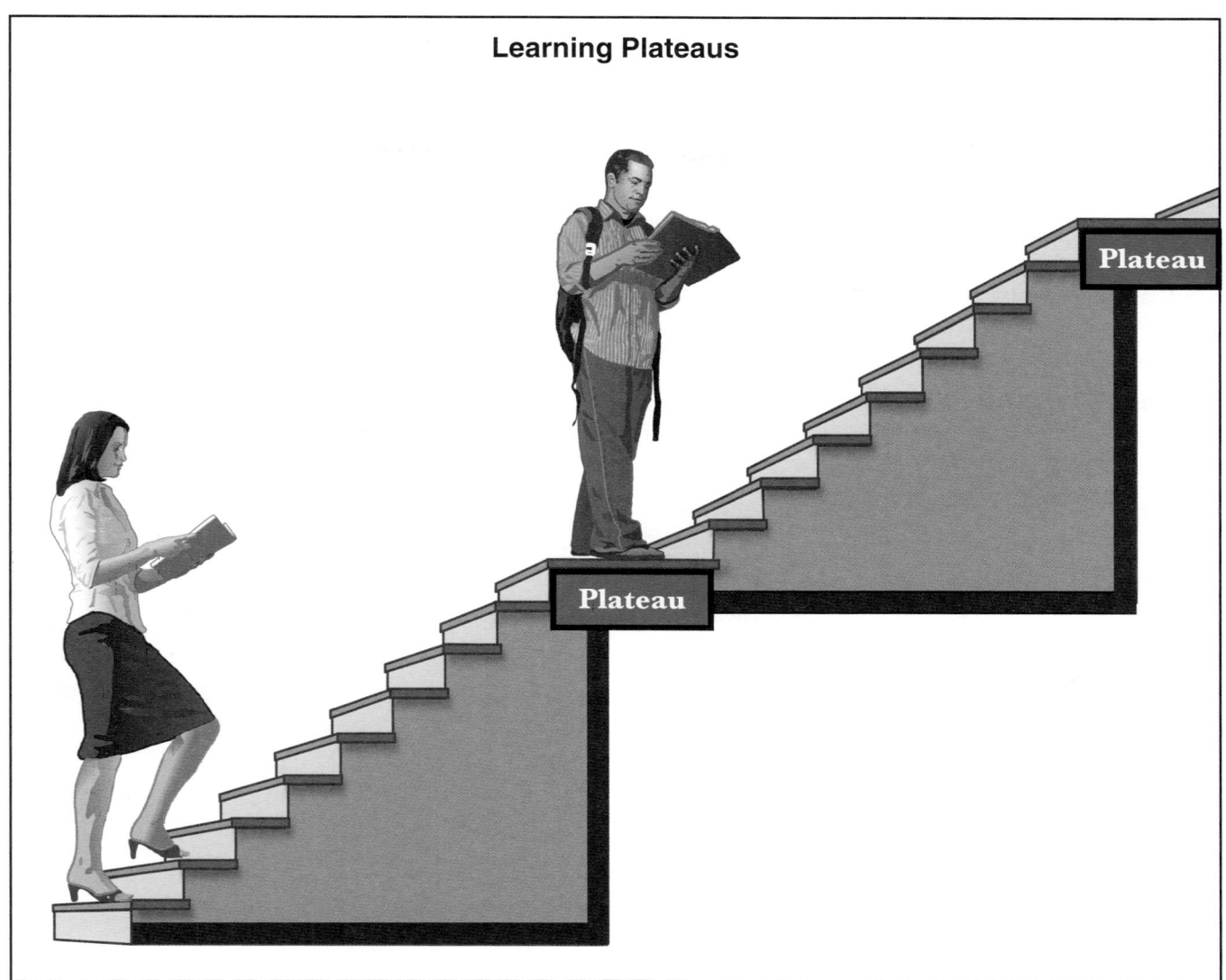

Learning Plateaus

Plateau

Plateau

Figure 7.13 Most students will encounter a learning plateau during their educational experience. For some the experience may be lengthy and frustrating, while others may not even notice the delay in upward progress.

tors must also consider that they may have failed to provide proper assistance. Instructors should review their instructional methods to ensure that they are able to communicate and demonstrate effectively.

Approaches to Teaching

The primary goal of instruction is to provide opportunities for all students to learn and successfully meet course goals and objectives. Opportunities to learn can be presented through two approaches to teaching: traditional and mastery. Most instructors are familiar with the traditional approach because it is the one typically used in schools and universities. However, it is generally *not* used in the

majority of fire and emergency services training programs. To meet the required fire service criteria or learning outcomes, the mastery approach is generally more applicable.

Each approach to teaching also has its own form of student evaluation or assessment. The outcome of traditional teaching is determined by a norm-referenced assessment, while the mastery learning approach is judged by a criterion-referenced assessment. An explanation of each of these approaches is included in the Approaches to Student Assessment section and Chapter 13, Student Progress Evaluation and Testing.

Traditional

The *traditional* approach to teaching is based on the presentation of information through lectures, readings, and audiovisuals. Students listen, read, take notes, and generally memorize information. While the traditional approach to teaching is *not* used for psychomotor skills training, it can be used for the teaching of theory or concepts such as leadership, management, or ethics. The characteristics of the traditional approach are as follows:

- *Content-based* — Lesson plans and curriculums are based on specific topics that the student must know and the instructor can teach.

- *Time-based* — Time required to teach the material is the same regardless of the learning speed of individual students.

- *Group-based* — Teaching is directed toward the learning ability of the average member of the class. Slow students may *not* have time to learn the material completely, and gifted or advanced students may become bored with the subject.

- *Delayed, general feedback* — Feedback on student accomplishments is directed to the class as a whole and usually occurs following examinations and projects.

- *Textbook/workbook* — Teaching is linked to the structure of a textbook or workbook and may *not* be flexible enough to satisfy the needs of students or the instructor.

- *Instructor-dependent* — Teaching is linked heavily to the instructor who is the primary resource for students.

- *General goals* — The approach is based on very general goals or learning outcomes.

- *Norm-referenced assessments* — Individual student success is based on the norm or average of the class. Students are graded against each other and *not* against an established level of proficiency. The current trend in classrooms at all levels is to use criterion-referenced evaluations that assess student success against an established standard. See Norm-Referenced Assessments and Criterion-Referenced Assessments sections.

NOTE: The term *traditional* is also used to refer to teaching that occurs in a classroom setting as opposed to electronic learning (e-learning) or distance learning. See Chapter 10, Instructional Delivery, for further information on each of these types of learning.

Mastery

Mastery is defined as a high-level or nearly complete degree of proficiency in the execution of a skill. The mastery approach to teaching, sometimes referred to as *competency-based learning* (CBL), requires that the student successfully master the learning objectives or outcomes of the lesson or course. When testing for mastery, instructors base student performance on criteria (standards) stated in learning objectives.

The basic task of instructors is to determine what is meant by mastery and search for methods and materials that enable the largest proportion of students to attain such mastery. The characteristics of the mastery approach are as follows:

- *Competency-based* — Primary focus is on the successful and accurate completion of the skills.

- *Performance-based* — Success is determined by the performance of the skills by the student.

- *Individual-based* — Training is individualized to meet the learning style of the student.

- *Immediate, specific feedback* — Instructors provide feedback to the individual student when the student performs the skill.

- *Modules and multimedia* — Courses and lessons are divided into blocks that are similar and supported by a variety of audiovisual training aids.

- *Instructor-supported* — Instructors help students learn the skill and become proficient at it.

- *Specific objectives* — Each course is constructed of learning objectives that combine to reach the final goal of the course.

- *Criterion-referenced assessments* — Success is based solely on the mastery of specific criteria at a predesignated level, usually 70 to 100 percent. See Criterion-Referenced Assessments section.

The mastery approach uses criterion-referenced teaching, learning, and assessments and focuses attention on learning objectives. Students who have problems reaching the desired criteria level on their initial efforts are given additional instruction, time, and opportunities to perform to the acceptable level. The learning objectives are written to establish the following criteria:

- Identify and clearly describe the learning outcome (behavior). *Example:* The student *will don an SCBA*.

- Define the important conditions by which the students will perform (conditions). *Example:* The student will don an SCBA *while wearing full personal protective equipment.*

- Define the criterion of acceptable performance (degree). *Example:* The student will don an SCBA while wearing full personal protective equipment *within 45 seconds.*

The mastery approach works very well in the fire and emergency services because the services are competency-based. Students keep working (learning) until they have acquired the necessary level of competency. This goal is achieved by creating learning objectives and delivery styles to permit this *mastery* to occur.

When the material is difficult or complex, instructors work more diligently to lift students to the mastery standard or spread the learning over a longer time period to allow for the more difficult *assimilation* of complex concepts. Finally, *no* student should proceed to new material until the basic requisite material is mastered.

Instructors and course developers should understand the mastery approach and realize that it has both advantages and disadvantages. The advantages outweigh the disadvantages, which can be overcome through planning.

Advantages
Some of the advantages of the mastery approach to teaching include the following:

- Students are prepared to advance to more complex knowledge or skills.

- Knowledge that the student possessed before the course can be used to gain mastery more quickly.

- Instructors must perform task analyses to ensure that they are prepared to teach the unit or lesson.

- Instructors must state the learning objectives before designating or designing student activities and projects.

- The responsibility for learning is focused on the student and increases the likelihood of success.

Disadvantages
Mastery has some associated disadvantages, too, which can be overcome. They include the following:

- Additional time must be available to ensure that all students master the subject.

- More effort is required on the instructor's part to teach to the individual learning speed of all the students in the class.

- Faster students may feel that the slower members of the class are holding them back.

- Several formative exams must be written and administered during the course.

- A wide variety of training materials must be available to meet the learning needs of all students.

Approaches to Student Assessment
Assessing or evaluating student success may be accomplished in two different ways: Traditional teaching may depend on the norm-referenced approach of assessment or the criterion-based assessment approach, while mastery teaching uses only the criterion-based assessment approach. Although the norm-reference approach has been useful in school- and university-based settings, it has limited usefulness in the fire and emergency services and is falling out of favor in most educational settings. Instructors may encounter this more traditional approach to evaluation in a few instances, but the more common approach in the fire and emergency services is the criterion-referenced assessment.

Norm-Referenced Assessments

The traditional approach to teaching is based on the *norm-referenced* assessment approach that measures the accomplishment of one student against that of another. At the end of an instructional unit, an exam is given, the results scored, and the scores translated into grades. These grades are often based on the distribution of scores within the class on an exam, which is presumed to be a normal or bell-shaped distribution **(Figure 7.14)**. This type of evaluation and assessment is rarely used in the fire and emergency services.

Criterion-Referenced Assessments

The term *criterion* refers to a standard on which a decision or judgment is based. The criteria that students must meet are stated in the course objectives that guide student performance. Instructors involve students in activities and practice that enable them to become competent in or master the knowledge and skills criteria stated in the course objectives.

A *criterion-referenced assessment* measures student performance by comparing it to the standard or criterion stated in the course objectives. At the point of testing, students should have mastered the criteria requirements **(Figure 7.15)**. Criterion-referenced assessment compares student performance with stated criteria, not with the performance of other students as in the case of the norm-referenced

assessment. Although each student's performance varies somewhat from another's, the performance is acceptable when it meets the conditions stated in the criteria.

Using the criterion-referenced approach, the test scores are translated to a *Pass* or *No Pass/Fail* grade. The grade is determined by whether the student's performance has met or failed to meet the prescribed standard or criterion as follows:

- *Pass* — Performance at or above the criterion
- *No Pass/Fail* — Performance below the criterion

For instance, the standard or criterion for performance on an end-of-instruction exam might be 70 percent. Students who achieve a score of 70 percent or more on the exam receive the grade of *Pass* and students who achieve a score of less than 70 percent receive a grade of *No Pass/Fail.*

A similar grading system may be used for psychomotor skills where a student is judged to have either passed or failed the manipulative skill test. For instance, a common manipulative skill test is an SCBA test. Typically students are required to accurately don an SCBA in a fixed amount of time such as 45 seconds. Using a skills

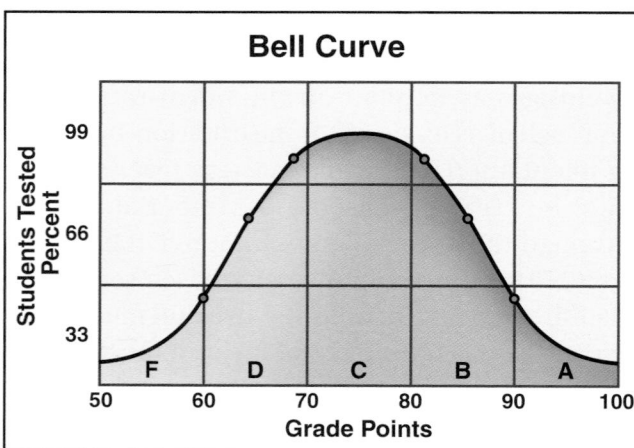

Figure 7.14 The Bell Curve (or Normal Distribution Chart) has been used in the traditional approach to student assessment but is rarely used in fire and emergency services training.

Figure 7.15 Instructors must observe and grade student performance of skills to determine whether students have mastered the skill. *Courtesy of Central Florida Fire Academy.*

checklist and a timer, students can be assessed for their ability to complete the skill correctly in 45 seconds.

Students who meet the criterion are given the grade of *Pass* and students who do *not* meet the criterion are given the grade of *No Pass/Fail.* In some skills, a single step may be so critical that *not* accomplishing it can result in a *No Pass/Fail* grade even though the rest of the skill was performed accurately.

Examinations used to certify personnel are used to determine mastery of a subject or topic. Personnel must have a complete and thorough knowledge of the subject and the ability to recall and apply the knowledge. Certification exams should *not* be given as end-of-course exams because most students will *not* have had time to develop mastery of the subject or topic.

Summary

Instructors who understand the principles of learning will have the foundations for developing the appropriate teaching style to meet the needs of their students, their organizations, and themselves. This understanding will allow them to be more flexible by matching their teaching style to the learning style of the individual student as well as matching it to the topic. The instructor will be able to develop not only effective teaching styles but also methods for motivating students to excel. Finally, acquiring this understanding allows an instructor to focus on the primary element of all education: the student.

Make it Meaningful

Ed Kirtley, Officer/Instructor Coordinator, Oklahoma Fire Service Training, has more tips from his Eleven Keys to Engaging Adult Students. Some that relate to principles of learning include the following:

- *Make it meaningful* — Adults search out (and tune into) learning experiences that have meaning for their lives. They want to learn about topics that are pertinent and will make their lives better. Either directly or indirectly through discussions and the objectives, you (as the instructor) must answer the following two questions that are in students' minds at the beginning of every presentation:

  — *How does this apply to me?* In other words, students must understand how the topic applies to them with their needs, their experiences, and their life situation.

  — *How will I benefit from this presentation?* or *What's in it for me?* Students must see some benefit from the presentation if you are to **actively engage them in the learning process**. Your goal is to create an environment where students are actively engaged rather than simply passively participating.

- *Discuss more — lecture less* — Adults need to learn through a sharing of experiences. In a sense, the sharing of experiences is an emotional connection with the educator. Discussion allows students to connect new information with information and experiences already stored in long-term memory.

Part A

General Knowledge and Skills

Chapter 8

Student Attributes and Behaviors

Figure 8.4 Instructors must be able to proportion their time so that all students receive the attention and assistance that they require for a successful learning experience. *Courtesy of Iowa Fire Service Training Bureau.*

timid or reserved; others are outspoken and try to impress the group by dominating the discussion. Students who are quiet (or nondisruptive) do *not* interrupt the lesson, but they may *not* be participating to the expected level. Disruptive students can jeopardize classroom management. Each type of student demands extra effort and special attention from the instructor.

Some individuals are labeled *problem students* when they are really only expressing different personalities. Different types of performance are indications of student ability and disability. Instructors must be aware that different social and cultural backgrounds, experiences, genders, and generational characteristics shape students and affect learning styles and abilities.

The educational and literacy levels of the student should be taken into consideration. *Educational level* is the number of years spent in school; *literacy level* is the level at which students can read and write. Many adults (and members of the fire and emergency services) return to college to take courses or pursue degrees with the intent of getting better jobs or promoting to higher ranks. Instructors may find that the educational level of students is higher now than in past years while (at the same time) the literacy level is declining.

After teaching the same subject several times, instructors will realize that each student group has different characteristics. This realization will cause instructors to change their presentation styles. The sections that follow describe some common student personalities that instructors may encounter in every audience. Instructors must be aware of, able to manage, and prepared to teach each type.

Individuals With Low Literacy Levels

The traditional definition of *literacy* has been based on any person who is 15 years or older and able to read and write. Because societies are becoming more complex and based on information and technology, the U.S. Workforce Investment Act of 1998 redefined literacy to mean *an individual's ability to read, write, speak in English, and compute and solve problems at levels of proficiency necessary to function on the job, in the family of the individual, and in society.*

Generally, fire and emergency services training divisions will *not* provide any form of remedial instruction in reading or writing. However, the instructor must be able to recognize that some students need additional assistance to overcome low literacy levels. Assistance may take the form of referrals to adult education programs, employee assistance programs (EAPs), or personal tutors.

Instructors should use visuals and other training aids rather than long lectures. Low literacy level students may have difficulty taking notes and keeping up with the material as it is presented. The instructor may also create, suggest, or select reading materials in textbooks, tests, and handouts that have the following features:

- Short sentences and paragraphs
- Double-spaced lines
- Directional headings and wide margins
- Type large enough to be read easily

Vocabulary should be simple, and all terms should be easily found in a glossary. When writing on an easel pad or marker board, the instructor

Figure 8.5 Instructors can help low literacy level students by using easels and other visual training aids and providing extra time for note taking. *Courtesy of Jocelyn Augustino, photographer, U. S. Federal Emergency Management Agency.*

should print using large letters rather than script or cursive writing **(Figure 8.5)**. When giving exams, the instructor should supply directions that are simple and to the point. Pictures, tables, graphs, and charts are helpful aids in illustrating and dividing large quantities of text. These aids may also be used in examinations.

Individuals With Learning Disabilities

Learning disabilities consist of a wide variety of disorders that may be neurological in origin and affect an individual's ability to understand, think, use the spoken or written word, perform mathemati-

cal functions, or perform fine psychomotor skills. It is estimated that 3 to 13 percent of the general population of the U.S. has some type of learning disability. Research also indicates that 30 to 80 percent of the low literacy level population includes individuals with learning disabilities.

Officially, the U.S. Government through the Americans with Disabilities Act (ADA) divides learning disabilities into three major categories:

1. ***Speech and language disorders*** — Difficulty producing speech sounds, using spoken language, or understanding what other people say

2. ***Academic skills disorders*** — Difficulty reading (dyslexia), writing (dysgraphia), and calculating (dyscalculia)

3. ***Miscellaneous learning disabilities*** — Difficulty performing fine motor skills (dyspraxia), learning nonverbal skills, and other difficulties

Students with learning disabilities have average to high intelligence but perform poorly on tests due to their particular disability. Students with any kind of learning disability are at a disadvantage. Instructors should look for the following indicators of learning disabilities in individuals:

- Problems with concentration

- Problems with memory

- Problems with auditory and visual perception

- Problems with oral language

- Difficulty in speaking, listening, and writing

- Problems in reading such as word recognition and comprehension

- Problems in mathematical areas such as calculating and reasoning

- Difficulty performing fine or precise psychomotor skills

While learning disabilities are serious barriers to learning, other impediments to learning may be present in students. These include visual or hearing impairments, color-blindness, or disadvantages created by economic, environmental, or cultural factors. Generally speaking, almost everyone has some impediment to learning, and almost everyone finds a unique way to compensate for that impediment. However, there are people whose these students with a feeling of success in their informal responses and participation before they are expected to initiate discussions or give presentations.

The instructor may also talk with these students during breaks to help them become comfortable with the learning process, teaching style, and course expectations. Instructors who use these simple methods of making students feel comfortable will help overcome shyness and encourage them to participate in the class.

Quiet or Bored

Many quiet students may be above average in ability but because of circumstances — such as uninteresting subject matter, unfamiliar terms, boredom, and long and technical lectures — they may drift mentally. Instructors can redirect attention by asking direct questions or beginning activities that require student participation rather than just listening. Instructors should be alert for the following signs of daydreaming and boredom:

- Glazed looks
- Gazing around the room
- Doodling
- Thumbing through materials *not* related to the subject

Uninterested

Students who are uninterested display little energy and attention. Curiosity in humans is inherent, and lack of interest is *not* natural. Instructors should be curious about the lack of interest in these students and check with their supervisors or other instructors to determine whether they have exhibited any personal or other problems. Instructors will want to know outcomes in order to plan strategies for working with these types of students. A supervisor or other instructor may indicate that a student had the following barriers to learning:

- Required counseling or tutoring in other courses
- Admitted to a class beyond the level of readiness
- Must address health, emotional, family, or learning problems before the student can make progress

Disruptive, Nonparticipating Students

Disruptive, nonparticipating students exhibit behavior that is inappropriate to a formal classroom setting and include those who sidetrack, distract, or stall class progress by diverting attention and interests from the lesson. Behaviors may include talkativeness and aggressiveness, indicating a lack of respect for the setting, instructor, or authority.

At the same time, these students may exhibit behavior that is intended to draw attention to them such as *showing off*. Not only does this behavior distract attention from the instructor and the topic, but it may also create an unsafe condition. In both cases, the instructor should act to correct the inappropriate behavior.

Instructors must manage these types of students with a certain amount of discipline. Instructors should use class time to pursue the lesson rather than allowing a disruptive individual to control it through inappropriate behavior. When initial, tactful methods of directing these students to cooperate fail and they do *not* cooperate, instructors should ask them to leave the session.

Instructors should tell disruptive students that cooperation and constructive participation is expected upon their return. Instructors can redirect the disruptive energy of these students by calling on them regularly so that they know they are expected to participate and be prepared for class.

Talkative and Aggressive

Talkative, aggressive, and extroverted individuals can monopolize a discussion. They talk so much that they prevent others from participating. The first approach for an instructor is to make a private appeal to the student. When this approach does *not* alter the student's behavior, the instructor may assign a special project to the student. While the disruptive student is occupied, the remainder of the group will have an opportunity to participate.

In almost every class, there is a small group who prefer to talk among themselves rather than participate in the current activity or discussion. In these situations, instructors must recapture the attention of the group. Instructors should tell the disruptive students that special problems can be discussed after class rather than taking time away from the whole class. It may be necessary to separate the group by having them move to different seats. With adults, this action is *not* usually necessary because in most cases they will cooperate with the instructor's requests to participate appropriately.

Show-Off

Individuals who like to *show off* use a group situation to perform and gain attention for themselves. Sometimes their performances help put other students at ease and get others to participate, but show-offs must know when to stop and share the floor. The class should be called to order and the main points of the discussion or skill reviewed as a means to redirect attention from the show-off. Other students in the class should be asked to respond. When the show-off tries to respond to all questions, the instructor should state that other students need an opportunity to respond first.

When this technique fails, a very direct and effective solution to this problem is to tell the show-off that the classroom is *not* the place for this type of behavior and disruptions of any kind will *not* be tolerated. The timeliness and manner in which an instructor delivers such an ultimatum determines its effectiveness. When students understand that cooperation is important and no alternatives are acceptable, instructors will have few if any problems. When problems persist, the instructor should always follow the organization's discipline policies and procedures.

The instructor should *not* tolerate any inappropriate behavior that creates an unsafe condition for students **(Figure 8.7)**. Although students should *not* be reprimanded in front of the class, this type of situation can be an opportunity to discuss safety violations and use the actions as examples of what can cause an accident, injury, or fatality. This example can provide a strong object lesson *not* only for the show-off but the rest of the class as well.

Figure 8.7 Safety is an essential element of all performance skills such as the ventilation of a roof shown in this photograph. Instructors should discourage students from showing off during any skills practice evolution because it could cause a dangerous situation.

Nondisruptive, Participating, Successful Students

Nondisruptive, participating, successful students are actively engaged in the learning process and are eager to contribute from their knowledge and experiences. The term is used to describe the majority of students in most fire and emergency services courses.

When other students demand too much of the instructor's time and attention, these students may be overlooked, causing them to become frustrated with the instructor, their classmates, or the course. Every opportunity should be taken to involve these students in class activities. It may also be helpful to enlist their assistance when working with some of the other types of students through peer teaching or mentoring.

Student Behavioral Management

Behavioral management can be a difficult skill for a new instructor to master. It is, however, one of the most important skills for an instructor to acquire and maintain. In an adult learning environment, some instructors believe that they do *not* need to perform behavioral management because *peer pressure* will control the classroom.

While it is a fact of human nature that the members of a group may respond to peer pressure, an instructor cannot shirk responsibility and depend information, the instructor can then carefully review the steps and coach the student through the steps again.

Often in delivering the verbal information followed by questioning — a technique to ensure understanding — instructors often give the standard reply of *OK* to all responses, even if they are off-track or clearly wrong. Instructors are sometime reluctant to discourage responses, so they accept all answers while tactfully trying to steer the group to the right conclusion. But taking a wrong answer and asking either why it is wrong or where it may fit appropriately in the lesson with what fact is a technique that allows students the following opportunities:

• Think and then analyze problems.

• Compare facts and ideas, and apply them to different situations.

• Critique and find solutions.

• Explore and discover new methods of application.

As instructors guide this type of discussion, they may find that they have covered more lesson material than they would have otherwise and students have truly learned the material. Students can then apply it appropriately in a variety of situations rather than in just staged classroom situations. This instructional method allows students to build their knowledge from what they discover and associate it with the class material and skills.

Providing Peer Assistance

In the learning environment, a *peer* is someone who is equal in status either socially or psychologically to another. *Peer assistance* refers to a process that involves having students assist other students in the learning process. Some students are intimidated or afraid to perform in front of an instructor until they feel confident in their abilities. These students feel more comfortable practicing with a peer.

Students who make good peer assistants are those who have grasped the knowledge and skill and can explain it well to others. They may also have background experiences that enable them to describe to another how certain classroom activities can be applied on the job. Peer assistants can

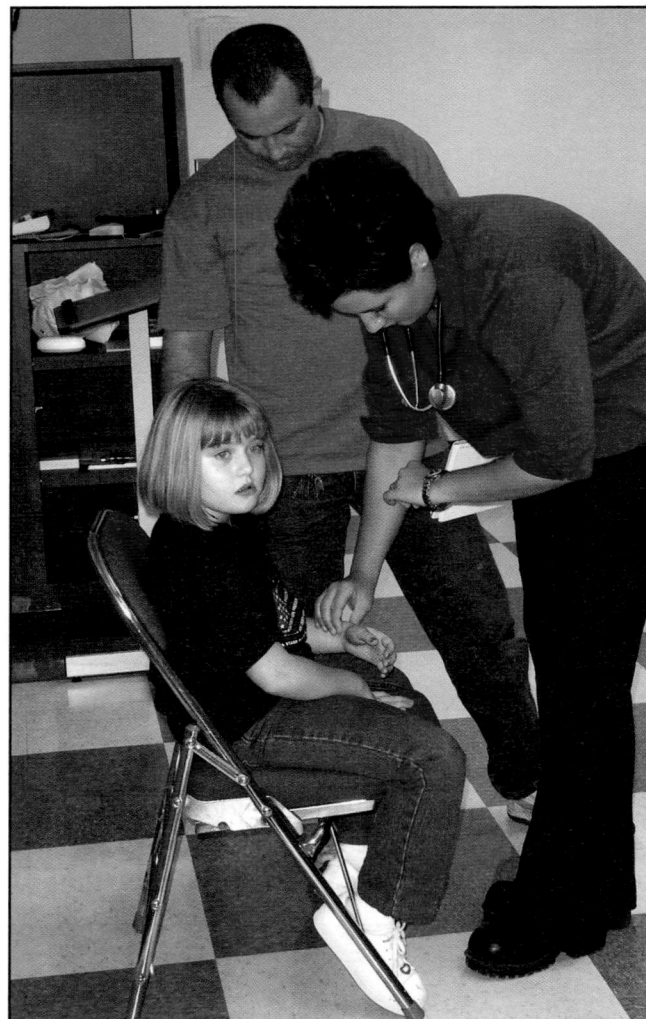

Figure 8.13 Peer assistance is a valuable tool that uses the knowledge and skills of advanced students to help their peers. *Courtesy of Alabama Fire College.*

work with other students who either may have difficulty in grasping concepts or learning skills or need more supervised practice time in a relaxed atmosphere (**Figure 8.13**).

Mentoring

Mentoring places a new student under the guidance of a more experienced professional or another student who acts as tutor, guide, and motivator. Mentoring situations occur outside the classroom, usually in the job environment. Many instructors have acted as mentors, either formally or informally. Instructors often guide the actions of new employees on the job, just as they guide the actions of new students in the learning environment or training evolution.

Typically, a mentor is usually someone other than the instructor who guides student actions in real experiences on the job. Mentors must be chosen carefully and selected for their experience, interest, patience, and communication abilities.

The primary purpose of mentoring is to prepare students for advancement within the organization through the direction of a positive role model. Mentoring programs enhance management skills, improve productivity, and encourage diversity. Instructors can mentor in the following ways:

- Serve as or provide role models for students.
- Provide guidance in career planning.
- Assist in gaining specialized training.
- Provide outside resources.
- Make challenging work assignments.
- Monitor the achievements of students.

Both mentors and students should be volunteers who are enthusiastic and supportive of the program. When mentoring is approached as a mandatory activity, the individuals involved may be resentful or participate only partially. In that case, the mentor may *not* provide the most positive role model. The accomplishments of both the mentor and the subordinate should be acknowledged throughout the process.

In some business texts it is suggested that the mentor should *not* be a direct supervisor to the subordinate. However, in the military, the concept of mentoring begins with the supervisor. According to the *U.S. Air Force Promotion Fitness Examination Guide*, a mentor is *a trusted counselor or guide*. The immediate supervisor or instructor is designated as the primary mentor (coach, counselor, guide, role model, etc.) for each student in the course. This designation in *no* way restricts the student's desire to seek additional counseling and professional development advice from other sources or mentors. Instructors must make themselves available to students who seek career guidance and counsel.

Controlling Disruptive Behavior

Disruptive behavior may be the result of instructor- or student-caused circumstances. One student or group of students may consistently cause disruptive behavior or it may be an isolated single event. Either way, the behavior distracts from the learning environment, may result in an unsafe practice, or wastes valuable time. Generally, student-originated disruptions may take the following forms:

- Arriving late
- Speaking out loud
- Talking with others off the subject
- Sleeping in class accompanied by snoring
- Showing off intentionally
- Interrupting others
- Sidetracking discussions
- Seeking attention
- Acting blatantly insubordinate and disrespectful

When these types of behavior occur, instructors are challenged to maintain their composure and control the atmosphere of the classroom. The *thing* being controlled may *not* necessarily be the behavior of a student but *the atmosphere of the classroom*. Adults usually resent any implication that someone else controls their behaviors, but instructors can *redirect* behaviors to beneficial outcomes when they manage situations appropriately.

Instructors should try to determine why some students behave in ways that disrupt the class. Although there is no real excuse for disruptive behavior, a student may believe that the behavior is legitimate. For instance, a student working a second job or overtime the day before class may fall asleep in class. Many adults who attend training classes have true concerns with competing commitments such as juggling family and work while finishing training requirements, worrying about money problems, and dealing with other similar events in their lives.

Students appreciate any concern an instructor shows because instructors who show concern also show respect for the individual. Most students return that respect by cooperating with instructors and fulfilling class requirements *to the best of their abilities*. The result is that an instructor can manage disruptive behavior and maintain control of the class with only a little effort at being flexible and humanistic.

Instructor-Caused

There are many reasons why students may display disruptive behavior. Some behavior may result from the actions of the instructor. Instructors may intentionally or unintentionally act in certain ways that cause unfavorable student reactions (see **Table 8.1**). Because instructor actions may stimulate student reactions, instructors must act appropriately to prevent any possible unfavorable student reactions.

Instructors must *never* attempt to intimidate a student physically, verbally, or emotionally. This intimidation demonstrates a lack of respect for students and results in a confrontation that could end in disaster. Exhibiting impatience with a student does *not* enforce the image of an instructor who is concerned with the student's learning experience. Impatience does *not* take into consideration the slow learner who needs additional time to develop an answer or even the gifted learner who may have many ideas to express. When the instructor is student-oriented, intimidation and impatience should *not* occur.

When instructors attempt to overcontrol students and classroom environments, the learning experience may become too stiff and structured for some student learning styles. Instructors should *not* rely on strict rules that may become barriers to learning. By being flexible and adjusting to the needs of students, the changing environment, and the variety of subject matter, an instructor can create a controlled yet healthy learning atmosphere.

Instructors who ramble through a lecture are generally unprepared for the class sessions, a fact that students will readily recognize. Lack of preparation also shows a lack of respect for students, the topic, and the learning experience. Preparation and practice are essential to good teaching. They also provide the basis for interesting and exciting lectures rather than dull ones. To prevent boredom, instructors must stimulate students to participate in the instruction and enjoy the experience.

Finally, good preparation and practice will also prevent sessions from running overtime. Students understand that a lecture may exceed the posted time limit occasionally due to unforeseen circumstances. However, they will resent instructors who perpetually exceed the time limit for *no* apparent reason other than attempting to include too much information into the session.

Student-Caused

Students may create some disruptive behavior for reasons other than as a response to the instructor. Students may bring their disruptive behaviors with them. A previous experience may have prepared these students to react inappropriately based on a perception of what the instructor might do. Students may *not* understand why they must attend the class. There may also be students who enjoy displaying their knowledge at the expense of the instructor. Finally, the instructor may be confronted with a student who wants or needs attention and uses disruptive behavior to gain it. In each of these situations, the instructor may have to rely on tactics that been developed by the education profession.

The student who does *not* understand why it is important to be in the class may exhibit boredom. One tactic instructors may use with bored, *Why am I here?* students is to plan the lesson with activities that guide students to discover exactly why they *are* there — activities that enable them to determine just *what is in it* for them.

This tactic requires matching the students' needs to the topic of the course. The instructor should ask these students to express their internal and external motivations as well as their professional needs. The instructor then helps students to determine the relationship between their needs and the course content for themselves.

Table 8.1 Unfavorable Student Reactions to Instructor Actions	
Instructor Actions	**Student Reactions**
Intimidates	Feels insecure
Shows impatience	Shows fear
Attempts to overcontrol	Rebels
Rambles without a goal	Shows no interest
Gives dull lectures	Feels unstimulated or bored
Runs overtime	Becomes fidgety

When it is necessary to regain the attention of students who are disrupting by talking among themselves on items other than the topic, instructors may try the tactic of calling on one of the individuals. Without trying to embarrass the person, the instructor makes a statement that summarizes the topic and asks a simple opinion question that directs the student's attention back to the lesson.

By this method, instructors are again letting students know that they are aware of the disruptive activity and requesting cooperation. Doing this more than once is *not* recommended.

Some students exhibit inappropriate or disruptive behavior by asking questions throughout the lecture. Sometimes students are truly curious and interested; other times their intent is to embarrass or discredit the instructor. Their intent may also be to display their own knowledge to their peers. The following list offers suggestions for dealing with these types of students:

- Show confidence in your role as content expert. Remember that these students would *not* be in the class if they were the experts.

- Tell the class you will get the information and get back to them if you are unsure of an answer. Then do it! Being responsive is more important than being perfect.

- Respond to the student, but continue to manage class time, and consider the interests of others when engaged in a dialogue with an individual.

- Always smile. A smile is disarming and indicates willingness to listen and discuss.

- Do *not* embarrass students when they expose their limitations publicly. In doing so, you can lose their respect and that of the rest of the class.

- Let participants know that their questions have merit, and then find some. Chances are that other students have the same questions and are too shy or embarrassed to ask, but they can contribute to finding the merit through an open discussion. Because of the positive reinforcement, everyone gets involved, all benefit from the discussion, and everyone grows comfortable with participating.

A student who is disruptive may be seeking needed attention, but instructors must be careful *not* to reward this behavior by paying too much attention to that student's actions. Some behaviors will simply stop; some will *not*. When it does *not*, the following L-E-A-S-T method of progressive discipline is suggested:

- *Leave it alone* — Notice whether the behavior goes away; it could be an example of an isolated occurrence.

- *Eye contact* — Look at the student long enough to make eye contact, which can be very effective. Eye contact lets the individual know that *I see what you are doing,* and the implied *now stop it* goes along with it.

- *Action* — Take action when the behavior continues. The type of action depends on the problem itself. The action is usually a comment stressing the importance of being attentive in class or directing a question to the problem student. Call on the individual and ask a question about the topic when the nonverbal cue was *not* enough to stop the behavior. In this subtle manner, instructors can communicate the knowledge that they are aware of how students are behaving.

- *Stop the class* — Stop the class and discuss the problem with the student because at this point the student is interrupting the class too often. Taking a break is the most tactful way of stopping a class.

- *Terminate the student* — Expel the student from the class when the discussion of the problem was *not* effective. The appropriate measures and documentation should be taken to issue a disciplinary action.

When students do *not* cooperate, instructors should take the appropriate measures to correct the problem. An advantage of being in a paramilitary organization such as the law enforcement, fire, and rescue services is that the instructor generally has the authority of an officer in the management of the classroom. Hopefully, this authority does *not* need to be used to maintain control of the classroom.

Summary

The student's learning experience is the primary concern of fire and emergency services instructors. That experience will provide the student with the knowledge necessary for a safe and productive career. Understanding various student characteristics, recognizing that students are individuals, and applying the tools necessary to manage all types of student behavior are essential to instructors.

Instructors should expand upon the information provided in this chapter by seeking additional information on adult students and contacting experts in the field. Additional resources provided by the human resources department or other agencies should be developed when necessary. Instructors should always remember that the student is the key element in the educational experience. Without the student, learning cannot occur.

Chapter 9

Preparation for Instruction

After reading this chapter, students will be able to —

1. Define a lesson plan.

2. Describe components of a lesson plan.

3. Distinguish among the steps in the four-step method of instruction.

4. Identify accurate statements about preparing to teach.

5. Discuss methods of ensuring course continuity.

6. Discuss methods of ensuring course consistency.

7. Identify types of classroom seating arrangements.

8. Identify accurate statements about controlling the indoor learning environment.

9. List considerations to address during the inspection and planning processes for outside instruction.

Chapter Contents

Lesson Plans
Definition
Components
Four-Step Method of Instruction

Instructor Preparation
Attitude for Learning
Advance Organization
Session Preparation
Session Logistics

Course Continuity and Consistency
Continuity
Consistency

Physical Setting
Classroom Environment
Outside Environment

Summary

Chapter 9
Preparation for Instruction

Most instructors cannot just appear in the classroom and begin teaching; neither can students just arrive for a class and begin learning. Both must prepare for the experience; both must have expectations and anticipations of what each wants to accomplish and how to accomplish it. Effective instructors take extensive preparatory steps to ensure that the learning experience is worthwhile, relevant, and interesting.

Taking time to properly prepare before the presentation will result in a learning experience that motivates students to think, question, and become involved in the learning experience. Once classes begin, instructors must prepare students for the learning experience.

This chapter discusses many important aspects of instructional preparation, including the following topics:

- *Lesson plans* — Understanding lesson plan components and importance of the four-step method of instruction used in lesson plan development

- *Instructor preparation* — Preparing to teach and preparing students to learn

- *Course continuity and consistency* — Maintaining *continuity* (ties each individual lesson plan together) and *consistency* (presents information that conforms to other information, standards, and accepted practices)

- *Physical setting* — Considering the learning environment (seating, lighting, climate, noise, learning aids, and whether the learning environment is inside or outside)

Instructor Tip: Observe Other Instructors

When teaching for the first time or before teaching a new class or topic, observe the methods of several other instructors. Watch how others manage student groups, present information, and demonstrate skills. Look for advantages and disadvantages of their presentation methods.

Think about which methods accomplish learning objectives and which methods appear to create problems and cause disruptions in learning and lesson organization. Draw conclusions about what methods seem to work best, and adapt those until you have the experience and confidence to develop your own special methods.

Lesson Plans

Basic to all teaching is the lesson plan, which is essentially a road map that guides the instructor through the topic. Lesson plans are generally developed by a Level II Instructor or purchased as part of an existing curriculum. However, all instructors must be familiar with the basic components of the lesson plan in order to use and alter it when necessary. A detailed discussion of lesson plan development is included in Chapter 14, Lesson Plan Development.

Planning what and how much of a topic will be taught is a prelude to instruction. Planning a lesson helps instructors to carefully think about and write what is to be taught and plan strategies for teaching. Most instructors cannot just walk into a classroom and begin teaching without some plan as to what they will do, where they will go with the information, and how they will get there. Teaching without a plan gives no guarantee that course objectives will be met or students will actually learn what is required by the course outcomes or NFPA job performance requirements (JPRs).

Using a lesson plan does *not* ensure fulfillment of objectives either, but it increases the odds of success. Without planning the lesson ahead of time, instructors may find that they are lacking important support equipment or supplemental materials, which means that they cannot teach or demonstrate information. The result for both instructors and students is that time is wasted because appropriate teaching and learning could *not* take place. This section defines the term *lesson plan,* provides a general overview of its main components, and describes the four-step method of instruction.

Definition

A *lesson plan* is an instructional device or tool that establishes the steps that an instructor will take to complete the various objectives and ultimate goal of the course. It states the information and skills that will be covered and time, space, equipment, supplies, and personnel required. A lesson plan clearly states what an instructor will accomplish with students during a particular lesson. It is a step-by-step guide for any type of presentation.

A lesson plan states all the steps and methods necessary for presenting the required knowledge or skills in the proper sequence. It also lists the appropriate support materials and indicates when they will be used. Instructors may use planning or objective pages to assist in lesson plan development. See **Figures 9.1 a (right) and b (p. 192)**. The lesson plan provides instructors with a teaching purpose and fulfills other important purposes and benefits as well.

Components

All instructors should be familiar with the components of a lesson plan. However, the specific components and the order they are listed in may vary depending on the format used by the local jurisdiction. The instructor should note also that lesson plans for cognitive topics differ slightly from lesson plans used for psychomotor topics. In the most basic format, lesson plans consist of the following components:

- ***Job or topic*** — Short descriptive title of the information covered. The title briefly describes or gives an indication of the lesson content. Topic titles are usually taken directly from the course outline.

- ***Time frame*** — Estimated *time* it takes to teach the lesson. Time frames may be set for each lesson objective so that the instructor has a better idea of how to set the pace of the lesson.

- ***Level of instruction*** — Desired learning *level* that students will reach by the end of the lesson, which may be based on NFPA JPRs or academically established taxonomy related to the appropriate learning domain.

- ***Learning objectives*** — Descriptions of the minimum acceptable *behaviors* that students must display by the end of an instructional period.

- ***Resources/materials needed*** — List of all items (including quantity) needed to teach the number of students in the course. This section of the lesson also includes any preparation, planning, or activities that an instructor needs to complete before delivering the lesson such as the following:

  — Determine the appropriate training site and seating arrangement.

  — Arrange for audiovisual training aids, props, and devices.

  — Reproduce handouts.

  — Acquire tools, apparatus, and other equipment.

  — Contact guest speakers.

  — List lesson *resources*. Include information on the following items:

    ○ Names of instructors or other personnel qualified to assist or provide logistical support

    ○ Textbooks and other instructional materials

    ○ Special equipment needs

  — Determine specific instructional methods and learning activities required to meet objectives.

Fire and Emergency Services Instructor
Lesson 2—Safety and the Training Function

Planning Page

PREPARATION

Lesson Overview
This lesson addresses the topic of safety as it relates to the training function. The instructor has a vital role in ensuring safety during training activities and in promoting safety in all activities. This lesson covers the instructor's role in safety, accident prevention and management, and resources for safety issues.

Skill Sheets/Assignment Sheets
This lesson does not have any corresponding skill or assignment sheets.

Equipment and Materials
Computer
Data Projector/screen

Audiovisual Aids
Lesson 2 PowerPoint® Presentation

Evaluation
Lesson 2 Quiz
Lesson 2 Written Test

REFERENCES

Fire and Emergency Services Instructor, 7th Ed. Stillwater, Oklahoma: IFSTA/Fire Protection Publications, 2005.

NFPA 1041 Standard for Fire Service Instructor Professional Qualifications, Quincy, Massachusetts: National Fire Protection Association, 2002.

Figure 9.1a Planning page example based on the one developed for Chapter 2, Safety and the Training Function.

— Select topic-specific training locations or change training locations to meet the requirements of the topic being taught.

- *Prerequisites* — List of information, skills, or previous requirements that students must have completed or mastered *before* entering this course or starting this lesson. *Differences:*

— *Cognitive lesson plan:* Prerequisites for the current lesson may have been addressed in a previous lesson The instructor may give out-of-class assignments for students to complete in order to be ready for this lesson.

— *Psychomotor lesson plan:* Prerequisites are essential for any skills-based training, especially training that involves live-fire training evolutions. For instance, students must be qualified in the use of self-contained breathing apparatus (SCBA) before any live-fire training.

Fire and Emergency Services Instructor
Lesson 2—Safety and the Training Function

Objectives

Course After completing this course, the student will be able to certify as an Instructor I, II, or III (depending upon the course taken) per the following:

NFPA 1041 Standard for Fire Service Instructor Professional Qualifications, 2002 Edition

Lesson After completing this lesson, the student will achieve an acceptable score, as defined by the student's training organization, on the Written Test.

Specific After completing this lesson, students will be able to—

1. Define accident.
2. List places where injuries and fatalities can occur.
3. List recommendations for casualty prevention. *[NFPA 1041: 5.4.3]*
4. List responsibilities of an organization's administration in preventing casualties. *[NFPA 1041: 5.4.3]*
5. List methods by which jurisdictions can reduce risk. *[NFPA 1041: 5.4.3]*
6. List areas in which the instructor has a role in creating and ensuring a safe work environment. *[NFPA 1041: 4.4.2, 4.4.5]*
7. Identify facts about the instructor's role in providing a safe training environment. *[NFPA 1041: 4.4.5, 5.4.3]*
8. List conditions under which the instructor may be responsible for teaching safety-related topics. *[NFPA 1041: 5.4.3]*
9. Identify facts about the instructor fulfilling the duties of the incident safety officer (ISO). *[NFPA 1041: 5.4.3]*
10. Identify facts about providing students with a positive, proactive safety role model.
11. List information students need to know in case of an accident.
12. Identify facts about accident prevention and management. *[NFPA 1041: 5.4.3]*
13. List the factors that contribute to accidents.
14. Identify the purposes of an accident investigation.
15. Describe the instructor's role in accident investigation.
16. Identify facts about accident analyses and mitigation. *[NFPA 1041: 4.4.2]*
17. Identify responsibilities of public and private agencies and organizations in the area of safety. *[NFPA 1041: 5.4.3]*

Figure 9.1b Objectives page example based on the one developed for Chapter 2, Safety and the Training Function.

- **References** — List of specific *references* and *resources* (textbooks and other instructional materials) on the lesson plan along with page numbers to refer to and review. References allow instructors to develop depth in the subject matter. *Differences:*

  — *Cognitive lesson plan:* Reference citations enable the instructor to qualify or verify information in case students ask unusual questions, question sources, or desire further information.

  — *Psychomotor lesson plan:* References can be especially important when instruction takes place at a remote training site.

- **Lesson summary** — Restatement or reemphasis of the key points (sometimes referred to as *conclusion*) of the lesson to clarify uncertainties, prevent misconceptions, increase learning, and improve retention. *Differences:*

  — *Cognitive lesson plan:* The lesson summary is usually included in the cognitive format.

  — *Psychomotor lesson plan:* The lesson summary may *not* always be included as a component in the psychomotor format.

- **Assignments** — Readings, practice, research, or other outside-of-class requirements for students. *Differences:*

  — *Cognitive lesson plan:* The use of assignments is determined by the lesson topic and needs of students.

  — *Psychomotor lesson plan:* Assignments consist of additional practice outside of class by students. Repeated and frequent practice ensures that students retain the skills and use them properly during emergency situations.

- **Lesson outline** — Summary of the information to be taught. It may be arranged into the four-step instructional method that is described in the following section.

- **Evaluations** — Type of evaluation instrument the instructor will use to determine whether students have met lesson objectives.

Four-Step Method of Instruction

One accepted instructional model for developing an effective lesson plan consists of four steps: preparation, presentation, application, and evaluation (**Figure 9.2, p. 194**). Development of a lesson plan includes the creation of the information or activities that will accomplish the requirements of each of these steps.

To assist the instructor candidate in learning the four-step method of instruction, this chapter and the following four chapters discusses each of the steps. This chapter focuses on instructor preparation. Student preparation is included in the chapters on presentation (Chapter 10, Instructional Delivery, and Chapter 11, Audiovisual Technology) and application (Chapter 12, Structured Exercises, Demonstrations, and Practical Training Evolutions).

The application step presents the use of structured exercises, demonstrations, and practical training evolutions as a means for reinforcing psychomotor skills. Finally, the evaluation step presents the student evaluation and testing instruments that the instructor is required to use (see Chapter 13, Student Progress Evaluation and Testing). Brief definitions and descriptions are in the sections that follow.

Preparation

The preparation step consists of two parts: *Preparing* the instructor to teach and *preparing* students to learn. Preparing students to learn (preparation) is the first formal part of the four steps of instruction. The instructor establishes lesson relevancy to the job by performing the following actions:

- Introduce the topic.
- Gain the students' attention.
- State the learning objectives.
- Motivate students by stating the reason the information is important to each of them and relating it to an aspect of their jobs.
- Prepare students to listen for key points by briefly stating the main topics that will be presented.

A useful acronym used to establish the relevance of the topic to students' jobs, safety, or needs is *ACID:* Attention, Curiosity, Interest, and Desire.

Four-Step Method of Instruction

Step 1 Preparation

Purpose
To prepare the instructor to teach and students to learn:

To prepare the instructor to teach:

1. Evaluate the audience.
2. Research topic and gather references and learning materials.
3. Create a lesson plan.
4. Create a physical learning environment.

To prepare students to learn:

1. Prepare the mind of students by creating:
   - Attention
   - Curiosity
   - Interest
   - Desire
2. Create a foundation for learning: Begin associating students' experiences with the lesson's contents.

How to Accomplish
Tested methods for preparing students to learn:

1. Generate curiosity by asking rhetorical questions or questions that cause students to relate personal experiences to the topic.
2. Create attention by telling a personal experience, analogy, or topic-related story.
3. Generate desire by citing the personal benefits associated with mastering the knowledge and skills.
4. Create interest by presenting new concepts, procedures, or equipment.
5. Create continuity by reviewing previous lessons.
6. Determine student knowledge by conducting diagnostic quizzes or pretests.

Step 2 Presentation

Purpose
To communicate content developed to change the behavior of students:

1. Present knowledge, new skills, concepts, or procedures to students.
2. Instruct, motivate, and educate students.

How to Accomplish
Tested methods for presenting knowledge and skills:

1. Select the appropriate presentation style for the audience, subject, and desired outcome.
2. Present lectures, demonstrations, and activities.
3. Use appropriate visual aids and props.
4. Explain procedures.
5. Emphasize key points.
6. Explain concepts, philosophies, principles, and implications.
7. Proceed from known to unknown and simple to complex.
8. Use textbooks and other reference materials.
9. Apply active learning principles.
10. Summarize key points and concepts at the end of the presentation.
11. Require students to take notes.

Step 3 Application

Purpose
To provide the opportunity for students to apply theory, critical thinking, critical decision-making, or psychomotor skills to practical situations:

1. Demonstrate skills-based knowledge through appropriate means.
2. Provide students with the opportunity to perform under supervision.
3. Involve students actively in the learning process.
4. Provide the opportunity to practice and master critical skills in a nonemergency learning environment.

How to Accomplish
Creative, organized, and tested methods for presenting and practicing practical skills:

1. Have students perform the task or activity under supervision.
2. Observe performances closely.
3. Check and correct errors.
4. Instill correct habits in students.
5. Check key points and safety points.
6. Develop discussions based on theory, decision-making, or skills application.
7. Conduct periodic skills tests.
8. Assign projects and activities.
9. Assign problems for students to resolve.

Step 4 Evaluation

Purpose
To evaluate the learning process:

1. Evaluate student understanding.
2. Evaluate teaching effectiveness.

How to Accomplish
Tested methods for evaluating the learning process:

1. Have students perform tasks unassisted.
2. Conduct performance tests.
3. Ask prepared questions.
4. Have students demonstrate and explain tasks.
5. Have students observe and critique other student performances.
6. Conduct final examinations.
7. Evaluate notebooks, projects, assignments, and activities.
8. Have students complete course and instructor evaluation forms.
9. Have instructors complete course evaluation forms.

Figure 9.2 The four-step method of instruction can be used as a basis for the lesson plan and includes the critical elements of preparation, presentation, application, and evaluation.

Successful instructors will develop introductory material that can generate one or more of the following traits in students:

- **Attention** — Attract students' attention by telling a brief story or analogy that relates to the topic. If the topic permits, a humorous story can gain attention as well as put the audience at ease.

- **Curiosity** — Arouse students' interest by asking a rhetorical question related to the topic. The question does *not* require an answer from the audience but is intended to make them think about possible answers.

- **Interest** — Create interest by describing the topic as something new or innovative. Showing a new tool or piece of equipment that students will be learning to use can generate interest.

- **Desire** — Stimulate students to want to learn because it will help them fulfill a personal need such as gaining a promotion or acquiring a needed skill **(Figure 9.3)**.

Each of these actions should meet the goal of creating a base on which to make the presentation. By relating the topic to previously learned information or past student experiences, instructors can show why the topic is important and how it will benefit students. Essentially, the preparation step is intended to motivate students to learn.

Figure 9.3 Enthusiasm is an effective tool that an instructor can use to create a desire in students to learn. *Courtesy of Central Florida Fire Academy.*

Presentation

In the second step (presentation), the instructor *presents* the information to be discussed using an orderly, sequential outline. *Presentation* can be combined with the next and most important step, *application*. The following items are listed with each key point on the outline:

- Teaching methods
- Learning activities
- Demonstrations and practices
- Instructional support materials such as audio-visuals, worksheets, and handouts to present the information to students and involve them in learning
- Summaries of key points and information given throughout the lesson plan and at the end of the lesson

Application

The third of the four steps of instruction (application) is where the instructor *provides opportunities* for learning through activities, exercises, discussions, work groups, skill practices, practical training evolutions, and similar learning activities. The purpose of the application step is to reinforce the student's learning. Most learning takes place during the application step, making this step critically important.

Application can be combined with presentation so that students can *apply* the *presented* information through activities that require thinking (the *psycho* part of *psychomotor*) to manipulative or skill (the *motor* part of *psychomotor*) activities. Typically, application is related to performing the operations or steps of a task, but *skills* do *not* refer solely to activity steps of using equipment. Students may demonstrate other skills such as the following:

- Give a presentation.
- Lead a group discussion or brainstorming session.
- Apply research methods.
- Demonstrate outlining and writing techniques.

Evaluation

The fourth step of instruction (evaluation) occurs when students demonstrate how much they have learned through a written, oral, or practical examination or test. In general, written tests are used to *evaluate cognitive* information; practical tests are used to *evaluate skill* ability **(Figure 9.4)**. Other types of tests may be used to evaluate other learning areas (see Chapter 16, Student Testing Instruments). The purpose of evaluation is to determine whether students achieved the lesson objectives or course outcomes.

Figure 9.4 The evaluation step permits instructors to determine how much students have learned and how effective the teaching process has been. *Courtesy of Louisiana State University, Fire and Emergency Training Institute (FETI)*

Instructor Preparation

Key to a successful teaching experience for instructors is *preparation*. Preparation time spent *outside* class is crucial to instructor accomplishments *inside* class. If instructors do *not* prepare, then class time can be wasted. Once instructors are familiar with the lesson plan components, then preparation for teaching can begin. To be prepared to teach, instructors must establish a learning attitude, organize the learning materials, schedule training sessions, prepare for the class session, and ensure that all logistical needs are met **(Figure 9.5)**.

Step 1 Preparation	
Purpose To prepare the instructor to teach and students to learn:	**How to Accomplish** Tested methods for preparing students to learn:
To prepare the instructor to teach:	1. Generate curiosity by asking rhetorical questions or questions that cause students to relate personal experiences to the topic.
1. Evaluate the audience.	
2. Research topic and gather references and learning materials.	2. Create attention by telling a personal experience, analogy, or topic-related story.
3. Create a lesson plan.	
4. Create a physical learning environment.	3. Generate desire by citing the personal benefits associated with mastering the knowledge and skills.
To prepare students to learn:	4. Create interest by presenting new concepts, procedures, or equipment.
1. Prepare the mind of students by creating: • Attention • Curiosity • Interest • Desire	5. Create continuity by reviewing previous lessons.
2. Create a foundation for learning: Begin associating students' experiences with the lesson's contents.	6. Determine student knowledge by conducting diagnostic quizzes or pretests.

Figure 9.5 The preparation step consists of two parts: instructor preparation and student preparation.

Attitude for Learning

To be effective, the instructor is responsible for establishing an atmosphere for learning in the classroom. Primary to the atmosphere of learning is the *enthusiasm* of both the instructor and students. Instructor actions and the apparent interest in the presentation have a great effect on establishing a productive learning atmosphere. The amount of enthusiasm projected by an instructor is directly related to the level of enthusiasm and interest exhibited by students.

One of the challenges of teaching is for instructors to maintain a positive level of enthusiasm in both themselves and their students. Students recognize enthusiasm and are affected by it because it is contagious. They use this enthusiasm to learn.

Some instructors confuse enthusiasm with *theatrics*. The job of an instructor is to convey new ideas, facts, and procedures, *not* to entertain. Research into classroom presentations indicates that a presentation that is very entertaining is *not* always very informative. There is no distinct line between being entertaining to maintain interest and being informative to impart knowledge.

The use of humor and entertaining stories can be effective when presenting information; however, they must be used appropriately and in moderation. There are no strict guidelines or rules that can be applied when using an entertaining approach to presentations.

Lacking specific formulas and theories, it is best for new instructors to carefully follow the lesson plans, take a *strictly business* approach at first, and then expand teaching techniques through practice and the use of various teaching methods and learning activities. The primary role of the Level I Instructor is to teach from a prepared lesson plan.

The instructor must teach so that learning takes place, *not* to perform so that amusement takes place. New instructors can also benefit from observing other instructors and teachers to determine how they maintain enthusiasm and use humor with various topics.

Advance Organization

Being organized is another attribute that contributes to the success of the new fire and emergency services instructor. Being organized can result in a variety of benefits such as the following:

- Increased instructor credibility
- Improved efficiency of classroom presentation
- More effective use of time, talent, and materials
- Reduced stress on the instructor

Instructor organization begins with the physical organization of the instructor's office or work area as well as the training division's resources and training aids storage. Files, lesson plans, handouts, report forms, and ancillaries (training aids) should be neatly stored and easily accessed. Guidelines for the filing and storage of these materials may be formalized in the division's standard operating procedures or guidelines (SOPs or SOGs).

The new instructor should review these procedures or guidelines to determine the appropriate methods. When *no* procedures or guidelines ex-

ist, the instructor should research organizational methods found in books, magazines, and on the Internet. Personal organization (at home, in the garage, and in officer spaces) has been a popular topic for many years, and these sources can provide many useful tips and suggestions.

The next step in being organized occurs when the instructor is assigned a topic to teach. At this point, the instructor should perform the following tasks:

- Review the lesson plan for the specific topic.
- Determine the audience size and composition.
- Review the learning objectives.
- Determine the required activities.
- Determine the time required to provide the instruction, perform the activities, and evaluate student performance.
- Locate and acquire the necessary resources and materials.
- Prepare the instructional area.
- Ensure that all equipment operates properly.
- Schedule outside speakers.

The final step to being well organized involves having an organized presentation. The instructor must be familiar with the topic, familiar with the operation of all training aids, and able to make logical, smooth transitions between sections of the material. For the new instructor, the best way to present an organized presentation is to practice the presentation.

Making a practice presentation helps the instructor recognize any points where adjustments need to be made. It also helps to build personal confidence and create enthusiasm for the topic. The best approach is to present the lesson to other instructors and ask them to provide suggestions and observations.

Session Preparation

A new instructor may be required to teach a topic for the first time. Even a veteran instructor may be required to develop a presentation on a new topic. To prepare for a new lesson, instructors must not only know *what* topic is to be taught but must also know *about* the topic to be taught. Knowing about the topic means that the instructor understands and has a working knowledge of the topic and is able to perform the skills associated with the topic.

Assuming that an instructor is capable of teaching a topic when that is *not* the case can result in an embarrassing and potentially disastrous learning experience. However, circumstances may arise when qualified instructors find themselves unprepared. Instructors should never acknowledge that they are unprepared to teach a topic. Such a statement destroys student confidence, instructor credibility, and any opportunity to motivate students.

At the same time, an instructor who is unqualified to teach a topic should *not* attempt to teach it. An unqualified instructor not only risks the safety of the students but also runs the risk of legal liability for providing possibly incorrect or inaccurate information.

Class preparation follows the same general steps previously discussed in the Advance Organization section. The most important preparation steps include the following:

- ***Read the lesson objectives*** — Become familiar with what the objectives require students to know and perform.

- ***Review the lesson plan*** — Use an organization's standard lesson guide to determine what material must be addressed, what time frame is required, and what assistance, materials, and equipment are needed.

- ***Check what equipment is needed*** — Be familiar with training aid materials and how to operate various pieces of equipment and use them for student activities **(Figure 9.6)**.

- ***Determine what skills must be taught*** — Practice the skill steps or at least review the steps mentally by looking at pictures, equipment, or handouts. Any instructor who lacks recent experience or practice in a skill must take time to review it or determine a method of presenting it so that the skill is understandable to students. Ideally, the instructor presents a skill to a mastery level.

- ***Review required lesson audiovisuals*** — Preview videotapes or slides to prepare for engaging students in related discussions and applications.

Figure 9.6 Instructors must be familiar with the props, equipment, and audiovisual training aids that they will be expected to use.

This step means being familiar with the lesson plan and knowing when and how audiovisuals are used.

- *Check documentation requirements* — Check on, arrange for, and have available and ready all handouts, rosters, and other reports and records before class begins.

Periodically, it may be necessary for an instructor to teach a class on short notice. For an experienced and well-organized instructor, this is generally *not* a problem. A new instructor, however, may feel the stress of having to adapt to a situation rapidly. The replacement instructor must make every effort to quickly prepare and deliver a lesson that makes the time in class worthwhile. The replacement instructor should attempt to apply the preparation steps mentioned before beginning the class.

Instructors who are put in the position of walking into the classroom with little opportunity for preparation should make the class session a *discovery zone* where everyone learns something. This situation may mean using each learning objective as an overview point and proceeding from there.

It may mean that the group learns or reviews the basic steps on whatever equipment or materials are available such as getting sections of rope and practicing knots or obtaining some mannequins and practicing cardiopulmonary resuscitation (CPR). The use of an appropriate audiovisual at the beginning of the session also gives the instructor time to further prepare for the session.

As instructors gain experience in a subject in a familiar course, the time it takes to prepare decreases. In the beginning, it is not unusual to spend 1 to 3 hours of preparation time for every hour of delivery time. For some courses, preparation time can extend to more hours or even days of scheduling, coordinating, and confirming that class and teaching needs are met.

Session Logistics

The term *logistics* as used in the fire and emergency services profession means *the procurement, distribution, maintenance, and replacement of material and personnel*. Fire and emergency services organizations usually have a division or individual who manages the logistics by providing the materials

Case Study: Instructor Preparation

You are preparing to teach your first class as a new instructor. Much of your preparation time is spent in reviewing details of the topic so that you can answer the questions that class members may have. You also want to prepare some handout materials that will help students study and learn the information and practice the skills. Answer the following questions:

1. What are some of *your* resources? Who can you ask or talk to about ideas, where to get materials, and what study aids are appropriate and effective for the type of class you are teaching?

2. What support tools, application components, and handouts would you develop for your first class? What information do you think would be appropriate for students to have so they can master the particular skills or learn the information more easily?

3. What is your organization's policy on out-of-class assignments? When they are not mandatory, do you have time in the course to cover all areas adequately? How else can you have the class master skills? When out-of-class assignments are required or expected, which ones would you assign to help students master skills?

and equipment required to meet the mission of the organization and its various divisions. Within the training division, each instructor is usually responsible for acquiring the logistical support required by the lesson plan.

Logistics can consume much of the time required for class preparation (**Figure 9.7, p. 200**). This situation is especially true with classes that have a lot of practical work like basic fire, rescue, and emergency medical technician (EMT) training courses along with law enforcement and highway safety training courses.

Logistics may also consume class time. The completion of some skills requires cleaning certain areas or restocking, refilling, or replacing certain items. The organization or the type of lesson plan may require that students perform such duties as the following:

Figure 9.7 Instructors must ensure that sufficient quantities of supplies are available when preparing to teach a class.

- Clean a spill.
- Return the classroom to order.
- Park vehicles in designated locations.
- Clean mannequins.
- Refill SCBA cylinders.
- Repack fire hose.
- Restock kits with supplies.
- Recharge battery-operated equipment.

Instructors must calculate the time it takes to perform these duties. Some duties are performed on class time as part of the required skills training; some duties are performed after class time so that the next class can begin promptly. Logistical needs may require several hours of preparation and restoration for classes with high equipment needs such as live-fire training, EMT training, or driver training for groups of 25 to 30 students.

For many instructors, logistics means *making arrangements* to have the materials and support they need to deliver training. The instructor is responsible for ensuring that all materials and equipment needed are determined and arranged for before the beginning of class. Organized instructors will have a checklist of necessary materials and equipment to ensure that nothing is forgotten. This list can be retained as part of the lesson-plan documentation used for future class sessions.

For those instructors who work in a training facility, there may be staff members to assist with maintenance, inventory control, and scheduling of equipment. The final responsibility always rests with the instructor who must take the time to ask for assistance, follow procedures when making requests or reservations, and follow up on those requests. Arriving early to get or assemble equipment and materials gives an instructor the opportunity to perform the following steps:

Step 1: Check for missing items.

Step 2: Review operations.

Step 3: Arrange room layout.

Step 4: Find replacements or make repairs.

Step 5: Revert to a *contingency plan* (also known as *Plan B*). Instructors must always have at least one contingency plan per lesson.

Course Continuity and Consistency

As instructors prepare each lesson, they must ensure that they maintain continuity and consistency throughout the course or curriculum. *Continuity* refers to the flow of information without interruption or change; *consistency* means that the information is not contradictory and conforms to the principles that the course is attempting to teach.

Continuity is generally present in professionally developed curriculums and should be present in all locally developed lesson plans and curriculums. However, continuity can be disrupted. Instructors should anticipate and prepare for all possible contingencies.

Fire and emergency services training courses contain segments that vary in length of time, lasting from only several hours to several weeks or months. Recruit or entry-level training courses may last from less than 2 to over 30 weeks, while a specialty course such as hazardous materials awareness may only require 40 hours or less of training (in some jurisdictions, awareness courses may only be 8 or 24 hours in length).

Some topics may be so specialized that they require external instructors provided by the state/ provincial, regional, or national training academy to teach a portion of the course. A challenge for the lead or primary instructor is to maintain some form of continuity and consistency within the course so that students can reasonably follow it.

Instructors may find it difficult to maintain continuity and even consistency in courses with the following or similar challenges:

- Multiple instructors
- Multiple activities
- Various student needs
- Potential schedule conflicts and changes
- Equipment failures

For these reasons, many courses include rules, procedures, and expectations for both instructors and students that provide a foundation to rely on and return to when even normal and expected class proceedings are disrupted.

Continuity

Continuity ensures that the information presented flows in a logical and understandable stream. Many factors can affect course continuity, but instructors can take steps to reduce their effects. Most of the steps can be included in the processes of session scheduling, preparation, and logistics. Instructors should always anticipate problems and prepare contingency plans for potential events such as the following:

- Instructor changes
- Weather variations
- Equipment and material variations
- Instructional resource variations
- Appropriate testing location variations
- Differences in learning styles

Instructor Changes

There are times when an instructor is *not* available to teach a scheduled class. Ideally, that instructor or instructor's supervisor contacts someone familiar with and experienced in teaching the lesson. Every time a different instructor teaches, it causes some amount of discontinuity in the class.

Another instance that causes discontinuity occurs when additional instructors must assist the lead course instructor in teaching a skills session. All instructors have their own personal perceptions, views, beliefs, and methods of teaching. It is possible that their ideas and methods may be different from those of the lead course instructor. The lead course instructor can maintain continuity by following these suggestions:

- ***Know fellow instructors*** — One of the many benefits of in-service training, meetings, conferences, and seminars is that instructors meet, exchange ideas, and make assessments of each other. If an instructor must call on another to substitute or assist in teaching a class, it will be someone whom the instructor knows and trusts, who has similar ideas and methods, and who has similar or better experience.

- ***Prepare the students*** — Ideal situations do *not* always occur, and the desired instructor substitute or assistant may *not* be available. Students become dependent on and familiar with the methods, attitudes, and personalities of *their* instructors and may *not* relate as well to a different one. Prepare students for different instructors in the following ways:

  — Give students some background on the substitute's experiences, knowledge, and teaching methods.

  — Introduce the substitute to the class when the person arrives.

  — Outline to the students, in front of the substitute, what the lesson plan is so that both students and the substitute know what is expected.

  — Prepare the supervisor or officer to provide the same information and introduction when it is not possible for the regular instructor to be present when the substitute arrives.

- ***Meet with substitute instructors or assistants to prepare for the class*** — Every instructor involved in teaching a class must prepare for it. The lead course instructor who arranges for a substitute or for assistants should meet with the substitute or assistants and perform the following activities **(Figure 9.8, p. 202):**

  — Outline the learning objectives and what must be accomplished in the lesson.

  — Assign specific duties or skills.

  — Show and orient each person to the teaching area or classroom.

Figure 9.8 To ensure consistency, substitute instructors must meet with the lead course instructor before the course starts. This time is an opportunity to review teaching methods, lesson plans, and course outcomes. *Courtesy of Iowa Fire Service Training Bureau.*

— Provide directions or assistance in locating and assembling equipment.

— Coordinate rest break and cleanup times.

— Perform any other duties needed to have a successful lesson.

Practicing the described actions regularly also has the benefit of providing continuity in instructor preparation and delivery. Classes run more smoothly, instructors perform more effectively, and students have the continuity they need to participate successfully in the learning process.

Weather Variations

Climate changes can have an adverse effect on training activities and schedules. Courses that are scheduled during the times of year when inclement weather is possible must have some flexibility built into them. Continuity may be challenged as instructors attempt to teach the same skills during the summer heat and winter cold. They must be able to adapt the skills to the existing weather while still remaining faithful to the specific skill requirements.

There has always been some debate on whether instructors should teach certain practical sessions in the extremes of hot, cold, wind, rain, or snow. One side of the issue declares that the reality is that *we fight fires and go on emergency medical services (EMS) calls in this weather, so why not train in this weather?*

The other side of the issue rebuts with the argument, *learning can't take place if the weather causes discomfort, concern, distraction, or safety hazards.* Also, emergency responses are necessary despite inclement conditions, whereas training activities are *not* emergencies. Proceeding with training in potentially hazardous conditions can expose students to unsafe conditions and the instructor and the organization to needless liability.

Both sides of the issue have merit, but instructors should *not* expect their students to learn skills effectively in any extreme weather conditions. When teaching psychomotor skills, the learning environment should *not* distract students from attending to the objectives of the lesson.

If instructors decide to schedule training during *realistic* weather conditions, then personnel safety must be taken into consideration. Students must be provided with the appropriate equipment, rehabilitation, and safety instruction when performing training during adverse environmental conditions.

Instructors should be aware that in some jurisdictions and situations there might be specific policies or labor/management contract provisions regarding weather conditions and training. In Florida, for instance, labor/management contracts have heat index provisions that limit training to days that have a heat index less than 100°F (38°C).

Equipment and Material Variations

The Session Logistics section discussed the importance of having equipment and materials available for classes. When scheduling equipment, an important factor in maintaining the continuity of the course is using the same type of equipment in the learning sessions that is used in the testing session and on the job.

When a group is to be tested on tying knots using a certain type and size of rope, for example, students should also practice tying knots with that type and size of rope. When students use a certain type of SCBA on the job, they should also be trained on the same or generically similar equipment (**Figure 9.9**). This procedure is not only fair, but it also makes testing valid and reliable (see Chapter 16, Student Testing Instruments).

Figure 9.9 Test validity and reliability depend on using equipment in testing that is the same as that used in training and at emergency incidents. *Courtesy of Maryland Fire and Rescue Institute (MFRI).*

Instructional Resource Variations

Instructional resources used in training include the information, product data, skills sheets, and references required to meet the lesson plan requirements. Continuity is maintained when this information is available to all course instructors when they are planning their course presentations.

As changes occur in the information or types of equipment that are used by the organization, instructors must adjust or update their references. Outdated information or procedures result in a loss of instructor credibility and can contribute to unsafe and inefficient practices.

Appropriate Testing Location Variations

When a course requires testing students on skills normally performed in particular places under certain conditions, students need to practice the skills in the same place under generically similar conditions during the training course. Ideally, testing conditions are similar to learning conditions, which are similar to job conditions. All should meet the requirements of the learning objectives, which are based on the job or task analysis. It is important for instructors to arrange for testing areas or facilities that are familiar to students.

Familiarity with the testing area also contributes to comfort. Adequate comfort levels enable students to demonstrate what they know and not be distracted by unfamiliar terrains, facilities, or environments. Organizations that have established valid and reliable testing policies and procedures understand the importance of *testing location* to training participants.

It is the responsibility of instructors to ensure that the places where the course will be taught and tested are available and that authorization is received from responsible persons. Continuity exists when the practice site is the same or similar to the test site.

Differences in Learning Styles

A barrier caused by differences in learning styles can create a challenge to instructors who are attempting to maintain course continuity. Ideally, instructors adapt lessons that include a variety of teaching methodologies so that all types of students are exposed to the material in a manner that enables them to learn through their preferred learning styles. Within every group of students, there are those who have the following characteristics:

- Those who are ready to learn
- Those who are *not* ready to learn

- Those who learn readily and easily
- Those who find it difficult to learn
- Those who learn quickly and can show others
- Those who need more time to learn the material or skill and need to be shown the steps several times

Instructors must adapt lessons with various activities and formats so that every student can gain the appropriate knowledge and skill and meet the lesson objectives. Many students do *not* know that there is more than one way to learn, and they may *not* learn successfully by using the only way they know. By using a variety of teaching methods, instructors expose students to different and possibly more successful ways of learning.

In the past, traditional teaching styles used by many training organizations depended upon a lecture-style format to provide cognitive information. Asking questions or using short written quizzes was generally used to check student understanding of the lectures or reading assignments. Students were expected to listen carefully to the instructor and take notes.

Over time, instructors began to add visual aids such as transparencies, slides, and videos. With visual aids, students are able to see an example of what is being said and can probably remember more of the information; but still, not everyone learns that way. Demonstration and skill-practice classes are best for those individuals who learn by doing; but again, not everyone learns that way.

In addition to the situations described in the preceding paragraphs, there are also occasions when the abilities of students do *not* match the target audience of the material to be presented. Students may be either ahead of the material or not ready for it. Instructors should begin by determining the gap between student abilities and the course material.

To maintain continuity, an instructor has to be flexible and adapt changes within the structure of the course based on the individual needs of students. By involving students in the process, the instructor can still ensure continuity of the overall course while meeting the needs of remedial or advanced students.

Remedial level. When a student's or group of students' knowledge base is beneath or lower than the level of the course material, instructors have to adjust the teaching pace and expectation. It may be necessary to spend more time on review or practice. Students may need a review of basic skills or knowledge before they are ready to progress to the new material in the lesson. Examples are as follows:

- Reviewing previous material or skills may delay the lesson agenda or course time frame initially but can allow students to feel more comfortable with their knowledge and abilities so that they feel ready to proceed.

- Using additional reading or study assignments for students to accomplish outside the class period may also help them advance in the class.

Advanced level. When a student's or group of students' knowledge base is advanced for the material, instructors should review the material with students to determine the appropriate level, and then assign problems or exercises at the advanced level. When the lesson includes some form of evaluation such as a test or demonstration of skills, instructors should have the students perform the evaluation. When there is still time available, the following options are available:

- Preview the next lesson and involve students in discussions or exercises to determine their levels of readiness.

- Have the group create exercises or scenarios and plan for the equipment they need to perform the exercises in the next lesson. Then arrange to have that equipment available for the next lesson. This option is available when it is not possible to move into the next lesson because of equipment limitations.

- Have participants work together in groups to create test questions complete with answer keys and text references. These tests can be used for study, debate, and discussion.

- Dismiss students early when they have completed all of these suggestions. Early dismissal may *not* be appropriate when the standard or training organization requires a minimum number of contact or skill hours for completion and certification.

Consistency

Consistency ensures that information is similar to the rest of the course content. When one piece of information differs from another similar piece of information, students will be confused. Instructors have to take time to determine which information is correct. Instructors and the training division lose credibility when the information has *not* been checked for accuracy and consistency. Consider consistency issues in the following areas:

- Safety factors
- Types of training material
- Resource materials
- Approaches to teaching
- Skill performances

Safety Factors

The purpose of *safety* is to avoid risk and prevent injuries to students and instructors during training. Safety is the primary responsibility of instructors and students who are engaged in training exercises. Both instructors and students must consistently adhere to safety policies and procedures. Consistency in application of safety procedures ensures that students will continue to follow the procedures during emergency incidents.

In addition, safety training is often required by the organization. Recognizing and addressing safety issues while planning and delivering instruction are two of the most important concerns of fire and emergency services instruction (see Chapter 2, Safety and the Training Function

Students learn from the examples provided by their instructors. When the lesson requires that students wear a protective hood during live-fire training, then all instructors involved in teaching live-fire training must also wear one. The same rule applies to using personal protective equipment (PPE). When instructors or standards require that students wear PPE on the fireground, then students need to wear it when they train.

Instructors must continuously demonstrate by example every safety feature, every time, and under every condition if they want students to learn and perform every safety practice. They must be consistent in their use of safety equipment and procedures to ensure that the safety message is apparent to students.

Skills and activities should be planned around the safest way of performing them. Instructors must inspect training classrooms and outdoor sites and then eliminate or reduce all potential hazards. Students must be taught to perform psychomotor skills in a safe manner. The repetition of the skills in a consistent manner helps create a safe behavioral pattern that students will continue to use after training is complete.

Finally, instructors must always err on the side of safety. Unsafe training activities must *not* be performed in the name of realism.

Types of Training Materials

Consistency in the types of materials used in training is also necessary. Fire-extinguishing agents, medical supplies, respiratory-protection equipment, and decontamination products should be identical to the types used in everyday and emergency activities. This consistency gives students the knowledge of how the product or material works and how it is packaged and looks.

Consistency also extends to the way that equipment and material is stored on the apparatus. Students perform more efficiently when they are familiar with a standard method of storing and accessing the equipment.

Resource Materials

During their teaching experiences, instructors collect information and materials from research materials, journals, the Internet, conferences, other training courses, and other instructors to use or adapt for use in their own courses. When using these types of information and materials, instructors must ensure that all sources can be cited to the appropriate credible resource or standard and are accepted by the sponsoring training organization.

Approaches to Teaching

Consistency must also exist between the instructors who are teaching the course. Planning meetings (used to ensure continuity) can also be a source of consistency. When instructors disagree on a particular fact, they should resolve it at this time and *not* in front of students.

When the inconsistency is a matter of personal preference and *not* a fact, instructors should decide which approach to use with students. When both opinions are equally valid, instructors should present them at the same time, explain the advantages and weaknesses of each opinion, and allow students to draw their own conclusions. This method provides an excellent teaching opportunity that demonstrates the wide variety of approaches to some topics.

Skill Performances

In some jurisdictions, there are very strict procedures/guidelines that must be followed that describe the way certain skills will be performed. Although there may be multiple ways to perform a particular skill such as raising a 24-foot (7.2 m) extension ladder for climbing, local SOPs/SOGs or state/provincial performance objectives may be very specific in how the skill will be performed. In these situations, consistency is even more important.

Physical Setting

Fire and emergency services training may occur at any location or in any environment. Wherever it occurs (either inside or outside), instructors must be able to control the learning environment to ensure that students are *not* distracted and able to concentrate on the learning experience. In addition, safety precautions must be taken into consideration to ensure a safe working and learning environment.

The learning environment may be at a training facility or remote site such as a fire station or acquired structure. The training may occur in a classroom setting, in wildland terrain, or next to a large body of water (**Figure 9.10**). Regardless of the location, instructors must evaluate the environment and do everything possible to remove distractions and potential hazards.

When training occurs in a classroom, fire station meeting room, or apparatus bay, instructors may have control over the following items:

• Room temperature

• Seating arrangements

• Sound levels for audiovisual equipment

Figure 9.10 Training can take place in many locations including wildland areas, rivers and lakes, and mountainous terrain. *Courtesy of San Ramon Valley Fire Protection District.*

• Sound levels of air-handling equipment and motor noises

• Lighting, both interior and exterior

• Accessibility of training props

When training occurs outside the classroom, instructors do *not* have the same level of direct control. Controls outdoors may include rescheduling sessions or relocating to an alternative location. Situations that may have an effect on outdoor training include the following:

• Weather conditions

• Noise and light levels

• Exposures

• Environmental laws and codes

Many of these concerns have been previously discussed in this chapter and Chapter 5, Instructional Facilities and Props. Instructors should become familiar with each type of situation and the methods used to reduce the distractions or potential hazards and improve the learning experience.

Classroom Environment

The advantage of working in a permanent classroom is that the environment rarely changes, and control over the environment is rather straightforward. Dedicated classrooms were originally designed for teaching and have built-in controls over noise, lighting, and temperature. Rooms in fire stations or other noneducational facilities may *not* have the same controls. Instructors must be prepared to adapt to the location to create the best learning environment. In both situations, the instructor should have control over the following elements:

- Seating
- Lighting
- Temperature
- Noise level
- Audiovisual equipment

Seating

The type and arrangement of student seating has an effect on how well students learn. Comfort is as important to learning as how well students can see and interact with the instructor and each other. Instructors rarely have the option of selecting the types of chairs used in training rooms. Some facilities are able to provide padded, comfortable chairs, but typically training rooms are filled with metal folding chairs. These types of chairs are comfortable only for a limited time. A long session in a metal chair can create a distraction for students. Individuals become more concerned with comfort and relief than absorbing information.

Frequent rest breaks, usually after every 45 to 50 minutes of instruction, allow students to stand, move around, stretch, and attend to other comfort needs. Trying to delay the break time for another 10 minutes in order to finish a segment of instruction may *not* accomplish anything. Participants are no longer interested in learning when they are distracted by comfort needs.

Related to the types of chairs is the arrangement of the chairs. When chairs are *not* permanently fixed to the floor (as they are in auditoriums), chair arrangements can and should vary. When the seating arrangement is *not* effective for the planned lesson, the instructor should change it. Many training facilities arrange their classrooms in the traditional rows format and require that the room be returned to that format. Instructors and students must respect the wishes and rules of the organization to return the room to its original arrangement when the lesson is finished.

Seating arrangements can influence how people learn and should match the instruction type. Several seating arrangement types (**Figure 9.11, p. 208**) that are commonly used in academic and training situations are as follows:

- *Fan* — Permits students to easily see and hear an instructor and also works effectively in small groups.

- *Classroom* — Permits students to see, hear, and interact with an instructor (traditional arrangement). Student interaction is limited and difficult, but the arrangement is applicable to any size of audience.

- *Auditorium or theater* — Arranges students in fixed seating that permanently faces the stage or lectern and permits only the interaction between students and instructor (similar to classroom-type seating). *Details:*

  — This style is used for medium-to-large-sized audiences but usually lacks a writing surface on which students can take notes.

  — It may also require a sound system so that all members of the audience can hear the instructor.

- *Conference* — Allows for total group discussion where limited or no small-group activities are required. It is most effective for small groups where students are seated around one table.

- *Chevron* — Permits students to see, hear, and interact with an instructor (similar to the traditional arrangement). Student interaction is limited and difficult.

- *Horseshoe or U shape* — Permits both instructor presentation and total group discussion but *not* small-group interaction. Used for small-to-medium-sized audiences and provides a clear view of an instructor who may be at the open or closed end of the *U* shape.

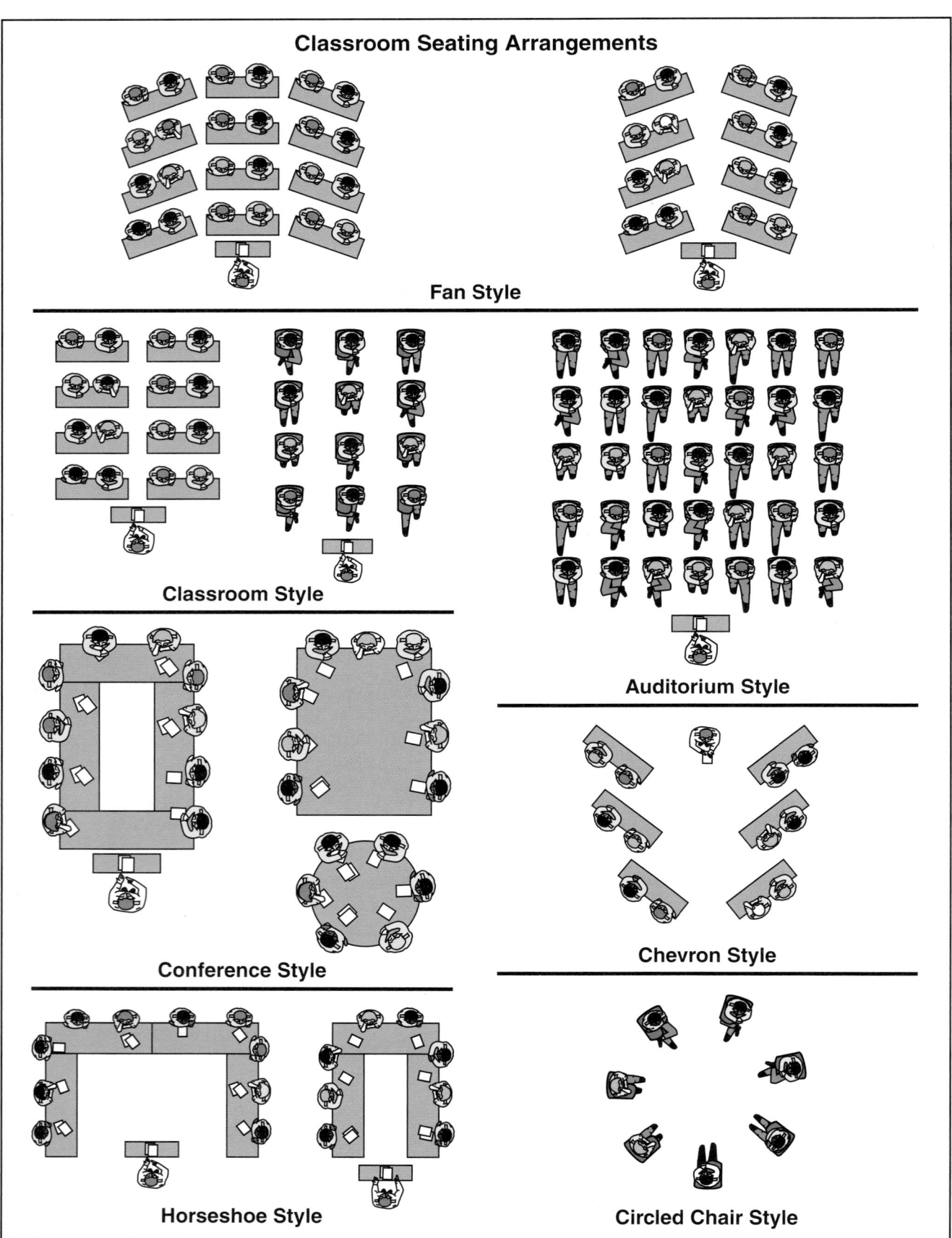

Figure 9.11 Illustration of the various seating types used in classroom situations. The instructor should select the type of seating that is most appropriate to the type of presentation that will be used for the topic being taught.

- **Hollow square** — Arranges tables into a square with seating along the outside of the square. It is effective for small-to-medium-sized groups and permits both instructor presentation and total discussion.

- **Round tables** — Provides space for meal functions, discussion groups, or small group meetings. The group size may be small around one table (conference type), or a group of tables may provide space for medium-to-large-sized groups. *Details:*

  — When an instructor is presenting from a position in front of the group, it may be difficult for students to comfortably see and hear the instructor.

  — Generally, 54 inches (1 372 mm) should be allowed between tables for movement.

- **Circled chairs** — Arranges chairs in a circle facing into the center of the circle, which is an open form designed to encourage group participation and discussion. The instructor (or facilitator) sits in the circle. It is best used for small-to-medium-sized groups where discussion is the primary method of teaching. It is *not* useful when students are expected to take notes.

Besides matching the instructional type, seating should ensure that students can see and hear the instructor and any audiovisual presentations given and also interact with other members of the class. Another important consideration when seating students at tables is the location of the table legs. Table legs can be both a physical obstruction and a learning distraction. When more seating is required, add additional tables rather than attempting to add more seats where table legs are located.

Another issue related to types of seating is the type of work surface, desktop, or table provided. Work surfaces vary and include the following:

- School desktops fixed to an individual chair
- Work surfaces that unfold over the student's lap from between auditorium-type seats
- Tables with varying depths that may accommodate a number of students on one or both sides or are arranged in a *U* or square shape
- Long conference tables
- Round tables

Instructors may *not* have the opportunity to choose the type of table or desktop surface for the classroom, and some training organizations may provide only desks or tables with small writing surfaces that do *not* accommodate an open notebook. Instructors should inspect the physical setting before beginning the class, arrange the seating (if possible) to accommodate the topic, and ask students to store any unneeded items on the floor or in a storage area to prevent cluttering the work surfaces.

Lighting

Training facilities typically have lighting that is designed for the learning experience. Lighting in permanent classrooms should consist of both fluorescent lights and incandescent lights. The primary source should be fluorescent because it causes less eyestrain and does *not* glare on reflective surfaces.

Dimmer switches that operate at low levels during audiovisual presentation should be available to control incandescent lighting. This low-light level permits students to see images on projector screens or computer monitors and still have enough light to take notes or read handouts. As a last resort, instructors may be able to unscrew lightbulbs that are directly above screens or computers so that images will *not* fade away but still allow students ample lighting to take notes.

The classroom should also be equipped with adjustable window blinds or room-darkening shades or curtains to control external light during daylight hours. With these features, instructors can easily regulate the amount of light in the room (**Figure 9.12, p. 210**).

When training must be provided in nonclassroom situations, instructors should inspect the room or area before class. The room may *not* permit the use of audiovisuals, and instructors may have to select a different format of instruction.

Temperature

The temperature of the classroom can create a distraction for students and instructors. Learning environments that are either too hot or too cold tend to preoccupy students as they attempt to make themselves comfortable. Generally, classroom

Figure 9.12 Window blinds and curtains should be closed to reduce ambient room light, eliminate glare, and improve the brilliance of projected images or television screens.

climate is a compromise between hot and cold. This compromise can be difficult to achieve because many heating, ventilating, and air-conditioning (HVAC) systems operate with an intensity that is *not* easily adjustable.

Instructor preparation may include operating the thermostat that regulates the HVAC equipment. The thermostat may be located in a room or hallway that is adjacent to the classroom. The location of the HVAC unit may be so close to the classroom that its operation provides a noisy distraction during the lesson. The unit may even need to be turned off when an instructor is trying

to present information. Under this condition, it is difficult to keep the physical climate at a comfortable level. In these situations, instructors need to do the following:

• Check climate controls before teaching in the facility.

• Determine whether controls can be adjusted and how to adjust them.

• Advise students on how to dress for comfort when the systems cannot be adjusted.

Ventilation in rooms and spaces located in old buildings that do *not* have central HVAC systems is another aspect that instructors need to consider. Windows may need to be opened and portable fans used to circulate room air. When temperature becomes a distraction, instructors may need to provide more frequent rest breaks for students.

Noise Level

Fire and emergency services personnel often work and attempt to be heard in environments with high noise levels caused by vehicle engines, pumps, sirens, radio transmissions, and shouting. Many fire and other emergency services organizations require the use of hearing protection as part of the PPE for use *on the job*. While these personnel may often have to work in a high-noise environment, they should *not* have to train in one.

Noise that overpowers the instructor distracts students from achieving the desired learning outcomes. A high level of noise is not only an annoyance and a distraction, it is a safety factor when working with power tools or giving instructions on how to operate equipment.

When inspecting the training facility, instructors can take actions to find, monitor, and eliminate or limit noise levels that originate from both inside and outside the classroom. These actions include lowering the volume on loudspeakers, radios, and pagers or turning them off. It may also be something as simple as closing the door to the hallway to stop noise from the hall coming into the classroom.

For students who are *in-service* or *on call* and responding to radios or pagers while attending the course, instructors can make arrangements with them before class sessions on how they will be alerted. Instructors can prepare other students for potential interruptions by informing them that some individuals may have to respond to calls during class sessions. This arrangement enables those in-service students to leave classes with as little distraction to others as possible.

Audiovisual Equipment

The idea of preparation to avoid or eliminate distractions also applies to the use of audiovisual equipment. Instructors who plan to use audiovisual equipment in their presentations must arrange ahead of time for its use. They should ensure that the appropriate equipment is available and functioning properly before the session. Both instructors and students will benefit when instructors take time to ensure that the equipment is in the classroom, is assembled and projects so that all can see, and operates properly.

How to Avoid Distractions When Using Audiovisual Equipment

- Do not stand between the audience and the projected image.
- Locate the projector so that it does *not* obstruct students' views.
- Ensure that the projected image fills the screen area without extending over the edges.
- Ensure that the projected image is *not* distorted.
- Locate the projector so that motor noise is at a minimum.
- Adjust the room light level to ensure that the projected image is bright while providing enough illumination for students to take notes.
- Use graphics that are clear, large, and visible from the most remote part of the viewing area.
- Elevate small props and demonstration items so that all students may view them clearly.

Instructors should preview a few overheads on the overhead projector or visual presenter or slides on the projector to make certain that they are in focus and can be seen from all parts of the room.

Videotapes should be previewed and cued to the appropriate position and the tracking control adjusted to ensure a good-quality image. Opening credits on videotapes can be distracting and time-consuming. When the videotape must be credited or referenced, give students handouts.

When using a computer and projector system, instructors should turn on the system, cue the PowerPoint® or other computer slide show, and test the show before class. The initial image may be used to welcome students or the system may be turned off until it is needed.

When using audiovisual equipment with which the instructor may not be familiar, it is important to have the facility staff provide instruction in the use of the equipment. Instructors should become familiar with the operation of the specific unit being used. Some information that the staff liaison should provide includes the following:

- Location of the on/off switch
- How to operate the focus and tracking controls (whether automatic or manual)
- How to operate the volume control
- Location of spare bulbs
- How to access staff support during the course or class period

Staff support is critical when an instructor is providing a course on closed-circuit television, interactive television, or computers (computer-based training). A test of all the equipment and remote receiving sites must be performed in advance. Broadcast airtime is valuable, and instructors cannot waste it trying to resolve problems with the system.

Instructors must always preview audiovisual aids before presenting the material. Instructors should check the material for accuracy, look for errors, determine points to emphasize and discuss, and identify information critical to the lesson. This preview also gives instructors an opportunity to develop handouts that have key points or questions that students must answer based on the presentation.

Before presenting the material in class, instructors should give students a preview, overview, or question sheet. Instructors may also wish to tell them what the media presentation is about, what to look for, and what questions to answer afterward. Audiovisual aids must have a point that relates to the lesson objectives. When the topic is *not* relevant to the lesson, students may feel that viewing it has been a waste of time. It may also create a distraction for students.

Other Classroom Considerations

Instructors should prepare for other classroom considerations such as the following:

- Locations of emergency exits, central alarm systems, and emergency lighting
- Locations and accessibility of electrical, phone, and cable outlets
- Visual distractions in the space
- Locations of comfort facilities
- Potential safety hazards

Power outlets. Before beginning a presentation in a remote location, instructors should locate any necessary electrical outlets, determine the need for extension power cords or power strips, and know where extension power cords are located. When extension cords are used, they should be within the length determined by the local fire code, usually 6 feet (1.8 m). *Never* overload a circuit by plugging too many pieces of equipment into one receptacle or power strip (**Figure 9.13**). It is a good habit for instructors to unplug all electrical equipment from outlets at the end of the class each day.

Locate telephone and cable television outlets in the presentation room. When they are *not* conveniently located, it may be necessary to rearrange the seating, move the television or lectern, or arrange for an extension cable.

Visual distractions. Items that attract the attention of students prevent them from focusing on the presentation. These items may be posters, photographs, maps, or other wall decorations that are *not* related to the lesson. They should be removed or covered before the session begins. Window blinds should also be closed.

Comfort facilities and emergency exits. Instructors should locate restrooms, water fountains, smoking areas, storm shelters, and exits before class and inform students of their locations during the introduction to the session. Provide informa-

Figure 9.13 Overloaded electrical outlets are dangerous, noncompliant with fire and electrical codes, and provide students with a bad safety example.

tion about disaster events when necessary. When refreshments are provided for the session, they should be located away from the classroom to reduce the temptation for students to move around the room during a presentation.

Safety hazards. Instructors must also eliminate any potential hazards that may result in accidents or injuries by planning and preparing ahead of time for using appropriate electrical outlets, extension power cords, and adapters. Critical safety concerns are protecting electrical cords and eliminating tripping hazards. For example, extension power cords should be taped to the floor or encased in a cover strip to prevent a tripping hazard (**Figure 9.14**). Instructors should also have the following information:

- Location of adapters for grounded plugs or power strips
- Condition of power cords (whether cords are frayed or worn or plugs are damaged)
- Location of the main breaker panel and identification of the circuit breaker that controls classroom receptacles
- Locations of timer-controlled automatic power switches that may turn off lights in the classroom during a presentation

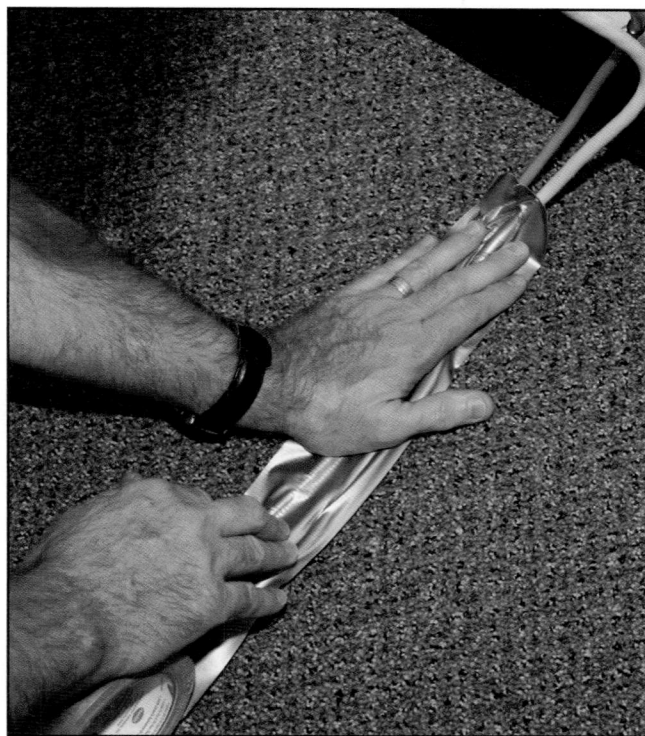

Figure 9.14 Electrical and computer cables should be secured to prevent tripping hazards.

Outside Environment

The outside learning environment can be a challenging place to teach. As part of the course preparation, instructors should visit and inspect the area that will be used for outside training. When training is to take place away from the training facility, photographs or videotapes of the area are helpful in planning and preparing for the training. For remote site training, it is also helpful for instructors to make a site map, indicating the following information (**Figures 9.15 a and b, p. 214**):

- Access routes
- Staging areas
- Traffic flow routes
- Potential exposure hazards
- Water runoff and drainage areas
- Sites of other physical conditions that may affect training

When training is performed at the training facility, instructors should inspect the area to determine the condition of the facility and training props and the need for repairs. Also determine the locations of simulated incidents, student parking

lots, apparatus staging, and observation seating (usually fixed position bleachers). Familiarity with the training area is essential to the safety of students. Potential considerations to address during the inspection and planning processes are as follows:

- *Weather conditions* — Climate-related factors include temperature, wind, precipitation, and humidity. Instructors cannot control these factors, but they should attempt to provide some means to lessen their effects on students. *Examples:*
  - Provide rehabilitation for students who are exposed to temperature extremes and high humidity.
  - Provide shielded observation and waiting areas to protect against strong winds and rain.
  - Provide cleats to add to soles of shoes or boots when ground surfaces are covered with ice and training cannot be cancelled or delayed.
  - Prohibit some operations such as the use of aerial devices or ground ladders during high wind or thunderstorms.

- *Terrain* — Terrain affects the location and use of aerial apparatus and ground ladders as well as access to the site and direction of water runoff. The initial inspection should determine areas that may create a safety or operational issue. Mark those areas appropriately. Inform students of any potential danger areas and areas that are *off-limits*.

- *Vehicle traffic* — Training operations that occur along public streets or in parking lots may be affected by vehicle traffic. When possible, limit or prohibit public access to the training area. Follow policies that regulate the use of safety cones and vests during training to enforce their use at emergency incidents. Involve law enforcement personnel also in the training scenario to both control traffic and become familiar with emergency scene operations.

- *Vehicle and machine noise* — Realistic training scenarios are just as noisy as actual emergency incidents. Use hearing protection (earplugs or earmuffs) during training operations. Turn off

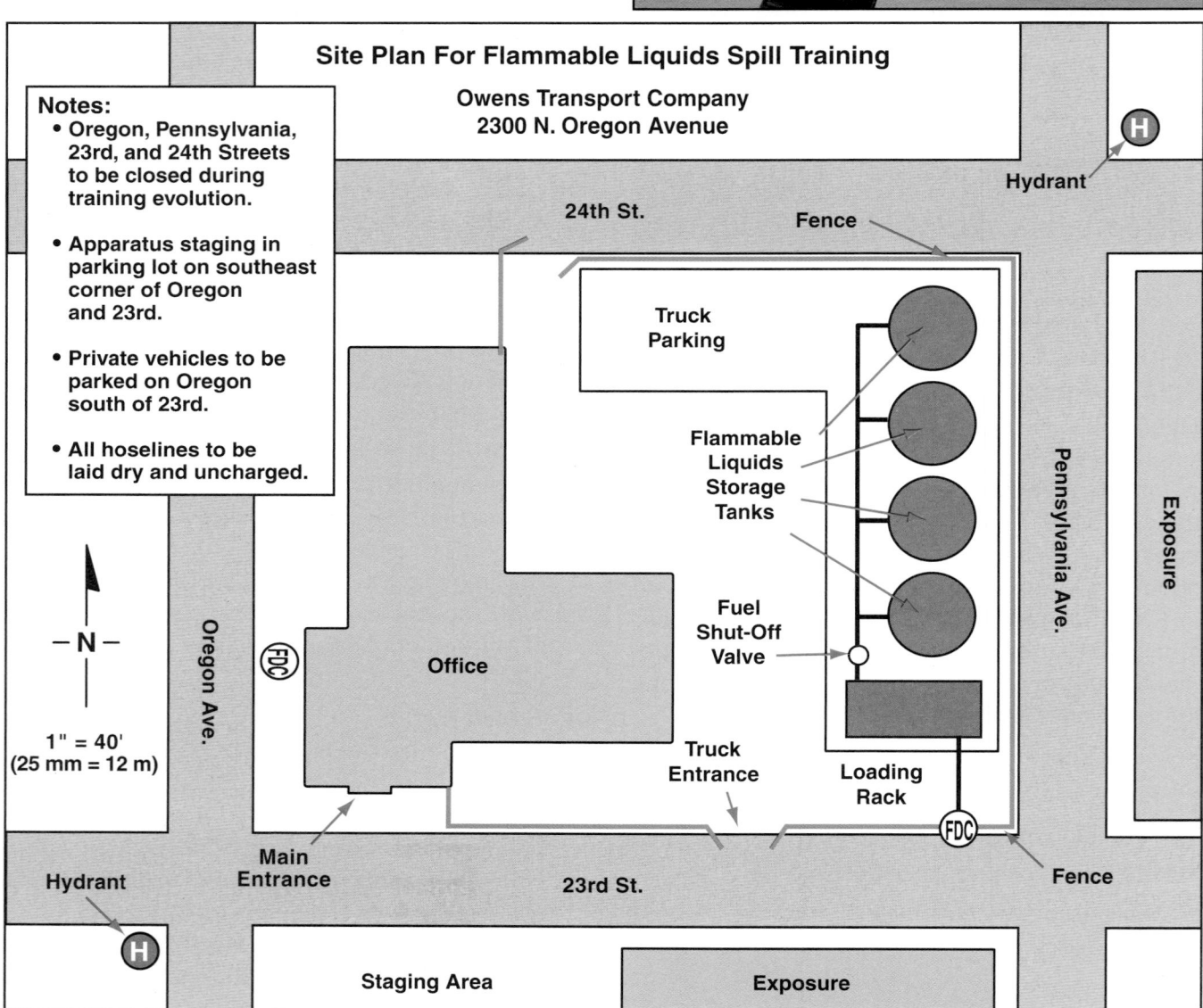

Figure 9.15a Instructors should visit remote training sites, including acquired structures, before planning an evolution. A sketch should be made of the site for assistance in planning.

Figure 9.15b The site plan should include information such as access routes, staging areas, and exposure hazards.

vehicle and machinery motors when instructors are giving instructions and procedures. When some noise cannot be controlled, use microphones and speaker systems so that students can properly hear instructors.

- *Light levels* — Exterior light can affect both teaching and safety. When the light is bright, students may *not* be able to see details because of reflected glare. When the light is low, shadows may conceal important details. Select a location and time of day that reduce the distractions caused by high or low light. Teaching at night training operations is particularly difficult. *Suggestions:*

  — Provide initial instruction in a well-lighted area, either indoors or under artificial illumination.

  — Provide sufficient lighting during the operation to prevent possible injuries from tripping and falling.

- *Site space* — When selecting a site for training or planning the type of training activity, instructors should consider the amount of training space required. Exterior space must be sufficient to provide student parking, apparatus staging, hose deployment, and incident development. When the space is too small for the proposed training, both training and safety are compromised.

- *Exposures* — The locations of exposed buildings and people need to be considered when live-fire training takes place (see Chapter 5, Instructional Facilities and Props). Identify exposures and consider wind direction and velocity as well as terrain and water runoff routes.

- *Environmental laws and codes* — Instructors must provide training within the limitations of national, state/provincial, and local environmental laws in addition to building and fire codes and zoning ordinances. See Chapter 2, Safety and the Training Function.

- *Access* — Whether training takes place at a training facility or remote site, access to the training area must be considered. This consideration is especially important when units remain in service during training. The site map created earlier indicates the location of access points, direction of traffic flow, and relationship to staging and incident areas. *Other considerations:*

  — Additional personnel may be required to control access to the site.

  — Whenever possible, provide at least two means of access.

At the beginning of any outdoor training session, instructors must provide an overview of the training scenario, indicating expected outcomes, safety issues, and unit or company or individual assignments. A walk-through of the area or structure must occur with emphasis on exit routes, control zones, and accountability practices. Demonstrate skills before the beginning of the training session.

Summary

Instructor preparation is essential to a successful, effective, and efficient learning experience. Both instructors and students benefit from good preparation. Instructors will benefit by having increased self-confidence, while students will have increased confidence in the ability and credibility of instructors. Neither will think that the teaching session has been a waste of time, and both will believe that the transfer of knowledge has been successful. Finally, both instructors and students will have the assurance that everything has been done to make the learning experience and environment as safe as possible during the training session.

Personal Preparation

Effective public speakers know the value of being prepared. Part of that preparation involves being physically and emotionally prepared to present a lecture or demonstration. Most speech communication courses and textbooks include lists of preparation steps for speakers to take. Some of those steps include the following:

- Know the audience and the purpose (topic) of the presentation.
- Rehearse the presentation.
- Visualize being successful.
- Practice using the visual aids and props.
- Take deep breaths to reduce stress.
- Be calm.
- Be rested.
- Eat a nutritious meal before making the presentation.
- Work from a lesson plan.
- Have a contingency plan available in the event of changes in the audience or environment.
- Be familiar with the learning environment and media equipment.
- Focus on the message and the audience.

Performing these steps will result in a professional presentation and eliminate any personal anxiety an instructor may have about making the presentation.

Part B

Instructor I Requirements

Chapter 10

Instructional Delivery

After reading this chapter, students will be able to —

1. Discuss types of instructional delivery methods.

2. List advantages and disadvantages of the lecture format.

3. List ways to overcome the disadvantages of the lecture format.

4. List guidelines for using visual aids in an illustrated lecture.

5. Identify accurate statements about the discussion presentation format.

6. Distinguish between advantages and disadvantages of the demonstration presentation format.

7. List guidelines for preparing for a demonstration.

8. Complete statements about demonstrating a skill.

9. Identify accurate statements about the multiple-instructor presentation format.

10. List reasons technology-based training is becoming increasingly popular.

11. Discuss types of technology-based training.

12. Distinguish between advantages and disadvantages of technology-based training.

13. Discuss security issues with technology-based training.

14. Identify accurate statements about self-directed learning and individualized instruction.

15. List the characteristics of effective speakers.

16. Identify guidelines for giving an effective presentation.

17. Discuss the importance of presenting appropriate attitudes, values, and beliefs in a classroom setting.

18. Describe the components of an oral presentation.

19. Distinguish among sequencing methods.

20. Discuss strategies to assist the instructor in applying instructional activities for active learning in the classroom.

21. List advantages of active learning.

22. List strategies for stimulating student interest.

23. Describe methods of reinforcing learning.

24. List the purposes of questions.

25. Identify guidelines for asking effective questions.

26. Distinguish among types of questions.

27. Discuss responding to student answers or new questions students may ask.

Chapter Contents

Instructional Delivery Methods
Instructor-Led Presentation Types
Technology-Based Training
Other Instructional Methods

Presentation Techniques
Characteristics of Effective Speakers
Nonverbal Elements
Presentation Preparation
Attitudes/Values Display

Presentation Organization Format
Methods of Sequencing

Instructional Methods for Active Learning
Strategies
Advantages
Motivational Techniques
Encouragement for Success
Reinforcement of Learning
Techniques for Questioning

Summary

Chapter 10
Instructional Delivery

Very few people are born with the ability to give oral presentations. Those who are, usually have personality traits that make them outgoing, gregarious, and desirous of being the center of attention. For the majority of people, presentation skills must be learned and practiced. Learning these skills generally begins in a high school speech class where students learn how to prepare and present a speech, develop the ability to speak with confidence, project their voices, and enunciate their words so that they are clearly understood.

This exposure to public speaking may lead some students to other courses in theater, oration, or debate. Most students, though, only take one basic speech course and then follow other interests that satisfy them more. Research has found that public speaking generates the greatest fear among most people.

Fire and emergency services personnel generally reflect the attitude of the majority of people when it comes to public speaking. They are confident of their abilities to fight fires or respond to crises, but they do *not* feel confident speaking before a large group or presenting a lecture. Nor are they trained in teaching methodology. The skills required to present information through any of the three learning domains — cognitive, psychomotor, or affective — are *not* included in Firefighter I and Firefighter II courses.

Therefore, fire and emergency services personnel who decide to or are assigned to teach other personnel must be taught the various methods of instructional delivery, presentation techniques, and instructional methods for active learning. Knowledge of these methods and techniques and associated skills can be acquired through college-level courses or classes taught through fire and emergency services training organizations and agencies.

This chapter provides the instructor candidate with the necessary basic skills to meet the job performance requirements (JPRs) of NFPA 1041, *Standard for Fire Service Instructor Professional Qualifications*, Level I, that relate to instructional delivery. However, instructors should continually work to expand and increase their knowledge in the areas of instructional delivery through continuing education and professional development.

The chapter focuses on the proper use of instructor-led presentations, including combining various methods that result in active learning (a contemporary concept of learning). In addition, the instructor's role in technology-based training is also discussed.

Instructional Delivery Methods

The presentation step of the four-step method of instruction builds on the preparation step introduced in Chapter 9, Preparation for Instruction. The purpose of the presentation step (present new skills, concepts, and procedures and instruct the student) is accomplished through lectures, demonstrations, and other presentation methods **(Figure 10.1, p. 220)**.

The use of audiovisual training aids in the presentation step is discussed in Chapter 11, Audiovisual Technology. Instructional methods that are associated with the application step are included in Chapter 12, Structured Exercises, Demonstrations, and Practical Training Evolutions.

Many methods for presenting information are available for instructors. Since the early 1990s, instructional delivery has changed and evolved through the increasing use of technology. Instructional delivery can be described as one of the following types:

- **Instructor-led training (ILT)** — Traditional instruction that depends on the direct transfer of knowledge from the instructor to the student.

- **Technology-based training (TBT)** — Electronic learning (e-learning) that uses methods such as Internet web-based instruction, interactive television (ITV), and other forms of computer-based electronically transferred knowledge.

- **Other instructional methods** — Variety of approaches to learning include self-directed learning and individualized instruction. Each of these methods may depend on portions of the ILT and TBT models for the transfer of knowledge.

Instructors must select the most appropriate method based on factors such as the audience and topic. These instructional delivery methods are *not* independent of one another, and effective instructors can incorporate more than one method into a presentation.

Instructor-Led Presentation Types

Traditional instructor-led presentation types are currently the most prevalent approaches to teaching (**Figure 10.2**). Instructor-led presentations have the advantage of being flexible, economical, and familiar to both students and instructors. Instructor-led presentation types include the following:

- Lecture
- Illustrated lecture
- Discussion
- Demonstration (in the cognitive domain)
- Multiple instructors

Demonstrations used to convey psychomotor skills and structured exercises such as role-playing and simulations are discussed in Chapter 12, Structured Exercises, Demonstrations, and Practical Training Evolutions.

Step 2 Presentation	
Purpose To communicate content developed to change the behavior of students:	**How to Accomplish** Tested methods for presenting knowledge and skills:
1. Present knowledge, new skills, concepts, or procedures to students. 2. Instruct, motivate, and educate students.	1. Select the appropriate presentation style for the audience, subject, and desired outcome. 2. Present lectures, demonstrations, and activities. 3. Use appropriate visual aids and props. 4. Explain procedures. 5. Emphasize key points. 6. Explain concepts, philosophies, principles, and implications. 7. Proceed from known to unknown and simple to complex. 8. Use textbooks and other reference materials. 9. Apply active learning principles. 10. Summarize key points and concepts at the end of the presentation. 11. Require students to take notes.

Figure 10.1 The presentation step: Communicating information to students in order to affect a change in behavior or attitude.

Figure 10.2 All adult students have experienced instructor-led training in some form.

Lecture

In the *lecture* format, the instructor provides, describes, and explains a topic through spoken words. The lecture format is an effective method for providing facts, rules and regulations, clarifications, examples, and definitions. With the lecture method, one speaker can reach people in any size group, ranging from one student (one-on-one) to large numbers of students in an auditorium.

Technology-based distance-learning courses allow the lecture method to extend beyond the limits of a single classroom and provide the message to students at distant sites. For these reasons, the lecture format can be very cost-effective — one instructor for dozens of students at multiple sites.

The time-efficiency of the presentation is another advantage of lectures. Many students can be taught at the same time while the instructor only prepares one presentation. The lecture format is familiar to students so they are aware of what to expect and what is expected of them.

Specific disadvantages of the lecture format (which usually involve one-way communication and a lack of student feedback) include the following:

- *Limited student/instructor interaction* — For students, listening to a lecture is like watching television: There is no interaction with the sender. The student listens, takes notes, and watches the instructor for additional information, usually in the form of nonverbal signals or visual aids. Beyond that, the instructor is expected to do all the work by making the information interesting and easy to understand.

- *Lack of student feedback* — In a strict lecture format, information only flows in one direction (from the sender to the receiver). From a communication standpoint, this format is *not* considered a communication process because there is no exchange of information in the form of feedback or return input from the receivers. The instructor must rely on nonverbal indicators for feedback that indicates student understanding. Nonverbal cues were discussed in Chapter 4, Effective Interpersonal Communication.

- *Limited senses involved in receiving the information* — Students receive the lecture information through only one sense — hearing. When an instructor is *not* a good public speaker, student acquisition and retention of material is limited to what is heard. Much of that material may be misunderstood, misperceived, or missed altogether while taking notes.

These disadvantages can be overcome with some effort on the part of the instructor in the following ways:

- *Generate student interaction* — Consider the following actions:
  — Pose questions to students and allow them to answer.
  — Permit students to ask questions of the instructor, which may occur either during the lecture or at the end of the session. *Timing considerations:*
    ○ While questions asked during the lecture can be linked directly to the information and lead to a discussion, the instructor may find that this approach is disruptive.
    ○ Questions at the end of the session may have the advantage of *not* disrupting the lecture but may also lack the relationship to the information. At the same time, the session may end before all student questions can be asked or answered.
  — Include discussions, illustrations, demonstrations, and structured exercises in the lecture.

- *Interpret nonverbal feedback* — Consider the following actions:
  — Stop lecturing and ask for questions from the audience.
  — Ask direct questions to determine understanding.
  — Apply effective listening skills (See Chapter 4, Effective Interpersonal Communication).
  — Use the same steps mentioned in the previous bullet to determine student understanding.

- *Consider limited senses* — Instructors who try to lecture about applications of technical equipment or processes often cannot provide adequate words to create appropriate visualizations in students' minds. *Suggestions:*

  — Avoid presenting too much information at once; it may be difficult for students to understand and write down new information.

  — Provide information in the lecture through other senses; people remember only a small portion of what they hear. Use illustrations or audiovisuals.

  — Provide supplemental information in the form of handouts and reference lists.

Few instructors use the strict lecture method today. Lectures alone can be boring to students who are used to the fast-paced visual and audio stimulation of television, videotapes, computers, and video games. The lecture method is appropriate when used in moderation or interspersed with other delivery methods.

Illustrated Lecture

What is called *lecture* in most classrooms is really an *illustrated lecture* — a presentation method that provides information directed toward the student's senses of sight and hearing. In this format, the instructor uses visual aids such as PowerPoint® presentations, illustrations on dry-erase boards or chalkboards, drawings, photographs, slides, transparencies, videotapes, films, models, and other aids to clarify details or processes (**Figure 10.3**).

Instructors often use visual aids to illustrate the main points of a lesson. The main points may resemble an outline that is based on the lesson plan. Whether on slides, transparencies, easel pads, or dry-erase boards/chalkboards, the visible outline shows the framework of the lecture. Students find that note-taking is easier when they can see the main points and these points remain visible while they write down information as the instructor inserts material into the outline. Also, when a subsequent point is *not* clear, students can easily refer back to previous points for clarification.

Instructors sometimes improperly use the illustration method as a substitute for a demonstration. An illustration may show a picture of a piece of

Figure 10.3 Instructors usually have multiple types of training aids available to them, including chalkboards, computer-projected images, and overhead protected images.

equipment, but it does *not* show the student how to use or operate the equipment. Illustrations can supplement a demonstration but they cannot take its place.

Additional information on the use of visual aids is included in Chapter 11, Audiovisual Technology. The following guidelines are helpful when using visual aids as illustrative teaching aids:

- Illustrate a single lesson objective in each visual.

- Make the visual large enough to be easily seen. Rearrange the seating if necessary.

- Hide visuals until the lesson topic calls for them to be displayed. Visual aids that are displayed early in a presentation can be a distraction by diverting student attention away from the lecture.

- Display steps in sequence individually when illustrating the steps in an operation. Displaying them all at once can be a confusing distraction. When all steps have been introduced, individual illustrations may be displayed together to allow students to see the relationship between them.

Discussion

In contrast to the one-sided lecture method of delivering instruction, the *discussion* method allows interaction between instructors and students. The instructor talks *with* the group rather than *to* the group. Group members participate by talking *with* the instructor and each other. During a discussion, instructors and students can interact in the following ways:

- Exchange views and ideas.

- Ask questions and receive answers.

- Provide examples based on experiences.

- Arrive at conclusions.

- Form a consensus.

- Accomplish the learning objectives of the lesson.

In order to be effective though, students must have a basic knowledge of the subject *before* the discussion begins. The discussion method is *not* a good format for introducing new material to inexperienced students. Discussions also work best for small groups of approximately 3 to 15 students **(Figure 10.4)**.

In large groups, students can be divided into small groups with either instructor or student facilitators leading the discussion in each group. When each group completes its task, the larger group is assembled, and the facilitators report any decisions made in the small groups.

Several categories of the discussion format exist. In each method, students play major roles in the discussions and activities, while the instructor role changes to that of facilitator. To be most effective, the room should be arranged so that students can see each other. See Chapter 9, Preparation for Instruction, for information on seating arrangements. Having eye contact with each other is essential to conducting an effective discussion.

Instructors must preplan all discussion formats and select the type best suited for the topic and time frame. Because discussions can be time-consuming, the instructor must ensure that the time is used efficiently and the topic is specific enough to provide students with the necessary information to conduct a discussion. The categories of the discussion format are as follows:

Figure 10.4 Small group discussions are most effective for groups ranging in size from 3 to 15 students. *Courtesy of Alabama Fire College.*

- *Guided* — The instructor presents a topic to a group, and the members of the group discuss ideas in an orderly exchange controlled or guided by the instructor. The intent of this type of discussion is to gain knowledge from other group members, modify their own ideas, or develop new ones. As facilitator, the instructor's role is to guide the discussion and meet the lesson objective(s) in the following ways:

  — Keep the discussion on the topic.

  — Add pertinent details.

  — Ask thought-provoking questions.

  — Analyze conversations to ensure understanding.

- *Conference* — This method directs group thinking toward the solution of a common problem. The goal of a conference is to have the group develop understanding and recognition of the topic. A successful conference cannot be spontaneous. It must be planned, have an agenda, have an established time and location, and have a stated purpose. In this method, instructors are facilitators *not* teachers. They do *not* tell the group how or what to think nor steer the results of the group's thinking in a personally preferred direction. *Details:*

  — A conference is effective in bringing about changes in student thinking, attitude, or behavior as students compare experiences, techniques, and beliefs with others. When a student hears the interpretation others have made of a similar experience, that person is often willing to adopt the attitude taken by the group.

— Students must be willing to share ideas and trust that the consensus of the group is better than the ideas of any single member.

— It is helpful for students to know the limits, scope, and purpose of the conference.

Instructor roles:

— Instructors influence the direction and outcome of the discussion by providing background information on the topic.

— The instructor must *not* enter into the discussion except to state or restate problems, ask questions, state cases, or summarize comments.

— Instructor roles may include controlling or eliminating bickering and irrelevant discussion, reconciling differences of opinion, and uniting students.

NOTE: The term *conference* is used for both a discussion format and a type of meeting that has the same purpose only on a larger scale.

Demonstration

A *demonstration* is the act of showing how to do something or how something operates or acts. It is a basic means for teaching manipulative skills, physical principles, and mechanical functions. It can be used effectively to show the operation of tools, equipment, or materials and show the results of their use.

In the cognitive domain, the demonstration is used to illustrate a concept that students are *not* expected to perform. In the psychomotor domain, the demonstration is used to illustrate modeling; that is, how to perform a task that students are expected to learn and repeat in the application step of the four-step instructional method (see Chapter 12, Structured Exercises, Demonstrations, and Practical Training Evolutions). The instructor demonstrates a task while explaining how and why it is performed **(Figure 10.5)**. This method communicates to both sight and hearing senses.

Figure 10.5 Instructors demonstrate the use of tools and equipment before allowing students to practice using them. *Courtesy of Alabama Fire College.*

When students practice the skill, they use psychomotor skills and add the sense of touch to their learning experiences. The following positive advantages can easily overcome any disadvantages when using demonstrations in both the cognitive and psychomotor domains:

- Students can receive feedback immediately.

- Instructors can readily observe a change in behavior.

- Students have a high level of interest when participating.

- Instructors can easily determine whether learning objectives have been met.

- Carefully supervised skills that students learn correctly in a safe environment give them confidence to perform the same skills on the job.

Some limitations to the demonstration method include the following:

- Instructors must plan for extensive preparation and cleanup times, especially when using such items as power tools, hose, breathing apparatus, and cardiopulmonary resuscitation (CPR) mannequins.

- Careful lesson planning is important because assembly and practice can use much of the class time.

- Large groups of students require extra equipment for practice as well as additional instructors for supervising, coaching, and ensuring that safety procedures are followed. It is imperative that instructors closely monitor students practicing potentially dangerous skills for the first time.

- Skills that must be performed or practiced outside depend on the weather. Instructors must have a contingency plan available in the event of inclement weather conditions.

Because of the hazardous nature of fire and emergency services, instructors must stress safety as every step of each skill is demonstrated. Many students want to be able to perform a skill quickly when they first learn it. Skill and speed only come with practice, and trying to perform new tasks without carefully learning the steps or developing coordination risks safety. Safety must be stressed during the demonstration of the procedure, during practice time, and during the final student evaluation.

To use the demonstration method effectively, instructors should follow a few guidelines. The following list is divided into two critical areas: (1) preparing for a demonstration and (2) demonstrating the skill.

Preparing for a Demonstration
• Know clearly what is to be demonstrated and its learning objective.
• Be proficient in every step of the demonstration by practicing in advance with all instructors who will be involved.
• Acquire all equipment and accessories, ensure that they work, and arrange them for use.
• Arrange the room or demonstration area so that all students can see and hear the demonstration.

Demonstrating the Skill
• Begin the demonstration by linking new information with the students' current knowledge.

- Explain what the demonstration will show the group how to do.

- Explain why the skill is important.

- Demonstrate the skill once at normal speed.

- Repeat the demonstration step by step while explaining each step slowly.

- Repeat the demonstration again while a class member or the group explains each step.

- Consider using a video camera and large-screen monitor when the group is large in order to allow students to see the process up close or observe small details.

- Allow students the opportunity to ask questions and clarify any misunderstandings.

- Ask for a student volunteer to demonstrate the skill while explaining the steps. Give reassurance by coaching and guiding the student through the process. Offer suggestions or corrections during the demonstration.

- Provide the opportunity for students to practice, and allow them to supervise and correct each other as they becomed skilled. Again, closely monitor student activities when students practice potentially dangerous skills for the first time.

- Reassemble the group and demonstrate the skill one more time at normal speed and/or one more time slowly as the group explains the steps as a summary. Relate the skill to the learning objective and performance on the job.

Multiple Instructors

Using multiple instructors is an arrangement in which a group of instructors (often with knowledge in a variety of topics or from different jurisdictions or organizations) cooperate to teach a single class or course. This presentation method has the advantage of giving students contact with more than one instructor during a lesson or course.

This method is an effective educational tool for instructors and a unifying force between organizations. A form of this method is called *team teaching*, which involves the simultaneous teaching by multiple instructors providing a more effective use of class time and smaller student-to-instructor ratios.

Figure 10.7 Students can benefit from computer-based training because of the wide variety of interactive presentations that are currently available.

- **_Web-based training (WBT)_** — As the name indicates, WBT is training/education delivered via the Internet or World Wide Web (WWW) or over a closed intranet/extranet (LAN/WAN) network. Any course that is described as *online* or *online learning* is a class that is conducted entirely through a web-based system. *Descriptions:*

  — *Browser-based training* is a term used to describe course material that requires a web browser to access, but may in fact be running from the Internet or a CD-ROM.

  — Some training courses can access information from both a web site as well as a CD-ROM. These courses are sometimes called *hybrids* or *hybrid-CD-ROMs.*

  — WBT may include an instructor/facilitator who provides course guidelines, manages discussion boards, delivers lectures, and evaluates student performance. When used with a facilitator, WBT offers some advantages of ILT while retaining the advantages of CBT.

  — *Blended electronic-learning (BeL)* is another form of WBT that is available to training divisions and agencies. It combines online learning courses that students complete independently with classroom-delivered instruction and hands-on, performance-based skills instruction. The online courses include the following:

  ○ Graphics-intensive CD-ROMs
  ○ Textbooks
  ○ Web-based evaluations and records management

  Students must successfully complete the online requirements before being admitted into the skills session. According to a report from the Office of Domestic Preparedness, BeL increases the following elements:

  ○ Learning by 56 percent
  ○ Learning consistency by 50 to 60 percent
  ○ Content retention by 25 to 50 percent

- **_Interactive Television (ITV)_** — ITV is used to link multiple classroom sites together and permits one instructor to reach more students (**Figure 10.8**). It is a popular approach to distance education. Students can interact with each other and the instructor. Each site is able to see, hear, and talk to the other sites.

Advantages and Disadvantages

TBT has both advantages and disadvantages for the organization and students. The organization should be aware of them before establishing a strictly technology-based program. Students should also be aware before enrolling in a TBT course because it may *not* be applicable to all learning styles.

Adult students who understand the importance of completing a course or degree program can usually overcome these disadvantages and have a successful learning experience. Instructors and their organizations are responsible for selecting appropriate teaching methods for course requirements and student needs.

Security

A major issue of concern with all TBT types is security. The instructor and students who are enrolled in the course must have access to the course web site or database. Security begins when students enroll or are assigned to a course or program. Each student is assigned a unique password that provides the necessary level of access. However, even student access is limited. Student access does *not* include the test bank of questions and answers, other student's grades, or archival material such as

Figure 10.8 Interactive television courses are effective methods of reaching a large audience that is distributed over a great distance.

Comparison of Traditional Classroom Delivery and Blended E-Learning Delivery

Traditional Delivery	Blended E-Learning Delivery
• *Sage on the Stage:* Instructor as authority	• *Guide on the Side:* Instructor as facilitator and director
• Instructor-led	• Student-led, instructor-directed
• 100-percent instructor delivered	• 60/40 mix: 60 percent self-paced with 40 percent instructor-led delivery
• Audiovisuals include videos, PowerPoint® slides, other visual aids	• Dependent on a variety of learning styles and methods
• Dependent on the instructor's ability and experience	• Web-ROM/Internet based
• Limited class size based on topic, facility, funding, student learning styles, and instructor delivery ability	• Content consistent and standardized

Advantages	Disadvantages
• Student travel time can be reduced or eliminated	• The student is isolated from other students and the instructor, eliminating the social contact that is normally part of classroom interaction.
• Students have the flexibility to complete course work on their own schedules.	• Students can lose interest and drop the course more easily.
• Associated costs to the student such as childcare expenses can be reduced.	• TBT requires a high level of student self-discipline and self-motivation.
• Learning is student-centered, which permits students to establish the pace, sequence, and style of learning that fits them.	• TBT requires students to have good writing skills.
• TBT permits quick and easy access to resources.	• TBT requires students to be comfortable with working on the Internet/intranet.

(Continued)

Advantages	Disadvantages
• TBT increases educational opportunities for students who may *not* be able to relocate or attend classroom sessions. • TBT reduces peer pressure or fear of interpersonal interaction. • TBT increases student exposure to thoughts, ideas, and worldviews of a wide range of students. • TBT teaches students to manage time and resources while taking courses. • Changes and updates to course material can be made in real time.	• TBT requires students to possess basic computer skills, including word-processing, Internet browser skills, and electronic mail (e-mail) software knowledge. • Course preparation and participation times are greater than classroom time. • Students lack the motivation that comes from classroom contact and interaction. • TBT requires an investment by the organization and students in technology systems. • Slow connection speeds and limited bandwidths can affect TBT efficiency and effectiveness. • Students require access to the WWW or Internet.

previous assignments or tests. Students will have access to the following information:

• Web site home page
• Links to additional resources
• Chat rooms
• Instructor's bulletin board that contains assignments, a syllabus, and other information
• Tests when they are assigned
• Individual student's grade sheet

The instructor must take precautions when corresponding with students. E-mail messages can be accidentally misdirected or sent to the entire class rather than an individual student. The instructor should always be careful of what is written in an e-mail message because of the possibility that the message may reach the wrong party. Instructor and student e-mail lists must be strictly controlled to ensure that they are *not* distributed to unauthorized persons or groups.

Other Instructional Methods

Changes in lifestyles, the inability to commit to a traditional class schedule, and the individual learning styles of diverse students have resulted in students, instructors, and educational institutions seeking additional methods of instruction.

CAUTION

Instructors must remember that electronic mail (e-mail) is *not* secure. Communications sent by e-mail may be misdirected, forwarded, altered, or distributed to unauthorized persons or sites. E-mail that is deleted from a computer or mailbox continues to exist. Confidential information such as student test results must never be transmitted via e-mail.

Self-directed learning and individualized learning are two methods for reaching students who would otherwise be unable to advance their educational experiences.

Self-Directed Learning

In *self-directed* or *independent learning*, individual students either are given or select a set of objectives to complete, but they do them at their own paces through their own methods of learning. Self-directed learning places the responsibility for achieving the course objectives solely on the student. An instructor is *not* involved in the delivery of the training, although one may act as a facilitator in some cases.

Instructors are available to answer questions, evaluate learning achievements, and guide the student, but the learning process is completely the student's responsibility. In self-directed learning, the instructor and the individual schedule several meetings to examine the progress of the independent study.

A key element of independent study is that individual students have much of the responsibility of how much they learn and how they learn it. However, this aspect of this type of instruction does *not* relieve the instructor of the responsibility of ensuring that the student accomplishes the intended tasks and skills in appropriate formats.

Quite often, this format of instruction so motivates students that they discover things above and beyond lesson requirements. Instructors should be aware that *not* all types of training programs, particularly basic-level skill programs, are suited to this type of instruction.

Self-directed learning may require the student to use TBT aids such as those listed in the Technology-Based Training section. It is the student's responsibility to either provide equipment necessary or have access to it in order to participate in the class.

Individualized Instruction

Because students possess a variety of learning styles, some of those styles may *not* enable a student to progress with a group. An alternative teaching method may be *individualized instruction:* The process of matching instructional methods with learning objectives and individual learning styles that enable a student to achieve lesson objectives. Individualized instruction offers a major advantage to students: It provides a successful learning format for students who could *not* normally succeed in the typical learning environment but could be successful given time and opportunity to learn.

Individualized instruction is a tool for an instructor to use in combination with other traditional methods, but it is *not* a substitute for the instructor. Individualized instruction does *not* imply *solitary* learning, the primary component of self-directed learning.

Individuals need to work with others to meet certain requirements and share experiences. They also work under the supervision of an instructor or mentor who ensures that they meet lesson or chosen individual objectives.

Variations of individualized instruction can be used to match instructional methods with learning objectives. For example, the instructor prescribes the learning objectives, but the student selects personal methods or techniques for accomplishing them. In another example, the instructor chooses fixed methods and techniques for meeting the learning objectives, and the methods and techniques chosen by the student are optional.

Individualized instruction is based on the following three premises:

- ***Student's needs and preferred learning style*** — The method of instructional delivery for individualized instruction is student-centered. It responds to the individual student, not the group or class.

- ***Learning objectives or competencies required by the occupation*** — Individualized instruction is competency-based, which means that it is based on the demands or requirements (competencies) of the occupation. It is also evaluation-based. It provides a system for frequent review of progress by diagnosing, prescribing, and evaluating achievement.

- ***Instructional strategies and media that fit the needs of the student*** — Because individualized instruction is individually paced, it is flexible in terms of the time taken to learn the objectives and the student's goals, which extend to the variety of methods and media used.

Many organizations are developing or using various individualized instruction methods in their training programs. Some of these instructional methods are as follows:

- ***Learning activity packets*** — Uses packets with sequenced activities and reading assignments. This method is the most familiar of the many types.

- ***Tutorial instruction*** — Provides one-on-one teaching-learning relationships with an instructor, another class member, or a peer.

- *Programmed learning* — Uses a systematic process of introducing information in small, sequential steps followed by questions that reinforce learning. This method either uses a workbook or is technology-based and requires computer access.
- *Other programs* — Requires access to cable television channels, telephones, and instructional workbooks.

Regardless of the methods used, frequent student-instructor contact is necessary. This contact enables the instructor to facilitate learning by evaluating progress, prescribing new learning objectives or different learning methods, and encouraging students. With individualized instruction, the instructor's role is different from the traditional role. The instructor manages learning resources, guides students, and interacts with them but is *not* the sole or primary resource for learning as in the traditional classroom.

Presentation Techniques

Presentation techniques apply not only to classroom situations but also to presentations given to superiors, administrative bodies, or the general public. They can apply to reports, public information, or public education. The ability to present information in a logical, informative, and interesting manner is basic to the duties of all instructor levels.

However, presentation techniques must be learned and practiced by the instructor candidate first so that the techniques can be effectively taught to others. The Level I certified instructor, either as a company officer or training officer, uses presentation skills more than any other position in the organization.

Presentation techniques consist of interpersonal and oral communication skills (see Chapter 4, Effective Interpersonal Communication), demonstration skills (see Chapter 12, Structured Exercises, Demonstrations, and Practical Training Evolutions), and the display of attitude and values. Each of these skills corresponds to the learning domains (cognitive, psychomotor, and affective).

Mastering effective communication skills permits instructors to clearly and concisely describe and explain information in ways that students can understand. The information may be in the form of a policy, process, theory, or procedure.

Along with the ability to explain how and why things happen, instructors must be able to demonstrate or show students the required procedures or skills. Showing procedures requires turning thoughts and words into actions and activities. Among the multitude of skills that must be demonstrated, instructors must be able to tie knots, operate power equipment, drive apparatus, advance hoselines, and apply bandages to name a very few (see Chapter 12, Structured Exercises, Demonstrations, and Practical Training Evolutions).

Finally, instructors must be able to transmit to students a professional attitude and the values and beliefs upon which the organization is established. This transmission may occur subtly while instructors present lectures or perform demonstrations by presenting role models to students. It may also be transmitted directly through the statement of specific values or beliefs during a lecture on the topic of ethics.

The sections that follow introduce the elements of good presentations, including the characteristics of effective speakers, the use of nonverbal communication, presentation preparation, and the delivery of attitudes and values. Accepted methods for organizing a presentation and sequencing the delivery of information are also given. The instructor candidate needs to expand on this knowledge and practice each of these methods to become proficient in them.

Characteristics of Effective Speakers

The first step toward becoming an effective public speaker is to identify the characteristics displayed by effective speakers. Analyses of effective speakers throughout history have shown that they all tend to have similar speaking traits or characteristics. Those characteristics that apply to the instructor in the classroom include the following:

- *Audience-centered* — The speaker knows the audience and adapts the topic, speech organization, presentation style, and personal appearance to this audience. This characteristic requires that the speaker learn as much as possible about the audience, determine what the audience needs to know about the subject, and determine the purpose of the presentation before the development of the speech. In the classroom, this characteristic becomes the task of matching the presentation style to the student's learning style.

- **Good development of ideas** — Effective speakers are also effective thinkers. They use their thinking skills to create interesting, appealing, and memorable ways of presenting their information. Some ways to make speeches interesting in the context of the lesson plan include the following:
  — Using relevant examples
  — Using appropriate humor
  — Telling stories to which the audience can relate
  — Using effective metaphors

- **Good organization of ideas** — Generally, instructors use either the persuasive or informative speech model in a classroom presentation. A well-organized persuasive speech, which is intended to alter a behavior or create an awareness of a problem, gains the audience's attention, provides the necessary background information, illustrates the situation, and offers a solution to the situation. An informative speech that is used to provide information on a topic may be organized either topically or according to the complexity of the subject.

- **Best choice of words** — Words (as much as any other part of the communication process) convey the message. The choice of the right words ensures that the message has a good chance of being understood. It is important to *not* speak above the intellectual level of the audience by using words they might *not* understand. It is just as important that the speaker *not* talk below the level of the audience, insulting their intelligence by being too basic.

- **Good delivery skills** — Effective speakers use more than words to convey the message. Enthusiasm for the subject is essential to communicating the message. It makes the audience want to listen and ensures that audience members do *not* let their minds drift and ignore

the speaker. Enthusiasm is conveyed in the following ways:
  — Eye contact
  — Facial expressions
  — Voice inflections (changes in tonal quality to emphasize ideas and thoughts)

- **Vocal characteristics** — Major elements are as follows:
  — *Volume (Projection):* How loud the voice is when speaking; used when trying to be heard in a large or noisy area. Instructors must be able to project their voices to the farthest part of the audience. When this projection is *not* possible, then a microphone and speaker system must be used.
  — *Rate (Variety or Variation):* Speed at which words are spoken. Research indicates that vocal delivery rates that are higher than the average rate of 130 to 150 words per minute are more persuasive than slower rates. Audience culture can affect the rate of speech that a person uses and is familiar with. Consideration of the audience is important to ensure that the speaker does *not* talk too fast to be understood.
  — *Inflection:* Variation in the pitch of the voice; used to emphasize important or critical information and provide clues to students about how they should interpret the information.

- **Vocal interferences** — Interferences or distractions that tend to clutter the speaker's presentation and detract from the content of the speech or conversation. *Examples:*
  — Interferences or filler words include sounds such as *uh, um,* or *er* and words such as *well, like,* and *you know.* Filler words can give the impression that a person is *not* educated or confident. These words have no real value in interpersonal or speech communications.
  — Students do *not* take instructors who use a lot of slang seriously.
  — Profanity is *always* unprofessional and may offend students and other instructors. Profanity can be considered an element of a *hostile environment.*

Presentation tips:

— Practicing a presentation before a meeting helps instructors recognize the presence of filler words and gain confidence in the material to be presented.

— Recording a presentation (either by audiotapes or videotapes) also helps speakers overcome the habit of using vocal interferences.

• ***Appropriate use of humor*** — Effective speakers use appropriate humor to create a relaxed atmosphere and get the attention of the audience. However, inappropriate humor that may offend members of the audience should be avoided. Humor that is appropriate in one setting may *not* be acceptable in another. The sensitivity of comments and actions must always be a consideration in any communication setting. Inappropriate humor that may have been considered acceptable in the past is no longer tolerated in progressive fire and emergency service organizations.

Nonverbal Elements

The nonverbal elements of speech were introduced in Chapter 4, Effective Interpersonal Communication. Nonverbal communication includes eye contact, facial expressions, gestures, posture, and poise and is an effective and important part of the communication process.

Because the listener or audience interprets the majority of the meaning from the nonverbal elements of the message, an instructor must consciously work to match the verbal and nonverbal elements to each other. When an instructor says *yes* while shaking the head side to side visually indicating *no,* students will become confused and distracted (**Figure 10.9**).

Presentation Preparation

Methods are available to help instructors identify distracting areas that need improvement, eliminate many annoying habits, and identify tendencies that distract from the delivery of the message. It is also important that instructors relax before a training session. The following list of presentation techniques can help instructors speak and communicate effectively:

• Practice the delivery of a presentation.

• Videotape the presentation and review it for distracting actions and speech patterns. Videotaping also enables instructors to experiment with different ways to present materials, which can increase instructional effectiveness (**Figure 10.10**).

Attributes of an Effective Speaking Voice

• ***Pronunciation*** — Correctly saying each pause, syllable, and accent. *Example: Fire* instead of *farr*

• ***Good grammar*** — Correct tense, possession, pronoun agreement, etc. *Examples: We* instead of *We is, I am not* instead of *I ain't,* and *We were* instead of *We is*

• ***Inflection*** — Variation of tone (pitch) of words, syllables, or phrases to emphasize important points. *Examples:* Have a *Great* day! Look at *That!*

• ***Variety*** — Changes in loudness, tone, and speaking rate that complement a presentation. *Examples:* Loud/soft volume, fast/slow speed, and high/low pitch

• ***Enunciation*** — Clearly emphasizing each syllable, accent, and pause (the opposite is slurring). *Examples: Got to* instead of *gotta, how are you*

doing, instead of *how you doin'* when *is* instead of *when's, going to* instead of *gonna,* and *yes* instead of *yeah*

• ***Projection*** — Being understood in the back of the room or teaching space through pronunciation, variety, loudness, enunciation, and proper grammar

Sounds, Words, Phrases and Gestures to Forget

• ***Sounds*** — Um, aah, and humm

• ***Crutch Words*** — Okay, now, basically, next, and yeah

• ***Phrases*** — You know, next we will, you are, and you are going to

• ***Gestures*** — Combing hair, jingling keys/coins, scratching, and/or rubbing

• ***Other words*** — Hope, think, plan, should, currently, about, wish, approximately, and almost

- Speak clearly and distinctly. Enunciate and clearly pronounce each word. Do *not* mumble or slur words together.

- Check the presentation materials to ensure that they are complete, in order, and correct for the topic.

- Use expressive voice inflection and add emphasis to words to transmit interest and excitement about what is expressed. Do *not* speak in a monotone.

- Govern the speaking pace or speed. Begin slowly with new information for new students and gradually increase speed as information becomes familiar and students understand it. Speak slowly for important points and when students need to take notes. Restate important points, and emphasize their importance with voice tone.

- Pause periodically so students can maintain their thoughts, think about what they heard, and ask questions. Do *not* feel pressured by silence. Students need time to think about and format responses.

- Use correct grammar. When using technical terms, abbreviations, and acronyms, define and explain them in context with the lesson. Avoid slang and expletives.

- Relax and speak in a conversational tone so listeners feel at ease and ready to receive information.

- Make eye contact with students while speaking. Eye contact reinforces the feeling that the speaker is interested in the students and concerned that they understand the message. Speakers who look at the wall or ceiling or out the window rather than at the students are *not* communicating with them.

- Get plenty of rest the night before a presentation.

- Select comfortable clothing in which to deliver a presentation, and always dress appropriately.

- Anticipate potential problems, and prepare to resolve them should they occur.

- Be yourself and use your own unique style, experiences, and abilities as a person.

- Use appropriate gestures to illustrate mental pictures or emphasize key points.

- Avoid distracting mannerisms such as the following:
  — Pacing around the floor
  — Playing with or tapping pens, pencils, and other items

Figure 10.9 Instructors must practice the correct use of appropriate nonverbal signals to emphasize the verbal portion of their presentations.

Figure 10.10 Instructors can benefit from videotaping their practice presentations and then reviewing the videos.

— Jingling keys or change

— Chewing gum, fingernails, matchsticks, or toothpicks

— Using filler words such as *OK, you know,* and *um* or *uh*

— Using the word *I* excessively

— Overusing *pet* words or fad phrases such as *24/7*

Attitudes/Values Display

The affective domain introduced in Chapter 7, Principles of Learning, involves the transmission of beliefs, values, and attitudes. The transmission can occur in two ways: through teaching and through personal actions. Teaching beliefs and values is similar to teaching cognitive knowledge. Instructors describe the belief or value, provide examples of correct and incorrect behavior, and explain the results of consequences of the behavior. Students can then discuss the examples and relate them to personal experiences. This approach could be used to introduce the organization's code of ethical conduct for instance.

The personal display of the belief, value, or attitude through the actions of the instructor is just as important as conveying information about a belief, value, or attitude. That display means that instructors who teach a subject like ethics must also adhere to the expected ethical behavior. By following ethical behavior, instructors provide students with a role model for them to follow. Students witness the actions and relate them to the words used to present the information.

Instructors who clearly present these aspects of the affective domain — attitude, values, and beliefs — convey important information and skills and set positive examples for students. Students can then internalize the information and develop the necessary skills while training and then correctly perform what they have learned later on the job.

Presentation Organization Format

Oral presentations generally consist of three parts: opening or introduction, body, and summary or conclusion. This format follows the basic concept of telling the listener or student the topic of the presentation, detailing the topic, and then stating what has been taught. In other words, follow the old axiom that states: *Tell them what you are going to tell them, tell them, and then tell them what you told them.*

All presentations should follow this general format. Within this format, the information can be presented in a variety of logical sequences (see Methods of Sequencing section). Descriptions of the three parts are as follows:

- ***Introduction*** — Use the opening of the presentation to get the attention of students. Introduce students to the topic and purpose of the presentation and tell them how it relates to them or their jobs. Also present a brief summary or outline of the main points to be discussed to help students remain focused on the topic.

- ***Body*** — Present the information by using a logical, sequencing approach along with supporting facts and information. Separate the body of a long presentation into smaller, easily understood segments. Ensure that each segment makes a single point or conveys one idea and has its own simple opening, body, and summary. Link segments by transition phrases in their summaries.

- ***Summary, closure, or conclusion*** — Review the objective of the presentation and how it is relevant to the overall goal of the course. Emphasize the main points and ideas of the presentation. Introduce the next lesson or the demonstration that is associated with the presentation. The conclusion should be a part of all lesson plans.

Methods of Sequencing

Teaching methodology and speech communication disciplines have established sequences for presenting information in a presentation. The sequence depends on the topic and the organization of the lesson plan. Generally accepted sequences for instructional delivery include the following:

- ***Known-to-unknown*** — Begin with material that students are familiar with or already know. From this point, lead students into the unfamiliar or what is unknown. This method is effective because it gives students an opportunity to base the learning experience on something they can recognize. For example, when introducing new tools or equipment, most students *know* that tools are aids for performing a job and the new tool will aid them to perform a particular job. How to use the tool to accomplish a job is *unknown* or new to them.

- *Simple-to-complex* — Begin by teaching the basic knowledge or skill and then introduce more difficult or complex knowledge as the lesson progresses. The basic knowledge and first steps of a skill are necessary foundations to mastering the more complex knowledge and skill. For example, instructors must be sure that students have mastered basic rope skills such as tying basic knots before moving on to more complex uses of rope such as assembling rigging and hauling systems. Without learning the simple (basic rope skills) first, learning the complex (assembling a hauling system) is *not* possible.

- *Whole-to-part* — Begin this sequence with an overview of the entire topic or a demonstration of the complete skill in real time. Next, divide the topic or skill into subsections or steps. Discuss, describe, or demonstrate each of the subsections or steps. Some instructors add another *whole* to the end by closing the lecture with a summary of the entire topic or a demonstration of the complete skill.

- *Part-to-whole* — Reverse the whole-to-part sequence. Begin by describing a part, such as the impeller of a pump, and then show how the part works with the larger unit, in this case the pump. Also relate how the part is important to the operation of the whole such as showing the relationship between the individual firefighter and the company, battalion, and organization.

- *Step-by-step* — Teach each step in order and then have students practice them in the same order. This sequence works best when teaching a process that is composed of individual steps. An example of knowledge taught in this manner would be one person picking up and setting a ground ladder.

- *Chronological* — Use a chronological sequence to teach history or the biographical life of an individual or organization. Highlight certain key events in the various stages of the event or life and describe the relationship of the events to each other. This sequence is used primarily for cognitive knowledge.

Instructors commonly use all of these sequences to present new material because they provide a solid foundation for the learning process. These sequences also help instructors outline the points that are essential to understanding the topic and mastering a skill. Educational professionals recommend that instructors use several checkpoints when preparing a lesson to enable them to check for understanding during the lesson. A short list of checkpoints include the following:

- Analyze the presentation to ensure that it is logical in its sequence.

- Show physical examples of unfamiliar objects or demonstrate unfamiliar processes.

- Diagram on a chalkboard, on a handout, or through other visual aids a complex set of ideas held together by some kind of structure (**Figure 10.11, p. 238**).

- Use demonstrations and modeling where possible, particularly cognitive modeling in which the instructor *thinks out loud* while performing the physical activities of demonstrating.

- Build motivation by pointing out the interest value or application possibilities of the new material. Stress aspects that interest students.

In all lessons, instructors must ensure that they introduce students to the key points, stress these points in the related parts of the lesson, and review and summarize them at the end of the lesson. Even though a lesson segment may be presented out of sequence from the outline, the lesson or segment must flow logically, using one of the sequential methods.

Instructional Methods for Active Learning

In the Instructional Delivery Methods section, the instructor candidate was introduced to the various instructor-led and technology-based approaches to teaching. In the past, teachers believed that it was only necessary to provide information in lectures, handouts, and textbooks and students would learn the information.

Figure 10.11 Dry marker boards enable instructors to illustrate complex ideas, concepts, or relationships.

Current research and teaching theory promotes the concept of *active learning* (also referred to as *active participation*) that is defined as using instructional activities that involve students in doing things and thinking about what they are doing **(Figure 10.12)**.

The following sections give strategies in applying instructional activities and list the advantages of active learning. In addition, guidance for instructors in motivating students, encouraging student success, and reinforcing learning is provided. Techniques for using questions as an element of active learning are also discussed.

Strategies

The following strategies have been developed to assist the instructor in applying instructional activities for active learning in the classroom:

- *Modify the traditional lecture method of instructional delivery* — Organize the lessons into small segments lasting from 12 to 18 minutes each. Research indicates that students can only absorb and retain so much information. While most instructors speak at a rate of 120 to 240 words per minute, students are only capable of taking notes at a rate of 20 words per minute. Research has determined that this approach can significantly improve student retention rates and test scores. *Small segment process:*

  — Speak slowly and emphasize key points.

  — Provide relevant examples and illustrations.

Figure 10.12 Active learning involves students in the learning process that includes applying and practicing psychomotor skills. *Courtesy of Alabama Fire College.*

  — Use visual aids as appropriate.

  — Allow students time to work in pairs or small groups at the end of each segment by letting them compare notes, ask questions of each other, and discuss the lecture material.

  — Start another short segment of lecture.

  — Give students 3 minutes at the end of the class lesson to write down everything they remember from the lesson **(Figure 10.13)**.

- *Intersperse the small lecture segments with discussion groups or skills practice times* — Permit students to either discuss the information or perform the skills that are related to the knowledge. The topic of the discussion or practice is the information that was contained in the lecture.

- *Provide a clear preview of the information that will be contained in the lecture* — Include a preview or outline in the introduction to the lesson. The overview should be short and precise and provide the following information:
  — Overall idea to be presented
  — Importance of the information to be learned
  — Outline of the structure of the content to be presented
- *Use effective presentation skills when delivering the lesson* — Use the following guidelines:
  — Stress important points. Write the points on the board, enumerate the points, pause or use vocal inflections, or simply state: *This is important.*
  — Include transitions (statements that tie two ideas together) between information because they permit a smooth flow in the information and connect what may otherwise be different ideas. Use transitions between the introduction and body and between the body and summary.
  — Refrain from using nonessential or irrelevant information. Information that is *not* related to the topic can be distracting and confusing for students.

Figure 10.13 Students must have time to write notes, highlight text, or copy diagrams during and at the end of a class session.

— Review frequently. Provide a brief review after the presentation of difficult or detailed information. Also, review material at the end of each short segment and end of the lesson. It may also be appropriate to review material again at the beginning of the next class period, especially if the material is related to the new lesson.

Advantages

The advantages of active learning have been established through research at all levels of education. Among the advantages that have been noted are the following:

- *Fosters improved student understanding* — Improved understanding results from small group discussions and the opportunity to reflect on the material presented in the lecture.
- *Improves student communication skills* — Improvement occurs through the interpersonal communication required to function in a small group. Students must learn to listen effectively, develop their positions on the topics, and discuss the information logically in the group.
- *Improves cooperation within a group* — Active learning helps to create a sense of teamwork and cooperation between students.
- *Places the responsibility for learning in the hands of the student* — Active learning increases the sense of ownership of the learning process on the part of the student.

When active learning is applied to TBT, these advantages are created through online chat groups and e-mail as well as periodic meetings. Additional advantages that occur with technology-based active training include the following:

- *Improves technology-usage skills* — Students are able to practice computer and Internet skills while performing course requirements.
- *Improves knowledge-management skills* — Students must use online information to complete the course requirements, which increases the skills that are required to function in a work environment that is becoming more dependent on easily accessible information.

Motivational Techniques

Students in fire and emergency services training programs include adults who bring their previous significant experiences to the learning experience. Because these adult students want to relate their experiences to the training, instructors need to plan lessons that allow students to integrate their experiences with new information. By getting students involved in the instruction, instructors stimulate and maintain student interest and achieve the goal of active learning.

Generating student interest is more than just causing students to pay attention — it is causing them to *desire* more information and understanding about the topic and *want* to participate in the learning process. Interested students are open and responsive and want to concentrate on what they are learning and retain it. As a result, they will also be more willing to actively participate in the active-learning process.

Generating interest is only the first step. Instructors must help students maintain interest throughout the lesson and the course. Fire and emergency services training can be repetitive because it often involves review of skills for accurate performance and recertification requirements.

Instructors need to show students a personal connection with the lesson. Maintaining interest can be accomplished by following several strategies. One set of educational professionals suggests the following strategies for maintaining interest:

- *Relate learning to student interests* — Material relevant to student experiences is important. By offering material that pertains to their professional goals, duties, and tasks, instructors expose students to experiences that arouse their curiosities and desires for understanding.

- *State clearly or demonstrate the advantages of the learning activity* — Learning activities that offer the possibility of gaining an advantage in life or on the job are interesting to students.

- *Use humor appropriately* — Humor has many attractive and stimulating qualities. Use it spontaneously; laugh *with* people but *not at* them. *Qualities:*

    — Offers enjoyment, unique perspective, and unpredictability
    — Makes people laugh
    — Makes learning interesting

- *Stimulate emotions* — People become interested in events that cause strong emotions such as anger, delight, affection, and sorrow. The experiences that students bring to training sessions evoke all of these emotions and can arouse interest when these experiences are incorporated into the lesson.

- *Explain and illustrate with examples, stories, analogies, and metaphors* — Examples allow students to focus on new learning by imagining in their minds how to perform an activity. Carefully chosen examples help students understand. Well-told and imaginative stories that are related to the topic can captivate students. Analogies and metaphors are ways of suggesting colorful likenesses between two completely different things. For example, an instructor might use an analogy: *Firefighters doing overhaul often act like a bull in a china shop. What can we do during overhaul to help preserve the victim's property?*

- *Use questions to stimulate interest* — Questions stimulate thinking and participation. With practice and experience, instructors can learn to pose well-timed, thought-provoking, appropriate, and quality questions that stimulate thought, encourage participation, and develop understanding. Questions are opportunities to stimulate students in either of two ways:

    — First, with interest, attention, and excitement because the student knows the answer and wants to use it

    — Second, with fear, uncertainty, curiosity, and interest because the student does *not* know the answer but wants to find out what it is

- *Use unpredictability and uncertainty with a sense of security and enjoyment* — When used appropriately, the unexpected can arouse interest. Unpredictability can be stimulating. The news media often use uncertainty and surprise to keep audience interest. Anticipating the unexpected is exciting when it is done so that it makes the audience feel safe and know that no one will be hurt. Instructors must plan these unexpected or surprise events to ensure safety and enjoyment during the learning process.

Words to Teach By

Your students have entrusted you with their most valuable possession, time. Don't you dare give them anything less than your best.

Be Prepared: Know your material, prepare your classroom, master your audiovisuals (including the machines), and have a backup plan.

Preview your video presentations. Use only those portions that are important to your lesson.

Be excited about what you teach; it's contagious!

Courtesy of Rod Smith, Training Chief, Lane County Fire District No. 1, Veneta, Oregon.

Encouragement for Success

Encouraging success is emotional coaching that assists students in completing tasks. Most people want to succeed and usually arrive at a training session with the desire to complete the course or curriculum successfully. The reasons students take a class were discussed in Chapter 8, Student Attributes and Behaviors. Generally, internal reasons include many kinds of motivators that fuel a desire for success such as the following:

- Keeping a job
- Getting a promotion or raise
- Gaining recognition
- Feeling important
- Joining a group (organization or club)

People want and need to succeed. Fear of failure is a major psychological barrier that prevents people from taking risks. This same fear may hold students back or cause them to believe that they *can't do a task*. Students find it difficult to dislike a class in which they are successful. Instructors can positively influence student attitudes and encourage their successes by offering the following instructional enhancements:

- *Provide quality instruction that helps students who try to learn* — Make the first experience with a new subject or topic safe, successful, and interesting. First impressions are important and have a lasting effect on future learning.

- *Provide evidence that student efforts make a difference* — Stress the importance of the amount and quality of effort needed for success in learning tasks before students begin. Students control the effort they put forth. Emphasizing the importance of effort, without threatening, accomplishes the following objectives:

  — Establishes student responsibility

  — Reduces feelings of helplessness

  — Increases perseverance

  — Generates feelings of pride and accomplishment

- *Provide continuous feedback about student progress* — Make the learning goals and evaluation criteria clear. Knowing what to expect and how they are progressing help students succeed. They need to know exactly what they are to learn and how well they are performing in preparation for testing. Instructors who provide learning and testing criteria, continuous and constructive feedback, and appropriate coaching and encouragement have confident and successful students. A verbal *pat on the back* can aid a student's self-esteem tremendously.

Reinforcement of Learning

Instructors reinforce learning by applying two different methods. The first approach involves reinforcing the information and its value by repeating, emphasizing, and reviewing it with the students. The second approach involves behavioral reinforcement that either encourages the student's attempts at learning and successful completion of the activity, skill, or exam or corrects incorrect skills or behavior.

Repetition

As mentioned, repetition is an integral part of active learning and the organization of the presentation. In lecture-type instructional delivery, it includes clearly stating the topic and learning

early in the session. Questions like these can help to create interest in the topic for discussion in the lesson.

- **Follow up answers** — The instructor can elicit further response by using techniques such as inviting elaboration, encouraging other class members to respond, or using silence. *Examples:*

    — In the first instance, once a student has answered the question, the instructor may state *Could you expand on your answer?* as a way of encouraging the student to go into greater depth or detail.

    — The instructor may also want to involve other students by asking them to provide an additional idea, fact, or experience to the answer that was already provided.

    — While most instructors are afraid of silence during a class, being deliberately silent can be an effective tool when asking questions. The instructor's silence can cause a student to elaborate on the initial answer.

New instructors should practice developing questions and include questions in their lesson plans or outlines. When there is extra time in a session, the questions can be used to help students focus on the key points of the presentation. Questions can also be used to start group discussions as time allows.

Question Types
The type of question depends on the specific answer or the direction an instructor wants to take the questioning. Instructors can use the following types of questions to start discussions, stimulate thinking, provide feedback on how training is being received, and enable students to assess their learning and complete their own learning gaps:

- **Rhetorical** — It is *not* the intent of this type of question to have only one correct answer or necessarily an oral response. Rather, rhetorical questions are used to stimulate thinking or motivate participants. This type of question is addressed to the entire group and often serves as an effective attention-getter. For example, an instructor might open a safety lesson by saying: *What are the most important pieces of*

equipment you will use on an emergency scene to protect yourself from injury or exposure? By the end of this lesson, you will know how to answer this question.

- **Closed** — This type of question has a limited number of possible answers. The instructor is able to anticipate and judge the accuracy of student responses. Example: *What is the definition of flashover?*

- **Open** — This type of question has many acceptable answers. The instructor has general criteria for judging the accuracy of an answer, although the student answer may be unexpected. Example: *What is one example of personal protective equipment?*

- **Direct** — The question is directed to one person in the class who is expected to respond. As mentioned previously in the guidelines, the instructor asks the question, waits 3 to 5 seconds, and then asks a specific student to provide the answer. This type of question is *not* frequently used with adult learners because it can put students on the spot. However, the direct question may be a technique the instructor may use to control an unruly student.

- **Overhead** — The instructor asks a question of the entire class, not just one student. Any member of the class is free to respond either spontaneously by calling out the answer or by raising a hand and waiting to be recognized. This technique is helpful in starting discussions or offering ideas or opinions. When no one offers the answer, the instructor can then direct the question to an individual. Instructors may also use this type of question and allow students to consult with each other in groups to produce the answer. This method can be an interesting diversion and a challenge to see which group correctly answers the question first.

- **Relay** — The instructor receives a question from a class member and sends it back to the class to answer. Using the relay question is a good way to open a discussion or start a debate. For either result, it stimulates thinking and participation.

- **Redirected** — This question may be used when a student asks a question that the instructor believes the individual should know. The instructor can ask the student to provide small amounts of information that taken together will answer the original question.

Instructor Responses

Instructors should prepare for student responses to questions they pose and understand the proper way of responding to those answers or new questions. Some basic guidelines for instructors are as follows:

- Use positive reinforcement when students are answering the instructor's question. For students who may answer the question correctly, reinforce their answer by replying *That is absolutely right! You obviously understand the topic.*

- Start by reinforcing the correct portion of an answer when a student answers a question partially correct. Redirect the question back to the student, ask another student in the class, or provide the answer to the question. The instructor's reply may be *You have the first two components correct, can we remember the third?*

- Do *not* let incorrect answers by students slip by without providing the correct answer or acknowledging that the student's answer was incorrect. Some students may not provide the correct answer to a question. It is important to provide the correct answer for the benefit of the student and the rest of the class. At the same time, correcting the student should *not* cause that person to cease participating in the class or be afraid to answer future questions. In this case, acknowledge the effort, redirect the question to others, or provide the answer to the question. A response could be *That is close. Maybe I didn't ask the question clearly. What I am asking is . . . .*

Answering students' questions is one of the most difficult things for instructors to do. Some students may pose questions that on the surface appear to be logical but are really complex, illogical, or off the topic. An instructor can respond to these types of questions in the following ways:

- Provide the answer to a question when the instructor is the best person to have the answer. When necessary, defer the question to a more knowledgeable source such as a senior instructor or administrator. Be aware that the question could be controversial or distract the class.

- Direct a question to another participant when there is a high probability that another participant will respond correctly. This approach can be used to generate group discussion.

- Defer questions that are beyond the scope of the course, or tell students that the answers will be provided later in the course materials.

- Defer questions that require time to research for the correct answer. Never bluff students by providing false or misleading information. Students usually can learn the truth, and then the instructor's credibility and integrity with the class is destroyed.

Summary

The fire and emergency services member who assumes the duties of instructor assumes a heavy responsibility. That person is responsible for training other members in the duties and tasks of a hazardous profession. To fulfill that responsibility, instructors must be able to provide training in a wide range of fire-and-emergency-services-related topics. At the same time, instructors must understand and apply instructional delivery techniques that make the information clear and easy to understand for any student.

Instructors must master presentation skills that may seem overwhelming at first and always frightening. Finally, instructors must provide a learning environment that meets the needs of students while meeting the requirements of the organization. This chapter provided an introduction to those teaching skills.

Active Training: A Tool for Improving Your Fire Service Training

The effectiveness of any fire department depends largely on the effectiveness of the department's training program. This is true whether it is a large metropolitan career or a small rural volunteer department. Unfortunately, there are few departments today that have the luxury of being able to provide the quantity of training needed to ensure that *all* firefighters have mastered *all* of their job skills.

One way to overcome this shortage of training time is to improve the *quality* of the training being delivered. A way to improve the quality of any training program is by applying the principles of active training.

Active training is *not* a new concept. Rather, it brings several of the principles of adult learning into a comprehensive approach to the design and delivery of training. Three components of active training are as follows:

- *Activity* — Involves keeping the students' minds working from start to finish in the class. For example, rather than listening to a lecture about strategy and tactics, students are drawn into a discussion about how to apply tactics to various fireground situations.

- *Variety* — Uses different instructional methods during delivery of the class or training evolution. A key instructional principle that most instructors are taught in any instructor course is that different people process information received during training in different ways such as the following:

  — *Visual learners:* Some students process information primarily through what they see.

  — *Auditory learners:* Others process information primarily through what they hear and read.

  — *Kinesthetic learners:* Still others process information primarily through what they experience.

  During instruction, you use all three approaches together so that *all* learners are able to more effectively process the information.

- *Participation* — Engages all students in the learning process. Students are *not* casual observers; they are active participants in what is being presented. Rather than listening to a lecture all day, the instructor asks students questions. The question *Why?* is asked routinely to generate discussion. Students are given an opportunity to have input into their learning experience by providing feedback to the instructor.

Courtesy of Ed Kirtley, Officer/Instructor Coordinator, Oklahoma Fire Service Training.

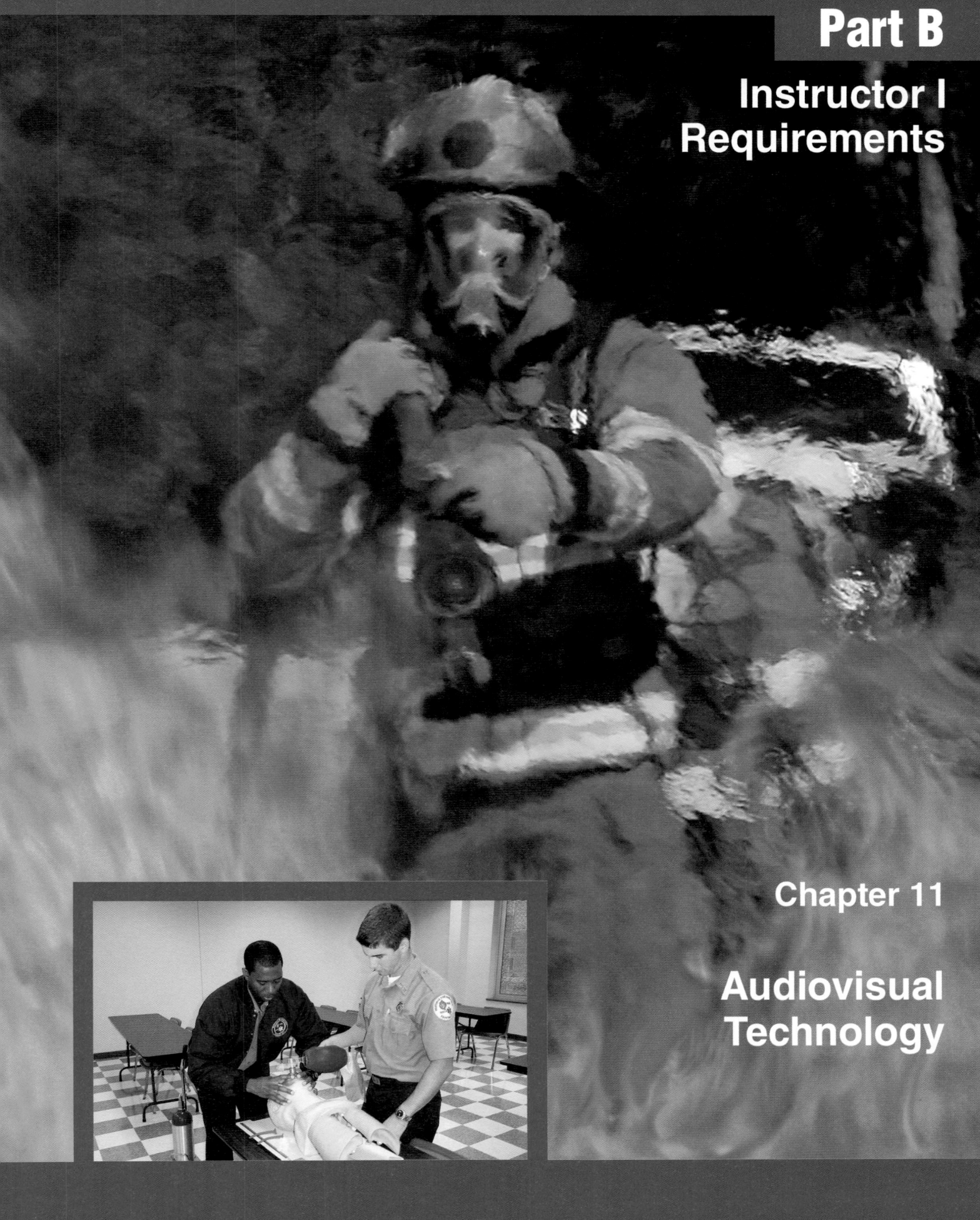

Part B

Instructor I Requirements

Chapter 11

Audiovisual Technology

After reading this chapter, students will be able to —

1. List benefits of using audiovisual training aids.

2. Identify accurate statements about factors to consider when selecting audiovisual training aids.

3. List guidelines for using audiovisual training aids.

4. Identify accurate statements about strategies for avoiding distractions when using audiovisual training aids.

5. List purposes of transitions.

6. List reasons transitions are used.

7. Describe a verbal transition and a nonverbal transition.

8. Identify guidelines for media transitions and animations.

9. List advantages of nonprojected audiovisual training aids over projected training aids.

10. Identify facts about nonprojected training aids.

11. List advantages and disadvantages of projected audiovisual training aids.

12. Identify accurate statements about front-screen and rear-screen projection devices.

13. Identify facts about projected audiovisual training aids.

14. Identify accurate statements about ancillary equipment.

15. List cleaning guidelines for audiovisual training aid devices.

16. List guidelines for the care of audiovisual training aids and devices.

17. Identify accurate statements about the maintenance of audiovisual training aid devices.

Chapter Contents

Audiovisual Training Aid Benefits

Audiovisual Training Aid Selection
Learning Objectives and Lesson Content
Required Student Performance
Class Size and Interaction
Pace of Learning
Practice Factors
Evaluative Factors
Budget Limitations

Audiovisual Training Aids Use and Development

Transitions in Presentations
Purposes
Timing
Types and Development

Audiovisual Training Aid Types
Nonprojected Training Aids
Projected Training Aids
Simulators
Ancillary Equipment

Cleaning, Care, and Maintenance

Summary

Chapter 11
Audiovisual Technology

Active learning includes the use of audiovisual training aids or other training aids to supplement lectures and demonstrations in instructor-led training. Audiovisual training aids are *not* substitutes for experienced, skilled instructors. Training aids should be used to enhance the lesson by providing information that appeals to the senses of sight and touch as well as that of hearing (**Figure 11.1**). Students learn and retain more information when it is provided by an appropriate combination of active learning-based delivery methods, like those outlined in Chapter 10, Instructional Delivery.

Instructors who lack confidence in their presentation skills may tend to rely on audiovisual training aids to replace their participation and fill class time. Instructors must *not* use audiovisual training aids as crutches or props. They must learn to use training aids effectively by integrating each element with the traditional presentation skills they already have. It should also be noted that PowerPoint® and other electronic presentation software packages do *not* replace the need for proper lesson development using traditional lesson plans.

Instructors must practice with the different types of audiovisual training aids, experiment with them, and learn how to use them to create interest in lesson topics. Most current fire and emergency services students have matured in the age of television, video games, and multimedia computing. They are accustomed to seeing fast-paced visual images and receiving information through sight, feel, and sound. They have a desire to learn information quickly and believe that education should be entertaining. Effective use of audiovisual training aids allows instructors to perform the following actions:

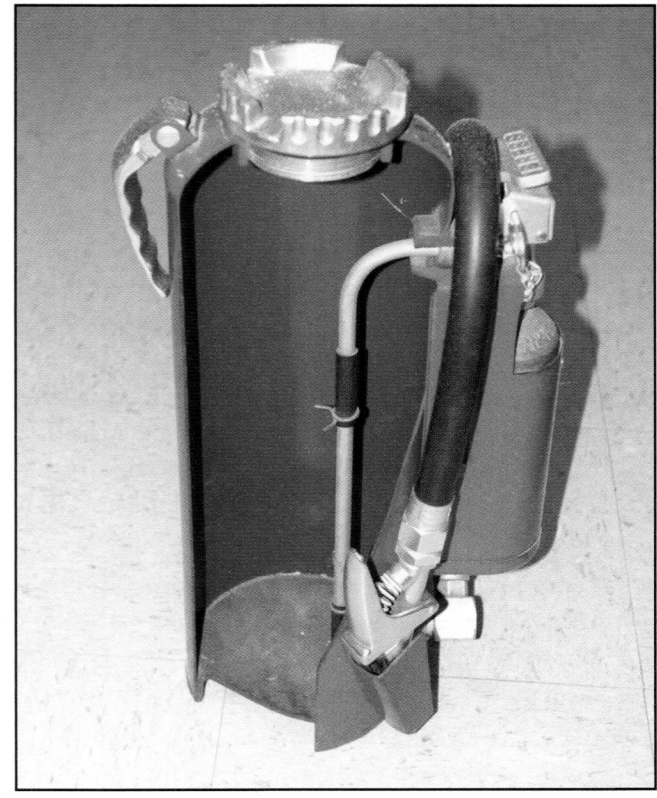

Figure 11.1 Through the active learning process, students can learn faster and retain more information by using detailed training aids such as this portable fire extinguisher cutaway.

- Satisfy many learning styles.
- Tailor instruction to individual needs.
- Design lesson plans to deliver messages through all three of those senses.

To assist the instructor candidate in meeting the requirements of NFPA 1041, *Standard for Fire Service Instructor Professional Qualifications,* for Instructor I, this chapter describes the various benefits and types of audiovisual technology that is currently available and commonly used for instructional delivery. It discusses the advantages and disadvantages of the various types so that instructors may consider which training aid is appropriate for a particular type of delivery.

The chapter also includes information on selecting the appropriate training aid or device, developing training aids, and using them effectively in the classroom. The creation, use, and importance of transitions are discussed as well. Suggestions for using, cleaning, caring for, and maintaining audiovisual training aids and devices are also included.

Audiovisual Training Aid Benefits

Many benefits of using audiovisual training aids have been presented in previous chapters. When included as part of an active learning instructional delivery, training aids perform the following functions:

- *Enhance student understanding* — Because 83 percent of all information is received visually, audiovisual training aids increase the ability of students to understand the information in a lesson.

- *Increase student acceptance* — Seeing an illustration or touching an item will help students accept the reality of the item more easily than simply hearing a description of it.

- *Add interest to a lecture* — An audiovisual training aid adds variety and interest to a lecture, providing the student with additional visual or tactile stimulation.

- *Clarify, prove, or emphasize a key point* — Students see the key point at the same time that they hear the description, thereby making the point clearer or more emphatic (important). A key point can be proven or validated by using illustrations of actual events or examples.

- *Enhance memory* — Audiovisual aids reinforce the information that is provided verbally in the lecture, making it easier to remember and retain. Research indicates that people remember 50 percent of the information that they see and hear at the same time.

- *Help students organize ideas* — Complex ideas or processes benefit from visually listing the components on a chart or board. Students can follow the lecture better when the words are associated with illustrations or outlines.

- *Gain and maintain students' attention* — Dramatic images can help get the attention of students and keep their attention throughout the lecture. Strong memorable illustrations, charts, graphs, or photographs remain with students and continue to bring back the words that were associated with them.

- *Illustrate a sequence of events or steps in a process* — Audiovisual training aids can establish a sequence of steps, the components of an assembly, or the steps of a theoretical process. They are especially helpful when the sequence is *not* one that can be demonstrated such as the circulation of blood in the body.

- *Save lecture time* — Because more information can be transferred to the student through the use of appropriate visual aids, lecture time can be reduced, making training more efficient.

With these benefits in mind, instructors must select the appropriate audiovisual training aid or device that best illustrates the topic, satisfies the required learning objective, and matches the learning styles of class members. Instructors should always remember that training aids should support the instructor's presentation but *not* replace it.

Audiovisual Training Aid Selection

Selecting the appropriate audiovisual training aids for use with a lecture or demonstration requires planning to make them work with the learning objectives and lesson content, ensuring that they have a purpose and are student-focused. Instructors should consider the following factors when selecting audiovisual training aids or devices:

- Learning objectives and lesson content
- Required student performance
- Class size and interaction
- Pace of learning

- Practice factors
- Evaluative factors
- Budget limitations

Learning Objectives and Lesson Content

The content of any audiovisual training aid that an instructor uses in a lecture or demonstration must be relevant to the desired learning objectives and lesson content. Instructors should review the lesson plan, determine the content and objectives, and then select the type of training aid that will satisfy as many of the benefits listed previously as possible.

When the source for the audiovisual training aid is a professionally produced curriculum or single item, it should be compared to the desired lesson plan outcome. It may be necessary to alter the training aid or use only the relevant portion of it.

For instance, when the lesson content concerns the behavior of fire and the learning objective is to understand the fire tetrahedron, then a simple transparency illustrating this theory is appropriate. When the illustration is part of a longer, more detailed video on fire development, it may be necessary to only use the appropriate short sequence within the video to satisfy the learning objective. When the instructor does *not* have an existing training aid, it is then necessary to create one using the technology that is available.

Required Student Performance

The use of standardized training curriculums in recent years has made it easier for instructors to select appropriate audiovisual training aids. Standards for professional competency that have been developed, published, and periodically updated are the bases for current fire and emergency services training and certification.

Textbooks, instructional deliveries, audiovisual training aids, and curriculums are developed to specifically satisfy the requirements of those standards. In many cases, standard development and curriculum development occur simultaneously or at least with some overlap. This timing allows current and NFPA-compliant materials to be available as soon as possible after the publication of the standards.

While some jurisdictions may be required by law to comply with these standards, others may have adopted locally developed training requirements based on local needs or ordinances. In either case, audiovisual training aids can help meet the established level of student performance.

Based on the lesson plan, training aids should be selected that most appropriately illustrate or demonstrate the knowledge that the student must possess when the course is completed. For instance, when a course is to help company officers become certified to command a multiple company operation, a computer-simulation program may be an effective training aid. When students are required to successfully perform cardiopulmonary resuscitation (CPR), then mannequins for training and evaluation are appropriate (**Figure 11.2**).

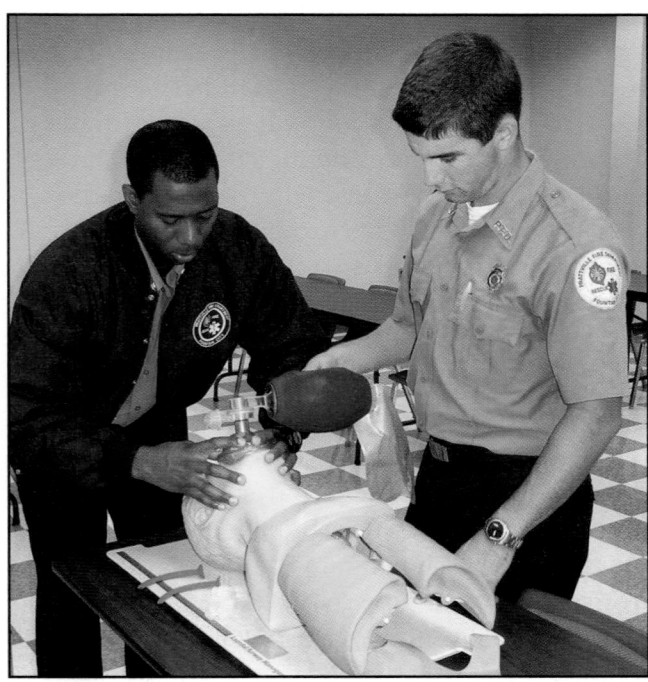

Figure 11.2 Mastery of a subject can be demonstrated with the use of a training aid such as a CPR mannequin. *Courtesy of Alabama Fire College.*

Class Size and Interaction

The size of a class and expected level of interaction are key factors in selecting audiovisual training aids. Class size and seating arrangement have a direct relationship with the size of the image the class is expected to view. For example, using an easel pad in front of an audience of 200 people seated in a large auditorium may *not* be appropriate. An overhead projector or visual presenter with a large projection screen is a better choice. On the other hand, when debriefing a group of 6 trainees after a practical training evolution, an easel pad or marker board may be ideal.

Teaching situations where instructors want to encourage student participation and interaction can influence the choice of training aids. Interaction with a large class may be limited by class size and arrangement to a question-and-answer period at the end of the presentation. Spontaneous diagrams on an easel pad or marker board can facilitate a highly participative coaching session in a small class.

Pace of Learning

Different audiovisual training aids can be effective when applied in different instructional environments. One factor in the suitability of a training aid to the environment is the intended pace of learning. When the expected pace of learning is high, training aids can be integrated into the lesson plan in such a way as to allow a class to move quickly through the information. For example, a video can quickly review the basics of an incident command system at the beginning of a lesson on the responsibilities of the division or group supervisor.

When the content of the lesson is primarily unfamiliar to students, training aids that allow an instructor to proceed at a slower pace are more appropriate. One strategy for teaching new material is to assign outside reading assignments from textbooks or self-study guides for completion before the beginning of class. The information is followed in class by guided discussions on marker boards or easel pads. Students can then view a video for review and reinforcement.

When students represent a variety of knowledge levels or experiences, a student-centered strategy can include a mixture of the two scenarios. Those students who are *not* yet at the required learning level can have access to self-study materials before joining the more advanced students at the appropriate time.

Practice Factors

It is always important to give students an opportunity to apply new knowledge and skills. To make the new application meaningful, practice time should be included in the lesson plan along with the training aids or props needed. In order to apply the knowledge and skills obtained from a lesson on tying knots or operating a power tool, for example, the students need the equipment and props so they can execute the steps.

The training aids required to apply nonphysical concepts or skills such as incident management, personnel supervision, problem solving, or accident or fire investigation may be more difficult to select. Training aids for prospective incident managers can include practice scenarios using the following methods or devices:

- Paper, marker boards, or easel pads
- Tabletop models
- Technology-based training (TBT) interactive and virtual reality equipment

Similarly, investigation skills can be applied by using case studies on paper, using computer-based scenarios, or staging an accident or incident scene for the student to physically investigate. Each of these examples requires that instructors carefully plan the use of audiovisual training aids into the lesson in order to give students meaningful application of their new knowledge and skills.

Evaluative Factors

A further consideration when selecting the appropriate audiovisual training aid is how a student's knowledge will be evaluated at the end of the course. The training aid used during the lecture may also be used as a testing tool. For example, the same CPR mannequin is usually used for the initial demonstration, student practice, and final evaluation. In a command course, the TBT simulation (or a similar one) can be used for both training and testing.

Using the same training aid for both ensures that the student is familiar with the prop or item during the skills evaluation. Care must be taken, however, to ensure that the continued use of a specific training aid does *not* create student performance tailored to the design and idiosyncrasies of the training aid, rather than promoting useful skill development.

Budget Limitations

Audiovisual training aid devices should also be cost-effective; that is, the benefit to the student and instructor must be greater than the purchase cost of the device, cost of upkeep and storage, and cost in time to develop the training aid. Generally, it is the last cost that is overlooked by instructors when they are preparing a slide presentation or creating a video. They may invest many hours in the creation of a slide presentation to illustrate a concept that is more easily understood through an oral presentation.

To determine cost-effectiveness, determine first the benefits of purchasing, developing, or using the training aid. Benefits may be determined by answering the following questions:

- Will the training aid increase student learning? If yes, how? If no, why not?

- How often will the training aid be used?

- How many students will use the training aid or be exposed to it?

- How will the training aid reduce instructor preparation time for future classes?

Determining the cost of purchasing or creating a training aid may also be determined by objectively answering the following questions:

- What does the training aid device cost?

- What are potential logistical costs in the form of maintenance, storage, or parts?

- How much will it cost to train instructors in the use of the device, who will provide the training, and how will training be funded?

- Is funding available for the training aid? If yes, how much is needed. If no, where can funding be found?

- How much development time will be required to create the training aid?

- Can the same results be attained by using an existing training aid instead of purchasing or creating a new one? If yes, which one. If no, why not?

The instructor should list the benefits in one column and costs in a second column and then compare the two. Some items such as the lack of funding or time may automatically prohibit the purchase or development of the training aid. When the benefit to student understanding of the subject is increased, then a means of overcoming the costs should be determined.

Audiovisual Training Aids Use and Development

Uses for audiovisual training aids generally match the benefits discussed previously. When selecting or developing a training aid, instructors should remember that good audiovisual training aids have the following purposes:

- Show abstract concepts through the use of charts or diagrams.

- Aid memory through the use of eye-catching, humorous, or colorful images.

- Illustrate reality through the use of plans, maps, photographs, or videos.

- Reinforce key points and exact information through the use of quotes, tables, or figures.

- Tie complex ideas together through diagrams, outlines, and headings.

- Compare information through the use of charts and graphs.

- Introduce the lesson through the use of a title slide or image.

- Summarize the lesson through a brief review of the material (**Figure 11.3, p. 254**).

- Illustrate an item through the use of artwork, photographs, or cutaway models.

- Define terms or words through the use of glossaries or examples.

- Provide motivation through images, logos, or slogans.

To create effective audiovisual aids, instructors should apply some generally accepted presentation practices or guidelines. These practices can apply to the creation of many visual images using slide (computer and film) presentations, easel pads, marker boards, and all audiovisual training aid devices. Guidelines include the following:

Summary

- Today's instructor has many responsibilities and challenges.
- Instructors must have the required knowledge to teach.
- Instructors must be positive role models and enthusiastic about teaching.

Instructor
1–1

Figure 11.3 The key points of a lesson can be effectively summarized on a transparency or slide.

- Keep visual aids simple and easy to understand.

- Allocate sufficient preparation time for the visual aids so that they convey the message and look professional.

- Rehearse with the training aids before giving a lecture or demonstration.

- Use only the necessary number of training aids; too many can be distracting.

- Create training aids that are large enough to be seen and read by all members of the class.

- Have a contingency plan available in case there is a failure with the audiovisual training aid device. Be prepared to repair or replace the projection equipment or materials in such an event.

- Ensure that slides, illustrations, or transparencies contain words that are simple and easy to read.

Regardless of the audiovisual training aids used, instructors must take measures to minimize distractions in the learning environment. Instructors should eliminate or minimize any auditory or visual stimuli that are *not* related to the topic. Some actions that help minimize distractions include adjusting ambient lighting, keeping window blinds closed to reduce glare, and/or coordinating with other personnel and operations to minimize pedestrian and/or vehicle traffic in the training area (**Figure 11.4**).

Figure 11.4 Instructors should prepare classrooms in training areas by reducing glare from windows and adjusting ambient light in the room.

Instructors must also consider how they actually use training aids. Inappropriate use of audiovisual training aids can actually create distractions. Techniques on how to avoid distractions when using specific types of audiovisual training aids are discussed as the training aids are introduced in later sections of this chapter. Some simple strategies for avoiding distractions include the following:

- *Introduce audiovisual training aids at the time they are to be viewed, heard, or manipulated* — As soon as the immediate relevance of audiovisual training aids are complete, withdraw them. For example, leaving a slide or transparency displayed on a screen while discussion continues on another point creates a distraction that may divide the attention of the class.

- *Avoid simultaneous use of multiple training aids unless they are carefully and strategically written into the lesson plan* — A common example is to pass a small item around the class for participants to examine. By the time it reaches the last person, it may no longer be relevant to the material the instructor is currently presenting. In the meantime, students' attentions have been divided between the instructor and the object in their hands or the wait for the object to get into their hands. *Alternatives:*

— Use a visual presenter (see Projected Training Aids section).

— Allow items to be viewed and handled by students following the lecture.

- ***Apply training aids in ways that emphasize the message not the equipment*** — This technique is especially important when using sophisticated electronic training aid devices such as multimedia projectors. Avoid the temptation to use every feature of a new program, system, or simulator. When students are paying more attention to flashing lights, overly showy slide transitions, and sound effects, they become distracted from the information in the lecture or training aid.

- ***Try to keep eye contact with students when using a visual aid*** — It is important to talk to the class *not* to the visual aid.

- ***Ensure that all students in the presentation room can hear audio training aid devices clearly*** — Low-volume presentations with devices such as radios, tape/compact disc (CD) players, and televisions can be very distracting and frustrating for students who are attempting to hear them. Accommodate students with hearing loss by locating them close to the speakers or increasing the volume.

- ***Display projected or nonprojected visual training aids above the eyelevel of seated students*** — Student seating may need to be adjusted to provide a clear field of vision for students throughout the classroom.

Transitions in Presentations

Training courses are composed of lessons on a specific topic. Each lesson is composed of a lecture, demonstration, and/or practical evolution that work together to create a learning experience for students. To work together effectively within the lesson, lectures, demonstrations, and evolutions must be connected in some logical manner. The *transition* is an important teaching element that is used to connect the parts of a lesson.

For continuity and consistency, the instructor uses transitions to move students from one portion of the lesson to the next without losing their attention. Transitions preview what will happen next or relate an upcoming concept or skill to a previous one. The instructor uses transitions in a lesson to create interest, keep attention, and create logical transitions from one part of the lesson to the next. The instructor should know why (purpose) transitions are needed, when (timing) to use them, how to determine the different types, and how to develop and include them in the lesson plan.

Purposes

The lesson plan should contain the location of the necessary transitions for the benefit of both experienced and inexperienced instructors. Besides motion pictures and plays, examples of transitions may be found in novels, manuals, television programs, and speeches. The purposes (why) of transitions are as follows:

- ***Maintain interest*** — Keep the viewer/reader interested in the story.

- ***Maintain continuity*** — Keep the information flowing in a steady, uninterrupted stream.

- ***Maintain consistency*** — Increase the consistency between seemingly unrelated topics such as transitions between lesson plans within a course.

- ***Establish relationships*** — Help tie parts of the topic together and show how they are related.

- ***Provide previews*** — Give the viewer/reader an idea of what to expect in the next portion of the material.

- ***Provide summaries*** — End the previous idea or topic.

Timing

When to use transitions is a question of timing. They are used when they are needed in the following ways:

- End one topic and begin another.
- End a complete lesson within a series or course.
- Start a new lesson within a series or course.
- Move from one teaching method into another.
- Provide rest breaks for students and instructors.

The length of time allotted to a transition varies according to the use. It may be as long as it takes for an instructor to summarize a topic, turn on a projector, or announce a rest break for the class **(Figure 11.5)**. Including the transition in the lesson plan helps establish the time required and prevents the lesson from continuing too long.

Figure 11.5 Students are more attentive when they are given periodic rest breaks during class sessions. *Courtesy of Alabama Fire College.*

Types and Development

Once the instructor has determined when to use transitions, it is time to determine what type of transition is needed and how to create them. Speech communication professionals teach two types of transitions for use in oral communication: verbal and nonverbal. These types may be used separately or together. With practice, the instructor can learn how to use and create them effectively and with variety. Another concern for the instructor is the use and creation of transitions in computer-generated media presentations.

Verbal Transitions

Transitions within a lecture must be as smooth as possible to ensure that students do *not* become distracted. Verbal transitions provide the summary and preview within a single sentence or two. Variations of the verbal transition include the following:

- ***Summary statement and preview*** — Example*: With an understanding of the operation of the components of the SCBA, our next step is to learn how to assemble them into a working system.*
- ***Review of the lesson or course agenda*** — Example: *Following the break, please assemble at the burn pit for a Class A foam demonstration followed by a practical evolution. This evolution will let you use the information that was presented in the lecture.*
- ***Change of media*** — Example: *This video will illustrate how rapidly a fire can develop in a controlled environment and demonstrate the theories of fire behavior that we have been discussing.*

Words or phrases that may be useful as transitions include *in addition to, in other words, as well, therefore, in summary,* and *not only.* The use of the words *finally* and *in conclusion* should be avoided in oral presentations. These last phrases give students permission to stop listening. Other methods of transitions are as follows:

- ***Repeat keywords or synonyms or pronouns in place of keywords*** — Repetition also emphasizes the importance of the word or phrase.
- ***Enumerate parts to ensure continuity*** — Use words such as *first, second, third,* etc. to establish the relationship between parts of an idea or process.
- ***Include questions*** — Rhetorical questions (ones that do not require an answer from the audience) help to establish a relationship between the information that has been provided and the information that follows. For instance, *Having discussed the effects of cavitation on the fire pump, you may be wondering what can be done to prevent it? This video discusses the topic.* The transition may also provide an opportunity to ask students questions or permit them to ask questions. Questions may lead to a planned or unplanned discussion period, depending on the topic and the level of student participation.

Nonverbal Transitions

Nonverbal transitions are usually used when instructors want to emphasize a point within a topic. They may consist of a change of facial expression, a pause, a change in vocal pitch or rate of speaking, a gesture, or physically moving from one point to another within the space. Nonverbal transitions must be smooth and *not* distracting.

Nonverbal transitions may also be used to move from one teaching method into another. These transitions may create some disturbance to student concentration because it involves an obvious change. Altering the light level, turning on audiovisual equipment, or assembling a model take time and cannot be accomplished effectively while the instructor is lecturing.

One approach is to have another instructor or aide assemble the equipment while the instructor answers questions or summarizes the topic. Another approach is to use the time for a rest break. This approach requires planning the timing of the break and transition to coincide.

Media Transitions and Animations

Presentations that use computer-generated slide shows involve the use of transitions between slides and animations within slides. New instructors have a tendency to overuse and abuse the animation effects that are part of these software programs. Guidelines for media transitions and animations include the following (**Figure 11.6**):

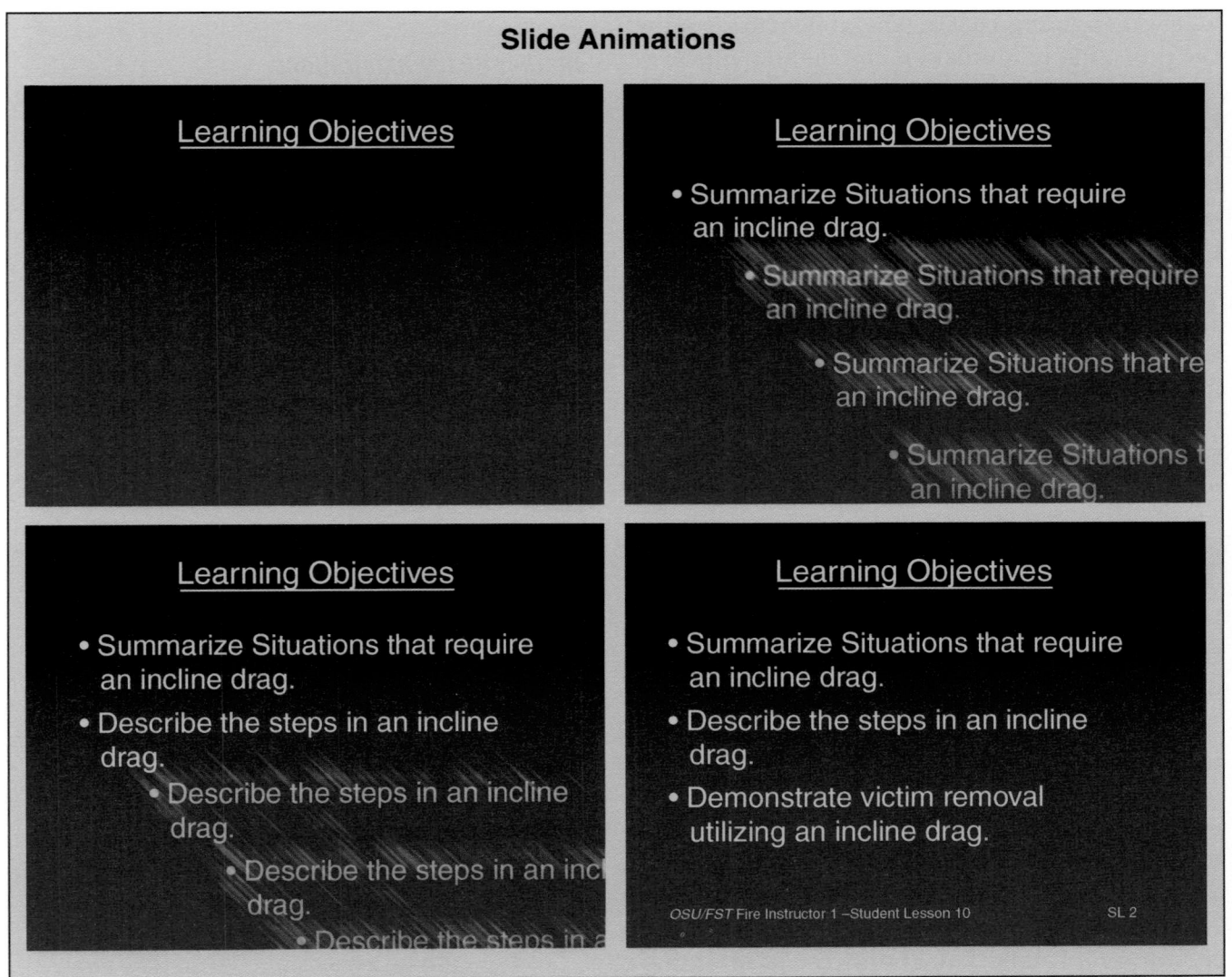

Figure 11.6 A sample of an effective slide animation using a simple background, one heading, and an interesting graphic that does *not* overpower the text. *Courtesy of Fire Service Training, Oklahoma State University.*

- Create one heading for each slide or image. Expand with subheadings or illustrations such as graphs, charts, photographs, or clipart.

- Keep backgrounds simple so that they do *not* conflict with the text or graphics.

- Use transitions and animations sparingly because they can overpower the message that a slide is attempting to convey.

- Use variety in the composition of the various elements on slides by interspersing graphs, charts, photographs, and clipart to create interest.

- Use one style of transition for the major topics and a different one for the subtopics.

Although it is tempting to create fancy, involved, and visually stimulating transitions and animations, the instructor should remember that these will be distracting, causing the student to focus on the transition or animation and *not* the information. The instructor should also refrain from using transitions and animations that involve too much motion. Finally, sound effects that are included in most software are *not* generally appropriate for training sessions and should *not* be used unless they are necessary to convey the message.

Audiovisual Training Aid Types

It is unlikely that a single training division or agency will possess all types of audiovisual training aids that are currently on the market. Many types perform similar functions, and some are economically out of reach of small training organizations. However, instructors should be familiar with the various types and their uses. Instructors who may be required to teach in facilities provided by other jurisdictions or organizations may have the opportunity to come into contact with some or all of these training aid types.

The sections that follow categorize audiovisual training aids and devices as nonprojected types, projected types, simulators, and ancillary equipment. Each category has several types of devices or equipment that are described.

Nonprojected Training Aids

Nonprojected audiovisual training aids offer several major advantages over projected aids. Nonprojected training aids do *not* depend on high levels of technology or technical skill. As a result, they are easier to use and less likely to malfunction during presentations. Generally, nonprojection-type equipment also costs less to purchase, is easy to create illustrations for, and is easy to maintain. Some training aids that use popular and easy-to-use nonprojected audiovisual equipment include the following:

- Marker board (chalkboard, dry-erase marker board, electronic or interactive board, and easel pad) illustrations

- Illustration or diagram displays

- Duplicated materials

- Models

- Audiotapes and CDs

- Casualty simulation training aids

Marker Board Illustrations

The easiest, most frequently used, and most versatile nonprojection-type equipment is a marker board (chalkboard, dry-erase marker board, electronic or interactive board, and easel pad) **(Figure 11.7)**. These items may be fixed or mounted to a wall, movable (on wheels or stands), or portable (folding and compact for travel). Instructors find these training aid devices useful for numerous instructional activities and rely on them as supplements and backup when more technical or complex training aid equipment fails.

Figure 11.7 Dry eraser boards have replaced most chalkboards in classrooms providing clean, easy-to-read, and dust-free working surfaces.

Many marker boards are made of an enameled surface on a thin sheet of steel, allowing instructors to use magnets as part of the display. Instructors can draw diagrams using markers of multiple colors and add magnets to represent fire apparatus, ambulances, or other objects.

Chalkboard. A chalkboard is the traditional mainstay of classroom education and remains a versatile and effective training tool. The advantages of a chalkboard are its low cost, low maintenance, high reliability, and high visibility. The wide availability of large-sized colored chalk (sidewalk chalk) makes it easy for instructors to vary their displays from the monochrome look of the usual white chalk on a black or green background. Some chalkboards also accept magnets. Chalkboards should be thoroughly erased between uses and periodically cleaned. *Disadvantages:*

- Once the presentation is produced, it must either be left in place or erased. When left in place, that portion of the chalkboard is no longer available for other uses. When erased, the presentation must be built from the beginning if needed again.

- The quantity of chalk dust that is released into the air and onto other surfaces can create a respiratory hazard and require frequent cleaning of surfaces.

Dry-erase marker board. This board is a non-electronic variation of the traditional *rewritable* classroom blackboard. The writing surface is white instead of black or green and made of a material that can be written on with colored markers (known as *dry-erase markers*). Dry-erase markers are easier to erase than the chalk used on a chalkboard (which sometimes requires a wet rag for thorough erasing). The dry-erase marker board has many of the same uses as the chalkboard: It is versatile, reliable, and easy to use. *Factors:*

- Instructors who have developed skills and an affinity for either the chalkboard or dry-erase marker board find it easy to transfer to the other.

- Dry-erase marker boards allow instructors to write or draw on the board with multiple color markers.

- Dry-erase markers leave colored marks that are erased with special erasers. If material is left on the board for more than a few minutes, a cleaning solution may be needed to completely remove all marks.

- It is important to use only dry-erase markers on marker boards. Using other types of markers may result in lengthy cleanups or may even necessitate replacing the board.

- Dry-erase markers are more expensive than regular markers used on easel pads. However, using dry-erase markers exclusively avoids the possibility of damaging a dry-erase marker board.

Electronic or interactive board. In electronic education technology and computer networks, an electronic or interactive board is one of several types of writable presentation display systems that can be used in a classroom or for videoconferencing **(Figure 11.8)**. These training aid devices generally fall into one of the following three categories:

- ***Electronic copyboard*** — Scans and prints a reduced-size copy of material drawn or printed on the board and is a versatile variation of the dry-erase marker board. An electronic copyboard is expensive, but its cost eventually may be reduced by increased demand and improved technology. This device is especially convenient

Figure 11.8 The use of electronic or interactive boards is increasing, although use is limited by the cost of the systems.

in cases where the instructor uses the board to develop a detailed plan or diagram for future use. Manufacturers provide copyboards in a variety of sizes including portable units that are the size of easel pads.

- **Peripheral board** — Transfers the information that is written on it into a digital file that is stored on an attached computer. Some peripheral boards can be attached to a projector that can be calibrated to the display, making the board interactive.

- **Interactive board** — Operates like a large touch-screen monitor that is synchronized to an attached computer and permits users to interact with the display, visit Internet sites, and access databases directly from the board. This board is the most expensive and sophisticated form of electronic marker board. *Details:*

  - The interactive board is either a rear-screen projection device, which means that the image is projected from behind the writing surface, or used as the screen for a data-projection system.

  - When the devices are rear-projected, images may *not* be as bright as what is needed in the classroom. To compensate for the short distances, mirrors refract the light to receive the image, which reduces the amount of light transmitted to the screen.

  - When funds allow, rear-projected boards should be equipped with a projector bulb with the highest available light output (lumens).

  NOTE: Projectors and bulbs are rated in *lumens,* a calculation used to determine the total amount of light leaving a projector or falling on the screen. The higher the amount of lumens, the brighter the image on the screen will be.

Easel pad. An easel pad is a large pad of paper mounted on an easel for display. Paper may be lined, unlined, or ruled for graphs. Various grades and colors are available. Easels can be wall-mounted, freestanding on the floor, or shortened for tabletop use. A wide variety of colored marker pens can produce attractive, interesting presentations. *Details:*

Instructor Tips: Using Marker Boards

- *Lightly* write any easily misspelled words or technical terms or *lightly* draw diagrams and other similar material on easel-pad paper or chalkboard in advance with a lead pencil. The pencil marks are visible to the instructor standing at the front of the class but not to students. Quickly trace over the pencil marks with chalk or marker. This technique ensures accuracy or quick reproduction of material in class.

- Draw complex or detailed diagrams in advance. Mark prepared material with instructions not to disturb if the classroom is to be used by other instructors in the interim. Keep diagrams covered until needed in order to avoid distracting the class. Use one of the following methods:
  - Cover material with a sliding section of a chalkboard or marker board.
  - Tape paper across material on boards.
  - Cover material on an easel pad with blank sheets or title sheets.

- Avoid speaking when facing boards or easel pads. Develop the skill of pausing while speaking when turned away from the students to write.

- Write only what is necessary. It is rarely necessary to transcribe verbatim every spoken word of a lesson. Using concise points minimizes the time needed to write while maximizing the space available.

- Use chalk or marker pen colors that contrast with the background. Contrasting colors means using light colors of chalk and dark colors of markers. For example, the use of yellow or light orange markers in a large classroom is *not* recommended because those colors are difficult to see.

- Write letters large enough to be seen at the back of the room. Experiment with letter size in advance. Remember that some students may be ten or twenty times further from the board or easel pad than the instructor.

- Bring chalk and marker pens of several colors when scheduled to teach in an unfamiliar location.

- Use manuscript (print) instead of cursive (written) letters **(Figure 11.9)**.

Figure 11.9 Instructors must print clearly and legibly so that students in all parts of the classroom can read the information.

- Instructors can easily transfer their chalkboard and marker-board skills to the easel pad.

- Some professionally prepared easel-pad presentations are available.

- A variation on the easel pad is the plastic static-cling sheet. These sheets can be produced in the same way as easel-pad paper sheets and mounted directly on a wall or board by static cling.

Illustration or Diagram Displays

Instructors can create interesting and informative lectures by displaying topical illustrations or diagrams that they have purchased or prepared in advance. Illustrations or diagrams that are prepared in advance save class time and provide consistency between similar class sessions. Illustrations and diagrams also address a variety of learning styles beyond those addressed by written or spoken words. Some examples of the benefits of using illustrations and display boards are as follows:

- Technical diagrams such as mechanical or electrical schematics illustrate and help explain troubleshooting or repair procedures.

- Maps or plan diagrams illustrate routes or aid in preplanning or debriefing incidents.

- Anatomical charts assist in explaining human anatomy and physiology in emergency medical services (EMS) classes.

- Flowcharts illustrate and help explain processes or procedures.

- Data charts such as pie charts or bar graphs illustrate common causes of injury, response types, or other statistical data.

- Photographs of incident scenes are invaluable in illustrating proper or improper procedures.

Illustrations can be mounted or created on poster board purchased from office or art supply companies. The boards are available in all colors and sizes up to 36 × 48 inches (914 mm by 1 219 mm). Maps may be mounted on rollers or hung flat from clips on chalkboards. Easels may also be used to support the mounted illustrations.

When displaying any of these types of training aids, it is important to remember the ability of such items to distract students. Avoid leaving illustrations and diagrams in view when they are *not* in use or relevant. Instructors should *not* attempt to hold illustrations in front of themselves while describing them. This practice is distracting and changes an instructor into an expensive easel.

Duplicated Materials

Duplicated materials (handouts) include any printed matter that instructors distribute before, during, or at the end of a class. Instructors should remember the copyright laws explained in Chapter 3, Legal and Ethical Considerations, and apply them appropriately. As with other audiovisual training aids, instructors must strategically plan their use in the lesson to gain maximum benefits. Examples with their benefits and suggested uses include the following:

- Distribute handouts of lecture material at the end of a presentation unless it is necessary for students to refer to or take notes on them during the class. This strategy avoids students dividing their attention between the handout and the instructor.

- Consider using handouts as precourse material when they contain the same material as the presentation. This method of early distribution has the additional advantage of advancing the achievable learning level of the class.

- Give self-study guides to students to assist them in working through textbooks or other learning materials at their own pace. Guides with self-quizzes offer review mechanisms that indicate areas of study where students can concentrate their efforts. Instructors can prepare the study guides or arrange to purchase them as part of a curriculum.

- Give assignments to students for completion within the class. Students can complete case studies, style inventories, or other in-class materials individually or in groups according to the lesson plan.

- Give activities such as research projects, practice applications of theory learned in class, or reviews of material presented by the instructor as take-home assignments.

- Provide note guides (outline or shell of the lesson) for students to fill with notes during class. When instructors design note guides into the lesson effectively, they help focus the attentions of students on the material presented. As students write their notes, they are attentive to the major points of the lesson that are reinforced.

Instructor Tips: Using Handouts

- Ensure that handouts are legible and complete. A photocopy of a photocopy of a fax copy may have poor-quality text or be askew on the page.
- Staple multiple pages. Students are less likely to lose or rearrange multiple-page handouts that have been stapled together in advance.
- Provide handouts with pages that are three-hole punched in advance unless they are bound otherwise.
- Include headers that contain the course name, instructor name, date, and page number on multiple-page handouts. Include codes that indicate the lesson also.
- Provide sufficient copies for all participants. Always print more than are required by the enrollment.
- Provide space on the handouts for taking notes.
- Be aware of and adhere to copyright laws.

Models

A model is an excellent medium for illustrating mechanical or spatial concepts. Students can clearly observe the types of relationships between parts of a model as they watch it function or manipulate it. Instructors can obtain many types of models or construct them at low cost, but some types (depending on their size and complexity) require a heavy investment of time and money. Some examples of models that are used as audiovisual training aids include the following:

- *Tabletop miniatures* — Miniatures of fire and emergency apparatus are routinely used along with model buildings to practice strategy and tactics. Tabletop models allow participants to enact a simulated incident in compressed time (for example, 5 minutes of simulation can represent 1 hour). Instructors can monitor a model town by video camera for display in other rooms. Advanced versions of tabletops may include smoke and flame effects that are static (non-moving) or that change continuously according to the inputs received by the instructor (**Figure 11.10**).

- *Cutaway models* — These models are of great value when students are learning the inner workings of mechanical systems such as valves or pumps. Instructors can often obtain cutaways at little or no cost by dismantling obsolete or surplus equipment. Some manufacturers may also have cutaway training models available.

- *Anatomical models* — These models are available in three dimensions, some of which have cutaway or take-apart features. These models benefit students who are developing their EMS skills and knowledge in such areas as the mechanisms of internal injuries. A life-size or even small-scale skeleton is also a good anatomical model.

- *Replicas or miniatures* — Replicas can demonstrate how actual equipment or devices are used. Examples are various types of cribbing and shoring assemblies based on actual designs (**Figure 11.11**). Students can see how the components are assembled and used before a practical training evolution is conducted.

Figure 11.10 Tabletop models are very popular and effective for training scenarios that involve multiagency responses. *Courtesy of Louisiana State University, Fire and Emergency Training Institute (FETI).*

Figure 11.11 Miniature scale models of large training props can be used for classroom familiarization before working with the actual prop.

- *Actual tools and equipment* — Actual equipment can also be used for demonstrations. For instance, an actual self-contained breathing apparatus (SCBA) is a better training aid to show key components than a transparency of the SCBA.

Audiotapes and Compact Discs

The ability to record and play sounds on audio-cassette tapes using a small, portable recording machine allows instructors to bring realism to many areas of training. In addition to classroom uses, audiotapes can be used by students to record and review lectures, dictate and review their own notes, or listen to prerecorded books on tape. Some examples of sounds that can be recorded for use in the classroom include the following:

- Engine and pump sounds (problem identification such as pump cavitation)

- Dispatch radio traffic (telecommunicator training or postincident critique)

- Heart, breathing, or blood-pressure sounds (EMS training)

Additional training material is available on CDs that may be played on portable players, computers, and digital versatile disc (DVD)/CD players or television combination units. New materials are constantly being added in the area of *books on tape,* a term that refers to material recorded on either audiotape or CD.

NOTE: The abbreviation CD that stands for compact disc, is generally associated with music recordings. The term may also be used to indicate data storage media as in CD-ROM (Compact Disc-Read-Only-Memory), CD-R (Compact Disc-Recordable), and CD-RW (Compact Disc-ReWritable).

Casualty Simulation Training Aids

Any medium that increases the realism of a simulation increases its value. Simulated casualties give tremendous benefits in increasing realism for EMS training involving hands-on applications **(Figure 11.12, p. 264)**. Instructors can simulate injuries using commercially available moulage kits and prostheses or by applying Plasticine® modeling paste, wax, and makeup.

Figure 11.12 Realism can be added to any training scenario involving trauma victims through the use of training mannequins that can simulate casualties. *Courtesy of Central Florida Fire Academy.*

Moulage kits typically contain plastic *wounds* that instructors can apply to a simulated casualty. Prostheses such as simulated amputated limbs, devices to simulate arterial bleeding, and other lifelike injury effects are also available. Minimal training is required to use moulage kits. The plastic wounds also have the advantage of being relatively quick to prepare and apply.

When a very realistic simulation is required, instructors can arrange to use personnel who are qualified as casualty simulators. Casualty simulators may be EMS instructors who have been trained to use Plasticine®, mortician's wax, makeup, prostheses, and simulated blood to produce *very* realistic wounds and other effects. The preparation process is more time-consuming than moulage but results in a higher degree of realism. For practical examinations or when simulations are captured on video for later use, the time invested is worthwhile.

For all cases of casualty simulation, it is important that instructors properly brief the individuals who are playing the roles of casualties on their injuries, the information they are to reveal to the rescuers, and any other pertinent scenario details. A realistic role-play helps enhance the lessons learned.

For mass-casualty disaster scenarios when the hands-on treatment is secondary to the bigger picture of response capacity and interorganizational liaison, simple moulage simulations are sufficient. See Simulators section for additional information.

Projected Training Aids

Projected audiovisual training aids offer many advantages: Images are vivid, multicolored, and visible to a large audience. These training aids stimulate multiple senses simultaneously. Some drawbacks are as follows:

- Large investment in audiovisual equipment
- Costly purchase of projected training-aid presentations
- Device placement obstructing the vision of some students in the classroom
- Distraction for some students by instructor operating the device
- Extensive time spent in creating presentations

Despite these factors, a certain level of audiovisual support is considered normal in the current instructional environment, and the expected level of support is increasing rapidly. Mixed-media training presentations are also very effective. Some projected audiovisual training devices/aids include the following:

- Video and multimedia projectors/large-screen images
- Visual presenters/displays
- Television/programs and video presentations

- Slide projectors/slides
- Overhead projectors/transparencies

With the exception of television, these training devices are generally front-screen projection devices; that is, the image is projected from the unit onto the face of a screen. This type of projection system has certain disadvantages including the following:

- Objects between the projector and the screen can block the image on the screen unless the projector is mounted from the ceiling.

- The image on the screen can be affected by light in the room or from windows, making it difficult to see.

- The image may only be visible when viewed directly in front of the screen. Students seated to the side may *not* be able to see the image clearly.

Some types of projection devices are rear-screen projectors. These are designed for use with special translucent screens that may be mounted over an opening in a wall. The projection device is located in a darkened room behind the opening. Rear-screen projection systems are permanent because they are incorporated into the design of the classroom. They are also more expensive than front-screen projection devices.

Instructor Tips: Using Projected Aids

- Dim the lights when using projected training aids when necessary. If possible, leave lights at a level where the projected image is clearly visible but students are still visible to the instructor. Create this level of visibility by dimming the light level only at the front where the screen or television is located. This light level provides sufficient light intensity to allow students to take notes.

- Maintain a backup set of training materials that can be used at a lower level of technology. For example, back up computer-generated presentations with overhead transparencies. Be prepared to present or demonstrate material if projection equipment fails.

- Keep a supply of spare projector bulbs, batteries for remote controls, extension cords, and anything else that may be needed in the event of equipment problems.

Video and Multimedia Projectors/Large-Screen Images

A *projection system* is a device for showing video, television, or computer images on a large screen. Projectors that are bright enough to display a quality video or computer-generated image in a classroom are affordable, portable, and versatile. Video projectors designed to accept input only from a videocassette recorder/player (VCR) or DVD player are smaller and less expensive than multimedia projectors.

Video projectors combine the best aspects of motion picture projectors (large, high-quality images) with those of television (near-silent operation with high-fidelity sound outputs). In addition, the portability of video projectors is similar to that of a VCR/DVD player allowing them to be easily moved between classrooms or taken to remote sites **(Figure 11.13)**. All features of the video source are available such as stop-motion, slow-motion, fast-forward, or reverse.

The only disadvantage in comparison to a television/VCR/DVD player combination is cost. While video projectors are more expensive than the average television, the price gap between large-screen televisions and video projectors is narrowing.

Figure 11.13 Portable video projectors permit instructors to take visual aids to remote classrooms and locations.

Multimedia projectors offer the same video projection capability as video projectors with the added capacity to display computer-generated images. The variety of uses of multimedia projectors is limited only by the capabilities of the presentation software. Presentations that contain sounds, video clips, data charts, animation, and photographs can be produced. Text can be introduced one point at a time with animated transitions between slides.

Multimedia projectors have uses beyond video and presentation software applications. For example, when a committee is meeting to develop or edit training documents such as a new policy or procedure, the document being considered can be projected for all to see. In this way, edits can be made as they are discussed, reducing the turn-around time between drafts of the document.

The sophistication of presentation software increases with the release of each new edition. Learning to use this instructional medium effectively is essential for instructors. Instructors should avoid the temptation to include every possible feature in the presentation. Making strategic and selective use of the software maximizes the benefits of multimedia presentations.

When selecting a video or multimedia projector for purchase, instructors should consider the following factors:

- Images must be bright enough to be seen in the classroom where the projector will be used. Displays in a darkened sales showroom may *not* project as well in the instructional environment.

- It is important to select a projector with the highest lumen rating. Consider the contrast ratio of the projector as well. An average contrast ratio is 500:1. Most projectors are rated in the 300/3,000:1 contrast ratio, which means that the blacks are 300 times darker than the whites (on a 300:1 model). In this case, true black may appear grayish. Projectors with 1,000:1 or 1,200:1 may provide better color images but also cost considerably more.

NOTE: *Contrast ratio* is a way of expressing the purity of colors in a projected image and is expressed as XXX:1. The higher the contrast ratio, the deeper and richer the colors will be.

- Replacement bulbs for multimedia projector bulbs are expensive, unlike overhead and slide projector bulbs. Bulbs with high lumens are even more expensive and have a lower amount of hour-life. It is *not* uncommon for most projector bulbs to cost between $250 and $500.

- Resolution of the video and computer-generated images must be high enough to produce a quality image at the size desired in the classroom.

- Sound output of the projector must have sufficient volume and fidelity for the intended use or external speakers must be added.

- Projectors must be compatible with the video and computer equipment that they are intended to support. Some projectors allow for multiple inputs for computers and video equipment.

Visual Presenters/Displays

Another audiovisual training device that can be used in many of the same ways as an overhead projector is the visual presenter. This device consists of a small video camera mounted vertically over a tabletop platform (**Figure 11.14**). Adjustable light units are mounted on either side of the platform. The platform also contains a light source to provide back lighting for transparencies.

Figure 11.14 The visual presenter combines the functions of the overhead projector and the transparency projector with computer-generated images and the video projector.

Live images of objects, documents, or transparencies that are placed on the platform are then displayed on a television monitor or through a multimedia projector. Some models also allow for external audio that can be used as a public announcement (PA) system in a small classroom.

An instructor who wants to project an item does *not* have to make a flat transparency when using a visual presenter. These units may also be linked to computers and distance learning networks to transmit images to remote sites.

Some examples of how this system could be used in the classroom include the following:

- Display a tool, material sample, or other item on the platform so that all students may view it at the same time.
- Display paper copies of documents without the need to make transparencies first.
- Display original photographs or illustrations without the degeneration that commonly occurs in duplication.
- Display images or text from books or magazines.
- Display transparencies like an overhead projector.

Television/Programs and Video Presentations

Television has tremendous potential as an audiovisual training aid device. Distance learning programs broadcast on community-access channels by cable, satellite, or closed circuit have the ability to reach large student audiences over vast distances. State or provincial authorities, postsecondary institutions, or any organization wishing to reach a diverse group of students can make effective use of televised lessons.

A video presentation has the advantage of stimulating multiple senses, specifically sight and sound. Video becomes a powerful instructional medium with the added effects of motion, animation, diagrams, and text. Videos are commercially available on a tremendous variety of fire and emergency services subjects.

Images captured on video may be stored or viewed on either analog or digital tapes or on DVDs. The current trend is toward the DVD format that permits the disc to be used in a DVD player connected to a television or computer.

The quality of affordable video recording and editing equipment has improved dramatically in recent years. It is possible for many organizations to produce very high-quality videos in-house. Different videotape formats are available, including video home system (VHS), super VHS (S-VHS), 8 mm, Sony Hi-8™, and digital. DVD-based cameras are also available. However, organizations must take into account that the time required to properly script, film, and edit a video may be as much as one hundred times the length of the finished product.

When using a video presentation in class, instructors should consider the following points:

- Always preview the video before showing it (**Figure 11.15, p. 268**).
- Emphasize key learning points/objectives before showing a video.
- Start the video before turning on the television set, and turn the set off before stopping the video. Some television sets automatically mute the sound and display a blue screen when not receiving a signal. Others display *snow* and a loud static noise that can be distracting and uncomfortable.
- Cue the video to the desired location in advance when showing only a portion of a tape or disc.
- Rewind a video immediately when showing it in its entirety or rewind at least as soon as a class is finished.
- Pause the video while it is playing when adding to or illustrating a teaching point. If the video must continue to illustrate the point, mute the sound. Do *not* attempt to talk over the soundtrack of a video.
- Do *not* leave the room while a class views a video. Instructors who leave during the showing of a video are *not* aware of any technical problems, classroom disruptions, or other issues that may occur in their absences.
- Do *not* use a video that takes more than half of the class session.
- Review key learning points/objectives after viewing a video.

Figure 11.15 Instructors must preview videotapes or compact discs before using them to ensure that they operate and are properly cued to the specific starting point.

Slide Projectors/Slides

Slide projectors and film-based slides are capable of producing the same types of images as overhead projectors and transparencies (see following section), but they have some different advantages. The images produced on a slide are generally of higher resolution (image quality) and project better to a large audience than transparencies.

Compatible film sizes that are available include 35 mm and 120/220 (also known as *2¼ × 2¼ inch [57 mm by 57 mm] square*). A film-based slide is an excellent medium for presenting a photograph. Many publishers of educational materials offer slide presentations in their catalogs.

The use of slide projectors is decreasing with the increasing use of computer-generated slide programs and visual presenters. Instructors may still find them in use, but support for slide projectors may *not* be available in the near future.

Overhead Projectors/Transparencies

The relatively low cost of overhead projectors along with the ability to produce high-quality transparencies (both black/white and color) on a computer printer make transparency presentations very popular and versatile training aids. Overhead projectors are common in most training environments **(Figure 11.17)**.

New models have the advantages of bright halogen bulbs and quiet operation. Current models of projectors can operate in a classroom without dimming the lights beyond the point where it becomes difficult to see the students. Portable models that are very compact are available, but generally they do *not* project as brightly as non-portable models.

Transparencies offer the following benefits to instructors:

Keystoning

Keystoning is an effect that occurs when the width of the projected image is wider at the top than at the bottom. Keystoning creates a distraction for students because of the distortion in the projected image. Lines are *not* parallel and the top and bottom of the image will be out of focus while the center is sharp. This distortion occurs because the projector is *not* perpendicular with the screen **(Figure 11.16)**.

Keystoning is a frequent occurrence when using overhead projectors, but it can also be an issue with slide projectors or ceiling-mounted video projectors. Slide projectors are less subject to keystoning than overhead projectors because they have a longer focal length.

Some portable projection screens may be equipped with a keystone eliminator that allows the angle of the screen to be adjusted at the top. Some newer model data projectors have an electronic keystone eliminator included, which allows the instructor to correct the keystone image on either a portable- or fixed-projection screen.

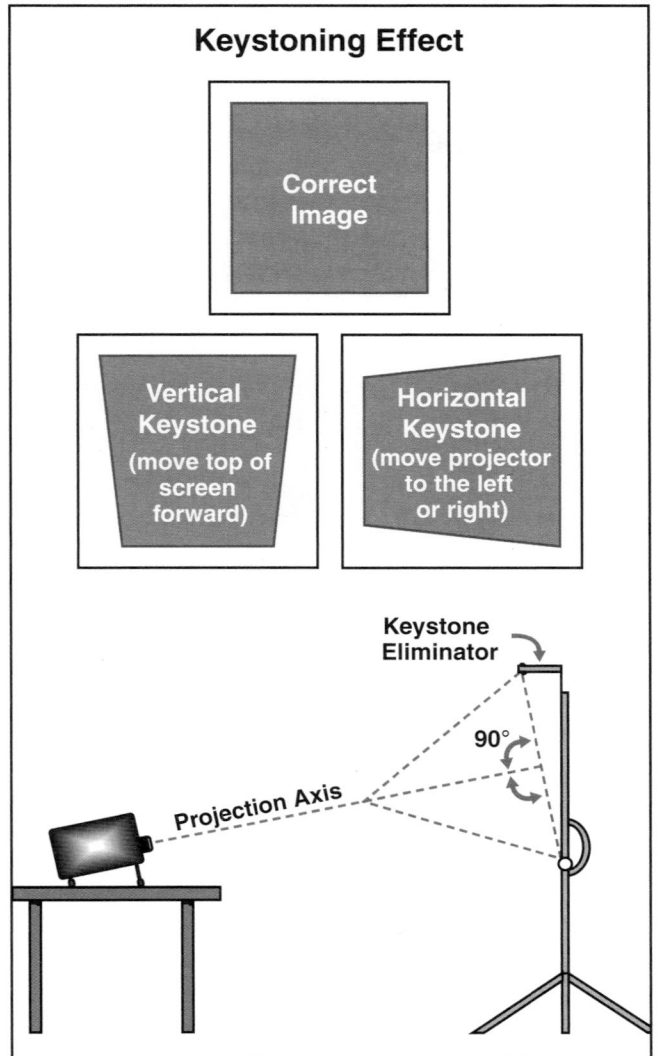

Figure 11.16 Instructors should be familiar with the operation of an overhead projector to prevent distortion known as *keystoning*.

- Instructors are in total control of the order and method of presentation of each overhead transparency.

- When asked a question relating to a transparency already shown, instructors can easily go back to it for review.

- Instructors can reveal bulleted lists one point at a time by placing an opaque sheet of paper between the transparency and projection surface. The paper can be moved to reveal each point in turn. The static cling between the transparency and the projection surface keeps the paper in place. The instructor can read all points directly from the transparency.

Figure 11.17 Most training organizations still use traditional overhead projectors for projecting illustrations onto screens.

Using overhead projectors does have a few disadvantages to consider. First, they have a very limited use in visual presentations. When the instructor needs to show materials with graphics, photos, or other types of illustrations, an overhead projector is *not* the best media to use. The resolution (detail and sharpness) available with transparencies is lower than with other types of media.

Second, using an overhead projector requires that the instructor come back to the projector (unless an assistant is in the classroom), making it difficult for instructors who like to move around the room during instruction. When there is a time gap between the displays of transparencies, instructors also need to turn off the projector to avoid a large bright, white screen.

Simulators

Simulators are training devices that represent systems, processes, or environments in which actual training would be unsafe, impractical, or prohibitively expensive. Examples are as follows:

- It is unsafe to practice search and rescue techniques in a structure that is on fire.

- It is impractical to use a defibrillator on live humans in an instructional environment.

- It is prohibitively expensive to fill high-rise apartment buildings with heat and smoke in order to study ventilation.

Simulators bring elements of reality to the instructional environment. The greater the degree of reality, the more effective the learning is. The following various types of simulators are available for fire and emergency services training:

- Electronic simulators
- Display boards
- Smoke simulators
- Computer simulations
- Virtual reality simulations
- Anatomical/physiological mannequins

Electronic Simulators

Electronic components are engineered to simulate a wide variety of situations and environments (**Figure 11.18**). For example, electronic simulations of a pump panel may include working gauges, realistic recorded sounds, and warning or trouble messages. Simulations that can be integrated into a tabletop tactical simulator include the following:

- Elements of communication systems
- Alarm/detection systems
- Ventilation fans
- Theatrical smoke machines
- Electric lights
- Miniature models
- Video cameras
- Projection and recording training aids

Display Boards

The component parts of systems can be mounted on display boards and used to simulate the operation of various systems. In this way, an instructor or student can manipulate a system without crawling under an apparatus chassis or into a machine. An example would be a display board mounted with the actual working parts of a vehicle air brake sys-

Figure 11.18 Electronic simulators can be effectively used to allow students to practice the use of equipment in a safe and comfortable environment.

tem. Students can practice maintenance inspections quickly and safely. Display boards can be constructed from parts removed from scrapped or salvaged vehicles.

Smoke Simulators

The movement of smoke through a building or area is critically important to fire and emergency services personnel. Smoke movement can be simulated or illustrated by using small-scale mechanical models of high-rise stairwells. Developments in computer modeling allow realistic simulations of smoke movement through complex structures such as shopping malls, tunnels, and high-rise buildings.

Computer Simulations

Computerized simulations of burning buildings, injured casualties, hostage scenarios, and other fire and emergency services applications are widely available. Because of the greater amounts of memory required for video and sound files, many of these simulations are being produced in CD-ROM and DVD formats. Some formats feature still photographs or illustrations with text. The more advanced DVD simulations feature high-quality, full-motion video and high-fidelity sound.

Low-cost fire simulation software can be purchased. With a little practice and creativity, instructors can create realistic tactical scenarios using their own photographs.

With the availability of CD-R and CD-RW technology, instructors now have the ability to produce instructional programming that may include video, text, photographs, and interactive feedback from the student. Other high-memory capacity storage media exist that may be used in the same manner.

Virtual Reality Simulations

Virtual reality simulations display fields of views as though students are parts of the simulated environments. Environments can be manipulated in response to inputs from students. Programmed changes occur based on the actions taken by students in relation to simulated scenarios.

Virtual reality simulations are continually improving in realism. These simulations are tremendous tools for reinforcing procedure-based or protocol-based skill sets such as incident management or EMS skills.

Most of these simulations are expensive and require an investment in equipment and software. This investment must be weighed against the instructional value offered by the increased realism of the product. Some simulations have built-in study materials and self-tests. In some cases, centralized training records and statistics are obtained directly from the simulation software when networked through an organization's computer network.

Anatomical/Physiological Mannequins

The degree of simulation offered by mannequins ranges from a simple representation of the human form to audible, visible, or palpable facsimiles of pulse, heart rhythm, reaction to defibrillation, ability to intubate or ventilate, and many other features. Mannequins are available to match any level of EMS training provided by the organization **(Figure 11.19)**. The skills of students become highly developed when the training closely simulates the services required on the job.

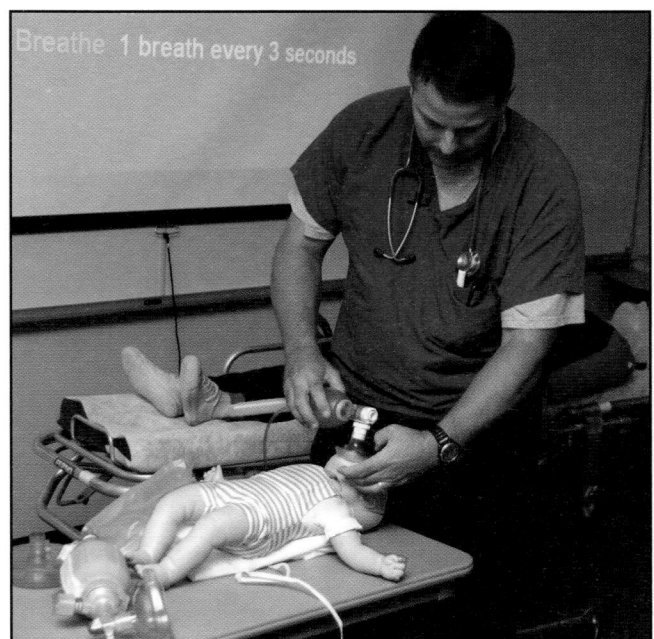

Figure 11.19 Most training organizations own or have access to CPR training mannequins.

Ancillary Equipment

Ancillary equipment consists of those devices such as televisions, projection screens, cameras, scanners, and video-capture devices that are used in support of audiovisual training aids. While television monitors and projection screens are used in presentations, the other items are used to create the images that compose the slides, transparencies, and electronic presentations.

Projected audiovisual training aids depend on images that have been created or obtained from a source. These sources include cameras (both still and video), scanners, and video-capture devices.

Although these devices are *not* used in the presentation of lectures or demonstrations, they are used to create the materials the instructor will use. Level I Instructors should be familiar with any equipment that they may be required to use or care for in the completion of their duties. Information on the various types of ancillary equipment may be found in Chapter 14, Lesson Plan Development.

Television Monitors

Television monitors can be used to present images from videos, visual presenters, or live presentations captured with video cameras. High-definition television (HDTV) provides images that are brighter and have greater clarity and quality than regular television. Large screen sizes also mean better viewing by large groups.

When using monitors, the guideline to consider for the correct screen size based on the audience size is 1 inch (25 mm) per person. For example, if the classroom can accommodate 20 students, the monitor screen should be a minimum of 20 inches (508 mm) on the diagonal dimension.

Projection Screens

Projection screens require a different projection formula than monitors. When using projection screens, a guideline to consider is the 2 by 6 Rule. This rule means that the front row should be no *closer* than twice the width of the projection from the screen, and the width of the front row should *not* be more than twice the width. The *6* part of the rule determines the distance from the back row to the screen. The back row should *not* be *farther* away than 6 times the width of the screen and also no wider than 6 times (**Figure 11.20**).

For example, for a 4-foot (1.2 m) projection, the front row should be no closer than 8 feet (2.4 m) and no wider than 8 feet (2.4 m). The back row should be no further than 24 feet (7.3 m) and the width of the back row should be no wider than 24 feet (7.3 m).

Cleaning, Care, and Maintenance

Audiovisual training aid devices require proper cleaning, care, and maintenance in the same ways that fire-fighting tools, apparatus, and equipment do. Instructors should make it a habit to inspect all training aids on a regular basis and before using them in class. The manufacturer of each training aid device should provide cleaning, care, and maintenance instructions when the item is delivered. These instructions should be filed for reference and a copy of specific instructions attached to the training aid device if possible.

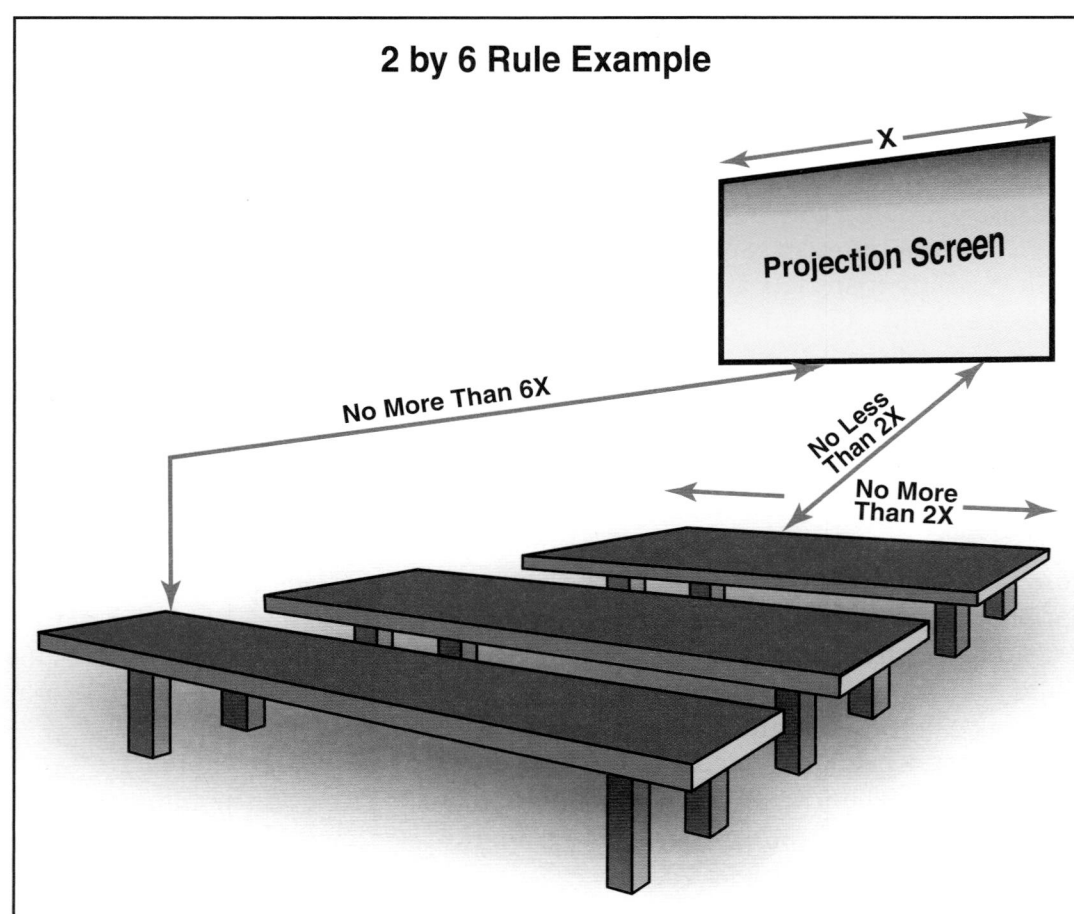

Figure 11.20
Illustration of the 2 by 6 Rule that is used to determine the minimum and maximum viewing distances that students should be from a projected image.

Cleaning

Keeping audiovisual training aid devices clean is a fairly simple process. Periodic cleaning is an opportunity to inspect the item for needed maintenance and determine the location and general condition of the item. Some cleaning suggestions include the following:

- Do *not* use abrasive cleaning agents on glass surfaces.
- Use manufacturer-recommended cleaning agents and procedures.
- Use a soft dust cloth to remove dust and fingerprints.
- Use a soft bristled brush to dust hard-to-reach areas inside equipment.
- Do *not* use solvents for cleaning training aid devices.
- Clean chalk and whiteboards completely when finished using them.
- Clean video and audio heads with appropriate cleaning device at recommended intervals.

Care

Proper care of training aids and devices can prevent damage, maintain cleanliness, and extend the useful life of audiovisual training aids and devices. Suggested care includes the following guidelines:

- Place dust covers over equipment when it is *not* in use (**Figure 11.21**).
- Store slide-in carousels or trays in covered boxes.
- Store slides in temperature-controlled areas.
- Do *not* place slides or transparencies in direct sunlight or near heat sources.
- Store mannequins properly in carrying cases or closed cabinets.
- Wrap power cords around carts or remove and store them separately.
- Use lens caps on all optical lenses (cameras and projectors).
- Store transparencies flat, separated by blank sheets of paper, in boxes or file folders.
- Store handouts in file folders.
- Store videotapes and audiotapes in climate-controlled areas.

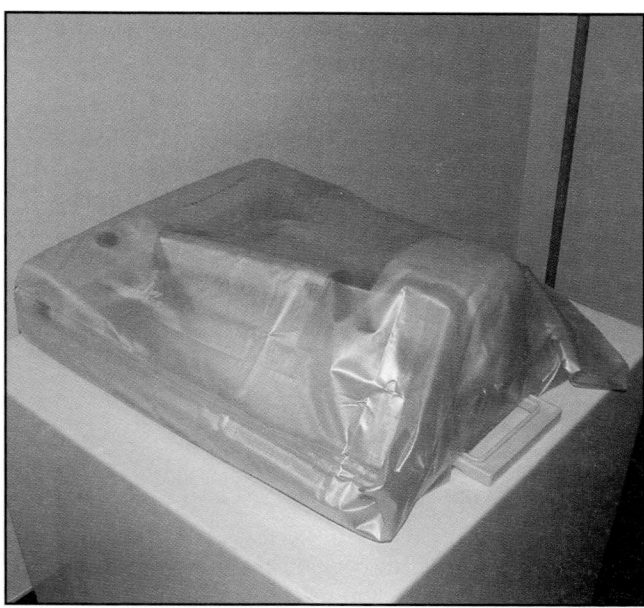

Figure 11.21 All training aids should be stored properly when not in use. This storage includes the use of dust covers that help to keep lenses, bulbs, and glass surfaces clean. *Courtesy of Elaine Johns.*

- Wear cotton gloves to handle transparencies and slides when sorting, cleaning, or storing them.
- Wear cotton gloves when touching optical lenses and replacing projection bulbs.
- Allow projectors sufficient cool-down time after the bulb is turned off. Many projectors have both *soft* and *hard* power buttons. Great care must be given to follow the manufacturer's guidelines, otherwise the fan may prematurely disengage, resulting in a greatly reduced bulb life span.
- Follow manufacturer's recommendations for use and storage of training aids and devices.
- Do *not* leave electronic equipment in vehicles when temperature extremes are expected.
- Do *not* leave electronic equipment or recording devices (videos, CD-ROMs, DVDs, or diskettes in direct sunlight in vehicles.

Maintenance

Only qualified repair personnel should perform specialized maintenance of training aid devices. Instructors who are familiar with the equipment may perform minor maintenance. Some types of maintenance include the following:

Because a laser reads CDs, CD-ROMs, and DVDs, they are generally resistant to fingerprints, dust, smudges, and scratches. However, surface contaminants and scratches can cause data errors. Coloring the outside edge of a CD/DVD (for filing and identification purposes) with a marker makes no difference in video or audio quality. Take the following steps when handling and using CDs, CD-ROMs, or DVDs:

- Treat the CD-ROM or DVD in the same way a music CD is supposed to be treated.
- Keep the disc clean, which will also keep the inside of the player clean.
- Never attempt to play a cracked disc — it could shatter and damage the player.

- Use a cleaning disc specially designed for CD/DVD players to clean the laser lens.
- Handle the CD/DVD at the hub (center) or outer edge. Do *not* touch the shiny surface.
- Store the disc in a protective case when it is *not* in use. Do *not* bend the disc when removing it from the case, and be careful to *not* scratch the disc when placing it in the case or player tray.
- Ensure that the disc is properly seated in the player tray before closing the tray.
- Keep CDs/DVDs away from hot equipment surfaces, direct sunlight, pets, small children, and other destructive forces. Magnetic fields have no effect on CDs/DVDs.

- ***Replace projector bulb*** — Always wear cotton gloves to prevent skin oil from covering the bulb surface or handle the bulb by the porcelain base only (**Figure 11.22**).
- ***Lubricate gears and moving parts*** — Follow manufacturer's recommendations.
- ***Unplug electrical power cords before opening any audiovisual equipment*** — Prevent possible electric shock.

- ***Tighten any loose screws or nuts*** — Do *not* over-tighten screws or nuts.
- ***Do not attempt specialized maintenance*** — Prevent further damage to the unit and possibly void any existing warranty.
- ***Periodically clean air filters in multimedia projectors*** — Prevent clogged air filters that cause cooling fans to work harder and decrease the life of the unit.

Summary

Properly used, audiovisual training aids and devices can create an active learning experience for any instructor. The instructor must know the benefits and limitations of the various types of equipment operated by the organization. How and when to use training aids to gain the greatest instructional benefit are import aspects in selecting the proper training aid to use. Instructors should also be familiar with the use of transitions in their presentations and how to effectively create them.

Finally, instructors must be able to clean, care for, and maintain the equipment assigned to the division. Audiovisual training aids are the instructor's tools just as nozzles and axes are the firefighter's tools.

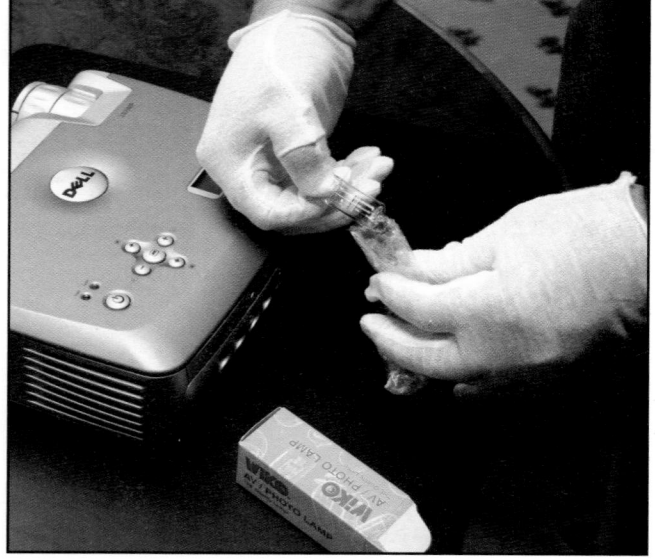

Figure 11.22 Gloves can be used to prevent skin oil from contacting high-intensity projection bulbs. The oil reduces the life of a bulb and may result in bulb failure.

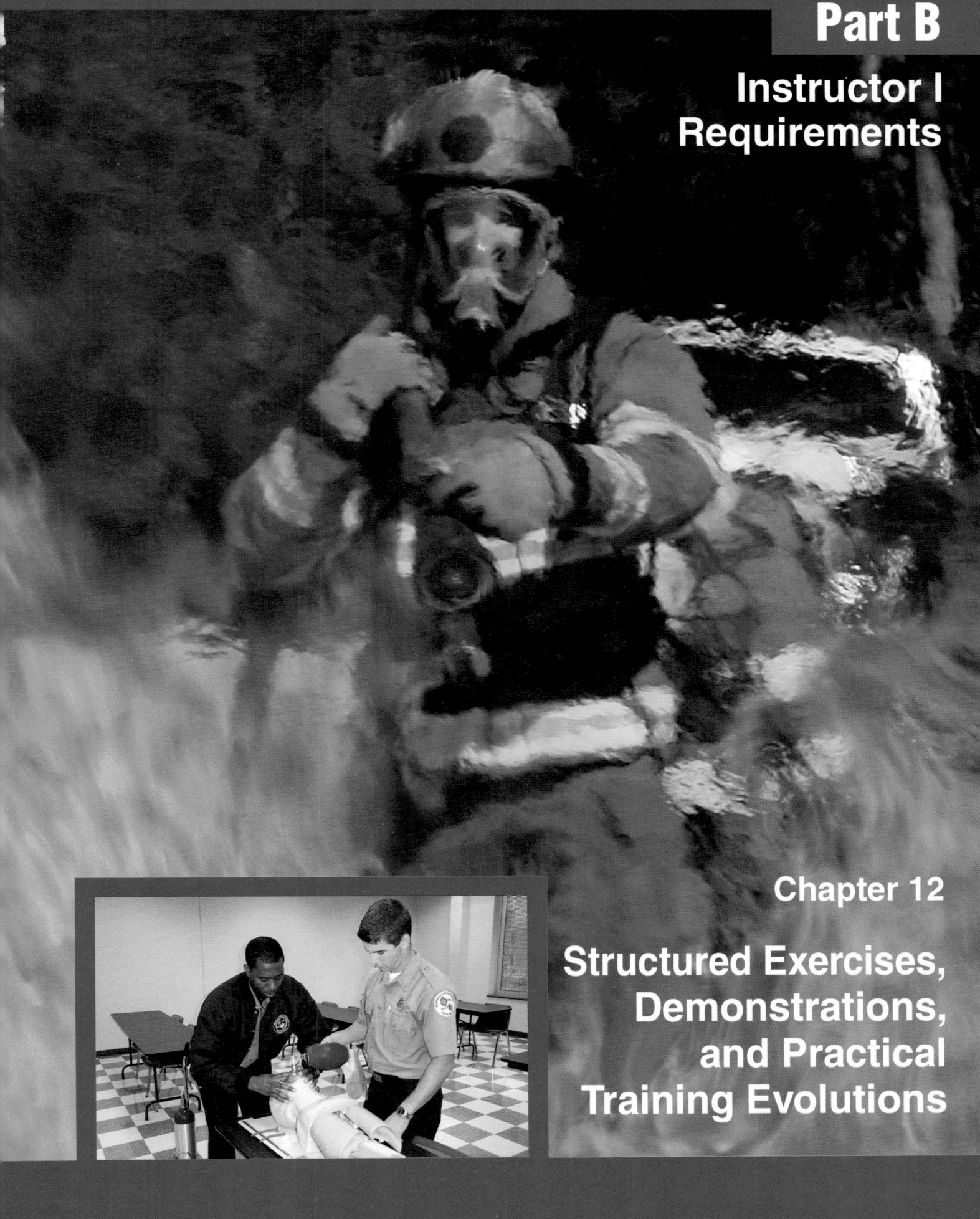

Chapter 12

Structured Exercises, Demonstrations, and Practical Training Evolutions

After reading this chapter, students will be able to —

1. Identify facts about structured exercises.

2. Explain the steps in a psychomotor skills demonstration.

3. Describe benefits of practical training evolutions.

4. List factors that the instructor must consider when preparing practical training evolutions.

5. List types of tasks or situations applicable to practical training evolutions.

6. Discuss locations used for practical training evolutions.

7. Identify accurate statements about factors to consider in planning practical training evolutions.

8. Identify guidelines for planning a practical training evolution.

9. List guidelines for ensuring the safety of students who participate in a practical training evolution.

10. Describe methods used to control an evolution.

11. Identify accurate statements about simple training evolutions.

12. Discuss complex training evolutions.

13. Explain the importance of live-fire training evolutions.

14. Identify accurate statements about small-fire training evolutions.

15. List guidelines for interior structural fire training.

16. Identify facts about exterior fire-suppression training.

17. Identify facts about technical training evolutions.

18. Identify accurate statements about instructor preparation when planning practical training evolutions.

Chapter Contents

Structured Exercises
Case Studies
Role-Plays
Brainstorming Sessions
Simulations
Field and Laboratory Experiences

Psychomotor Skills Demonstrations

Practical Training Evolutions
Training Locations
Evolution Planning

Safety and Health Considerations
Evolution Control
  Simple Training Evolutions
  Complex Training Evolutions
Fire-Suppression Training Evolutions
  Small Fires
  Interior Structural Fires
  Exterior Fires
Technical Training Evolutions
Instructor Preparation

Summary

Chapter 12
Structured Exercises, Demonstrations, and Practical Training Evolutions

The application step of the four-step method of instruction provides the student with the opportunity to perform an activity or skill under the supervision of an instructor **(Figure 12.1)**. This step contains elements of the presentation step because both have the purpose of changing student behavior. The application step can be used to teach both cognitive and psychomotor skills through various activities. To teach cognitive knowledge, structured exercises such as case studies, role-playing, brainstorming, simulations, and field or laboratory experiences are used. These exercises help students understand concepts and apply them to scenarios that model actual situations.

Demonstrations of psychomotor skills consist of an illustrated lecture, followed by a guided practice, and finally an unguided performance of a skill that the student will be expected to use on the job. Finally, practical training evolutions are used for individual, single-unit, multiunit, and multiagency training. This chapter includes each of these approaches to the application of knowledge and skills in fire and emergency services training.

Structured Exercises

Structured exercises include a variety of instructional methods that actively involve the students in the learning process. Structured exercises include but are not limited to the following:

- Case studies
- Role-plays
- Brainstorming sessions
- Simulations
- Field and laboratory experiences

Step 3 Application

Purpose	How to Accomplish
To provide the opportunity for students to apply theory, critical thinking, critical decision-making, or psychomotor skills to practical situations:	Creative, organized, and tested methods for presenting and practicing practical skills:
1. Demonstrate skills-based knowledge through appropriate means. 2. Provide students with the opportunity to perform under supervision. 3. Involve students actively in the learning process. 4. Provide the opportunity to practice and master critical skills in a nonemergency learning environment.	1. Have students perform the task or activity under supervision. 2. Observe performances closely. 3. Check and correct errors. 4. Instill correct habits in students. 5. Check key points and safety points. 6. Develop discussions based on theory, decision-making, or skills application. 7. Conduct periodic skills tests. 8. Assign projects and activities. 9. Assign problems for students to resolve.

Figure 12.1 The application step allows students to perform and practice the skills that have been taught in the presentation step.

Case Studies

A *case study* is a description of a real or hypothetical problem that an organization or an individual has dealt with or could deal with. When selecting or developing a case study, the instructor should ensure that the problem is similar to one that students will face in performing their duties. Typically, a case study reviews and discusses detailed accounts of past events and then allows students to analyze the situation, evaluate the situation, and synthesize possible answers to the problem.

This method helps develop a student's ability to analyze situations and examine facts to reach a conclusion. It provides opportunities to form and discuss ideas and perform problem-solving exercises by using the problems faced by participants in the event. The instructor establishes an environment that provides students with time to review, research, and discuss the situation. Face-to-face or electronic communication between students must also be established to encourage student interaction.

Because students must have the past experiences and education to analyze the situation and relate it to their own experiences, case studies are best used for fire and emergency services officers rather than lower ranked personnel. Students must be willing and able to communicate and defend their suggestions to other members of the group.

Whether an instructor locates an existing case study or develops a hypothetical one, the following development process should be used:

- ***Identify a story or event*** — The example must relate to the learning objective students are expected to achieve. Therefore, when the learning objective involves an understanding of decision-making, the example should then involve a situation where people had to make a decision. The example, in this case, might involve a crisis situation involving fire attack or a management situation involving a discipline problem.

- ***Research the story or event*** — The instructor must locate as much information on the event as possible and ensure that it is readily available to students for their analyses. *Examples:*

  — When the event occurred locally, the instructor may choose to interview participants to gain an insight into their decision-making process. This information can be used following student presentations to compare the actual approach to the students' suggestions.

  — When the story is hypothetical, the instructor should then research similar actual events and use pertinent elements to create the fictional event.

- ***Develop the case study outline*** — An outline provides students with all the facts in the story and ties the details and visual aids (if any are used) to the timeline of the story. Key elements in the outline should include those that had a direct effect on the outcome of the event.

- ***Determine presentation factors*** — The instructor must establish a time frame for presenting the story, allowing students time to analyze it and present their suggestions. Case studies must have an established time frame because the presentations and discussion can consume time when they are left open-ended. Presentation formats, visual aids, and the question-and-answer process must also be determined.

- ***Writing the case study and collecting the exhibits*** — The final step includes the following actions:

  — Write the story.

  — Write questions that students must answer to guide their research and analyses.

  — Prepare slide, transparency, or electronic visual aids.

  — Prepare the case study overview that contains all the rules for analyzing the story (time frame, exhibits, etc.).

Examples of case studies can come from the following groups:

- Private business community

- Local, regional, state/provincial, or national training agencies

- Professional training associations

- Other government agencies

Practical case studies can be based on National Institute for Occupational Safety and Health (NIOSH) investigations and warnings. Stories that may be of assistance can be found in NFPA and other trade journals.

Case Study: Career Fire Fighter Dies After Falling From Tailboard and Being Backed Over by Engine (California)

NIOSH Fire Fighter Fatality Investigation Report, May 20, 2005

Incident Summary

On August 14, 2004, a 25-year-old female career firefighter (the victim) died when she apparently fell from the tailboard and was backed over by an engine. The victim and her crew had been released from the scene of a residential fire. Other apparatus blocked the road, so the victim's crew began backing to an intersection approximately 300 feet (91 m) away in order to proceed forward. The victim took her position standing on the tailboard as directed by departmental policy, and notified the driver to begin backing by pushing an electronic signaling button located on the rear panel of the engine.

NOTE: The fire department policy was for a firefighter to serve as the Tailboard Safety Member to ride on the tailboard and guide the driver whenever the apparatus needs to back by pressing a signal button located on the rear engine panel. The Tailboard Safety Member would push the button once to stop, twice to go forward, and three times to go back. The signal button would sound a bell in the cab and a red light would also flash correspondingly on the dash.

As also directed by departmental policy, the Captain was acting as the Traffic Control Officer and guiding the backing operation from behind the apparatus in the road on the driver's side by using hand signals. When the Captain turned and walked into the intersection to stop cross-traffic, the victim apparently fell from the tailboard and was run over by the engine. Members on the scene provided advanced life support, and the victim was transported to a local hospital where she was pronounced dead.

Discussion Questions

1. Were appropriate safety measures in effect at the time of the incident?

2. Were those safety measures in use at the time of the incident?

3. What NFPA standards can be applied to this incident?

4. What could have been done to prevent this type of fatality?

5. What changes could be made in the following areas: technology, policy, training, or national standard?

See **Appendix K** for a complete copy of this NIOSH investigation report.

Role-Plays

In *role-plays*, students portray characters and act the roles assigned to them in scenarios. This method provides an opportunity to practice actions that prepare students for situations they may encounter while fulfilling their duties (**Figure 12.2, p. 280**). Role-plays can be used in training personnel for a variety of tasks or situations such as public safety telecommunication personnel who must receive and dispatch calls during emotionally intense times or public information officers who interact with citizens.

Role-playing is particularly helpful when the aspects of the affective domain (values, beliefs, and emotions) need to be taught or reinforced. The basics of interpersonal communication can be taught through the role-play method. The following areas are considered when planning a role-play lesson:

- Ensure that scenarios apply to the course materials, and clearly explain learning objectives.

- Explain the purpose of the activity at the beginning of the role-play, and ensure that students fully understand the results that are expected.

- Ensure that students understand the scenario, character roles, and time frame of the role-play.

- Involve all students in some part of the role-play activity, whether acting, critiquing, taking notes, or observing.

- Limit the actual role-play to a few who play the roles, and assign activities directed toward a summary discussion and conclusion to the rest of the group. It is possible to supervise only one group at a time.

Figure 12.2 Role-play can take many forms, including permiting students to experience difficult situations they may face during actual emergency operations. *Courtesy of Alabama Fire College.*

- Encourages application of knowledge and practicing of skills
- Permits students to practice under less anxiety or stress
- Facilitates identification of critical features of interpersonal relations
- Identifies multiple approaches to a problem
- Increases the development of empathy through substituted experience
- Helps develop critical consciousness
- Provides a quick, economical, and easily available resource
- Prepares students for emotionally challenging events such as dealing with trauma patients

While there are advantages to role-play, the following disadvantages are possible:

- Preparation can be very involved and time-consuming. Consider using case studies as the basis for role-play scenarios, which reduces the preparation time for both.
- A role-play can take time to perform and may result in students digressing from the topic when they are bored, uninterested, or see no value in the activity. Fully explain all activities and the importance of them as well as how they relate to the students' work-related duties.
- A role-play depends on the ability of students to involve themselves in the characters and scenario, which depends on the internal motivation of each student. Instructors can influence student motivation to some extent. Remind students that role-play is the closest they will come to real-life encounters in a controlled setting. Students can react and act without fear of permanently damaging a relationship or becoming embarrassed by their actions.

- Have several role-plays for a large group to provide many (if not all) individuals the opportunity to act a role.

- Monitor the role-play throughout the scenario to ensure that students are engaged and not overreacting to the scene.

At the end of the role-play, the instructor must debrief students and observers. This debriefing gives students an opportunity to explain their feelings and actions in the role-play and further understand the objective of the activity. The instructor should summarize the scenario and reinforce the importance of any positive behavior that was exhibited.

The advantages of role-play include the following:

Brainstorming Sessions

In the *brainstorming* method, a group of students is given a problem or situation and time to determine a solution to it **(Figure 12.3)**. Brainstorming is an effective teaching method when participants have adequate knowledge of the subject matter. Management and administrative personnel also effectively use brainstorming to generate possible solutions for problems facing the organization. The rules of brainstorming apply to both teaching and problem-solving situations. Effective brainstorming sessions require the performance of the following activities:

- **Record all ideas** — The purpose of brainstorming is to allow individuals to think creatively within a group and express their ideas openly.

- **Allow everyone to speak** — Everyone should participate and stay on topic. Do *not* allow one or two strong personalities to dominate the process or wander from the issue.

- **Encourage creative ideas** — There are no wrong ideas; ideas generate discussions.

- **Respect each member of the group** — Mutual respect is essential; without it, members will *not* participate or provide suggestions.

- **Encourage piggybacking** — One individual's suggestion may spark ideas from other persons, which eventually enables the group to produce a solution to a problem.

- **Evaluate and prioritize issues after ideas are exhausted** — After all ideas are recorded, select the top five or ten ideas to discuss or resolve.

Figure 12.3 Brainstorming sessions allow students to use creative ideas to solve problems. *Courtesy of Iowa Fire Service Training Bureau.*

- **Act as facilitator** — The instructor is *not* an active participant in the process. The instructor answers questions, keeps the group on topic, and summarizes the results.

Simulations

Training *simulations* are activities that allow students to participate in scenarios that represent real-life situations. They may take many forms, including practical training evolutions described later in this chapter and computer-based training (CBT) that was presented in Chapter 10, Instructional Delivery. Simulations permit students to experience a situation and see the results of their decisions without the negative results that can occur at an actual emergency.

A simulation may include elements of the role-play approach as students take on assigned duties and interact with one another. A tabletop emergency management drill is an example of a simulation that is economical and effective **(Figure 12.4)**. Confined-space rescue training that permits actual operations in a simulated hazardous environment is an example of a practical training evolution. CBT permits individual students to operate apparatus pump panels, simulate command of structure fires, and even attack a computer-created structure fire. The key to all simulations is to ensure that they

Figure 12.4 Tabletop training simulators are very effective in multiagency training exercises. The simulation allows students to have an overall view of an incident, see how available resources are deployed, and learn how to coordinate with other agencies to control the incident.

effectively reflect the equipment, procedures, protocols, and situations that students will encounter on duty.

Field and Laboratory Experiences

Field and laboratory experiences involve elements of the demonstration and simulation methods where students have the opportunity to inspect, use, test, and evaluate equipment or processes either in actual installations or laboratory settings. In the field, students are typically given a tour of an installation such as a fire detection and suppression system in a building. They may be permitted to observe a systems test or see the steps required to replace a component.

In a laboratory, students can see models of equipment such as cutaway apparatus engines or pumps or sprinkler control valves. They may perform chemistry experiments to simulate fire behavior or fire spread in an enclosed space (**Figure 12.5**). The instructor explains the equipment

Figure 12.5 Laboratory-type tests can be used to simulate fire development, the elements of the fire tetrahedron, or the use of extinguishing agents within a small, controlled space.

or process, demonstrates the steps required, and observes students as they repeat the skills. Students may work independently or in groups. One approach can include giving the students a problem such as a defective SCBA regulator and asking them to solve the problem.

Psychomotor Skills Demonstrations

Planning, preparation, and practice are essential to a successful skills demonstration. The instructor who does *not* appear proficient at a skill will lose credibility with students and waste valuable training time by having to repeat or correct skill steps. Skills demonstrations begin with giving the following information:

- An explanation of the skill
- Why it is important
- How it relates to other skills
- How many people are required to perform it
- When it should be performed

This explanation is followed by a demonstration of the skill performed at a normal rate of speed. The skill is next performed slowly with the instructor explaining each step. Students should be encouraged to ask questions after the step-by-step portion of the demonstration. This slow-speed demonstration may be repeated several times until students can verbalize the steps to the instructor before the instructor performs them. Students are then ready to practice the skill themselves. The slow-speed demonstration is the transition between the presentation step and the application step.

Students practice the steps while being guided and coached by instructors. Next, students work in small groups, continuing to practice the skill as they critique and coach each other (**Figure 12.6**). Once or twice during a practice session, instructors may need to demonstrate the entire skill and show the entire skill one more time at the end of the session. Instructors must show the skill steps correctly and in sequence. Students should be encouraged to practice skills during rest breaks, during free time, and at the beginning of the next training session. When students have perfected the skill, they are ready for evaluation.

Figure 12.6 Students practice skills in small groups under the supervision of an instructor. *Courtesy of Louisiana State University.*

Practical Training Evolutions

Practical training evolutions are essential for providing safe and efficient fire and emergency services to the public. Therefore, they are key elements in any fire and emergency services organization's training program. Practical training evolutions fulfill the following two primary requirements for the emergency services organization:

- Evolutions fulfill the written requirements for *hands-on* training that are found in applicable NFPA standards and Occupational Safety and Health Administration (OSHA) regulations and mandated by professional associations and local jurisdictions that have authority over the training function.

- Practical training evolutions permit students to apply the knowledge and practice the skills they have learned in the classroom.

Fire and emergency services instructors are responsible for developing, supervising, and conducting practical training evolutions. Instructors must provide training in controlled environments where students can learn a new skill or improve an existing one.

For the new entry-level firefighter, practical training evolutions permit the application of knowledge and skills learned through lectures and demonstrations under near realistic conditions. For experienced firefighters, live-fire and other technical training evolutions provide opportunities to develop additional skills and increase skill-performance levels.

In addition, realistic practical training evolutions promote enthusiasm, morale, and team spirit among fire and emergency service responders. Practical training evolutions are also an opportunity for personnel and units from various agencies, organizations, and jurisdictions to train together for potential joint operations. Factors that the instructor must consider when preparing practical training evolutions include the following:

- Best location for the type of training evolution
- Evolution planning and control requirements
- Safety and health considerations
- Instructor preparation

For planning purposes, practical training evolutions may be divided into fire suppression and technical training (non-fire-suppression activities) categories. The list of practical training evolutions mirrors the tasks generally performed by personnel in fire and emergency services organizations. Evolutions provide training in the following types of tasks or situations:

- Fire suppression
  - Interior
  - Exterior
  - Flammable liquids
- Technical training
  - Vehicle and apparatus operations
  - Hazardous materials
  - Technical rescue
  - Emergency medical training
  - Counterterrorism operations
  - Disaster management

A practical training evolution is the final step in a process that many fire and emergency services training organizations have used for years. This process can be visualized as a staircase that leads the student to the completion of the training course or curriculum. Each step depends on the successful completion of the previous step. At the same time, the stress that the student feels increases just as the stress at an emergency incident increases.

This process provides the student not only with increasing complexity of skills and combination of skills but also the physical and emotional stress that a real incident creates.

Training Locations

The locations used for practical training evolutions can be as varied as the types of evolutions. As mentioned in Chapter 5, Instructional Facilities and Props, training evolutions may be held at either permanent training facilities or remote sites. Many fire and emergency services organizations have access to permanent facilities within their state/province. Permanent training facilities usually contain permanent and portable props required for a variety of training such as the following:

- Burn and smoke buildings
- Drill towers
- Flammable/combustible liquids pits
- Vehicle driving courses

Instructors should develop a list of potential facilities, including those owned by the jurisdiction, local colleges and vocational/technical schools, and regional and state/provincial training agen-

---

WARNING!

Instructors must be familiar with and adhere to the following requirements when planning evolutions and selecting training locations:

- NFPA 1403, *Standard on Live Fire Training Evolutions*
- Occupational Safety and Health Administration (OSHA), federal, state/provincial, and local laws and ordinances that pertain to environmental protection
- All jurisdictional policies and procedures that regulate fire and emergency services training

---

cies. After compiling a comprehensive list of facilities, the types of training props available, and the names of facility representatives, instructors can plan the types of evolutions that can be performed at each location. Next, instructors can arrange with individual representatives to schedule and coordinate the use of each facility.

Remote training sites may include a wide variety of locations and types that may meet the organization's needs. Similar to the list compiled about permanent facilities, instructors then compile a list of available remote sites, including location, name of owner/representative, availability (access and time), water supply source, and possible types of training evolutions that the site could support. Examples of potential remote training sites and possible training uses include the following:

- *Parking lots* — Driver/operator training, supply and attack hose deployment, and vehicle extrication
- *Highway entry and exit ramps* — Highway incidents that require the use of traffic control devices, coordination with other agencies, hazardous materials spill control supplies, and vehicle extrication equipment **(Figure 12.7)**
- *Subdivisions under construction* — Driver/operator training and building construction training
- *Abandoned/condemned structures* — Live-burn evolutions, ventilation, and forcible entry
- *Military or government-owned reservations* — Wildland fire suppression, off-road driver/operator training, and joint military fire department training
- *Airports* — Aircraft crash/fire/rescue training, driver/operator training, and foam fire-suppression training
- *Grain elevators/silos* — Technical and rope rescue training
- *Industrial sites* — Technical and rope rescue, hazardous materials spill control, and fire-suppression training as well as joint-training evolutions with the local industrial fire brigade
- *Open wildlands* — Wildland fire-suppression and off-road driver/operator training (may involve joint activity with controlled burns) **(Figure 12.8)**

Figure 12.7 Highway entry and exit ramps can be used for training on safety procedures and the placement of traffic control markers. Caution must be used constantly, and law enforcement agencies must be involved in the training exercise.

Figure 12.8 Highways and open grassland can be used for training in establishing helicopter landing zones.

- *Structures under demolition* — Building collapse and confined-space rescue
- *Vehicle salvage yards* — Vehicle extrication
- *Parking garages* — Standpipe operations and high-angle rescue
- *Warehouses and aircraft hangars* — Large area search, rapid intervention, hoseline deployment, and tactical simulation

Some of these remote sites will be available for repeated use while others will provide only a onetime training opportunity. In all cases, the appropriate permission to gain access and train on any remote site must be obtained in advance from the property owners or their agents.

Both permanent facilities and remote-site training locations must meet the requirements for environmental protection regarding water runoff, soil contamination, and air pollution. Instructors must consult the agencies responsible for these environmental regulations and determine the required precautions and permits. Instructors must also monitor weather conditions to ensure that wind, lightning, limited visibility, icing, and temperature extremes do not increase risks to participants.

Finally, instructors must adhere to the requirements of NFPA 1500, *Standard on Fire Department Occupational Safety and Health Program,* and NFPA 1403, *Standard on Live Fire Training Evolutions,* regarding safety during live-burn training exercises. Safety is the primary concern during any and all practical training evolutions.

Evolution Planning

When planning practical training evolutions, instructors must take many factors that contribute to a safe and effective learning experience into consideration. These factors include the following:

- *Safety* — This factor cannot be overemphasized in planning training. Instructors must balance the level of realism in the training evolution with the level of risk to the safety and health of students. In all cases, safety must take precedence over realism. Safety means not only the use of proper personal protective equipment (PPE) but also planning the evolution with safety as a key component.

- *Learning objective/outcome* — The practical training evolution must result in students meeting the learning objective of the lesson or course. When the evolution does *not* meet this criterion, it is a waste of time and effort. A lesson plan must be created to help define the learning objectives and outcomes.

- *Justification* — Meeting the learning objective is just one justification for the evolution. The training must meet other criteria too, including the following:
  - Cost/benefit
  - Legal requirements
  - Community perception
  - Allotment of resources

- **Supervision** — Every training evolution must be supervised and monitored by the course instructors. Instructors should remember that the larger the evolution, the more instructors required for supervision. For example, NFPA 1403 requirements for live-fire training evolutions specify that the instructor-to-student ratio shall *not* exceed 1 to 5.

- **Resources/logistics** — The instructor's plan must provide for all the resources necessary to perform the tasks and complete the evolution. This factor is especially critical for evolutions that occur at remote sites. *Requirements:*
  - Water supply quantities must be calculated based on the requirements of NFPA 1142, *Standard on Water Supplies for Suburban and Rural Fire Fighting.*
  - Apparatus, tools, extinguishing agents, and personnel must be available at the site.
  - Rest and rehabilitation resources for all participants as well as emergency medical resources must be planned for and brought to the site **(Figure 12.9)**.
  - Sufficient time must be provided to complete the evolution.

- **Weather** — The weather factor has been mentioned previously. Simply stated, instructors must plan to hold evolutions when the weather will *not* be a distraction or create a safety hazard and be prepared to alter their plans when the weather becomes inclement.

- **Legal requirements** — Legal considerations include those laws, regulations, or standards that require the training to occur and those that limit, constrain, or prohibit training evolutions. The legal requirements that place limitations on training evolutions include the following:
  - Environmental laws
  - Zoning regulations
  - Building and fire codes
  - Ownership rights

See Chapter 3, Legal and Ethical Considerations, and Chapter 5, Instructional Facilities and Props, for details. Legal requirements that cause the training to occur define the following elements:

Figure 12.9 Training exercises that involve high-risk training or temperature extremes must include the establishment of a rehabilitation section for students. *Courtesy of Iowa Fire Service Training Bureau.*

  - Type of training that must take place
  - Minimum amount of time that must be used for training
  - Evaluation criteria used to determine whether training was successful

- **Incident command system (ICS)** — In order for a training evolution to mirror the actual events that take place at an emergency incident, an evolution must adhere to an accepted command structure. Whether the evolution is intended to involve a single company, multiple companies, or multiple agencies and jurisdictions, the National Incident Management System (NIMS) ICS must be established and followed.

- **Coordination** — Coordination with outside agencies, organizations, and jurisdictions as well as the civilian population in the area of the training is essential. Instructors should include representatives of these groups in the planning process for best results.

- **Exposures** — Both permanent training facilities and remote training locations have exposures that must be considered when planning a practical training evolution. Exposure protection must be provided during all live-fire evolutions. *Other considerations:*

— The movement of smoke and fire embers on wind currents may affect residents living in the area.

— Water runoff could contaminate drinking water supplies or create a slipping or skidding hazard.

• *Evaluation/critique* — Lesson plans should include an opportunity for instructors and participants to evaluate evolutions and their performances. Evaluations provide the following benefits:

— Assists students in attaining proficiency and addressing weaknesses

— Assists the training division in determining the effectiveness of the particular evolution

— Assists instructors in determining their own effectiveness in teaching and supervising a practical training evolution

— Provides models for all participants to become familiar with when they are involved in emergency incident critiques **(Figure 12.10)**

The role of the instructor changes depending on the type of students involved in the training. When the evolution involves new entry-level students, the instructor remains in the role of *teacher* while also acting as a *supervisor*. In this situation the instructor may be an active participant in the evolution, acting in the role of company officer and directing the activities of the students.

When students are experienced fire and emergency services personnel, the role of the instructor shifts from *teacher* to that of *monitor* or *facilitator*. Experienced fire and emergency service personnel respond best to training evolutions that help them overcome problems they have encountered in their professional lives. In the monitor or facilitator context, the instructor arranges a training evolution so that students can achieve the following results:

• Develop their own abilities.

• Test new ideas.

• Reinforce or develop new skills.

• Avoid behaviors that should be eliminated.

Figure 12.10 Training does not *end* with the completion of the training evolution. More knowledge can still be gained during the post-training incident critique.

High-Hazard Training

High-hazard training implies that training involves activities that are potentially risky. Consider risk-management factors when planning training of this type. Examples of high-hazard training include the following:

• Live-fire exercises

• Hazardous materials exercises

• High- and low-angle rope rescue

• Confined-space rescue (including aboveground and below-grade scenarios)

• Evolutions that require the use of power tools and equipment

• Dive, surface-water, and swift-water rescue training

Risk Management Factors

Before demonstrating skills with associated risks, instructors should consider the following risk management questions. When instructors cannot answer these questions satisfactorily or positively, they should consider another method of demonstration.

• What aspects of demonstrating the skill could be dangerous to both the instructor and students? What precautions must be taken? What safety equipment is required?

• Is the demonstration necessary? Is this type of demonstration approved by the sponsoring organization? Is there another way to demonstrate the risky skill such as showing videotapes?

• Are additional instructors needed to supervise participants? Should special emergency units stand by? What aspects of the environment can be controlled? Which ones cannot? How can these aspects be resolved or accommodated?

Experienced fire and emergency service responders are generally task-oriented and cooperative students. They enjoy working as a team or group and accomplishing an assigned task with others. This orientation has important implications for planning practical evolutions. The instructor should apply the following guidelines when planning a practical evolution and establishing the desired learning outcomes for experienced personnel during company drills:

- Give each student the opportunity to have input and influence the outcome. Students must know their roles and the desired learning objectives of the training evolution.

- Do *not* assign too many students to specific tasks. Keep all students busy, and eliminate or greatly reduce *stand-around time.*

- Provide a safe staging area for students and an observation area for nonparticipants.

- Maintain a suitable instructor-to-student ratio. The exact ratio varies with the type of evolution, although the guideline ratio given earlier may be used as a gauge.

- Assign a safety officer to monitor all training activities. Having a safety officer is a requirement of NFPA 1500 and good fire service practice **(Figure 12.11)**.

- Assign an instructor or experienced staff member to act as fuel-control officer when using liquefied petroleum gas (LPG), natural gas, or flammable/combustible liquid-fed live-fire training props. The sole duty of this officer is to turn off the flow of fuel to the prop in the event of an emergency or at the termination of the evolution.

- Ensure that students have the necessary skill levels and knowledge needed for the particular training evolution. For example, a student who is *not* familiar with the specialized knots needed for high-angle rescue requires additional training before participating in such a course or training evolution. *Factors:*
  - Prerequisites may have to be satisfied before students are allowed to participate in an evolution.
  - A complete review of each individual's training record will reveal those who are qualified to participate in advanced exercises.

Figure 12.11 A qualified instructor or the organization's safety officer should be assigned the duties of incident safety officer at all training activities. *Courtesy of Alabama Fire College.*

  - This review will encompass job performance requirements and prerequisite skills and knowledge.

- Design the practical evolution so that a positive outcome is possible. Assigning a task that is very difficult or impossible to accomplish provides a limited learning experience.

- Provide a summary of what has been learned and what can be carried into the operational environment and actual emergency setting.

- Record the training evolution if possible to assist with the critique and for future use as a visual training aid.

When planning is complete, instructors should schedule the use of the training facility or remote site based on availability. The training schedule also takes into consideration the availability of students based on outside demands and operational requirements.

Safety and Health Considerations

Ensuring the safety of students who participate in practical training evolutions begins before the training occurs. As mentioned earlier, ensuring safety first begins with the planning of the training evolution. Second, students' safety depends partially on their physical well-being. It is the instructor's responsibility to determine that students are in good health and physically and emotionally capable of performing the tasks included in evolutions.

According to NFPA statistics, the majority of training related fatalities are the result of heart attacks created by stress from evolutions. To prevent these fatalities, instructors must take the following precautions:

- Determine that each student is in good health. A medical examination and release should be required before a person can participate in strenuous training evolutions.

- Determine that students are emotionally able to perform the tasks required. When students are afraid of heights or confined spaces, there is the risk that they will freeze in place and require rescue or they might panic and injure another student while attempting to escape the situation.

- Ascertain that each student is in good physical condition. Students who are physically *out of shape* may *not* be able to finish the training due to exhaustion or fatigue. Someone who becomes tired increases the chance of being injured or inflicting injury on another student.

- Monitor students carefully during strenuous practical training evolutions. An exercise should *not* be so demanding that learning is difficult or impossible. Even when the physical demand is carefully measured, the effect of extreme heat or cold on students must be considered. Rest and rehabilitation facilities must be provided for all participants.

- Do *not* allow the length of an exercise to interfere with students' abilities to learn and succeed at their tasks. A student who is physically exhausted will be mentally exhausted and unable to focus on the required activities. Exhausted students are more likely to perform unsafe acts.

Instructors must be familiar with the safety and health requirements outlined in NFPA 1500 and the duties and responsibilities for both health and safety officer (HSO) and incident safety officer (ISO) found in NFPA 1521, *Standard for Fire Department Safety Officer*. Additional safety information for live-fire training is provided in NFPA 1403.

As stated earlier, ensuring safety begins with taking a complete survey of the training facility or location (especially acquired structures) where the evolution is to take place. The instructor should complete an inspection of all equipment permanently installed or brought to the site of the evolution. Damaged equipment can interfere with the evolution, create a distraction, and also potentially cause injuries.

Inspections of PPE, personal alert safety system (PASS) devices, self-contained breathing apparatus (SCBA), and other safety items required by a student's organization are always performed before beginning the evolution. By emphasizing the care and use of PPE and other safety equipment, an evolution can achieve a behavioral objective that can be applied by students to everyday responsibilities (**Figure 12.12**).

A personnel accountability system must be used for all evolutions that involve high-risk training evolutions such as the following:

- Interior and wildland fire suppression

- Confined-space search and rescue

- Dive rescue, surface-water rescue, and swift-water rescue

- Large-scale multiple company operations

Figure 12.12 Instructors must always wear full personal protective equipment (PPE) during training exercises that require it. The PPE must be clean and in good condition not only for safety sake but also as a proper example for students. *Courtesy of Alabama Fire College.*

The system normally used by the organization should be used during the evolution. The instructor, working with the ISO, must ensure that all students are trained in the accountability system and protocol. No student or instructor who is *not* accounted for in the system should be allowed to enter the area nearest the fire or hazardous materials incident (hot zone) or participate in the evolution.

Evolution Control

Both simple and complex practical training evolutions must be controlled. Controlling an evolution involves the following elements:

- *Supervising* — Instructors provide direct supervision over students to ensure that the correct skills are used safely during the evolution.

- *Monitoring* — Instructors observe the progress of the evolution to ensure that all lesson objectives are performed and accomplished.

- *Teaching* — When appropriate, instructors use the evolution to teach by including related or new information for students.

- *Managing* — Instructors apply the elements of the NIMS ICS to control the evolution as though it was an actual emergency situation.

To effectively control a practical training evolution, the ratio of active students to instructors must *not* exceed the ability of the instructors to perform these tasks. As introduced previously, the guideline ratio of 5 students to 1 instructor can generally be applied to most practical training evolutions. As the size or complexity of the evolution increases, additional instructors may be required.

Simple Training Evolutions

Simple training evolutions involve small numbers of students performing a single task that requires only a few skills. Examples include the following:

- Lifting and setting a ground ladder
- Using a portable fire extinguisher
- Lifting and moving patients
- Forcing entry through a door
- Taking and recording patients' vital signs
- Deploying and advancing an attack hoseline
- Driving and parking a fire apparatus (**Figure 12.13**)

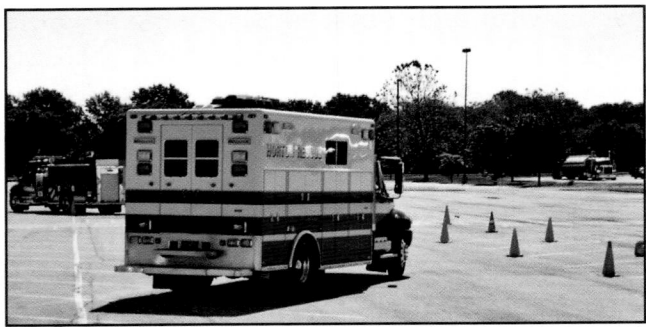

Figure 12.13 Driver/operators can practice maneuvering fire apparatus or ambulances on closed driving courses to build their confidence and skills in vehicle operation. *Courtesy of Iowa Fire Service Training Bureau.*

These types of training evolutions may involve from one to five active students and require only one or two instructors for supervision. The evolution is repeated until each student is able to perform it without error. When more than one student is involved, they rotate positions so each has the opportunity to experience and practice each part of the skill.

The instructor begins an evolution by performing the following actions:

- Explain the learning objectives or outcomes.

- Demonstrate the evolution, which may require the use of an experienced group of responders to perform the evolution for students to observe when the evolution involves more than one student.

- Relate the evolution to the classroom lecture.

- Emphasize the safety requirements for the evolution.

While monitoring the evolution, the instructor should immediately stop and correct any performance weaknesses or errors. The sooner corrections are made, the more likely students are to recognize the problem and adjust their behaviors. Safety infractions are always acknowledged and corrected immediately.

Simple training evolutions should be performed as though students were involved in a real emergency incident, which means that the appropriate PPE is worn during the evolution. All policies and procedures that would affect personnel are applied during the training evolution, including the NIMS

ICS. Practical training evolutions should also be practiced with both the minimum and maximum levels of staffing that the organization requires.

For instance, when an engine company is staffed by one person who may arrive at the incident ahead of the rest of the crew, that scenario should be part of the training. When a company is normally staffed by four people but has a minimum level of three, both scenarios should be practiced. By following these suggestions, students will practice and learn the skills they are required to use when they are on duty.

Complex Training Evolutions

Any practical evolution that involves multiple teams of fire or emergency services responders automatically demands the use of the NIMS ICS. With such a system, instructors, students, and observers are accounted for and kept under control. Evolutions that are complex, involve more students or agencies, or may involve dangers inherent in the exercise itself demand incident management.

The NIMS ICS model adopted by many jurisdictions in North America is based on NFPA 1561, *Standard on Emergency Services Incident Management System*. It provides guidance and direction for the management and control of all types of emergency incidents ranging from single company responses to multiple agency and jurisdiction incidents.

In 2004, the U.S. government adopted ICS as part of NIMS, and it must be used by all federal agencies or agencies that receive federal funding. Additional information on the NIMS ICS model and its application may be found in the Model Procedures Guide series developed by the National Fire Service Incident Management Consortium and published by Fire Protection Publications and the NIMS document itself.

The use of NIMS ICS during practical training evolutions has two benefits: First, and most importantly, it helps ensure the safety and accountability of students. Second, it has the additional benefit of acquainting students with the operation of the system. Students can take this training experience and apply what they have learned at the scene of an actual emergency. Instructors should adapt the NIMS ICS to fit the requirements of the particular

type of evolution. In the case of any evolution that holds the potential for injuries, the use of an incident management system is an absolute necessity.

The duties and tasks assigned in the NIMS ICS may be performed by instructors or experienced students. When students are used to fill the positions, instructors are assigned to observe and monitor their activities **(Figure 12.14)**. Some of the important functions or positions that are assigned by the NIMS ICS and used during training are as follows:

- *Incident safety officer (ISO)* — Ensures the safety of all participants and advises the instructor or student incident commander (IC) on safety-related issues
- *Logistics officer* — Provides the materials and supplies required to perform the evolutions and ensures that adequate breathing air, fire-suppression agents, fuel, and rehabilitation/ emergency medical services (EMS) resources are available during the evolution
- *Staging officer* — Manages the staging area for multiple company/agency evolutions
- *Division/branch/sector officer* — Manages or supervises participants in the various locations around the site; special sector officer controls

Figure 12.14 Instructors should monitor the incident command post to ensure that proper procedures are followed.

and manages the classroom or assembly area where students receive final instructions, briefings, or postincident critiques

- *Communications officer* — Monitors operational communications to ensure that correct protocol is used and listens for potential problems involving participants

All practical training evolutions that involve interior fire fighting must include the establishment of a rapid intervention team or crew (RIT/RIC). Training evolutions that involve basic training for entry-level students require that the RIT/RIC be composed of experienced firefighters or instructors. Evolutions for experienced personnel can involve experienced students to provide them with experience in establishing and staffing this position.

Controlling the evolution is critical when multiple agencies or jurisdictions are involved. Because each agency or jurisdiction may have differing protocols or operational procedures, planning must include efforts to coordinate the activities of the various groups. The NIMS ICS model assists instructors in coordinating this type of training evolution. Clear-text (plain English) communication is essential for control. Agreement on this issue and

others must be resolved before the joint training evolution is held. Additionally, training outcome and judging criteria must be established.

Fire-Suppression Training Evolutions

Live-fire training is an important part of both entry-level and experienced firefighter training. Entry-level personnel learn new skills and experienced personnel develop, improve, or alter previously learned skills. In many communities with strict building- and fire-code enforcement, modern construction, and active public fire and life safety awareness programs, the number of fires has been reduced significantly.

The decrease in actual fire-fighting incidents and the assignment of entry-level personnel to EMS duties has resulted in fewer opportunities for personnel to experience live-fire situations. Therefore, the practical training evolutions involving live-fire situations may be the only experience some personnel receive. Live-fire training evolutions can involve the following categories:

- Small fires involving small amounts of fuel
- Interior structural fires
- Exterior fires, including transportation fires, wildland fires, flammable/combustible liquid fires, and large-quantity Class A materials fires

NFPA 1403, *Standard on Live Fire Training Evolutions*

NFPA 1403 states that before being permitted to participate in live-fire training evolutions, the student shall have received training to meet the performance objectives for Fire Fighter I in NFPA 1001, *Standard for Fire Fighter Professional Qualifications,* related to the following subjects:

(1) Safety

(2) Fire Behavior

(3) Portable Extinguishers

(4) Personal Protective Equipment

(5) Ladders

(6) Fire Hose, Appliances, and Streams

(7) Overhaul

(8) Water Supply

(9) Ventilation

(10) Forcible Entry

See the following chapters and sections in NFPA 1403:

- Chapter 4, Acquired Structures, Section 4.1.1
- Chapter 5, Gas-Fired Training Center Buildings, Section 5.1.1
- Chapter 6, Non-Gas-Fire Training Center Buildings, Section 6.1.1
- Chapter 7, Exterior Props, Section 7.1.1
- Chapter 8, Exterior Class B Fires, Section 8.1.1

———————

List reprinted with permission from NFPA 1403, *Standard on Live Fire Training Evolutions,* Copyright © 2002, National Fire Protection Association, Quincy, MA 02269. This reprinted material is not the complete and official position of the National Fire Protection Association on the referenced subject, which is represented only by the standard in its entirety.

All live-fire training evolutions must meet the requirements of the appropriate sections of the current NFPA 1403. Experience indicates that noncompliance with this standard has resulted in injuries and fatalities for which instructors were held responsible. In October, 2004, the Centers for Disease Control and Prevention from the U.S. National Institute for Occupational Safety and Health issued a Workplace Solutions document titled *Preventing Deaths and Injuries to Fire Fighters during Live-Fire Training in Acquired Structures* that outline the precautions to take when engaging in live-fire training (see **Appendix L**).

Small Fires

The majority of fires involve small quantities of fuel. Entry-level students and industrial fire brigade members are trained in the use of portable handheld fire extinguishers to control all classes of fires (**Figure 12.15, p. 294**). The training evolution usually takes place outside in an area where the spread of fire is limited or nonexistent.

Fuel may include Class A materials in the form of shipping pallets or Class B materials contained in small burn pans. Similar LPG- or natural gas-supplied burn pans are also available.

Instructors demonstrate the appropriate procedure based on the type of fuel and extinguisher and students then repeat the procedure, practicing it until they are proficient. In all cases, a backup extinguishing system must be present, usually in the form of an experienced crew with a charged attack hoseline.

Case History: Volunteer Fire Fighter Dies and Two Others Are Injured During Live-Burn Training (New York)

NIOSH Fire Fighter Fatality Investigation Report, October 31, 2002

On September 25, 2001, a 19-year-old male volunteer firefighter (the victim) died and two male volunteer firefighters (Firefighter No. 1 and Firefighter No. 2) were injured during a multiagency, live-burn training session. The victim and Firefighter No. 1 were playing the roles of firefighters who had become trapped on the second level of the structure. The training became reality when the fire was started and progressed up the stairwell, accelerated by a foam mattress that was ignited on the first floor.

Firefighter No. 1 and the victim were recovered from the second-level front bedroom where they had been placed for the training. Firefighter No. 2 jumped from a second-level window in the rear bedroom. The victim was unresponsive when removed from the structure. Advanced life-saving procedures were initiated on the victim en route to the local hospital where he was pronounced dead. Firefighter No. 1 and Firefighter No. 2 suffered severe burns and were airlifted to an area burn unit.

NIOSH investigators concluded that to minimize the risk of similar occurrences, fire departments should perform the following procedures:

- Ensure that no one plays the role of victim inside the structure during live-burn training.

- Ensure that a certified instructor is in charge of the live-burn training and a separate safety officer is appointed and has the authority to intervene and control any aspect of the operation.

- Ensure that a designated ignition officer lights only one training fire at a time and a charged hoseline is present while igniting the fire.

- Ensure that standard operating procedures (SOPs) are developed and followed.

- Ensure that all firefighters participating in live-burn training have previously achieved a minimum level of basic training.

- Ensure that before conducting live-burn training, a preburn briefing session is conducted and an evacuation plan and signal are established for all participants.

- Ensure that fires used for live-burn training are *not* located in any designated exit paths.

- Ensure that the fuels used in live-burn training evolutions have known burning characteristics and the structure is inspected for possible environmental hazards.

Additionally, states should develop a permitting procedure for live-burn training to be conducted at acquired structures. States should ensure that all of the requirements of NFPA 1403 have been satisfied before issuing the permit. See **Appendix M** for a complete copy of this NIOSH investigation report.

Figure 12.15 Basic skills learned in Firefighter I training include the selection, care, and use of handheld fire extinguishers. *Courtesy of Central Florida Fire Academy.*

Interior Structural Fires

Interior structural fire training may occur in purpose-built live-fire structures or acquired structures. Each of these facilities was discussed in detail in Chapter 5, Instructional Facilities and Props. The purpose-built structures should be equipped with temperature sensors to monitor the rate of temperature rise within the unit. Fuel sources may be LPG, natural gas, or flammable/combustible liquid or Class A materials such as untreated lumber or straw. All interior structural fire training evolutions must meet the requirements of NFPA 1403.

Students must have the requisite Firefighter I training and wear full PPE (**Figure 12.16**). All NIMS ICS requirements must be adhered to, including personnel accountability. A RIT/RIC unit must be organized and staffed. Students or instructors may *not* act as victims within the burn structure, and only one designated ignition officer (wearing full PPE) may start the fire. Ignition of the fuel must start at the most remote point in the structure and work towards the exit.

Exterior Fires

Exterior fire-suppression training may include evolutions that simulate transportation fires, flammable/combustible liquids fires, wildland fires, and large quantities of Class A materials fires. They

Figure 12.16 Students and instructors must wear full PPE when they are engaged in interior structural fire fighting training.

may take place at a permanent training facility or at a remote site and involve single or multiple company or agency training.

Transportation fires. Transportation fires may occur in all types of air, sea, or land craft. They can be as small as an engine compartment fire in an automobile or as large as a fire in the cargo compartment of a ship. The burning material may be Classes A, B, or D and may have been ignited by Class C fuels or other sources. Training usually occurs with single or multiple company evolutions. Generally, these types of incidents are duplicated using permanent training props that are contained in burn pits and fueled by LPG, natural gas, or flammable/combustible liquids. Valves located outside the pit and supervised by a fuel-control officer are used to turn off fuel supplies. An ignition officer is designated to start the fire using an approved ignition device.

Flammable/combustible liquid fires. Simulating fires in flammable/combustible liquid, LPG, and natural gas storage, production, and pipeline

Figure 12.17 All flammable/combustible liquid fire training requires students to wear full PPE. *Courtesy of Central Florida Fire Academy.*

facilities is usually restricted to purpose-built props located at permanent training facilities (**Figure 12.17**). Requirements, as mentioned in Chapter 5, Instructional Facilities and Props, include piped fuel supplies, control valves, product- and water-containment diking, high-capacity water supplies, and water-decontamination capabilities. Evolutions generally involve multiple company training, although small props (such as a *Christmas tree)* can be used for single company training. All flammable/combustible liquid fire training evolutions must conform to NFPA 1403 requirements and use a NIMS ICS structure.

Wildland fires. Training fire and emergency services personnel to control and eliminate wildland and urban-interface (areas where structures mix with wildland fuels) fires can take two approaches: The first approach includes specialized training for organizations that have the sole responsibility for protecting forests and wildland areas. The second is training for structural firefighters who may be responsible for limited areas of wildland or areas that include the urban interface. In some areas of North America, the training for both groups is the same: Focus on the extreme dangers that wildland fires can pose. In other areas, structural firefighters may only receive limited training, involving off-road driving and pumping skills, fire attack, and exposure protection.

Training evolutions vary, depending on the skills required to meet the local dangers that wildland fires create. The very nature of wildland fires makes them unpredictable and highly hazardous. Training is essential to ensure the safety of firefighters, and safety is a major consideration during this type of training.

Large-quantity Class A material fires. All jurisdictions have the potential for large-quantity Class A material fires. Potential sites include lumberyards, refuse dumps, automobile salvage yards, tire dumps, paper recycling sites, and even apartment complexes that are under construction. In general, fires in these types of sites generate a great deal of heat, create exposure hazards, require large quantities of water and/or foam extinguishing agents, and consume time and personal energy to control. Creating training evolutions to match these hazards is difficult, although not impossible. Training evolutions can focus on the following topics:

- Initiating exterior attack tactics
- Deploying and using large attack hoselines
- Deploying and using master stream appliances
- Deploying and pumping large diameter or multiple supply hoselines
- Pumping and drafting skills
- Selecting and applying Class A foam extinguishing agents

Simulating the large-quantity hazard can involve a controlled burn of a structure scheduled for demolition or burning a medium-sized pile of untreated wood pallets or bales of hay. Considerations including the effects of weather, smoke and embers movement toward exposures, and environmental requirements must be taken into account. Full PPE must also be required as well as the use of a NIMS ICS command structure.

Technical Training Evolutions

The expanding role of fire and emergency services in protecting life and property has increased the demand for technical training evolutions involving activities other than fire suppression. This technical training is required to introduce students to new skills and keep current skill levels and performance competencies high. Examples of technical training evolutions include the following:

- **Emergency vehicle operations** — All personnel who drive emergency vehicles must be trained and certified. This training involves defensive driving skills, pump operations, aerial device operations, auxiliary power equipment operation, spotting and locating at the scene, preventive care and maintenance, and emergency response techniques **(Figure 12.18)**. Training may occur on the following surfaces:
  - Purpose-built driving course at the training facility
  - Simulated courses arranged on parking lots
  - Public streets and thoroughfares

- **Vehicle extrication** — Training involves the use of power and hand tools to remove a victim trapped in a wrecked vehicle. Training may occur at a training facility, fire station, or at a vehicle salvage yard. Salvaged aircraft fuselages may also be used by organizations that respond to commercial airports.

- **Emergency medical or triage operations** — Mass casualties are simulated, and training is coordinated between rescuers, medical aid workers, and hospitals. Training generally occurs as part of a major disaster drill involving numerous agencies and jurisdictions.

- **Agricultural equipment rescue operations** — Derelict agricultural equipment is arranged to simulate victims pinned underneath or with limbs caught in machinery. Mannequins are used to simulate victims. Power and hand tools are used to perform the rescue tasks. Training is similar to the vehicle extrication training.

- **Machinery and industrial extrication** — Training is similar to vehicle extrication and agricultural equipment rescue operations training. Evolutions may occur in factories or plants where old equipment is being dismantled.

- **Surface-water, swift-water, and dive rescues** — Training evolutions may involve the use of lifelines, boats, helicopters, or swimmers. Surface-water, swift-water, and dive rescue operations may occur in swimming pools, ponds, lakes, streams, or rivers. All participants must use proper safety equipment, including personal flotation devices **(Figure 12.19)**.

- **Building collapse search and rescue operations** — Typically, only large agencies and organizations will have purpose-built technical rescue simulations. Small organizations may be able to locate and use vacant commercial structures or structures that are in the process of demolition. Collapse conditions can be simulated, although caution must be taken to ensure that the work

Figure 12.18 Besides learning to drive fire apparatus, driver/operator candidates must develop skills involving pump operation, aerial device operation, and vehicle preventive maintenance. *Courtesy of Central Florida Fire Academy.*

Figure 12.19 Surface-water and dive rescue training evolutions require the use of task-specific PPE. In this example, students wear wet suits and personal flotation devices. *Courtesy of Alabama Fire College.*

area is safe. Small sections of concrete pipe or wall sections can be used for cutting and breaching evolutions.

- *Hazardous materials operations* — Evolutions that simulate hazardous materials spills can take place at a training facility, at industrial sites, at rail or marine facilities, or on access-controlled roadways.

- *Aboveground/below-grade operations* — Basements in structures that have outside access (doors or windows) can be used for this type of training.

- *Trench shoring and rescue operations* — Temporary trenches can be dug and shored where space and codes permit. Consider soil conditions, permit requirements, weather conditions, and access limitations. If necessary, shoring can occur in an aboveground space lined with permanent concrete walls.

- *Ice rescues* — Training must occur when the water is sufficiently frozen to support the weight of students. Lifelines, thermal protection, and personal floatation devices are mandatory for this type of training. Possible training sites include thoroughly frozen bodies of water, ice-skating arenas, and hockey rinks. Ice rescue is one of the more difficult training evolutions to simulate.

- *Power tool and equipment operations* — This training may initially be provided by the manufacturer's technical representatives. Once instructors are certified, they provide the training to operational personnel. Depending on the type of tool or equipment, the training evolution may involve vehicle extrication, structural ventilation, water removal, emergency scene lighting and generator operations, or cutting and breaching of walls/floors.

- *Confined-space entry operations* — Confined spaces can be simulated through the construction of mazes made of wood, canvas, or tables. Students wearing full PPE and SCBA facepieces covered with blackout materials crawl through the maze. Evolutions can also occur in vacant buildings where students with their vision obscured must find their way along corridors and into rooms to locate victims **(Figure 12.20)**.

Figure 12.20 Confined-space training evolutions require students to wear either structural PPE or clothing designed specifically for work in narrow, confined areas. Self-contained breathing apparatus (SCBA) or supplied-air respiratory equipment is always required. *Courtesy of Central Florida Fire Academy.*

- *Counterterrorism operations* — Counterterrorism training can include many of the previously mentioned props or locations. The training scenario can be multijurisdictional and occur on many levels. For instance, upper management personnel can be involved in strategic training using a tabletop model while operational units are deployed to locations that simulate the result of a terrorist attack such as a hazardous chemical release or building collapse.

- *Disaster management operations* — Disaster management training operations are similar to the counterterrorism operations training and involve both strategic and operational level exercises. The operational level scenario could include mass casualties and the disruption of communication and public services as a result of a tornado or earthquake.

Although these training evolutions are dissimilar in some ways, they may share the following directives:

- Training may be mandated due to government requirements.

- In some cases, funding sources (grant-issuing agencies) may require training to meet the grant requirements.

- Training requirements may be part of a manufacturer's contract when supplying certain types of equipment.

- The knowledge and skills required to perform these tasks at emergency scenes is very specialized. Emergency responders are *not* authorized to attempt the tasks without adequate training or certification.

- Instructors who provide the training must be qualified in the specific field.

- The duty of the lead instructor is to arrange for suitable training sites with the advice and assistance of these qualified instructors.

- Planning and coordination between the local training staff and qualified instructors are essential to a successful training evolution.

Each technical training evolution involves its own set of safety requirements. These requirements must be clearly established and satisfied before actual training begins. The instructor or group of instructors who provides this specialized training is also responsible for coordinating all safety measures with the lead instructor in a cooperative effort.

Additional federal or state/provincial regulations may apply for this specialized training. For example, a permit required for confined-space operations may be required in similar training evolutions.

Instructor Preparation

Effective and safe practical training evolutions require thorough instructor preparation. Fire and emergency services instructors will have completed the required basic entry-level training and served for some time in a position that includes emergency response functions. The experience that they gain performing the skills and tasks of responders provides a firm foundation for teaching practical training evolutions.

However, over time instructors may have adopted behavior habits or altered accepted procedures that work for them but are *not* appropriate for new personnel. Therefore, instructors should receive a refresher course before instructing students or supervising practical training evolutions.

One approach is to require new instructors to participate in an entry-level training course, either with new personnel or other instructor candidates. This approach permits a new instructor to learn the skills the way they are to be taught. It also exposes them to the teaching and classroom management of senior, more experienced instructors.

Before the beginning of any training course, new instructors should practice the skills and evolutions they are responsible for teaching. This practice is done under the supervision of a senior instructor. Immediately before teaching a particular skill or managing a practical training evolution, new instructors should practice the skill again to ensure that the steps are correct and clearly in their minds.

Instructors who are responsible for a training evolution should meet before the event and discuss individual assignments and procedures. Each instructor should be assigned a specific task such as ignition officer, ISO, staging officer, and so on. Communication protocol should be established and proper training radio frequencies assigned. This level of coordination is particularly important when multiple agencies or jurisdictions are involved in providing or participating in the training.

The more experienced instructors become, the more confident they will be in their abilities to perform the assigned skills and evolutions. Periodic refresher classes should be provided for all instructors to ensure that their skill levels are still adequate.

Summary

Familiarity with practical training evolutions is essential for the fire and emergency services instructor. Practical training evolutions are parts of the variety of teaching methods used to teach the application of cognitive and psychomotor skills.

The methods include structured exercises that involve the student in the subject such as role-plays and simulations, demonstrations that explain the steps that compose tasks, and practical training evolutions that permit students to apply the psychomotor skills.

Combined with the presentation skills mentioned previously, understanding the selection of suitable training locations, how to plan the appropriate evolution, and how to enforce safety and health requirements will ensure a successful learning experience for students. Using and teaching the use of incident command concepts will not only ensure safety during the training evolution but also stress the importance of using them during emergency operations. Instructors provide students with the opportunity to apply, reinforce, practice, and correct the skills that are basic to all fire and emergency services operations.

Train with Rapid Intervention Crews

Practical training evolutions provide an opportunity for fire and emergency responders to train in the use of rapid intervention crews (RICs). When non-live-fire training evolutions are practiced, the establishment and deployment of a RIC can be part of the training scenario.

Attack crews can be assigned the role of a lost or trapped unit within a dangerous atmosphere. The RIC is activated and its response and actions are judged against the required criteria.

During live-fire training evolutions, the establishment of a RIC is mandatory. During these training scenarios, the RIC functions in the same way that it would during an actual emergency. Crew members may be assigned limited duties as they would at an emergency incident, but they must be ready to respond immediately when needed.

Generally, depending on the local protocol, the RIC is located in the staging area (at or near the command post) or near the operations center. When a large-area or multiagency incident is simulated, multiple RIC units may be required and placed at various points of entry into the dangerous or hot zone.

Training with RIC units as part of the practical training evolution is also an opportunity to determine the type and quantity of tools and equipment that crew members should have with them. While NFPA has established the minimum tools necessary for rapid intervention, it is the local jurisdiction's responsibility to determine any additional equipment that may be required to meet local situations.

Most organizations will *not* have the luxury of having a single company dedicated to rapid intervention activities. Therefore, every unit will have the potential responsibility of acting as a RIC during training and at emergencies. Similar RIC tools and equipment will have to be available for all units.

Part B

Instructor I Requirements

Chapter 13

Student Progress Evaluation and Testing

After reading this chapter, students will be able to —

1. Identify terms related to testing and evaluation.

2. Explain the purpose of student evaluations and testing.

3. Define criterion-referenced and norm-referenced tests.

4. Distinguish among prescriptive, formative, and summative tests.

5. Identify accurate statements about oral tests.

6. Identify facts about written tests.

7. Identify accurate statements about performance tests.

8. Identify guidelines for administering written tests.

9. Identify guidelines for administering performance tests.

10. Identify accurate statements about scoring oral, written, and performance tests.

11. Identify accurate statements about reporting grades.

12. List guidelines regarding test security.

13. Identify facts about feedback.

Chapter Contents

Formal Evaluations Through Testing
Test Types
Test Administration
Test Scoring
Grade Reporting
Test Security

Feedback
Positive Feedback
Negative Feedback
Feedback Applications

Summary

Chapter 13
Student Progress Evaluation and Testing

The final step in the four-step method of instruction is evaluation **(Figure 13.1)**. Instructors evaluate the progress that students make during a course or class through observation and testing. While evaluation may be formal, it should always result in feedback to students. The feedback provides students with a clear idea of what has been learned, what should have been learned, and what still needs to be learned.

Evaluating student progress or performance requires a stated performance criterion. Determining whether the criterion has been met or not involves direct instructor observation or the use of testing instruments. Instructors observe students by watching them practice skills, respond to questions, participate in discussions, or participate in practical training evolutions. Test instruments include quizzes, written reports or research papers, oral tests, written tests, and timed skill performance tests.

Tests may be developed internally by the organization or purchased from a test-writing organization. In either case, tests must be valid and reliable based on the organization's job requirements or course or class learning objectives.

Before proceeding in this chapter the instructor should understand the following terms that are important regarding the testing process:

- *Evaluation* — Process used to assess a student's achievements (fulfillment of the course or lesson requirements) and/or the effectiveness of learning experiences. The assessment is made against a defined criteria or standard. Evaluations can assess both the learning process and the student's achievement of course learning outcomes.

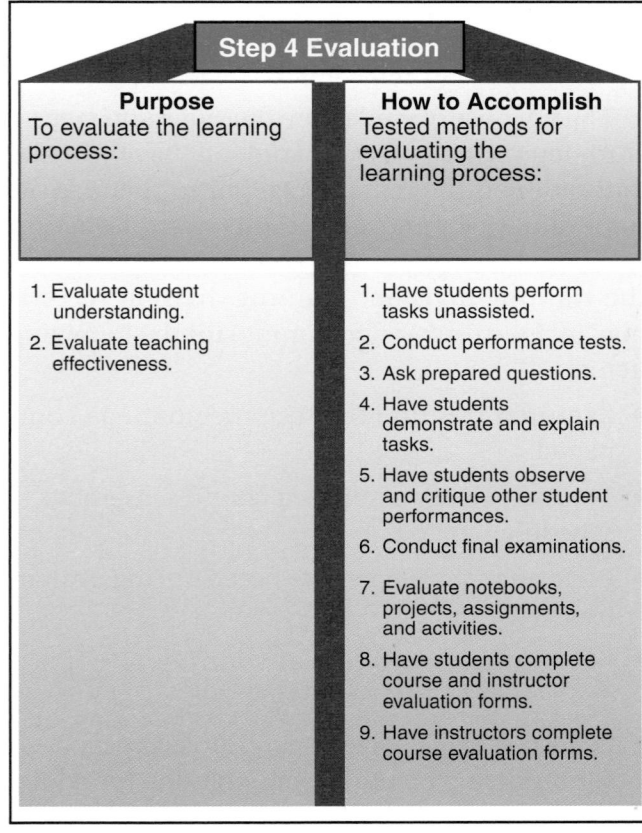

Figure 13.1 The evaluation step of the four-step method of instruction is used to determine how well students have learned the information presented in the course.

- *Testing* — Process of evaluation that implies standardization in which the student is compared against a defined criteria or standard. It includes a basis or means to determine the degree to which students learned what was intended for them to learn.

- *Validity* — Extent to which a test measures what it was designed to measure. Does the test, in fact, evaluate the criterion that it purports to test? For example:

— Did the student learn the objectives or did the student guess the right answers?

— Did the student learn the objectives, but due to poor test design, the student was unable to identify the correct answers?

- **Reliability** — Condition that ensures that the test is dependable by providing the same results every time it is administered. Does the test, in fact, yield the same results each time it is given? For example, if a test were given to a student repeatedly, would the student score the same each time? Scoring the same would be difficult because students learn from tests and would score better on subsequent tests.

The purpose of student evaluations and testing is to determine how well students have learned and retained the material taught to them. Written evaluations and test results are retained in personnel files or training records maintained by the training division. Training division records may include (but are *not* limited to) the following items:

- Required training that the member has completed

- Training that was missed that the member is scheduled to take

- Performance deficiencies noted during evaluations

- Recommended remedial training to correct deficiencies based on testing

- Reports of skill deficiencies observed by supervisor or during emergency operations (provided by company officer or supervisor)

This information is analyzed to determine the progress each student has made and whether additional training is required. The information may also be the basis for determining a student's aptitude to acquire advanced-level or specialized training.

This chapter focuses on the formal evaluation and testing duties of Level I Instructors as defined in NFPA 1041, *Standard for Fire Service Instructor Professional Qualifications*. Level I instructors are responsible for performing the following duties:

- Administering oral, written, and performance examinations

- Scoring examinations and determining grades

- Reporting examination results to the administration of the training division or organization

- Providing security for testing materials and processes

- Providing feedback to students based on both informal and formal evaluations

Test development and selection are responsibilities of Level II instructors and are addressed in Chapter 16, Student Testing Instruments. However, an overview of available test types is included in this chapter to introduce them to Level I Instructors.

Formal Evaluations Through Testing

The formal evaluation of student progress is determined through testing. *Testing* is a method of measuring the results of learning (**Figure 13.2**). The purpose of measuring learning is to determine the degree to which students learned what the instruction intended for them to learn based on learning objectives. Testing is also used as a tool to determine promotion eligibility or readiness to progress to another level in a training curriculum or course or within an organization.

Level I Instructors are responsible for administering, scoring, grading, reporting, and providing security for student testing. Level I Instructors should also be aware of the various types of tests. Test development is discussed in the Level II Instructor portion of this manual.

Test Types

Rarely will one type of test be suitable for all purposes. To choose the type of test that is the best measure of learning, instructors must be aware of and familiar with the various tests and their classifications (interpretation, purpose, and administration). These classifications group tests based on related factors. Within each classification, distinctions are made among the various types of tests. A simple classification helps instructors distinguish among tests and select one that best suits the measurement purpose.

Figure 13.2 Testing criteria may involve the element of time. Students must perform to an established level of proficiency within a defined time period. *Courtesy of Central Florida Fire Academy.*

Interpretation Classification

This test classification is based on interpreting test results and includes the following two types:

- *Criterion-referenced tests* — Compare performance against appropriate minimum standards.

- *Norm-referenced tests* — Rate student performance compared to other students based on broad sampling.

These two test types represent distinct types of tests and give administrators, educational institutions, and instructors flexibility to match curriculum and course goals with the best method of evaluating student performance. Further information is included in the Level II Instructor portion of this text.

Purpose Classification

The purpose classification is based on the reasons a test is given and the point at which they are given during instruction. Test types include prescriptive, formative, and summative.

Prescriptive (pretest). Prescriptive tests are given at the beginning of instruction to establish a student's current level of knowledge in order to measure the following two placement elements.

- *Readiness* — When measuring readiness, the test answers the question: *Does the student have the skills needed to perform in the course?* If not, the training division should offer remedial activities or require the student to acquire more job experience.

- *Placement* — When determining placement, the test answers the question: *Has the student already achieved the behavioral objectives?* If so, the student moves on to the next course or unit of instruction. If not, the student can attend the class.

Prescriptive tests that measure readiness include each prerequisite skill required for entry into the class or course. The test items are usually easy and criterion-referenced. Prescriptive tests that determine placement of students provide a representative sample of test items. The items generally have a wide range of difficulty and are norm-referenced.

Formative (progress). Formative tests are often viewed as quizzes, pop tests, or question/answer periods in class that are given throughout the course or unit of instruction. These tests typically measure improvement and give the instructor and students feedback on learning progress. When measuring improvement, the test answers the question: *Is the student achieving the objectives?* Tests include the most important behavioral objectives or all of them if possible. Each test item matches the level of difficulty of the corresponding behavioral objective and thus is criterion-referenced.

Summative (comprehensive). Summative tests measure student achievement in an entire area on a number of topics covered over a long period of time such as a semester or other major segment of a course. They test general mastery of a broad academic field and are typically given in the middle (midterm) or at the end of instruction (final). When measuring comprehensive knowledge and skills, the test answers the question: *Has the student achieved the course objectives?*

Examples of comprehensive tests given for a training course are the written and/or practical exams given at the midpoint or end of emergency medical technician (EMT), basic fire fighting, or driver/operator courses. Students who are tested must demonstrate comprehensive knowledge and skills learned in all areas from the beginning to the testing point (midterm or end) of the course.

Administration Classification

The administration classification is based on various ways that test questions are administered or answered. Test types include oral, written, and performance. Determining which test type to use is based on the type of learning that is being evaluated. At the same time, instructors must remember that some students may respond better to one type of test than to another.

Therefore, instructors should use variations of all three types during the course in order to get an accurate evaluation of student learning. An average of the scores provided by the three types of tests will indicate the true learning outcomes of the students.

Oral. During oral tests, the student generally gives verbal answers to spoken questions. Oral tests are usually given one-on-one between a student and an instructor **(Figure 13.3)**. Oral tests are *not* commonly used in the fire and emergency services, but they may be useful under certain circumstances. In the case of oral tests used for officer candidate evaluations, an oral test may be given to each individual officer candidate by an assessment board composed of experts in the profession. Situations that may justify the use of oral tests include the following:

- When a student cannot read at the level to which a test is written

- When a student must demonstrate the ability to respond under pressure

- When the test is used to supplement performance tests to determine whether a student knows the reasoning behind the tasks performed

- At the beginning of the class period to determine whether assigned reading has been accomplished

- At the beginning of the class period to provide a pretest and an introduction to the topic to be presented

- As a component of a comprehensive examination in an officer candidate course or promotional process

- When determining student understanding at the end of a lesson

The two types of questions used for oral tests are as follows:

- ***Closed question*** — When the purpose of the test is to determine knowledge, then the question should be *closed*, requiring only a single brief answer.

- ***Open question*** — When the purpose is to determine how a student responds under pressure, then the question should judge both accuracy and presentation. In this case, the question should be *open*, permitting longer answers that may lead to further questions. See Techniques for Questioning section in Chapter 10, Instructional Delivery.

When giving oral tests, instructors or assessment board members must listen carefully to an individual's responses. This practice prevents misunderstandings because people phrase answers differently even though they mean or are trying

Figure 13.3 The use of oral test questions helps determine how well students can respond under pressure.

to say the same thing. Instructors and assessment board members should also *not* give facial expressions that may mislead a student one way or another.

Instructors or assessment board members should consider the test's purpose and carefully create appropriate questions. They should write the answers down and state them back to the student to ensure that they were recorded correctly. Oral tests should never be used as the sole means of evaluating students for terminal performance or officer candidates for promotion.

Written. Written tests evaluate the accomplishment of cognitive and affective learning objectives and may be *subjective* (based on individual perceptions) or *objective* (based on facts). They are useful for measuring retention and understanding of technical information. Technical subject examples include fire chemistry, laws and ordinances, hydraulic principles, and medical protocols. Written tests may have numerous question types. Variations of the basic types exist, but most test question types include the following:

- *Multiple-choice* — Single question followed by multiple possible answers of which only one is correct. The remaining answers, called *distracters,* must be reasonable answers. If distracters are obviously incorrect or unreasonable, then students can guess the correct answer.

- *True/false* — Statement that requires students to determine whether it is true or false. Students have a fifty-fifty chance of guessing the correct answer.

- *Matching* — Series of words, dates, events, or items is listed in one column. A second column contains the definition or related information necessary to describe each item. Extra definitions may be used as distracters, providing additional answers to choose from.

- *Fill in the blank/completion* — Question consists of a statement that is either missing a word (or several words) or incomplete. Students must add the missing word (or words) or complete the sentence.

- *Short-answer* — Question that requires a brief answer to a specific question. Questions may ask students to list items, describe a process, or explain a procedure.

- *Essay* — Question that requires a lengthy, sometimes subjective, answer. It may be used to determine the student's ability to evaluate or analyze a situation or recall a sequence of events or facts.

Written tests may be administered by posting the questions on a marker board, reading them aloud, or reproducing them on a question sheet **(Figure 13.4)**. Answers may be written on a blank page, on a formal answer sheet, or in spaces provided on the question sheet. The legibility of students' handwriting can be a factor when instructors score answer sheets. Tests that require students to circle, check, or fill in a block reduce the potential for misinterpretation based on handwriting. Answer sheets that can be read, scored, and recorded electronically/mechanically can be used when available.

The increasing popularity and availability of computers provides a further method for administering written tests. Students take the written test on a computer in a testing center or computer lab. The computer-testing program scores the results and posts them to the appropriate student file in the test databank. Computer testing permits the use of all forms of written tests plus scenarios that require the student to evaluate a situation and determine the correct response. Computer-administered tests are also necessary for web-based or Internet training programs.

Figure 13.4 Written tests may consist of a variety of types of test instruments and usually have a time limit imposed on them. *Courtesy of Iowa Fire Service Training Bureau.*

Performance. In performance tests students are required to perform a skill, task, or evolution rather than talk or write about it. Students are required to perform the psychomotor skill as it would be performed on the job, and they are tested on their present abilities or attainments rather than their potentials. Performance tests must be based on standard criteria and performance objectives. When preparing to administer a performance test, instructors should perform the following tasks:

- Determine the materials, tools, or equipment that students need to perform the skills or activities. Ensure that single-use materials are available in appropriate quantities for the testing situations.

- Ensure that tools and equipment are working properly and consistently **(Figure 13.5)**. Review the operation of equipment with all instructors and test evaluators (instructors or members of the organization who are proficient in performing the skill being tested).

- Determine the number of test evaluators needed to observe and measure (by checklist) the performances of students.

- Prepare checklists of objective skills with appropriate time limits and assigned points or sequences to enable evaluators to verify that they observed students complete the listed performance requirements.

Figure 13.5 The instructor must ensure that tools and equipment used in performance tests are clean, operational, and consistent with the type of tools used during training.

The purpose of performance checklists based on objectives is to avoid or minimize inaccurate measurements due to the subjectivity or personal feelings and impressions of test evaluators. *Subjectivity* is a kind of analysis, method, description, or judgment in which people differ because their values, experiences, opinions, attitudes, preferences, biases, and perceptions are different. These characteristics give every individual different attitudes and ideas about how a task should be accomplished. Some test evaluators may find it difficult to completely lay aside their personal attitudes and neutrally judge the performance of the students.

Test Administration

Administration of a test begins before the test is given. Instructors tell students about the test type and content, how they can prepare for the test, and what they must bring to class for the test (paper, pencil, pen, notes, books, etc.). Students are notified in an informative and motivating manner well in advance of the test date. The course syllabus should also contain the dates and times of major tests or periodic quizzes. Instructors should remember suggested guidelines for administering written and performance tests. On the day of the test, the instructor ensures that the environment aids students in testing effectively and the quality of their performance is not influenced by adverse conditions such as the following:

- Poor lighting

- Uncomfortable seating

- Noises

- Extreme heat or cold temperatures

- Other potential barriers to performance

Written Tests

Some suggested guidelines for instructors when administering written tests (before, during and after) are as follows:

- ***Before the test***

  — Ask the administration or agency to determine whether there are any specific instructions or protocol for administering the test.

  — Report to the assigned testing location 15 minutes before testing begins.

— Maintain security of tests at all times.

— Rearrange classroom seating when necessary so that it is conducive for taking written tests.

— Eliminate loud talking or noises outside the room.

— Ensure that all distractions are eliminated from the testing room.

— Number all tests and answer sheets as well as each page within the tests, and account for all tests and pages at the end of the test.

— Ensure that all cellular phones, personal digital assistants (PDAs), and pagers are turned off and put away **(Figure 13.6)**.

— Ensure that no student notes (written or in electronic/digital form) are brought into the testing room unless they are specifically noted on the examination cover sheet. Allowable notes must be printed, typed, or handwritten.

- *During the test*
  - Ensure that the environment remains quiet and safe for students.
  - Ensure that all backpacks, purses, books, and any other items *not* necessary for testing are placed at the front of the room and remain off desks throughout the examination.
  - Ensure that when students leave the room to use the rehabilitation facilities (restroom, refreshment area, etc.), they do *not* take the test instrument or paper with them.
  - Maintain a supply of extra paper and course evaluation forms in the room.
  - When testing aides are available, have them assist with difficult students, difficult situations, or other duties such as issuing and collecting tests and evaluation forms.
  - Ensure that students are *not* cheating. Walk around the room or monitor the area from a desk.
  - Ensure that students have completed the answer sheet correctly when they finish the test. Accept students' test forms and answer sheets when they are complete.

Figure 13.6 For security and to ensure fairness during testing, cell phones, pagers, and personal digital assistants (PDAs) must be turned off. Calculators may only be used if all students are permitted to use them.

- *After the test*
  - Review the test (when appropriate) with students to clarify any objectives they may *not* have understood.
  - Do *not* allow students to change their answers once answer sheets have been submitted.
  - Maintain security of tests and answer sheets after the test and while scoring tests, determining grades, and recording grades.
  - Return test materials to the proper authority when *not* given scoring and grading responsibilities.

Performance Tests

Some suggested guidelines when administering performance tests are as follows:

- *Before the test*
  - Ensure that the subject matter of the test matches the subject matter that is being tested.
  - Provide students with adequate practice time before the test begins.
  - Provide rehabilitation facilities (restroom, refreshment area, etc.) for students, instructors, test evaluators, and observers.

— Ensure that tests are *not* biased through wording, timing, or unattainable criteria.

— Include all test administration rules in the introductory instructions.

— Give specific instructions and tell students the time limits for each test.

— Explain the purpose of each test.

— Encourage students to ask questions when there is something they do *not* understand.

- *During the test*

— Give the test to each student in exactly the same manner.

— Record students' scores on performance checklists as testing progresses.

- *After the test* — Keep all test scores confidential.

Test Scoring

Once tests have been administered, instructors collect answer sheets or performance checklists and score them. The sections that follow provide accepted guidelines for scoring each of the three types of tests: oral, written, and performance. Instructors must remember that the scoring process must be objective and based on established criteria. The results must be kept confidential.

Oral Tests

Scoring oral tests depends on the purpose of the test and type of question asked. As mentioned previously, the questions may be closed or open. When scoring closed questions, students' answers must accurately match required answers. When more than one answer is possible, each possible answer must then be considered correct and given equal value. Instructors should mark the written copy of the oral answers as correct or incorrect, add the correct answer, and cite the location of the information by page number or lecture title.

Open questions are more subjective to score because they depend not only on content accuracy, but also on how students answered the question. Possible scoring guidelines include answering the following questions:

- Did the student support theory with appropriate examples?

- Was the answer logically organized and understandable?

- Did the student answer within the allotted time when a time limit was imposed?

- Were answers complete and detailed?

Written Tests

Written tests can be scored either by hand or an electronic/mechanical-scoring device. Tests administered on computers are scored automatically, and the results are posted to student files in the course database. While the electronic/mechanical scorer is easy and fast to use, it can be costly to purchase and require the use of specific types of answer forms (**Figure 13.7**). Errors can occur with the electronic/mechanical scorer, requiring the instructor to rescore the tests by hand. Some guidelines for scoring written tests by hand include the following:

- Score one question at a time on short-answer or essay exams. This guideline improves scoring consistency and permits instructors to identify any questions that have resulted in a large number of incorrect answers.

- Scan several responses before marking any answers when scoring essay or short-answer tests. This guideline is especially valuable when variations on answers are possible.

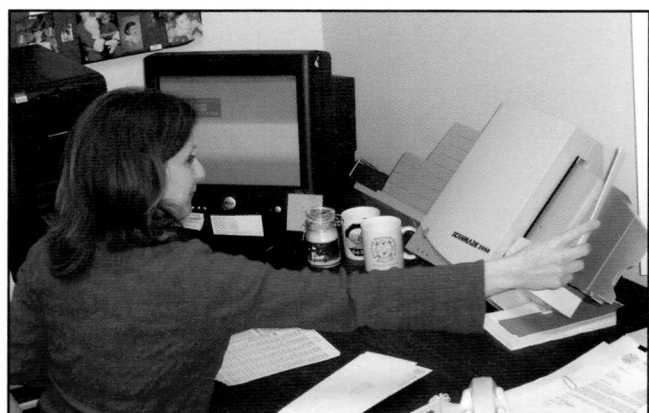

Figure 13.7 Electronic scoring devices may be linked to computers that are used to store and analyze student test results. *Courtesy of Alabama Fire College.*

- Add comments to essay or short-answer questions to indicate what is missing or congratulate the student on exceptionally good work. Scoring is an extension of teaching, and this guideline acts as positive reinforcement and motivation for students.

- Be specific, avoid negative or sarcastic comments, and try to provide suggestions for improving the answer when making comments.

- Shuffle the papers before scoring the next question after scoring one set of questions on all the tests. This guideline helps offset the potential fatigue that instructors can experience and reduce the potential for scoring errors.

- Do *not* attempt to score large numbers of tests at one time. Take breaks or work on other projects between sets of papers.

- Use lines or arrows to indicate what word or portion of the answer to which a comment refers.

- Inform students about the meaning of scoring marks that are used in essay or short-answer question tests.

- Identify a maximum of three strengths and three weaknesses of an answer when scoring an essay or short-answer question. More than three can discourage the student.

Instructors who teach distance-learning courses need to take into consideration the limited contact they have with their students. Some factors to consider are as follows:

- The time it takes for test papers and written assignments to travel between students and instructors is increased, which results in longer than usual times between the submission of tests or assignments and their return to students. Online courses do not have this time delay.

- Over the length of a course, student improvement takes longer because it takes longer for feedback to reach the students. Instructors have to work diligently to provide effective and timely feedback to the students.

- The lack of direct contact between students and instructors places an additional demand on scoring. Scoring criteria, marking and comment notations, and instructor comments must be clear, concise, and constructive. Students should have no doubt about what is expected or how to correct weaknesses in a test answer or assignment.

- When depending on fax (originally acronym for *facsimile*) transmissions of tests, remember that most are in black and white. Some color inks are not legible following the transmission. Select ink and writing style that are readable by students.

Performance Tests

Scoring performance (psychomotor) tests can be very subjective. Instructors or test evaluators may each have their own opinion on how a particular evolution or activity should be performed. To overcome this subjectivity, the training division should do the following two things:

- Train instructors or test evaluators in the steps of the skills to be tested, which is especially important when instructors represent a variety of jurisdictions.

- Develop checklists for each skill that is tested and use them for scoring students' performances. Checklists ensure that the instructors are scoring the same step and students are performing consistently (**Figure 13.8, pp. 312 and 313**). Fire and emergency services skills must be accomplished completely and accurately because there is no margin of error during an emergency.

When possible, use multiple instructors or test evaluators to observe each student during the test. Multiple observers result in a more consistent and accurate score of a student's performance. The instructors or test evaluators should come to a consensus and mark the checklist accordingly. When there is a disagreement, a student may be required to perform the skill again or explain to the evaluators how or why the activity is performed.

Scoring laboratory performance may include the following two approaches:

- Instructors may use a checklist (like the one used for psychomotor skills) to score students based on observation.

- Students may be required to complete a laboratory report form, indicating the project, process, observations, and results.

Break a Door Lock
Checklist

Name_____ **Date** _____

JOB STEPS	ATTEMPT NO.		
	1	2	3

Using a K-Tool

1. Size up the situation. _— — —

   a. Status/location of fire _— — —

   b. Windows in/near door _— — —

2. Try the door. _— — —

3. Examine the lock to determine the type of staple and metal. _— — —

4. Select the appropriate tool for lock type. _— — —

5. Adjust your protective gear. _— — —

   a. Lowering faceshield, if not wearing SCBA _— — —

   b. Donning gloves _— — —

6. Using the driver, force the K-tool behind the ring and face of the lock cylinder. _— — —

7. Insert a prying tool into the metal loop on the front of the K-tool. _— — —

8. Pry the cylinder from the door using the K-tool as a fulcrum. _— — —

9. Move the locking bolt to the open position. _— — —

   a. Inserting either end of key tool into hole made by removed cylinder (lock hub) _— — —

   b. Manipulating and rotating tool until bolt moves to open position _— — —

       Note: If, for any reason, this method fails, insert the straight end of the K-tool through the cylinder hole, and drive the lock off the door with an axe.

                                      Time (Total) _— — —

EVALUATOR'S COMMENTS

_____

_____

_____

Page 1 of 2

Figure 13.8 Checklists are used to ensure consistency between evaluators when scoring psychomotor tests.

JOB STEPS	ATTEMPT NO.		
	1	2	3

Using an A-Tool

1. Size up the situation.   — — —

   a. Status/location of fire   — — —

   b. Windows in/near door   — — —

2. Try the door.   — — —

3. Examine the lock to determine the type of staple and metal.   — — —

4. Select the appropriate tool for lock type.   — — —

5. Adjust your protective gear.   — — —

   a. Lowering faceshield, if not wearing SCBA   — — —

   b. Donning gloves   — — —

6. Using the driver, force the jaws of the A-tool around and behind the protruding rim of the cylinder.   — — —

7. Gouge the wood around the cylinder with A-tool chisel head for a better bite if necessary.   — — —

8. Pry the cylinder from the door, using the A-tool's curved head as a fulcrum.   — — —

9. Move the locking bolt to the open position.   — — —

   a. Inserting either end of key tool into hole made by removed cylinder (lock hub)   — — —

   b. Manipulating and rotating tool until bolt moves to open position   — — —

   Note: If, for any reason, this method fails, insert the straight end of A-tool through the cylinder hole, and drive the lock off the door with an axe.   — — —

                          Time (Total)   — — —

EVALUATOR'S COMMENTS

_____

_____

_____

Page 2 of 2

Figure 13.8 *Continued*

In both cases, students must be given a clearly stated set of objectives and the scoring criteria. Instructors should provide immediate feedback while observing the project, especially when safety is a concern. Instructor comments on laboratory report forms should adhere to the same scoring criteria used for written tests or reports. All instructors in the training division should develop a consistent scoring criterion that is valid and objective and adhere to it consistently.

Certification Testing

Instructors need to be aware that the testing required in courses is part of the learning process. In essence, this testing is the final opportunity an instructor has with students to ensure that they understand the learning objectives. Course testing exams are different from certification exams that are *not* part of the learning process.

Certification testing should measure mastery. One cannot expect mastery at the conclusion of a course. Organizations who use certification exams at the end of a course are putting students at an extreme disadvantage and, in most cases, there is no opportunity for the evaluator to provide a review of the exam or other feedback.

Grade Reporting

Once instructors have scored oral, written, or performance tests, the scores must be recorded and reported in accordance with local procedures. Because fire and emergency services students are graded against a set of specific criteria and *not* against each other, grades are recorded in individual student records and used as feedback for students. Care must be taken to accurately record the grades in student records.

A student's individual test scores should be added together to determine a final grade for the course. Students who fail to achieve the minimum required grade should *not* be certified as having completed the training.

Testing records are private and confidential. Only instructors, training division administrators, and the student should have access to student training records. Testing results should be retained in individual student files for the period required by local ordinance, policy, or law and then destroyed. Privacy of student records (as mentioned in Chapter 3, Legal and Ethical Considerations) shall be maintained based on department/agency policies and applicable laws.

Reporting test results to the training division or organization's administration is necessary for the following two reasons:

- The organization must know whether a student has achieved the required certification to effectively perform a duty or task.

- The test results for all participants in a course provide the training division or administration with an idea of the effectiveness of the course or curriculum. When test results indicate an abnormal number of students did *not* pass the course, the teaching style, course curriculum, or testing system should then be reevaluated and altered as appropriate.

Test Security

Security of oral, written, performance, and computer-administered tests is essential to an effective training program. While the security of the test results has been stressed to comply with privacy requirements, security of testing instruments is equally important to prevent cheating. Cheating on tests presents special problems for instructors — problems that may be reduced by using a suggested set of guidelines as follows:

- Protect test security by regularly revising test questions and answer sheets.

- Take care in writing, duplicating, and storing test materials.

- Number and inventory test sheets, booklets, and answer sheets following each use.

- Use secure data storage systems to prevent unauthorized access to tests or grades.

- Regulate the presence of cellular phones, pagers, programmable calculators, PDAs, or handheld computers in the classroom during tests. They could be used to access information for use on tests.

- Be aware of suspicious student activities that are symptoms of cheating:
  — Students looking (wandering eyes) around the room.
  — Answers written on clothing, skin, shoes, or papers lying on the floor near the test taker's desk.
  — Students talking to each other during the test.
  — Students leaving the room during the test.
  — Identical incorrect answers or sequences of answers on multiple test sheets.
- Remain in the room during the test and be aware of how students are taking the test.
- Use three or more different tests for the same exam to prevent copying during the test. Altering the placement of questions or the wording of questions can assist in creating different tests. Care must be taken in distributing and retrieving tests as well as in scoring answer sheets.
- Use questions that require essay, completion, or short-answer responses to prevent the cheating that can occur with true/false or multiple-choice questions.
- Maintain security over all old test sheets and destroy outdated testing materials.
- Do *not* rely on questions published in the textbook or study guide.
- Limit access to computer-administered tests by requiring students to use assigned passwords.

Although cheating may never be completely eliminated, fire and emergency services instructors can actively work to minimize it. All attempts should be made to decrease the opportunity for cheating.

At the beginning of a course, instructors should review the organization's code of ethics and establish a connection between cheating and unethical activities. Ground rules, complete with personal responsibility and consequences, should be established for students. *Plagiarism,* a form of cheating that involves using materials in reports or research papers that were originally written by others, should be defined for students.

Instructors must stress that all forms of cheating will be taken seriously with zero tolerance when cheating is discovered. Instructors must be prepared to take action when cheating occurs. Eliminating the perceived need to cheat can also reduce cheating. Students are less likely to feel a need to cheat in the following situations:

- Course material is useful and desirable.
- Assignments are relevant to the student's goals or duties.
- Students receive positive feedback and assistance from instructors.
- Gaining knowledge is more important to students than attaining a grade.

Feedback

Instructors continually give *feedback* to their students. Instructor feedback may be based on informal or formal evaluations. Informal evaluations occur daily through the interaction between instructors and students. These evaluations provide immediate feedback to students and help enforce learning as it occurs.

Informal evaluations processes take the form of coaching, counseling, and mentoring, which were discussed in Chapter 4, Effective Interpersonal Communication, and in Chapter 8, Student Attributes and Behaviors. The continual contact that informal evaluations provide between student and instructor give both an accurate idea of the progress a student is making in the course and what is expected by the instructor.

Formal feedback is the result of the evaluation and testing process. Instructors discuss the test results with students privately, explaining the positive and negative results of the student's test scores. In some cases, an entire class or group of students may be given feedback on the test results. This situation occurs when the performance being tested involves teams or multiple groups of people. An example of a group receiving feedback is the posttraining critique used for multiunit or multiagency training.

Positive Feedback

Positive feedback stresses the strengths of a student's attempt at completing an activity or performance evaluation. Positive feedback results in the following student behavior changes:

- Becoming or remaining motivated
- Changing or correcting inappropriate behavior
- Acquiring new beliefs, values, or attitudes
- Improving skills and knowledge
- Increasing self-confidence, awareness, and esteem
- Feeling accepted into the organization and profession

To accomplish these positive results, instructors must ensure that feedback has the following elements:

- Prompt and timely
- Encouraging **(Figure 13.9)**
- Specific (focused on one skill or behavior) on what is correct or incorrect and how incorrect skills or behaviors can be corrected if necessary
- Clear and easily understood
- Objective and focused on the action and *not* the student
- Relevant to the action, behavior, or knowledge

Figure 13.9 Instructors should provide positive feedback to encourage students and assure them of their accomplishments. *Courtesy of Alabama Fire College.*

Feedback can have its greatest influence on students when it causes them to compare their performance with the expected criteria-based performance. Students should be permitted to diagnose their own strengths and weaknesses and determine the best way to reach the expected level of performance. Students should also be permitted to help in determining how to correct a skill or behavior. These procedures help students learn how to analyze personal performance and make an appropriate decision.

Negative Feedback

Instructors should be aware that feedback could have a negative result when it is *not* provided correctly. Negative results can occur when feedback has the following elements:

- Too vague or general, leaving the student to wonder what can be done to correct the skill or behavior
- Subjective (*not* based on fact or specific criteria) or directed at the individual and *not* the skill or behavior
- Late in delivery; for example:
  — Positive feedback loses its sincerity or importance when it is delayed.
  — Negative feedback is disconnected from the action and seems unimportant.
- Critical of the student and *not* focused on correcting the skill or behavior
- One-sided with instructors providing the criticism and solution

Feedback Applications

While the general considerations for informal feedback apply to informal student evaluations, instructors should also apply them to formal evaluations. Formal evaluations based on tests give instructors the opportunity to use errors for reinforcing knowledge, skills, and attitudes that were addressed on the test. The following two approaches can be taken:

- ***Counsel individually with students to discuss the test*** — Individual counseling permits instructors the time to help a student understand the correct answers to missed questions and for instructors to determine whether a student's learning or studying styles were barriers to success **(Figure 13.10)**. Remedial instruction or practice can be recommended for the student or alterations in the presentation or testing methods can be made to assist the student in reaching the desired goal.

- ***Review incorrect answers with the entire class*** — Class review of the questions answered incorrectly on the test is an opportunity to review and reinforce the correct answers. *Examples:*

  — Questions that were answered incorrectly by a majority of students can be used for group discussions.

  — Instructors may find class reviews helpful in altering a question so that it is easier to understand.

  — The group may review performance tests, and additional practice can be assigned to ensure that skills are learned properly.

Summary

Student progress evaluation and testing provide instructors and training divisions with some indications of how well students are learning and how well instructors are teaching. Instructors must be able to recognize the various forms of formal stu-

Figure 13.10 It is important to discuss test results with students and help them overcome any barriers that may be affecting their learning experiences.

dent evaluation, types of tests and their uses, and methods for performing the evaluations. Critical skills for the Level I Instructor to master include properly administering, scoring, and securing tests and determining and reporting grades. Finally, the instructor must be able to use the test results to give students helpful, accurate, and timely feedback that is valuable to their learning experiences.

Student Tests as Feedback

Student tests are opportunities to provide positive feedback to students. Feedback may consist of notes written on the test to indicate that a student's efforts have been recognized and appreciated. The instructor may also use the test as an opportunity to speak privately with a student when the results do not meet the instructor's expectations.

Some guidelines for student test feedback include the following:

- Be prompt.
- Be encouraging.
- Be specific.
- Be clear and unambiguous.
- Focus on how the student can improve.
- Ask students how they believe they can improve.
- Ask how you can help the student.
- Compare test results with the desired criteria.
- Avoid using criticism when giving feedback.
- Use open-ended questions that will help students express how they feel about the results.

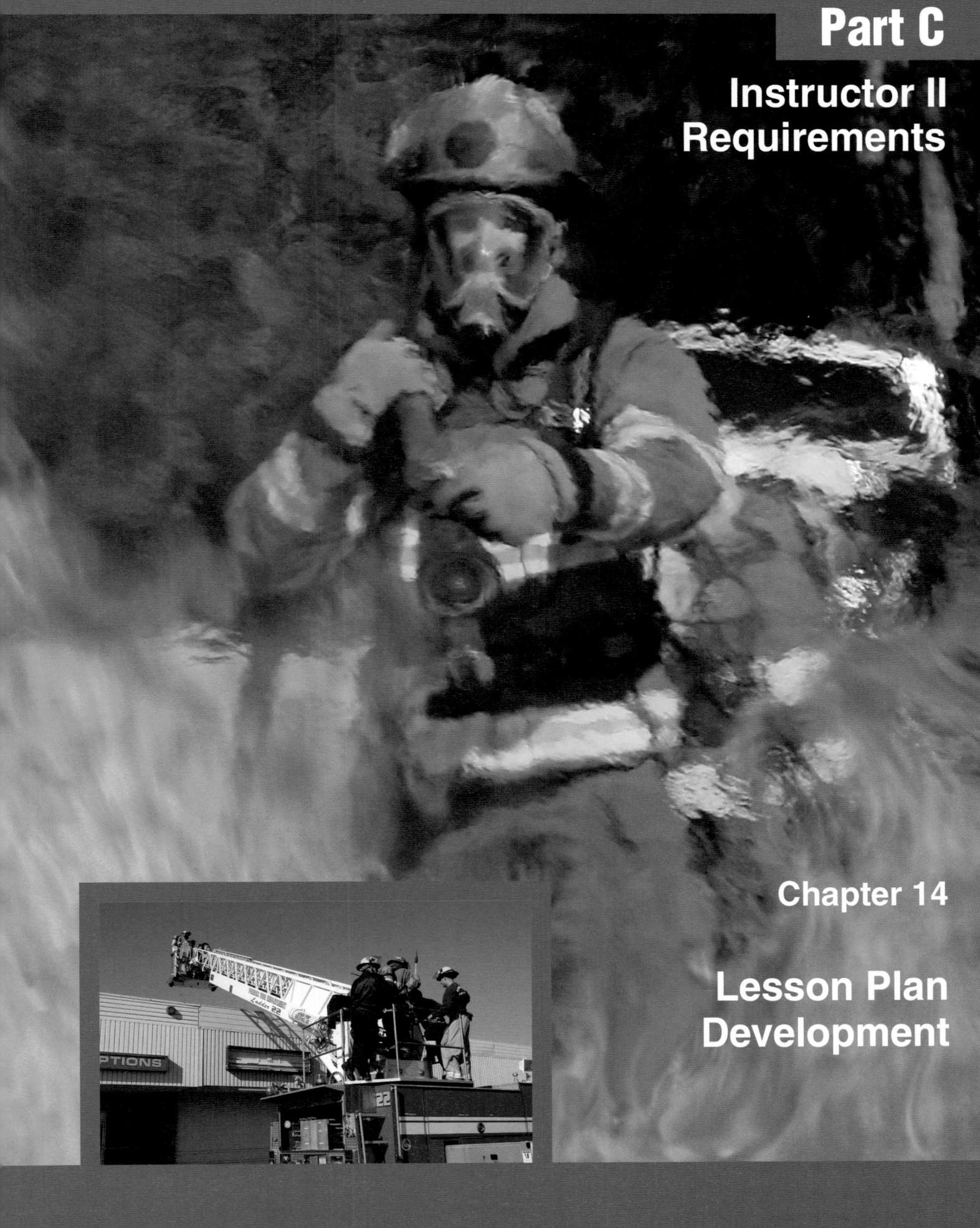

Part C
Instructor II Requirements

Chapter 14

Lesson Plan Development

After reading this chapter, students will be able to —

1. Define a lesson plan.

2. List the purposes and benefits of lesson plans.

3. Identify facts about parts and components of a lesson plan.

4. List the key purposes of learning objectives.

5. Explain the three components of a learning objective.

6. Identify guidelines for writing learning objectives.

7. Discuss types of lesson plans and formats for lesson plans.

8. Complete statements about creating a lesson plan.

9. List reasons why a lesson plan may need modifications.

10. Identify ancillary components of a lesson plan.

11. Identify guidelines for developing effective visual aids.

12. Identify facts about equipment used to create audiovisual training aids.

13. Discuss evaluating and revising a lesson plan.

Chapter Contents

The Lesson Plan and Its Components
Purposes and Benefits
Parts and Components

Learning Objectives
Development
Action Verbs

Lesson Plan Types and Formats

Lesson Plan Creation

Lesson Plan Modification or Adaptation

Ancillary Components
Information Sheet
Skills Sheet
Worksheet
Study Sheet
Assignment Sheet

Audiovisual Components
Development Guidelines
Equipment

Lesson Plan Evaluation and Revision

Summary

NFPA 1041, *Standard for Fire Service Instructor Professional Qualifications,* divides the assigned duties for fire and emergency services instructors into three categories or levels. For an instructor to certify at each level, that person must complete the requirements of the previous level. Thus far, this manual has provided general information that is necessary for all three levels (Part A) and information that is specific to the Level I Instructor (Part B). Beginning with this chapter and continuing through Chapter 19, Supervision and Management, the required knowledge for the Level II Instructor (Part C) is presented.

Even though NFPA 1041 divides the duties among the three levels, it should be obvious that similar divisions do *not* always exist in the fire and emergency services in North America. In many small volunteer, combination, and career organizations, a single instructor may be required to perform the functions of all three NFPA instructor levels. This requirement may be the result of limited staffing, limited funding, or organizational structure.

Therefore, an instructor who is certified as Level I may be required to develop lesson plans and evaluate courses. When this situation occurs, the instructor should attempt to certify to the higher level as soon as possible. Certifying to the appropriate level not only provides the instructor with the necessary knowledge but also relieves the officer of potential liabilities that are associated with performing duties beyond the current certification level.

Basic to the duties of the Level II Instructor is the ability to develop and modify lesson plans. This chapter provides the Level II Instructor candidate with the necessary information needed to develop and modify lesson plans, including the following elements:

- Lesson plan component identification
- Learning objective development and recognition
- Lesson plan types and formats
- Lesson plan creation
- Lesson plan modification or adaptation
- Ancillary component development
- Audiovisual component development
- Lesson plan evaluation and revision

Other knowledge requirements, including instructional methods and techniques, characteristics of adult students, and types and application of instructional media have been discussed in previous chapters. Information on basic research and outlining techniques and resource needs analysis are included in subsequent chapters.

The development of lesson plans is based on the creation of the course or unit plan that is part of curriculum development. The training division/agency may purchase a curriculum that has been developed by an outside organization or create it internally. Generally, the creation of internal curriculums is the duty of a Level III Instructor, which is included in Part D of this manual.

The Lesson Plan and Its Components

A *lesson plan* is an instructional document that outlines the information and skills to be taught (a prelude to instruction) and makes effective use of available resources (personnel, time, space, and

Figure 14.1 Psychomotor skills such as advancing a hoseline, operating a fog stream nozzle, or extinguishing a structure fire are described in detail in the lesson plan. *Courtesy of Alabama Fire College.*

materials) **(Figure 14. 1)**. The definition expands further by adding the following elements:

- State clearly what an instructor will accomplish with students during a particular lesson.

- Provide a step-by-step guide for any type of presentation by stating all the steps and methods necessary for presenting the required knowledge or skills in the proper sequence for the correct application of a skill or topic.

- List the appropriate support materials and indicate when they will be used.

- Provide instructors with a teaching purpose and fulfill other important purposes and benefits as well.

Just as driver/operators need maps when responding to emergencies in their response area, instructors need a lesson plan to guide them through a course or curriculum. Effective instructors systematically and carefully plan for productive use of their instructional time and resources. Designing and implementing lesson plans become two of the primary roles that Level II Instructors perform.

Instructors need to make careful decisions about the strategies and methods they employ to help students move systematically toward the lesson objectives and goals. The effective instructor also needs to develop a plan to provide direction toward the attainment of the lesson and course objectives.

The more organized an instructor is, the more effective the teaching and learning are. Writing detailed lesson plans is a large part of being organized. Lesson plans provide instructors with the learning objectives, testing criteria, training aids, materials, and teaching style required for the particular lesson. When lesson plans are developed to meet the available resources, they help instructors meet the needs of students.

Before learning how to develop a lesson plan, an instructor must understand its purposes and benefits. Students can easily recognize an instructor who lacks the knowledge, skills, and abilities needed to teach a class. As a result, the instructor and training program can lose credibility.

Purposes and Benefits

Lesson plans have the following multiple purposes and benefits to students, instructors, and administrators:

- Provide uniformity by standardizing the instruction and enabling instructors to provide the same information in a similar format each time the lesson is taught, which makes teaching easier. Lesson uniformity also ensures the administration of a cadre of employees who perform consistently and to the requirements of the actual job.

- Give a clear path for both instructors and students to follow. Sequential, orderly instruction makes learning interesting and worthwhile. The more effective a lesson plan is at providing a clear route to achieving the learning objectives, the more effective the instructor. The clearer the route is, the easier it is for the student to learn, be successful, and stay motivated.

- Ensure continuity when more than one instructor must teach from them. Establish continuity through appropriate sequences in the following ways:
  — Introduce the material.
  — Guide students through practical training evolutions to meet objectives.

— Guide students through a summary of the key learning points.

- Provide documentation for the training division and the organization's administration in the following ways:

  — Indicate teaching/learning information, methods and activities, and time frames for lessons.

  — Provide documentation of the amount and type of materials, equipment, and other resources needed to teach the lesson, which in turn, provides justification for the budget requests involving material and equipment purchases.

- Provide a document for developing test and evaluation requirements in the following ways:

  — Show the material that was taught (based on the objectives).

  — Verify that the information presented is appropriate for testing.

  — Establish the testing criteria.

Instructor Tip: Review Lesson Plans

Gather and review other lesson plans created and used by the organization or other instructors. Look for the points that The Lesson Plan and Its Components section addresses. Consider the answers to the following questions:

- Do these lesson plans fulfill the definition, meet the purposes, and provide the benefits described?

- Do these plans provide a clear path for instruction and learning?

Part of the instructor role is preparing a plan for teaching, which means that when using already-prepared lesson plans, instructors may have to add information so that the plan succeeds for them and their classes during instruction.

Parts and Components

In the most basic format, lesson plans should contain the following components that are organized into each of the following three parts (**Figure 14.2, pp. 324–327**):

Part 1: *Preparation information*—Contains the following components:

- *Job or topic* — Short descriptive title of the information covered. The title should briefly describe or give an indication of the lesson content. Topic titles are usually taken directly from the course outline.

- *Time frame* — Estimated *time* it takes to teach the lesson. Time frames may be set for each objective so that the instructor has a better idea of how to set the pace of the lesson. Time estimates can allow for variations in class size, experience level of students, etc.

- *Level of instruction* — Desired learning *level* that participants will reach by the end of the lesson, which may be based on NFPA job performance requirements (JPRs) or academically established taxonomy related to the appropriate learning domain. Many approaches to establishing the level of instruction are available.

- *Learning objective* — Description of the minimum acceptable *behavior* that a student must display by the end of an instructional period.

- *Resources/materials needed* — List of all items (including quantity) needed to teach the number of participants in the course. This section of the lesson also includes any preparation, planning, or activities that an instructor needs to complete before delivering the lesson such as the following:

  — Determining the appropriate training site (psychomotor lesson plan) and seating arrangement

  — Arranging for audiovisual training aids and devices

  — Reproducing handouts

  — Acquiring tools, apparatus, and other equipment (psychomotor lesson plan)

  — Contacting guest speakers (cognitive lesson plan)

1. Preparation

Topic:	Ground Ladders
Time:	1 hour
Level of Instruction:	Application
Learning Objective:	Inspect a ladder as part of a maintenance schedule.
Resources Needed:	Ladder to be inspected — ladder should be old enough to show some wear and tear Stick of chalk for marking defects Two sawhorses **Important:** Set up ladder on sawhorses in demonstration area before class begins.
Prerequisites:	Completion of ladder lifts and carries, as tested in Skill Sheets 9-2 through 9-8
References:	NFPA 1001, Fireground Operations 5.3.6 *Essentials of Fire Fighting*, Chapter 9
Summary:	Regular and proper cleaning of ladders is more than a matter of appearance: Dirt or debris from a fire may collect and harden, making the ladder sections inoperable. Ladders should be cleaned and inspected after each use. They should also be inspected on a regular monthly basis.
Assignment:	Additional practice, if needed
Comments:	If time permits, consider showing the video *Ground Ladders*.

Figure 14.2 Lesson plans exist in many physical formats but all should contain the same information.

Firefighter I — Student Lesson 9

2. Lesson Outline

A. Maintenance

1. Keep ground ladders free of moisture.
2. Do not store or rest ladders in a position where they are subjected to exhaust or engine heat.
3. Do not store ladders in any area where they are exposed to the elements.
4. Do not paint ladders except for the top and bottom 12 inches (300 mm) of the beams for purposes of identification or visibility.

B. Cleaning ladders

1. Clean ladders after every use and before inspecting.
2. Use a soft-bristle brush and running water for cleaning.
3. Wipe the ladder dry, checking for defects.

C. General maintenance, inspection, and repair

1. Maintenance means keeping ladders in a state of usefulness or readiness
2. Repair means either restoring or replacing that which has become inoperable.
3. Ladders meeting NFPA 1931 are marked by the manufacturer with a certification label on the ladder beam.
4. All firefighters should be capable of performing routine ladder maintenance.
5. Only trained ladder repair technicians should perform ladder repairs.

Page 2 of 4

Figure 14.2 *Continued*

6. Firefighters should clean ladders after each use; dirty ladders cannot be properly inspected.

7. Firefighters should inspect ladders after each use and monthly.

8. There are two methods of determining whether metal ladders have been exposed to high temperatures.

   a. Water boils when sprayed on the ladder

   b. Heat indicator label has changed color

9. Only trained fire service personnel or an approved testing organization should service test fire service ground ladders.

D. Inspecting specific ladder types

   1. Ground ladders

      a. Check heat sensor labels on metal and fiberglass ladders for a color change indicating heat exposure.

      b. Check rungs for snugness and tightness.

      c. Check bolts and rivets for tightness.

      d. Check welds for any cracks or apparent defects.

      e. Check beams and rungs for cracks, splintering, breaks, gouges, checks, wavy conditions, or deformation.

   2. Wood ladders/ladders with wood components

      a. Look for areas where the varnish finish has been chafed or scraped.

      b. Check for darkening of the varnish (indicating exposure to heat).

      c. Check for dark streaks in the wood (indicating deterioration of the wood).

Figure 14.2 *Continued*

   3. Roof ladders

      a. Make sure that the roof hook assemblies operate with relative ease.

      b. Check for signs of rust, deformities, and looseness of parts.

   4. Extension ladders

      a. Make sure the pawl assemblies work properly.

      b. Look for fraying or kinking of the halyard.

      c. Check the snugness of the halyard cable when the ladder is in the bedded position.

      d. Make sure the pulleys turn freely.

      e. Check the condition of the ladder guides and for free movement of the fly sections.

      f. Check for free operation of the pole ladder staypole toggles and check their condition.

   E. Summary

      Summarize lesson by reviewing:
      - Names of ladder parts
      - Maintenance and inspection guidelines

Part 3. Evaluation

Distribute and administer Chapter 9 Written Test to evaluate candidate mastery of the cognitive content of the lesson.

Administer Chapter 9 Performance Test at scheduled time. Record competency ratings on competency profile.

Page 4 of 4

Figure 14.2 *Continued*

— Listing lesson *resources*. Include information on the following items:

  ❍ Names of instructors or other personnel qualified to assist or provide logistical support

  ❍ Textbooks and other instructional materials

  ❍ Special equipment needs

— Determining specific instructional methods and learning activities required to meet objectives

— Selecting topic-specific training locations or changing training locations to meet the requirements of the topic being taught

- *Prerequisites* — List of information, skills, or previous requirements that students must have completed or mastered *before* entering this course or starting this lesson. *Differences:*

  — *Cognitive lesson plan:* Prerequisites for the current lesson may have been covered in a previous lesson. The instructor may give out-of-class assignments for students to complete in order to be ready for this lesson. An example of a prerequisite would be to understand fire behavior before taking a lesson on fire-extinguishment theory.

  — *Psychomotor lesson plan:* Prerequisites are essential for any skills-based training, especially training that involves live-fire training evolutions. For instance, students must be qualified in the use of self-contained breathing apparatus (SCBA) before any live-fire training.

- *References* — List of specific *references* and *resources* on the lesson plan for review along with page numbers to refer to; for example, textbooks and other instructional materials for the instructor to develop depth in the subject matter. *Differences:*

  — *Cognitive lesson plan:* Reference citations enable the instructor to qualify or verify information in case students ask unique questions, question sources, or desire further information.

  — *Psychomotor lesson plan*: References can be especially important when instruction takes place at a remote training site.

- *Lesson summary* — Restatement or reemphasis of the key points (sometimes referred to as *conclusion*) of the lesson to clarify uncertainties, prevent misconceptions, increase learning, and improve retention.

- *Assignments* — Reading, practice, research, or other outside-of-class requirements for students. *Differences:*

  — *Cognitive lesson plan:* Use of assignments is determined by the lesson topic and needs of the students.

  — *Psychomotor lesson plan:* Assignments consist of additional practice outside of class by students. Repeated and frequent practice ensures that students retain the skills and use them properly during emergency situations.

- *Comments (optional)* — General comments, references to ancillary components (assignment/activity sheets), and reminders for the instructor.

Part 2: *Lesson outline* — Contains the information and skills that are to be taught using the four-step method format: preparation, presentation, application, and evaluation; lists each step and includes the activities performed by the instructor to complete each step.

Part 3: *Evaluation* — Contains the type of performance evaluation that the instructor plans to use to determine whether students have met lesson objectives. *Differences:*

— *Cognitive lesson plan:* Include written or oral test items that test knowledge of the learning objectives. Role-plays, discussions, research projects, or other assignments may also be used to determine the level of understanding attained by the student.

— *Psychomotor lesson plan:* Ensure that performance skills accurately reflect the ability of the student to perform the required task. State the level of success, that is, the degree of success such as 100-percent mastery, 70-percent mastery, or pass/fail.

It is the training organization's responsibility to determine the components to use in their lesson plans. However, the parts and components listed are the most important and need to be considered.

Learning Objectives

This section gives a detailed explanation of learning objectives and their use in developing a lesson plan, describes how to develop or write learning objectives, and explains how to use action verbs. In Chapter 7, Principles of Learning, the definitions of learning outcomes and learning objectives were briefly described. Learning outcomes are discussed later in the manual as they relate to curriculum development. Definitions are as follows:

- *Learning outcomes* — Statements that specify what students will know or be able to do once learning is complete. They are usually expressed in terms of the three learning domains: cognitive, psychomotor, or affective. Learning outcomes are based on the needs assessment that defines the duties, jobs, and tasks that a student will be required to perform as a member of the organization. Learning outcomes are generally broad, while learning objectives may be more specific.

- *Learning objectives* — Specific statements (also referred to as *performance objectives* or *competencies*) that describe desired learning results. These statements describe what students will be able to do or demonstrate knowledge of at the conclusion of instructional activities. Written learning objectives represent the learning outcomes and, therefore, learning objectives and learning outcomes are directly related.

A Reminder About Terminology

Learning objectives, instructional objectives, performance objectives, behavioral objectives, specific objectives, enabling objectives, terminal objectives, course objectives, course outcomes, learning outcomes — all these different terms are bound to confuse instructors! While some education professionals may argue that there are differences between these terms, the terms ultimately indicate desired student performance. Although terminology is important, the instructor should focus on what is most important: the desired student performance.

Learning objectives focus on the outcomes or results of instruction. They need to be specific and measurable. Learning objectives are basic components in instructional development and have the following key purposes:

- Provide a foundation for instructional design and aid in overall course development. They help instructors select content and instructional materials and develop an appropriate instructional strategy.

- Provide a basis for measuring and evaluating student learning through appropriate assessment and testing.

- Inform students of expected performance standards and criteria.

- Allow instructors flexibility in teaching and makes teaching more efficient. When instructors are given objectives that students must attain, instructors can become flexible in helping students reach those objectives. Stating objectives can also make teaching more efficient by focusing on important content.

Learning objectives may have other important purposes within the fire and emergency services organization such as establishing promotional criteria. Learning objectives also help ensure consistency across instruction. For example, a training division/agency may have several instructors who teach the same course. When each instructor adheres to the same learning objectives, intended student outcomes should be the same.

Learning objectives are meant to help the instructor facilitate instruction. Therefore, the learning objective must work for the instructor, training division/agency, and organization. A sound objective is one that clearly communicates intended student outcomes. By understanding the construction of effective learning objectives, instructors will be able to recognize the intended learning domain and emphasis.

When a learning objective appears to be inappropriate or too subjective, instructors should modify or alter it accordingly. Additional information on modifying learning objectives is provided later in the Lesson Plan Modification or Adaptation section.

Development

Learning objectives can be developed or written in various ways. Although each individual instructor may approach writing learning objectives with a different perspective, all learning objectives should communicate the intended learning outcome and be clearly stated, measurable, specific, and detailed.

Several accepted models for writing learning objectives are available. One of the most widely used models was developed by Robert F. Mager in the early 1960s and continues to help define the role of learning objectives in training. Because of its simplicity and consistency, the Mager Model is used in this manual and its associated curriculum. According to Mager, learning objective statements should contain the following three components:

- *Conditions description* — Describe the situation, tools, or materials required for a student to perform a single specific action or behavior. *Example*:
  - *Learning objective: Given an adult cardiopulmonary resuscitation (CPR) training mannequin*, administer CPR.
  - *Condition:* The CPR training mannequin is necessary for the performance of administering CPR.
- *Performance (behavior) statement* — Identify what the student is expected to do. The behavior must be stated in observable terms

and begin with clear action verbs such as *recall, identify, list, label, describe,* or *state* (among others). *Examples:*
  - *Learning objective: Describe* the safety precautions used when ventilating a pitched roof with a power saw.
  - *Performance (behavior):* The student verbally or in writing describes the safety precautions for ventilating a roof.
- *Standards criteria* — State the acceptable level of student performance. Standards provide the measurable criteria for evaluating student performance and may include a statement about the degree of accuracy or a time limit for completion. *Example*:
  - *Learning objective:* Given photos of extrication tools, *identify (label)* 90 percent of the tools accurately.
  - *Criterion*: The standard requires 90-percent accuracy.

Standards may also be set at a specific level such as 70 percent for the organization. Instructors may want learning objectives that deal with safety issues and/or critical tasks to require students to perform at 100-percent accuracy.

A current trend in training is to omit the conditions and standards statements from the learning objective. This trend is based on two assumptions: First, it is assumed that the conditions consist of normal working environments, equipment, and situations. Second, it is assumed that the standards criterion is complete mastery or requires 100-percent accuracy.

In addition to the components in the Mager Model, the learning objective statement may also be student-centered so that the learning objective focuses on the student as the person displaying the observable behavior. The learning objective may be written to include the phrase *the student will . . . ,* although the active participation of the student is understood when the phrase is *not* used.

In addition to these basic components, effective learning objectives should adhere to the following guidelines:

- Avoid vague terminology such as *understand, know, comprehend,* or *learn*. For example, *Understand the principles of fire behavior* does *not* indicate a measurable outcome. Learning objectives must contain an action verb and a specific description of the lesson content. A measurable outcome example: *State the principles of fire behavior.*

- Make learning objectives short and focused on a single outcome. Example: *Match U.S. Department of Transportation (DOT) symbols to their meanings.*

- Make learning objectives specific and objective, not vague and subjective. Example: ***Apply** a dressing to an open wound on a victim.*

- Base course development on learning objectives. They can be used like an outline for determining the following elements:

  — Evaluation requirements

  — Course content

  — Course activities

Action Verbs

Because effective learning objectives depend on the use of the appropriate action verb, instructors should create or locate a list of verbs for use with the various learning domains and required emphasis. Note that some words are applicable to a variety of learning domains and emphasis. Some appropriate action verbs for use in the cognitive domain include those in **Table 14.1, p 332.**

Lesson Plan Types and Formats

Learning objectives are essential to any lesson plan, but they are *not* the only components of a detailed written lesson plan. The type of instruction presented in a course may be from the cognitive, psychomotor, or affective domains. For simplicity, only two lesson plan types are presented: one for cognitive lesson plans involving the presentation of technical information and the other for psychomotor lesson plans involving the teaching of manipulative or physical skills.

Learning in the affective domain usually involves behavioral changes and evolves naturally from these two types. The sections that follow outline the two types of lesson plans and formats that instructors may use when writing lesson plans.

Table 14.1
Useful Words for Expressing Objectives

Knowledge: Level 1.0			
Arrange	Label	Order	State
Define	List	Recall	Select
Describe	Match	Recognize	
Distinguish	Name		
Identify			

Comprehension: Level 2.0			
Choose	Differentiate between	Indicate	Restate
Classify	Discriminate	Interpret	Review
Compare	Discuss	Locate	Select
Convert	Estimate	Recognize	Sort
Describe	Express	Report	Tell
Determine	Identify	Respond	Translate

Application: Level 3.0			
Apply	Explain	Modify	Predict
Calculate	Illustrate	Operate	Produce
Choose	Implement	Perform	Schedule
Compute	Interpret	Plan	Sketch
Construct	Measure	Prepare	Solve
Demonstrate	Manipulate	Practice	Use

Analysis: Level 4.0		Synthesis: Level 5.0		Evaluation: Level 6.0	
Analyze	Diagram	Arrange	Organize	Appraise	Evaluate
Appraise	Differentiate	Assemble	Plan	Argue	Judge
Calculate	Discriminate	Collect	Predict	Assess	Measure
Categorize	Distinguish	Compose	Prepare	Attack	Predict
Choose	Draw conclusions	Construct	Produce	Choose	Rate
Compare	Estimate	Create	Propose	Compare	Revise
Conclude	Evaluate	Design	Revise	Conclude	Score
Contrast	Examine	Develop	Set up	Contrast	Select
Deduce	Identify	Formulate	Summarize	Defend	Support
Detect	Inspect	Generate	Synthesize	Determine	Value
Determine	Interpret	Manage	Write	Estimate	
Develop	Predict	Modify			
Diagnose	Solve				

Types

Two basic types of lesson plans are used in fire and emergency services training: cognitive and psychomotor. While they are similar, there are differences as discussed in the sections that follow. Both lesson plan types may include a detailed time schedule for the lesson. Created in chart form, this schedule may include the lesson outline, teaching location (when more than one is used during the lesson), instructor activities, student activities, and specific time frames. See **Table 14.2** for samples of two course time schedule formats.

Cognitive Lesson Plans

Cognitive lesson plans contain all of the components mentioned earlier and address the knowl-

Table 14.2
Course Time Schedule Formats

Sample 1

Lesson Outline	Location	Instructor Activity	Student Activity	Time
Introduction	Classroom C	Lecture	Listen	8:00–8:30 a.m.
Video presentation	Classroom C	Monitor	Watch	8:30–9:15 a.m.
Break				9:15–9:30 a.m.
Discussion of video	Classroom C	Facilitate	Participate	9:30–10:30 a.m.
Practice evolutions	Drill Tower	Observe	Practice	10:30 a.m.–12 noon

Sample 2

Four-Day Format	Estimated Time
Day 1	
Section 1: Roles and Responsibilities	4 hours
Section 2: Creating and Modifying Lesson Plans	4 hours
Day 2	
Section 2: Creating and Modifying Lesson Plans	8 hours
Day 3	
Section 2: Creating and Modifying Lesson Plans	8 hours
Day 4	
Section 3: Analyzing Evaluations and Tests	4 hours
Section 4: Supervising Instruction	2 hours

Saturday-Sunday Format	
First Weekend:	
Saturday	
Section 1: Roles and Responsibilities	4 hours
Section 2: Creating and Modifying Lesson Plans	4 hours
Sunday	
Section 2: Creating and Modifying Lesson Plans	8 hours
Second Weekend:	
Saturday	
Section 2: Creating and Modifying Lesson Plans	8 hours
Sunday	
Section 3: Analyzing Evaluations and Tests	4 hours
Section 4: Supervising Instruction	2 hours
Class Time	**25.5 hours**
Activity Time	**4.5 hours**
Total Time	**30.0 hours**

edge lessons delivered by instructors. The majority of lesson plans developed for the cognitive domain include student activities that may require some type of psychomotor skill, but not necessarily to the degree found in psychomotor lesson plans. Ancillary components, discussed later, include information, work, and study sheets.

Psychomotor Lesson Plans

In addition to lesson plan parts and components that are common to both cognitive and psychomotor lesson plan formats, a psychomotor lesson plan also has a *skills sheet* component. This sheet lists a task and divides it into its parts by listing the operations (steps) and key points.

Curriculum developers and/or instructors can develop a skills sheet for each of the psychomotor skills listed or discussed in the course outline. These sheets provide instructors and students with sequences and details needed to teach and learn the knowledge and skills of a task. Skills sheets, as well as other materials that are used with the lesson plans, are described in the Ancillary Components section.

Formats

A variety of formats can be used to write a lesson plan. Three that may be suited to fire and emergency service instructors are as follows:

- *Outline major points* — Includes only the major statements or words in the outline. This format is best used by very experienced instructors who have a wealth of knowledge regarding the topic. It may *not* serve inexperienced instructors or Level I Instructors as well when they do not have a lot of knowledge in the subject matter (**Figure 14.3, p. 334**).

- *Detailed outline* — Condenses the information in the lesson plan; written more in a paragraph format instead of the short statements of keywords. It may be a distraction for experienced instructors because they do *not* need this much information and may consider this style too complicated or distracting from which to teach. However, it may be an advantage to inexperienced instructors who need additional information in the lesson plan (**Figure 14.4, p. 335**).

- *Major points with explanatory material* — Presents the lesson in a two-column format with major points discussed in one column and explanatory information in the other column, which may be more of the information found in the detailed outline. This type of lesson plan format can serve both experienced and inexperienced instructors because all of the information is present (**Figure 14.5, p. 337**).

Fire Instructor **Student Lesson 7**

Lecture/ Discussion **I. Introduction**

A. Administrative Details
1. Fire alarm.
2. Exits from the classroom.
3. Student roster.

B. Instructor Introduction

Easel

1. Name of instructor.
2. Experience in the fire service.
3. Experience with the use of fire hoses.
4. Training and certifications.

C. Motivation of Students

1. The most common hose roll is the straight roll. Every fire fighter will have to perform the roll following incidents, training exercises, testing hose, etc.

2. A fire fighter must be able to perform the roll so the hose is rolled evenly, without kinking, and with the correct coupling on the outside of the roll.

D. Lesson Goal

1. At the end of the lesson, the recruit fire fighter will be able to successfully perform a straight hose roll.

E. Learning Objectives
1. Describe the purpose of the straight roll.
2. Demonstrate the straight hose roll.

Page 1 of 1

Figure 14.3 Lesson plans may be prepared in an outline format. Adapted from Fire Service Training, Oklahoma State University.

**Lecture/
Discussion**

    I.   **Introduction**

        A.   Administrative Details

            1.   Fire alarm.

            2.   Exits from the classroom.

            3.   Student roster.

        B.   Instructor Introduction

Easel

> Print your name and contact information on an easel. Reveal the sheet during your introduction so that students will have the correct spelling of your name and your contact information in case they need assistance following the lesson.

            1.   Name of instructor.

            2.   Experience in the fire service.

            3.   Experience with the use of fire hoses.

            4.   Training and certifications.

        C.   Motivation of Students

> It is critical that the students understand and appreciate the need to be able to properly roll a joint of hose using a straight roll. Review the following key points about performing a straight hose roll. If possible, share a personal experience or an anecdote that illustrates the importance of being able to safely and quickly roll a joint of hose.

Figure 14.4 A sample of a detailed lesson plan that contains more information than the outline format. Adapted from Fire Service Training, Oklahoma State University.

1.   The most common hose roll is the straight roll. Every fire fighter will have to perform the roll following incidents, training exercises, testing hose, etc.

> The straight hose roll is generally used for hose that is going to be put in storage (especially rack storage), returned to quarters for washing, or loaded back on the apparatus at the fire scene. When the roll is completed, the female end is exposed, with the male end protected in the center of the roll.
>
> A variation of this method is to begin the roll at the female coupling so that when the roll is completed, the male coupling is exposed. This is often done to denote a damaged coupling or piece of hose. A tag is usually attached to the male coupling indicating the type and location of the damage.

2.   A fire fighter must be able to perform the roll so the hose is rolled evenly, without kinking, and with the correct coupling on the outside of the roll.

D.   Lesson Goal

1.   At the end of the lesson, the recruit fire fighter will be able to successfully perform a straight hose roll.

E.   Learning Objectives

1.   Describe the purpose of the straight roll.

2.   Demonstrate the straight hose roll.

> **ASK: Are there any questions about the learning objectives or the goal of the lesson?**
>
> Answer any questions or concerns. Once any questions have been addressed proceed to Section II.

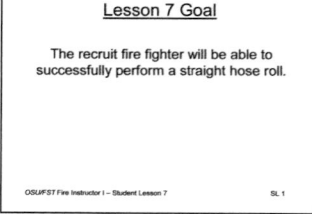

Lesson 7 Goal

The recruit fire fighter will be able to successfully perform a straight hose roll.

OSU/FST Fire Instructor I – Student Lesson 7   SL 1

Learning Objectives

• Describe the purpose of the straight hose roll.
• Demonstrate the straight hose roll.

OSU/FST Fire Instructor I – Student Lesson 7   SL 2

Page 2 of 2

Figure 14.4 *Continued*

Fire Instructor   Student Lesson 7

I. Introduction

    A. Administrative Details

        1. Fire Alarm

        2. Classroom exits

        3. Student Roster

    B. Instructor introduction

        1. Name of instructor

        2. Fire Service Experience

        3. Experience with the use of Fire hoses.

        4. Training and certifications

    C. Student motivation

        1. The most common hose roll is the straight roll. Every fire fighter will have to perform the roll following incidents, training exercises, testing hose, etc.

        2. A fire fighter must be able to perform the roll so the hose is rolled evenly, without kinking, and with the correct coupling on the outside of the roll.

II. Presentation

    A. Purpose of a Straight Hose Roll

Easel

> Print your name and contact information on an easel. Reveal the sheet during your introduction so that students will have the correct spelling of your name and your contact information in case they need assistance following the lesson.

> It is critical that the students understand and appreciate the need to be able to properly roll a joint of hose using a straight roll. Review the following key points about performing a straight hose roll. If possible, share a personal experience or an anecdote that illustrates the importance of being able to safely and quickly roll a joint of hose.

Data Projector
PowerPoint® Slide

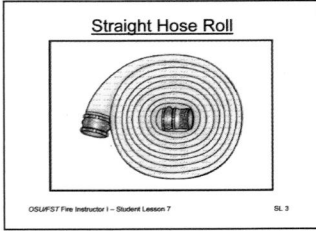

Straight Hose Roll

OSU/FST Fire Instructor I – Student Lesson 7   SL 3

Page 1 of 1

Figure 14.5 The two-column format combines elements of both the outline and detailed formats. Adapted from Fire Service Training, Oklahoma State University.

Lesson Plan Creation

A lesson may vary in length from a few minutes to several hours, depending on the desired learning objectives. When instructors create a lesson plan, determining the performance outcomes is the first step. The required performance outcomes lead to the writing of the learning objectives. The subsequent steps generated by the learning objectives develop then into a lesson plan, all of which assist the instructor in preparing to teach the lesson or course. When creating a lesson plan, instructors should perform the following steps:

Step 1: *Identify the expected performance outcomes* — Analyze the job to identify all of the expected job performances that a person would perform when doing the job.

Step 2: *Divide performance outcomes into tasks* — Use the NFPA JPRs when using NFPA's performance outcomes.

Step 3: *Divide tasks into the steps required to accomplish outcomes* — Divide the tasks into the basic knowledge and skills steps required to perform each task. Use this list to identify the essential knowledge and skills required to perform the task.

Step 4: *Write lesson objectives for each task* — Write an objective for each task or performance outcome and for all of the required knowledge and skills that a person must learn.

Step 5: *Write test items for each lesson objective* — Write the test items that will be used to evaluate the level of knowledge and skills that the person possesses to be successful in performing the job.

Step 6: *Determine the order for instructing the material* — Identify the order in which the knowledge and skills will be taught to develop the instructional outline. Identify the prerequisite and corequisite knowledge and skills.

Step 7: *Research information to support instruction* — Use sources such as the following:

  — Standard operating guidelines and procedures

  — Current literature

  — Current accepted practices

  — National consensus standards

Step 8: *Write the outline* — Develop the lesson plan, using any one of the following formats:

  — Outline with major points

  — Detailed outline

  — Major points with explanatory information (considered the best type of format for the fire and emergency services Level I Instructor to use)

Step 9: *Develop lesson activities* — Identify appropriate instructional techniques/methods for delivering the lesson. Develop activities and insert them into the lesson to reinforce objectives and provide students the opportunity to apply what they have learned.

Step 10: *Identify and develop instructional aids to support instruction* — List all the appropriate media, props, equipment, materials, facilities, costs, and time that will be required to present the lesson.

Step 11: *Write or develop the preparation section/component of the lesson plan* — Include title, level of instruction, list of instructional references, list of resources required including human, physical, and instructional elements.

Step 12: *Write ancillary and reference materials*

  — Identify and develop assignments (when required).

  — Develop course and instructor evaluation instruments used to determine the effectiveness of the course.

  — Write a bibliography of references referred to in writing the lesson plan.

  — Use the appropriate form and style for citing references, for example, American Psychological Association (APA) or Modern Language Association (MLA) documentation methods.

Step 13: *Write the lesson summary* — Emphasize important, critical, or key information from the lesson or review or preview information. Provide a means for bringing the lesson to a close.

Lesson Plan Modification or Adaptation

Training divisions and agencies either create lesson plans based on local needs or purchase commercially available curriculums that contain prepared lesson plans. Even though these lesson plans may include all the component parts and information listed in the preceding sections, an instructor may still be required to modify or adapt the plan to the needs of a specific class or situation.

The instructor should review the lesson plan to determine if any modifications to the format or content are required. Components may need modifications for the following reasons:

- Ensures complete coverage and effective use of available resources

- Includes current information or changes in operating policies and procedures

- Addresses certain groups or introduces information specific to a group

When creating a lesson plan, instructors start with the learning outcomes as the first step. To modify a lesson plan, it is necessary to start at the same point. Subsequent steps to modifying or adapting a lesson plan again guide instructors through the preparation stage necessary for teaching a lesson or course. Because the steps are similar, the instructor should adhere to the steps listed in the Lesson Plan Creation section when modifying or adapting a lesson plan.

The instructor should maintain records of any modifications or alterations to the lesson plans. Curriculum content and lesson plans should be reviewed by the training division or agency periodically to determine that the materials are current and that all instructors are familiar with the modifications that have been made. Old versions of curriculums or lesson plans should be retained in archives for future reference and as documentation that the organization has met the training requirements at a given time in its history.

Ancillary Components

In addition to the items listed in The Lesson Plan and Its Components section for each type of lesson plan, there are supporting or ancillary materials that should be included with each lesson plan. Ancillary components include informational handouts and study guides, skills sheets, work or activity sheets, and assignment sheets. The purpose of these materials is to provide students with background or resource information that is *not* available in the text nor easily copied from copyrighted standards or lengthy protocols.

In addition, some ancillary components list performance steps that students can follow while practicing skills or evolutions. The overall purpose of ancillary materials is to enable students to apply, study, and practice the lesson content.

Ancillary components are aids that an instructor can use as desired; however, they often serve as important and useful instructional adjuncts as well as helpful guides that reinforce learning. The following sections describe several types of ancillary components including information, skills, work, study, and assignment sheets.

Information Sheet

An *information sheet* is a type of handout or fact sheet that provides additional background information on a topic supplemental to the information provided in the text or other course resources **(Figure 14.6, p. 340)**. The information may be in the form of detailed text or an outline that summarizes key ideas. The handout may also list information references or include suggestions for further research.

Information sheets should be designed to encourage students to learn. See steps for developing information sheets in information box. Information sheets are usually created for one of the following reasons:

- The information is unavailable to some students because texts or other learning resources are limited.

- To get the information, students would have to find and consult a number of texts, which may be difficult to obtain and would be time-consuming.

- The information is *not* available in any text.

Information Sheet 1B-1
Accidents & Injuries

ACCIDENTS

Accidents are unplanned events that may result in bodily injury, illness, or physical or property loss. H. W. Heinrich of the Travelers Insurance Company devoted the greater portion of his life to the study of industrial accidents and their prevention. Heinrich proposed that there were five factors involved in an accident sequence:

1. Social environment
2. Human factors
3. Unsafe acts or conditions
4. Accident
5. Injury

He found that the last factor in the sequence, an injury, was always preceded by an accident. But, in order for an accident to occur, some unsafe act had to be committed or some unsafe condition had to exist. The unsafe act or condition was invariably caused by the human factor. In turn, the human factors responsible resulted from inherited characteristics or social and environmental conditioning. Heinrich called his findings the Domino Theory because like a row of end-standing dominoes, the activation of one factor precipitated the activation of the next, and the next, eventually resulting in an accident or injury.

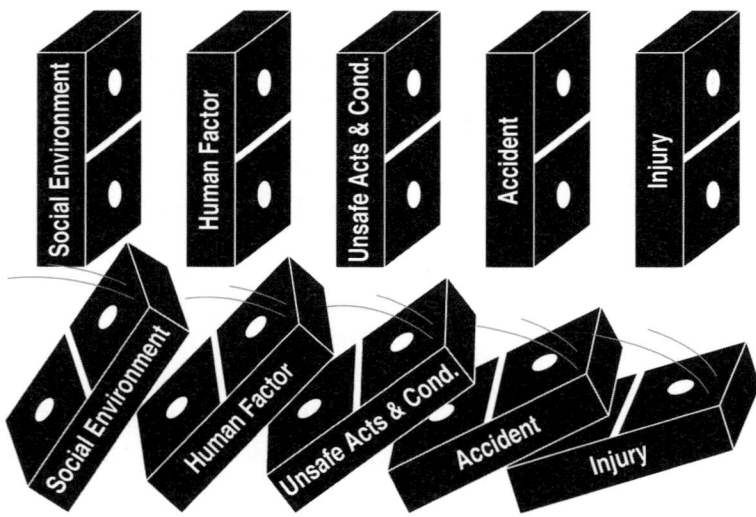

In Heinrich's Domino Theory, the emphasis on accident (and thus injury) control is in the middle of the sequence — at the unsafe act or mechanical or physical hazard. If this act or hazard is removed, the sequence is interrupted and the injury cannot occur.

Figure 14.6 An information sheet (first page) can provide additional material to students.

Information Sheet

Step 1: Create a title that indicates the subject area and relates the title to the lesson.

Step 2: Introduce the information with a brief description that explains its importance, relating it to the appropriate portion of the primary text or part of the lesson. Present the information in a form that creates interest in the student to read, study, and learn it.

Step 3: Present the information in the most appropriate form so that it is easy to read and follow. Include appropriate charts, tables, or illustrations on the form, or place them on separate pages; label them for easy referral.

Step 4: Develop test questions based on the information sheet so students can assess whether they have achieved the lesson objectives. Test questions should stress important points in the information sheet and enable the instructor to check student comprehension. Make the questions thought provoking, and develop a sufficient number to address the information.

Skills Sheet

Step 1: List the task to be performed (this task becomes the title).

Step 2: Divide the page into columns.

Step 3: Head the left column *operations* or *performance units* where the instructor lists the actual psychomotor skills.

Step 4: Head the next column *key points* or *knowledge units* where the instructor lists pieces of knowledge without which the operations cannot be safely or accurately performed.

Step 5: List the steps of the task in sequence under *operations,* using action verbs (such as *grasp, push, turn, lift, don,* etc.).

Step 6: List cautions, warnings, safety factors, and conditions essential for performing the task operations under *key points.*

Skills Sheet

A *skills sheet* divides a task into parts by listing the operational steps and their key points or steps for completing each operation **(Figure 14.7, p. 342)**. The purpose of skills sheets is to provide instructors and students with the sequences and details necessary to teach and learn a task that includes both psychomotor skills and knowledge.

The *operation (performance unit)* is a step or the smallest aspect in performing a task. A *key point (knowledge unit)* is a step that is part of the process of completing the task and may include information that aids in knowing or understanding operations that enable the student to perform the task correctly. Students can use a skills sheet to prepare for a performance evaluation.

Skill operations that students need to be able to perform based on knowledge are listed on the left side of the page; key points that students need to know in order to perform a task are listed in another column. A completed skills sheet lists the step-by-step procedures for doing a job in sequence and the key points that the instructor must stress and demonstrate while teaching the task. See steps for developing a skills sheet in the information box.

Students typically practice skills with the guidance of instructors, but instructors cannot supervise every student during every practice activity. Skills sheets provide the skill steps students need to know and practice and allow them to practice in groups on their own as they coach each other, discuss and think about the activities, and develop higher level (analytical and synthesis) cognitive skills. These self-practice exercises allow students to prepare for performance evaluations where they perform without instructor guidance, exercise thinking skills, and perform at the mastery level for an evaluator **(Figure 14.8, p. 343)**.

Worksheet

A *worksheet* or *activity sheet* provides students opportunities to apply rules, analyze and evaluate objects and situations, or use multiple skills while completing activities. Instructors create student worksheets from the information content of the lesson plan **(Figure 14.9, p. 345)**. Any worksheets

Skills Sheet 1
Replace a Hose Gasket

Name_____Date_____

Evaluator _____Competency Rating_____

References	*NFPA 1001*, Prevention, Preparedness, and Maintenance 5.5.4 ***Essentials***, pages 405, 406 and 439
Prerequisites	None
Introduction	Before any piece of equipment is placed on the apparatus, it should be in top operating condition. Hose couplings are vital for attaching hose to other hose and nozzles. If they or their gaskets are damaged, they can hinder the mission and endanger firefighters' lives.
Equipment & Personnel	• One firefighter in protective clothing • Hoses with male, female, and sexless couplings • Replacement gaskets of appropriate types and sizes

OPERATION	KEY POINTS	ATTEMPT NO. 1 2 3
Replace a Hose Gasket		
1. Remove and discard old or damaged gasket.	In proper receptacle	__ __ __
2. Pick up new gasket.	Between middle finger and thumb	__ __ __
3. Fold loop upward.	With index finger.	__ __ __
4. Place gasket into swivel	a. Large loop first	
	b. Smoothing as necessary to seat.	__ __ __
	Time (Total)	__ __ __

EVALUATOR'S COMMENTS

_____

_____

_____

Figure 14.7 A skills sheet can give students the sequences and details necessary to learn a task.

Skills Sheet 2
Inspect Hose Couplings

Name_____Date_____

Evaluator _____Competency Rating_____

References	NFPA 1001, Prevention, Preparedness, and Maintenance 5.5.4 Essentials, pages 405, 406 and 439
Prerequisites	None
Introduction	Before any piece of equipment is placed on the apparatus, it should be in top operating condition. Hose couplings are vital for attaching hose to other hose and nozzles. If they or their gaskets are damaged, they can hinder the mission and endanger firefighters' lives.
Equipment & Personnel	• One firefighter in protective clothing • Hoses with male, female, and sexless couplings • Replacement gaskets of appropriate types and sizes

OPERATION	KEY POINTS	ATTEMPT NO. 1 2 3

Inspect Hose Couplings

1. Inspect the male couplings.Meets the following criteria: ___ ___ ___
    a. Tight on hose or appliance
    b. Undamaged threads
    c. Not out of round
    d. Free of burrs
    e. Clean

2. Inspect the female couplings. Meets the following criteria: ___ ___ ___
    a. Tight on hose or appliance
    b. Undamaged threads
    c. Not out of round
    d. Free of burrs
    e. Clean
    f. Free-spinning swivel
    g. Swivel gasket undamaged, pliable, and clean

Page 1 of 2

Figure 14.8 A performance evaluation sheet may be used for assessing psychomotor skills.

OPERATION	KEY POINTS	ATTEMPT NO. 1	2	3
3. Inspect the sexless couplings.	Meets the following criteria: a. Tight on hose or appliance b. Not edged c. Free of burrs d. Clean e. Free-spinning swivel f. Swivel gasket undamaged and clean g. Swivel gasket in place h. Undamaged connecting lugs	___	___	___
	Time (Total)	___	___	___

EVALUATOR'S COMMENTS

____

____

____

Page 2 of 2

Figure 14.8 *Continued*

Worksheet 12A-1
Select the Proper Nozzle and Hose for Given Fire Attack Situations

Name_____ Date_____

Evaluator _____Competency Rating_____

Reference	*NFPA 1001*, Fireground Operations 5.3.10A
Prerequisites	None
Introduction	Firefighters must know the different sizes and uses for the various hoses and nozzles used in the fire service. Just as a carpenter knows that a particular type of saw or screwdriver is right for a specific job, so too should the firefighter be able to choose the hose and nozzle type appropriate for the fire situation on hand.
Directions	Select the correct nozzle and hose for each of the situations described below. Write your answers in the blanks.
Activity	**Situation 1:** Wildland fire

a. Nozzle selected

_____

b. Hose size/type selected

_____

Situation 2: Residential structure; fire confined to two bedrooms
a. Nozzle selected

_____

b. Hose size/type selected

_____

Situation 3: Large, fully involved warehouse
a. Nozzle selected

_____

b. Hose size/type selected

_____

Figure 14.9 A worksheet (first page) contains activities that students are expected to complete as a means of applying information that has been presented in class or a reading assignment.

that the instructor develops must support the learning objectives and provide activities that enable students to meet those objectives.

Completing a worksheet may also be a learning objective that requires students to participate in activities that include and apply knowledge or skills acquired in previous learning objectives. Worksheets can be used to generate discussions on a topic and generally contain optional activities. Worksheets may *not* require scoring or grading by the instructor.

Worksheets that require students to exercise abilities in the affective domain may support more than one learning objective in which more than knowledge and skill must be developed or demonstrated. Recall that the affective domain has students change or adjust, develop, practice, and adapt attitudes, values, beliefs, and appreciations. Use the steps in the information box to develop a worksheet

Worksheet

Step 1: Create a title that reflects the subject or topic, and relate it to the lesson.

Step 2: List all the materials and resources that students need in order to complete the activity. List titles and page numbers of books, journals, or other reference material. Provide enough information so that students can locate resources quickly and easily.

Step 3: Write a brief introduction that arouses interest and motivates students to complete the activity. Discuss the skill or activity, and explain how it relates to the topic or training area and the lesson objectives. Explain how and why the activity is important and relevant to the job and how the activity helps students master the skill.

Step 4: Provide clear directions that explain how to complete the worksheet.

Step 5. Provide answers or solutions on a separate page. The answer sheet may be given either with the worksheet or after the worksheet is completed.

Study Sheet

A *study sheet* is an instructional document designed to arouse student interest in a topic and explain to students the specific areas to study. Instructors may want to distribute study sheets for students to use during instruction or for them to use as self-study aides. It is also helpful to include a self-study test with the study sheet, which enables the instructor to measure and provide feedback on how well students understood the material (**Figure 14.10**). Use the steps in the information box to create a study sheet:

Study Sheet

Step 1: Create a title that reflects the subject or topic, and relate it to the lesson.

Step 2: List all the materials and resources that students need to complete the study sheet. List titles and page numbers of books, journals, or other reference material. Provide enough information so that students can locate resources quickly and easily.

Step 3: Write a brief introduction that arouses interest and motivates students to complete the study sheet.

Step 4: Design the study sheet to present the study information in a format that enables students to use and learn the material.

Step 5: Put a study-sheet test (if one is included) on a separate sheet of paper.

Step 6: Design study questions to make students think and assess understanding of all aspects of the topic. Include enough questions to thoroughly address the material.

Assignment Sheet

An *assignment sheet* contains information about a specific activity or project that the student is expected to perform without supervision (**Figure 14.11, p. 348**). The activity may occur within the class period or outside of class. Generally, an assignment sheet contains the three components of the Mager Model (performance, conditions, and

Chapter 12 — Fire Hose
Lesson 12B — Laying, Carrying, & Advancing Hose

Study Sheet

This study sheet is intended to help you learn the material on caring for hose and on laying, carrying, and advancing hose in Chapter 12 of ***Essentials of Fire Fighting***, Fourth Edition, pages 402 through 406 and 413 through 422. You may use it for self-study, or you may use it to review material that will be covered in the lesson and chapter review tests. The numbers in parentheses are the pages in ***Essentials*** on which the answers or terms can be found.

CHAPTER VOCABULARY

Be sure that you know the chapter-related meanings of the following terms and abbreviations. Use a dictionary or the glossary in ***Fire Service Orientation and Terminology*** if you cannot determine the meaning of the term from its context.

- Forward hose lay *vs.* reverse hose lay (*423*)
- Intake hose *vs.* supply hose (*422, 427*)
- Soft-sleeve hose *vs.* hard-suction (sleeve) hose (*427*)
- Split hose lay (*428*)
- Standpipe (*431*)

STUDY QUESTIONS & ACTIVITIES

1. What are the usual basic causes of hose damage? (*399*)

   ____

   ____

   ____

2. What is the most important factor affecting the life of fire hose? (*399*)

   ____

   ____

3. Detail specific ways that fire hose may be damaged, and then list recommended practices to prevent these damages. (*399 – 401*)

   a. Mechanical damage ______________________________

   ____

   Prevention practices ______________________________

   ____

   ____

Figure 14.10 A study sheet (first page) may be used as a self-study test for students to determine how much of the reading assignment is understood.

Awareness-Level First Responder
Lesson 2
Assignment Sheet 2

Objective 10: Locate hazard information in the current edition of the ERG.

Name _____ **Date** _____

References	*NFPA 472, 4.2.3; Hazardous Materials for First Responders*, 3rd ed.; *Emergency Response Guidebook*

References   *NFPA 472, 4.2.3; Hazardous Materials for First Responders,* 3rd ed.; *Emergency Response Guidebook*

Prerequisites   None

Introduction   The *Emergency Response Guidebook* is primarily a guide to aid first responders in quickly identifying the specific or generic hazards of the materials involved in an emergency incident, so that they may protect themselves and the general public during the initial response phase of the incident.

                       The *ERG* assists responders in making initial decisions upon arriving at the scene of a hazardous materials incident. It is designed primarily for use at a haz mat incident occurring on a highway or railroad, so there may be limited value in its application at fixed facility locations.

Directions   Using the current edition of the *ERG*, answer the following questions. Always refer to the current edition to ensure up-to-date information.

1. What is the definition of oxidizer?

   _____

   _____

2. On which orange-bordered Guide page will you find information for Titanium trichloride, pyrophoric?

   _____

3. What is the UN/NA identification number for nitrous oxide, compressed?

   _____

Figure 14.11 An assignment sheet (first page) describes an activity or project that students are expected to perform.

criteria) and some of the same material listed for the lesson plan (see information box). Assignment sheets differ from worksheets in that the assignment is a requirement and results in a graded activity.

Assignment Sheet

Step 1: Create a title that reflects the subject or topic, and relate it to the lesson.

Step 2: List all the materials and resources that students need to complete the assignment. List titles and page numbers of books, journals, or other reference material. Provide enough information so that students can locate resources quickly and easily.

Step 3: Write a brief introduction that arouses interest and motivates students to complete the assignment.

Step 4: Design the assignment sheet to present the information in a format that enables students to use and learn the material.

Step 5: Include the scoring and grading criteria for the assignment.

Step 6: Describe the form (if necessary) that the final product (essay, table, graphic, etc.) should be in as well as the format (handwritten, typed, model, etc.) and the required date for completion.

Audiovisual Components

In addition to creating lesson plans, the Level II Instructor may also be required to create or select audiovisual components for use with the lesson plan. The instructor should be familiar with the guidelines for developing effective visual aids as well as the types of equipment used to generate the images used in the visual aids.

Development Guidelines

Effective visual aids depend on the application of guidelines that have resulted from many years of effort. Trainers in the private business sector as well as professional educators have determined the best ways to present information to students. Key guidelines include the following (**Figure 14.12**):

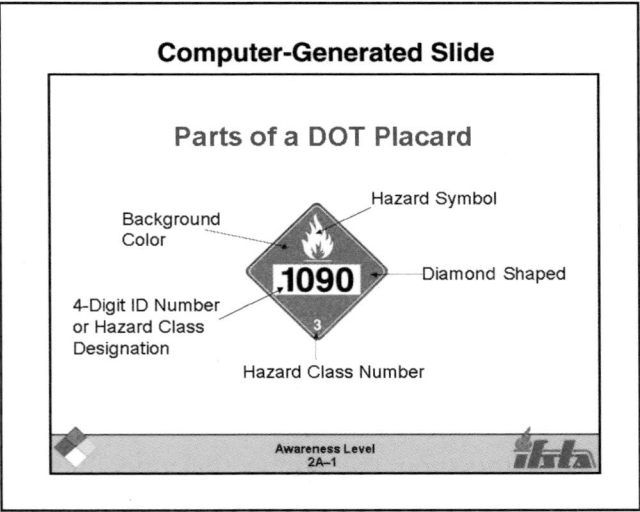

Figure 14.12 This computer-generated slide illustrates the points mentioned in the text for an effective visual aid.

- Use typefaces or fonts that are readable, consistent, and large enough to read at a distance. Font size depends on the size of the presentation room and projection screen. One guideline is to *never* use less than a 24-point size.

- Follow the *6 by 6 Rule*: Use a maximum of 6 lines down and 6 words across the viewing area.

- Limit the text to phrases, *not* complete sentences. The text helps the audience focus on the key points of the presentation. The oral presentation expands on these phrases.

- Create one heading for each slide or image. Expand with subheadings or illustrations such as graphs, charts, photographs, or clipart.

- Keep the backgrounds simple so they do *not* conflict with the text or graphics.

- Use contrasting colors between backgrounds and text.

- Keep the background color compatible with the text and graphics. Do *not* select colors that clash or distract the attention of the audience.

- Use effects (transitions and animations) sparingly because they can overpower the message that a slide or image is attempting to convey.

- Use variety in the composition of the various elements on slides or images by interspersing graphs, charts, photographs, and clipart to create interest.

- Use parallel structure on each slide or image: Start phrases with nouns and start bullets with verbs, which make points easier to link together.

- Use handouts of slides or images as necessary. Handouts can be particularly helpful when presenting complex or detailed concepts. The audience can make appropriate notes using handouts based on the slides or images; however, handouts can also become distractions by giving the audience something to look at other than the presentation.

Instructors should remember that guidelines are provided to assist in the creation of effective visual aids. There may be situations where the guidelines can be altered so that the change results in a more understandable or attractive image.

Equipment

Although instructors may *not* have all the equipment described here for the creation of audiovisual training aids, they should be familiar with what is available. Cameras, both still and video, scanners, video capture devices, and video editing equipment and software provide the instructor with the opportunity to create or modify effective training aids.

Cameras

Cameras capture images of people, equipment, and activities as they occur. The images may be captured on film or digitally in electronic memory. The image format may also be still or in motion **(Figure 14.13)**. For the purpose of categorizing these various types and formats, cameras are divided into traditional and digital photography.

Traditional photography. *Traditional photography* is the recording of images on film. The equipment used is a still camera, using 35 mm, 2¼ (57 mm), or larger film sizes, or a motion picture camera, recording on 8, 16, or 35 mm reels of film. Film may be black and white, color negative (used to produce prints), and color transparency (slides). Motion picture cameras are still in use by commercial film companies but rarely found in use by training organizations or individuals. Traditional photography is still popular, although it is being steadily replaced by digital photography.

Figure 14.13 Instructors should be familiar with the operation, use, and limitations of the photographic equipment owned by the organization. The equipment may include film or digital still cameras and video cameras.

Traditional photography requires the use of a photo-processing company or the operation of a processing laboratory within the organization. Film, processing, and printing costs can be high due to the cost of materials and labor. The advantage of traditional photography is the fact that the original negative can be used to reprint images for later use. Also, large format negatives produce high-resolution (quality) images that can be enlarged to sizes that can cover a billboard.

Digital photography. Digital photography has gained in popularity in the past decade. Both still and motion pictures can be captured in digital formats. Some still digital cameras can record short-motion segments, and some digital video cameras can capture still images. The amount of images or video that a camera can hold depends on the size of the memory chip or tape and the resolution of the individual images.

Digital photography has the advantage of not requiring the use of a photo processor in order to produce a useful image. Instructors with access to a digital camera and a computer can take high-quality photographs and integrate them into documents within minutes.

The greatest disadvantage of digital photography is the storage of the image. When images are stored on a computer hard drive, they can be lost if the computer *crashes*, wiping out the memory and files on the unit. All images (and files) should be stored on compact disc-read-only-memory

(CD-ROM), digital videodisc (DVD) storage files, or universal serial bus (USB) Portable Flash Drive (also known as *Thumbdrive*™ or *Jumpdrive*®) to prevent such a loss (**Figure 14.14**).

In addition, images that are stored in one format today may not be retrievable in 5 years due to changes in photo software. The rapid pace of computer technology has caused some government agencies to continually transfer images and files from older formats to current formats.

Scanners

A *scanner* is a peripheral computer device that allows photographs, slides, transparencies, diagrams, or illustrations to be digitized for integration into a presentation, into a document, or for storage on a CD-ROM or DVD (**Figure 14.15**). The quality of the image depends on the resolution of the scanner and the original item. The higher the resolution, the larger the size of the file created. This factor must be considered when using scanned images.

The desired end result, for example a projected image, may require very-high resolution. Printed materials such as a black and white photo in a training manual may *not* reproduce with the quality required for a projected image.

Another application of scanners is optical character recognition (OCR). This technology differentiates between text and graphics by creating a text file from a scanned document. Instructors can save a great deal of time by scanning existing documents through OCR as opposed to retyping them.

Video Capture Devices

An option for creating digital images is a *video capture device*. This medium can take an individual frame or short segment of a video and digitize it for use in a document or presentation. High-resolution analog images from a reasonably priced 8-mm video camera can be incorporated as video clips or still images into presentations.

This device can also be used to capture images from television broadcasts. The quality of the resulting image depends on the quality of the original image, broadcast signal reception, and recording equipment. As mentioned in Chapter 3, Legal and Ethical Considerations, copyright laws protect all copying of broadcast or commercially produced materials.

Video Editing Devices

Rapid advances in computer technology have made it possible for instructors to create custom training videotapes and DVDs quickly and economically. The process is known as *digital* or *desktop video editing* and uses the computer, video camera, video

Figure 14.14 Digitally produced photographic images may be stored on a variety of devices. A photo manipulation program can be used to enhance, correct, label, or categorize the images in the computer.

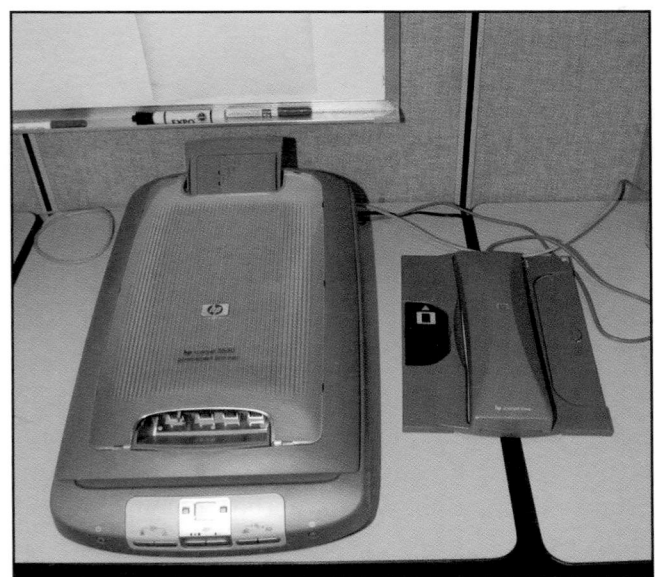

Figure 14.15 A scanner is a copying device that permits the instructor to copy, enhance, and store old film-based photo images in digital formats on the computer.

capture device, and special editing software. Video images are stored on the computer's hard drive, manipulated using the software, and copied onto DVDs using a compact disc (CD)/DVD burner. The manipulation permits the video to be edited in the following ways:

- Reduced in length
- Enhanced with sound
- Divided into chapters with text slides in between
- Accessed from the Internet/intranet
- Incorporated into presentations with other types of media

Editing Digital Images

Regardless of the device used to create or import them, digital images can be edited on a computer by using graphic or word-processing software. The following options are available for editing digital images:

- Cropping for size and shape
- Enlarging
- Reducing
- Labeling
- Enhancing
- Correcting color, contrast, and brightness
- Repairing damages to the image
- Highlighting
- Transmitting by electronic mail (e-mail) or other electronic means

Lesson Plan Evaluation and Revision

Evaluations that are specific to a particular course include those that *evaluate* the knowledge and skills of the students, the performance of the instructor, and the effectiveness of the lesson plan. Student evaluations consist of the written, oral, and skills examinations discussed in Chapter 13, Student Progress Evaluation and Testing. Instructor evaluations are discussed in Chapter 15, Instructor and Course Evaluations. Lesson plan effectiveness is discussed in this section.

Figure 14.16 The effectiveness of the instructional process can be determined by evaluating the psychomotor skills of students.

Administrators, employers, course or curriculum developers, and instructors can judge whether the course or curriculum accomplished its objectives by reviewing and assessing the results of instruction and learning (**Figure 14.16***)*. Following the evaluation of the course or curriculum, it may be necessary to revise the lesson plans to correct any deficiencies that are discovered.

Evaluation

The evaluations used to determine the performance of both the student and the instructor can also assist in determining the effectiveness of the lesson plan. The following process assists the instructor in evaluating a lesson plan:

Step 1: *Review the student evaluations*—Analyze results. *Situations:*

— When the majority of students met the evaluation criteria, lesson plan alterations may *not* be required.

— When the majority of students did *not* perform satisfactorily, a review of the instructor and course evaluations may help determine the cause.

— To determine the cause of unsatisfactory performances, review the students' training records and interview those who did *not* meet the criteria.

Step 2: *Review the instructor and course evaluations* — Look for a consistency in comments concerning the presentation style. *Considerations:*

— Determine whether factors concerning the facility such as lighting, noise, or temperature could have created a barrier to learning.

— Determine whether any external factors could have affected the teaching or learning environment.

Step 3: *Review the lesson plan* — Determine whether the learning objectives are clear, concise, and attainable. *Factors:*

— Audiovisual training aids and devices are appropriate to the topic (**Figure 14.17**).

— Time frame is sufficient to cover the required material in sufficient detail.

— Testing criteria are appropriate to the topic and teaching style.

— Testing criteria and learning objectives were properly explained to the students.

— Support materials and personnel were adequate to meet the lesson plan requirements.

— Instructor was familiar with the topic and lesson plan.

— Unforeseen elements (such as weather, equipment malfunction, or site conditions) caused a problem in the presentation.

When it is determined that there is a problem with the lesson plan, the instructor and/or training division should revise it. Revisions should be made only when they are warranted by the evaluation and are cost- and time-effective.

Revision

Revising a lesson plan generally follows the steps shown in the Lesson Plan Modification or Adaptation section. The evaluation should provide a definite list of revisions to be made. The instructor should make the revisions, and then compare the

Figure 14.17 The instructor is responsible for determining the appropriate audiovisual training aids or props for the topic being taught. This instructor is using a computer, data projector, and linked computer terminals to teach a course in report writing.

revised lesson plan to the revision list and course curriculum requirements. It may be necessary to further refine the changes to meet all requirements.

The revised lesson plan should be reviewed by other instructors, the training division or agency administration, or other experts. When possible, it should be presented to the original group of students to determine whether the revisions were effective. Effectiveness is determined through the evaluation process outlined previously.

Summary

Of all the knowledge and skills that an instructor should possess or acquire, developing effective lesson plans may be one of the most important. This skill includes the creation of clear, concise, attainable, and measurable learning objectives. Learning objectives provide not only the outline for the lesson but they are also the criteria for evaluating student performance.

Instructors who attempt to work without a lesson plan run the risk of being ineffective in the classroom. They may also waste their time and the time of students, provide inaccurate or incorrect information, or simply lose the attention of students. At the same time instructors should remember that good instructors who develop highly structured and detailed plans rarely adhere to them in lock-step fashion. Such rigidity may hinder, rather than help, the learning process.

The components of the lesson plan should be thought of as guiding principles to be applied as aids (but *not* blueprints) to systematic instruction. Precise preparation must allow for flexible delivery. During actual classroom interaction, the instructor needs to make adaptations and add artistry to each lesson plan and classroom presentation.

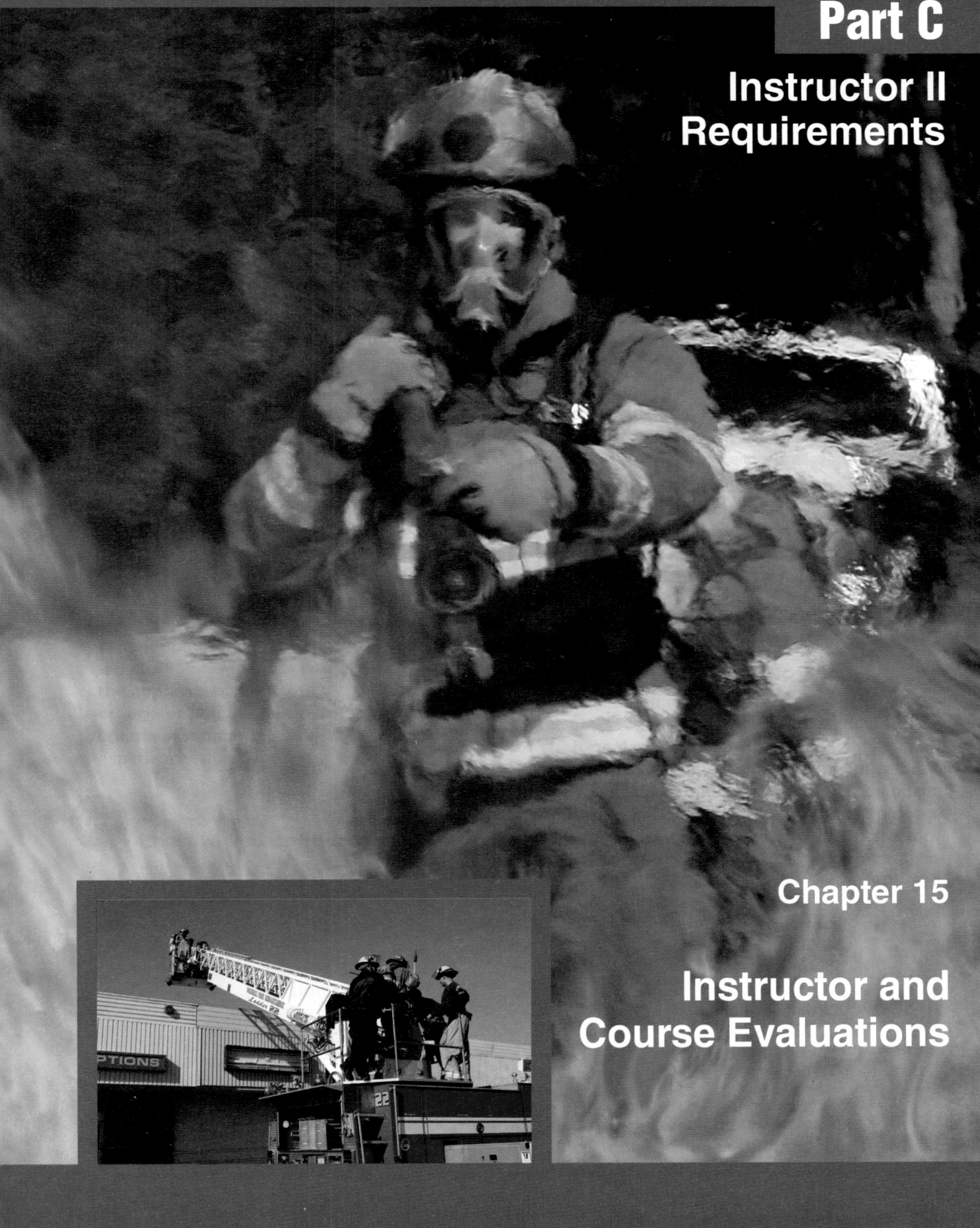

Part C

Instructor II Requirements

Chapter 15

Instructor and Course Evaluations

- Personality of either the instructor or the student

- Preconceived idea held by the student

- How frustrated or pressured the student feels at the time the form is completed

Sufficient time should always be provided for students to complete the survey at the end of the session or course. *Never* send the survey home with students and expect them to return it. Research indicates that there is a very low rate of return on this type of survey.

Student surveys of instructor performance should include questions on the following instructor characteristics:

- Preparation

- Presentation skills

- Knowledge of the subject

- Interest and enthusiasm for the subject

- Ability to answer questions from students

- Interaction with students **(Figure 15.4)**

- Concern for students

Figure 15.4 One indication of the effectiveness of an instructor is how well that person interacts with students. *Courtesy of Iowa Fire Service Training Bureau.*

- Strengths (both interpersonal and instructional)

- Weaknesses (both interpersonal and instructional)

- Time-management skills

- Whether students would take another class with this instructor

The completed student surveys should be gathered and forwarded to the instructor's supervisor. The answers from all the surveys should be compiled and reviewed to determine the effectiveness of the instructor. When apparent weaknesses are consistently mentioned on the forms, a counseling session with the instructor should be scheduled to determine an appropriate solution.

The need to provide anonymity for students is very important when they complete evaluations on instructors who may be from the same department/agency (in-house training). The training division/agency should develop a policy that requires the instructor to leave the room while evaluations are being completed and appoint a volunteer to be responsible for collecting the completed evaluations and sealing them in an envelope for the instructor **(Figure 15.5)**.

Organizations that have this type of policy should also provide a through summary report to the instructor. Students should *not* be permitted to sign the evaluation forms.

Figure 15.5 Student volunteers are used to collect instructor evaluation forms.

Course/Lesson Evaluations

Sometimes instructors only use student test results to evaluate the effectiveness of a course or lesson. However, there are many other types of data that collectively give a more complete picture of the effectiveness of the teaching/learning process. The following two kinds of evaluation provide an approach for looking at the process and the product of the instructional process:

- *Formative evaluation*—Looks at the process of course development and instruction

- *Summative evaluation*—Looks at the product and evaluates reactions to the course and instructional methods

In both cases, it is important that the evaluation process is useful to planners and decision makers; therefore, data collection must be accurate. Evaluation instruments should always be easy to administer, and results should be easy to report. Planning the evaluation approach is very important.

Considerations for Planning

To get the most from a course/lesson evaluation, the instructor must plan the approach by thinking through and answering the following questions:

- How did students feel about the training? What did they learn? How did training affect their attitudes and behavior? What were the organizational results?

- How can items addressed be answered? Will information gathering be administered by paper-and-pencil tests, questionnaires, or surveys? Will tests require students to demonstrate their new knowledge and skills in role-plays, simulations, or actual performances? If not, why?

- What are the objectives of the training course or curriculum? Are the evaluation criteria based on these objectives? If not, why?

- Do the criteria indicate improvement between expected and actual performance when measured against the results of the needs analysis? If not, why?

- What data sources are already available to help measure results (productivity reports, daily log sheets, and training and personnel records)?

- What alternative methods for gathering data are available (interviews and on-site observations)?

- What are the best and most cost-effective methods for measuring the results of training? Are there less costly, more efficient ways of administering the evaluation? If so, what are they? If not, why?

In evaluating the instructional process, it is critical that the training organization or agency make clear to anyone involved *what* is to be evaluated and *why*. Answering *what* and *why* clarifies and guides how evaluation is to be conducted and eliminates misunderstanding. A thorough evaluation includes analyzing the following essential areas of the instructional process and answering the questions related to each area:

- *Reaction* — Were students satisfied with the course? If not, why? Were instructors and management officials satisfied with the learning that occurred? If not, why?

- *Knowledge*—What new knowledge did students acquire and demonstrate?

- *Skills* — What new skills did students acquire and demonstrate?

- *Attitudes* — How has the training changed students' opinions, values, and beliefs?

- *Transfer of learning* — How has the training affected the ways students perform on their jobs?

- *Results* — How has the training contributed to accomplishing organizational goals and objectives?

Formative Evaluations

A *formative evaluation* is the ongoing, repeated checking during course development and during instruction to determine the most effective instructional content, presentation methods, training aids, and testing techniques. Two ways to conduct formative evaluations are field tests and observations. Formative evaluations answer questions such as the following:

- Does the course provide the appropriate information and learning format? If not, why?

Figure 15.6 The formative evaluation can help to determine whether the instructor has selected the appropriate method for teaching a particular topic. For instance, a demonstration may be the more effective means for teaching the use of an extrication tool.

- Is the instructor teaching the right content and using the most appropriate methods to facilitate learning? If not, why? **(Figure 15.6)**
- Have students learned in the most efficient way possible? If so, how? If not, why?

Field Test

The course objectives or outcomes serve as the primary criteria against which judgments are made. Objectives are developed before the course is designed. Course design and how it works with the objectives are field-tested in a *pilot course* before the course is finalized. A *field test* is the process of teaching the course on a trial basis to determine whether the following components are addressed:

- Sequence of material facilitates learning.
- Teaching methods and aids are appropriate to the objectives and effective in teaching the material.
- Objectives can be met within the designated time frame.
- Testing procedures are adequate and appropriate for the course objectives.
- Course can be revised before using it on a regular basis when necessary.

Observation

Evaluation is *not* a static, one-time event; it occurs at all times throughout development and instruction. Just as testing occurs throughout instruction, course evaluation occurs before, during, and after instruction. Instructors can gather different kinds of data, most of which are based on observation, during the course. The instructor wants to be attentive to the following factors:

- Student interest in the subject
- Level of student participation
- Student reaction to exercises and activities
- Level of student questions and comments
- Level of student frustration
- Level of student sense of achievement
- Student test results

With feedback received during the course, instructors can change or modify instructional methods to meet the needs of the students. In some cases, it will be clear that a course needs to be changed on a permanent basis. The judgment of instructors is critical when making decisions about a curriculum or course that is under development.

Summative Evaluations

A *summative evaluation* is an end-of-the-course appraisal that commonly measures learning by some form of objective or subjective evaluation instrument. It is also used to evaluate the reactions of students and instructors to each other and the course. Some examples of how summative or reaction evaluations are gathered include observing and reporting unexpected learning outcomes or performing follow-up surveys of students, their supervisors, and their instructors. Surveys can ask about the effectiveness of the course, its activities, and its job relevance. Summative evaluations answer the following questions:

- Have students learned what is needed to perform their work duties on their jobs? If not, why?

- Was instruction effective so that it met learning/performance objectives? If not, why?

- Were instructional activities relevant to job tasks? If not, why?

Evaluating a training course or lesson involves determining the satisfaction of the students with the course or topic. Students who participate in an *effective* training course/lesson appreciate the time they spend there and the information they learn. Likewise, students are the first to recognize a training course/lesson that is ineffective or inappropriate and will make their displeasures known (**Figure 15.7**).

Like the student evaluation of the instructor, the evaluation of the course/lesson can be very subjective. The course/lesson evaluation form should contain questions that focus students on their perceptions of their learning experience and the learning environment. The course/lesson evaluation form should include questions that provide information on the following elements:

- Effectiveness of the course/lesson objectives

- Length of the course/lesson

- Course/lesson scheduling

- Classroom environment (lighting, noise, seating, temperature, etc.)

- Overall impressions of the course/lesson

- Types of visual training aids used and their effectiveness

- Student expectations of the course/lesson

- Value of the course/lesson

- Relationship of the course/lesson to students' duties or job

- Safety-related concerns or issues

Figure 15.7 Although student course evaluations may be very subjective, students are eager to express their feelings about the value of the learning experience. *Courtesy of Iowa Fire Service Training Bureau.*

The answers on most survey forms for instructors and courses/lessons usually provide the respondent with the opportunity to answer on a continuum from *very satisfied* to *very dissatisfied.* Assigning numerical values from *1 (poor)* to *5 (best)* can provide the ability to statistically average the responses of a single class or multiple classes (**Figure 15.8, pp. 366 and 367**).

All surveys should have space for open-ended answers or comments. General comments permit students to express more complete thoughts that may not be represented by a numerical value or specific question. Students should *not* be required to sign their survey form, although a signature line may be provided as *optional* in the event the student wishes to be contacted in order to voluntarily provide additional information.

Supervisory Personnel Surveys

The training course/lesson evaluation process also includes surveys of supervisory personnel such as incident commanders (ICs), supervisors, and division managers within the organization. These supervisory personnel work with the individuals who complete the training course/lesson. They are aware of any changes in the skills, behaviors, and attitudes that these individuals display on the job following completion of the course. Supervisory personnel provide invaluable information about the successes and results of training courses.

These survey forms can be distributed to the appropriate supervisory personnel within a few weeks of completion of the course/lesson or posted

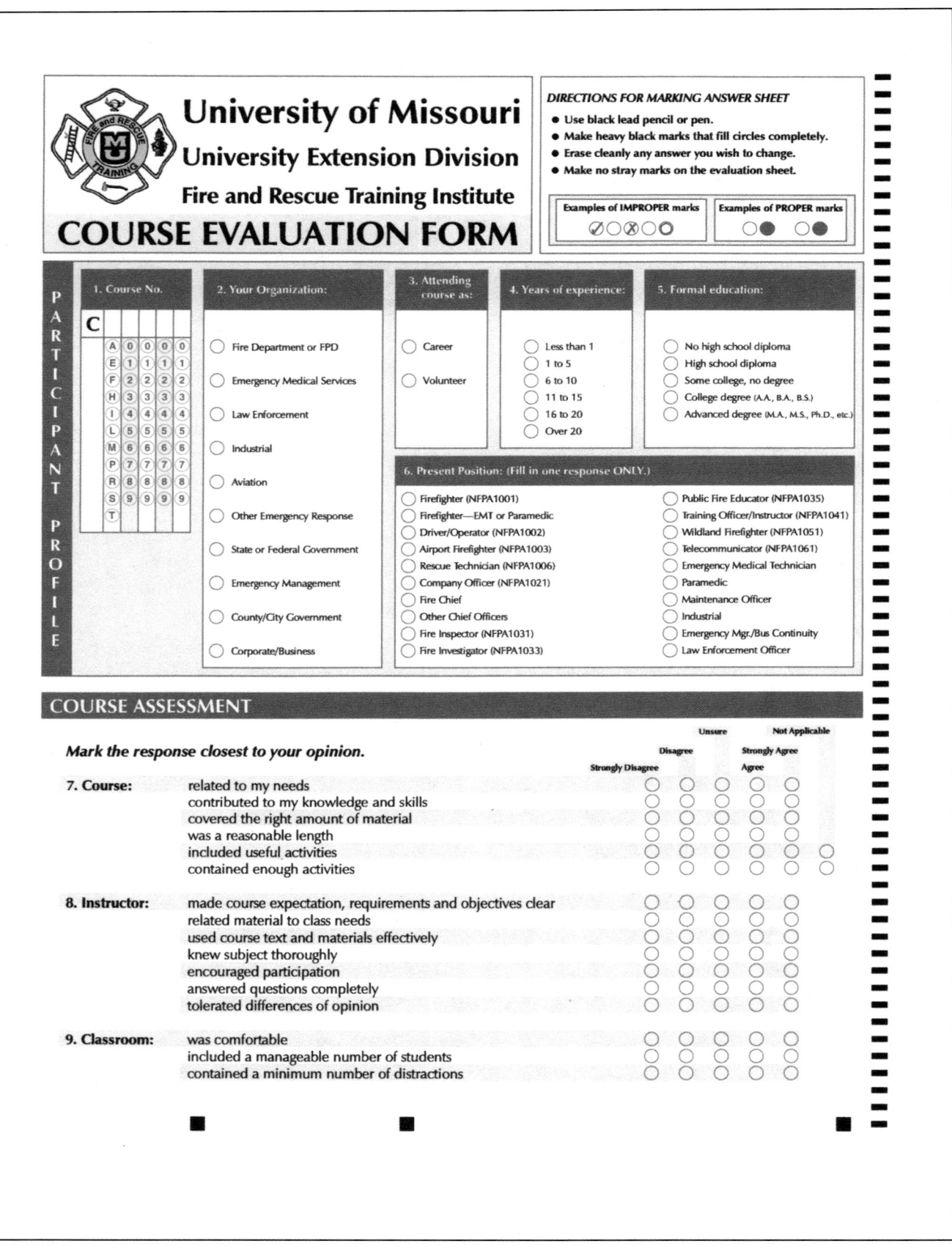

Figure 15.8 A course evaluation survey form should include both specific questions that are easy to evaluate and open-ended questions that permit students to express opinions freely. *Courtesy of Fire and Rescue Training Institute, University of Missouri.*

COURSE ASSESSMENT (continued)

Mark the response closest to your opinion.

		Strongly Disagree	Disagree	Unsure	Agree	Strongly Agree	Not Applicable
10. Outside Activities:	included a manageable number of students	○	○	○	○	○	
	adequate/enough equipment available	○	○	○	○	○	
	activities performed were realistic	○	○	○	○	○	
	activities performed were relevant to the course objectives	○	○	○	○	○	
	adequate opportunity given to perform the activities	○	○	○	○	○	
	no outside activities	○	○	○	○	○	○
11. Visual materials were:	related to the course	○	○	○	○	○	
	good quality	○	○	○	○	○	
	in appropriate number	○	○	○	○	○	
	easy to see	○	○	○	○	○	
12. Printed materials were:	well organized	○	○	○	○	○	
	complete	○	○	○	○	○	
	readable (printed well)	○	○	○	○	○	

SUGGESTIONS

13. How could the course content or structure be improved?

14. How could the instructor improve the class delivery?

15. How could the classroom be improved?

16. How could outside activities be improved?

17. How could the audiovisual materials be improved to increase learning?

18. How could the printed materials be improved to increase learning?

Please feel free to use additional blank paper, if additional comments are needed.

CHECK FRONT PAGE TO MAKE SURE YOU HAVE COMPLETED ALL QUESTIONS.

SCANTRON CUSTOM FORM NO. F-15591-UOMFRT   **Thank you for your cooperation.**   ©SCANTRON CORPORATION 2001 ALL RIGHTS RESERVED   PC2 1901-254-5 4 3 2 1

Figure 15.8 *Continued*

Part II: Supervisor and Department Statistics

1. How many years have you been in Fire and Emergency Services?

○ Less than one year
○ 1 - 5 years
○ 6 - 10 years
○ 11 - 15 years
○ 16 - 20 years
○ More than 20 years

2. How long have you been this employee's supervisor?

○ less than one year
○ 1 - 5 years
○ More than 5 years

3. Approximately how many members are there in your department?

○ 1 to 25   ○ 201 to 500
○ 26 to 50   ○ 501 to 1000
○ 51 to 100   ○ 1001 to 2000
○ 101 to 200   ○ More than 2000

4. What percent of your department has had NFA training? *(For example, fill in bubbles 1, 0, 0 if the percent is 100; and fill in bubbles 0, 5, 0 if the percent trained at NFA is 50%)*

First digit of percent	⓪ ①
Second digit of percent	⓪ ① ② ③ ④ ⑤ ⑥ ⑦ ⑧ ⑨
Third digit of percent	⓪ ① ② ③ ④ ⑤ ⑥ ⑦ ⑧ ⑨

5. Please estimate the size of the population served by your department/organization.

○ Under 2500   ○ 10,000 - 24,999
○ 2,501 - 4,999   ○ 25,000 - 49,999
○ 5,000 - 9,999   ○ 50,000 - 99,999
           ○ 100,000 or more

6. Have you ever attended NFA sponsored courses? (Mark as many as apply.)

○ Yes, NFA Direct Delivery/SWP class(es)
○ Yes, NFA Regional Delivery class(es)
○ Yes, NFA Off-Campus Hazmat class(es)
○ Yes, NFA Resident class(es) at Maryland
○ Yes, other NFA classes
○ No, I have never attended NFA classes

If you have never attended NFA classes, is this because you think the course(s) would . . . (Mark all that apply.)

○ Not be up to your expectations?
○ Have material that is too dated?
○ Take too much away from your work time?
○ Require too much traveling?
○ Be more useful if offered online?
○ Conflict with family responsibilities?
○ Other: _____

---

1. What changes, if any, have you seen in your employee as a result of attending the NFA training class?

_____
_____
_____

2. Has the attendee proposed any organizational changes since the training? If so, please describe them, and indicate how these changes have impacted your department.

_____
_____
_____

3. Please tell us what you think are the new, emerging issues in the fire/emergency services field that should be topics for future NFA courses.

_____
_____
_____

4. Additional comments?

_____
_____
_____

Thank you for completing this questionnaire. Please return it to the National Fire Academy in the postage paid envelope provided.

001306

DO NOT MARK IN THIS AREA

FF, 95-58, NOV 02   SCANTRON CUSTOM FORM NO. F-8872-NETC © SCANTRON CORPORATION 2003 ALL RIGHTS RESERVED PC8 1603 553 5 4 3 2 1

Figure 15.9 *Continued*

Step 3: *Document and report results to superiors*
— *Actions:*

— Keep daily records of training activities.

— Maintain individual training records.

— Retain class test results and results of analyses.

— Provide written progress reports to management that outline recommendations in Steps 1 and 2.

Summary

Level II Instructors generally have the responsibility of supervising other instructors in the training division. This responsibility includes evaluating the job-performance duties of each subordinate as well as evaluating the courses and lessons that the instructors are responsible for teaching. To fulfill this responsibility, the instructor-supervisor must be trained in the following elements:

- Use of evaluation techniques

- Administration of the organization's personnel evaluation program

- Development of evaluation forms and surveys

- Use of information gained from student evaluations of instructors and courses

The instructor-supervisor may also be required to create the requisite evaluation form. The skills required must be fully understood and practiced to produce accurate and applicable information that can be used to improve instructor presentations and training division courses.

Online Course and Instructor Surveys

In the traditional classroom, students complete course and instructor surveys at the end of the course or class period. The primary advantage to this timing is that all surveys will be completed and accounted for. A disadvantage is the lack of time that students have to provide a full and accurate evaluation of the course. Most are anxious to leave the class and return to the station or their homes. Students are also influenced by what has occurred during that class session. In addition, students who are absent on the day the survey is completed miss an opportunity to express their views.

In the virtual classroom of online instruction, the survey provides many advantages over the traditional method. Online surveys can be used for both online and traditional courses as long as all students have access to a computer that is linked to the Internet. Some advantages to online surveys are as follows:

- Data are compiled electronically, reducing human error and time involvement.

- Results are available rapidly.

- Data can be quickly converted to graphic illustrations of the survey results.

- Students may complete the survey at their leisure (although a time frame must be imposed if the surveys are to be available when they are required).

- The amount of paper that traditional surveys require is reduced.

- Course data can be easily and quickly compared to the results generated in other classes.

- The time generally required to complete the survey in class is removed, thereby adding to actual instruction time.

To be successful, online surveys must have the following characteristics:

- Surveys must be completed in a specified time period.

- Although anonymous, surveys must have some type of tracking method to ensure that they are all completed.

- The information in the surveys must be secure to prevent tampering or altering the responses.

- Surveys must provide students with the same opportunities found in traditional surveys to answer objectively and subjectively.

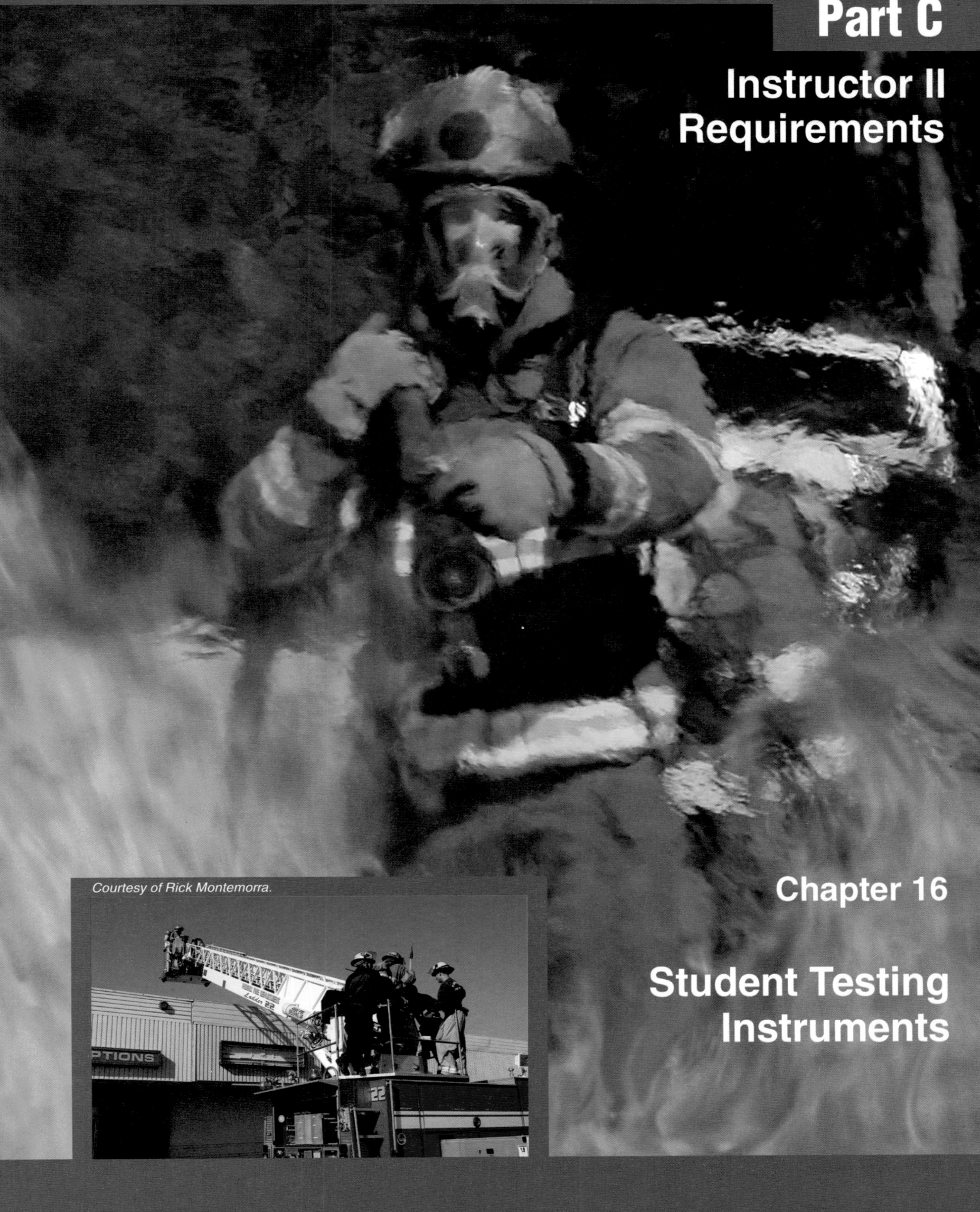

Part C

Instructor II Requirements

Courtesy of Rick Montemorra.

Chapter 16

Student Testing Instruments

After reading this chapter, students will be able to —

1. List the steps in test planning.

2. Identify facts about determining test purpose and type.

3. Identify accurate statements about identifying and defining learning objectives.

4. Identify facts about preparing test specifications.

5. Discuss matching test items to learning objectives.

6. Identify testing language and comprehension barriers.

7. Identify factors that give clues to test answers.

8. Identify accurate statements about selecting the proper level of test item difficulty.

9. Identify facts about determining the appropriate number of test items.

10. List characteristics that ensure test usability.

11. Discuss test validity and reliability.

12. List the three basic types of test instruments.

13. Identify facts about common considerations for all tests.

14. Explain the differences between objective and subjective tests.

15. Identify accurate statements about components of multiple-choice test items.

16. Identify guidelines for constructing multiple-choice test items.

17. List advantages and disadvantages of multiple-choice test items.

18. Identify guidelines for creating true-false test items.

19. Distinguish between advantages and disadvantages of true-false test items.

20. Identify guidelines for creating matching test items.

21. List advantages and disadvantages of matching test items.

22. Identify guidelines for creating short-answer/completion test items.

23. List advantages and disadvantages of short-answer/completion test items.

24. List guidelines for creating an essay test item.

25. Distinguish between advantages and disadvantages of essay test items.

26. Identify guidelines for creating an interpretive exercise.

27. Distinguish between advantages and disadvantages of interpretive exercises.

28. Discuss oral tests.

29. List advantages and disadvantages of oral tests.

30. Identify guidelines for creating performance tests.

31. Distinguish between advantages and disadvantages of performance tests.

32. Define scoring and grading.

33. Discuss the criterion-referenced grading system.

34. Identify accurate statements about scoring methods.

35. Identify facts about test item and result analyses.

36. List corrective techniques for skewed test results.

Chapter Contents

Test Planning Steps
  Determine Test Purpose and Type
  Identify and Define Learning Objectives
  Prepare Test Specifications
  Construct Appropriate Test Items

Test Instruments
  Common Considerations for All Tests
  Written Test Types
  Oral Tests
  Performance (Skills) Tests

Test Data Collection
  Criterion-Referenced Grading System
  Scoring Methods

Test Item and Result Analyses
  Validity and Reliability Components
  Statistical Test Result Analysis
  Test Item Analysis
  Corrective Techniques

Summary

Chapter 16
Student Testing Instruments

Training programs, curriculums, courses, and lessons are *not* complete without a method to measure that learning actually occurred. Common measurement terms and processes used in the teaching field include *evaluation* and *testing*. Selecting the appropriate term is often based on the type of measurement.

As mentioned in the previous chapter, the act of *evaluating* involves establishing the worth or value of an item, person, program, process, or organization based on the desired outcome. Evaluating learning refers to methods of identifying the effects and judging the effectiveness of learning experiences, courses, or complete curriculums. Evaluation is *terminal*, meaning that it is the measurement of the end product or outcome of learning.

The term *evaluation* is sometimes used interchangeably with the term *assessment*. Assessment refers to the processes used to determine the knowledge, skills, and abilities of a student by observation and the application of special activities such as quizzes, examinations, oral tests, and similar testing devices. Assessment can also include measuring student knowledge levels before and after the learning experience — a valuable part of an evaluation process. Assessment is a broad term, which reflects the kind of testing and measuring that instructors must do.

A *test* is a means by which the absence, presence, amount, or nature of some student quality or ability is observed or inferred and appraised or measured. All of the measurement terms have the same goal: measuring student knowledge, attitudes, and skills. To some extent, tests assess changes in attitudes, values, and beliefs. Therefore,

the use of both pretests and posttests can establish the extent to which a student's attitudes, values, or beliefs have changed.

Historically, the term *testing* has implied that the testing instrument was a paper-and-pencil measurement tool. Paper-and-pencil testing involved the student reading the test questions from a sheet and answering them with the use of a pencil and test booklet or answer sheet. The result was scored by hand or an electrical/mechanical scoring device and used to assign a grade.

Paper-and-pencil testing has been the traditional form of testing in the fire and emergency services and continues to be used for determining cognitive learning achievements. Coupled with psychomotor skills testing by observation, paper-and-pencil testing provides a means of determining whether a student is ready to move to the next level of learning.

The current trend in testing is to determine student status with a wide variety of measuring devices. A variety of testing methods also measure the many important kinds of learning that cannot be measured appropriately by paper-and-pencil tests or assessments alone. One of the more recent trends is computer-based testing that can replace the paper-and-pencil method. A computer provides a wide variety of testing possibilities based on the learning styles of students and the learning outcome needs of the organization.

Many organizations use professionally prepared tests that may be part of a purchased curriculum or are acquired separately from a commercial test preparation company. Because commercially prepared tests are *not* validated and may lack reliability, training organizations must validate and certify the tests locally. This validation requires determining the reliability of the test items based on local requirements.

These prepared tests are validated and checked for reliability, but they may *not* always accurately test specific jurisdictional criteria and policies or reflect instructional methods and learning styles. For these reasons, instructors may often find that they need to develop test questions or entire tests in order to appropriately measure the learning that has taken place in their courses.

Because creating a test is *not* an easy process, this chapter discusses the importance of knowing how to plan tests, including what to consider when creating tests, and how to select and develop the appropriate evaluation tool from the many common instruments. This chapter also describes the common considerations used in all types of test instruments.

Other important aspects of this chapter are how to interpret test data once they are collected and how instructors use the data once a test is given and scored. The Level II Instructor candidate should review the information in Chapter 13, Student Progress Evaluation and Testing, which includes information on administering student tests.

Test Planning Steps

The key to designing effective tests is careful planning. Planning ensures that instructors and training organizations can measure the appropriate learning outcomes, include an adequate sample of the intended learning outcomes, and have the type of evidence needed to make sound instructional decisions. Test planning includes the following four steps:

Step 1: Determine test purpose and type.

Step 2: Identify and define learning objectives or learning outcomes.

Step 3: Prepare test specifications.

Step 4: Construct appropriate test items.

Constructing appropriate test items (Step 4) can be fairly easy when the instructor pays attention to and completes the first three steps of the planning process. The sections that follow describe the four test planning steps.

Terminology

The terms *test item* and *question* are often used synonymously; however, they are different. *Test item* is a generic term for all types of statements or lists to which students must respond. *Question* is a type of test item that is denoted by the use of a question mark *(?).* A question is just one type of test item along with true/false statements, fill-in-the-blank statements, completion statements, and matching lists. In this manual, the term *test item* is used to include all of these types of statements or lists.

Determine Test Purpose and Type

As mentioned earlier, the primary purpose of testing is to determine the amount of learning that has resulted from instruction. Instruction must be based on learning objectives and, therefore, the test must match those objectives. When an objective requires performance of a psychomotor skill, instructors must demonstrate the skill and allow students to practice it **(Figure 16.1)**. The test must evaluate each student's performance of that skill and *not* require a cognitive written test on it.

However, there are other considerations when determining the purpose of a test. Test developers must ask: *Is the test to assess student performance against a set criterion or rank individual performance against other students?* The answer to that question determines whether test developers create a criterion-referenced or norm-referenced test.

The majority of tests written for fire and emergency services personnel are criterion-based, using criteria that have been established through the following sources:

- Adoption of NFPA professional qualifications standards

- Federal, state/provincial, or local requirements

- Other professionally accepted requirements

Norm-referenced tests should *not* be used as end-of-course or certification tests, although they may be used for promotional examinations for the purpose of ranking applicants. A review of the test classification definitions given in Chapter 13, Student Progress Evaluation and Testing, is as follows:

Figure 16.1 Evaluations measure how well students have learned the course material. *Courtesy of Kenneth Krulish, Jr.*

- *Criterion-referenced tests* — Compare performance against appropriate minimum standards.
- *Norm-referenced tests* — Rate student performance compared to other students based on broad sampling.

Test developers must consider other relevant factors when determining the type of test to use in measuring learning. When planning tests, the instructor should consider the following factors:

- Whether the test is designed to determine readiness for instruction or placement in the appropriate instructional level (prescriptive or placement test)
- Whether the test is designed to measure improved progress or identify learning problems that are hampering progress (formative or progress test)
- Whether the test is designed to diagnose or determine student-learning difficulties (diagnostic test)
- Whether the test is designed to rate terminal performance (summative or comprehensive test)

All four types of tests listed have common characteristics and often an overlap exists between the categories. For instance, summative test questions may be included in a formative test to determine whether unit objectives have been learned before advancing to another unit within the course. **Table 16.1, p. 378,** describes the characteristics of each of the four types of tests.

The purpose of a test also depends on the learning domain that is being tested. Therefore, the instructor must also consider the following factors when planning tests:

- Whether the test measures technical knowledge retention and recall in the cognitive domain, which requires the use of written or oral tests
- Whether the test measures manipulative skills in the psychomotor domain, which requires the use of performance or skill tests
- Whether the test measures behavioral changes in attitude, values, or beliefs in the affective domain, which requires written, oral, or performance tests

Identify and Define Learning Objectives

Once the purpose and type of test has been determined, the instructor must identify and define the learning objectives that are required to achieve the test purpose. Learning objectives are generally created in a hierarchal format with the course or learning outcomes at the top stated in very general terms, followed by more specific

Table 16.1
Test Types Characteristics

All Test Types			
• Objective • General results		• Replicable (Reliability) • Valid Methodology (Validity)	
Prescriptive Test	**Diagnostic Test**	**Formative Test**	**Summative Test**
• *Definition:* Test given before course • *Purpose:* Completes areas of need • Determines the current level of student knowledge and skills • Determines the areas where the student needs additional knowledge or skills • Uses scoring of test items for placement purposes • Uses questions based on course prerequisite knowledge and skills • Determines knowledge (criterion-referenced) • Determines placement in class (norm-referenced)	• *Definition:* Test given before or at the beginning of course • *Purpose:* Finds areas of need • Determines weaknesses in the student's ability to learn • Provides results that are evaluated but *not* graded • Uses questions based on prerequisite knowledge and skills • Determines student testing abilities by using multiple types of test items	• *Definition:* Test given during course • *Purpose:* Determines student progress, strengths, and weaknesses • Uses objective test items • Evaluates a small quantity of material over a short period of time • Uses norm- or criterion-referenced test items • Focuses on the process of learning	• *Definition:* Test given at the end of course • *Purpose:* Evaluates success of both teaching and learning • Uses objective test items • Uses norm- or criterion-referenced test items • Evaluates a large quantity of material over a long period of time • Focuses on the products of learning

learning objectives for each subunit and lesson (**Figure 16.2**). Lesson objectives are the most detailed and the test questions are specifically written to address them.

Course planners (who are generally Level III certified instructors) establish learning outcomes for the proposed course to provide instructors with targets or goals toward which they can develop lesson plans, create learning objectives, and direct their instruction. Course outcomes establish the desired general results of a particular course.

Course outcomes also provide testing and evaluation requirements or criteria. For example, when a course is designed to develop the ability to perform a series of tasks, instructors must determine whether students who have completed the course can actually perform those tasks.

One of the models available for creating domain specific tests was developed by Dr. Benjamin Bloom* in 1956. The model consists of a comprehensive and systematic method for classifying the learning outcomes for each of the domains. As presented in Chapter 7, Principles of Learning, Bloom divided the learning outcomes for the cognitive domain into six categories. Within each category, further divisions were established as follows:

● *Knowledge* — Ability to remember previously learned information; includes the following:

— Specifics and specific facts

— Terms

— Ways and means of dealing with specific facts

— Conventions

— Trends and sequences

— Classifications and categories

— Criteria

— Methodologies

— Universals and abstractions

— Principles and generalizations

— Theories and structures

- *Comprehension* — Ability to understand the meaning of the information; includes the following:
  - *Translation:* Ability to convert from one form to another
  - *Interpretation:* Ability to explain or summarize information
  - *Extrapolation:* Ability to extend the meaning of the information beyond the given data
- *Application* — Ability to put information to use in actual situations
- *Analysis* — Ability to divide the information into its most basic components; includes the following:
  - *Elements:* Ability to identify the parts of the whole
  - *Relationships:* Ability to identify relationships between the basic components
  - *Organizational principles:* Ability to identify the organization of the structure or information
- *Synthesis* — Ability to assemble component parts into a larger body of information; does the following:
  - Produces a unique communication
  - Produces a plan or set of operational steps
  - Develops a set of abstract relations
- *Evaluation* — Ability to judge the value or worth of the information based on a set of definite criteria; does the following:
  - Develops judgments based on internal evidence
  - Develop judgments based on external criteria

The level of difficulty increases from the beginning of the categories and within each category. The teaching process is based on this hierarchy, moving the student from the simplest information to the more complex. Testing would naturally follow this progression too.

---

* From Benjamin S. Bloom, et al., *Taxonomy of Educational Objectives.* Published by Allyn and Bacon, Boston, MA. Copyright © 1984 by Pearson Education, Adapted by permission of the publisher.

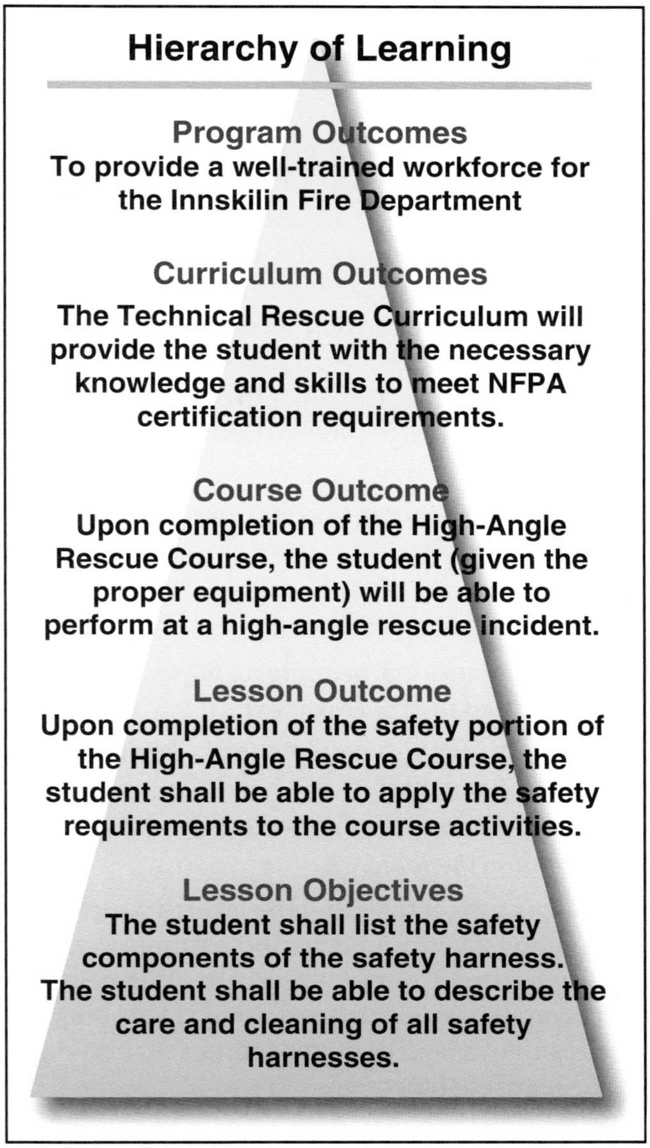

Hierarchy of Learning

Program Outcomes
To provide a well-trained workforce for the Innskilin Fire Department

Curriculum Outcomes
The Technical Rescue Curriculum will provide the student with the necessary knowledge and skills to meet NFPA certification requirements.

Course Outcome
Upon completion of the High-Angle Rescue Course, the student (given the proper equipment) will be able to perform at a high-angle rescue incident.

Lesson Outcome
Upon completion of the safety portion of the High-Angle Rescue Course, the student shall be able to apply the safety requirements to the course activities.

Lesson Objectives
The student shall list the safety components of the safety harness. The student shall be able to describe the care and cleaning of all safety harnesses.

Figure 16.2 Course outcomes depend on the accomplishment of learning objectives found in each lesson of the course.

The first step in defining the learning outcomes is to list the terminal or final outcomes desired (or required) for the course. These outcomes are stated in general terms such as the following:

Upon completion of this course, students will be able to demonstrate that they:

1. *Know the meanings of commonly used terms.*
2. *Know specific facts relating to the topic.*
3. *Know basic procedures for applying the topic.*

4. *Comprehend the principles regarding the topic.*

5. *Apply the principles of the topic in practice.*

To further define each of these general requirements, more specific learning objectives are written in clear, concise terms that have observable results. The learning objectives contain action verbs that describe the expected student performance for the instructor or test evaluator to observe. Specific, topic-related test items are based on these learning outcomes and objectives. An example of learning objectives for one of the previous learning outcomes is as follows:

1. *Know the meanings of commonly used terms.*
   A. *Identify the correct definitions of the terms.*
   B. *Identify the meanings of the terms when used in proper context.*
   C. *Distinguish between terms on the basis of meaning.*
   D. *Select appropriate terms when describing the topic.*

Learning objectives and the level to which each student must be trained are indications of what is to be measured. Course planners base all measurements on what students are directed to accomplish as a result of a course of instruction that is taught to the learning objectives.

Learning objectives also provide students with a self-assessment tool. By having a list of the learning objectives with the lesson or course outline, students are able to determine whether they are accomplishing the requirements of each learning objective as they complete the course of instruction. They are also better prepared for success in comprehensive final or summative tests.

Prepare Test Specifications

Test specifications are the roadmaps or blueprints for the construction of valid tests that accurately describe the level of learning that is being measured. Test specifications also ensure that a representative sampling of questions are created to determine student understanding of the learning objectives and course outcomes.

Although there are a variety of procedures for developing test specifications, this chapter focuses on the two more commonly used procedures for norm-referenced and criterion-referenced tests: table of specifications and test planning sheet. To assist in the test planning process, the instructor must also determine the number of test items that can be included on a test in a specified period of time.

Table of Specification

One of the most commonly used tools for creating norm-referenced tests is the two-way chart or grid known as the *table of specifications*. Other terms used to define the same chart are *test blueprint*, *formal specifications*, *master chart*, or *matrix of content and behaviors*.

The table is created before writing the test or, more appropriately, when planning the lesson or course. Each column of the chart lists the learning objectives or skills levels being tested. Each row of the chart lists the key concepts or content of the test being measured (**Table 16.2**). The *cells* or boxes created by the intersection of the columns and rows contain numbers that represent the number of test items to be devoted to each learning objective and concept. Determining the number of test items (questions) is discussed later in the Test Item and Result Analyses section.

According to some educational authorities, the table of specifications should represent the following six major elements:

1. Balance between the desired goals for the test
2. Balance between the levels of learning
3. Test format
4. Total number of test items
5. Number of test items for each goal and learning level
6. Learning objectives for each goal

The table of specifications should contain the following items:

- *Table heading* — Contains the name or title of the lesson/course, the time period allotted for taking the test, and the date the test is to be administered.

- *Subject matter digest* — Defines the subject or topic to be tested in a brief paragraph. It ensures

Table 16.2
Table of Specifications

Firefighter I Course

Student Lesson 7: __Fire Hose__   Test Date: ____10/28/2005____
Time Allotted: __90 minutes__   Test Developed by: ____J. Fortney____

At the end of the lesson, the recruit firefighter will be able to successfully identify, use, store, and care for fire service hose.

Topic	Number of Test Items							
	Learning Objectives							
	Knowledge (1)			Comprehension (2)			Application (3)	Total
	Terms	Facts	Criteria	Translation	Interpretation	Extrapolation		
Types of Hose	5	5	5					15
Use of Hose	5		5	5			15	30
Storage of Hose	5			5	5		15	30
Care of Hose		5	5				10	20
Cleaning of Hose			5	5	5		10	25
Test Item Total	15	10	20	15	10		50	120

that the material presented in the lesson/course and tested for in the final exam meet the established criteria or objectives.

- *Learning objectives* — Lists objectives across the top of the table and includes the major titles such as *Knows, Comprehends, Applies, Analyzes, Synthesizes,* or *Evaluates*. The topic and level of learning determine which titles are used.

- *Learning objectives, subheadings* — Lists the more specific objectives being tested for in the row just below the learning objectives. For instance, under *Knows,* the subheadings might be *Terms, Specifics, Facts, Criteria,* etc. Test items are developed for each of these subheadings.

- *Content/concepts*—Lists general descriptions of the information being tested for in the left-hand column of the table. For instance, the topic may be listed as *Principles of Fire Behavior* or *Elements of the Fire Tetrahedron*.

- *Number of test items* — Lists the number of questions for each topic and learning objective in each cell.

- *Total number of test items* — Gives the number of test questions for each topic and learning objective in the right-hand column and the bottom row of the table. The cell in the lower right-hand corner is the total of the items in the column or row.

Creating the table of specifications while planning the lesson or course helps instructors determine which topics and learning objectives are the most important to teach and test for. The most desirable outcome is to test for all the stated learning objectives on each topic. However, there is one major constraint that prohibits this outcome: time. It may *not* be possible to adequately administer a test that contains a large number of test items.

Time Requirements
A general set of testing guidelines based on the average time required to complete a test item is included in the key information box, p. 382. In addition to other factors, these guidelines should be used in determining the number of test items for each test.

Determining Testing Times for Various Types of Test Items

- **True-false (true answer)** — 15 seconds
- **True-false (false answer)** — 30 to 45 seconds
- **Seven-item matching** — 60 to 90 seconds
- **Multiple choice** (four responses)
  - *Knowledge level:* 30 seconds
  - *Application level:* 60 seconds
- **Problem solving, analysis, synthesis, or evaluation** — 30 to 60 seconds
- **Short-answer** — 30 to 60 seconds
- **Essay** — 60 seconds for each point that must be covered

Time limits restrict the number of test items that may be included in a test. Although long tests are more reliable than short tests, the validity of the test is *not* directly related to the test length. Long tests are only more reliable when all the test items are reliable. At the same time, an overly long test may lack the reliability of an appropriately crafted short test.

When time is a restrictive factor, constructing a test that samples each objective is an acceptable approach. When the instructor uses sampling, the plan must be documented. The most critical objectives must be tested and the less critical objectives tested in rotation (that is, tested on a series of tests during the lesson or course).

Test Planning Sheet

The learning domain that is being tested determines whether the table of specification should be used. The most likely used version of the table of specifications is the simple *test planning sheet*. The test planning sheet can be created as a form that the instructor completes for each topic, lesson, or course (**Figure 16.3**).

One of the functions of the test planning sheet is to specify the levels of learning in each content area and the number of test items for each topic and learning objective. In criterion-referenced tests, one test item for each objective may be enough. Using the following steps allows the instructor to easily develop a test planning sheet:

Test Planning Sheet
Firefighter I Course
Rope Lesson

Purpose of Test: __Summative__   Type of Test: __Written__
Number of Test Items: __50__   Time Allotted: __50 minutes__
Test Date: __10/28/2005__   JPR: __4.3.2__
Test Developed by: _____   J. Fortney

| Total | Training Level | Number of Test Items | | | Total |
| | | Testing Level | | | |
		Knowledge (1)	Comprehension (2)	Application (3)	
Types	1	10			10
Knots	1	5			5
Hoisting	2		5	5	10
Security	2		5	5	10
Safety	3	5	5	5	15
Test Item Total		20	15	15	50

Figure 16.3 A test planning sheet is based on the levels of learning defined by the specific learning objective of the lesson.

Step 1: Identify the levels of learning and the content material to be tested.

Step 2: Determine the relative importance of the content material at each level of learning.

Step 3: Ensure that all objectives are tested with an appropriate number of test items.

Contents of the test planning sheet include the following items:

- **Planning sheet header** — Gives the lesson/course name and the following information:
  - *Purpose of the test:* Formative or summative (for instance, a quiz to determine progress or a unit final exam)
  - *Type of test:* Written, oral, or skills
  - *Test items total:* Appropriate number
  - *Test time allotted:* Maximum time for completing test
  - *Test date:* When to be administered
  - *Test developer's name:* Person responsible for test creation
  - *Job performance requirement number:* When applicable

- **Body of text** — Items include the following:

  - *Left column:* Place the task or topic to be tested.

  - *Next column:* Place the training level (1, 2, or 3) of each task or topic.

  - *Remaining columns:* Indicate the testing levels: Knowledge (1), Comprehension (2), and Performance (3). Place the number of test items that correspond to the task or topic in each column. Enter the total of these test items into the appropriate space. Ensure that the training level and testing level are the same.

While the test planning sheet covers the entire lesson or course, some educational professionals advocate creating a single sheet for each set of test items that meet a specific task or topic. This approach may be very time-consuming and result in several pages of specifications. However, the result is a very detailed guideline of the student performance criteria for the lesson or course.

Construct Appropriate Test Items

After determining the purpose and type of test, identifying the specific learning objectives, and preparing the test specifications, test developers and instructors are ready to meet the challenge of matching the specifications with individual test items. Writing effective tests requires the instructor to perform the following tasks:

- Match test items to learning objectives.
- Eliminate testing language and comprehension barriers.
- Avoid giving clues to test answers.
- Select proper level of test item difficulty.
- Determine appropriate number of test items.
- Ensure test usability (ease of testing and scoring).
- Ensure validity and reliability.

Match Test Items to Learning Objectives

Instructors should write test items that provide a measure of the intended learning outcome stated in the course and lesson objectives. For example, when the objective is to convert metric measurements (International System) to U.S. measurements (Customary System), a test item requiring students to identify metric numbers or add a set of metric numbers would be testing on items other than what is required by and included in the stated lesson objective. A more appropriate test item would ask students to use the correct conversion formula to convert meters into feet or yards.

Eliminate Testing Language and Comprehension Barriers

Instructors must compose test items that eliminate or at least minimize language and comprehension barriers to taking the test. One approach is to use words that students would use during training or on the job. Some barriers to test taking include the following:

- Higher reading level than the student audience possesses
- Lengthy, complex, or unclear sentences
- Vague directions
- Unclear graphic materials
- Archaic or obsolete words or terms (for example, *carbon copy*)

Avoid Giving Clues to Test Answers

Instructors should write test items that do *not* give clues on how to answer the question correctly. Some areas to avoid include the following:

- Word associations that give away the answer
- Plural or singular verbs or use of the words *a* or *an* that may hint at the answer or eliminate an answer
- Words that make some answers more likely (such as *sometimes*) or less likely (such as *always* or *never*)
- Answers consistently placed in the same location (such as the Choice B answer in multiple-choice questions) or consistently long correct answers (such as making all true statements longer than false statements)
- Words and materials routinely copied verbatim from the textbook
- Stereotypical answers
- Test items that give the answer to other test items

Select Proper Level of Test Item Difficulty

Test item difficulty is determined by whether the test is norm-referenced or criterion-referenced. Norm-referenced tests rank the members of the class. Criterion-referenced tests determine how well the individual student has achieved the learning objectives established for the lesson or course.

Norm-referenced tests must include test items that have a wide range of difficulty. Test items with better discrimination (appropriate difficulty) help distribute the scores. The desired test result is a wide spread of test scores. Test items that are easily answered by the majority of students are eliminated from the test.

The most desirable test items are those with an average or greater level of difficulty, that is, test items that can be answered correctly by half or less of the class members. This level of difficulty ensures that the test discriminates among the students and creates a gap between the high- and low-scoring members.

Criterion-referenced test items determine how well all students have learned the material. Tests are designed to match the clearly defined learning objectives established for the lesson or course. The learning objectives may be based on criteria such as the NFPA job performance requirements (JPRs) or government-established criteria such as that found in the *Emergency Responder Guidelines* from the Office for Domestic Preparedness (ODP).

When the learning objective is easy, the test item should then be easy. Likewise, when the learning objective is difficult, the test item should reflect the same level of difficulty.

Determine Appropriate Number of Test Items

The number of test items is the key to comprehensiveness in test writing. Determining the number of test items depends on a number of factors such as the following:

- Purpose of the test
- Types of test items or performance items
- Reliability level of the test to accurately determine student abilities

A test should be constructed so that it can measure students' abilities in all phases of a course. It should be complete without unnecessary details. The greater the number of reliable test items, the greater the reliability of the test to accurately assess students' knowledge, skills, and abilities will be. However, it must also fit within the constraints posed by the length of time available for administering the test. Determining the appropriate number of test items to include on a test may be accomplished by using either an established set of guidelines or a mathematical approach.

Regardless of how the final number of test items is determined, the distribution should accurately reflect the importance of the information being tested and amount of emphasis and time given to the subject in class. Learning objectives that are considered the most important by the instructor or required by the certification process should have the greatest number of test items.

Some educational professionals believe that the total time spent teaching a topic should be the baseline for determining the emphasis placed on the topic in the test. The instructor may use either the guideline or mathematical approach to determine the appropriate number of test items for a test.

Guideline approach. Educational recommendations for criterion-referenced tests are ten items per learning level. This number ensures that each level of learning is adequately measured. Do *not* confuse

Discriminate Versus Bias

Note that all norm-referenced and criterion-referenced tests discriminate between students. However, no tests should be biased toward one group or individual. In this use of the words, *discriminate* means that the difficulty is based on the student's ability to learn and retain the knowledge. *Bias* means that the words or cultural references are unknown or difficult to understand for a group or individual because of ethnic, economic, social, or cultural influences and background.

the number of items per level with the suggestion of creating at least one test item per learning objective. (Many objectives are written at the same level of learning.) For practical considerations, the number of items must match the time allowed for testing. When developing a test, use the testing time guidelines in the key information box in the Time Requirements section, p. 382.

Besides the consideration of available time for administering a test, questions involving comprehension and application require more time than those questions that test knowledge. To gain a comprehensive set of test results, it may be necessary to combine or cluster test items on a single topic and include a sampling of the knowledge, comprehension, and application testing levels.

Student learning styles also affect test development. Slow-thinking students also require more time to complete most types of questions. In this situation, the criterion-referenced test must be developed with the slow-thinking student in mind.

Mathematical approach. This approach to determining the number of test items to use involves comparing the results from two mathematical computations. The first computation is based on the division of teaching time allotted to a specific learning objective by the total amount of time allotted to the course. The second computation is based on dividing the number of points assigned to the specific learning objective to the total number of points possible on the test. The results are then compared to one another. The process can be separated into the following three steps:

Step 1: Determine the percentage of time that was spent teaching the learning objective based on the total instructional time for the topic. *Example:*

— *Learning Objective 1:* Explain the fire tetrahedron. Teaching time: 60 minutes

— *Total Teaching Time*: Principles of Fire Behavior. Teaching time: 300 minutes

— *60/300 = 0.20 or 20 percent:* Therefore, 20 percent of the test items should involve the fire tetrahedron.

Step 2: Determine the percentage of points assigned to the learning objective based on the total number of points possible on the test.

— *Learning Objective 1:* Explain the fire tetrahedron. Points: 20

— *Total Teaching Time:* Principles of Fire Behavior. Total Points: 100

— *20/100 = 0.20 or 20 percent:* Therefore, 20 percent of the total points possible should be generated by questions concerning the fire tetrahedron.

Step 3: Compare the results of Steps 1 and 2. They should be within ± 2 percent. When the results are *not* within this range, then the number of test items should be altered to reach the appropriate comparison range.

When this process is used during the development of the test specifications, alterations can be made in the amount of time the instructor allocates to the specific learning objective. When the process is used when developing the test items, then the alterations must be made in the number of test items or the assessment value (points) for each item.

Ensure Test Usability

Fire and emergency services tests should be usable by both instructors and students. Usability should be a contributing factor in the development of locally created tests and selection of third-party developed tests. A test that burdens the instructor with the mechanics of administrating or scoring is an obstacle to effective testing. A test that is difficult to understand creates a barrier to success for students. Therefore, tests must have the following usability characteristics:

• ***Easy to administer*** — Tests should contain simple and clear directions because they may be administered by personnel with limited training in test administration. This characteristic is especially important for tests that are administered by company officers in the field or those performance (skills) tests that are observed and assessed by a number of personnel. Errors in the administration of tests can negatively affect their validity and reliability.

- **Easy to take** — Effective tests include clear and complete directions for students and explain exactly what they are to do. The test developer should provide sample test questions and answer examples for students.

- **Sufficient time for administration** — Test length should be sufficient to provide accurate assessment of student learning. Therefore, the length of time for taking the test must meet this criterion. Tests should be long enough to obtain valid and reliable results, but no longer. A guideline for the overall length of an assessment test is 20 to 60 minutes.

- **Cost-effective** — Although not as important as other characteristics, the cost of test development or test acquisition is a consideration. It is better to purchase a validated and reliable test from a third-party organization than attempt to develop a test that may result in false or legally questionable test items or results.

- **Available comparable forms** — Some test-preparation firms offer a variety of tests on the same subjects or learning objectives. The availability of a variety of tests is an advantage that adds to the flexibility in developing instructional materials. It permits the use of a variety of textbooks, skills sheets, or other ancillary materials. It also provides increased validity and reliability for the results.

- **Easy to score** — An answer sheet or simple test form aids the instructor in quickly scoring tests. The design of the answer sheet should make the scoring easy by placing the answer spaces in a single column to the left of the appropriate question or on a single answer sheet in two to four columns. Columns should *not* be crowded. Other easy-to-score methods include mechanical/electronic scoring devices that permit the answers sheets to be rapidly scored, graded, and recorded.

Ensure Validity and Reliability

The two most important conditions of a well-designed test are validity and reliability. *Validity* is the extent to which a test measures what it is

supposed to measure. It is built into the test by selecting an ample number of test items for each learning level and content area. The best way to ensure validity of the course content is to take the following steps:

Step 1: Identify and define the content of the course/lesson and the learning objectives to be measured.

Step 2: Develop a table of specifications that specifies the sample of test items to be used.

Step 3: Design a test that matches the specifications.

Reliability is the consistency and accuracy of test measurement. A reliable test has the following characteristics:

- Clear directions

- Lack of bias that may discriminate against a student or group of students

- Clear, well-written test items

- Specific scoring criteria

Devoting attention to each of the test characteristics, analyzing a test each time it is given, and discarding or rewriting test items that do *not* meet requirements aid in improving test reliability. Any test that cannot give consistent and accurate scores does *not* measure what it is required to measure. Reliability is an essential condition of validity, but it is *not* the only condition.

Five Steps for Ensuring Test Reliability

Step 1: Select a representative sample of learning objectives.

Step 2: Select enough test items to represent the skills required in the learning objective.

Step 3: Select test-item formats that reduce the potential for guessing.

Step 4: Use only the number of test items that a student can complete in the available time.

Step 5: Determine methods to maintain positive student attitudes toward testing.

Test Instruments

The three learning domains — cognitive, psychomotor, and affective — each contain several levels of learning that enable instructors to teach in progressive steps and for students to proceed from simple to advanced knowledge, skills, and attitudes. There are also different levels of training courses — beginning, intermediate, and advanced — each of which requires different levels of knowledge and skills.

These factors make the task of developing appropriate tests a challenge. It is important, however, for test developers and instructors to select the appropriate testing instrument for the appropriate learning levels and types of programs, objectives, and students.

Instructors must understand the common considerations for all types of tests and the types of test instruments available to them. Each type has advantages, disadvantages, and test construction considerations. The three basic types of test instruments are as follows:

- **Written tests** — Test cognitive (knowledge) ability.
- **Oral tests** — Test cognitive and communication abilities.
- **Performance tests** — Test psychomotor skill ability.

Common Considerations for All Tests

When designing tests, some points that are considerably important for uniform testing are commonly overlooked. The most significant consideration for test design is that all test items must be referenced to a learning objective. In turn, these learning objectives are the teaching points that are found in credible sources such as national standards, organization policies, and textbooks.

Test designers must also give consideration to test format, arrangement, item difficulty, and instructions. Methods of ensuring test security, ease of test administration, and reporting test results are also important.

Format

Considerations for the physical test format makes test administration, test taking, and test scoring easier (**Figure 16.4, p. 388**). The following elements should be included in any test format:

- Spaces for the date and the student's name on the test sheet unless separate answer sheets are provided
- Test title or label
- Numbered tests or different test versions, which aid in reporting scores and maintaining security
- Clear, easy-to-follow instructions at the beginning of the test and each test section that starts a different test format (multiple-choice, matching, true-false, or fill-in-the-blank)
- Sample test item and answer demonstrating how the test is to be taken
- Consecutive numbering of test items
- Single spacing within test items
- Double spacing between test items
- Point value of each test item (for example, multiple-choice: 1 point; short-answer: 2 points; true-false items: 1 point)
- Commonly understood terms; for example, do *not* use abbreviations unless they are placed in parentheses following the common term

Test Item Arrangement

After the test items are prepared, they are arranged on the test instrument in a logical way. They can be grouped either by learning domain outcome (such as knowledge, comprehension, or application) or type of test item (such as multiple-choice, matching, or short-answer).

In either case, it is recommended that the test items be placed in a sequence of increasing difficulty from simple to complex. This placement allows students to answer some easy test items at the beginning of the test, gain confidence, move on to the moderately difficult test items, and then be challenged by more difficult test items toward the end of the test or section. When arranging test items, the instructor must be careful to *not* reveal the answer to subsequent test items in the wording of other items.

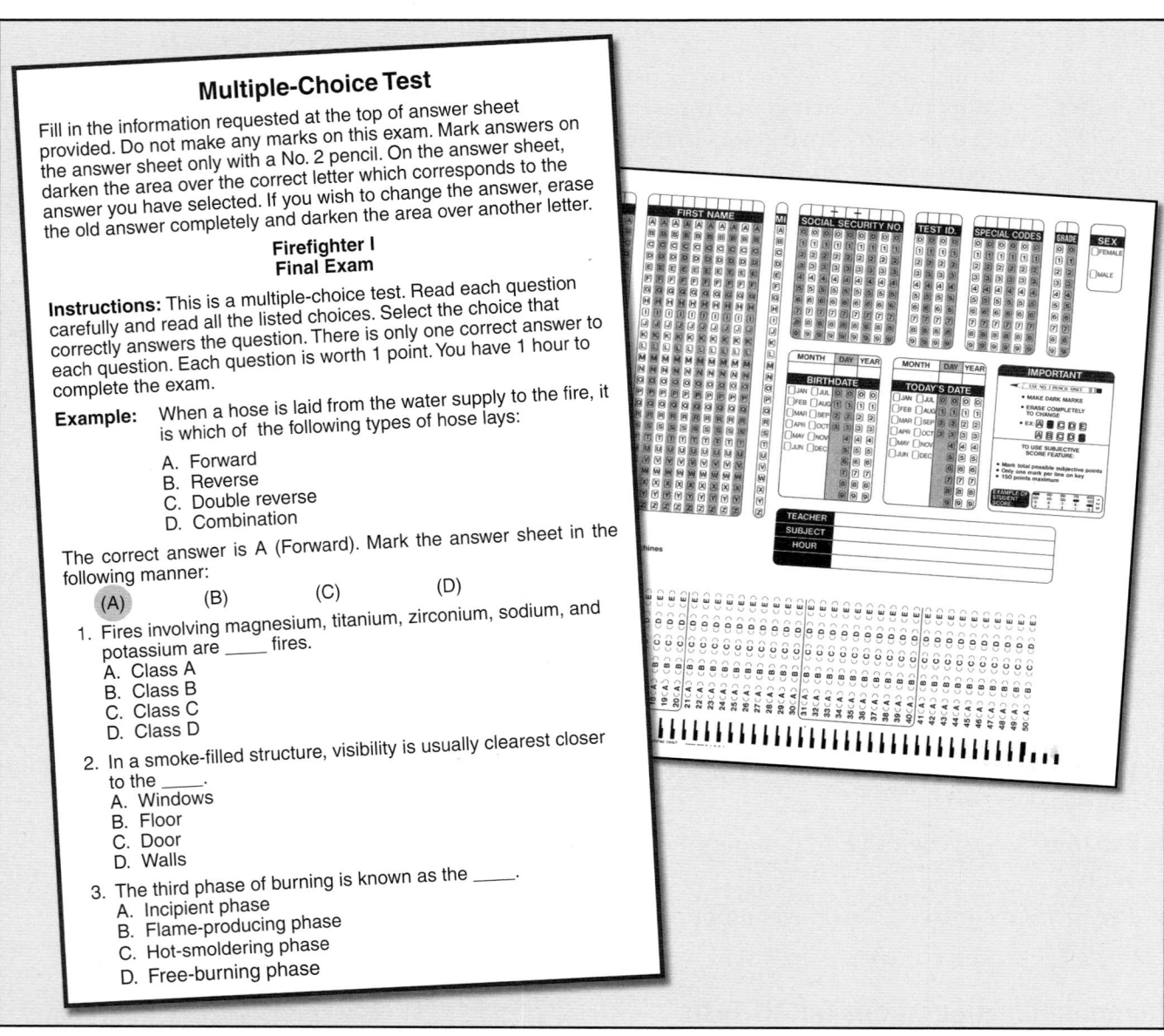

Figure 16.4 Test formats should include space for the date, student name or identification number, test title, consecutively numbered test items, instructions, and a space for test answers when a separate answer sheet is not provided. *Courtesy of Maryland Fire and Rescue Institute.*

Test Item Difficulty

Test item difficulty is based on the learning level of the lesson. The levels found in Bloom's Taxonomy (see Figure 7.5 in Chapter 7, Principles of Learning) may be categorized as follows:

- *Basic* — Divided into two levels

  Level 1: Knowledge

  Level 2: Comprehension

- *Intermediate* — Followed by two more levels

  Level 3: Application

  Level 4: Analysis

- *Advanced* — Followed by the final two levels

  Level 5: Synthesis

  Level 6: Evaluation

The test items within each level have varying degrees of difficulty based on the topic. The instructor begins by creating test items that evaluate the student's ability at the appropriate level. The actual determination of test item difficulty, however, will *not* occur until the test has been taken and scored. At that time, the number of students who correctly or incorrectly answered a question in relation to other questions will determine the level of difficulty. The questions can then be rearranged for future testing.

Tests that depend on test item organization from simple to difficult are called *powered tests,* which are designed to evaluate the performance level of students. Time limits for powered tests are established to permit the majority if not all of the students to complete the test.

An alternative approach is the *speeded test* that assesses the student's ability to perform a test within a specific time. Performance or skills tests generally have established time limits for completion of the task. Speeded tests are *not* recommended for written or oral type tests in fire and emergency services training.

Test Item Difficulty

Difficulty is the percentage of test takers that got an item correct. Conventional wisdom suggests evaluating item difficulty using the following scale:

- *Easy* — 75 percent or above
- *Average* — 50 percent
- *Difficult* — 25 percent and below

However, for most practical applications, the following scale is recommended:

- *Too easy* — 90 percent or above
- *Appropriate* — 65 to 85 percent
- *Too difficult* — 60 percent and below

A test that is comprised of items that have an average difficulty of 70 to 75 percent will yield a mean score in that 70 to 75 percent range, which is the usual standard for passing an exam.

Instructions

An effective test should include instructions on how to complete it. Instructions should be brief, clear, and to the point. The general instructions provided at the beginning of the test should explain the following items:

- Purpose of the test
- Method and means for recording answers

- Suggestion on whether to guess when undecided on an answer (in some cases, incorrect answers are penalized more than *not* answering the question)
- Amount of time available to complete the test

In tests with multiple parts based on test items grouped by type (such as sections of multiple-choice, matching, true-false, etc.), the specific instructions at the beginning of each section should be included. In addition to the method for answering the specific types of questions, the instructions should indicate the amount of time the student should spend on each section **(Figure 16.5)**.

It is also good policy for instructors to read all instructions to the class, point out any variances with different sections of the test, and ask then whether there are any questions. This policy is particularly important for performance or skills tests and should include the scoring, timing, and evaluation criteria for each type of skill.

Firefighter I Final Examination

General Instructions:
This test is the final comprehensive examination for the Firefighter I course. The test consists of multiple-choice, true-false, matching, and short-answer test items. Each type of test item has its own instructions: *Read them carefully.* The student will use the attached answer sheet to record the answers. Blank answers will be counted as an incorrect answer. Use a soft-lead (No. 2) pencil to record the answers in the appropriate spaces. The total time allowed for the test is 4 hours. A break will be permitted halfway through the examination.

Part I: Multiple-Choice
This section consists of 50 multiple-choice questions. Read each question carefully and select the best answer for each question or statement. There is only one correct answer for each question. Each test item is worth 1 point. This section of the test will last 1 hour.

Figure 16.5 Test instructions should be clear and concise and include the amount of time students have to complete the test.

Written Test Types

The purpose of written tests is to measure student understanding and retention of technical information and evaluate student accomplishment of the cognitive learning objectives. Depending on their types, the desired test results, and their construction, written test items may be objective or subjective. Test developers must distinguish between the following test items and determine the most appropriate use for them:

- *Objective* — Measures cognitive learning, but objective test items are often limited to the low cognitive learning levels of recall and recognition because these levels lend themselves easily to the objective test format. Objective test items can also be used to measure high levels of cognitive learning such as interpretation and analysis. Construct test items carefully. *Examples:*

  — An objective test item that asks students to choose the correct function for a tool from among four listed functions requires only that a student recognize the correct function.

  — The test item that presents a problem and asks students to choose the best tool for solving the problem requires a student to interpret and analyze.

- *Subjective* — Measures effectively the high cognitive levels of analysis, evaluation, and interpretation because subjective test items allow students the freedom to organize, analyze, revise, redesign, or evaluate a problem. A subjective test item has no single correct answer. How correct or appropriate a response is varies with each student's solution to the stated problem. *Examples:*

  — Subjective test items are used most often in officer training courses. Most of the training at this level involves intellectual, problem-solving skills. Students must be able to demonstrate high cognitive skills to meet high-level job performance requirements.

  — Subjective test items are also effective in specialized training courses in areas such as hazardous materials and emergency medical services.

Five test item types are used in written test instruments. Three (multiple-choice, true-false, and matching test items) are objective and tend to be the most popular for fire and emergency services testing. The remaining test items (short-answer/completion and essay) are subjective and generally used for high levels of cognition such as analysis, synthesis, and stating personal judgments and opinions.

One final type of test instrument, the interpretive exercise, uses combinations of the five test item types and may be either objective or subjective. Advantages and disadvantages of each test item or test type are included with the descriptions of each test type.

> **CAUTION**
> Questions that are published in study guides, test preparation guides, and textbooks or manuals should *not* be used for certification or terminal examinations. These types of questions are *not* validated and are only used as student resources for determining understanding of the material in the specific textbook or manual.

Multiple-Choice

A test consisting of well-constructed multiple-choice test items is one of the most versatile of the objective test types. This type of test can measure a variety of student abilities and adapts to most types of subject matter. Multiple-choice test items are *not* easy to construct. In order to perform as described, they must be clear and test to the learning level desired. Once constructed, they are quick and easy to score.

A multiple-choice test item consists of either a question or an incomplete statement, commonly referred to as the *stem*. Following the stem is a list of several possible responses referred to as *choices* or *alternatives*. The student is asked to read the stem and select the correct response from the list of choices or alternatives. The correct choice in each item is known as the *answer*, and the remaining choices are called *distracters*.

The obvious purpose of distracters is to discriminate between those students who know a lot versus those who know only a little and are uncertain of the correct answer. Distracters are *not* meant to trick, confuse, or mislead students (**Figure 16.6, p. 392**).

When creating multiple-choice tests and test items, it is important to include the following components:

- Write the stem in the form of a direct question or an incomplete sentence that asks and measures only one learning objective.

- Write a clear, brief stem that contains most of the wording (rather than placing repeated words in the choices).

- Write positive statements, but if and when negative statements are used, underline (or italicize) or emphasize negative words in bold. Example: *Which of the following is <u>not</u> a part of the fire tetrahedron:*

- List at least four choices: the answer and three plausible, attractive distracters.

- Create choices with phrases in parallel form and grammatically consistent with the stem.

- Place correct answers in varied positions among the A, B, C, and D choices.

- Place each choice on separate, indented lines and in a single column.

- Begin responses with capital letters when the stem is a complete question.

- Begin responses with lowercase letters when the stem is an incomplete sentence.

Other possible formats for designing multiple-choice questions depend on the training division's style preference and whether the organization uses a computer-generated, test-creator program. This program automatically sets spacing between the choice letters (A, B, C, and D) and the choice sentence. Placing periods after responses may depend on style preference or whether the response finishes an incomplete sentence or fills in a blank in the stem.

While assuring that all the components listed are included in multiple-choice tests, test developers should be aware of the following guidelines (**Figure 16.7, p. 393**):

- Do *not* include choices that are obviously wrong or humorous.

- Construct the stem and choices to avoid grammatical clues to the correct answer such as using the words *a* and *an* or singular and plural word endings at the end of the stem that direct students to choose a response that matches the tense and case of the stem.

- Make all choices close to the same length; the correct response should *not* be longer or shorter than the distracters.

- Avoid using the phrases *all of the above* and *none of the above* as the fourth choice if possible.

- Do *not* test trivial ideas or information.

- Use correct grammar and punctuation.

Many of the rules for writing the various types of test items apply to more than one type of test item. The instructor should be aware of the rules and apply them accordingly. The information box checklist can be helpful for applying the rules to test items.

Multiple-Choice Test Item Checklist

❏ Information is important — *not* trivial.

The test item is intended to test the following:

❏   Knowledge

❏   Comprehension

❏   Application

❏ The stem is a complete question or sentence fragment that is punctuated properly.

❏ There is one, clearly correct answer.

❏ Three distracters are clearly incorrect but reasonable.

❏ Four responses are approximately the same length and punctuated properly.

Advantages. A major advantage of multiple-choice test items is the ability to measure achievement, complex learning objectives, and various types of knowledge. These measurements are advantages only when the test is constructed with clear, unambiguous test items. Well-written test items take time to carefully plan and thoughtfully word. Instructors should remember that a test item

Awareness-Level First Responder
Lesson 2A

Lesson 2A Quiz

Name ______________________________ **Date** ______________

Select the best answer for each of the following multiple-choice questions. Print the letter of the correct answer in the space provided to the left of the question. Each question is worth 5 points. Thirty (30) minutes are allowed to complete the test.

_______ 1. Which of the following is a purpose of a pre-incident survey?

A. Ensure legal protection
B. Reduce number of personnel needed
C. Identify cost of clean-up
D. Identify possible access/egress difficulties

_______ 2. Which of the following should the LERP identify?

A. Likely routes for bicycle and pedestrian traffic
B. Likely routes for commuter travel
C. Likely routes for extremely hazardous substance transport
D. Likely routes for livestock transport

_______ 3. Which of the following refers to packaging, other than that on a vessel or barge, in which materials are loaded with no intermediate form of containment?

A. Primary packaging
B. Secondary packaging
C. Bulk packaging
D. Nonbulk packaging

_______ 4. What materials are included in UN/DOT hazard Class 1?

A. Explosives
B. Gases
C. Flammable liquids
D. Corrosive substances

_______ 5. What materials are included in UN/DOT hazard Class 2?

A. Explosives
B. Gases
C. Flammable liquids
D. Corrosive substances

Figure 16.6 Multiple-choice test items generally consist of a minimum of four possible answers. The type of answer sheet depends on the method used to score the answers such as electronic, mechanical, or by hand (like the test shown here requires). The test item construction and the answer sheet should match.

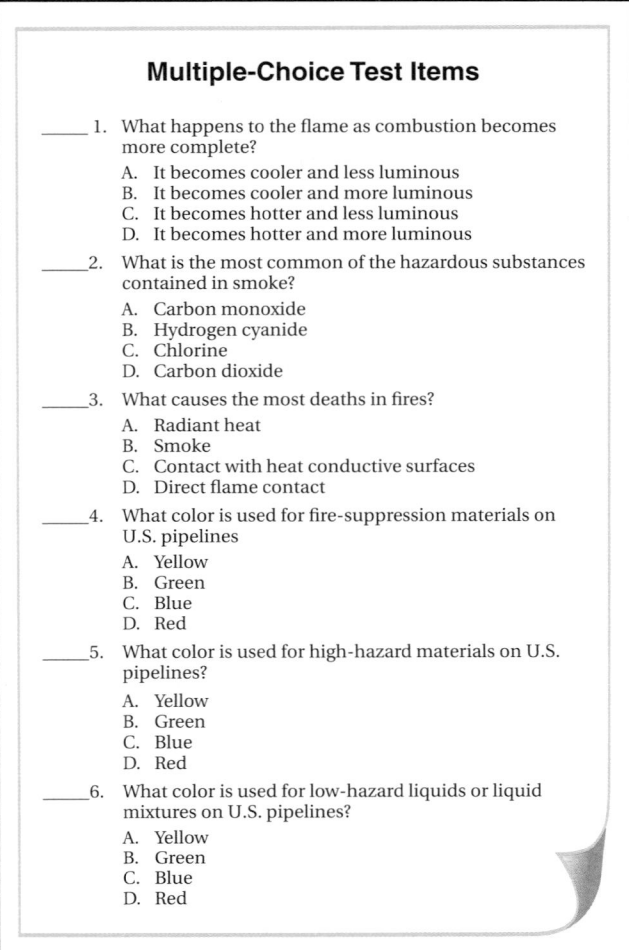

Multiple-Choice Test Items

_____ 1. What happens to the flame as combustion becomes more complete?
    A. It becomes cooler and less luminous
    B. It becomes cooler and more luminous
    C. It becomes hotter and less luminous
    D. It becomes hotter and more luminous

_____ 2. What is the most common of the hazardous substances contained in smoke?
    A. Carbon monoxide
    B. Hydrogen cyanide
    C. Chlorine
    D. Carbon dioxide

_____ 3. What causes the most deaths in fires?
    A. Radiant heat
    B. Smoke
    C. Contact with heat conductive surfaces
    D. Direct flame contact

_____ 4. What color is used for fire-suppression materials on U.S. pipelines
    A. Yellow
    B. Green
    C. Blue
    D. Red

_____ 5. What color is used for high-hazard materials on U.S. pipelines?
    A. Yellow
    B. Green
    C. Blue
    D. Red

_____ 6. What color is used for low-hazard liquids or liquid mixtures on U.S. pipelines?
    A. Yellow
    B. Green
    C. Blue
    D. Red

Figure 16.7 Multiple-choice test items should contain correct grammar and punctuation.

that is clear to the test developer or instructor is _not_ always clear or have the same meaning to students. Having at least four choices limits the possibility of correctly guessing to 25 percent instead of the 50 percent possible in true-false tests.

**Disadvantages.** As useful, common, and favored as multiple-choice tests are, they have some of the following disadvantages:

- These tests are _not_ as well suited as essay tests for measuring some cognitive skills such as the ability to organize and present ideas.

- It can be very difficult to construct multiple-choice tests that include different difficulty-level test items that measure a variety of learning levels.

- It is often difficult to create enough appropriate and plausible distracters for each stem.

- It is possible for students to guess the correct answer, yet _not_ know the material.

True-False

Probably the best known of the objective tests is the _true-false_ or _alternative-response_ test. Though considered relatively easy to construct, true-false tests are also the most abused, and their quality is often doubted. The true-false test item usually consists of a single statement that the student is required to recognize as either true or false.

The difficulty in constructing this type of test is creating a statement that is completely true or completely false. True statements should be created based on true facts, while false statements should be created based on common misconceptions of the facts (**Figure 16.8**).

True-False Tests

Example 1:

Identify accurate statements about fuel characteristics. Circle the word _TRUE_ before each correct statement, and the word _FALSE_ before each false statement.

TRUE   FALSE   1. The shape and size of a fuel affects its ignitability.

TRUE   FALSE   2. As a fuel's surface-to-mass ratio decreases, its ignitability increases.

TRUE   FALSE   3. When a solid fuel is in a vertical position, fire spread is more rapid than when it is in a horizontal position.

TRUE   FALSE   4. Liquid fuels have physical properties that increase the difficulty of extinguishment and the hazard to personnel.

TRUE   FALSE   5. Volatility is the ease with which a liquid gives off vapor.

Example 2:

Identify accurate statements about fuel characteristics. Place a check mark under the column marked _TRUE_ for each correct statement and under the column marked _FALSE_ for each false statement.

TRUE   FALSE

_____ _____ 1. The shape and size of a fuel affects its ignitability.

_____ _____ 2. As a fuel's surface-to-mass ratio decreases, its ignitability increases.

_____ _____ 3. When a solid fuel is in a vertical position, fire spread is more rapid than when it is in a horizontal position.

_____ _____ 4. Liquid fuels have physical properties that increase the difficulty of extinguishment and the hazard to personnel.

_____ _____ 5. Volatility is the ease with which a liquid gives off vapor.

Figure 16.8 Traditional true-false test items are difficult to create because they must be either totally true or totally false, a condition that is hard to attain.

Alternative-Response Questions

The alternative-response question is based on the concept that the question has only one correct answer out of two possible choices. Although the true-false test item is the most common, other options include *agree-disagree*, *yes-no*, or *right-wrong*.

Another approach is to use the alternative-response to determine whether the student can categorize information based on topics such as *awareness-operational*, *Level I-Level II*, or *line-staff*. These alternatives can overcome some of the disadvantage to the true-false approach that exists when the student can guess the answer and has a 50-50 chance of getting it correct **(Figure 16.9)**.

Alternative-Response Test Item

Objective 6:

Distinguish between a chemical and a biological incident. Write *C* before characteristics of a chemical incident and *B* before characteristics of a biological incident. *(1 point each, 4/5)*

_____ 1. May have a unique odor and color

_____ 2. Symptoms are noticeable either within minutes or hours

_____ 3. Symptoms may take days or even weeks to appear

_____ 4. No odor or color

_____ 5. May spread beyond the initial contamination because of the activities of affected individuals

---

Figure 16.9 Alternative-response test items provide the instructor with additional variety for the true-false approach to test items.

In addition to the traditional true-false test items, there are also modified true-false test items. The modified test item asks the student to explain why an item is false when that is the answer chosen. The modified version tests learning at a higher level than the traditional true-false test **(Figure 16.10)**.

When creating true-false tests and test items, instructors should consider the following guidelines:

- Write the words *True* and *False* at the left margin when answers are to be marked on the test paper.

- Write instructions that direct students to draw a circle around the answer they select rather than have them write the letter *T* or *F*, the symbol + or -, or the word *yes* or *no*.

- Create a sufficient number of test items to provide reliable results. More items are needed than the number used for multiple-choice items. A large number of test items minimize the possibility of guessing the correct answer.

- Distribute an equal number of true and false test items randomly throughout the test.

- Do *not* use specific determiners (words that indicate a specific answer) that provide unwarranted clues. Words such as *usually, generally, often*, or *sometimes* are most likely to appear in true statements. The words *never, all, always*, or *none* are more likely to be found in false statements.

- Avoid creating test items that could trick or mislead students into making a mistake.

- Do *not* use double-negative test items; they are very confusing to students and do *not* accurately measure knowledge, only cleverness at interpreting the test items.

- Avoid using personal pronouns such as *you* in test items.

- Do *not* use *command statements* in test items. These types of statements usually incorporate other *don'ts* as well. For example, the statement *You must always wear gloves when caring for a patient* uses the personal pronoun *you* and the qualifier *always* in a command statement.

- Do *not* use test items that test trivia or obscure facts. Tests do *not* need to measure insignificant or common knowledge.

- Develop test items that require students to think about what they have learned, rather than merely remember it.

Building Construction and the Fire Service
Lesson 1
Lesson 1 Quiz

Name _____ **Date** _____

Tue/False

Write *True* or *False* before each of the following statements. Correct those statements that are false.

_____ 1. The laws of physics and chemistry that govern fire behavior never change.

_____

_____

_____

_____ 2. Automatic suppression systems have little value when impediments exist to their complete control of a fire.

_____

_____

_____

_____ 3. A high fire load does not necessarily result in an equivalent structural load.

_____

_____

_____

_____ 4. A building's actual construction type is obvious from its external appearance.

_____

_____

_____

Figure 16.10 Modified true-false tests are used to test higher levels of learning than the traditional true-false test by asking students to explain why an answer is false when that is the answer chosen.

- Avoid using unusually long or short test items because the length may often be a clue. Test developers tend to write true test items consistently longer than false ones because they are trying to justify them as true.

- Create brief and simply stated test items that deal with a single concept rather than lengthy and complex ones. It is *not* necessary to include humorous or absurd statements when testing for knowledge.

- Create test item based on facts or common misconceptions without quoting information verbatim from the textbook — the most common mistake made when writing true-false test-items.

Advantages. Although true-false tests are *not* popular with test developers, instructors should consider the following advantages:

- Test items can be adapted to sample a wide range of subject matter and can be brief enough so that students can answer a large number in a short time.

- The traditional test format is easy to score, but the modified format takes longer.

- True-false test items can promote student interest and motivation and introduce points for discussion.

Disadvantages. While true-false test items have a reputation for being easy to construct, it is usually because items are often taken verbatim from textbook statements and altered somewhat to make them false. It is easier to construct poorly written true-false statements than good ones. Disadvantages are as follows:

- It is difficult to avoid creating test items with ambiguities or construct test items that are either completely true or completely false without making the correct answer obvious.

- It is easy for students to guess the item correctly without knowing anything about the subject matter. With only two choices, they have a 50 percent chance of selecting the correct answer.

- From the students' standpoint, true-false test items do *not* give them the opportunity to demonstrate what they really know or can do.

Matching

Instructors should clearly explain the matching exercise in the instructions when creating matching tests and test items. Instructions should indicate whether a response could be used more than once. The content of a matching test item must consist of similar material, items, or information.

A matching test item consists of two parallel columns of words, phrases, images, or a combination. The student is required to match each *problem statement* (word, phrase, or image) in one column with the response in the other column to which it is most closely related.

Matching test items are variations of multiple-choice test items. They are relatively easy to construct, can be objective, and are easy to score. They are especially applicable for testing *who, what, where,* and *when* types of subject matter.

Some test items can use illustrations, photographs, or images. Some examples of matching test items are shown in **Figure 16.11** and **Figure 16.12**. A partial list of test items that can be easily made into matching test items includes the following:

- *Short questions* — With answers
- *Events* — With dates
- *Parts* — With their functions
- *Terms* — With their definitions
- *Objects* — With their names
- *Machines or tools* — With their uses
- *Problems* — With their solutions
- *Causes* — With their effects

It is important to consider the following guidelines for matching tests and matching test items:

- Avoid placing each group of problem statements (words, phrases, or images) and the list of responses on more than one page. Responses are brief, but problem statements are usually longer and appropriately detailed.

- Prepare at least five but *not* more than seven problem statements. When a mechanically scored answer sheet is used, the problem statements for each matching section are limited to five so that answers can be recorded in the *A* through *E* spaces on the answer sheet.

Figure 16.11 Matching test items are objective and easy to construct and score.

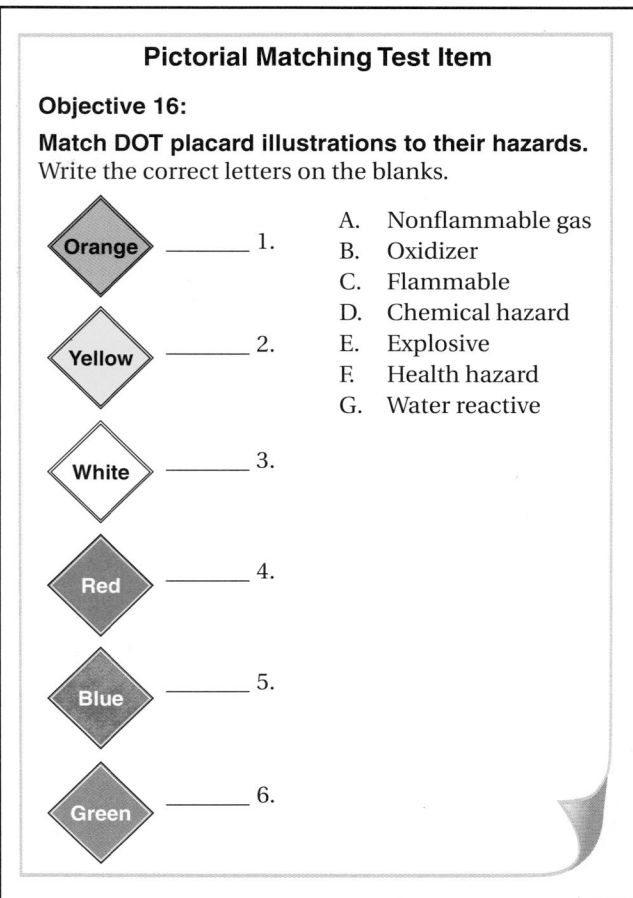

Figure 16.12 Test items that include pictures that students match with a name or its function can be used in preparation for practical training evolutions.

- Prepare one more response than problem statements. The extra response requires more precise knowledge from the student and reduces selection by elimination.

- Arrange problem statements and responses into two columns: problem statements on the left side of the page and responses on the right. Columns may be titled with appropriate headings (for example, Tools and Uses, Symptoms and Treatments, etc.). *Details:*

  — Number the problem statements. Place an answer line to either the left or right of each number unless an answer sheet is used.

  — Use letters for each response (*A, B, C,* etc.)

- Arrange responses in a systematic manner such as alphabetically, chronologically, or numerically (in ascending or descending order).

- State whether a response may be used once, more than once, or not at all. Ideally, only one response is the correct answer for each problem statement. However, the use of additional responses (acting as distracters) or using a response more than once can reduce the chance that the student can guess the correct answer.

- Avoid giving clues to answers in either problem statements or responses.

- Do *not* include responses that are obviously wrong.

Advantages. When choosing among the many objective test types, instructors should consider the advantages of matching test items. Properly constructed matching test items minimize the chance of guessing correctly, are relatively easy to construct, and can cover a large amount of factual material in a compact space.

Disadvantages. As with all types of tests, there are a few drawbacks to matching tests. Measurement of knowledge is limited because the problem phrases used must be short. Matching tests are considered inferior to multiple-choice tests in measuring high levels of instruction. For this reason, a test should include a mix of several test formats instead of all matching items.

Short-Answer/Completion

The short-answer/completion test is subjective. Unlike the previous objective test types, it does *not* include the answer on the test sheet. It requires the student to supply the answer. Students must recall previous learning, apply principles, understand methods or procedures to determine the correct answer and insert it into the answer space (**Figure 16.13** and **Figure 16.14**). Test items are constructed similarly to the multiple-choice test item, but without the alternatives from which to select.

The short-answer test item is a question to which an answer is required. The completion item is an incomplete statement with key words omitted (the key word may be at the end of the statement or represented by an underlined blank space within the statement).

When creating short-answer/completion tests, instructors should consider the following guidelines:

- Create short, concise, and direct statements so that only one answer is possible.

- Avoid long, involved statements with a string of blanks to fill; they tend to be confusing.

- Start with a direct question and change it to an incomplete statement.

- Ensure that the answer to be supplied is a key point in the lesson.

- Arrange the statement in order to place the blanks at or near the end of the sentence.

- Indicate when answers can be used more than once when a list of choices is provided.

- Avoid statements that call for answers with more than one word, phrase, or number.

- Eliminate unnecessary clues such as variations in the length of the blanks for answers or the use of the words *a* or *an* preceding the blank.

Advantages. Short-answer/completion tests are flexible and commonly used in measuring *who, what, when, where,* and *how* information. They

---

Short-Answer Test Items

1. In degrees Celsius, the freezing point of water is _____.

2. In degrees Celsius, the boiling point of water is _____.

3. In degrees Fahrenheit, the freezing point of water is _____.

4. In degrees Fahrenheit, the boiling point of water is _____.

5. The minimum concentration of fuel vapor and air that supports combustion is the _____.

6. The concentration of fuel vapor and air above which combustion cannot take place is the _____.

Figure 16.13 The short-answer test item is considered subjective because there may be more than one correct answer. The instructor must decide whether the student has provided enough information to determine the answer is correct.

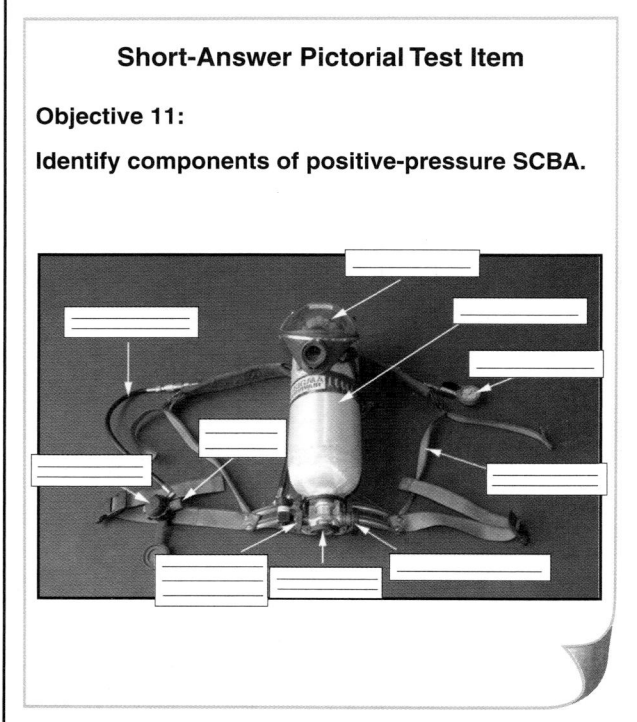

Short-Answer Pictorial Test Item

Objective 11:

Identify components of positive-pressure SCBA.

Figure 16.14 The short-answer pictorial test item may provide an illustration that requires the student to evaluate a situation and determine a response.

---

are also useful in measuring a student's ability to solve mathematical and similar problems. One of the most important advantages of short-answer/completion test items is that students must supply the answer, which minimizes the possibility that they can guess the correct answer.

Some short-answer/completion tests provide the correct answers in a list of words or phrases. However, partial knowledge, which might enable the student to choose the correct answer from this list of choices, is usually insufficient to enable the student to guess correctly on a short-answer/completion item.

Disadvantages. Because a variety of answers may appear and must be considered for total or partial credit, this type of test may be difficult to score. Misspelled words may also make it difficult to determine whether the answer is correct or the student was making a poor attempt at guessing. Short-answer/completion tests cannot be machine scored. Other disadvantages of short-answer/completion tests include the following:

- These tests have limitations of measurement or an inability to measure complex achievement.

- It is difficult to design the items so that only one answer is correct and at the same time be clear to students which term is to be used for the answer. *For example:*
  - When the short-answer/completion statement says *The primary responsibility of the company officer is to* _____, students could supply any one of the following words: *supervise, manage, lead,* or *delegate* among others.
  - It must be clear which answer is required or the instructor must give credit for any answer that means the same thing.

Essay

Like the short-answer/completion test item, the essay is a subjective form of test. Students express analyses, methods, descriptions, and judgments based on their own values, opinions, attitudes, preferences, biases, and perceptions that may be different or vary from those of other students and instructors.

An essay test item allows students to write an extended piece of nonfiction information on a topic or question created by the instructor or test developer (**Figure 16.15, p. 400**). Students are expected to demonstrate the ability to analyze the topic, organize ideas and information, and argue or explain concepts clearly. Although essay test items are generally easy to construct, instructors should consider the following guidelines:

- Create and follow a plan for selecting test topics.

- Write an outline of the acceptable responses to set parameters and use as a guide for scoring student responses.

- Define clearly the task to be completed when responding to each question.

- Give thorough and specific directions that designate the time to be spent on each question or the length of each response.

- Provide sufficient time for students to respond to all questions.

Advantages. This type of test eliminates guessing because the student must know the material in order to respond to the question. Creative students like this type of test because it allows them to express and explain all they know, whereas objective-type tests restrict creative students' abilities to justify their answers. Essay test items are easy to create and test important skills in the higher learning levels of analysis, synthesis, and evaluation. Essay test items provide opportunities for debating points and reinforcing knowledge when they are reviewed.

Disadvantages. Although essay tests provide students the opportunity to express their knowledge at the higher learning levels, these test items are difficult to evaluate or assess fairly because instructors may have a different opinion than the student or may have stressed a different point than the one perceived by the student. As a result, the answers may contain a variety of opinions and perceptions on the topic that instructors must analyze, interpret, compare with the required information, and evaluate based on that comparison. Additional disadvantages are as follows:

Awareness-Level First Responder

Comprehensive Exam

Answer the following questions completely in the space provided. Each question is worth 10 points. Allow a maximum of 10 minutes for each question.

1. Explain the difference between initial isolation distances and protective action distances.

_____

_____

_____

_____

_____

_____

_____

_____

_____

2. Describe the limitations of using the senses to determine the presence or absence of hazardous materials.

_____

_____

_____

_____

_____

_____

_____

_____

_____

_____

Figure 16.15 Essay test items are generally used to determine the highest levels of learning and require students to analyze, organize, or explain a concept.

- Essays are time-consuming, both for students to complete and instructors to score.

- Writing ability and penmanship may become barriers to both students and instructors.

- Students who have difficulty writing or write slowly will be at a disadvantage in a timed test.

- Students may be self-conscious about weaknesses in writing or spelling, which will prevent them from performing adequately.

- Instructors may find it difficult to read the students' response, which affects the ability to score essays accurately.

Interpretive Exercises

While each type of written test has its advantage, there are times when complex-learning outcomes must be tested. *The interpretive exercise* is an effective method for testing learning outcomes that involve comprehension, application, analysis, synthesis, and evaluation.

The exercise consists of introductory material that may be a paragraph of text describing a situation or scenario, numerical data, illustration, graph, table, chart, diagram, or map, followed by a series of test items. Computer scenarios, audiovisual recordings, or models may also be used as introductory material.

Test items may be multiple-choice, true-false, short-answer/completion, matching, or essay. Students read the texts or look at the illustrations and then answer the questions posed in the test items.

Instructors should apply the following rules when creating an interpretive exercise:

- Ensure that paragraphs, illustrations, graphs, tables, maps, or charts are relevant to the learning objective that is being measured.

- Ensure that introductory material is as brief and concise as possible.

- Apply the rules for effective test item construction for each type of test item.

- Use test items that require the same type of performance that is listed in the test specifications for the various learning objectives.

- Create new introductory material that is unfamiliar to students. For example, create a scenario that requires them to apply a set of learned responses from a similar situation.

- Ensure that the answer to the test item is *not* contained in the introductory material.

- Ensure that the test items cannot be answered without the introductory material.

- Use a variety of test item types in sufficient quantity to provide a good sample of a student's ability to interpret the introductory material.

Advantages. Advantages of interpretive exercises include the following:

- Material may be tested in great depth.

- Complex levels of learning may be tested.

- Knowledge may be tested in realistic methods by using models, illustrations, or other visual aids.

- The testing process becomes interesting and appealing to all student learning styles.

Disadvantages. Disadvantages of interpretive exercises include the following:

- Introductory material and test items are complex and difficult to construct.

- Test items must accurately match learning objectives and criteria.

- Exercises require a high level of student reading ability.

- Exercises require longer test time than other test types.

Oral Tests

Oral tests were described in Chapter 13, Student Progress Evaluation and Testing. During oral tests, students generally give verbal answers to spoken questions. Oral tests are usually given one-on-one between an instructor and a student. Oral tests are *not* commonly used in the fire and emergency services, but oral test questions may be useful under certain circumstances **(Figure 16.16, p. 402)**.

As mentioned in Chapter 13, Student Progress Evaluation and Testing, the types of questions used for oral tests are either closed or open. When the purpose of the test is to determine knowledge,

Figure 16.16 The ability to accurately describe a procedure or an item may be determined with an oral test question.

then the questions should be *closed*, requiring only a single brief answer. When the purpose is to determine how a student responds under pressure, then the question should judge both accuracy and presentation. In this case, the questions should be *open*, permitting longer answers that may lead to further questions.

Instructors or test evaluators must make every effort to put individuals at ease and in comfortable situations so that adverse emotions and environments do not influence oral responses. Three areas that provide more detail on oral tests include the following:

- *Development* — Base oral questions on standard criteria and performance objectives. Developers must ensure that questions clearly state what students are to describe.

- *Validation* — Validate oral tests by asking the questions to other faculty, experts, and students in other training programs before using them on actual testing candidates. Revise inappropriate questions and update questions as needed to meet changing or updated criteria.

- *Evaluation* — State the question, carefully listen to and consider the response, assess knowledge

based on objectives and standards, and score the response based on what is expressed compared to the knowledge required.

Advantages

Oral tests have similar advantages to performance tests that are discussed in the Performance (Skills) Tests section. Advantages include the following:

- *Validity* — An oral test is the only valid method of measuring students' ability to verbally communicate ideas, concepts, or processes.

- *Reliability* — A properly constructed oral test using specific criteria is a reliable measure of students' communication skills.

- *Observation* — Instructors or test evaluators can observe individual differences in judgment, thought, and approach to problems. An oral test can demonstrate the ability of students to communicate under pressure.

Disadvantages

Oral tests have some disadvantages, which is the case with all types of tests. Disadvantages include the following:

- *Unreliability* — Scores may be unreliable because of test evaluator subjectivity. Reliability is proportionate to how well the evaluator identifies the key points in the oral response and compares them with the specified criteria. Lack of definitive rating or grading criteria adds to evaluator subjectivity and reduces reliability.

- *Inefficiency of time* — Oral tests are time-consuming. Each student is tested individually and must be given sufficient time to respond to each test item.

- *Difficulty* — It is difficult to eliminate subjectivity and ensure consistency between individual test takers.

Performance (Skills) Tests

Performance or skills tests measure an individual's proficiency in performing a job, task, or evolution that requires achieving a psychomotor objective. This type of test holds test-takers to either a speed standard (timed performance) or quality standard (minimum acceptable product or process standard) or both.

Figure 16.17 Basic skills such as the use of a portable fire extinguisher can be evaluated with performance tests.

Performance tests are the most direct means of determining how well an individual can do a job. Some examples of performance tests include those that require demonstrating care of tools and equipment, driving and operating apparatus, and performing emergency care steps and techniques (**Figure 16.17**).

The purpose of performance tests is to give students an opportunity to demonstrate their proficiency under controlled conditions after appropriate practice or drill sessions. Instructors can make valid and reliable judgments about student performance only when testing conditions are controlled.

Instructors and test developers should consider the following guidelines when creating performance tests:

- *Specify performance objectives to be measured* — Construct test items based on those objectives. Each test item should require the performance of a number of basic skills, which allows a broad sampling without consuming the time necessary to test performance of each separate basic skill. For example, a test item that requires ventilating a pitched roof also requires students to demonstrate use of ground and roof ladders, cutting tools, safety ropes, and hoselines.

- *Select rating factors on which the test will be judged* — Rate students against a standard, *not* against the performance of other students (**Figure 16.18, p. 404**). Design a rating form and include such items as the following:

  — Student's approach to a stated job or procedure

  — Care shown in handling tools, equipment, and materials

  — Demonstration of accuracy

  — Time required to complete a job or procedure safely

- *Prepare directions that clearly explain the test situation to students* — Supplement a written set of instructions with an oral explanation and give students the opportunity to ask questions if necessary so students understand what is expected of them.

- *Try a new performance test on other instructors before using it on students* — Conduct a trial test to measure validity and uncover problems that can be corrected.

- *Use more than one test evaluator* — Request other instructors or officers to be test evaluators. For certification testing, use more than one test evaluator. Avoid using instructors who taught the class to evaluate the groups that they taught. Provide instructions to evaluators about what they are to look for during the test and how to use the rating scales and forms. Calculate an average score from all evaluators for each student or student team. *Examples:*

  — A student or team who receives three scores of 97, 94, and 94 percent from three evaluators receives an average score of 95 percent.

  — Scoring for performance tests that are criterion-referenced are typically pass/fail or satisfactory/unsatisfactory, although this scoring may be coupled with a minimum-points-earned requirement.

- *Follow established procedures during performance test administration* — Ensure that all necessary apparatus and equipment are ready before beginning the tests. A test evaluator must use the same equipment throughout the test for testing students, follow the same sequence of tasks for all students, and rate each student on the same basis. All distractions must be eliminated from the testing area so that evaluators can concentrate on observing and evaluating

COMMONWEALTH OF VIRGINIA
VIRGINIA DEPARTMENT *of* FIRE PROGRAMS
FIREFIGHTER LEVEL I
INDIVIDUAL PRACTICAL SKILLS CHECK SHEET

Full Name: _____ SSN#_____-___-_____ FDID _____

INSTRUCTIONS:

Student completes identification line on the check sheet and keeps the form during practical testing. When all test sites have been completed this form is to be returned to Test Supervisor.

Instructor dates each practical skill and checks the appropriate box reflecting whether the student passed or failed. If student fails, the instructor is to fill out reason for failure.

No retest for practical skills will be given during the initial test site.

PRACTICAL SKILL	DATE	PASS	FAIL	EVALUATORS SIGNATURE

INSTRUCTOR WILL NOTE BELOW WHICH SKILL WAS FAILED, COMPLETE REASON FOR FAILURE, AND SIGN THE NOTE.
THE STUDENT WILL BE ADVISED OF A RETEST DATE AND LOCATION FOLLOWING THE COMPLETION OF ALL PRATICAL TESTING.

PRACTICAL SKILL	REASON FOR FAILURE	EVALUATORS SIGNATURE

Additional Remarks : _____

_____

_____

_____

Figure 16.18 The performance test-rating sheet is used to score student performance in a specific practical evolution based on stated criteria but *not* on the performance of other students. *Courtesy of Virginia Department of Fire Programs.*

student performances and students can concentrate on demonstrating proficient performances.

- **Make a score distribution chart after tests have been administered** — Evaluate students with low scores. Those students who have difficulty in performing manipulative skills must receive immediate attention.

- **Rotate team members to every position for team evaluation ratings** — Ensure that each student is observed and evaluated in each position in an evolution.

Advantages

Performance or skills tests provide many advantages to the instructor and the organization, including the following:

- **Validity** — A performance test is the only valid method of measuring a student's achievement and ability to perform manipulative skills.

- **Reliability** — A properly constructed performance test using specific criteria is a reliable measure of performance when coupled with an appropriate rating scale.

- **Observation** — Evaluators can observe individual differences in judgment and approach to problems. Some individuals may *not* be able to express themselves orally or in writing. However, they may be able to perform a job as well as or better than other students.

- **Student motivation** — Performance tests are excellent means of motivating students. Knowing that they are expected to demonstrate skill abilities in performance tests usually motivates students to spend in-class and out-of-class time practicing productively to prepare and develop comfort levels for their skills.

- **Sense of accomplishment** — Students who successfully complete well-prepared and carefully administered performance tests will be proud of their accomplishments.

- **Job related** — Students recognize that the psychomotor skills they are being tested for are directly related to the performance of their duties as fire and emergency services personnel.

Disadvantages

Instructors should be aware that there are disadvantages to this type of test, including the following:

- **Unreliability** — Scores may be unreliable because of test evaluator subjectivity. Reliability is proportionate to how well the evaluator identifies the skills observed and compares them with the criteria specified. Lack of definitive rating criteria adds to evaluator subjectivity and reduces reliability.

- **Inefficiency of time and resources** — Performance tests are both time- and resource-consuming. This type of test also requires more instructors and test evaluators to observe, monitor, and evaluate students during the progress of the test.

- **Difficulty** — It is difficult to test each individual in team evolutions, eliminate subjectivity, and provide consistent conditions for each individual or team because the test may take many hours.

Test Data Collection

During the lesson and course development process, instructors (or test developers) determine which learning objectives are important and how to test students on their understanding of those objectives. As test items are created, they should be given values in the form of points per test item. Generally, each item should be worth 1 point on a test.

However, instructors may be limited in the number of test items that may be included for each learning objective. Therefore, additional points may be assigned to more important test items, which is the act of *weighting* the question. For instance, when instructors are limited to one question for a learning objective that may require five, then the one question would be weighted with the greater value of 5 points.

The value points provide instructors with the necessary data for analyzing the quality of test items, learning abilities of the students, and success of the lesson or course in communicating the learning objectives to students. First, however, the data must be collected in a useable form. Collecting data consists of scoring and grading test items. Instructors must understand the meaning and use of the following two terms:

- **Scoring** — Act of identifying which answers are right and which are wrong. Example: The instructor uses an answer key to score a multiple-choice test.

- **Grading** — Act of assigning a value to the score. Example: The instructor determines that a score of 75 points is a *C* grade. This grade is based on the total number of points available on the test.

Because scoring is a fairly hollow exercise when it doesn't lead to a grade, both activities can be considered as the two parts of grading. Generally two accepted grading systems are used in the educational profession: criterion-referenced and norm-referenced. Obviously, the two grading systems conform to the theories for learning objective and test development.

There are also variations of these systems that rely on elements of both. Because norm-referenced testing is *not* used in fire and emergency services training, it is *not* addressed in this section. However, scoring methods are discussed.

Criterion-Referenced Grading System

The *criterion-referenced grading system* requires instructors to measure the student's test results against an established standard or criteria that states what the student is expected to learn. In this system, the competition is between the student and mastery of a defined body or level of knowledge or skills. Using the criterion-referenced grading system can result in the majority of students either passing or failing the lesson or course.

In fire and emergency services training, meeting the established criteria and mastering the knowledge and skills are essential to the safety of personnel and the citizens they protect. Some instructors argue that no less than 100-percent mastery should be required in emergency services training. Others may establish a mastery level of 70 percent or above, which is similar to the system used in colleges and universities. In some cases, grading a psychomotor skill includes one or more critical functions that must be performed with

100-percent mastery, while other steps may be completed with a minimum of 70-percent mastery **(Figure 16.19)**.

This grading system depends heavily on its relation to the learning objectives. The initial lesson and course development must generate accurate and appropriate learning objectives. The test items must then be developed to match the value placed on each learning objective. As a tool for determining the quality of the teaching in a lesson or course, the criterion-referenced grading system provides data that show how well instructors communicated the knowledge to students and how well they understood it.

It is the responsibility of the training division or agency to establish the required level of achievement for its students. It is the responsibility of instructors to perform the following procedures:

- Adhere to the required level of achievement.

- Create lessons and courses that meet the required level.

- Develop tests and test items that reflect the learning objectives.

- Grade the tests based on the established level.

Figure 16.19 Critical skills such as donning respiratory protection equipment may require 100-percent mastery on evaluation tests. *Courtesy of Iowa Fire Service Training Bureau.*

The required level may be based on nationally established criteria such as the requirements for respiratory protection found in the U S. *Code of Federal Regulations (CFR)*, third-party criteria such as the NFPA standards, or locally developed criteria such as the departmental code of ethics.

With the criterion-referenced grading system, there is a danger that instructors might set an expected level of achievement that is unrealistically high or low and inconsistent with the level of the division or agency. The result would be a test that students perceive as inappropriate and unfair.

Scoring Methods

When completed, the tests and activities used in the lesson or course examination must be scored. Test scores are meaningless unless measured against a predetermined scale. A score of 66 points is excellent if the total possible is 70, but it is usually considered a failing score if the total possible is 100.

Regardless of whether a score is recorded as a numeric or letter grade, it must be meaningful. When students earn scores in several areas or for different activities, instructors must have a method of combining all scores to determine a final score. Several methods are appropriate and also contribute to analyzing test items and results. Composite scoring, point systems, and a class participation rating scale are discussed in the sections that follow.

Composite Scoring and Point Systems

The basis of scoring and assigning grades should be a *composite* (mixture) of various lesson/course activities and other factors. Instructors establish specific values for activities such as assignments, projects, quizzes, examinations, and participation. Other less obvious learning objective factors that can be scored come from the affective learning domain such as attitude, cooperation, and ethical conduct.

Composite scoring used for criterion-referenced tests is based on a *point system*. During the lesson/course development, instructors establish point values for each course activity. Instructors then add the points to determine the total points earned by a student during the course.

Several ways are available to use composite scoring. The following example uses a particular percentage based on a point spread. In norm-referenced testing, the total points earned by a student can be converted to a letter grade such as the following:

- 85–100 percent of possible points = A
- 75–84 percent of possible points = B
- 65–74 percent of possible points = C
- 50–64 percent of possible points = D

In criterion-referenced testing (also called *competency testing and pass-fail*), the point values can be converted to a *mastery or nonmastery classification* such as the following:

- 85–100 percent of possible points = Mastery (competency/pass)
- 84 percent or less of possible points = Nonmastery (noncompetency/fail)

NOTE: In some jurisdictions, percents below 70 are considered *F (failing)*. Instructors must comply with the grade system used in their jurisdictions.

Instructors must be as objective as possible in scoring and grading and must *not* be influenced by factors that are unrelated to the student's achievement. Instructors must be prepared to defend any score or grade given. Developing a standard system of scoring and grading and then adhering to it serves to increase objectivity, consistency, fairness, and reliability.

Class Participation Rating Scale

A class participation rating scale documents the active participation of students in a class and rates this participation. In the example shown in **Figure 16.20, p. 408,** the instructor circles the number that best describes the student's participation in class activities

Judgment by the instructor is subjective and determined by consciously observing students during class sessions. Instructors should realize when assessing participation levels that some students are more aggressive than others. This aggressiveness may make the docile students appear unusually introverted. Instructors must compare and evaluate each class member as an individual.

Student Class Participation Form

Student Name _____   Class session _____

The numbers represent the following values:

5 = Excellent
4 = Good
3 = Acceptable
2 = Needs improvement
1 = Not acceptable

1. To what degree does the student participate in class discussions?

    1   2   3   4   5

2. To what degree is the student's comment related to the discussion topic?

    1   2   3   4   5

3. To what degree does the student pose thoughtful questions on the discussion topic?

    1   2   3   4   5

Figure 16.20 A class participation form records the daily activities of students during discussions, practice sessions, and assignments.

Simultaneously, instructors should compare each student to other class members. The use of this type of rating scale can reduce some of the subjectivity by establishing the specific actions that instructors should use to judge performance.

Test Item and Result Analyses

Testing is a measurement process that determines whether learning has occurred. Giving a test is only part of the process. Scoring and analyzing the results are also necessary parts of testing. The primary purpose of analyzing test results is to improve the teaching/learning process. Performing some simple test results analyses provides instructors, test developers, and organizations with information on test validity and reliability.

The results of a test analysis identify test items that may need altering, rewording, or restructuring to make them more easily understood and significant to the learning objectives being tested.

Instructors can perform some simple analyses to assess the effectiveness of test items. A list of corrective actions is also provided to help an instructor determine how to alter test items that require attention.

Validity and Reliability Components

When test results are *not* valid or reliable, they have no meaning. As defined previously, *validity* is the degree to which a test measures what it was designed to measure. *Reliability* is the consistency of test scores from one measurement to another. Reliability is a condition of validity.

In other words, if test scores differ on a test given one day from a test covering the same material given the next day, then the test scores are *not* reliable. If the scores differ, they cannot be said to measure what they were designed to measure and thus are *not* valid. Therefore, reliability is necessary for validity.

Validity has different meanings when interpreting the results of criterion-referenced and norm-referenced tests. In both types of tests, validity means the extent to which the test measures student achievement of the learning objectives. In criterion-referenced tests, validity refers to the measurement of mastery or nonmastery by a student as compared against the established learning objectives. In norm-referenced tests, validity refers to the measurement or grade of the individual student compared against other students in the class.

Reliability also has different meanings when interpreting test results. Reliability of criterion-referenced tests means the consistency of results in classifying mastery or nonmastery of an individual. In contrast, reliability of norm-referenced tests means the consistency of results among a group of students. The type of test — criterion-referenced or norm-referenced — should be specified and designed by intent *not* by accident.

Statistical Test Result Analysis

Some methods of analyzing test results are generally referred to as *statistics* or *statistical analysis*. Statistics are nothing more than ways of organizing, analyzing, and interpreting test scores. The elementary statistical methods described here use simple arithmetic skills that instructors already possess. The only new element is the introduction of new terms.

Raw scores consist of the points a student receives on a test or other graded activity. If a student answers 38 items correctly out of 40 test questions, then the raw score is 38. A raw score is easily converted to a percentage score. The instructor computes a percentage score by adding the number of correct answers and dividing by the total possible answers. In the example given, the percentage score is 95 percent, which is computed by taking the raw score of 38 correct answers and dividing it by 40 total possible answers.

The raw score is of little value in norm-referenced tests unless it is converted into some type of calculated score that shows how it compares to other scores from the same test in the same class. This method of comparing student scores to other student scores is called *ranking of scores*. The simplest method is to list all scores from highest to lowest (or lowest to highest), which gives a quick visual identification of how many students scored what points. Once ranking is done, it is easy to see the range of scores and the *median* (middle score) and *mode* (common score).

To determine the *mean* (average score), total all scores and divide by the number of individuals testing. It is not unusual for the mean, median, and mode to be the same or close to the same number (often within 1 to 3 points). With these basic arithmetic calculations, instructors can quickly calculate basic statistics for any group of testing scores as shown in **Figure 16.21**.

In the example given, the instructor may decide that the 84 score is the average or *C* range. Scores above 84 are ranked as *B* and *A*; scores below 84 are ranked as *D* and *E* or *F*. Another option is to *curve* the scores and decide that 84 is the *B* score; every score above 84 is an *A*, and scores below it are *C, D,* and *E* or *F*. For many certification exams, scores cannot be curved, and 70 percent is considered mastery or passing. As mentioned earlier, 100 percent may also be considered mastery.

Test Result Analysis Chart

1. List raw scores (21 scores): 76, 62, 84, 95, 98, 93, 84, 88, 89, 84, 84, 83, 84, 81, 78, 83, 84, 97, 79, 69, 78.

2. Rank scores from lowest to highest: 62, 69, 76, 78, 79, 80, 82, 83, 83, 84, 84, 84, 84, 84, 84, 88, 89, 93, 95, 97, 98.

3. Range of scores is easily seen: 62 to 98.

4. Total of all scores: 1,756.

5. Divide total of all scores by total number of scores to get the mean or average score: *1,756 ÷ 21 = 83.6 (rounded to 84)*.

6. The middle score of the 21 scores is 84 (the eleventh score, which has ten scores before and after it). When there is an even number, the middle score is the average of the two middle scores. If there were one less score in this example, the middle score would still be 84. (If the middle scores were 82 and 83, the average score would be 82.5, even if there is not an actual score of 82.5. This score is an *anchor point* to determine the mean.)

7. The mode or most common score is 84 since there were six scores of 84. There may be several modes in a range of scores.

Figure 16.21 An example of a simple analysis technique that can be applied to the calculation of test results.

Test Item Analysis

A *test item analysis* allows instructors to use systematic methods to assess the quality of an item on a test. Three relatively simple measures of quality can be computed when using a multiple-choice test item format: difficulty index, discrimination index, and distracter analysis. Analyses of other test formats such as short-answer and essay require reliance on proper test item construction. Descriptions of the three measures used for multiple-choice items are in the sections that follow.

Difficulty Index

Most of the time, instructors are interested in measuring a student's *minimal competency* in an area, and thus they rely on criterion-referenced tests. Ideally, an item's difficulty should be similar to the test's *criterion level*. *Difficulty* is a simple proportion of how many students selected the correct answer.

For example, 7 of 14 students responded appropriately to the correct item answer. The proportion of students getting the answer correct is then 0.5 or 50 percent ($7 \div 14$). Because the instructor expects the item to perform similarly to the test where a criterion level of 0.7 or 70 percent was established as demonstrating minimal competency, this result shows the test item is too difficult. While this item information is helpful in examining how well items perform, it does *not* tell the instructor whether those students who answered it correctly were the ones who performed well on the test overall.

When using a difficulty index with criterion-referenced tests, any number less than 0.5 is too difficult. Likewise, any number above 0.9 is too easy. The best result would be 0.7. As shown in the example, proportions are sometimes expressed as percentages (50 percent rather than 0.5).

Discrimination Index

For a test to be valid and reliable, test items should discriminate between students who did well on the test from those who performed poorly. To calculate the discrimination index, an instructor can follow the following five steps:

Step 1: Arrange tests papers from highest to lowest scores.

Step 2: Divide the papers so that the highest (passing) scorers are in one group and the remaining lower scorers are in a second group.

Step 3: Count the number of students who correctly answered the test item in each group.

Step 4: Place the information in a table. *Example:*

Test Item 1

Options	A	B	C*	D
High scorers	1	2	6	1
Low scorers	2	3	3	2

*Correct answer is C.

Step 5: Calculate a discrimination index, using the example in Step 4: Number in high group correct (6) minus number in low group correct (3) divided by total number in high group (10) equals the discrimination index as follows:

$$(6 - 3) \div 10 = 0.3$$

The difficulty index for this example test item is determined by dividing the total number of correct answers (9) by the total number of students taking the test (20) or 0.45. The difficulty index in the example indicates that the test item is too difficult to meet the 0.70 criterion for topic mastery. It is also evident that the test item would require some revision based on the standard for discrimination. For test item discrimination, it would be desirable for the indices to follow the following standards:

- Test item needs no revision — 0.40 and above
- Test item needs some revision — 0.21 to 0.39
- Test item needs substantial revision — 0.00 to 0.20
- Test item needs substantial revision — Any negative number

NOTE: Proportions are sometimes expressed as percentages (40 percent rather than 0.40).

For good test items, the discrimination index should always be a positive number and as large as possible. When the discrimination value for test items is a negative number, the item does *not* discriminate in a meaningful manner. Using the discrimination and difficulty indices along with the distracter analysis for items can provide the instructor with very valuable information about how well the test performs.

Distracter Analysis

Many tests use multiple-choice, true-false, or matching items to measure the level of student learning. *Distracter analysis* is the simple process of examining responses for each test item to determine the distribution of responses. *Item quality* refers to the effectiveness of the distracters. Distracters that are *not* selected by any test taker need revision.

For example, assume a multiple-choice test item has four possible responses: *A, B, C,* and *D* with *D* being the correct response to the test item. The instructor determines how many students correctly answered D as well as how many answered the other possible responses. The results show 2 students answered A, 5 answered B, none answered C, and 7 answered D.

Clearly all students recognized the response for C was incorrect, thus suggesting that this distracter was too easy and *not* a good option for a response to the question. By examining which distracters are *not* selected (or inappropriately selected), the instructor can begin to rewrite and improve poor distracters, thus improving the quality of the test item.

Test Item Analysis Guide

Once a test item analysis has been completed, the instructor needs to follow up by implementing the required changes. While there are many ways to implement changes, one process uses the following steps:

Step 1: Ensure that the answer key for the test item is correct.

Step 2: Evaluate the distracters and see whether they are viable. There should only be one correct answer. Correct any errors in the distracters.

Step 3: Ensure the content in the lesson plan is sufficient and accurate to provide the student with the necessary information to answer the question correctly.

Step 4: Research instructor evaluation forms if possible to find whether there have been any discrepancies or changes in instructor presentation or lesson content.

Corrective Techniques

Test results may sometimes appear *skewed* (distributed mostly toward one end of a scale rather than evenly distributed). When an entire class scores poorly or the scores are skewed toward the lower end of the scale, the instructor should perform a careful analysis to determine the reasons for poor testing performance. Corrective actions can be immediate or long range and also simple or complex. Some procedures that instructors can take to correct skewed test scores are as follows:

- ***Throw out poor test items and recalculate the score*** — Take this action after carefully evaluating the test item and determining that its content or structure was misleading to students.

- ***Review the test analysis, adjust the test items, and give the test again*** — Adjust test items by rewording to make them clearer or change the wording in distracters, for example.

- ***Teach the lesson again and retest*** — Take this action when it appears that certain critical information was *not* taught or was *not* clear to students during the program.

Other possibilities are to review the instruction, circumstances of the instruction, and testing situations. Any of these factors may have confused, misled, or distracted the students in testing effectively. Adjust the instruction, teach the lesson again, and administer the test as necessary when there were critical circumstances. When two or more identical classes are held at the same time, another corrective analysis technique is to compare test results of all classes, then determine the appropriate steps to take.

Summary

Evaluating student performance depends on accurately designed test instruments that match the learning objectives of the lesson or course. Those test instruments must be valid and reliable. The Level II Instructor must understand and apply the concepts of test item development, grading, and analysis to ensure that objectives are met, students have learned the material, and teaching processes are effective.

General Test Item Reliability and Validity Considerations

The following are suggestions to further improve instructor-created test items:

1. Create test items and examinations before beginning a unit.

2. Ensure that the test is correlated with course learning objectives. Use a table of specifications when developing examinations.

3. Provide clear directions for each section of the test.

4. Arrange test items from simple to complex.

5. List point values for each section of the examination.

6. Vary the test item types.

7. Group test item types together.

8. Leave spaces between test items to facilitate easy reading.

9. Ensure appropriate reading level is used.

10. Consider allowances for students with special needs.

11. Vary the cognitive levels using verbs that require high levels of understanding, application, analysis, synthesis, and evaluation, for example.

12. Provide sufficient time for all students to finish.

13. Review test items for possible bias or insensitivity.

15. Calculate and consider indices of difficulty and discrimination when possible.

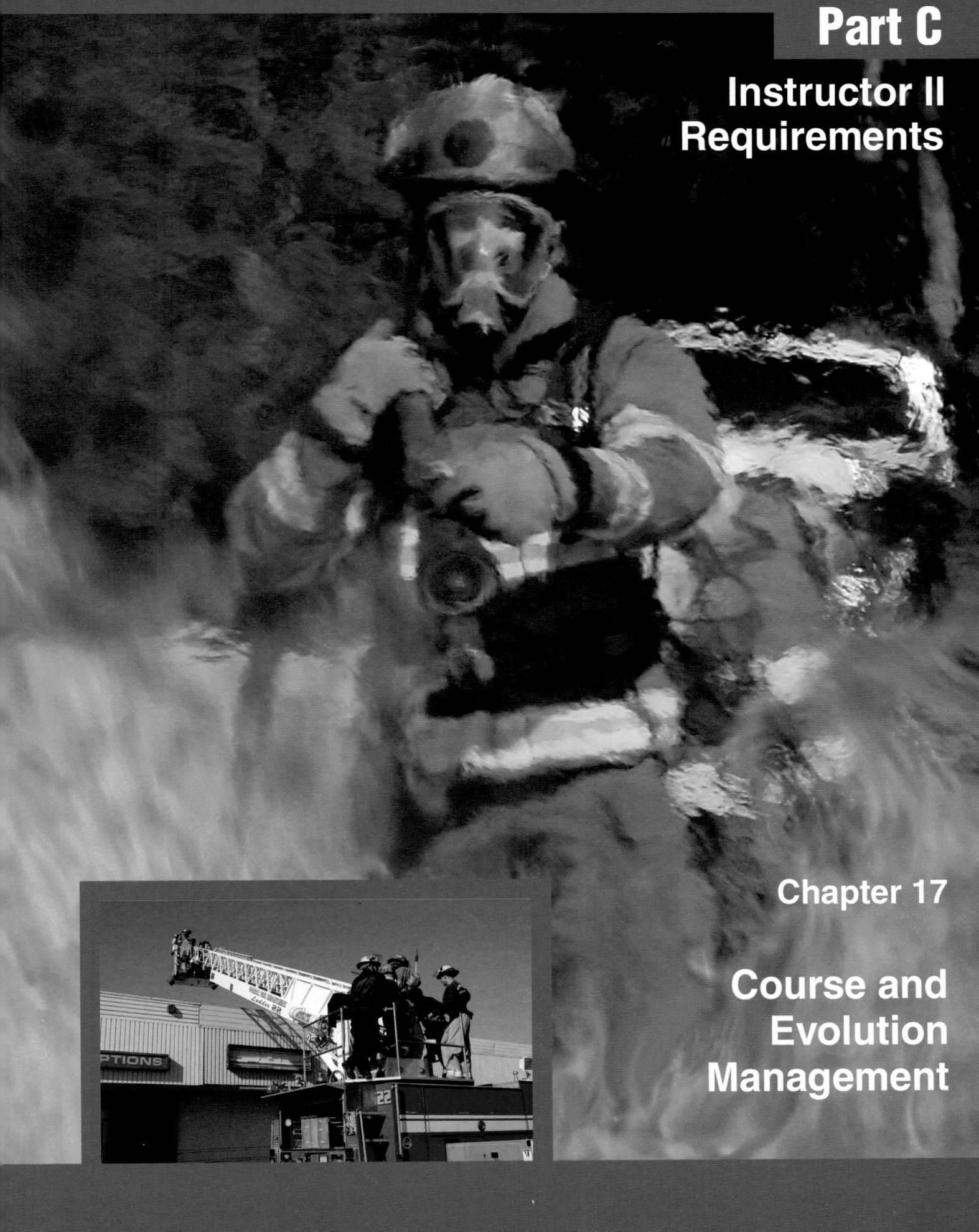

Part C

Instructor II Requirements

Chapter 17

Course and Evolution Management

After reading this chapter, students will be able to —

1. Identify accurate statements about discussions.

2. Distinguish between advantages and disadvantages of discussions.

3. List actions to take in preparing for classroom discussions.

4. Identify accurate statements about large group discussions and small group discussions.

5. Distinguish among techniques used to regulate and direct the outcome of a discussion.

6. Discuss leadership for large and small group discussions.

7. Discuss the Incident Command System (ICS).

8. Distinguish among ICS functions.

9. List ICS components.

10. Identify facts about evolution planning.

11. Discuss multiagency training evolutions.

12. Discuss implementation, supervision, and evaluation of practical training evolutions.

Chapter Contents

Transition Usage

Discussion Management
Discussion Format
Preparation Planning
Large Group Discussions
Small Group Discussions
Techniques
Leadership Skills

Training Evolution Management
Incident Command System Duties and Functions
Incident Command System Components
Evolution Planning
Multiagency Training Evolutions
Implementation
Supervision
Evaluation

Summary

Chapter 17
Course and Evolution Management

When fire and emergency services instructors advance to the NFPA Level II Instructor position, it is expected that they will have spent a sufficient amount of time teaching both classroom and practical skills lessons under the supervision of experienced instructors. It is also possible that a single member of an organization has been selected to serve as the only instructor or training officer for the organization. This individual may be placed in the unenviable position of having to learn and apply the duties, knowledge, and skills of all three instructor levels.

Besides the duties listed in the previous three chapters, additional duties that are assigned to the Level II Instructor include the following:

- Understanding, applying, and developing transitions between various teaching methods

- Leading discussion-type training

- Managing practical training evolutions based on the National Incident Management System-Incident Command System (NIMS-ICS) **(Figure 17.1)**

Before reading the rest of this chapter, the instructor candidate should review the previous chapters on safety and the training function (Chapter 2), principles of learning (Chapter 7), student attributes and behaviors (Chapter 8), preparation for instruction (Chapter 9), instructional delivery (Chapter 10), audiovisual technology (Chapter 11), and structured exercises, demonstrations, and practical training evolutions (Chapter 12). The information in those chapters is basic to the material presented in this chapter.

Figure 17.1 The Incident Command System must be applied to all types of hazardous training scenarios.

Transition Usage

Instructors at both Level I and Level II are required to use effective transitions between media types and presentation methods. In the development of lesson plans, the Level II instructor should include recommended transitions as a guide for other instructors using the lesson plans. This section is a review of the transitional information found in Chapter 11, Audiovisual Technology, and includes the purpose of transitions, when to use them (timing), and transitional development.

Transitions are important elements in all presentations. They connect the various parts of a presentation and help the student recognize the relationship between cognitive, psychomotor, and behavioral topics. The lesson plan should contain the location of the necessary transitions for the benefit of both experienced and inexperienced instructors. An instructor may find examples of transitions in motion pictures, plays, novels, manuals, television programs, and speeches.

When to use transitions is a question of timing. The time allotted to a transition varies according to the use. The transition can be as long as it takes for the instructor to summarize a topic, turn on a projector, or provide a rest break for the class. Including transitions into the lesson plan helps establish the time required and prevents the lesson from continuing too long (**Figure 17.2**).

Once an instructor has determined when to use a transition, it is time to determine what type of transition is needed: *verbal* or *nonverbal*. These types may be used separately or together. With practice, instructors can learn how to use them effectively and with variety. Another concern for instructors is developing transitions in computer-generated presentations.

Transitions within a lecture must be as smooth as possible to ensure that students do *not* become distracted. Verbal transitions provide the summary and preview with a single sentence or two. The transition can also be used to gain student feedback by asking questions over the previous information or establish a connection by asking questions that lead into the next presentation.

A nonverbal transition is usually used when the instructor wants to emphasize a point within a topic. Nonverbal transitions must *not* be distracting. The nonverbal transition may also be used to move from one teaching method into another. This transition may create some disturbance to student concentration because it involves an obvious change. Turning on audiovisual equipment or assembling a model takes time and cannot be accomplished effectively while the instructor is lecturing.

One approach is to have another instructor or aide assemble the audiovisual equipment or visual aids while the instructor answers questions or summarizes the topic (**Figure 17.3**). Another approach is to use the assembly time for a rest break. This approach requires ensuring the timing of the break and transition coincide.

Presentations that use the computer-generated slide shows involve the use of transitions between slides. New instructors have a tendency to overuse

Figure 17.2 Transitions should be indicated on lesson plans and explained to new instructors so that they are aware of them.

Figure 17.3 An advantage of multiple instructors is that while one is teaching another other can be preparing for the next activity or demonstration.

and abuse the transition effects that are parts of these software programs.

Although it is tempting to create fancy, involved, and visually stimulating transitions, instructors should remember that these are distracting and cause students to focus on transitions and *not* the information. Instructors should also refrain from using transitions that involve too much motion. Finally, sound effects that are included in most software packages are generally *not* appropriate for training sessions and should *not* be used unless they are necessary to convey the message.

Discussion Management

A *discussion* is an organized, possibly unstructured, two-way dialog between members of a group. Discussions may involve students in a class setting, participants in a conference, or staff members as part of a workgroup. Members of the group consider a topic, issue, or problem and exchange information based on personal knowledge, experience, values, and beliefs.

The result of a discussion may be a solution to a problem, a decision, or the increase in personal knowledge. Discussions can be effective tools in the discovery learning process for adult students.

There are two types of discussions: large group discussions (also known as *full-class discussions*) and small group discussions (**Figures 17.4 a and b**). Instructors will find both types valuable when developing conferences and courses. When an

Figures 17.4 a and b
Discussions groups may consist of (a) large numbers of students or (b) small numbers of students. *Photo b Courtesy of Iowa Fire Service Training Bureau.*

facilitate or lead the discussion in each of the small groups. Students have a tendency to be more open in expressing ideas and opinions in the presence of peers than in front of instructors. Small group discussions work best when the following situations are present:

- The task is structured.
- Students are experienced in working with others.
- The outcome is clearly defined.
- Students have time to prepare for the discussion.

The instructor should prepare for the small group discussion by performing the following actions:

- *Start simple* — Select a relatively easy, uncontroversial topic for the first discussion and place a short duration on the time for it.
- *Define group goals* — Define goals for the group, which may include the following:
  - Generate a new process or policy or create a plan for completing a task.
  - Choose an appropriate course of action to solve a problem.
  - Negotiate a dispute and gain a consensus agreement.
  - Perform an activity in competition with other groups.
- *Establish time frames* — Establish time limits during planning to assist groups in staying on track and not wasting time. Divide the time between research (if necessary), discussion, and summary. Let the group know when each of these landmarks is about to occur.
- *Gather closing summaries* — Reconvene small groups into the larger group when each group has completed its work. At this time, the facilitator or recorder for each group presents the small group's conclusions and summarizes the discussion. *Instructor tasks:*
  - Post conclusions for the entire group to see and then move into a large group discussion.
  - Be prepared to summarize the results of all the reports generated by the individual groups by connecting the important points made by each.

Techniques

A variety of techniques may be used to regulate and direct the outcome of a discussion. These techniques apply to both large and small group discussions and include the following:

- *Debate* — Select a controversial topic and ask students to debate the pros and cons of the topic. Use this technique with students who are more experienced in both the topic and discussion format. Select members of the group may be asked to research the topic in advance and present both sides of the issue at the beginning of the debate.
- *Brainstorm* — Accept all ideas and then discuss the relative merits of each. Basic to this approach is the concept that *there are no bad ideas*. Rank the ideas from best to worst. Brainstorming requires students to use creative thinking to propose a solution to a problem based on their knowledge and experience.
- *Use nominal group process* — Allow students to experience the process used in organizational decision-making because they will use it on the job. This technique is more structured than brainstorming and requires that ideas be more realistic. *Steps:*
  - Begin the session by having students write a list of the pros and cons of the topic.
  - Have students present their lists to the group, each speaking in order until all have commented (**Figure 17.5**).
  - Gather, examine, discuss, and rewrite comments as necessary.
  - Have the group select the top five considerations.
  - Have the instructor summarize the findings.
- *Use agenda-based process* — Create an agenda of topics or key points and provide it to students. Students may be assigned to research some or all of the key points and prepare a report to give to the group. In the discussion, students may ask questions or express opinions on the reports. This discussion technique is very structured and may be used with other teaching formats.

Figure 17.5 The ideas generated by each student are written on newsprint and posted for other members of the group to read and make comments. *Courtesy of Jocelyn Augustino, photographer, U. S. Federal Emergency Management Agency.*

Leadership Skills

Both large and small group discussions require leadership on the part of the instructor or group facilitator. Discussion leadership involves being aware of the content and the process at the same time. Being aware of the content requires the instructor or facilitator to be mindful of the following elements:

- Points raised by students
- Questions that are asked (and answered)
- Ideas that are offered
- Goals that are being met

The instructor must also be aware of the process, which includes who is and is *not* participating, how involved students are in the discussion, and whether the discussion is on track. Leading a discussion requires that an instructor or facilitator assume the following roles:

- *Director* — Move the discussion along and do *not* allow it to bog down in trivia or sidetrack to another issue.

- *Gatekeeper* — Ensure that all students have an opportunity to speak and no one dominates the discussion.

- *Timekeeper* — Remind students of the time remaining for discussion or summary.

Other activities that exhibit leadership skills include the following:

- Open the discussion with the topic or problem to be solved.

- Paraphrase student contributions to ensure that the information is completely understood.

- Question students to ensure that students understand their own positions as well as the position of others.

- Act as a resource for additional information and statistics.

- Restate and clarify student comments.

- Summarize the results of the discussion.

Instructors who plan small group discussions should take the time to develop these discussion leadership skills in students who will facilitate the groups. Role-playing can be an effective method for teaching the small group discussion process.

Training Evolution Management

Any practical evolution that involves multiple teams of fire or emergency services responders automatically requires the establishment of a formal command and control system. The Incident Command System (ICS) was introduced in Chapter 12, Structured Exercises, Demonstrations, and Practical Training Evolutions. ICS provides the structure to manage the activities of the evolution and account for instructors, students, and observers.

Evolutions that are complex and involve a large number of students or more agencies or may involve dangers inherent in the exercise itself demand incident management. It is the responsibility of the Level II Instructor to be familiar with and implement the procedures of the ICS adopted by the local jurisdiction or organization **(Figure 17.6, p. 422).**

The ICS model adopted by many jurisdictions in North America is based on NFPA 1561, *Standard on Emergency Services Incident Management*

Figure 17.6 Before each training session, the lead instructor familiarizes the rest of the instructors with the learning outcomes and training process to be used. *Courtesy of Andrew Haag, Senior Rescue Instructor, New South Wales Fire Brigade.*

System. It provides guidance and direction for the management and control of all types of emergency incidents ranging from single company responses to multiple agency and jurisdiction incidents.

In March 2004, the U.S. government officially adopted ICS as part of the National Incident Management System (NIMS), and it must be used by all federal agencies or agencies that receive federal funding. Additional information on the NIMS ICS model and its application may be found in the NIMS document itself and the *Model Procedures Guide* series developed by the National Fire Service Incident Management Consortium and published by Fire Protection Publications.

The use of ICS during practical training evolutions has two benefits: First and most importantly, it ensures the safety and accountability of students. Second, it has the additional benefit of acquainting students with the operation of the system. Students can take this training experience and apply what they have learned at the scene of an actual emergency. Instructors should adapt ICS to fit the requirements of the particular type of evolution. It is especially important to use ICS in the case of any evolution that holds the potential for injuries.

The Level II Instructor must know the ICS used in the local jurisdiction in order to teach it and to implement it during practical training evolutions. This knowledge includes the following topics:

- Duties and functions of each command staff position

- Components of the system

- ICS-based training evolution planning

- Multiagency training evolution development

- Training evolution implementation and supervision

- Evaluation evaluation once it is terminated

Incident Command System Duties and Functions

The duties and tasks assigned in ICS may be performed by instructors or experienced students **(Figure 17.7)**. When students are used to fill the

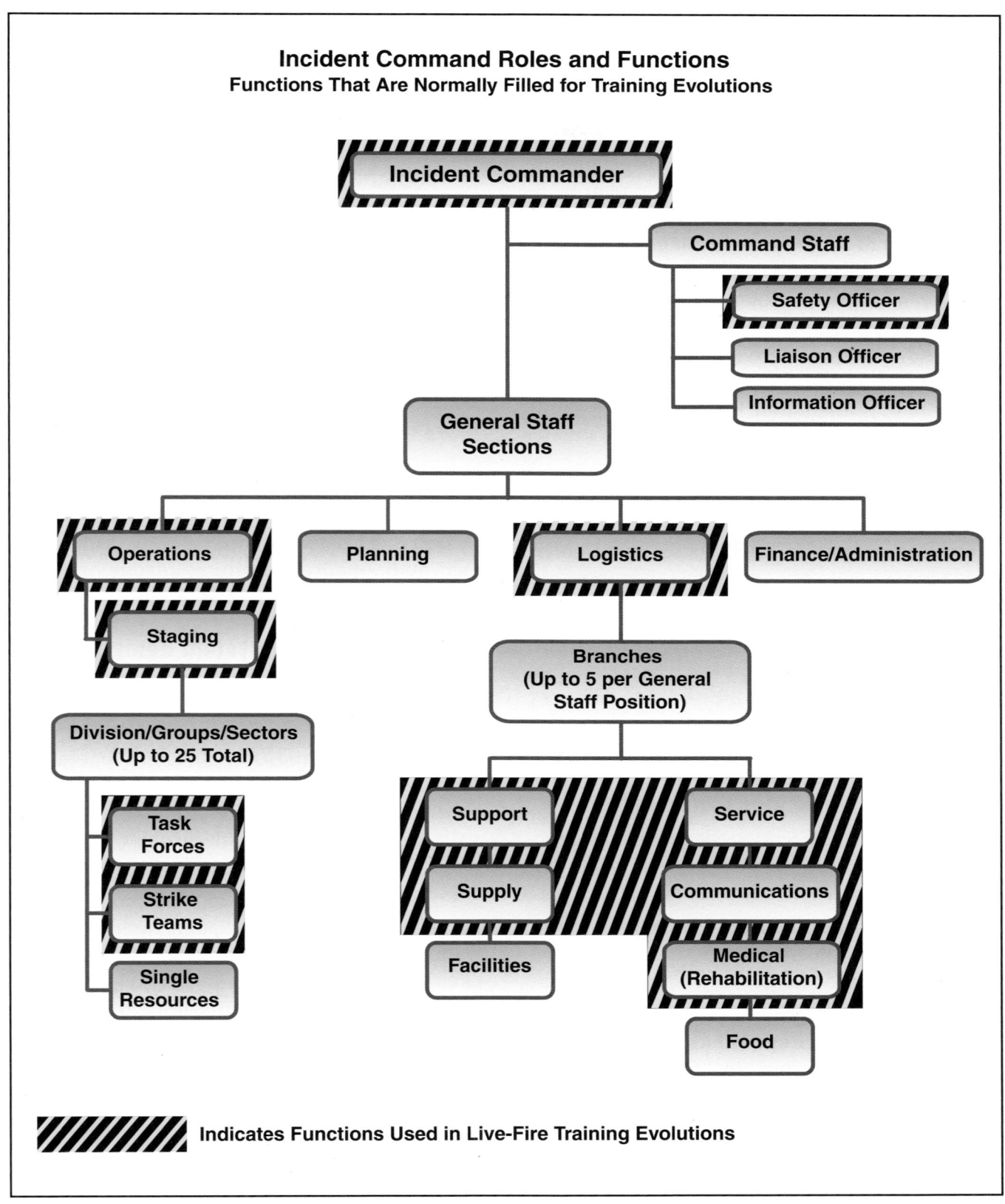

Incident Command Roles and Functions
Functions That Are Normally Filled for Training Evolutions

- Incident Commander
- Command Staff
  - Safety Officer
  - Liaison Officer
  - Information Officer
- General Staff Sections
  - Operations
    - Staging
      - Division/Groups/Sectors (Up to 25 Total)
        - Task Forces
        - Strike Teams
        - Single Resources
  - Planning
  - Logistics
    - Branches (Up to 5 per General Staff Position)
      - Support
        - Supply
        - Facilities
      - Service
        - Communications
        - Medical (Rehabilitation)
        - Food
  - Finance/Administration

////// Indicates Functions Used in Live-Fire Training Evolutions

Figure 17.7 Basic Incident Command System roles and duties.

positions, instructors are assigned to observe and monitor their activities. Some of the important functions or positions that are assigned by the ICS and used during training are as follows:

- **Incident commander (IC)** — Manages all incident operations and is primarily responsible for formulating the incident action plan (IAP) and coordinating and directing all incident resources to implement the plan and meet its goals and objectives

- **Incident safety officer (ISO)** — Ensures the safety of all students, advises the instructor or student IC on safety-related issues, creates the incident safety plan (ISP), and has the authority to immediately halt any unsafe act or practice

- **Logistics officer** — Provides the materials and supplies required to perform the evolutions and ensures that adequate breathing air, fire-suppression agents, fuel, and rehabilitation/emergency medical services (EMS) resources are available during the evolution

- **Staging officer** — Manages the staging area for multiple company/agency evolutions

- **Division/group/branch officer** — Manages or supervises students in the various locations around the site, including classroom or assembly area where students receive final instructions, briefings, or postincident critiques

  NOTE: While NIMS does *not* use the term *sector*, some forms of the model use it in addition to those listed.

- **Communications officer** — Monitors operational communications to ensure that correct protocol is used and listens for potential problems involving students

All practical training evolutions that involve interior fire fighting must include the establishment of a rapid intervention team/crew (RIT/RIC). Training evolutions that involve basic training for entry-level students require that the RIT/RIC be composed of experienced firefighters or instructors. Evolutions for experienced personnel can involve experienced students to provide them with experience in establishing and staffing this position.

In addition, instructors and students need to exercise proper radio discipline and follow all protocols. They should also confine transmissions to essential information and keep them as brief as possible. Personnel transmitting long messages need to pause at frequent intervals to allow others to transmit with high-priority traffic. Obviously, emergency transmissions always have priority over other traffic, and others need to avoid transmitting whenever anyone declares they have emergency traffic.

Local protocols dictate how messages are phrased, but in ICS everyone should be called by the ICS position they occupy. For example, regardless of who the IC is, that person is always called *IC* or *Command.*

During practical training evolutions that involve multiple agencies, it is essential that differences in communication styles, protocol, and frequencies be corrected before a joint training evolution is held. Additionally, the training outcome and judging criteria must also be established.

Incident Command System Components

Operational ICS builds from the ground up and is the basic operating system for all incidents within a jurisdiction. The transition from a small-scale incident to large and/or multiagency operations requires minimal adjustment for any of the agencies involved. By design, ICS can grow from a small-scale incident to a large-scale incident, depending on the needs of the incident.

Likewise, training evolutions can be designed to develop in complexity so that the evolution of ICS training is as realistic as possible. The following components work together interactively to provide the basis for clear communication and effective operations:

- Common terminology
- Modular organization
- Integrated communications
- Unified command structure
- Consolidated action plans
- Manageable span of control
- Predesignated incident facilities
- Comprehensive resource management

Evolution Planning

The instructor who is assigned the task of planning a practical training evolution should base the exercise on the ICS model. When students are entry-level personnel, the model provides them with the experience of operating in a managed emergency environment. Experienced students have the opportunity of applying what they have learned and being evaluated on their ability to fulfill the ICS requirements. In both cases the model ensures greater scene safety and personnel accountability.

Because all ICS emergency operations require the use of an IAP, the planning of practical training evolutions should also start with one. The written IAP provides a working lesson plan for the evolution. The instructor determines the type of practical training exercise, determines the overall strategy for dealing with the evolution, and establishes the objectives for meeting that strategy.

The IAP contains all tactical and support activities required for the control of the training evolution. The plan is divided into operational periods consisting of specific time intervals. Generally, operational periods may be as short as 2 hours and as long as 24 hours. The duration of the operational periods may vary depending on the following factors:

- Complexity and type of training evolution
- Estimated time to terminate the training evolution
- Number of agencies and units involved
- Environmental and safety considerations

Training evolutions may be planned to last as long as is necessary to achieve the required learning objectives. Long duration evolutions require logistical support that is the same as that required of actual emergency incidents **(Figure 17.8)**. Like operational IAPs, training evolution IAPs usually contain the following elements:

- *Incident objectives* — Clearly stated and measurable objectives to be achieved in a specific time interval, in other words, learning objectives
- *Organization* — Description of the ICS table of organization, including the units and agencies that are involved

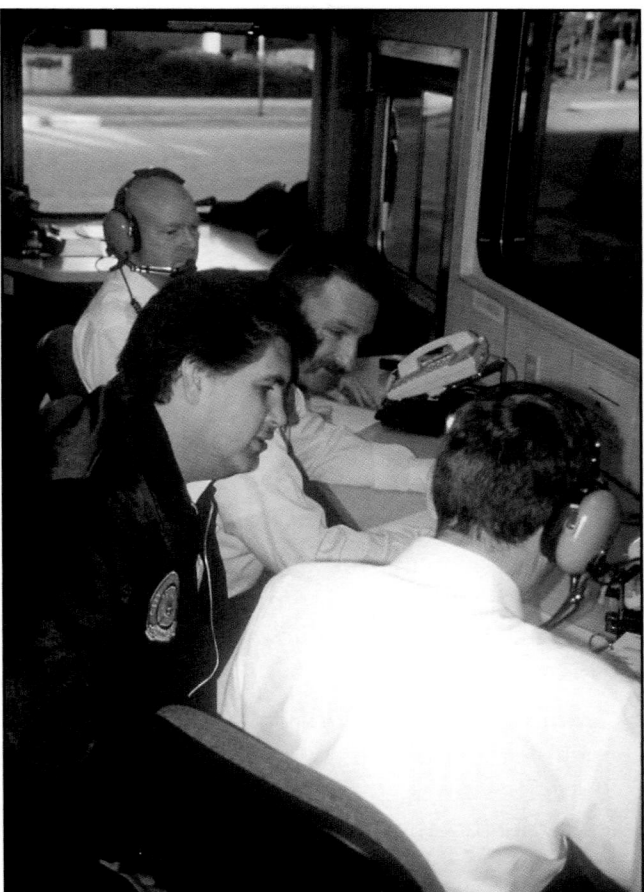

Figure 17.8 Large-scale training scenarios should include a command post and a logistics support area. The use of these ICS components helps students learn what to expect during real incidents. *Courtesy of Rick Montemorra.*

- *Assignments* — Specific unit tactical assignments divided by branch, division, and group, which includes the assignment of instructors or experienced personnel
- *Support materials* — Site plans, access or traffic plans, locations of support activities (staging, rehabilitation, logistics, etc.), and similar resources
- *Safety message* — Information concerning personnel safety at the training incident, which may be part of the ISP developed by the ISO (the instructor may wish to develop this message during the planning stage or assign it to the instructor or student responsible for incident safety)

NOTE: In high-hazard training, it is probably a good idea to develop a site-safety plan before the training activity.

During a practical training evolution, the IAP is maintained at the incident command post and updated or revised as warranted or at the end of the specified time interval. At the end of the training evolution, the plan is used as part of the postincident analysis and critique. It provides the evaluation instrument for both the students' learning achievements and training evolution effectiveness.

Multiagency Training Evolutions

The instructor may be assigned the task of planning and supervising a multiagency practical training evolution. An effective planning strategy includes involving instructors or representatives from other participating agencies in the planning process. When planning a multiagency training evolution, the group should consider the following elements:

- *Training to agreed standards* — Training should include the use of similar equipment, terminology, procedures, and processes. It also includes ensuring that the ICS procedures adopted by the various agencies are similar.

- *Exercising management functions* — Each agency and unit must know its responsibility, role, and authority at a multiagency training evolution. Students must be assigned based on skills and ability.

- *Gaining and maintaining proficiency in assigned tasks* — Students must be thoroughly trained in the duties that they are expected to perform. Continuing practice is essential to maintaining high skill levels.

- *Exercising operational functions* — Exercising is the constant practice of using all the tools and equipment that will be required at an emergency incident. The multiagency training evolution should be a regular event that occurs frequently.

- *Practicing pre-incident planning through multiagency drills* — Evolution planning should result in a full-scale drill with the participating agencies (**Figure 17.9**). This drill is an opportunity to monitor the effectiveness of the training and proposed response. Consider the following factors:

— Drills need to focus on the activities that occur at the command and operational levels; however, large-scale training of this type is costly and can be unproductive unless it is properly planned, conducted, and evaluated.

— Command scenarios (either on tabletops or in the form of computer-generated simulations) can assist managers in solving large-scale situations. These solutions can then be applied in a single exercise involving representatives of the various agencies and units.

Implementation

The ICS model is implemented at all training incidents involving live-fire and high-risk training evolutions. By using the ICS model, the instructor accomplishes two goals: First, using the model ensures that the practical training evolution is as safe as possible and that all students are accounted for during the evolution. Second, continuous use of the model during training ensures that students will accept it and use it during actual emergency operations.

For training purposes, the model should be used at all types of training evolutions whether they involve live fire or not. Students and instructors will then become familiar with the various roles and procedures that ICS uses.

Supervision

The instructor who is in charge of the practical training evolution cannot physically monitor all aspects of the exercise alone. ICS provides the additional personnel necessary to supervise each branch, group, or division and provide the IC (either a student or the lead instructor) with the information necessary to manage the training evolution.

When students are used to fill the ICS positions, they should be under the direct supervision of a qualified instructor or fire officer. While authority for the various functions can be delegated to students who are learning the roles, the ultimate responsibility for the function rests with the supervising instructor.

Figure 17.9 Multiagency training drills have become increasingly important because the threat of terrorism has increased in North America along with the rest of the world.

Evaluation

At the termination of the practical training evolution, a postincident critique or analysis should be held **(Figure 17.10, p. 428)**. The postincident critique fulfills the following purposes:

- Evaluates student skills and learning

- Evaluates the practical training evolution

- Determines safety problems that need to be corrected

- Determines the effectiveness of the organization's ICS model

- Trains students in the postincident critique process

- Evaluates the instructor's supervision and teaching skills

When the critique determines that students have *not* attained the learning objectives for the evolution, further training should be provided and the evolution restaged. When the evaluation determines that the evolution did *not* provide the level of training necessary to meet the learning objectives, then the evolution should be redesigned to provide that level.

When ICS or safety problems are discovered, they should be corrected immediately before the evolution is used again. When the instructor did *not* provide the supervision or teaching required, then additional professional development should be provided.

Along with the IAP and ISP, the postincident critique should be used to generate a report on the training evolution. That report should contain the

Figure 17.10 Posttraining incident critiques permit students to review scenarios and discuss ways to improve performances.

recommendations for changes to the evolution and be sent to the organization's leadership. All reports should be maintained in the organization's record system.

Summary

Level II Instructors are not only responsible for presenting training courses, they are also responsible for developing specialized aspects of training (evolutions) and supervising their use. They must be familiar with the various methods for transitioning between training methods, know how to implement large and small group discussions, and know how to plan, implement, supervise, and evaluate practical training evolutions that require the use of the NIMS ICS model. As an instructor gains experience in these areas, that experience is passed on to subordinates.

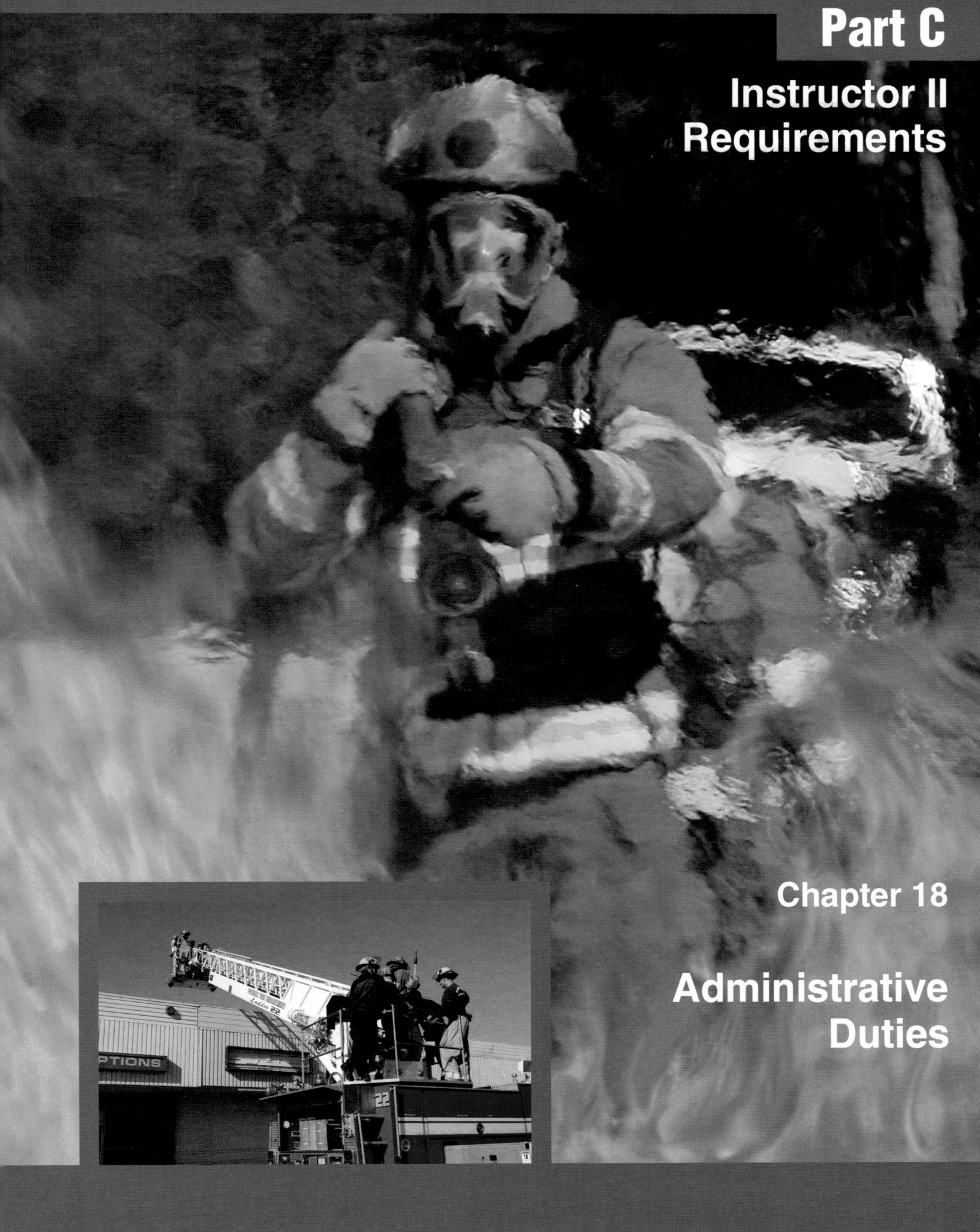

Part C

Instructor II Requirements

Chapter 18

Administrative Duties

After reading this chapter, students will be able to —

1. Identify facts about data collection and information types.

2. List sources of information for the fire and emergency services instructor.

3. Distinguish between primary, secondary, and tertiary literature.

4. Discuss using the Internet as a research tool.

5. Discuss how the fire and emergency services instructor can use information provided by various sources.

6. List the characteristics of valid data or sources.

7. Discuss reference material citations.

8. Distinguish between types of analyses.

9. Complete statements about steps in the analysis process.

10. List the three main functions of budgets for government.

11. Distinguish between characteristics of capital budgets and operating budgets.

12. Discuss sources of funds.

13. Identify facts about the budget development process.

14. List characteristics of an effective purchasing process.

15. Identify facts about the purchasing process.

Chapter Contents

Research Process
Data Collection
Information Sources
Validity
Reference Material Citations

Analysis Process
Types
Steps
Application

Budget Preparation and Development
Budget Types

Sources of Funds
Budget Development Process

Purchasing Process
Determine Needs
Conduct Research
Evaluate Equipment
Review Product Data
Conduct Purchasing Process
Evaluate and Revise the Process

Summary

Chapter 18
Administrative Duties

Besides developing and presenting instructional material, the Level II Instructor is also assigned duties associated with the administration of the training division. These duties include the following:

- Instructional resource management

- Staff management (See Chapter 19, Supervision and Management)

- Facilities management (See Chapter 19, Supervision and Management)

- Record and report management (See Chapter 6, Report Writing and Record Keeping)

This chapter concentrates on the knowledge and skills that are required to perform instructional resource duties. They include the following:

- ***Research process*** — Applying techniques to both administrative and instructional duties

- ***Analysis process*** — Applying skills to conduct needs analysis, which is basic to developing lessons and courses

- ***Budget preparation and development*** — Applying knowledge to create program and division budgets

- ***Purchasing process*** — Applying general knowledge required for procuring equipment, materials, apparatus, and facilities used for training

Research Process

Research consists of basic detective work where facts, data, and evidence are collected. It is basic to the development of lesson plans and training courses and performance of most administrative duties. Information is used for budget development, program development, personnel evaluation, pur-

Figure 18.1 Selecting and recommending an item for purchase requires that the instructor use the research process to gather as much information as possible about it.

chasing process development, and factual support of training content **(Figure 18.1)**. To be effective at researching a topic, an instructor must know what to look for, where to look for it, how to determine the validity of the data that are collected, and how to cite the sources of data.

Data Collection

The type of data to be collected depends on the use of the data. For example, when the training program involves teaching how to inspect residential sprinkler systems, the data collected might include information on the following items:

- Applicable ordinances adopted by the jurisdiction

- Types and designs of systems in use in the jurisdiction

- NFPA sprinkler design requirements
- Organizational records and reports on sprinkler activation during residential fires
- Specific fatality fire incident reports in unprotected structures

Sometimes it is difficult to determine what to exclude as well as what to include within the search parameters. In this example, commercial sprinkler systems or information on other types of fire-suppression systems would be unnecessary to support the topic.

Based on a personal understanding of their own skills and abilities, instructors may decide to do the research personally, delegate the research project to another member of the division/agency, or hire a consultant or research specialist. Hiring an outside consultant may only occur when administrative decisions concerning facilities or equipment are involved. Factors that assist in this decision include the following:

- Knowledge of research methodology
- Time available
- Importance of the project
- Complexity of the project
- Funds available to hire a specialist

The first step of the data-gathering process is to identify the topic that is to be researched. List all possible topics that are similar to the main topic. Next list the various types of data that may support the topic such as internal reports, regional or national reports, legislation, NFPA standards, product reviews, cost estimates, and so on. Then list the possible sources for each information type.

Index cards can be used to record this information and the sources. Information can also be placed in a computer database for easy retrieval and sorting. Information types may include the following:

- **Expert opinions** — Statements by credible experts in a particular field or someone who has analyzed or experienced a similar situation. The instructor's personal knowledge is an acceptable starting point when looking for this type of information.

- **Trends** — Patterns that can be traced over time and used to forecast the future. Trends may be developed from raw data such as hazardous materials incident rates; however, raw data must be the same type for each entry on the timeline.

- **Models** — Frameworks composed of accepted practices that an organization can adapt to its own needs such as a model building or fire code.

- **Similar situations** — Information from interviews with other people on how they handled particular situations or courses. Sources for this type of research include industry journals, newspaper articles, or peers in professional organizations.

- **Data** — Raw numbers such as response times or average staffing for units.

- **Examples** — Representative images of situations, processes, items, or models that a researcher can use to illustrate concepts. A good example can be used to create a *benchmark;* that is, something that is considered an informal standard or goal that an organization is attempting to attain. An organization can determine how well it has done in reaching or surpassing the standard by using benchmarks.

- **Analyses** — Third-party testing laboratories, universities, and other organizations continually evaluate equipment, procedures, and trends and then produce written analytical reports of the behavior of those items. The resulting reports can provide researchers with objective reviews without having to perform the testing themselves.

- **Recommended/suggested practices** — Suggestions on how to do something; usually based on scientific research or trial-and-error experiences of other people. The Hazen-Williams Water Flow Tests are examples of this type of information because they provide a basis for determining nozzle pressures on hoselines.

- **Industry standards** — Generally accepted methods for accomplishing some task or function (similar to recommended practices). For example, generally accepted accounting practices are the basis for all bookkeeping and accounting functions, while NFPA provides the industry standards for fire and life safety. Other types of standards are developed by engineering and scientific testing organizations such as the American Society of Mechanical Engineers (ASME) or the member organizations accredited by American National Standards Institute (ANSI).

- *Legal requirements* — Laws, codes, ordinances, and decrees that are legally binding requirements created at most levels of government to ensure the safety and welfare of a society. In the U.S., the *Code of Federal Regulations (CFR)* applies to many areas of the fire and emergency services while the Americans with Disabilities Act (ADA) affects the design of public facilities to ensure access for people with physical impairments.

- *Sources of funds* — Supplemental funding bases from sources besides tax revenues. At some point, most fire and emergency service organizations need to have information on types of grants and loans, where to find them, how to apply for them, and how to administer them.

Information Sources

With the knowledge of what to look for, the next step is to start locating information sources. However, an instructor needs to be prepared to seek assistance from a professional research firm when necessary. The savings in time, effort, and frustration can easily offset the cost of hiring a research organization that specializes in the particular field of research. Budget constraints may affect this option as a tool.

Finding information sources, or where to look, depends a great deal on the topic that is being researched. In general, data may be located from the following sources:

- Internet
- Government agencies
- Libraries
- Educational institutions **(Figure 18.2)**
- Professional organizations
- Testing and standards organizations
- Vendors/manufacturers
- Nonprofit organizations

The greatest challenge in locating reliable data is determining the credibility of the source. It is a mistake to *believe everything one reads in the paper* because most information (regardless of the source) is biased in some way. Some examples are as follows:

- Information provided by a government agency may be written in such a way as to justify that agency's actions such as increasing taxes or proposing a noise abatement ordinance.

- Information obtained from vendors tends to show the positive results of using their products rather than providing an unbiased view such as the one provided by third-party testing agencies.

- The Internet is the least credible of all sources because the primary source for the information may have been lost or altered. Authorship of online articles should always be questioned.

Figure 18.2 A major source of research data may be acquired from universities and colleges. Some of the information will be the result of original research performed by faculty members while other information may be found in the library archives.

When researching information, it is a good practice to use the accepted guidelines for determining reliability and creditability of research material. The following terms are used to describe types of research source material that an instructor may find:

- **Primary literature** — Source material that was written by someone who had direct knowledge of the event or topic. The material is original and considered to be the most credible type of literature to use. Example: An eyewitness account of the Triangle Shirtwaist fire written by the first-arriving fire officer.

- **Secondary literature** — Source material that is based on primary literature but written or compiled by someone who was *not* present at the event. This type of literature is also acceptable as long as the primary source material was accurately recorded and evaluated. Example: A history book specifically about the Triangle Shirtwaist fire that quotes or refers to the primary source document.

- **Tertiary literature** — Literature that has been twice removed from the original source. This literature is usually *not* a good reference source and may contain errors of translation, interpretation, or context. Example: A newspaper or magazine article based in part on the history book.

Internet

The creation and development of the Internet has greatly increased the amount of information that is easily available to instructors. Finding it, however, is still a challenge. Some information is proprietary such as a manufacturer's formula for Class A foam concentrate. Other information is considered vital to national security and access to it is restricted. At the same time, information may be located in obscure files or under a variety of names, causing the researcher additional frustration.

Searching the Internet is similar to looking in the index of a book. The researcher has to know the exact word or combination of words to look for in order to get the most accurate result. Internet *search engines* are vehicles that are used to locate information on the World Wide Web. Most search engines are limited to the organizations that supply them with information; that is, a search engine only goes to a limited number of sources when searching for the requested information.

In recent years, search engines have been created that can search the databases of other search engines, thereby multiplying the potential sources. By entering a word or combination of words, the researcher can locate sources based on the number of times the words are used and in what relationships. The resulting pages show the requested words in bold type allowing the researcher to determine the relationship of the words to each other and the value of the recommended web site. Some search engines can translate web pages into English from other languages such as German and Spanish.

Once a search engine provides a list of sources, it is simply a matter of going to each site and looking for the desired information. It may be necessary to use the site's internal search engine to further search for the material. When the information is located, a researcher can bookmark the page on the computer, print a copy of the page, or select, copy, and paste the information to a word-processing document for filing and later analysis.

Many information sources are available on the Internet. It is quite possible to do all of the necessary research from an instructor's home or office. However, it is important to remember that *not* all of the information found on the Internet is accurate, valid, and current. Chat rooms and message boards are the least accurate or credible sites for information because authors of the information can remain anonymous. When evaluating Internet resources, an instructor needs to look at the authority, scope/content, design, functionality, and cost for the use of the specific site in question.

Authority. Verify the authority of information found on Internet sites by considering the following items:

- Determine who is producing or sponsoring the document or site by examining the headers, footers, and the site address.

- Be aware of misleading Universal Resource Locators (URLs) that are *not* accurate for the type of site the author claims it to be.

- Recognize that the domains *.edu, .org, .gov,* and *.mil* are generally more reliable and have higher quality information than *.com* domains.

- Read the *About This Page* or *About This Company/ Organization* link for more information on the sponsoring organization.

- Look for clues to the author of a document such as links to that person's home page.

- Look for a *date stamp* to see when the information was created or last updated.

- Send an electronic mail (e-mail) message to the creator of a page (when an address is provided), and ask about the author's experience, education, background, etc.

- Look for a reason to believe that this person/ organization/company/institution would be an authoritative source for the document topic.

- Consider the credibility of a referring organization when it located the document.

Scope/content. Determine the scope and content of the Internet resource by answering the following questions:

- What is the purpose of the document/site? Does the site provide new information? Does the site link to additional information? Does the site explain or sell a product or service?

- Who is the intended audience? Fire and emergency services professionals? Peers? The general public?

- How comprehensive is this resource? How important is comprehensiveness?

- How current is the information? Is currency important for the particular topic?

- Does the information appear to be presented as *fact* or *opinion*?

- Does the affiliation of an organization/company/institution to the resource present a potential for bias? Does it lend more credibility to the content?

- Are there other resources that present the same information? If so, how do they compare with this one?

Design. In evaluating design, consider both the aesthetic and functional aspects of how the resource is displayed such as answering the following questions:

- How readable/printable is the information displayed?

- Does the use of graphics, animated graphics interchange format (GIF), JavaScript, sound files, etc. enhance or inhibit the use of the resource? Are there text-based alternatives for the graphics?

- Are consistent and helpful design features used throughout the resource?

Functionality. This area of evaluation focuses on the Internet characteristics of the site and includes the issues presented by the following questions:

- Is the server frequently busy or unavailable?

- Are the pages, content, and design changing constantly, making it difficult or unreliable to use?

- Do links to other resources appear to be regularly maintained?

- What is the effect of graphics, animated GIF, etc. on download time of the pages associated with the resource?

- What additional plug-ins (accessory programs) or help applications are necessary in order to make the most effective use of the resource?

Cost. Because not all information is free on the Internet, include an individual cost versus benefit analysis in any evaluation process for such resources. Advantages/disadvantages are as follows:

- *Advantages* — The resource has the potential of being available anywhere, anytime, and anyplace for any person.
  - It can be independent from the computer operating system, especially when it uses a web browser.
  - The information provided is often updated frequently.
  - There may be less operational and information storage cost for the resource library.

- *Disadvantages* — The search interface may lack sophistication.
  - There are problems associated with providing assistance to remote users.

— There is less control over the system's availability because it is no longer maintained locally.

— There may be technical issues that have to be addressed/resolved at the resource library such as privacy protection and information access.

Government Agencies

Canadian and U.S. national government agencies at all levels are the best sources of raw data on fire and emergency services topics. State/provincial agencies are also excellent sources for information related to occurrences within their jurisdictions. Laws, ordinances, and statutes that affect fire and emergency services exist at national, state/provincial, and local levels. Additional examples are as follows:

• The U.S. government maintains data of fire and emergency responses through the National Fire Incident Reporting System (NFIRS) and on fire equipment failures through the National Institute for Occupational Safety and Health (NIOSH).

• Agencies responsible for transportation, manufacturing, and natural resources maintain information on incidents that occur on highways, airways, and railways and in ship channels, factories, and national forests and grasslands.

• The Centers for Disease Control and Prevention (CDC) and the World Health Organization (WHO) can provide information on health and wellness topics.

• Federal and state/provincial agencies that are responsible for homeland defense and emergency management such as the following can provide both information and funds for fire and emergency services **(Figure 18.3)**:

— U.S. Federal Emergency Management Agency (FEMA) and U.S. Fire Administration (USFA) within the U.S. Department of Homeland Security (DHS)

— Public Safety and Emergency Preparedness Canada (PSEPC)

— Similar state/provincial agencies

• The U.S. federal government also funds research into fire and life-safety hazards through agencies such as the National Institute of Standards and Technology (NIST).

• Government agencies are also sources for funding grants as well as instructions on how to apply for them.

As is the case with all information collected by the government, it is subject to manipulation, biased analysis, dated material, and incorrect collection and recording procedures. In some cases, data that is supposed to be collected never gets to the agency responsible for it, which makes it difficult to accurately forecast or analyze a trend. Access to many governmental agencies is now available through the Internet, although some data may be available only through secure web sites.

Libraries

Libraries are located at all levels of government, within educational institutions, and in some third-party organizations. Many are accessible through the Internet or through other libraries. A few are specific to the fire service for research such as the U.S. National Fire Academy Learning Resource Center or the Fire Protection Publications Library at Oklahoma State University. Library reference sections can be valuable sources for information. In addition, library reference staff can assist in the research process.

Because libraries are widely networked and have sharing agreements, materials that are *not* available locally can be acquired from other libraries through interlibrary loans. This service is available at most libraries. Material can be checked out for 3 to 4 weeks rather than the usual 2 weeks for local materials. Many libraries also have computers that are dedicated to Internet research. Fire and emergency services organizations that lack this capability may wish to locate a library that has it.

Educational Institutions

Vocational schools, community colleges, and universities are other sources of information. The libraries within these institutions are usually linked to public libraries and archives. Most higher education institutions maintain access

Figure 18.3 Documents such as the technical report, *Emergency Responder Injuries and Fatalities,* prepared for the U.S. National Institute for Occupational Safety and Health (NIOSH) by the Rand Corporation are updated periodically and can be used to establish trends and make projections. *Courtesy of RAND Corporation, Cover of "Emergency Responder Injuries and Fatalities," Copyright RAND, 2004.*

to electronic databases for research purposes. In addition, many of these institutions have research projects underway or individual professors doing research that may be of benefit when researching topics ranging from fire science to social/political issues. Educational institutions are also sources for assistance in applying for and obtaining funding grants.

Professional Organizations

Fire and emergency services professional organizations are also sources for data, information, and model programs. Among these organizations are the following:

- International Society of Five Service Instructors (ISFSI)
- International Association of Fire Chiefs (IAFC)
- Canadian Association of Fire Chiefs (CAFC)
- International Association of Fire Fighters (IAFF)
- Canadian Volunteer Fire Fighters Association (CVFFA)
- National Volunteer Fire Council (NVFC)
- International Association of Black Professional Fire Fighters (IABPFF)
- Women in the Fire Service (WFS)

- African American Women in the Fire Service (AAWFS)
- Black Women in the Fire Service (BWFS)
- Women Chief Fire Officers (WCFO)
- National Association of Hispanic Fire Fighters (NAHFF)
- North American Fire Training Directors (NAFTD)
- Fire Department Safety Officers Association (FDSOA)
- American Society of Safety Engineers (ASSA)
- Canadian Society of Safety Engineers (CSSE)
- International Association of Arson Investigators (IAAI)
- National Association of Emergency Medical Technicians (NAEMT)
- Training Resources and Data Exchange (TRADE)

State/provincial-level organizations associated with these groups may also be able to assist in the gathering of data. Membership may be required to take advantage of the services offered by these organizations.

Information is also available from the Volunteer Fire Insurance Service (VFIS), an organization that provides educational material through its subsidiary, the Emergency Services Education and Consulting Group (ESECG). The International Fire Service Training Association (IFSTA) is another source for information both through its research library and technical editors. The Congressional Fire Services Institute (CFSI) and the Home Fire Sprinkler Coalition are both sources of information.

Another source that may not be directly associated with the fire and emergency services but is still an excellent source of information is the International City/County Management Association (ICMA). It has a variety of publications and can provide information on local government, public management, human resources, and trends in laws that affect employment practices.

Testing and Standards Organizations
Third-party testing and certification organizations provide statistics on the quality of equipment and products and the ability of that equipment or product to perform a specific task. Most fire and emergency services personnel are familiar with the testing that is performed by Underwriters Laboratories Inc. (UL), Underwriters' Laboratories of Canada (ULC), FM Global (formerly Factory Mutual), and other similar organizations.

Test results, specifications, and performance criteria are available from these organizations, and they may assist in writing specifications or establishing testing criteria for internal equipment evaluations.

NFPA maintains data on fire-related losses, injuries, deaths, fire causes, and other fire- and safety-related topics. In addition, they create consensus standards.

Vendors/Manufacturers
Product specifications and performance standards are available from individual vehicle, equipment, and material vendors and manufacturers. Professional association sources include the Fire and Emergency Manufacturer's and Services Association (FEMSA), Fire Apparatus Manufacturers Association (FAMA), National Emergency Equipment Dealers Association (NEEDA), and Ambulance Manufacturers Division of the National Truck Equipment Association (NTEA).

Any information provided by a vendor or manufacturer needs to be compared to information from other vendors and information from third-party testing organizations. It is wise to obtain all information in writing rather than verbally. Regardless of the source, retain all information obtained in a file as supporting evidence for the project or decision that is being researched.

Nonprofit Organizations
Nonprofit organizations that have safety-related missions are also excellent sources of information for instructors. Most of these organizations have the mission of reducing injuries and deaths due to accidents by educating the population in proper safety activities. Some of those groups include the following:

- Home Safety Council (HSC)
- Association of State and Territorial Health Officials (ASTHO)

- National Safe Kids Campaign®
- Other public safety councils at federal, state/provincial, and local levels

Validity

Instructors must determine how valid or accurate the data are before using any of it to create a budget, program, or lesson. Validity is based on how authentic, real, genuine, or truthful something is. Determining the validity of the data collected requires the application of the analysis process. Valid data or sources have the following four characteristics:

- *Credibility* — Author's credentials, quality controls used in collecting the data, and reputation of the source for providing reliable information
- *Accuracy* — How detailed, factual, comprehensive, and up to date the information is
- *Reasonableness* — How objective, fair, balanced, and free from bias and fallacies the information is
- *Support* — Quality of the documentation and research methodology used to develop the data

Reference Material Citations

An instructor may be required to adhere to a certain citation style, depending on how the material is used. Citations are used in research papers, books, articles, and electronic media to indicate the source of quotes, statistics, and other information that is *not* original to the writer. At the same time, citations used in lesson plans can assist the instructor who is using the lesson plan to answer student questions or refer the student to the source material. There are many accepted citation styles. The instructor should be familiar with the style used by the organization and use it consistently.

Three popular citation styles include the American Psychiatric Association (APA), Modern Language Association (MLA), and Chicago styles. An example of each for a book with a single author is shown as follows:

- *APA style* — Covey, S. R. (1990). *Principle-Centered Leadership.* New York: Fireside.

- *MLA style* — Covey, Stephen R. *Principle-Centered Leadership.* New York: Fireside, 1990.
- *Chicago style* — Covey, Stephen R. *Principle-Centered Leadership.* New York: Fireside, 1990.

While the examples for MLA and Chicago styles are identical, other citation formats for articles, online material, and motion pictures may differ. The instructor should consult the style guide in use by the organization or select the style that seems most appropriate and use it consistently.

Analysis Process

Analysis is the process of methodically examining the various parts of an item, project, or incident. This analysis is then used to determine how the item or project works or how an incident occurred. Analysis implies an objective study of the widest array of facts, statistics, or data. It involves looking at each piece or component to determine how it interacts with other parts and how they work together to create the whole. Analysis may require looking at the facts repeatedly to try to make all the pieces fit, much like assembling a massive jigsaw puzzle.

A very graphic example of the analysis of an incident is the meticulous review of firefighter fatalities that have occurred during live-fire training. Each available piece of physical evidence was collected and inspected to determine how the incidents occurred. Participants and witnesses were interviewed to determine the sequence of events. Radio transmission logs and incident action and safety plans were used to determine the planned actions as well as the real actions that took place. When all of the various elements were analyzed, the information was gathered into final reports that were evaluated to determine the root cause of the incidents (**Figure 18.4, p. 440**).

Decisions that are based on solid analysis have a strong foundation and are defendable against speculation and criticism. Therefore, it is important to understand the types of analyses that an instructor may be required to do, the general steps in the analytical process, and the application of these steps to the various tasks assigned to the instructor.

Figure 18.4 Fire cause determination performed by fire investigators relies on the basic analysis process. *Courtesy of Iowa Fire Service Training Bureau.*

Types

There are numerous types of analyses, many more than the fire and emergency services instructor will be called upon to perform. Analysis types that benefit the instructor are those that concern cost/benefit, process, policy, program, needs, task, and risk.

Cost/Benefit

Cost/benefit analysis is based on the relationship between the effort (cost) and the result (benefit). To be successful or effective, the benefit must match or exceed the cost to justify the program, process, or purchase. Public officials sometimes refer to this benefit as *return on investment*. It can be applied to the purchase of a new piece of equipment, staffing, facility construction (design or location), and many other situations. One example of a cost/benefit analysis would be comparing the cost of purchase,

installation, maintenance, testing, and user training for a new breathing air compressor to the cost of an annual contract with an outside vendor to supply the same service.

Two other elements of the cost/benefit analysis are cost avoidance and financial consequences. *Cost avoidance* occurs when a person or organization takes action that will prevent a future expense. The action can be as simple as scheduling periodic oil changes on an apparatus, which prevents the need to replace a burned-out engine or retire an apparatus earlier than projected. *Financial consequences,* on the other hand, are costs that will occur by *not* taking a specific action or by purchasing a high-maintenance piece of equipment.

Process

Process analysis involves looking at each step in a process and determining the best way to do it. Process analysis usually occurs when a system or process is first established. It may also be performed when a process is evaluated and determined to be ineffective or inefficient. Examples of processes include the planning process, communication process, or steps used to open a concealed space with an axe. Historically, Frederick W. Taylor, an engineer and efficiency expert of the early 20th century, applied process analysis to develop efficient methods for performing physical labor and organizing businesses.

Policy

Policy analysis occurs when current policies (or the resulting problems caused by the lack of them) are analyzed for effectiveness and enforcement. This analysis usually takes place when an organization is experiencing some type of internal difficulty. This process may take up to a year and require the use of an outside agency such as the authority's legal department or human resources department. Generally, though, when the problems are *not* severe, the fire or emergency services organization can form an internal committee or task force to provide the analysis.

Program

A *program analysis* determines the most efficient ways to provide a program or service by looking at each program component. It may occur before program implementation or periodically during the life of a program. It usually takes about six months to analyze a program.

Needs

A *needs analysis* or assessment determines the types of services that an organization is currently delivering and comparing them to the services that will be needed in the future. Changes in equipment or technology, mandated training, personnel changes, legal concerns, and observations at emergency scenes as well as requests from the public may indicate needs that exist. The differences between actual service delivery and desired service delivery require reevaluations of the effectiveness of current deliveries.

Task

A *task analysis* determines the physical activities that members of the organization must perform as part of their assigned duties. A task analysis can be the basis for making decisions that include the creation of the following elements:

- Job-related hiring criteria
- Physical fitness programs
- Practical skills evolutions
- Training courses and lesson plans

The instructor, sometimes in conjunction with the health and safety officer, may be responsible for performing task analyses for the organization.

Each individual task or job performed by personnel in the line of duty is listed **(Figure 18.5)**. These tasks are then divided into steps that can be used to develop skills sheets and lesson plans.

Risk

A *risk analysis* determines the likelihood of an event occurring such as a major fire or natural disaster, the type and severity of heart attacks for firefighters, or the potential for terrorist attacks on the community or a portion of the community. The risk is defined in the following terms:

- Type
- Location
- Frequency
- Severity

The cost of mitigating the risk (actions taken to prevent or lessen the severity of an incident) is added to the analysis along with the cost of recovery following the incident. For instance, a community that is located in an area with rivers or large bodies of water may have a flooding hazard and may require a rescue boat and trained water-rescue crews **(Figure 18.6)**.

Steps

The steps in the analysis process advance from specific items to general items; that is, from the smallest part or element to the complete topic, item, program, or process. Once the results of the analysis are known and collected, they can be evaluated for worth and a decision can be made

Figure 18.5 The task analysis is used to create lesson plans, skills sheets, and testing methods for the tasks that fire and emergency services personnel must perform. *Courtesy of Andrew Haag, Senior Rescue Instructor, New South Wales Fire Brigade.*

Figure 18.6 Many fire and emergency service organizations in North America maintain trained rapid water rescue units. *Courtesy of Jason Parks, photographer, U.S. Federal Emergency Management Agency.*

based on the outcome. The steps may vary slightly depending on the application. In general, however, the steps needed to accomplish the analysis process are as follows:

Step 1: Determine each of the components that compose the larger item, program, or process.

Step 2: Follow a systematic process each time an evaluation is made, using the same steps so that they become familiar.

Step 3: Try to remain objective and *not* jump to a conclusion before all the facts are known.

Step 4: Go over all the various components and look for a pattern or relationship between them.

Step 5: Seek the advice of others by discussing the analysis with them or involving them in the process.

Step 6: Attempt to look at the item, program, or process from the viewpoint of others who will be affected by it, which would include internal (employees) and external (citizens) customers.

Step 7: Set the analysis aside for a short time and take a break unless there is a definite deadline for completion. This action allows for a fresh view and may generate a new approach.

Step 8: Try to develop at least two approaches to the problem so that multiple approaches can be evaluated for effectiveness and value. This approach generates a minimum of three options: the best, compromise, and status quo (no action at all).

Application

Some analytical models are available in both paper hardcopy and computer program forms. These models may be applied to the following issues:

- Budget evaluation and preparation
- Specifications development
- Long-range planning
- Risk analysis

Budget Preparation and Development

The term *budget* can be defined as a planned quantitative allocation of resources for specific activities. Therefore, in the broadest of definitions, it is the allocation of all resources to the completion of a task. In this manual, budget refers to the narrower financial budget that lists both the proposed expenditures and the expected revenue sources. Resources include (among others) the following:

- Time
- Space
- Equipment
- Facilities
- Apparatus
- Personnel
- Funding
- Research

Developing and managing budgets are highly specialized skills that are usually performed by financial officers who work for the jurisdiction. Some large fire and emergency services organizations may have internal budget departments that are staffed by nonemergency employees and managed by an instructor. Volunteer departments may have an accountant or financial advisor as part of the governing board. No matter the arrangement, Level II Instructors should have knowledge of the budget process that is used by their organizations.

According to the job performance requirements of NFPA 1041, *Standard for Fire Service Instructor Professional Qualifications*, Level II Instructors must have knowledge of budget management that includes being able to perform the following tasks:

- Prepare a budget.
- Develop a budget management system.
- Allocate resources.
- Develop and maintain a budgetary records system.

To accomplish these tasks, an instructor must understand the types of budgets normally used in public administration, the types of revenue sources available, and the budget-development process itself. State/provincial and local laws and ordinances vary, but the basic budgetary theory between jurisdictions remains the same.

Budget Types

The budgets of governmental jurisdictions are more than a list of proposed expenditures and expected revenue. These budgets perform three vital functions for government by (1) describing and identifying the relationship between different tasks, (2) providing assistance in the decision-making process, and (3) clarifying political power. In addition, most budgets perform the following functions:

- Anticipate future expenditures based on the goals and objectives of the jurisdiction or organization.

- Review the effectiveness of the past budget performance.

- Establish and reinforce governmental policy.

- Assign responsibility for the accomplishment of the goals and objectives.

It is important for all instructors to participate in the budget process both to share the workload and reduce the chances that something is omitted. Once a budget is approved, it is difficult to purchase anything that was *not* requested.

In general, two types of budgets are used by public organizations: capital budgets (major purchases) and operating budgets (recurring expenses) (**Figures 18.7 a and b**). The two budgets are normally separated for a number of reasons including the following:

- *Funding* — Separation ensures that the funds will *not* be used for other expenditures.

  - *Capital budgets:* Funded by one-time, earmarked funds. One source of funds is the sale of bonds for the purchase of capital items.

  - *Operating budgets:* Funded from general revenue sources such as property or sales taxes that are then assigned to the various departments, programs, or categories (personnel, training, etc.).

- *Decision-making process*

  - *Capital budgets*: Involve a listing of all potential projects and ranking them in order of priority. As a project is funded and completed, it leaves the list and a new one is added.

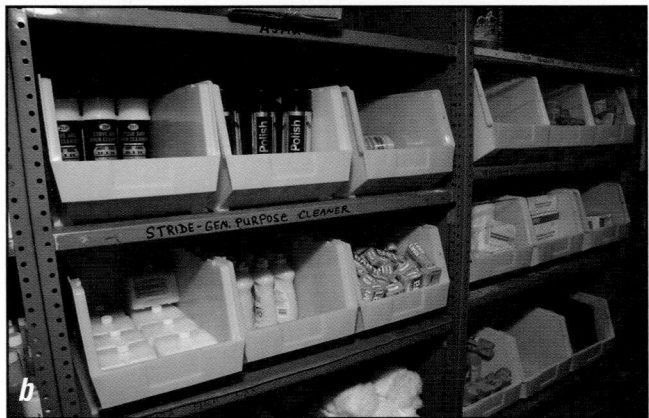

Figure 18.7 Funds allotted in emergency services budgets are divided into two main categories: (a) capital budgets, which are used for single purchase items such as apparatus, and (b) operating budgets, which consist of recurring costs such as personnel costs, services, or materials.

  - *Operating budgets*: Generally do *not* require ranking because the programs they fund usually continue from year to year.

- *Planning and implementing time frames* — Operating budgets do *not* require the high level of monitoring that capital budget projects require.

  - *Capital budgets*: Involve a longer development time and may require many years for completion. Detailed planning is critical to prevent costly errors that result in change orders to the project documents.

  - *Operating budgets*: Generally developed over a period of 6 months before adoption of a new budget.

A Level II Instructor may be responsible for preparing budget requests to obtain the items needed to provide the organization's mandated training, excluding personnel services (sometimes called *personnel costs*). This responsibility usually involves the relatively simple process of updating the requests from the previous year's budget to reflect the current needs.

The requests from the training division are combined with requests from the rest of the organization to form a single budget request. A percentage is usually added to the request that represents the rate of inflation based on the federal government's cost-of-living estimate.

Capital

A *capital budget* includes projected major purchases — items that cost more than a certain specified amount of money and are expected to last more than 1 year, usually 3 or more years. Fire apparatus and vehicles, equipment, and facilities are typical capital items.

Many jurisdictions have multiyear capital improvement plans or projects (CIPs) for these and other major investments. A typical CIP may include a multiyear plan for replacing apparatus or equipment or building a new training center. When a CIP exists, each year's capital budget represents that year's portion of the expenditures included in the CIP.

The revenue for capital purchases may be provided from a variety of sources. It may be a set percentage of the annual revenues used to operate the jurisdiction. These funds are shared between the various departments. The final decision on what is purchased is made by the governing body based on the justification provided by the representatives of the departments.

Another source may be a special tax that is dedicated to capital purchases such as the multiyear CIP mentioned or a dedicated sales tax. Special grants, assessments, or bond issues may also provide the necessary funds.

Operating

Unlike the capital budget that is used to pay for one-time, long-term purchases, the organization's *operating budget* is used to pay for the recurring expenses of the day-to-day operation of the fire and emergency services organization. The largest, single item in the operating budget of most career organizations is personnel costs — salaries and benefits.

In many organizations, personnel costs, sometimes called *personal services,* represent as much as 90 percent of the operating budget. Considering that fringe benefits cost some jurisdictions an amount equal to 50 percent of base salary, it is easy to understand why the personal services category represents such a high percentage of the operating budget.

The operating budget also pays for station utilities, office supplies, apparatus and vehicle fuel, janitorial supplies, and countless other items that are needed to function on a daily basis. Contract services for the maintenance of apparatus and facilities are also a part of the operational budget.

Sources of Funds

All governmental jurisdictions depend on some type of revenue to provide the services that citizens require. The majority of jurisdictions depend on revenue from property, sales, or income taxes or a combination of these taxes as the primary source of revenue. Trust funds, enterprise funds, bond sales, grants/gifts, or fundraising may supplement or replace this revenue (**Figure 18.8**).

Although instructors may *not* have any control over the majority of these funding sources, they can be directly involved in grants/gifts and fundrais-

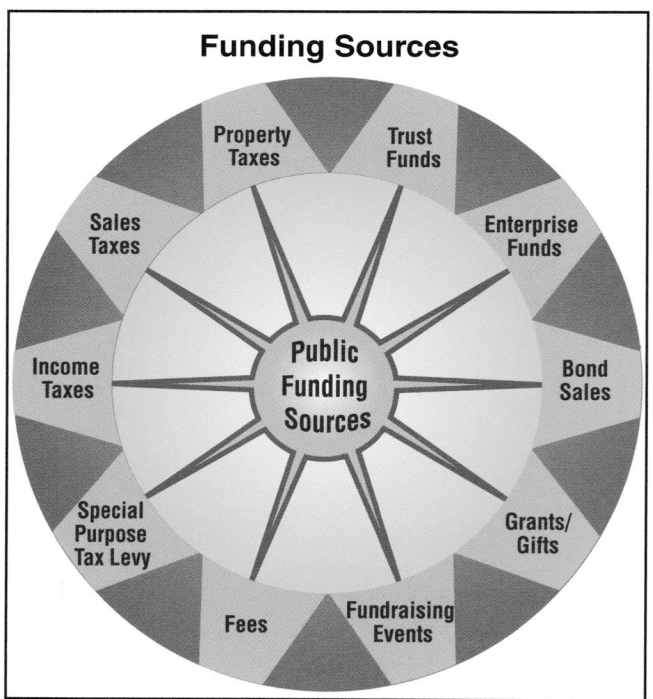

Figure 18.8 Many funding sources exist for public services.

ing. Instructors who write grants or are responsible for accepting gifts must be aware of the budget and reporting rules of the local/state/provincial and national authorities.

Grants/Gifts

Many fire and emergency services organizations supplement their general budgets with grants and gifts. These grants and gifts are either private or corporate donations or subsidies from the national or state/territorial/provincial governments to these organizations to meet specific needs. For example, in some states a portion of all fire insurance premiums paid into the insurance industry is returned to local fire and emergency services organizations to pay for training and training-related materials.

In many jurisdictions, service clubs and other civic organizations have donated funds to purchase specialized equipment such as hydraulic rescue tools or semiautomatic defibrillators. It is important that funds donated for capital purchases are used for that purpose only — and *not* for operating expenses.

Grants are available from both governmental and nongovernmental organizations (NGO) for specific purposes. U.S. governmental grants such as those provided by the USFA or other parts of DHS or Department of Transportation (DOT) are intended to provide local emergency responders with the training and equipment necessary to deal with a variety of incidents. NGOs or nonprofit organizations provide grant money to fund programs such as civilian cardiopulmonary resuscitation (CPR) training through the fire and emergency services organizations.

Obtaining grants can be challenging, especially for small organizations, due to the application process. Grant writing is very specialized and requires a skilled professional grant writer if it is to be successful. Instructors would be wise to either assign the task to staff members who have the skills and time necessary to perform the task or contract it to a professional service.

While many grants are based on specific needs, such as hazardous materials training, other government-supported programs operate largely through consolidated funding streams, normally referred to as *block grants*. Under this methodology, funding is made available for defined purposes but with minimum conditions.

The use and support for block grants have increased in recent years. They meet the need for flexibility at the program level. Block grant funding minimizes the bureaucratic aspects of the budgeting process, wherein those outside the performance chain are presumed to be accountable for fund expenditures.

The increasing use of block grants recognizes that those who do the work and spend the funds are accountable, responsible, and best qualified to make such decisions. At the same time, block grants ensure community involvement in the application process. An example of a program funded by a block grant is a senior citizen safety awareness program that provides education as well as smoke detectors or fire extinguishers to participants.

Fundraising

Fundraising is most often an activity of volunteer or combination emergency services organizations that must supplement or provide their own operating revenue. It usually takes the form of social events, bingo, raffles, requests for donations, or other local events. Some organizations have annual bean or pancake suppers that act as public relations events as well as fundraisers. Fundraising activities have the added benefit of publicizing the organization and providing an opportunity for fire and life safety education (**Figure 18.9**).

Figure 18.9 Fundraising activities can be combined with public fire and life safety events that benefit both the organization and the community. *Courtesy of Iowa Fire Service Training Bureau.*

Budget Development Process

Instructors working together with chief officers, company officers, other staff members, and citizen representatives create the annual budget. To help ensure successful adoption, both internal and external customers should be involved in the process. Because the process is involved and also ongoing, it should be divided into understandable steps. In general, the following six steps are in the budget process:

Step 1: Plan

Step 2: Prepare

Step 3: Implement

Step 4: Monitor

Step 5: Evaluate

Step 6: Revise

Plan

Throughout the year, instructors who are responsible for budget preparation should keep records and make notes on the implementation of the training division's current budget. Depending on local conditions or legal requirements, the budget process begins in earnest 3 to 5 months before the end of the current fiscal year. At this point, the jurisdiction should have a fairly clear idea of estimated revenues, based upon tax projections, expected grants and subsidies, expected fees for services, bond sales, and other sources.

Budget planning is part of the strategic planning process. The financial resources necessary to implement elements of the strategic plan must be determined in order to include them in the budget process. A budget project management team may be composed of representatives from both internal/external customers to assist with the following functions:

- Evaluate the effectiveness of the current budget.

- Determine funding requirements to meet the annual objectives of the strategic plan.

- Analyze any trends that may affect the budget such as taxpayer unrest.

Prepare

Estimated revenues from all sources are translated into preliminary budget priorities by the finance and revenue department of the jurisdiction. The chief of the department may be informed of general fiscal conditions and what parameters to work with during departmental budget planning and preparation. The jurisdiction may require that the department submit the same budget as the current year with an adjustment for inflation.

It is also possible that the chief may be told to submit a budget that reflects an across-the-board increase or decrease of a specified percentage. In any case, the personnel responsible for preparing the organization's budget request must begin work on the budget-request proposal.

An important point relating to preparing budget requests is that requests should *not* be inflated or overestimated. To help taxpayers and their elected representatives make informed decisions about how tax revenues are spent, fire and emergency services organization officers have a responsibility to make every budget request as accurate and realistic as possible and present that in a format expected by administrators and elected officials.

At this point, the chief and administrative staff members must decide the level and type of services the department can and should provide during the upcoming year. In most cases, the organization's budget request reflects the same services and service levels as the previous year. However, there may be a need to add new services or delete existing services because of a change in the needs of the service area.

The decisions regarding services and service levels must be translated into concrete program proposals, and a funding request must be developed for each program. Each program must be described in terms of personnel, equipment, and material needs as well as other costs. Instructors are responsible for describing training programs and developing the funding request for each one.

All requests should be kept as simple as possible. The simplest, most direct language should be used. In the narrative description of the services and their funding requirements, the language should be such that anyone can understand it — no acronyms or fire and emergency services jargon.

Those who ultimately decide to approve or disapprove these requests may have little or no knowledge of fire and emergency services terms. When a request is to be disapproved or reduced, it should be done on the merits of the program — not because the request could not be understood.

The systems model can be an effective tool in the preparation of the organization's budget. It can provide a visual model of the desired output, the throughput, and the required input in the form of all resources. Those resources can be translated into monetary values to match the costs associated with the output (**Figure 18.10**).

Some jurisdictions require that specific types of program justification forms be used in the budget development process. Instructors must be familiar with the forms that relate to training programs and the information required to complete them.

Request justification. Justifying a budget request requires documentation and supporting evidence that proves to even the most casual listener that the request is valid. Thorough research is the basis for this documentation. This information is not only used to justify the budget request, it is also the information that was used to prepare the budget initially. Accurate research and internal records maintenance provide a strong base for both activities. Sources to be researched include the following:

- *Organizational financial history* — Primary source of data to support the budget request based on the actual cost of providing the services required by the jurisdiction. This history includes (but is not limited to) the cost of fuel, maintenance, utilities, parts, training, operating supplies, and a multitude of other expenditures.

It can be used to justify the operating budget or a capital request such as the replacement of an apparatus or vehicle.

- *Market studies* — Surveys of similar service areas and organizations that provide a foundation for personnel salary increases, changes in benefits, or the hiring of additional personnel.

- *Actual equipment, material, or service costs* — Information available from vendors, which reflect the average cost of an item or product. It may also be based on existing contracts that the jurisdiction has for materials or services.

- *Government economic reports* — Reports that provide an idea of the cost-of-living increase based on inflation or the estimated revenue potential for the service area.

- *Insurance information* — Information available through the state/territorial/provincial insurance commission. Also includes fire-related claims, insurance premiums, Insurance Services Office (ISO) rating figures, and projections based on service levels.

- *Governmental mandates* — Documentation essential when higher levels of government place requirements on local services and then fail to provide adequate funding.

- *Contractual requirements* — Labor/management contracts and contracts for services that an organization is obligated to provide such as mutual or automatic aid response.

Request draft. In most jurisdictions, funding requests for capital items are separated from those for operating expenses. Even though these two categories must be separated, they are submitted as part of the same organizational budget request. Once all this data are compiled and translated into specific requests for specific programs and activities, the first draft of the budget request is finished.

Systems Model Approach Applied to the Training Function

Inputs	Throughputs	Outputs	Outcomes
Bond Sales	Purchase Process	Live-Fire Simulator	Number of personnel trained per year

Figure 18.10 The systems model approach can be used to illustrate the budget process.

Because this request will be thoroughly scrutinized along with the requests from every other department in the jurisdiction, its chances for approval are increased when the document is as complete and correct as possible. Therefore, before it is submitted for external review by the jurisdiction, prudent administrators insist that each departmental budget request go through a diligent internal review first.

Internal review. In this context, *internal* refers to the fire and emergency services organization as well as the parent organization to which it may be assigned such as the department of public safety. The fire and emergency services organization's budget request is thoroughly reviewed by the parent organization's administrator, the chief of the department, or their respective staffs.

At this stage of the process, the budget is critically reviewed to determine whether the data available justify the request. It is also an opportunity to consider alternative approaches to providing the same services or alternative sources of revenue. Potential questions that may be asked by the governing body should be considered and answers developed based on sound arguments.

External review. After a thorough internal review, the fire and emergency services organization's budget is incorporated into the combined budget request for the entire public safety department. This document is then submitted to the jurisdiction's governing body for an external review — the final review that the budget request document receives.

The governing body of the jurisdiction schedules one or more public hearings so that citizens of the jurisdiction can have input into the decisions on the budget. The budget may be sent back to the administrator to be revised in light of citizen concerns.

Approval. The governing body then considers both revenues and expenditures and may adjust either or both to balance the budget and meet the needs of citizens. When the concerns of citizens have been addressed and the budget is in balance, the governing body approves the budget, and it becomes law.

Once the budget has been approved, the administrator, department heads, division managers, and supervisors (company officers) now have the funds with which to turn the vision reflected in the budget into reality. They must next use their administrative and managerial skills to implement the budget.

Implement

Once the budget is adopted, the chief of the department and the rest of the organization's personnel use the budgeted funds to implement the programs and activities that provide the services approved by the jurisdiction. In addition to important fiscal details, the approved and adopted budget represents a plan for the organization's operation for the fiscal year. This information should be communicated by the administration to all members of the organization.

The budget tells those who must function within its limitations when new personnel can be hired, staff cuts will be necessary, vacant positions can be filled, and new equipment can be purchased. In addition, the budget requests that were approved or disapproved may provide an indication about how the jurisdiction perceives the services provided by the organization — or they may simply reflect fiscal reality.

The budget message should include any specific praise or criticism of the organization's operation by the jurisdiction. While the praise may be gratifying, the criticism may be more valuable. When criticism is viewed objectively, it can serve as a way to focus future priorities and performance within the fire and emergency services organization.

Monitor

The budget process does *not* end with the implementation of the budget. It must be monitored to determine its effectiveness and prevent a budgetary crisis in the event of a change in the economic environment. Typically, the individual departments within the jurisdiction are only informed of the expenditures of their allotted budgets.

Most jurisdictions print and distribute monthly account statements that indicate the account balance in each program, line item, or category of the budget. This statement allows the chief officer or instructor who is responsible for budget administration within the training division to track the purchasing trends and ensure that the accounts are *not* overspent.

With the addition of computer-based accounting programs, this monitoring control can become a more frequent check performed on a monthly, weekly, or daily basis with feedback provided to budget managers (**Figure 18.11**). In addition, many organizations now keep such budget accounting information in electronic form on computer servers accessible to department managers. This electronic form provides more current information and eliminates the need for much of the printing and distribution that was done in the past.

Evaluate

Evaluating the effectiveness of the budget is part of the monitoring process. When applied to the purchase of materials, an evaluation can be as simple as determining that the proper amount and quality of materials are available in a reasonable amount of time. When applied to programs and performance, evaluation requires a cost/benefit analysis that compares the total effort necessary to produce the desired results.

The individual project manager, the chief of the department, or an auditor assigned by the jurisdiction may perform evaluations. The results of the evaluation can be used to justify program changes, additional funding for programs, or elimination of a program that is deemed cost-prohibitive.

Revise

There is always the possibility that a budget will have to be revised during the budget cycle. Causes may include the following:

- Decrease in revenues
- Increase in operating costs
- Underestimated actual costs
- Increase in service requirements
- Change in labor/management agreements
- Unforeseen or catastrophic occurrences
- Unfunded governmental mandates

Because budget expenditures must be in line with actual revenue, the most likely result will be to revise the cost of operation or capital purchases. The process for revising the budget is defined by the local ordinance or policy.

Records should be maintained on all changes and revisions in the budget during the cycle. Records are necessary for improving the accuracy of future budget preparation and provide a history of the current budget.

Typical Monthly Operating Budget Report

Report for July 2005

Account Number	Title	July Expenditures	July Encumbered	July Balance Remaining	Approved Monthly Allowance	Current Year to Date	Current Year Total
1002003001230	Janitorial	$ 5,000	$ 2,000	$ 1,000	$ 8,000	$ 35,000	$ 96,000
1002003001231	Tools	1,000	1,500	500	3,000	15,000	36,000
1002003001232	Supplies	5,000	2,000	3,000	10,000	40,000	4,000
1002003001233	Professional Services	4,000	2,500	1,000	7,500	21,000	90,000
1002003001234	Training	3,000	4,000	2,000	9,000	40,000	108,000
1002003001235	Personal Protective Equipment	10,000	5,000	5,000	20,000	120,000	240,000
Total		$28,000	$17,000	$12,500	$57,500	$271,500	$654,000

Figure 18.11 A budget report may be generated by the finance department on a daily, weekly, or monthly basis.

Purchasing Process

A budget provides an organization with the funds necessary to perform its assigned mission. Part of this mission is to purchase materials, equipment, and apparatus necessary to perform that mission. Purchasing may be the responsibility of a supply, apparatus, or logistics chief; nonuniformed employee; or member of the jurisdiction's central purchasing department. A Level II Instructor may be responsible for purchasing materials or equipment that is specific to the organization's training needs.

Purchasing involves two important concepts that an instructor must understand: authority and responsibility. The organization may provide an instructor with a certain amount of authority to make purchasing decisions. For example, an instructor may be able to purchase training materials costing less than $500 without approval from a supervisor or using a bid process. The organization gives the instructor this authority. Instructors may also be able to authorize the purchase of bid items that may cost in the thousands of dollars.

However, with authority comes responsibility. It is the instructor's responsibility to ensure that the organization receives the exact materials that were ordered. Because many suppliers maintain a reduced inventory, they may substitute other items for the same price. The instructor must ensure that the substituted item is acceptable.

While large fire and emergency services organizations may have internal purchasing capabilities, small organizations may rely on a centralized purchasing department within the jurisdiction. In either case, the purchasing process possesses certain characteristics. The process for selecting and procuring apparatus, equipment, and materials must be objective, logical, methodical, and repeatable. Descriptions are as follows:

- An *objective* process must be based on fact — *not* emotion.

- It must have a *logical*, stepping-stone pattern that allows each decision to be based firmly on the preceding decision.

- *Methodical* means that it adheres to an existing, well-established pattern that has been used successfully by other organizations.

- Finally, it must be *repeatable* by future personnel who are given the task of providing logistical support through this process.

The selection and procurement process model provided in this chapter is applicable for all types of apparatus, equipment, personal protective equipment, and some types of expendable materials. The process steps include the following:

Step 1: Determine the needs of the department/organization.

Step 2: Conduct research on the equipment, manufacturers, and any applicable standards/regulations.

Step 3: Evaluate and field-test proposed equipment.

Step 4: Review product data.

Step 5: Conduct the purchasing process.

Step 6: Evaluate purchasing process and revise when necessary.

The instructor who is responsible for purchasing training-related equipment or materials directly from vendors or who generates purchase requests to be filled by the central supply should apply the steps listed as necessary to ensure that the proper supplies are provided. These steps apply to both capital items and operating equipment and materials, although purchasing procedures may vary as indicated later in this section.

Determine Needs

A needs assessment takes place once during the budget preparation process and again before purchasing the approved equipment and materials. Once a list of equipment and materials is developed, it is necessary to research the quality and quantity that is available for purchase and vendors who can provide them. The organization's needs may be determined in a variety of ways such as the following:

- ***Perform a needs assessment*** — Evaluate needs based on the programs and services provided by the organization to the jurisdiction. Each program manager (suppression, prevention, training, etc.) can provide a list of the equipment and materials required to complete the programs during the fiscal year based on past experience and future projections. Compatibility of equipment should also be noted **(Figure 18.12)**.

Figure 18.12 Equipment that is purchased specifically for training must be the same as the equipment assigned to and used by emergency response units. *Courtesy of Kenneth Krulish, Jr.*

- *Review the standards and regulations that mandate the purchase of specific types of equipment* — Review the legal mandates created by the local, state/territorial/provincial, or federal governments for the operation of a fire and emergency services organization.

- *Review the current purchases* — Indicate the effectiveness of the current equipment and materials in meeting the organization's service requirements. Determine whether the correct quantities of materials are available in a timely fashion.

- *Perform a hazards analysis of the response area* — Focus on any changes in the service area and the need for changes in programs, services, or equipment.

- *Determine the amount of funds available in each budget account* — Determine whether an account contains sufficient funds to purchase the required quantity of materials. It may be necessary to locate additional funds, transfer funds from unused accounts, or cancel the associated training.

Conduct Research

The time required to conduct research depends on the type of equipment or materials that are to be purchased. The instructor must provide sufficient time to gather and evaluate the information. Expendable items such as janitorial supplies may require only a review of product literature, while personal protective equipment may require from a few months to a year for research. The research process for capital purchases may include the following actions:

- Survey other jurisdictions.
- Review manufacturers' business histories.
- Request references.
- Review standards and regulations.
- Review industry trends.
- Compare various products.
- Determine equipment compatibility.
- Review purchasing ordinances and laws.
- Develop a request for proposal (RFP).

Survey Other Jurisdictions

Research can begin by surveying fire and emergency service organizations in other jurisdictions about the type of equipment or material that they use. Survey topics should include the following:

- Types of equipment used
- Problems encountered with the equipment
- Ability of the equipment to meet specifications
- Equipment service or maintenance difficulties
- After-sales support by manufacturers

When the training divisions of the various organizations participate in joint training, equipment compatibility should then be considered.

Review Manufacturers' Business Histories

A review of the business histories of the various manufacturers and vendors representing them should be performed. Annual reports, articles in trade journals, financial statements, and business reports published by companies like Dunn and Bradstreet can provide an image of the organization and some insight into the company's ability to supply the system or equipment. The share of the market that the manufacturers hold and why they have that share should be considered.

Request References

References from other equipment purchasers are also an important source of information. The instructor should request a list of the most recent purchasers of the particular equipment similar to the type under consideration from the manufacturers. Other organizations within the area, including both public and private purchasers, can provide these references.

Review Standards and Regulations

All applicable standards and regulations should also be reviewed. These standards and regulations include not only the equipment's operational requirements but also the design and testing requirements. This review allows an instructor to develop specifications that meet or exceed the standards and regulations. A thorough understanding of the relevant standards and regulations also allows the instructor to better evaluate the products that are submitted for evaluation.

Review Industry Trends

Manufacturers are continuously making changes in the design of fire and emergency services equipment to meet changes in the standards/regulations. In addition, changes are made to improve the equipment based on internal research projects. Therefore, an instructor must review the latest industry trends in equipment design. Trade journals, trade shows, and press releases by the manufacturers' marketing divisions provide opportunities to stay abreast of current developments. In some cases online Internet sites have product reviews that may assist in the decision-making process.

Compare Various Products

Competition is very strong among fire protection equipment manufacturers (**Figure 18.13**). Unlike the automobile industry, there are few fire protection equipment manufacturers and limited customers. Therefore, an instructor must compare the various products based on the following factors:

- Similar characteristics
- Sales and technical support
- Parts availability
- Length of time before equipment may become obsolete or have a major design change

Figure 18.13 Trade shows are excellent opportunities for instructors to view new and innovative equipment and materials. *Courtesy of Iowa Fire Service Training Bureau.*

- Available warranties and warranty support
- Local manufacturer representation
- Manufacturer's ability to fill orders within a specified time frame
- Service records of vendor and manufacturer

This information can be entered into a matrix or database for ease of comparison. Competition in the marketplace can be used to an organization's advantage in negotiating the terms of contracts.

Determine Equipment Compatibility

Information gained during the needs assessment relating to compatibility can now be applied to the equipment under consideration. Compatibility includes both physical compatibility and how the equipment is used. The equipment must meet the operational procedures of the organization without drastic changes in training and operational procedures.

For example, when the organization is issuing individual respiratory protection facepieces that can be used with both self-contained breathing apparatus (SCBA) and supplied-air respirator (SAR) units, compatibility concerns must be included in the evaluation. At the same time, the purchase of A-frame folding ladders when the operational standard calls for 24-foot (7.3 m) extension ladders will have a negative effect on ladder operations and training.

Review Purchasing Ordinances and Laws

Once all of the essential data has been collected, the instructor should review the purchasing ordinances and laws of the jurisdiction. Most jurisdictions are bound by state/territorial/provincial purchasing requirements. Involving members of the jurisdiction's legal, finance, or purchasing departments in the process prevents any errors in the development of specifications or bid development.

Develop Request for Proposal

When the jurisdiction permits, it is a good idea to develop a RFP before sending bid notices. A RFP defines the needs of the organization and allows manufacturers or their authorized distributors to decide whether they can meet bid specifications. A RFP must have the following components:

- Specific schedule outline
- Bid dates and delivery dates
- Provisions for supplying equipment for scheduled evaluations
- Training dates for maintenance technicians and instructors

A RFP also allows the jurisdiction to have control over the companies that can bid based on the response to the RFP and participation in prebid meetings. The RFP process reduces the number of bidders to those companies that are capable of meeting the bid specifications. Companies are eliminated from consideration in the following situations:

- Cannot meet delivery deadlines
- Cannot provide the required performance bonds
- Lack the established financial support to complete the contract
- Have a documented history of contract violations

Before writing the RFP, an instructor should consult both legal counsel and the authority's purchasing laws to determine what kinds of controls can legally be placed on bids or bidders. The selection of bidders may *not* be subjective or arbitrary. A sample RFP is found in **Appendix N,** Sample Request for Proposal.

NOTE: Fire and emergency services organizations cannot be subjective or arbitrary in the selection of bidders for fire protection equipment, apparatus, or materials. Open and fair purchasing laws regulate all governmental organizations. Instructors must respect these laws and operate within them.

Once a specific product is determined to be the most appropriate for the organization, it can be established as the *standard* for the organization. Thus the organization does *not* have to rewrite specifications the next time identical equipment needs to be purchased.

Another approach is to establish a renewable contract in the bid specifications. The contract may be negotiated for 1 year with three subsequent annual renewals based on a set increase for inflation when both parties agree. However, due to rapid changes in the standards/regulations for respiratory protection, protective clothing, and apparatus, the purchasing organization must be prepared to rewrite the specifications based on recent changes. Contract language should also reflect this possibility.

Evaluate Equipment

The RFP should contain language requiring a physical evaluation of fire protection equipment and accessories that each manufacturer is planning to submit for bid. This physical evaluation is an opportunity for the organization to test the proposed equipment in controlled training exercises and actual daily operations **(Figure 18.14)**.

The physical evaluation, like the prebid conference, should be a requirement for participation in the official bid process. Companies that do *not* participate should *not* be certified to continue the bidding process. Each manufacturer should be required to provide a specified number of units, usually enough to outfit at least one company.

Before the actual evaluations, the manufacturer must provide training for personnel participating in the testing of the equipment. A manufacturer's sales or technical representative should be present during the equipment evaluations to answer questions or provide additional training.

Figure 18.14 Field tests of equipment that is being considered for purchase are important for determining how well it will function under actual operational conditions.

The physical evaluation should include both training evolutions and actual field tests. Therefore, the RFP must specify the total amount of time that the units are needed for evaluation, the specific date and time for the training evolutions, and language releasing the department/organization from responsibility for any damage or wear to the units.

Regardless of the types of training evolutions, an instructor must have an objective grading system for the equipment. Criteria should be established and points assigned based on the equipment's ability to meet the standard or regulation. The grades may be numerical from *best to worst* or terms such as *excellent, good, fair,* or *poor.* A comments section should be included on the grade form for any additional information or opinions by the users.

A sample form for the evaluation of respiratory protection equipment is included in **Appendix O,** Equipment Evaluation Form. For example, respiratory protection evaluation criteria may include (but are not limited to) the following factors:

- Maneuverability
- Flexibility
- Effect on vision
- Ease of donning
- Ease of doffing
- Effect on workload
- Comfort
- Durability
- Ease of operation
- Compatibility with operational procedures

Once the controlled training evaluations are complete, the units used for evaluation should be assigned to active emergency response companies. Depending on the activity level of the companies, this portion of the evaluation may take a month or more. Equipment evaluation forms should be supplied for personnel to complete after each use.

Field evaluations under actual use conditions provide additional data for the instructor and also allow personnel who will be using the final product an opportunity to have a part in the selection process. Therefore, personnel other than those who participated in the controlled training evaluations should be selected to conduct field tests.

The information gained from the physical evaluations must be compiled and analyzed by the instructor. All grading forms and comments should be retained in the specifications files in case the final purchase decision is questioned. The importance of maintaining thorough and complete records cannot be overemphasized.

Review Product Data

Once field evaluations are complete, the instructor can consider other facts about the various equipment or materials. Some areas of concern and factors to consider are as follows:

- **Features** — List the various features and accessories available with the particular equipment.

- **Durability** — Answer the following questions: How sturdy is the equipment? Are plastic parts easily broken? Will the equipment stand up to rough treatment?

- **Lifecycle cost** — Include the initial purchase price (which may have to be estimated based on the list price) and the cost of annual maintenance, parts, and support amortized over the life expectancy of the equipment to determine lifecycle cost.

- **Maintenance requirements** — Determine maintenance requirements by considering the manufacturer's suggested maintenance schedule, the level of technician certification and training, and whether maintenance can be done in-house or by a contract vendor approved by the manufacturer **(Figure 18.15)**.

- **Infrastructure** — Answer the following questions: What is the existing infrastructure that supports the current brand of equipment? What changes or investments are required to redesign the equipment maintenance facility, modify existing systems, and retrofit apparatus mounting hardware?

When all of the data are collected and reviewed, the instructor selects the equipment that best meets the established needs of the training division. Units that do *not* meet the criteria should

Figure 18.15 Maintaining equipment to the manufacturer's recommended standard can add to the organization's annual operating budget requirements. Maintenance may be performed internally or contracted externally to a qualified vendor. *Courtesy of Cherry Hill (NJ) Fire Department.*

be eliminated from consideration. The instructor must be fully aware of purchasing ordinances or laws in the event that specifications are too restrictive and legally prohibited.

When specific equipment is determined to meet the organization's needs, thereby precluding an open-bid process, a variance or exemption from the approved purchasing process may be required from the jurisdiction's purchasing and legal departments. See Create Bid Specifications section for more information.

Conduct Purchasing Process

The purchasing procedure for fire protection equipment depends on the process adopted and regulated by the authority having jurisdiction (AHJ). Most equipment such as SCBA, SAR systems, ventilation fans, and power extrication tools are considered capital purchases and must have funds specifically allocated for those purposes. Other items such as the following may be purchased from operating funds:

- High efficiency particulate air (HEPA) masks
- Equipment parts
- Air-purifying respirator (APR) cartridges
- Hand tools
- Equipment accessories
- Janitorial supplies

the specific requirements listed down the side and individual bidders listed across the top. Values can be assigned to each requirement and inserted into the corresponding box, depending on whether or not the bidder exceeded, met, or failed to meet the specification.

Once the grid is complete, the scores are added. When certain specifications outweigh others, the scoring can be weighted in favor of the more important specification. For example, a buddy-breathing accessory or integrated personal alert safety system (PASS) device on a respiratory protection unit would receive more points than a carrying case or neck strap.

Scoring must be equitable and well documented. In most jurisdictions in the U.S., this material may be subject to the Freedom of Information Act and outside review.

Award Purchase Contract

After the instructor has reviewed the bids and made a recommendation to the training division manager or department chief, the bid must be awarded by the jurisdiction. Usually the legal department writes a contract, and the AHJ awards the bid to the winning supplier. The contract binds both the supplier to meet the specifications and the jurisdiction to pay for the goods or services.

Administration of the contract is the responsibility of the purchasing department on behalf of the emergency services organization that receives the goods or services. The emergency services organization is responsible then for the following actions regarding the purchased equipment, materials, or apparatus:

- Accept
- Test
- Inventory
- Store
- Maintain
- Place into service

Evaluate and Revise the Process

Once the purchasing process is complete, it should be evaluated for its effectiveness. When a change in the process is indicated, then a revision should be made within the limitations of the jurisdiction's purchasing laws and ordinances.

Summary

The Level II Instructor may find that administrative responsibilities are both challenging and interesting. Preparing budget requests, purchasing equipment and materials, conducting research, and performing analyses require the application of many different skills other than those required of a classroom teacher. At the same time, many of the organizing and planning skills developed as a teacher can also be applied to administrative duties. For some instructors who love teaching, the disadvantage of taking on additional administrative duties is the lack of available teaching time.

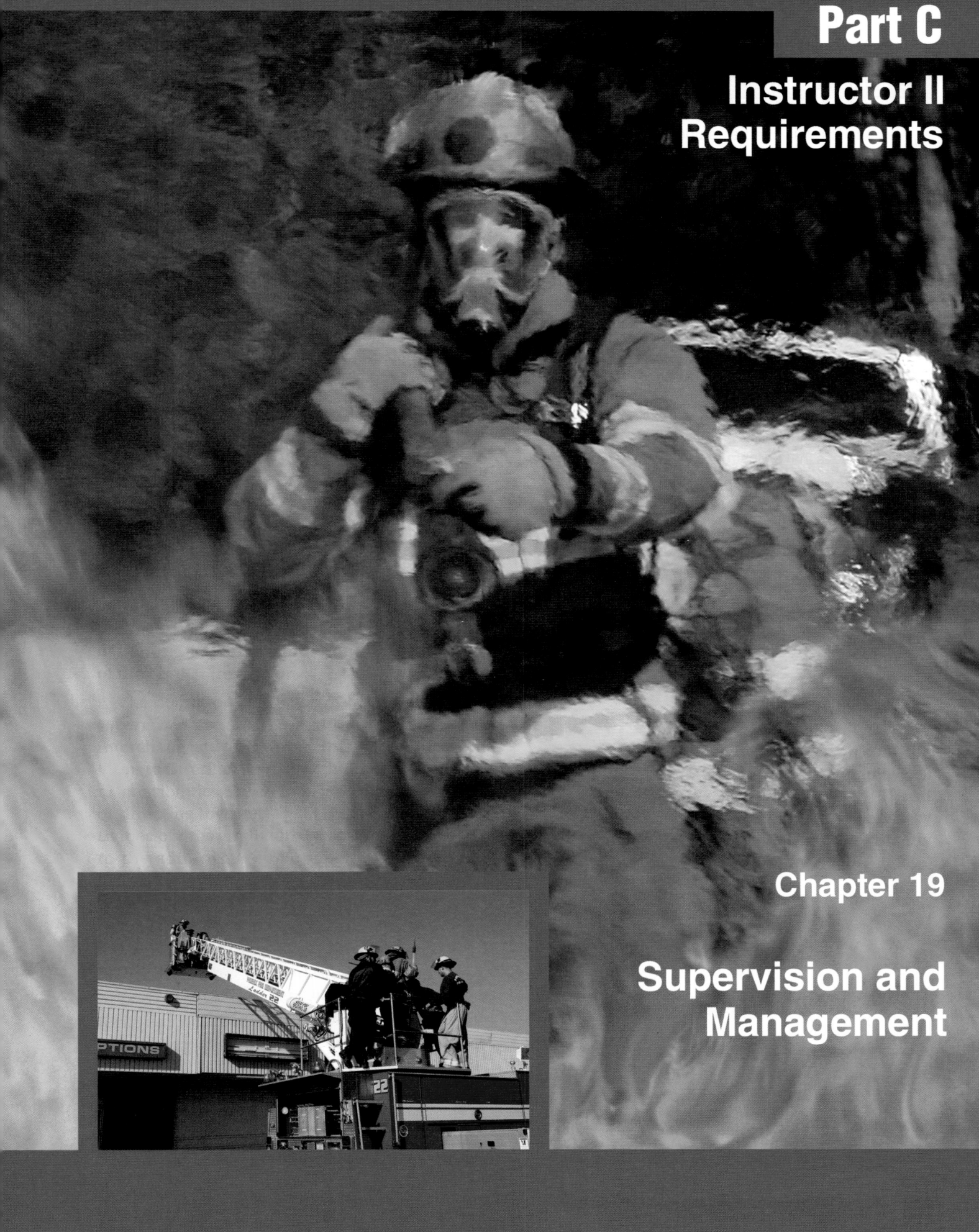

Chapter 19

Supervision and Management

the common goal. In addition, supervisors who involve the employees in the process of establishing the objectives will find that their employees have more incentive to fulfill the objectives.

Involving Employees in the Process

Supervisors can involve employees in the process of establishing goals and objectives in any one of the following three methods:

- ***Simply require the employee to accomplish a specific task in a specific manner*** — Method based on the concept that the supervisor knows the best method to perform the task, has all the information necessary to make the decision, and the employee is thoroughly trained in performing the task as required. This traditional method has been followed in the military, the fire service, and in business during much of the past century. *Other elements:*

  — In a crisis situation where time is critical and reaction must be immediate, this autocratic method may still be an option.

  — However, regular use of this method for non-emergency tasks can serve as a disincentive and lead to employee resentment.

- ***Delegate tasks*** — Method that allows the employee to select the specific method for accomplishing the task. It is similar to the first method, but involves giving the employee the authority to accomplish the task and accepting the fact that the employee is capable of deciding how to do it. *Advantages:*

  — Delegation of authority helps to promote an atmosphere of team spirit within the workgroup.

  — It also gives the employee a sense of value and self-respect, while allowing the supervisor more time and energy to deal with more urgent problems.

- ***Give members of the workgroup an opportunity based on democratic principles to establish goals and objectives during the planning stage*** — Method where the chief of the department and the senior management team establish the organizational goals initially. This group determines the major objectives for each division or branch for a specific time period. Each division

or branch manager meets then with the members of their workgroup and communicates the objectives that apply to them. In some cases, objectives that are assigned to one division or branch affect the operation of another division or branch. *Process example:*

— The decision to purchase a compressed-air foam system apparatus affects the training division, logistics division, and finance division as well as the operations division.

— The formation of an ad hoc committee of division managers may be needed to oversee the project and coordinate efforts.

— The management team of each division or branch then establishes the objectives necessary to perform the following actions:

  ○ Develop specifications.

  ○ Provide funding.

  ○ Complete training and testing.

  ○ Develop operational procedures in the time frame determined by the department/organization.

— Each member of each workgroup is involved through a brainstorming process that depends on the knowledge and skills of each member.

— The supervisor is a member of the team and also facilitator and coach, guiding the team on to the objective.

Creating an Effective Team

Each supervising instructor is responsible for a workgroup that is completing specific objectives within the department/organization based on the organizational function of the various divisions of the organization (**Figure 19.3**). Workgroup characteristics are as follows:

- Varies in size from as few as five people to as many as the entire division or branch

- Forms the basis for the department/organization's table of organization when sizes are larger than twelve people and have subunits with their own supervisors

- Needs necessary facilities, equipment, and other resources to accomplish its assigned tasks

Figure 19.3 Workgroups are used to make decisions and monitor policies or processes within an organization.

It is the responsibility of the individual instructor to create a team from a workgroup. *Teambuilding* is the process of overcoming inherent differences within the workgroup such as age, experience, rank, job classification, education, gender, ethnicity, religion, politics, and personal interests.

The members of a team must go beyond individual differences and learn to think in terms of the group as a whole. This task is *not* an easy one because the majority of members have matured following the cultural norms that emphasize the importance of the individual rather than the group.

The instructor has to guide the group on the journey from disjointed individuals to a cohesive team. According to research by B. W. Tuckman, that journey passes through the following four stages of development:

1. *Forming* — Employees are uncertain of their roles in the group in this initial stage. They are *not* certain that they can trust or work with the other members. As relationships within the group grow, trust and respect develop, and members begin to see themselves as a part of the group. This phase is critical within the team-development process and one in which the instructor can have a significant effect. Training and information on diversity issues must also be provided to team members.

2. *Storming* — Conflict may result at this stage as members jockey for leadership or attempt to exert their own individual influences over the group.

3. *Norming* — The group establishes its own sets of norms and values that each member accepts and adheres to during this stage. The members become closer and more cohesive. The instructor again must be aware of team norms and values as much as possible to make sure that those norms do *not* violate the sense of decency.

4. *Performing*— The supervisor works to maintain the team spirit in this final stage as the group moves toward accomplishing objectives. At this point, the group is a true team. The instructor must monitor progress in this area as well because team members can develop certain behaviors and attitudes that can work to destroy the team concept. *Factors:*

   — It is critical for leaders to insist that team members act as equals and treat each other as equals.

   — It is critical to team growth that all the team members participate fully in team activities.

   — The end result is when everyone *plays in the game* and is happy and involved in most cases.

The process of teambuilding occurs within new organizations, within individual units as personnel promote and transfer, within temporary committees, and in associations with people normally outside the department/organization. The instructor can create an effective team by adhering to the following basic principles:

- Tell members how they fit into the team, what is expected of them, what the objectives are, and how accomplishing the objectives will affect them.

- Have frequent planning meetings with the team to determine progress, explain deviations from the plan, resolve problems, and commend accomplishments.

- Work with individual team members to establish personal goals and objectives. Make certain that they understand what is expected of them, what responsibilities and authority they have, and that they can and should ask for assistance when necessary.

- Encourage team members to make suggestions or provide solutions for problems. Members need to understand the brainstorming process of problem solving so that the team does not stifle member participation. When a suggestion is valid and valuable, publicly acknowledge the contribution. When it is *not,* explain privately to the individual why it will *not* work or cannot be implemented.

- Encourage team members to be open and honest in their comments in order to foster an atmosphere of trust and respect within the group.

- Allow the team to establish measurements for success, allowing members to determine whether the team and team members are successful. The supervisor will then have fair and equitable guidelines on which to base awards or discipline.

- Ensure that teams are composed of people of differing backgrounds. Diversity of membership assists in obtaining balanced team decisions. Furthermore, team diversity is the single greatest tool for combating *groupthink* (self-deception and forced conformity).

- Be sensitive to the diverse nature of the team and understand the cultural background of each team member. Value team members for their experience, background, intelligence, knowledge, and skills. Mutual respect is an important part of team development.

- Understand that team members have other concerns and obligations and recognize the effect that family, health, finances, and nonwork-related situations could have on employees. Within the limitations of the organization's personnel policy and procedures, assist employees in meeting objectives while still supporting outside concerns. *Examples:*

  — When difficulties in the private lives of employees start to have negative effects on the workgroup, intervene with care.

  — When there are problems of a personal nature, refer employees to the appropriate EAP, human resources department, or other behavioral counseling services for assistance.

Creating Job Interest within a Team

An instructor can create job interest within a team in a number of ways such as the following:

- ***Empowering employees*** — A form of delegation that is based on the concept of giving decision-making power to employees instead of having the supervisor retain it; therefore, employees take responsibility for their actions and decisions. It requires the supervisor to relinquish some authority and have confidence in the employee's skills, judgment, and abilities. It also helps to build self-esteem and motivation within the employee. By empowering employees, the supervisor is helping to increase their self-image and productivity. *Examples:*

  — Utilizing special talents of an employee can both empower and involve the employee in a project more deeply.

  — Personal skills such as photography, calligraphy, computer skills, or other hobbies may be a means for allowing employees to add more to the project.

  — Empowerment gives the employee a vested interest in the organization. As an internal customer, the employee's success is directly linked to the success of the organization and vice versa.

- ***Rewarding employees*** — Most supervisors do *not* have authority to grant raises, give time off, or provide any type of monetary rewards for employees, but that does *not* mean that they cannot provide rewards and incentives for good work within the team. *Incentives* are those things earned through effort or participation, and they are critical as motivational techniques in volunteer and combination departments/organizations. *Examples:*

  — Make public acknowledgements of accomplishments.

  — Hold group gatherings or parties to create a unit cohesiveness and spirit.

  — Make positive statements on the skills and abilities of team members to improve self-esteem.

  — Make appropriate comments on the employee's job performance evaluation, which can result in future monetary rewards.

The size or value of the incentive is *not* the critical part of providing incentive for an accomplishment; it is the mere fact that the instructor made an effort to acknowledge an individual's contribution to a group or project. Reward and award programs are critical to the volunteer staffing component. *Incentive elements:*

— A department/organization should have a series of reward and award programs. The instructor should be aware of those programs that are available and use them.

— The receiving of rewards and awards must be earned. When a person is presented with a reward or award that is *not* truly earned, disrespect is shown to that individual as well as the other individuals that did deserve the recognition.

— It is important to make the rewards as soon as possible following the accomplishment. Delaying the award or reward lessens its value.

- *Celebrating accomplishments* — When objectives are met, celebrate their accomplishment as soon as possible. This celebration signals the completion of the project as well as shows the team that their contributions are important **(Figure 19.4)**. Announce the completion of the project to the rest of the department/organization and congratulate the participants on the results.

Figure 19.4 The accomplishments of individuals, small groups, or organizations should be celebrated as soon as possible.

Responsibilities

All supervisors have nine major responsibilities to an organization regardless of its type. By accomplishing each of these responsibilities, an instructor can ensure an efficient and stable organization. Several of these responsibilities are discussed in the sections that follow. The nine responsibilities are listed as follows:

1. Set a clear and positive example for subordinates.

2. Receive assignments and complete tasks or objectives efficiently and effectively.

3. Promote and maintain health and safety policies within the workplace.

4. Develop an environment of cooperation and teamwork.

5. Promote skills development, skills maintenance, and skills improvement in employees.

6. Maintain discipline.

7. Promote the pursuit of educational and professional opportunities.

8. Promote credentialing and certification as opportunities to enhance an individual's professionalism.

9. Maintain files and records and prepare reports.

Completing Tasks

Completing a task requires the application of planning, organizing, controlling, and evaluating skills, which are outlined as follows:

- The plan for task completion must be established and communicated to employees.

- The schedule must be realistic with attainable objectives **(Figure 19.5, p. 468)**.

- Employees must be organized to work as a team with the objective or goal in focus.

- As much responsibility and authority as possible must be delegated to the employees, which give them a sense of ownership in the project. However, final responsibility and authority must always remain with the supervising instructor.

- The supervising instructor is responsible for evaluating the quality and completion of the task, which means that the supervising instructor

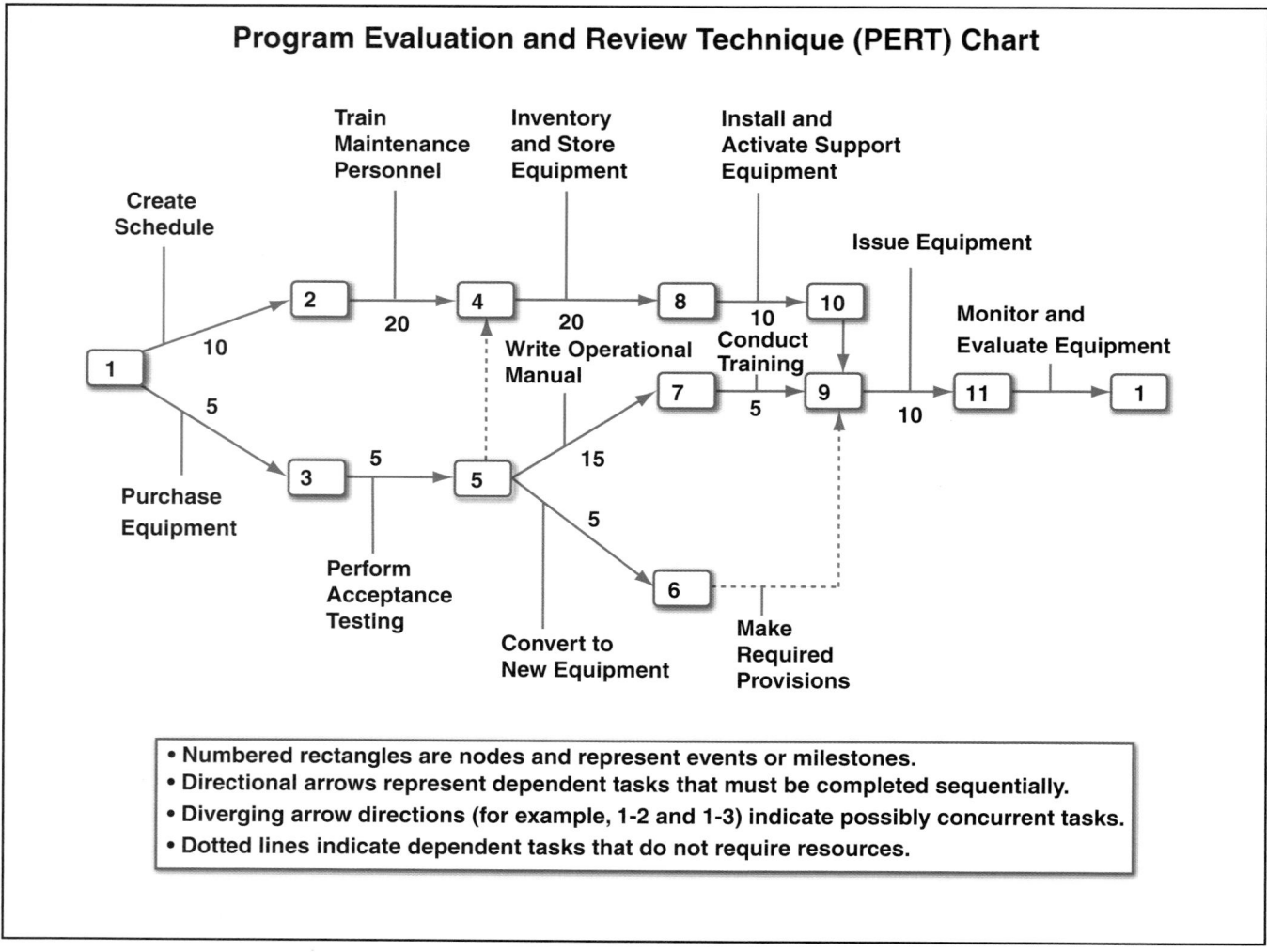

Figure 19.5 Program Evaluation and Review Technique (PERT) Charts are effective ways of illustrating projects and establishing completion dates and responsibilities.

must monitor the progress to determine whether the plan is being followed or whether a change must be made to resolve unforeseen difficulties.

Building Teamwork and Cooperation

Ensuring teamwork and cooperation within the organization are also responsibilities of the supervisor. Creating an atmosphere where teamwork is expected at all times takes interpersonal skills that include the following:

- Building morale
- Focusing on the objective
- Developing mutual respect
- Mitigating conflict
- Acknowledging accomplishments

At the same time, cooperation between a workgroup and other workgroups (both within the organization and externally) is important. A workgroup must think of itself as a team within a larger team that has one goal: Accomplish the organization's mission.

Developing Skills

An employee in the fire and emergency services rarely performs the same task all the time. Changes in assignments, promotions, and the addition of new technology all require that employees learn new skills. It is the responsibility and duty of the supervisor to provide the skills training necessary to complete new tasks.

Sometimes the instructor can provide that training directly. Otherwise, educational opportunities must be developed, located, or provided from other sources. Succession and career planning must be developed to assist employees in developing an attainable and successful career path.

Maintaining Positive Examples/Attitudes

An instructor should always maintain a positive attitude toward superiors, peers, subordinates, and students. This attitude should be reflected through personal actions that set an example for others to follow. Part of this example is having respect for others, which will create mutual respect between members of the workgroup. When respect for others is lost, it is very difficult to regain it.

Maintaining Records and Reports

All supervisors are responsible for the maintenance of records and reports such as daily timesheets, performance evaluations, injury and exposure report forms, and training reports. These records must be accurate, complete, timely, and confidential (where necessary). All records have the potential of becoming legal documents and most, with the exception of medical records, may become public.

Leadership Elements

Regardless of the rank held by the supervisor, that individual must be a leader at all times. The supervising instructor leads by example and must adhere to a standard of ethical, moral, and legal behavior that will motivate the workgroup to do the same. In addition, some key elements must be part of the instructor's supervisory style such as the following:

- Encourage employee participation in the decision-making process.
- Delegate or involve team members in planning.
- Respect the judgment of employees.
- Teach, enforce, and follow health and safety rules.
- Be a coach and mentor to employees.
- Show consideration for diversity within the workgroup.
- Acknowledge accomplishments.
- Treat each member of the workgroup fairly and equitably.

- Intervene in the private lives of the members of the group only when problems are affecting the workplace.
- Keep accurate records.
- Keep lines of communication open at all times.
- Do *not* contribute to or allow situations that make other people feel uncomfortable or impose upon their personal dignity.

Above all, the supervisor must be consistent in the application of these elements. A lack of consistency will ultimately undermine the instructor's authority and ability to lead and create relationships within the department/organization that take energy, time, effort, and attention to repair and distract from the primary goals of the organization.

Methods and Styles of Management

As defined earlier, managing is the act of controlling, monitoring, or directing a project, program, system, resource, or organization through the use of authority, discipline, or persuasion. To be an effective manager, an instructor must understand the various management functions that managers perform, recognize the skills necessary to manage, and understand the management of change within the organization.

As a manager, the instructor is responsible for achieving the training division's goals and objectives through the effective and efficient use of its resources. Those resources are generally considered to be as follows:

- *Human* — Personnel assigned to the training division
- *Financial* — Funds that are allocated to the organization and, subsequently, to each division or branch for the completion of its assigned tasks
- *Physical* — Facilities, apparatus, tools, equipment, extinguishing agents, and daily operating materials of the department/organization that are required to perform the tasks (**Figure 19.6, p. 470**)

Figure 19.6 Instructors are responsible for managing training facilities, props, and equipment and ensuring that they are clean, safe, and in working order.

- *Information* — Data that are compiled by the department/organization concerning its operation such as incident reports, attendance reports, exposure reports, and injury reports to name a few; also includes the following:
  — Demographics of the community
  — Political environment, economic climate, and trends in the fire and emergency services industry
  — Systems and processes used to manage the organization's information
- *Time* — Time required for completion of any project, which competes with the time required for other projects; must be invested wisely and prioritized with priority given to the most important projects

Although these resources are different from each other, general management concepts and theories can be applied to each of them. The following sections introduce the functions and skills required for managing resources as well as programs and projects.

Functions

Instructors need to have a basic knowledge of management and their part in the management process. It is a generally accepted business prin-

ciple that the management process includes the following four functions:

1. *Planning* — Setting goals and objectives and determining the direction the organization or unit will take to achieve those results. Planning involves both the broadest view of the organization (creation of the mission statement) and the narrowest (development of tactical plans for accomplishing a specific objective).

2. *Organizing* — Coordinating tasks and resources to accomplish the goals and objectives; accomplished by the following functions:
   — Establishing the internal structure of the department/organization that creates divisions of labor
   — Coordinating the allocation of resources
   — Taking responsibility for tasks and flow of information within the department
   — Staffing (filling of positions with qualified people); also includes recruiting, hiring, training, evaluating, compensating, supporting, and retaining personnel

3. *Leading* — Influencing, inspiring, and motivating employees to achieve the goals and objectives; also referred to as *directing* in some business definitions. Leading is considered a proactive approach to managing.

4. *Controlling* — Establishing and implementing the mechanisms to ensure that objectives are attained. Includes the following functions:
   — Setting performance standards
   — Measuring and reporting the actual performance
   — Comparing the performance standard with the actual performance
   — Taking preventive or corrective action to close the gap between the two levels of performance

Skills

Proper application of the management functions requires an instructor to possess certain management skills. Most instructors have the basic training necessary to perform the operational tasks of the fire and emergency services. Years of experience and education also provide a sound foundation to perform as a manager. Management skills that are required to be an effective manager include the following:

- **Technical skills** — Methods and techniques required to perform certain tasks as a manager such as the following:
  - Computer skills
  - Knowledge of laws, codes, and ordinances
  - Report writing
  - Other skills that will be used to prepare budgets or develop specifications

- **Interpersonal communication skills** — Interpersonal skills that include the ability to work with other people and supervise subordinates. success or failure often hinges on the ability to communicate (**Figure 19.7**).

- **Conceptual and decision-making skills** — Skills that include the ability to understand abstract ideas and solve problems through a variety of ways; also the ability to understand the organization as a whole and recognize how the various parts are interrelated.

Resource Scheduling

An important responsibility of the Level II Instructor is that of scheduling resources and instructional delivery. Training resources are all the elements

that are required to present a course or program, including human (personnel), financial (funds), physical (facilities and materials), information (data), and time. See Methods and Styles of Management section for descriptions. Scheduling is influenced by numerous factors, including the following:

- **Governmental mandates** — Requirements exist not only for the type of training but also the minimum amount of time for each topic. It may even appear that the time required for mandated training exceeds the time available to provide the mandated training.

- **Instructor availability** — Availability is especially applicable in volunteer or combination organizations where the instructor must fulfill multiple roles in addition to training.

- **Facility availability** — Facilities must be reserved in advance of training by organizations that depend on outside sources for classroom and training space.

- **Minimum staffing levels** — Training must be planned in career or combination organizations so that it will *not* reduce the minimum level of personnel or units required for emergency responses.

- **Work schedules** — Vacations, holidays, and sick leaves must be considered when planning training sessions. Alternative sessions must be provided for members who are unable to attend the initial courses (**Figure 19.8**).

Figure 19.7 One of the most important skills that an instructor can have is the ability to communicate with students, subordinates, superiors, peers, and the public. *Courtesy of Andrew Haag, Senior Rescue Instructor, New South Wales Fire Brigade.*

Figure 19.8 Providing the various training courses that are required by law means establishing a schedule that makes the most effective use of all resources.

- *Student availability* — Training in volunteer and combination organizations must be provided when the largest number of students is available. Employment work schedules, personal obligations, and other barriers to training must be considered.

- *Funds* — Funds must be available to pay instructors, purchase materials, or rent training aids or space. Training may have to be postponed until budgeted funds are available.

- *Environment* — Adverse environmental conditions may create a safety hazard for students, so training should not occur during those conditions. In that respect, training schedules depend on the weather. At the same time, training that is weather-related, such as ice rescue, should be planned to take advantage of appropriate weather conditions **(Figure 19.9)**.

Once critical factors have been determined and resolved, the instructor should follow a sequence of steps to create a training schedule for the division or agency. These steps may be applied to a single course, a series of courses within a program, or the entire organization. Each of the following steps is repeated for each course or element of a program:

Figure 19.9 Some types of training such as ice rescue require planning and coordination. *Courtesy of Iowa Fire Service Training Bureau.*

Step 1: Determine needs.

Step 2: Determine requirements.

Step 3: Determine availability.

Step 4: Coordinate training.

Step 5: Create a schedule.

Step 6: Publish the schedule.

Step 7: Revise the schedule.

Determine Needs

The initial step in establishing a training schedule is to determine the organization's training needs. The instructor should create a list of training courses or programs required to provide the minimum level of training. The schedule should reflect both the short-term and long-term needs of the organization; that is, an annual schedule for immediate training and a 3- to 5-year schedule to establish recurring training needs and projected training needs.

Recurring needs involve recertification or annually mandated training. Projected training needs are based on increases in service levels, expansion of coverage areas, or retirements that will require hiring new personnel.

When faced with competing training requirements, the instructor should prioritize the requirements into one of the following three priority training levels:

Priority 1: *Training to meet any certification, recertification or relicensing requirements for members of the organization* — Training may include the following:

- Certification or recertification for emergency medical technicians (EMTs)

- Hazardous materials responder competency requirements mandated by state/provincial statutes

- Federally mandated emergency responder respiratory protection recertification.

- Continuing education requirements that the organization may require to maintain mastery for company personnel.

Priority 2: *Training that is required to meet organizational goals determined by the organization or jurisdiction* — For example, an organization may want to expand its ability to respond to technical rescue incidents. One priority in a given year would be to certify all emergency responders to the Operations Level of structural collapse and a select group of individual emergency responders to the Technician Level.

Priority 3: *Training that is not mandated or required but would be nice to complete* — While an organization may have required all emergency responders to meet the Operations Level of structural collapse, resources may also allow it to certify everyone at the Technician Level. Other types of Priority 3 training may include the following:

- Attending state or national conferences

- Providing additional training for the benefit of the organization that is not attached to any of the organizational goals for a particular year.

Determine Requirements

The local jurisdiction or other governmental authority usually mandates required training. Required training includes the following elements:

- Specific topics to be taught

- Certification or testing criteria

- Minimum number of contact or teaching hours

The instructor should determine the required training, amount of time to be allocated to each course, and sequence in which the courses must be taught. Because governmental mandates have a tendency to change over time, the instructor should research the requirements annually.

Determine Availability

Determining the availability of instructors, facilities, and students may occur at two different times. First, availability of instructors and facilities should be determined before creating the training sched-

ule. This determination can be made through the use of surveys that state the required training and time allocations. Instructors and facility managers complete the surveys, indicating the best times for providing the training.

The availability of students may be determined either in a general manner before creating the schedule or specifically after the schedule is created. In general, personnel and units from career and combination organizations are available throughout their work cycles. The challenge is in scheduling training while maintaining minimum staffing or response requirements. Training may be provided in the evenings and on weekends or by closed-circuit television to the stations as an alternative to weekday training.

Volunteer organizations usually schedule training in the evenings and on weekends and make attendance a mandatory part of membership in the organization (**Figure 19.10**). However, specialized or individual training may require that volunteers attend training sessions provided during the day by other agencies. This scheduling places a burden on students and requires flexibility and creativity on the part of both students and the organization.

Consideration must also be given to holidays and annual leave/vacation patterns in the local jurisdiction. Instructors and students tend to take annual leave around major holidays such as the

Figure 19.10 Volunteer and combination departments must plan training sessions when students are available such as evenings and weekends. *Courtesy of Dave Coombs.*

Revise the Schedule

Both short- and long-term training schedules require revisions. The reasons for making such revisions may include the following:

- Illness
- Inclement weather
- Lack of funds
- Lack of equipment or materials
- Lack of facilities
- Unforeseen situations
- Changes in the time required to present courses
- Creation of newly mandated courses

The instructor or training staff should review the schedule periodically and make the necessary alterations. These changes should also be added to the projected 3- and 5-year schedules. Changes to the schedule should be made available to the teaching staff and members of the organization **(Figure 19.12)**.

Summary

Developing the skills necessary to be an effective supervisor, manager, or leader can be challenging for any instructor. Although principles can be learned in courses, seminars, and workshops or through reading books and articles, these skills must be practiced to become part of the instructor's personal traits. Selecting a role model or mentor that can provide insight into these skills is an effective way to supplement the acquired knowledge. Practice will also help the instructor to become proficient in managing personnel, programs, and projects and in creating cost-efficient training schedules.

Figure 19.12 Adverse weather can disrupt training schedules. Contingency plans should be in place to ensure that the best use of training resources may occur. *Courtesy of Iowa Fire Service Training Bureau.*

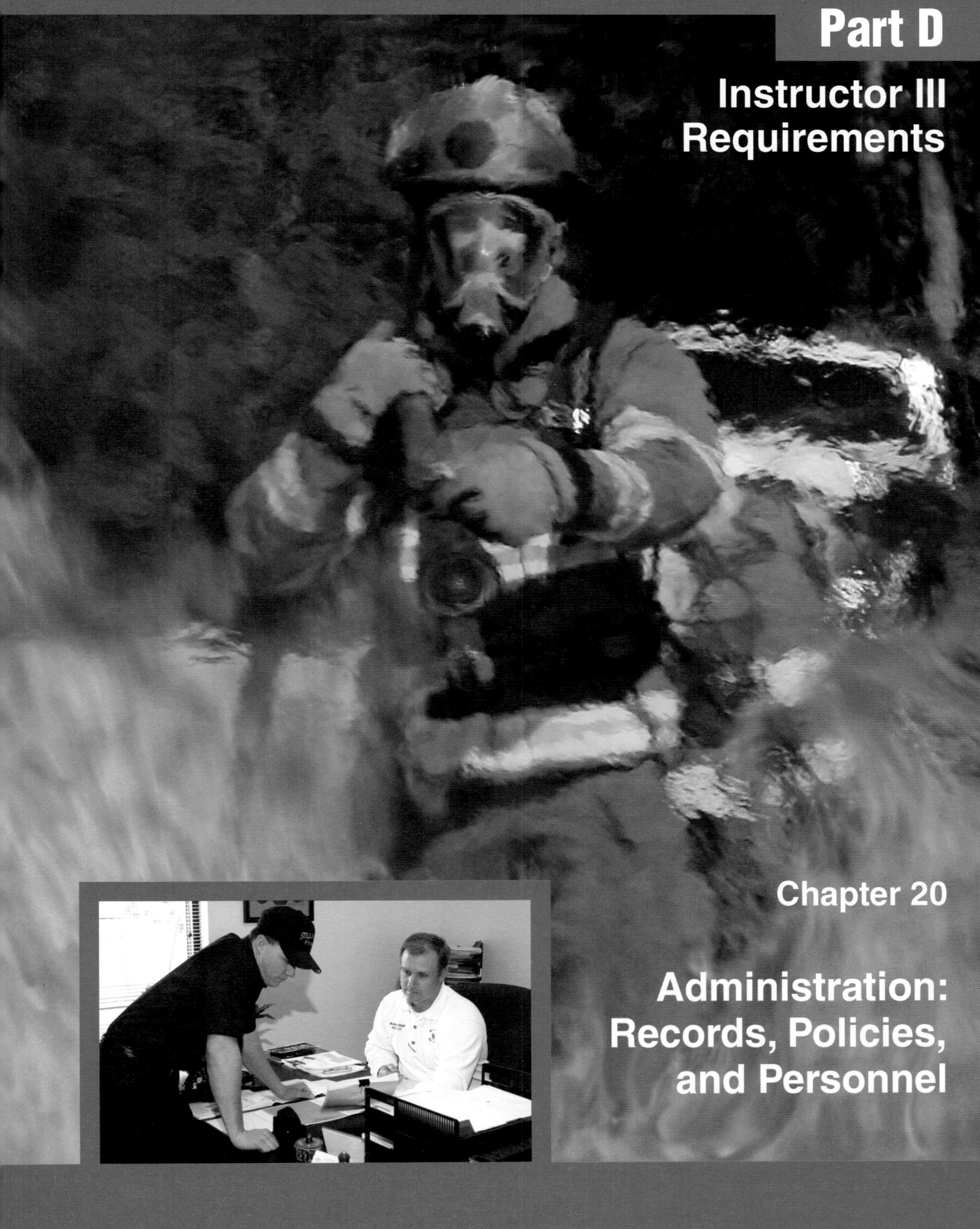

Part D

Instructor III Requirements

Chapter 20

Administration: Records, Policies, and Personnel

After reading this chapter, students will be able to —

1. Discuss records management.

2. List information that should be included in records to ensure complete documentation.

3. List functions of the records-management system.

4. Discuss records-management system types.

5. Identify components of a records-management system.

6. List benefits of keeping accurate training records.

7. Identify information to be gathered for a training records system.

8. List types of training documented in training records.

9. Discuss access to training records.

10. Discuss the development of standardized forms.

11. List characteristics of effective policies.

12. Describe procedures and guidelines.

13. Describe the steps for determining the need for a new policy, procedure, or guideline.

14. Discuss the revision process for policies, procedures, or guidelines.

15. Identify facts about the adoption process for a policy, procedure, or guideline.

16. Identify accurate statements about standards in the fire and emergency services.

17. List rules for making the transition to a higher rank.

18. Discuss staff selection.

19. List advantages of the personnel evaluation program.

20. Identify guidelines for personnel evaluations.

21. Discuss the personnel evaluation process.

22. List actions the supervisor should take to ensure a successful formal evaluation.

23. Discuss the concept of a 360-degree feedback evaluation.

24. List legal factors that influence the evaluation process.

Chapter Contents

Records Management
System Types
System Components
Training Records
Forms Development

Development of Training Policies
Policies
Procedures and Guidelines
Need for New Policy, Procedure, or Guideline

Revision Process
Adoption Process
Standards

Human Resources Management
Supervision
Staff Selection
Personnel Evaluations

Summary

Chapter 20
Administration: Records, Policies, and Personnel

The majority of fire and emergency services instructors who certify to NFPA 1041, *Standard for Fire Service Instructor Professional Qualifications,* criteria may remain Level I or Level II Instructors throughout their training careers. Because there are fewer Level III positions available, the possibility of advancement is limited in most states/provinces, organizations, or agencies. However, the knowledge that is required for Level III certification is still valuable for all instructors.

Therefore, the chapters in Part D of this manual serve two purposes: (1) to provide information for training divisions and agencies that teach Level III courses and (2) to provide a reference source for current instructors who must understand and apply some of the requirements normally assigned to a Level III Instructor.

The Level III Instructor may be responsible for the management of the training program as determined by the authority having jurisdiction (AHJ). The instructor may have this responsibility as the head of the organization or as a member of the senior staff **(Figure 20.1)**. To effectively fulfill this responsibility, the Level III Instructor must be able to do the following:

- Successfully attain Instructor II certification.
- Develop comprehensive training curriculums and programs for use by single or multiple organizations.
- Conduct an organizational needs analysis.
- Develop training goals and implementation strategies.

Figure 20.1 The management of the training function is assigned to a certified Level III instructor in some emergency services organizations.

- Administer policies and procedures for the management of instructional resources, staff, facilities, records, and reports.
- Develop a program evaluation plan.

NFPA 1041 does *not* assign rank requirements to each instructor level, although it states that the training program manager may be either a uniformed officer or civilian. Generally, the training program manager will probably be a chief officer (Fire Officer Level III). Each AHJ is given the flexibility to develop an organizational structure that meets its unique needs while still conforming to the certification requirements.

According to NPFA 1041, a fire and emergency services training program manager should understand and be able to perform the following functions:

- Develop budgets.
- Manage purchasing processes.
- Develop specifications.
- Manage resources.
- Manage personnel.

The skills that are required to perform these functions include the following:

- Instruction management
- Program evaluation
- Training needs analysis
- Schedule development
- Goal setting
- Information networking with other training agencies
- Technical writing
- Effective verbal and written communications

Some of these topics have been discussed in previous chapters that give general requirements or Level II Instructor requirements while others may be found in the IFSTA **Chief Officer** manual, second edition. The remaining chapters in this manual discuss analysis and evaluation methods and program and curriculum development. This chapter specifically discusses records management, training policies development, and human resources management.

Records Management

Records management includes the planning, controlling, directing, organizing, training, and conducting of other managerial activities required for maintaining an organization's records. It also involves the creation, maintenance, use, and disposition of the organization's records. A successful records-management program results in the proper documentation of the policies and transactions of the organization and effective and economical management of its operations.

The information stored in the records can be used for many purposes including the development or alteration of policies and procedures. The raw data alone cannot support any recommendation.

Statistical analysis, the use of raw numbers to establish trends and relationships, must be applied to the data. The results can be used to formulate training policies, mandate safe practices, or change procedures.

Statistical analyses can also provide indications of the efficiency of an instructional delivery system. Efficiency from a training standpoint can have several different measurement instruments such as cost of course, enrollment number, and cost per instructional hour.

The organization must create and preserve adequate and proper documentation of its activities in a records-management system that supports operational needs, protects individual rights, and allows accountability. Additional information on record keeping may be found in Chapter 6, Report Writing and Record Keeping.

To ensure complete documentation, records should include the following information:

- Proper identification of document originators
- Proper identification of document recipients
- Appropriate dates of document origination
- Any other information required to meet the organization's needs

In addition, the records-management system should be able to perform the following functions:

- Organize and index records in a manner that properly preserves, retrieves, uses, and disposes of the material.
- Provide accessibility to all appropriate staff.
- Provide security from unauthorized access or tampering.
- Distinguish records from nonrecord material and personal papers.
- Apply the records disposal schedule.

The instructor should be familiar with the two types of records management systems, the components of the systems, what training records include, and how to develop forms that are used in the collection of information for the training records. The sections that follow provide information on each of these subjects.

System Types

Records-management systems may be manual or automated. A *manual system* involves the physical collection, organization, storage, preservation, and disposal of hardcopy records and materials. These records may include reports, forms, maps, graphs, illustrations, audio/video tapes, or photographs. An *automated system* utilizes the electronic storage of data on tapes, discs, or other electronic media. Either type of system must be able to perform the following functions:

- Organize records.
- Index records.
- Allow authorized staff members to access the records.

Records-management systems may be in the following formats:

- *Paper or physical* — Includes forms, written reports, maps, graphs, photographs, etc.
- *Micrographic* — Duplicates photographically images of documents that may be accessed using a microfilm reader (**Figure 20.2**).
- *Electronic* — Maintains digital records of documents or images on electronic media.

System Components

Records-management systems consist of more than the software applications designed to manage the records. The system is composed of the following items:

Figure 20.2 Although microfilm technology is rapidly being replaced by digital copying of documents, it is still used for copying and storing photographic images of records.

- *People* — Personnel who are trained in the operation of the system.
- *Policies* — Codified statements that define the system, the data to be gathered, and how data are stored, accessed, analyzed, and disposed of.
- *Procedures* — Methods used to meet the requirements of the policies.
- *Tools* — Record-keeping instruments designed to manage and control the records over time. These instruments include disposal schedules, thesauri, access and security classification schemes, etc.
- *Technology* — Software, hardware, physical storage, and disposal equipment.
- *Ongoing supporting education* — Personnel training required to manage changes in the system.
- *Maintenance* — System support that ensures that the system continues to operate correctly and efficiently and is available in the event the system experiences a malfunction.

Training Records

The effective and efficient management of training records is essential to a successful training program. Accurate records provide an organization with a long-term inventory of its training activities as well as support in legal proceedings and management reviews by outside agencies such as the Insurance Services Office (ISO).

In addition to the elements of inventories, legal records, and management reviews, the benefits of keeping accurate training records also include the following:

- Training documents may be reviewed by appropriate or authorized parties when necessary.
- Records identify training areas that are emphasized as well as areas that require more attention.
- Records provide documentation of required training completion.
- Information in records can be used for planning training programs and scheduling training.
- Records can be used in defense of legal challenges in cases of accidents, fatalities, or injuries.

In addition, federal, state/provincial, or local laws require that organizations maintain certain training records. U.S. governmental agencies, such as the Occupational Safety and Health Administration (OSHA) or Environmental Protection Agency (EPA), may require training records of personnel who are exposed to hazardous chemicals and infectious disease and records for respiratory protection training programs. These requirements, in effect, make training records legal documents.

In developing or improving a records system for a training program, training managers must consider what information to gather for the records. Important information to be gathered for any training records system include the following:

- Student attendance rosters **(Figure 20.3)**

- Topics taught at each session

- Lesson plans, workbooks and texts, tests, attendance sheets, videotapes, and other program-event documentation and processes

Figure 20.3 Attendance records must be maintained for all legally mandated courses.

- Evaluation/testing scores of students when applicable

- Dates of each training session

- Names of instructors for each training session

- Descriptions of instructors' qualifications

- Any other information deemed appropriate by the organization such as employee identification numbers and locations of the training sessions

The type and format of training records may vary widely depending upon the specific needs of the organization. NFPA 1401, *Recommended Practice for Fire Service Training Reports and Records*, provides examples of different training forms as well as other helpful information on the design and procedures for effective management of training records. The format of records may also depend on the type of training for which information is being gathered **(Figure 20.4)**.

Training managers will likely collect information for some of the following types of training:

- Daily training delivered by a training division

- Company training delivered by a company officer or qualified member of the emergency response unit or fire company

- Organizational training delivered to all members of an organization

- Self-study by an individual

- Individual training provided by an organization

- Special training received outside the organization

State/provincial and federal governments generally have specific laws that direct record maintenance and in some cases the information that is gathered and stored in these records. For example, many organizations no longer use an employee's Social Security number for records identification. The practice of using other identification methods reduces the opportunity for improper use or identity theft.

Training records may also be considered part of an individual's personal, private employment file — a fact that requires an organization to limit access to training records. Even when a law does

Virigina Department of Fire Programs

Standard Roll Call Form

Hours and
Subject Codes

COURSE _____

LOCATION_____

SCHOOL NUMBER _____

STUDENT NAME (Print Clearly)	Social Security #	Date of Birth	FDID#				CAREER M	F	VOL M	F

Figure 20.4 Collecting, organizing, and archiving training course materials and documents completed by students are essential ingredients in the management of training programs. An example of a typical course sign-in sheet is shown. *Courtesy of Virginia Department of Fire Programs.*

not require this practice, organizations should develop and adopt policies that limit access to training records only to those personnel with a legal need to know.

Other information that is protected by law is an individual's evaluation/testing scores. In the U.S., the Family Education and Privacy Act prohibits the release of this type of information. Similarly, the Canadian province of Ontario has the Municipal Freedom of Information and Protection of Privacy Act (MFIPPA) that places the responsibility on instructors to know their duties and responsibilities under the applicable legislation within their jurisdictions.

The old practice of posting test scores and other personal information on bulletin boards is no longer allowed. Scores and personal data are considered privileged information and are available only to management and a few other designated personnel with authorization and a specific need to know.

While many organizations develop their own training records systems, there are many commercial software programs available for keeping training records. Computer software programs improve the efficiency of records management and make it easy to record, access, and process training information. The cost of such software may limit its availability, but the software can be cost-effective by developing an effective records system through the organization of files.

Regardless of the system that an organization uses, authorized personnel must be able to easily retrieve information contained in the records and protect it from general access. Laws may require organizations to maintain training records for a specified time period. Training managers or personnel responsible for maintaining training records must be aware of and follow local and state or provincial requirements.

Forms Development

Standardized forms ensure that information that is mandated by law and stored in the records-management system is consistent and complete. Forms are based on the type of information that is outlined in the organization's policies or legal requirements of various governmental agencies.

When the Level III Instructor is required to create a form for gathering a particular type of data, the policies and legal requirements should be researched first. At the same time, the instructor should determine whether forms that gather the same information already exist or are provided by other levels of government.

The widespread use of computers makes the creation of forms such as record maintenance forms very easy. Forms such as course attendance sheets may be simple word documents that are printed and filled in by hand. Forms may be created into

data sheets that have fields that are filled in by the instructor and compiled on a spreadsheet (**Figure 20.5**).

In any case, forms should have fields that are consistent with other training forms used by the organization. For instance, Field 1 may always contain the date, Field 2 may always contain the instructor's name, Field 3 may always contain the student's name, and so on. The more consistent the assignment of data to specific fields, the easier the form will be to use and the easier the information will be to locate, analyze, and store.

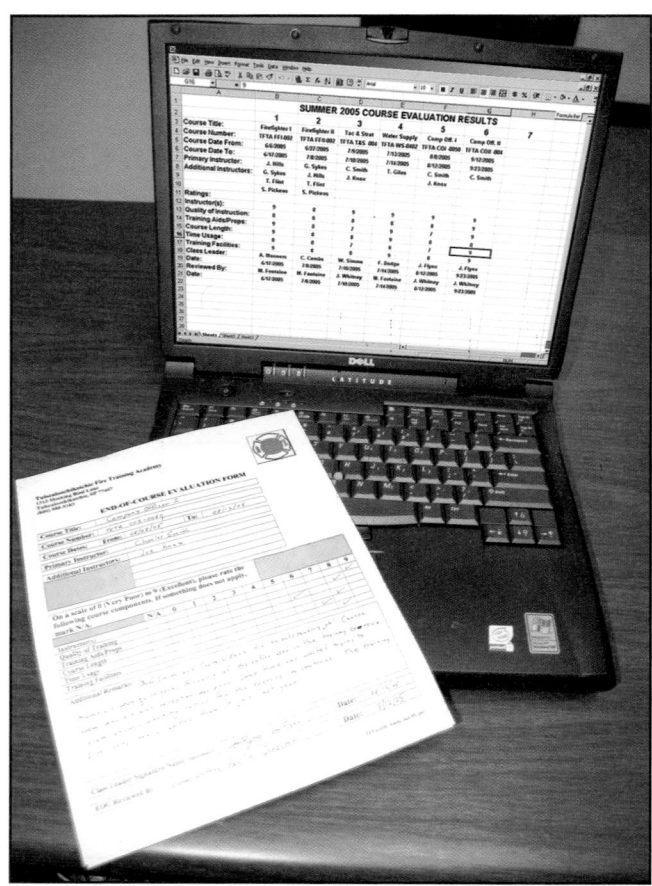

Figure 20.5 Information may be entered onto forms in a computer or written by hand. When a signature is required, both forms must be printed, signed, and dated.

Development of Training Policies

For the effective and efficient operation of any fire and emergency services organization, written policies, procedures, and guidelines are essential. They place into writing the expectations of the organization based on the organizational model and strategic and operational plans. Policies, procedures, and guidelines are known by a variety of names including *standard operating procedures (SOPs), standard operating guidelines (SOGs), administrative policies and procedures,* and simply *policies and procedures.*

Regardless of the title, the documents must contain information that is current and appropriate. Therefore, the organization should have a process to perform the following functions:

- Evaluate the need for new policies, procedures, and guidelines.

- Revise existing policies, procedures, and guidelines.

- Adopt policies, procedures, and guidelines.

In addition, the organization should be familiar with the consensus standards that are available and the process for adopting them into law.

Policies

A *policy* is a guiding principle or rule that organizations develop, adopt, and use as a basis or foundation for decision-making. Policies help organizations address specific issues or problems. Training policies serve to guide an organization's training function on a day-to-day basis and are often accompanied by procedures for fulfilling the requirements of the policies. For policies to be effective, they must have the following characteristics **(Figure 20.6)**:

- Well-written

- Adopted through a process that provides critical feedback

- Explicitly supported by the organization's administration and training manager

In some cases, policies are developed at the local level. In other cases, organizational training policies are based upon state, provincial, or federal laws or standards. For example, in the U.S. the *Code of Federal Regulations (CFR)* identifies specific requirements for the training of personnel who respond to hazardous materials incidents.

These federal regulations often serve as the basis for locally adopted training requirements. Sometimes, these regulations, such as Title 29

Figure 20.6 Organizational policies guide personnel in many tasks such as performing procedures and making decisions. Policies may include guidelines on canceling classes due to inclement weather, selecting texts or videotapes for use in a training course, or wearing respiratory protection equipment when exposed to hazardous atmospheres. *Courtesy of Rick Montemorra.*

(Respiratory Protection) CFR 1910.134, require the development of local policies and procedures. A resource for developing local policies are some of the NFPA standards such as NFPA 1201, *Standard for Providing Emergency Services to the Public,* and NFPA 1500, *Standard on Fire Department Occupational Safety and Health Program.*

Procedures and Guidelines

Training managers are responsible for ensuring that instructors comply with training policies. Instructors also need directions or methods by which they can comply with policies. To facilitate this compliance, training managers develop procedures and guidelines that delineate steps to follow and outline what latitude can be used to make decisions. Procedures and guidelines may either accompany policies or exist independently from them. They are both essential management tools for a training program. Consider the following definitions and explanations:

- *Procedure* — Identifies the steps that must be taken to fulfill the intent of a policy and is written to support a policy. For example, a policy may state that *all live-fire training evolutions must be conducted in compliance with NFPA 1403, Standard on Live Fire Training Evolutions.* The procedures accompanying this policy list steps the instructor takes to ensure the policy is achieved, including such criteria as the following:

— Establish the Incident Command System (ICS) based on the National Incident Management System (NIMS) model.

— Inspect the training structure.

— Provide a safety officer for evolutions.

— Require use of appropriate protective equipment.

— Use qualified instructors who are knowledgeable in fire behavior.

An advantage of adopting well-defined procedures is consistency in implementing the policy **(Figure 20.7)**. Procedures are essential in programs where adherence to policy is a critical factor such as the following:

— Implementing safety precautions during training

— Hiring or evaluating personnel

— Acquiring structures

- *Guideline* — Identifies a general philosophy unlike a policy or procedure that provides a clear rule or step-by-step process. Guidelines may be part of a policy or exist independently. They provide direction with latitude for achieving the overall goal of the guideline or policy. *Examples:*

— An organization may have a policy for conducting training in inclement or extreme weather conditions.

— Included in the policy are guidelines that give instructors information so that they may make decisions on when it is appropriate to either cancel or reschedule training.

— The information in the guidelines gives instructors the *parameters (leeway)* they need in considering all factors involved before making a decision.

Need for New Policy, Procedure, or Guideline

When deciding whether an issue requires a policy, procedure, or guideline, the instructor considers the goal to be achieved. When a specific rule or philosophy is needed that allows no variance, a

Figure 20.7 Procedures define the steps that must be used to perform critical functions that may be associated with a policy.

policy is the answer. When a step-by-step outline is required for an administrative task or training operation, a procedure is the answer. When a general philosophy is needed that provides direction but allows the instructor to use some discretion, a guideline is most appropriate.

The steps for determining the need for a new policy, procedure, or guideline are as follows:

Step 1: *Identify the problem or requirement for a policy, procedure, or guideline* — Determine whether a policy or procedure is actually necessary to address the problem **(Figure 20.8)**. Some problems may be best addressed on an individual basis that will *not* require a formal policy.

Step 2: *Collect the data to evaluate the need* — Determine whether data is quantitative or qualitative. Data may come from personnel interviews, product literature, or activity reports.

Step 3: *Select the evaluation model* — Determine whether an evaluation model is goals-based, process-based, or outcomes-based.

Step 4: *Establish a timetable for making the needs evaluation* — Determine length of time required to evaluate the problem. The length of time needed depends on the complexity of the problem and amount of information that must be evaluated.

Step 5: ***Conduct the evaluation*** — Follow the recommended steps for the model that is most appropriate for the problem.

Step 6: ***Select the best response to the need*** — Determine the best policy, procedure, or guideline to solve the problem. Remember that this determination may include no policy, procedure, or guideline at all.

Step 7: ***Select alternative responses*** — Select a second-best choice when a contingency is indicated. External influences may make it necessary to select a policy, procedure, or guideline other than the first choice. Personal safety, however, should *not* be compromised.

Step 8: ***Establish a revision process or schedule*** — Create a revision process as part of the policy, procedure, or guideline. Revision may be a general process for all policies, procedures, or guidelines or one that is specific to the policy that has been selected.

Step 9: ***Recommend the policy, procedure, or guideline that best meets the need*** — Determine whether the recommended policy, procedure, or guideline needs to be formally adopted by the jurisdiction because policies, procedures, or guidelines may have the effect of law. Formal approval requires that the policy, procedure, or guideline be supported by documentation (**Figure 20.9**).

Figure 20.8 The creation of a policy, procedure, or guideline may be the result of behaviors that caused accidents. For instance, a policy requiring that apparatus responding to an emergency must stop at all controlled intersections may be required if there is an increase in apparatus collisions at those locations. *Courtesy of Tulsa (OK) Fire Department.*

Revision Process

To ensure that policies, procedures, or guidelines are flexible to meet potential or unexpected changes in the operating environment and organizational requirements, a process for revising them should be established. The revision process is included in the policy or procedures manual

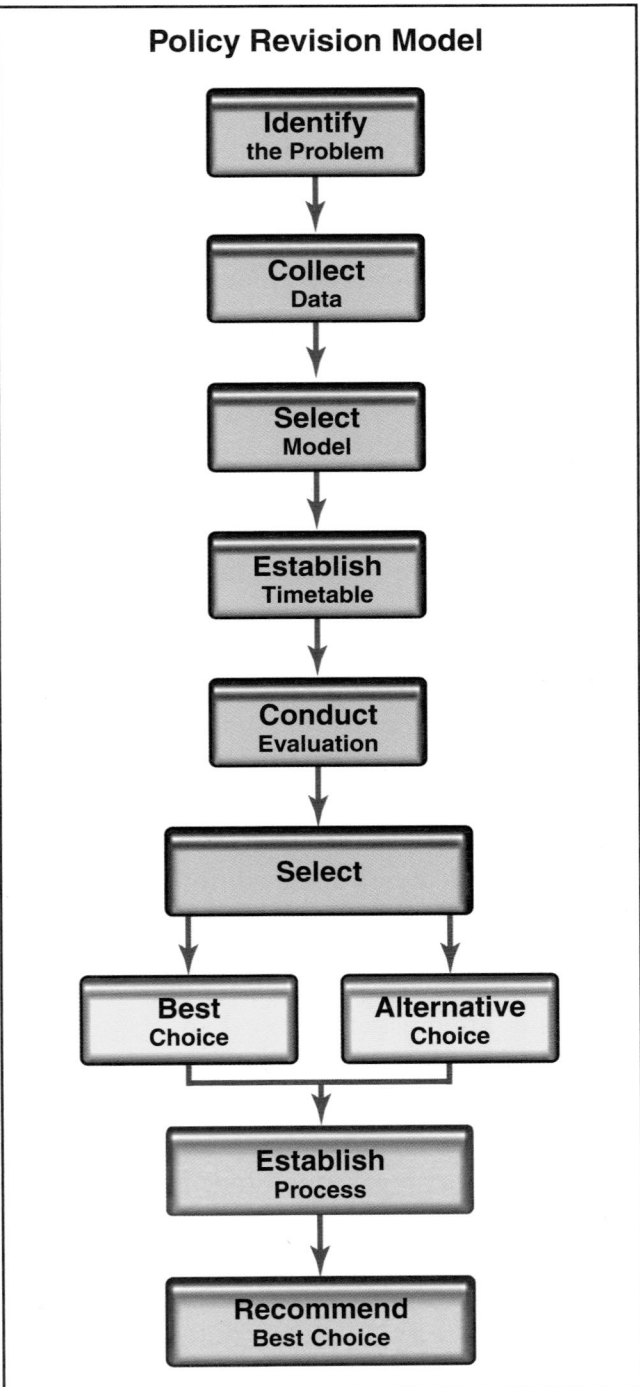

Figure 20.9 A flowchart can be used to illustrate the process for developing a policy, procedure, or guideline.

and is based on the answers to the following questions:

- What is the provision for revising the policy, procedure, or guideline on a specific time schedule?

- What conditions or circumstances would cause the policy, procedure, or guideline to need to be revised?

- How should the policy, procedure, or guideline be revised: completely, partially, or not at all (abandoned)?

Indications that a policy, procedure, or guideline needs to be revised may include the following:

- Internal/external customer complaints

- Increase in policy infractions

- Injuries or property loss due to a failure of the procedure

- Lack of consistency caused by varying interpretations of guidelines

- Change in the resources used to accomplish the task

- Change in the problem that the policy or procedure was intended to solve

When it becomes apparent that the policy, procedure, or guideline must be revised, replaced, or abandoned, the actual process steps are the same as those used for the creation of a new policy, procedure, or guideline. See the steps in Need for New Policy, Procedure, or Guideline section.

Like most elements of the administrative function, the policies, procedures, or guidelines of the training organization must be continually monitored for effectiveness. Policies, procedures, and guidelines are most effective when they are considered dynamic documents; that is, documents that are subject to constant scrutiny, review, and revision.

Responsibility for the monitoring of all policies and procedures rests with the chief officers of the organization. They should be familiar with the contents, applications, and effects of the policies they use to manage the organization. They should also be aware of the proper procedures for performing the tasks assigned to them and members of their command. Infractions and unauthorized alterations of the policies, procedures, or guidelines should be noted and reported for the purpose of reinforcing the existing policies, procedures, or guidelines or revising them to meet changing conditions.

Adoption Process

Before a policy, procedure, or guideline can be used in the management of a training program, the training manager or staff must develop it and follow organization policy for having it adopted. *Adoption* is the process by which the chief and/or designated administrators review, amend, and approve the policy, procedure, or guideline. If this document is to have credibility and be effective in day-to-day operations, it is essential that it go through a formal adoption process.

The adoption process begins well before a final version is put on paper. Consider the following adoption process steps:

Step 1: Identify a need.

Step 2: Develop a draft document.

Step 3: Submit the draft for organizational review.

Step 4: Adopt the document.

Step 5: Publish the document.

Step 6: Implement the document's contents.

Step 7: Evaluate its effectiveness.

Identify Need

First, it must be evident that there is a need for a policy, procedure, or guideline. A need becomes apparent when a challenge arises or there is a change in the scope or structure of a training program. Needs can be identified by the following methods:

- *Record and maintain documents on issues, challenges, and incidents that occur during training and refer to them when researching information for a needs analysis* — When there are frequent incidents of heatstroke during summer drills, for example, a policy, procedure, and/or guideline may be needed for the following issues:

  — Addressing weather conditions

  — Hydrating students

— Taking breaks during training

— Rescheduling classes

- ***Communicate with other training organizations and share information regarding training issues, challenges, and incidents*** — Learning from other organizations can contribute to the safety of all training activities. Sometimes the need for a policy, procedure, or guideline becomes evident through training challenges that other organizations experience. *Examples:*

  — During the past quarter century, numerous fatal training fires in acquired structures have been well publicized. Investigations of these incidents have shown that the fatalities and injuries were preventable.

  — Becoming aware of these incidents had positive results: Organizations developed and adopted strict policies on live-fire training in acquired structures and burn buildings.

Develop Draft Document

After a need is identified, an individual or committee develops a draft of the document. Use the following steps:

- Determine whether a policy, procedure, or guideline is the most appropriate for the issue or incident or all three are needed. Always select the least restrictive type of document. Use similar existing policies, procedures, or guidelines as references when possible.

- Make the wording in the document clear, concise, and easy to follow. Use appropriate terms, and follow proper organizational format.

- Include the date the document becomes effective if adopted.

- List the person or unit responsible for managing the new rule and any other policy, procedure, or guideline to which it is related. *Requirements:*

  — *Policy* must also state to whom or what it applies and the specific rules of application.

  — *Procedure* must contain the steps to follow and the policy to which it applies.

  — *Guideline* must include to whom or what it applies and the guideline statement.

- Conduct research on the legalities of the rule because the documented issue or incident likely has potential legal implications. *Process:*

  — Determine whether the issue or incident is addressed in existing organizational policies.

  — Review NFPA standards that address the issue or incident.

  — Seek similar issue or incident resolutions from other organizations.

- Submit the draft document to the organization's legal counsel for review. It is the training manager's responsibility to ensure that any document is legally and administratively valid before leaving the draft step in the adoption process.

Submit Draft for Review

Next, submit the draft document for organizational review and comment. Review and comment opportunities are especially important for those documents that are controversial or affect multiple groups in an organization. For example, a proposed policy on attendance at training sessions certainly affects students more than instructors or program administrators.

A critical consideration about feedback on draft documents is the fact that those affected by a new rule may *not* always support the change. Their lack of support does *not* necessarily mean that the rule is *not* worthwhile or needed. Ultimately, it is the training manager and the organization's chief executive officer who are held accountable to the obligations of providing safe and effective operations in the training program.

When a rule is required to meet those obligations, then it is appropriate to adopt one, even when it is *not* popular with members of the organization. Use the following review process steps:

Step 1: Provide personnel an opportunity to respond with feedback and input on any document that affects them. An important point is that the draft document does *not* need to be reviewed by *all* personnel, but it should be reviewed by the chief officers responsible for managing the fire and emergency services responders affected by the rule and also representative personnel who will be affected.

Step 2: Provide a comment period for the draft document, and review all comments.

Step 3: Evaluate comments, and amend draft document as necessary.

Adopt Document

Once feedback has been evaluated and the document has been amended if necessary, the policy, procedure, or guideline is ready for adoption. The appropriate manager or administrator endorses the document. When it is a policy for the training program, for example, the training manager endorses it. When it is a broader policy affecting the entire organization, the endorsement must come from the organization's chief executive officer. An endorsement demonstrates to organizational personnel that the rule has official sanction.

Publish Document

Once the document has all the necessary signatures, it is time to publish the policy, procedure, or guideline. Anyone potentially affected by the rule must be informed of the change. Memos often inform personnel, but when the document is implementing a substantial change or addressing a critical issue, the best method for communicating the new rule is a face-to-face meeting with personnel and supervisors **(Figure 20.10)**. The face-to-face method provides the following opportunities for personnel:

- Ask questions.
- Gain clarification.
- Ensure understanding.

Regardless of the method used, it is essential to inform everyone with an interest in the rule. Without this communication, it is likely that neither supervisors nor subordinates will follow the contents of the document.

Implement Document's Contents

Experience has shown that the lack of proper implementation of policies, procedures, and guidelines is the primary cause for the failure of personnel to accept and adhere to the contents of those documents. The main intent of most of these documents is to create a change in behavior. To

Figure 20.10 To be effective, policies must be communicated to the personnel that they affect. Communication is best done in a face-to-face meeting that permits the employee to ask questions and gain clarification of the new policy. *Courtesy of Rick Montemorra.*

ensure that personnel learn, adopt, and practice these changes, they must be educated about the new policy, procedure, or guideline.

Acceptance of the changes requires that personnel know the reason for the change, understand the benefits of the change, and accept that the change is an improvement over the previous situation or process. Other requirements of the implementation step include providing the necessary equipment, support, and training required by the new policy, procedure, or guideline.

For instance, if a policy is adopted that prohibits the use of tobacco products in the fire station during working hours, the following steps should be taken to implement the prohibition:

Step 1: Communicate the new policy.

Step 2: Train supervisors in the implementation and enforcement of the new policy.

Step 3: Educate personnel about the benefits to health and hygiene of *not* using tobacco.

Step 4: Provide a designated smoking area in a well-ventilated portion of the station.

Step 5: Post *No Smoking* or *Smoking in Designated Areas Only* signs as appropriate.

Step 6: Provide employee assistance programs to help personnel stop using tobacco products.

Step 7: Remove built-in ashtrays from the station.

Implementation of any policy, procedure, or guideline must be consistent, fair, and documented. Credibility of the new requirements as well as the administration that supports them can be destroyed when personnel perceive that implementation and enforcement are inconsistent.

Evaluate Effectiveness

When the policy, procedure, or guideline is implemented, it must be monitored for effectiveness. Chief officers, managers, and supervisors can observe the new requirement in use and determine its effectiveness based on the established criteria. When it is apparent that the new requirement is *not* providing the intended change, the process should be evaluated to determine whether the policy, procedure, or guideline was correctly developed.

Interviews with personnel who are affected by the change may indicate that additional education, support, or changes are required to gain full acceptance. Monitoring of the policy, procedure, or guideline should continue. A periodic review should be performed to determine whether the document requires revision, replacement, or abandonment based on changes in the operating environment.

Standards

Organizations adopt *standards* to provide the basis for performance or operational requirements. Every day, training managers make decisions based on standards. They are key elements to any training program.

The most common standards used by fire and emergency services organizations in North America are those from NFPA. These standards address many issues including professional qualifications, firefighter health and safety programs, and organizational structure. Some of the more commonly used NFPA standards that affect the training function are listed in the information box (p. 492).

Other standards used in the fire and emergency services include governmental standards and regulations. Many of the policies and requirements for hazardous materials programs are found in federal laws. Also, most states and provinces have specific requirements for emergency medical services (EMS) training and certification. An organization's training program must comply with the standards that apply to the subjects taught.

Most standards reflect state/provincial or national norms for fire and emergency services. For example, professionals from appropriate fire and emergency services organizations develop NFPA standards through a consensus process. NFPA members have the opportunity then to either ratify or reject the proposed standards. This process ensures that standards reflect the needs and current practices of the fire and emergency services.

When a standard is accepted and followed, it becomes the accepted *standard of care* by the group publishing it. Standards promulgated by NFPA are considered minimum standards against which an organization could possibly be judged, regardless of whether or not that organization adopts the

NFPA Standards: Fire and Emergency Services

- NFPA 472, *Standard for Professional Competence of Responders to Hazardous Materials Incidents*
- NFPA 473, *Standard for Competencies for EMS Personnel Responding to Hazardous Materials Incidents*
- NFPA 600, *Standard on Industrial Fire Brigades*
- NFPA 1001, *Standard for Fire Fighter Professional Qualifications*
- NFPA 1002, *Standard for Fire Apparatus Driver/ Operator Professional Qualifications*
- NFPA 1003, *Standard for Airport Fire Fighter Professional Qualifications*
- NFPA 1021, *Standard for Fire Officer Professional Qualifications*
- NFPA 1031, *Standard for Professional Qualifications for Fire Inspector and Plan Examiner*
- NFPA 1033, *Standard for Professional Qualifications for Fire Investigator*
- NFPA 1035, *Standard for Professional Qualifications for Public Fire and Life Safety Educator*
- NFPA 1041, *Standard for Fire Service Instructor Professional Qualifications*

- NFPA 1051, *Standard for Wildland Fire Fighter Professional Qualifications*
- NFPA 1061, *Standard for Professional Qualifications for Public Safety Telecommunicator*
- NFPA 1201, *Standard for Providing Emergency Services to the Public*
- NFPA 1401, *Recommended Practice for Fire Service Training Reports and Records*
- NFPA 1403, *Standard on Live Fire Training Evolutions*
- NFPA 1404, *Standard for Fire Service Respiratory Protection Training*
- NFPA 1500, *Standard on Fire Department Occupational Safety and Health Program*
- NFPA 1521, *Standard for Fire Department Safety Officer*
- NFPA 1710, *Standard for the Organization and Deployment of Fire Suppression Operations, Emergency Medical Operations, and Special Operations to the Public by Career Fire Departments*
- NFPA 1720, *Standard for the Organization and Deployment of Fire Suppression Operations, Emergency Medical Operations, and Special Operations to the Public by Volunteer Fire Departments*

standard. In essence, the consensus of organizations considers that NFPA standards carry the weight of law.

Many standards can affect an organization's training program, so it is advisable for training managers to learn about those standards that affect their particular organizations. When an organization participates in a state or provincial fire and life safety education certification program, for example, the training manager should review NFPA 1035, *Standard for Professional Qualifications for Public Fire and Life Safety Educator* (**Figure 20.11**).

A recent example of the adoption of a standard into law occurred in Florida. In response to three fatalities that occurred during two live-fire training incidents, the state adopted NFPA 1403 as a state law. By 2007, all live-fire training must be conducted at a certified training center. Acquired

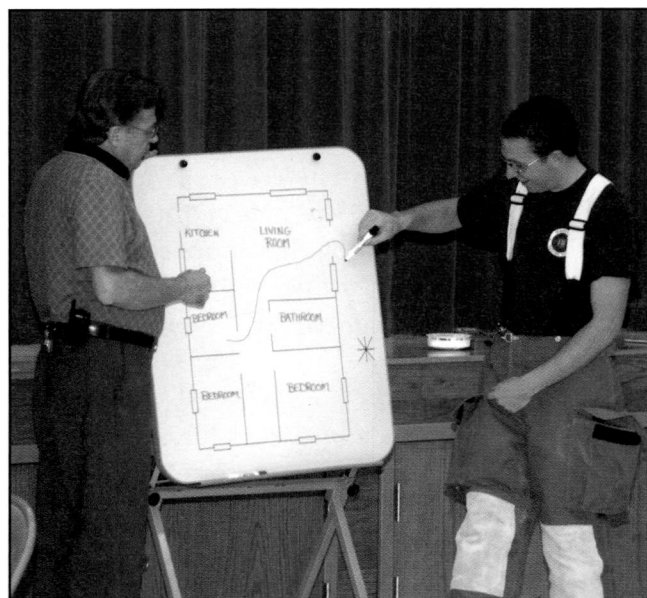

Figure 20.11 NFPA standards provide directions for many fire and life safety activities including public education programs.

structures must meet the requirements of the standard and a certified live-fire instructor must be on site during the training evolution.

When there is an NFPA or other standard used for identifying either organizational training requirements or operations, the organization should formally adopt it. Adopting the standard gives it formal *power* in the organization and allows the training manager to enforce the requirements set forth in the standard.

Of course, adoption also allows the training manager to hold organizational personnel accountable for meeting the requirements in the standard. The adoption process would be the same as that used for adopting policies, procedures, or guidelines.

Human Resources Management

When a Level III Instructor is assigned the role of training manager, the instructor may relinquish the responsibility for teaching and assume the responsibility for supervising subordinate instructors and the staff that supports them. This responsibility means that the Level III Instructor must be familiar with the human resources policies and procedures that the local jurisdiction adheres to.

The instructor may have full authority in all of these areas or may only have limited authority. Those policies may include the following:

- Hiring procedures
- Promotional processes
- Transfer policies
- Employee termination
- Employee discipline
- Employee evaluations

The sections that follow discuss the general concepts of general human resources guidelines regarding supervision, staff selection, and personnel evaluations. The instructor should always seek the assistance of the jurisdiction's human resources department or legal department when dealing with specific personnel matters.

Supervision

Most Level III Instructors have had experience supervising personnel at the fire company level, small groups of around four people, or other in-structors. The experience gained at this lower level creates the foundation for supervising larger and more complex groups. As a supervisor, the Level III Instructor has the following five basic challenges that are common to most supervisory positions:

- Anticipating problems
- Facilitating the development of group goals or objectives by involving members of the group
- Fostering a team atmosphere or environment through the use of sound team development and management techniques
- Involving members of the group in establishing goals and objectives
- Motivating group members through dedication, positive attitude, commitment, and perseverance, which then lead to empowering, rewarding, coaching, mentoring, and celebrating accomplishments

In addition, the training manager provides an example to the group by demonstrating sound leadership characteristics. The sections that follow discuss the supervisory challenges and the responsibilities that the Level III Instructor will assume as training manager.

Challenges

As a supervisor, the Level III instructor must be able to overcome the challenges identified in Chapter 19, Supervision and Management, in addition to new challenges associated with accepting the responsibility of a higher level of supervision. A person's first-level supervisor plays a very important role in creating an environment in which performance and behavioral expectations are identified and mentored.

Making the transition from a Level II to Level III Instructor creates a variety of personal challenges for the new training manager. As mentioned in Chapter 19, Supervision and Management, one of the greatest of these challenges is the change of relationships when former peers become subordinates.

The IFSTA **Chief Officer** manual provides six rules for making the transition to a higher rank. Those same rules (paraphrased here) can apply to the transition to Level III Instructor or training manager regardless of whether the person promotes from within or is hired from outside the organization. The rules are as follows:

- **Commit to the position** — Learn about it, be interested in it, and be dedicated to it.

- **Show loyalty to the organization** — Support the leadership team and political authority. Do *not* openly criticize the organization, management, or decisions that are made.

- **Support all types of education and training** — Seek opportunities to learn and also provide education and training to other members of the organization. All supervisors, regardless of their level, perform the following three roles simultaneously:

  — Stewards of the position that they hold

  — Teachers of those they supervise

  — Students of the positions to which they aspire

- **Guard conversations** — Be careful to *not* say anything that would bring dishonor onto a person, a position, or the organization. Do *not* disclose information that is confidential, particularly information concerning subordinates.

- **Accept criticism graciously and accept praise, honors, and advancement modestly** — Admit mistakes and errors and take responsibility for them. Do *not* take the credit for the accomplishments of others.

- **Lead by example** — Realize that example is the key to successful leadership of any organization. This rule cannot be stressed too much. It is founded on a consistent adherence to a set of moral, ethical, and social values.

Responsibilities

All supervisors have the nine major responsibilities to an organization described in Chapter 19, Supervision and Management. By accomplishing each of these responsibilities, the training manager can ensure an efficient and stable organization. An especially important one is to promote and maintain health, wellness, and safety policies within the workplace **(Figure 20.12)**.

The instructor-supervisor should consider these responsibilities in relationships with other persons both inside and outside the organization and as

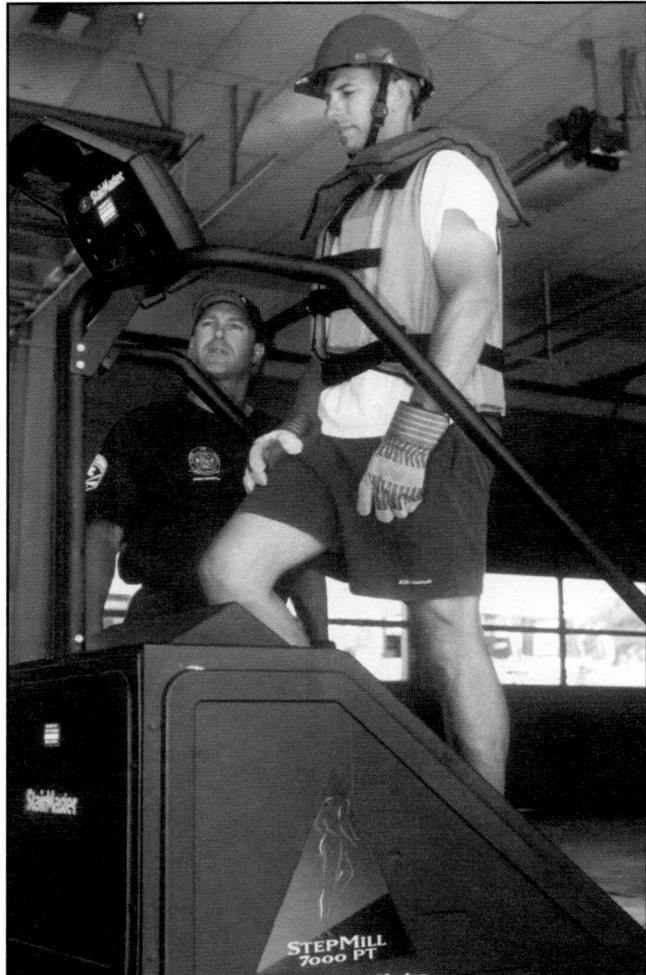

Figure 20.12 The training manager is responsible for ensuring that personnel assigned to the training division comply with the organization's health, wellness, and safety policies. *Courtesy of Rick Montemorra.*

the basis for daily decision-making. Like a code of conduct, the instructor should adhere to these both in principle and in fact.

Staff Selection

Effective instructors are the foundations upon which effective training programs are built. Effective instructors can teach, lead, motivate, inspire, and change the attitudes of an organization. However, organizations often invest too little effort and consideration in the selection of competent instructors. Selecting competent instructors is a key management function of training managers.

In addition, determining whether instructor roles are short-term or long-term aids in the selection process. When the instructor is only going to teach one course or topic, then the role may be considered short-term. When the instructor is expected to perform the function for an extended period such as 5 years, then the role is long-term and the selection criteria will be different.

Next, the training manager should determine the instructors' roles in the organization and the qualifications they need to teach the training programs. Establishing their positions in the organizational structure gives importance to the instructor role. Instructors, whether long- or short-term, are critical parts of program planning. Other components of staff selection include the following:

- Qualifications
- Position advertising
- Internal/external sources
- Recruitment and training
- Applications and interviews
- Employee orientation

Qualifications

Instructors also act as intermediaries between administration and personnel in training. Instructors not only teach job knowledge and skills, but they are active in applying knowledge and skills on the job at various ranks or positions in the organization. Their experiences are critical components to their qualifications.

Few instructors are qualified to teach all the topics required in a modern fire and emergency services curriculum. Rather, instructors tend to specialize in certain areas and become proficient in teaching knowledge and skills specific to their areas of experience and expertise. The training manager should base instructor selection upon the topics to be taught and the designated instructor roles in the organization and training program.

In addition to topic expertise, instructors must have credibility with the personnel being trained. Personnel perceive that instructors have credibility when they display technical proficiency and evidence of formal training and education and demonstrate instructional experience. Credibility is also indicated by rank, reputation, and respect among members of the organization.

When determining instructor qualifications, establishing credibility in technical proficiency and professional experience in the subject to be taught are important factors.

When instructors have neither skill nor credibility in the desired teaching areas, they will *not* be effective (**Figure 20.13**).

Instructors must be effective communicators along with having technical credibility. Topic expertise and credibility are only effective in training when instructors are able to transmit knowledge and demonstrate skills in methods that program participants can understand and apply (see Chapter 1, Challenges of Fire and Emergency Services Instruction).

Along with the technical qualifications, an instructor must also be qualified and certified. Qualifications can be based on legally adopted or nationally recognized certification standards. For example, fire instructors should meet the Instructor I requirements of NFPA 1041. When no personnel meet these requirements, training managers need to provide instructor-training programs. Training, program resources, and information are generally available from local, state, or provincial training organizations.

Figure 20.13 Effective instructors must be technically proficient in the skills they are required to teach. *Courtesy of Iowa Fire Service Training.*

Position Advertising

After instructor roles and qualifications are determined, the training manager must advertise or market the position to prospective candidates both inside and outside the organization. Too often instructors are selected from a small group because the majority of internal personnel who may be eligible for an instructor position are unaware of the open position. All eligible personnel must be made aware of openings.

An organization may have policies or other requirements (such as required rank or service time) that limit the number of applicants, but these requirements must also be advertised so that interested personnel may choose an appropriate course of action. When the position involves a change in working conditions (increase in pay, change in hours of work, or other benefits), personnel policies or union/management agreements may require that the process follow a specific set of steps.

Internal/External Sources

Sources for potential instructors may be either internal or external to the organization. Internally, all company-level personnel who have been required to certify to the Level I Instructor requirements are primary sources. Other sources include former instructors, personnel responsible for public fire and life safety education, or public information officers.

Knowledge of adult education can be very helpful even when the individual is *not* completely familiar with the requirements of the fire and emergency services. Outside the organization, sources include the following:

- Professional educators
- Recent college graduates with a degree in education
- Retired educators
- Members of other fire and life safety organizations
- People involved in training in private industry

Recruitment and Training

Volunteer and combination departments have the further challenge of recruiting instructors who have full-time jobs or other commitments. The administration of the department must look at the cost-effectiveness of recruiting and training a part-time instructor as opposed to using the courses provided by the state/provincial training agency or National Fire Academy to train department personnel (**Figure 20.14**).

When there is a shortage of qualified applicants, the organization should provide instructor training so personnel who wish to teach can improve their skills. Training managers are responsible for ensuring that the instructors they use are competent. To ensure competence, provide opportunities for instructor training and the development of current and potential instructors.

Applications and Interviews

While a position is being advertised, interested people submit applications. The training manager or a selection committee reviews the applications and selects the most qualified to interview. Ideally, and in order to observe and evaluate an applicant's qualifications, the interview process includes an instructional scenario in which the candidate demonstrates the desired abilities and qualifications.

This scenario activity gives the training manager or selection committee an opportunity to see all candidates simulating the job they would perform if selected. Many potential instructors have great

Figure 20.14 Emergency services organizations that do not maintain a training division can rely on state/provincial or national training agencies. Courses are available in all basic and advanced topics and some are available in distant learning formats. *Courtesy of Alabama Fire College.*

résumés but cannot effectively communicate or demonstrate effective teaching methods. Training managers should select instructors based on organizational needs.

Employee Orientation

Once a selection has been made and the successful candidate is hired, the training manager orients the new instructor. Orientation includes defining the instructor's teaching role. Instructors must have a clear understanding of the job before they enter the classroom or arrive at the drill ground. The new instructor needs to know the following information:

- Topics to teach
- Policies of the training program to promote and enforce
- Instructional support to expect
- Limitations to expect
- Authority and responsibility

Instructors in volunteer departments must also be aware of the time commitment that the position of instructor demands. This commitment includes professional development, travel, lesson preparation, and lesson delivery.

Personnel Evaluations

As managers and supervisors, Level III Instructors must periodically evaluate the personnel who work for them. The *formal* personnel evaluation program is necessary to maintain complete and documented personnel files. Formal personnel evaluations occur in the following situations:

- When employees are hired or recruited as a member of a volunteer organization
- Continually during the probationary employment period
- Annually as part of a performance review
- For promotional purposes
- For disciplinary or termination purposes

The preferred approach to personnel evaluations is the *informal* approach, which involves providing feedback to the employee on the quality of work that that person is performing. It allows the supervisor to correct performance and behavioral problems quickly and provides the employee with the knowledge that the supervisor is genuinely concerned. This type of personal interaction also allows the employee to ask for assistance, make suggestions, and learn more about the job.

The informal personnel evaluations then become the basis for the formal periodic performance review. Performance objectives that were agreed upon in the informal evaluation are included in the formal review to indicate that they have been accomplished. The personnel evaluation program has the following advantages:

- Creates a permanent record of an employee's achievements for the purpose of awards, promotions, transfers, discipline, and termination
- Shows whether additional training is needed; if so, new programs can be developed to address the deficiency when it appears to be widespread
- Gives the supervisor more familiarity with the personnel being evaluated
- Motivates personnel to improve
- Gives higher levels of management more awareness of the abilities of lower level managers and supervisors
- Illuminates the specific talents of individuals that may be used in other areas of the organization (**Figure 20.15**)
- Improves the efficiency of both employees and the organization as a whole

Figure 20.15 Personnel evaluations are an opportunity for supervisors to identify specific talents that subordinates have and channel those talents into areas that can benefit from them.

All personnel evaluations need to be timely; that is, they need to occur when the need becomes apparent. The informal approach allows for this situation to happen. When an employee is performing at or above the anticipated level, then personal recognition instills pride in the employee. When there is a need to correct a work habit that is *not* meeting the required standard, then the immediate attention to the issue lessens the effect of the work habit and prevents any future problems associated with the act.

In addition, when it becomes apparent that an employee is either unable or unwilling to meet the minimum employment standard, then termination proceedings need to be considered. Failing to terminate an employee when the reasons are warranted (especially during the probationary period) results in a number of unwanted situations such as the following:

- Causes other employees to view the supervisor or organization as being inconsistent with established policies
- Creates resentment within the work force and the impression that the organization is unwilling to deal with this type of situation
- Sends the message to other employees that nothing will happen to them when they, too, break rules, regulations, policies, and/or procedures

The periodic job-performance evaluation is an opportunity to generate positive change in the organization. The training manager can accomplish this change by focusing on the positive accomplishments of the employee, involving the employee in setting goals and objectives, and creating an atmosphere in which the employee can feel comfortable and accepted. Fire and emergency services personnel should also be familiar with the concept of a 360-degree feedback evaluation.

Regardless of the type of organization, personnel evaluations have specific characteristics with which the instructor should be familiar. In addition, the instructor should also be aware of the evaluation process that the local authority has adopted and legal considerations that accompany all personnel evaluations. Each of these topics is addressed in the sections that follow.

Characteristics

Personnel evaluations have specific characteristics. These characteristics can be used to generate guidelines that should be adhered to. When these guidelines are applied properly to the process, then personnel evaluations can be effective tools in the management of the organization. These guidelines are as follows (**Figure 20.16**):

- *Timely* — Conduct evaluations in a timely manner. This characteristic is especially true of performance evaluations that are linked to a specific incidence of unsatisfactory performance.

- *Clearly stated criteria* — State goals and objectives clearly and concisely. Maintain written job-performance criteria for review at each successive evaluation.

- *Nondiscriminatory* — Apply job-performance standards regardless of gender, race, ethnicity, age, or other classifications.

- *Consistency* — Apply job-performance standards equally throughout the organization based on the type of job or duty performed.

- *Thorough records* — Maintain thorough and complete records of each evaluation in the employee's personnel file. Give a copy of the evaluation to the employee; however, these records are *not* public so it is important to maintain confidentiality.

- *Trained supervisors* — Properly train instructors or supervisors who are required to perform personnel evaluations.

- *Objectivity* — Overcome personal bias and base the evaluation on established criteria. Objectivity is essential in personnel evaluations.

Process

The personnel evaluation process begins with an initial meeting between the training manager and the new instructor or staff member. At this point, the training division's expectations for the job performance of the employee are established. Performance standards are outlined and agreed upon by both parties.

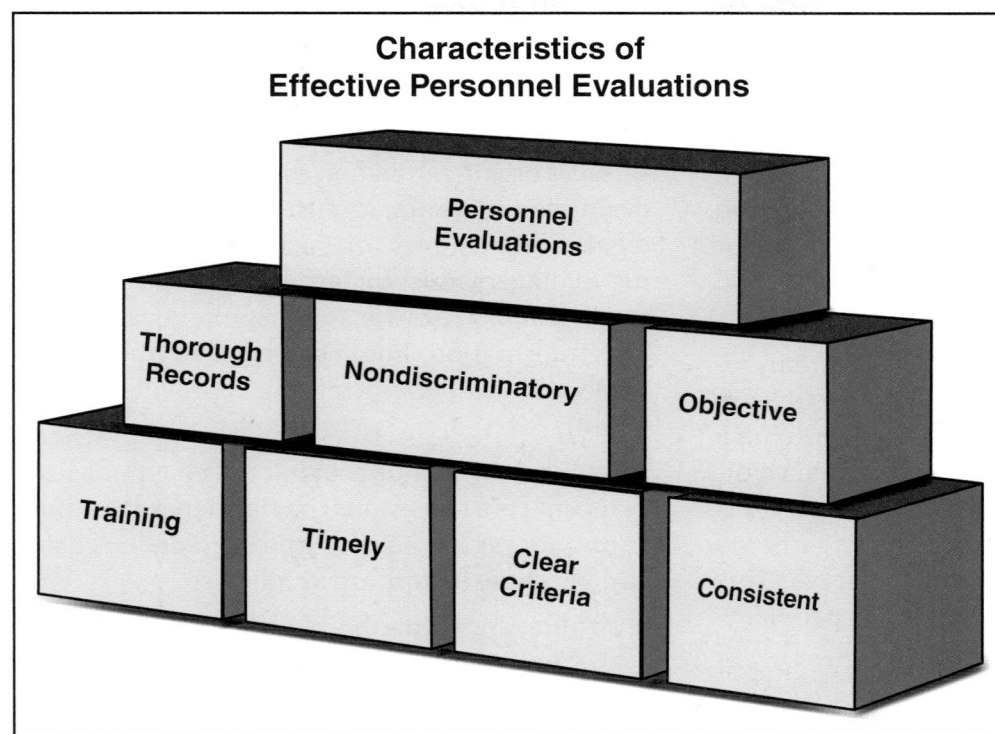

Characteristics of Effective Personnel Evaluations

Figure 20.16 Personnel evaluations should include certain characteristics.

Some fire and emergency services organizations have a probationary period for new instructors or staff members. The job-performance expectations that were established initially provide the basis for performance evaluations during this probationary period. The training manager or supervisor must continually monitor the job performance of new instructors or staff members and provide appropriate feedback.

Feedback may be either additional information about what is expected or praise for meeting or exceeding expectations. This probationary period can be difficult when the supervisor does *not* provide enough information or when the new instructor fails to ask questions or clarify misunderstandings.

Periodic Job-Performance Evaluations

Following the probationary period, periodic job-performance evaluations are established on an annual basis. These evaluations are opportunities for both the training manager and instructor to review the quality of work and established performance goals and objectives. The current trend in personnel evaluation is to provide continuous feedback to the employee. The formal evaluation

is then used to reinforce continuous feedback. To ensure that evaluations are successful, supervisors should take the following actions:

- Ensure that the employee is aware of the relationship of the position in the organization, authority the position has, and responsibilities assigned to the position.

- Allow the employee to contribute to the establishing or altering of performance goals and objectives.

- Conduct the evaluation like a formal interview: Select a predetermined time in the privacy of the evaluator's office and prohibit interruptions. There should be no surprises regarding performance or expectations of the employee during this interview.

- Include the signatures of both the supervisor and employee on the final evaluation form to indicate that the employee has received the evaluation. The employee's signature does *not* necessarily indicate agreement with the content of the evaluation. It simply indicates that the comments of the evaluator were reviewed with the employee.

Feedback Evaluations: 360-Degree Concept

Fire and emergency services personnel should also be familiar with the concept of a 360-degree feedback evaluation. It is similar to the type of size-up that occurs at an emergency incident when the incident commander (IC) requests situation reports from all sides of the incident. The need for tactical changes becomes apparent quickly, and the IC then responds accordingly.

When the concept is applied to the human resources program, the process and the results are similar. The information used in the performance evaluation is gathered from people who have direct professional contact with the person who is being evaluated. The information that is gathered is based on the performance they observe. This evaluation would include the following people:

- Peers
- Subordinates
- Employees
- Members of other agencies
- Members of the public who are in reasonably constant contact with the individual

Responses must remain confidential to protect the people who are providing the information. It also ensures that they will speak freely and *not* hesitate to provide constructive criticism.

Feedback should also be supported by a plan for the improvement of any behaviors that are perceived to be below standard. Evaluations and the interpretation of results should be administered and performed by a professional trained in this technique. Some of the ways to help an individual improve to meet the performance expectations are as follows:

- Coaching
- Mentoring
- Continuing education
- Training in specialized skills

Legal Considerations

Personnel evaluations must adhere to the guidelines provided by the local AHJ, state/province, and federal governments. When a fire or emergency services organization first establishes a personnel evaluation program, it must research the various legal requirements for such a program. Training managers must be familiar with all statutory requirements relevant to personnel evaluations. This information should be provided when initial personnel evaluation training is provided by the organization.

Some of the factors that have been emphasized in recent court decisions that influence the evaluation process are similar to the guidelines listed earlier. These factors are as follows:

- Evaluations must be significantly related to the work behavior or skills that the employee is assigned to perform. The individual cannot be judged on tasks that are not assigned or the person is not trained to perform.

- Evaluations must include definite identifiable criteria based on the quality or quantity of work or on specific performances that are supported by a documented record.

- Evaluations must be objective and not based on subjective observations.

- Evaluations must be supported by documentation.

Summary

The tasks and responsibilities of a Level III Instructor can be very challenging. New skills and knowledge have to be acquired to permit the instructor to effectively supervise personnel and manage administrative assignments. Among those responsibilities discussed in this chapter were records management, training policy development, and personnel or human resources management. The remaining administrative responsibilities are discussed in the chapters that follow.

Part D

Instructor III Requirements

Chapter 21

Analysis and Evaluation

After reading this chapter, students will be able to —

1. Identify types of analyses.

2. Complete statements about the steps needed to accomplish the analysis process.

3. Discuss using a planning model.

4. Complete statements about the evaluation process.

5. Identify characteristics of prospective and retrospective evaluations.

6. Explain the difference between qualitative and quantitative evaluations.

7. Discuss the evaluation of a fire and emergency services organization.

8. Discuss the evaluation of fire and emergency services programs.

9. Explain the three major components of training program evaluation.

10. List the six areas that should be addressed in a thorough evaluation of the instructional process.

11. Discuss formative evaluations.

12. Discuss summative evaluations.

13. Discuss steps to take after reviewing evaluation results.

Chapter Contents

Analysis Process
    Types
    Process Steps
    Application

Evaluation Process
    General Methodology
    Application Skills

Evaluation Plans
Course and Instructional Design Evaluations
    Considerations for Planning
    Formative Evaluations
    Summative Evaluations (Reaction Surveys)
    Evaluation Results

Summary

Chapter 21
Analysis and Evaluation

The Level III Instructor must be able to determine the types of training that the division or agency must provide to meet the organization's needs. Therefore, the instructor must understand the analysis process and how to apply it to the training function.

This determination begins with a needs analysis that determines the gap between the type of training currently being provided and the type of training required. After the organization's needs have been determined, the instructor can perform a task analysis to determine the specific steps or tasks that compose each job that members of the organization perform to provide the required services for the response area.

The instructor must also be able to evaluate the quality of the training program, curriculum, or lesson. While the terms *analysis* and *evaluation* are sometimes used to mean the same thing, they are in fact two approaches to determining how something works and how effective it is. An *analysis* is used to determine how the training program will work, and an *evaluation* is used to determine how well the training program has worked.

The concept of analysis was introduced as it applies to Level II Instructors in Chapter 18, Administrative Duties. This chapter provides the Level III Instructor with overviews of both analysis and evaluation and their uses in planning training programs, curriculums, and instructional designs.

Analysis Process

Analysis is used to determine how an item, a program, or a project works or how an incident occurred. Analysis implies an objective study of the

Analyzing Vs. Evaluating
- *Analyzing* is the process of methodically examining the various parts of an item, project, program, or incident.
- *Evaluating* is establishing the worth or value of each part or the sum total of the whole based on the desired outcome, which therefore determines how effective or efficient an item, program, or process is compared to a benchmark or established set of criteria.

widest array of facts, statistics, or data. It involves looking at each piece or component to determine how it interacts with other parts and how they work together to create the whole. Analysis may require looking at the facts repeatedly to try to make all the pieces fit, much like assembling a massive jigsaw puzzle.

A very graphic example of analyzing an incident is the meticulous review of the *Challenger* and *Columbia* space shuttle tragedies by the U.S. National Aeronautics and Space Administration (NASA). Each available piece of debris, computer data, and physical evidence was reviewed and examined to determine how the incidents occurred. When all of the various parts were analyzed, the information was gathered into final reports that were evaluated to determine the root cause of the incidents (**Figure 21.1, p. 504**).

Obviously, analysis precedes drawing any conclusions or making a decision. Conclusions based on solid analyses have strong foundations and are defendable against speculation and criticism. Therefore, it is important to understand the types of analyses that an instructor or training manager

Figure 21.1 Government agencies perform detailed and thorough analyses to determine the causes of major disasters such as the loss of the space shuttle *Columbia. Courtesy of Mark Wolfe, photographer, U.S. Federal Emergency Management Agency.*

may be required to perform, general steps in the analytical process, and application of these steps to the various tasks assigned to that instructor, including both needs and task analyses.

Types

There are numerous types of analyses, many more than the instructor or fire and emergency services training manager will be called upon to perform. Those analysis types that benefit the training manager are those that concern the following topics:

- Cost/benefit
- Process
- Policy
- Program
- Need
- Task
- Risk

Cost/Benefit

A *cost/benefit analysis* is based on the relationship between the effort (cost) and the result (benefit). To be successful or effective, the benefit must match or exceed the cost to justify the program, process, or purchase. Public officials sometimes refer to this benefit as *return on investment*. It can be applied to the following functions:

- Purchase of a new piece of equipment
- Employee staffing
- Facility construction, design, or location
- Many other situations

One example of a cost/benefit analysis would be comparing the cost of developing a course curriculum internally or purchasing one from an external source.

Process

A *process analysis* involves looking at each step in the process and determining the best way to do it. Process analysis usually occurs when a system or process is first established. It may also be performed when a process is evaluated and determined to be ineffective or inefficient. Examples of processes include the planning process, communication process, or steps used to open a concealed space with an axe.

Policy

A *policy analysis* occurs when current policies (or the resulting problems caused by the lack of them) are analyzed for effectiveness and enforcement. This analysis usually takes place when an organization is experiencing some type of internal difficulty. This process may take up to a year and require the use of an outside agency such as the authority's legal department or human resources department.

Generally, though, when the problems are *not* severe, the fire or emergency services organization can form an internal committee or task force to provide the analysis. For instance, an organization that is experiencing an increase in back injuries may decide to analyze the problem to determine whether a lifting policy would reduce injuries or another solution would be more cost-effective.

Program

A *program analysis* is used to determine the most efficient ways to provide a program or service by looking at each program component. It may occur before program implementation or periodically during the life of a program. It usually takes about 6 months to analyze a program.

For instance, to analyze a training program, each component (including mandated courses; entry-level courses; instructor certification; and facilities, props, and materials requirements) would be studied. As part of the program analysis, need, task, and cost/benefit analyses will also be conducted.

Need

A *needs analysis* or *assessment* is conducted to determine the types of services that an organization is currently delivering and compare them to the services that the community desires. The gap between the actual service delivery and the desired service delivery requires a reevaluation of the effectiveness of the current delivery **(Figure 21.2)**. See Chapter 22, Program and Curriculum Development, for a detailed discussion of needs analysis.

For instance, the fire department/organization may decide, based on a community needs analysis, to provide emergency medical services (EMS). The training division would perform an internal needs analysis to determine the types of medical programs currently offered.

This needs analysis would illuminate the gap between current offerings and the courses required to support the new medical service to be provided by the organization. Further, a cost/benefit analysis may be required to determine whether it is more effective to create the training program internally or contract it to another agency or organization such as a community college.

Task

A *task analysis* (often also called *job analysis* and *occupational analysis*) is a systematic appraisal of duties of a specific job or jobs, which identifies and describes all component tasks of that job or jobs. A task analysis enables program developers to design appropriate training courses for entry-level and current personnel who must learn certain tasks to perform a job.

A task analysis contains several components that enable analyzers to divide and identify every aspect of a job. It is important to determine the starting and ending point of each job and task and divide each into logical components. See Chapter 22, Program and Curriculum Development, for a detailed discussion of task analysis.

Figure 21.2 The construction of high-rise buildings within a jurisdiction creates a need for additional equipment and changes in strategy and tactics caused by the increased building height and modern fire protection systems. *Courtesy of OSU College of Engineering, Architecture, and Technology.*

For instance, the job of ventilating a roof might include the following tasks:

- Removing tools from the apparatus
- Placing a ladder against the building
- Climbing the ladder while carrying an axe
- Determining the proper place to ventilate
- Using the axe to cut the hole in the roof

For servicing the pumping apparatus, tasks might include changing the oil, checking fluid levels, replacing engine belts, and checking lights.

Risk

A *risk analysis* is applied to the likelihood of an event occurring such as a major fire or natural disaster, the type and severity of heart attacks for firefighters, or the potential for terrorist attacks on a community or a portion of a community. The risk is defined in terms of the following factors:

- Type
- Location
- Frequency
- Severity

The cost of mitigating the risk (actions taken to prevent or lessen the severity of an incident) is added to the analysis (such as the cost of recovery following the incident). For instance, a community that is located in an area where severe tornados are frequent may establish an early warning system, train emergency responders in search and rescue, and perform joint agency training drills to prepare for the potential destruction caused by severe weather **(Figure 21.3)**.

A computer software program that assists in developing a risk analysis is the Risk, Hazard, and Value Evaluation (RHAVE) Program. The program was developed jointly between the International Association of Fire Chiefs (IAFC) and the U.S. Fire Administration (USFA) and is available from both IAFC and USFA. The program can help communities develop objective, quantifiable risk-reduction policies.

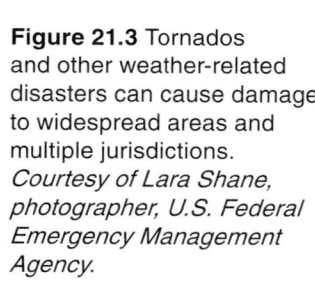

Figure 21.3 Tornados and other weather-related disasters can cause damage to widespread areas and multiple jurisdictions. *Courtesy of Lara Shane, photographer, U.S. Federal Emergency Management Agency.*

Process Steps

The steps in the analysis process move from specific items to general items; that is, from the smallest part or element to the complete subject item, program, or project. Once the results of the analysis are known and collected, they can be evaluated for worth and a decision can be made. The steps may vary slightly depending on the application. In general, however, the steps needed to accomplish the analysis process are as follows:

Step 1: Determine each of the components that compose the larger item, program, or process.

Step 2: Follow a systematic process each time an evaluation is made, using the same steps so that they become familiar.

Step 3: Remain objective and do not jump to a conclusion before all the facts are known.

Step 4: Review all of the various components and look for a pattern or relationship between the components.

Step 5: Seek the advice of others by discussing the analysis with them or involving them in the process.

Step 6: Look at the item, program, or process from the viewpoint of others who will be affected by it, which would include both service providers and customers.

Step 7: Set the analysis aside for a short time and take a break unless there is a definite deadline for completion. This action allows for a fresh view and may generate a new approach.

Step 8: Develop at least two approaches to the problem so that multiple approaches can be evaluated for effectiveness and value. This approach generates a minimum of three options:
— Best
— Compromise
— Status quo (no action at all)

Application

Some analytical models are available in both paper hardcopy and computer program forms. These models may be applied to such issues as budget evaluation and preparation, specifications development, station-location determination, long-range planning, and needs and risk analyses.

Whether planning a training program, a course of instruction or a single lesson, a helpful device called a *decision* or *planning model* can be used for selecting the following items:

● Appropriate methods of instruction

● Most direct routes or appropriate methods to reach course goals

● Intermediate points that measure instruction and learning

● Budgets to cover costs

● Numerous other course-planning processes that direct successful programs

When using a planning model to work toward a well-defined goal, it is possible to *map out* and measure progress during the planning process and along the route to reach selected goals and determine when the desired outcome has been met. Chapter 22, Program and Curriculum Development, examines the planning model and its application to training program and curriculum or instructional development.

Identifying needs, setting training goals to meet those needs, and designing training and planning instruction to achieve those goals determine program or course outcomes. These first steps are typical processes used to develop new courses or programs of instruction. The steps are also performed or reviewed each time instructors prepare a lesson.

Just as program developers plan ways to meet goals within a program of instruction, instructors do the same as they prepare to teach. Developers and instructors ensure that instructional methods, course materials, training aids, evaluation instruments, exercises, and drills work to meet the program goals and performance objectives that are identified in the plan of instruction. At the same time, developers and instructors ensure that the program of instruction is presented safely and efficiently.

Evaluation Process

While analyzing is determining how the various parts of the whole work and fit together, *evaluating* is establishing the worth or value of each of those parts (or the whole) based on the desired outcome. Evaluation determines how effective and efficient a person, an item, a program, or a project is compared to a benchmark or established set of criteria.

While analysis is objective, evaluation is subjective because it depends on the knowledge and experience of the evaluator. Although *evaluation* is defined as the appraisal of persons, programs, courses, projects, or organizations in relation to stated criteria or standards, the interpretation of the criteria or standards is subject to personal bias. Level III Instructors have already experienced the process through the application of evaluation instruments (tests) to determine how well students have learned information and in the development of student, instructor, and course evaluation instruments **(Figure 21.4)**.

Figure 21.4 Course evaluations completed by students or participants can be very subjective. Evaluation instruments must be carefully prepared in order to provide the most objective opinion possible.

Effective Versus Efficient

Although *effective* and *efficient* are sometimes used interchangeably, they have two separate and distinct meanings as follows:

- **Effective** — An action, activity, or item that produces the desired result or meets an intended purpose, which could be considered *doing the right thing*

- **Efficient** — Results that are produced with a minimum of effort, waste, or expense; that is, the minimum cost for the maximum effect

NFPA 1041, *Standard for Fire Service Instructor Professional Qualifications,* requires the Level III Instructor to be able to create a program evaluation plan. Therefore, the instructor must have a working knowledge of evaluation methodology including the types of evaluations, evaluation skills, and the application of the methodology to organizations, programs, and courses. Although the instructor should have been exposed to the methodology used to evaluate student learning, the sections that follow discuss the process as it is applied to programs and organizations.

General Methodology

A wide variety of evaluation methods or models exist in science, industry, business, and education. *Evaluation methodology* is the use of statistics and other methods to determine the efficiency, effectiveness, quality, and coverage of a program, policy, or activity. Some models are extremely technical and specific to the topic that is being evaluated such as those used by NASA or the aviation industry. Others are general in nature such as the process used to evaluate educational programs.

In all cases, the models share some basic steps. Research indicates that a typical process of evaluation contains the following general guidelines:

- Set criteria by identifying the problems or issues that must be addressed.

- Develop revision strategies and priorities.

- Determine what data is currently available for evaluation.

- Determine what new data will have to be collected for evaluation.

- Identify the evaluation model that will be most effective.

- Determine completion time necessary for the evaluation.

- Identify the personnel who will be responsible for making the evaluation.
- Conduct the evaluation.
- Analyze the results of the evaluation, and develop conclusions based on the results.
- Establish alternate responses.
- Prepare final reports on the evaluation based on the various audiences of those reports.

Some of the characteristics of evaluation are similar to the characteristics found in planning. Evaluation is part of the planning process. Several evaluation types and methods are available to conduct the evaluation process.

Evaluation Types

One generally accepted division of evaluation methodology is whether it is *prospective* or *retrospective*. When the intent of the evaluation is to improve a program, isolate any evident weaknesses, or understand the program's strengths and build on them, then the evaluation is *prospective* or *formative* (see Course and Instructional Design Evaluations section). When the intent of the evaluation is to assess the achievements or outcome of the program, then it is a *retrospective* or *summative* evaluation. Both types are complementary, and one element of the summative evaluation involves a formative evaluation. Descriptions are as follows:

- ***Prospective or formative evaluation*** — Features are as follows:
  - Provides an ongoing process
  - Allows the program or project to be altered while it is operating
  - Provides a look into the future (prospective)
  - Evaluates strengths and weaknesses with the intention of improving the program
  - Develops habits
  - Shapes the direction of professional development
  - Relies on feedback
  - Evaluates the effectiveness of similar past events

- ***Retrospective or summative evaluation*** — Features are as follows:
  - Concerns the overall effectiveness of the program
  - Generates new programs or projects
  - Provides a look into the past (retrospective)
  - Documents the achievements of the program
  - Documents habits that were relied upon by students
  - Shows the results of variations on the traditional approach
  - Relies on evidence
  - Depends on any information developed through the formative evaluations

An easily relatable example of each of these is the evaluation of an emergency incident. During the event, the incident commander (IC) continually performs a formative evaluation of the situation. When the incident is over, a summative evaluation in the form of the postincident analysis takes place. In the context of training, formative evaluations occur periodically during a course of instruction, while summative evaluations occur at the end of courses.

Evaluation Methods

Whether the type of evaluation selected is prospective/formative or retrospective/summative, the data may be collected by evaluation methods based on quality and quantity. Qualitative evaluation is a more subjective form of evaluation, while quantitative is more objective. Definitions are as follows:

- ***Qualitative evaluation*** — Based most often on nonnumeric analysis (although it may have numeric evaluations assigned to the values); that is, whether the item, project, or program meets the perceived values established for the item, project, or program. It is difficult to tabulate into neat, precise categories. Data are usually gathered through the following methods:
  - Open-ended questions
  - Interviews of students
  - Content analysis

— Student observations

— Nonstudent observations

- *Quantitative evaluation* — Based on a numeric or statistical analysis; specific numeric criteria are established and the item, program, or project is judged against them. Quantitative evaluation works best when information is gathered from a large number of respondents. In this case, information gathered locally may be judged against statistics gathered on a national level. *Details:*

  — Data are gathered from questionnaires that contain yes/no questions, checklists, or preference scales.

  — The limit that is placed on the respondent's answers may also prevent any fresh concepts from being developed.

  — Survey responses are also typically limited, usually around a 50-percent return rate.

Well-known examples in the fire and emergency services are the qualitative and quantitative fit-testing protocols used with respiratory protection facepieces. Qualitative fit testing involves the subjective judgment of the person being tested to determine whether the test chemical is entering the facepiece. Quantitative testing involves the use of test sensors within the facepiece to determine the amount of chemical that has entered compared to a maximum acceptable level **(Figure 21.5)**.

Figure 21.5 Respiratory protection facepiece fit testing may be either qualitative or quantitative, depending on the testing protocol used in the test.

Application Skills

Everyone uses evaluation skills informally on a daily basis. In most cases, it is on a very subjective and subconscious level. Decisions on what to have for lunch, what television show to watch, or what type of bath soap to buy are all based on formative, qualitative evaluations. Some daily evaluations are quantitative, though. Comparing the price of similar products or the comparison of fuel costs as opposed to fuel octane ratings is based on known, quantifiable amounts.

The formal application of evaluation skills, however, tends to be conscious activity that may be more objective than subjective. The sections that follow apply the evaluation process to organizations such as a training division or agency and to programs such as a training course or curriculum.

Organizations

The evaluation of a fire and emergency services organization is an ongoing process. It begins with the establishment of the organization, its mission statement, its authority, its responsibilities, and services to be provided. The performance-based evaluation uses specific standards such as those created by NFPA or established by a local board or authority.

Overall performance of the organization, which includes the internal divisions or branches of the department, is judged against the accepted criteria. The evaluation of the training division or agency is part of the overall performance of the parent organization.

Organizational evaluations may be conducted internally, by an outside agency, or by a third party. Internal evaluation is a quality-control measure that is part of the planning process. Outside agencies that may evaluate the organization include the local jurisdiction, state/territory/province, or national government. The third-party evaluation may be conducted by organizations such as the following:

- International City/County Management Association (ICMA)

- Insurance Services Office (ISO)

- Commission on Fire Accreditation International (CFAI) (a joint venture between IAFC and ICMA)

- Commission on Ambulance Accreditation Services (CAAS)

These organizations provide a process that allows jurisdictions or organizations to be evaluated on the quality of fire and emergency services that are available. The evaluation process used by the National Fire Academy (NFA) for organizations is based on the systems approach and includes the following elements **(Figure 21.6)**:

- *Input* — Resources such as personnel, equipment, and finances that are devoted to the specific activity that is being measured. Resources are stated in quantities such as the following:

  — Amount of money allotted for training

  — Number of instructors

  — Number of courses taught

  — Number of hours per class

- *Process* (may also be referred to as *transformation* or *thru-put*) — Change that occurs to resources; any activity that resources are used for such as training, purchasing, or hiring.

- *Output* — Quantity of services that are the result of input and process. Quantity may be stated in the following means:

  — Number of students enrolled

  — Hours of training provided

  — Number of certification requirements met

- *Output efficiency* — Input divided by the output (such as the amount of money allotted divided by the number of hours of training provided), which results in a cost per instructional hour of training.

- *Outcome* — Results of the process such as the ISO rating reduction due to training.

- *Intermediate Outcome* — Factors that are expected to directly change an outcome; may include an increased number of enrollments or hours of training.

The results of organizational performance evaluations, either internal or external, help the leadership of the department/organization improve services and adjust to potential changes in the expected services. Evaluations are viewed as management tools that result in positive changes.

Programs

Fire and emergency services organizations provide a wide variety of both internal and external programs. *Internal programs* include training, professional development, health and wellness, and equipment/facility maintenance to name a few. *External programs* are the result of community expectations and are derived from the mission statement of the organization. They include (but are not limited to) emergency medical assistance, fire suppression, public education, inspections, plans review, and code enforcement.

Each of these internal and external programs must be evaluated periodically to ensure its effectiveness. Three generally accepted types of evaluations used for programs are as follows:

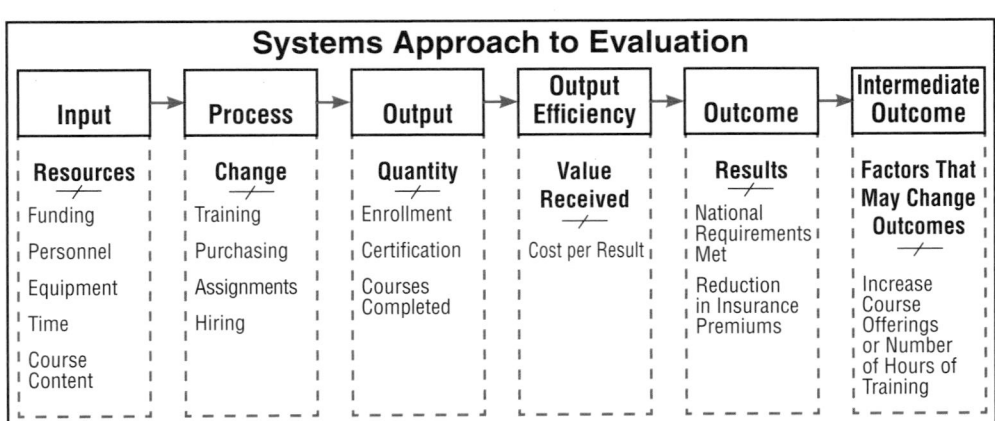

Figure 21.6 The systems model approach used by the National Fire Academy includes six elements: input, process, output, output efficiency, outcome, and intermediate outcome.

- *Goals-based evaluations* — Determine how well a program is meeting the original goals or objectives that were established for it.

- *Process-based evaluations* — Determine how a program actually works and highlight its strengths and weaknesses; particularly useful for long-standing programs or when a program is determined to be inefficient and complaints are being generated about it.

- *Outcomes-based evaluations* — Identify the benefits to a community or consumer of the service. The term *outcome* refers to the actual benefits enjoyed by the community such as reduced fire loss or improved quality of life.

These evaluations may be formative or summative (see Evaluation Methods and Course and Instructional Design Evaluations sections). The method may be either quantitative or qualitative, depending on the data available. In any case, the evaluation results need to be made public to the people who are affected by the program. Any changes need to be implemented as soon as possible.

Any of these types of evaluations can be applied to the activities of the training division or agency. Because the training program is an internal program, the consumers of the service are the emergency and nonemergency members of the organization.

Evaluation Plans

The basic framework for all types of evaluations should be maintained in a written evaluation plan that contains the step-by-step process for the various types of evaluations. The plan ensures that the process is conducted in the same manner each time it is implemented. The plan needs to contain enough information for anyone to understand and follow it.

When the appropriate evaluation plan is applied to a program, project, or item, it can be used as the basis for the evaluation report; that is, it can act as the outline upon which the information is developed. Records must be kept on all formal evaluations. Not only is this mandated in some jurisdictions, it is also good business practice.

When applied to the training program, a complete evaluation plan must include a review of behavioral objectives and test results in order to make a decision about whether the results are a true measure of the objectives. This review process enables instructors and program developers to meet the primary purpose of evaluation, which is to improve the teaching/learning process. Many evaluation techniques are available to assess learning levels and to determine how instruction can be changed to enhance learning.

The evaluation process outlined in the evaluation plan systematically collects information for the purpose of making decisions. Training program evaluation has three major components: criteria, evidence, and judgment.

In evaluating learning levels, instructors must have well-defined behavioral objectives (*criteria*) and results of tests or observations (*evidence*). Based on these two components, instructors can make decisions (*judgments*) on whether the results (*evidence*) indicate accomplishment of the behavioral objectives (*criteria*) that were set at the beginning of the program.

Each component must be present in order to have a complete evaluation process. For example, when there is no learning objective, there is no way to judge the test result because there is no criterion to measure evidence of accomplishment. When no one can make a decision or judgment about how well learning objectives and test results match, then no effective evaluation takes place.

Evaluation is used for many other purposes such as the following:

- Discover weaknesses in learning as well as in instruction.

- Diagnose causes of learning problems or weaknesses.

- Establish guidance or recommendations for further study.

- Assign grades.

- Make administrative decisions about students, instructors, and courses.

Course and Instructional Design Evaluations

Instructional design is composed of the analysis of training needs, the systematic design of teaching/learning activities, and the assessment of the teaching/learning process. As training requirements change, the instructional process changes. When the design of teaching/learning activities is no longer effective, the instructional process must change.

Change is the reason for continuous assessment of the teaching/learning process. Instructors must always be alert to ways of improving or updating instruction or even eliminating instruction that is no longer needed. In a changing world of instructional needs, content, methods, and techniques, instructors must remain flexible.

Often, instructors use only test results for evaluation. But there are many other types of evidence that collectively give a more complete picture as to whether the teaching/learning process was successful. The following two kinds of evaluation provide an approach for looking at the process and product of the instructional process:

- *Formative evaluation* — Looks at the process of course development and instruction
- *Summative evaluation* — Looks at the product and evaluates reactions to the course and instructional methods

In both cases, it is important that the evaluation process is useful to its users, thus data collection must be accurate. Evaluation instruments, as mentioned previously, should always be easy and practical to administer, and results should be easy to report. Planning the approach is also important.

Considerations for Planning

To get the most from a course evaluation, the instructor must plan the approach by thinking through and answering the following questions:

- How did students feel about the training? What did they learn? How did training affect their attitudes and behavior? What were the organizational results?
- How can items addressed be answered? Will information gathering be administered by paper-and-pencil tests, questionnaires, or surveys? Will tests require students to demonstrate their new knowledge and skills in role-plays, simulations, or actual performances?
- What are the objectives of the training program? Are the evaluation criteria based on these objectives?
- How do criteria indicate improvement between expected and actual performance when measured against the results of the needs analysis?
- What data sources are already available to help measure results (productivity reports, daily log sheets, and training and personnel records)?
- What alternative methods for gathering data are available (interviews and on-site observations)?
- What are the best and most cost-effective methods for measuring the results of the training? Are there less costly, more efficient ways of administering the evaluation?

In evaluating the instructional process, it is critical that the training organization makes clear to anyone involved what is to be evaluated and why. Answering *what* and *why* clarifies and guides how evaluation is to be conducted and eliminates misunderstanding. Include the following six essential areas in a thorough evaluation of the instructional process. Answer the questions related to each area.

1. *Reaction* — How did students indicate satisfaction with the course? How did instructors and management officials indicate satisfaction with the learning that occurred?
2. *Knowledge* — What new knowledge did students acquire and demonstrate?
3. *Skills* — What new skills did students acquire and demonstrate?
4. *Attitudes* — How has training changed students' opinions, values, and beliefs?
5. *Transfer of learning* — How has training affected the ways students perform on their jobs?
6. *Results* — How has training contributed to accomplishing organizational goals and objectives?

Formative Evaluations

Formative evaluation is the ongoing, repeated checking during course development and during instruction to determine the most effective instructional content, methods, aids, and testing techniques **(Figure 21.7)**. Two ways to conduct formative evaluations are field-testing and observation. Formative evaluations provide yes or no answers to the following questions (among others):

- Does the course provide the appropriate information and learning format?

- Is the instructor teaching the right content and using the most appropriate methods to facilitate learning?

- Have students learned in the most efficient way possible?

Field-testing. The course objectives serve as the primary criteria against which a judgment is made. Objectives are developed before the course is designed. Course design and how it works with the objectives is field-tested in a pilot program before the course is finalized. A *field test* is the process of teaching the course on a trial basis to determine whether the following components are addressed:

- Sequence of material facilitates learning.

- Teaching methods and aids are appropriate to the objectives and effective in teaching the material.

- Objectives can be met within the designated time frame.

- Testing procedures are adequate and appropriate for the course objectives.

- Course can be revised before using it on a regular basis when necessary.

Observation. Evaluation is *not* a static, one-time event; it occurs at all times throughout development and instruction. Just as testing occurs throughout instruction, course evaluation occurs before, during, and after instruction. Instructors can gather different kinds of evidence (most of which is observational) during the course **(Figure 21.8)**. The instructor wants to be attentive to the following factors:

- Student interest in the subject

- Level of general participation

- Student reaction to exercises and activities

- Level of student questions and comments

- Level of student frustration

- Level of student sense of achievement

- Test results

With feedback received during instruction, instructors can change or modify instructional methods to meet the needs of the class. In some cases, it

Figure 21.7 Formative testing is used repeatedly during an instructional course to ensure that instruction is appropriate and satisfies the course learning objectives. *Courtesy of Iowa Fire Service Training Bureau.*

Figure 21.8 Formative tests evaluate the effectiveness of the teaching process while it occurs. Instructors observe students performing skills to determine the level of their sense of achievement.

will be clear that a course needs to be changed on a permanent basis. The judgment of instructors is critical when making decisions about a program that is under development.

Summative Evaluations (Reaction Surveys)

A *summative evaluation* is an end-of-the-course appraisal. This type of evaluation commonly measures learning by some form of objective or subjective test, but it is also used to evaluate the reactions of students and instructors to each other and to the course.

Some examples of how summative or reaction evaluations are gathered are by observing and reporting unexpected learning outcomes or by performing follow-up surveys of students, their supervisors, and their instructors about the effectiveness of the program, its activities, and its job relevance. Summative evaluations provide yes or no answers to the following questions:

- Have program students learned what is needed to perform their work duties on their jobs?

- Was instruction effective so that it met performance objectives?

- Were instructional activities relevant to job tasks?

Instructors and program developers gather evidence from the following two critical sources:

- **Test results** — Measure the degree of learning that has occurred (see Chapter 16, Student Testing Instruments)

- **Course feedbacks from students** — Describe students' opinions of and reactions to the success of the course materials and the instruction

Instructor assessment of the program content and relevance is also an important source of feedback. In addition, supervisor input on program relevance to job tasks is considered when evaluating a training program.

The final course evaluation (feedback) is an important part of the entire evaluation procedure and determines whether the instructional process met the course objectives. As a course of study or period of training ends, instructors may feel unsure of how well they taught and how much students learned. An in-depth evaluation of the course by

students is helpful in letting instructors know how satisfied students were with the program, learning activities, and outcome **(Figure 21.9)**.

Instructors also look for comments from their peers and supervisors. During field-testing of a program as well as during finalized course deliveries, course developers, topic experts, other instructors, and instructor supervisors often attend sessions to determine whether the following elements are being met:

- Program plans are meeting objectives.

- Sessions are working well and within the time frame designated.

- Training is job relevant.

In addition to giving instructors information on how well they and their students met program objectives, final evaluations help discover areas where student involvement needs to be increased. Final evaluations also give input on the effectiveness of course materials, teaching techniques, and training aids.

Instructors must plan when the course evaluation form is distributed to students. When courses extend over a period of time, instructors may solicit feedback at the course midpoint so that they have information that will guide them in making course adjustments to meet student needs. For many courses, the evaluation form is usually distributed during the last lesson of the program.

Figure 21.9 Instructors use course evaluations to determine the effectiveness of their teaching styles, the satisfaction of students, and whether the instructional process met the established learning objectives.

Unless the form asks for comments regarding the final exam, the instructor may plan to distribute it just before the final exam is administered. Distribution at this point ensures that there is adequate time to complete the evaluation form and student performances or scores on the final exam or performance evaluation do *not* influence comments on the course.

Evaluation Results

The evaluation process helps instructors and management determine what would be changed to ensure that learning occurs in the easiest and most efficient way possible for students. Evaluations help guide the adjustment of the final program product. With the help of these evaluations and course reactions, developers can ensure a successful program.

Unless the results collected from tests and course feedback are used to make some decisions about future instruction, then any time, money, and effort expended on the evaluation process are wasted. After reviewing the evaluations (whether tests or feedback), instructors and program developers should take the following three steps:

Step 1: *Determine causes for student failure*
— *Examples:*

- Course objectives were inappropriate.
- Course outline and materials did *not* match objectives.
- Instructional methods and aids did *not* facilitate learning.
- Presentation style hampered learning.
- Learning environment was *not* conducive to learning.
- Evaluation techniques were *not* valid or reliable.
- Personal or logistical problems inhibited learning.
- Student learning problems were revealed.

Step 2: *Identify actions to correct deficiencies*

- Revise course objectives.
- Modify the course outline and materials to match objectives.
- Change instructional methods/aids to facilitate learning.
- Improve presentation style to foster learning.
- Enhance the learning environment to promote learning.
- Alter evaluation techniques to produce valid and reliable instruments.
- Provide support for students and offer referral services.
- Provide extra learning opportunities such as learning activity packets, individual or pair assignments, group study, or one-on-one tutoring.

Step 3: *Document and report results to superiors*

- Keep daily records of training activities.
- Maintain individual training records.
- Retain class test results and results of analyses.
- Provide written progress reports to management that outline recommendations in Steps 1 and 2.

Evaluations can also be used in the review of material and overall evaluation of the training program. Some agencies refer to this as their Customer Approval Rating (CAR) or Customer Satisfaction Rating (CSR). It is easy to manage this process when the information is provided in a computer database. Small departments can manage this process manually.

The examples in the information box show the use of the overall CAR. From this data an organization can look at areas of the course that may need improving such as instructor competency. Each category has been assigned a value. Some categories such as the outdoor factor in the Case Law course may *not* apply.

Course Performance Ratings Examples

Course Title and Overall Customer Approval Rating (CAR)			
Farm Accident Rescue		**Farm Machinery Rescue: Technician**	
Total Courses: 1		Total Courses: 1	
CAR	3.53	CAR	3.36
Instructor	3.59	Instructor	3.67
Classroom	3.40	Classroom	2.90
Outdoor	3.50	Outdoor	3.07
Visuals	3.63	Visuals	3.63
Print	3.60	Print	3.53
Completing the NFIRS* Report and Writing Incident Reports		**Fire and Emergency Case Law**	
Total Courses: 1		Total Courses: 1	
CAR	2.60	CAR	3.40
Instructor	2.70	Instructor	3.41
Classroom	2.47	Classroom	3.70
Outdoor	2.22	Outdoor	NA
Visuals	2.75	Visuals	3.18
Print	2.73	Print	3.57

*NFIRS = National Fire Incident Reporting System

Source: *Courtesy of Fire and Rescue Training Institute, University of Missouri.*

Summary

By learning the general theories of analysis and evaluation, the instructor or training manager can apply them to a wide array of duties. Not only can the training program be analyzed to determine the need for changes but new training and emergency equipment can be analyzed to determine their value or cost-effectiveness. Personnel, programs, projects, and courses can be evaluated to determine if they are meeting the criteria that were set for students to attain. Both analysis and evaluation are valuable skills for any member of the fire and emergency services to learn, understand, and apply.

Responsibility for Ensuring a Successful Training Program

The effectiveness of fire and emergency services training program belongs to each member of the organization. Beginning with senior management and extending to the newest recruit, every level must assess, to the best of their ability and responsibility, how well the needs of the organization (and the community) are being met by the training function. Personnel at each level should consider what their responsibility in the success of the process is and be prepared to provide input through the evaluation process to guarantee success.

Senior Management
- Be aware of the need for and value of training to the organization.
- Recognize the importance of involving the training division manager in senior management meetings.
- Involve training personnel in the decision-making process.
- Have knowledge of and support for training program, curriculum, and course development.
- Maintain active participation in training activities and events.
- Require the performance of formative and summative training evaluations and require regular summary reports.
- Make policy and strategic decisions based on results of the training.

Training Division Manager
- Manage the training division effectively.
- Support the strategic organization's planning process.
- Implement all mandated training programs, curriculums, and courses.
- Ensure the development, adoption, and maintenance of training evaluation systems.
- Ensure the preparation of regular reports for senior management.
- Maintain frequent, relevant contact with senior management.
- Be a liaison with line supervisors to determine the effectiveness of current training and the need for new training programs.

Instructor
- Develop training materials that meet the learning objectives of the program, curriculum, or course.
- Identify the current knowledge and skills level of students before the start of the course.
- Create or acquire the necessary resources to enable students to learn the required knowledge and skills to meet the course learning objectives.
- Monitor the learning process continually throughout the program, curriculum, or course.
- Create and administer student evaluation instruments that accurately determine the effectiveness of the learning process and the knowledge acquired by the students.
- Modify or adapt the learning process to meet the changing needs of students and the organization.

Line Supervisor
- Identify the jobs, tasks, and subordinate training needs.
- Be actively involved in the training program and evaluation development.
- Provide constant support for the training program.
- Discuss the new knowledge and skills with the subordinate following the completion of the training program or course.
- Monitor the application of new knowledge and skills by the subordinate.
- Ensure the prompt completion of all posttraining course surveys.

Student
- Be involved in the planning and design of training programs, curriculums, and courses.
- Be actively involved in the planning and design of the training evaluation process.
- Take an interest and active part in appropriate training programs or activities.
- Apply the knowledge and skills learned in training programs or courses.
- Support the evaluation process by accurately completing and returning training evaluation surveys.

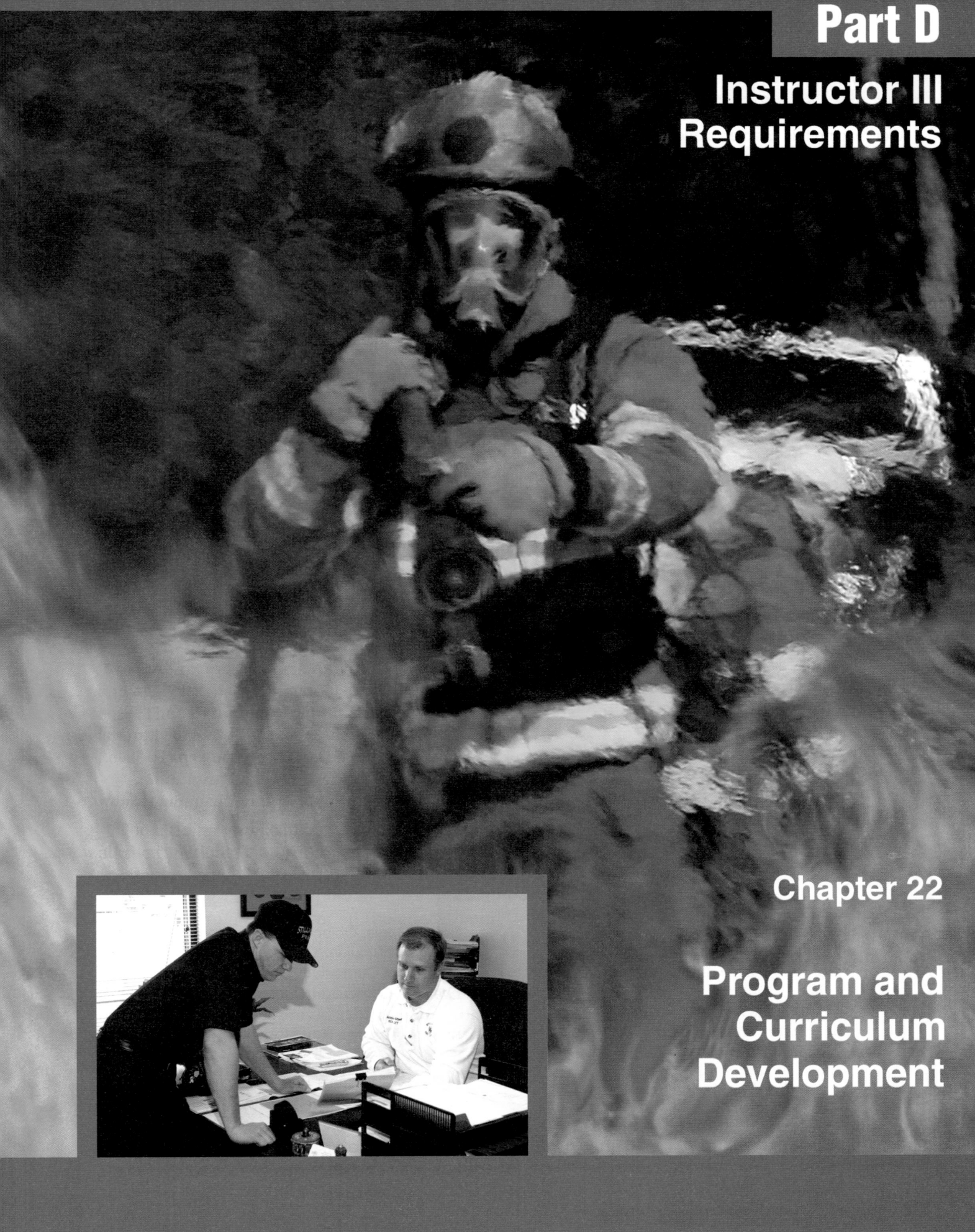

Part D

Instructor III Requirements

Chapter 22

Program and Curriculum Development

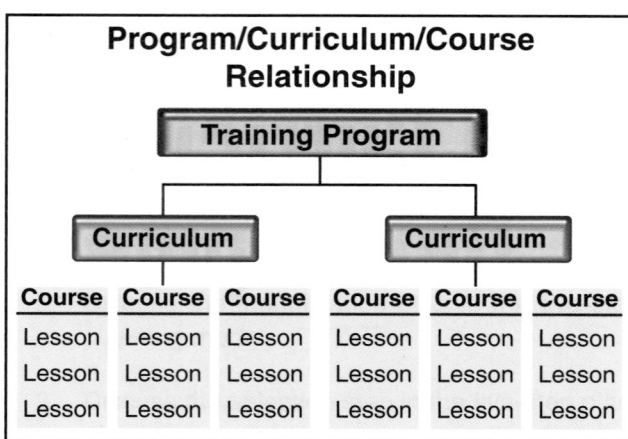

Program/Curriculum/Course Relationship

Figure 22.1 A tree diagram can illustrate the relationship between programs, curriculums, courses, and lessons.

This chapter describes how instructors, course planners and developers, and training managers can use the five-step model for instructional planning. This model is applied then to the design of new training programs, curriculums, and courses and the revision of existing programs, curriculums, and courses.

Sample Planning Model

One common model includes five steps that guide instructors through the processes of *identification, selection, design, implementation,* and *evaluation.* This type of model is usually presented graphically to illustrate the relationships of the component parts. The purpose of this five-step model (or any other similar program-planning model) is to provide program, curriculum, and course planners with a systematic approach to instructional design. Other multistep models are similar, including the ADDIE Model that is used in many educational institutions (see information box).

Following a planning model is helpful in developing programs and curriculums because it provides an outline or guide that assists Level III Instructors in reaching the program goal as well as the learning outcomes described in the course and learning objectives found in the lesson plans. It is an efficient and effective method for ensuring that students are provided with the information required to meet the learning outcomes or certification criteria that have been established or adopted.

ADDIE Model

In general, the ADDIE Model shares the same steps with the five-step process and differs only in terminology. The ADDIE Model consists of the following steps:

Step 1: *Analyze* — Determine the components of the learning process, including the audience, environment, time, funding, technology, topic, course outcomes, etc.

Step 2: *Design* — Perform the systematic method of research, planning, developing, evaluating, and managing the instructional process.

Step 3: *Develop* — Develop the tools and processes used to create instructional material, including lesson plans, audiovisual training aids, and props.

Step 4: *Implement* — Establish the timeline and procedures for training instructors and students and presenting the course.

Step 5: *Evaluate* — Use a systemic process to determine the quality and effectiveness of the program, course, or learning

The five-step planning model includes the following steps:

Step 1: *Identify* — Perform a needs analysis to determine the training program, curriculum, or course required to meet the organization's needs and jurisdictional mandates. Use this step to also determine the need for alterations to existing programs, curriculums, or courses when deficiencies are found in the evaluate step. Step 1 is the Analyze Step of the ADDIE Model.

Step 2: *Select* — Choose the type of training that will meet the requirements. Choose the goals, outcomes, and learning or performance objectives. Step 2 is a portion of the Design Step of the ADDIE Model. This step includes performing the following actions:

— Establish goals.

— Develop course outcomes and learning objectives.

Step 3: *Design* — Design a program, curriculum, or course that will meet the requirements. Step 3 is the final portion of the Design Step plus the Develop Step of the ADDIE Model. This step includes performing the following actions:

— Group similar objectives.

— Develop lesson plans.

— Sequence lessons into courses.

— Sequence courses into a curriculum.

— Create student, course, and instructor evaluation instruments.

Step 4: *Implement* — Perform a pilot presentation of the course or curriculum. Add the course/curriculum to the training schedule when it meets the identified needs. Step 4 is the Implement Step of the ADDIE Model.

Step 5: *Evaluate* — Determine the effectiveness of the course or curriculum in meeting the requirements. Conduct evaluations following the initial pilot test and following each presentation of the course. Step 5 is the Evaluate Step of the ADDIE Model. Base evaluations on the following:

— Student testing instruments

— Course evaluation surveys

— Instructor evaluation surveys

The five-step planning model can be represented as a circular path or as a flowchart (**Figure 22.2** and **Figure 22.3**). The results of the evaluation may indicate gaps in the instruction that still remain. When the gaps are identified, a new analysis is used to begin the cycle again.

Courses may be revised, replaced, or removed from the curriculum when the identification and evaluation steps indicate that they no longer provide the desired outcomes. At the same time, curriculums may also be altered, replaced, or abandoned when the evaluations indicate such an action is necessary.

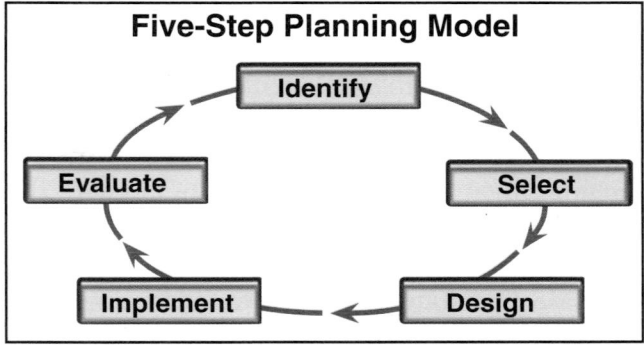

Figure 22.2 The five-step planning process may be represented as a circular path creating a never-ending process.

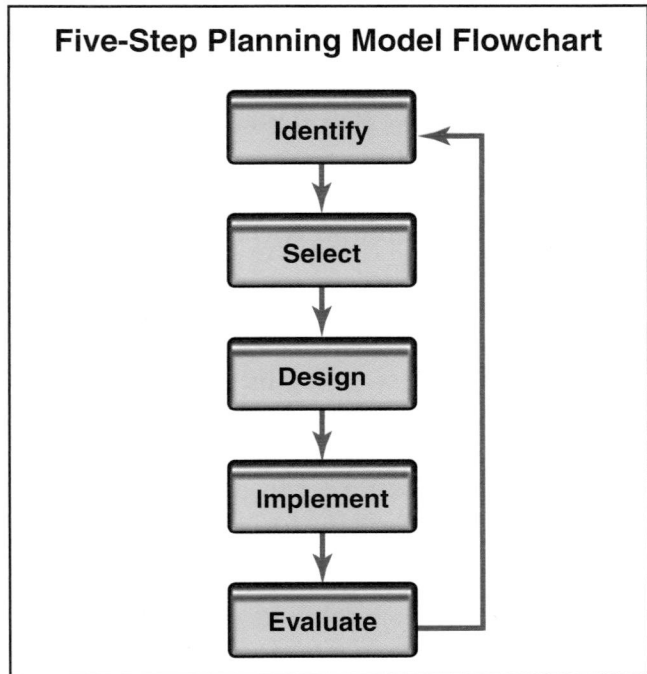

Figure 22.3 A flowchart may also be used to represent the planning process.

Training Program and Curriculum Design

It would be very rare for an instructor to be assigned the task of developing an entire training program. Existing fire and emergency services organizations either have a training program in place or rely on state/provincial training agencies to provide the required training. The training program may consist of basic firefighter certification training (Level I), advanced firefighter training (Level II), driver/operator training, officer training, and specialized training (to name a few).

It is more likely that the Level III Instructor would be assigned the task of identifying a need for training and creating a curriculum/course caused by an internal or external change to the organization. For instance, an expanding service area that includes an aging population combined with the loss of an emergency medical services (EMS) provider may cause a fire department to expand and add EMS. Or a state/provincial or federal mandate may require the fire department to provide technical rescue services based on a perceived need.

To address these changes, an instructor applies the appropriate planning model for the creation of the required training curriculum. The instructor performs each step — identify, select, design, implement, and evaluate — to fulfill the requirements. The sections that follow expand on each of those steps and illustrate them with the hypothetical need for a Technical Rescue Curriculum. The examples are found within the text at the appropriate locations.

Identify Needs

The identification step begins with the realization that a change in the organization's operating environment has occurred, requiring a change in the organization's service delivery. The realization may come in the following forms:

- Mandate (such as a law)
- Request from a stakeholder group (such as a governing body)
- Evaluation (such as a critical course evaluation)
- Event (such as the loss of services provided by another agency)

For example, one of the requirements in meeting the requirements of the National Incident Management System (NIMS) is credentialing of first responders as to their qualifications to respond to a weapons of mass destruction (WMD) incident. Adoption of NIMS at the federal level becomes the motivation to change service delivery and training at the local levels.

When it is apparent that change is required or that different or additional services are required, the organization must perform a needs analysis to determine how the current service level and capability differ from the new requirement or how much and what type of training is required to ensure that the organization can provide the new level of service. This analysis is a function of the administration of the organization and may include representatives from all divisions of the organization (**Figure 22.4**).

The processes that are available to the instructor for identifying needs include the needs analysis, job performance requirements, task analysis, and cost/benefit analysis. In addition, the instructor should have an understanding of the hierarchy of work that organizes various levels of work and is essential to the creation of curriculum, courses, and lessons.

Figure 22.4 A needs analysis can begin with an inspection of the organization's response equipment to determine the types of tools and equipment used to provide the current level of services.

Needs Analysis

The needs analysis may identify, for instance, that the fire and emergency services organization lacks credentials to provide any technical rescue services as mandated by NIMS. This needs analysis is the responsibility of the Level III Instructor or division manager and may involve other members of the training division.

With thoughtful questioning, carefully designed surveys, and in-depth research, a needs analysis accomplishes several functions such as the following:

- Defines where personnel or organizations are at a designated time and where they need to be in the future in terms of knowledge, skills, and attitudes

- Determines whether a need exists and indicates whether the need is for training, equipment to perform a task, administrative policies or commitment, or a change in procedures

- Identifies specific individuals, workgroups, or organizations who need training, equipment, or procedure change

- Identifies a method to achieve desired levels of knowledge, skills, or attitudes

To determine the needs in the areas of knowledge, skills, or attitudes, the instructor identifies the need by analyzing the following items:

- Operational reports
- Injury records
- Accident reports
- Results of promotional exams
- Personnel, operation, and training records
- Other resources

Various methods are used to determine individual training needs or readiness for a training curriculum or course such as the following:

- *Pretest* — Type of test used by organizations to determine the current level of training or skill of potential students. Pretests help instructors in making decisions on what to include in the curriculum/course content that will enable students to reach desired levels of competence or mastery **(Figure 22.5)**.

- *Prerequisite training or skill level requirement* — Minimum level of knowledge or skill *(prerequisite)* for personnel in certain types of jobs and students before they enter certain training courses. The following elements may be used to determine whether a person has the necessary knowledge or skills to be admitted to a course:

— Completion of specific courses

— Training certification

— Professional development points

— Verification of ability on a pretest for the required knowledge

Regardless of the technique used to determine training needs, instructors need to know the current knowledge or skill level of the organization's members before proceeding with curriculum or course development. Otherwise the level or complexity of the instruction may be inappropriate for some or even all of the curriculum/course students. Based on the national mandate and the organization's needs analysis, an instructor should use the analysis process to determine the training requirements that will be the basis for the required curriculum (such as a Technical Rescue Curriculum).

Figure 22.5 Student knowledge and ability may be determined through pretests given to students before their admittance to a course.

Job Performance Requirements

When evaluating existing training materials, instructors determine knowledge, skill, or attitude levels that a training curriculum/course expects students to begin and end with. To effectively and efficiently develop and present a curriculum/course, instructors must have a defined and desired starting point and an ending point in the educational and training process.

Starting and ending points are often determined by the skills that personnel must learn and perform on their jobs. Program planners often start their needs analysis by identifying and reviewing national standards and determining minimum *job performance requirements (JPRs)* or performances required for a specific job based on those standards.

JPRs are grouped according to job *duties* (functional areas of responsibility within a job). After determining JPRs, planners evaluate resources and select training objectives that will be used in designing and implementing the revision of existing programs and curriculums or developing new program curriculums.

Professional qualifications standards can be used for the following purposes:

- Designing and evaluating training
- Certifying personnel
- Measuring and critiquing on-the-job performances
- Defining hiring practices
- Setting organizational policies, procedures, and goals

Professional qualifications standards are often written in the JPR format and organized by areas of responsibility (duties). The list of JPRs for each duty defines what an individual should be able to do in order to successfully perform that duty. The standard containing each duty and its JPRs define and describe the job, giving instructors and planners an end point around which to design and teach a training curriculum.

Hierarchy of Work

Many terms are used to describe the work people do, the components of their work, and how each component interacts with the others. The following hierarchy of work defines each of the common terms and places them in order from large to small:

- *Occupations*—Career or professional categories such as the following:
  - Law enforcement
  - Fire and emergency services

  - Education
  - Medicine
- *Blocks* — Division of occupation that includes related tasks with common factors such as the following:
  - Police departments (which have street officers, detectives, and undercover officers)
  - Fire departments (which have firefighters, technicians, and hazardous materials specialists)
  - EMS departments (which have first responders, emergency medical technicians [EMTs], and paramedics)

A block may be an administrative division within a political authority, as described above, or a division within a department such as a fire department that has the following divisions:

- Public education
- Training
- Fire suppression
- Patient care
- Equipment maintenance

- *Jobs (duties)* — Grouping of similar functions within a block, for example:
  - Fire suppression includes ventilation and overhaul.
  - Patient care includes the following functions:
    - ○ Conducting an assessment
    - ○ Performing cardiopulmonary resuscitation (CPR)
    - ○ Using an automated external defibrillator (AED)
    - ○ Performing patient immobilization
- *Tasks* — Combination of steps performed in a job; a task results in the completion of an objective. It has an identifiable beginning, an action (either psychomotor or cognitive), and a result or end (sometimes referred to as a product). The task identifies a component of knowledge and skills of an occupation such as the tasks of performing CPR, which require skills and knowledge in the following:

— Opening the airway

— Checking for a pulse

— Ventilating

— Compressing the chest

- *Task steps (performance steps)* — Steps required to perform each task. For example, a step explains how hands are placed to perform head-tilt, chin-lift maneuvers. Knowledge and skill requirements are also listed. Steps become enabling objectives that are written as action statements and listed to *enable* the student to *perform* the task or behavior.

- *Key points/outline facts* — Main ideas taken from the list of steps and developed into outline form detailing cognitive information and/or psychomotor motor skills and/or behavior.

Task Analysis

A *task analysis* is a detailed review of each physical task or job that is performed by emergency personnel. Each task is divided into steps that are required to complete it. In order to perform a task analysis, the instructor must first collect information on the specific tasks that compose the job or duty. Instructors can use either formal or informal methods to collect information as follows:

- *Formal methods*
  - Carefully designed and executed surveys
  - Opinion polls
  - Checklists
  - Observations
  - Psychological profiles
  - Research analyses
  - Tests

- *Informal methods*
  - Conversations
  - Casual observations of activities and habits
  - Other unobtrusive measures

The information is then used to determine the steps that compose the task. The following four methods can determine the order in which steps must be accomplished:

- *Hierarchical* — Method of arranging tasks in order of operation (sequential)

Task Analysis Worksheet

Using a task analysis worksheet, complete a worksheet for several tasks so that you can provide your class with samples. Have several groups in the class complete task analysis worksheets for several tasks and allow them to compare their results. This activity gives the class opportunities to practice, discuss, and reason why the components fit into certain categories and what flexibility there may be in creating a task analysis **(Figure 22.6)**.

Task Analysis Worksheet

Occupation: _____

Block: _____

Job: _____

Tasks: _____

Performance Steps: Individual steps that are required to complete the task listed above.	Key Points: Individual steps stated in outline form, including cognitive and behavioral points.

1.	I.
	  A.
	    1.
	    2.
	  B.
	    1.
	    2.

2.	II.
	  A.
	    1.
	    2.
	  B.
	    1.
	    2.

3.	III.
	  A.
	    1.
	    2.
	  B.
	    1.
	    2.

Figure 22.6 Sample task analysis worksheet form used in the fire service.

- *If and then* — Method of completing one action or determining the existence of a condition before deciding on the next appropriate action or step

- *Model based* — Model used for professional tasks when the steps for performing the tasks are vague or difficult to define

- *Cognitive* — Critical decision-based approach that focuses on the psychological processes that underlie the physical task

The method that is used most often is the hierarchical task analysis. In this method, the steps are arranged in sequence from first to last. The method may be used for a simple task (depicted in a linear fashion) or a complex task that may contain a combination of simple tasks, some performed simultaneously (**Figure 22.7**).

Steps that are considered key points are used to create the teaching outline for the task. Some steps may require the student to make a decision before performing the step. Decisions may be based on safety concerns or cause and effect considerations. For instance, before raising a ground ladder, the student must determine whether overhead obstructions or electrical power lines are present.

Cost/Benefit Analysis

As part of the needs analysis, the instructor should also perform a cost/benefit analysis. The cost of creating a curriculum or providing the training internally should be estimated and compared to the cost of purchasing an existing curriculum or contracting with an external agency to provide the training.

In some instances, it may be more cost-effective to purchase an existing curriculum or use training available from state/provincial or national agencies or other sources. For instance, CPR classes may be available from the local American Red Cross or American Heart Association office.

Select Goals, Objectives, and Resources

When data collected in the needs analysis identifies training as a means of correcting a problem, the process of planning instruction then proceeds to the selection step that includes selecting goals, objectives, and resources.

Goals

The instructor must determine the curriculum/course *goal:* a statement of the desired effect of the curriculum/course. However, a goal is *not* an objective because it does *not* state the performance level of the student, only what the curriculum/course will enable the student to do. Examples are as follows:

- *Curriculum goal* — The Technical Rescue Curriculum will provide students with the necessary knowledge and skills to meet NFPA certification requirements.

- *Course goal* — The High-Angle Rescue Course will provide students with the knowledge and skills to operate at the rope technician level (**Figure 22.8**).

Neither goal contains student performances, conditions, or standards that students must meet. The performances, conditions, or standards are found in the course and lesson objectives.

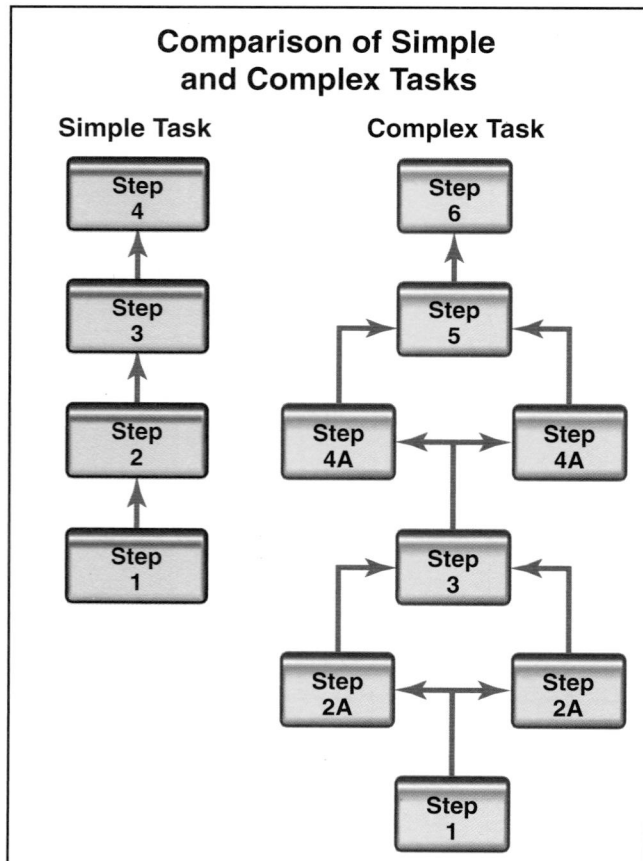

Figure 22.7 Example of the hierarchical task analysis model.

Figure 22.8 The goal of a high-angle rescue course is to have graduates certify at the rope technician level based on the adopted criteria. *Courtesy of Central Florida Fire Academy.*

Objectives

Learning objectives (also referred to as *performance objectives* or *competencies*) address specific knowledge to learn and apply, skills to perform and master, or performance to meet. Performance standards or skills may be dictated by outside entities such as NFPA or legislation, for example, Title 29, *Code of Federal Regulations (CFR) 1910.120, Hazardous Waste Site Operations and Emergency Response.* Learning or performance objectives are narrowly focused interim measurable accomplishments that lead to attaining the desired goal.

Learning objectives must clearly support the educational goals — the destination or end point — of the training curriculum/course. Subject matter experts who can clearly identify the knowledge, skills, and attitudes to be performed or exhibited and evaluated will develop the task analysis that corresponds to each task stated in the objectives. As tasks are developed, instructors determine the resources needed to appropriately complete the tasks and ensure that these resources are acquired for the training curriculum/course.

Objectives are classified as course and content objectives and become part of the course outline. Descriptions are as follows:

- **Course objectives** (also referred to as *terminal objectives* or *course outcomes)* — General statements of what the student will be able to do at the completion of a course. There is one objective for each course. For example, upon completion of the High-Angle Rescue Course, students (given the proper equipment) will be able to perform at a high-angle rescue incident.

- **Content objectives** — Learning and performance objectives that are associated with each lesson within a course. There are usually multiple objectives in each lesson. For example, one of the objectives may be stated as follows: Upon completion of the Safety Lesson of the High-Angle Rescue Course, students (given the proper equipment) will be able to use proper safety precautions and equipment.

Course Objectives/Outcomes

Each course objective/outcome or terminal objective should have the following characteristics:

- Understandable by instructors, students, members of the organization, and accrediting agencies

- Appropriate to the topic area and certification standard

- Capable of capturing the knowledge and skills expected of students

- Supportive of the use of a range of teaching and learning styles, evaluation instruments, and training resources

- Observable, measurable, and reportable to ensure that learning achievements are properly evaluated

In order to guide instruction effectively, Level III Instructors select, revise, or develop learning and performance objectives based on the Mager Model previously discussed in Chapter 14, Lesson Plan Development. Learning objectives should contain each of the following three components:

1. **Conditions description** — Describe one specific action or behavior that the student is expected to perform and the situation, tools, or materials provided to perform it. *Example*:

    — *Learning objective*: Given rescue rope and ascenders, *ascend* a fixed rope safely and efficiently.

    — *Condition*: Rescue rope and ascenders are necessary to ascend (climb) a rope.

2. **Performance (behavior) statement** — Identify what the student is expected to do. The behavior must be stated in observable terms and begin with clear action verbs such as *recall, identify, list, label, describe,* or *state* among others. *Examples*:

    — *Learning objective*: Describe the purposes for rappelling.

    — *Performance (behavior)*: The student describes the purposes for rappelling.

3. **Standards (degree) criteria** — State the acceptable level of student performance. Standards provide the measurable criteria for evaluating student performance and may include a statement about the degree of accuracy or a time limit for completion among others. *Example*:

    — *Learning objective*: Given photos of basic high-angle rescue hardware, *identify (label)* 90 percent of the hardware accurately.

    — *Criterion*: The standard is 90-percent accuracy.

Another element to consider is the person who must perform the skill or action, although it is *not* always included in the learning objective statement. See the following example:

Identify the student clearly — Who is to perform the objective? It may be the generic student or a specific firefighter, chief, hazardous materials technician, EMT, pump operator, etc. Examples:

Learning objective: Given photos of basic high-angle rescue hardware, *(the student will)* identify 90 percent of the hardware accurately.

Student: The student will perform to the criterion.

Objectives designate a level of instruction based on a model such as Bloom's Taxonomy. The evaluation of learning must be consistent with the level of instruction defined in the objectives. When an objective requires students to learn at the cognitive domain level three (application), the instruction and evaluation must be to that level and *not* a more advanced level (see **Table 22.1, right,** and **Table 22.2, p. 532**).

The various objectives of a course require instructors to teach and students to perform at different levels in one or more of the learning domains. These levels are determined by the results of the needs analysis. When decisions regarding the level of instruction and learning domain have been made, then the performance objectives can be written.

Instructors must evaluate and select objectives for completeness and consistency with the level of instruction and learning domain. Instructors further evaluate objectives during the course to ensure that they achieve the change in student performance required by the needs analysis.

Several objectives may compose a single goal. In the training function, objectives describe the intended end result of instruction — what students will know and be able to do — rather than the instructional process and what instructors will teach. Specifically, objectives perform the following functions:

- Steps necessary to achieve the stated goal

- Guide for selecting or designing curriculum materials, content, methods, and activities

- Measurement to determine whether skill or knowledge requirements were met and instruction was successful

- Basis for student testing and evaluation

- Guide that enables students to organize learning efforts toward completing requirements to reach goals

Table 22.1
Examples of Verbs and Their Corresponding Learning Levels (Cognitive Domain)

Learning Levels	Samples of Corresponding Verbs
Basic Levels	
Knowledge (Level 1) Ability to recall or recognize information	**Recall, List, Label, State, Recognize (communication or situation previously presented), Quote, Define, Name, Show, Identify**
	Illustration: The student quotes the formula for computing the area of a rectangle: $A = L \times W$. The student labels the sides of a rectangle.
Comprehension (Level 2) Ability to understand or use information within a limited context.	**Restate, Interpret, Explain in your own words, Illustrate, Discuss, Describe, Compare, Demonstrate, Give an example of your own**
	Illustration: The student can explain that in the formula given, A stands for area, L stands for length, and W stands for width. The student can give an example of a similar area that is also rectangular in shape.
Intermediate Levels	
Application (Level 3) Ability to use abstractions in particular concrete situations.	**Apply a rule, guideline, or principle; Calculate; Measure; Use; Manipulate; Predict trends, outcomes, or results; Solve problems**
	Illustration: Given a rectangle 4 inches (100 mm) long and 3 inches (75 mm) wide, the student can calculate that the area of the rectangle is 12 square inches (77 cm²). Given other examples of different sized rectangles, the student can solve the problems of finding the areas.
Analysis (Level 4) Ability to break information into its parts to clarify relationships.	**Test; Check; Inspect; Analyze; Determine conditions, properties, and aspects; Verify; Divide; Classify; Organize; Deduce; Choose**
	Illustration: For a given rectangle, the student recognizes the properties of the rectangle and determines that if either the length or width is increased, area will also increase. The student verifies this property by checking the calculations.
Advanced Levels	
Synthesis (Level 5) Ability to create a new communication or concept through the examination of other communications or situations.	**Create; Design; Compare; Describe; Develop (new information, not recital); Produce; Plan; Formulate; Devise; Support; Write; Report**
	Illustration: Knowing the formula for the area of a rectangle, the student can develop a formula for computing the area of a parallelogram. The student can describe steps taken in these calculations.
Evaluation (Level 6) Ability to use standards and criteria to make judgments.	**Rank, Evaluate, Judge, Defend, Critique, Choose (based on standards), Diagnose, Appraise, Recommend, Decide, Justify**
	Illustration: The student chooses from a list which formula for determining the area of a right triangle is correct. The student performs a self-appraisal on ability to select formulas.

Table 22.2
Performance Terms for Behavioral Objectives

Term	Description	Example
Describe *Synonyms:* discuss, define, tell how	Reports essential properties or characteristics of objects or events	**Describe** the eight-step problem-solving process.
Define *Synonyms:* describe, delineate	Provides a description that gives a precise meaning or basic traits	**Define** *scalar.*
Identify *Synonyms:* mark, match, choose, recognize	Selects a named, described, or pictured item orally or by pointing to it, picking it up, labeling it, or marking it	**Identify** ventilation tools in the given illustration.
Name *Synonyms:* describe, delineate	Supplies a title for objects, people, processes, events, or principles	**Name** the type of heat generated by splitting or combining atoms.
List *Synonyms:* write, arrange	Recalls similar objects or events and records in a methodical or systematic arrangement	**List** all of the types of splints carried on the ambulance.
Order *Synonyms:* arrange in order, list in order, sequence	Arranges, rearranges, lists in sequence, or places in order	**List in order** the phases of negotiation.
Differentiate *Synonyms:* distinguish, discriminate	Recognizes as different and separates into kinds, classes, or categories	**Differentiate** among hazard classes the following chemicals.
Classify *Synonyms:* sort, arrange, group	Puts into groups having common attributes, uses, characteristics, or functions	**Classify** forcible entry tools according to their uses.
Construct *Synonyms:* draw, make, build, design, create	Makes an object, verbal statement, or drawing	**Construct** a floor plan for a pre-incident survey.
Apply *Synonym:* use	Uses a stated relationship or principle to perform a task or answer a problem	**Apply** the progressive system to properly discipline an employee.
Demonstrate *Synonyms:* show, perform, (any of various appropriate action verbs)	Performs operations necessary to carry out a specified procedure	**Demonstrate** the ability to properly place a roof ladder. **Show** how to properly dispose of personal protective equipment.

To be complete and effective, objectives must meet certain requirements. They must clearly state a measurement so instructors and students can compare it to a scale or criterion. They must have a terminal or end point so instructors and students know when each objective is completed. They also must state and require an observable behavior change so instructors and students can see learning, improvement, and success **(Figure 22.9)**.

Resources

One of the components of the lesson plan is a statement of the conditions under which the skill or behavior will be performed. When a student is to remove an extension ladder from an apparatus, carry the ladder to a wall, and extend the ladder into a second-story window, then all those conditions must be present; that is, an extension ladder, apparatus, and a two-story structure.

These conditions are, then, resources that the instructor must arrange for in advance of the training. The resources must match those that the student will use to be evaluated with at the end of the training and also those that are used at emergency incidents. For instance, when students will be using a specific type or model of respiratory protection equipment when assigned to a fire company, training and evaluation should then take place with the same type or model **(Figure 22.10)**.

Design Curriculum/Course

Once the type and quantity of required training has been identified, an instructor designs a curriculum/course that will meet those requirements. To design a curriculum, an instructor must perform the following tasks:

- Group similar objectives.
- Develop lesson plans.
- Sequence lessons into courses.
- Sequence courses into a curriculum.
- Create student, course, and instructor evaluation instruments.

Figure 22.9 A basic component of learning objectives is that skills and behavior must be observable and based on clearly stated criteria. *Courtesy of Iowa Fire Service Training Bureau.*

Figure 22.10 The type of respiratory protection used for training and evaluation must be the same as the equipment used at emergency incidents.

Group Similar Objectives

Similar objectives are grouped together and paired with the steps in the task analysis. This procedure ensures that objectives match the skills and are in the proper sequence to accomplish the task and therefore the job. Examples of similar objectives are as follows:

- Upon completion of the Safety Lesson of the High-Angle Rescue Course, students (given the proper equipment) will be able to use proper safety precautions and equipment.

- Upon completion of the Safety Lesson of the High-Angle Rescue Course, students (given the proper equipment) will be able to identify safety equipment.

- Upon completion of the Safety Lesson of the High-Angle Rescue Course, students (given the proper equipment) will be able to select the appropriate safety equipment.

Develop Lesson Plans

At this point, the outline for a lesson plan is basically complete. The required knowledge or skills are listed in the outline, and they provide the same information that must be presented to the students. By adding a few component parts provided in the following list, the lesson plan is complete **(Figure 22.11, pp. 535 and 536):**

- **Preparation section** — *Front-end* piece that prepares the student for learning. In this section, the instructor performs the following functions:

  - Provides a motivational statement that gets students' attention and interest

  - States the objective so students know what they are to do in this lesson

  - Lists the overview points so students know the key points to notice

- **Presentation section** — Part that is the outline taken from the key-points section of the task analysis. In this section, the instructor performs the following functions:

  - Introduces each topic (taken from the list of overview points)

  - Uses appropriate curriculum methods to discuss or demonstrate

  - Uses curriculum materials effectively

  - Relates known or familiar information and tasks to unknown or new and unfamiliar information and tasks.

- **Application section** — Part that works together with the presentation section. An instructor who presents effectively not only *tells* information but also *shows* how it is applied. The application section provides opportunities for students to practice applying the information or skill.

- **Evaluation section** — Part that reviews main points and checks for student understanding of the topics discussed, demonstrated, applied, and practiced. Various types of evaluation instruments can also be used at points during the lessons or course to measure knowledge and skill. Tests and evaluations can be one or more types such as the following:

  - Written or practical

  - Diagnostic

  - Comprehensive

Sequence Lessons into Courses

Once the lessons are created for the required learning objectives, they must be sequentially grouped to create a course. The lessons must be placed in order so that the most basic knowledge is taught first. Subsequent lessons build on the basic knowledge until the student is able to perform the final course outcome or objective **(Figure 22.12, p. 537)**. A student should *not* advance to a higher level if the current level of learning has *not* been mastered.

Sequence Courses into Curriculum

Likewise, courses are placed into a sequence that is logical and progressive **(Figure 22.13, p. 537)**. In the case of courses, the sequence may be more flexible than the sequence of lessons. Courses may be completed over a period of time with only a few prerequisites. However, courses must be completed satisfactorily before the following events occur:

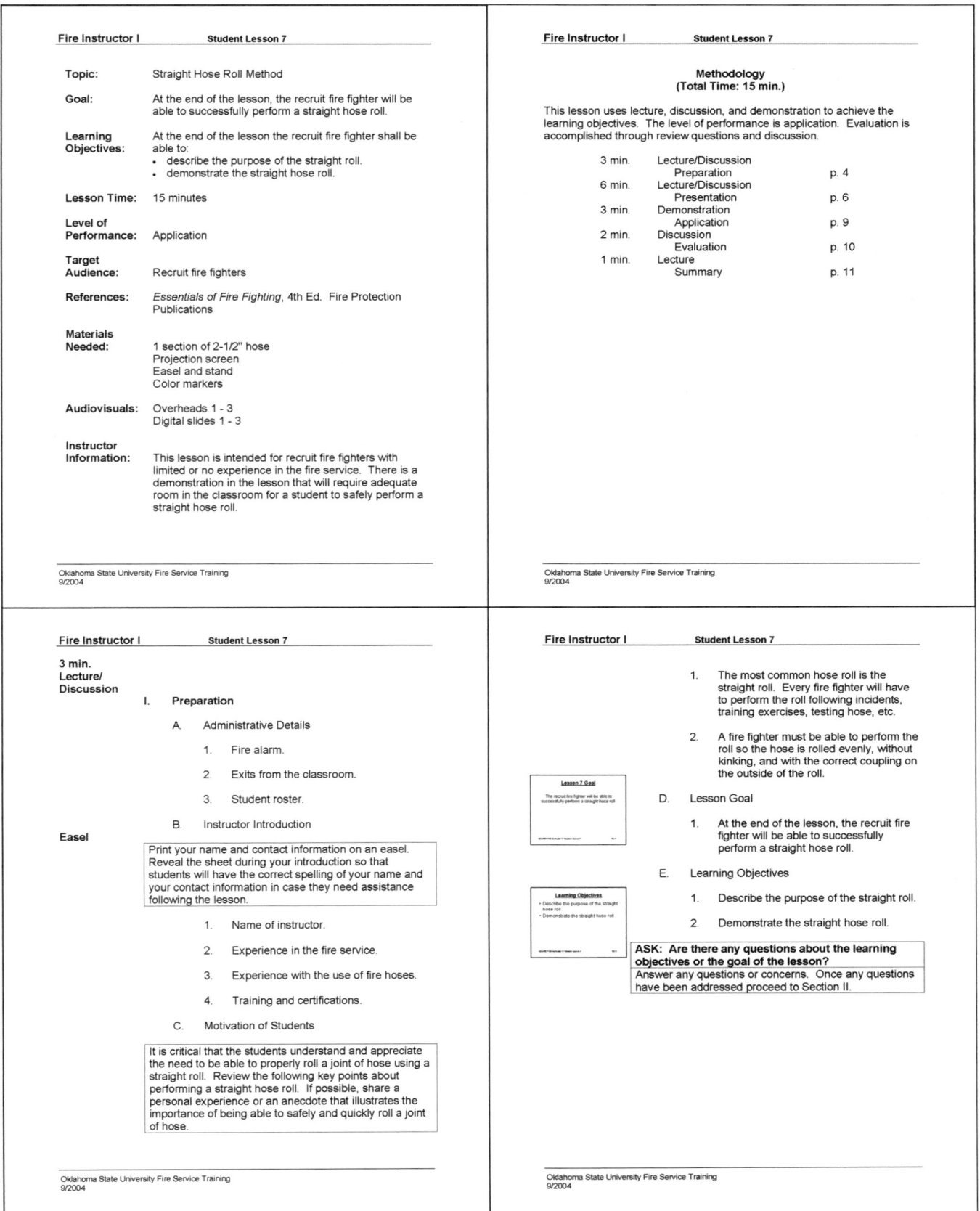

Figure 22.11 A sample lesson plan including the preparation, presentation, application, and evaluation sections. *Courtesy of Fire Service Training, Oklahoma State University.*

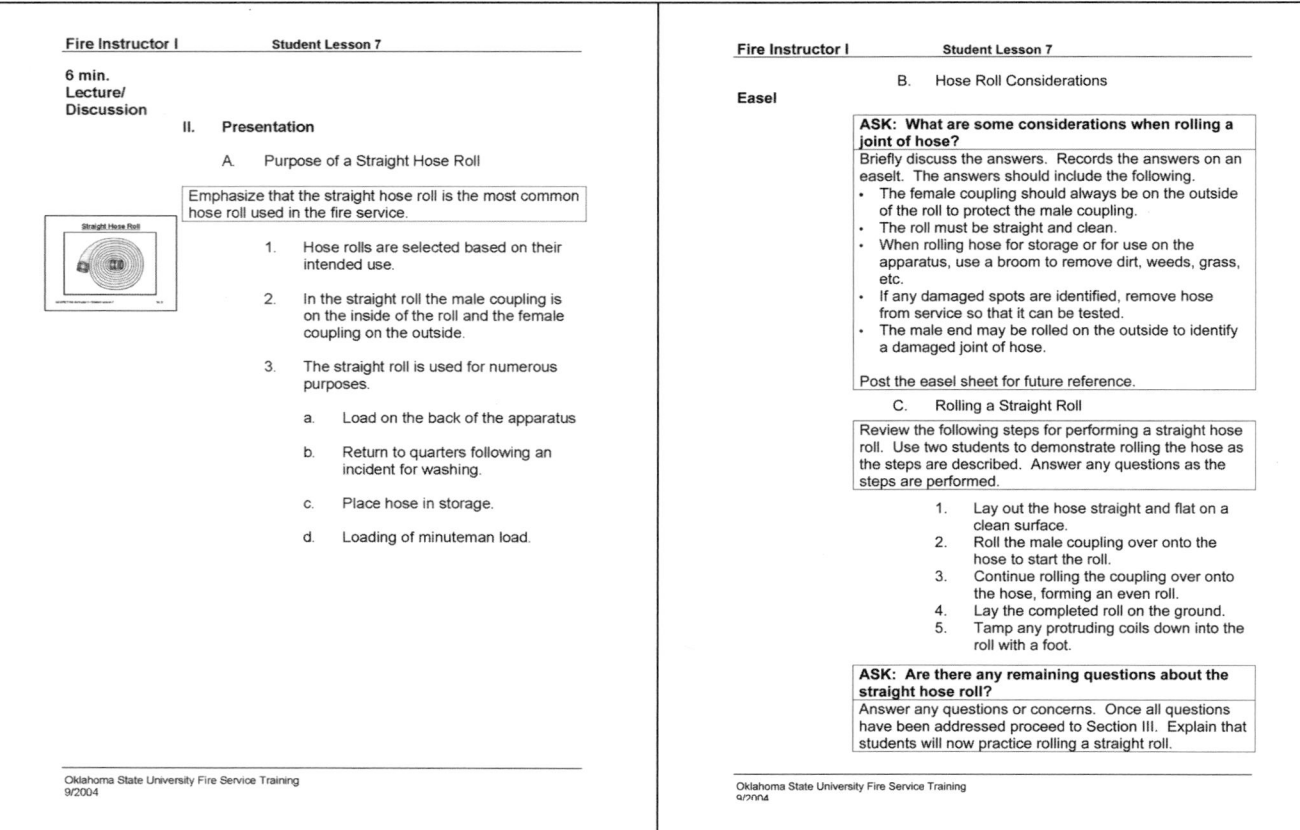

Figure 22.11 *Continued*

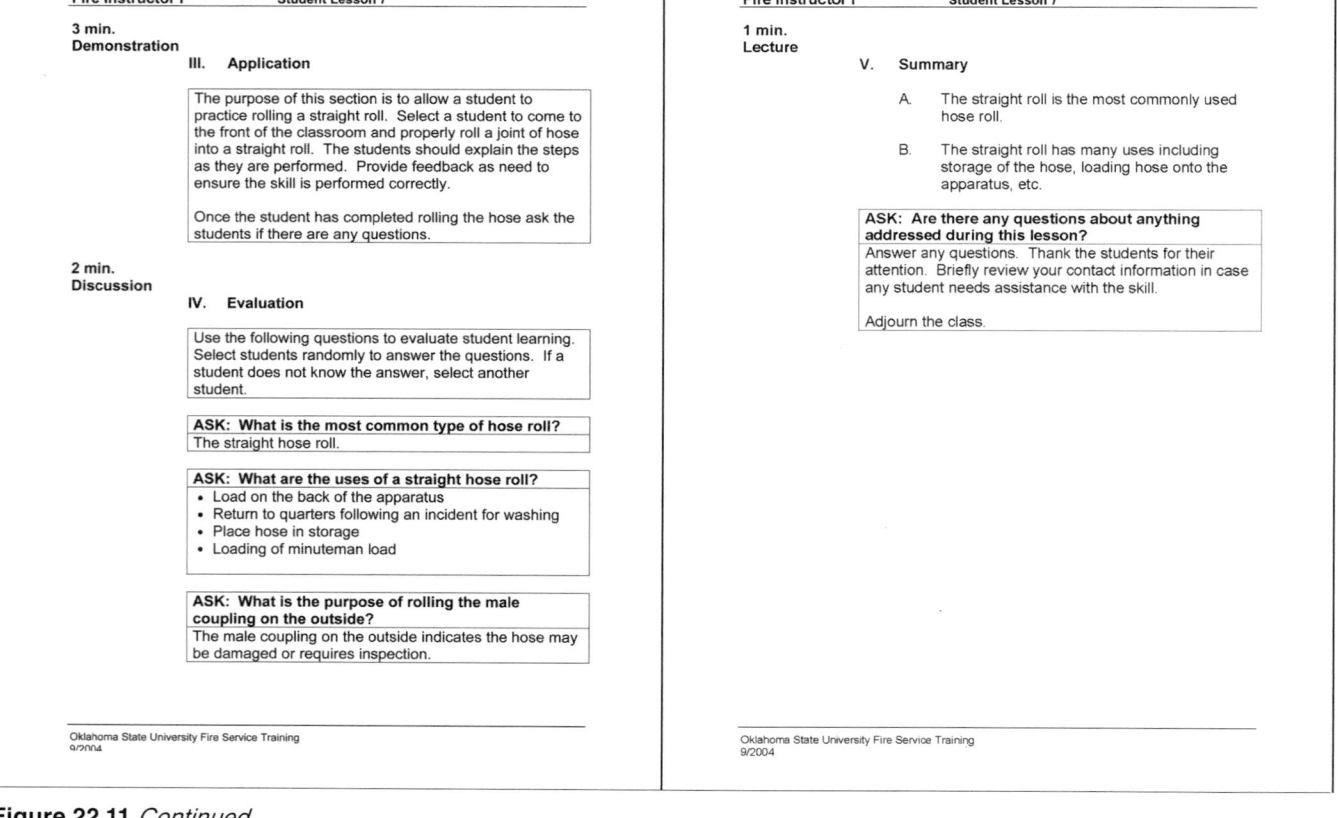

Figure 22.11 *Continued*

Lesson Sequence Example
High-Angle Rescue Course
Lessons:

- Understanding the High-Angle Environment
- Personal Protective Equipment
- Rope and Related Equipment
- Knots
- Equipment Care and Use
- Safety Issues
- Anchoring
- Rappelling
- Basic Ascending
- Victim Removal

Figure 22.12 The sequence of lessons is based on providing simple information and skills first and progressing then to more complex concepts and applications.

- Curriculum is considered complete.
- Students' efforts are validated.
- Certificates are awarded.

Create Evaluation Instruments

Evaluation instruments serve many roles and are more than just tests for students at the end of a course. Organizations are interested in evaluations on the curriculum/courses themselves and instructors who teach them as well as on the accomplishments of the students who participate in these courses. Evaluations identify curriculum and course strengths and weaknesses in areas such as the following:

- Time allotted
- Equipment used or needed
- Instructor and student expectations
- Instructional methods used
- Learning environments used
- Evaluation methods used

For instructors, evaluations provide an assessment of themselves and their teaching methods. For students, evaluations provide feedback on their knowledge and skill level and assess needs for further study or practice.

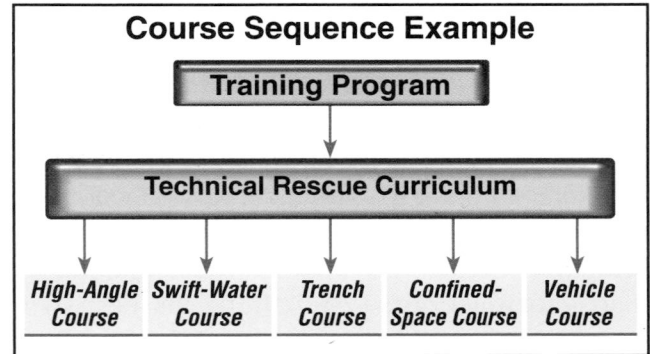

Figure 22.13 The sequence of courses in a curriculum may not be based on an established order although students must complete a course before being admitted to any of the others.

From evaluations of student performance, instructors and training managers receive feedback on test validity and reliability as well as on the effectiveness of the instructor and course. Low test scores do *not* always mean that the student did *not* learn. In those respects, evaluations provide information for examining and analyzing reasons for failure and determining areas to adjust and improve (**Figure 22.14**). Low scores could also mean one of the following situations has occurred:

Figure 22.14 Student evaluations not only determine the amount of knowledge that the student has learned but also the effectiveness of the teaching process and validity/reliability of testing instruments. *Courtesy of U.S. Department of Defense.*

- Instructor did *not* teach to the objectives.
- Course was *not* suited to the level of the student.
- Evaluation instrument (test) was *not* valid.

Refer to Chapter 13, Student Progress Evaluation and Testing, for a detailed presentation of the development of testing instruments. See Chapter 15, Instructor and Course Evaluations, for the instruments and process used for evaluating instructors and courses.

Implement Curriculum/Course

Throughout the process of instructional design, program developers must be aware of the reality of implementing the training curriculum/course. When instructors have completed the initial design steps through the final writing of lesson plans and development of evaluation instruments, their next logical step is to implement the curriculum.

Implementation requires a complete delivery system, including procedures such as the following:

- Acquire funding and facilities.
- Determine instructor and student time requirements.
- Find qualified instructors or train them.
- Determine and create appropriate training aids or materials.

The Level III Instructor must confirm, for example, that the curriculum or course can be presented in the existing facility. The location, design, and equipment of a facility directly affect the kinds of activities that instructors can conduct and students can perform to achieve course objectives.

Before implementation begins, instructors perform a detailed formative evaluation. Ideally, formative evaluations have been in progress throughout the design phase. These evaluations include the following items:

- Reviews by peers or supervisors
- Consultations with subject-matter experts
- Reviews by prospective instructors
- Any other steps that perform the following functions:

— Helps to ensure the quality of the curriculum or course

— Monitors the curriculum or course continually to ensure its focus on meeting performance objectives

Once everyone is satisfied that the formative evaluation and ensuing corrections indicate that the course is ready to move forward, instructors can take the necessary steps to implement the training curriculum/course. Implementation actions typically include the following steps:

Step 1: Obtain final course approval.

Step 2: Assemble, create, or select appropriate training aids or materials.

Step 3: Schedule facilities and equipment.

Step 4: Qualify instructors.

Step 5: Establish appropriate training records systems or databases.

Step 6: Schedule and announce the curriculum or course.

Step 7: Select students.

Step 8: Present a pilot version of the course.

Each organization or jurisdiction may have different requirements for obtaining curriculum or course approval for implementation. Instructors may conduct a detailed presentation showing the approval authorities how a course supports organizational learning goals and achieves the learning objectives (through instructional methods and learning activities and with appropriate training materials). The presentation gives information on the financial and time commitments that the organization will have to invest by providing details on facilities and equipment required and instructor and student hours necessary.

When a course is required by defined standards, information on how it meets those standards and what records must be kept to satisfy certification processes assist the decision makers in reaching a favorable conclusion. With approval, the process of scheduling classes and selecting students can easily follow.

Most of these steps have been discussed in previous chapters. However, selecting qualified instructors, developing or selecting appropriate training aids, and presenting a pilot course are included for the benefit of the instructor and curriculum developer.

Select Qualified Instructors

When the course has been approved, qualified instructors must be selected. In many cases, the person most qualified to teach a course is the one that assisted in its development. In other cases, the most qualified person may *not* be an instructor but someone who is a subject matter expert (SME) in the topic to be taught. For instance, an emergency room doctor may be selected to teach a course in emergency trauma care.

Certified Level I or Level II Instructors, however, should teach courses that are specific to the fire and emergency services. Specialized topics, such as confined-space rescue, require instructors who are certified in the topic as well as instructor-certified **(Figure 22.15)**.

Create or Select Appropriate Training Aids

Finally, the appropriate training aids are created or selected for the specific courses. The training aids should assist the student in learning the concepts and mastering the skills outlined in the objectives.

Figure 22.15 Specialized training such as trench or confined-space shoring requires that qualified and certified instructors teach the courses. *Courtesy of Alabama Fire College.*

See Chapter 11, Audiovisual Technology, for a discussion on types of training aids and Chapter 5, Instructional Facilities and Props, for information on props used in skills development.

Present a Pilot of the Course

The first delivery of a course is a pilot presentation. The purposes of a pilot course are as follows:

- Verifies course content
- Determines the adequacy of facilities, props, materials, logistics support, and audiovisual training aids
- Determines the adequacy of course design and time allotment

Evaluations of the course are based on feedback received from instructors, observers, and students as well as student performance on evaluation instruments. These evaluations are also opportunities to evaluate the effectiveness of the evaluation process and instruments.

Alterations are made to correct any problems that are discovered in the course evaluations. A pilot course is also an opportunity for instructors to become familiar with course content and presentation requirements.

Evaluate Curriculum/Course

Instructors and students can perform a summative evaluation at the end of each course to determine whether the course met the educational goals of the organization. This evaluation answers the following questions:

- Did students meet performance objectives?
- Was training conducted as designed and within the resources allocated?

There are many ways to accomplish summative evaluations. Examples include the following:

- Students' scores on written tests or performance tests
- Students' behaviors observed in the field
- Feedback from students and instructors
- Feedback from field supervisors

As the course continues, a summative evaluation is performed after every course presentation. The trends identified in student performance help evaluators judge whether the course was successful (meets organizational training goals) and determine whether the course continues or needs further adjustments. In order to accurately measure the improvement in student performance, curriculum/course evaluators need to compare the postcourse performance to the performance level observed in the needs analysis and pretests.

In addition to evaluating students' performances and whether they meet course learning objectives and JPRs, there must be an evaluation system for course materials and instructor performance. A system for evaluating instructor performance is an important aspect of evaluating training. A detailed discussion on student evaluations is in Chapter 15, Instructor and Course Evaluations.

Evaluate Course Materials

Both instructors and students should have input into the assessment of teaching and learning materials (textbooks, study materials, audiovisual aids, props, etc). The results should answer the following questions:

- Did the materials support the objectives?
- Were the materials relevant or applicable to job requirements?

Evaluate Instructor Performances

An excellent course design with appropriate training materials can be jeopardized by one or more instructors whose teaching skills are not adequate. When establishing instructor evaluation instruments, ensure that they answer the following questions:

- How well does the instructor know the subject being taught?
- How enthusiastic is the instructor for the topic and teaching?
- How well does the instructor provide the knowledge necessary to meet the lesson and course objectives?
- How well is the instructor prepared?
- How well is the instructor organized?
- How well does the instructor relate to or interact with students?

- How well does the instructor respond to and answer student questions?

During the presentation of a course, a course instructor should be periodically evaluated by more experienced instructors with subject-matter expertise. Student input is also an important component in instructor evaluation. Students can complete carefully designed course-feedback instruments that elicit objective responses (**Figure 22.16**). The results of instructor evaluations may show the need for either enhanced instructor development or only the need for appropriate instructor orientation, particularly when new courses are being introduced.

Curriculum/Course Revision

The evaluation of the training curriculum/course may determine the need for revision of the curriculum/course. The instructor or training manager should regularly assess the need for curriculum revision to improve student learning or provide students with opportunities to learn that do *not* currently exist. Revisions may be necessary because of changes in operational standards, department protocols, new technologies, or standards of appropriate accrediting bodies.

When planning revisions, the instructor should take the following actions:

- Determine whether the revision is *mission appropriate* for the department/organization, training division, or agency. Does the proposed revision help and support the organization to meet its mission statement or goal? If not, then the revision should *not* be made or the curriculum/course should be altered so that it does meet the mission statement or goal.
- Involve other branches or divisions of the department/organization that may be affected by the proposed changes.
- Involve the entire training division or agency membership in the development process.
- Evaluate the existing resources and potential needs regarding staffing, funding, time, technology, equipment, props, and facilities.
- Communicate clearly to the organization the reason for the proposed revision as well as the anticipated results of the change.

- Create clear, concise revision proposals that meet the criteria for any new curriculum or course.
- Apply the five-step planning model to the revision of the curriculum or course.

Periodic evaluations of all curriculums and courses should be scheduled to determine whether they still meet the original needs of the organization. It is also important to determine whether changes caused by unauthorized revisions have

---

Student Evaluation of Instruction

Instructor Name: _____   Date: _____

Course Title: _____   Course Location: _____

Directions: Read the entire sheet BEFORE marking responses. Place an X in the space that most accurately represents your opinion of the instructor's ability. It is not necessary to sign your name. Your opinion is important so the course may be improved.

Instructor Knowledge of Topic:
( )   ( )   ( )   ( )
Very well informed   Well informed   Limited background   Poorly informed

Preparation:
( )   ( )   ( )   ( )
Always prepared   Usually prepared   Sometimes prepared   Unprepared

Presentation:
( )   ( )   ( )   ( )
Stimulating   Adequate   Routine   Dull

Attitude Toward Students:
( )   ( )   ( )   ( )
Very considerate   Considerate   Somewhat intolerant   Inconsiderate and rude

Explanations:
( )   ( )   ( )   ( )
Very clear   Clear   Confused   Faulty

Composure or Manner:
( )   ( )   ( )   ( )
Always composed   Usually composed   Easily upset   Highly insecure

Instructor Organization:
( )   ( )   ( )   ( )
Well organized   Usually well-planned   Somewhat unplanned   Often disorganized

Assignments:
( )   ( )   ( )   ( )
Very clear   Usually clear   Somewhat vague   Always vague

Examination Questions:
( )   ( )   ( )   ( )
Clear, relevant   Adequate   Often confusing   Irrelevant and unclear

Grading Methods:
( )   ( )   ( )   ( )
Always fair   Usually fair   Inconsistent   Biased

Enthusiasm for Topic and Course:
( )   ( )   ( )   ( )
Very enthusiastic   Somewhat enthusiastic Indifferent   Negative

Figure 22.16 Evaluation forms that students complete at the end of a course should be accurate and easy to understand to ensure that students will complete them.

occurred in the courses over time. The current course outcomes may *not* resemble those of the original course design.

Summary

Analyzing and planning instruction can include tasks ranging from planning a single course to developing a training program, curriculum, or course for the entire organization. The training manager must understand the analysis process in order to be able to determine the types of training required to meet the organization's needs.

An understanding in the application of planning models, including the five-step method, is also important for the training manager to have. This planning model can be applied to instructional development, course development, and program development. Each of these components is essential to the knowledge base required for any instructor who is responsible for the role of training manager.

Appendix A
NFPA Job Performance Requirements (JPRs) with Chapter and Page References

NFPA 1041 JPR Numbers	Chapter References*	Page References
4.2	5, 6	101–115, 119–134
4.2.1	6	119–134
4.2.2	5, 9	101–115, 189–196
4.2.3	6	119–134
4.3.1	8, 9, 10	163–186, 189–215, 219–245
4.3.2	5, 7, 8, 9, 12	101–115, 137–159, 163–186, 189–215, 277–299
4.3.3	9, 11	189–193, 196–200, 249–274
4.4.1	10	219–245
4.4.2	2, 9, 10, 11, 12	35–57, 206–215, 219–232, 249–274, 277–299
4.4.3	4, 7, 8, 9, 10, 11, 12	85–97, 137–159, 163–186, 189–215, 219–245, 249–274, 277–299
4.4.4	9, 12	189–215, 277–299
4.4.5	2, 8, 9, 12	35–57, 163–186, 189–215, 277–299
4.4.6	11	249–274
4.4.7	11	249–274
4.5.2	3, 13	61–82, 303–317
4.5.3	13	303–317
4.5.4	4, 6, 8, 13	85–97, 119–125, 178–182, 303–317
4.5.5	4, 8, 13	85–97, 178–182, 303–317
5.2.2	5, 19	101–115, 461–476
5.2.3	5, 11, 18	101–115, 258–285, 442–449
5.2.4	18	442–458
5.2.5	3, 6	61–77, 125–134
5.2.6	4, 10, 15, 19	85–97, 232–245, 357–362, 461–469
5.3.2	7, 8, 9, 14, 18	137–158, 163–186, 189–196, 321–324, 431–439

NFPA 1041 JPR Numbers	Chapter References*	Page References
5.3.3	7, 8, 9, 11, 14, 18	137–158, 163–186, 189–196, 249–274, 321–324, 431–439
5.4.2	2, 7, 9, 10, 11, 12, 17	35–57, 137–159, 219–245, 249–274, 277–299, 415–428
5.4.3	2, 3, 12, 17	35–57, 61–77, 277–299, 415–428
5.5.2	13, 16	303–317, 375–411
5.5.3	15	357–371
5.5.4	16	375–411
6.2.2	6, 20	125–134, 480–484
6.2.3	6, 20	119–125, 484–493
6.2.4	20	493–500
6.2.5	20, 21	497–500, 508–517
6.2.6	18, 21	450–458, 508–517
6.2.7	4, 10, 21	85–97, 232–237, 508–517
6.3.2	8, 14, 18, 21, 22	163–175, 321–354, 431–439, 503–507, 521–542
6.3.3	6, 7, 8, 18, 22	119–125, 137–159, 163–175, 431–439, 521–542
6.3.4	6, 7, 18, 22	119–125, 137–159, 431–439, 521–542
6.3.5	6, 22	119–125, 521–542
6.3.6	22	521–542
6.3.7	7, 10, 22	137–159, 219–245, 521–542
6.5.2	6, 20	125–134, 480–484
6.5.3	15, 21	357–371, 508–517
6.5.4	15, 21	357–371, 508–517

* Instructor Chapter Titles:

Part A General Knowledge and Skills
1: Challenges of Fire and Emergency Services Instruction
2: Safety and the Training Function
3: Legal and Ethical Considerations
4: Effective Interpersonal Communication
5: Instructional Facilities and Props
6: Report Writing and Record Keeping
7: Principles of Learning
8: Student Attributes and Behaviors

Part B Instructor I Requirements
9: Preparation for Instruction
10: Instructional Delivery
11: Audiovisual Technology

12: Structured Exercises, Demonstrations, and Practical Training Evolutions
13: Student Progress Evaluation and Testing

Part C Instructor II Requirements
14: Lesson Plan Development
15: Instructor and Course Evaluations
16: Student Testing Instruments
17: Course and Evolution Management
18: Administrative Duties
19: Supervision and Management

Part D Instructor III Requirements
20: Administration: Records, Policies, and Personnel
21: Analysis and Evaluation
22: Program and Curriculum Development

Appendix B
Leadership Styles

Leading is the act of controlling, directing, conducting, guiding, and administering through the use of personal behavioral traits or personality characteristics that motivate employees to the successful completion of the organization's goals (part of the management process). As a supervisor, manager, and role model, an instructor is expected to exhibit leadership traits and characteristics.

According to one survey, leadership is one of the top five skills that employers look for when hiring new personnel; others are communication, technical, teamwork, and interpersonal skills. When combined with these skills, leadership produces real results that benefit the organization and the community.

Leaders are committed to a vision, one that is expressed as a result and not as an activity. They develop relationships that help to accomplish a vision by sharing it with others and seeking their input on how best to attain that vision.

Finally, leaders have a high level of personal integrity that is at the core of all decisions and actions. Ethical leadership not only considers what is best for the organization but also what is best for the community. There are rare instances when doing what is best for the organization as a whole may *not* be in the best interest of the community or personnel.

In these situations, the ethical decision would put the priority on what is best for the community. The result of a vision-driven leadership style that is shared and based on integrity is an exceptional contribution to the training division, the department/organization, the community, and society.

Leadership is also an important part of the management process because it means the difference between an organization that is reactive to a situation and one that is proactive, meeting challenges as they develop and *not* after they occur. In order to develop one's leadership ability, it is important for an instructor to have a general understanding of the various theories and styles of leadership.

Four general theories or approaches to describing leadership have developed in the past century. It cannot be overemphasized that to become an effective leader, an instructor must be flexible enough to choose the appropriate leadership style to fit the situation or occasion. These approaches to leadership are based on the following elements:

- Traits
- Behaviors
- Situations
- Principles

Leadership Traits

Throughout the 1900s, sociologists, psychologists, and organizational theorists attempted to determine the specific character traits that make a person an effective leader. During a period of 70 years, more than 300 studies were done to pinpoint traits that were consistently found in all leaders. No single trait was found in all the cases.

In 1971, Edwin Ghiselli conducted a study of leadership traits that isolated the following six traits that were important for effective leadership:

1. *Supervisory ability* — Applying the four functions of management to accomplish the objectives through the efforts of others

2. *Decisiveness* — Solving problems and making informed decisions

3. *Intelligence* — Using common sense, logic, and reason in making decisions

4. *Self-assurance* — Demonstrating self-confidence and self-esteem when making decisions

5. *Initiative* — Accomplishing goals and objectives with a minimum of supervision

6. *Desire for professional success* — Working hard in order to gain additional responsibility within the organization

Additional traits that have been attributed to effective leaders by other theorists include the following:

- *Integrity* — Applying a set of morals or values consistently to the decision-making process and doing the right thing

- *Personal security* — Knowing that the leader is secure in the position and does *not* feel threatened by subordinates, peers, or the political environment

- *Sense of priority* — Determining what must be accomplished first and maintaining focus on the outcome

- *Vision* — Having a dream or concept of the way things can or should be

- *Industriousness* — Accomplishing seemingly insurmountable tasks

- *Interpersonal skills* — Communicating ideas and getting along with others

- *Empowerment* — Sharing authority and responsibility with other members of the organization

- *Innovation and creativity* — Seeking new and imaginative methods continuously for accomplishing the mission of the organization

- *Consistency* — Applying procedures, policies, rewards, and discipline evenly and fairly over time

- *Preparedness* — Being always prepared for any potential situation and having contingency plans in place to resolve it

- *Living in the future* — Anticipating change and meeting it in a proactive manner (concerned with *what will be* more than *what has been*)

Most of these traits cannot be taught in a classroom or learned by reading a book. Traits are developed by consciously observing role models and then applying those leadership traits through practice. Successful leaders in private industry,

political leaders, military leaders, athletic leaders, social activists, and religious leaders all provide examples of some if not all of the traits.

Historical examples abound in the pages of biographies as well as the stylized characters of folk stories. Because of the importance of leadership, many volumes are available that focus on the individuals who have demonstrated leadership traits, how they used those traits, and the effect they had on organizations or situations.

Behavioral Leadership

The theory of behavioral leadership developed in the 1940s and includes several styles. Each of these styles (including, among others, the *basic leadership styles*, *two-dimensional leadership styles*, and *contemporary leadership styles*) may be the result of the presence (or lack of) some of the leadership traits listed previously. Three behavioral leadership styles are described in the sections that follow

Basic Leadership Style

The basic style, which may be the most familiar, categorizes leaders into three groups: autocratic, democratic, and laissez-faire. The basic leadership styles are then described as follows:

- *Autocratic* — Tells subordinates what to do and how to do it with little or no input from them. When this is the dominant leadership style used, this type of leader will have significant challenges from subordinates. This style is appropriate for emergency operations but *not* nonemergency operations or daily operations.

- *Democratic* — Includes employees in the decision-making process and allows them to work with the least amount of supervision necessary.

- *Laissez-faire* — Leaves employees to make all the decisions and does *not* supervise them at all. In French the term literally means *to allow to do.*

Two-Dimensional Leadership Style

This style is a theory based on independent studies done at Ohio State University and the University of Michigan in the late 1940s. It is represented by a four-quadrant chart that compares the degree of job structure to the degree of employee consideration (also referred to as *job-centered* and *employee-centered*). Depending on the amount of emphasis placed on getting the job done through an autocratic approach or allowing employees full authority as in the laissez-faire approach, this type of leadership style can be plotted on a graph (**Figure B.1**).

The four two-dimensional leadership styles are described as follows:

- *Telling* — Autocratic approach
- *Selling* — Refined autocratic approach that involves convincing members that the task is appropriate and justified
- *Participating* — Relies on input from members in determining how the task should be accomplished
- *Delegating* — Leader sets limits and allows members to determine how the task will be accomplished

Contemporary Leadership Category

These styles include the following leadership theories that are currently popular in the field of management studies:

- *Charismatic* — Inspires employee loyalty and creates an enthusiastic vision that others work to attain. Leaders have strong personalities, and it is sometimes difficult to separate the personality of the leader from that of the organization. When the leader dies or leaves the organization, it is difficult to find a replacement that can live up to the image of the charismatic leader.

- *Transformational* — Depends on continuous learning, innovation, and change within the organization. This leader works to involve employees in the change process, challenges employees to attain their full potential, and creates employee satisfaction and growth while still meeting organizational goals. True transformational leadership is a rare quality, yet it can be

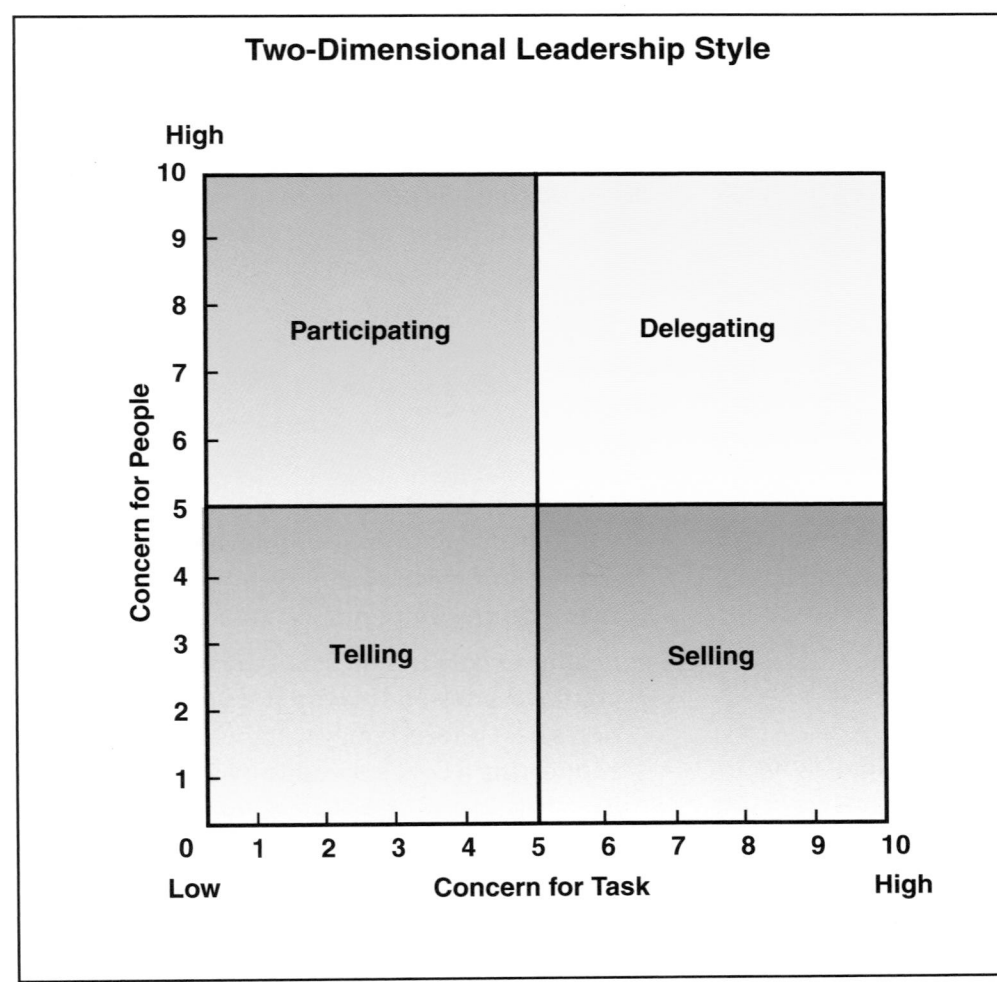

Figure B.1 Model of two-dimensional leadership style theory.

found at different organizational levels. These leaders are often identifiable by their dedicated followers.

- **Transactional** — Involves an exchange between a manager and employees in which employees perform tasks effectively in exchange for rewards provided by the manager. This style is often used by first-line supervisors and middle-level managers.

- **Symbolic** — Holds common values and beliefs that are based on a strong organizational culture. Leadership starts at the top of the organization and extends downward to the first-line supervisor. Employees and subordinates have full faith and trust in the leadership of the organization. The leaders are viewed as infallible. The difficulty associated with this type of leadership is that employees fail to question leadership decisions or speak out when management makes apparent errors.

Situational Leadership

Situational leadership is a category that includes a variety of theories and methods that were intended to address the shortcomings of both the trait and behavioral approaches. In the case of the fire and emergency services, an instructor should select the most effective leadership style depending on the situation.

This selection would compare to an incident command situation where the initial leadership style may be the autocratic approach. As more personnel become available, the style may shift to participatory as members of the command staff provide the necessary information to deal with the situation. However, the formation of a protective clothing evaluation committee, for example, may be more democratic. The members of the committee are provided with general guidelines and then delegated with the responsibility of evaluating the clothing.

Situational leadership allows an instructor to be flexible in selecting the style that best suits the situation and the employees who are involved. The leader is expected to examine each situation and choose the appropriate action to accomplish the task. The ability and willingness of members to comply are also factors that influence the choice of styles. Not all employees are skilled or knowledgeable enough to be involved in every participatory management situation. Each member will have a different commitment level based upon the readiness level for which they have been trained.

Also, some employees resent the totally autocratic approach and rebel through various means. The instructor must have a sound understanding of subordinates or students and their abilities and be knowledgeable enough to use the style best suited to the situation.

Leadership theorists attempted to determine the appropriate style of leadership based on the type of situation. Two models within this category are the leadership continuum and situational leadership.

Leadership Continuum Model

This model is used to determine which leadership style (ranging from autocratic to participatory leadership) to use. The model can be applied to the fire and emergency services when each style is appropriately applied to the correct situation.

Traditional leaders tend to be autocratic at all times. Leaders that embrace empowerment understand that it is possible to move along the continuum (line), using the most effective and efficient leadership style based on the specific situation.

The weakness of this leadership model is that it requires the leader to be a good judge of situations and people in order to select the appropriate style of leadership. The following leadership styles list begins from the autocratic end of the continuum:

- Leader makes the decision and announces it without discussion or employee involvement; may be applied to an emergency scene situation that requires immediate action

- Leader makes the decision and then sells it to employees based on why it is in the organization's best interest; may work when the leader is supporting a decision made by a higher authority

- Leader presents ideas to members and invites their questions; can be used when the leader has made a decision and simply wants to clarify it to the membership

- Leader presents a tentative decision to members that is subject to change; can be used when some member participation is desired such as duty assignments

- Leader presents the problem to members, asks for suggestions, and then makes the decision based on the best recommendation; a form of participatory management that allows members to provide alternative ideas while allowing the leader to make the final selection

- Leader defines limits on a decision and asks members to make the decision; an example of the consensus process that may be used to develop facility specifications

- Leader sets the limitations and allows members to make all decisions without interference; requires the leader and members to agree upon the limitations and for the leader to feel comfortable empowering subordinates with the decision-making process

Situational Leadership Model

This model is based on matching the leadership style to the maturity of the members of the workgroup or subordinates (approach developed by Paul Hersey and Ken Blanchard as an extension of the Ohio State University study mentioned earlier). The term *maturity* used in this context does not refer to age or emotional stability but rather to the competence, commitment, technical ability, and willingness of the subordinates to do the task.

The maturity of the employee (also referred to by Hersey/Blanchard as the *follower readiness*) is based on the following two elements:

- First is the *ability* (determined by knowledge, skills, and experience) of the employee to perform the task.

- Second is the *willingness* of the employee to perform the task. Commitment and motivation determine the willingness level.

The authors established four readiness levels based on these two elements **(Figure B.2)**. Based

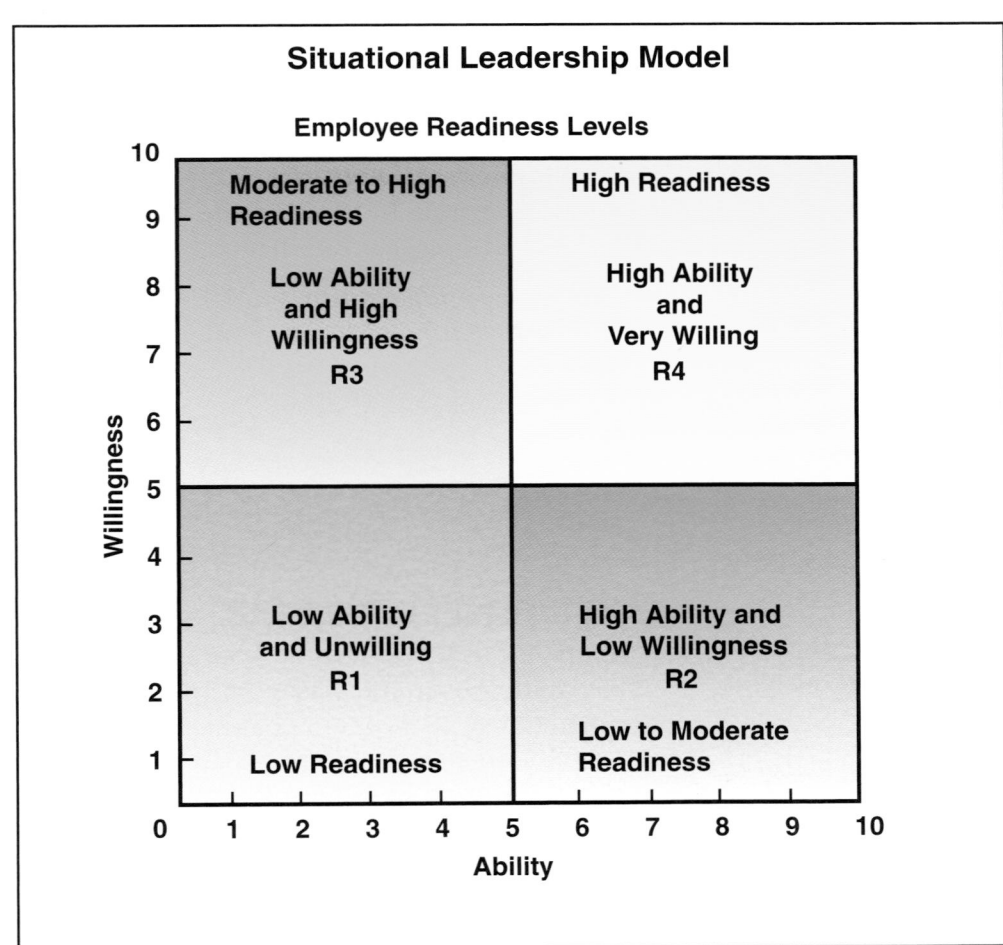

Figure B.2 Four levels of employee readiness in the situational leadership model.

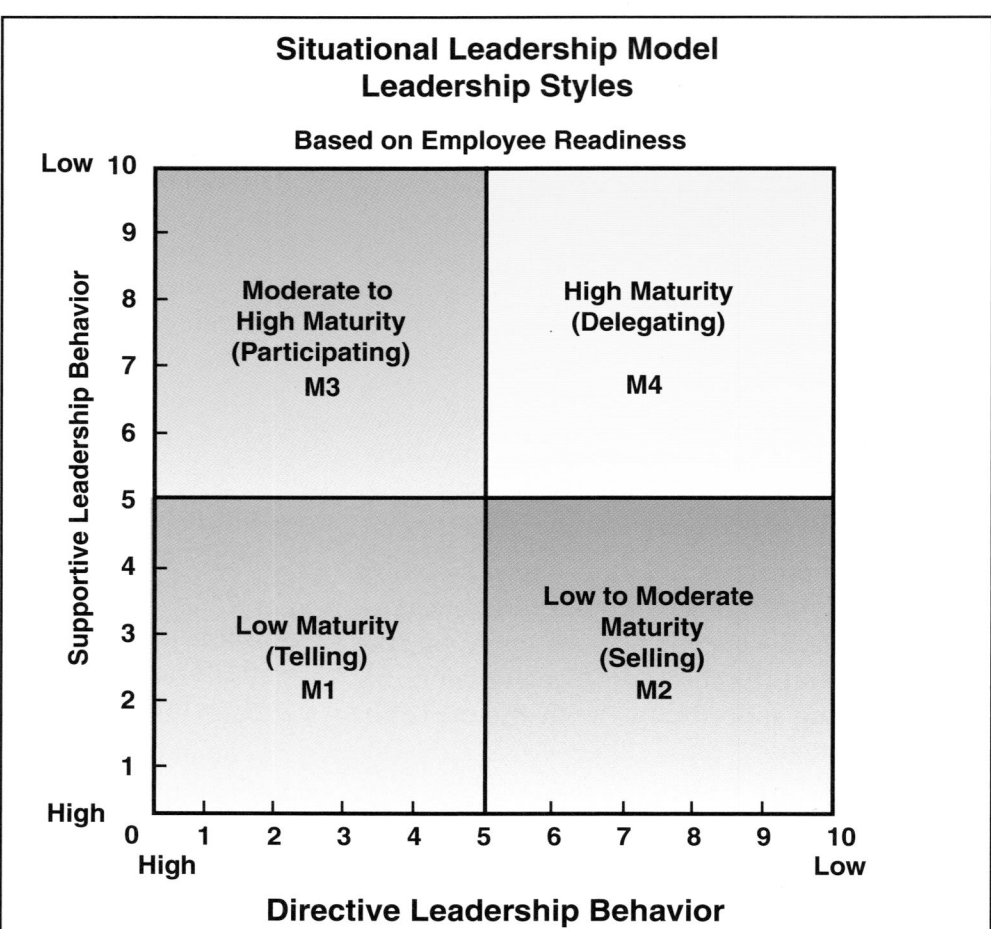

Figure B.3 Four leadership styles based on employee readiness in the situational leadership model.

on these four levels of readiness, the leader may then decide to use one of the four leadership styles that follow (**Figure B.3**).

- *Low readiness (R1)* — Employee is unable and unwilling to perform the task, resulting in an insecure feeling.

- *Low-to-moderate readiness (R2)* — Employee is unable but willing to perform the task and displays a confident appearance.

- *Moderate-to-high readiness (R3)* — Employee is able but unwilling to perform the task, resulting in an insecure feeling.

- *High readiness (R4)* — Employee is able and willing to perform the task and displays a highly confident attitude.

Leadership styles can also be based on maturity levels as follows:

- *Low maturity (M1)* — Leader uses the *telling* or autocratic style.

- *Low-to-moderate maturity (M2)* — Leader uses the *selling* style by making the decision and coaching employees on what to do.

- *Moderate-to-high maturity (M3)* — Leader uses the *participating* style, allowing employees to participate in the decision-making process.

- *High maturity (M4)* — Leader uses the *delegating* or fully democratic style, giving employees the freedom to make and carry out the decisions.

Principled Leadership

This theory of leadership developed during the 1980s and 1990s and is based on the writings of Stephen Covey. Referred to as either *principled* or *principle-centered* leadership, it focuses on the use of basic values or principles to lead an organization. It suggests that there are certain core ethical values that the individual holds and transfers to others in the organization.

These values may be the foundation for the organization's mission statement or code of ethics. In any case, they must be held by other members of the organization for principled leadership to be effective. The theory states that the leader uses these values to guide internal and external personal relations, make decisions, create policy, and determine success. Examples of these values, which are parts of the Leadership Traits theory, include the following:

- Integrity
- Excellence
- Respect for the individual
- Harmony
- Loyalty
- Faith
- Honesty
- Courage

Appendix C
Instructor Resources

Professional Organizations and their Publications

Training & Development
American Society for Training and Development, Inc. (ASTD)
1640 King Street
Alexandria, VA 22313
Phone 703-683-8100
www.astd.org

Instruct-O-Gram and *The Voice*
International Society of Fire Service Instructors (ISFSI)
2425 Highway 49
Pleasant View, TN 37146
Phone 800-435-0005
www.isfsi.org
info@isfsi.org

Domain
National Association of EMS Educators (NAEMSE)
Foster Plaza 6, 681 Andersen Drive
Pittsburgh, PA 15220
Phone 412-920-4775
www.naemse.org
naemse@naemse.org

Safety-Gram
Fire Department Safety Officers Association (FDSOA)
P.O. Box 149
Ashland, MA 01721-0149
Phone 508-881-3114
www.fdsoa.org
fdsoa@fdsoa.org

Periodicals

Educational Leadership
Association for Supervision and Curriculum Development (ASCD)
1703 N. Beauregard Street
Alexandria, VA 22311
Phone 800-933-2723 (press 2)
www.ascd.org

Speaking of Fire
Oklahoma State University
Fire Protection Publications
930 N. Willis
Stillwater, OK 74078-8045
Phone 800-654-4055
www.ifsta.org

Training Magazine
Lakewood Publications, Inc.
Lakewood Building, 50 S. Ninth Street
Minneapolis, MN 55402
Phone 800-328-4329
traininmag@aol.com

Vocational Education Journal
American Vocational Association, Inc.
1410 King Street
Alexandria, VA 22314

Other Resources

Division of Adult Education and Literacy
Office of Vocational and Adult Education
U.S. Department of Education
4090 MES
400 Maryland Avenue S.W.
Washington, DC 20202-7240
Phone 202-205-5451
www.ed.gov/about/offices/list/ova/pi/AdultEd/index.html

Learning Disabilities Association of America (LDA)
4156 Library Road
Pittsburgh, PA 15234
Phone 412-341-1515
Publications available in Spanish
www.ldaamerica.org
info@ldaamerica.org

Libraries

Fire Service Programs Library
Oklahoma State University
930 N. Willis Street
Stillwater, OK 74078
Phone 405-744-7046
www.ifsta.org

National Fire Academy Learning Resource Center
16825 South Seton Avenue
Emmitsburg, MD 21727
Phone 800-638-1821
www.lrc.fema.gov
netclr@dhs.gov

National Institute of Standards and Technology (NIST)
100 Bureau Drive, Stop 1070
Gaithersburg, MD 20899
Phone 301-975-6478
www.nist.gov
inquiries@nist.gov

Worcester Polytechnic Institute
100 Institute Road
Worcester, MA 01609
Phone 500-831-5000
Online Resource Library
www.wpi.edu

Standards

National Fire Protection Association (NFPA)
1 Batterymarch Park
Quincy, MA 02169
Phone 800-344-3555
www.nfpa.org

New York Firefighter and Code Enforcement Standards and Education Committee
Department of State Office of Fire Prevention and Control (OFPC)
41 State Street
Albany, NY 12231
Phone 518-474-6746
www.dos.state.ny.us/fire/firewww.html

American National Standards Institute (ANSI)
1819 L Street, N.W., Suite 600
Washington, DC 20036
Phone 202-293-8020
www.ansi.org

Appendix D
Emergency Incident Casualty Statistics

A report published in March, 2004, by RAND® Worldwide provides an interesting overview of fire and emergency responder casualties for the previous year. The report indicates that injuries during emergency operations amounted to approximately 88,000 injuries, half of the total fire and emergency responder injuries reported per year. Of these emergency operations injuries, 2,000 injuries were potentially life threatening.

The types of injuries included trauma, cuts and bruises, burns, asphyxiation, and thermal stress. The majority of injuries occurred during fire attack and search/rescue activities. Personnel involved in emergency medical activities were most likely to suffer sprains, strains, back injuries, and exposures to infectious or communicable diseases.

According to information provided by the U.S. Fire Administration (USFA) in 2003, the leading cause of fatalities to firefighters was heart attack resulting from physical stress, accounting for 44 percent of all deaths. Trauma (including internal and head injuries) was the second leading cause of fatal injuries at 27 percent. Asphyxia and burns combined accounted for 20 percent of fatalities.

Based on the information in this report, firefighters under the age of 35 are more likely to be killed by traumatic injuries than they are to die of medical causes (such as heart attack or stroke). After age 35, the proportion of deaths due to traumatic injuries decreases, and proportion of deaths due to heart attacks, strokes, and other medical causes rises steadily.

The majority of firefighter fatalities (57 percent) were members of rural or municipal volunteer fire agencies (including combination departments). Full-time career personnel account for 33 percent of firefighter fatalities; yet they compose approximately only 26 percent of the American fire service.

Numerically, more volunteer firefighters are killed than career personnel, yet career personnel are killed at a rate disproportionate to their representation in the fire service.

In many fire and emergency services organizations, emergency medical services (EMS) responses account for between 50 and 80 percent of emergency-response volume. These incidents result in only 3 percent of firefighter fatalities. Trauma accounts for the deaths of 50 percent of firefighters who were involved in EMS operations at the time of their fatal injuries; another 38 percent involved in EMS operations died from heart attacks.

USFA also determined the type of duty that was being performed at the time of the fatality. Of those firefighters killed while en route to an incident, 85 percent were volunteers. For firefighters killed while performing in-station duties, 69 percent were career personnel; the majority of those deaths were the result of heart attacks. These variations can be attributed to differences between career and volunteer agencies.

Generally, unless they are on a call or other fire-department business, career personnel are required to be in the fire station for the duration of their shifts, which is generally between 10 and 24 hours long. Volunteers spend more time away from the station and are more likely than career firefighters to respond from locations other than the fire station. Volunteers will more often respond using privately owned vehicles (POVs) and account for a high percentage of accidental deaths involving motor vehicle accidents.

Since 1984, motor-vehicle-related accidents involving fire and emergency services personnel have accounted for between 20 and 25 percent of fire and emergency responders' fatalities annually. One quarter of firefighters or emergency responders who died in these accidents were killed in POVs because of the large number of volunteers who respond to incidents in their personal vehicles.

According to USFA statistics, the type of emergency apparatus most often involved in fatal collisions included mobile water tenders (tankers), engines/pumpers, and aircraft. More firefighters were killed in tender/tanker collisions than in engines and ladder apparatus combined. About 27 percent of fatalities involved in motor vehicle accidents were ejected from the vehicle at the time of the collision, but only 21 percent of firefighters or emergency responders were reportedly wearing seatbelts before the collision.

Appendix E

NIOSH Training Fatality Report: 2003

F2002 34 — Fire Fighter Fatality Investigation and Prevention Program

Death in the line of duty...

A Summary of a NIOSH fire fighter fatality investigation   June 16, 2003

Career Lieutenant and Fire Fighter Die in a Flashover During a Live-Fire Training Evolution - Florida

SUMMARY

On July 30, 2002, a 32-year-old male career Lieutenant (Victim #1) and a 20-year-old male career fire fighter (Victim #2) died while participating in a live-fire training evolution. A flashover occurred several minutes after the fire had been lit in the acquired vacant structure while both of the victims were performing a simulated search and rescue. The Lieutenant and the fire fighter were both transported by ambulances to a local hospital where they were pronounced dead. NIOSH investigators concluded that, to minimize the risk of similar occurrences, fire departments should

- *ensure that the fuels used in live-fire training have known burning characteristics and the structure is inspected for possible hazards prior to the training*

- *ensure that ventilation is closely coordinated with interior operations*

- *ensure that fires are not located in designated exit paths*

- *ensure that a method of fireground communication is established to enable coordination among the Incident Commander and fire fighters*

- *ensure that Standard Operating Guidelines (SOGs) specific to live-fire training are developed and followed*

- *consider using a thermal imaging camera during live-fire training*

Additionally, States should consider

- *developing a permitting procedure for live-fire training to be conducted at acquired structures. States should ensure that all the requirements of NFPA 1403 have been met before issuing the permit*

Incident Scene

The **Fire Fighter Fatality Investigation and Prevention Program** is conducted by the National Institute for Occupational Safety and Health (NIOSH). The purpose of the program is to determine factors that cause or contribute to fire fighter deaths suffered in the line of duty. Identification of causal and contributing factors enable researchers and safety specialists to develop strategies for preventing future similar incidents. The program does not seek to determine fault or place blame on fire departments or individual fire fighters. To request additional copies of this report (specify the case number shown in the shield above), other fatality investigation reports, or further information, visit the Program Website at
www.cdc.gov/niosh/firehome.html
or call toll free 1-800-35-NIOSH

Career Lieutenant and Fire Fighter Die in a Flashover During a Live-Fire Training Evolution - Florida

INTRODUCTION

On July 30, 2002, a 32-year-old male career Lieutenant (Victim #1) and a 20-year-old male career fire fighter (Victim #2) died while participating in a live-fire training evolution. On July 31, 2002, the U.S. Fire Administration (USFA) notified the National Institute for Occupational Safety and Health (NIOSH) of these fatalities. On September 9-12, 2002, three safety and occupational health specialists from the NIOSH Fire Fighter Fatality Investigation and Prevention Program investigated the incident. NIOSH investigators interviewed the officers and fire fighters involved in this incident, and they met with representatives from the International Association of Fire Fighters and the Office of the State Fire Marshal. The NIOSH investigators reviewed the fire department's standard operating guidelines (SOGs), photographs of the incident scene, training records of the victims, reports completed by the State Fire Marshal's Office, and the death certificates.

This combination department is comprised of 135 career and 93 volunteer fire fighters, has 12 fire stations, and serves a population of approximately 100,000 in an area of about 1,450 square miles.

Training. The department requires all personnel to meet the State fire fighter requirements and have a minimum of National Fire Protection Association (NFPA) Firefighter Level I and II (480 hours) certification, and Emergency Medical Technician (EMT) I certification. The department also requires 40 hours of refresher training annually. Victim #1 had 9 years of fire-fighting experience, including 5 years as a Lieutenant. Victim #1 met the State and department requirements and had approximately 1,000 hours of fire-fighter training. Victim #2 met

the State and department requirements, which he had completed on April 24, 2002. He began serving as a career fire fighter with the department on July 22, 2002, and had completed two tours[a] of duty with the department before the incident.

Personal Protective Equipment. At the time of the incident, both of the victims were wearing their full array of personal protective clothing and equipment, consisting of turnout gear (coat and pants), helmet, Nomex ® hood, gloves, boots, and a Self-Contained Breathing Apparatus (SCBA) with a Personal Alerting Safety System (PASS) integrated into the air pack. During the NIOSH interviews, the participants reported not hearing the PASS devices sounding when the victims were found. The SCBA with integrated PASS devices were significantly damaged during the incident and were not examined by the investigators.

Structure. The structure was a vacant single-family, single-story, ordinary concrete block dwelling (approximately 1,600 square feet) with a pitched-style roof with asphalt shingles (Photo1). Several years earlier a garage or carport had been converted into a bedroom. The structure contained three bedrooms, two bathrooms, a living room, and a kitchen (Figure 1). The structure had a total of 10 windows, 4 on the A-Side and 3 each on the B-Side and C-Side.

The converted bedroom, used as the burn room (approximately 24 by 15 square feet) during the live-fire training, was where the live-fire was ignited and where both victims were found (Photo 2). The floor in the burn room was covered with an indoor/outdoor-type carpeting with a urethane foam padding, and a scuttle hole[b] in the ceiling had been

---

[a]   Each tour consists of working a 24-hour shift
[b]   Opening in the ceiling of the structure, fitted with removable cover for the purpose of providing access and ventilation to the cockloft or roof.

Page 2

Career Lieutenant and Fire Fighter Die in a Flashover During a Live-Fire Training Evolution - Florida

covered to prevent fire extension. According to the Office of the State Fire Marshal, several of the rooms in the structure had some furnishings (e.g., a televison set, an easy chair, a set of twin beds), and the floor was carpeted throughout the structure.

Fuel. The fuel used to generate the live-fire for the training consisted of approximately five wooden pallets, a bale of straw, and a twin-size urethane foam mattress. Other fuels in the burn room included carpeting, foam urethane padding, hollow core closet doors, wood molding, wall-mounted headboards, and painted gypsum board on the walls and ceiling.

Weather. The air temperature was 84 to 88 degrees Fahrenheit and the wind was calm. Weather conditions did not appear to be a factor in this incident.

Fire Analysis. Upon a request from NIOSH, the National Institute of Standards and Technology (NIST) developed a fire analysis of the incident. The purpose of the fire analysis is to help demonstrate the growth and the fire's reaction when different variables are introduced. The complete fire analysis will be available for viewing on-line in the near future at http://www.fire.nist.gov.

INVESTIGATION

On July 30, 2002, a 32-year-old male career Lieutenant (Victim #1) and a 20-year-old male career fire fighter (Victim #2) died while participating in live-fire training. The victims' combination department was leading the training with a career department participating. At approximately 0900 hours, personnel arrived at the training site, and the Instructor-in-Charge/Incident Commander (IC) gave them their assignments. The following personnel, listed according to their assignments, participated in the live-fire training exercise:

Instructor-in-Charge/Incident Commander (IC) (Officer)
Search and Rescue Team (Lieutenant/Victim #1 and Fire Fighter/Victim #2)
Ignition Officer/Interior Safety (1 Fire Fighter)
Interior Safety (3 Fire Fighters)
Rapid Intervention Team (RIT) (2 Fire Fighters)
Attack Line 1 (Officer and 2 Fire Fighters)
Attack Line 2 (Officer and 1 Fire Fighter)
Exterior Ventilation (Fire Fighter)
Pump Operator (Fire Fighter)

Before the start of the training, the IC and the participants walked through the structure so that the IC could give them a preburn briefing (Photo 1 and Figure 1). The IC pointed out the ingress and egress routes, and he told them that a mannequin dressed in fire fighter bunker gear would serve as a simulated rescue victim in the training exercise. He did not tell the participants that the mannequin would be located in the kitchen area. The IC told the participants that the live-fire would be built inside a closet on the northwest corner of the burn room. The participants helped put the fuel–wooden pallets and straw–inside and outside of the closet.

At approximately 1010 hours, the Ignition Officer/ Interior Safety used a road flare to ignite the items in the closet and radioed the IC that the fire had been lit. When the Ignition Officer/Interior Safety left the burn room, the live-fire was producing some flames, and the smoke had diminished visibility in the room (Photo 2). To produce a larger fire, some of the fire fighters retrieved a twin-size mattress from another bedroom and put it on the live-fire in the burn room.

The Ignition Officer/Interior Safety and one of the participants who was acting as Interior Safety assumed their position in the hallway outside the burn room while the other two Interior Safety fire fighters staged in the living room. At approximately 1011 hours, the Ignition Officer/Interior Safety radioed the IC that they were ready to begin the first training evolution. The IC ordered the search and rescue team (Victim #1 and Victim #2) to enter the structure.

Page 3

Career Lieutenant and Fire Fighter Die in a Flashover During a Live-Fire Training Evolution - Florida

Victim #1 and Victim #2 crawled through the front door (A-side) and performed a right-hand search to look for the simulated victim. A very brief time later, after receiving orders from the IC, the crew on Attack Line #1 entered the structure through the front door (A-side) with a charged 1 3/4-inch hoseline.

While Victim #1 and Victim #2 were conducting a search of the living room where two of the interior safety fire fighters were positioned, Victim #1 was overheard giving instructions on searching techniques to Victim #2. After both of the victims performed their search in the living room, they crawled down the hallway to the burn room, followed by one of the interior safety fire fighters from the living room. *Note: Conditions in the structure at this time were heavy smoke with very little visibility.*

As both victims were conducting their search, one of the victims collided with one of the interior safety fire fighters in the hallway outside the burn room. The interior safety fire fighter in the hallway identified himself to the victims as one of the interior safety personnel and instructed them to continue their search. The interior safety fire fghter that had followed both of the victims from the living room into the hallway told one of the other interior safety fire fighters in the hallway outside the burn room that he was going to look for the crew with the first attack line. Victim #1 was overheard in the burn room asking Victim #2 if the entire room had been searched and receiving an affirmative response.

As the interior safety fire fighter went back down the hallway to look for the first attack line crew, he encountered them entering the hallway, and he told them to put some water on the fire. He then headed back toward the burn room followed by the crew

from Attack Line #1. Once he reached the section of hallway outside the burn room, he asked one of the interior safety fire fighters in that area for the location of both victims. Receiving a reply that they were out, he then asked a second time if both victims were out of the burn room and received an affirmative response. He left to search for both the victims in the bedrooms on the B-Side and the kitchen on the C-Side.

At approximately 1013 hours, the IC radioed Attack Line #1 that the window in the burn room was going to be vented, and the exterior ventilation person broke out the window. When the window (56 inches in height by 42 ½ inches in width and made of 1/4-inch-thick plate glass) was vented, it emitted very heavy black smoke followed a few seconds later by intense flames. According to the Office of the State Fire Marshal, and the fire analysis performed by NIST, a flashover[c] is believed to have occurred in the burn room after the window was broken. *Note: According to NIST, the fire analysis of the incident indicates that the gases were so fuel rich in the burn room that it took the fire seconds to mix with the oxygen and flashover.* Attack Line #1, positioned at the doorway of the burn room, began applying water in short-flow increments into the room. At approximately 1014 hours, the IC ordered the crew of Attack Line #2 to enter the structure with the second 1 3/4-inch hoseline. He then attempted to make radio contact with the victims. At approximately 1015 hours, Attack Line #1 radioed the IC that water was being applied to the fire. One of the interior safety fire fighters that was positioned in the hallway outside the burn room began to feel like he was getting steamed as a result of the water being applied to the fire. As he crawled down the hallway, he told the Ignition Officer/Interior safety in

---

[c] A flashover is defined by the International Fire Service Training Association (IFSTA) as a stage of fire at which all surfaces and objects within a space have been heated to their ignition temperature, and flame breaks out almost at once over the surface of all objects in the space.

Page 4

Career Lieutenant and Fire Fighter Die in a Flashover During a Live-Fire Training Evolution - Florida

that area that he needed to leave. When he entered the living room, visibility improved, and he was able to stand and walk out of the structure. As he exited on the A-Side, he told the IC that he had gotten hot and steamed. At approximately 1016 hours, the IC radioed the crews inside and told them to let him know if the roof needed to be vented. Meanwhile, the exterior ventilation person went to remove a gable vent on the D-Side.

After completing his search for both victims in the bedrooms on the B-side and kitchen on the C-Side, the interior safety fire fighter discovered the simulated rescue mannequin in the kitchen. Realizing that the victims had not performed a search in that area, he left the structure and asked the IC if the victims had come out. Receiving a negative response, he reentered the structure to perform another search for both victims. At approximately 1017 hours, the IC radioed the victims to report in for accountability, with no response. At approximately 1018 hours, the IC attempted to contact the victims again on the radio.

Returning from ventilating the gable on the D-Side, the exterior ventilation fire fighter looked into the burn room window and saw a white helmet lying on the floor. The conditions in the burn room were reported as heavy fire and smoke. He reached into the window and retrieved the helmet, which was within arm's reach, and gave it to the IC. *Note: The white helmet caused some confusion because all the participants were wearing yellow helmets. The helmet was yellow, but exposure to the heat had turned it white.* After experiencing a lot of heat and getting steamed, the Ignition Officer/Interior Safety assigned to the hallway outside the burn room exited the structure. He informed the IC of the intense heat, told the IC that he did not know the location of the victims, and advised that a personnel accountability report (PAR) needed to be done.

At approximately 1019 hours, the IC called on the radio to ask who was missing a helmet. An interior safety fire fighter assigned to the living room radioed a request to the IC for D-Side to be ventilated. The IC directed ventilation to be performed by the exterior ventilation fire fighter, who interpreted the request as C-Side and ventilated that side. The IC radioed a request for status reports from Attack Lines #1 and #2 and the victims. At approximately 1020 hours, Attack Line #2 entered the burn room and radioed that they were applying water on the fire. The IC called by radio for a PAR and sent in the RIT to search for both victims. The RIT entered the structure with the third 1 3/4-inch hoseline and went to the hallway outside the burn room. At approximately 1021 hours, the IC received a PAR from Attack Lines #1 and #2, but he did not receive any response from the victims. Attack Line #2 radioed the IC that they had knocked down the fire in the burn room and that they did not find any fire extension in the ceiling. The IC radioed Attack Line #2 to ask if they had seen the victims, and they said no. In the hallway the RIT met some fire fighters who informed them that the fire was under control and that the burn room was clear. The number of fire fighters in the hallway made it difficult to move, so one of the RIT members went to the bedrooms on the B-Side and the kitchen area on the C-Side to search for the victims.

At approximately 1023 hours, the IC radioed orders to evacuate the structure and commanded the air-horn blasts to be sounded. After hearing the evacuation air horns, the Attack Line #2 crew began to leave the burn room when they saw what they thought was the simulated mannequin lying facedown on the floor next to the closet where the fire had been ignited. As they attempted to move the mannequin, they realized that it was actually Victim #1. The Ignition Officer/Interior Safety walked over to the A-Side and climbed through the window into

Career Lieutenant and Fire Fighter Die in a Flashover During a Live-Fire Training Evolution - Florida

the burn room. *Note: Conditions in the burn room were reported as white smoke or steam emitting from the floor area.*

At approximately 1024 hours, a call was radioed from the burn room to report that a fire fighter was down. The Ignition Officer /Interior Safety, a fire fighter from the RIT, and the crew from Attack Line #2 removed Victim #1 through the window in the burn room. The IC radioed a request for two ambulances to respond to the scene. After inquiring about the location of the other victim, one of the interior safety fire fighters reentered to perform a search. After searching the kitchen and bathroom areas (C-Side), he entered the burn room and shone his flashlight around the room. Observing a helmet lying in the middle of the floor, he went to it and discovered Victim #2 lying on the floor next to the window on A-Side. To get the attention of fire fighters outside, he threw his helmet out the window. Fire fighters outside the structure helped remove Victim #2 through the window. At approximately 1027 hours, the IC radioed to dispatch that they had one fire fighter with burns and another fire fighter being removed from the building. Both of the victims were transported via ambulances to a local hospital where they were pronounced dead.

CAUSE OF DEATH

The death certificates listed the cause of death for both victims as smoke inhalation and thermal injuries.

RECOMMENDATIONS/DISCUSSION

Recommendation #1: Fire departments should ensure that the fuels used in live-fire training have known burning characteristics.[1]

Discussion: Fuels for training fires should have known burning characteristics, and the quantities used should be the minimum necessary that are controllable and able to create the desired fire conditions. The NFPA

notes that fuel materials shall be used only in the amounts necessary to create the desired fire size. Pressure-treated wood, rubber, plastic, and straw or hay treated with pesticides or harmful chemicals should not be used. According to the NFPA, the fuel load shall be limited to avoid conditions that could cause an uncontrolled flashover or backdraft. According to NIST, the fire analysis of the incident indicates that the carpet, the foam padding, the hollow core wood doors and the mattress added to the fuel load and the speed of the fire development. The structure should be inspected to identify and remove materials that could contribute to rapidly spreading fires and create an environmental or health hazard.

Recommendation #2: Fire departments should ensure that ventilation is closely coordinated with interior operations.[2-5]

Discussion: Chapter 10 of *Essentials of Fire Fighting*, 4th edition, states that "ventilation must be closely coordinated with fire attack." Fire can quickly spread in a structure, causing problems such as flashover, a backdraft, or an explosion. Ventilation timing is extremely important and must be carefully coordinated between interior operating crews and ventilation crews. Ventilation is necessary to improve a fire environment so that fire fighters can perform such duties as search and rescue and approach a fire with a hoseline for extinguishment. Incident command should determine if ventilation is needed and where ventilation is needed. The type of ventilation should be determined, based on evaluation of the structure and the location of any interior crews. Proper venting of heat, smoke, and combustible gas/air mixtures from buildings can reduce the possibility of dangerous situations that confront fire fighters.

Recommendation #3: Fire departments should ensure that fires are not located in designated exit paths.[1]

Career Lieutenant and Fire Fighter Die in a Flashover During a Live-Fire Training Evolution - Florida

Discussion: During a training exercise, every effort must be made to ensure the exit paths are free from obstructions. To provide a protected area of travel, fires should not be located in the vicinity of exit paths. Once the closet area in the burn room was ignited, the fire continued to increase in size, which produced fire, heat and smoke in the exit path of the only doorway in the room.

Recommendation #4: Fire departments should ensure that a method of fireground communication is established to enable coordination among the Incident Commander and fire fighters.[1]

Discussion: The NFPA Standard 1403, 2-4.9, notes that communication shall be established between the Incident Commander and fire fighters performing any interior operations, sector leaders, and the safety officer. Proper communication is a must at any incident site. Portable radios should be used to keep all personnel on the scene in communication with the Incident Commander. The use of a portable radio that is located in a radio coat or pants pocket impairs the performance of the unit. Portable radios should be held or used with a microphone and speaker attached to the lapel of the coat, which allows the fire fighter to monitor and transmit a clear message. In this incident, Victim #1 had a portable radio; however, it was kept in the pocket of his bunker coat. Victim #2 did not have a portable radio. During the NIOSH interviews, several of the interior safety fire fighters acknowledged that they were unable to hear their radios during the incident because their radios were in their pants or bunker coat pockets.

Recommendation #5: Fire departments should ensure that Standard Operating Guidelines (SOGs) specific to live-fire training are developed and followed.[6]

Discussion: Standard operating guidelines (SOGs) should be developed specifically for training fires and include areas such as facility inspection, fuel materials, RIT operations, SCBA, water supply, and hoseline operations. These SOGs will then form the foundation as to how the training will be conducted. The SOG should be in written form and be included in the overall risk-management plan for the fire department. If these procedures are changed, appropriate training should be provided to all affected members.

Recommendation #6: Fire departments should consider using a thermal imaging camera during live-fire training situations.[7-9]

Discussion: Thermal imaging cameras may assist fire fighters by allowing them to see through blinding smoke and in zero visibility conditions. With the help of a thermal imaging camera, training instructors, interior safety officers, and fire fighters may observe and critique participants, ensuring that they develop good foundational skills in areas including accountability, conducting effective search patterns, and handling a hose. A thermal imaging camera may be an excellent tool to enhance training.

Advances in technology allow a thermal imaging camera to be equipped with a wireless video transmitter to provide an instructor, Incident Commander, or other training participants who are outside the structure with the opportunity to observe training activities. Thermal imaging technology allows the instructor and interior safety officers to monitor heat and fire conditions inside the structure, which could help to keep the participants safe. Of course, fire departments must always remember that thermal imaging cameras have limitations and that technology does not replace or alter basic safety procedures and fire-fighting tactics.

Page 7

Career Lieutenant and Fire Fighter Die in a Flashover During a Live-Fire Training Evolution - Florida

Additionally, States should consider the following:

Recommendation #7: Develop a permitting procedure for live-fire training to be conducted at acquired structures. States should ensure that all the requirements of NFPA 1403 have been met before issuing the permit.[1,10]

Discussion: NFPA 1403, *Standard on Live Fire Training Evolutions*, is the guideline for conducting live-fire training evolutions at approved training centers, and in this case, acquired structures. Approved training centers have burn buildings that are specifically designed for repeated live-fire training evolutions. The structures that are acquired for live-fire training are usually in disrepair and were never designed for live-fire training. Any building that is acquired for live-fire training must go through an inspection process to identify and eliminate any hazards or potential hazards that may be present to the participants, the public, and the environment. An application for permit procedure that is overseen by the State through local officials or a State fire marshal would help ensure safety. If training facilities with approved burn buildings are available, then live-fire training exercises should not be conducted in acquired structures.

REFERENCES

1. NFPA [2002]. NFPA 1403, standard on live fire training evolutions. Quincy, MA: National Fire Protection Association.

2. Dunn V [1988]. Collapse of burning buildings, a guide to fireground safety. Saddle Brook, NJ: Fire Engineering Books and Videos.

3. Brunacini, A V [1985]. Fire command. Quincy, MA: National Fire Protection Association.

4. Dunn V [1992]. Safety and survival on the fireground. Saddle Brook, NJ: Fire Engineering Books and Videos.

5. International Fire Service Training Association [1995]. Essentials of fire fighting. 4th ed. Stillwater, OK: Oklahoma State University, Fire Protection Publications.

6. NFPA [1997]. NFPA 1500: standard on fire department occupational safety and health program. Quincy, MA: National Fire Protection Association.

7. FEMA/USFA [2001]. Report on the assistance to firefighters grant program for year 2001. Federal Emergency Management Agency/United States Fire Administration, October 9, 2001.

8. FEMA/USFA [2002]. Assistance to firefighters grant program applicant workshop materials, Federal Emergency Management Agency/United States Fire Administration, January 15, 2002.

9. Richardson M [2001].Thermal triage. Fire Chief Magazine, September 2001.

10. Carter H [2000]. Why did he have to die? Firehouse.com, May 26, 2000, http://server.firehouse.com/carter/2000/052600.html.

INVESTIGATOR INFORMATION
This incident was investigated by Nancy T. Romano, Jay Tarley, and Stephen Berardinelli Jr., Safety and Occupational Health Specialists, NIOSH, Division of Safety Research, Surveillance and Field Investigation Branch.

Page 8

*Career Lieutenant and Fire Fighter Die in a Flashover During a Live-Fire Training
Evolution - Florida*

Photo 1. Front of structure used for live-fire training

Career Lieutenant and Fire Fighter Die in a Flashover During a Live-Fire Training Evolution - Florida

Photo 2. Burn room in the structure

Career Lieutenant and Fire Fighter Die in a Flashover During a Live-Fire Training Evolution - Florida

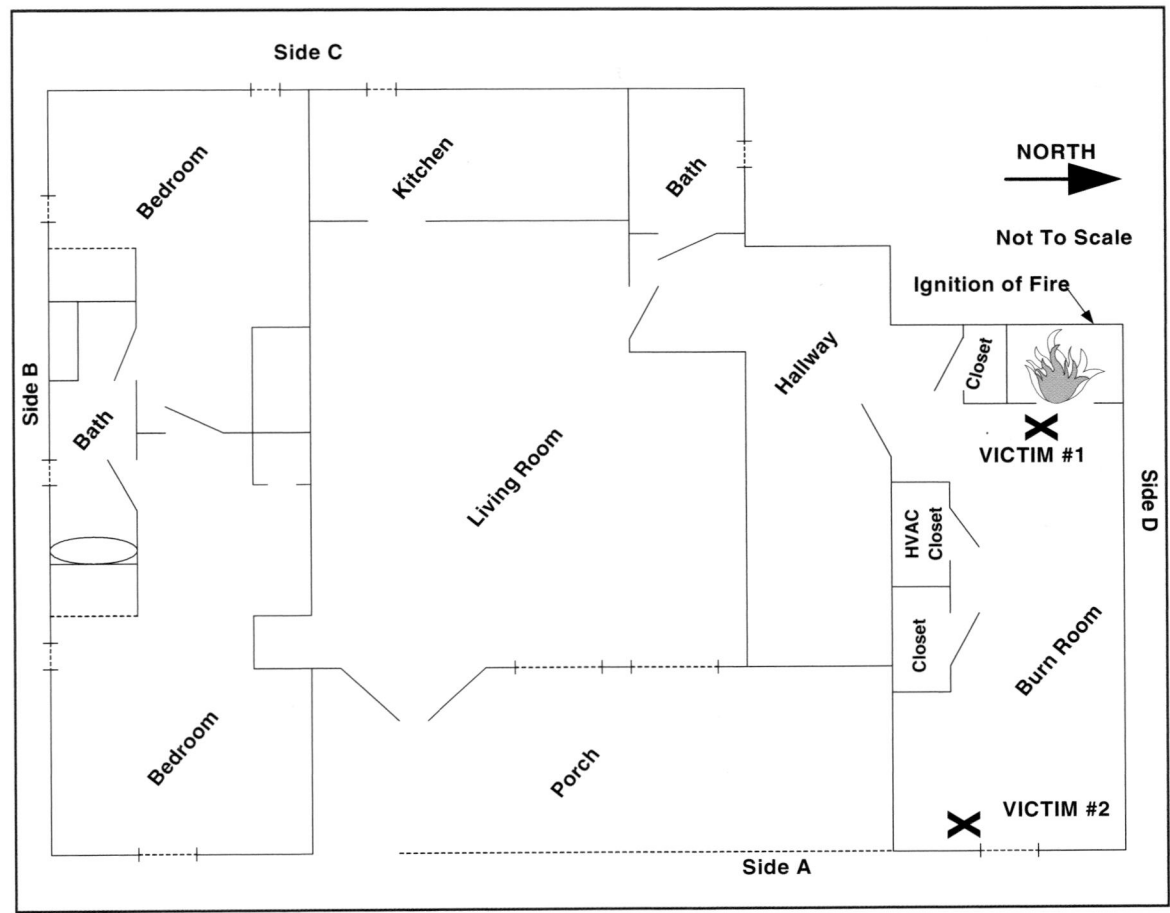

Figure 1. Floor plan; overhead view of structure

U. S. Department of Health and Human Services
Public Health Service
Centers for Disease Control and Prevention
National Institute for Occupational Safety and Health
4676 Columbia Parkway, MS C-13
Cincinnati, OH 45226-1998

OFFICIAL BUSINESS
Penalty for private use $300

**Delivering on the Nation's promise:
Safety and health at work for all people
through research and prevention**

Appendix F
Risk-Management Formulas

The following formulas may be used to calculate the frequency or incident rate and the severity of incidents.

The Occupational Safety and Health Administration (OSHA) calculates the frequency (incident rate) as follows:

$$N/EH \times 200{,}000 = IR$$

Where:

$\quad$ N $\;=\;$ number of injuries and/or illnesses

$\quad$ EH $\;=\;$ total hours worked by all employees during the calendar year

$\quad$ 200,000 $\;=\;$ base for 100 full-time equivalent employees (provides *standardization between agencies and companies*)

$\quad$ IR $\;=\;$ incident rate

OSHA calculates the severity as follows:

$$LWD/EH \times 200{,}000 = S$$

Where:

$\quad$ LWD $\;=\;$ loss work days

$\quad$ EH $\;=\;$ total hours worked by all employees during the calendar year

$\quad$ 200,000 $\;=\;$ base for 100 full-time equivalent employees

$\quad$ S $\;=\;$ severity rate

Another method is to assign values to the frequency and severity in the following formula:

$$R = S \times IR$$

Where:

$\quad$ R $\;=\;$ risk

$\quad$ S $\;=\;$ severity

$\quad$ IR $\;=\;$ incident rate

Assessment of Severity

8.	Extreme	Multiple deaths or widespread destruction may result from hazard.
7.	Very High	Potential death or injury or severe financial loss may result.
6.	High	Permanent disabling injury may result.
5.	Serious	Loss time injury greater than 28 days or considerable financial loss.
4.	Moderate	Loss time injury of 4 to 28 days or moderate financial loss.
3.	Minor	Loss time injury up to 3 days.
2.	Slight	Minor injury resulting in no loss of time or slight financial loss.
1.	Minimal	No loss of time injury or financial loss to organization.

Assessment of Incident Rate

7.	Frequent	Occurs weekly.
6.	Very Likely	Occurs once every few months.
5.	Likely	Occurs about once a year.
4.	Occasional	Occurs annually in the United States.
3.	Rare	Occurs every 10 to 30 years.
2.	Exceptional	Occurs every 10 to 30 years in the United States.
1.	Unlikely	May occur once in 10,000 years within the global fire service.

Appendix G
Incident Command System Forms

The following NIMS-ICS forms are available from numerous Internet sites in PDF format. Although there are approximately 26 forms available to assist in the establishment of an incident command, this appendix contains only 9 forms that may be the most useful to instructors. The forms are public domain and may be copied or accessed from other sources on the Internet. The forms contained here are as follows:

ICS-201	Incident Briefing
ICS-202	Incident Objectives
ICS-203	Organization Assignment List
ICS-204	Assignment List
ICS-205	Incident Radio Communications Plan
ICS-206	Medical Plan
ICS-208HM	Site Safety and Control Plan (Hazardous Materials Specific)
ICS-209	Incident Status Summary
ICS-215G	Operational Planning Worksheet (Generic)

INCIDENT BRIEFING	1. INCIDENT NAME	2. DATE PREPARED	3. TIME PREPARED

4. MAP SKETCH

ICS 201 5-94	PAGE 1	8. PREPARED BY (NAME AND POSITION)

7. SUMMARY OF CURRENT OBJECTIVES AND ACTIONS

CURRENT OBJECTIVES:

CURRENT ACTIONS:

ICS 201 **5-94**	PAGE 2	

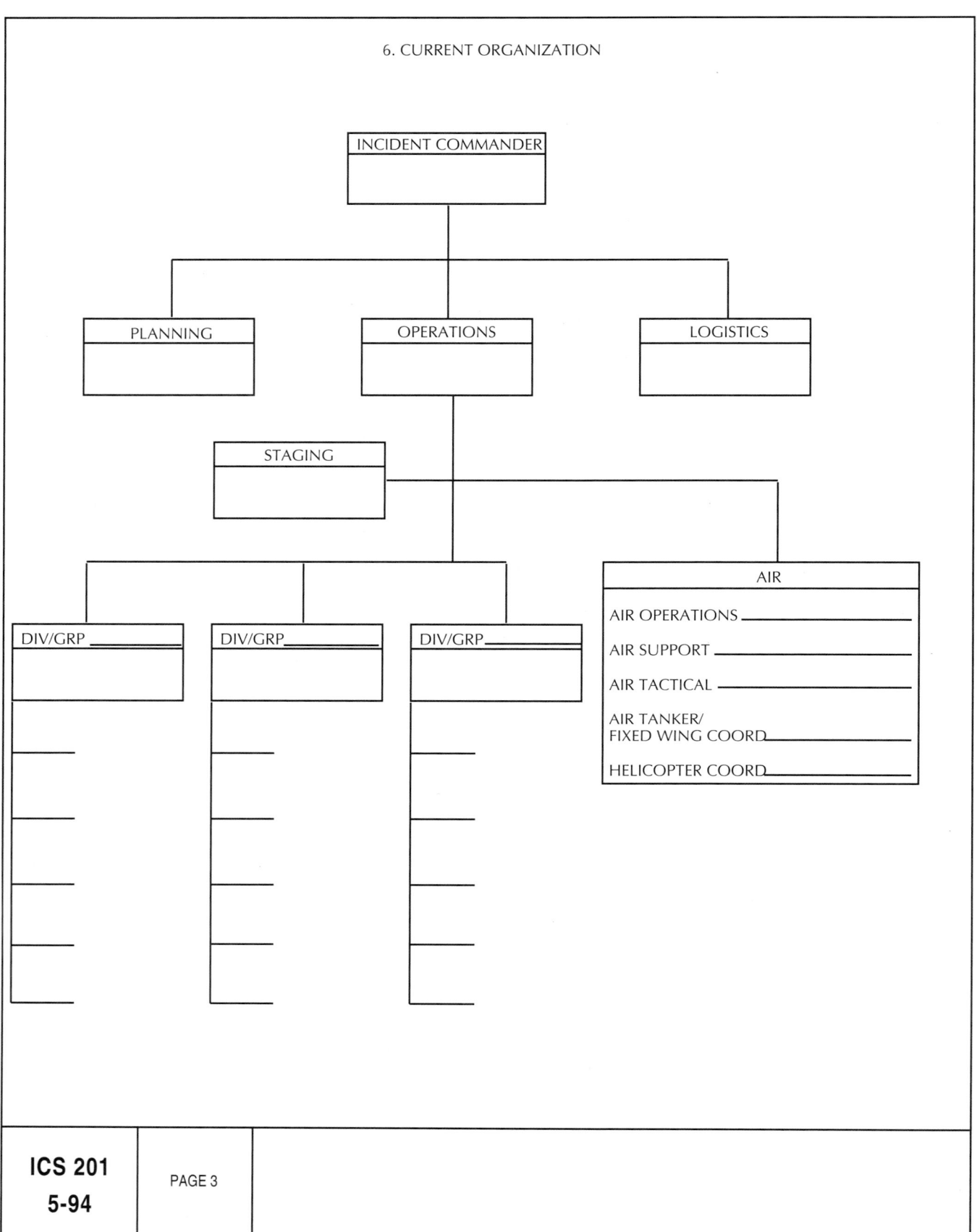

6. CURRENT ORGANIZATION

INCIDENT COMMANDER

PLANNING

OPERATIONS

LOGISTICS

STAGING

DIV/GRP

DIV/GRP

DIV/GRP

AIR

AIR OPERATIONS

AIR SUPPORT

AIR TACTICAL

AIR TANKER/
FIXED WING COORD.

HELICOPTER COORD.

ICS 201
5-94

PAGE 3

5. RESOURCES SUMMARY				
RESOURCES ORDERED	RESOURCE IDENTIFICATION	ETA	ON SCENE ✓	LOCATION/ASSIGNMENT

ICS 201

5-94

PAGE 4

INCIDENT OBJECTIVES	1. INCIDENT NAME	2. DATE PREPARED	3. TIME PREPARED

4. OPERATIONAL PERIOD (Date/Time)

5. GENERAL CONTROL OBJECTIVES FOR THE INCIDENT (Include Alternatives)

6. WEATHER FORECAST FOR OPERATIONAL PERIOD

7. GENERAL/SAFETY MESSAGE

8. ATTACHMENTS (✔ IF ATTACHED)

☐ ORGANIZATION LIST (ICS 203) ☐ MEDICAL PLAN (ICS 206) ☐ _____

☐ DIVISION ASSIGNMENT LISTS (ICS 204) ☐ INCIDENT MAP ☐ _____

☐ COMMUNICATIONS PLAN (ICS 205) ☐ TRAFFIC PLAN ☐ _____

ICS 202 **3-80**	9. PREPARED BY (Planning Section Chief)	10. APPROVED BY (Incident Commander)

11-9-I300-VG

ORGANIZATION **ASSIGNMENT LIST**	**ICS 203**	1. INCIDENT NAME	2. DATE PREPARED	3. TIME PREPARED

POSITION	NAME	4. OPERATIONAL PERIOD (DATE/TIME)

5. INCIDENT COMMANDER AND STAFF

INCIDENT COMMANDER	
DEPUTY	
SAFETY OFFICER	
INFORMATION OFFICER	
LIAISON OFFICER	

6. AGENCY REPRESENTATIVES

AGENCY	NAME

7. PLANNING SECTION

CHIEF	
DEPUTY	
RESOURCES UNIT	
SITUATION UNIT	
DOCUMENTATION UNIT	
DEMOBILIZATION UNIT	
TECHNICAL SPECIALISTS	

8. LOGISTICS SECTION

CHIEF	
DEPUTY	

a. SUPPORT BRANCH

DIRECTOR	
DEPUTY	
SUPPLY UNIT	
FACILITIES UNIT	
GROUND SUPPORT UNIT	

b. SERVICE BRANCH

DIRECTOR	
DEPUTY	
COMMUNICATIONS UNIT	
MEDICAL UNIT	
FOOD UNIT	

9. OPERATIONS SECTION

CHIEF	
DEPUTY	

a. BRANCH I - DIVISIONS/GROUPS

BRANCH DIRECTOR	
DEPUTY	
DIVISION/GROUP	
DIVISION/GROUP	
DIVISION/GROUP	
DIVISION/GROUP	
DIVISION/GROUP	

b. BRANCH II - DIVISIONS/GROUPS

BRANCH DIRECTOR	
DEPUTY	
DIVISION/GROUP	
DIVISION/GROUP	
DIVISION/GROUP	
DIVISION/GROUP	
DIVISION/GROUP	

c. BRANCH III - DIVISIONS/GROUPS

BRANCH DIRECTOR	
DEPUTY	
DIVISION/GROUP	
DIVISION/GROUP	
DIVISION/GROUP	
DIVISION/GROUP	
DIVISION/GROUP	

d. AIR OPERATIONS BRANCH

AIR OPERATIONS BR. DIR.	
DEPUTY	
AIR TACTICAL SUPERVISOR	
AIR SUPPORT SUPERVISOR	
HELICOPTER COORDINATOR	
AIR TANKER/ FIXED WING COORDINATOR	

10. FINANCE/ADMINISTRATION SECTION

CHIEF	
DEPUTY	
TIME UNIT	
PROCUREMENT UNIT	
COMPENSATION/CLAIMS UNIT	
COST UNIT	

PREPARED BY (RESOURCES UNIT)

ICS 203	**5/94**

1. BRANCH	2. DIVISION/GROUP	ASSIGNMENT LIST	ICS 204 (5-94)

3. INCIDENT NAME	4. OPERATIONAL PERIOD
	DATE
	TIME

5. OPERATIONS PERSONNEL

OPERATIONS CHIEF		DIVISION/GROUP SUPERVISOR	
BRANCH DIRECTOR		AIR TACTICAL SUPERVISOR	

6. RESOURCES ASSIGNED THIS PERIOD

RESOURCE DESIGNATOR	LEADER	NUMBER PERSONS	TRANS. NEEDED	DROP OFF PT./TIME	PICK UP PT./TIME

7. CONTROL ASSIGNMENT (S)

8. SPECIAL INSTRUCTIONS/SAFETY MESSAGE

9. DIVISION/GROUP COMMUNICATION SUMMARY

FUNCTION		FREQ.	SYSTEM	CHAN.	FUNCTION		FREQ.	SYSTEM	CHAN.
COMMAND	LOCAL				SUPPORT	LOCAL			
	REPEAT					REPEAT			
DIV/GROUP TACTICAL					GROUND TO AIR				

PREPARED BY (RESOURCE UNIT LEADER)	APPROVED BY (PLANNING SECTION CHIEF)	DATE	TIME

INCIDENT RADIO COMMUNICATIONS PLAN

	1. INCIDENT NAME	2. DATE/TIME PREPARED	3. OPERATIONAL PERIOD DATE/TIME
SYSTEM/CACHE	CHANNEL	FUNCTION	FREQUENCY	ASSIGNMENT	REMARKS

4. PREPARED BY (COMMUNICATIONS UNIT)

ICS 205   2-95

MEDICAL PLAN	1. INCIDENT NAME	2. DATE PREPARED	3. TIME PREPARED	4. OPERATIONAL PERIOD

5. INCIDENT MEDICAL AID STATIONS

MEDICAL AID STATIONS	LOCATION	PARAMEDICS YES	NO

6. TRANSPORTATION

A. AMBULANCE SERVICES

NAME	ADDRESS	PHONE	PARAMEDICS YES	NO

B. INCIDENT AMBULANCES

NAME	LOCATION	PARAMEDICS YES	NO

7. HOSPITALS

NAME	ADDRESS	TRAVEL TIME AIR	GRND	PHONE	HELIPAD YES	NO	BURN CENTER YES	NO

8. MEDICAL EMERGENCY PROCEDURES

ICS 206 5-94	9. PREPARED BY (MEDICAL UNIT LEADER)	10. REVIEWED BY (SAFETY OFFICER)

SITE SAFETY AND CONTROL PLAN ICS 208 HM	1. Incident Name:	2. Date Prepared:	3. Operational Period: Time:

Section I. Site Information

4. Incident Location:

Section II. Organization

5. Incident Commander:	6. HM Group Supervisor:	7. Tech. Specialist - HM Reference:
8. Safety Officer:	9. Entry Leader:	10. Site Access Control Leader:
11. Asst. Safety Officer - HM:	12. Decontamination Leader:	13. Safe Refuge Area Mgr:
14. Environmental Health:	15.	16.

17. Entry Team: (Buddy System) Name:	PPE Level	18. Decontamination Element: Name:	PPE Level
Entry 1		Decon 1	
Entry 2		Decon 2	
Entry 3		Decon 3	
Entry 4		Decon 4	

Section III. Hazard/Risk Analysis

19. Material:	Container type	Qty.	Phys. State	pH	IDLH	F.P.	I.T.	V.P.	V.D.	S.G.	LEL	UEL

Comment:

Section IV. Hazard Monitoring

20. LEL Instrument(s):	21. O_2 Instrument(s):
22. Toxicity/PPM Instrument(s):	23. Radiological Instrument(s):

Comment:

Section V. Decontamination Procedures

24. Standard Decontamination Procedures:	YES:	NO:

Comment:

Section VI. Site Communications

25. Command Frequency:	26. Tactical Frequency:	27. Entry Frequency:

Section VII. Medical Assistance

28. Medical Monitoring:	YES:	NO:	29. Medical Treatment and Transport In-place:	YES:	NO:

Comment:

Section VIII. Site Map	
30. Site Map:	↑

Weather ❑   Command Post ❑   Zones ❑   Assembly Areas ❑   Escape Routes ❑   Other ❑

Section IX. Entry Objectives

31. Entry Objectives:

Section X. SOP S and Safe Work Practices

32. Modifications to Documented SOP s or Work Practices:	YES:	NO:

Comment:

Section XI. Emergency Procedures

33. Emergency Procedures:

Section XII. Safety Briefing

34. Asst. Safety Officer - HM Signature:	Safety Briefing Completed (Time):
35. HM Group Supervisor Signature:	36. Incident Commander Signature:

INSTRUCTIONS FOR COMPLETING THE SITE SAFETY AND CONTROL PLAN
ICS 208 HM

A Site Safety and Control Plan must be completed by the Hazardous Materials Group Supervisor and reviewed by all within the Hazardous Materials Group prior to operations commencing within the Exclusion Zone.

Item Number	Item Title	Instructions
1.	Incident Name/Number	Print name and/or incident number.
2.	Date and Time	Enter date and time prepared.
3.	Operational Period	Enter the time interval for which the form applies.
4.	Incident Location	Enter the address and or map coordinates of the incident.
5 - 16.	Organization	Enter names of all individuals assigned to ICS positions. (Entries 5 & 8 mandatory). Use Boxes 15 and 16 for other functions: i.e. Medical Monitoring.
17 - 18.	Entry Team/Decon Element	Enter names and level of PPE of Entry & Decon personnel. (Entries 1 - 4 mandatory buddy system and back-up.)
19.	Material	Enter names and pertinent information of all known chemical products. Enter UNK if material is not known. Include any which apply to chemical properties. (Definitions: ph = Potential for Hydrogen (Corrosivity), IDLH = Immediately Dangerous to Life and Health, F.P. = Flash Point, I.T. = Ignition Temperature, V.P. = Vapor Pressure, V.D. = Vapor Density, S.G. = Specific Gravity, LEL = Lower Explosive Limit, UEL = Upper Explosive Limit)
20 - 23.	Hazard Monitoring	List the instruments which will be used to monitor for chemical.
24.	Decontamination Procedures	Check NO if modifications are made to standard decontamination procedures and make appropriate Comments including type of solutions.
25 - 27.	Site Communications	Enter the radio frequency(ies) which apply.
28 - 29.	Medical Assistance	Enter comments if NO is checked.
30.	Site Map	Sketch or attach a site map which defines all locations and layouts of operational zones. (Check boxes are mandatory to be identified.)
31.	Entry Objectives	List all objectives to be performed by the Entry Team in the Exclusion Zone and any parameters which will alter or stop entry operations.
32 - 33.	SOP s, Safe Work Practices, and Emergency Procedures	List in Comments if any modifications to SOP s and any emergency procedures which will be affected if an emergency occurs while personnel are within the Exclusion Zone.
34 - 36.	Safety Briefing	Have the appropriate individual place their signature in the box once the Site Safety and Control Plan is reviewed. Note the time in box 34 when the safety briefing has been completed.

INCIDENT STATUS SUMMARY
FS-5100-11

1. Date/Time	2. Initial ☐ Update ☐ Final ☐	3. Incident Name	4. Incident Number

5. Incident Commander	6. Jurisdiction	7. County	8. Type Incident	9. Location	10. Started Date/Time

11. Cause	12. Area Involved	13. % Controlled	14. Expected Containment Date/Time	15. Estimated Controlled Date/Time	16. Declared Controlled Date/Time

17. Current Threat	18. Control Problems

19. Est. Loss	20. Est Savings	21. Injuries Deaths	22. Line Built	23. Line to Build

24. Current Weather WS Temp WD RH	25. Predicted Weather WS Temp WD RH	26. Cost to Date	27. Est. Total Cost

28. Agencies

29. Resources Kind of Resource	SR	ST	SR	ST	SR	ST	SR	ST	SR	ST	SR	ST	SR	ST	SR	ST	SR	ST	SR	ST	SR	ST	TOTALS SR	ST
ENGINES																								
DOZERS																								
CREWS Number of Crews:																								
Number of Crew Personnel:																								
HELICOPTERS																								
AIR TANKERS																								
TRUCK COS.																								
RESCUE/MED.																								
WATER TENDERS																								
OVERHEAD PERSONNL																								
TOTAL PERSONNEL																								

30. Cooperating Agencies

31. Remarks

32. Prepared by	33. Approved by	34. Sent to: Date Time By

ICS 209   NFES 1333

General Instructions

Completion of the Incident Status Summary will be as specified by Agency or municipality. Report by telephone, teletype, computer, or facsimile to the local Agency or municipality headquarters by 2100 hours daily on incidents as required by Agency or municipality (reports are normally required on life threatening situations, real property threatened or destroyed, high resource damage potential, and complex incidents that could have political ramifications). Normally, wildland agencies require a report on all Class D (100 acres plus) and larger incidents (unless primarily grass type in which case report Class E (300 acres or larger). The first summary will cover the period from the start of the incident to 2100 hour the first day of the incident, if at least four hours have elapsed; thereafter the summary will cover the 24 hour period ending at 1900 (this reporting time will enable compilation of reporting data and submission of report to local agency or municipality headquarters by 2100 hours) daily until incident is under control. Wildland fire agencies will send the summary to NIFC by 2400 hours Mountain Time.

1. Enter date and time report completed (mandatory).
2. Check appropriate space (mandatory).
3. Provide name given to incident by Incident Commander or Agency (mandatory).
4. Enter number assigned to incident by Agency (mandatory).
5. Enter first initial and last name of Incident Commander (optional).
6. Enter Agency or Municipality (mandatory).
7. Enter County where incident is occurring (optional).
8. Enter type of incident, e.g. wildland fire (enter fuel type), structure fire, hazardous chemical spill, etc. (mandatory).
9. Enter legal description and general location. Use remarks for additional date if necessary (mandatory).
10. Enter date and zulu time incident started (mandatory - maximum of six characters for date and four characters for time).
11. Enter specific cause or under investigation (mandatory).
12. Enter area involved, e.g. 50 acres, top three floors of building, etc. (mandatory).
13. Enter estimate of percent of containment (mandatory).
14. Enter estimate of date and time of total containment (mandatory).
15. Enter estimated date and time of control (mandatory).
16. Enter actual date and time fire was declared controlled (mandatory).
17. Report significant threat to structures, watershed, timber, wildlife habitat or other valuable resources (mandatory).
18. Enter control problems, e.g. accessibility, fuels, rocky terrain, high winds, structures (mandatory).
19. Enter estimated dollar value of total damage to date. Include structures, watershed, timber, etc. Be specific in remarks (mandatory).
20. Enter estimate of values saved as result of all suppression efforts (optional).
21. Enter any serious injuries or deaths which have occurred since the last report. Be specific in remarks (mandatory).
22. Indicate the extent of line completed by chains or other units of measurement (optional).
23. Indicate line to be consturcted by chains or other units of measurement (optional).
24. Indicate current weather conditions at the incident (mandatory).
25. Indicate predicted weather conditions for the next operational period (mandatory).
26. Provide total incident cost ot date (optional).
27. Provide estimated total cost for entire incident (optional).
28. List agencies which have resources assigned to the incident (mandatory).
29. Enter resource information under appropriate Agency column by singe resource or stike team (mandatory).
30. List by name those agencies which are providing support (e.g. Salvation Army, Red Cross, Law Enforcement, National Weather Service, etc. mandatory).
31. The Remarks space can be used to (1) list additional resources not covered in Section 28/29; (2) provide more information on location; (3) enter additional information regarding threat control problems, anticipated release or demobilization, etc.(mandatory).
32. This will normally be the Incident Situation Status Unit Leader (mandatory).
33. This will normally be the Incident Planning Section Chief (mandatory).
34. The ID of the Agency entering the report will be entered (optional).

ICS 209

NFES 1333

OPERATIONAL PLANNING WORKSHEET (Generic)

1. Incident Name

2. Date Prepared / Time Prepared

3. Operational Period (Date/Time)

4. Division/ Group/ Staging or Other Location	5. Work Assignments	6. Resources By Type (Show Strike Teams as ST)		7. Overhead	8. Special Equipment	9. Supplies	10. Reporting Location	11. Requested Arrival Time
		Req.						
		Have						
		Need						
		Req.						
		Have						
		Need						
		Req.						
		Have						
		Need						
		Req.						
		Have						
		Need						
		Req.						
		Have						
		Need						
		Req.						
		Have						
		Need						
		Req.						
		Have						
		Need						
		Req.						
		Have						
		Need						
		Req.						
		Have						
		Need						
		Req.						
		Have						
		Need						

12.
Total Resources Required — Single Resources / Strike Teams
Total Resources on Hand — Single Resources / Strike Teams
Total Resources Needed — Single Resources / Strike Teams

13. Prepared by (Name and Position)

2-98

ICS 215-G

Appendix H
OSHA State-Plan States and Non-State-Plan States

State-Plan States	Non-State-Plan States
Alaska	Alabama
Arizona	Arkansas
California	Colorado
Connecticut (state and local government employees only)	Delaware
	District of Columbia
Hawaii	Florida
Indiana	Georgia
Iowa	Guam
Kentucky	Idaho
Maryland	Illinois
Michigan	Kansas
Minnesota	Louisiana
Nevada	Maine
New Mexico	Massachusetts
New York (state and local government employees only)	Mississippi
	Missouri
North Carolina	Montana
Oregon	Nebraska
Puerto Rico	New Hampshire
South Carolina	New Jersey
Tennessee	North Dakota
Utah	Ohio
Vermont	Oklahoma
Virginia	Pennsylvania
Virgin Islands	Rhode Island
Washington	South Dakota
Wyoming	Texas
	West Virginia
	Wisconsin

Training Organization Code of Ethics

This sample code of ethics is based on a variety of sources including existing codes for fire service organizations and educational institutions. The following code outlines the activities of a training organization or agency.

Code of Ethics

The purpose of the _____ Fire and Emergency Services Training (Organization/Division/Agency) is to prepare personnel through training and education for a safe and successful career in the fire and emergency services and as a member of the _____ Department/Division/Agency. This goal shall be promoted and emphasized by every instructor, administrator, and staff member according to the ethical principles consistent with professional conduct by:

- Promoting the highest standards of personal integrity.

- Being honest, respectful, and straightforward in dealing with students, peers, supervisors, and citizens.

- Avoiding any conflict of interest that may bring disgrace upon the division/ department/agency or the individual.

- Placing the public's and the employees' safety and welfare above all other concerns.

- Providing training and education to promote safety in the occupational conduct and habits of members of this organization/division/agency and other emergency services providers whose training is entrusted to this organization/division/ agency.

- Ensuring the training and education offered by our instructors is delivered fairly and equitably to all.

- Respecting the needs of peers and subordinates to assist them in the development of their abilities, skills, and talents to achieve their full potential.

- Offering encouragement to those individuals who are striving to improve themselves, the organization/division/agency, and the fire and emergency services.

- Fostering creativity and being open to innovations that improve the performance of the members' to assist them in meeting their responsibilities and fulfilling their duties.

Appendix J
Structural Live-Fire Training Forms

Fire and emergency services use NFPA 1403 *Standard on Live Fire Training Evolutions* (2002) as a guideline in developing policies that establish procedures for conducting all live-fire training evolutions. Included in this appendix are several examples from the Gainesville (Florida) Fire Rescue Department (sample notification letter to area residents and agreement form) and the Virginia Department of Fire Programs (evolution checklist). These emergency services organizations have compiled a number of forms that are useful in planning and conducting live-fire training evolutions. These sample forms might be adapted for local or can serve also as a guideline to help develop new forms.

Sample forms include the following:

- Notification Letter to Area Residents
- Agreement to Destroy Structure and Release
- Live-Fire Evaluation Checklist
- Live-Burn Accountability Form

Forms courtesy of Gainesville (FL) Fire Rescue Department and Virginia Department of Fire Programs.

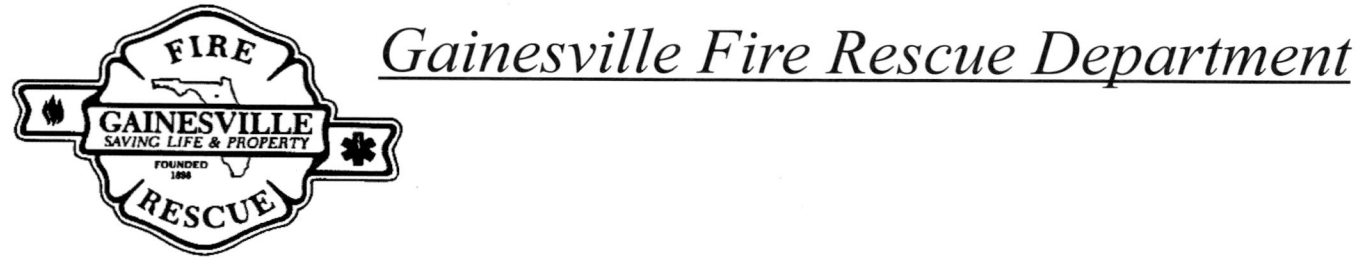

IMPORTANT NOTICE

The City of Gainesville Fire Rescue Department has a training program designed to help our firefighters maintain their skills as well as train on new equipment and fire fighting techniques. In order to do this we routinely burn vacant houses to simulate true working conditions. Since this is a common practice around the country the National Fire Protection Association (NFPA) has developed a standard for Fire Department Training Burns, NFPA 1403. This standard is designed to maintain a safe training environment and is strictly adhered to by the City of Gainesville Fire Rescue Department.

You may see a number of fire department apparatus in your neighborhood. There is nothing to be concerned about as we are running training evolutions.

Due to the smoke generated by a burning house, we request that you keep your windows and doors closed on the following date(s):

We anticipate completion by the end of the day.

We also request that you avoid parking on the street so that fire apparatus can have easy access to the building.

Sincerely,

Gainesville Fire Rescue Training Bureau

Updated 11/25/98

PO Box 490 • Gainesville, Florida 32601-0490 • 352.334.5078 • Fax: 352.334.2529

Gainesville Fire Rescue Department

AGREEMENT TO DESTROY STRUCTURE
AND RELEASE

THIS AGREEMENT entered into this _____ day of _____, 19__, by and between the City of Gainesville, hereinafter called the "City," and _____ called "Owners."

W I T N E S S E T H:

WHEREAS, Owners are the owners of certain property located within the City of Gainesville, which property contains a structure the Owners wish to have destroyed, and

WHEREAS, the City of Gainesville Fire Rescue Department is willing to destroy the structure as part of a training exercise for its employees.

NOW, THEREFORE, in consideration of the mutual premises and agreements herein contained and other good and valuable consideration, the parties do hereby mutually agree as follows:

1. The City of Gainesville Fire Rescue Department agrees to destroy the structure located on the property owned by the Owners, the property and structure being more particularly described as follows:

2. The Owners agree to allow the structure to be destroyed in the course of a training exercise conducted by the City of Gainesville Fire Rescue Department.

3. The Owners hereby warranty that they are in fact the sole owners of the structure and/or property described herein and, by affixation of the signatures hereunder, attest to the fact. The Owners further certify that there are no outstanding or unsatisfied mortgages, liens, claims or any other type of encumbrances on or against the above described property or structure.

4. The Owners further certify that no claim for loss under any insurance policy will be made because of damage, or because of destruction of the structure, as a result of the Fire Rescue Department's training activities at said structure. The Owners further certify that as of _____ _____, 19__, there is no effective insurance policy covering the structure described in paragraph one (1) under which the activities described herein by the City would constitute a claim.

Page 1 of 3

5.	Upon completion of said destruction, the Owners agree to remove any and all debris remaining on the property. The Owners hereby acknowledge that the City's activities in razing, demolishing, and destroying the structure described in paragraph one (1) will, except as described in paragraph six (6), result in the structure being wrecked and reduced to ruin. What remains of the structure will be worthless rubble and debris, which could constitute a danger to persons entering the premises and should be expeditiously removed by the Owners.

6.	If for any reason whatsoever the City of Gainesville Fire Rescue Department finds or determines that it cannot begin or complete the destruction of said structure, the Owners, upon notification of the Fire Rescue Department's inability or unwillingness to destroy or complete destruction of said structure, agree to expeditiously complete the destruction and debris removal of said structure or otherwise restore the property to such condition as to meet the minimum building and/or housing codes in effect within the government having jurisdiction.

7.	The Owners understand and acknowledge their continuing control over, and liability for, damages occurring on or about the property described in Paragraph one (1) above; except during the actual training exercise authorized herein. It is specifically understood that the City's liability during the training exercise does not include the settling of ash on surrounding property. The training exercise shall be conducted between _____ and _____ _____. When the training is concluded, control over, and sole liability for damages occurring on or about the premises shall automatically revert to the Owners, unless notification to the contrary is made by the City.

8.	The Owners agree to indemnify and save harmless the City of Gainesville, the City of Gainesville Fire Rescue Department, its officers, agents and employees from and against any and all claims, suits, actions, damages or causes of action arising out of the destruction of the structure described herein or the fact that any representation made herein was false when made, for any personal injury, loss of life, or damage to property sustained in or about the owned property by reason of the destruction of the structure located thereon except those injuries, losses or damages solely attributable to the gross negligence of the City, its agents and employees, and for and against any orders, judgments or decrees which may be entered thereon and from and against all costs, attorney's fees, expenses and liabilities incurred in or about the defense of such claims and investigation thereof.

9.	Nothing contained in this contract shall be interpreted as a waiver of the City's sovereign immunity granted under Section 768.28, Florida Status

Page 2 of 3

PO Box 490 • Gainesville, Florida 32601-0490 • 352.334.5078 • Fax: 352.334.2529

IN WITNESS WHEREOF, we the undersigned have set our hands and seals first   written above.

CITY OF GAINESVILLE, FLORIDA

By_____

City Manager

Approved as to form and legality:

By_____

City Attorney

WITNESSES: OWNERS:

_____   _____

_____   _____

SWORN TO AND SUBSCRIBED before me this _____day of _____, 19__.

_____

Notary Public

My Commission Expires:

_____

Updated 08/24/98

Page 3 of 3

PO Box 490 • Gainesville, Florida 32601-0490 • 352.334.5078 • Fax: 352.334.2529

PERMITS/DOCUMENTS/INSURANCE

[ ] Permission to burn building
[ ] Proof of Clear Title
[ ] Certificate of Insurance Cancellation
[ ] Acknowledgement of post-burn property condition
[ ] Local Burn Permit received
[ ] Permission obtained to use local water source(s)
[ ] Notification to appropriate emergency service dispatch office of date, time, and location of live fire training
[ ] Notification to all affected agencies/departments (Police, Fire, Sheriff, VDOT, Forestry, DEQ)
[ ] Notification made to owners for structure and adjacent properties of date, time, and location of live fire training
[ ] Assistance for Traffic Control, training ground security
[ ] Liability Insurance obtained covering damage to other property
[ ] Written Evidence of **pre-requisite training** obtained from all participating students
[ ] Written documentation of supervisory and instructional personnel on qualifications as stipulated by NFPA 1403 and the Authority Having Jurisdiction (AHJ)

PRE-BURN PLANNING

[ ] Pre-burn planning
　　[ ] Site Plan Drawing of structure or facility
　　[ ] Floor Plan detailing all rooms and exits
　　[ ] Location of Command Post
　　[ ] Position of all apparatus
　　[ ] Position of all hose and backup lines
　　[ ] Location of Emergency escape routes
　　[ ] Location of emergency evacuation assembly area
　　[ ] Location of ingress and egress escape routes for emergency vehicles

[ ] Available water supply determined
[ ] Required fire flow determined for the burn structure and exposure buildings
[ ] Required reserve flow determined (50% of fire flow)

[ ] Pumping Apparatus meets or exceeds the required fire flow for the building and exposures
[ ] Separate water sources established for attack and backup hose lines
[ ] Periodic weather reports obtained
[ ] Parking areas designated and obtained
　　[ ] apparatus
　　[ ] ambulance
　　[ ] Police/Sheriff's vehicles
　　[ ] Press vehicles
　　[ ] Private vehicles
[ ] Operations area established and perimeter Marked
[ ] Communications frequencies established, equipment obtained

BUILDING PREPARATION

[ ] Building Inspection to determine structural integrity
[ ] All utilities disconnected (acquired structure)
[ ] Highly combustible interior wall and ceiling coverings removed
[ ] All holes in walls and ceilings patched/covered
[ ] Ventilation openings of adequate size precut for each separate roof area
[ ] Windows checked and operated, opened or closed, as needed
[ ] Doors checked and operated, opened or closed, as needed
[ ] Building components checked and operated: (burn buildings)
　　[ ] roof scuttles
　　[ ] automatic ventilators
　　[ ] mechanical equipment
　　[ ] lighting equipment
　　[ ] manual and automatic sprinklers
　　[ ] standpipes
[ ] Stairways made safe with railings in place
[ ] Chimney (if applicable) checked for stability
[ ] Fuel tanks and closed vessels removed or adequately vented
[ ] Unnecessary inside and outside debris removed
[ ] Porches and outside steps made safe
[ ] Cisterns, wells, cesspools, and other ground openings identified, fenced or filled.

[ ] Hazards from toxic weeds, hives, and vermin
eliminated
[ ] Hazardous trees, brush, and surrounding
vegetation removed

BUILDING PREPARATION (Continued)

[ ] Exposures such as buildings, trees, and utilities
removed or protected
[ ] All extraordinary exterior and interior hazards
remedied
[ ] Fire "sets" prepared
  [ ] Class "A" materials only
  [ ] **NO** flammable/combustible liquids
  [ ] No contaminated materials

PRE-BURN PROCEDURES

[ ] All participants briefed:
  [ ] Building layout
  [ ] Crew and Instructor assignments
  [ ] Safety rules
  [ ] Building evacuation procedures
  [ ] Evacuation signal (demonstrate)
[ ] All hose lines checked:
  [ ] Sufficient size for the area of fire
Involvement
  [ ] Charged and flow tested
  [ ] Supervised by qualified instructors
  [ ] Adequate number of personnel
[ ] Necessary tools and equipment positioned
[ ] Participants checked:
  [ ] approved full protective clothing
  [ ] self contained breathing apparatus
  [ ] adequate SCBA air volume
  [ ] all equipment properly donned

POST-BURN PROCEDURES

[ ] All personnel accounted for
[ ] Remaining fires overhauled, as needed
[ ] Building inspected for stability and hazards
Where more training is to follow (see Section B.3,
Building Preparation)
[ ] Training critique conducted
[ ] Records and reports prepared, as required:
  [ ] account of activities conducted
  [ ] list of instructors and assignments

[ ] list of other participants
[ ] documentation of unusual conditions or
events
[ ] documentation of inquiries incurred and
treatment rendered
[ ] documentation of changes or deterioration
of training center burn building
[ ] acquired building release
[ ] student training records
[ ] certificates of completion
[ ] Building and property releases to owner, release
document signed

Completed by: (Printed Name)

Completed by: (Signature)   Date

Reviewed by: (Printed Name)

Reviewed by: (Signature)   Date

Virginia Department of Fire Programs

Location: _____ Date: _____ School No.: _____

Live Burn Accountability

Individual Name: _____ **Department:** _____
Emergency Contact: _____ **Allergies:** _____
Known Medical Problems: _____

Note: Remember to keep crews well hydrated during time in staging or rehabilitation

VITAL SIGNS	B/P	RESP.	PULSE	TEMP.	SKIN	TAKEN BY:
Base Line						
Post Entry #1						
Post Entry #2						
Post Entry #3						
Post Entry #4						
Post Entry #5						
Post Entry #6						
Post Entry #7						

PERSONNEL/TURNOUT GEAR INSPECTION:

Coat: _____ Pants: _____ Helmet: _____ Boots: _____

Gloves: _____ Hood: _____ SCBA: _____ Pass: _____

Accountability: _____ Problems with Personnel/Gear: _____

TRAINING LEVEL: The above named individual meets the following training Job Performance Requirements (JPR). These NFPA 1001 JPR subjects are listed in the appendix of NFPA 1403.

Safety   Fire Behavior   Portable extinguishers
Personal Protective Equipment   Ladders   Fire Hose, Appliances, and
Overhaul   Water Supply   Ventilation
                                   Forcible Entry

I _____ certify that I have received the above training prior to entering the Live Fire Training being offered here. I also certify the above information is true.
Signature: _____ ____/____/_____
               (Legible Signature)   (Date)

I _____ certify that _____ has received the above training prior to entry into the Live Fire Training being offered, I also certify the above information is true.

Signature of
Dept. Official: _____ **Title:** _____ **Date:** ___/___/___

Signature of Lead Instructor: _____ **Date:** ___/___/___

Signature of Safety Officer: _____ **Date:** ___/___/___

Appendix K

NIOSH Firefighter Fatality Report: 2005

F2005 01

NIOSH
Fire Fighter Fatality Investigation and Prevention Program

Death in the line of duty...

A summary of a NIOSH fire fighter fatality investigation	*May 20, 2005*

Career Fire Fighter Dies After Falling From Tailboard and Being Backed Over by Engine - California

SUMMARY

On August 14, 2004, a 25-year-old female career fire fighter (the victim) died when she apparently fell from the tailboard and was backed over by an engine. The victim and her crew had been released from the scene of a residential fire. The road was blocked by other apparatus, so the victim's crew began backing to an intersection approximately 300 feet away in order to proceed forward. The victim took her position on the tailboard as the "Tailboard Safety Member" and signaled the driver to begin backing. A Captain acting as the "Traffic Control Officer" guided the backing operation from the road on the driver's side, behind the apparatus, by using hand signals. When the Captain turned and walked into the intersection to stop cross-traffic, the victim apparently fell from the tailboard and was run over by the engine. Members on the scene provided advanced life support and the victim was transported to a local hospital where she was pronounced dead. NIOSH investigators concluded that, to minimize the risk of similar occurrences, fire departments should:

- *modify existing policies to prohibit members from riding on the tailboard or any exposed position when the vehicle is in motion*

- *develop, implement, and periodically review standard operating procedures for backing fire apparatus*

- *consider equipping apparatus with safety equipment such as mirrors, automatic sensing devices, and/or video cameras to assist with backing operations*

INTRODUCTION

On August 14, 2004, a 25-year-old female career fire fighter (the victim) died when she apparently fell from the tailboard and was backed over by her engine. On August 16, 2004, the U.S. Fire Administration (USFA) notified the National Institute for Occupational Safety and Health (NIOSH) of the fatality. On January 5 through January 7, 2005, a Safety and Occupational Health Specialist from the NIOSH Division of Safety Research investigated the incident. Meetings were conducted with officers of the fire department. Interviews were conducted with officers and fire fighters who were at the incident scene. The NIOSH investigator reviewed the department's standard operating procedures (SOPs), the fire department's incident report, the victim's training records, photographs, and drawings of the incident site. The incident site was also visited and photographed.

Tailboard of Engine 273

The Fire Fighter Fatality Investigation and Prevention Program is conducted by the National Institute for Occupational Safety and Health (NIOSH). The purpose of the program is to determine factors that cause or contribute to fire fighter deaths suffered in the line of duty. Identification of causal and contributing factors enable researchers and safety specialists to develop strategies for preventing future similar incidents. The program does not seek to determine fault or place blame on fire departments or individual fire fighters. To request additional copies of this report (specify the case number shown in the shield above), other fatality investigation reports, or further information, visit the Program Website at
www.cdc.gov/niosh/firehome.html
or call toll free **1-800-35-NIOSH**

*Career Fire Fighter Dies After Falling From Tailboard and Being Backed Over by Engine
- California*

Department

The career department involved in this incident is comprised of 3,250 uniformed fire fighters. The department serves a population of approximately 6 million residents in a geographic area of about 250 square miles.

Training

The State requires all career fire fighters to complete training equivalent to National Fire Protection Association (NFPA) Level I. The fire department provides all new recruits with a 15-week training course conducted at the city's fire academy. The victim had approximately 3 months of experience after graduating from the academy.

Equipment

Engine 83 (Officer, driver/operator, 2 fire fighters)
Engine 100 (Officer, driver/operator, 2 fire fighters)
Engine 273 (Officer, driver/operator, victim, fire fighter)
Engine 293 (Officer, driver/operator, 2 fire fighters)
Truck 73 (Officer, driver/operator, 3 fire fighters)
Truck 93 (Officer, driver/operator, 3 fire fighters)
Rescue Ambulance 93 (Officer, driver/operator, 3 fire fighters)
B10 (Battalion Chief, firefighter/staff assistant)

Weather

The conditions were clear and sunny, with light winds and temperatures in the low 90's. The relative humidity was 49 percent.

INVESTIGATION

On August 14, 2004, a 25-year-old female career fire fighter (the victim) died when she apparently fell from the tailboard and was backed over by an engine. At 1254 hours, Central Dispatch received a call of a reported structure fire and dispatched four engines, two trucks, an ambulance, and a battalion chief. At 1259 hours, crews arrived on the scene and encountered a one room fire in a one story, single-family dwelling. Crews were assigned to fire attack, search and rescue, roof operations, interior truck operations, and searching for extension. The victim's crew, among the last to arrive at the scene, placed a smoke ejector at the front door, donned their self-contained breathing apparatus (SCBA), and entered the structure. The crew pulled ceiling using pike poles for approximately two minutes searching for fire extension into the attic. The attack operations were successful and a knockdown was declared at 1305 hours as the fire was contained to the room of origin.

The victim's crew exited the structure and returned to their apparatus to remove their turnout coats and SCBA. They remained in their turnout pants and wore their brush jackets to conduct overhaul. The victim used an axe for approximately 10 minutes on the roof while clearing a ventilation hole.

The crew returned to their apparatus, removed their gear, and rested for a few minutes as they drank water. The Incident Commander released the victim's crew from the incident at approximately 1330 hours, and because of other apparatus blocking the road, they were forced to back up to leave the fireground (see Photo #1).

The victim took her position standing on the tailboard as the "Tailboard Safety Member," and as directed by department policy, notified the driver to begin backing up by pushing an electronic signaling button located on the rear panel of the engine. *Note: The fire department policy is for a fire fighter to ride on the tailboard and guide the driver whenever the apparatus is backing by pressing a signal button located on the rear engine panel. The "Tailboard Safety Member" would push the button once to stop, twice to go, and three times to back-up (see Photo #2 and Photo #3). The signal button would sound a bell in the cab and a red light would also flash correspondingly on the dash (see Photo #4).* A Captain, as directed by department policy, acted as the "Traffic Control Officer" and guided the backing operation from behind the apparatus, in the road on the driver's side, by using hand signals.

Page 2

Career Fire Fighter Dies After Falling From Tailboard and Being Backed Over by Engine - California

The driver backed-up the engine at idle speed as they proceeded toward an intersection where they could turn to go forward. The intersection was approximately 300 feet from where the engine had been parked. The Captain turned and walked into the intersection to stop cross traffic. At approximately 1343 hours, the Captain turned back around and did not see the victim. He proceeded across the rear of the engine to the passenger side while he heard a crashing noise. The driver saw the Captain cross behind him and looked over to see him in the passenger's side mirror. As he was looking in the passenger side mirror, the victim's boots came into view on the road through the windshield and he simultaneously heard the Captain yelling to stop. He immediately stopped and rushed to provide assistance to the victim approximately 60 feet from the intersection. Advanced life support was initiated and the victim was transported to a local hospital at 1355 hours where she was pronounced dead shortly thereafter.

CAUSE OF DEATH
The medical examiner lists the cause of death as multiple blunt force injuries.

RECOMMENDATIONS/DISCUSSIONS
Recommendation #1: Fire departments should modify existing policies to prohibit members from riding on the tailboard or any exposed position when the vehicle is in motion.

NFPA 1500 states "All persons riding in fire apparatus shall be seated and belted securely by seat belts in approved riding positions and at any time the vehicle is in motion. Standing or riding on tail steps, sidesteps, running boards, or any other exposed position shall be specifically prohibited."[1]

The department involved in this incident had a policy that required a member titled the "Tailboard Safety Member," to ride on the tailboard and act as a spotter whenever the apparatus was backing. The spotter would face toward the rear while backing and communicate to the driver with an electronic signaling button located on the rear panel. A member riding in a standing position on the outside of the apparatus cannot be secured to

provide any means of protection from a collision or a fall from the apparatus. For an unknown reason, the victim fell from the apparatus and was run over.

Recommendation #2: Fire departments should develop, implement, and periodically review standard operating procedures for backing fire apparatus.

Backing a fire apparatus is a challenge regardless of the conditions and should be avoided whenever possible. If backing is unavoidable, then spotters should be used to safely direct the operation from outside the vehicle. When backing the apparatus, all members (excluding the driver and tiller person) should dismount and act as spotters for the backing operation.[2] Spotters should not be permitted to ride the apparatus from an exposed position such as the tailboard.

The spotters should discuss a backing plan (consistent with the SOP) with the driver and agree on the communication or warning process prior to beginning. Communication could be verbal, by a remote electronic signaling device, hand signals, or radio. The vehicle should not be moved until the spotters are in position and have communicated their approval to start backing. Once the backing begins, the spotters should remain visible to the driver. Spotters who are not in their turnout gear should always wear high visibility reflective vests. At least one spotter should be positioned at the left rear corner and operate as the primary spotter. Whenever the driver cannot see the primary spotter, the backing operation should immediately stop.

Recommendation #3: Fire departments should consider equipping apparatus with safety equipment such as additional mirrors, automatic sensing devices, and/or video cameras to assist with backing operations.

Operating a fire apparatus in reverse involves risk of injury as well as equipment damage.[3] Fire apparatus could be equipped or retrofitted with additional mirrors, commercially available video cameras, or sensing devices. This would help to alleviate some of the risk involved with backing

Page 3

Fatality Assessment and Control Evaluation
Investigative Report #F2005-01

Career Fire Fighter Dies After Falling From Tailboard and Being Backed Over by Engine
- California

operations; however, these devices cannot take the place of spotters, who are not riding on the apparatus, but assisting and directing the driver while backing.

INVESTIGATOR INFORMATION

This incident was investigated by Jay Tarley, Safety and Occupational Health Specialist, Division of Safety Research, NIOSH.

REFERENCES

1. NFPA [1997]. NFPA 1500, standard on fire department occupational safety and health programs. Quincy, MA: National Fire Protection Association.
2. Phoenix Fire Department [1993]. M.P. 205.08A 05/93-R: standard signals for backing of fire apparatus. Phoenix, AZ: Phoenix Fire Department.
3. U.S. Fire Administration [2003]. Safe operation of fire tankers. Emmitsburg, MD. Federal Emergency Management Agency FA-248.

Career Fire Fighter Dies After Falling From Tailboard and Being Backed Over by Engine - California

LOCATION OF VICTIM

ENGINE'S LOCATION PRIOR TO BACKING

~280 FEET

FIRE LOCATION

NOT TO SCALE

Photo 1. Recreated incident scene

Career Fire Fighter Dies After Falling From Tailboard and Being Backed Over by Engine - California

Photo 2. Demonstration of victim's position and function just prior to incident

Career Fire Fighter Dies After Falling From Tailboard and Being Backed Over by Engine
- California

Photo 3. Push button on rear panel of engine with operating instructions

Photo 4. Red light on dash that flashes when the electronic signal button is pushed

Page 7

U. S. Department of Health and Human Services
Public Health Service
Centers for Disease Control and Prevention
National Institute for Occupational Safety and Health
4676 Columbia Parkway, MS C-13
Cincinnati, OH 45226-1998

OFFICIAL BUSINESS
Penalty for private use $300

**Delivering on the Nation's promise:
Safety and health at work for all people
through research and prevention**

NIOSH/CDC Workplace Solutions
Live-Fire Training Report

WORKPLACE SOLUTIONS

From the National Institute for Occupational Safety and Health

Preventing Deaths and Injuries to Fire Fighters during Live-Fire Training in Acquired Structures

Summary

Fire fighters are subjected to many hazards when participating in live-fire training. Training facilities with approved burn buildings should be used for live-fire training whenever possible. However, when acquired structures are used for live-fire training, NIOSH strongly recommends that fire departments follow the national consensus guidelines in NFPA 1403, standard on live-fire training evolutions [NFPA 2002a] to reduce the risk of injury and death. These guidelines are summarized in the recommendations in this document.

Description of Exposure

Live-fire training exercises are a crucial element in the structural fire fighting curriculum. Live-fire training is often conducted in burn buildings designed and approved for such training. Unlike burn buildings, acquired structures are obtained from a private property owner and are not designed or intended for live-fire applications. Several factors associated with live-fire training in acquired structures create safety concerns for fire departments: insufficient or unstable structural components (i.e. floors, railings, stairs, chimneys, and ceilings), limited access to entry and exit paths, hidden combustible materials, debris, and inadequate ventilation [NFPA 2002a].

During 1983–2002, 10 fire fighters died as a result of injuries while participating in live-fire training exercises at acquired structures [Fahy 2003]. During 2000–2002, the NIOSH Fire Fighter Fatality Investigation and Prevention Program investigated three incidents involving four fire fighters who sustained fatal traumatic injuries while participating in live-fire training in acquired structures [NIOSH 2000, 2001, 2002]. Two of these cases are described below.

Case Studies

Case 1

A volunteer fire fighter (the victim) died and two other fire fighters were injured during a live-fire training exercise in a two-story duplex. The victim and anoth-

DEPARTMENT OF HEALTH AND HUMAN SERVICES
Centers for Disease Control and Prevention
National Institute for Occupational Safety and Health

er fire fighter played the role of trapped fire fighters under a table on the second floor. The victim did not have any formal training, and the other fire fighter had been with the department for about 1 year. A burn barrel on the second floor was not producing enough smoke, so the instructor lit a second flare to ignite a foam mattress sleeper sofa next to the stairs on the first floor. The fire rapidly progressed up the stairway, trapping the fire fighters on the second floor. The trapped fire fighters were recovered from their original position and removed from the structure. The victim was unresponsive, and advanced life-saving procedures were initiated en route to the local hospital where he was pronounced dead. The cause of death was listed as asphyxia due to smoke inhalation [NIOSH 2001].

Case 2

A career lieutenant and a career fire fighter died while participating in live-fire training at an acquired vacant structure. The fire was built in a closet with five wooden pallets and bales of straw as fuel. To produce a larger fire, fire fighters added a twin-sized urethane foam mattress to the fire. The search and rescue team (the two victims) entered the structure to "rescue" a mannequin. The fire intensified, and smoke filled the burn room and the hallway. The Incident Commander (IC) ordered ventilation so a window was broken. Heavy smoke followed by intense flames were emitted. A flashover is believed to have occurred seconds after the window was vented. (Flashover is when all surfaces and objects in a space have been heated to their ignition temperatures.) The IC and fire fighters on the scene did not realize that the victims were in the burn room at the time of the flashover. Failing to contact the two victims by radio, the IC sent in the Rapid Intervention Team. Approximately 10 minutes after the flashover, the IC called for an accountability check on the radio and receiving no response from the victims, he sounded the air horns to evacuate the structure. The attack crew then found one of the victims lying on the floor next to the closet where the fire had been ignited. The second victim was found lying next to the window of the burn room. The victims were both transported by ambulances to a local hospital where they were pronounced dead. The cause of death for both was smoke inhalation and thermal injuries [NIOSH 2002].

Controls

Whenever possible, NIOSH recommends that training facilities with approved burn buildings be used for live-fire training. To minimize risks when participating in live-fire training, NIOSH recommends that fire departments comply with NFPA 1403 [NFPA 2002a], including the following precautions:

Instructors

- Ensure that the instructor in charge is aware of his or her responsibility for overall coordination of the training and compliance with NFPA 1403.

- Ensure that instructors are qualified to provide live-fire training. Verify instructor [NFPA 2002b] and officer qualifications [NFPA 2003a] through national certifying agencies such as the National Professional Qualifications Board, the International Fire Service Accreditation Congress, or through a State fire board or commission.

Site Set Up

- Ensure that the acquired structure is adequate and safe to be used for live-fire training. Use Appendix B of NFPA 1403 as a checklist for pre-burn planning, building preparation, and pre-burn/post-burn procedures.

- Develop, implement, and train fire fighters in standard operating procedures (SOPs) for live-fire training.

- Conduct a pre-burn briefing session for all participants, and establish an evacuation plan and signal.

- Ensure that a sufficient water supply is available.

- Ensure that the fuels used in the live-fire training have known burning characteristics.

- Inspect the structure for possible environmental hazards.

- Do not use flammable or combustible liquids in live-fire training.

- Do not set fires for live-fire training in any designated exit paths.

- Do not allow anyone to play the role of victim inside the structure during live-fire training.

- Establish a method of fire ground communication among the IC and fire fighters.

- Ensure that proper ventilation is in place before the onset of a controlled burn and is coordinated with interior operations.

- Ensure that backup personnel are standing by with equipment, ready to provide assistance or rescue.

- Ensure that all fire fighters participating in live-fire training have had minimum basic training.

- Ensure that each fire fighter is equipped with NFPA-compliant full protective clothing, a NIOSH approved self-contained breathing apparatus (SCBA), and a personal alert safety system (PASS).

- Establish rehabilitation operations at training exercises that pose the risk of fire fighters exceeding a safe level of physical or mental endurance [NFPA 2003b].

Site Safety

- Appoint a separate, adequately trained safety officer that has the authority to intervene in any aspect of the live-fire training.

- Ensure that all participants are accounted for when entering and exiting the building.

- Assign only one person as the ignition officer. Ensure that he or she is not a fire fighter participating in the training.

- Ensure that the ignition officer lights only one training fire at a time.

- Ensure that a charged hose line is present while igniting the fire.

- Use a thermal imaging camera during live-fire training situations to observe fire fighters and monitor heat conditions for safety.

Training Participants

- Follow Standard Operating Procedures (SOPs) established by the department.

- Use NFPA-compliant full protective clothing, an SCBA, and a PASS device, as provided by the department.

- Do not enter a hazardous environment alone. Enter only as a team of two or more.

- Be familiar with the fire department's evacuation plan and signal.

States

- Ensure that acquired structures that will be used in live-fire training are inspected to identify and eliminate hazards.

- Develop a procedure to issue permits to use inspected acquired structures for live-fire training.

- Check NFPA 1403 for voluntary guidelines on issuing permits [NFPA 2002a].

Acknowledgments

The principal contributors to this publication were Jay Tarley and Carolyn Guglielmo, NIOSH.

References

NFPA [2002a]. NFPA 1403, standard on live fire training evolutions. Quincy, MA: National Fire Protection Association.

NFPA [2002b]. NFPA 1041, standard for fire service instructor professional qualifications. Quincy, MA: National Fire Protection Association.

NFPA [2003a]. NFPA 1021, standard for fire officer professional qualifications. Quincy, MA: National Fire Protection Association.

NFPA [2003b]. NFPA 1584, recommended practice on the rehabilitation of members operating at incident scene operations and training exercises. Quincy, MA: National Fire Protection Association.

NIOSH [2000]. Volunteer assistant chief dies during a controlled-burn training evolution—Delaware. Cincinnati, OH: U.S. Department of Health and Human Services, Public Health Service, Centers for Disease Control and Prevention, National Institute for Occupational

Safety and Health, DHHS (NIOSH) Publication No. F2000–27. Fire Fighter Fatality Investigation Report F2000–27. [www.cdc.gov/niosh/face200027.html]

NIOSH [2001]. Volunteer fire fighter dies and two others are injured during live-fire training—NY. Cincinnati, OH: U.S. Department of Health and Human Services, Public Health Service, Centers for Disease Control and Prevention, National Institute for Occupational Safety and Health, DHHS (NIOSH) Publication No. F2001–38. Fire Fighter Fatality Investigation Report F2001–38. [www.cdc.gov/niosh/face200138.html]

NIOSH [2002]. Career lieutenant and fire fighter die in flashover during a live-fire training evolution—FL. Cincinnati, OH: U.S. Department of Health and Human Services, Public Health Service, Centers for Disease Control and Prevention, National Institute for Occupational Safety and Health, DHHS (NIOSH) Publication No. F2002–34. Fire Fighter Fatality Investigation Report F2002–34. [www.cdc.gov/niosh/face200234.html]

Fahy R (rfahy@NFPA.org) [2003]. NFPA Live-fire training deaths. Personal communication email message to Jay Tarley (jst9@cdc.gov), February 10, 2003.

For More Information

The information in this document is based on fatality investigations and expert review. More information about the Fire Fighter Fatality Investigation and Prevention Program is available at www.cdc.gov/niosh/firehome.html

To receive more information about occupational safety and health topics, contact NIOSH at

NIOSH
Publications Dissemination
4676 Columbia Parkway
Cincinnati, OH 45226–1998

Telephone: 1–800–35–NIOSH (1–800–356–4674)
Fax: 513–533–8573 ▪ E-mail: pubstaff@cdc.gov

or visit the NIOSH Web site at www.cdc.gov/niosh

For a monthly update on news at NIOSH, subscribe to NIOSH eNews by visiting www.cdc.gov/niosh/eNews.

Preventing Deaths and Injuries to Fire Fighters during Live-Fire Training in Acquired Structures

Mention of any company or product does not constitute endorsement by NIOSH. In addition, citations to Web sites external to NIOSH do not constitute NIOSH endorsement of the sponsoring organizations or their programs or products. Furthermore, NIOSH is not responsible for the content of these Web sites.

As part of the Centers for Disease Control and Prevention, NIOSH is the Federal agency responsible for conducting research and making recommendations to prevent work-related illnesses and injuries. All Workplace Solutions are based on research studies that show how worker exposures to hazardous agents or activities can be significantly reduced.

DHHS (NIOSH) Publication No. 2005–102

SAFER • HEALTHIER • PEOPLE™

October 2004

DEPARTMENT OF HEALTH AND HUMAN SERVICES
Centers for Disease Control and Prevention
National Institute for Occupational Safety and Health
4676 Columbia Parkway
Cincinnati, OH 45226–1998

NIOSH Training Fatality Report: 2002

Death in the line of duty...

A Summary of a NIOSH fire fighter fatality investigation *October 31, 2002*

Volunteer Fire Fighter Dies and Two Others Are Injured During Live-Burn Training - New York

SUMMARY

On September 25, 2001, a 19-year-old male volunteer fire fighter (the victim) died and two male volunteer fire fighters (Fire Fighter #1 and Fire Fighter #2) were injured during a multi-agency, live-burn training session. The victim and Fire Fighter #1 were playing the role of fire fighters who had become trapped on the second-level of the structure. The training became reality when the fire was started and progressed up the stairwell, accelerated by a foam mattress that was ignited on the first floor. Fire Fighter #1 and the victim were recovered from the second-level front bedroom where they had been placed for the training. Fire Fighter #2 jumped from a second-level window in the rear bedroom. The victim was unresponsive when removed from the structure. Advanced life saving procedures were initiated on the victim en route to the local hospital where he was pronounced dead. Fire Fighter #1 and Fire Fighter #2 suffered severe burns and were airlifted to an area burn unit.

NIOSH investigators concluded that to minimize the risk of similar occurrences, fire departments should

- *ensure that no one plays the role of victim inside the structure during live-burn training*

- *ensure that a certified instructor is in charge of the live-burn training and that a separate safety officer is appointed and has the authority to intervene and control any aspect of the operation*

- *ensure that only one training fire is lit at a time by a designated ignition officer and that a charged hoseline is present while igniting the fire*

- *ensure that Standard Operating Procedures (SOPs) are developed and followed*

- *ensure that all fire fighters participating in live-burn training have achieved a minimum level of basic training*

- *ensure that before conducting live-burn training, a preburn briefing session is*

Site of the Incident

The **Fire Fighter Fatality Investigation and Prevention Program** is conducted by the National Institute for Occupational Safety and Health (NIOSH). The purpose of the program is to determine factors that cause or contribute to fire fighter deaths suffered in the line of duty. Identification of causal and contributing factors enable researchers and safety specialists to develop strategies for preventing future similar incidents. The program does not seek to determine fault or place blame on fire departments or individual fire fighters. To request additional copies of this report (specify the case number shown in the shield above), other fatality investigation reports, or further information, visit the Program Website at
www.cdc.gov/niosh/firehome.html
or call toll free 1-800-35-NIOSH

Volunteer Fire Fighter Dies and Two Others Are Injured During Live-Burn Training - New York

conducted and an evacuation plan and signal are established for all participants

- ensure that fires used for live-burn training are not located in any designated exit paths

- ensure that the fuels used in the live-burn training evolutions have known burning characteristics and the structure is inspected for possible environmental hazards

Additionally,

- *States should develop a permitting procedure for live-burn training to be conducted at acquired structures. States should ensure that all the requirements of NFPA 1403 have been met before issuing the permit.*

INTRODUCTION

On September 25, 2001, a fire fighter (the victim) died and two fire fighters (Fire Fighter #1 and Fire Fighter #2) were injured while participating in a multi-agency, live-burn training session. The victim and Fire Fighter #1 were playing the role of fire fighters who had become trapped in a structure on the second level.

On September 27, 2001, the United States Fire Administration notified the National Institute for Occupational Safety and Health (NIOSH) of this incident. On December 4-5, 2001, two safety and occupational health specialists and the section chief from the NIOSH Fire Fighter Fatality Investigation and Prevention Program investigated this incident. Interviews were conducted with the Chief, the Assistant Chiefs, and fire fighters of the departments from the district involved in the training session. The department that was operating the training was disbanded. Copies of their standard operating procedures were not available for review. The training records of the victim and injured fire fighters were reviewed.

The fire district involved in this multi-agency training session operated from four volunteer stations and was comprised of 102 active members. The district serves a population of approximately 25,000 in a geographic area of about 25 square miles. The victim had been a volunteer fire fighter for just a few weeks and had not received any formalized training before the incident. Fire Fighter #1 was reported to have received Basic Fire Fighting Essentials, Maze Training, and Live Tower Training, but no documentation was provided during the investigation. Fire Fighter #2 was documented to have completed Fire Fighting Essentials, Pump Operator, Commanding the Initial Response, Apparatus Operator, and Hazardous Materials First Responder Operations. The site was a two-story, side-by-side duplex. Vacant and in disrepair, the duplex was scheduled for demolition in the near future by the owner.

INVESTIGATION

At approximately 1845 hours, Fire Fighter #1, Fire Fighter #2, the victim, the 1st Assistant Chief, and the 2nd Assistant Chief were on the scene discussing the plan for a rescue drill during live-burn training. The 1st Assistant Chief was the instructor. The 2nd Assistant Chief was a Safety Officer for the west unit of the duplex. Fire Fighter #2 was a Safety Officer for the east unit and the Ignition Officer. The following apparatus were on the scene before the start of the training:

Engine #451 equipped with a 1,000-gallon water tank
Engine #3 equipped with a 1,000-gallon water tank
Heavy Rescue #449
Rescue #1
Truck #459
10,000-gallon water tanker (building owner's)

The training scenario was designed to include two fire fighters who had become trapped while

Page 2

Volunteer Fire Fighter Dies and Two Others Are Injured During Live-Burn Training - New York

conducting a search for an infant in a bedroom located on the second floor of a duplex apartment. *Note: The fire fighters that were used to simulate victims during this training session will be referred to as the "trapped fire fighters" throughout this report.* Engine #451 was to hook up to the owner's water tanker on site and have two 1 3/4" handlines stretched to the structure, one handline to the rear entrance and one handline to the front entrance of the east unit. Engine #3 and Heavy Rescue #449 were then dispatched to stage approximately 3/4 of a mile away to practice their response to the scene. The scenario included blocking the door to the stairs of the unit (east unit) leading to the "trapped fire fighters" to simulate that the stairs had collapsed. The responding units would have to deploy a rapid intervention team (RIT) which would then be forced to access the second floor via the stairs on the other side of the duplex. Once on the second floor, the RIT would breach the wall leading to the other apartment to conduct a search for the "trapped fire fighters"and the infant. *Note: The wall on the second floor separating the two units had been breached during earlier training sessions.* The "trapped fire fighters" (Fire Fighter #1 and the victim) were placed in the front bedroom with some debris scattered about the floor and a Ping-Pong table placed upon them to simulate a real entrapment. *Note: This was reportedly the first time the victim had worn a self-contained breathing apparatus (SCBA) in a fire condition. Fire Fighter #1 had approximately 1 year with the department and minimal experience with an SCBA in fire conditions.* A burn barrel was to be used to produce smoke and simulate fire from the back bedroom of the east duplex.

The 2nd Assistant Chief was positioned with a 20-pound fire extinguisher on the second floor of the west unit to guide the RIT up the stairs and through the breach in the wall. He was to ensure the RIT did not go through an opening in the back wall of the

west unit. Fire Fighter #2 was on the second floor of the east unit where he was to place the "trapped fire fighters" in the front bedroom, light the burn barrel in the back bedroom, and guide the RIT if necessary (Diagram #1). The Chief arrived on the scene and did a walkthrough of the upstairs to ensure safety and to make sure no accelerants were used in the burn barrel. He then proceeded to the front of the duplex and took over outside command as requested by the 1st Assistant Chief, who had interior command from the first floor of the burn unit (Diagram #2).

Fire Fighter #2 struck a flare and lit the burn barrel on the second floor and radioed to the Chief at approximately 1855 hours that it was lit. He then positioned himself in the hallway to guide the RIT if necessary. The barrel was not producing smoke, so Fire Fighter #2 went to the back bedroom to assist in the process. During this time, the 1st Assistant Chief struck another flare on the first floor and lit the foam mattress of a sleeper sofa that was extended adjacent to the open side of the stairs.

Fire Fighter #2 heard the second flare being struck and went to investigate. In a matter of seconds, the flames began to roll across the ceiling, up the stairs, and out the front windows of the burn unit, producing what was described as a thick, "steamy" smoke. The 2nd Assistant Chief was cut off from the east unit by the fire extending up the stairwell. He exited via a ladder through an opening in the back wall of the west unit. The 1st Assistant Chief went out the back of the structure to locate a handline. Unable to locate a handline in the back of the structure, he searched for a handline at the front of the structure. *Note: No handlines had been stretched from Engine #451 before the start of the training evolution.* Flames were now extending out of the first-floor bay window into the front bedroom. He then pulled 200 feet of 1 3/4 inch preconnect off Engine #451 and advanced the line to the rear of the structure.

Page 3

*Volunteer Fire Fighter Dies and Two Others Are Injured During Live-Burn Training -
New York*

Fire Fighter #2 went to retrieve the "trapped fire fighters" from the front bedroom where flames were already coming through the windows from downstairs. Fire Fighter #2 grabbed the two "trapped fire fighters" and led them to the stairwell, which was fully engulfed. Fire Fighter #2 lost his fire gloves in the process, exposing the leather gloves he had worn underneath. The leather gloves immediately burned and adhered to his skin. He and the "trapped fire fighters" became separated. Fire Fighter #2 made it to the back bedroom where the burn barrel was located. Conditions in the back bedroom were extremely smoky with little heat. Fire Fighter #2 frantically searched for the window that had been boarded shut to aid in the smoke conditions. He was able to pry the window open with his hands, and he jumped from the second floor just as the 1st Assistant Chief arrived with the handline.

The two staged engines proceeded to the scene under normal driving conditions as planned for the training operations. Once on the scene, they were immediately informed that this was no longer a drill, that two fire fighters were down on the second floor, and that one fire fighter had jumped from the second-story window. Due to the circumstances, both engines deployed a RIT team. The first RIT made forcible entry through the front door of the east unit and proceeded up the stairs to the front bedroom. They immediately found Fire Fighter #1 and dragged him down the stairs by his turnout gear to the lawn in front of the duplex. The second RIT proceeded to the front bedroom and found the victim. They dragged the victim to the front of the duplex for immediate assistance. *Note: Both the victim and Fire Fighter #1 were found wearing their facepieces. Burn injuries to the faces of both fire fighters indicated that their masks had been removed during the fire's progression.* The victim was unresponsive when removed from the structure. Advanced life saving procedures were initiated on the victim en route to the local hospital where he

was pronounced dead. Fire Fighter #1 and Fire Fighter #2 suffered severe burns and were airlifted to an area burn unit.

CAUSE OF DEATH
The cause of death was listed as asphyxia due to smoke inhalation.

RECOMMENDATIONS AND DISCUSSION
Recommendation #1: Fire departments should ensure that no one plays the role of victim inside the structure during live-burn training.[1]

The National Fire Protection Association Standard 1403, 2-4.13, notes that individuals shall not play the role of a victim inside the building. Rescue operations should be conducted by using mannequins instead of fire fighters, just as the mock baby was used to simulate the infant.

Recommendation #2: Fire departments should ensure that a certified instructor is in charge of the live-burn training and that a separate safety officer is appointed and has the authority to intervene and control any aspect of the operation.[1]

Fire departments should comply with the National Fire Protection Association Standard 1403, which notes that all instructors shall be deemed qualified to deliver fire-fighter training by the authority having jurisdiction. The instructor-in-charge should be a certified instructor who oversees all aspects of the training session. Their responsibilities include planning and coordinating all training activities, monitoring activities, structure inspections, briefing and assigning instructors and support personnel, and ensuring adherence to the directives. The authority having jurisdiction in this area does not have any requirements or procedures in place for determining if an instructor is qualified to provide fire-fighter training as outlined in NFPA 1041, *Standard for*

Page 4

Volunteer Fire Fighter Dies and Two Others Are Injured During Live-Burn Training - New York

Fire Service Instructor Professional Qualifications.

NFPA Standard 1403 further states that safety officers shall be appointed for all training sessions and have no other duties to interfere with their safety responsibilities for all persons on the scene. The safety officer should eliminate unsafe conditions, prevent unsafe acts, coordinate lighting of fires with instructor-in-charge, ensure personal protective equipment compliance, ensure all participants are accounted for before and after each evolution. The safety officer must have the authority to intervene and control all aspects of the operation. One of the safety officers during this incident also had the responsibility of the ignition officer to light the burn barrel on the second floor.

A person who is not a student should be designated as the ignition officer to control the material being burned. The fire should be ignited by the ignition officer in the presence of and under the direct supervision of the safety officer.

Recommendation #3: Fire departments should ensure that only one training fire is ignited at a time by a designated ignition officer and that a charged hoseline is present while igniting the fire.[1]

One person, who is not participating in the training, should be assigned the duty of ignition officer and light the fire as instructed by the instructor-in-charge. The safety officer should be in the presence of, and have direct supervision over, the ignition officer when the fire is lit. A charged hoseline should be present when igniting the fire.

Recommendation #4: Fire departments should ensure that Standard Operating Procedures (SOPs) are developed and followed.[2]

Standard operating procedures (SOPs) should be developed addressing emergency-scene operations such as Training Fires, RIT Operations, SCBA, Water Supply, and Hoseline Operations. These SOPs will then form the foundation as to how the training will be conducted. The SOP should be in written form and included in the overall risk-management plan for the fire department. If these procedures are changed, appropriate training should be provided to all affected members.

Recommendation #5: Fire departments should ensure that all fire fighters participating in live-burn training have achieved a minimum level of basic training.[1]

To ensure safety during live-burn training, all fire fighters should have a minimum level of basic training. As stated in NFPA 1403, 2-1.2, the fire fighter student shall have received training to meet the performance objectives for Fire Fighter 1 of the following sections of NFPA 1001, *Standard for Fire Fighter Professional Qualifications:*
Section 3-3 Safety
Section 3-5 Fire Behavior
Section 3-6 Portable Extinguishers
Section 3-7 Personal Protective Equipment
Section 3-11 Ladders
Section 3-12 Fire Hose, Appliances and Streams
Section 3-16 Overhaul
Section 3-19 Water Supply

Recommendation #6: Fire departments should ensure that before conducting live-burn training, a preburn briefing session is conducted and an evacuation plan and signal are established for all participants.[1,2]

All participants should attend a preburn briefing before conducting the live-burn training session to discuss all facets of the training. The instructor in charge of the training should present the briefing session using the preburn plan to detail all aspects of the operation. The characteristics of the training area

Page 5

Volunteer Fire Fighter Dies and Two Others Are Injured During Live-Burn Training - New York

and structure should be addressed to include such items as crew assignments and the designation and layout of ingress/egress routes in the event of emergency. An evacuation plan should be established and an audible evacuation signal be demonstrated to all participants in an interior live-burn training evolution. It is imperative that all participants are familiar with the layout of the structure. All participants should conduct a walk-through of the structure before any training evolutions are initiated.

Recommendation #7: Fire departments should ensure that fires used for live-burn training are not located in any designated exit paths. [1]

During a training exercise, every effort must be made to ensure the exit paths are free from obstructions. To provide a protected area of travel, fires should not be located in any exit paths. These areas should be closely monitored to ensure that fire does not spread during the training exercise. The sofa bed was located at the bottom of the stairs leading to the front exit. The front exit was blocked to simulate that the stairs had collapsed for the responding RIT. Once the sofa bed was lit, the fire immediately traveled into the exit path using the stairway as a chimney. To enhance the smoke conditions for the evolution, the windows on both floors were boarded over or partially covered to minimize ventilation. When the fire entered the exit path, the training exercise became a working structure fire.

Recommendation #8: Fire departments should ensure that the fuels used in the live-burn training have known burning characteristics and the structure is inspected for possible environmental hazards. [1]

Fuels for training fires should have known burning characteristics, and the quantities used should be the minimum necessary that are controllable and able to create the desired fire conditions. The structure should be inspected to identify and remove materials that could

contribute to rapidly spreading fires and create an environmental or health hazard. The structure must also be inspected to provide for physical safety of the participants in the training. NFPA 1403, 2-2.10, identifies the following items that should be addressed:

- Floors, railings, and stairs shall be made safe.
- Special attention shall be given to potential chimney hazards.
- All walls and ceilings shall be intact or patched.
- Debris creating or contributing unsafe conditions shall be removed.
- Low-density combustible fiberboard and unconventional interior finishes shall be removed.
- Extraordinary weight above the training area shall be removed, or the area below it shall be rendered inaccessible.
- An adequate ventilation opening(s) shall be made in the roof.
- Utilities shall be disconnected.
- Consideration shall be given to potential hazards of toxic weeds, insect hives, and vermin.
- All forms of asbestos shall be removed by an approved asbestos removal contractor.

Additionally,

Recommendation #9: States should develop a permitting procedure for live-burn training to be conducted at acquired structures. States should ensure that all the requirements of NFPA 1403 have been met before issuing the permit. [1,3]

Discussion: NFPA 1403, *Standard on Live Fire Training Evolutions*, is the guideline for conducting live-burn training evolutions at approved training centers, and in this case, acquired structures. Approved training centers have burn buildings that are specifically designed for repeated live-burn training evolutions. The structures that are acquired for live-burn training are usually in disrepair and were

Page 6

*Volunteer Fire Fighter Dies and Two Others Are Injured During Live-Burn Training -
New York*

never designed for live-burn training. Any building that is acquired for live-burn training must go through an inspection process to identify and eliminate any hazards, or potential hazards, that may be present to the participants, the public, and the environment. An application for permit procedure that is overseen by the state through local officials or a State representative would help ensure safety. If training facilities with approved burn buildings are available, then live-burn training exercises should not be conducted in acquired structures.

REFERENCES

1. NFPA [1997]. NFPA 1403, standard on live fire training evolutions. Quincy, MA: National Fire Protection Association.

2. NFPA [1997]. NFPA 1500, standard on fire department occupational safety and health program. Quincy, MA: National Fire Protection Association.

3. Carter H [2000]. Why did he have to die? Firehouse.com, May 26, 2000, http:// server.firehouse.com/carter/2000/052600.html

INVESTIGATOR INFORMATION

This incident was investigated by Jay Tarley and Tom Mezzanotte Safety and Occupational Health Specialists, and Robert Koedam, Section Chief, Trauma Investigations Section, Surveillance and Field Investigations Branch, Division of Safety Research, NIOSH.

*Volunteer Fire Fighter Dies and Two Others Are Injured During Live-Burn Training -
New York*

Photo. Sleeper Sofa Adjacent to Stairwell

Volunteer Fire Fighter Dies and Two Others Are Injured During Live-Burn Training -
New York

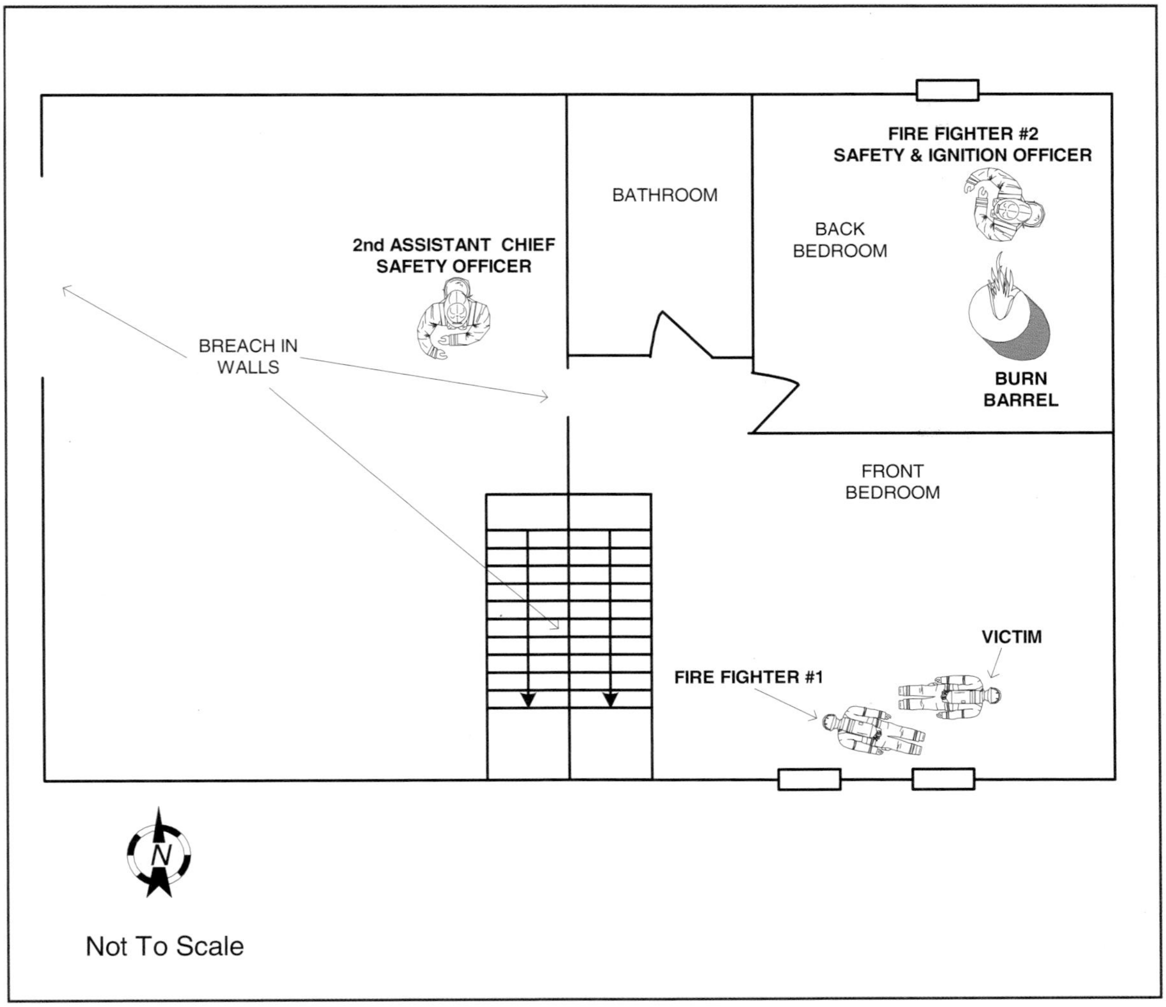

BATHROOM

FIRE FIGHTER #2
SAFETY & IGNITION OFFICER

BACK
BEDROOM

2nd ASSISTANT CHIEF
SAFETY OFFICER

BURN
BARREL

BREACH IN
WALLS

FRONT
BEDROOM

VICTIM

FIRE FIGHTER #1

N

Not To Scale

Diagram 1: Second Floor Aerial View

Volunteer Fire Fighter Dies and Two Others Are Injured During Live-Burn Training - New York

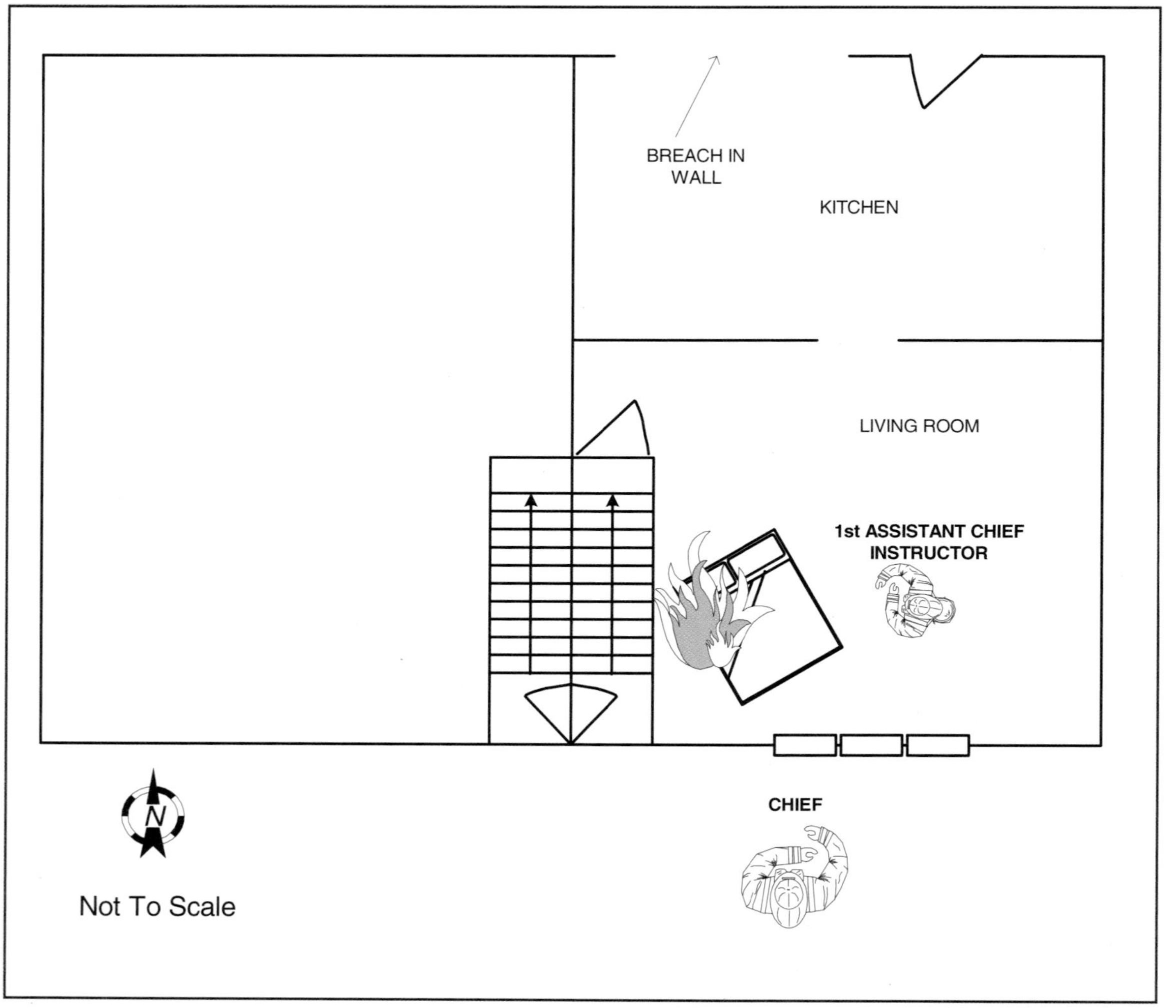

BREACH IN
WALL

KITCHEN

LIVING ROOM

1st ASSISTANT CHIEF
INSTRUCTOR

CHIEF

N

Not To Scale

Diagram 2: First Floor Aerial View

Appendix N
Sample Request for Proposal

Introduction

The _____ Department is pursuing the evaluation and subsequent purchase of SCBA. To accomplish this, the department is requesting SCBA meeting the specifications shown in this request for proposal.

Through each of the major steps of the evaluation process, the SCBA evaluated will be assigned points based on a point system in the categories as follows:

SCBA Provider Support	30 points
Actual and/or Simulated Use Conditions	35 points
Classroom/Maintenance	35 points

Throughout the evaluation process each evaluation team member will review the features of the SCBA submitted and complete an evaluation form. The forms will be tabulated and totaled in each category.

The evaluation process will begin with distributor presentations and training of firefighters who are assigned to evaluate the SCBA. At the time of the presentation, the supplier must submit _____ SCBA meeting the specifications shown in this request for proposal and at least one spare cylinder for each SCBA to be used by the department for the evaluation period.

Each supplier is requested to complete the attached questionnaire and return it to:

_____

(Department Contact Person and Address)

The completed questionnaire should be returned no later than_____.

Pre-Qualification Questionnaire

All questions will be answered in detail on a separate sheet.

1. Location of Corporate/Business Headquarters:

    Company Name:
    Street:
    City, State, Zip:
    Phone:
    FAX:
    SCBA Supplied:

2. Location of the nearest office or distribution center with repair capabilities. Prompt facilitation of repairs will be a critical factor in pre-qualification. Describe in this section your ability to effectively perform maintenance service and repair functions.

   Company Name:

   Name of Person in Charge:

   Street:

   City, State, Zip:

   Phone:

   FAX:

3. Provide contact individuals, titles, and phone numbers of persons within your organization who will be responsible for supporting the department through the evaluation process as well as subsequent use and maintenance of SCBA.

4. How long has your firm been in the business of supplying SCBA and service?

5. What major fire department or industrial SCBA owner does your firm currently support? How many SCBA does this department/company own? How long has your firm supported this customer?

6. Indicate the approximate number of self-contained breathing apparatus sold during each of the past two years.

7. Indicate the approximate number of self-contained breathing apparatus overhauled/serviced during each of the past two years.

8. Will you furnish a finance program for this purchase? If so, include details of program.

9. Indicate if you will provide facepiece fit testing, equipment identification, and record format. Please provide details of how each process is conducted.

10. Will you furnish a written guarantee that sufficient replacement apparatus and/or replacement parts and components will be available at your facility if requested within a minimum 24-hour period?

11. Will your firm provide support including training and technical information for the evaluation units and subsequent purchased SCBA?

12. Will you provide a written copy of the manufacturer's warranty on the entire SCBA unit? State length of standard warranty and portions of unit covered as well as all requirements for the department to remain within warranty compliance.

13. Provider must state estimated ability to meet current and future NFPA standards.

14. Include any information that may be of interest to the _____ Department in this process.

15. Prospective provider must submit "Current Customer Profile" to allow the _____ Department full range of communication with current distributor customers.

Appendix O
Equipment Evaluation Form

Rank _____   Name _____

Date _____   Location _____

      (1)   Strongly Disagree
      (2)   Disagree
      (3)   No Opinion or Not Applicable
      (4)   Agree
      (5)   Strongly Agree

1. The SCBA was easy to don.   1   2   3   4   5

_____

_____

2. After donning, the SCBA fit comfortably.   1   2   3   4   5

_____

_____

3. The facepiece is easy to don.   1   2   3   4   5

_____

_____

4. The facepiece and head harness do *not* interfere with head protection.   1   2   3   4   5

_____

_____

5. It is easy to breathe with the regulator undocked from the facepiece.   1   2   3   4   5

_____

_____

6. The regulator is easy to dock/undock and remains secure.   1   2   3   4   5

_____

_____

7.	It is easy to breathe with air flowing.	1	2	3	4	5

_____

8.	The purge/bypass is easy to operate.	1	2	3	4	5

_____

9.	It is easy to determine when *my* PASS device activates.	1	2	3	4	5

_____

10.	The PASS device is easy to reset.	1	2	3	4	5

_____

11. I felt balanced wearing the SCBA while:

A.	Walking	1	2	3	4	5
B.	Climbing Ladder	1	2	3	4	5
C.	Crawling	1	2	3	4	5
D.	Raising arms and pulling	1	2	3	4	5

_____

12.	The air pressure gauge is easy to read.	1	2	3	4	5

_____

13.	The low air alarm is easy to hear and identify.	1	2	3	4	5

_____

14.	The cylinder valve is easy to turn off.	1	2	3	4	5

_____

15.	The cylinder is easy to change.	1	2	3	4	5

_____

16. Communication is clear with the
    facepiece on.   1   2   3   4   5

    _____

    _____

17. The communication system is clear.   1   2   3   4   5

    _____

    _____

Total Points _____ / 100 possible

Glossary

Glossary

A

Abstract — *See* Executive Summary.

Accident Investigation — Fact-finding rather than fault-finding procedure that looks for causes of accidents, which leads to analyzing causes in order to prevent similar accidents.

Accident — Sequence of unplanned or uncontrolled events that produces unintended injury, death, or property damage; the results of unsafe acts by persons who are unaware or uninformed of potential hazards, are ignorant of safety policies, or fail to follow safety procedures. *Also see* Hazard.

ACCP — Abbreviation for Association Canadienne des Chef de Pompiers.

ADA — Abbreviation for Americans with Disabilities Act.

ADDIE — Acronym for a planning model that includes the Analysis, Design, Development, Implementation, and Evaluation steps. Used in program, curriculum, and course design.

Administrative Law — Body of law created by an administrative agency in the form of rules, regulations, orders, and decisions to administer regulatory powers and duties of the agency. *Also see* Legislative or Statutory Law.

Adult Education — Specialized area of the teaching profession that provides knowledge and skills to students who are generally older than 18 years of age.

Affective (Attitude) Domain — Learning domain that involves emotions, feelings, and attitudes. *Also see* Domain.

Affirmative Action Policies — Employment programs required by federal statutes and regulations designed to correct past and current discriminatory practices in hiring and promoting members of underutilized and minority groups.

Affirmative Action Programs — Employment programs designed to remedy discriminatory practices in hiring and promoting of members of underutilized and minority groups.

AHJ — Abbreviation for Authority Having Jurisdiction.

American National Standards Institute (ANSI) — Voluntary, private, nonprofit membership standards-setting organization that examines and certifies existing standards and new standards with the mission of making the U.S. economy more competitive in the world market.

American Society for Public Administration (ASPA) — Professional society representing all areas of public service and advocates greater effectiveness in government.

American Society for Testing and Materials (ASTM) — Voluntary standards-setting organization that establishes characteristics and performance criteria for materials, products, systems, and services.

American Society of Safety Engineers (ASSE) — Professional safety organization composed of members who manage, supervise, and consult on safety, health, and environmental issues in industry, insurance, government, and education.

Americans with Disabilities Act (ADA) — U.S. federal law that prohibits discrimination against a qualified individual with a disability in application, hiring, advancement, discharge, compensation, job training, and other terms, conditions, and privileges of employment; prohibits asking certain questions of job applicants, including those about medical history, workers' compensation or health insurance claims, absenteeism due to illness, mental illness, and past treatment for alcoholism.

Analysis — Ability to divide information into its most basic components. *Also see* Analyzing, Task Analysis, Hazard/Risk Analysis, and Task-Item Analysis.

Analyzing — Process of methodically examining the various parts of an item, project, program, or incident.

Andragogy — Study of adult education and its methods of teaching and learning.

ANSI — Acronym for American National Standards Institute.

Application — Lesson plan component where the instructor provides opportunities for students to practice or apply cognitive information to skills learned in a lesson; also the ability to put information to use in actual situations.

Assessment — Process used to determine the knowledge, skills, and abilities of a student by observation and application of special activities including quizzes, examinations, oral tests, and similar testing devices. *Also see* Test.

Assignment — Work that must be performed by students outside class in order to reach a skill level, meet an objective, and/or prepare for the next lesson.

Assignment Sheet — Document that contains information about a specific activity or project that a student is expected to perform without supervision.

ASPA — Abbreviation for American Society for Public Administration.

ASSE — Abbreviation for American Society of Safety Engineers.

ASTM — Abbreviation for American Society for Testing and Materials.

Attending — Element of the listening process that involves paying attention to a message, focusing on the speaker (sender), and ignoring other distractions. *Also see* Message and Listening.

Authority Having Jurisdiction (AHJ) — Organization, office, or individual responsible for approving equipment, an installation, or a procedure.

B

B.C.E. — Abbreviation for Before the Common Era.

Before the Common Era (B.C.E.) — Term used to designate the time period before the Common Era (C.E.); replaces the previously used B.C. *(before Christ)*, and covers the period of history before the birth of Christ.

Behavioral Objective — Description of the minimum acceptable behavior that a student must perform by the end of an instructional period.

Block — Division of an occupation that includes related tasks with common factors.

Brainstorming — Teaching method in which a group of students is given a problem or situation and then given time to determine a solution to it.

Buckley Amendment — *See* Privacy Act.

Budget — Planned quantitative allocation of resources for specific activities. In this manual, budget refers to the narrower financial budget that lists both the proposed expenditures and expected revenue sources. *Also see* Capital Budget and Operating Budget.

C

CAFC — Abbreviation for Canadian Association of Fire Chiefs.

CAI — Abbreviation for Computer-Assisted Instruction.

Canadian Association of Fire Chiefs (CAFC/ACCP [Association Canadienne des Chef de Pompiers]) — Professional organization representing fire and emergency services chief officers in Canada.

Canadian Centre for Occupational Health and Safety Administration (CCOHC) — Canadian federal agency responsible for workplace health and safety issues; similar to U.S. Occupational Safety and Health Administration (OSHA).

Capital Budget — Budget that includes funds for projected major purchases — items that cost more than a certain specified amount of money and are expected to last more than 1 year, usually 3 or more years. *Also see* Operating Budget and Budget.

Cardiopulmonary Resuscitation (CPR) — Application of rescue breathing and external cardiac compression used on patients in cardiac arrest to provide an adequate circulation and oxygen to support life.

Case Law — *See* Judiciary Law.

Case Study — Description of a real or hypothetical problem that an organization or an individual has dealt with or could deal with.

CBE — Abbreviation for Computer-Based Education.

CBI — Abbreviation for Computer-Based Instruction.

CBL — Abbreviation for Computer-Based Learning.

CBRNE — Abbreviation for Chemical, Biological, Radiological, Nuclear, and Explosive.

CBT — Abbreviation for Computer-Based Training.

CCOHC — Abbreviation for Canadian Centre for Occupational Health and Safety Administration.

CDC — Abbreviation for U.S. Centers for Disease Control and Prevention.

CD-ROM — Abbreviation/acronym for compact disc-read-only memory.

Centers for Disease Control and Prevention (CDC) — U.S. government agency responsible for the collection and analysis of data regarding disease and health trends.

Certified — Condition in which a person has successfully completed specific criteria and has been designated as capable of performing specific functions, duties, or tasks.

CFR — Abbreviation for U.S. *Code of Federal Regulations.*

Chemical, Biological, Radiological, Nuclear, or Explosive (CBRNE) Device — *See* Weapons of Mass Destruction.

Clarity — Ability to precisely and clearly explain concepts and processes through a systematic presentation of material.

Clear-Text — Use of plain English (or language) in radio communications transmissions; replaces ten-signal or agency-specific coded systems.

CMI — Abbreviation for Computer-Managed Instruction.

Coaching — Process in which instructors direct the skills performance of students by observing, evaluating, and making suggestions for improvement; also used by supervisors to assist subordinates in improving work or personal habits and skills.

Code — Body of law established either by legislative or administrative agencies with rule-making authority; designed to regulate (within its scope) the topic to which it relates.

Code of Ethics — Organized group of ethical behavior guidelines that govern day-to-day activities of a profession, an organization, or an individual.

Code of Federal Regulations (CFR) — Formal name given to the books or documents containing the specific U.S. regulations provided by law; the complete body of federal law.

Cognition — General concept that refers to all forms of knowing, including perceiving, imagining, reasoning, and judging.

Cognitive Domain — Learning domain that emphasizes thought rather than feeling or movement and involves the learning of concepts and principles.

Cognitive Evaluation — Assessment of knowledge that shows cognitive or knowing level by requiring that students respond appropriately to questions on various types of tests. *Also see* Test, Assessment, and Evaluation.

Communication — Two-way process of transmitting and receiving some type of message. *Also see* Message, Receiver, and Sender.

Compact Disc-Read-Only Memory (CD-ROM) — Electronic media data storage device.

Comprehension — Ability to understand the meaning of information.

Comprehensive Test — Type of summative test typically given in the middle (midterm exam) or at the end (final exam) of instruction that measures terminal performance of students in a course and whether they have achieved course objectives. *Also see* Summative Test and Test.

Computer-Assisted Instruction (CAI) — Instruction that uses a computer to provide multimedia training, including tutorial, simulations, games, and remedial training; does *not* involve the use of web-based or limited-area network/wide-area network (LAN/WAN) connections.

Computer-Based Education (CBE) — Education delivered on interactive multimedia devices such as CD-ROM and digital versatile disc (DVD). Also called *computer-based instruction* or *computer-based learning. Also see* Computer-Based Training and Computer-Managed Instruction.

Computer-Based Instruction (CBI) — *See* Computer-Based Education.

Computer-Based Learning (CBL) — *See* Computer-Based Education.

Computer-Based Training (CBT) — Training delivered on interactive multimedia devices such as CD-ROM and digital versatile disk (DVD). *Also see* Computer-Based Education and Computer-Managed Instruction.

Computer-Managed Instruction (CMI) — All instruction delivered on interactive multimedia devices such as compact disc-read-only memory (CD-ROM) and digital versatile disk (DVD). *Also see* Computer-Based Training and Computer-Based Education.

Consistency — Concept that information is *not* contradictory and conforms to the principles that a course is attempting to teach.

Continuity — Flow of information without interruption or change.

Controlling — Management process for establishing and implementing mechanisms to ensure that objectives are attained.

Copyright Law — Legal document that protects the works of artists, photographers, and authors and gives them exclusive rights to publish their works or determine who may publish or reproduce them.

Counseling — Advising students or subordinates on their educational progress, career opportunities, personal anxieties, or sudden crises in their lives; broad term used for a variety of procedures designed to help individuals adjust to certain situations and means of either redirecting students or eliminating learning interferences.

Course — Series of lessons that lead to the completion of a discipline or certification.

CPR — Abbreviation for Cardiopulmonary Resuscitation.

Criterion (s), Criteria (pl) — Standard(s) on which a decision or judgment is/are based.

Criterion-Referenced Test — Assessment in which a student's test performance is compared with some absolute standard or criterion of performance, *not* with the performance of other students. *Also see* Norm-Referenced Test and Test.

Curriculum — Series of courses in which students are introduced to skills and knowledge required for a specific discipline.

D

Demographics — Data related to population: size, components of change, and characteristics such as age, education, sex, income, etc.

Demonstration — Act of showing how to perform a procedure or activity or how an item operates, works, or acts.

Department of Homeland Security (DHS) — Administrative body of the executive branch of the U.S. federal government responsible for the security of the nation against terrorist attacks. Similar state agencies also exist to assist in coordinating efforts on a local level.

Department of Transportation (DOT) — Administrative body of the executive branch of the state/provincial or federal government responsible for transportation policy, regulation, and enforcement.

DHS — Abbreviation for U.S. Department of Homeland Security.

Difficulty — Term used to describe how difficult or easy a test item is based on the percentage of test takers that answer a test item correctly. *Also see* Test-Item Analysis and Test.

Digital Versatile Disc (DVD) — Electronic media storage disc used for storing and replaying videos or movable images.

Disability — Term used in connection with workers' compensation acts; composite of actual incapacity to perform the usual tasks of one's employment and the resulting wage loss as well as the physical impairment of the body that may or may not be incapacitating.

Discrimination (in Testing or Discrimination Index) — Measure of the extent to which any test item is answered correctly by students being tested who do well or poorly on a test as a whole and therefore discriminates between them. Ideally, test items that do *not* discriminate would be omitted from revised versions of the test. *Also see* Test-Item Analysis.

Discussion — Organized, possibly unstructured, two-way dialog between members of a group.

Diversity — Condition of being different or having differences; recognizing, valuing, and using those differences in employees and subordinates to make the organization more efficient and effective.

DOT — Abbreviation for Department of Transportation.

Duty — Obligation that one has by law or contract.

DVD — Abbreviation for Digital Versatile Disc.

E

EAP — Abbreviation for Employee Assistance Program.

Education — Acquisition of knowledge, usually through academic means such as college or university courses; instruction that emphasizes knowledge-based learning objectives that are *not* tied to a specific job as opposed to training where learning objectives are tied to a specific job.

EEO — Abbreviation for Equal Employment Opportunity.

EEOC — Abbreviation for U.S. Equal Employment Opportunity Commission.

Effective — Efforts or conditions that produce the desired result or meets its intended purpose, which could be considered *doing the right thing.*

Efficient — Condition that exists when results are produced with a minimum of effort, waste, or expense; that is, minimum cost for maximum effect.

E-Learning — Abbreviation for Electronic Learning.

Electronic Learning (E-Learning) — All types of education, training, and instruction that is provided via an electronic system such as computers, television, World Wide Web, or intranet.

Electronic Mail (E-Mail) — Form of electronic communication based on Internet and intranet connections between computer systems.

E-Mail — Abbreviation for Electronic Mail.

Emergency Medical Services (EMS) — Publicly or privately funded immediate medical care that extends hospital emergency room treatment into the community in order to provide care to the victims of illness and injury as quickly as possible.

Emergency Medical Technician (EMT) — Qualified provider of basic life support medical care.

Empathy — Ability to understand the feelings and attitudes of another person.

Employee Assistance Program (EAP) — Program designed to provide employees with counseling services ranging from financial counseling to substance-abuse programs and domestic-violence prevention.

EMS — Abbreviation for Emergency Medical Services.

EMT — Abbreviation for Emergency Medical Technician.

Environmental Protection Agency (EPA) — U. S. government agency that creates regulations and enforces laws designed to protect air, water, and soil from contamination.

EPA — Abbreviation for U.S. Environmental Protection Agency.

Equal Employment Opportunity (EEO) — Process required by law in the U.S. that requires fair and equitable access to jobs through the hiring and promotional process.

Equal Employment Opportunity Commission (EEOC) — U.S. government agency that reviews and enforces fair hiring and promotional standards.

Equal Employment Opportunity Laws — Laws that apply to protected groups of individuals who have experienced past workplace discrimination.

Ethics — Philosophical principles that are used to determine correct and proper behavior by members of a society. Sometimes called *moral philosophies.*

Evaluating — Act of establishing the worth or value of each part or the sum total of the whole based on the desired outcome, which therefore determines how effective or efficient an item, program, or process is compared to a benchmark or established set of criteria. In the communication process, it is the act of critically analyzing a message to determine how factual it really is; the receiver (or listener) must be able to separate facts from opinions. *Also see* Evaluation, Communication, Receiver, and Message.

Evaluation — Process used to assess a student's achievements (fulfillment of the course or lesson requirements) and/or the effectiveness of learning experiences; also, a lesson-plan component where an instructor assesses student learning through various types of assessment methods. *Also see* Assessment, Testing, Lesson Plan, and Test.

Executive Summary — Brief review of the key points in a report, a technical paper, a list of specifications, or an analysis; also called *abstract.*

F

FAA — Abbreviation for U.S. Federal Aviation Administration.

Fact — Verifiable piece of data that can be used to support the decision-making process.

Fax — Term that refers to the act of sending (verb) a copy of a document via the telephone system; also used as a noun to mean the item that is transmitted; originally an acronym for *facsimile.*

FDSOA — Abbreviation for Fire Department Safety Officers Association.

Federal Aviation Administration (FAA) — Subdivision of the U.S. Department of Transportation that is responsible for the regulation of civil aviation.

Federal Emergency Management Agency (FEMA) — U.S. federal agency responsible for emergency preparedness, mitigation, and response activities including natural, technological, and attack-related emergencies; part of the U.S. Department of Homeland Security (DHS).

Feedback — In the communication process, responses that clarify and ensure that a message was received and understood by the receiver (or listener); also used to mean comments by an instructor to a student regarding the student's abilities or achievements. *Also see* Communication, Receiver, and Message.

FEMA — Abbreviation for U.S. Federal Emergency Management Agency.

Field Test — Process of teaching a course on a trial basis.

Fire Department Safety Officers Association (FDSOA) — Fire service professional organization whose mission is to promote safety standards and practices in the fire, rescue, and emergency services community.

Foreseeability — Legal concept that reasonable people should be able to foresee the consequences of their actions and take reasonable precautions.

Formative Test — Periodic test that typically measures improvement and gives an instructor and students feedback on their learning progress during a course rather than at the end. *Also see* Test and Summative Test.

G

Gifted Student — Term generally applied to children and youth who have great natural abilities or talents. *Also see* Slow Student.

Grading — Act of assigning a value to a score. *Also see* Scoring, Ranking of Scores, and Raw Score.

H

Hazard — Condition, substance, or device that can directly cause an injury or loss; usually refers to the source of a risk. *Also see* Accident and Risk.

Hazard/Risk Analysis — Determines the potential safety threats that may be encountered during training and emergency operations; the analysis process identifies potential problem areas and is the foundation for a risk-management plan. *Also see* Hazard, Risk, and Risk-Management Plan.

Health and Safety Officer (HSO) — Member of the fire and emergency services organization who is assigned and authorized by the administration as the manager of the health and safety program and performs the duties, functions, and responsibilities found in NFPA 1521, *Standard for Fire Department Safety Officer.*

Heating, Ventilating, and Air-Conditioning (HVAC) — Air-handling system within a building consisting of fans, ducts, dampers, and other equipment necessary to make the system function.

High-Hazard Training — Training that involves activities that are potentially risky. Training that includes certain known risks and potential unknown risks. *Also see* Hazard and Risk.

Home Safety Council (HSC) — National nonprofit organization dedicated to preventing home-related injuries through national programs, partnerships, and the support of volunteers by educating people of all ages how to be safer in and around their homes.

HSC — Abbreviation for Home Safety Council.

HSO — Abbreviation for Health and Safety Officer.

HVAC — Abbreviation for Heating, Ventilating, and Air-Conditioning.

I

IAFC — Abbreviation for International Association of Fire Chiefs.

IAFF — Abbreviation for International Association of Firefighters.

IAP — Abbreviation for Incident Action Plan.

IC — Abbreviation for Incident Commander.

ICMA — Abbreviation for International City/County Managers Association.

ICS — Abbreviation for Incident Command System.

IFSAC — Abbreviation for International Fire Service Accreditation Congress.

IFSTA — Abbreviation for International Fire Service Training Association.

ILT — Abbreviation for Instructor-Led Training.

IMS — Abbreviation for Incident Management System.

Incident Action Plan (IAP) — Written or unwritten plan for the disposition of an incident; establishes the strategic goals and tactical objectives of the operation or scenario for a specific time period.

Incident Commander (IC) — Person in charge of the incident command/management system and responsible for the management of all incident operations during an emergency.

Incident Command System (ICS) — Process that provides for a systematic development of a complete, functional command organization and increases the effectiveness of fire and emergency services organizations; also provides the base for multiagency and multijurisdictional incident management systems. It is part of the National Incident Management System (NIMS). Also called *Incident Management System (IMS).*

Incident Management System (IMS) — *See* Incident command System.

Incident Safety Officer (ISO) — Member of the Incident Command System (ICS) Command Staff responsible for monitoring and assessing safety hazards and unsafe conditions during an incident, and developing measures for ensuring personnel safety.

Incident Safety Plan (ISP) — Plan based on the Incident Commander's (IC's) strategy and tactics as described in the incident action plan (IAP) and the type of hazard involved at the incident.

Information Management — *See* Records Management.

Information Sheet — Type of handout or fact sheet that provides additional background information on a topic supplemental to the information provided in the text or other course resources.

Information Technology (IT) — All forms of technology used to create, store, exchange, and use information (including business data) in its various forms such as conversations, still images, motion pictures, and multimedia presentations.

Instruction — *See* Teaching/Instruction.

Instructional/Interactive Television (ITV) — Television-based system used to link multiple classroom sites together and permits one instructor to reach more students.

Instructor Information—Component of the lesson plan that lists lesson resources such as personnel, texts, references sources, instructional methods, learning activities, training locations, etc.

Instructor-Led Training (ILT) — Traditional instruction that depends on the direct transfer of knowledge from the instructor to the student.

Insurance Services Office (ISO) — Private national organization that evaluates and establishes insurance rates for communities based on fire protection services available to them.

Integrity — Personal quality that is based on the values and morals of an individual.

Intelligence Quotient (IQ) — Ratio of tested mental age to chronological age, usually expressed as a quotient multiplied by 100.

Interference — In the communication process, those factors that prevent the receiver from fully receiving a message; may be created by either internal or external sources. *Also see* Communication, Receiver, and Message.

International Association of Fire Chiefs (IAFC) — Professional organization that represents the interests of fire and emergency services chief officers.

International Association of Fire Fighters (IAFF) — Professional organization that represents the interests of fire and emergency services personnel through professional development and labor/management relations.

International City/County Managers Association (ICMA) — Professional and educational organization that provides technical and management assistance, training, and information resources to members and the local government community.

International Fire Service Accreditation Congress (IFSAC) — Nonprofit organization that accredits both fire service certification programs and higher education fire-related degree programs.

International Fire Service Training Association (IFSTA) — Nonprofit educational association that develops and provides training materials to the fire and emergency services internationally.

International Society of Fire Service Instructors (ISFSI) — Professional organization that represents the interests of fire and emergency services instructors internationally.

Interpersonal Communication — Communication that takes place between two people who have established a relationship; occurs on a daily basis in the lives of all people who live in groups.

IQ — Abbreviation for Intelligence Quotient.

ISFSI — Abbreviation for International Society of Fire Service Instructors.

ISO — Abbreviation for Incident Safety Officer.

ISO — Abbreviation for Insurance Services Office.

ISP — Abbreviation for Incident Safety Plan.

IT — Abbreviation for Information Technology.

ITV — Abbreviation for Instructional/Interactive Television.

J

Job — Grouping of similar functions within a block in a task analysis. *Also see* Analysis and Task Analysis.

Job Performance Requirement (JPR) — Statement that describe the performance required for a specific job.

JPR — Abbreviation for Job Performance Requirement.

Judicial Legislation — *See* Judiciary Law

Judiciary Law — Usually the result of a legal precedent or a judicial decision; decisions that serve as rules for future determinations in similar cases; also known as *judicial legislation* or *case law*.

K

Keystoning — Effect that occurs when the width of a projected image is wider at the top than at the bottom.

Kinesics — Use of body motion and position in the nonverbal component of the communication process. *Also see* Communication and Nonverbal Cue.

Knowledge — Ability to remember previously learned information.

L

LAN — Acronym for Local-Area Network.

Law — Legal document that sets forth rules that govern a particular type of activity; also used to mean a rule or body of rules of conduct inherent in human nature and essential to the operation of society; used broadly and commonly to address many legal concepts.

Leadership — Art of influencing and directing people to accomplish a mission or task. *Also see* Leading and Motivation.

Leading — Act of controlling, directing, conducting, guiding, and administering through the use of personal behavioral traits or personality characteristics that motivate employees to the successful completion of an organization's goals. *Also see* Leadership and Motivation.

Learning — Active process in which students progress through a series of mental steps to bring about a change in behavior; relatively permanent and observable change in a person's behavior that is the result of interaction with the environment.

Learning Disability — Consists of a wide variety of disorders that may be neurological in origin and affect an individual's ability to understand, think, or use the spoken or written word.

Learning Domain — Distinct sphere or area of knowledge, such as cognitive, psychomotor, or affective. *Also see* Cognitive Domain, Affective Domain, and Psychomotor Domain.

Learning Method — Way an individual thinks or processes information.

Learning Objective — Specific statement that describes desired learning result (competency) necessary to complete a learning outcome. *Also see* Learning Outcome.

Learning Outcome — Statement that specifies what students will know or be able to do once learning is complete. *Also see* Learning Objective.

Learning Style — Consistent way a person gathers and processes information.

Legislative or Statutory Law — Legal document made by federal, state/provincial, or local legislative bodies that pertain to civil and criminal matters. *Also see* Administrative Law.

Lesson — Planned and organized learning experience that is developed to guide students through a course of study. *Also see* Lesson Plan

Lesson Plan — Instructional document that outlines the information and skills to be taught (prelude to instruction); makes effective use of available resources (personnel, time, space, and materials). *Also see* Lesson and Level of Instruction.

Level of Instruction — Lesson plan component that states the learning level that students will reach by the end of the lesson; may be based on the taxonomy of learning domains or performance of job requirements. *Also see* Lesson Plan.

Liability — Broad, comprehensive term that describes legal responsibility. *Also see* Negligence and Vicarious Liability.

Local-Area Network (LAN) — Electronic system of computers that are connected together to form an intranet within an organization. *Also see* Wide-Area Network (WAN).

Liquefied Petroleum Gas (LPG) — Confined gas that at normal temperatures exists in both liquid and gaseous states.

Listener — *See* Receiver.

Listening — Active process that includes receiving, attending, understanding, remembering, evaluating, and responding to a message from a speaker (sender). *Also see* Attending, Remembering, Sender, Receiver, and Message.

Literacy — Individual's ability to read, write, speak in English, and compute and solve problems at levels of proficiency necessary to function on the job, in the family of the individual, and in society.

Live-Fire Training — Training activity that involves a simulated fire-suppression activity. May take place in a purpose-built structure, acquired structure, or in the open.

Logistics — Procurement, distribution, maintenance, and replacement of material and equipment.

LPG — Abbreviation for Liquefied Petroleum Gas.

M

Management — Administration and control of projects, programs, systems, resources, or organizations. *Also see* Managing.

Managing — Act of controlling, monitoring, or directing a project, program, system, or organization through the use of authority, discipline, or persuasion. *Also see* Management.

Manipulative Performance Test — Type of test that measures the student's ability and proficiency in performing a job or evolution that requires them to handle equipment or materials in a coordinated, step-by-step process; measures learner or employee achievement of a psychomotor objective and holds the test-taker to either a speed standard (timed performance) or quality standard (minimum acceptable product or process standard) or both. *Also see* Test and Performance Evaluation.

Mastery — High-level or nearly complete degree of proficiency in the performance of a skill based on criteria stated in objectives.

Materials — In the training process, equipment and other instructional support tools required for teaching a lesson or course.

Mean — Average of a set of scores; found by adding the set of scores (values) and dividing by the total number of scores. *Also see* Median and Mode.

Median — Middle score in a set of scores (values) that are arranged or ranked in size (order) from high to low. *Also see* Mean and Mode.

Medium — In the communication process, path that the message takes between the sender and receiver. *Also see* Communication, Sender, Receiver, and Message.

Memory — Individual record or past mental and sensory experience; some aspects can be measured by the individual's ability to recall, recognize, and relearn.

Mentor — Trusted and friendly adviser or guide for someone who is new to a particular role. *Also see* Mentoring.

Mentoring — Activity that matches a mentor with a new student or employee to provide guidance, motivation, and a positive role model for the new person. *Also see* Mentor.

Message — In the communication process, information or idea transmitted and received through all or most of the senses. *Also see* Communication.

MFIPPA — Abbreviation for Municipal Freedom of Information and Protection of Privacy Act.

Mitigation — Act of making less severe or intense; process of finding solutions to reduce the severity of hazards or emergencies.

Mode — The most frequent score (value) in a set of scores. *Also see* Mean, and Median.

Moral Philosophies — *See* Ethics.

Motivation — Internal state or condition that activates and directs behavior toward a goal. *Also see* Leadership and Leading.

Municipal Freedom of Information and Protection of Privacy Act (MFIPPA) — Canadian law that ensures public access to information under the control of government and nongovernment institutions while, at the same time, ensuring privacy for individuals whose records are held by those institutions.

N

National Board on Fire Service Professional Qualifications (Pro Board) — Certification and accreditation organization with the purpose of establishing an internationally recognized means of acknowledging professional achievement in the fire and emergency services; primary goal is the accreditation of organizations that certify uniform members of career and volunteer public fire departments.

National Fire Academy (NFA) — Educational component of the U.S. Fire Administration (USFA) providing training to members of the fire and emergency services nationally.

National Fire Incident Reporting System (NFIRS) — U.S. government agency that collects and analyses information about fires in the U.S.

National Fire Protection Association (NFPA) — Nonprofit educational and technical association devoted to protecting life and property from fire by developing fire protection standards and educating the public.

National Incident Management System (NIMS) — Process that provides for the systematic establishment of a complete, functional command organization for multiagency incidents that involve the U.S. government as well as state and local agencies. *Also see* Incident Command System (ICS).

National Institute for Occupational Safety and Health (NIOSH) — U.S. government agency of the Centers for Disease Control and Prevention (CDC) that helps ensure that workplaces and associated equipment are safe; also investigates workplace injuries, reports results, and makes recommendations.

National Volunteer Fire Council (NVFC) — Nonprofit membership association representing the interests of the volunteer fire, emergency medical services (EMS), and rescue services; serves as the information source regarding legislation, standards and regulatory issues that affect the volunteer emergency services.

Needs Assessment — Survey of the types of services required or desired by the community or service area.

Negligence — Breach of duty where there is a responsibility to perform. *Also see* Liability.

NFA — Abbreviation for U.S. National Fire Academy.

NFIRS — Abbreviation for National Fire Incident Reporting System.

NFPA — Abbreviation for National Fire Protection Association.

NIMS — Abbreviation for the National Incident Management System.

NIOSH — Abbreviation for U.S. National Institute for Occupational Safety and Health.

Nonverbal Cue — Message without words often transmitted in gestures, posture or body language, eye contact, facial expression, tone of voice, and appearance. *Also see* Message, Communication, and Kinesics.

Norm-Referenced Test — Student's test performance compared with the performance of other students; grade is dependent on the average performance and variability of performance among the others in the group. *Also see* Criterion-Referenced Test and Test.

NVFC — Abbreviation for National Volunteer Fire Council.

O

Objective Test — Test or test item designed so that all qualified test developers agree on the correct answer; test item and its answer are based on course objectives that were developed from some selected criteria or standard. Types include multiple-choice, matching, true-false, and short-answer/completion. *Also see* Subjective Test, Test-Item Analysis, and Test.

Occupation — Career or professional category used in task analysis. *Also see* Task Analysis.

Occupational Safety and Health Administration (OSHA) — U.S. federal agency that develops and enforces standards and regulations for occupational safety in the workplace.

On-the-Job Training — Situation where workers can develop the skills needed for average job performance after a short demonstration of the skill, through experience, or brief instruction.

Operating Budget — List of funds that are used to pay for the recurring expenses of the day-to-day operation of the fire and emergency services organization. *Also see* Capital Budget and Budget.

Opinion — Generalization that may *not* be verifiable without additional data.

Oral Test — Test or form of assessment in which students are tested, usually individually, in face-to-face discussion with the examiner or group of examiners, often in conjunction with written and/or skills testing. *Also see* Test, Performance Evaluation, and Manipulative Performance Test.

Ordinance — Local law that applies to persons, things, and activities in a jurisdiction and has the same force and effect as legislative or statutory law. *Also see* Legislative or Statutory Law.

Organizing — Activity that involves coordinating tasks and resources to accomplish established goals and objectives.

OSHA — Abbreviation for U.S. Occupational Safety and Health Administration.

P

Paralanguage or Vocalics — Vowel sound or tone used to create the verbal message in the communication process. *Also see* Communication and Message.

Pedagogy — Principles, methods, and profession for teaching children and youth.

Peer — Someone who is equal in status either socially or psychologically to another.

Peer Assistance — Process that involves having students assist other students in the learning process.

Percentage Score — Refers to the percent of test items that are answered correctly. *Also see* Test-Item Analysis.

Performance Evaluation — Assessment of skills that shows the level of student performance or ability to perform skill steps for a particular task or job. *Also see* Manipulative Performance Test, Assessment, and Skills Sheet.

PERT — Acronym for Program Evaluation and Review Technique.

Planning — Act of setting goals and objectives and determining the direction an organization or unit will take to achieve those results.

Powered Test — Test designed to evaluate the performance level of students; time limit is established to permit the majority, if not all, students to complete the test. *Also see* Test.

Preparation — Lesson plan component where the instructor provides preliminary information that will motivate and prepare the student to learn; also refers to the preparation that the instructor makes before teaching. *Also see* Lesson Plan.

Prerequisite — Knowledge, information, skill, or previous requirement that students must have completed or mastered before entering a course or beginning a lesson.

Prescriptive Test — Test given before or at the beginning of instruction to measure learning readiness and determine student placement. Also called *pretest. See* Test, Formative Test, and Summative Test.

Presentation — Lesson plan component where the instructor provides to, shares with, demonstrates

to, and involves students in the lesson information. *Also see* Lesson Plan

Pretest — *See* Prescriptive Test.

Privacy Act — Prohibits invasion of a person's right to privacy or unwanted publicity; restricts access to personal information such as personnel files and student grades; guarantees access to records only by the covered student or eligible parent or guardian; prohibits disclosure of personal information without consent. Also called *Buckley Amendment.*

Pro Board — Unofficial name for the National Board on Fire Service Professional Qualifications.

Profession — Vocation that requires specialized knowledge and long, intense preparation that includes (1) learning scientific, historical, or scholarly principles that apply to specific skills, processes, and methods; (2) maintaining high standards of personal achievement and conduct; and (3) committing to continued study and educational advancement.

Program Evaluation and Review Technique (PERT) Chart — Chart that plots a project and evaluates the success of each step; depicts the individual tasks, time required for each task, and interrelationship or dependency of the various steps with each other.

Progress Test — Test that may be written or oral used as a diagnostic device to measure the progress or improvement of students throughout a course and helps guide instructors and students in deciding what areas need more emphasis or learning time. Also called *quiz. Also see* Test.

Projection System — Audiovisual device for showing video, television, or computer images on a large screen.

Promulgate — To officially develop, file, publish, announce, and put into effect a law, ordinance, rule, or regulation.

Psychomotor Domain — Learning domain that refers to skills involving knowledge learned through the senses that is applied to physical movement. *Also see* Domain.

Q

Qualified — Person who meets the proper standards, requirements, training, and certifications to perform a task or fill a position.

Quiz — *See* Progress test.

R

Ranking of Scores — Process of arranging a number of scores (values) in order from high to low; process that makes it easy to determine median and mode. *Also see* Median, Mode, Mean, Grading, Raw Score, and Scoring.

Rapid Intervention Crew (RIC) — Two or more fully equipped and immediately available firefighters designated to stand outside the hazard zone ready to enter and affect rescue of firefighters inside if necessary. Also called *rapid intervention team (RIT)*

Rapid Intervention Team (RIT) — *See* Rapid Intervention Crew.

Raw Score — Score on a test that has *not* yet been statistically processed to make it comparable with other scores. *Also see* Ranking of Scores, Test, Grading, and Scoring

Reasonable Accommodation — Making facilities readily accessible to and usable by individuals with disabilities.

Receiver — In the communication process the individual who receives the message and decodes or interprets it. Also called *listener*. *Also see* Communication and Message.

Record — Permanent account of known or recorded fact that is used to recall or relate a past event or action taken by an individual, unit, or organization. *Also see* Record Keeping.

Record Keeping — Storage of records and reports accumulated by an organization. Also known as information management. *Also see* Record and Records Management.

Records Management — Process of planning, controlling, directing, organizing, training, and conducting other managerial activities required for maintaining an organization's records. Also known as *information management*. *Also see* Record and Record Keeping.

Reference — Citation, bibliography, or resource used in developing, planning, and researching course or lesson information.

Regulation — Rule or similar directive issued by an administrative agency.

Reliability — Condition that ensures that a test item is dependable by providing the same results every time it is administered. *Also see* Test-Item Analysis.

Remembering — Element of the listening process that involves retaining the message in the receiver's memory. *Also see* Listening, Receiver, and Message.

Report — Written or verbal accounting of an event based on facts surrounding the incident, response, or activity.

Responding — In the communication process, the action of the receiver who completes the process, which means an exchange of roles has occurred (the receiver becomes the sender and vice versa). *Also see* Communication, Receiver, and Sender.

RIC — Abbreviation for Rapid Intervention Crew.

Risk — Exposure to a hazard that may result in injury, loss of life, or loss of property. *Also see* Hazard/Risk Analysis and Risk-Management Plan.

Risk-Management Plan — Written plan that identifies and analyzes the exposures to hazards, selects appropriate risk-management techniques to address exposures, explains how to implement chosen techniques, and explains how to monitor the results of those techniques.

RIT — Abbreviation for Rapid Intervention Team.

Role Model — Individual who others look to as an example while learning or adopting a new role or job; the part an instructor plays, image an instructor portrays, and actions an instructor demonstrates to students, peers, and subordinates.

Role-Play — Activities in which students portray characters and act the roles assigned to them in hypothetical scenarios.

S

Safety Guidelines — Rules, regulations, or policies created and/or adopted by an organization that list steps or procedures to follow that will aid in reducing or eliminating accidents or injuries. Also called *safety plan*.

Safety Plan — *See* Safety Guidelines.

Sarcasm — Use of language that may be insulting, demeaning, or scornful of others.

Schema (s), Schemata (pl) — Refers to conceptual or knowledge structure(s) (mental map[s]) in the human memory system that is/are used to interpret information that is presented to the senses by the external environment.

Scoring — Act of identifying which answers to test items are correct and which are incorrect. *Also see* Ranking of Scores, Test-Item Analysis, and Raw Scores.

Semantics — Study of meaning in words and symbols; refers to language, word meanings, and meaning changes due to context, all of which may be affected by individual background, knowledge, and experience.

Sender — In the communication process, the person who originates a message by encoding or turning thoughts and mental images into words. Also referred to in some speech communication texts as *speaker*. *Also see* Communication and Message.

Sensitivity — Ability to view the learning environment from a student perspective and recognize the barriers to learning and communication; involves having a personal interest in people.

Simulation — Activity that allows students to participate in a scenario that represents a real-life situation.

Simulator — Any training device that represents a system, process, or environment in which actual training would be unsafe, impractical, or prohibitively expensive.

Sincerity — Personal quality of being open and truthful.

Skills Sheet — Instructional document that divides a task into parts by listing the operational steps and their key points or steps for completing each operation.

Slow Student — Individual with borderline intelligence, which is defined as the minimum intelligence required for a person to function normally and independently in the world. *Also see* Gifted Student.

SOG — Abbreviation for Standard Operating Guideline.

SOP — Abbreviation for Standard Operating Procedure.

Speaker — *See* Sender.

Speeded Test — Test that assesses the student's ability to perform a test within a specific time. *Also see* Powered Test and Test.

Standard — Any rule, principle, criterion, or measure established by authority.

Standard of Care — Degree of care that a reasonably prudent person should exercise in similar or the same circumstances.

Standard Operating Guideline (SOG) — Standard method, procedure, or rule in which a fire and emergency services organization operates to perform a routine function; usually contained in a written policy and procedures handbook. Also called *standard operating procedure*.

Standard Operating Procedure (SOP) — *See* Standard Operating Guideline.

Statutory Law — *See* Legislative Law.

Study Sheet — Instructional document designed to arouse student interest in a topic and explain specific areas to study.

Subjective Test — Test in which different but equally qualified instructors will respond differently in judging the quality of a student's work (subjectivity) and therefore award different scores; measures high cognitive levels; common types are essay and term paper. *Also see* Test and Objective Test.

Substantive Right — Right everyone has such as right to equal enjoyment of fundamental rights, privileges, and immunities.

Summary — Lesson plan component where the instructor restates or reemphasizes key points with students by asking questions and guiding review by having them recall relationships, make comparisons, draw conclusions, etc. *Also see* Lesson Plan.

Summative Test — Measurement of student achievement in an entire area on a number of topics covered during a course. *Also see* Comprehensive Test, Formative Test, and Test.

Supervision — Act that includes the processes of directing, overseeing, and controlling the activities of other individuals who are assigned to a particular supervisor.

Synthesis — Ability to assemble component parts into a larger body of information.

T

Task Analysis — Detailed review of each physical task or job that is performed by emergency personnel; each task is divided into steps that are required to complete it. *Also see* Analysis, Hazard/Risk Analysis, and Test-Item Analysis.

Taxonomy — Classification system in which each separate class of items is given a name and contains items that are more like one another than like items in other classes. Examples are the Dewey Decimal System and Bloom's Taxonomy of Objectives for the Cognitive Domain.

TBT — Abbreviation for Technology-Based Training.

Teaching/Instruction — Method of transferring knowledge by giving information through various forms of communication in a systematic manner. *Also see* Traditional Instruction and Training.

Technology-Based Training (TBT) — Electronic learning (e-learning) that uses methods such as Internet web-based instruction, instructional interactive television (ITV), and other forms of computer-based electronically transferred knowledge. *Also see* Electronic Learning.

Test — Any means by which the absence, presence, amount, or nature of some quality or ability is observed or inferred and appraised or measured in a student. *Also see* Assessment, Evaluation, Objective Test, Subjective Test, Norm-Referenced Test, Criterion-Referenced Test, Formative Test, Summative Test, Prescriptive Test, Powered Test, Speeded Test, Progress Test, Comprehensive Test, Written Test, Oral Test, Manipulative Performance Test, and Testing.

Testing — Process of evaluation that implies standardization in which the student is compared against a defined criteria or standard; includes a basis or means to determine the degree to which students learned what was intended for them to learn. *Also see* Test, Evaluation, Criterion-Referenced Test, and Assessment.

Test-Item Analysis — Process that allows instructors to use systematic methods to assess the quality of a test item. *Also see* Test, Analysis, and Testing.

Test Planning Sheet — Form that lists and specifies the number of test items to be written and at what levels of learning in each content area. *Also see* Test.

Time Frame — Lesson plan component that lists the estimated time it will take to teach a lesson. *Also see* Lesson Plan.

Traditional Instruction — Approach to teaching based on the presentation of information through lectures, readings, and audiovisuals. *Also see* Teaching/Instruction and Training.

Training — Instruction that emphasizes job-specific learning objectives and traditional skills-based instruction as opposed to only knowledge-based education. It is primarily the transfer of knowledge regarding vocational or technical skills. *Also see* Teaching/Instruction, Knowledge, Training Agency, and Traditional Instruction.

Training Agency — State, provincial, regional, or national organization that provides fire and emergency services training. *Also see* Training, Training Division, and Training Program.

Training Aid — *See* Training Prop.

Training Division — Division, bureau, branch, or section within a fire and emergency services organization that is primarily responsible for providing internal training. *Also see* Training, Training Agency, and Training Program.

Training Program — Function of the training division or agency; consists of all training and educational activities that are provided by the division or agency to meet certification, legal, or local requirements for fire and emergency services organizations. *Also see* Training, Training Agency, Training Aid, and Training Division.

Training Prop — Permanent structure or portable device used to simulate specific types of emergency situations and teach fire and emergency related-subjects. Sometimes called *training aid*. *Also see* Training and Training Program.

U

Underwriters Laboratories Inc. (UL) — Independent fire research and testing laboratory that certifies equipment and materials. *Also see* Underwriters' Laboratories of Canada.

Underwriters' Laboratories of Canada (ULC) — Canadian branch of Underwriters Laboratories Inc. (UL). *Also see* Underwriters Laboratories Inc.

UL — Abbreviation for Underwriters Laboratories Inc.

ULC — Abbreviation for Underwriters' Laboratories of Canada.

Understanding — Element of the listening process that consists of the receiver decoding the message and assigning meaning to it. *Also see* Message, Receiver, and Listening.

U.S. Fire Administration (USFA) — Agency of the U.S. Department of Homeland Security (DHS) whose mission is to reduce life and economic losses due to fire and related emergencies through leadership, advocacy, coordination, and support.

USFA — Abbreviation for U.S. Fire Administration.

V

Validity — Extent to which a test or any assessment technique measures the student qualities (knowledge and skills) that it is designed to measure. *Also see* Test and Assessment.

Vicarious Liability — Liability imposed on one person for the conduct of another based solely on the relationship between the two persons. Indirect legal responsibility for acts of another (liability of an employer for acts of an employee). *Also see* Liability and Negligence.

W

WAN — Acronym for Wide-Area Network.

WBT — Abbreviation for Web-Based Training.

Weapons of Mass Destruction (WMD) — Weapons that cause large-scale destruction; generally use chemical, biological agents, radiological, nuclear, or explosive (CBRNE) devices.

Web-Based Training (WBT) — Training or education delivered via the Internet or World Wide Web (WWW) or over a closed intranet/extranet (LAN/WAN) network. *Also see* Training, Education/Instruction, World Wide Web, Local-Area Network, and Wide-Area Network.

World Wide Web (WWW) — Information system using the Internet to access information stored on computers worldwide. *Also see* Web-Based Training.

Wide-Area Network (WAN) — Set of widely separated computers connected together such as the Internet. *Also see* Local-Area Network (LAN).

WMD — Abbreviation for Weapons of Mass Destruction.

Worksheet — Sheet that lists tasks to accomplish, guides activities, and enables students to apply cognitive information in order to practice and develop skills.

Written Test — Test that typically assesses or measures cognitive knowledge, commonly by pencil and paper but may also be given by computer. *Also see* Test and Testing.

WWW — Abbreviation for World Wide Web.

Suggested Readings

Suggested Readings

Leadership

Compton, Dennis. *When in Doubt, Lead!* Oklahoma State University: Fire Protection Publications, 1999.

Compton, Dennis. *When in Doubt, Lead . . . Part 2.* Oklahoma State University: Fire Protection Publications, 2000.

Compton, Dennis. *When in Doubt, Lead! Part 3.* Oklahoma State University: Fire Protection Publications, 2002.

Covey, Stephen R. *The Seven Habits of Highly Effective People.* New York: Simon and Schuster, 1990.

Covey, Stephen R. *Principle-Centered Leadership.* New York: Simon and Schuster, 1992.

Covey, Stephen R. *The Eighth Habit: From Effectiveness to Greatness.* New York: Simon and Schuster, 2004.

Linsky, Martin, and Ronald A. Heifetz. *Leadership on the Line: Staying Alive Through the Dangers of Leading.* Boston: Harvard Business School Press, 2002.

Northouse, Peter Guy. *Leadership: Theory and Practice.* Thousand Oaks, CA: Sage Publications, 1997.

Communication Skills

Beebe, Steven A., and Susan J. Beebe. *Public Speaking: An Audience-Centered Approach.* Needham Heights, MA: Pearson, Allyn and Bacon, 2002.

Brill, Laura. *Business Writing Quick & Easy,* 2nd Edition. New York: AMACOM Books, 1989.

Devito, Joseph A. *The Interpersonal Communication Book,* 10th Edition. Needham Heights, MA: Pearson, Allyn and Bacon, 2003.

Markel, Mike. *Technical Communication,* 6th Edition. New York: St. Martin's Press, 2001.

Pearsall, Thomas E. *The Elements of Technical Writing.* Boston: Allyn and Bacon, 2001.

Robey, Cora L. *New Handbook of Basic Writing Skills.* Ft. Worth, TX: Harcourt College Publishers, 2001.

Wood, Julia T. *Everyday Encounters: An Introduction to Interpersonal Communication.* Florence, KY: Wadsworth Publishing, 2001.

Basic Administrative Skills

Bruce, Andy. *Project Management.* New York: Dorling Kindersley, 2000.

— *Fire Data Analysis Handbook,* Federal Emergency Management Agency, U.S. Fire Administration, Washington, DC: U.S. Government Printing Office, 1995.

Lussier, Robert N. Ph.D. *Management Fundamentals: Concepts, Applications, Skill Development,* 2nd Edition. Mason, OH: Thomson South-Western Publishers, 2003.

Maira, Arun, and Peter Scott-Morgan. *The Accelerating Organization: Embracing the Human Face of Change.* New York: McGraw-Hill, 1997.

Wallace, Mark. *Fire Department Strategic Planning: Creating Future Excellence.* Fair Lawn, NJ: Fire Engineering Books and Videos, PennWell Publishing Company, 1998.

Weiss, Joseph W., and Robert K. Wysocki. *Five-Phase Project Management: A Practical Planning and Implementation Guide.* Boulder, CO: Perseus Books Group, 1992.

Wysocki, Robert K., Robert Beck, Jr., and David B. Crane. *Effective Project Management,* 2nd Edition. New York: John A. Wiley and Sons, Inc., 2000.

Management and Supervision

Collins, Jim. *Good to Great: Why Some Companies Make the Leap . . . and Others Don't.* New York: HarperCollins, 2001.

Compton, Dennis, and John Granito, Editors. *Managing Fire and Rescue Services.* Washington, DC: International City/County Mangers Association, 2002.

Gaynor, Gerard H. *What Every New Manager Needs to Know.* New York: AMACOM Books, 2003.

Hersey, Paul. *Management of Organizational Behavior: Leading Human Resources,* 8th Edition. Upper Saddle River, NJ: Prentice Hall, 2000.

Logic, Ethics, and Decision-Making

Badaracco, Joseph L. *Defining Moments: When Managers Must Choose Between Right and Right.* Boston: Harvard Business School Press, 1997.

— *Harvard Business Review on Decision-Making.* Boston: Harvard Business School Press, 2001.

Janing, Judy, and Gordon M. Sachs. *Achieving Excellence in the Fire Service.* Upper Saddle River, NJ: Prentice-Hall, 2002.

Klein, Gary. *Sources of Power: How People Make Decisions.* Cambridge: Massachusette Institute of Technology Press, 1998.

Human Resources

Blanchard, Kenneth H., Paul Hersey, and Dewey E. Johnson. *Management of Organizational Behavior: Utilizing Human Resources.* Upper Saddle River, NJ: Prentice Hall, 1996.

Chetkovich, Carol. *Real Heat: Gender and Race in the Urban Fire Service.* New Brunswick, NJ: Rutgers University Press, 1997.

Compton, Dennis. *Mental Aspects of Performance for Firefighters,* 2nd Edition. Oklahoma State University: Fire Protection Publications, 2004.

Edwards, Steven T. *Fire Service Personnel Management.* Upper Saddle River, NJ: Prentice-Hall, 2000.

Gaston, James M., and Dr. Riley Harvil. *Fire Officer Coaching.* Oklahoma State University: Fire Protection Publications, 2005.

Macoby, Michael. *The Gamesman.* New York: Bantam Doubleday Dell Publishing Group, 1977.

— *Many Faces, One Purpose: A Manager's Handbook on Women in Firefighting.* Federal Emergency Management Association and U.S. Fire Administration, date unknown.

— *Retention and Recruitment in the Volunteer Fire Service: Problems and Solutions.* National Volunteer Fire Council and U.S. Fire Administration, Final Report, 1998.

Snook, Jack W., Jeffery D. Johnson, Daniel C. Olsen, and John Buckman. *Recruiting, Training, and Maintaining Volunteer Firefighters,* 3rd Edition. West Linn, OR: Emergency Services Consulting Group, 1998.

Community Relations

Brunacini, Alan. *Essentials of Fire Department Customer Service.* Oklahoma State University: Fire Protection Publications, 1996.

— *Fire Risk Analysis: A Systems Approach.* Emmitsburg, MD: National Fire Academy, 1984.

Instructional Development and Presentations

Anderson, Lorin W., and David Krathwohl, Editors. *A Taxonomy for Learning, Teaching and Assessing.* New York: Longman, 2001.

Baden, Clifford. *Adult Learning in Associations: Models for Good Practice.* Washington, DC: American Society of Association Executives, 1998.

Bloom, Benjamin S., M. B. Englebert, E. J. Furst, W. H. Hill, and D. R. Krathwohl, Editors *Taxonomy of Educational Objectives: The Classification of Educational Goals. Handbook I: Cognitive Domain.* New York: McKay, 1956.

Cantonwine, Sheila. *Safety Training That Delivers – How to Design and Present Better Technical Training.* Des Plaines, IL: American Society of Safety Engineers, 1999.

— *Fire and Life Safety Educator.* Oklahoma State University: International Fire Service Training Association, 1997.

Gagne, Robert, Leslie Briggs, and Walter Wager. *Principles of Instructional Design,* 4th Edition. Fort Worth, TX: Harcourt Brace Jovanovich College Publishers, 1992.

Gronlund, Norman Edward. *How to Construct Achievement Tests.* Englewood Cliffs, NJ: Prentice-Hall, 1988.

Gronlund, Norman Edward. *Stating Objectives for Classroom Instruction.* New York: MacMillan Publishing Company, 1985.

Hassell-Corbiell, Rives. *Developing Training Courses: a Technical Writer's Guide to Instruction Design and Development.* Tacoma, WA: Learning Edge Publications, 2001.

Hunter, Madeline C. *Enhancing Teaching.* New York: MacMillan College Publishing Company, 1994.

Kemp, Jerrold E. *Planning for Effective Technical Training.* Englewood Cliffs, NJ: Educational Technology Publications, 1994.

Khan, Badrul H., Editor. *Web-Based Instruction.* Englewood Cliffs, NJ: Educational Technology Publications, 1997.

Knowles, Malcolm Shepherd. *The Modern Practice of Adult Education.* Englewood Cliffs, NJ: Educational Technology Publications, 1980.

Knowles, Malcolm Shepherd. *The Adult Learner.* Houston, TX: Gulf Publishing Company, 1990.

Mager, Robert F. *Measuring Instructional Results,* 3rd Edition. Atlanta, GA: Center for Effective Performance, Inc., 1997.

Mager, Robert F., and Peter Pipe. *Analyzing Performance Problems,* 3rd Edition. Atlanta, GA: Center for Effective Performance, Inc., 1997.

Noe, Raymond A. *Employee Training and Development.* Boston: McGraw-Hill, 2002.

Piskurich, Geoge M., Editor. *The American Society for Training and Development (ASTD) Handbook of Instructional Technology.* New York: McGraw-Hill, 1993.

Powers, Bob. *Instructor Excellence: Mastering the Delivery of Training.* San Francisco: Jossey-Bass Publishers, 1992.

Emergency Operations

Brunacini, Alan. *Fire Command.* Oklahoma State University: Fire Protection Publications, 2002.

Carter, Harry, Ph.D. *Fire Fighting Strategy and Tactics.* Oklahoma State University: Fire Protection Publications, 1998.

— *Incident Management System Model Procedures Guide for Structural Firefighting.* National Fire Service Incident Management System Consortium and Oklahoma State University: Fire Protection Publications, 2000.

— *Incident Management System Model Procedures Guide for High-Rise Firefighting.* National Fire Service Incident Management System Consortium and Oklahoma State University: Fire Protection Publications, 2003.

— *Incident Management System Model Procedures Guide for Structural Collapse and US&R Operations.* National Fire Service Incident Management System Consortium and Oklahoma State University: Fire Protection Publications, 1998.

Klaene, Ben, and Russell Sanders. *Structural Fire Fighting.* Batterymarch Park, Quincy, MA: National Fire Protection Association, 2002.

Marks, Michael E. *Emergency Responder's Guide to Terrorism. A Comprehensive Real-World Guide to Recognizing and Understanding Terrorist Weapons of Mass Destruction.* Chester, MD: Red Hat Publishing, 2003.

Phelps, Burton, and Robert Murgallis. *Command and Control: ICS, Strategy Development, and Tactical Selections.* Oklahoma State University: Fire Protection Publications, 2001.

Phelps, Burton, and Robert Murgallis. *Command and Control 2: ICS, Strategy Development, and Tactical Selections.* Oklahoma State University: Fire Protection Publications, 2004.

Smith, James P. *Strategic and Tactical Considerations on the Fireground.* Upper Saddle River, NJ: Prentice-Hall, 2002.

Safety

Fanning, Fred. *Basic Safety Administration: A Handbook for the New Safety Specialist.* Des Plaines, IL: American Society of Safety Engineers, 2003.

Kipp, Jonathan D., and Murrey E. Loflin. *Emergency Incident Risk Management: A Safety and Health Perspective.* New York: John Wiley and Sons, 1996.

Krieger, Gary R., and John F. Montgomery, Editors. *Accident Prevention Manual for Business and Industry*, 12th Edition. Itasca, IL: National Safety Council, 2001.

Stowell, Frederick M. *Fire Department Safety Officer.* Oklahoma State University: International Fire Service Training Association, 2001.

Index

A

Aboveground/below-grade operations, 297
Abstract (executive summary), 123, 125
Abstract learning method, 146
Acceptance of instructors, 17
Access to the training area, 215
Accidents
    analyses, 50–52
    check records for injury trends, 49, 51
    contributing factors, 48–49
    defined, 35
    investigations, 50
    management, 47, 48–53
    mitigation, 52–53
    prevention, 47–48
    Standard on Training for Initial Emergency Scene Operations
        (NFPA 1410), 55
ACID acronym, 193, 195
Acquired training structures
    environmental conditions, 113
    fuel usage, 115
    inspections, 114
    instructor responsibilities, 114
    live-fire trainings, 112–113
    structural conditions, 113–114
    water supply, 115
Action verbs, 331, 332
Active learning
    advantages of use, 239
    audiovisual technology. *See* Audiovisual technology
    behavioral reinforcement, 242
    defined, 238
    discussion groups or skills practices, 238
    effective presentation skills, 239
    encouraging success, 241
    learning reinforcement, 241–242
    motivational techniques, 240–241
    preview of information, 239
    questioning, 240, 242–245
    repetition, 241–242
    small segment process, 238, 239
    strategies, 238–239
    words to teach by, 241
Activity sheet (worksheet), 341, 345–346
ADA (Americans with Disabilities Act), 65–66, 171
ADD (attention deficit disorder), 172
ADDIE model, 522–523
ADHD (attention deficit hyperactivity disorder), 172
Administration
    analysis, 439–442
    budgets, 442–449
    classification testing, 306–308
    human resources, 493–500
    laws, 64, 67
    Level III certification, 479–480
    offices, 104, 105
    purchasing, 450–458
    records. *See* Records management
    research, 431–439
    testing, 308–310
    training policy development, 484–493
Adult education, 10
Advanced level, learning style, 204

Advertising for positions, 496
Affective (attitude) learning domain
    instructional delivery, 236
    learning levels, 142
    overview, 141, 144–145
Affirmative action policies, 66
Age Discrimination in Employment Act, 65
Age of adult students, 166–167
Agenda-based discussion process, 420, 421
Aggressive, talkative students, 174–175
Agricultural equipment rescues, 296
AHJ. *See* Authority having jurisdiction
Aircraft incident training area, 109–110
Airport firefighter professional qualifications (NFPA 1003), 492
Alternative-response (true/false) test, 307, 393–396
American National Standards Institute (ANSI), 56
American Society for Testing and Materials (ASTM), 56
American Society of Safety Engineers (ASSE), 57
Americans with Disabilities Act (ADA), 65–66, 171
Analysis
    accident, 50–52
    administration, 439–442
    Analysis of Emergency Responder Injuries and Fatalities, 45
    application, 442, 507
    checklist, 27
    cost/benefit, 440, 504, 528
    defined, 439, 503
    distracter, 410–411
    evaluation vs., 503
    job, 140–141, 505–506
    learning outcome, 379
    level of learning, 143
    needs, 441, 505
    occupational, 505–506
    policy, 440, 504–505
    process, 440, 504
    process steps, 507
    program, 440–442, 505
    purpose, 503
    records, 133
    research data, 432
    risk, 441, 506
    steps, 441–442
    task. *See* Task analysis
Analysis of Emergency Responder Injuries and Fatalities, 45
Analytical models, 507
Anatomical mannequins, 271
Anatomical models, 262
Ancillary components of lesson plans, 339–348
Ancillary equipment, 271–272
Andragogy, 138
ANSI (American National Standards Institute), 56
Application learning outcome, 379
Application level of learning, 143
Archived records, 128
Aristotle, 149
Arnold, Charles, 138–139
ASSE (American Society of Safety Engineers), 57
Assessment. *See also* Evaluation
    criterion-referenced, 158–159
    defined, 375
    norm-referenced, 158

Assignment sheet, 346, 348
Association, law of learning, 147
ASTM (American Society for Testing and Materials), 56
Atmosphere, environmental issues, 76–77
Attendance records, 68, 130
Attending, listening skill, 95
Attention deficit disorder (ADD), 172
Attention deficit hyperactivity disorder (ADHD), 172
Attitude
    as accident factor, 49
    attitude (affective) learning domain. *See* Affective (attitude)
      learning domain
    instructional delivery, 236
    and motivation, 149
Audience recognition, reference checklist, 29–30
Audience-centered speakers, 232–233
Audio learning style, 145
Audiotapes, 263
Audiovisual technology
    ancillary equipment, 271–272
    avoiding distractions, 211, 254–255
    benefits of use, 250
    budget limitations, 253
    cameras, 349–350
    care, 272, 273
    class size and interaction, 251–252
    in classrooms, 211–212
    cleaning, 272, 273
    evaluative factors, 252–253
    guidelines for use, 253–254
    learning objectives and lesson content, 251
    learning pace, 252
    in lesson plans, 348–351
    maintenance, 272, 273–274
    nonprojected training aids, 258–264
    overview, 249–250
    practice factors, 252
    projected training aids, 264–269
    purposes, 253, 254
    required student performance, 251
    scanners, 350–351
    selection for courses, 539
    simulators, 269–271
    transitions in presentations, 255–258
    video capture devices, 351
    video editing devices, 351
Auditorium or theater seating arrangement, 207, 208
Audits of records, 127–128
Authority having jurisdiction (AHJ)
    defined, 63
    equipment purchases, 455
    examples, 63–64
Autocratic leadership style, 16–17

B

Baby Boom Generation, 163, 166, 167
Backdraft indicators, 38
Balanced leader continuum, 16–17
Behavioral management of students
    coaching, 176, 178, 180–182
    counseling, 176, 177–178, 179
    mentoring, 176, 182–183
    overview, 175–176
    peer assistance, 176, 182
    reviewing policies, 176–177
Behavioral reinforcement, 242
BeL (blended electronic-learning), 228, 229–230
Benchmark examples, 432

Bidding for purchases, 453–454, 456–458
Blended electronic-learning (BeL), 228, 229–230
Block grants, 445
Blocks, hierarchy of work, 526
Bloom, Benjamin, 139, 141, 378–379, 388, 530
Bluffing vs. honesty, 20–21
Body of oral presentation, 236
Bonds for funding, 456
Book organization, 2–3
Bored students, 174
Bottom-line mentality, 78
Brainstorming, 280–281, 420
Browser-based training, 228
Buckley Amendment, 66
Budgets. *See also* Funds and resources
    audiovisual aid limitations, 253
    capital, 443, 444, 456
    defined, 442
    evaluation, 449
    functions, 443
    implementation, 448
    Level II Instructor functions, 442
    monitoring, 448–449
    operating, 443, 444, 456
    operating budget report example, 449
    planning, 446
    preparation, 446–448
    records, 128
    revision, 449
    sources of funds, 444–445
Burn pans, 112

C

CAI (computer-assisted instruction), 227
Cameras
    digital photography, 350
    editing digital images, 351
    traditional photography, 349–350
Canadian Centre for Occupational Health and Safety (CCOHC), 54
Capital funds, 443, 444, 456
Case history
    flashover live-fire training accident, 37
    example, 5
    live-burn training deaths, 293
    training records, 129
Case law, 67. *See also* Judiciary law
Case study
    defined, 277
    development process, 278
    ethical decisions, 81
    example, 5
    firefighter killed in accident, 279
    instructor behaviors, personality, and effectiveness, 22
    instructor preparation, 199
    outline, 278
    purpose, 278
    roles and responsibilities, 27
    safety on the training ground, 43
    structured exercises, 277–279
    student characteristics and learning styles, 164
Casualty
    case history, 37
    prevention, 37–39
    simulation training aids, 263–264
    statistics, 35–36
    during training, 36–37

Cautions
    e-mail security, 230
    example, 5
    study guides, 390
CBE (computer-based education), 227
CBI (computer-based instruction), 227
CBL (competency-based learning), 156–157
CBL (computer-based learning), 227
CBT (computer-based training), 227–228
CCOHC (Canadian Centre for Occupational Health and Safety), 54
CD (compact disc), 255, 263, 274
CDC (Centers for Disease Control and Prevention), 54, 436
CD-ROM (compact disc-read-only-memory), 263, 270–271, 274
Centers for Disease Control and Prevention (CDC), 54, 436
Certification testing, 314
CFR (Code of Federal Regulations), 433, 485, 529
CFSI (Congressional Fire Services Institute), 438
Chalkboards, 259
Challenges of instructors
    changes, 24
    cooperative relationships, 24
    course schedules, 25, 26
    diverse students, 23
    effective characteristics, 16–20
    funds and resources, 25
    instructor obligations, 10–14
    management directives, 24
    multiple priorities, 23
    organizational apathy, 23
    organizational promotion, 24
    overview, 9–10
    professional development, 25
    qualified instructor recruitment, 26
    reference checklist, 27–30
    role models, 14–16, 45–47
    safe training environments, 24–25
    teaching traits, 20–22
Changes
    factors, 12
    multiple, 24
Characteristics of effective instructors
    conflict-resolution skills, 20
    desire to teach, 18
    empathy, 20
    enthusiasm, 18–19
    fairness, 20
    ingenuity, creativity, and flexibility, 20
    interpersonal skills, 17–18
    leadership abilities, 16–17, 469, 470
    motivation, 19
    personal integrity, 20
    preparation and organization, 19
    subject and teaching competencies, 18
Checklists
    analysis, 27
    audience recognition, 29–30
    challenges of instructors, 27–30
    diversity, 28–29
    instructional facilities and props, 27–28
    legal requirements, 29
    Level I Instructor, 312–313
    reference. *See* Reference checklist
Chevron seating arrangement, 207, 208
Chief officer, responsibilities, 9
Christmas trees, 112
Chronological sequencing, 237
Circled chairs seating arrangement, 208, 209
Citations of reference materials, 439

Civil Rights Act, 64–65
Clarity, interpersonal skill, 17
Class A material fires, 295
Class participation rating scale, 407–408
Class size and audiovisual technology, 251–252
Classrooms
    audiovisuals, 211–212, 254
    comfort facilities, 212
    disruptive behavior, 183
    emergency exits, 212
    lighting, 209, 210
    noise level, 210–211
    overview of needs, 104
    permanent training facilities, 104
    power outlets, 212
    safety, 212–213
    seating, 207–209
    temperature, 209–210
    visual distractions, 212
Clear-text, 87, 292
Closed questions, 244, 306, 401–402
CMI (computer-managed instruction), 227
Coaching, 176, 178, 180–182
Code, defined, 62
Code of ethics, 79–80. *See also* Ethics
Code of Federal Regulations (CFR), 433, 485, 529
Cognitive (knowledge) learning domain
    analysis learning outcome, 379
    application learning outcome, 379
    comprehension learning outcome, 379
    demonstration, 224
    evaluation learning outcome, 379
    knowledge learning outcome, 378
    learning outcomes, 378–379
    lesson plans, 191, 193, 328–329, 332–333
    overview, 141–143
    performance terms, 532
    synthesis learning outcome, 379
    task analysis, 528
    verbs and learning levels, 531
    written tests, 390
Collapse. *See* Structural collapse
Combustible liquids training area, 109–110, 111, 294–295
Communications
    clear-text, 87, 292
    cultural concept of words, 90–91
    feedback, 86, 88
    information sharing, 489
    infrastructure requirements, 103
    instructor obligations to students, 11
    instructor skills, 85
    interference, 86, 88–89
    interpersonal skills, 15, 16
    listening skills, 94–97
    medium or channel, 86, 87, 88
    message, 86, 87
    NIMS ICS officer, 292
    nonverbal component. *See* Nonverbal communications
    obsolete terms and their replacements, 91
    officers, 424
    oral, 15
    overview, 85–86
    paralanguage or vocalics, 92
    presentation techniques, 232–237
    purposes, 89
    receiver (listener), 86, 87
    sender (speaker), 86, 87
    skills of management, 471

Communications (continued)
    Standard for Professional Qualifications for Public Safety
      Telecommunicator (NFPA 1061), 492
    verbal component, 90–92
    verbal skills improvement, 91–92
    written, 15
Compact discs (CDs), 255, 263, 274
Compact disc-read-only-memory (CD-ROM), 263, 270–271, 274
Competence of responders (NFPA 472, NFPA 473), 492
Competency of instructors, 18
Competency-based learning (CBL), 156–157
Complaints vs. solutions, 21–22
Completion (fill in the blank) tests, 307, 398–399
Composite scoring, 407
Comprehension learning outcome, 379
Comprehension level of learning, 143
Comprehensive barriers on tests, 383
Computers. *See also* Internet
    analytical models, 507
    browser-based training, 228
    computer-assisted instruction (CAI), 227
    computer-based education (CBE), 227
    computer-based instruction (CBI), 227
    computer-based learning (CBL), 227
    computer-based training (CBT), 227–228
    computer-managed instruction (CMI), 227
    RHAVE software, 506
    simulations, 270–271
    software programs, 127
    testing, 307
Concrete objects learning method, 146
Cone of learning, 150–151, 152
Conference
    discussion presentation format, 223–224
    seating arrangement, 207, 208
Confined spaces
    entry operations training, 297
    rescue training areas, 108
Conflict-resolution skills, 20
Confucius, 81–82, 137
Congressional Fire Services Institute (CFSI), 438
Consistency of instructors, 17
Consistency of lesson
    defined, 200
    purpose, 205
    resource materials, 205
    safety factors, 205
    skill performances, 206
    teaching approaches, 205–206
    training materials, 205
    transitions in presentations, 255
Continuity of lesson
    advanced level, 204
    defined, 200
    equipment and material variations, 203
    instructor changes, 201–202
    learning style differences, 203–204
    remedial level, 204
    resource variations, 203
    testing location variations, 203
    transitions in presentations, 255
    weather variations, 202
Control by management, 470
Cooperative relationships, 24
Copyright laws and permissions
    copying materials, 73–74
    infringement, 73
    invasion of privacy, 74–75
    permissions, 74–75

    purpose, 73
    restrictions, 75
    rights of individuals, 75
    text and symbol, 73
    where and who factor, 74
CORP Business, The 30 Management Principles of the U.S. Marines,
    148
Corrective maintenance, 129
Cost/benefit analysis, 440, 504, 528
Cost-effectiveness of audiovisual aids, 253
Counseling, 176, 177–178, 179
Counterterrorism operations, 297
Course. *See also* Curriculum
    consistency, defined, 189
    continuity, defined, 189
    defined, 521
    evaluations. *See* Course evaluations
Course evaluations
    for curriculum, 539–540, 541
    field test, 364
    formative, 363–364
    observation, 364
    performance ratings examples, 517
    pilot course, 364
    planning, 363
    results, 368, 371
    summative, 363, 364–368, 369–370
Creativity of instructors, 20
Criterion-referenced tests
    grading system, 406–407
    number of test items, 385
    reliability, 408
    test interpretation, 305, 377
    test item difficulty, 384
    uses for, 376
    validity, 408
Cultural demographics of adult students, 168–169
Curriculum. *See also* Program and curriculum development
    defined, 521
    evaluation, 539–540, 541
    implementation, 538–539
    revisions, 540–542
    sequencing, 534, 537
Cutaway models, 262

D
Data collection
    for research, 431–433
    for testing, 405–408
Data interpretation, 133
Debate technique in discussions, 420
Decontamination of equipment and water, 103–104
Delivery of lessons. *See* Instructional delivery
Democratic leadership style, 16–17
Demographics of adult students
    age, 166–167
    culture, 168–169
    educational background, 169
    ethnicity, 168–169
    gender, 167–168
    overview, 165–166
Demonstrations
    defined, 224
    instructor-led presentation, 224–225
    psychomotor skills, 224, 277, 282–283
    purpose, 277
Department of Homeland Security-Federal Emergency
    Management Agency (DHS-FEMA), 54

Desire to teach, 18
DHS-FEMA (Department of Homeland Security-Federal
   Emergency Management Agency), 54
Diagnostic test, 378
Diagram displays, 261
Difficulty index of tests, 409–410
Digital versatile disks (DVDs), 363, 267, 270–271, 274
Direct questions, 244
Director, in discussion groups, 421
Disabled person, defined, 65
Disaster management operations, 297
Discovery zone, 199
Discriminate vs. bias, 384
Discrimination index of tests, 410
Discussion presentation format
   advantages and disadvantages of use, 418
   agenda-based process, 420, 421
   brainstorm, 280–281, 420
   conference, 223–224
   debate, 420
   discussion, defined, 417
   guided, 223
   large group (full-class), 417–418, 419–420
   leadership skills, 421
   nominal group process, 420, 421
   overview, 223–224
   preparation planning, 419
   purpose, 418
   small group, 417–418, 419–420
Display boards, 270
Disruptive behavior
   classroom atmosphere, 183
   forms, 183
   instructor-caused, 184
   nonparticipating students, 174–175
   student-caused, 184–185
Distance-learning courses, 221
Distracter analysis, 410–411
Disuse, law of learning, 147
Diversity
   instructor challenges, 23
   reference checklist, 28–29
   of students, 23
Division/branch/sector officer, 291–292, 424
Dot coms, 166, 167
Drill towers, 105
Driver/operator education, 52
Driving courses, 105
Dry-erase marker board, 259
Duplicated materials, 261–262
DVDs (digital versatile discs), 263, 267, 270–271, 274

E

Easel pad, 260–261
Education
   of adult students, 10, 169
   continuing education of instructors, 13–14
   defined, 9, 140
   level, 170
   public education, 10
Educational institutions, research information resource, 436–437
EEOC (Equal Employment Opportunity Commission), 64–65
Effect, law of learning, 147
Effective vs. efficient, 357, 508
E-learning, 228, 229–230
Electronic boards, 259–260
E-mail security, 230

Emergency Services Education and Consulting Group (ESECG),
   438
Emergency vehicle operations, 296
Empathy of instructors, 20
Employees. *See* Human resources management
Empowering employees on a team, 466
EMS personnel competency (NFPA 473), 492
Enthusiasm
   of instructors, 18–19
   theatrics vs., 196–197
Environment
   accident factor, 48
   acquired structures, 113
   atmosphere, 76–77
   Environmental Protection Agency (EPA), 76
   fuel for training exercises, 77, 115
   infrastructure requirements, 103
   laws and codes, 215
   legal issues, 76–77
   live-fire training, 77
   practical training evolution considerations, 285
   scheduling consideration, 472
   soil, 77, 285
   water, 76, 285
EPA (Environmental Protection Agency), 76
Equal Employment Opportunity Commission (EEOC), 64–65
Equal Pay Act of 1993, 65
Equipment
   ancillary, 271–272
   audiovisual training aids, 349–351. *See also* Audiovisual
      technology
   budgeting for costs, 447
   compatibility assessment before purchase, 453
   decontamination, 103
   evaluation before purchase, 454–455
   during practical training evolutions, 289
   variations, 203
ESECG (Emergency Services Education and Consulting Group),
   438
Essay tests, 307, 399–401
Ethics
   bottom-line mentality, 78
   code of ethics, 79–80
   components, 78–79
   defined, 61
   exploitive mentality, 78
   IAFC code of ethics, 12
   instructor obligations to the organization, 12
   issues, 80–82
   moral philosophies, 61
   overview, 61, 77
   personal code of ethics example, 80
   personal justifications, 79
   personal traits, 78
   program, 79–80
   unethical conduct, 78
   violation of standards, 78
Ethnicity of adult students, 168–169
Evaluation. *See also* Testing; Assessment
   administration classification, 306–308
   analysis vs., 503
   application skills, 510–512
   budgets, 449
   course performance ratings examples, 517
   course/lessons. *See* Course evaluations
   for courses, 513–517
   defined, 303, 375, 503, 508
   effective vs. efficient, 508

Evaluation (continued)
   equipment, before purchase, 454–455
   feedback, 315–317, 500, 515
   formal, 497
   formative. *See* Formative evaluations
   formative (progress) testing, 305, 378
   four-step process of learning, 196, 303–304
   goals-based, 512
   Incident Command System, 427–428
   informal, 497, 498
   instructor, 304, 357–362, 508
   interpretation classification, 305
   job-performance, 499
   learning outcome, 379
   legal considerations, 500
   lesson plan, 193, 351–352
   level of learning, 143
   listening skill, 96
   methodology, 508–510
   observation, 514–515
   oral tests, 402
   organizations, 510–511
   outcomes-based, 512
   personnel, 497–500
   PERT (Program Evaluation, and Review Technique) chart, 131, 468
   plans, 512
   of policies, 491
   practical training evolutions, 287, 427–428
   process-based, 512
   program and curriculum development, 537–538, 539–540, 541
   programs, 511–512
   prospective or formative, 509
   purpose, 304, 512
   purpose classification, 305–306
   qualitative, 509–510
   quantitative, 510
   of records, 133
   results, 516
   retrospective or summative, 509
   RHAVE (Risk, Hazard, and Value Evaluation) Program, 506
   of risk, 39
   summative. *See* Summative evaluation
   of supervisors, 358
   systems approach, 511
Evolutions. *See* Practical training evolutions
Executive summary, 123, 125
Exercise, law of learning, 146–147
Experience, andragogy assumption, 138
Expert opinions, 431–433
Expertise of instructors, 17
Exploitive mentality, 78
Exposure reports, 69
Exterior fire training, 294–295
Exterior safety precautions, 47
External programs, 511–512
External reviews, 448
Eye contact
   during audiovisual presentations, 255
   in communication, 92, 93
   presentation techniques, 235
   progressive discipline, 185

F
FAA (Federal Aviation Administration), 101
Facial expression in communication, 92, 93
Facilities and props. *See* Instructional facilities and props
Fairness
   of instructors, 20
   interpersonal skill, 17–18

Family Education and Privacy Act, 127, 483
Family Educational Rights and Privacy Act of 1974, 66, 69
Fan style seating arrangement, 207, 208
FDSOA (Fire Department Safety Officer Association), 57
Federal Aviation Administration (FAA), 101
Feedback
   applications, 316–317
   coaching, 181–182
   in communications, 86, 88
   on evaluations, 315–317, 500, 515
   in lecture presentation format, 221
   negative, 316
   positive, 316
Field experiences, 282
Field test of course, 364
Field-testing, 514
Fill in the blank (completion) tests, 307, 398–399
Fire apparatus driver/operator professional qualifications (NFPA 1002), 492
Fire departments
   occupational safety and health program. *See* NFPA 1500
   safety officer standard. *See* NFPA 1521
   standards (NFPA 1710, NFPA 1720), 492
Fire Department Safety Officer Association (FDSOA), 57
Firefighter professional qualifications (NFPA 1001), 492
Fire inspector qualifications (NFPA 1031), 492
Fire Instructor I certification checklist, 312–313
Fire investigator qualifications (NFPA 1033), 492
Fire officer professional qualifications (NFPA 1021), 1, 40, 492
Fire service instructor professional qualifications. *See* NFPA 1041
Fire suppression, practical training evolutions, 283, 292–295
Fires. *See* Live-fire training
Five-step planning model, 522–523
Flammable liquids training area, 109–110, 111, 294–295
Flexibility of instructors, 20
FM Global (Factory Mutual), 438
Foreseeability of potential injury events, 70, 72
Formative (progress) testing, 305, 378
Formative evaluations
   for courses, 363, 513, 514–515
   defined, 363, 514
   features, 509
   field-testing, 514
   observation, 514–515
   purpose, 363–364
Forming stage of team development, 465
Four-step process of learning
   application, 195, 277. *See also* Demonstrations; Practical training evolutions; Structured exercises
   background, 139
   evaluation, 196, 303–304. *See also* Evaluation
   instructor preparation, 196. *See also* Instructor preparation
   preparation, 193, 195
   presentation step, 219–220. *See also* Instructional delivery
   steps, 193, 194
Freedman, David, *CORP Business, The 30 Management Principles of the U.S. Marines*, 148
Fuels for training exercises, 77, 115, 288
Funds and resources. *See also* Budgets
   bonds, 456
   budgets, 444–445
   financial management, 469
   fundraising, 445
   grants, 445, 456
   instructor challenges, 25
   managing, 469
   operating, 443, 444, 456

for purchases, 450, 456
researching sources, 433
for scheduling, 472

G

Gantt chart, 131
Gatekeepers, in discussion groups, 421
Gen Xers, 166, 167
Gender of students, 167–168
Gestures in communication, 93
Gifted students, 172, 173
Gifts, 445
Global learning method, 146
Goals
    goal-based evaluation, 512
    program and curriculum development, 528–529
    supervision, 463–464
    workgroup, 463–464
Government
    agency safety guidelines, 53–54
    federal agency research information resource, 436
    federal legislative (statutory) law, 64
    local departments and organizations, 66–67
    local legislative (statutory) law, 66, 67
    local safety and health agencies, 54–55
    state/provincial legislative (statutory) law, 66
    state/provincial safety and health agencies, 54–55
Grants for funding, 445, 456
Groupthink, 466
Guide, defined, 63
Guide for Land-Based Fire Fighters Who Respond to Marine Vessel Fires (NFPA 1405), 110
Guide to Building Fire Service Training Centers (NFPA 1402), 55, 101, 106
Guided discussion presentation format, 223
Guidelines, document requirements, 489

H

Hall, R. M., 168
Handouts, 261–262
Harassment under the EEOC, 64
Hazard
    defined, 42
    hazard-risk analysis, 41–42
    high-hazard training, 287, 425
    prioritizing, 51
Hazardous materials
    EMS personnel competency, 492
    practical training evolutions, 297
    responder competency (NFPA 472, NFPA 473), 492
    training area, 109–110
Hazen-Williams Water Flow Tests, 432
Health and fitness
    for accident reduction, 52
    for practical training evolutions, 288–290
    Standard on Health-Related Fitness Programs for Fire Fighters (NFPA 1583), 55
Hierarchical task analysis, 527, 528
Hierarchy of learning, 379
Hierarchy of work, 526–527
High-angle rescue training area, 109
High-hazard training, 287, 425
Hiring records, 68
History
    case history. *See* Case history
    IFSTA (International Fire Service Training Association), ii
    training, 1–2
Holistic learning method, 146

Hollow square seating arrangement, 209
Home Fire Sprinkler Coalition, 438
Honesty vs. bluffing, 20–21
Horseshoe or U-shape seating arrangement, 207, 208
Human accident factor, 49
Human resources management. *See also* Personnel
    applications and interviews, 496–497
    characteristics of personnel evaluations, 498
    employee orientation, 497
    human resources, defined, 469
    internal or external sources for instructors, 496
    legal considerations, 500
    personnel evaluations, 497–500
    position advertising, 496
    qualifications, 495
    recruitment, 496
    staff selection, 494–497
    supervision, 493–494
    terminations, 498
    training, 496
Humor
    appropriate use of, 234, 240
    positive vs. offensive, 22
Hybrid-CD-ROMs, 228
Hyperactive, 152
Hypoxia, 152

I

IAFC (International Association of Fire Chiefs), code of ethics, 12
IAP. *See* Incident action plan
Ice rescues, 297
ICMA (International City/County Management Association), 438
ICS. *See* Incident Command System
If and then task analysis, 528
IFSTA. *See* International Fire Service Training Association
Illustrated lecture presentation format, 222
Illustration displays, 261
ILT. *See* Instructor-led training
IMS. *See* Incident Management System
Incentives, 466–467
Incident action plan (IAP)
    evolution planning, 425
    mitigation activities, 52
    safety considerations, 41, 42
Incident Command System (ICS). *See also* NIMS ICS
    components, 424
    defined, 3
    evaluation, 427–428
    evolution planning, 286, 425–426
    implementation, 426
    multiagency training evolutions, 426, 427
    purpose, 421, 422
    roles and functions, 422–424
    supervision, 426
Incident commander (IC) duties, 424
Incident Management System (IMS), defined, 3. *See also* NFPA 1561
Incident reports, 69
Incident safety officer (ISO)
    accident investigations, 50–51
    duties, 44–45, 424
    NIMS ICS, 291
Individualized instruction, 231–232
Industrial fire brigades (NFPA 600), 492
Industry standards, 432–433
Industry trends, 452

Information boxes
alternative-response questions, 394
assignment sheet, 348
audiovisual equipment distractions, 211
certification testing, 314
example, 5
executive summary, 125
Fire Fighter I performance objectives (NFPA 1001), 292
handouts, 262
high-hazard training, 287
information sheet, 341
job performance and learning objectives, 331
management, 470
multiple-choice tests, 391
paragraph and table information, 123
personal code of ethics example, 80
relating new information to known information, 152
report-writing responsibilities, 120
risk-management plan development, 39
skills sheet, 341
training function, 9
using CDs, CD-ROMs and DVDs, 274
using marker boards, 260
using projected aids, 265
voice attributes, 234
worksheet, 346
writing styles, 123
Information sharing, 489
Information sheets, 339–341
Information sources for research
credibility, 433–434, 439
educational institutions, 436–437
government agencies, 436
Internet, 434–436
libraries, 436
nonprofit organizations, 438–439
primary literature, 434
professional organizations, 437–438
secondary literature, 434
tertiary literature, 434
testing and standards organizations, 438
vendors/manufacturers, 438
Infrastructure requirements
breathing air supply, 102, 103
communication systems, 103
environmental controls, 103
equipment decontamination area, 103
fuel source, 102
location, 102
security, 104
staging area, 102–103
water decontamination system, 103–104
water supply, 102
weather monitoring, 103
Ingenuity of instructors, 20
Initial emergency scene operational standard (NFPA 1410), 55
Inspections of facilities and props, 42–43
Inspiration vs. intimidation, 22
Instructional delivery
active learning, 237–245
attitudes/values display, 236
effective speakers, 232–234
individualized instruction, 231–232
instructor-led training. See Instructor-led training
nonverbal elements, 234
organization, 236
overview, 219
preparation, 234–236

self-directed (independent) learning, 230–231
sequencing, 236–237, 238
techniques, 232–237
technology-based training. See Technology-based training
Instructional facilities and props. See also Training props
acquired structures, 112–115
Guide to Building Fire Service Training Centers (NFPA 1402), 55, 101, 106
infrastructure requirements, 102–104
inspections, 42–43
management, 469–470
mobile training facilities, 106–108
overview, 101
permanent facilities, 104–106
reference checklist, 27–28
repairs, 42–43
safety, 27
selection for courses, 539
Standard on Live Fire Training Evolutions. See NFPA 1403
training props, 108–112
Instructor evaluations
advantages of program, 358
characteristics, 358–359
formal, 359–360
informal, 359
instruments, 361
overview, 357–358
performance, 359–360
by students, 361–362
supervisors, 358
uses for, 361
Instructor preparation
attitude for learning, 196–197
case study, 199
logistics, 199–200
organization, 197
overview, 189
session preparation, 197–199
step 1, 196
Instructor-caused disruptive behavior, 184
Instructor-led training (ILT)
demonstration, 224–225
discussion, 223–224
illustrated lecture, 222
lecture, 221–222
multiple instructors, 225–227, 416
overview, 220
Insurance, budgeting for, 447
Intensity, law of learning, 148
Interactive boards, 259–260
Interactive television (ITV), 228, 229
Interference in communications, 86, 88–89
Interior safety precautions, 47
Interior structural fire training, 294
Internal programs, 511–512
Internal reviews, 448
International Association of Fire Chiefs (IAFC), code of ethics, 12
International City/County Management Association (ICMA), 438
International Fire Service Training Association (IFSTA)
history, ii
research data source, 438
training materials, 2
Validation Conference, ii
International Society of Fire Service Instructors (ISFSI), 57
Internet
cost, 435–436
design, 435
dot coms, 166, 167

e-mail security, 230
    functionality, 435
    information authority, 434–436
    scope/content, 435
    search engines, 434
Interpersonal communication. *See* Communications
Interpersonal skills
    clarity, 17
    communication, 15, 16
    fairness, 17–18
    sensitivity, 17
Interpretation classification test, 305
Interpretative exercises, 401
Intimidation vs. inspiration, 22
Introduction to oral presentation, 236
Invasion of privacy, 74–75
Inventory records, 128–129
ISFSI (International Society of Fire Service Instructors), 57
ISO. *See* Incident safety officer
Item quality, 410
ITV (interactive television), 228, 229

J
Job analysis, 140–141, 505–506
Job performance evaluations, 499
Job performance records, 130
Job performance requirements (JPRs), 526
Jobs, hierarchy of work, 526
JPRs (job performance requirements), 526
Judicial legislation, 67
Judiciary law, 64, 67

K
Key information
    balanced leader continuum, 16
    barriers to listening, 97
    broaden instructional background, 14
    check records for injury trends, 49
    discriminate vs. bias, 384
    editing digital images, 351
    effective vs. efficient, 357
    example, 5
    gender terminology, 168
    hazards and risks, 42
    item analysis guide, 411
    keystoning, 268–269
    knowing safety policies and guidelines, 45
    lesson plan terminology, 329
    observe other instructors, 15
    overview of symbols, 4–6
    proper equipment use, 53
    review lesson plans, 323
    safety precautions, 47
    terminology confusion, 141
    test item difficulty, 389
    test reliability, 386
    test terminology, 376
    testing times, 382
Key points, hierarchy of work, 527
Keystoning, 268–269
Kinesics, 92–93
Kinesthetic learning style, 145
Knowledge learning domain. *See* Cognitive (knowledge) learning
    domain
Knowledge learning outcome, 378
Knowledge level of learning, 143
Knowles, Malcolm, 138
Known-to-unknown sequencing, 236–237

L
Laboratory experiences, 282
Lack of knowledge or skill as accident factor, 49
Ladder, lifting safety, 41
Laird, Dugan, 149
Laissez-faire leadership style, 16–17
Language barriers on tests, 383
Large group discussions, 417–418, 419–420
Large-quantity Class A material fires, 295
Law. *See also* Legal requirements; Regulation
    administrative, 64, 67
    Age Discrimination in Employment Act, 65
    Americans with Disabilities Act, 65–66, 171
    Buckley Amendment, 66
    budgeting for governmental mandates, 447
    case law, 67
    Civil Rights Act, 64–65
    Code of Federal Regulations, 433, 485, 529
    defined, 63–64
    environmental, 215
    Equal Pay Act of 1993, 65
    Family Education and Privacy Act, 127, 483
    Family Educational Rights and Privacy Act of 1974, 66, 69
    judiciary, 64, 67
    legislative (statutory), 64–67
    Municipal Freedom of Information and Protection of Priacy
      Act, 69, 483
    Occupational Safety and Health Act of 1970, 53
    Office of Privacy Commissioner of Canada privacy laws, 127
    purchasing, 453
    scheduling and government mandates, 471
    U.S. Workforce Investment Act of 1998, 170
Leadership abilities, 16–17, 469, 470
Leading, defined, 461
Learning
    activity packets, 231
    defined, 139
    disabilities, 171–172
    informal, 140
    objectives. *See* Learning objectives
    orientation, andragogy assumption, 138
    outcomes, 140, 378–379
    principles. *See* Learning principles
    test planning objectives, 377–380
    types, 139–140
Learning objectives
    audiovisual technology, 251
    conditions description, 530
    defined, 140
    expressive terms, 332
    matching to test items, 383
    overview, 329–331
    performance statement, 530
    program and curriculum development, 528–533
    standards criteria, 530
    test specifications, 381
Learning principles
    affective (attitude), 141, 142, 144–145
    andragogy, 138
    association, 147
    cognitive (knowledge), 141–143
    development, 137–139
    disuse, 147
    domains, 141–145
    effect, 147
    exercise, 146–147
    four-step process, 139. *See also* Four-step process of learning

Learning principles (continued)
    intensity, 148
    laws of learning, 146–148
    learning obstacles, 153–154
    mastery learning theory, 139
    mastery teaching approach, 156–157
    memory, 151–153. *See also* Memory
    methods, 145–146
    motivation, 148–149
    pedagogy, 137–138
    plateaus (leveling-off) points, 153, 154–155
    primacy, 147–148
    psychomotor (skills), 141–144, 180–181. *See also* Psychomotor
      (skills) learning domain
    readiness, 138, 146
    recency, 147
    student assessment, 157–159
    student frustrations, 154
    styles, 145, 165, 203–204
    teaching approaches, 155–157
    terminology, 139–141
    theories, 137–139, 149–151
    traditional teaching approach, 156
Lease or lease/purchases, 456
L-E-A-S-T method of progressive discipline, 185
Lecture presentation format, 221–222, 250
Legal requirements. *See also* Law
    applications, 67–68
    copyright laws and permissions, 73–75
    environmental issues, 76–77
    instructor knowledge of, 61–62
    liability, 70–73
    overview, 61
    personnel evaluations, 500
    during practical training evolutions, 286
    records, 127, 133
    records management, 68–70
    reference checklist, 29
    research data collection, 433
    students' rights, 75
    terminology, 62–64
Legislative (statutory) law, 64–67. *See also* Law
Lesson, defined, 521
Lesson evaluations. *See* Course evaluations
Lesson plan
    ancillary components, 339–348
    assignment sheet, 346, 348
    assignments, 193
    audiovisual components, 348–351
    benefits of use, 322–323
    cognitive, 191, 193, 328–329, 332–333
    components, 190–191, 193, 323–329
    consistency, 200, 205–206, 255
    continuity, 200–204, 255
    creation of, 338–339
    curriculum development, 534, 535
    defined, 190, 321–322
    evaluation, 193, 351–352
    example, 191, 324–327
    formats, 333–337
    four-step method of instruction, 193–196
    information sheet, 339–341
    learning objectives, 329–331, 332
    level of instruction, 190
    modifications, 339
    NFPA 1041 standard, 321
    objectives, 190, 192
    outline, 193
    overview, 189–190

    prerequisites, 191
    psychomotor, 328–329, 333
    purposes, 322–323
    references, 193
    resources needed, 190–191
    reviewing, 323
    revision, 352–353
    skills sheet, 333, 341, 342–344
    study sheet, 346, 347
    summary, 193
    time frame, 190
    topic, 190
    worksheet, 341, 345–346
Level I Instructor
    checklist, 312–313
    evaluation and testing, 304
    functions, 3, 9–10
    legal requirements, 62
    record keeping, 125
    report-writing responsibilities, 120
Level II Instructor
    budgets, 442
    functions, 3, 9–10
    legal requirements, 62
    record keeping, 125
    report-writing responsibilities, 120
    supervision, 461–462
Level III Instructor
    analysis, 503
    certification, 479–480
    evaluations, 357, 508
    functions, 3–4, 9–10
    human resources management, 493–500
    legal requirements, 62
    record keeping, 125
    report-writing responsibilities, 120
    supervision, 461
Liability
    defined, 70
    foreseeability, 70, 72
    live-fire training, 70–71
    negligent acts, 70
    reduction of risk, 72–73
    vicarious liability, 71–72
Libraries, research information resource, 436
Life experiences of students, 164
Lighting
    in classrooms, 209, 210
    outside environment, 215
Linear learning method, 146
Liquefied petroleum gas (LPG) props, 112
Listening skills, 94–97
Literacy level, 170–171
Live-fire training
    acquired structures, 112–115
    environmental issues, 77
    exposures, 215
    exterior fires, 294–295
    firefighter death, 293
    flammable/combustible liquids, 294–295
    flashover accident case history, 37
    interior structural fires, 294
    large-quantity Class A materials, 295
    liability issues, 70–71
    practical training evolutions, 283, 292–295
    Preventing Deaths and Injuries to Fire Fighters during Live-Fire
      Training in Acquired Structures, 293, 609
    simulators, 107–108, 111

small fires, 293, 294
Standard on Live Fire Training Evolutions. See NFPA 1403
structures, 106, 110–111
transportation fires, 294
wildland fires, 106, 295
Locke, John, 149
Logistics officer, 291, 424
Logistics preparation, 199–200
Long-term memory, 153
LPG (liquefied petroleum gas) props, 112

M
Machinery extrication, 109, 296
Mager, Robert, 139
Mager, Robert F., learning objectives model, 330
Maintenance and storage structures, 105
Maintenance records, 129–130
Management
    accident, 47, 48–53
    defined, 461, 469
    directives, 24
    financial, 469
    functions, 470
    human resources. *See* Human resources management
    records, 480–484
    skills, 470–471
    of time, 470
Mannequins, 271
Maritime incident training area, 110, 111
Marker board illustrations
    chalkboard, 259
    dry-erase marker board, 259
    easel pad, 260–261
    electronic or interactive board, 259–260
    overview, 258–259
    tips for using, 260
Mastery learning theory, 139
Mastery teaching approach, 156–157
Matching tests, 307, 396–397
Materials for lessons
    American Society for Testing and Materials (ASTM), 56
    consistency, 205
    continuity, 203
    copying, 73–74
    handouts, 261–262
    IFSTA training materials, 2
    permissions for copyrighted materials, 74–75
    restrictions on copyrighted materials, 75
Mazes, 112
Media transitions and animations, 257–258
Medical examination records, 68
Medical operations, 296
Medical program standard for fire departments (NFPA 1582), 52
Medium or channel in communications, 86, 87, 88
Memory
    audiovisual aids, 250
    long-term, 153
    mental schema, 151
    remembering, 95–96, 151
    sensory, 151
    short-term (working), 153
Mentoring, 176, 182–183
Message in communications, 86, 87
MFIPPA (Municipal Freedom of Information and Protection of Privacy Act), 69, 483
Millenniums, 166, 167
Miniatures, 262–263

Mitigation after accidents, 52–53
Mobile training facilities, 106–108
Models
    actual tools and equipment, 263
    ADDIE, 522–523
    analytical, 507
    anatomical, 262
    cutaways, 262
    five-step planning, 522–523
    ICS. *See* Incident Command System
    planning, 507
    program and curriculum development, 522–523
    releases, 74
    replicas or miniatures, 262–263
    research, 432
    systems approach to training function, 447
    tabletop miniatures, 262
    task analysis, 528
    training aids, 262–263
Monitoring training activities, 43–44
Moral philosophies, 61. *See also* Ethics
Motivation
    active learning, 240–241
    adult students, 148, 164–165
    andragogy assumption, 138
    defined, 140
    encouraging success, 241
    of instructors, 19
    learning principle, 148
    relationship to learning, 148–149
    triggers, 148
Moulage kits, 263–264
Multiagency training evolutions, 426, 427
Multimedia projectors, 266
Multimedia training, 227
Multiple instructors, 225–227, 416
Multiple-choice tests, 307, 390–393
Municipal Freedom of Information and Protection of Privacy Act (MFIPPA), 69, 483

N
NASA (National Aeronautics and Space Administration), 503, 504
National Aeronautics and Space Administration (NASA) analysis of *Challenger* and *Columbia*, 503, 504
National Fire Academy (NFA), 2, 511
National Fire Incident Reporting System (NFIRS), 436
National Fire Protection Association (NFPA). *See also specific NFPA standard*
    purpose, 55–56, 491–493
    standards listing, 55, 492
National Fire Service Incident Management System Consortium Model Procedures Committee, 3
National Incident Management System (NIMS)
    ICS. *See* NIMS ICS
    ICS and IMS terminology, 3
    requirements for use, 422
    weapons of mass destruction credentialing, 524
National Institute for Occupational Safety and Health (NIOSH), 53, 436
Needs analysis, 441, 505
Needs assessment, defined, 140
Nexters, 166, 167
NFA (National Fire Academy), 2, 511
NFIRS (National Fire Incident Reporting System), 436
NFPA. *See* National Fire Protection Association
NFPA 472, *Standard for Professional Competence of Responders to Hazardous Materials Incidents*, 492

NFPA 473, *Standard for Competencies for EMS Personnel Responding to Hazardous Materials Incidents*, 492
NFPA 600, *Standard on Industrial Fire Brigades*, 492
NFPA 1001, *Standard for Fire Fighter Professional Qualifications*, 492
NFPA 1002, *Standard for Fire Apparatus Driver/Operator Professional Qualifications*, 492
NFPA 1003, *Standard for Airport Fire Fighter Professional Qualifications*, 492
NFPA 1021, *Standard for Fire Officer Professional Qualifications*, 1, 40, 492
NFPA 1031, *Standard for Professional Qualifications for Fire Inspector and Plan Examiner*, 492
NFPA 1033, *Standard for Professional Qualifications for Fire Investigator*, 492
NFPA 1035, *Standard for Professional Qualifications for Public Fire and Life Safety Educator*, 492
NFPA 1041, *Standard for Fire Service Instructor Professional Qualifications*
  audiovisual technology, 249
  budgets, 442
  contents, 55
  evaluation and testing, 304, 357
  instructional delivery, 219
  instructional facilities and training props, 101
  legal requirements, 62
  Level III certification, 479–480
  levels of duties, 321
  listing, 492
  program and curriculum development, 521
  program evaluation plan, 508
  purpose, 1
  record keeping, 125
  records management, 481
  report-writing responsibilities, 120
  safety, 40
NFPA 1051, *Standard for Wildland Fire Fighter Professional Qualifications*, 492
NFPA 1061, *Standard for Professional Qualifications for Public Safety Telecommunicator*, 492
NFPA 1142, *Standard on Water Supplies for Suburban and Rural Fire Fighting*, 102, 115, 286
NFPA 1201, *Standard for Providing Emergency Services to the Public*, 485, 492
NFPA 1401, *Recommended Practice for Fire Service Training Reports and Records*, 68, 126, 492
NFPA 1402, *Guide to Building Fire Service Training Centers*, 55, 101, 106
NFPA 1403, *Standard on Live Fire Training Evolutions*
  acquired structures, 113
  casualty prevention, 37
  contents, 55
  Fire Fighter I performance objectives, 292
  fuel usage, 115
  instructional facilities, 101
  listing, 492
  practical training evolutions, 285, 286
  training policies, 485
NFPA 1404, *Standard for Fire Service Respiratory Protection Training*, 492
NFPA 1405, *Guide for Land-Based Fire Fighters Who Respond to Marine Vessel Fires*, 110
NFPA 1410, *Standard on Training for Initial Emergency Scene Operations*, 55
NFPA 1500, *Standard on Fire Department Occupational Safety and Health Program*
  contents, 55
  listing, 492
  monitoring training activities, 43
  policy development, 485
  practical training evolutions, 285
  risk-management plan development, 39
  smoke buildings, 106
NFPA 1521, *Standard for Fire Department Safety Officer*
  contents, 55
  duties, 40, 44–45
  listing, 492
  in practical training evolutions, 289
NFPA 1561, *Standard on Emergency Services Incident Management System*
  contents, 55
  Incident Command System (ICS) model, 421–422
NFPA 1582, *Standard on Comprehensive Occupational Medical Program for Fire Departments*, 52
NFPA 1583, *Standard on Health-Related Fitness Programs for Fire Fighters*, 55
NFPA 1584, *Recommended Practice on the Rehabilitation of Members Operating at Incident Scene Operations and Training Exercises*, 40, 55
NFPA 1710, *Standard for the Organization and Deployment of Fire Suppression Operations, Emergency Medical Operations, and Special Operations to the Public by Career Fire Departments*, 492
NFPA 1720, *Standard for the Organization and Deployment of Fire Suppression Operations, Emergency Medical Operations, and Special Operations to the Public by Volunteer Fire Departments*, 492
NIMS. *See* National Incident Management System
NIMS ICS
  during complex training evolutions, 291–292
  evolution control, 290
  functions, 291–292
  NFPA 1561 standards, 291
  during simple training evolutions, 290–291
NIOSH (National Institute for Occupational Safety and Health), 37, 53, 278, 436
Noise level in classrooms, 210–211
Nominal group discussion process, 420, 421
Nondisruptive, nonparticipating students, 173–174
Nondisruptive, participating, successful students, 175
Nonprofit organizations, research information source, 438–439
Nonprojected training aids
  audiotapes, 263
  casualty simulation training aids, 263–264
  compact discs, 263
  duplicated materials, 261–262
  illustration or diagram displays, 261
  marker board, 258–261
  models, 262–263
Nonverbal communications. *See also* Communications
  communication improvement, 93
  kinesics, 92–93
  in lecture presentation format, 221
  presentation, 234
Nonverbal transitions, 257, 416
Norming stage of team development, 465
Norm-referenced tests
  reliability, 408
  test interpretation, 305, 377
  test item difficulty, 384
  uses for, 376
  validity, 408
Notes
  compact discs, 263
  conferences, 224
  failing test scores, 407
  high-hazard training, 425

example, 6
projectors, 260
proportions, 410
purchasing laws, 453
sectors, 424
student individuality, 168

O
Objective written tests, 390
Objectives
audiovisual aids, 251
learning. *See* Learning objectives
lesson plan, 190, 192
practical training evolutions, 285
program and curriculum development, 529–533
supervision, 463–464
Obligations
adult education, 10
to the organization, 12
to the profession, 13
public education, 10
to students, 10–12
to themselves, 13–14
Observation evaluation, 514–515
Observing other instructors, 15
Occupational safety and health program. *See* NFPA 1500
Occupational analysis, 505–506
Occupational Safety and Health Act of 1970, 53
Occupational Safety and Health Administration (OSHA), 53–54
Occupations, hierarchy of work, 526
Office of Privacy Commissioner of Canada, privacy laws, 127
Open questions, 244, 306–307, 401–402
Open records act exemptions, 70
Operating funds, 443, 444, 456
Oral tests
administration classification, 306
closed question, 401–402
open question, 401–402
purpose, 387, 401, 402
scoring, 310
Ordinances, local government, 66
Organization
apathy of instructors, 23
instructional delivery, 236
instructor characteristic, 19
instructor obligations, 12
instructor preparation, 197
management, 470
promotion by instructors, 24
OSHA (Occupational Safety and Health Administration), 53–54
Outline facts, hierarchy of work, 527
Outside learning environment, 213–215
Overhead projectors/transparencies, 268–269
Overhead questions, 244

P
Paralanguage or vocalics, 92
Parking areas at training facilities, 104
Part-to-whole sequencing, 237
PASS (personal alert safety system) devices, 43, 52
Pedagogy, 137–138
Peer assistance, 176, 182
Performance (psychomotor) testing
administration of, 309–310
advantages, 405
disadvantages, 405
guidelines for tests, 403, 405
instructor evaluations, 359–360

purpose, 308, 387, 403
rating sheet, 404
scoring, 311–314
test instruments, 402–405
Performing stage of team development, 465
Peripheral board, 260
Permanent training facilities
administrative offices, 104, 105
classrooms, 104
development and expansion, 104, 105
drill towers, 105
driving courses, 105
live-fire buildings, 106
maintenance and storage structures, 105
parking areas, 104
practical training evolutions, 284, 285
smoke buildings, 106
specialized props, 106
training props, 108–111
water rescue training areas, 106
wildland training areas, 106
Permissions for copyright materials, 74–75
Personal integrity of instructors, 20
Personal alert safety system (PASS) devices, 43, 53
Personnel. *See also* Human resources management
accountability, 52
file privacy, 69
records, 130
PERT (Program Evaluation and Review Technique) chart, 131, 468
Photography
digital photography, 350
editing digital images, 351
photograph privacy requirements, 74–75
traditional photography, 349–350
Physical limitations as accident factor, 49
Physical setting
classroom environment, 207–213
outside environment, 213–215
overview, 189, 206
Physiological mannequins, 271
Piggybacking of ideas, 281
Pilot course, 364
Plan examiner qualifications (NFPA 1031), 492
Planning
budgets, 446
course evaluations, 513
discussion presentations, 419
five-step model, 522–523
ICS model for evolutions, 425–426
management, 470
models, 507
program and curriculum development, 522–523
test. *See* Test planning
Plateaus (leveling-off) points in learning, 153, 154–155
Point system test scoring, 407
Poise in communication, 93
Police power, 64
Policy
analysis, 440, 504–505
document requirements, 489
training. *See* Training policy development
Political bottom line, 78
Pork-barrel projects, 78
Portable training props, 111–112, 284–285
Positive reinforcement, 245
Posture in communication, 93
Power tool and equipment operations, 297

Practical training evolutions
 complex training evolutions, 291–292
 controls, 290–292
 evaluation, 287, 427–428
 fire suppression, 283, 292–295
 ICS model, 286, 425–426
 instructor preparation, 298
 learning outcomes, 288
 management, 421–428
 objectives, 285
 planning safe training scenarios, 285–288
 purpose, 277, 283
 safety, 285, 288–290, 425
 simple training evolutions, 290–291
 technical training, 283
 technical training evolutions, 283, 295–298
 training locations, 284–285
Preparation
 course continuity and consistency, 189, 200–206
 instructional delivery, 234–236
 instructor characteristic, 19
 instructor preparation, 189, 196–200
 lesson plans, 189–196, 323, 328
 physical setting, 189, 206–215
 practical training evolutions, 298
Prerequisite training, 525
Prescriptive tests, 305, 378
Pretest, 525
Preventing Deaths and Injuries to Fire Fighters during Live-Fire Training in Acquired Structures, 293, 609
Preventive maintenance, 129
Primacy, law of learning, 147–148
Primary literature, 434
Priorities, multiple, 23
Privacy
 Family Education and Privacy Act, 127, 483
 Family Educational Rights and Privacy Act of 1974, 66, 69
 invasion of privacy, 74–75
 Municipal Freedom of Information and Protection of Privacy Act, 69, 483
 Office of Privacy Commissioner of Canada, 127
 of records, 69, 74–75, 127, 483
 of tests, 314–315
Procedure, document requirements, 489
Process analysis, 440, 504
Process steps analysis, 507
Profession, defined, 10
Professional organizations
 for research data, 437–438
 for safety information, 57
Professionalism
 development by instructors, 25
 of instructors, 13
Program analysis, 440–442, 505
Program and curriculum development
 cost/benefit analysis, 528
 course sequence, 534, 537
 curriculum implementation, 538–539
 definitions, 521
 designing curriculum/course, 533–538
 evaluation, 537–538, 539–540, 541
 goals, 528–529
 group similar objectives, 534
 hierarchy of work, 526–527
 job performance requirements, 525–526
 learning objectives, 529–533
 lesson plans, 534

 lesson sequence, 534, 536
 needs analysis, 524–525
 needs identification, 524–528
 overview, 521–522
 pilot presentation, 539
 planning model, 522–523
 resources, 533
 revisions, 540–542
 task analysis, 527–528
Program Evaluation and Review Technique (PERT) chart, 131, 468
Programmed learning, 232
Progress evaluation and testing. *See* Evaluation
Projected training aids
 drawbacks, 264
 keystoning, 268–269
 overhead projectors/transparencies, 268–269
 projection screens, 272
 projection systems, 265–266
 slide projectors/slides, 268, 416–417
 television, 267–268
 tips for using, 265
 video presentations, 267–268
 visual presenters/displays, 266–267
Promotional examinations, 68
Props. *See* Facilities and props
Prospective evaluation, 509
Psychomotor (skills) learning domain
 coaching, 180–181
 demonstrations, 224, 277, 282–283
 learning levels, 142
 lesson plan application, 195
 lesson plans, 191, 193, 328–329, 333
 overview, 141, 143–144
 performance testing. *See* Performance (psychomotor) testing
 weather variations, 202
Public education, 10
Public fire and life safety educations qualifications (NFPA 1035), 492
Public safety telecommunicator qualifications (NFPA 1061), 492
Purchasing
 authority, 450
 bidding, 453–454, 456–458
 budgeting, 450, 456
 conducting research, 451–454
 equipment evaluation, 454–455
 needs assessment, 450–451
 process, 455–458
 purchase contracts, 457
 responsibility, 450
 review product data, 455
Purpose classification, 305–306
Purpose of book, 1

Q
Qualified individual with disability, 65
Qualitative evaluation, 509–510
Quantitative evaluation, 510
Questions
 alternative-response, 394
 closed, 244, 306, 401–402
 direct, 244
 open, 244, 306–307, 401–402
 overhead, 244
 redirected, 244–245
 relay, 244
 rhetorical, 244, 256
 techniques, 240, 242–245, 256
Quiet students, 174

R

RAND Worldwide report, 45
Rapid intervention teams or crews (RITs or RICs), 52, 53, 292, 424
Reaction surveys, 515–516
Readiness to learn
    andragogy assumption, 138
    law of learning, 146
Reasonable accommodations, 65–66
Receiver (listener) in communications, 86, 87
Recency, law of learning, 147
Recommended Practice for Fire Service Training Reports and Records (NFPA 1401), 68, 126, 492
Recommended Practice on the Rehabilitation of Members Operating at Incident Scene Operations and Training Exercises (NFPA 1584), 40, 55
Records
    archived, 128
    attendance, 68, 130
    audits, 127–128
    benefits of accurate records, 127
    budget, 128
    case history, 129
    contents, 127
    data interpretation, 133
    defined, 119
    evaluation, 133
    exposure reports, 69
    hiring records, 68
    incident reports, 69
    information uses, 125
    inventory, 128–129
    job performance, 130
    legal requirements, 127, 133
    liability, 70–73
    maintenance, 129–130
    management. *See* Records management
    medical examinations, 68
    open records act exemptions, 70
    personnel, 130
    privacy, 69, 74–75, 127
    project completion, 133
    promotional examinations, 68
    public access, 69–70
    recommendations (NFPA 1401), 68, 126, 492
    record keeping, defined, 119
    retention length, 69
    revision, 133
    software programs, 127
    storage systems, 131–132
    supervisory, 469
    system development, 130–133
    system plan, 131
    training records, 68, 69, 126, 481–484
Records management
    automated system, 481
    defined, 480
    electronic, 481
    forms, 484
    information to include, 480
    manual system, 481
    micrographic, 481
    paper or physical, 481
    statistical analyses, 480
    system components, 481
    training records, 481–484
Recruitment of qualified instructors, 26
Redirected questions, 244–245

Reference checklist
    analyses, 27
    audience recognition, 29–30
    diversity issues, 28–29
    facilities, props, acquired structures, 27–28
    legal requirements, 29
Regulation. *See also* Law
    defined, 62, 67
    example, 62, 63
Rehabilitation of incident scene members, 286. *See also* NFPA 1584
Relay questions, 244
Reliability of tests
    criterion-referenced tests, 408
    defined, 304, 408
    norm-referenced tests, 408
    oral tests, 402
    performance tests, 405
Remedial level, learning style, 204
Remembering, listening skill, 95–96, 151. *See also* Memory
Remote sites for practical training evolutions, 284
Repairing facilities and props, 42–43
Repetition in active learning, 241–242
Replicas, 262–263
Report writing
    executive summary, 123, 125
    functions, 120
    information structure, 120
    instructor responsibilities, 120
    organization, 121, 122
    overview, 119–120
    proofreading, 121
    report development, 123, 124
    technical accuracy, 121
    writing style, 123
Reports
    defined, 119
    exposure reports, 69
    recommendations (NFPA 1401), 68, 126, 492
    supervisory, 469
    writing. *See* Report writing
Request for proposal (RFP), 453–454
Rescue/extrication training area, 108–109
Research
    data collection, 431–433
    defined, 431
    information sources, 433–439
    models, 432
    for purchases, 455–458
    reference material citations, 439
    trends, 432
    validity, 439
Resources
    consistency of materials, 205
    funds. *See* Funds and resources
    for lesson planning, 190–191
    practical training evolutions, 286
    program and curriculum development, 533
    scheduling, 471–476
    variations in materials, 203
Respiratory protection, 52–53, 102–103, 492
Responding, listening skill, 96
Responsibility of instructors, 17
Restrictions on copyrighted materials, 75
Retention length records, 69
Retrospective evaluation, 509
Revision of records, 133
Rewarding employees on a team, 466–467
RFP (request for proposal), 453–454

RHAVE (Risk, Hazard, and Value Evaluation) Program, 506
Rhetorical questions, 244, 256
RICs (rapid intervention crews), 52, 53, 292, 424
Risk
    analysis, 441, 506
    control, 39
    defined, 42
    evaluation, 39
    high-hazard training, 287
    identification, 39
    monitoring and follow-up, 39
    reduction of liability risk, 72–73
    Risk, Hazard, and Value Evaluation (RHAVE) Program, 506
    risk-management plan, 37–39
RITs (rapid intervention teams), 52, 53, 292, 424
Role model of instructors, 14–16, 45–47
Role-plays, 279–280
Roles and responsibilities, case study, 27
Round table seating arrangement, 209

S
Safety
    accident management, 47, 48–53
    accident prevention, 47–48
    casualty prevention, 37–39
    casualty statistics, 35–36
    in the classroom, 212–213
    environmental laws and codes, 215
    equipment training, 53
    facilities and props, 27
    federal government agencies, 53–54
    incident safety officer duties, 44–45
    instructor as role model, 45–47
    instructor challenge, 24–25
    instructor obligations to students, 11–12
    instructor responsibilities, 35
    instructor's role, 39–47
    lesson consistency, 205
    planning safe training scenarios, 41–42
    plans, 46–47
    practical training evolutions, 285, 288–290, 425
    professional organizations and associations, 57
    reinforcement, 46
    scheduling, 472
    standards-writing organizations, 55–56
    state/provincial and local safety and health agencies, 54–55
    teaching topics, 44
    training casualties, 36–37
    training environment, 40–44
    on the training ground, 43
Safety officer
    ISO. *See also* Incident safety officer
    Standard for Fire Department Safety Officer. See NFPA 1521
Sandler, B. R., 168
Sarcasm, defined, 21
Sarcasm vs. sincerity, 21
Scanners, 350–351
Schedules
    availability of resources, 473–474
    challenges of scheduling, 25, 26
    coordination of training, 474
    course time schedule formats, 332, 333
    creation of, 474
    determining requirements, 473
    need determination, 472–473
    publishing, 475
    resources, 471–476
    revisions, 476

Scope of book, 1
Scoring methods for tests
    class participation rating scale, 407–408
    composite scoring and point systems, 407
    ease of scoring, 386
    oral tests, 310
    performance tests, 311–314
    raw scores, 409
    scoring, defined, 406
    written tests, 310–311
Seating arrangements, 207–209, 251–252
Secondary literature, 434
Security
    technology-based training, 228, 230
    of tests, 314–315
    of training area, 104
Self-concept, andragogy assumption, 138
Self-confidence
    of adult students, 165
    of instructors, 17
Self-directed (independent) learning, 230–231
Self-presentation, nonverbal communication, 92
Sender (speaker) in communications, 86, 87
Senses
    information gathering, 149–151
    limited, in lecture presentation format, 221, 222
Sensitivity, interpersonal skill, 17
Sensory memory, 151
Sequencing, 236–237, 238
Sequential learning method, 146
Shaler, Rhoberta, 85
Short-answer tests, 307, 398–399
Short-term (working) memory, 153
Show-off students, 174, 175
Shy individuals, 173–174
Sidebar information
    example, 4
    NFPA standards listing, 55
    obsolete terms and their replacements, 91
    strategic initiatives, 36
    words to teach by, 241
Simple-to-complex sequencing, 237
Simulations
    casualty simulation training aids, 263–264
    defined, 281
    structured exercises, 281–282
Simulators
    anatomical/physiological mannequins, 271
    computer, 270–271
    defined, 269
    display boards, 270
    electronic, 270
    live-fire training, 107–108, 111
    smoke, 270
    virtual reality, 271
Sincerity, defined, 21
Sincerity vs. sarcasm, 21
Site space for training, 215
Situation accident factor, 48
Skewed test results, 411
Skills
    of management, 470–471
    performances, 206
    psychomotor learning domain. *See* Psychomotor (skills) learning domain
    skills sheet, 333, 341, 342–344
Slide projectors/slides, 268, 416–417
Slow learners, 172–173

Small group discussions, 417–418, 419–420
Smoke buildings, 106
Smoke simulators, 270
Social Security number privacy, 69
Socrates, 137
Software programs, 127
Soil, environmental issues, 77, 285
Solutions vs. complaints, 21–22
Span of control concept, 461–462
Speakers, characteristics, 232–234
Specification, table of, 380–381
Staging officer, 291, 424
Standard, defined, 62–63
Standard for Airport Fire Fighter Professional Qualifications (NFPA 1003), 492
Standard for Competencies for EMS Personnel Responding to Hazardous Materials Incidents (NFPA 473), 492
Standard for Fire Apparatus Driver/Operator Professional Qualifications (NFPA 1002), 492
Standard for Fire Department Safety Officer. See NFPA 1521
Standard for Fire Fighter Professional Qualifications (NFPA 1001), 492
Standard for Fire Officer Professional Qualifications (NFPA 1021), 1, 40, 492
Standard for Fire Service Instructor Professional Qualifications. See NFPA 1041
Standard for Fire Service Respiratory Protection Training (NFPA 1404), 492
Standard for Professional Competence of Responders to Hazardous Materials Incidents (NFPA 472), 492
Standard for Professional Qualifications for Fire Inspector and Plan Examiner (NFPA 1031), 492
Standard for Professional Qualifications for Fire Investigator (NFPA 1033), 492
Standard for Professional Qualifications for Public Fire and Life Safety Educator (NFPA 1035), 492
Standard for Professional Qualifications for Public Safety Telecommunicator (NFPA 1061), 492
Standard for Providing Emergency Services to the Public (NFPA 1201), 485, 492
Standard for the Organization and Deployment of Fire Suppression Operations, Emergency Medical Operations, and Special Operations to the Public by Career Fire Departments (NFPA 1710), 492
Standard for the Organization and Deployment of Fire Suppression Operations, Emergency Medical Operations, and Special Operations to the Public by Volunteer Fire Departments (NFPA 1720), 492
Standard for Wildland Fire Fighter Professional Qualifications (NFPA 1051), 492
Standard on Comprehensive Occupational Medical Program for Fire Departments (NFPA 1582), 52
Standard on Emergency Services Incident Management System. See NFPA 1561
Standard on Fire Department Occupational Safety and Health Program. See NFPA 1500
Standard on Health-Related Fitness Programs for Fire Fighters (NFPA 1583), 55
Standard on Industrial Fire Brigades (NFPA 600), 492
Standard on Live Fire Training Evolutions. See NFPA 1403
Standard on Training for Initial Emergency Scene Operations (NFPA 1410), 55
Standard on Water Supplies for Suburban and Rural Fire Fighting (NFPA 1142), 102, 115, 286
Standards, development of, 491–493
Standards-writing organizations
    American Society for Testing and Materials (ASTM), 56
    NFPA. *See* National Fire Protection Association
    professional organizations and associations, 57
    purpose, 55
    Underwriters Laboratories Inc. (UL or ULC), 56
Statistical test result analysis, 408–409
Statutory (legislative) law, 64–67
Step-by-step sequencing, 237
Stereotypes in communications, 91
Storming stage of team development, 465
Strategic initiatives, 36
Structural collapse
    practical training evolutions, 296–297
    training area, 108
Structured exercises
    brainstorming, 280–281
    case studies, 277–279
    field and laboratory experiences, 282
    purpose, 277
    role-plays, 279–280
    simulations, 281–282
Structures. *See* Acquired structures
Students
    adult responsibilities, 165
    aggressive, 174–175
    behavioral management, 175–185
    characteristics, 163–169
    confidence, 165
    demographics, 165–169
    disruptive behavior, 184–185
    as individuals, 169–175
    instructor evaluation surveys, 361–362
    instructor obligations, 10–12
    learning styles, 165
    life experiences, 164
    motivation, 164–165
    progress evaluation and testing. *See* Evaluation
    rights of, 75
    student learning surveys, 368
Study sheet, 346, 347
Subjective testing, 308, 390
Substantive rights, 75
Summary of oral presentation, 236
Summative (comprehensive) testing, 305–306, 378
Summative evaluation
    for courses, 363, 364–368, 369–370, 513
    for curriculum, 539–540, 541
    features, 509
    reaction surveys, 515–516
Supervision
    anticipating problems, 462–463
    celebrating accomplishments, 467
    challenges, 462–467
    completing tasks, 467–468
    defined, 461
    employee involvement, 464
    goals and objectives, 463–464
    leadership elements, 469
    Level III Instructor functions, 493–494
    positive attitudes, 469
    records and reports, 469
    responsibilities of supervisors, 467–469
    rewarding employees, 466–467
    skill development, 468–469
    span of control, 461–462
    team effectiveness, 464–466
    teamwork and cooperation, 468
Supervisor evaluations, 358
Supervisory personnel surveys, 365, 368

Surveys
  instructor evaluations by students, 361–362
  reaction, 515–516
  sample employer survey, 369–370
  student learning surveys, 368
  supervisory personnel, 365, 368
Symbolic learning method, 146
Synthesis learning outcome, 379
Synthesis level of learning, 143
Systems approach to evaluation, 511
Systems model approach to training function, 447

T
Table of specification, 380–381
Tabletop miniatures, 262
Talkative students, 174–175
Task analysis
  cognitive, 528
  defined, 140–141, 505
  formal methods, 527
  hierarchical, 527, 528
  if and then, 528
  information methods, 527
  model based, 528
  program and curriculum development, 527–528
  purpose, 441, 505–506
  training scenarios, 41
  worksheet, 527
Tasks, hierarchy of work, 526–527
TBT. *See* Technology-based training
Teaching
  approaches, 155–157, 205–206
  defined, 140
  team teaching, 225–227
  traits. *See* Teaching traits
Teaching traits
  case study, 22
  honesty vs. bluffing, 20–21
  inspiration vs. intimidation, 22
  positive humor vs. offensive humor, 22
  sincerity vs. sarcasm, 21
  solutions vs. complaints, 21–22
Team teaching, 225–227
Teams. *See* Workgroup
Technical training, practical training evolutions, 283, 295–298
Technology-based training (TBT)
  active learning, 239
  advantages and disadvantages of use, 228
  computer-based training, 227–228
  distance-learning courses, 221
  increased use of, 227
  overview, 220
  security, 228, 230
Television
  monitors, 271–272
  projection screens, 272
  as training aid, 267–268
Temperature in classrooms, 209–210
Terminating personnel, 498
Terminating students, 185
Terrain, impact on training, 213
Terrorism, counterterrorism operations, 297
Tertiary literature, 434
Test instruments
  format, 387, 388
  instructions, 389
  level of difficulty, 388–389
  oral. *See* Oral tests

  performance (skills) tests, 402–405
  test item arrangement, 387
  written. *See* Written tests
Test item analysis, 409–411
Test planning
  clues to answers, 383
  determining test purpose and type, 376–377, 378
  guideline approach to number of test items, 385
  learning objectives, 377–380
  level of difficulty, 384
  mathematical approach to number of test items, 385
  number of test items, 384–385
  reliability of test, 386
  table of specification, 380–381
  test items, 383–386, 409–411
  test planning sheet, 382–383
  test specifications, 380–383
  time requirements, 381–382
  usability of test, 385–386
  validity of test, 386
Testing. *See also* Evaluation
  administration, 308–310
  administration classification, 306–308
  American Society for Testing and Materials (ASTM), 56
  certification, 314
  closed question, 244, 306, 401–402
  commercially prepared, 375–376
  completion (fill in the blank), 307
  computer-testing, 307
  corrective techniques, 411
  criterion-referenced. *See* Criterion-referenced tests
  data collection, 405–408
  defined, 303, 304, 305, 375
  diagnostic, 378
  essay, 307, 399–401
  formative, 305, 378. *See also* Formative evaluations
  grade reporting, 314
  Hazen-Williams Water Flow Tests, 432
  instruments. *See* Test instruments
  interpretation classification, 305
  locations, 203
  matching, 307, 396–397
  multiple-choice, 307, 390–393
  norm-referenced. *See* Norm-referenced tests
  open question, 244, 306–307, 401–402
  oral. *See* Oral tests
  performance. *See* Performance (psychomotor) testing
  placement, 305
  planning. *See* Test planning
  prescriptive, 305, 378
  pretest, 525
  privacy, 314–315
  purpose classification, 305–306
  readiness, 305
  reliability. *See* Reliability of tests
  scoring. *See* Scoring methods for tests
  security, 314–315
  short-answer, 307, 398–399
  skewed test results, 411
  statistical test result analysis, 408–409
  student progress. *See* Evaluation
  subjective, 308, 390
  summative (comprehensive), 305–306, 378
  test item analysis, 409–411
  test score privacy, 69
  true/false, 307, 393–396
  validity, 408
  written. *See* Written tests

Testing and standards organizations, research information source, 438

Theatrics vs. enthusiasm, 196–197

360-degree feedback evaluation, 500

Time management, 470

Timekeeper, in discussion groups, 421

Timid students, 173–174

Title VI of the Civil Rights Act, 65

Title VII of the Civil Rights Act, 64–65

Tool as communication example, 90

Tools and equipment demonstrations, 263

Trade shows, 452

Traditional teaching approach
    active learning, 238
    blended e-learning delivery vs., 228, 229–230
    characteristics, 156
    methodology, 156, 204

Traditionalists, 166, 167

Training
    defined, 9, 140
    evolutions. *See* Practical training evolutions
    function, 9
    Guide to Building Fire Service Training Centers (NFPA 1402), 55, 101, 106
    history, 1–2
    importance of, 4
    policies. *See* Training policy development
    program, defined, 521
    records, 68, 69, 126, 481–484
    Trends and Hazards in Firefighter Training, 37

Training policy development
    adoption, 488–491
    characteristics of policies, 485
    determining need for new policies, 486–487, 488–489
    draft document, 489–490
    evaluation of effectiveness, 491
    guidelines, 486
    implementation, 490–491
    overview, 484–485
    policy, defined, 485
    procedures, 485–486
    publication of document, 490
    revision, 487–488
    standards listing, 491–493

Training props. *See also* Instructional facilities and props
    confined space, 108
    flammable/combustible liquids and hazardous materials, 109–110
    Guide to Building Fire Service Training Centers (NFPA 1402), 55, 101, 106
    high-angle rescue, 109
    LPG (liquefied petroleum gas), 112
    overview, 108
    permanent structures, 108–111
    portable, 111–112, 284–285
    structural collapse, 108, 296–297
    trench rescue, 108
    vehicle and machinery extrications, 109, 296

Transitions in presentations
    continuity and consistency, 255
    defined, 239
    media transitions and animations, 257–258
    multiple instructors, 225–227, 416
    nonverbal transitions, 257, 416
    purposes, 255
    slide transitions, 257, 416–417
    timing, 255–256, 416
    verbal transitions, 256, 416

Transportation
    fire training, 294
    incident training area, 109–110
    vehicle extrication, 109, 296
    vehicle traffic and noise, impact on training, 213, 214

Trenches
    rescue training areas, 108
    shoring and rescue operations, 297

Trends
    industry, 452
    research, 432
    Trends and Hazards in Firefighter Training, 37

Triage operations, 296

True/false tests, 307, 393–396

Trustworthiness of instructors, 17

Tuckman, B. W., 465

Tutorial instruction, 231

2 by 6 rule of projection screens, 272

U

UL (Underwriters Laboratories Inc.), 55, 56, 438

ULC (Underwriters' Laboratories of Canada), 55, 56, 438

Understanding, listening skill, 95

Underwriters Laboratories Inc. (UL), 55, 56, 438

Underwriters' Laboratories of Canada (ULC), 55, 56, 438

Uninterested students, 174

USFA (U.S. Fire Academy), 36, 37, 49, 54

U.S. Fire Academy (USFA), 36, 37, 49, 54

U.S. Workforce Investment Act of 1998, 170

V

Validity
    criterion-referenced tests, 408
    defined, 303–304, 408
    norm-referenced tests, 408
    oral tests, 402
    performance tests, 405

Vehicle extrication, 109, 296

Vehicle traffic and noise, impact on training, 213, 214

Vendors
    research for purchasing, 452
    research information source, 438

Verbal communication, 90–92

Verbal transitions, 256, 416

VFIS (Volunteer Fire Insurance Service), 438

Vicarious liability, 71–72

Video
    capture devices, 351
    editing devices, 351
    presentations, 267–268
    projectors, 265

Virtual reality simulations, 271

Visual learning style, 145, 204

Visual presenters/displays, 266–267

Vocal characteristics of speakers, 233

Vocal interferences of speakers, 233–234

Voice attributes, 234

Volunteer fire departments
    recruitment, 496
    standards (NFPA 1720), 492
    Volunteer Fire Insurance Service (VFIS), 438

W

Wall and door assemblies for training, 112

Warnings
    example, 5
    live-fire trainings, 102, 111
    practical training evolutions, 284
    training prop safety standards, 112

Water
    adequate supplies for training operations, 102
    decontamination system, 103–104
    environmental issues, 76, 285
    ice rescues, 297
    maritime incident training area, 110, 111
    practical training evolutions, 296
    rescue training areas, 106
    *Standard on Water Supplies for Suburban and Rural Fire
        Fighting* (NFPA 1142), 102, 115, 286
    supplies in acquired structures, 115
WBT (web-based training), 228
Weapons of mass destruction credentialing, 524
Weather
    acquired structures, 113
    monitoring devices, 103
    during practical training evolutions, 285, 286
    scheduling impact, 476
    variations, impact on training, 202, 213
Web-based training (WBT), 228
Whirlpool Corporation vs. Marshall, 67
WHO (World Health Organization), 436
Whole-to-part sequencing, 237
Wildlands
    firefighter qualifications (NFPA 1051), 492
    training areas, 106, 295

Workgroup
    celebrating accomplishments, 467
    defined, 462
    employee involvement, 464
    empowering employees, 466
    forming stage of team development, 465
    goals and objectives, 463–464
    norming stage of team development, 465
    performing stage of team development, 465
    rewarding employees, 466–467
    storming stage of team development, 465
    team effectiveness, 464–466
Worksheets, 341, 345–346, 527
World Health Organization (WHO), 436
Writing reports. *See* Report writing
Written tests
    administration, 308–309
    alternative-response (true/false), 307, 393–396
    essay, 307, 399–401
    interpretative exercises, 401
    interpretive exercise, 390
    matching, 307, 396–397
    multiple-choice, 307, 390–393
    objective, 390
    purpose, 307, 387
    scoring, 310–311
    short-answer/completion, 307, 398–399
    subjective, 390
    true/false, 307, 393–396

Index by Nancy Kopper